The United States in LITERATURE

AMERICA READS **CLASSIC EDITION**

AMERICA READS

CLASSIC EDITION

BEGINNINGS IN LITERATURE
Alan L. Madsen
Sarah Durand Wood
Philip M. Connors

DISCOVERIES IN LITERATURE
L. Jane Christensen
Edmund J. Farrell

EXPLORATIONS IN LITERATURE
Nancy C. Millett
Raymond J. Rodrigues

PATTERNS IN LITERATURE
Edmund J. Farrell
Ouida H. Clapp
Karen J. Kuehner

TRADITIONS IN LITERATURE
Helen McDonnell
James E. Miller, Jr.
Russell J. Hogan

THE UNITED STATES IN LITERATURE
The Red Badge of Courage edition
Three Long Stories edition
James E. Miller, Jr.
Kerry M. Wood
Carlota Cárdenas de Dwyer

ENGLAND IN LITERATURE
Macbeth edition
Hamlet edition
John Pfordresher
Gladys V. Veidemanis
Helen McDonnell

CLASSICS IN WORLD LITERATURE
Kerry M. Wood
Helen McDonnell
John Pfordresher
Mary Alice Fite
Paul Lankford

The authors and editors wish to thank the following consultants for reading and teaching editorial material and proposed selections for America Reads.

■ Barbara E. Anderson, Junior Level Coordinator and Teacher, James B. Conant High School, Hoffman Estates, Illinois

■ Anita Arnold, Chairman, English Department, Thomas Jefferson High School, San Antonio, Texas

■ Pat Dudley, Principal, Jane Long Elementary School, Abilene ISD, Abilene, Texas

■ Dr. V. Pauline Hodges-McLain, Coordinator, Language Arts, Jefferson County Public Schools, Golden, Colorado

■ Rance Howe, English/Language Arts Consultant K-12, Anoka-Hennepin ISD 11, Coon Rapids, Minnesota

■ Lisbeth Johnson, English Teacher, Capital High School, Olympia, Washington

■ Daniel Lane, Supervisor of Humanities, Holmdel Twp. Public Schools, Holmdel, New Jersey

■ May Lee, English Teacher, Baldwin Senior High School, Baldwin, New York

■ Richard T. Martin, English Department Chairman, Burrillville Junior-Senior High School, Harrisville, Rhode Island

■ Barbara McCormick, Systemwide Chairman of English, Greenville Public Schools, Greenville, Mississippi

■ James McCullough, English Teacher, Carmel High School, Mundelein, Illinois

■ Cathy Nufer, Teacher, Grade 6, Elm School, Hinsdale, Illinois

■ Marlyn Payne, Teacher, Grade 7, Nichols Middle School, Evanston, Illinois

■ Sally P. Pfeifer, English Department Chair, Lewis and Clark High School, Spokane, Washington

■ James B. Phillips, Instructor in English and Reading, Norwood Senior High School, Norwood, Massachusetts

■ John Pratt, Language Arts Chairperson, Edison High School, Stockton, California

■ Cora Wolfe, English Department Chairperson, Antelope Union High School, Wellton, Arizona

The United States in LITERATURE

AMERICA READS   **CLASSIC EDITION**

James E. Miller, Jr.
Kerry M. Wood
Carlota Cárdenas de Dwyer

CLASSIC EDITION
S F

S C O T T,   F O R E S M A N

Scott, Foresman and Company   Editorial Offices: Glenview, Illinois
Regional Offices:
Sunnyvale, California   Tucker, Georgia   Glenview, Illinois   Oakland, New Jersey   Dallas, Texas

DISCARDED

LAMAR UNIVERSITY LIBRARY

James E. Miller, Jr. Helen A. Regenstein Professor of Literature and former Department Chairman, University of Chicago. Visiting professor at the Sorbonne, Paris 1984–85 and 1986. Fulbright Lecturer in Naples and Rome, Italy, 1958–1959, and in Kyoto, Japan, 1968. Chairman, Commission on Literature, National Council of Teachers of English, 1967–1969. Guggenheim Fellow, 1969–1970. President, NCTE, 1970. Author of *Quests Surd and Absurd; Word, Self, and Reality; T. S. Eliot's Personal Waste Land;* and *The American Quest for a Supreme Fiction.*

Kerry M. Wood English teacher at Woodside High School in Woodside, California. Formerly: coordinator of the Advanced Placement English program, Sequoia Union High School District, California. Consultant of the University of California Bay Area Writing Project. Teacher of a course in Scholastic Aptitude Test preparation for College Admissions Preparatory Service on the San Francisco Peninsula.

Carlota Cárdenas de Dwyer English teacher at Thomas C. Clark High School, San Antonio. Editor of the *Journal of the San Antonio Council of Teachers of English* (1985–1986). Formerly: member of the Executive Committee of the Conference on College Composition and Communication and of the Task Force on Racism and Bias of the National Council of Teachers of English.

Cover: Thomas Eakins, detail of *Sailboats Racing on the Delaware* (1874). Philadelphia Museum of Art. Given by Mrs. Thomas Eakins and Miss Adeline Williams

Pronunciation key and dictionary entries are from *Scott, Foresman Advanced Dictionary* by E. L. Thorndike and Clarence L. Barnhart. Copyright © 1988 Scott, Foresman and Company.

ISBN: 0–673–27071–8 (Three Long Stories)
ISBN: 0–673–27072–6 (*The Red Badge of Courage*)

Copyright © 1989
Scott, Foresman and Company, Glenview, Illinois.
All Rights Reserved. Printed in the United States of America.

This publication is protected by Copyright, and permission should be obtained from the publisher prior to any prohibited reproduction, storage in a retrieval system, or transmission in any form or by any means, electronic, mechanical, photocopying, recording, or otherwise. For information regarding permission, write to: Scott, Foresman and Company, 1900 East Lake Avenue, Glenview, Illinois 60025.

3 4 5 6 7 8 9 10   RRC   98 97 96 95 94 93 92 91 90 89

CONTENTS

UNIT 2   LITERARY NATIONALISM   *1800–1840*

UNIT 3   AMERICAN CLASSIC   *1840–1870*

THINKING CRITICALLY ABOUT LITERATURE

UNIT 4   VARIATIONS AND DEPARTURES   *1870–1915*

THINKING CRITICALLY ABOUT LITERATURE

UNIT 5 THE MODERN TEMPER *1915–1945*

UNIT 6   MODERN DRAMA

THINKING CRITICALLY ABOUT LITERATURE

UNIT 7   NEW FRONTIERS   *1945–*

The Classic Edition of *The United States in Literature* is available in two versions, one containing *The Red Badge of Courage*, the other, Three Long Stories.

READING LITERATURE

COMMENTS

READER'S NOTES

THEMES IN AMERICAN LITERATURE

THE STORY OF AMERICAN ENGLISH

HANDBOOK OF LITERARY TERMS

WRITER'S HANDBOOK

GLOSSARY OF LITERARY TERMS   *952*

PREVIEW

★*The United States in Literature* has eight units, six of them arranged chronologically, that present a survey of major American writers over the past four centuries. Alternate editions offer either *The Red Badge of Courage* by Stephen Crane or three long stories by Henry James, Edith Wharton, and Willa Cather.

UNIT ORGANIZATION

Every unit begins with a time line showing major events from history, the Presidents' administrations, and landmarks in American literature. This is followed by a unit preview. Next, a background article provides political and social history, so that the works of literature can be read in a more meaningful context.

Author biographies precede each selection or group of selections. Each biography portrays a writer and his or her works in the appropriate historical setting.

Many selections contain **footnotes** to define and pronounce words or to help clarify passages. A **date** on the right following a selection indicates the publication of the work. If there is a date on the left, it indicates the year the author wrote the work. The abbreviation c. with a date means "approximate."

Think and Discuss questions follow each selection or group of selections. They are divided into three levels: *Understanding, Analyzing,* and *Extending.* You may find it helpful to study the questions as a guide before you read a selection.

Many selections are preceded by a **handbook reference** that directs you to an article in the Handbook of Literary Terms at the back of the text. There you will learn about or review a literary term before you read the selection. Then, following the selection, **Applying/Reviewing** questions about that literary term help ensure that you understand the literary techniques involved. After a term has been introduced, it may appear in boldface type in the editorial material accompanying subsequent selections.

Vocabulary exercises focus on selected words in a piece of writing and help you learn or review techniques for determining the meanings of unfamiliar words as well as for increasing your vocabulary. You may be tested on the words in these exercises.

Thinking Skills exercises will help you learn to think about literature in new ways by *classifying, generalizing, synthesizing* (putting together parts and elements to form new ideas), and *evaluating.*

Composition assignments and ideas follow most selections. You can refer to the Writer's Handbook at the back of this text for more help with some of these assignments.

Enrichment sections occasionally provide ideas for class projects, research, and speaking and listening activities.

OTHER FEATURES

Five types of articles occur from time to time throughout this text.

Comment articles provide interesting sidelights on a work, an author, or a period. (See, for example, "America on the Eve of Discovery," page 12.)

Reader's Note articles provide help in reading certain works, or present a critical insight into an author's technique or style. (See, for example, "Patterns," page 502.)

A **Themes in American Literature** article in each unit explores major themes in the writings of different periods. (See, for example, "Moral Struggle" on page 253.)

The Story of American English articles, also appearing in each unit, discuss the development of the language and provide useful insights about why we speak as we do. (See, for example, page 658.)

A **Reading Literature** article in each unit provides hints on reading types of literature. (See "Reading a Poem" on page 166.)

A **Reading Literature Skillfully** exercise follows a subsequent selection in each unit, highlighting a particular reading skill.

UNIT REVIEWS

Each unit ends with a review entitled **Thinking Critically About Literature.** It is divided into three parts.

In the **Concept Review** appears a short work typical of the period, accompanied by sidenotes to guide your reading. Questions then measure your understanding of the work and review applicable literary terms that you have studied in the unit.

In the **Content Review,** classifying, generalizing, synthesizing, and evaluating questions help you review the selections in the unit.

A **Composition Review** provides topics for writing about the period or the literary genres you have studied.

END-OF-BOOK MATERIAL

The **Handbook of Literary Terms** contains brief lessons about the important terms you need in order to understand and discuss the literature. Handbook references preceding selected writings refer you to specific articles, to be studied before reading the selections.

The **Writer's Handbook** contains lessons on the writing process and on writing about various types of literature. Some composition assignments will refer you to these lessons.

A **Glossary of Literary Terms** provides definitions and examples of many terms in addition to those taught in the Handbook.

A dictionary-type **Glossary** contains all words featured in Vocabulary exercises, plus other words you will encounter in your reading.

By studying four centuries of American literature, you can recognize influences that have helped shape the society you now live in. In addition, you read these works to discover what they can teach us about ourselves—where we have come from and where we are going—as well as for the genuine enjoyment they continue to offer.

HE NEW LAND 1500–1800

1500	1550	1600

HISTORY AND THE ARTS

Bubonic plague rages in England • • Mayflower Compact

• Balboa reaches Pacific Ocean

Harvard College founded •

• Reformation begins in Germany

First printing press in America •

Spanish found St. Augustine •

Massachusetts law requires public schools •

Jamestown founded • • Pilgrims settle Plymouth

Dutch open trading port at Albany •

African slaves imported to Jamestown •

MONARCHS AND PRESIDENTS

• 1558–1603 Elizabeth I

• 1603–1625 James I

• 1625–1649 Charles I

LITERATURE

• Smith: *The General History*

Bay Psalm Book •

Woven cradle used on the *Mayflower* in 1620

Embroidered wedding shoes (c. 1730)

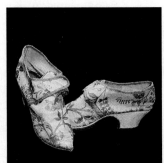

Teapot decorated with anti-Stamp Act slogan (1765)

UNIT

1650	1700	1750	1800

• King Philip's War   • Franklin starts first circulating library

• Charles I beheaded   Frederick the Great begins reign (Prussia) •   • Franklin's kite experiment

  (England)   • Salem witch trials   • French and Indian War begins

  Puritan reign begins   Father Serra establishes California missions •   Population •

               Battles of Lexington and Concord •   of U.S.

                                     5,308,483

                           Constitutional Convention •

                           French Revolution begins •

• 1649–1660   • 1685–1689 James II   • 1714–1727 George I

  Commonwealth   • 1689–1694 William III   • 1727–1760 George II

     • 1660–1685   and Mary II   • 1760–1820 George III

       Charles II   • 1702–1714 Anne   1789–1797 George Washington •

     1694–1702 William III •   1797–1801 John Adams •

• Bradstreet: *The Tenth Muse*   • Mather: *Wonders of*   • Byrd: *A History of the Dividing Line*

   • Bradford: *The History*   *the Invisible World*   • First *Poor Richard's*   • Franklin begins

     of Plymouth Plantation   *Almanack*   his *Autobiography*

                 • *Boston News Letter,*   • Paine: *Common*

Knight: *The Journal of Madame Knight* • first successful American newspaper   *Sense* • Paine:

       Edwards: "Sinners in the Hands of an Angry God" •   Declaration of •   *Rights*

                                       Independence   *of Man*

John Singleton Copley, *Paul Revere* (c. 1768–1770)

Inkstand used in signing the Declaration and Constitution

Rising sun chair used at the Constitutional Convention

PREVIEW

UNIT 1   THE NEW LAND   1500–1800

Authors

Christopher Columbus
Navajo
Pima
Quechuan, Dakota, Ojibwa
Dekanawidah
Alvar Núñez Cabeza de Vaca
Robert de La Salle

John Smith
William Bradford
Sarah Kemble Knight
William Byrd II
Cotton Mather
Jonathan Edwards
Anne Bradstreet

Edward Taylor
Phillis Wheatley
Philip Freneau
Benjamin Franklin
Michel-Guillaume Jean de Crèvecoeur
Thomas Jefferson
Thomas Paine

Features

Comments: America on the Eve of Discovery
    Oral Literature
Reading a Historical Narrative
Comments: On the Iroquois Constitution
    Offer of Help by Canassatego
    La Salle II
    The First Settlers
    Types of Colonial Literature
    Witchcraft as Seen Through the Ages
    The Mystery of the Flying Spider
    The Tenth Muse
Reader's Note: "Huswifery"
Themes in American Literature: An Overview
Comment: "As Poor Richard Says . . . "
The Story of American English

Application of Literary Terms

simile   rhyme
imagery   extended metaphor
metaphor   heroic couplet
allusion   tone
satire   style
paradox

Reading Literature Skillfully

fact/opinion

Vocabulary Skills

antonyms   context   dictionary

Thinking Skills

classifying   synthesizing
generalizing   evaluating

Composition Assignments Include

Being a Historical Character
Writing a Humorous Satire
Analyzing a Theme
Writing an Outline
Developing an Extended Metaphor
Writing a Literary Letter
Writing to Persuade
Writing to Defend Your Position

Enrichment

Participating in a Discussion
Oral Reading
Oral Report

Thinking Critically About Literature

Concept Review
Content Review
Composition Review

THE NEW LAND   1500–1800

BEGINNINGS

America's independence from Great Britain was proclaimed in 1776, a little over two centuries ago. But America's beginnings stretch back 150 years and more before independence, during which time various British colonies developed and flourished, linked mainly through the mother country. The writings of this colonial period were tied closely to the life, work, and belief of those who gave up the old world for the new, and were busy carving a country out of a wilderness.

During the fifteenth century, the stability of Medieval Europe gave way to the ferment of the Renaissance. Europeans, who were experiencing a surge of creative energy seen in such technological accomplishments as the cannon and the printing press, were gazing toward new horizons in art, religion, and politics, as well as in geography. Well before the English settled in America, other Europeans had established interests in the North American continent, most noticeably the gold-seekers of Spain and the fur traders and fishermen of France. Soon to follow was a continuous stream of other immigrants that began to flow toward the ancient American civilization already on the continent.

In noting European "discoveries" of America, we must remember that any such claims were predated by those of the inhabitants who had come from Asia and controlled the land for 30,000 years or so before European exploration began. Nonetheless, Europeans, who marveled at the fabulous cities of the Aztec, Mayan, and Incan Empires, did make claims and sent back reports of discovery along with glowing accounts of tropical paradises, men-

acing forests, endless plains, vast mountain ranges, exotic plants and animals, and tremendous wealth. The original Americans and the Europeans-becoming-Americans changed each other, eventually incorporating values and lifestyles totally different from those of either feudal Europe or America before Columbus.

After more than two centuries of the shaping of new societies on both continents of America, the French immigrant Michel-Guillaume Jean de Crèvecoeur would ask: "What, then, is the American, this new man?" Crèvecoeur, examining British North America, went on to give his answer (see his "What Is an American?" included in this unit). But then, as now, no definition could indicate the complexity of people from all continents mingling and clashing in the formation of a New Land. The selections in this unit are chosen to give some idea of that diversity, yet also to suggest some common elements of the North American experience. Such shared characteristics include a fascination with the wilderness, which was potent to the imagination of original Americans and settlers alike; a devotion to fair government, seen both in the Iroquois Constitution and the Declaration of Independence; and an abiding concern with practical affairs, which was essential in the times of exploration, colonization, and revolution.

THREE GEOGRAPHICAL GROUPS

Any attempt to describe the colonists in terms of a national identity is necessarily limiting, given the extremes imposed by various religions, different geographical areas, and contrasting lifestyles. Indeed, the colonists were as diverse as were their reasons for coming to the New World. Although their differences were by no means confined to geographical boundaries, these differences can best be explained by looking at the three basic colonial areas: New England, the Southern Colonies, and the Middle Colonies.

To the New England Colonies came the Puritans. The first to settle (in Plymouth) were the Pilgrims, who wished to separate from the Church of England. Later, nonseparatist Puritans came to Massachusetts Bay. The Puritans were called by that name because they had attempted to reform or "purify" the Church of England by simplifying the forms of worship and by abolishing ritual. Believing that God had chosen at the time of their birth those who were to be saved or damned, the Puritans adhered to a strict code of morality and proper behavior. Centered in the towns in New England with their most important colonies in Massachusetts, these colonists turned to the forests and the sea for their livelihood, establishing industries in shipbuilding, trading, and fishing. Puritans believed that God's laws can be understood only through studying the Bible—hence, their emphasis on reading and education in general and the popularity of the sermon as a literary form.

In contrast to the Puritans of New England, the Planters of Virginia and the Southeast were farmers, some of whom established large plantations that depended on a huge work force of white bond servants and African slaves. Thus evolved a rural way of life, based largely on the cash crop of tobacco, and a planting aristocracy. The Southern colonists produced less writing than their New England counterparts. While religion was an integral part of life for the Southerner, it was by no means the dominating influence it was for the Puritans. The perspective of the Southern gentleman can best be seen in the diary entries of William Byrd, the most prominent of the Southern writers, which gave only a closing mention to God after listing the social events, business, and routines of the day.

Between New England to the northeast and the Southern Colonies were the Middle Colonies of Pennsylvania, Delaware, New Jersey, and New York, nicknamed the "bread colonies" because grain was the major crop. Ethnically diverse and culturally mixed, these colonies included Dutch, Swedish, German, and French-Huguenot refugees. Centrally located with access to the great inland waterways, the area thrived in agriculture, manufacturing, and commerce. Religious toleration, practiced throughout these Middle Colonies, was the cornerstone of Pennsylvania, where Quakers and other religious groups lived according to the principles of simplicity, truth, and peace. Here the settlers lived amica-

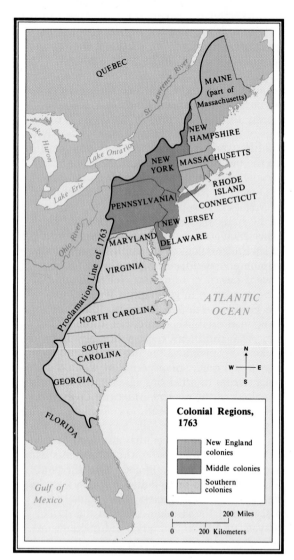

Colonial Regions, 1763

New England colonies

Middle colonies

Southern colonies

0   200 Miles

0   200 Kilometers

bly with the Indians from whom they had purchased plots of land. And here, under the leadership of William Penn, the people achieved self-government. By 1750 the Quaker city of Philadelphia had become the unofficial colonial capital—the site twenty-six years later for the signing of the Declaration of Independence.

EXPLORERS AND NATIVE AMERICANS

Columbus, a Genoese navigator, combined facts and rumors from Arabic, Jewish, Portuguese, Irish, and even ancient Greek maps and writings, and convinced Ferdinand and Isabella of Spain to fund a quest for the western route to Asia. When he found the "new" land in 1492, he thought it to be the coast of India, and so its varied inhabitants received the misleading name of "Indians." His famous letter announcing the discovery of America, included in this unit, describes these inhabitants of the New World.

The sixteenth century was the golden age of the explorer. The earliest penetrations of the North American wilderness, like the journey of Cabeza de Vaca, recorded here, were accomplished by a few intrepid French and Spanish soldiers and Catholic missionaries who followed wilderness trails from the St. Lawrence River to the mouth of the Mississippi and from Florida to California. Cabeza de Vaca's ordeal is one of the greatest adventures in American exploration. His record, despite the perils and hardships described, lured Coronado and others to seek in vain the fabled Seven Golden Cities of Cibola—which were actually cliff-towns of Pueblo farmers.

In 1681 Robert de La Salle, a French explorer, traveled from the Great Lakes down to the mouth of the Mississippi, claiming for France the Mississippi, the rivers that entered into it, and all the land watered by these rivers. The entire area he called Louisiana, in honor of King Louis XIV of France. The account that appears in this unit, based on his reports, acknowledges his indebtedness to the Indians who lived along his travel route.

During the 1500s and the 1600s, accounts of these voyages and narratives of exploration flowed from the New World back to the Old,

and were avidly read, as they are read today, as stories of high adventure, great risk, and derring-do. Among European readers of all these early accounts were scientists and philosophers who wondered about the social development of humankind outside the structures of so-called civilized society. Were the Indians barbaric beings or noble primitives? Evidence, not always reliable, mounted on both sides. Skeptics concluded that the natives were brutal barbarians; idealists imagined them noble savages. Conflicting philosophies and political theories were based on both conceptions.

The earliest display of American diversity appears in the distinct cultures and languages of Native Americans. The farming pueblo communities of the Southwest cherished stability and communal solidarity. Mounted buffalo hunters of the plains, on the other hand, displayed individualistic tendencies as they moved frequently in pursuit of game. Yet as diverse as these cultures were, they shared a fundamental sense of a divine order that regulates the universe. And they also shared a belief in the power of language to control the mysterious forces that preside over the world and shape human destiny. Their poems, like "The War God's Horse Song" (Navajo) or "A Dancing Song" (Pima), were sung or chanted in ritualistic ceremonies aligning the participants with hidden energies of nature and the universe.

The Iroquois Constitution, like that of the United States, looks to a stable political order and emphasizes the duties, rather than the privileges, of leadership. Like the Puritans, Native Americans revered education, but it was to be an education designed on their own principles. Canassatego, speaking for the Iroquois in 1744, declined an invitation to allow young Iroquois to be educated in English fashion at the College of William and Mary. His wry counter offer appears in this unit.

PIONEERS AND SETTLERS

The chronicles of Cabeza de Vaca stimulated the imagination and the ambition of Englishmen like Sir Walter Raleigh and John Smith. When Smith founded the first permanent English settlement in 1607, the Spanish had long been settled at St. Augustine (1565) and were moving into New Mexico. Smith's own *True Relation* (1608) is the earliest firsthand narrative of the English settlement of the New World. His various books were composed to attract future settlers, to furnish economic reports for investors in colonial ventures, and to provide news and information for the curious back in England. And, as such, they succeeded. Before their journey to America, the Puritans carefully studied Smith's *Description of New England* (1616).

The leading force in early New England was William Bradford, author of *The History of Plymouth Plantation* and governor of Plymouth, Massachusetts, for thirty-one successive terms. Bradford's grave, dignified style expresses the Puritans' sense that their divine mission permeated all aspects of life. This powerful feeling generated the variety of journals, histories, and sermons that comprised most New England prose. Exuberant prayers and sermons incorporated much of the creativity we now associate with drama, fiction, and poetry.

Although the works of Sarah Kemble Knight display the Puritan virtues of wisdom, shrewdness, and self-discipline, her *Journal* of 1704 reveals a quick wit that Puritans generally suppressed. Her keen powers of observation and staunch independence make her works lively reading.

William Byrd, a sharp observer like Knight, was a typical Virginia aristocrat, as much at home in the literary salons of London as in the Virginia backwoods that he helped survey. His polished, witty style, his learned allusions, and, above all, his fascination with human and natural curiosities rather than with divine order represent the contrast between New England and Southern writers, a contrast that extended into succeeding periods.

DIVINES AND POETS

Creative energies of the Puritans were generally directed into religion, and some of the most distinguished writers were divines, or ministers. One of the best known was Cotton Mather, whose learned books include the strange *Wonders of the Invisible World*, which describes in fascinating detail a number of witch trials held in the late 1600s in Salem, Massachusetts. The witchcraft hysteria diminished as suddenly as it had developed. But Mather's reputation was tarnished by his wholehearted belief in witchcraft, even though he did not support the executions.

The greatest of the Puritan theologians was Jonathan Edwards. His sermon, "Sinners in the Hands of an Angry God," is considered the most passionate and terrifying sermon of the time. He was at first a leader, then a critic of the religious revival known as "The Great Awakening" (1739–40). By the time of this movement, religious fervor was already yielding to the political ferment that led to the Revolution.

While poetry was not a common vehicle for Puritan expression, it finds a genuinely moving voice in the innovative poems of Anne Bradstreet and in the intricate verses of Edward Taylor. The works of both these New England poets reveal an emotional depth and sensitivity not usually associated with the Puritans. In addition, these poems reflect a wide-ranging imaginative dimension operating within the strict constraints of Puritan piety, as when Taylor portrays God as "Might Almighty" who "in this bowling alley bowled the sun."

In New England, the latter eighteenth century saw the creation of imaginative literature to replace literature written solely for practical, religious, or political ends. There was enough leisure for the production and reading of literature written not only to instruct but also to delight and entertain. Once printing presses became common throughout the Colonies, their use was no longer confined to printing utilitarian materials. First came newspapers, then fiction, and finally poetry that was no longer limited to pious purposes. The slave-girl Phillis Wheatley astonished her owners—and the age—by developing into an accomplished poet. Although Wheatley and other American writers borrowed their literary forms and standards from Europe, they struck a distinctively American note in their writings.

That American voice echoed clearly in the poetry of Philip Freneau, especially in his patriotic poems written in support of America in the Revolutionary War. But he is remembered today for his nature lyrics, such as "The Wild Honeysuckle," in which he draws wistful parallels between a flower's life and human existence. Sometimes called the "Father of American Poetry," Freneau marked the advent of the Romantic period in American literature.

PHILOSOPHERS AND STATESMEN

Many changes were taking place during the second half of the eighteenth century in America, and even greater changes were forthcoming. The spirit of liberty was being kindled; schools were being established; commerce was thriving; and the population was multiplying at enormous rates. The preachers, theologians, and religious poets who had spoken for their times were being replaced by a new breed—philosophers, statesmen, pamphleteers, and poets dedicated to politics or nature—who focused on the material, rational world rather than the spiritual one. The independent thinking that had led to the colonization of America began to show itself in literature, most notably in the works of Franklin, Jefferson, and Crèvecoeur.

The major writer of this period was Benjamin Franklin, who embodied the aspirations, deeply felt in the fledgling country, for both literary and political independence. The excerpt from his *Autobiography* on how to attain "Moral Perfection" is based on the rationalist's confidence in self and the certainty of progress. Franklin's optimism, shrewd common sense, plain speaking, and down-to-earth humor are considered by some critics to be the keynotes of American literature.

The work that figured most prominently in shaping nationhood was Thomas Jefferson's Declaration of Independence. It may justly be called the single most significant literary, as well as political, work of eighteenth-century America. In it is the core of American identity and expression. It serves as a climax to the unit in casting light on the theme running through most of the works in this unit—the riddle of identity. It is a riddle that will puzzle and inspire most American writers to come.

THINKING ABOUT GRAPHIC AIDS
Using the Time Line

The time line on pages xx–1 gives the chronological sequence of historical and literary events of this period. As you read the time line, keep in mind that although one event precedes another, it does not necessarily bear a relationship to it. For example, although the Battle of Lexington followed Franklin's kite experiment, it in no way resulted from it. Two time-line events, however, may bear a cause-effect relationship. For example, the settling of Plymouth Colony in 1620 alienated the neighboring Indians and eventually led to King Philip's War in 1675.

Answer the following items by determining what, if any, relationships exist between items in the time line.

1. Find two items in the time line that were possible only after the printing press was introduced in America.
2. Could the founders of Jamestown have read any colonial newspapers?
3. Could an account of Franklin's kite experiment have appeared in his *Autobiography?*
4. Name two countries with colonies in America before the British settled at Plymouth.
5. Who of the following may have known about Harvard College: Columbus, Father Serra, Byrd?

Using the Map

Use the map on page 4, which shows the colonial regions as they appeared in 1763, to answer the following items.

1. In an effort to limit westward colonization and separate colonists from Indians, the English government declared a north-south barrier. Find the barrier on the map.
2. One history text observes that in 1760 a Georgia farmer was linked by the ocean to Europe more easily than by the land to Maine. Using the map and what you know about travel conditions during this time, explain the statement.

BIOGRAPHY

Christopher Columbus
1446–1506

Statue of Christopher
Columbus by Carlo
Brioschi

Born in Genoa, Italy, Christopher Columbus went to sea at an early age and later settled in Portugal after his ship was sunk by French privateers. It was first to the Portuguese that Columbus applied for support in his attempt to reach Asia by sailing west. His bid was unsuccessful. Finally, after months of negotiations, Columbus succeeded in enlisting the support of Ferdinand and Isabella, King and Queen of Spain, for his exploration. He set sail on August 3, 1492, and on October 12 he sighted and claimed a number of islands he believed to be off the coast of India. These islands included what are now known as the Bahamas, Cuba, and Haiti. This discovery launched the entire exploration and settlement of the Americas and gave Spain title to the New World.

Columbus made a total of four voyages to the New World, but gradually fell out of favor with his sponsors, was imprisoned for a time, and eventually died in poverty. He believed to the end that he had reached the coast of India.

Columbus's letter, excerpted here, was probably written at sea in early 1493. It initiated a long tradition of works that describe the New World as a wondrous place, offering to Europeans riches, renewal, and the fulfillment of a dazzling dream.

A Spectacle of Great Beauty

Christopher Columbus

These islands are of a beautiful appearance and present a great diversity of views. They may be traversed in any part, and are adorned with a great variety of exceedingly lofty trees, which to appearance never lose their foliage, for I saw them as verdant and flourishing as they exist in Spain in the month of May, some covered with flowers, others loaded with fruit, according to their different species and their season of bearing, the whole offering a spectacle of great beauty. The nightingale and countless other birds were singing, although it was the month of November when I visited this delightful region. . . .

The inhabitants of both sexes, in Espanola and all the other islands which I saw or heard of, go naked as they were born, all except a few females who wear at the waist a green leaf, a portion of cotton, or bit of silk which they manufacture for this purpose. . . .

They possess no iron, and they neither use nor are acquainted with weapons, to the exer-

Christopher Columbus, *Journal of First Voyage to America*. New York: Albert & Charles Boni, 1924, pp. 211–218. Reprinted by permission of William F. Boni.

Edward Moran (1829–1901), detail of *The Debarkation of Columbus, Morning of October 12, 1492.* United States Naval Academy Museum

cise of which indeed they are not at all adapted, not by reason of any corporal deficiency, as they are very well shaped, but on account of their great timidity. Instead of arms they have canes dried in the sun, to the largest ends of which they fix a piece of wood sharpened at the end; of these, however, they have not the courage to make much use. I have in many instances sent two or three of my men to their towns to communicate with the inhabitants, when the Indians would tumultuously rush out, and seeing our people drawing near, run away with such haste that the father would abandon his child, and the child his father. This timidity was not owing to any violence or injury we offered them, as I was in the practice of making presents of cloth and other things to all the natives whom I met, but arose from their natural mildness and want of courage. Notwithstanding this, as soon as they have thrown aside their fear, and consider themselves in safety, they are very ingenuous and honest, and display great liberality with whatever they possess.

They never refuse to give any thing away which is demanded of them, and will even themselves entreat an acceptance of their property. They exhibit a great friendship towards every one, and will give whatever they have for a trifle or nothing at all. I forbade my men to purchase any thing of them with such worthless articles as bits of earthenware, fragments of platters, broken glass, nails, and thongs of leather, although when they got possession of any such thing they valued it as highly as the most precious jewel in the world. . . .

They are not idolaters, but believe that all power and goodness is in heaven, and that I had proceeded from that place with my ships and men; under this notion they received me at my first arrival as soon as they had banished their fear. They are not stupid and indolent, but acute and sagacious. Those of them who navigate the seas among those islands give singular accounts of what they have observed upon their voyages, but have never seen people who wear clothes, nor any ships similar to ours. On my arrival I took

by force from the first island a few of the Indians, in order that we might become acquainted with one another's language, and to gain a knowledge of what their country contained. These were of singular use to us, as we came to understand each other in a short time by the help of words and signs. I have them still with me, and they continue in the belief that we have come from heaven. This information they published wherever we arrived, exclaiming in a loud voice, "Come! Come! and see the celestial people." Upon this call, the natives would come thronging to us, after having banished the fear which seized them at first, men, women and children, old and young, crowding the roads and bringing us victuals and drink, with the utmost affection and reverence. . . .

In every one of these islands there are a great number of canoes, each one made of a solid log, of a narrow shape, somewhat resembling our *fustas*,[1] but swifter in the water; they are navigated solely by oars. They are of different sizes, the most of them containing seats for eighteen rowers. With these they carry on a commerce among these islands which are innumerable. I saw some of these canoes with seventy or eighty rowers. Throughout these islands there is no diversity in the appearance of the people, their manners or language, all the inhabitants understanding one another, a very favorable circumstance in my opinion, to the design which I have no doubt is entertained by our king, namely to convert them to the holy Christian faith, to which as far as I can perceive they are well disposed. . . .

Each of the natives, as far as I can understand, has one wife, with the exception of the King and Princes, who are permitted to have as many as twenty. The women appear to do more labor than the men. Whether there exists any such thing here as private property I have not been able to ascertain, as I have observed that an individual has been set to distribute to the others, in partic-

---

1. *fusta* (fus'tə), a vessel rigged with a triangular sail. [*Spanish*]

ular, food and such things. I found no ferocious sanguinary people in these parts, as some seem to have imagined the people here to be, but they are a very mild and friendly race. Their color is not black like that of the Ethiopians. Their hair is lank and hanging down. They do not inhabit those parts where the sun's rays are very

1493

powerful, as the heat is excessive here, the latitude being apparently twenty-six degrees. On the summits of the mountains the cold is great, but they do not suffer any incommodity from it, by being accustomed to the climate, and by the use of hot meats and drinks which they consume very prodigally.

THINK AND DISCUSS
Understanding
1. How do the natives behave when they see Columbus's men approaching? Where do the inhabitants think that Columbus and his men have come from?
2. Briefly describe the country and its people, as Columbus sees them.
3. What evidence indicates that the natives are generous?

Analyzing
4. What elements in Columbus's description of the New World would inspire readers in the Old World to want to visit these new-found lands?
5. What in his observations might lead Columbus to consider the natives skilled in practical matters?
6. Does Columbus have reason to fear attack from the natives? Explain.
7. What are some differences between Columbus's religion and way of life and those of the inhabitants?
8. What indications are there that Columbus considers his a superior culture and tries to impose it on the inhabitants?

Extending
9. Do you think Columbus appears to understand these inhabitants? Explain.

COMPOSITION
Being a Historical Character
Pretend you are the King of Spain or his minister writing instructions for Columbus on a second voyage to America. In three paragraphs, indicate three areas in which you want more information about the new-found land and its inhabitants and explain the reasons for your interest. Consider possible queries about food, agricultural methods, family life, language, social structure, methods of governing, and forms of education.

Describing Modern American Society
People gather ideas about earlier cultures from, among other things, the reports of explorers such as Columbus. Modern societies often seal time capsules, to be found by later generations, that reveal aspects of their culture. Imagine that you were to enclose in a time capsule 6 feet by 6 feet objects (perhaps a book, a mechanical device, a picture, or painting, and some clothes) that you feel represent America at the end of the twentieth century. Choose at least four such items and devote a paragraph to each, describing how these objects are expressive of our culture. In a final paragraph, make some general comments about our society. Direct your writing to a historian living one hundred years from now. See "Writing About a Period or Trend" in the Writer's Handbook.

Comment

America on the Eve of Discovery by John Bakeless

It is interesting to think of the vast continent as it lay for a few hours before dawn in the darkness of that moonlit October night [1492] and of its unconcerned inhabitants, still ignorant of that momentous instant. In Mexico, only a few hundred miles west of San Salvador, where Columbus landed, the Aztec civilization was at its height of grace, cruelty, and power, though already showing faint signs of corruption at its heart.

In the southwestern United States, where dawn was at that moment not yet ready to break, the peaceful Indians of the Pueblos would wake to the life they had been living for at least a thousand years, worshipping the rain-gods with ceremonial dances, harvesting their crops, managing their irrigation, fearing nothing. Were not their painted deserts a protection? Undisturbed in their majesty, giant redwoods that had been growing when Rome was still an empire looked through the fogs toward the Pacific waves breaking on the California coast. Northward, on the Columbia [River], Chinook and Klamath [Indian tribes of the American Northwest] had relaxed from the ardors of the salmon fishing. From the Rockies to the forests of Pennsylvania, black, gigantic buffalo herds were beginning to stir in the morning and think of grass and forage. Wolf, cougar, lynx, weasel, wildcat, fox were nearly ready to den up for their daytime rest. Between the Mississippi and the Pacific, the giant grizzlies prowled, lords of plain and mountain, certain of their power, contemptuous of the frail creatures who, with bows and arrows, occasionally disturbed them briefly. And over it all, through the autumn night, swept the miraculous millions of the migrant birds. . . .

To all appearance, the life of the whole great continent that fateful October morning in 1492 was wholly unchanged. Save on one insignificant island, there was no stir that day and no excitement. Yet the arrival of these three small ships, bobbing in the warm blue waves off San Salvador, meant that all this life of plains, mountains, lakes, and forests was now an insubstantial pageant soon to fade.

John Bakeless. *The Eyes of Discovery.* Philadelphia: J. B. Lippincott Company, 1950, pp. 12–14.

American Indian Poetry

It has been estimated that when Columbus "discovered" America, there were over six hundred different Indian cultures in what is now the United States, speaking several hundred different dialects. Poems included here come from a variety of tribes. The Navajo, largest Indian nation in the United States, are an Apache-related people who today occupy an extensive area in and about northeastern Arizona. Pima are village farmers who have lived from ancient prehistoric times along the valleys of the Gila and Salt rivers in the region that is now Phoenix, Arizona. Ojibwa (pronounced ō jib′wā or ō jib′wə; another name for Chippewa) live on the shores of Lake Superior and Lake Huron. Quechuan (kech′wän) is the name used today—their own name—for the Colorado River people formerly known as the Yuma. Dakota is the real name of the Sioux, who are chiefly associated with the high plains of the West.

American Indians accumulated a rich body of literature in which poetry played a central role. They relied on the sacred power of language to help them through life, creating and chanting poems whenever they felt the need to align themselves with, or appeal to, the mysterious powers that governed all aspects of daily experience.

Thus their poetry served a multitude of functions—celebrating, praising, explaining, mourning, communicating, remembering. Native Americans used poetry to help them in hunting, in planting, in harvesting, in dancing, in making war, in overcoming trouble, in observing life, in confronting death.

Poetry, like property, was communally shared. Any member of the tribe could create a poem, but it then became a possession of the tribe, to be used by all. Often the recitation was by a group, chanting in unison to the accompaniment of a drum. Repetition of phrases and lines, as in song, was therefore common.

Poems such as those included here tell a great deal about the people who wrote them and about their culture. These people celebrated nature and saw enchantment in everyday occurrences. The images, or word pictures, are generally drawn from the natural world—a world both beautiful and mystical: the Holy Wind, white light winking, a singing bush, a horse with legs "like quick lightning." Why does a commonplace animal assume mythic proportions as it does in "The War God's Horse Song"? To answer, one must understand how the introduction of the horse by the Spanish in sixteenth-century Mexico drastically changed the nomadic lives of the Navajo. The horse, presented as never thirsty and bridled by a rainbow, was nothing short of miraculous to these people.

As you read these poems, try to visualize them as part of a ceremony or chant, accompanied by music, dancing, and elaborate costumes.

The War God's Horse Song

Navajo

I am the Turquoise Woman's son

On top of Belted Mountain beautiful horses
slim like a weasel

My horse has a hoof like striped agate
5   his fetlock is like fine eagle plume
his legs are like quick lightning

My horse's body is like an eagle-feathered arrow

My horse has a tail like a trailing black cloud

I put flexible goods on my horse's back

10   The Holy Wind blows through his mane
his mane is made of rainbows

My horse's ears are made of round corn

My horse's eyes are made of stars

My horse's head is made of mixed waters
15   (from the holy waters)
         (he never knows thirst)

My horse's teeth are made of white shell

The long rainbow is in his mouth for a bridle
with it I guide him

20   When my horse neighs
different-colored horses follow

When my horse neighs
different-colored sheep follow

I am wealthy from my horse

25   Before me peaceful
Behind me peaceful
Under me peaceful
Over me peaceful
Around me peaceful
30   Peaceful voice when he neighs
I am everlasting and peaceful
I stand for my horse

From *The Navajo Indians* by Dane and Mary Roberts Coolidge.
Copyright 1930 by Dane and Mary Roberts Coolidge. Reprinted by
permission of Houghton Mifflin Company.

Quincy Tahoma, detail of *In the Days of Plentiful* (1946). Philbrook Institute of Art, Tulsa

THINK AND DISCUSS

Understanding

1. Find lines that illustrate each of the following qualities in the horse: swiftness, beauty, supernatural powers.

Analyzing

2. What do you think is meant by the following line: "I am wealthy from my horse" (line 24)?
3. What do you think the speaker means by the last line of the poem: "I stand for my horse"?

Extending

4. On what occasion do you think this poem was sung? Why would a song to a butterfly or a grasshopper have been less effective for this occasion?

APPLYING: Simile

See Handbook of Literary Terms, p. 886.

A **simile** is a figure of speech—language used in a nonliteral way—that makes a direct comparison, usually with the words *like* or *as*, between two basically unlike things that have something in common (heart like a bird; a face as gray as his dusty uniform). Note how the similes in "The War God's Horse Song" compare parts of the horse to things in nature.

1. Why do you think that the three similes in lines 4–6 are clustered together?
2. How might the horse's body resemble an "eagle-feathered arrow"? its tail, a "trailing black cloud"?
3. Restate lines 12 and 13 in the form of similes.

A Dancing Song

Pima

Dizzy I run into the bog water
there tadpoles sing among the reeds
tadpoles wearing girdles of bark
           there singing

5 In the evening land a very blue dragonfly
hanging on the water top
touching in his tail

There I run in rattling darkness
cactus flowers in my hair
10 in rattling darkness

                  darkness rattling
running to that singing place

Firefly Song

Ojibwa

Flickering firefly
              give me light
              light
once more before I sleep

5 Dancing firefly
              wandering firefly
              light
once more before I sleep

White light sailing
10   white light winking
just once more before I sleep

THINK AND DISCUSS
Understanding
1. Cite examples of repetition in both poems.

Analyzing
2. How are the feelings and situations of the speakers in each poem alike and how are they different?

APPLYING: Imagery **H🖋**
See Handbook of Literary Terms, p. 891.

    The term **imagery** refers to concrete words or details that appeal to the senses of sight, sound, touch, smell, and taste, or to internal feelings. Imagery creates word pictures that make a work vivid, clarify its meaning, and communicate its atmosphere by evoking in the reader emotional associations.

1. Find imagery that appeals to two different senses in "A Dancing Song."
2. In what sense might the darkness be described as "rattling"? (Note how this image appeals to two different senses.)
3. In "Firefly Song," why is "white light winking" an appropriate image to describe a firefly? Why would this be an unsuitable image to describe a dragonfly or bee?

COMPOSITION

Writing an Imaginative Description

Take a walk during which you find and observe an object: it may be moving, growing, or merely existing. Write a one-paragraph description for your journal in which you go beyond physical portrayal to make imaginative comparisons. For example, you might find an oddly shaped rock that resembles an animal, a squirrel with a tail like a conductor's baton, or a field of flowers that appear to be attending a convention.

Analyzing a Poem

Write a four-paragraph essay for your classmates in which you focus on how the similes and images from nature reveal the speaker's feelings for his horse in "The War God's Horse Song." Before you begin to write, list words and phrases from the poem that you wish to use in your essay. The first paragraph should include a thesis statement about the effects achieved by the use of imagery and simile. Devote the second and third paragraphs, respectively, to a discussion of the use of simile and imagery throughout the poem, citing specific examples. In the final paragraph, speculate on what the horse may have meant to the speaker, judging from the language he uses to describe it. See "The Writing Process" in the Writer's Handbook.

Three Fragments

Quechuan, Dakota, Ojibwa

QUECHUAN:　The water bug is drawing
　　　　　　　the shadows of the evening
　　　　　　　　　toward him on the water

DAKOTA:　　You cannot harm me
　　　　　　　you cannot harm
　　　　　　　　　one who has dreamed a dream like
　　　　　　　　　　mine

OJIBWA:　　The bush is sitting under a tree and
　　　　　　singing

THINK AND DISCUSS
Analyzing

1. How does the second fragment differ from the first and last?
2. What might have prompted the speech of the second fragment?
3. The water bug and the bush seem to be doing impossible things in fragments one and three. What are these things?

Comment

Oral Literature

Literature has been transmitted and preserved orally in many cultures. For example, English folk ballads were passed through generations from singer to singer. Perhaps the most famous examples of oral literature are the Greek epics, the *Iliad* and the *Odyssey*, finally written down by Homer some time between the twelfth and the ninth centuries B.C.

Although early Native Americans had no written language, they had a strong belief in the sacredness of words. One scholar, William Brandon, has written, "Life [for the Indians] was a mystical adventure, and making up songs and singing them its most important business. Much of this was a wholly religious activity, in which poetry . . . transformed the soul to an awareness of the beauty and holiness of the 'permanent real.' " It was the spoken—or chanted—word that performed ritualistically and magically for them.

In the Native American oral tradition, the poems (or songs) were sung or chanted, often by a group. Words were few but carefully selected, and frequently repeated. No doubt these features facilitated memorization of the poetry, thus preserving it from one ritual to another.

From the time the white explorers and settlers arrived in the New World, Native American literature began to be recorded. Often in the early days, missionaries used European alphabets to copy down the sounds. More recently, Native American singers have been recorded on disk and tape. Effective translation requires not only a knowledge of Indian languages, but also a sensitivity attuned to poetic effects: in short, a sound scholar with the soul of a poet.

BIOGRAPHY

Dekanawidah

15th Century

Dekanawidah (de′kä nä wē′dä) is considered the founder of the Iroquois Confederation, ruling over the area that is now the state of New York. The Confederation, a union of fifty males who were selected by female clan leaders, met each fall. This union of Native Americans was most powerful during the 1600s and 1700s and came to comprise six nations. The Iroquois Constitution, like much Native American writing, includes concepts of personal and political conduct and recognizes the supremacy of a divine power.

See METAPHOR in the Handbook of Literary Terms, page 887.

from The Iroquois Constitution

Dekanawidah

 am Dekanawidah, and with the Five Nations confederate lords I plant the Tree of the Great Peace. . . . I name the tree the Tree of the Great Long Leaves. Under the shade of this Tree of the Great Peace we spread the soft white feather down of the globe thistle as seats for you, Atotarho and your cousin lords. There shall you sit and watch the council fire of the confederacy of the Five Nations. Roots have spread out from the Tree, and the name of these roots is the Great White Roots of Peace. If any man of any nation shall show a desire to obey the laws of the Great Peace, they shall trace the roots to their source, and they

William N. Fenton, ed., *Parker on the Iroquois*, Book III, 30–31, 49, 38–39, 32.

E. L. Henry, *Johnson Hall* (1903). Sir William Johnson (1715–1774) holding council with the Iroquois in the province of New York. Collection of Mr. John B. Knox

shall be welcomed to take shelter beneath the Tree of the Long Leaves. The smoke of the confederate council fire shall pierce the sky so that all nations may discover the central council fire of the Great Peace. I, Dekanawidah, and the confederate lords now uproot the tallest pine tree and into the cavity thereby made we cast all weapons of war. Into the depth of the earth, down into the deep underearth currents of water flowing into unknown regions; we cast all weapons of war. We bury them from sight forever and plant again the Tree.

We do now crown you with the sacred emblem of the antlers, the sign of your lordship. You shall now become a mentor of the people of the Five Nations. The thickness of your skin will be seven spans, for you will be proof against anger, offensive action, and criticism. With endless patience you shall carry out your duty, and your firmness shall be tempered with compassion for your people. Neither anger nor fear shall find lodgment in your mind, and all your words and actions shall be tempered with calm deliberation. In all your official acts, self-interest shall be cast aside. You shall look and listen to the welfare of the whole people, and have always in view, not only the present but the coming generations—the unborn of the future Nation.

The Onondaga lords shall open each council by expressing their gratitude to their cousin lords, and greeting them, and they shall make an address and offer thanks to the earth where men dwell, to the streams of water, the pools, the springs, the lakes, to the maize and the fruits, to the medicinal herbs and the trees, to the forest trees for their usefulness, to the animals that serve as food and who offer their pelts as clothing, to the great winds and the lesser winds, to the Thunderers, and the Sun, the mighty warrior, to the moon, to the messengers of the Great Spirit who dwells in the skies above, who gives all things useful to men, who is the source and the ruler of health and life.

Then shall the Onondaga lords declare the council open.

1570

THINK AND DISCUSS
Understanding
1. What personal qualities does Dekanawidah stress as important for the new rulers?
2. What kinds of greetings should make up an opening ceremony (20a, 2)?

Analyzing
3. What ideas regarding personal conduct and belief in a supreme being are reflected in the speech?

Extending
4. Do you think the personal qualities of leaders stressed by Dekanawidah might be relevant for world leaders today? Why or why not?

APPLYING: Metaphor H2
See Handbook of Literary Terms, p. 887.

A **metaphor** is a figure of speech (language used in a nonliteral way) involving a comparison between two basically unlike things. Unlike a simile, a metaphor uses no connective such as *like* or *as*. "Love is unpredictable" is a literal statement. "Love is a roller coaster" restates the same idea as a metaphor. Although fundamentally different, love and a roller coaster can both have abrupt turns and unexpected twists. Like all figurative language, metaphors force associations that help us see things in a new light.

1. To what does Dekanawidah compare the Iroquois Constitution? What are some of the labels used in the first paragraph to develop this comparison?
2. Why is the tree metaphor appropriate?

Reading A HISTORICAL NARRATIVE

Historical narratives are nonfiction prose accounts about real people, places, and events. The historical narratives in this unit were written by the explorers, adventurers, and settlers who came to America at its beginning. They often kept diaries or journals to record their encounters and struggles in a wilderness that was variously frightening, spectacular, mystifying, and formidable. When they found time later, these early Americans used their private records as a basis for historical accounts that were shared with an eager European audience. As you read the historical narratives in this unit, you will glimpse the way America was seen by these early Americans—people who lived out their lives of loneliness or camaraderie, longing or fulfillment, as they cleared the path for future Americans. In order to gain full benefit from reading these narratives, keep in mind the following guidelines.

Determine the purpose of each work. Is it mainly to entertain, to persuade, to explain, or merely to describe? Note that although a humorous tone serves Sarah Kemble Knight well in her entertaining account, such a tone would be inappropriate in Columbus's description. Word choice is likewise colored by the author's purpose. Words repeated in John Smith's promotional piece—*pleasure, pretty, pleasing*—would be out of place in a narrative such as William Bradford's. Instead, Bradford uses words such as *bitterly, desperate, dangerous, furious,* and *dreadful* to explain the grim workings of providence.

Consult the biographies to determine the various backgrounds of writers. In doing so, you will be better able to understand the vantage point, motives, and cultural orientation of these writers. For example, a reader should be able to distinguish between the motives of Robert de La Salle, who was laying claim to American territory for France, and those of Bradford, whose goal was to find religious freedom.

Use the graphic aids provided. Consult the map on page 27 to determine the routes these explorers and adventurers took and the regions where they settled. The time line (pages xx–1) will serve to put these works and writers into the context of the period in which they lived.

Try to distinguish fact from opinion in these works. Each writer brings certain beliefs and preconceptions to his or her work. For example, Bradford regards the hair-raising incidents encountered on the *Mayflower* as evidence of God's justice, rather than as purely natural disasters. When Columbus observes the "timidity" of the native inhabitants or notes that they lacked "courage to make much use" of weapons, he is judging a people whom he considers outside the structures of so-called civilized society.

Understand that these narratives lay the groundwork for later American literature. There are certain basic ingredients common to every good story that appear in these early works. The elements of conflict, surprise, suspense, climax, and resolution that characterize later fiction appear in these historical narratives. Although the characters have not been fleshed out, many of these narratives contain the kernels of a plot that could be developed into a compelling modern short story or novel.

Look for parallels to modern life. Recognize that the writers of these narratives were flesh-and-blood people who provide insights into our lives. Although products of a unique and rather far removed era, these writers had hopes and defeats, dreams and despair, similar to ours. We read these works today because the writers were shrewd, keen-eyed observers of the passing human scene. They teach us how to endure, how to conquer, how to adjust, and, occasionally, how to laugh. Whatever we can learn from them may help us operate more effectively in the twentieth century.

Comment

Benjamin Franklin on the Iroquois Constitution

Thomas Jefferson is said to have studied the Constitution of the Iroquois when it came time to frame the United States Constitution. Earlier, in 1754, when Benjamin Franklin was pleading the cause of political union of the American colonies at Albany, New York, Franklin referred to the Iroquois Confederation. Note his ironic labeling of the Iroquois as "ignorant savages."

"It would be a strange thing if Six Nations of ignorant savages should be capable of form-ing a scheme for such a union, and be able to execute it in such a manner as that it has sub-sisted for ages and appears indissoluble; and yet that a like union should be impracticable for ten or a dozen English colonies, to whom it is more necessary and must be more advantageous, and who cannot be supposed to want an equal understanding of their interests."

Albert Henry Smyth, ed., *The Writings of Benjamin Franklin*. Vol. IV, 182.

Charles Willson Peale (1741–1827), detail of his portrait of Benjamin Franklin. Historical Society of Pennsylvania

BIOGRAPHY

Alvar Núñez Cabeza de Vaca
1490–1560

Frederic Remington, *Cabeza de Vaca in the Desert* (1905). De Vaca is the middle figure.

In 1527 Cabeza de Vaca (kä bā′thä de vä′kä) shipped as treasurer on an expedition from Spain to the New World, reaching Florida in 1528. Because of a series of misfortunes, the expedition was dissolved and de Vaca was among those later shipwrecked on an island off the Texas coast. The group was taken captive by Indians, but de Vaca escaped. With Esteban (es te′bän), a Moor, as companion, he wandered for some eight years over a large section of the Southwest before reaching northwest Mexico. He published his account, entitled *The Shipwrecked Men*, in 1542, describing his startling adventures in a part of the New World then unknown and mysterious to Europeans. The following excerpt is from this account.

After returning from Mexico to Spain, de Vaca was appointed governor of Paraguay. In 1540, he led another epic journey through the Amazonian jungles to Paraguay, but the Paraguayan colonists revolted and de Vaca was shipped back to Spain in chains. He was tried and exiled to Africa, but was later pardoned and lived out his retirement in Spain, writing accounts of his various journeys.

Cabeza de Vaca's family acquired its name in an interesting manner. During a battle in the thirteenth century, an ancestor named Alhaja helped the Spanish forces by marking a crucial mountain pass with the head of a cow. In gratitude, the king ennobled the family, and they changed their name to Cabeza de Vaca (head of a cow).

from The Narrative of His Journey

Alvar Núñez Cabeza de Vaca

The Indians bring us food.

At sunrise the next day, the time the Indians appointed, they came according to their promise, and brought us a large quantity of fish with certain roots, some a little larger than walnuts, others a trifle smaller, the greater part got from under the water and with much labor. In the evening they returned and brought us more fish and roots. They sent their women and children to look at us, who went back rich with the hawkbells and beads given them, and they came afterwards on other days, return-

Frederick W. Hodge, ed., "The Narrative of Alvar Núñez Cabeza de Vaca," *Spanish Explorers in the Southern United States 1528–1543*. New York: Charles Scribner's Sons, 1907, pp. 45–48, 52–54.

ing as before. Finding that we had provision, fish, roots, water, and other things we asked for, we determined to embark again and pursue our course. Having dug out our boat from the sand in which it was buried, it became necessary that we should strip, and go through great exertion to launch her, we being in such a state that things very much lighter sufficed to make us great labor.

Thus embarked, at the distance of two cross-bow shots in the sea we shipped a wave that entirely wet us. As we were naked, and the cold was very great, the oars loosened in our hands, and the next blow the sea struck us, capsized the boat. The assessor[1] and two others held fast to her for preservation, but it happened to be far otherwise; the boat carried them over, and they were drowned under her. As the surf near the shore was very high, a single roll of the sea threw the rest into the waves and half-drowned upon the shore of the island, without our losing any more than those the boat took down. The survivors escaped naked as they were born, with the loss of all they had; and although the whole was of little value, at that time it was worth much, as we were then in November, the cold was severe, and our bodies were so emaciated the bones might be counted with little difficulty, having become the perfect figures of death. For myself I can say that from the month of May past, I had eaten no other thing than maize, and sometimes I found myself obliged to eat it unparched; for although the beasts[2] were slaughtered while the boats were building, I could never eat their flesh, and I did not eat fish ten times. I state this to avoid giving excuses, and that everyone may judge in what condition we were. Besides all these misfortunes, came a north wind upon us, from which we were nearer to death than life. Thanks be to our Lord that, looking among the brands we had used there, we found sparks from which we made great fires. And thus were we asking mercy of Him and pardon for our transgressions, shedding many tears and each regretting not his own fate alone, but that of his comrades about him.

At sunset, the Indians thinking that we had not gone, came to seek us and bring us food; but when they saw us thus, in a plight so different from what it was before, and so extraordinary, they were alarmed and turned back. I went toward them and called, when they returned much frightened. I gave them to understand by signs that our boat had sunk and three of our number had been drowned. There, before them, they saw two of the departed, and we who remained were near joining them. The Indians, at sight of what had befallen us, and our state of suffering and melancholy destitution, sat down among us, and from the sorrow and pity they felt, they all began to lament so earnestly that they might have been heard at a distance, and continued so doing more than half an hour. It was strange to see these men, wild and untaught, howling like brutes over our misfortunes. It caused in me as in others, an increase of feeling and a livelier sense of our calamity.

The cries having ceased, I talked with the Christians,[3] and said that if it appeared well to them, I would beg these Indians to take us to their houses. Some, who had been in New Spain,[4] replied that we ought not to think of it; for if they should do so, they would sacrifice us to their idols. But seeing no better course, and that any other led to a nearer and more certain death, I disregarded what was said, and besought the Indians to take us to their dwellings. They signified that it would give them delight, and that we should tarry a little, that they might do what we asked. Presently thirty men loaded themselves with wood and started for their houses, which were far-off, and we remained with the others until near night, when, holding us up, they carried us with all haste. Because of the extreme coldness of the weather, lest any one should die or fail by the way, they caused four or five very large fires to be placed at intervals, and at each they warmed us; and when they saw that we had

---

1. *assessor,* the expedition's legal advisor.
2. *beasts,* horses.
3. *Christians,* other Spaniards stranded on the island.
4. *New Spain,* Spanish name for colonial Mexico.

regained some heat and strength, they took us to the next so swiftly that they hardly let us touch our feet to the ground. In this manner we went as far as their habitations, where we found that they had made a house for us with many fires in it. An hour after our arrival, they began to dance and hold great rejoicing, which lasted all night, although for us there was no joy, festivity nor sleep, awaiting the hour they should make us victims. In the morning they again gave us fish and roots, showing us such hospitality that we were reassured, and lost somewhat the fear of sacrifice.

What befell us among the people of Malhado.[5]

On an island of which I have spoken, they wished to make us physicians without examination or inquiring for diplomas. They cure by blowing upon the sick, and with that breath and the imposing of hands they cast out infirmity. They ordered that we also should do this, and be of use to them in some way. We laughed at what they did, telling them it was folly, that we knew not how to heal. In consequence, they withheld food from us until we should practice what they required. Seeing our persistence, an Indian told me I knew not what I uttered, in saying that what he knew availed nothing; for stones and other matters growing about in the fields have virtue, and that passing a pebble along the stomach would take away pain and restore health, and certainly then we who were extraordinary men must possess power and efficacy over all other things. At last, finding ourselves in great want we were constrained to obey; but without fear lest we should be blamed for any failure or success.

Their custom is, on finding themselves sick to send for a physician, and after he has applied the cure, they give him not only all they have, but seek among their relatives for more to give. The practitioner scarifies over the seat of pain, and then sucks about the wound. They make cauteries with fire, a remedy among them in high repute, which I have tried on myself and found benefit from it. They afterwards blow on the spot, and having finished, the patient considers that he is relieved.

Our method was to bless the sick, breathing upon them, and recite a Pater-noster and an Ave-Maria,[6] praying with all earnestness to God our Lord that He would give health and influence them to make us some good return. In His clemency He willed that all those for whom we supplicated, should tell the others that they were sound and in health, directly after we made the sign of the blessed cross over them. For this the Indians treated us kindly; they deprived themselves of food that they might give to us, and presented us with skins and some trifles.

So protracted was the hunger we there experienced, that many times I was three days without eating. The natives also endured as much; and it appeared to me a thing impossible that life could be so prolonged, although afterwards I found myself in greater hunger and necessity. . . .

1542   1907

---

5. *Malhado* (mäl häd′ô), Bad Luck Island. [*Spanish*]
6. *Pater-noster* (pä′ter näs′ter) . . . *Ave-Maria* (ä′vä mə rē′ə), the Lord's Prayer and the Hail Mary. [*Latin*]

THINK AND DISCUSS
Understanding
1. What happens to the members of Cabeza de Vaca's expedition who cling to the capsized boat for safety?

2. How do the native inhabitants treat the surviving members of the expedition?

3. What is the general condition of the Spanish explorers? Describe some of their greatest difficulties once they reach America.

4. How do the Indians customarily treat their sick?

5. What do Cabeza de Vaca and his companions do to heal the sick?

Analyzing

6. Cabeza de Vaca observes various aspects of the lives of the Indians. What aspects does he describe and what seems to govern his selection?

7. What does Cabeza de Vaca's account reveal about his personality and the qualities that enable him to survive?

Extending

8. On the basis of his narrative, what might readers of the sixteenth century have concluded about the life and character of the native inhabitants in the New World?

COMPOSITION

Describing a Character

From your understanding of Cabeza de Vaca's character after reading this selection, write a three-paragraph sketch of him for your classmates in which you describe three prominent traits. Decide whether he is timid or brave, skeptical or religious, passive or active, and withdrawn or outgoing.

Putting Yourself in the Narrative

At times in Cabeza de Vaca's narrative, the behavior of the Indians surprises the members of his expedition—for example, when they begin their loud lament at the misfortunes of the Spaniards, or when they hold an all-night celebration after the rescue and retreat to warm shelter. Assume you are a member of the de Vaca expedition and are writing a letter of three paragraphs to a friend back in Spain. Relate one of these incidents and describe your feelings as the Indians surprise you by their behavior.

Comment

Offer of Help by Canassatego

At treaty talks in 1744, the Iroquois leader Canassatego (kä′näs sä tä′gō) made the following reply to an offer from the Virginia government to educate some Iroquois youths at the College of William and Mary. Note Canassatego's tone, or attitude toward his audience.

"We know you highly esteem the kind of Learning taught in these Colleges, and the maintenance of our young Men, while with you, would be very expensive to you. We are convinced, therefore, that you mean to do us Good by your Proposal; and we thank you heartily. But you who are so wise must know that different Nations have different Conceptions of things; and you will not therefore take it amiss, if our Ideas of this kind of Education happens not to be the same with yours. We have had some experience of it. Several of our young People were formerly brought up in the Colleges of the Northern Provinces;[1] they were instructed in all your Sciences; but, when they came back to us, they were bad Runners, ignorant of every means of living in the Woods, unable to bear either Cold or Hunger, knew neither how to build a Cabin, take a deer, or kill an enemy, spoke our language imperfectly, were therefore neither fit for Hunters, Warriors, nor Counsellors, they were totally good for nothing. We are however not the less obliged for your kind Offer, tho' we decline accepting it; and to show our grateful Sense of it, if the Gentlemen of Virginia shall send us a Dozen of their Sons, we will take great care of their Education, instruct them in all we know, and make Men of them."

---

1. *Northern Provinces*, New Hampshire and Massachusetts, which were ruled by officers appointed by the King.

Albert Henry Smyth, ed., *The Writings of Benjamin Franklin*, Vol. X, 98–99.

BIOGRAPHY

Robert de La Salle

1643–1687

George P. A. Healy (1813–1894), detail of *Cavalier Sieur de La Salle.* Chicago Historical Society

Eager when a child to follow the religious life of a Jesuit, La Salle was eventually lured from France by the promise of adventure and discovery in the New World. He began his explorations in Canada, and ultimately fulfilled his ambition of following the Mississippi River all the way through the great center of the unexplored continent to the Gulf of Mexico. Reaching the mouth of the Mississippi in April, 1682, he claimed the entire area for France, calling it Louisiana after King Louis XIV. Ultimately, La Salle was empowered to govern Louisiana, from Lake Michigan to the Gulf of Mexico.

His last voyage to the mouth of the Mississippi was doomed when some ships were captured by the Spanish and others were lost through shipwreck. After landing in Texas, La Salle and his men attempted to reach their goal overland. But his men turned mutinous and murdered him in 1687.

It is believed that *Relation of the Discoveries and Voyages . . .* was pieced together and adapted from La Salle's letters. In the excerpt presented here, La Salle, who is exploring the Illinois River, recognizes his dependence upon the help of the Indians along the way. Compare the route of La Salle with those of Columbus and de Vaca (see map below) who preceded him by nearly two centuries.

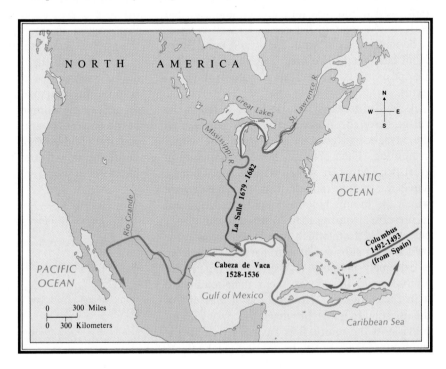

Making Peace with the Illinois Indians

Robert de La Salle

Throughout the rest of December, M.[1] de La Salle continued his journey along the Illinois River; and finally, after having traveled one hundred and twenty or one hundred and thirty leagues from Lake Illinois, and killed along the river two bullocks and a large number of turkeys, he reached the Illinois village on the first of January, 1680. This village is situated in forty degrees of latitude, on a somewhat marshy plain, upon the right bank of the river, which is at this point as wide as the Seine[2] at Paris, and is diversified by some very fine islands. The village contains four hundred and sixty lodges, built like long arbors, and thatched with double mats of flat reeds, so well sewn as to be impervious to wind, snow, and rain. Every cabin has four or five fires, and about every fire are one or two families, living all together on good terms.

As he had foreseen, M. de La Salle found the village deserted. According to their custom, all the Savages had gone away to spend the winter in hunting. Their absence, however, put him in great perplexity. He was in want of food, but he dared not supply himself from the Indian corn which the Illinois hide in trenches underground to preserve it during their absence in the chase, on returning from which they make use of it for seed and for subsistence until harvest. This store is extremely precious to them, and no greater offense could be offered them than to disturb it in their absence. However, as it was out of the question to go farther down the river without provisions, the prairie fires having driven all the game out of the country, he decided to take thirty

minots[3] of Indian corn, hoping that he might find some means of satisfying the Illinois.

With this new supply, he reembarked on the same day, and for four days descended the river, which runs south by west. Toward the close of the fourth day, while traversing a small lake formed by the river, they noticed wreaths of smoke, which told them that the Savages were encamped near by. On the fifth, about nine o'clock in the morning, a number of pirogues[4] were seen on both sides of the river, and about eighty lodges swarming with Illinois, who did not catch sight of the canoes until they had doubled a point behind which was the encampment, at a distance of half a gunshot. The French were in light canoes, in single file, all armed, and letting themselves float with the stream.

According to the custom of these nations, M. de La Salle caused the first cry to be raised, as if to inquire whether it should be peace or war, for it is of great importance to exhibit resolution at the outset. Instantly the old men, the women, and the children took flight through the woods bordering the stream; the warriors flew to arms, but with so much confusion that the canoes had

---

1. M., French *Monsieur*, roughly equivalent to English *Mr.*
2. Seine (sān), river flowing from eastern France into the English Channel.
3. minot (mī'nət), an old French measure of 39 liters or 8 3/4 gallons.
4. pirogue (pə rōg'), boat made of a single great tree trunk, hollowed out, and capable of carrying forty or fifty people.

Melville B. Anderson, translator, *Relation of the Discoveries and Voyages of Cavalier de La Salle from 1679 to 1681, the Official Narrative.* Chicago: The Caxton Club, 1901, pp. 85–89.

George Catlin, detail of *La Salle Claiming Louisiana for France, April 9, 1682.* (1847–8). National Gallery of Art, Washington

touched the bank before they were aware. M. de La Salle was the first to leap ashore, and he might have defeated the Savages in the disorder in which they were; but this not being his aim, he halted his men in order to restore confidence to the Illinois. One of their chiefs, who was on the other side of the river, and had noticed that M. de La Salle had refrained from firing upon seven or eight Savages, who might easily have been killed, began a harangue to check the young men, who were about to shoot arrows across the river. Those encamped on the side on which the French had disembarked, recovering from their first consternation, sent two of their chiefs to display the calumet[5] of peace from the top of a hill; soon those on the other side did the same, and then M. de La Salle gave them to understand that he accepted peace. Their joy was as great as their fear had been strong—that of some having been such that they were three days in returning from their hiding places.

After the rejoicings, the dancing, and the feasting in which the rest of the day was spent, M. de La Salle called together the chiefs of the villages from both sides of the river. First making them a present of tobacco and some hatchets, he began by saying that he had convoked them for the consideration of a matter which he wished to explain before speaking of anything further. He was aware, he said, how essential to them was their reserve of corn; nevertheless, he continued, his need of food upon his arrival at their village, and the lack of game in the land, had compelled him to take a certain amount of Indian corn, which was now in the canoes and still untouched. If they would let him have it, he would give them in exchange the hatchets and other things they had need of; if, on the other hand, they could not dispense with it, they were free to take it back; but if they were unable to provide him with the provisions necessary for the subsistence of himself and his men, he would go to their neighbors, the Osages, of whom he could buy food, in return for which he would leave with them the blacksmith whom he had brought, who would repair their hatchets and other tools.

M. de La Salle addressed the Illinois in this manner, because he knew they would not fail to be jealous of the advantages which the French might bring to their neighbors, especially the advantage of having a blacksmith, of whose services they stood themselves in extreme need. They therefore accepted with many signs of gladness the payment offered for the Indian corn; they gave him still more, and entreated him to establish himself among them. He answered that he would willingly do this, but that, as the Iroquois were subjects of the King,[6] and consequently his brethren, he could not wage war against them. He therefore exhorted the Illinois to make peace with the Iroquois, to which end he would use his influence; and promised that if, despite his remonstrances, that proud nation should attack them, he would defend them, provided they would permit him to build a fort where he could stand out against the Iroquois with the few Frenchmen he had; and that he would even furnish the Illinois with arms and munitions, provided they would not use these against the nations living under the protection of the King.

He added that it was his purpose to bring other Frenchmen, who would secure them from the insults of their enemies, and would furnish them with everything they required; that the only impediment was the length and difficulty of the road; that, in order to overcome this obstacle, he purposed to build a great canoe to sail down to the sea, so as to bring them all sorts of goods by this shorter and easier route. This undertaking being, however, an expensive one, he desired first to be informed whether indeed their river was navigable to the sea, and whether there were other Europeans living near its mouth.

They replied that they accepted all his proposals, and would aid him so far as in them lay.

---

5. *calumet* (kal′yə met), a long-stemmed tobacco pipe smoked as a token of peace.
6. *Iroquois . . . King.* This is probably a reference to the Mohawks, who were once part of the Iroquois Confederacy. After they were converted by French missionaries, they withdrew from the Confederacy in 1670 and took the part of the French against their former confederates.

Then they made a description of the great River Colbert, or Mississippi, telling him wonders of its breadth and beauty, assuring him that it was everywhere open and easy of navigation, and that no Europeans were settled near its mouth. But what more than all else convinced M. de La Salle that this river is navigable was their mention of four nations referred to in the *Relation of the Journey in Florida of Ferdinando de Soto*[7]—namely, the Tula, the Casquia, the Chickasaw, and the Aminoia[8] nations. They added that slaves from the country near the seacoast, whom they had taken in war, had told them of seeing ships which fired volleys resembling thunder; but that these ships had effected no settlement on the coast, for had this been done they themselves would not have failed to go thither to trade, the sea being at a distance of but twenty days' journey in their pirogues.

1680   1879

---

7. *Ferdinando de Soto*, Spanish explorer (1500?–1542), who landed in Florida, pushed westward, and discovered the Mississippi River (1541), encountering the Indian tribes listed by La Salle.
8. *Tula* (tü′lə), *Casquia* (kä skē′ə), *Chickasaw* (chik′ə sô), *Aminoia* (ä mē noi′yə).

THINK AND DISCUSS

Understanding

1. Why does La Salle hesitate to take the corn he needs for his party when he comes upon it in the seemingly abandoned Illinois village?
2. How does La Salle avoid conflict on encountering the Indians?

Analyzing

3. How does La Salle persuade the Illinois Indians to let him have the corn?
4. How does La Salle win over the Indians, inspiring them to tell what they know about the Mississippi River and the people he will encounter on navigating it to its mouth?

Extending

5. If La Salle were alive today, what do you think he would be doing for a living?

COMPOSITION ◄━●

Defending Your Position

Assume that you are a Native American listening to La Salle's offer to trade certain things in exchange for the corn he has already taken from the Illinois village. You form a group to hear him out and then withdraw to decide what to do. Make a list of all the arguments for agreeing with and another list of all the arguments for disagreeing with La Salle. After studying the pros and cons, make up your mind and write a two- or three-paragraph defense of your vote.

Writing a Diary Account

Assume you are a member of La Salle's party. On your first encounter with the Indians, you raise your rifle, but on La Salle's order, you refrain from firing. Write a journal account of three or more paragraphs describing your feelings at the time and at the subsequent events you witness. Describe your attitude toward your leader throughout this episode.

Comment

La Salle II

On August 11, 1976, nearly 300 years after La Salle's historic trip through the Great Lakes and down the Mississippi River to the Gulf of Mexico, a group of students from Larkin High School in Elgin, Illinois, set out to trace the explorer's route. The trip, which took nearly 8 months, involved 2 years of planning and preparation. Students constructed canoes and seventeenth-century gear, including utensils, tools, bone buttons, hand-stitched moccasins, muskets, and wool garments. To prepare for the physical demands of the trip, students underwent rigorous workouts on the school's football field.

The group of 23 voyagers included 16 students, Reid Lewis, the Larkin French teacher who organized the trip, and 6 other adults. Like their predecessors, those on the La Salle II trip experienced fatigue, ice-clogged rivers, and bad weather (the winter of 1976 was one of the most severe on record). The group ate fare such as peas, oatmeal mush, and fried bread—all cooked over fires started with flint and steel. Even in subzero weather, they slept in sleeping bags under their canoes. Ice forced the group to portage 525 miles overland to Chester, Illinois; and in Gary, Indiana, bad weather caused them to continue on foot, sending their canoes ahead.

On April 3 the expedition reached its destination, New Orleans. The trip offers proof that the spirit of adventure and the ability to survive that characterized the early settlers still motivate people in the final decades of the twentieth century.

Route of La Salle II Expedition

1. August 11, 1976: Expedition leaves the Montreal suburb of La Salle.

2. September 9–21: Voyagers portage 36 miles from Toronto to Holland River, Ontario.

3. October 21: Expedition enters Lake Michigan.

4. November 4: A canoe carrying 4 voyagers overturns near Washington Island, Wisconsin.

5. December 19: Because of bad weather, expedition continues on foot, sending canoes ahead.

6. January 12, 1977: Four crew members are injured by a truck near Hebron, Indiana.

7. February 14: Expedition returns to water near Chester, Illinois.

8. April 3: Voyagers reach the Gulf of Mexico.

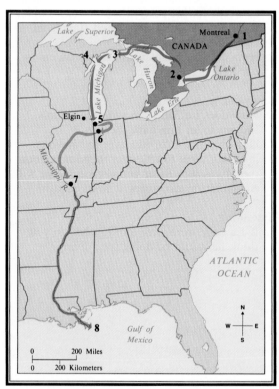

Captain John Smith was a soldier of fortune who had adventures in Europe and Africa before sailing to the New World to establish the first British colony in America, Jamestown. Because of a difficult and hazardous voyage, only 105 of the original party of 143 landed at Jamestown, Virginia, in 1607. Captain Smith was held prisoner by Indians for a time and, according to legend, was sentenced to death and rescued by Pocahontas, daughter of Chief Powhatan (pou'ə tan').

Captain Smith remained in America until 1609, serving as president of the council of Jamestown. During his administration, the settlement began to recover from disease and starvation, strengthened their defenses, and planted crops. In 1608 he wrote *A True Relation*, the first English book written in America. But the book that sparked the most intense interest in the New Land was his *Description of New England* (1616). Quite promotional in nature, it lured colonists to America in search of the good life that had eluded them in the old country. The following excerpt, titled "The New Land," is taken from this work. In 1609, suffering from a severe gunpowder wound, he returned to England, where he continued to promote Virginia until his death in 1631.

The New Land

John Smith

Who can desire more content, that hath small means, or but only his merit to advance his fortunes, than to tread and plant that ground he hath purchased by the hazard of his life? If he have but the taste of virtue and magnanimity, what to such a mind can be more pleasant, than planting and building a foundation for his Posterity, got from the rude earth, by God's blessing and his own industry without prejudice to any? If he have any grain of faith or zeal in Religion, what can he do less hurtful to any, or more agreeable to God, than to seek to convert those poor Savages to know Christ, and humanity, whose labors with discretion will triple requite thy charge and pains? What so truly suits with honor and honesty, as the discovering things unknown, erecting Towns, peopling Countries, informing the ignorant, reforming things unjust, teaching virtue and gain to our native Mother-Country, a kingdom to attend her; find employment for those that are idle because they know not what to do: so far from wronging any, as to

From *A Description of New England* (1616) in Captain John Smith's *Works, 1608–1613*, edited by Edward Arber, Birmingham: The English Scholar's Library, No. 16, 1884.

Prosperous new land. Rare Book Division. The New York Public Library, Astor, Lenox and Tilden Foundations

cause Posterity to remember thee; and remembering thee, ever honor that remembrance with praise? . . .

Here nature and liberty afford us that freely, which in England we want, or it costeth us dearly. What pleasure can be more, than (being tired with any occasion ashore, in planting Vines, Fruits, or Herbs, in contriving their own grounds to the pleasure of their own minds, their Fields, Gardens, Orchards, Buildings, Ships, and other works, etc.) to recreate themselves before their own doors in their own boats upon the Sea; where man, woman and child, with a small hook and line, by angling, may take divers sorts of excellent fish, at their pleasures? And is it not pretty sport, to pull up two pence, six pence, and twelve pence,[1] as fast as you can haul and veer a line? He is a very bad Fisher [that] cannot kill in one day with his hook and line, one, two, or three hundred Cods: which dressed and dried, if they be sold there for ten shillings a hundred, though in England they will give more than twenty, may not both the servant, the master, and merchant, be well content with his gain? If a man work but three days in seven, he may get more than he can spend unless he will be excessive.[2] Now that Carpenter, Mason, Gardener, Tailor, Smith, Sailor, Forgers, or what other, may they not make this a pretty recreation though they fish but an hour in a day, to take more than they can eat in a week? Or if they will not eat it, because there is so much better choice, yet sell it, or change it, with the fishermen or merchants for anything they want. And what sport doth yield a more pleasing content, and less hurt and charge than angling with a hook; and crossing the sweet air from Isle to Isle, over the silent streams of a calm Sea? Wherein the most curious may find pleasure, profit, and content.

Thus, though all men be not fishers, yet all men, whatsoever, may in other matters do as well. For necessity doth in these cases so rule a Commonwealth, and each in their several functions, as their labors in their qualities may be as profitable, because there is a necessary mutual use of all.

For Gentlemen, what exercise should more delight them, than ranging daily these unknown parts, using fowling and fishing, for hunting and hawking?[3] And yet you shall see the wild hawks give you some pleasure, in seeing them stoop[4] (six or seven times after one another) an hour or two together, at the schools of fish in the fair harbors, as those ashore at a fowl; and never trouble nor torment yourselves, with watching, mewing,[5] feeding and attending them; nor kill horse and man with running and crying, "See you not a hawk?" For hunting also, the woods, lakes and rivers afford not only chase sufficient, for any that delights in that kind of toil or pleasure; but such beasts to hunt, that besides the delicacy of their bodies for food, their skins are so rich, as

they will recompense thy daily labor with a Captain's pay.

For laborers, if those that sow hemp, rape, turnips, parsnips, carrots, cabbage, and such like, give twenty, thirty, forty, fifty shillings yearly for an acre of ground, and meat, drink, and wages to use it, and yet grow rich; when better, or at least as good ground may be had and cost nothing but labor; it seems strange to me, any such should there grow poor.

My purpose is not to persuade children from their parents; men from their wives; nor servants from their masters; only such as with free consent may be spared: But that each parish, or village, in City, or Country, that will but apparel their fatherless children of thirteen or fourteen years of age, or young married people that have small wealth to live on, here by their labor may live exceeding well: provided always, that first there be a sufficient power to command them, houses to receive them, means to defend them, and meet provisions necessary for them; for any place may be over-lain[6] and it is most necessary to have a fortress (ere this grow to practice[7]) and sufficient masters, (as, Carpenters, Masons, Fishers, Fowlers, Gardeners, Husbandmen, Sawyers, Smiths, Spinsters,[8] Tailors, Weavers, and such like) to take ten, twelve, or twenty, or as there is occasion, for Apprentices. The Masters by this may quickly grow rich; these may learn their trades themselves, to do the like, to a general and an incredible benefit, for King and Country, Master and Servant.

1616

---

1. *pence* (pens), pennies, the basic coins of the old British currency.
2. *excessive* (ek ses′iv), wasteful.
3. *using fowling . . . hawking.* Smith suggests hunting wild fowl and fishing can substitute for the English gentlemen's usual sports of hunting game and catching birds with trained hawks.
4. *stoop,* swoop of a hawk toward its prey.
5. *mewing,* putting hawks in cages when they are shedding their feathers.
6. *over-lain,* probably "beseiged."
7. *ere . . . practice,* before an attack occurs.
8. *Spinsters,* spinners of wool.

THINK AND DISCUSS
Understanding
1. According to Smith, how easy and profitable is fishing in the New World?
2. What appeal does Smith make to hunters?
3. According to Smith, what awaits a farmer in America?
4. Smith says in the final paragraph that he does not want to persuade certain people to come but does want to persuade others. What kinds of people is he trying to attract?

Analyzing
5. In the first paragraph, Smith asks a series of questions that he knows will stimulate interest in coming to America. What are the particular desires to which Smith appeals?
6. How does Smith make fishing in America seem so attractive, aside from its ease and profitability?
7. What appears to be Smith's purpose in listing eleven specific crafts of skills in the last paragraph?

Extending
8. What is the overall picture of America that Smith presents? How does it differ from an overall description of America today?
9. Imagine that John Smith were living at the end of the twentieth century. Where would he live? What would be his hobbies? What kind of job would he have?

THINKING SKILLS
Classifying
To classify is to arrange similar ideas or things into groups or categories, according to some system. For example, language can be classified as literal or figurative, and figurative language can be further classified into simile, metaphor, personification, and so on.

1. Smith promotes America as a land of abundant food and a place full of employment and recreational opportunities. Write the following heads in columns: *Sport, Vegetables, Employment.* Then list under these heads as many things as possible that Smith mentions in his account.
2. In the second paragraph, Smith mentions "Vines, Fruits, or Herbs . . . Fields, Gardens, Orchards, Buildings, Ships." Think of three heads under which to classify these items and write at least two items under each head.

COMPOSITION ◄━◼
Writing an Advertisement
Imagine that you are a colonial travel agent who is trying to encourage people to come to Jamestown, just as John Smith did. Using comments from the selection, write an advertisement of at least two paragraphs in your own words that persuades others to join you in the New Land. You may wish to begin your advertisement with a series of questions, as Smith does, or you may wish to use exaggeration. Use modern English in your ad. See "Writing to Persuade an Audience" in the Writer's Handbook.

Writing to Inform
Assume that a pen pal in another country has requested information about the United States and, specifically, about your city and state. Write a letter of explanation, devoting a paragraph each to subjects such as the following: fashions, food, schools, recreation, jobs for teenagers. In the final paragraph of your letter, make some general observations about contemporary life in your city.

Comment

The First Settlers

One historian observed about the early colonial period, "Few expeditions returned to their European backers any profit, many of them suffered disaster, virtually all of them encountered something repellent in the way of climate, soil, wild beasts, wild Indians, or hostile whites."[1] Nevertheless, European immigrants did settle in the New World and are responsible for the American existence that we have today. Two early British settlements—Jamestown, Virginia (1607), and Plymouth, Massachusetts (1620)—serve to illustrate what made early colonial existence so hazardous.

The first settlers who landed at Jamestown were financed by a group of London investors who wanted to increase their economic opportunities by developing settlements in the New World. Three ships carrying 143 men and boys left England in December 1606, in search of gold and a route to the Indies. Five months later, after a difficult voyage, the ships landed on the coast of Virginia, laying out a settlement they called Jamestown in honor of their king. The site that the settlers chose turned out to be a swampy peninsula full of polluted water and infested by malaria-carrying mosquitoes. Time that could have been better spent building shelters and planting crops was wasted looking for gold and for a nonexistent passage to Asia. In addition, most of the men that the London Company had sent to the New World were "gentlemen" who had come unprepared to work and were unsuited to life in the wilderness. The Indians, whom they had presumed would be a source of cheap labor, refused to work and retaliated against the European encroachment with raids. Plagued with sickness and unable to provide for themselves, only 38 of the original colonists survived the first winter. Between 1608 and 1609 about 500 new settlers joined the colony, but only 60 of them survived the winter of 1609 by subsisting on plants, nuts, and fish. Faced with extinction, the colonists decided to return to England. Only the timely arrival of a ship carrying supplies and more settlers caused them to stay. The Jamestown settlement continued to struggle to establish itself throughout the next decade.

In 1620, the Pilgrims, a group that opposed the rites of the Church of England and separated from the other Puritans, decided to establish a colony in the New World. Unlike their predecessors in Jamestown, these people sought religious freedom rather than profit. They had no money and had borrowed to pay their fares for the voyage. Their ship, the *Mayflower*, left England in September 1620, and arrived at Plymouth in November 1620. Fortunately, they chose a better location than the Jamestown settlers had, one with good water and land that had already been cleared by the Native Americans. Even so, of the 102 people who had landed, one-half did not live through the winter. In the spring, however, their chances of survival improved as their food supply increased.

More successful than the other two groups were the Puritans who arrived a thousand strong in 1630, settling in what is Boston today. Unlike the impoverished Pilgrims, the Puritans were a group of prosperous landowners, ministers, and merchants. They came in 17 good ships, loaded with food, clothing, and livestock—a dramatic contrast to the Pilgrims who had preceded them in the decrepit *Mayflower*. Like the Pilgrims, they sought religious freedom, but they also wished to create the perfect society, where church and state were one. Interpreting the Bible literally, they withstood hardships with an unwavering faith that every occurrence was the result of the will of God.

With the success of the Jamestown and Plymouth colonies, the development of the United States, as we know it today, was underway.

---

1. Howard Mumford Jones, *O Strange New World*. New York: The Viking Press, 1964, p. 69.

Born of a farmer and a tradesman's daughter, William Bradford began to educate himself at an early age, reading in several languages and becoming a serious student of the Bible while still in his teens. At eighteen, he and a Separatist group who broke away from the Church of England escaped to Leyden, Holland, to avoid religious persecution. After eleven years of exile, these Pilgrims set out on the *Mayflower* for America, landing on the New England coast at Plymouth in December, 1620. Finally they had reached a land where they could worship freely.

Bradford was elected governor of the Massachusetts colony—an office to which he was re-elected thirty times. His account of the colony, written in simple, unadorned language known as the Puritan Plain Style, was titled *The History of Plymouth Plantation*. This account supplied a valuable source of information to colonial historians. The work then disappeared for nearly a century, until it was rediscovered in London. Bradford's history, from which the following excerpt is taken, chronicles the life and fortunes of a people inspired by faith and armed with dauntless courage and resourcefulness in the face of countless obstacles.

from The History of Plymouth Plantation

William Bradford

Of Their Voyage, and How They Passed the Sea; and of Their Safe Arrival at Cape Cod

eptember 6. These troubles being blown over, and now all being compact together in one ship, they put to sea again with a prosperous wind, which continued divers days together, which was some encouragement unto them; yet according to the usual manner, many were afflicted with seasickness. And I may not omit here a special work of God's providence. There was a proud and very profane young man, one of the seamen, of a lusty, able body, which made him the more haughty; he would always be contemning the poor people in their sickness and cursing them daily with grievous execrations; and did not let to tell them that he hoped to help to cast half of them overboard before they came to their journey's end, and to make merry with what they had; and if he were by any gently reproved, he would curse and swear most bitterly. But it pleased God before they came half seas over, to smite this young man with a grievous disease, of which he died in a desperate manner, and so was himself the first that was thrown overboard. Thus his curses light on his own head, and it was an astonishment to all his fellows for they noted it to be the just hand of God upon him.

After they had enjoyed fair winds and weather for a season, they were encountered many times with cross winds and met with many fierce storms with which the ship was shroudly[1] shaken, and her upper works made very leaky; and one of the main beams in the midships was bowed and cracked, which put them in some fear that the ship could not be able to perform the voyage. So some of the chief of the company, perceiving the mariners to fear the sufficiency of the ship as appeared by their mutterings, they entered into serious consultation with the master and other officers of the ship, to consider in time of the danger, and rather to return than to cast themselves into a desperate and inevitable peril. And truly there was great distraction and difference of opinion amongst the mariners themselves; fain would they do what could be done for their wages' sake (being now near half the seas over) and on the other hand they were loath to hazard their lives too desperately. But in examination of all opinions, the master and others affirmed they knew the ship to be strong and firm underwater; and for the buckling of the main beam, there was a great iron screw the passengers brought out of Holland, which would raise the beam into his place; the which being done, the carpenter and master affirmed that with a post put under it, set firm in the lower deck and otherways bound, he would make it sufficient. And as for the decks and upper works, they would caulk them as well

---

1. ***shroudly,*** an old form of *shrewdly* that means "harshly."

From *Of Plymouth Plantation*, by William Bradford, edited by Samuel Eliot Morison. Copyright 1952 by Samuel Eliot Morison. Reprinted by permission of Alfred A. Knopf, Inc.

as they could, and though with the working of the ship they would not long keep staunch, yet there would otherwise be no great danger, if they did not overpress her with sails. So they committed themselves to the will of God and resolved to proceed.

In sundry of these storms the winds were so fierce and the seas so high, as they could not bear a knot of sail, but were forced to hull[2] for divers days together. And in one of them, as they thus lay at hull in a mighty storm, a lusty young man called John Howland,[3] coming upon some occasion above the gratings was, with a seele[4] of the ship, thrown into sea; but it pleased God that he caught hold of the topsail halyards which hung overboard and ran out at length. Yet he held his hold (though he was sundry fathoms under water) till he was hauled up by the same rope to the brim of the water, and then with a boat hook and other means got into the ship again and his life saved. And though he was something ill with it, yet he lived many years after and became a profitable member both in church and commonwealth. In all this voyage there died but one of the passengers, which was William Butten, a youth, servant to Samuel Fuller, when they drew near the coast.

But to omit other things (that I may be brief) after long beating at sea they fell with that land which is called Cape Cod, the which being made and certainly known to be it, they were not a little joyful. After some deliberation had amongst themselves and with the master of the ship, they tacked about and resolved to stand for the southward (the wind and weather being fair) to find some place about Hudson's River for their habitation. But after they had sailed that course about half the day, they fell amongst dangerous shoals and roaring breakers, and they were so far entangled therewith as they conceived themselves in great danger; and the wind shrinking upon them withal, they resolved to bear up again for the Cape and thought themselves happy to get out of those dangers before night overtook them, as by God's good providence they did. And the next day they got into the Cape Harbor[5] where they rid in safety. . . .

. . . Being thus arrived in a good harbor, and brought safe to land, they fell upon their knees and blessed the God of Heaven who had brought them over the vast and furious ocean, and delivered them from all the perils and miseries thereof, again to set their feet on the firm and stable earth, their proper element. And no marvel if they were thus joyful, seeing wise Seneca[6] was so affected with sailing a few miles on the coast of his own Italy, as he affirmed, that he had rather remain twenty years on his way by land than pass by sea to any place in a short time, so tedious and dreadful was the same unto him.

But here I cannot but stay and make a pause, and stand half amazed at this poor people's present condition; and so I think will the reader, too, when he well considers the same. Being thus passed the vast ocean, and a sea of troubles before in their preparation (as may be remembered by that which went before), they had now no friends to welcome them nor inns to entertain or refresh their weather-beaten bodies; no houses or much less towns to repair to, to seek for succor. It is recorded in Scripture as a mercy to the Apostle[7] and his shipwrecked company, that the barbarians showed them no small kindness in refreshing them, but these savage barbarians, when they met with them (as after will appear), were readier to fill their sides full of arrows than otherwise. And for the season it was winter, and they that know the winters of that country know them to be sharp and violent, and subject to cruel and fierce storms, dangerous to travel to known places, much more to search an unknown coast. Besides, what could they see but a hideous and desolate wilderness, full of wild beasts and wild men—and what multitudes there might be

---

2. *to hull,* to drift with the wind using very little sail.
3. *John Howland.* Howland became an influential member of the Massachusetts Bay Colony.
4. *seele,* the pitch or roll of a ship.
5. *Cape Harbor,* Provincetown Harbor at the tip of Cape Cod.
6. *Seneca,* a famous Roman poet and tragedian.
7. *a mercy to the Apostle.* The allusion is to Paul's shipwreck on Malta (see Acts 28:2).

of them they knew not. Neither could they, as it were, go up to the top of Pisgah[8] to view from this wilderness a more goodly country to feed their hopes; for which way soever they turned their eyes (save upward to the heavens) they could have little solace or content in respect of any outward objects. For summer being done, all things stand upon them with a weather-beaten face, and the whole country, full of woods and thickets, represented a wild and savage hue. If they looked behind them, there was the mighty ocean which they had passed and was now as a main bar and gulf to separate them from all the civil parts of the world. If it be said they had a ship to succor them, it is true; but what heard they daily from the master and company? But that with speed they should look out a place (with their shallop) where they would be, at some near distance; for the season was such as he would not stir from thence till a safe harbor was discovered by them, where they would be, and he might go without danger; and that victuals consumed apace but he must and would keep sufficient for themselves and their return. Yea, it was muttered by some that if they got not a place in time, they would turn them and their goods ashore and leave them. Let it also be considered what weak hopes of supply and succor they left behind them, that might bear up their minds in this sad condition and trials they were under; and they could not be very small. It is true, indeed, the affections and love of their brethren at Leyden was cordial and entire towards them, but they had little power to help them or themselves; and how the case stood between them and the merchants at their coming away hath already been declared.

What could now sustain them but the Spirit of God and His grace? May not and ought not the children of these fathers rightly say: "Our fathers were Englishmen which came over this great ocean, and were ready to perish in this wilderness; but they cried unto the Lord, and He heard their voice and looked on their adversity,"[9] etc. "Let them therefore praise the Lord, because He is good: and His mercies endure forever," "Yea, let them which have been redeemed of the Lord, shew[10] how He hath delivered them from the hand of the oppressor. When they wandered in the desert wilderness out of the way, and found no city to dwell in, both hungry and thirsty, their soul was overwhelmed in them. Let them confess before the Lord His loving-kindness and His wonderful works before the sons of men."[11]

1620   1856

---

8. *Pisgah.* Moses led the Hebrews up Mt. Pisgah near the Dead Sea to view the Promised Land (Numbers 21:18–20).
9. *He . . . adversity.* Deuteronomy 26:5, 7.
10. *shew* (shō), variant of *show*.
11. *"Yea, let them . . . before the sons of men,"* Psalms 107:1–5, 8.

THINK AND DISCUSS
Understanding
1. According to the first paragraph, how does the "profane young man" experience "the just hand of God upon him"?
2. Describe the voyage on ship, citing three events that affected the journey.
3. What are three difficulties Bradford and his group encounter upon reaching land?

Analyzing
4. How does the fate of the young man, as related in the first paragraph, differ from that of John Howland?
5. In the sixth paragraph, Bradford describes "this poor people's present condition" upon arriving on the shores of the New World. What elements in the description might evoke sympathy in the reader?

6. Although the outlook for the Pilgrims seems very bleak at the end of this excerpt, what sustains them?

Extending

7. If Bradford were living today, would he side with those who want to preserve wild land or with those who want to develop it?

APPLYING: Allusion
See Handbook of Literary Terms, p. 878.

An **allusion** is a reference to a person, place, or event, real or fictitious, that a reader is expected to recognize. Drawn from areas such as literature, mythology, history, culture, or religion, allusions clarify the meaning or enhance the effect of a work. Bradford alludes to the Roman poet Seneca's terrible seasickness in order to dramatize the same malady, as suffered by the Pilgrims. Bradford also makes a number of biblical allusions, which are footnoted in the text.

1. Why is the allusion to the Apostle Paul's shipwreck on Malta appropriate?
2. What is the difference between the situation of Bradford's group and that of the Hebrews, as indicated in the allusion to Pisgah?

VOCABULARY
Antonyms

Each numbered item consists of a word in capital letters, followed by five lettered words. Choose the antonym, or word that is most nearly *opposite* in meaning to the word in capital letters.

1. PROFANE: (**a**) bad; (**b**) undesirable; (**c**) sacred; (**d**) likable; (**e**) popular
2. REPROVE: (**a**) praise; (**b**) correct; (**c**) indicate; (**d**) change; (**e**) analyze
3. EXECRATION: (**a**) denial; (**b**) pronouncement; (**c**) love; (**d**) criticism; (**e**) scorn
4. PROVIDENCE: (**a**) laziness; (**b**) immaturity; (**c**) spirit; (**d**) neglect; (**e**) humor
5. SMITE: (**a**) attack; (**b**) caress; (**c**) injure; (**d**) lift; (**e**) verify

COMPOSITION
Writing About an Interview

Interview someone (a relative, a friend, or a neighbor) who left another country to settle in America. Take notes on the following: conditions that caused this person to emigrate; experiences on the journey; whether or not life in America fulfilled the person's expectations. Then use these notes to develop three paragraphs. In a fourth paragraph, compare these experiences to those of Bradford and the first Pilgrims. In a fifth and final paragraph, make some observations about these two immigrant experiences. Assume your essay will be a feature in an eleventh-grade American history textbook.

Analyzing a Historical Account

A primary motivation for the Pilgrims in sailing to America on the *Mayflower* was the search for religious freedom. Write an essay of four or five paragraphs analyzing Bradford's account carefully, showing how the various references to God serve to reveal the nature and depth of his religious beliefs. The final paragraph should present a generalization about the importance of religion in sustaining the Pilgrims in adversity. See "Writing About a Period or Trend" in the Writer's Handbook.

ENRICHMENT
Participating in a Discussion

One class member should locate a copy of the Mayflower Compact and study it. Two other students should study the Iroquois Constitution (page 19) and the Declaration of Independence (page 92). These three students will then form a panel to discuss the significance of the individual documents and their effect on U.S. citizens today. After its presentation, the panel should invite class members to ask questions and offer their own ideas.

Comment

Types of Colonial Literature

The types of colonial literature and the subjects they covered were as diverse as the people who helped settle the country. There was the *New England Primer*, for example, almost the only textbook used in the primary schools for two centuries. It was often revised, sometimes in amusing ways, as when references to King George had to be taken out because matters between the colonies and the mother country had become strained. Illustrated with woodcuts, the primer combined religious teaching with subjects ordinarily taught in school.

The most popular poem of the period was *The Day of Doom* (1662), written by a preacher named Michael Wigglesworth. This long poem of 224 stanzas described in vivid detail the terrible miseries sinners would undergo in hell.

The first book to be printed in the United States was a collection of Psalms that appeared in Cambridge, Massachusetts, in 1640. This collection, translated into meter to be sung during Puritan worship, was adopted as a hymn by the churches in Massachusetts Bay Colony. Thus it came to be known as *The Bay Psalm Book*. The Puritans wanted a translation of the Psalms that was "pure," literal, accurate, and closer in meaning to the original Hebrew text. That they sacrificed the elegance and grace of previous translations in favor of plainness can be seen in these lines from the Twenty-Third Psalm:

The Lord to mee a shepheard is,
 want therefore shall not I.
Hee in the folds of tender-grasse,
 doth cause mee down to lie.

A colonial best seller, the book was revised and enlarged, going through fifty editions. Only ten of the original seventeen hundred copies are known to be in existence.

Various colonial authors gained prominence by writing of their convictions and experiences. One such writer, Nathaniel Ward, railed against religious toleration and what he considered female frivolity. He may appear to the modern reader to be more a misogynist than a humorist in the following lines:

The world is full of care, much like unto a
 bubble,
Women and care, and care and Women, and
 Women and care and trouble.

Judge Samuel Sewall, a dignified and learned judge, published *The Selling of Joseph*, an early anti-slavery tract read by abolitionists more than a century after its publication in 1700. In addition, he kept a diary, setting down careful notes on the ill-fated courtship of a Madame Winthrop. He observed how he made presents to Madame's servant and kinsfolk and what each present cost; how sometimes Madame gave him cake and canary wine and sometimes did not; and how at length he went to a party to which she was not invited and she gave a party to which she did not ask him, thus ending the long courtship.

John Eliot, the "Apostle of the Indians," went on many missionary journeys and wrote a book called *The Daybreaking If Not the Sunrising of the Gospel with the Indians of New England*. In the early 1660s Eliot, the first clergyman to preach to Native Americans in their own tongue, translated the Bible into the language of the Massachusetts Indians.

Many colonial works were written by women, although few names survive other than those of Anne Bradstreet, Sarah Kemble Knight, and Phillis Wheatley. Mary Rowlandson wrote a thrilling story of her captivity among the Indians (1682). Esther Edwards, daughter of the famed colonial preacher, Jonathan Edwards, wrote charming diary entries, such as the following one on her cat: "I doubt if she has much divinity about her unless it is the sparks of electricity when she is rubbed the wrong way."

BIOGRAPHY

Sarah Kemble Knight
1666–1727

Sarah Kemble Knight was a person of many accomplishments—most of them uncommon for a woman of her time. In Boston, where she spent most of her life, she managed a shop, ran a boardinghouse, and taught school. The young Ben Franklin is reported to have been one of her pupils. Knight gained considerable knowledge of law by preparing court records and other legal documents. Occasionally, she used her legal knowledge in settling estates. In 1712 Knight moved to Connecticut, where she acquired property, farmed, and had a place of entertainment that was probably an inn. When she died in 1727, she left a considerable estate, proof of her ability as a businesswoman.

When Knight traveled from Boston to New York in 1704 to settle an estate, she went on horseback because stagecoaches were not yet common. The following excerpt from her journal of the five-month journey has been partly modernized, though some archaic spellings have been retained to give the flavor of the original.

 See SATIRE in the Handbook of Literary Terms, page 905.

Traveling in the New Land

Sarah Kemble Knight

hen we had Ridd about an how'r, we come into a thick Swamp, which, by Reason of a great fog, very much startled me, it being now very Dark. But nothing dismay'd John: He had encountered a thousand and a thousand such Swamps, having a Universal Knowledge in the woods; and readily answered all my inquiries, which were not a few.

In about an how'r, or something more, after we left the Swamp, we come to Billinges,[1] where

I was to lodge. My Guide dismounted and very complaisantly help't me down and showed the door, signing to me with his hand to go in; which I gladly did—But had not gone many steps into the Room, ere I was interrogated by a young lady I understood afterwards was the Eldest daughter of the family, with these, or words to this pur-

---

1. Billinges, probably a colonial village south of Boston.

From *The Journal of Madam Knight* by Sarah Kemble Knight. Albany: Frank Little, 1865.

pose: "Law for me—what in the world brings You here at this time a night?—I never see a woman on the Road so dreadful late, in all the days of my versall[2] life. Who are You? Where are You going? I'm scar'd out of my wits"—with much now of the same kind. I stood aghast, preparing to reply, when in comes my Guide—to him Madam turn'd Roaring out: "Lawful heart; John, is it You?—how de do! Where in the world are you going with this woman? Who is she?" John made no Answer but sat down in the corner, fumbled out his black Junk,[3] and saluted that instead of Debb; she then turned agen to me and fell anew into her silly questions, without asking me to sit down.

I told her she treated me very rudely, and I did not think it my duty to answer her unmannerly Questions. But to get rid of them, I told her I come there to have the Post's[4] company with me to-morrow on my Journey, etc. Miss star'd awhile, drew a chair, bid me sit, and then run upstairs and puts on two or three Rings (or else I had not seen them before), and returning, set herself just before me, showing the way to Reding,[5] that I might see her Ornaments, perhaps to gain the more respect. But her Granam's new-rung sow,[6] had it appeared, would [have] affected me as much.

I paid honest John with money and dram[7] according to contract, and dismissed him, and pray'd Miss to shew me where I must Lodge. She conducted me to a parlour in a little back Leanto, which was almost filled with the bedsted, which was so high I was forced to climb on a chair to git up to the wretched bed that lay on it; on which having Stretch't my tired Limbs, and lay'd my head on a Sad-colour'd pillow, I began to think on the transactions of the past day.

Tuesday, October the third, about eight in the morning, I with the Post proceeded forward without observing any thing remarkable; and about two, afternoon, Arrived at the Post's stage, where the western Post met him and exchanged Letters. Here, having called for something to eat, the woman brought in a twisted thing like a cable, but something whiter; and laying it on the board,

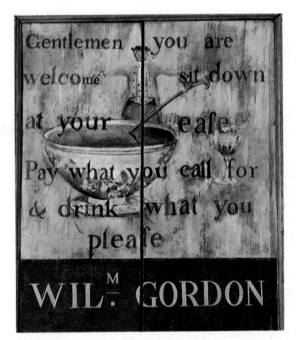

Inn sign.
Connecticut Historical Society

tugg'd for life to bring it into a capacity to spread; which having with great pains accomplished, she serv'd in a dish of Pork and Cabbage, I suppose the remains of Dinner. The sause was of a deep Purple, which I thought was boil'd in her dye Kettle; the bread was Indian,[8] and every thing on the Table service agreeable to these. I, being hungry, got a little down; but my stomach was soon cloy'd, and what cabbage I swallowed serv'd me for a Cud the whole day after.

Having here discharged the Ordinary[9] for self and Guide (as I understood was the custom),

---

2. *versall* (vèr′səl), an archaic word meaning "individual."
3. *black Junk*, tobacco.
4. *Post*, messenger carrying the mail.
5. *showing . . . Reding*, an idiom meaning "to make a display of oneself."
6. *Granam's new-rung sow*, Grandmother's sow with a ring through its snout.
7. *dram*, small drink of whiskey.
8. *bread was Indian*, bread made from Indian corn.
9. *discharged the Ordinary*, paid the bill.

about three, afternoon, went on with my third Guide, who Rode very hard; and having crossed Providence Ferry, we come to a River which they generally Ride thro'. But I dare not venture; so the Post got a Lad and Cannoo to carry me to t'other side, and he rid thro' and Led my hors. The Cannoo was very small and shallow, so that when we were in, she seem'd ready to take in water, which greatly terrified me, and caused me to be very circumspect, sitting with my hands fast on each side, my eyes steady, not daring so much as to lodge my tongue a hair's breadth more on one side of my mouth than t'other, nor so much as think on Lot's wife,[10] for a wry thought would have overset our wherry. But was soon put out of this pain, by feeling the Cannoo on shore, which I as soon almost saluted with my feet; and Rewarding my sculler, again mounted and made the best of our way forwards. The Road here was very even and the day pleasant, it being now near Sunset. But the Post told me we had near fourteen miles to Ride to the next Stage (where we were to Lodge). I ask't him of the rest of the Road, foreseeing we must travel in the night. He told me there was a bad River we were to Ride thro', which was so very fierce a hors could sometimes hardly stem it: But it was but narrow, and we should soon be over. I cannot express the concern of mind this relation set me in: no thoughts but those of the dangerous River could entertain my Imagination; and they were as formidable as various, still Tormenting me with blackest Ideas of my Approaching fate—Sometimes seeing myself drowning, otherwhiles drowned, and at the best like a Holy Sister just come out of a Spiritual Bath in dripping Garments.

Now was the Glorious Luminary with his swift Coursers arrived at his Stage,[11] leaving poor me with the rest of this part of the lower world in darkness, with which we were soon Surrounded. The only Glimmering we now had was from the spangled Skies, whose Imperfect Reflections rendered every Object formidable. Each lifeless Trunk, with its shatter'd Limbs, appear'd an Armed Enemy; and every little stump like a Ravenous Devourer. Nor could I so much as

discern my Guide, when at any distance, which added to the terror.

Thus, absolutely lost in Thought, and dying with the very thoughts of drowning, I come up with the Post, who I did not see till even with his hors: he told me he stop't for me; and we Rode on very deliberately a few paces, when he entered a Thicket of Trees and Shrubs, and I perceived by the hors's going we were on the descent of a Hill, which, as we come nearer the bottom, 'twas totally dark with the Trees that surrounded it. But I knew by the going of the hors we had entered the water, which my Guide told me was the hazardous River he had told me of; and he, Riding up close to my side, Bid me not fear—we should be over immediately. I now rallied all the Courage I was mistress of, knowing that I must either Venture my fate of drowning, or be left like the Children in the wood.[12] So, as the Post bid me, I gave reins to my Nag; and sitting as Steady as just before in the Cannoo, in a few minutes got safe to the other side, which he told me was the Narragansett country.[13]

Here we found great difficulty in Traveling, the way being very narrow, and on each side the Trees and bushes gave us very unpleasant welcome with their branches and boughs, which we could not avoid, it being so exceeding dark. My Guide, as before so now, put on harder than I, with my weary bones, could follow; so left me and the way behind him. Now returned my distressed apprehensions of the place where I was: the dolesome woods, my Company next to none, going I knew not whither, and encompassed with terrifying darkness; the least of which was enough to startle a more Masculine courage. Added to which the Reflections, as

---

10. *Lot's wife.* In the Bible, Lot's wife was turned into a pillar of salt when she looked back at Sodom (Genesis 19:26).

11. *Glorious Luminary* (lü′mə ner′ē) . . . *Stage.* The sun went down.

12. *Children in the wood,* a fairy tale, in which two young children die in the forest where they have been left by their greedy uncle.

13. *Narragansett* (nar′ə gan′sət) *country,* Earea around the town of Narragansett in southern Rhode Island.

in the afternoon of the day, that my Call was very questionable, which till then I had not so Prudently as I ought considered. Now, coming to the foot of a hill, I found great difficulty in ascending; but being got to the Top, was there amply recompenced with the friendly Appearance of the Kind Conductress of the night, just then advancing above the Horisontal Line. The Raptures which the Sight of that fair Planet produced in me, caus'd me, for the moment, to forget my present wearyness and past toils; and Inspir'd me for most of the remaining way with very diverting thoughts, some of which, with the other occurrences of the day, I reserved to note down when I should come to my Stage. My thoughts on the sight of the moon were to this purpose:

Fair Cynthia,[14] all the Homage that I may
Unto a Creature, unto thee I pay;
In Lonesome woods to meet so kind a guide,
To me's more worth than all the world beside.
Some Joy I felt just now, when safe got o'er
Yon Surly River to this Rugged shore,
Deeming Rough welcomes from these
     clownish Trees,
Better than Lodgings with Nereidees.[15]
Yet swelling fears surprise; all dark appears—
Nothing but Light can dissipate those fears.
My fainting vitals can't lend strength to say,
But softly whisper, O I wish 'twere day.
The murmur hardly warm'd the Ambient air,
Ere thy Bright Aspect rescues from despair:
Makes the old Hag[16] her sable mantle loose,
And a Bright Joy do's through my Soul diffuse.

The Biostero's Trees now Lend a Passage Free,
And pleasant prospects thou giv'st light to see.

From hence we kept on, with more ease than before: the way being smooth and even, the night warm and serene, and the tall and thick Trees at a distance, especially when the moon glar'd light through the branches, fill'd my Imagination with the pleasant delusion of a Sumptuous city, fill'd with famous Buildings and Churches, with their spiring Steeples, Balconies, Galleries and I know not what; Grandeurs which I had heard of and which the stories of foreign countries had given me the Idea of.

Here stood a Lofty church—there is a steeple
And there the Grand Parade—O see the people!
That Famous Castle there, were I but nigh,
To see the moat and Bridge and walls so high—
They're very fine! says my deluded eye.

Being thus agreeably entertain'd without a thought of anything but thoughts themselves, I on a sudden was Rous'd from these pleasing Imaginations, by the Post's sounding his horn, which assured me he was arrived at the Stage, where we were to Lodge: and that musick was then most musickal and agreeable to me.

1704   1825

---

14. **Fair Cynthia,** Greek goddess of the moon.
15. **Nereidees** (nə rē′ə dēz′), Greek sea nymphs.
16. **the old Hag,** evil female spirit, here the night.

THINK AND DISCUSS
Understanding
1. Describe the reception Madame Knight receives at the inn in Billinges. How does she respond to this reception?
2. What does the innkeeper's daughter do, to Knight's surprise?

3. Describe the room in the inn where Knight spends the night.

Analyzing
4. What elements of Knight's journal make it lively and engaging?

5. Cite examples of humor in Knight's description of her stay in Billinges.
6. What personal qualities does Knight reveal when she speaks with the woman at Billinges, and later, when she is in the small boat crossing the river?
7. How does the style of the poem beginning "Fair Cynthia" differ from the rest of Knight's diary?
8. What has caused the author's change in mood at the end of her journal account?

Extending
9. If you were to travel from Boston to New York today (or between any major American cities), how would your experiences differ from Madame Knight's? Would the trip be as interesting? Explain.

APPLYING: Satire H🖊
See Handbook of Literary Terms, p. 905.

Satire is a technique that ridicules some human weakness or social shortcoming. The purpose of satire is often to bring about a change. Some satires are gentle and good-natured, while others are scornful and bitter. Often exaggeration is used to heighten the effect of satire.

1. What does Knight satirize about the innkeeper's daughter?
2. What does Knight satirize about her bedroom at Billinges and her lunch the next day on the road?
3. Do you think Knight's satire is designed to bring about reform or merely to enliven her account? Explain.

VOCABULARY
Context
When you encounter a word whose exact meaning you are unsure of, you can often guess its meaning from its *context*, the way it is used in a sentence. Choose one of the following words, which appear in Knight's account, to complete each sentence. Use context clues to help you make a choice. The words are *apprehensions, complaisantly, circumspect, formidable, sumptuous,* and *homage*.

1. Although she had many _____ about the trip, Knight looked confident as she embarked on the journey.
2. The man dressed in a frivolous manner, although his behavior otherwise seemed very _____.
3. Judging from the _____ meal she has prepared, I would assume that Millie is an excellent cook.
4. Climbing upstairs can be a _____ task for a child who has just learned to walk.
5. She treated me so_____ that I wrote to her supervisor about her courtesy.
6. He tipped his hat—a gesture of _____ that seemed comically out of place at a rock concert.

COMPOSITION ◀▬▶
Writing a Humorous Satire
Write a four-paragraph essay in which you use humor to satirize an aspect of human nature, such as a love of material goods, a passion for TV or movies, or a reluctance to take advice. Assume your essay will be submitted as a feature article for a magazine such as *Reader's Digest*. Document your article with examples from everyday life. Consider using exaggeration to achieve a humorous effect. Keep in mind that your purpose is to entertain rather than to reform.

Writing a Character Sketch
Write a four-paragraph character sketch of Madame Knight for your classmates. Support your generalizations about her personality by citing specific aspects of her behavior revealed in her journal. Concentrate on three traits (one paragraph for each) and conclude with a paragraph speculating on what her poem reveals about her.

Detail of portrait attributed
to Hans Hysing (1678–1752).
Virginia Historical Society

Although born in Virginia Colony, William Byrd II spent almost half his life in England, first as an infant sent to avoid the danger of attack by Indians, and later as a student. On his father's death in 1704, Byrd inherited 26,000 acres near Williamsburg, Virginia (which he eventually increased to 179,000 acres). When he was not abroad, he lived the life of a genteel country planter.

An avid student of literature, Byrd read Greek, Latin, Hebrew, and French, and had a library of 3,600 volumes—one of the largest private collections of the time in America. Appointed receiver-general of the King's revenues. Byrd represented Virginia three times at the court of England. In addition, he was a member of the King's Council, the top governing body in the colony.

For a good part of his life, Byrd kept a secret diary in shorthand, which was not decoded and published until the twentieth century. Through this diary, Byrd's life emerges as a rich mixture of social visits, reading, business matters, merriment, religion, and domestic encounters.

As a member of the Virginia plantation aristocracy, Byrd belonged to the commission that surveyed the dividing line between North Carolina and Virginia. The commissioners and surveyors, representing both states, intended to determine the long-disputed boundary between these states. The notes he made during this expedition were not meant for publication, but were printed almost a century after his death. The following selection is from his account.

Bears

William Byrd II

he grapes we commonly met with were black, tho' there be two or three kinds of white grapes that grow wild. The black are very sweet, but small, because the strength of the vine spends itself in wood; tho' without question a proper culture would make the same grapes both larger and sweeter. But, with all these disadvantages, I have drunk tolerably good wine prest from them, tho' made without skill. There is then good Reason to believe it might admit of great improvement, if rightly managed.

From *William Byrd's Histories of the Dividing Line Betwixt Virginia and North Carolina*. Originally published by the North Carolina Historical Commission. Published 1967 by Dover Publications.

Glen Loates, detail of *Black Bear* (1969).
Private collection

Our Indian kill'd a Bear, of two years old, that was feasting on these grapes. He was very fat, as they generally are in that season of the year. In the fall, the flesh of this animal has a high relish, different from that of the other creatures, tho' inclining nearest to that of Pork, or rather of Wild Boar.

A true Woodsman prefers this sort of meat to that of the fattest Venison, not only for the *Hautgout*[1] but also because the fat of it is well tasted, and never rises in the stomach. Another proof of the goodness of this meat is, that it is less apt to corrupt than any other we are acquainted with. As agreeable as such rich diet was to the men, yet we who were not accustom'd to it, tasted it at first with some sort of squeamishness, that animal being of the Dog-kind; tho' a little use soon reconcil'd us to this American Venison. And that its being of the Dog-kind might give us the less disgust, we had the example of that ancient and polite People, the Chinese, who reckon Dog's flesh too good for any under the quality of a mandarin.[2]

This Beast is in truth a very clean feeder, living, while the season lasts, upon acorns, chestnuts and chinkapins,[3] wild honey and wild grapes. They are naturally not carnivorous, unless hunger constrains them to it, after the mast is all gone, and the products of the woods quite exhausted.

They are not provident enough to lay up any hoard, like the Squirrels, nor can they, after all, live very long upon licking their paws, as Sir John Mandevil[4] and some Travellers tell us, but are forced in the winter months to quit the mountains, and visit the inhabitants.

Their errand is then to surprise a poor Hog at a pinch to keep them from starving. And to shew that they are not flesh-eaters by trade, they devour their prey very awkwardly.

They don't kill it right out, and feast upon its blood and entrails, like other ravenous Beasts, but having, after a fair pursuit, seiz'd it with their paws, they begin first upon the rump, and so devour one collop after another, till they come to the vitals, the poor Animal crying all the while, for several minutes together. However, in so

---

1. *Hautgout* (ō gü'), highly seasoned flavor. [*French*]
2. *mandarin* (man'dər ən), a high-ranking public official in the Chinese Empire.
3. *chinkapin* (chink'ə pin), a dwarf chestnut.
4. *Sir John Mandevil* (man'də vil'), the pen name of an author of a fourteenth-century travel book.

doing, Bruin acts a little imprudently, because the dismal outcry of the Hog alarms the neighbourhood, and 'tis odds but he pays the forfeit with his Life,[5] before he can secure his retreat.

But Bears soon grow weary of this unnatural diet, and about January, when there is nothing to be got in the woods, they retire into some cave or hollow tree, where they sleep away two or three months very comfortably. But then they quit their holes in March, when the Fish begin to run up the rivers, on which they are forced to keep Lent,[6] till some fruit or berry comes in season.

But Bears are fondest of chestnuts, which grow plentifully toward the mountains, upon very large trees, where the soil happens to be rich. We were curious to know how it happen'd that many of the outward branches of those trees came to be broke off in that solitary place, and were inform'd that the Bears are so discreet as not to trust their unwieldy bodies on the smaller limbs of the tree, that would not bear their weight; but after venturing as far as is safe, which they can judge to an inch, they bite off the end of the branch, which falling down, they are content to finish their repast upon the ground. In the same cautious manner they secure the acorns that grow on the weaker limbs of the oak. And it must be allow'd that, in these instances, a Bear carries Instinct a great way, and acts more reasonably than many of his betters, who indiscreetly venture upon frail projects that won't bear them.

1728   1841

---

5. *forfeit . . . Life,* pay the penalty with a loss of life.
6. *Lent,* the Christian season of penance.

THINK AND DISCUSS

Understanding
1. What are the qualities of the wild black grapes mentioned by Byrd in the first paragraph?
2. According to Byrd, what does bear meat taste like, and why does the "true woodsman" prefer it to venison?
3. What is the bear's usual food, according to Byrd?

Analyzing
4. How would you characterize Byrd's attitude toward the bears?
5. In which of their actions does Byrd feel that the bears are cautious and even calculating?
6. What humanlike qualities does Byrd ascribe to the bears?
7. Is there any point in the account where you feel sympathy for the bears? If so, describe.
8. Who are the bears' "betters" mentioned in the last sentence? Explain the meaning of the sentence.

Extending
9. Would Byrd have been a "survivor" in today's culture? Explain.

COMPOSITION
Describing an Animal
In an essay of at least four paragraphs, written for a magazine, describe an animal that seems to display humanlike qualities, such as intelligence, a sense of humor, or loyalty. To prepare for this assignment, closely observe an animal—a pet, a neighborhood visitor, or an animal on a TV show or commercial. In your final paragraph, make some general observation about what this animal can teach human beings about themselves.

Outlining
Byrd has somewhat systematically described for us the bear as he has come to know it through observation. Construct an outline of his description, showing the order in which Byrd deals with various aspects of his subject.

Cotton Mather came from a long and distinguished line of clergymen; his grandfather was Richard Mather, his father Increase Mather, both important colonial leaders and writers. Graduated from Harvard at the age of fifteen, Mather soon began his career as minister at the Old North Church of Boston, a position he held until his death. He married three times and fathered fifteen children, surviving all but two of them. Preaching and writing without cease, he produced more than four hundred books. Pious, pedantic, proud, and neurotic, he was a remarkably learned man, skilled in seven languages and well-read in history, philosophy, and theology. His library contained around two thousand volumes—an extensive collection for that time and second only to William Byrd's library in Virginia.

All his work was written in an ornate, highly allusive style, with extravagant use of archaic or old-fashioned words and expressions. His masterpiece is *Magnalia Christi Americana* (A History of Christ's Church in America, 1702). But his most curious book is *The Wonders of the Invisible World* (1693), from which the following excerpt is taken, in which he makes a biblical defense of the existence of witchcraft in New England during this period.

Mather was not alone in his belief in witchcraft. Such belief was universal in the seventeenth century, throughout Europe and America. In the early 1690s, a kind of hysteria swept New England, and in 1692 nineteen people were hanged and one was pressed to death (by use of heavy stones) for allegedly practicing witchcraft. Many more confessed, and still more were jailed. Mather had a keen interest in the phenomenon, and attended the trials and executions. His account of the trial of Martha Carrier, who was found guilty and executed on August 19, 1692, is included here. Mather did not approve of the executions but instead believed that the witches should repent. The witchcraft hysteria faded, followed by a communal sense of guilt and regret at the executions.

The Trial of Martha Carrier

Cotton Mather

I.

Martha Carrier was indicted for bewitching certain persons, according to the form usual in such cases, pleading *not guilty* to her indictment. There were first brought in a considerable number of the bewitched persons, who not only made the Court sensible of an horrid witchcraft committed upon them, but also deposed that it was Martha Carrier, or her shape, that grievously tormented them by biting, pricking, pinching, and choking of them. It was further deposed that while this Carrier was on her examination before the Magistrates, the poor people were so tortured that every one expected their death upon the very spot, but that upon the binding of Carrier they were eased. Moreover, the look of Carrier then laid the afflicted people for dead, and her touch, if her eye at the same time were off them, raised them again: which things were also now seen upon her trial. And it was testified that upon the mention of some having their necks twisted almost round, by the shape of this Carrier, she replied, *It's no matter though their necks had been twisted quite off.*

II. Before the trial of this prisoner, several of her own children had frankly and fully confessed not only that they were witches themselves, but that this their mother had made them so. This confession they made with great shows of repentance, and with much demonstration of truth. They related place, time, occasion; they gave an account of journeys, meetings, and mischiefs by them performed and were very credible in what they said. Nevertheless, this evidence was not produced against the prisoner at the bar, inasmuch as there was other evidence enough to proceed upon.

III. Benjamin Abbot gave his testimony that last March was a twelvemonth, this Carrier was very angry with him, upon laying out some land near her husband's. Her expressions in this anger were that she would stick as close to Abbot as the bark stuck to the tree, and that he should repent of it afore seven years came to an end, so as Doctor Prescot should never cure him. These words were heard by others besides Abbot himself, who also heard her say she would hold his nose as close to the grindstone as ever it was held since his name was Abbot. Presently after this he was taken with a swelling in his foot, and then with a pain in his side, and exceedingly tormented. It bred into a sore, which was lanced by Doctor Prescot, and several gallons of corruption ran out of it. For six weeks it continued very bad, and then another sore bred in the groin, which was also lanced by Doctor Prescot. Another sore then bred in his groin, which was likewise cut and put him to very great misery. He was brought until death's door and so remained until Carrier was taken and carried away by the Constable, from which very day he began to mend and so grew better every day and is well ever since.

Sarah Abbot, his wife, also testified that her husband was not only all this while afflicted in his body, but also that strange, extraordinary, and unaccountable calamities befell his cattle, their death being such as they could guess at no natural reason for.

IV. Allin Toothaker testified that Richard, the son of Martha Carrier, having some difference with him, pulled him down by the hair of the head. When he rose again, he was going to strike at Richard Carrier, but fell down flat on his back to the ground and had not power to stir hand or foot until he told Carrier he yielded; and then he

Cotton Mather, *The Wonders of the Invisible World.* London: John Russell Smith, 1862.

T. H. Matteson, detail of *The Trial of George Jacobs for Witchcraft, 1692* (1855). Essex Institute

saw the shape of Martha Carrier go off his breast.

This Toothaker had received a wound in the wars and he now testified that Martha Carrier told him he should never be cured. Just afore the apprehending of Carrier, he could thrust a knitting needle into his wound, four inches deep; but presently, after her being seized, he was thoroughly healed.

He further testified that when Carrier and he sometimes were at variance, she would clap her hands at him, and say he should get nothing by it; whereupon he several times lost his cattle by strange deaths, whereof no natural causes could be given.

V. John Rogger also testified that upon the threatening words of this malicious Carrier, his cattle would be strangely bewitched, as was more particularly then described.

VI. Samuel Preston testified that about two years ago, having some difference with Martha Carrier, he lost a cow in a strange preternatural, unusual manner; and about a month after this, the said Carrier, having again some difference with him, she told him he had lately lost a cow and it should not be long before he lost another, which accordingly came to pass; for he had a thriving and well-kept cow, which without any known cause quickly fell down and died.

VII. Phebe Chandler testified that about a fort night before the apprehension of Martha Carrier, on a Lordsday, while the Psalm was singing in the Church, this Carrier then took her by the shoulder and, shaking her, asked her where she lived. She made her no answer, although as Carrier, who lived next door to her father's house, could not in reason but know who she was. Quickly after this, as she was at several times crossing the fields, she heard a voice that she took to be Martha Carrier's, and it seemed as if it was over her head. The voice told her she should within two or three days be poisoned. Accordingly, within such a little time, one-half of her right hand became greatly swollen and very painful, as also part of her face: whereof she can give no account how it came. It continued very bad for some days; and several times since, she has had

a great pain in her breast and been so seized on her legs that she has hardly been able to go. She added that lately, going well to the House of God, Richard, the son of Martha Carrier, looked very earnestly upon her and immediately her hand, which had formerly been poisoned as is above-said, began to pain her greatly, and she had a strange burning at her stomach, but then was struck deaf, so that she could not hear any of the prayer or singing till the two or three last words of the Psalm.

VIII. One Foster, who confessed her own share in the witchcraft for which the prisoner stood indicted, affirmed that she had seen the prisoner at some of their witch-meetings and that it was this Carrier who persuaded her to be a witch. She confessed that the devil carried them on a pole to a witch-meeting, but the pole broke, and she hanging about Carrier's neck, they both fell down, and she then received an hurt by the fall, whereof she was not at this very time recovered.

IX. One Lacy, who likewise confessed her share in this witchcraft, now testified that she and the prisoner were once bodily present at a witch-meeting in Salem Village; and that she knew the prisoner to be a witch and to have been at a diabolical sacrament and that the prisoner was the undoing of her and her children by enticing them into the snare of the devil.

X. Another Lacy, who also confessed her share in this witchcraft, now testified that the prisoner was at the witch-meeting in Salem Village, where they had bread and wine administered unto them.

XI. In the time of this prisoner's trial, one Susanna Sheldon, in open court, had her hands unaccountably tied together with a wheel-band, so fast that without cutting, it could not be loosened. It was done by a specter, and the sufferer affirmed it was the prisoner's.

Memorandum. This rampant hag, Martha Carrier, was the person of whom the confessions of the witches and of her own children, among the rest, agreed that the devil had promised her she should be *Queen of Heb.* **1693**

THINK AND DISCUSS
Understanding
1. What qualities of a witch does Martha Carrier seem to exhibit while being examined by the magistrates (in I)?
2. Summarize the testimony of Martha Carrier's children (in II).
3. Was the evidence of her children used against Martha Carrier? Explain.

Analyzing
4. How might the charge made by Allin Toothaker against Richard Carrier be rationally explained?
5. How does Phebe Chandler's testimony (in VII) suggest that Martha Carrier and her son Richard worked together in their witchcraft?
6. How does the testimony of Foster and the two Lacys (in VIII–X) differ from the testimony of previous witnesses?
7. What aspect of Susanna Sheldon's appearance before the court is stressed as particularly convincing?

Extending
8. What rational explanation might be given for Abbot's illness and recovery?

THINKING SKILLS
Evaluating
To evaluate is to make a judgment based on some kind of standard. For example, a critic sees a movie and writes a review that includes judgments about how well written, directed, and acted it is, compared to all the other movies he or she has seen.

1. Evaluate the evidence presented in the cases of Benjamin Abbot (in III) and Foster (in VIII). Do you think that the testimony of these people is convincing?
2. Read the Comment "Witchcraft as Seen Through the Ages." Judging from this article and from Mather's account, which of the following do you consider the most responsible for the Salem trials: superstition, universal evil, the need for a scapegoat, personal vengeance? Give reasons for your choice.

COMPOSITION
Proving Your Identity in a Courtroom
Imagine that you have been accused of being a Martian and are on trial. Brainstorm with a classmate about the kinds of questions a judge would likely ask you and the answers you would give to prove that you are a human being from Earth. List six questions and answers that could form a courtroom dialogue. Once you have written this dialogue, you might want to present it with your classmate to the class, having them decide whether or not you have proven your identity.

Describing a Historical Event
Research one of the following topics: the Salem witch hunts, the California Gold Rush of 1849, the McCarthy hearings of the 1950s, the flying saucer sightings of the post-War decades. Then write an essay of at least four paragraphs for your classmates, explaining the causes of this event, movement, or phenomenon and the outcome. See "Writing About a Period or Trend" in the Writer's Handbook.

ENRICHMENT
Oral Reading
Look up Arthur Miller's play, *The Crucible* (1953), which is based on the Salem witch trials of 1692. Choose a scene that offers parallels to Mather's account of the Martha Carrier trial. See especially the witchcraft scene that ends Act 3. Your teacher will assign parts to be prepared and delivered.

Oral Report

Some class members may form two groups of three students each. The first group should research the activities of Senator Joseph McCarthy during the early 1950s. The second group should read *The Crucible* by Arthur Miller in its entirety. Working together, these groups will first give a summary of the play, then an explanation of the McCarthy era, and, finally, discuss ways in which Miller's play was as much about his own time as about the 1600s.

Comment

Witchcraft as Seen Through the Ages

Many people have attempted to explain what kindled the hysteria of Salem in 1692. One historian (Mary K. Matossian, University of Maryland) has argued (in *American Scientist*, 1982) that it is likely those who felt themselves bewitched were suffering delusions from eating rye grains, contained in breads, that had become diseased through a fungus called *ergot*. Victims of the disease of ergotism have fits, see visions, and complain of being pricked or bitten—symptoms resembling those of the Salem "witches." Ergotism has a similar effect on animals and could thus explain the bewitched behavior of Salem's dogs, two of whom were executed along with the human victims. Matossian's findings have been disputed and remain only a theory.

The idea of witchcraft has had a peculiar fascination for the American literary imagination. In the mid-nineteenth century, Nathaniel Hawthorne, descendant of a judge who had officiated at the trials, based his story "Young Goodman Brown" (Unit 3) on descriptions in Cotton Mather's accounts. In this story, all people in the community partake in witchcraft because everyone on earth shares "one stain of guilt, one mighty blood spot."

Arthur Miller is another American writer who recognized that witch hunts—attempts to blame a scapegoat for all the ills of society—can occur during any era. In the early 1950s, Senator Joseph McCarthy conducted a search for those he considered radicals and communists, both in and out of government. As a result, many innocent people suffered damaged reputations or loss of jobs. Miller's play *The Crucible* (1953), though set in the Puritan period, is a commentary on the McCarthy witch hunts.

Another twentieth-century writer who examined the Salem witch trials was Stephen Vincent Benét, who made the following observation in an essay titled "We Aren't Superstitious":

It is well for us to consider Salem. It was a town, like another, and a strange madness took hold of it. But is it stranger madness to hang a man for witchcraft than to hang him for the shape of his nose or the color of his skin? We are not superstitious, no. Well, let us be sure we are not. For persecution follows superstition and intolerance as fire follows the fuse. And, once we light that fuse, we cannot foresee where the fire will burn or what it will consume—any more than they could in Salem, so many years ago.

From *We Aren't Superstitious* by Stephen Vincent Benét. Copyright 1937 by Esquire, Inc. Copyright © renewed by Thomas C. Benét, Rachel Benét Lewis and Stephanie Benét Mahin. By special permission to use Abridgement. Reprinted by permission of Brandt & Brandt Literary Agents, Inc.

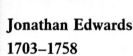

Among the most eminent theologians that America has produced, Jonathan Edwards was born in Connecticut in a long line of Puritan ministers. He was strictly educated in the Calvinistic faith, which emphasized innate human corruption and the doctrine of the elect (people do not win salvation through good works but are "elected" by God for salvation—or damnation). A child prodigy, Edwards entered Yale University at thirteen and graduated at sixteen.

In 1729 he followed his grandfather into the ministry of Northampton, Massachusetts. His powerful preaching helped spark a major religious revival called the Great Awakening that spread through New England in the 1730s and 1740s. Edwards presented a dramatic figure on the pulpit—a tall, spare man with piercing eyes and thin, set lips who, according to a minister who was present, could cause "such a breathing of distress and weeping, that the preacher was obliged to speak to the people and desire silence that he might be heard." The power of Edwards's sermons, achieved largely through effective use of metaphor, can be seen in the excerpt from "Sinners in the Hands of an Angry God," which is included here.

Edwards's strong beliefs and forceful sermons offended some members of his congregation, and in 1751 he resigned over doctrinal differences and moved to Stockbridge, Massachusetts, a frontier settlement, where he became missionary to the Indians. In January of 1758 he became president of the College of New Jersey, later to become Princeton. Three months later he died of smallpox, a disease common in the colonies.

from Sinners in the Hands of an Angry God

Jonathan Edwards

he wrath of God is like great waters that are dammed for the present; they increase more and more and rise higher and higher, till an outlet is given; and the longer the stream is stopped, the more rapid and mighty is its course when once it is let loose. 'Tis true that judgment against your evil work has not been executed hitherto; the floods of God's vengeance have been withheld; but your guilt in the meantime is constantly increasing, and you are every day treasuring up more wrath; the waters are continually rising and waxing more and more mighty; and there is nothing but the mere pleasure of God that holds the waters back, that are unwilling to be stopped, and press hard to go forward. If God should only withdraw his hand from the floodgate, it would immediately fly open, and the fiery floods of the fierceness and wrath of God would rush forth with inconceivable fury, and would come upon you with omnipotent power; and if your strength were ten thousand times greater than it is, yea, ten thousand times greater than the strength of the stoutest, sturdiest devil in hell, it would be nothing to withstand or endure it.

The bow of God's wrath is bent, and the arrow made ready on the string, and justice bends the arrow at your heart and strains the bow, and it is nothing but the mere pleasure of God, and that of an angry God, without any promise or obligation at all, that keeps the arrow one moment from being made drunk with your blood.

Thus are all you that never passed under a great change of heart by the mighty power of the Spirit of God upon your souls; all that were never born again and made new creatures, and raised from being dead in sin to a state of new and before altogether unexperienced light and life (however you may have reformed your life in many things, and may have had religious affections, and may keep up a form of religion in your families and closets and in the house of God, and may be strict in it), you are thus in the hands of an angry God; 'tis nothing but his mere pleasure that keeps you from being this moment swallowed up in everlasting destruction.

However unconvinced you may now be of the truth of what you hear, by and by you will be fully convinced of it. Those that are gone from being in the like circumstances with you, see that it was so with them; for destruction came suddenly upon most of them; when they expected nothing of it, and while they were saying, Peace and Safety. Now they see that those things that they depended on for peace and safety were nothing but thin air and empty shadows.

The God that holds you over the pit of hell much as one holds a spider or some loathsome insect over the fire, abhors you, and is dreadfully provoked; his wrath toward you burns like fire; he looks upon you as worthy of nothing else but to be cast into the fire; he is of purer eyes than to bear to have you in his sight; you are ten thousand times so abominable in his eyes as the most hateful and venomous serpent is in ours. You have offended him infinitely more than ever a

Passages from Jonathan Edwards reprinted by permission of Hill and Wang, a division of Farrar, Straus and Giroux, Inc. Excerpts adapted and abridged from *Jonathan Edwards* by Clarence H. Faust and Thomas H. Johnson. Copyright 1935, © 1962 by Hill and Wang, Inc.

Rubbing from a minister's gravestone

else, that you did not go to hell the last night; that you were suffered to awake again in this world after you closed your eyes to sleep and there is no other reason to be given why you have not dropped into hell since you arose in the morning, but that God's hand has held you up. There is no other reason to be given why you have not gone to hell since you have sat here in the house of God, provoking his pure eyes by your sinful wicked manner of attending his solemn worship. Yea, there is nothing else that is to be given as a reason why you don't this very moment drop down into hell.

O sinner! Consider the fearful danger you are in. 'Tis a great furnace of wrath, a wide and bottomless pit, full of the fire of wrath, that you are held over in the hand of that God whose wrath is provoked and incensed as much against you as against many of the damned in hell. You hang by a slender thread, with the flames of divine wrath flashing about it, and ready every moment to singe it and burn it asunder; and you have no interest in any Mediator, and nothing to lay hold of to save yourself, nothing to keep off the flames of wrath, nothing of your own, nothing that you ever have done, nothing that you can do, to induce God to spare you one moment. . . .

1741

stubborn rebel did his prince; and yet it is nothing but his hand that holds you from falling into the fire every moment. 'Tis ascribed to nothing

---

THINK AND DISCUSS
Understanding
1. To what does Edwards compare God's wrath in the first paragraph?

Analyzing
2. Edwards introduces two **metaphors** for God's wrath in paragraphs two and five. Describe what is being compared in each.
3. According to these metaphors, the flood waters are ready to pour, the arrow to fly, the spider to drop and burn. What stops them?

4. In paragraph three, what is the distinction Edwards draws between those who escape and those who are condemned by God's wrath?

Extending
5. What can you deduce about the religious convictions of the average member of Edwards's congregation?
6. Would Edwards be an effective preacher today? Why or why not?

VOCABULARY
Dictionary
Use your Glossary to answer these questions.

1. Edwards characterizes God as *omnipotent*. What does he mean?
2. Sinners are compared to "*loathsome* insects." What kinds of insect are these?
3. What characteristics of humanity does Edwards find *abominable*?
4. Edwards says his listeners are hanging by a thread. What will happen when this thread comes *asunder*?
5. Edwards says that the waters are *waxing*. What does this mean?

COMPOSITION
Describing a Place
In an essay of three or four paragraphs, describe for your class a dangerous or terrible place, real or imaginary. Create your own images, similes, and metaphors to make this place seem vivid.

Writing to Persuade
In a persuasive essay of three paragraphs, urge a person or group to change their behavior. Suggest a different mode of behavior, using examples to illustrate the advantages of this new behavior over the old.

The Mystery of the Flying Spider

Many of Jonathan Edwards's early writings show a strong intellectual curiosity as well as a scientific aptitude. At the age of eleven he wrote an essay entitled "Of Insects," which is based on his discovery of the nature of the movement through the air of "flying spiders." He opened the essay (the spelling and punctuation have been modernized): "Of all insects no one is more wonderful than the spider. . . . I know I have several times seen, in a very calm and serene day . . . multitudes of little shining webs and glistening strings of a great length and at such a height as that one would think they were tacked to the sky by one end were it not that they were moving and floating. And there very often appears at the end of these webs a spider floating and sailing in the air with them. . . ."

The young Edwards proceeded to do what any good scientist would do: he found a spider and observed it closely and repeatedly until he had discovered the secret of the mystery of the spider's flight: "I repeated the trial over and over again till I was fully satisfied of [the spider's] way of working . . . they would go from tree to tree or would sail in the air, let themselves hang down a little way by their web and then put out a web at their tails which being so exceeding rare when it first comes from the spider as to be lighter than the air so as of itself it will ascend in it (which I know by experience). The moving air takes it by the end and by the spider's permission pulls it out of his tail to any length. And if the further end of it happens to catch by a tree or anything, why there's a web for him to go over upon, and the spider immediately perceives it and feels when it touches. . . . And this very way I have seen spiders go from one thing to another I believe fifty times at least since I first discovered it. But if nothing is in the way of these webs to hinder their flying out at a sufficient distance and they don't catch by anything, there will be so much of it drawn out into the air as by its ascending force there will be enough to carry the spider with it. . . ." Thus the spider flies!

A contemporary poet, Robert Lowell, has written a poem based on this youthful and brilliant account of the flying spider. The poem, in which Edwards is portrayed as the speaker, serves as a point of departure in revealing the clergyman's character. See "Mr. Edwards and the Spider" in Unit 7.

BIOGRAPHY

Anne Bradstreet
1612?–1672

Curious and intellectually active as a child, Anne Bradstreet received a more comprehensive education than was common for young women of the time. At sixteen, she married Simon Bradstreet, a young graduate of Cambridge, and two years later in 1630 the couple sailed west and arrived in America with the first group of Massachusetts Bay settlers. Both her father and her husband became governors of the colony.

In spite of the demands made on her as housewife, mother of eight, and busy hostess, Bradstreet found time to write poems. Her first volume, appearing in London in 1650, was titled *The Tenth Muse Lately Sprung Up in America.*

Running as a dominant theme through all her poems is the strong Puritan faith that sustained her in life's hardships. But many of her most interesting poems were written out of her everyday experience, concentrating on topics such as her eight children, her husband, or her house. Contemporary poet Adrienne Rich praises works such as "Upon the Burning of Our House" for their "life-giving strokes of personal fact."

Modern stained glass from St. Botolph's Church, Boston (Lincolnshire), England

 See PARADOX in the Handbook of Literary Terms, page 898.

To My Dear and Loving Husband

Anne Bradstreet

If ever two were one, then surely we.
If ever man were loved by wife, then thee;
If ever wife was happy in a man,
Compare with me ye women if you can
5 I prize thy love more than whole mines of gold,
Or all the riches that the East doth hold.
My love is such that rivers cannot quench,
Nor ought but love from thee give recompense.
Thy love is such I can no way repay;
10 The heavens reward thee manifold, I pray.
Then while we live, in love let's so persever,
That when we live no more we may live ever.

1678

THINK AND DISCUSS

Understanding

1. To what things does the speaker compare her husband's love?
2. According to line 8, what is the only thing that can be fairly exchanged for the speaker's love?
3. How can her husband's love for her be repaid (lines 9–10)?

Analyzing

4. Puritan poetry is better known for its religious than for its love themes. Yet "To My Dear and Loving Husband" is an intensely felt love poem from a wife to her husband. Discuss the ways in which the first four lines build intensity of feeling in the poem.

APPLYING: Paradox H⅂

See Handbook of Literary Terms, p. 898.

A **paradox** is a statement that seems contradictory although it actually has valid meaning. A paradoxical statement often made about modern art or architecture is "less is more" (the less ornamented, the more functional and effective). The last line of Bradstreet's poem contains a paradox.

1. Explain how these lovers may "live ever" when they "live no more."
2. What do these paradoxes reveal about Bradstreet's ideas of both love and death?

 See RHYME in the Handbook of Literary Terms, page 902.

Upon the Burning of Our House

July 10th, 1666

Anne Bradstreet

In silent night when rest I took,
For sorrow near I did not look,
I waken'd was with thund'ring noise
And piteous shrieks of dreadful voice.
5 That fearful sound of fire and fire,
Let no man know is my desire.

I, starting up, the light did spy,
And to my God my heart did cry

To strengthen me in my distress
10 And not to leave me succorless.
Then coming out beheld a space,
The flame consume my dwelling place.

And, when I could no longer look,
I blest his Name that gave and took,
15 That laid my goods now in the dust:
Yea so it was, and so 'twas just.

(continued)

It was his own: it was not mine;
Far be it that I should repine.

He might of all justly bereft,
20 But yet sufficient for us left.
When by the ruins oft I past,
My sorrowing eyes aside did cast,
And here and there the places spy
Where oft I sat, and long did lie.

25 Here stood that trunk, and there that chest;
There lay that store I counted best:
My pleasant things in ashes lie,
And them behold no more shall I.
Under thy roof no guest shall sit,
30 Nor at thy table eat a bit.

No pleasant tale shall e'er be told,
Nor things recounted done of old.
No candle e'er shall shine in thee,
Nor bridegroom's voice ere heard shall be.
35 In silence ever shalt thou lie;
Adieu, adieu; all's vanity.

Then straight I gin my heart to chide,
And did thy wealth on earth abide?
Didst fix thy hope on mould'ring dust,
40 The arm of flesh didst make thy trust?
Raise up thy thoughts above the sky
That dunghill mists away may fly.

Thou hast an house on high erect,
Fram'd by that mighty Architect,
45 With glory richly furnished,
Stands permanent tho' this be fled.
It's purchased, and paid for too
By him who hath enough to do.

A prize so vast as is unknown,
50 Yet, by his gift, is made thine own.
There's wealth enough, I need no more;
Farewell my pelf,[1] farewell my store.
The world no longer let me love,
My hope and treasure lies above.

1678

_____

1. *pelf,* money or riches, thought of as bad or degrading.

THINK AND DISCUSS
Understanding
1. What are the speaker's initial feelings, presented in lines 1–10, on discovering the fire?
2. What reasoning does the speaker use in line 17 to explain that the fire was "just"?
3. What things will the speaker miss, according to lines 29–35?
4. In lines 37–42 the speaker's attitude changes. With what questions does she chide, or scold, herself?

Analyzing
5. What two homes does the speaker refer to in the poem? Who owns them? Explain.

6. Explain what the speaker means in line 36 by "all's vanity."

Extending
7. Today, we try to find logical explanations for unfortunate disasters. What explanations and concerns might a modern person who has lost all his or her possessions in a fire have about this disaster?

APPLYING: Rhyme HT
See Handbook of Literary Terms, p. 902.
The pattern of **rhyme** —words having the same sounds in their stressed syllables—at the end of lines in a poem is called *rhyme scheme*. This pattern can be charted by labeling the

first rhyme, *a* (and all words that rhyme with it); the second rhyme, *b*; the third rhyme, *c*; and so on. Stanza one is charted this way:

In silent night when rest I took,	*a*
For sorrow near I did not look,	*a*
I waken'd was with thund'ring noise	*b*
And piteous shrieks of dreadful voice.	*b*
That fearful sound of fire and fire,	*c*
Let no man know is my desire.	*c*

Note that each pair of lines not only rhymes but has the same rhythm. Such lines are called *couplets.*

1. One of these couplets ends with words that do not rhyme exactly. (These words may have been pronounced as rhymes in Bradstreet's time.) What are these words?
2. Chart the rhyme scheme of the second and third stanzas.
3. Which lines in the third stanza should be labeled *a?*

The Tenth Muse

In 1650 Anne Bradstreet's brother-in-law, "less wise than true," published a book of her poems in London, without her knowledge or consent, titled *The Tenth Muse Lately Sprung Up in America. Severall Poems, compiled with great variety of Wit and Learning, full of delight. Wherein especially is contained a compleat discourse and description of the Four Elements, Constitutions, Ages of Man, Seasons of the Year. Together with an exact epitome of the Four Monarchies, viz. The Assyrian, Persian, Grecian, Roman. Also a Dialogue between Old England and New, concerning the late troubles. With divers other pleasant and serious Poems. By a Gentlewoman in those parts.* Readers of the day, aware of the nine muses (goddesses of poetry, song, etc.) in Greek mythology, realized that the reference to Bradstreet as an upstart muse in a new country may have been ironic. Her brother-in-law himself felt obliged to emphasize two points to legitimize her poems:

". . . I doubt not but the reader will quickly find more than I can say, and the worst effect of his reading will be unbelief, which will make him question whether it be a woman's work, and ask, Is it possible? If any do, take this as an answer from him that dares avow it; it is the work of a woman, honored, and esteemed where she lives, for her gracious demeanor, her eminent parts, her pious conversation, her courteous disposition, her exact diligence in her place, and discreet managing of her family occasions; and more than so, these poems are the fruit but of some few hours, curtailed from her sleep, and other refreshments. . . ."[1]

Bradstreet herself recognized that any woman who sought a profession other than that of housewife in Puritan New England would meet with disapproval. In lines from one of her poems, she acknowledges those who condemn female poets:

I am obnoxious to each carping tongue
Who says my hand a needle better fits.
A poet's pen all scorn I should thus wrong
For such despite they cast on female wits:
If what I do prove well, it won't advance,
They'll say it's stol'n, or else it was by chance.[2]

1. John Woodbridge, as cited in *Anne Bradstreet,* "The Tenth Muse" by Elizabeth Wade White. New York: Oxford University Press, 1971, p. 255.
2. Anne Bradstreet, Stanza V. "The Prologue."

BIOGRAPHY

Edward Taylor

1645?–1729

The most talented American poet of the early period, Edward Taylor was born in England and came to America in his early twenties. He attended Harvard and after graduation became a physician and pastor of a church in a frontier Massachusetts town, Westfield, remaining there for fifty-eight years, until his death in 1729. Although he was a prolific poet, only a few of his friends were aware that he wrote at all.

His poems were generally forgotten until the twentieth century, when a few were printed in 1939. His genius was then recognized, and his complete poems were published in 1960. He is the only American poet of the metaphysical school, a group of seventeenth-century British poets, such as John Donne, who were fond of using complex intellectual metaphors, called "conceits." His poetry is characterized by its religious themes and its use of simple objects and situations from everyday experience. But Taylor is remarkably imaginative in his use of metaphor, making his a genuinely original poetic voice.

"Huswifery" is essentially a prayer, beginning "Make me, O Lord," and ending with a vision of glory that serves as an "Amen." The title refers to common domestic tasks performed by Puritan housewives— spinning and weaving. Composed entirely of interrelated metaphors, the poem compares cloth making to God's granting of salvation. Taylor, who was familiar with the terms and processes used in cloth making, recognized that they lent themselves to portraying God as a Master Weaver who clothes His people in grace. All of the obscure words and phrases in this poem, generally related to parts of the spinning wheel or loom, are defined in the Reader's Note following the poem. All these items were, in Taylor's day, household terms.

Huswifery

Edward Taylor

Make me, O Lord, Thy spinning-wheel complete.
   Thy holy Word my distaff make for me;
Make mine affections Thy swift flyers neat;
   And make my soul Thy holy spool to be;
5   My conversation make to be Thy reel,
   And reel the yarn thereon spun of Thy wheel.

Make me Thy loom then; knit therein this twine;
   And make Thy Holy Spirit, Lord, wind quills;
Then weave the web Thyself. The yarn is fine.
10   Thine ordinances make my fulling mills.
   Then dye the same in heavenly colors choice,
   All pinked with varnished flowers of paradise.

Then clothe therewith mine understanding, will,
   Affections, judgment, conscience, memory,
15 My words and actions, that their shine may fill
   My ways with glory and Thee glorify.
   Then mine apparel shall display before Ye
   That I am clothed in holy robes for glory.

1685   **1937**

Thomas Eakins (1844–1916), detail of
Spinning. Private collection

"Huswifery" from *The Poems of Edward Taylor*, edited by Donald
E. Stanford. Copyright © 1960 by Donald E. Stanford. Reprinted
by permission.

"Upon What Base?" from *The Poetical Works of Edward Taylor*,
Thomas H. Johnson, editor. (Princeton Paperback, 1966) Copyright
Rockland 1939; Princeton University Press, 1943. Reprinted by
permission of Princeton University Press.

Reader's Note

"Huswifery"

"Huswifery" is an elaborate comparison between cloth making and God's granting of salvation through grace. This type of intellectual comparison between two very dissimilar things, called a *conceit*, extends throughout the poem.

In stanza one, the speaker asks to be made God's spinning wheel, equating each part of the wheel with some element in his spiritual life. The *distaff*, the stick which holds the raw flax or wool, is equated with God's *holy Word*. The comparison suggests that God's Word, the Bible, is essential in anchoring the raw material of the speaker's soul in its quest for grace. The *flyers*, which twist the raw material into threads, resemble the speaker's *affections*, or emotions; the *spool*, onto which the twisted threads are first wound, is like the speaker's *soul*; and the *reel*, which holds the finished thread, is likened to the speaker's *conversation*, or social behavior. In this stanza, then, God's work upon the speaker has progressed: one stage of salvation through grace has been completed.

In stanza two, the speaker asks to be made God's *loom*, a machine used for weaving thread into cloth. God, the Weaver, winds, or turns, the *quills* (hollow reeds onto which the yarn is wound), thus converting the threads into the *web* of cloth. God's *ordinances* (laws and sacraments) will cleanse the cloth, just as *fulling mills* did in Taylor's day. Then the cloth can be decorated and dyed (*pinked*) with bright (*varnished*) flowers.

In the final stanza, the speaker asks God to robe all his faculties, words, and actions in this newly spun cloth. Thus glorified in this beautiful robe, the speaker can in turn give glory to God.

In asking first to be made God's spinning wheel, then to be made His loom, and finally to be clad in Divine robes, the speaker is offering his entire existence and life to be placed in the service of God. Every dedicated Puritan minister (like Edward Taylor) would desire to make such an offer, but few could write such an ingenious and powerful poem in the process.

THINK AND DISCUSS
Understanding
1. What is huswifery? (Refer to the last paragraph of Taylor's biography, if necessary.)
2. What verb is repeated throughout the first two stanzas? Who is the subject of this verb? the object?

Analyzing
3. What is the effect of the imperative form of verbs used throughout this poem?
4. Why do you think that the poem is divided into three stanzas?
5. What is the speaker requesting of God, particularly in the final stanza?

APPLYING: Extended Metaphor HⱫ
See Handbook of Literary Terms, p. 887.
You have learned that a metaphor is a comparison between two basically unlike things that have something in common (page 20). An **extended metaphor** is one that is developed throughout an entire work or a significant part of it.

1. What object or process is described in each stanza of "Huswifery"? How are they related?
2. What is God's role and what is the speaker's role in the activities represented by these metaphors?

Upon What Base?

Edward Taylor

Upon what base was fixed the lathe wherein
He turned this globe and rigolled it[1] so trim?
Who blew the bellows of His furnace vast?
Or held the mold wherein the world was cast?
5 Who laid its cornerstone? Or whose command?
Where stand the pillars upon which it stands?
Who laced and filleted[2] the earth so fine
With rivers like green ribbons smaragdine?[3]
Who made the seas its selvage,[4] and its locks

10 Like a quilt ball within a silver box?[5]
Who spread its canopy? Or curtains spun?
Who in this bowling alley bowled the sun?
Who made it always when it rises set
To go at once both down, and up to get?
15 Who the curtain rods made for this tapestry?
Who hung the twinkling lanterns in the sky?
Who? Who did this? Or who is He? Why, know
It's only Might Almighty this did do.

1682   **1939**

THINK AND DISCUSS
Understanding
1. To what kinds of earthly craftsmen does the speaker compare God in this poem?
2. What aspects of the earth's beauty does the speaker describe in lines 7–11?

Analyzing
3. What is the basic question asked in this poem? What is the answer?
4. Why might line 12 surprise a modern reader? Explain its meaning.

Extending
5. What information about life in colonial New England do Taylor's poems provide?

COMPOSITION ◄══
Developing an Extended Metaphor
    Think of a metaphor to reflect a personal quality or feeling. Develop this metaphor as fully as possible in a diary entry.

Writing a Question-Poem
    Write a poem of at least 12 lines, similar in format to "Upon What Base?" The poem should consist of a series of questions, ending with an answer. Try to use vivid images, and at least one metaphor in your poem, which should be directed to a student literary magazine.

---

1. *rigolled* (rig′əld) *it,* shaped and grooved it so that its various parts fitted snugly together.
2. *filleted,* edged.
3. *smaragdine* (smə rag′din), having the deep green color of emeralds.
4. *Who made . . . selvage* (sel′vij), "Who made the seas the edges or border of the land?"
5. *locks . . . box,* landlocked lakes that look like balls of quilting materials in a silver-colored sewing box.

In 1761, a slave ship arrived in Boston from the west coast of Africa. An eight-year-old girl from that ship was purchased at the auction block by John Wheatley, a successful tailor, and given the name Phillis Wheatley. Educated by her new family, she displayed a keen intelligence and quickly mastered English and Latin. By the age of thirteen, she had written her first poem. Shortly thereafter, the poem was published, and she became something of a celebrity in Boston society, reading her poems for drawing-room audiences.

Unable to find a Boston publisher for her prodigy, Mrs. Wheatley arranged for London publication of *Poems on Various Subjects, Religious and Moral* in 1773. Then she sent Phillis, accompanied by the Wheatleys' son, to England, where she was honored as "The Sable Muse." Upon her return to Boston, Phillis was given her freedom, six months before Mrs. Wheatley's death in March, 1774.

Living amidst the turmoil of revolutionary Boston, Wheatley continued to write poetry, much of it espousing freedom and patriotism. In 1775, she wrote a poem to George Washington, who was then commander of the American armies in the Revolutionary War. So pleased was Washington with the tribute that he invited Wheatley to visit him at the Continental Army Camp. But always her poetry expressed Wheatley's Christian faith, as in the poem that follows.

Wheatley married John Peters, another free black, who later was imprisoned for debt. Her three children died in infancy, the last shortly after the thirty-year-old Wheatley died, alone and poor, but uncomplaining.

The quality of her poems, which were modeled on works of eighteenth-century English poets, makes them noteworthy in themselves. That such poetry was written by a young woman, who spoke no English when she was taken into slavery, at a time when educational opportunities for women and blacks were limited, makes Wheatley unique in American letters.

To S. M., A Young African Painter on Seeing His Works

Phillis Wheatley

To show the lab'ring bosom's deep intent,
And thought in living characters to paint,
When first thy pencil did those beauties give,
And breathing figures learnt from thee to live,
5 How did those prospects give my soul delight,
A new creation rushing on my sight!
Still, wondrous youth! each noble path pursue;
On deathless glories fix thine ardent view:
Still may the painter's and the poet's fire,
10 To aid thy pencil and thy verse conspire!
And may the charms of each seraphic theme
Conduct thy footsteps to immortal fame!
High to the blissful wonders of the skies
Elate thy soul, and raise thy wishful eyes.
15 Thrice happy, when exalted to survey
That splendid city, crowned with endless day,
Whose twice six gates on radiant hinges ring:[1]
Celestial Salem[2] blooms in endless spring.
Calm and serene thy moments glide along,
20 And may the muse[3] inspire each future song!
Still, with the sweets of contemplation blessed,
May peace with balmy wings your soul invest!
But when these shades of time are chased away,
And darkness ends in everlasting day,
25 On what seraphic pinions shall we move,
And view the landscapes in the realms above!
There shall thy tongue in heavenly murmurs flow,
And there my muse with heavenly transport glow;
No more to tell of Damon's[4] tender sighs,
30 Or rising radiance of Aurora's[5] eyes;
For nobler themes demand a nobler strain,
And purer language on the ethereal plain.
Cease, gentle Muse! the solemn gloom of night
Now seals the fair creation from my sight.

1773

S. M., Scipio Moorhead, slave-servant of the Reverend John Moorhead, Boston.

1. *city . . . ring*, Revelation 21:10–12: The wall of the heavenly city "had twelve gates, and at the gates twelve angels, and names written thereon, which are the names of the twelve tribes of Israel."
2. *Salem*, Jeru*salem*.
3. *muse*, the spirit believed to inspire a poet or an artist in the act of creating a work.
4. *Damon*, an idealized shepherd-singer of love in pastoral poetry, was falsely accused and imprisoned and nearly lost his life for his friend Pythias.
5. *Aurora*, Roman goddess of dawn.

From *Early Negro American Writers*, edited by Benjamin Brawley. Published by The University of North Carolina Press.

THINK AND DISCUSS
Understanding
1. What, according to the first six lines, does the speaker admire in S. M.?
2. What do we learn about S. M. in lines 9 and 10?
3. What is the "splendid city" (line 16)?

Analyzing
4. In lines 23–24, what is suggested by "shades of time" and "darkness"?
5. In line 24, to what does "everlasting day" refer?
6. In line 26, what **images** does the word *landscapes* evoke?
7. In lines 27–32, the poet envisions S. M. gone to heaven. How does his art differ there?
8. In the last two lines, what brings about a change in the poet's feelings?

APPLYING: Heroic Couplet HⱫ
See Handbook of Literary Terms, p. 884.

A special kind of couplet is called the **heroic couplet,** which consists of two consecutive rhyming lines of iambic pentameter. A line of *iambic pentameter* is made up of five *feet* (or units of rhythm); each foot has an unstressed syllable followed by a stressed one. The stressed syllables can be indicated with the symbol ´, the unstressed syllables with the symbol ˘. The feet can be indicated with a slash. The result looks like this.

To shŏw / the lá/b'rĭng bŏs/ŏm's deép /
   ĭntént,
Ănd thóught / ĭn lĭv/ĭng chár/ăctĕrs / tŏ paínt,

1. Note that some couplets in this poem end with words that have similar sounds but do not rhyme exactly, such as *intent/paint.* Find two other word pairs that do not rhyme exactly.

2. A closed heroic couplet is one that ends with a complete stop and whose meaning is complete within the two lines. Reread lines 1–6 and 29–34. Which couplets are closed?
3. Look at both of Anne Bradstreet's poems (pages 62 and 63). Which poem is written in heroic couplets?

COMPOSITION ◀━●
Analyzing a Painting
Write an essay of four paragraphs for an art magazine, discussing your impressions of the painting on pages 9 or 94. To prepare for writing this essay, first examine the painting closely, noting the use of color, the mood or atmosphere, the theme of the work, and anything else you consider important. Devote a paragraph to each aspect of the painting you wish to discuss. Finally, explain why this painting seems appropriate for a unit titled The New Land.

Analyzing a Theme
Wheatley's poem can be considered a comment on each of the following themes: artistic endeavor, the plight of the slave, or the need for religious faith. Choose one of these themes and write an essay of at least three paragraphs, using lines from the poem or from Wheatley's biography to illustrate this theme. If you have a student literary magazine, submit your article to it. See "Writing About Theme" in the Writer's Handbook.

Philip Freneau, (frə nō′) whose poetry is closely identified with the American Revolution, was born in New York and attended Princeton University. It was there that his poetic talent became known, with the publication of a collection titled *The Rising Glory of America*, written with a fellow student. Freneau's life was a series of adventures—as a schoolteacher, sailor, sea captain, West Indian adventurer, and editor. During the Revolutionary War, Freneau enlisted in the militia and, while serving on an American privateer (a privately owned and armed vessel commissioned by the government to engage in war), was taken prisoner. Later freed, Freneau wrote a poem about the episode titled "The British Prison Ship."

As a newspaper editor with strong political leanings, he managed to antagonize Washington, who referred to him as "that rascal Freneau." Yet Jefferson thought highly of Freneau's partisan paper, the *National Gazette*, saying that it had "saved our constitution which was galloping fast into monarchy."

Freneau's poems seem to divide naturally into two groups: those devoted to politics and freedom and those given over to nature and romantic fancy. The latter group, which includes "The Wild Honeysuckle," comprise nearly all of his best works. In the summer of 1786, Freneau wrote "The Wild Honeysuckle" after he stopped to meditate on the plant with white, fragrant blossoms which he found growing in the wilds of South Carolina. Neglected in its time, it is considered the best American nature poem of the eighteenth century and points the way to later poets such as William Cullen Bryant (see Unit 2).

The Wild Honeysuckle

Philip Freneau

Fair flower, that does so comely grow,
Hid in this silent, dull retreat.
Untouched thy honied blossoms blow,
Unseen thy little branches greet:
5   No roving foot shall crush thee here,
    No busy hand provoke a tear.

By Nature's self in white arrayed,
She bade thee shun the vulgar eye,
And planted here the guardian shade,
10 And sent soft waters murmuring by;
    Thus quietly thy summer goes,
    Thy days declining to repose.

Smit with those charms, that must decay,
I grieve to see your future doom;

15 They died—nor were those flowers more gay,
The flowers that did in Eden bloom;
    Unpitying frosts, and Autumn's power
    Shall leave no vestige of this flower.

From morning suns and evening dews
20 At first thy little being came:
If nothing once, you nothing lose,
For when you die you are the same;
    The space between, is but an hour,
    The frail duration of a flower.

1786

Philip Freneau, "The Wild Honeysuckle" from *The Poems of Philip Freneau*. Princeton, N.J., Princeton University Library, 1902.

The term "wild honeysuckle" has been used to describe a variety of plants. In Freneau's time it referred to the swamp azalea shown here.

THINK AND DISCUSS
Understanding
1. According to stanza 1, what causes the honeysuckle to remain untouched?
2. How has nature favored the wild honeysuckle, according to stanza 2?

Analyzing
3. What words and phrases create a happy, restful atmosphere in stanzas 1 and 2? What words and phrases create a somber atmosphere that suggests death in the third stanza?
4. What causes the poet to adopt a reflective attitude in the final stanza?
5. In the last stanza, the poet appears somewhat reconciled to the fate of the wild honeysuckle. Discuss.
6. In the last stanza, and particularly the last two lines of the poem, the poet suggests a relationship between the life of the flower and the life of human beings. Explain the relationship.

THINKING SKILLS
Generalizing
To generalize is to draw a general conclusion from particular information. For example, you can make some broad observations about an author's philosophy and style by studying his or her works.

1. Make a general statement about death, based on lines 21 and 22 of "The Wild Honeysuckle."
2. Given the fact that Freneau is said to be more representative of the nineteenth century than the eighteenth, what might you expect of nineteenth-century poetry?

COMPOSITION ◄●▬
Describing an Object Imaginatively
Try an experiment in which you closely examine some object, such as a flower, weed, rusting can, broken bottle, or empty matchbook. In at least three paragraphs, describe the item for your friends. Indicate what seems ordinary about it, what is unique, and what thought it inspires in you about human experience, society, life, or fate.

Writing About a Poem
Write a five-paragraph essay on "The Wild Honeysuckle" for a reference book on poetry. The first four paragraphs should explain what each of the four stanzas appears to be saying. In the last paragraph, speculate about how the life of the flower is suggestive of human life.

An Overview

American literature of the colonial period reflects the practical concerns of a people attempting to survive in a wilderness. Mainly factual prose and a bit of poetry, the works show immediate concerns of the early settlers—conveying information, persuading readers, recording events, describing landscapes, and invoking God. While these early works might be considered a literature of struggling endurance rather than a literature of imaginative leisure, they compensate for what they lack in grace, style, and artistic balance by their vividness, power, and charm. Moreover, the colonial sermons, diaries, letters, travel narratives, and historical accounts provide a valuable source of firsthand information in recording the life, ideals, rigors, and progress in settling a new land. In addition, these works supply insight into the colonial imagination and introduce themes that, in the New World environment, become uniquely American.

To understand American literature, we should note the recurring themes that appear from earliest times to the present. These themes, though grounded in the American experience, have universal appeal. What makes them uniquely American? No doubt it is a combination of many things: the infinite promise of an undeveloped land; the drive and determination of people seeking freedom or adventure; the moral underpinnings of a Puritan ethic; the challenge of abandoning old ways for new; the lure of an ever receding frontier; and the restless movement in search of a fulfilled life, to name a few.

Every country has its ideals, but America is particularly identified with a dream. One critic said that America was "a fable waiting to be agreed upon"—that is, a land designed to fulfill many people's preconceptions and ideals. One recurring theme, the *American Dream,* is an original blend of the spirit of enterprise, the longing for an ideal, the passion for liberty—all impulses that led to the founding and settling of our country. The American Dream which, in the words of John Smith, involves a land where one can "live exceeding well," spans many centuries, from the gilded expectations Columbus had for a virgin continent, to the quest of the Pilgrims for social and religious freedom, to the launching pads and moon walks of our present century. As you read the selections in this book, notice how the American Dream always looks to the future as it is adapted and refined throughout the ages, appearing in fantasy versions such as science fiction (set in a technological wonder world); or turning into its dark opposite, the *American Nightmare* (set in a technological nether world).

Note also the many other themes that reappear in different dress during different literary periods: *The Search for Identity; Individualism; Freedom; The Journey; Initiation; The Frontier; Moral Struggle; Rebellion vs. Conformity.*

In order to establish an *Identity,* the colonists had to define their place in the New World, their connections with England, and their relationship with God. This search for identity takes the form of a personal quest as Benjamin Franklin strives toward moral perfection. To Canassatego, identity is established largely through an appropriate education, while Jonathan Edwards sees identity as formed and tempered by "the just hand of God." Closely linked to identity is the theme of *Individualism*—the special factor that enabled Crèvecoeur to define an American. One critic observed that when the settlers put down roots in the new land, "Yankee sap began to flow in American veins," making a new breed of people. Many elements contributed to this individualism, among them the sense of personal accountability before God that resulted from the Protestant Reformation, and the self-sufficiency required in settling an untamed land.

Freedom meant many different things to early Americans and appeared imminently attainable in a new land devoid of the shackles of tradition. For John Smith it meant the spirit of adventure and the openness to possibility in the challenges of a new beginning. For Benjamin Franklin it signified the right to overcome humble origins by using one's native abilities and pluck. For Thomas Jefferson it pointed to the overthrow of political tyranny. But for black slaves freedom was unattainable, however conceived. Even for the talented poet Phillis Wheatley, the strictures of the slave society prevailed over the compassion of her "owners."

The Journey, a recurring motif throughout this unit, can be found in the accounts of La Salle, Columbus, Smith, and Bradford. On a literal level, these journeys embody the hardships that immigrants encountered as they traveled from one land to another. But the colonists' journeys were figurative as well—a nation of people first at sea, then transplanted, arriving at a destination that was as spiritual as it was physical.

Initiation is a theme that takes a variety of forms in colonial literature, from the young Navajo brave who celebrates the independence of the world made possible by his bonding with his horse, to the young Ben Franklin who discovers much of his unacknowledged self through his experiment in achieving moral perfection. But aside from the personal initiations that appear in individual selections is the underlying motif of a nation that is itself coming of age, suffering from growing pains, and establishing its independence.

Many aspects of *The Frontier*, or the land, are portrayed in this unit—its newness, its untapped wealth, its brutality, its availability, and its tremendous beauty. Crèvecoeur differentiates Americans in terms of their geographical proximity to the sea or the frontier. John Smith recognizes that the land affords an opportunity for "planting and building a foundation for . . . Posterity." Selections by Columbus and La Salle record the successes and failures of those who tried to impose order on an untamed land. The frontier has many faces in early American writing. Occasionally, in the form of an infinitely bountiful nature, it offers a subject for speculation, as it does with Freneau's wild honeysuckle and Edwards's flying spider. But more frequently the frontier represents the wilderness, and appears in the light of its cruel or benevolent effect on settlers' lives.

The theme of *Moral Struggle*—or Good vs. Evil—is particularly evident in the Puritan world where God and Satan, virtue and vice, waged constant battle. Witchcraft, for Mather and his contemporaries, was a manifestation of the powers of the Devil, while the fire-and-brimstone sermons of Jonathan Edwards established God's power, if not His mercy. Today, Americans, perhaps more than other people, continue to see the world as a place of passionate moral struggle, constantly testing the individual and the national commitment to virtue and moral right.

Rebellion vs. Conformity has been a theme in American experience from the beginning. The colonists were in rebellion against the religious and political restraints of the old country in their flight to the new. Yet as they developed their own sometimes rigid customs and laws, they expected a conformity that caused many to rebel anew. The Declaration of Independence was, of course, a supreme act of national rebellion. The subsequent adoption of the American Constitution represented a remarkable agreement among the individual colonies to conform to the just principles of a federal government. The future would, of course, bring other rebellions together with other attempts to impose conformity.

Although it is difficult to assess eighteenth-century literature in the light of modern literary standards, these early works provide essential information to the student of modern literature. From these origins one can extract the fundamental material, organized around certain basic themes, that provides American literature with its distinctive voice. As you read selections throughout this book, watch for these themes to resurface. Note that each unit includes an essay that explores a major theme in American literature.

BIOGRAPHY

Benjamin Franklin
1706–1790

Detail of portrait by Charles Willson Peale (1741–1827)

Self-educated and self-made, Benjamin Franklin led a rich and active life that nearly spanned the eighteenth century. Universally recognized as a superb diplomat and celebrated wit, Franklin was also a scientist, a musician, a philosopher, and the inventor of, among other things, the glass harmonica, the "Franklin" stove, and bifocal glasses.

Born the son of a Boston tallow maker, Franklin became at the age of twelve a printer's apprentice to his brother, who had just brought back a press from England. Under the pen name of Silence Dogood, Franklin wrote a number of satiric pieces for his brother's newspaper, the *New England Courant*. At the age of seventeen, he headed for Philadelphia, where he acquired his own printing shop. In 1730, he created a character who came to be known as Poor Richard, and *Poor Richard's Almanack* continued for the next twenty-five years. Both Silence Dogood and Poor Richard were ancestors of a long and popular line of humorous philosophers, including Mark Twain and Will Rogers.

The growth of his printing company and some wise investments enabled Franklin to retire when he was forty-four and devote his time to inventions and scientific experiments. His findings established him as the leading scientist of the Western Hemisphere and caused his election to the exclusive Royal Society in London.

It was only natural that a man of Franklin's talents should be sought out for public office. The Pennsylvania legislature sent him to London in 1757 to represent Pennsylvania in its disputes with the mother country. Between 1768 and 1770 three more of the colonies asked Franklin to represent them, and he quickly became the chief spokesman for the colonies as a whole. By 1775 he had given up his once strong hope for reconciliation with England and returned to America where he was elected to the Second Continental Congress. He was appointed to the committee to frame the Declaration of Independence.

In 1776 he sailed to France to obtain military assistance for the colonies. His quick wit and worldly wisdom made him extremely popular there, and he secured the support of both France and Spain and eventually helped negotiate the Treaty of Paris (1783), by which England recognized American independence. While abroad, he wrote *The Autobiography*, which explains the regimen of self-education that he so rigorously pursued.

Although he was old and ill when he returned to America in 1785, he served as a delegate to the Constitutional Convention (1787) and continued his work with many humanitarian and scientific societies. It has been said of Franklin, "In the adolescence of America, he was the representative American."

Moral Perfection

from The Autobiography

Benjamin Franklin

It was about this time I conceived the bold and arduous project of arriving at moral perfection. I wished to live without committing any fault at any time; I would conquer all that either natural inclination, custom, or company might lead me into. As I knew, or thought I knew, what was right and wrong, I did not see why I might not always do the one and avoid the other. But I soon found I had undertaken a task of more difficulty than I had imagined. While my care was employed in guarding against one fault, I was often surprised by another; habit took the advantage of inattention; inclination was sometimes too strong for reason. I concluded, at length, that the mere speculative conviction that it was our interest to be completely virtuous, was not sufficient to prevent our slipping; and that the contrary habits must be broken, and good ones acquired and established, before we can have any dependence on a steady, uniform rectitude of conduct. For this purpose I therefore contrived the following method.

In the various enumerations of the moral virtues I had met with in my reading, I found the catalog more or less numerous, as different writers included more or fewer ideas under the same name. Temperance, for example, was by some confined to eating and drinking, while by others it was extended to mean the moderating every other pleasure, appetite, inclination, or passion, bodily or mental, even to our avarice and ambition. I proposed to myself, for the sake of clearness, to use rather more names, with fewer ideas annexed to each, than a few names with more ideas; and I included under thirteen names of virtues all that at that time occurred to me as necessary or desirable, and annexed to each a short precept, which fully expressed the extent I gave to its meaning.

These names of virtues, with their precepts, were:

1. Temperance

Eat not to dullness: drink not to elevation.

2. Silence

Speak not but what may benefit others or yourself; avoid trifling conversation.

3. Order

Let all your things have their places; let each part of your business have its time.

4. Resolution

Resolve to perform what you ought; perform without fail what you resolve.

5. Frugality

Make no expense but to do good to others or yourself; *i.e.*, waste nothing.

6. Industry

Lose no time; be always employed in something useful; cut off all unnecessary action.

From *The Writings of Benjamin Franklin*, edited by Albert Henry Smyth (1905–1907).

7. Sincerity

Use no hurtful deceit; think innocently and justly, and, if you speak, speak accordingly.

8. Justice

Wrong none by doing injuries, or omitting the benefits that are your duty.

9. Moderation

Avoid extremes; forbear resenting injuries so much as you think they deserve.

10. Cleanliness

Tolerate no uncleanliness in body, clothes, or habitation.

11. Tranquillity

Be not disturbed at trifles, or at accidents common or unavoidable.

12. Chastity

Rarely use venery but for health or offspring, never to dullness, weakness, or the injury of your own or another's peace or reputation.

13. Humility

Imitate Jesus and Socrates.[1]

My intention being to acquire the *habitude* of all these virtues, I judged it would be well not to distract my attention by attempting the whole at once, but to fix it on one of them at a time; and, when I should be master of that, then to proceed to another, and so on, till I should have gone through the thirteen; and, as the previous acquisition of some might facilitate the acquisition of certain others, I arranged them with that view, as they stand above. *Temperance* first, as it tends to procure that coolness and clearness of head, which is so necessary where constant vigilance was to be kept up, and guard maintained against the unremitting attraction of ancient habits, and

the force of perpetual temptations. This being acquired and established, *Silence* would be more easy; and my desire being to gain knowledge at the same time that I improved in virtue, and considering that in conversation it was obtained rather by the use of the ears than of the tongue, and therefore wishing to break a habit I was getting into of prattling, punning, and joking, which only made me acceptable to trifling company, I gave *Silence* the second place. This and the next, *Order*, I expected would allow me more time for attending to my project and my studies. *Resolution*, once become habitual, would keep me firm in my endeavours to obtain all the subsequent virtues; *Frugality* and *Industry* freeing me from my remaining debt, and producing affluence and independence, would make more easy the practice of *Sincerity* and *Justice*, etc., etc. Conceiving then, that, agreeably to the advice of Pythagoras in his *Golden Verses*,[2] daily examination would be necessary, I contrived the following method for conducting that examination.

I made a little book, in which I allotted a page for each of the virtues. I ruled each page with red ink, so as to have seven columns, one for each day of the week, marking each column with a letter for the day. I crossed these columns with thirteen red lines, marking the beginning of each line with the first letter of one of the virtues, on which line, and in its proper column, I might mark, by a little black spot, every fault I found upon examination to have been committed respecting that virtue upon that day.

I determined to give a week's strict attention to each of the virtues successively. Thus, in the first week, my great guard was to avoid every the least offence against *Temperance*, leaving the other virtues to their ordinary chance, only marking every evening the faults of the day. Thus, if in the first week I could keep my first line,

1. *Socrates* (sok′rə tēz′), 469?-399 B.C., Greek philosopher who lived humbly.
2. *Pythagoras* (pə thag′ər əs) . . . *Golden Verses*, a Greek philosopher (582?–500? B.C.), whose practical sayings are known as the *Golden Verses*.

TEMPERANCE.						
EAT NOT TO DULLNESS. **DRINK NOT TO ELEVATION.**						
	S.	M.	T.	W.	T.	F.	S.
T.							
S.	★	★		★		★	
O.	★★	★	★		★	★	★
R.			★		★		
F.		★			★		
I.			★				
S.							
J.							
M.							
C.							
T.							
C.							
H.							

marked *T*, clear of spots, I supposed the habit of that virtue so much strengthened, and its opposite weakened, that I might venture extending my attention to include the next, and for the following week keep both lines clear of spots. Proceeding thus to the last, I could go through a course complete in thirteen weeks, and four courses in a year. And like him who, having a garden to weed, does not attempt to eradicate all the bad herbs at once, which would exceed his reach and his strength, but works on one of the beds at a time, and, having accomplished the first, proceeds to a second; so I should have, I hoped, the encouraging pleasure of seeing on my pages the progress I made in virtue, by clearing successively my lines of their spots, till in the end, by a number of courses, I should be happy in viewing

a clean book, after a thirteen weeks' daily examination.

The precept of *Order* requiring that *every part of my business should have its allotted time,* one page in my little book contained the following scheme of employment for the twenty-four hours of a natural day.

The Morning.
Question. What good shall I do this day?

5
6
7 — Rise, wash, and address *Powerful Goodness!*[3] Contrive day's business, and take the resolution of the day; prosecute the present study, and breakfast.

8
9
10
11 — Work.

Noon.
12
1 — Read, or overlook my accounts, and dine.

2
3
4
5 — Work.

Evening.
Question. What good have I done today?

6
7
8
9 — Put things in their places. Supper. Music or diversion, or conversation. Examination of the day.

Night.
10
11
12
1
2
3
4 — Sleep.

I entered upon the execution of this plan for self-examination, and continued it with occa-

---

3. *Powerful Goodness,* God.

sional intermissions for some time. I was surprised to find myself so much fuller of faults than I had imagined; but I had the satisfaction of seeing them diminish. To avoid the trouble of renewing now and then my little book, which, by scraping out the marks on the paper of old faults to make room for new ones in a new course, became full of holes; I transferred my tables and precepts to the ivory leaves of a memorandum book, on which the lines were drawn with red ink, that made a durable stain, and on those lines I marked my faults with a black-lead pencil, which marks I could easily wipe out with a wet sponge. After a while I went through one course only in a year, and afterward only one in several years, till at length I omitted them entirely, being employed in voyages and business abroad, with a multiplicity of affairs that interfered; but I always carried my little book with me.

My scheme of *Order* gave me the most trouble; and I found that, though it might be practicable where a man's business was such as to leave him the disposition of his time, that of a journeyman printer, for instance, it was not possible to be exactly observed by a master, who must mix with the world, and often receive people of business at their own hours. *Order,* too, with regard to places for things, papers, etc., I found extremely difficult to acquire. I had not been early accustomed to it, and, having an exceeding good memory, I was not so sensible of the inconvenience attending want of method. This article, therefore, cost me so much painful attention, and my faults in it vexed me so much, and I made so little progress in amendment, and had such frequent relapses, that I was almost ready to give up the attempt, and content myself with a faulty character in that respect; like the man who, in buying an ax of a smith, my neighbor, desired to have the whole of its surface as bright as the edge. The smith consented to grind it bright for him if he would turn the wheel; he turned, while the smith pressed the broad face of the ax hard and heavily on the stone, which made the turning of it very fatiguing. The man came every now and then from the wheel to see how the work went

on, and at length would take his ax as it was, without farther grinding. "No," said the smith, "turn on, turn on; we shall have it bright by-and-by; as yet, it is only speckled." "Yes," says the man, *"but I think I like a speckled ax best."* And I believe this may have been the case with many, who, having, for want of some such means as I employed, found the difficulty of obtaining good and breaking bad habits in other points of vice and virtue, have given up the struggle, and concluded that *"a speckled ax was best"*; for something, that pretended to be reason, was every now and then suggesting to me that such extreme nicety as I exacted of myself might be a kind of foppery in morals, which, if it were known, would make me ridiculous; that a perfect character might be attended with the inconvenience of being envied and hated; and that a benevolent man should allow a few faults in himself, to keep his friends in countenance.

In truth, I found myself incorrigible with respect to *Order;* and now I am grown old, and my memory bad, I feel very sensibly the want of it. But, on the whole, though I never arrived at the perfection I had been so ambitious of obtaining, but fell far short of it, yet I was, by the endeavor, a better and a happier man than I otherwise should have been if I had not attempted it; as those who aim at perfect writing by imitating the engraved copies, though they never reach the wished-for excellence of those copies, their hand is mended by the endeavor, and is tolerable while it continues fair and legible.

It may be well my posterity should be informed that to this little artifice, with the blessing of God, their ancestor owed the constant felicity of his life, down to his seventy-ninth year in which this is written. What reverses may attend the remainder is in the hand of Providence; but, if they arrive, the reflection on past happiness enjoyed ought to help his bearing them with more resignation. To *Temperance* he ascribes his long-continued health, and what is still left to him of a good constitution; to *Industry* and *Frugality,* the early easiness of his circumstances and acquisition of his fortune, with all that knowledge that enabled him to be a useful citizen, and obtained for him some degree of reputation among the learned; to *Sincerity* and *Justice*, the confidence of his country, and the honorable employs it conferred upon him; and to the joint influence of the whole mass of the virtues, even in the imperfect state he was able to acquire them, all that even-ness of temper, and that cheerfulness in conversation, which makes his company still sought for, and agreeable even to his younger acquaintance. I hope, therefore, that some of my descendants may follow the example and reap the benefit.

1784   1887

THINK AND DISCUSS

Understanding

1. According to the first paragraph, why does Franklin work out a deliberate method for achieving moral perfection?
2. Why does Temperance lead the list?
3. Why does Silence appear second on the list?
4. What moral virtue does Franklin find the most difficult to acquire? Why?

Analyzing

5. Citing examples from his *Autobiography*, explain to what degree you think Franklin possessed each of the following qualities: honesty; humility; self-discipline; a sense of humor.
6. Franklin uses the speckled ax and the weeding of a garden to illustrate pit-falls in trying to achieve moral perfection. What point is he making in each of these **metaphors?**

Extending

7. In what way does *The Autobiography* reinforce the notion of Franklin as a self-made man?
8. What do you think Jonathan Edwards would feel was wrong with Franklin's approach to achieving morality?

COMPOSITION ◀●▬

Writing a Self-Examination

Make a list of virtues, in order, that could lead to your self-improvement. In a four-paragraph essay, written as part of a book on self-improvement, explain why you have selected these particular virtues and why you have put them in the order you have chosen.

Analyzing Character

Reread Franklin's biography and the excerpt from *The Autobiography* with an eye to what they reveal about Franklin's character and personality. See also your answer to question 5 under Analyzing. Choose four traits—reasoning ability, orderliness, humility or pride, self-discipline or self-indulgence, a sense of humor, or others—and write an essay of four paragraphs for your teacher about Franklin's character, citing examples that support your observations.

"As Poor Richard Says . . ." by Benjamin Franklin

Never leave that till tomorrow, which you can do today.

He that riseth late must trot all day, and shall scarce overtake his business at night; while Laziness travels so slowly, that Poverty soon overtakes him.

Sloth, like rust, consumes faster than labor wears; while the used key is always bright.

The sleeping fox catches no poultry, and there will be sleeping enough in the grave.

It would be thought a hard government that should tax its people one-tenth part of their time, to be employed in its service. But idleness taxes many of us much more.

Help, hands, for I have no lands; or, if I have, they are smartly taxed.

At the workingman's house hunger looks in, but dares not enter.

Then plough deep while sluggards sleep, and you shall have corn to sell and to keep.

Early to bed, and early to rise, makes a man healthy, wealthy, and wise.

Handle your tools without mittens; remember, that the cat in gloves catches no mice.

It is true there is much to be done, and perhaps you are weak-handed; but stick to it steadily, and you will see great effects; for constant dropping wears away stones.

Methinks I hear some of you say, "Must a man afford himself no leisure?" I will tell thee, my friend, what Poor Richard says, "Employ thy time well, if thou meanest to gain leisure."

Leisure is time for doing something useful: this leisure the diligent man will obtain, but the lazy man never.

Fly pleasures, and they will follow you.

Now I have a sheep and a cow, everybody bids me good morrow.

 See TONE in the Handbook of Literary Terms, page 915.

A Witch Trial at Mount Holly

Benjamin Franklin

aturday last, at Mount Holly, about eight miles from this place (Burlington, N.J.) near three hundred People were gathered together to see an Experiment or two tried on some Persons accused of Witchcraft. It seems the Accused had been charged with making their Neighbors' Sheep dance in an uncommon manner, and with causing Hogs to speak and sing

From the *Pennsylvania Gazette*, Oct. 22, 1730.

Psalms, etc., to the great Terror and Amazement of the king's good and peaceable Subjects in this Province; and the Accusers, being very positive that if the Accused were weighed in scales against a Bible, the Bible would prove too heavy for them; or that, if they were bound and put into the river they would swim;[1] the said Accused, desirous to make Innocence appear, voluntarily offered to undergo the said Trials if two of the most violent of their Accusers would be tried with them. Accordingly the time and place was agreed on and advertised about the Country. The Accusers were one Man and one Woman; and the Accused the same. The Parties being met and the People got together, a grand Consultation was held, before they proceeded to Trial, in which it was agreed to use the scales first; and a Committee of Men were appointed to search the Men, and a Committee of Women to search the Women, to see if they had any thing of weight about them, particularly pins. After the scrutiny was over a huge great Bible belonging to the Justice of the Place was provided, and a lane through the Populace was made from the Justice's house to the scales, which were fixed on a Gallows erected for that Purpose opposite to the house, that the Justice's wife and the rest of the Ladies might see the Trial without coming amongst the Mob, and after the manner of Moorfields[2] a large ring was also made. Then came out of the house a grave, tall Man carrying the Holy Writ before the supposed Wizard etc., (as solemnly as the Sword-bearer of London before the Lord Mayor[3]) the Wizard was first put in the scale, and over him was read a Chapter out of the Books of Moses,[4] and then the Bible was put in the other scale, (which, being kept down before, was immediately let go); but, to the great surprise of the spectators, flesh and bones came down plump, and outweighed that great good Book by abundance. After the same manner the others were served, and their Lumps of Mortality severally were too heavy for Moses and all the Prophets and Apostles. This being over, the Accusers and the rest of the Mob, not satisfied with this Experiment, would have the Trial by Water. Accordingly a most solemn Procession was made to the Millpond, where both Accused and Accusers being stripped (saving only to the Women their shifts), were bound hand and foot and severally placed in the water, lengthways, from the side of a barge or flat, having for security only a rope about the middle of each, which was held by some in the flat. The accused man being thin and spare with some difficulty began to sink at last; but the rest, every one of them, swam very light upon the water. A Sailor in the flat jumped out upon the back of the Man accused thinking to drive him down to the bottom; but the Person bound, without any help, came up some time before the other. The Woman Accuser being told that she did not sink, would be ducked a second time; when she swam again as light as before. Upon which she declared that she believed the Accused had bewitched her to make her so light, and that she would be ducked again a Hundred Times but she would duck the Devil out of her. The Accused Man, being surprised at his own swimming, was not so confident of his Innocence as before, but said, "If I am a Witch, it is more than I know," The more thinking part of the spectators were of opinion that any Person so bound and placed in the water (unless they were mere skin and bones) would swim, till their breath was gone, and their lungs filled with water. But it being the general Belief of the Populace that the Women's shifts and the garters with which they were bound helped to support them, it is said they are to be tried again the next warm weather, naked.

1730

---

1. *swim,* float.
2. *Moorfields,* an English resort near London that has a walk for promenades.
3. *Sword-bearer . . . Lord Mayor,* an official who, in processions, carries the sword of state before the mayor of London.
4. *Books of Moses,* the first five books of the Bible: Genesis, Exodus, Leviticus, Numbers, and Deuteronomy.

THINK AND DISCUSS
Understanding
1. What two tests for witchcraft are described in the selection?
2. Who underwent these two tests? What were the results of these tests?

Analyzing
3. On what incorrect assumptions are the two tests based?
4. This selection appeared originally as a news article. At what points does the story inform the reader of the "five W's" of news reporting: who, what, where, when, and why?

Extending
5. On the basis of this account, do you think Franklin believed in witches? Did he believe in the witch tests? Explain.

APPLYING: Tone H⫐
See Handbook of Literary Terms, p. 915.

The **tone** of a literary work expresses the author's attitude toward his or her subject or audience. Although Franklin's news story was supposed to be a purely factual account, it contains words and details that indicate his attitude about witchcraft and the means used to detect it. His tone clearly reveals his opinion of the effectiveness of the witchcraft tests.

1. What words and details does Franklin use in this account to indicate that the people in this province and the spectators at the trial feared witchcraft? What details indicate that they believed witches could be detected through these tests?
2. What word would you use to describe Franklin's attitude about witchcraft and the tests used to detect witches? What phrases in the news story indicate this attitude?

COMPOSITION ◀●▬
Writing to a Newspaper
As a reader of the newspaper in which Franklin's piece has appeared, write a letter of three paragraphs or more requesting detailed information about the sheep dancing and the hogs speaking and singing psalms. Assume a tone that is skeptical, amused, or humorous. For example, you might inquire whether the sheep waltzed together or did individual interpretative dances, or if the talking hogs had discernible accents or sang the psalms with musical accompaniment.

Explaining a Belief or Superstition
Even today, some people refuse to walk under a ladder, some will not stay on the thirteenth floor of a hotel, and some believe Friday the thirteenth is an unlucky (and dangerous) day. Write an essay of at least four paragraphs describing a strange belief or superstition, prevalent today or long ago. To gather information, you might interview someone, explain beliefs that you yourself hold, or do some library research on superstitions. In your final paragraph, try to arrive at some explanation or speculation about how this superstition came to be, or about the way it serves to answer human needs or account for events that are otherwise inexplicable. Assume that your essay will be published in a psychology magazine.

BIOGRAPHY

Michel-Guillaume Jean de Crèvecoeur[1]
1735–1813

Born in France, Michel-Guillaume Jean de Crèvecoeur was educated in England and at nineteen sailed for Canada to become a map maker with the French army. Eventually he settled on a frontier farm in New York. Unwilling to join either party in the Revolution, he set sail in 1780 for England to await the end of the war. Crèvecoeur returned to America only to discover his home had been burned and his wife killed during an Indian raid. After spending seven years as French consul, he took a leave of absence in 1790, sailed for Europe, and never returned. His circle of literary friends included not only French writers, but also Benjamin Franklin, then American Minister to France.

In his most celebrated work, *Letters from an American Farmer*, Crèvecoeur showed his admiration for the independent and self-reliant American farmer. Such a farmer served as the *persona*, or assumed voice, for his letters. Ostensibly directed to the farmer's friend, these letters were, in fact, a literary creation directed to a much larger audience— Europeans with an appetite for information about America. In fashioning the *literary letter*, Crèvecoeur adopted a personal tone with an American flavor, drawing freely from two genres familiar to the European audience. From the essay, he adapted techniques of presenting facts and expressing opinions; from the epistolary novel (consisting of letters written by fictional characters) he adapted techniques of creating character and incident. Throughout these letters, Crèvecoeur portrayed "individuals of all nations [that] are melted into a new race," offering fresh hope and renewed possibility in the New World.

---

1. *Michel-Guillaume Jean de Crèvecoeur* (mi shel′ gē yōm′ jän də krev′kèr)

What Is an American?

Michel-Guillaume Jean de Crèvecoeur

hat, then, is the American, this new man? He is either an European or the descendant of an European; hence that strange mixture of blood, which you will find in no other country. I could point out to you a family whose grandfather was an Englishman, whose wife was Dutch, whose son married a French woman, and whose present four sons have now four wives of different nations. He is an American, who, leaving behind him all his ancient prejudices and manners, receives new ones from the new mode of life he has embraced, the new government he obeys, and the new rank he holds. He becomes an American by being received in the broad lap of our great Alma Mater. Here individuals of all nations are melted into a new race of men, whose labors and posterity will one day cause great changes in the world. Americans are the western pilgrims who are carrying along with them that great mass of arts, sciences, vigor, and industry which began long since in the East; they will finish the great circle. The Americans were once scattered all over Europe; here they are incorporated into one of the finest systems of population which has ever appeared, and which will hereafter become distinct by the power of the different climates they inhabit. The American ought therefore to love this country much better than that wherein either he or his forefathers were born. Here the rewards of his industry follow with equal steps the progress of his labor; his labor is founded on the basis of nature, self-interest; can it want a stronger allurement? Wives and children, who before in vain demanded of him a morsel of bread, now, fat and frolicsome, gladly help their father to clear those fields whence exuberant crops are to arise to feed and to clothe them all, without any part

being claimed, either by a despotic prince, a rich abbot, or a mighty lord. Here religion demands but little of him: a small voluntary salary to the minister and gratitude to God; can he refuse these? The American is a new man, who acts upon new principles; he must therefore entertain new ideas and form new opinions. From involuntary idleness, servile dependence, penury, and useless labor, he has passed to toils of a very different nature, rewarded by ample subsistence. This is an American.

British America is divided into many provinces, forming a large association scattered along a coast of 1,500 miles extent and about 200 wide. This society I would fain examine, at least such as it appears in the middle provinces; if it does not afford that variety of tinges and gradations which may be observed in Europe, we have colors peculiar to ourselves. For instance, it is natural to conceive that those who live near the sea must be very different from those who live in the woods; the intermediate space will afford a separate and distinct class.

Men are like plants; the goodness and flavor of the fruit proceeds from the peculiar soil and exposition in which they grow. We are nothing but what we derive from the air we breathe, the climate we inhabit, the government we obey, the system of religion we profess, and the nature of our employment. Here you will find but few crimes; these have acquired as yet no root among us. I wish I were able to trace all my ideas; if my ignorance prevents me from describing them properly, I hope I shall be able to delineate a few of the outlines; which is all I propose.

From *Letters from an American Farmer*. The New American Library of World Literature, Inc.

Nineteenth-century ceramic statues.
The National Gallery, Washington

Those who live near the sea feed more on fish than on flesh and often encounter that boisterous element. This renders them more bold and enterprising; this leads them to neglect the confined occupations of the land. They see and converse with a variety of people; their intercourse with mankind becomes extensive. The sea inspires them with a love of traffic, a desire of transporting produce from one place to another, and leads them to a variety of resources which supply the place of labor. Those who inhabit the middle settlements, by far the most numerous, must be very different; the simple cultivation of the earth purifies them, but the indulgences of the government, the soft remonstrances of religion, the rank of independent freeholders, must necessarily inspire them with sentiments, very little known in Europe among a people of the same class. What do I say? Europe has no such class of men; the early knowledge they acquire, the early bargains they make, give them a great degree of sagacity. As freemen, they will be litigious; pride and obstinacy are often the cause of lawsuits; the nature of our laws and governments may be another. As citizens, it is easy to imagine that they will carefully read the newspapers, enter into every political disquisition, freely blame or censure governors and others. As farmers, they will be careful and anxious to get as much as they can, because what they get is their own. As northern men, they will love the cheerful cup. As Christians, religion curbs them not in their opinions; the general indulgence leaves every one to think for themselves in spiritual matters; the law inspects our actions; our thoughts are left to God. Industry, good living, selfishness, litigiousness, country politics, the pride of freemen, religious indifference, are their characteristics. If you recede still farther from the sea, you will come into more modern settlements; they exhibit the same strong lineaments, in a ruder appearance. Religion seems to have still less influence, and their manners are less improved.

Now we arrive near the great woods, near the last inhabited districts; there men seem to be placed still farther beyond the reach of government, which in some measure leaves them to themselves. How can it pervade every corner, as they were driven there by misfortunes, necessity of beginnings, desire of acquiring large tracks of land, idleness, frequent want of economy, ancient debts; the reunion of such people does not afford a very pleasing spectacle. When discord, want of unity and friendship, when either drunkenness or idleness prevail in such remote districts, contention, inactivity, and wretchedness must ensue. There are not the same remedies to these evils as in a long-established community. The few magistrates they have are in general little better than the rest; they are often in a perfect state of war; that of man against man, sometimes decided by blows, sometimes by means of the law; that of man against every wild inhabitant of these venerable woods, of which they are come to dispossess them. There men appear to be no better than carnivorous animals of a superior rank, living on the flesh of wild animals when they can catch them, and when they are not able, they subsist on grain. He who would wish to see America in its proper light and have a true idea of its feeble beginnings and barbarous rudiments must visit our extended line of frontiers, where the last settlers dwell and where he may see the first labors of settlement, the mode of clearing the earth, in all their different appearances, where men are wholly left dependent on their native tempers and on the spur of uncertain industry, which often fails when not sanctified by the efficacy of a few moral rules. There, remote from the power of example and check of shame, many families exhibit the most hideous parts of our society. They are a kind of forlorn hope, preceding by ten or twelve years the most respectable army of veterans which come after them. In that space, prosperity will polish some, vice and the law will drive off the rest, who, uniting again with others like themselves, will recede still farther, making room for more industrious people, who will finish their improvements, convert the log house into a convenient habitation, and rejoicing that the first heavy labors are finished, will change in a few years that hitherto barbarous country into a fine, fertile, well-regulated district. Such is our progress; such is the march of the Europeans toward the interior parts of this continent. In all societies there are off-casts; this impure part serves as our precursors or pioneers; my father himself was one of that class, but he came upon honest principles and was therefore one of the few who held fast; by good conduct and temperance, he transmitted to me his fair inheritance, when not above one in fourteen of his contemporaries had the same good fortune.

Forty years ago, this smiling country was thus inhabited; it is now purged, a general decency of manners prevails throughout, and such has been the fate of our best countries.

Exclusive of those general characteristics, each province has its own, founded on the government, climate, mode of husbandry, customs, and peculiarity of circumstances. Europeans submit insensibly to these great powers and become, in the course of a few generations, not only Americans in general, but either Pennsylvanians, Virginians, or provincials under some other name. Whoever traverses the continent must easily observe those strong differences, which will grow more evident in time. The inhabitants of Canada, Massachusetts, the middle provinces, the southern ones, will be as different as their climates; their only points of unity will be those of religion and language. . . .

1782

THINK AND DISCUSS

Understanding
1. According to the first paragraph, what does the American leave behind? What new things does the American embrace, obey, and hold?
2. Why are men like plants, according to the third paragraph?
3. Into what three groups does Crèvecoeur divide Americans?

Analyzing
4. What adjectives would you use to describe the author's attitude toward the frontiersman? Explain.
5. What happens to the frontiersman when the "more respectable army of veterans" takes over the frontier?

Extending
6. What ways of life described in the essay are no longer part of present-day America?
7. Crèvecoeur introduces the idea of America as a melting pot. Reread the first half of his

opening paragraph. Has history proven the theory true or false? Give examples from contemporary life to prove your point.

8. In Crèvecoeur's time the possibility for westward expansion seemed limitless. What attitudes toward the land itself might be bred by such a belief?

READING LITERATURE SKILLFULLY
Fact/Opinion

A **statement of fact** can be proved to be true or false. A **statement of opinion** expresses someone's judgment or way of thinking about something. Opinions are often indicated by words such as *best, silly,* or *should*. Although statements of opinion cannot be proved true or false, they can be supported or explained. In order for an opinion to be valid, it must be supported with sufficient evidence.

A **mixed statement** is one that expresses part fact and part opinion. The following is a mixed statement:

Red River, a marvelous historical narrative, was written in 1874 by a Civil War veteran named Ned Sackville.

What word expresses an opinion? What parts of the sentence can be proved true or false? Where could you find such proof?

The following sentences are from "What Is an American?" Decide which is a statement of fact, which is a statement of opinion, and which is a mixed statement.

1. "The Americans were once scattered all over Europe; here they are incorporated into one of the finest systems of population which has ever appeared. . . ."
2. "There men appear to be no better than carnivorous animals of a superior rank. . . ."

3. "British America is divided into many provinces, forming a[n] . . . association scattered along a coast of 1,500 miles extent and 200 wide."

COMPOSITION
Writing a Literary Letter

Write a literary letter of at least three paragraphs, assuming a persona, or voice, other than your own. Comment on a recent event or some aspect of contemporary American life. Direct your letter to a nationally known figure. Keep in mind, however, that you are actually addressing a wider audience, perhaps the nation at large or a citizens' action group. In the final paragraph, ask questions of your audience and try to arrive at some conclusion.

Writing About New Frontiers

Think about frontiers that are still open to exploration today. Such a frontier may be physical (space exploration), scientific (advancements that improve or extend life), or psychological (discoveries about the mind). Choose one such frontier and in an essay of at least four paragraphs, explain to a classmate how this area is being explored in the twentieth century. In the final paragraph, make some predictions about future exploration in this area.

BIOGRAPHY

Thomas Jefferson
1743–1826

Detail of portrait by
Rembrandt Peale (1805).
Independence National
Historical Park Collection

When speaking at a dinner for Nobel prizewinners, John Kennedy described the assembly as "the most extraordinary collection of talent, of human knowledge, that has ever been gathered together at the White House, with the possible exception of when Thomas Jefferson dined alone."

A Virginia planter and aristocrat, a graduate of William and Mary College, an accomplished architect, and a lawyer by profession, Jefferson served first in the Virginia House of Burgesses and was one of the Virginia representatives to the Second Continental Congress. At the Congress Jefferson reluctantly agreed to attempt a draft of a document declaring colonial independence. The resulting Declaration of Independence remains his masterpiece.

He subsequently served as governor of Virginia, minister to France, Secretary of State, Vice-President, and finally President from 1801 to 1809. On retiring from the presidency, Jefferson devoted much time to founding and building the University of Virginia, laying the plans for a curriculum that offered a broadly liberal education.

He died on July 4, 1826, the fiftieth anniversary of the Declaration, and was buried at his home in Monticello, Virginia. He wrote his own epitaph: "Here was buried Thomas Jefferson, Author of the Declaration of American Independence, of the Statute of Virginia for Religious Freedom, and Father of the University of Virginia."

See STYLE in the Handbook of Literary Terms, page 912.

The Declaration of Independence

Thomas Jefferson

hen, in the course of human events, it becomes necessary for one people to dissolve the political bands which have connected them with another, and to assume, among the Powers of the earth, the separate and equal station to which the Laws of Nature and of Nature's God entitle them, a decent respect to the opinions of mankind requires that they should declare the causes which impel them to the separation.

We hold these truths to be self-evident: that

all men are created equal; that they are endowed by their Creator with certain unalienable Rights; that among these are Life, Liberty, and the pursuit of Happiness. That, to secure these Rights, Governments are instituted among Men, deriving their just powers from the consent of the governed—That, whenever any Form of Government becomes destructive of these ends, it is the Right of the People to alter or abolish it, and to institute new Government, laying its foundation on such Principles, and organizing its Powers in such form, as to them shall seem most likely to effect their Safety and Happiness. Prudence, indeed, will dictate that Governments long established should not be changed for light and transient causes; and, accordingly, all experience hath shown that mankind are more disposed to suffer, while evils are sufferable, than to right themselves by abolishing the forms to which they are accustomed. But, when a long train of abuses and usurpations, pursuing invariably the same Object, evinces a design to reduce them under absolute Despotism, it is their right, it is their duty, to throw off such Government, and to provide new Guards for their future security. Such has been the patient sufferance of these Colonies, and such is now the necessity which constrains them to alter their former Systems of Government. The history of the present King of Great Britain is a history of repeated injuries and usurpations, all having in direct object the establishment of an absolute Tyranny over these States. To prove this, let Facts be submitted to a candid world:

He has refused his Assent to Laws the most wholesome and necessary for the public good.

He has forbidden his Governors to pass Laws of immediate and pressing importance, unless suspended in their operation till his Assent should be obtained; and, when so suspended, he has utterly neglected to attend to them.

He has refused to pass other Laws for the accommodation of large districts of people, unless those people would relinquish the rights of Representation in the Legislature; a right inestimable to them, and formidable to tyrants only.

He has called together legislative bodies at places unusual, uncomfortable, and distant from the depository of their Public Records, for the sole purpose of fatiguing them into compliance with his measures.

He has dissolved Representatives Houses repeatedly for opposing, with manly firmness, his invasions on the rights of the people.

He has refused for a long time after such dissolutions to cause others to be elected; whereby the Legislative Powers, incapable of Annihilation, have returned to the People at large for their exercise; the State remaining, in the meantime, exposed to all the dangers of invasions from without, and convulsions within.

He has endeavored to prevent the Population of these States; for that purpose obstructing the Laws for Naturalization of Foreigners; refusing to pass others to encourage their migrations hither, and raising the conditions of new Appropriations of Lands.

He has obstructed the Administration of Justice by refusing his Assent to Laws for establishing Judiciary Powers.

He has made Judges dependent on his Will alone for the tenure of their offices, and the amount and Payment of their salaries.

He has erected a multitude of New Offices, and sent hither swarms of Officers to harass our People and eat out their substance.

He has kept among us, in times of Peace, Standing Armies, without the Consent of our legislatures.

He has affected to render the Military independent of and superior to the Civil Power.

He has combined with others to subject us to a jurisdiction foreign to our constitution, and unacknowledged by our laws: giving his Assent to their Acts of pretended Legislation:

For quartering large bodies of armed troops among us;

For protecting them, by a mock Trial, from Punishment for any Murders which they should commit on the Inhabitants of these States;

For cutting off our Trade with all parts of the world;

Robert Edge Pine, detail of *Congress Voting Independence* (1788).
Historical Society of Pennsylvania

For imposing Taxes on us without our Consent;

For depriving us, in many cases, of the benefits of Trial by Jury;

For transporting us beyond Seas to be tried for pretended offenses;

For abolishing the free System of English Laws in a neighboring Province,[1] establishing therein an Arbitrary government, and enlarging its Boundaries, so as to render it at once an example and fit instrument for introducing the same absolute rule into these Colonies;

For taking away our Charters, abolishing our most valuable Laws, and altering, fundamentally, the Forms of our Governments;

For suspending our own Legislatures, and declaring themselves invested with Power to legislate for us in all cases whatsoever.

He has abdicated Government here by declaring us out of his Protection, and waging War against us.

He has plundered our seas, ravaged our Coasts, burnt our towns, and destroyed the Lives of our People.

He is, at this time, transporting large Armies of foreign Mercenaries to complete the works of death, desolation, and tyranny, already begun with circumstances of Cruelty and Perfidy scarcely paralleled in the most barbarous ages, and totally unworthy the Head of a civilized nation.

He has constrained our fellow Citizens, taken Captive on the high Seas, to bear Arms against their Country, to become the executioners of their friends and Brethren, or to fall themselves by their Hands.

He has excited domestic insurrections amongst us, and has endeavored to bring on the inhabitants of our frontiers the merciless Indian Savages, whose known rule of warfare is an undistinguished destruction of all ages, sexes, and conditions.

In every stage of these Oppressions, We have Petitioned for Redress, in the most hum-

---

1. *a neighboring Province.* After capturing Quebec, the English in 1774 imposed its rigid French laws on British colonists living in former French domains.

ble terms: Our repeated Petitions have been answered only by repeated injury. A Prince, whose character is thus marked by every act which may define a Tyrant, is unfit to be the ruler of a free People.

Nor have We been wanting in attentions to our British brethren. We have warned them, from time to time, of attempts by their legislature to extend an unwarrantable jurisdiction over us. We have reminded them of the circumstances of our emigration and settlement here. We have appealed to their native justice and magnanimity, and we have conjured them, by the ties of our common kindred, to disavow these usurpations, which would inevitably interrupt our connections and correspondence. They, too, have been deaf to the voice of justice and of consanguinity. We must, therefore, acquiesce in the necessity which denounces our Separation, and hold them, as we hold the rest of mankind—Enemies in War—in Peace, Friends.

WE, THEREFORE, the REPRESENTATIVES of the UNITED STATES of AMERICA, in GENERAL CONGRESS Assembled, appealing to the Supreme Judge of the world for the rectitude of our intentions, Do, in the Name and by the Authority of the good People of these Colonies, solemnly PUBLISH and DECLARE, That these United Colonies are, and of Right ought to be, FREE AND INDEPENDENT STATES; that they are Absolved from all Allegiance to the British Crown, and that all political connection between them and the State of Great Britain is, and ought to be, totally dissolved; and that, as FREE AND INDEPENDENT STATES, they have full Power to levy War, conclude Peace, contract Alliances, establish Commerce, and to do all other Acts and Things which INDEPENDENT STATES may of right do. And, for the support of this Declaration, with a firm reliance on the Protection of Divine Providence, we mutually pledge to each other our Lives, our Fortunes, and our Sacred Honor.

1776

THINK AND DISCUSS
Understanding
1. What has made this Declaration necessary, according to the first paragraph?
2. What, according to the second paragraph, are among the unalienable rights of people? Under what circumstances may a government be changed or abolished? Where does this government get its power?
3. Name some of the abuses of which the makers of the Declaration declare George III guilty.
4. What does this document "publish and declare" in the final paragraph?

Analyzing
5. Why do you think Jefferson says "the pursuit of Happiness" rather than merely "Happiness"?

6. After listing the colonists' grievances (paragraphs three–twenty-nine), Jefferson makes clear the fact that they have tried using peaceful means to draw the king's attention to their plight. What is the purpose of this statement?
7. What is the purpose of the last paragraph?
8. Is the **tone** of the last paragraph in keeping with that of the body of the Declaration? Why or why not?
9. What emotional effect is conveyed in the final sentence? What particular words, by both their sounds and meanings, contribute to the creation of this effect?

APPLYING: Style H7
See Handbook of Literary Terms, p. 912.

Style is the way writers use language to fit their ideas and to reach their audience. The purpose of the Declaration of Independence was to convince the world at large that the American colonies had good reason to break away from England. Jefferson, who recognized the power of appropriate language to bring about action, adopted a serious, persuasive **tone** and used words that were formal and forceful. In addition, he used the techniques of *parallelism* (phrases and sentences that are similar in structure) and *repetition* in order to emphasize his point.

1. Jefferson uses the words *invariably* instead of *always, relinquish* instead of *give up, consanguinity* instead of *blood ties.* What effect would the substitution of these simpler terms have had on the Declaration?
2. What parallel phrases does Jefferson use to present the "repeated injuries and usurpations" of the King? What is the effect of this use of parallelism?
3. What is the overall effect of words such as the following: *plundered, ravaged, tyranny, cruelty, perfidy, barbarous?*

THINKING SKILLS
Synthesizing

To synthesize is to put together parts and elements so as to form a whole, a new pattern or structure not evident before. Synthesis can involve personal experience and imagination. For example, in the 1920s when writer Gertrude Stein referred to her contemporaries as the Lost Generation, she was synthesizing the effects of war on an uprooted, disillusioned group of American writers.

1. Create a descriptive name for the people of the colonial period. Like Stein's label, your name should consist of an adjective followed by a noun.
2. Imagine that Jefferson has written a document titled A Request for Independence and adopted a friendly tone, rather than a demanding one. Speculate on the effectiveness of such a document, giving reasons for your opinion.

COMPOSITION
Writing to Persuade

Most of us have strong feelings about something, whether it's nuclear disarmament or environmental pollution. Write a four- or five-paragraph advertisement for a widely read magazine, persuading the readers to support your cause. You may want to discuss how far state and local governments should take censorship, alternatives other than grades for evaluating an education, or the effect a generation of children raised in day-care centers will have on the future of the country.

Writing to Defend Your Position

Imagine that you are one of the writers of the Declaration of Independence. You have gone back to England to explain the self-evident truths set forth in the first part of the second paragraph. In a three- or four-paragraph essay, defend these truths and explain why they justify a separation from England.

ENRICHMENT
Participating in a Discussion

Thomas Jefferson's original version of the Declaration of Independence called for the abolishment of slavery. Look up this original version of the Declaration and read aloud the parts that were eventually cut from it. Discuss in a small group whether the passages should have been cut—especially if it had meant that some states would not have signed and there might have been no Declaration at all. Make a report to the class on the results of your research and discussion.

The Story of American English

From the moment the Pilgrims set sail for the New World on the *Mayflower,* the language they spoke and wrote became molded by the pressures of change. The language of Elizabethan England that the settlers brought with them often proved inadequate for functioning in a wilderness, confronting wild animals, strange plants, and new exotic foods. It was to be measured, too, against unwritten languages used by the native inhabitants who were already adapted to life in America.

The early settlers, as Thomas Jefferson would later point out, faced "new circumstances . . . which . . . called for new words, new phrases, and the transfer of old words to new objects." From the Indians they met as they moved west, the settlers borrowed words to name the *raccoon, chipmunk, skunk, possum, moose;* the *catalpa, hickory, pecan, persimmon, squash;* the *moccasin, canoe, tomahawk, wigwam.* And today, the names of many of our mountains, rivers, and cities—*Appalachian, Mississippi, Ohio, Manhattan, Chicago*—echo the original Indian languages.

Many new words were developed by giving an old English word a new meaning, or by simply making new combinations of old words. For example, as the colonists moved inland, they passed through *foothills* and climbed *notches* or *gaps,* separating one *watershed* from another, often navigating *rapids.* They listened to the *bullfrog* on the *pond* and the *katydid* and picked a *johnny-jump-up* growing near the *basswood* tree. After they made a *clearing,* they built a *log cabin* on the top of a *bluff* overlooking a *creek.*

The British were not the only foreign settlers bringing their language to the New World. Indeed, the Spanish had arrived first, settling in Mexico, and then moving north into what is now the American Southwest and California.

The French settled in Canada and began their explorations of the Mississippi River down to the Gulf of Mexico. The Dutch re-created their Old World way of life in the Hudson Valley. As English encountered these other European tongues, it adapted by borrowing and absorbing. The following words from the Dutch are commonly used today: *cookie, cole slaw, waffle, sleigh, caboose, stoop* (porch), *boss, dumb, snoop, Yankee,* and *Santa Claus.* From the French, American English took words such as the following: *chowder, jambalaya* (a Creole shrimp dish), *brioche* (a bread roll), *shanty, cent, dime, sashay, prairie, gopher,* and *pumpkin.* Spanish proved a rich resource, supplying words such as *chile, tamale, lariat, lasso, corral, vigilante, alligator,* and *mesa.*

But the English did not always see the additions to the language as an enrichment. One visitor to Georgia in 1735 called the use of the term *bluff* "barbarous English." And Jefferson's coinage *belittle* outraged some who cried: "Spare our mother-tongue."

No one was more influential in defining the American language than Noah Webster, who saw a national language as a way to deepen the bonds among the widely scattered and strongly individualistic people of a new nation. To this end, Webster published in 1783 *The American Spelling Book,* a combination speller, primer, and reader. He clarified pronunciation by a new system of syllable division and simplified American spelling by eliminating foreign elements and silent letters. Thus, we have *color* for *colour, wagon* for *waggon, fiber* for *fibre, tire* for *tyre,* and *risk* for *risque.* Webster spoke for many of the nation's founders when he wrote: "The reasons for American English being different than English English are simple: As an independent nation, our honor requires us to have a system of our own, in language as well as government."

THINKING CRITICALLY
ABOUT LITERATURE

UNIT 1   THE NEW LAND   1500–1800

■ CONCEPT REVIEW

The selections at the end of each unit in *The United States in Literature* illustrate many of the important ideas and literary terms found in the period you have just studied. The selection is accompanied by notes and questions designed to help you think critically about your reading. Page numbers in the notes refer to an application of a literary skill. A more extensive discussion of these terms is in the Handbook of Literary Terms.

The American Crisis is the title given to sixteen pamphlets that Paine wrote from December, 1776, to December, 1783, to boost the sagging spirits of colonists during the Revolution. This excerpt from the first pamphlet, published on December 19, 1776, remains the most famous.

from The American Crisis

Thomas Paine

These are the times that try men's souls: The summer soldier and the sunshine patriot will in this crisis, shrink from the service of his country; but he that stands it NOW, deserves the love and thanks of man and woman. Tyranny, like hell, is not easily conquered; yet we have this consolation with us, that the harder the conflict, the more glorious the triumph. What we obtain too cheap, we esteem too lightly:—'Tis dearness only that gives everything its value. Heaven knows how to put a proper price upon its goods; and it would be strange indeed, if so celestial an article as FREEDOM should not be highly rated. Britain, with an army to enforce her tyranny, has declared that she has a right (*not only to*) TAX but "to BIND *us in* ALL CASES WHATSOEVER," and if being *bound in that manner* is not slavery, then is there not such a thing as slavery upon earth. Even the expression is impious, for so unlimited a power can belong only to GOD. . . .

I have as little superstition in me as any man living, but my secret opinion has ever been, and still is, that God Almighty will not give up a people to

■ **Tyranny . . . triumph:** Note how Paine develops the concept of tyranny in this **simile** (page. 15).
■ **the harder . . . too lightly:** Paine's **style** (page 96), with its *parallelism* and *balance*, lends eloquence to his appeal.

■ Note the appeal to God as on the side of the peace-loving.

military destruction, or leave them unsupportedly to perish, who have so earnestly and so repeatedly sought to avoid the calamities of war, by every decent method which wisdom could invent. Neither have I so much of the infidel in me, as to suppose that he has relinquished the government of the world, and given us up to the care of devils; and as I do not, I cannot see on what grounds the king of Britain can look up to Heaven for help against us: a common murderer, a highwayman, or a housebreaker, has as good a pretense as he. . . .

I once felt all that kind of anger, which a man ought to feel against the mean principles that are held by the Tories: A noted one, who kept a tavern at Amboy, was standing at his door, with as pretty a child in his hand, about eight or nine years old, as I ever saw, and after speaking his mind as freely as he thought was prudent, finished with this unfatherly expression, *"Well! give me peace in my day."* Not a man lives on the continent but fully believes that a separation must some time or other finally take place, and a generous parent should have said, *"If there must be trouble, let it be in my day, that my child may have peace,"* and this single reflection, well applied, is sufficient to awaken every man to duty. Not a place upon earth might be so happy as America. Her situation is remote from all the wrangling world, and she has nothing to do but to trade with them. A man can distinguish himself between temper and principle, and I am as confident, as I am that GOD governs the world, that America will never be happy till she gets clear of foreign dominion. Wars, without ceasing, will break out till that period arrives, and the continent must in the end be conqueror; for though the flame of liberty may sometimes cease to shine, the coal can never expire. . . .

The heart that feels not now is dead; the blood of his children will curse his cowardice, who shrinks back at a time when a little might have saved the whole, and made *them* happy. I love the man that can smile in trouble, that can gather strength from distress, and grow brave by reflection. 'Tis the business of little minds to shrink; but he whose heart is firm, and whose conscience approves his conduct, will pursue his principles unto death. My own line of reasoning is to myself as straight and clear as a ray of light. Not all the treasures of the world, so far as I believe, could have induced me to support an offensive war, for I think it murder; but if a thief breaks into my house, burns and destroys my property, and kills or threatens to kill me, or those that are in it, and to *"bind me in all cases whatsoever"* to his absolute will, am I to suffer it? What signifies it to me, whether he who does it is a king or a common man; my countryman or not my countryman; whether it be done by an individual villain, or an army of them? If we reason to the root of things, we shall find no difference; neither can any just cause be assigned why we should punish in the one case and pardon in the other. . . .

1776

■ The **tone** (page 86) is intense, urgent, and filled with the sense of immediate crisis.
■ **infidel** (in′fə dəl): person who does not believe in religion.

■ **Tory:** an American who favors British rule of the colonies.

■ The Amboy anecdote humanizes the abstract argument.

■ Note that a generous parent elects strife so that his child will have peace.

■ **flame . . . expire:** This **metaphor** (page 20) reinforces the enduring qualities of liberty.

■ Paine classifies people into those with little minds and those with firm hearts.

■ Note how Paine generalizes from particular examples.

■ Note that the *we* is an attempt to bring the reader in on the side of the writer.

THINK AND DISCUSS
Understanding
1. How, according to Paine in the first paragraph, do people determine the value of what they obtain?
2. What is Paine's "secret opinion" revealed in the second paragraph?
3. In what sense does the King of England resemble a "common murderer, a highwayman, or a housebreaker"?

Analyzing
4. Who are the "summer soldier" and "sunshine patriot" mentioned in paragraph one?
5. In the tavern anecdote of paragraph three, why is "Give me peace in my day" called an "unfatherly expression"?
6. In the first sentence of paragraph four, what does the heart represent?

Extending
7. To convince the people of the justice of the Revolution, to what human qualities does Paine appeal throughout this selection? Evaluate the effectiveness of this appeal.

REVIEWING LITERARY TERMS
Style
1. Paine writes, "What we obtain too cheaply, we esteem too lightly." Imagine that he had instead written, "Things that we don't work for are not valued." What qualities of the original does this paraphrase lack?

Simile
2. Explain the appropriateness of the following simile: "My own line of reasoning is to myself as straight and clear as a ray of light."

Metaphor
3. What kinds of people are indicated by the "summer soldier" and the "sunshine patriot"?
4. Paine writes, "The *heart* that feels not now is dead." Why is *heart* a more effective word here than *mind?*

Tone
5. Think of two words to describe the tone of this excerpt. Use examples from the text to explain why you have chosen these words.

■ CONTENT REVIEW

THINKING SKILLS
Classifying
1. Make a chart with the titles of eight selections from the unit listed down the side and the following heads across the top: *Food, Travel, Superstitions, Views of Government,* and *Religious Beliefs.* For each selection, place a check mark under each head that describes information contained in the selection.
2. The authors in this unit had a variety of occupations, as revealed in their biographies and works. Skim the unit and classify the authors under the correct heading: *Explorer, Housewife, Farmer, Clergyman, Statesman.*

Generalizing
3. What types of journeys do the writers in this unit describe? List different types of journeys, noting spiritual as well as physical ones.
4. Discuss at least six kinds of adversity that the colonial writers describe. Along with each type of adversity, discuss the physical, emotional, or spiritual aids these writers enlist to cope with this adversity.

5. Reread the Iroquois Constitution and the Declaration of Independence. What does each reveal about the ideals of the people who created it?

Synthesizing

6. Choose one work from the unit and speculate on how a modern writer would update, improve, or harm the original.

7. If you could travel back in time to the colonial period, what invention would you take to help improve the quality of life? How would it change things?

Evaluating

8. Which four selections in this unit do you think, in combination, give the most representative picture of colonial life? Which two selections do you think give the least insight into this period? Give brief reasons for your choices.

9. Some people believe that the quality of American literature has improved with time. Of the works collected here, which two or three do you consider to be the best literature? Why?

10. Given the accounts of Cabeza de Vaca, Columbus, and Crèvecoeur, along with the biographical details you have read about Anne Bradstreet, Phillis Wheatley, and Sarah Kemble Knight, explain what role you think women and non-white men played in colonial life.

■ COMPOSITION REVIEW

Choose one of the following topics for a composition.

Writing to Inform

As a reporter for an eighteenth-century newspaper, write a three-paragraph article that will give prospective European travelers an accurate answer to the question, "What is an American?" Review two or three selections in this unit for ideas and specific examples.

Translating into Modern Style

Much early American writing is characterized by complicated sentence structure and formal vocabulary. Choose either the first three paragraphs of "Sinners in the Hands of an Angry God" or the first two paragraphs of the Declaration of Independence and translate the selection into a modern style of writing. Don't change the ideas or the order of the ideas. Assume you are writing for immigrants who have just become citizens of America.

Writing a Formal Essay

"The dominant interests of the revolutionary writers were political and social, while the interests of early colonial writers were mainly religious and economic." Using the quoted sentence above as a thesis statement, write a four-paragraph essay for your classmates comparing and contrasting the goals of revolutionary and colonial writers. Begin by making a list of political and social goals of the revolutionary writers (Franklin, Crèvecoeur, and Jefferson) and another list of the religious and economic goals expressed by other writers in this unit. Organize your lists into a cohesive essay that compares and contrasts the two.

ITERARY NATIONALISM

1800	1805	1810	1815	1820

HISTORY AND THE ARTS

- War of 1812
- Louisiana Purchase   "The Star-Spangled Banner" composed •
- Work begins on Erie Canal
- Napoleon becomes Emperor (France)
- First textile factory, Lowell, Massachusetts
- Lewis and Clark expedition
- Washington, D.C., becomes U.S. capital   First Atlantic crossing by an American steamship •
- Missouri Compromise •
- Beethoven finishes *Fifth Symphony* (Austria) •
- Construction begins on Cumberland Road
- Importation of slaves outlawed •
- Steamboat service begins on Mississippi

PRESIDENTS' ADMINISTRATIONS

- 1801–1809 Thomas Jefferson
- 1809–1817 James Madison
- 1817–1825 James Monroe

LITERATURE

- Bryant: "Thanatopsis" •
- Irving: *The Sketch Book* •
- Paine: *Letters to the Citizens*
- Irving: *Knickerbocker's History of New York*
- History of Lewis and Clark expedition published

Whale's tooth scrimshaw

Detail of appliquéd quilt by Sarah Warner (c. 1800)

Pennsylvania German dish decorated with courtship scene

1800–1840

UNIT

1825	1830	1835	1840

- First public high school, Boston
  - Monroe Doctrine
    - Bolshoi Ballet founded (Russia)
- "Trail of Tears," forced migration of Cherokees •
- Victoria begins reign (England) •
- Mt. Holyoke, first women's college •
  - American Anti-Slavery Society founded
- Indian Removal Act •
  - The Erie Railroad established
  - Nat Turner's slave revolt in Virginia
    - 2,800 miles of railroad in operation •
    - U.S. population passes 17 million •

- 1825–1829 John Quincy Adams
  - 1829–1837 Andrew Jackson
- 1837–1841 Martin Van Buren

- *The Saturday Evening Post* first published
  - Emerson: *The American Scholar* •
  - Noah Webster: *American Dictionary of the English Language*
- Cooper: *The Last of the Mohicans* •
  - Poe: *Tamerlane and Other Poems*
  - Cooper: *The Pathfinder* •
  - *Freedom's Journal*, first black newspaper
  - Hawthorne: *Twice-Told Tales* •
  - *The Dial*, a quarterly magazine, published •
    - Holmes: *Poems*

Railroad poster (1837)

Hand-painted chest made of pine (c. 1840)

Robert Lindneux (born 1891), detail of *The Trail of Tears*

PREVIEW

UNIT 2   LITERARY NATIONALISM   1800–1840

Authors

Washington Irving
James Fenimore Cooper
William Cullen Bryant
Henry Wadsworth Longfellow

Oliver Wendell Holmes
John Greenleaf Whittier
Fanny Kemble
Edgar Allan Poe

James Russell Lowell
James W. C. Pennington

Features

Reader's Note: Romanticism
Themes in American Literature:
    The Search for a Voice
Reader's Note: Bryant and Romanticism
Comment: Longfellow at Home
The Story of American English
Comment: The Facts Behind "The Cask of
    Amontillado"
Reading a Poem
Reader's Note: "To Helen"
Comment: Of the Sorrow Songs

Composition Assignments Include

Writing a News Article
Writing a Folk Tale
Stating an Opinion
Observing Contemporary Life
Evoking a Mood
Analyzing a Character
Writing About Irony
Writing About Author's Technique
Imitating a Poetic Style
Interpreting a Poem
Writing a Dialogue

Application of Literary Terms

stereotype   personification
anastrophe   irony
synecdoche   characterization
theme   sound devices
rhythm

Enrichment

Oral Reading
Research
Memorizing Poetry

Thinking Critically About Literature

Concept Review
Content Review
Composition Review

Reading Literature Skillfully

author's purpose

Vocabulary Skills

antonyms   dictionary
etymology   context

Thinking Skills

generalizing
evaluating

LITERARY NATIONALISM 1800–1840

At the beginning of the nineteenth century, the United States had a population of just over 5 million and claimed 889,000 square miles of land. By midcentury both the population and the territory had almost quadrupled. Through various treaties, purchases, and wars, the frontier was extended from the Northwest Territory to Oregon, from Louisiana to the Rocky Mountains, and in the Southwest from Texas to California. Eastern cities expanded rapidly and other cities such as St. Louis and Cincinnati experienced phenomenal growth. Chicago grew from a mud flat of 250 inhabitants to a thriving city of nearly 100,000 in scarcely more than a generation.

Perhaps even more amazing was the spectacular increase in wealth due to the rapid expansion of shipping, trade, manufacture, and agriculture. Eli Whitney's invention of the cotton gin caused thousands of acres in the South to be cultivated. New England ships voyaged farther and farther until they carried freight on all the seven seas. After the War of 1812, factories were built along the waterways of New England and the Middle Atlantic states.

WESTWARD EXPANSION

As settlers attempted to move west of the Appalachian Mountains, they encountered great difficulties crossing the mountain barrier. Once they settled, they could not ship their products back East for sale. Congress, aware of the urgent need for good public roads, passed an act that provided for the construction of the Cumberland Road, begun in 1811. This road initially connected Cumberland, Maryland, on the Potomac River, to Wheeling, Ohio, on the Ohio River, and was later extended to Vandalia, then the capital of Illinois. The construction of

an artificial waterway, the Erie Canal, connecting the Hudson River with Lake Erie, began in 1817 and was completed in 1825. By 1840, 3,000 miles of canals existed in the United States, which, in conjunction with roads and navigable rivers, created a vastly improved transportation network north of the Ohio River.

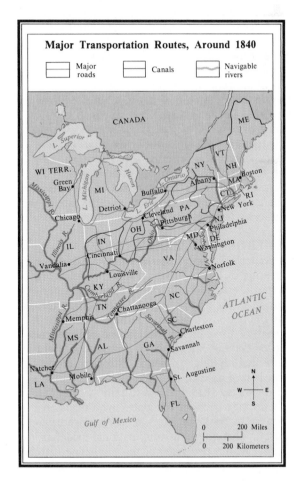

Major Transportation Routes, Around 1840

Such tremendous growth, however, was not without its devastating effects. Westward expansion was catastrophic for the Indians who, as a result of the War of 1812, were defeated in the South and Northwest, dispossessed, and forced to move beyond the Mississippi River to "Indian country." With the invention of the cotton gin, there was an increased need for cheap labor, and the subject of slavery became the greatest national issue of this era. In addition, many people, both white and black, suffered from poverty, lack of food, and exploitation.

Certain writers of the day were especially sensitive to these social disorders. John Greenleaf Whittier and James Russell Lowell in particular espoused human and civil rights, and much of their work is infused with a zealous spirit of reform. The abolition movement, which grew strong in the 1830s, produced a flood of writing, much of it by black writers, slave and free. *Freedom's Journal,* the first black newspaper, was founded in 1827, and in 1829 David Walker issued his *Appeal* for a war of black independence. Some of the finest products of this movement are represented here by the spirituals and by James Pennington's narrative of his life as a slave. The spirituals, some of which were sung to pass coded messages among slaves, were eloquent expressions of the yearning for freedom. Songs of a different sort were springing up to chronicle the westward movement ("The Kansas Emigrants"), the spread of the railroads, the loneliness of the cowboy, and the fate of the miners ("Clementine").

EMERGING LITERARY VOICES

Material growth fostered cultural expansion, creating a climate in which writers could forge a new literature—a literature typically American in theme and setting and often characterized by the nation's mood of youthful optimism. It was time for a literary declaration of independence—for the emergence of imaginative literature that no longer imitated European models but blazed its own trail.

As late as 1819 an English critic wrote: "In the four quarters of the globe, who reads an American book? or looks at an American picture?" This question stung national pride. Ironically, within two years of this challenge, three

distinctively American works appeared: *The Sketch Book* (1819–1820) by Washington Irving; *The Spy* (1821) by James Fenimore Cooper; and the *Poems* of William Cullen Bryant (1821). These works won high esteem and a large readership among Europeans, and a Golden Age of literature was launched in America.

Washington Irving, the first professional American writer, eventually gained the respect of the English, who were at first reluctant to recognize his literary genius. Although he was never totally free of European influences, much of his writing is uniquely American in its themes, good-humored presentation of American eccentricities, and special feeling for setting and local custom. He wrote highly complimentary biographies of Christopher Columbus and George Washington, but his greatest contributions were his fanciful creations of Rip Van Winkle, Ichabod Crane, and a host of other figures that soon became part of American folklore.

After *The Spy*, a novel of the American Revolution, James Fenimore Cooper wrote *The Leatherstocking Tales* (*The Deerslayer* is one of these novels), which depict his romanticized vision of the "noble savage," the heroic frontiersman, and the unsurpassed beauty of the American wilderness. Though authors have delighted in poking fun at Cooper (Mark Twain called his characters "corpses," his Indians "cigar-store," and his dialogue "book talk"), he is still among the most widely translated and most popular of American authors.

Poems by William Cullen Bryant included "Thanatopsis," written when Bryant was only seventeen, and "To a Waterfowl." The volume marked the first published verse of stature by an American. Bryant's skillful lyrics and his abiding theme of nature in New England settings have earned for him the reputation of one of America's greatest nature poets.

Some of the best-known poets of this period have been called the "Fireside Poets," so named probably because of the congeniality and gentle persuasiveness of their finest verse. These poets (Longfellow, Lowell, Whittier, and Holmes), all from New England, celebrated the virtues of home, family, and democracy. In their best verse, they display a simple diction, a courageous love of freedom, and a keen eye for the natural beauties of their eastern locale. Writings of the long-lived Fireside Poets, like these poets' own lives, spanned the century. Works such as *Snowbound* and "The Chambered Nautilus," which were written after the National Period, have been included in this unit since they reflect the spirit of this era.

Henry Wadsworth Longfellow immortalized historical figures such as Miles Standish and Paul Revere and made the fictional characters Hiawatha and Minnehaha part of the American heritage. His poem "A Psalm of Life" is an optimistic and quotable acknowledgment of the immortality of the soul.

James Russell Lowell, a man of wit and imagination, championed in essays, speeches, and poems (such as "Stanzas on Freedom") humanitarian causes, especially the abolition of slavery. His poetry, like that of his Puritan predecessors, was often moralistic.

John Greenleaf Whittier, like so many of the poets of his time, was primarily a public rather than a private poet—an orator for the people's interest, not a quiet voice speaking to the private self. Like Lowell, he wrote poems in support of the abolition movement, but his most enduring contribution to American letters is *Snowbound*, a reminiscence that captures the people and the rural New England setting of his youth.

In both verse and prose, Oliver Wendell Holmes was often informal. He wrote numerous verses like "The Ballad of the Oysterman," in which he employed a mock-epic tone, ballad stanzas, and heroic couplets. "I hold it to be a gift of a certain value," he wrote to Lowell, "to give that slight passing spasm of pleasure which a few ringing couplets often cause, read at the right moment." Yet he abandoned his light tone in "The Chambered Nautilus" as he pondered the soul's immortality.

Dramatically different from the Fireside Poets was Edgar Allan Poe, who wrote poems noted for their otherworldly atmosphere and haunting musical effects—poems which, once read, could fasten themselves in the mind with their hypnotic rhythms and rhymes. Perhaps his greatest single contribution, aside from per-fecting the short story as a new literary form, is the creation of the detective story.

Perhaps the myth of the frontiersman symbolizes the essence of this period; for the ever expanding frontier gave an optimistic sense of destiny that largely shaped the people and the literature of a youthful America. And the writers of this era remain the pioneers of our literature.

THINKING ABOUT GRAPHIC AIDS
Using the Time Line

The time line on pages 102–103 gives the chronological sequence of historical and literary events of this period. As you read the time line, note how certain items reflect trends or movements of the period. For example, Nat Turner's revolt and the formation of the American Anti-Slavery Society indicate an increasingly active protest against slavery. Think of broad heads under which you could classify different time-line items.

1. List the following heads in separate columns on a sheet of paper: *Improved Transportation, Progress in Education, Geographical Expansion, Injustices to Native Americans.* Under each head, list time-line items that fit under the classification.
2. By the 1840s the Canal Age was ending. What entry appearing on the time line suggests the cause of its demise?

Using the Map

Use the map on page 105, which shows major transportation routes around 1840, to answer the following items.

1. What do you think was the most commonly used way in 1840—water or road—for the South to transport cotton to coastal ports?
2. Trace the water routes that lead most directly from Natchez to Pittsburgh.

Reader's Note

Romanticism

Though the writers of the National Period displayed a remarkable degree of independence from the main currents of European literature, the influences of the Old World were nonetheless apparent in most of the works they produced. Nineteenth-century writing, both here and abroad, was dominated by the spirit of Romanticism, a movement that flourished in Europe and had as its manifesto the *Lyrical Ballads*, written in 1798 by the British poets William Wordsworth and Samuel Taylor Coleridge. Romanticism was a reaction against Classicism, the dominant philosophy of the Age of Reason, which stressed reason, clarity, balance, and order as valued by the ancient Greeks and Romans. Unlike Classicism, Romanticism championed imagination and the emotions.

In a broad sense, Romanticism was an attitude toward nature, humanity, and society that espoused freedom and individualism. Echoing the ideals of equality set forth in the Declaration of Independence, Romanticism offered a parallel to the growing sense of nationalism.

Many trends make up the Romantic Movement, particularly the following: (1) an emphasis on imagination as a key to revealing the innermost depths of the human spirit; (2) a great interest in the picturesque and exotic aspects of the past; (3) an enthusiasm for portraying national life and character; (4) the celebration of the beauty and mystery of nature; (5) a focus on the individual; (6) a fascination with the supernatural and the gothic; (7) a sense of idealism.

Romanticism was not confined to literature. With the new emphasis on individual dignity and human rights came attempts at social reforms such as the feminist movement and abolitionism. The gothic revival in architecture adopted medieval building styles whose design, which included pointed arches and flying buttresses, carried the eye and the imagination upward and beyond. American music, though still in its artistic infancy, borrowed Romantic motifs from abroad. Painting, especially that produced by the group known as the Hudson River School, depicted the sweeping grandeur of American landscapes. One such work, *Thanatopsis* by Asher Durand (page 131), with its breathtaking panorama of natural beauty, captures the Romantic awe of nature that is portrayed in many of the literary and artistic works in this unit.

Romanticism characterized the works of America's first group of great imaginative writers—Irving, Cooper, Bryant, and Poe. Out of this tradition emerged immortal literary creations such as Cooper's Deerslayer and Chingachgook, men molded by the frontier wilderness, and Rip Van Winkle and Tom Walker, figures drawn from a national past and from German legend. The eminently Romantic works of Bryant (see Reader's Note, page 133) looked to nature and to the past to reveal qualities of the human spirit.

Although he did not share the spirit of idealism of the three other writers, Poe drew from many aspects of the Romantic tradition. In creating the bizarre plots and tormented characters for his short stories and poems, he borrowed from European gothic romances—horror stories and investigations of the supernatural, the most famous of which is Mary Shelley's *Frankenstein* (1818). Poe's preoccupation with the dark, irrational side of the imagination pointed toward later writers such as Herman Melville and Nathaniel Hawthorne, whose works explore the motives and actions of tormented souls.

By the second half of the nineteenth century, American Romanticism was yielding to the philosophy of Transcendentalism, which, like the earlier movement, upheld the goodness of humanity, the glories of nature, and the importance of the individual. Later literary movements were offshoots of Romanticism, adding to and refocusing elements to meet the needs of another age. Even today American writers display Romantic qualities as they probe the national character and celebrate nature.

BIOGRAPHY

Washington Irving

1783–1859

Detail of a portrait of Irving at twenty-seven by one of his friends, John Wesley Jarvis (1780–1840). Sleepy Hollow Restoration, Tarrytown, New York

When Washington Irving was born, his mother reportedly said, "George Washington's work is ended, and the child shall be named for him." The name was appropriate for several reasons. Young Irving's birth occurred in New York on April 3, 1783, five months before peace was established between Great Britain and the colonies. Like his namesake, Washington Irving was also a father of America—a literary patriarch who was the first famous man of letters in the new nation. Significantly, the last work published before Irving's death in 1859 was the fifth volume of his excellent biography, *The Life of George Washington*.

As a youth, Washington Irving rejected the strict religious upbringing imposed by his Scottish Presbyterian father. He enjoyed the emerging arts of nineteenth-century America—music, literature, and especially the theater. He frequented a nearby theater, watching the drama until nine o'clock, when he hurried home for family prayers. After prayers, he escaped through a bedroom window, climbed down the roof, and returned to the theater to see the end of the play.

Irving attended a series of schools until he left the classroom for good at sixteen, claiming to have learned as little as his teachers allowed. He decided to pursue a legal profession, but once he had passed the bar he found "the dull routine of a lawyer's office" unappealing. Witty, urbane, handsome, and friendly, he enjoyed a life of leisure in the company of other youths who formed a club calling itself "The Nine Worthies."

In 1807 and 1808 Irving and his friends began to publish a periodical called *Salmagundi* (after a spicy appetizer), which offered impudent and amusing portrayals of the society, politics, and personalities of New York. Soon Irving decided to write a novel that spoofed the past history of his native city. Although the resulting book, *Knickerbocker's History of New York*, offended some members of society, its high spirits, humor, imagination, and good-natured irreverence established it as a youthful masterpiece. Moreover, in embodying the local settings, customs, and people of America in a work of literature, Irving was contributing to a national literature.

In 1815 he went to England, attempting to save his family's import business, which had suffered financial upsets from the War of 1812. Not until the firm was forced into bankruptcy in 1818 did Irving decide that he must support himself by writing. In 1819 and 1820 *The Sketch Book* was sent in installments to America, where it was highly praised by readers and critics alike, and eventually published in book form in England. Although most of the collection involved essays about the charm of English life and manners, it is mainly remembered for two stories, "The Legend of Sleepy Hollow" and "Rip Van Winkle." Irving followed the success of *The Sketch Book* with many other books—legends, folk tales, biographies, and histories.

The Devil and Tom Walker

Washington Irving

 few miles from Boston in Massachusetts, there is a deep inlet, winding several miles into the interior of the country from Charles Bay, and terminating in a thickly wooded swamp or morass. On one side of this inlet is a beautiful dark grove; on the opposite side the land rises abruptly from the water's edge into a high ridge, on which grow a few scattered oaks of great age and immense size.

Under one of these gigantic trees, according to old stories, there was a great amount of treasure buried by Kidd the pirate. The inlet allowed a facility to bring the money in a boat secretly and at night to the very foot of the hill; the elevation of the place permitted a good lookout to be kept that no one was at hand; while the remarkable trees formed good landmarks by which the place might easily be found again. The old stories add, moreover, that the devil presided at the hiding of the money, and took it under his guardianship; but this, it is well known, he always does with buried treasure, particularly when it has been ill-gotten. Be that as it may, Kidd never returned to recover his wealth, being shortly after seized at Boston, sent out to England, and there hanged for a pirate.

About the year 1727, just at the time that earthquakes were prevalent in New England, and shook many tall sinners down upon their knees, there lived near this place a meager, miserly fellow, of the name of Tom Walker. He had a wife as miserly as himself; they were so miserly that they even conspired to cheat each other. Whatever the woman could lay hands on, she hid away; a hen could not cackle but she was on the alert to secure the new-laid egg. Her husband was continually prying about to detect her secret hoards, and many and fierce were the conflicts that took place about what ought to have been common property.

They lived in a forlorn-looking house that stood alone, and had an air of starvation. A few straggling savin trees, emblems of sterility, grew near it; no smoke ever curled from its chimney; no traveler stopped at its door. A miserable horse, whose ribs were as articulate as the bars of a gridiron, stalked about a field, where a thin carpet of moss, scarcely covering the ragged beds of pudding stone, tantalized and balked his hunger; and sometimes he would lean his head over the fence, look piteously at the passer-by, and seem to petition deliverance from this land of famine.

The house and its inmates had altogether a bad name. Tom's wife was a tall termagant, fierce of temper, loud of tongue, and strong of arm. Her voice was often heard in wordy warfare with her husband; and his face sometimes showed signs that their conflicts were not confined to words. No one ventured, however, to interfere between them. The lonely wayfarer shrunk within himself at the horrid clamor and clapper-clawing;[1] eyed the den of discord askance; and hurried on his

---

1. *clapper-clawing*, an argument accompanied by scratching and slapping.

way, rejoicing, if a bachelor, in his celibacy.

One day that Tom Walker had been to a distant part of the neighborhood, he took what he considered a shortcut homeward, through the swamp. Like most shortcuts, it was an ill-chosen route. The swamp was thickly grown with great gloomy pines and hemlocks, some of them ninety feet high, which made it dark at noonday and a retreat for all the owls of the neighborhood. It was full of pits and quagmires, partly covered with weeds and mosses, where the green surface often betrayed the traveler into a gulf of black, smothering mud; there were also dark and stagnant pools, the abodes of the tadpole, the bullfrog, and the water snake, where the trunks of pines and hemlocks lay half-drowned, half-rotting, looking like alligators sleeping in the mire.

Tom had long been picking his way cautiously through this treacherous forest, stepping from tuft to tuft of rushes and roots, which afforded precarious footholds among deep sloughs; or pacing carefully, like a cat, along the prostrate trunks of trees, startled now and then by the sudden screaming of the bittern, or the quacking of wild duck rising on the wing from some solitary pool. At length he arrived at a firm piece of ground, which ran out like a peninsula into the deep bosom of the swamp. It had been one of the strongholds of the Indians during their wars with the first colonists. Here they had thrown up a kind of fort, which they had looked upon as almost impregnable, and had used as a place of refuge for their squaws and children. Nothing remained of the old Indian fort but a few embankments, gradually sinking to the level of the surrounding earth and already overgrown in part by oaks and other forest trees, the foliage of which formed a contrast to the dark pines and hemlocks of the swamp.

It was late in the dusk of evening when Tom Walker reached the old fort, and he paused there awhile to rest himself. Anyone but he would have felt unwilling to linger in this lonely, melancholy place, for the common people had a bad opinion of it, from the stories handed down from the time of the Indian wars, when it was asserted that the savages held incantations here and made sacrifices to the evil spirit.

Tom Walker, however, was not a man to be troubled with any fears of the kind. He reposed himself for some time on the trunk of a fallen hemlock, listening to the boding cry of the tree toad, and delving with his walking staff into a mound of black mold at his feet. As he turned up the soil unconsciously, his staff struck against something hard. He raked it out of the vegetable mold, and lo! a cloven skull, with an Indian tomahawk buried deep in it, lay before him. The rust on the weapon showed the time that had elapsed since this deathblow had been given. It was a dreary memento of the fierce struggle that had taken place in this last foothold of the Indian warriors. "Humph!" said Tom Walker as he gave it a kick to shake the dirt from it.

"Let that skull alone!" said a gruff voice. Tom lifted up his eyes and beheld a great black man seated directly opposite him, on the stump of a tree. He was exceedingly surprised, having neither heard nor seen anyone approach; and he was still more perplexed on observing, as well as the gathering gloom would permit, that the stranger was neither Negro nor Indian. It is true he was dressed in a rude half-Indian garb, and had a red belt or sash swathed around his body; but his face was neither black nor copper color, but swarthy and dingy, and begrimed with soot, as if he had been accustomed to toil among fires and forges. He had a shock of coarse black hair that stood out from his head in all directions, and bore an ax on his shoulder.

He scowled for a moment at Tom with a pair of great red eyes.

"What are you doing on my grounds?" said the black man, with a hoarse, growling voice.

"Your grounds!" said Tom, with a sneer, "no more your grounds than mine; they belong to Deacon Peabody."

"Deacon Peabody be damned," said the stranger, "as I flatter myself he will be, if he does not look more to his own sins and less to those of his neighbors. Look yonder, and see how Deacon Peabody is faring."

Tom looked in the direction that the stranger pointed and beheld one of the great trees, fair and flourishing without, but rotten at the core, and saw that it had been nearly hewn through, so that the first high wind was likely to blow it down. On the bark of the tree was scored the name of Deacon Peabody, an eminent man who had waxed wealthy by driving shrewd bargains with the Indians. He now looked around, and found most of the tall trees marked with the name of some great man of the colony, and all more or less scored by the ax. The one on which he had been seated, and which had evidently just been hewn down, bore the name of Crowninshield; and he recollected a mighty rich man of that name, who made a vulgar display of wealth, which it was whispered he had acquired by buccaneering.

"He's just ready for burning!" said the black man, with a growl of triumph. "You see I am likely to have a good stock of firewood for winter."

"But what right have you," said Tom, "to cut down Deacon Peabody's timber?"

"The right of a prior claim," said the other. "This woodland belonged to me long before one of your white-faced race put foot upon the soil."

"And pray, who are you, if I may be so bold?" said Tom.

"Oh, I go by various names. I am the wild huntsman in some countries; the black miner in others. In this neighborhood I am known by the name of the black woodsman. I am he to whom the red men consecrated this spot, and in honor of whom they now and then roasted a white man, by way of sweet-smelling sacrifice. Since the red men have been exterminated by you white savages, I amuse myself by presiding at the persecutions of Quakers and Anabaptists;[2] I am the great patron and prompter of slave dealers, and the grand master of the Salem witches."[3]

"The upshot of all which is, that, if I mistake not," said Tom sturdily, " you are he commonly called Old Scratch."

"The same, at your service!" replied the black man, with a half-civil nod.

Such was the opening of this interview, according to the old story; though it has almost too familiar an air to be credited. One would think that to meet with such a singular personage, in this wild, lonely place, would have shaken any man's nerves; but Tom was a hard-minded fellow, not easily daunted, and he had lived so long with a termagant wife that he did not even fear the devil.

It is said that after this commencement they had a long and earnest conversation together, as Tom returned homeward. The black man told him of great sums of money buried by Kidd the pirate, under the oak trees on the high ridge, not far from the morass. All these were under his command, and protected by his power, so that none could find them but such as propitiated his favor. These he offered to place within Tom Walker's reach, having conceived an especial kindness for him; but they were to be had only on certain conditions. What these conditions were may be easily surmised, though Tom never disclosed them publicly. They must have been very hard, for he required time to think of them, and he was not a man to stick at trifles when money was in view.

When they had reached the edge of the swamp, the stranger paused. "What proof have I that all you have been telling me is true?" said Tom. "There's my signature," said the black man, pressing his finger on Tom's forehead. So saying, he turned off among the thickets of the swamp, and seemed, as Tom said, to go down, down, down, into the earth, until he totally disappeared.

When Tom reached home, he found the black print of a finger burned, as it were, into his forehead, which nothing could obliterate.

The first news his wife had to tell him was the sudden death of Absalom Crowninshield, the rich

---

2. **Anabaptists** (an'ə bap'tists), members of a Protestant sect which originated in the 1500s. Quakers and Anabaptists were persecuted in the Massachusetts colony.
3. **Salem witches**, defendants in the Salem witch trials of 1692.

buccaneer. It was announced in the papers with the usual flourish that "A great man had fallen in Israel."[4]

Tom recollected the tree which his black friend had just hewn down and which was ready for burning. "Let the freebooter roast," said Tom; "who cares!" He now felt convinced that all he had heard and seen was no illusion.

He was not prone to let his wife into his confidence; but as this was an uneasy secret, he willingly shared it with her. All her avarice was awakened at the mention of hidden gold, and she urged her husband to comply with the black man's terms, and secure what would make them wealthy for life. However Tom might have felt disposed to sell himself to the devil, he was determined not to do so to oblige his wife; so he flatly refused, out of the mere spirit of contradiction. Many were the quarrels they had on the subject; but the more she talked, the more resolute was Tom not to be damned to please her.

At length she determined to drive the bargain on her own account, and if she succeeded, to keep all the gain to herself. Being of the same fearless temper as her husband, she set off for the old Indian fort toward the close of a summer's day. She was many hours absent. When she came back, she was reserved and sullen in her replies. She spoke something of a black man, whom she met about twilight hewing at the root of a tall tree. He was sulky, however, and would not come to terms; she was to go again with a propitiatory offering, but what it was she forbore to say.

The next evening she set off again for the swamp, with her apron heavily laden. Tom waited and waited for her, but in vain; midnight came, but she did not make her appearance; morning, noon, night returned, but still she did not come. Tom now grew uneasy for her safety, especially as he found she had carried off in her apron the silver teapot and spoons, and every portable article of value. Another night elapsed, another morning came; but no wife. In a word, she was never heard of more.

What was her real fate nobody knows, in consequence of so many pretending to know. It is one of those facts which have become confounded by a variety of historians. Some asserted that she lost her way among the tangled mazes of the swamp, and sank into some pit or slough; others, more uncharitable, hinted that she had eloped with the household booty, and made off to some other province; while others surmised that the tempter had decoyed her into a dismal quagmire, on the top of which her hat was found lying. In confirmation of this, it was said a great black man, with an ax on his shoulder, was seen late that very evening coming out of the swamp, carrying a bundle tied in a check apron, with an air of surly triumph.

The most current and probable story, however, observed that Tom Walker grew so anxious about the fate of his wife and his property that he set out at length to seek them both at the Indian fort. During a long summer's afternoon he searched about the gloomy place, but no wife was to be seen. He called her name repeatedly, but she was nowhere to be heard. The bittern alone responded to his voice, as he flew screaming by; or the bullfrog croaked dolefully from a neighboring pool. At length, it is said, just in the brown hour of twilight, when the owls began to hoot, and the bats to flit about, his attention was attracted by the clamor of carrion crows hovering about a cypress tree. He looked up and beheld a bundle tied in a check apron and hanging in the branches of the tree, with a great vulture perched hard by, as if keeping watch upon it. He leaped with joy; for he recognized his wife's apron and supposed it to contain the household valuables.

"Let us get hold of the property," said he consolingly to himself, "and we will endeavor to do without the woman."

As he scrambled up the tree, the vulture spread its wide wings and sailed off screaming into the deep shadows of the forest. Tom seized the checked apron, but, woeful sight! found nothing but a heart and liver tied up in it!

---

4. *Israel,* Massachusetts. The Puritans of Massachusetts regarded their colony as the Promised Land (Israel).

John Quidor (1801–1881), detail of *The Devil and Tom Walker*. This painting is one of seventeen that Quidor did on tales from Irving. Cleveland Museum of Art

Such, according to this most authentic old story, was all that was to be found of Tom's wife. She had probably attempted to deal with the black man as she had been accustomed to deal with her husband; but though a female scold is generally considered a match for the devil, yet in this instance she appears to have had the worst of it. She must have died game, however; for it is said Tom noticed many prints of cloven feet deeply stamped upon the tree, and found handfuls of hair that looked as if they had been plucked from the coarse black shock of the woodsman. Tom knew his wife's prowess by experience. He shrugged his shoulders as he looked at the signs of a fierce clapper-clawing. "Egad," said he to himself, "Old Scratch must have had a tough time of it!"

Tom consoled himself for the loss of his property with the loss of his wife, for he was a man of fortitude. He even felt something like gratitude toward the black woodsman, who, he considered, had done him a kindness. He sought, therefore, to cultivate a further acquaintance with him, but for some time without success; the old blacklegs played shy, for whatever people may think, he is not always to be had for calling for; he knows how to play his cards when pretty sure of his game.

At length, it is said, when delay had whetted Tom's eagerness to the quick, and prepared him to agree to anything rather than not gain the promised treasure, he met the black man one evening in his usual woodsman's dress, with his ax on his shoulder, sauntering along the swamp and humming a tune. He affected to receive Tom's advances with great indifference, made brief replies, and went on humming his tune.

By degrees, however, Tom brought him to business, and they began to haggle about the terms on which the former was to have the pirate's treasure. There was one condition which need not be mentioned, being generally understood in all cases where the devil grants favors; but there were others about which, though of less importance, he was inflexibly obstinate. He insisted that the money found through his means should be employed in his service. He proposed, therefore, that Tom should employ it in the black traffic; that is to say, that he should fit out a slave ship. This, however, Tom resolutely refused; he was bad enough in all conscience, but the devil himself could not tempt him to turn slave trader.

Finding Tom so squeamish on this point, he did not insist upon it, but proposed, instead, that he should turn usurer, the devil being extremely anxious for the increase of usurers, looking upon them as his peculiar people.

To this no objections were made, for it was just to Tom's taste.

"You shall open a broker's shop in Boston next month," said the black man.

"I'll do it tomorrow, if you wish," said Tom Walker.

"You shall lend money at two percent a month."

"Egad, I'll charge four!" replied Tom Walker.

"You shall extort bonds, foreclose mortgages, drive the merchants to bankruptcy——"

"I'll drive them to the devil," cried Tom Walker.

"You are the usurer for my money!" said blacklegs with delight. "When will you want the rhino?"[5]

"This very night."

"Done!" said the devil.

"Done!" said Tom Walker. So they shook hands and struck a bargain.

A few days' time saw Tom Walker seated behind his desk in a countinghouse in Boston.

His reputation for a ready-moneyed man, who would lend money out for a good consideration, soon spread abroad. Everybody remembers the time of Governor Belcher,[6] when money was particularly scarce. It was a time of paper credit.[7] The country had been deluged with government bills, the famous Land Bank[8] had been established; there had been a rage for speculating; the people had run mad with schemes for new settlements, for building cities in the wilderness; land jobbers[9] went about with maps of grants, and townships, and El Dorados,[10] lying nobody knew where, but which everybody was ready to purchase. In a word, the great speculating fever which breaks out every now and then in the country had raged to an alarming degree, and everybody was dreaming of making sudden fortunes from nothing. As usual the fever had subsided; the dream had gone off, and the imaginary fortunes with it; the patients were left in doleful plight, and the whole country resounded with the

---

5. *rhino* (rī′nō), money. [*Slang*]
6. *Governor Belcher,* Jonathan Belcher, who governed Massachusetts from 1730 to 1741.
7. *paper credit,* assets that existed on paper but were actually of no value.
8. *Land Bank,* a scheme to relieve the shortage of gold in Massachusetts by establishing a bank whose resources rested on real-estate mortgages.
9. *land jobbers,* people who bought tracts of undeveloped land as a speculation and sold them to others.
10. *El Dorado,* imaginary country, abounding in gold, searched for by Spaniards in the sixteenth century. The name now applies to any place where riches can be had easily and quickly.

consequent cry of "hard times."

At this propitious time of public distress did Tom Walker set up as usurer in Boston. His door was soon thronged by customers. The needy and adventurous, the gambling speculator, the dreaming land jobber, the thriftless tradesman, the merchant with cracked credit—in short, everyone driven to raise money by desperate means and desperate sacrifices hurried to Tom Walker.

Thus Tom was the universal friend of the needy, and acted like a "friend in need"; that is to say, he always exacted good pay and good security. In proportion to the distress of the applicant was the hardness of his terms. He accumulated bonds and mortgages; gradually squeezed his customers closer and closer; and sent them at length, dry as a sponge, from his door.

In this way he made money hand over hand; became a rich and mighty man, and exalted his cocked hat upon 'Change.[11] He built himself, as usual, a vast house, out of ostentation; but left the greater part of it unfinished and unfurnished, out of parsimony. He even set up a carriage in the fullness of his vainglory, though he nearly starved the horses which drew it; and as the ungreased wheels groaned and screeched on the axletrees, you would have thought you heard the souls of the poor debtors he was squeezing.

As Tom waxed old, however, he grew thoughtful. Having secured the good things of this world, he began to feel anxious about those of the next. He thought with regret on the bargain he had made with his black friend, and set his wits to work to cheat him out of the conditions. He became, therefore, all of a sudden, a violent churchgoer. He prayed loudly and strenuously, as if heaven were to be taken by force of lungs. Indeed, one might always tell when he had sinned most during the week by the clamor of his Sunday devotion. The quiet Christians who had been modestly and steadfastly traveling Zionward,[12] were struck with self-reproach at seeing themselves so suddenly outstripped in their career by this new-made convert. Tom was as rigid in religious as in money matters; he was

a stern supervisor and censurer of his neighbors, and seemed to think every sin entered up to their account became a credit on his own side of the page. He even talked of the expediency of reviving the persecution of Quakers and Anabaptists. In a word, Tom's zeal became as notorious as his riches.

Still, in spite of all this strenuous attention to forms, Tom had a lurking dread that the devil, after all, would have his due. That he might not be taken unawares, therefore, it is said he always carried a small Bible in his coat pocket. He had also a great folio Bible on his countinghouse desk, and would frequently be found reading it when people called on business; on such occasions he would lay his green spectacles in the book, to mark the place, while he turned round to drive some usurious bargain.

Some say that Tom grew a little crack-brained in his old days, and that, fancying his end approaching, he had his horse new shod, saddled and bridled, and buried with his feet uppermost; because he supposed that at the last day the world would be turned upside down in which case he should find his horse standing ready for mounting, and he was determined at the worst to give his friend a run for it. This, however, is probably a mere old wives' fable. If he really did take such a precaution, it was totally superfluous; at least so says the authentic old legend, which closes his story in the following manner.

One hot summer afternoon in the dog days, just as a terrible black thundergust was coming up, Tom sat in his countinghouse in his white cap and India silk morning gown. He was on the point of foreclosing a mortgage, by which he would complete the ruin of an unlucky land speculator for whom he had professed the greatest friendship. The poor land jobber begged him to grant a few months' indulgence. Tom had grown

---

11. '*Change,* the Exchange, or the financial center of Boston, where merchants, traders, and brokers do business.
12. *Zionward,* toward heaven. Zion, originally the hill in Jerusalem on which the temple stood, is often used to typify heaven.

testy and irritated, and refused another day.

"My family will be ruined and brought upon the parish,"[13] said the land jobber.

"Charity begins at home," replied Tom; "I must take care of myself in these hard times."

"You have made so much money out of me," said the speculator.

Tom lost his patience and his piety. "The devil take me," said he, "if I have made a farthing!"

Just then there were three loud knocks at the street door. He stepped out to see who was there. A black man was holding a black horse, which neighed and stamped with impatience.

"Tom, you're come for," said the black fellow, gruffly. Tom shrank back, but too late. He had left his little Bible at the bottom of his coat pocket, and his big Bible on the desk buried under the mortgage he was about to foreclose; never was sinner taken more unawares. The black man whisked him like a child into the saddle, gave the horse the lash, and away he galloped, with Tom on his back, in the midst of the thunderstorm. The clerks stuck their pens behind their ears, and stared after him from the windows. Away went Tom Walker, dashing down the streets, his white cap bobbing up and down, his morning gown fluttering in the wind, and his steed striking fire out of the pavement at every bound. When the clerks turned to look for the black man, he had disappeared.

Tom Walker never returned to foreclose the mortgage. A countryman, who lived on the border of the swamp, reported that in the height of the thundergust he had heard a great clattering of hoofs and a howling along the road, and running to the window caught sight of a figure, such as I have described, on a horse that galloped like mad across the fields, over the hills, and down into the black hemlock swamp toward the old Indian fort; and that shortly after, a thunderbolt falling in that direction seemed to set the whole forest in a blaze.

The good people of Boston shook their heads and shrugged their shoulders, but had been so much accustomed to witches and goblins and tricks of the devil in all kinds of shapes, from the first settlement of the colony, that they were not so much horror-struck as might have been expected. Trustees were appointed to take charge of Tom's effects. There was nothing, however, to administer upon. On searching his coffers, all his bonds and mortgages were found reduced to cinders. In place of gold and silver, his iron chest was filled with chips and shavings; two skeletons lay in his stable instead of his half-starved horses, and the very next day his great house took fire and burned to the ground.

Such was the end of Tom Walker and his ill-gotten wealth. Let all griping money brokers lay this story to heart. The truth of it is not to be doubted. The very hole under the oak trees whence he dug Kidd's money is to be seen to this day; and the neighboring swamp and old Indian fort are often haunted on stormy nights by a figure on horseback, in morning gown and white cap, which is doubtless the troubled spirit of the usurer. In fact, the story has resolved itself into a proverb, and is the origin of that popular saying, so prevalent throughout New England, of "The Devil and Tom Walker."

1824

---

13. **brought upon the parish,** forced to depend upon public charity for support.

THINK AND DISCUSS
Understanding
1. What words and phrases in paragraphs three and five describe Tom and his wife? How would you describe their marriage?
2. For what reasons does Tom's wife make two trips to the swamp? What are some of the stories that attempt to explain her fate?
3. What must Tom do in exchange for the pirate's treasure?
4. Why does Tom eventually become "a violent churchgoer"? How else does he try to cheat the devil?

5. What indicates that Tom is taken by surprise when the devil claims him at the end of the story? What happens to Tom's possessions?

Analyzing

6. What do the trees in the wooded swamp represent? Why have names been scored on these trees?
7. Irving describes land speculation as a "fever" and the speculators as "patients." What do you think he is saying through these **metaphors** about the love of money?
8. What is the "one condition which need not be mentioned" that is understood to be part of all contracts made with the devil?
9. "The Devil and Tom Walker" is a *folk tale*. In such tales, the tone is generally humorous; the main characters are types rather than individual personalities; and many events are unbelievable and ascribed to the supernatural or to hearsay ("it is said," "some asserted"). Find and discuss examples of these three characteristics in Irving's story.
10. What elements of Romanticism (see Reader's Note, page 108) can you find in this story?

Extending

11. Some tales about pacts with the devil end tragically for their heroes, illustrating the moral that one should never sell one's soul. Explain whether or not "The Devil and Tom Walker" is a tragedy. What, if any, is the moral?

APPLYING: Stereotype H𝕋
See Handbook of Literary Terms, p. 883.

A **stereotype** is a fixed, generalized idea about a character or situation. Stereotyped characters, also called stock characters, are broadly drawn with no individualizing qualities. Such characters conform to standardized mental pictures and behave in predictable patterns. Stereotypes that appear throughout literature are the clever detective, the female in distress, and the absent-minded professor. Plots (the last-minute rescue of the hero) and settings (the eerie ruins of a castle) may also be stereotyped.

1. What stereotype does Tom fit? his wife?
2. In what way is the plot stereotyped?
3. Cite examples of other literary works that contain stereotypes.

VOCABULARY
Antonyms

Each adjective in the first column below has an antonym, or word with an opposite meaning, in the second column. Copy the first word in the first column on a sheet of paper; then choose its antonym from the second column and write it on the same line. Continue in the same way with the other words. You may use a dictionary if necessary.

parsimonious	simple
propitiatory	rare
ostentatious	pliant
inflexible	antagonistic
superfluous	false
ill-gotten	generous
melancholy	necessary
authentic	joyous
testy	patient
prevalent	honestly acquired

COMPOSITION ◄▬▭
Writing a News Article

Imagine you are a reporter for a newspaper in the town where Tom Walker lived. Write a news story of at least three paragraphs about Tom's disappearance. Answer the questions *who, what, where, when, why,* and *how.* Maintain an objective tone and use a headline and a lead sentence that attract attention.

Writing a Folk Tale

Write a folk tale of at least four paragraphs in which a character or characters exhibit a particular vice or weakness that eventually causes their downfall. Make sure your story has the qualities of a folk tale: a humorous tone, stereotyped characters, and events that are ascribed to the supernatural or to hearsay. Be prepared to read your tale aloud to the class, trying it out first on a friend to see if everything makes sense and sounds smooth.

BIOGRAPHY

James Fenimore Cooper
1789–1851

When James Fenimore Cooper was a year old, his family moved from his birthplace, Burlington, New Jersey, to an enormous estate in what is now Cooperstown in upstate New York. Though the boy lived in a fine manor house on a thousand-acre tract, his home was surrounded by wilderness, and in many ways his was the life of a frontier boy. He learned to use the bow and arrow, to ride horseback, to fish, and to shoot. As a youth, he heard about Native Americans who not long before had lived in the forests, and he even encountered some members of the Oneida tribe who still camped in the woods. Such boyhood experiences formed the background for many of his novels.

After a brief stay at Yale (he reportedly was expelled for having tied a donkey to his tutor's chair) and three years in the Navy, Cooper married and settled down as a gentleman farmer in New York. One evening, he flung aside a dull English novel, claiming to his wife that he could write a better book himself. Thus began his career as a novelist. But his first effort was a rather dull book with genteel English characters and English settings of which Cooper knew next to nothing. Fortunately, he chose more familiar subjects for his next novels—the Revolutionary War (*The Spy*); the New York frontier (*The Leatherstocking Tales*); and the sea (*The Pilot*). Despite the romantic excesses, the melodrama, the sometimes stilted dialogue, and the occasional indifference to craft and detail, there was a vitality and energy to his narratives that made him a magnificent storyteller. Within a few years he was famous even in Europe, and by the end of his career he had completed thirty-three novels as well as volumes of social comment, naval history, and travel description.

The Deerslayer, from which "A Rescue" is taken, was the last and per-haps finest novel in Cooper's five-part adventure saga, *The Leatherstocking Tales*. As America's first internationally famous novelist, Cooper devel-oped not only the adventure tale, a new literary mode for America, but also one of the most memorable and often imitated heroes in our fiction: Natty Bumppo, frontiersman, who in various novels assumes the names of Deerslayer, Hawkeye, Pathfinder, and Leatherstocking.

Many elements typical of Cooper's fiction can be found in "A Rescue." These include the brave, faultless hero; the loyal Indian companion; the encounter with physical danger; physical danger as a test of prowess; and, of course, the hairbreadth rescue.

The events of *The Deerslayer*, from which the following selection is taken, occur between 1740 and 1745. Natty Bumppo, the young "Deer-slayer," has been reared by the Delaware Indians. He therefore has been trained in the ways of the forest and of the Indians. His closest friend is a young Delaware chief, Chingachgook (chin gach'gok), who is engaged to an Indian girl named Hist. This girl has been stolen by the Hurons and adopted into their tribe. In attempting her rescue, Deerslayer has himself been captured by the Hurons.

A Rescue

from **The Deerslayer**   **James Fenimore Cooper**

It was one of the common expedients of the savages, on such occasions, to put the nerves of their victims to the severest proofs. On the other hand, it was a matter of Indian pride to betray no yielding to terror or pain, but for the prisoner to provoke his enemies to such acts of violence as would soonest produce death. Many a warrior had been known to bring his own sufferings to a more speedy termination, by taunting reproaches and reviling language. . . . This happy expedient of taking refuge from the ferocity of his foes in their passions was denied Deerslayer, however, by his peculiar notions of the duty of a white man; and he had stoutly made up his mind to endure everything in preference to disgracing his color.

No sooner did the young men understand that they were at liberty to commence than some of the boldest and most forward among them sprang into the arena, tomahawk in hand. Here they prepared to throw that dangerous weapon, the object being to strike the tree as near as possible to the victim's head without absolutely hitting him. This was so hazardous an experiment that none but those who were known to be exceedingly expert with the weapon were allowed to enter the lists[1] at all, lest an early death might interfere with the expected entertainment. In the truest hands, it was seldom that the captive escaped injury in these trials; and it often happened that death followed even when the blow was not premeditated. In the particular case of our hero, Rivenoak[2] and the older warriors were apprehensive that the example of the Panther's fate[3] might prove a motive with some fiery spirit. . . . This circumstance, of itself, rendered the ordeal of the tomahawk doubly critical for the Deerslayer. . . .

The first youth who presented himself for the trial was called the Raven, having as yet had no opportunity of obtaining a more warlike sobriquet. He was remarkable for high pretension rather than for skill or exploits, and those who knew his character thought the captive in imminent danger when he took his stand and poised the tomahawk. Nevertheless, the young man was good-natured, and no thought was uppermost in his mind other than the desire to make a better cast than any of his fellows. . . . Still, our hero maintained an appearance of self-possession. He had made up his mind that his hour was come, and it would have been a mercy, instead of a calamity, to fall by the unsteadiness of the first hand that was raised against him.

After a suitable number of flourishes and gesticulations that promised much more than he could perform, the Raven let the tomahawk quit his hand. The weapon whirled through the air with the usual evolutions, cut a chip from the sapling to which the prisoner was bound, within a few inches of his cheek, and stuck in a large oak that grew several yards behind him. This was decidedly a bad effort, and a common sneer proclaimed as much, to the great mortification of the young man. On the other hand, there was a general but suppressed murmur of admiration at the steadiness with which the captive stood the trial. The head was the only part he could move, and this had been purposely left free, that the tormentors might have the amusement, and the

---

1. *enter the lists,* join in the contest. This is a phrase borrowed from the jousting tournaments of the Middle Ages.
2. *Rivenoak* (riv′ən ōk′), a Huron chief who wanted Deerslayer to join his tribe.
3. *the Panther's fate.* Deerslayer had killed the Panther, a Huron warrior, with his tomahawk.

tormented endure the shame, of dodging and otherwise attempting to avoid the blows. Deerslayer disappointed these hopes by a command of nerve that rendered his whole body as immovable as the tree to which he was bound. Nor did he even adopt the natural and usual expedient of shutting his eyes. . . .

The Raven had no sooner made his unsuccessful and puerile effort than he was succeeded by Le Daim-Mose,[4] or the Moose, a middle-aged warrior, who was particularly skillful in the use of the tomahawk, and from whose attempt the spectators confidently looked for gratification. This man had none of the good nature of the Raven, but he would gladly have sacrificed the captive to his hatred of the palefaces generally, were it not for the greater interest he felt in his own success as one particularly skillful in the use of this weapon. He took his stand quietly but with an air of confidence, poised his little ax but a single instant, advanced a foot with a quick motion, and threw. Deerslayer saw the keen instrument whirling toward him, and believed all was over; still he was not touched. The tomahawk had actually bound the head of the captive to the tree by carrying before it some of his hair, having buried itself deep beneath the soft bark. A general yell expressed the delight of the spectators, and the Moose felt his heart soften a little toward the prisoner, whose steadiness of nerve alone enabled him to give this evidence of his consummate skill.

Le Daim-Mose was succeeded by the Bounding Boy, or Le Garçon qui Bondi,[5] who came leaping into the circle like a hound or a goat at play. . . . Nevertheless he was both brave and skillful, and had gained the respect of his people by deeds in war as well as success in the hunts. . . . The Bounding Boy skipped about in front of the captive, menacing him with his tomahawk, now on one side and now on another and then again in front, in the vain hope of being able to extort some sign of fear by this parade of danger. At length Deerslayer's patience became exhausted by all this mummery, and he spoke for the first time since the trial had actually commenced.

"Throw away, Huron!" he cried, "or your tomahawk will forget its arr'nd.[6] Why do you keep loping about like a fa'an[7] that's showing its dam how well it can skip, when you're a warrior grown, yourself, and a warrior grown defies you and all your silly antics? Throw, or the Huron gals will laugh in your face."

The last words aroused the "Bounding" warrior to fury. The same nervous excitability which rendered him so active in his person made it difficult to repress his feelings, and the words were scarcely past the lips of the speaker than the tomahawk left the hand of the Indian. Nor was it cast without goodwill, and a fierce determination to slay. Had the intention been less deadly, the danger might have been greater. The aim was uncertain, and the weapon glanced near the cheek of the captive, slightly cutting the shoulder in its evolutions. This was the first instance in which any other object than that of terrifying the prisoner and of displaying skill had been manifested; and the Bounding Boy was immediately led from the arena and was warmly rebuked for his intemperate haste, which had come so near defeating all the hopes of the band.

To this irritable person succeeded several other young warriors, who not only hurled the tomahawk but who cast the knife. . . . Several times Deerslayer was grazed, but in no instance did he receive what might be termed a wound. The unflinching firmness with which he faced his assailants . . . excited a profound respect in the spectators. . . .

Rivenoak now told his people that the paleface had proved himself to be a man. He might live with the Delawares, but he had not been made woman with that tribe. He wished to know whether it was the desire of the Hurons to proceed any further. Even the gentlest of the

---

4. *Le Daim-Mose* (lə da'mōz'), "the moose deer." Many Hurons were called by names the French had given them.
5. *Le Garçon qui Bondi* (lə gär sōN'kē bôN di'), "the boy who bounds." [*French*]
6. *arr'nd*, errand.
7. *fa'an*, fawn.

females, however, had received too much satisfaction in the late trials to forego their expectations of a gratifying exhibition; and there was but one voice[8] in the request to proceed. The politic chief, who had some such desire to receive so celebrated a hunter into his tribe as a European minister had to devise a new and available means of taxation, sought every plausible means of arresting the trial in season; for he well knew if permitted to go far enough to arouse the more ferocious passions of the tormenters, it would be as easy to dam the waters of the great lakes of his own region as to attempt to arrest them in their bloody career. He therefore called four or five of the best marksmen to him and bid them put the captive to the proof of the rifle, while, at the same time, he cautioned them touching the necessity of their maintaining their own credit by the closest attention to the manner of exhibiting their skill.

When Deerslayer saw the chosen warriors step into the circle with their arms prepared for service, he felt some such relief as the miserable sufferer who had long endured the agonies of disease feels at the certain approach of death. . . .

The warriors prepared to exhibit their skill, as there was a double object in view: that of putting the constancy of the captive to the proof, and that of showing how steady were the hands of the marksmen under circumstances of excitement. The distance was small, and, in one sense, safe. But in diminishing the distance taken by the tormentors, the trial to the nerves of the captive was essentially increased. The face of Deerslayer, indeed, was just removed sufficiently from the ends of the guns to escape the effects of the flash, and his steady eye was enabled to look directly into their muzzles. . . .

Shot after shot was made, all the bullets coming in close proximity to the Deerslayer's head, without touching it. Still, no one could detect even the twitching of a muscle on the part of the captive, or the slightest winking of an eye. . . . When five or six had discharged their bullets into the trees, he could not refrain from expressing his contempt.

"You may call this shooting, Mingos,"[9] he exclaimed, "but we've squaws among the Delawares, and I have known Dutch gals on the Mohawk, that could outdo your greatest indivors. Ondo these arms of mine; put a rifle into my hands; and I'll pin the thinnest warlock in your party to any tree you can show me, and this at a hundred yards—aye, or at two hundred, if the object can be seen—nineteen shots in twenty—or, for that matter, twenty in twenty, if the piece is creditable and trusty!"

A low, menacing murmur followed this cool taunt; the ire of the warriors kindled at listening to such a reproach from one who so far disdained their efforts as to refuse even to wink when a rifle was discharged as near his face as could be done without burning it. Rivenoak perceived that the moment was critical; and, still retaining his hope of adopting so noted a hunter into his tribe, the politic old chief interposed in time, probably, to prevent an immediate resort to that portion of the torture which must necessarily have produced death. . . .

"I see how it is," he said. "We have been like the palefaces when they fasten their doors at night, out of fear of the red man. They use so many bars that the fire comes and burns them before they can get out. We have bound the Deerslayer too tight; the thongs keep his limbs from shaking, and his eyes from shutting. Loosen him; let us see what his own body is really made of."

The proposal of the chief found instant favor; and several hands were immediately at work cutting and tearing the ropes of bark from the body of our hero. In half a minute Deerslayer stood free from bonds. . . . Deerslayer, by rubbing his limbs, stamping his feet, and moving about, soon regained the circulation, recovering all his physical powers as if nothing had occurred to disturb them.

---

8. *there was but one voice*. All of the Hurons spoke together in agreement.
9. *Mingos* (min'gōz), a name scornfully applied by the Delawares to their enemies.

Frank Schoonover, *The Deer Stalker* (1920). Private collection

It is seldom men think of death in the pride of their health and strength. So it was with Deerslayer. Having been helplessly bound, and, as he had every reason to suppose, so lately on the very verge of the other world, to find himself so unexpectedly liberated, in possession of his strength, and with a full command of limb, acted on him like a sudden restoration to life, reanimating hopes that he had once absolutely abandoned. . . . The change was so great that his mind resumed its elasticity; and, no longer thinking of submission, it dwelt only on the devices of the sort of warfare in which he was engaged. . . .

The honor of the band was now involved in the issue; and even the female sex lost all its sympathy with suffering, in the desire to save the reputation of the tribe. The voices of the girls, soft and melodious as nature had made them, were heard mingling with the menaces of the men; and the wrongs of Sumach[10] suddenly assumed the character of injuries inflicted on every Huron female. Yielding to this rising tumult the men drew back a little, signifying to the females that they left the captive, for a time, in their hands, it being a common practice on such occasions for the women to endeavor to throw the victim into a rage by their taunts and revilings, and then to turn him suddenly over to the men in a state of mind that was little favorable to resisting the agony of bodily suffering. . . .

But Deerslayer's mind was too much occupied to permit him to be disturbed by the abuse of excited hags; and their rage necessarily increasing with his indifference, as his indifference increased with their rage, the furies soon rendered themselves impotent by their own excesses. Perceiving that the attempt was a complete failure, the warriors interfered to put a stop to this scene. . . . Fragments of dried wood were rapidly collected near the sapling; the splinters which it was intended to thrust into the flesh of the victim, previously to lighting, were all collected; and the thongs were already produced to bind him to the tree. . . .

Suddenly a young Indian came bounding through the Huron ranks, leaping into the very center of the circle in a way to denote the utmost confidence or a temerity bordering on foolhardiness. Five or six sentinels were still watching the lake at different and distant points; and it was the first impression of Rivenoak that one of these had come in with tidings of import. Still, the movements of the stranger were so rapid, and his war dress, which scarcely left him more drapery than an antique statue, had so little distinguishing about it, that, at the first moment, it was impossible to ascertain whether he were friend or foe. Three leaps carried this warrior to the side of Deerslayer. . . . Then he turned and showed the astonished Hurons the noble brow, fine person, and eagle eye of a young warrior in the paint and panoply of a Delaware. He had a rifle in each hand, the butts of both resting on the earth, while from one dangled its proper pouch and horn. This was Killdeer,[11] which even as he looked boldly and in defiance on the crowd around him, he suffered to fall back into the hands of the proper owner. The presence of two armed men, though it was in their midst, startled the Hurons. Their rifles were scattered about against the different trees and their only weapons were their knives and tomahawks. Still, they had too much self-possession to betray fear. . . .

"Hurons," the stranger said, "this earth is very big. The great lakes are big, too; there is room beyond them for the Iroquois; there is room for the Delawares on this side. I am Chingachgook, the son of Uncas, the kinsman of Tamenund. That paleface is my friend. My heart was heavy when I missed him. Come, let us say farewell, and go on our path."

"Hurons, this is your mortal enemy, the Great Serpent of them you hate!" cried Briarthorn.[12] "If he escape, blood will be in your moccasin prints from this spot to the Canadas. . . ."

---

10. **Sumach** (sü′mak *or* shü′mak), the sister of the Panther.
11. **Killdeer**, Deerslayer's rifle.
12. **the Great Serpent . . . Briarthorn.** The Great Serpent is Chingachgook, and Briarthorn is a Delaware traitor who had joined the Hurons.

As the last words were uttered, the traitor cast his knife at the naked breast of the Delaware. With a quick movement Chingachgook avoided the blow, the dangerous weapon burying its point in a pine. At the next instant a similar weapon glanced from the hand of the Serpent, and quivered in the recreant's heart. . . . Briarthorn fell, like a dog, dead in his tracks. . . . A common exclamation followed, and the whole party was in motion. At this instant a sound unusual to the woods was heard, and every Huron, male and female, paused to listen. . . . The sound was regular and heavy, as if the earth were struck with beetles. Objects came visible among the trees of the background, and a body of troops was seen advancing with measured tread. They came upon the charge, the scarlet of the King's livery shining among the bright green foliage of the forest. . . .

A general yell burst from the enclosed Hurons; it was succeeded by the hearty cheers of England. Still, not a musket or rifle was fired, though that steady, measured tramp continued, and the bayonet was seen gleaming in advance of a line that counted nearly sixty men. The Hurons were taken at a fearful disadvantage. On three sides was the water, while their formidable and trained foes cut them off from flight on the fourth. Each warrior rushed for his arms, and then all on the point, man, woman, and child, eagerly sought cover. In this scene of confusion and dismay, however, nothing could surpass the discretion and coolness of Deerslayer. He threw himself on a flank of the retiring Hurons. . . . Deerslayer watched his opportunity, and finding two of his recent tormentors in range, his rifle first broke the silence of the terrific scene. The bullet brought down both at one discharge. This drew a general fire from the Hurons, and the rifle and war cry of the Serpent were heard in the clamor. Still the trained men returned no answering volley. . . . Presently, however, the shrieks, groans, and denunciations that usually accompany the use of the bayonet followed. That terrible and deadly weapon was glutted in vengeance. The scene that succeeded was one of those of which so many have occurred in our own times, in which neither age nor sex forms an exemption to the lot of a savage warfare.

1841

THINK AND DISCUSS
Understanding
1. Describe the "ordeal of the tomahawk" that Deerslayer is forced to endure.
2. Besides the tomahawk, what other weapons are used to test Deerslayer's nerve?
3. How does Deerslayer earn the respect of the Hurons?

Analyzing
4. What virtues and faults do the Deerslayer and the Hurons share?
5. Explain how the character traits of the Deerslayer and the Hurons determine the events of the story.

6. By what means does the order of events create suspense?
7. What do you learn about Deerslayer from his behavior? from the attitudes that Rivenoak, the Moose, and the Bounding Boy display toward him? from the descriptions of his feelings provided by the author?

Extending
8. Does the relationship of Deerslayer and his faithful friend Chingachgook remind you of that of any other fictional pairs? Name as many similarly paired characters as you can from books, movies, and television series.

VOCABULARY
Dictionary

Answer the questions that follow this passage. You may need to consult a dictionary.

In *The Deerslayer* Cooper writes: "The first youth who presented himself for the trial was called the Raven, having as yet had no opportunity of obtaining a more warlike *sobriquet*."

1. What is a *sobriquet*?
2. Does the word rhyme with *coquette* or *croquet*?
3. List some of the sobriquets that Cooper employs.
4. Choose four of the following sobriquets and explain to what or whom each refers.

Old Hickory	Old Glory
redcoat	Bard of Avon
John Bull	Jolly Roger
iron horse	staff of life

THINKING SKILLS
Evaluating

Cooper's contemporary, poet James Russell Lowell, called some of Cooper's characters "clothes upon sticks." Evaluate Lowell's statement in the light of "The Rescue."

1. Do you think that the characters in this excerpt are one-dimensional, or **stereotypical,** or do they appear to be realistic? Explain.
2. What aspects of the plot and setting might be considered stereotypical?

COMPOSITION ◄━●
Explaining a Sobriquet

You, your family members, or your friends may have sobriquets based on an individual trait. Explain one such sobriquet in three paragraphs directed to a classmate. You may want to explain how the name was acquired, whether or not it was deserved, if it was eventually outgrown, or whether another name would have been more appropriate. Decide what tone can best express your ideas. You may, for example, adopt a tone that is humorous, angry, or reflective.

Writing a Speech

Imagine that you are Rivenoak, delivering a speech to his fellow Hurons that urges them to make Deerslayer an honorary member of their tribe. Base your argument on the actions of Deerslayer as described in "A Rescue." Try to capture the flavor of Native American oratory by using the speech of Dekanawidah (page 19) as a model.

The Search for a Voice

"The Americans have no national literature, and no learned men. . . . The talents of our transatlantic brethren show themselves chiefly in political pamphlets. The Americans are too young to rival in literature the old nations of Europe." Thus said the *British Critic* in 1819. But within the next generation, the works of Irving, Cooper, and Poe appeared, and America began to speak with its own voice. True, this voice had, at times, a foreign accent, but the tones were unmistakably American and the echoes far-reaching.

In the beginning of the nineteenth century, many American authors, in trying to find a voice, imitated those of British authors. Irving's early works, significantly signed with the pseudonym Jonathan Oldstyle, were patterned on the essays popularized in England by Addison and Steele. Longfellow's narrative poems followed a longstanding epic tradition. Irving's Rip Van Winkle and Ichabod Crane were direct borrowings from German legends, and many of Poe's short stories, including "The Cask of Amontillado," were based on European gothic romances. Bryant's "Thanatopsis" was originally considered a British forgery because of its polished use of blank verse, a form popular in England since before Shakespeare's time. Even Cooper's frontier hero Leatherstocking was considered by some to be a European knight transplanted on democratic soil. In fact, all American literature of the time might be considered a transplant, since the best of authors distill from existing literature forms and subjects that can best serve them.

But the outcome of these borrowings was a national literature clearly stamped with the scenes and exuberance of a youthful continent —a literature rich in native character and tradition. The settings and themes of this literature ranged from the rigors of frontier existence and the beauties of New England rural life, to the picturesque, idyllic life around the Hudson River. Such literature awakened a European interest in the life of American regions and earned an international reputation for the writers of the adolescent nation. Unlike their Puritan predecessors, writers of the National Period emphasized enjoyment of the present world rather than the promise of the afterworld. Factual writing, designed to inform or to persuade readers, gave way to imaginative writing, designed to entertain.

Moreover, in finding their voice, American writers began to develop new forms, memorable characters, and distinct styles. The rambling sketches that introduced Rip Van Winkle and Ichabod Crane to American literature broke ground for a new American form, the short story. Later, Poe shaped and developed this genre, introducing another offspring, the detective story, and immortalizing the crafty supersleuth Dupin. Cooper's Leatherstocking was clearly an American product—a character whose actions and personality were determined by the mountains, streams, and prairies of his forest surroundings. The lighter tones of the national voice could be heard in the works of Irving and Holmes, as they introduced the extravagant American humor later popularized by writers such as Mark Twain. And Longfellow and Irving provided the young nation with a body of legend and lore drawn from America's history, making names such as Hiawatha and Knickerbocker household words.

America's literary revolution took much longer than her War of Independence. Authors still generally looked abroad for their models, but they found their subject matter largely in American scenes. At midcentury the uniquely American voice was only beginning to be heard. It remained for the immensely talented Walt Whitman and Emily Dickinson in poetry and Nathaniel Hawthorne, Herman Melville, and Mark Twain in prose to transform the raw and rich tones of American voices into a stirring literary language.

Often regarded as America's first eminent poet, William Cullen Bryant was a Puritan who could trace his ancestry back to a settler in Plymouth Colony. As a youngster in western Massachusetts, he lived among the apple trees, rocky fields, and deep woods of the Berkshire Hills—surroundings that awakened in the future poet a love of nature and later provided the chief subjects of his verse. His interest in nature, along with that of Irving and Cooper, helped to establish the new Romantic Movement in America.

At fourteen, Bryant gained attention with a poetic lampoon on one of President Jefferson's laws. But Bryant's first enduring verse revealed his Puritan ancestry. Because of his father's meager income, he was forced at seventeen to drop out of Williams College after a few months of study. As he contemplated the future at the onset of the gloomy New England winter, he began a poem to express the solemn mood with which he faced life. The first draft of "Thanatopsis" was pushed into a pigeonhole of his father's desk. Six years later, the elder Bryant submitted his son's poem to the editor of the newly established *North American Review*. The editor, on consulting a friend, was warned, "You have been imposed on; no one on this side of the Atlantic is capable of writing such verses." Dr. Bryant removed his doubts, and the contribution was accepted, with the result that its publication in 1817 established the young man's position as the leading American poet.

Meanwhile, giving up all hope of college, Bryant turned to law as the most direct path to self-support. Tradition holds that on the seven-mile walk to his first law office Bryant noticed a lone waterfowl winging south through cold December skies. By the time the frustrated poet had completed his journey, he had composed in his head "To a Waterfowl," which the English author Matthew Arnold called "the most perfect brief poem in the language."

Though he found the constant bickering of the law courts distasteful, he became a successful attorney. At the same time his poetical reputation steadily grew. A pamphlet containing twelve poems issued in 1821 spread his fame to England, and by 1825 several contributions to a short-lived periodical maintained his eminence above contemporary American poets. This distinction brought him an attractive offer to enter journalism in New York, where he joined the staff of the *New York Evening Post* and soon advanced to the editor's chair.

During the next fifty years he raised the *Post* to a position of national prominence while he himself gained a reputation as a champion of liberal causes, especially that of the abolitionist movement. His reputation as a speaker on public occasions also mounted. Even on the last active day of his life, in his eighty-fourth year, he worked at his desk until it was time to deliver an oration in Central Park. The hot sun beating down on his bare head caused a dizziness after the ceremonies. As he went up the steps of his home, he fell, struck his head, and never regained consciousness.

Thanatopsis

William Cullen Bryant

   To him who in the love of Nature holds
Communion with her visible forms, she speaks
A various language; for his gayer hours
She has a voice of gladness, and a smile
5 And eloquence of beauty, and she glides
Into his darker musings with a mild
And healing sympathy that steals away
Their sharpness ere he is aware. When thoughts
Of the last bitter hour come like a blight
10 Over thy spirit, and sad images
Of the stern agony, and shroud, and pall,
And breathless darkness, and the narrow house[1]
Make thee to shudder and grow sick at heart—
Go forth, under the open sky, and list
15 To Nature's teachings, while from all around—
Earth and her waters, and the depths of air—
Comes a still voice—
                        Yet a few days, and thee
The all-beholding sun shall see no more
In all his course; nor yet in the cold ground,
20 Where thy pale form was laid with many tears,
Nor in the embrace of ocean shall exist
Thy image. Earth, that nourished thee, shall claim
Thy growth, to be resolved to earth again,
And, lost each human trace, surrendering up
25 Thine individual being, shalt thou go
To mix forever with the elements,
To be a brother to the insensible rock
And to the sluggish clod which the rude swain
Turns with his share and treads upon. The oak

Thanatopsis (than'ə top'sis), in Greek, means "a view of death."
1. *the narrow house,* the grave.

30 Shall send his roots abroad and pierce thy mold.
    Yet not to thine eternal resting place
Shalt thou retire alone; nor couldst thou wish
Couch more magnificent. Thou shalt lie down
With patriarchs of the infant world—with kings,
35 The powerful of the earth—the wise, the good,
Fair forms, and hoary seers of ages past,
All in one mighty sepulcher. The hills
Rock-ribbed and ancient as the sun; the vales
Stretching in pensive quietness between;
40 The venerable woods; rivers that move
In majesty; and the complaining brooks
That make the meadows green; and, poured round all
Old Ocean's gray and melancholy waste—
Are but the solemn decorations all
45 Of the great tomb of man. The golden sun,
The planets, all the infinite host of heaven,
Are shining on the sad abodes of death
Through the still lapse of ages. All that tread
The globe are but a handful to the tribes
50 That slumber in its bosom. Take the wings
Of morning, pierce the Barcan wilderness,[2]
Or lose thyself in the continuous woods
Where rolls the Oregon,[3] and hears no sound
Save his own dashings—yet the dead are there;
55 And millions in those solitudes, since first
The flight of years began, have laid them down
In their last sleep—the dead reign there alone.
So shalt thou rest, and what if thou withdraw
In silence from the living, and no friend
60 Take note of thy departure? All that breathe
Will share thy destiny. The gay will laugh
When thou are gone, the solemn brood of care
Plod on, and each one as before will chase
His favorite phantom; yet all these shall leave
65 Their mirth and their employments, and shall come
And make their bed with thee. As the long train
Of ages glides away, the sons of men,
The youth in life's green spring, and he who goes
In the full strength of years, matron and maid,
70 The speechless babe, and the gray-headed man—

---

2. *Barcan wilderness,* the desert land of Cyrenaica (sir′ə nā′ə kə) in northern Africa.
3. *the Oregon,* the old name for the Columbia River.

Asher Brown Durand, *Landscape—Scene from "Thanatopsis"* (1850).
The Metropolitan Museum of Art

Shall one by one be gathered to thy side,
By those who in their turn shall follow them.

   So live, that when thy summons comes to join
The innumerable caravan which moves
75 To that mysterious realm, where each shall take
His chamber in the silent halls of death,
Thou go not, like the quarry slave at night,
Scourged to his dungeon, but, sustained and soothed
By an unfaltering trust, approach thy grave
80 Like one who wraps the drapery of his couch
About him, and lies down to pleasant dreams.
1811   **1817**

THINK AND DISCUSS

Understanding

1. What is "the last bitter hour" (line 9) and to what can one turn at this time, according to the poem?
2. What process is described in lines 22–29?
3. Why are those who die not alone (lines 31–37)?
4. What are the "solemn decorations" of the tomb (lines 37–45)? What words and **images** in these lines suggest peacefulness and comfort?
5. Who are some members of the "innumerable caravan" mentioned in line 74?
6. What, according to lines 78 and 79, will sustain and sooth those who approach death? What picture of death does the **simile** in lines 80 and 81 provide?

Analyzing

7. How does the poem answer the question posed in lines 58–60?
8. The poet mentions the Barcan wilderness and the Oregon River. What purpose do you think these **allusions** serve?
9. How does the description of death in the final lines of the poem differ from that provided in lines 8–13?
10. Summarize in your own words Bryant's view of death.

Extending

11. Do you think the ideas expressed in "Thanatopsis" are consoling or disturbing? Explain.

APPLYING: Anastrophe H◨
See Handbook of Literary Terms, p. 880.

Anastrophe is the inversion of the usual word order in a sentence. A poet who says, "Sad was I" is reversing the normal sentence order of subject-verb-complement ("I was sad"). Such manipulation of a sentence can be used for emphasis or to preserve rhythm and rhyme.

1. Look at the inverted word *thee* in the clause "and thee/ The all-beholding sun shall see no more" (lines 17–18). Rearrange these words to fit a subject-verb-object pattern.
2. Change the word order (not the words) in lines 31–32 ("Yet not . . . alone") to fit a common sentence pattern.
3. How do these rephrasings affect the poem?

THINKING SKILLS

Generalizing

You can generalize, or draw broad conclusions, about a work by examining different elements in the work. Study the picture on page 131. What elements in it capture the spirit of Romanticism? Consider the subject, the use of color, the mood, and the overall impression conveyed by the picture. Why do you consider it a better illustration of "Thanatopsis" than a picture of a grave scene?

COMPOSITION ◀━●

Writing About a Reunion

In "Thanatopsis" Bryant speaks of death as a grand reunion with all those who have died at an earlier time. Imagine that you are about to enter the afterlife. Write a composition of three or four paragraphs for a friend telling what people—friends, relatives, historical figures—you would be most interested in getting together with. What questions would you ask? What mysteries would you seek answers to?

Stating an Opinion

Suppose that someone close to you has died and that you have been asked to do a reading of "Thanatopsis" at the funeral or burial service. Write a response, directed to the person conducting the service, in which you state your opinion as to the appropriateness or inappropriateness of this poem. If you feel the poem would not be suitable, suggest another poem, explaining why you feel it would be a better choice.

Bryant and Romanticism

"Thanatopsis," Bryant's meditation on death, is a Romantic vision of nature, as it reflects the human spirit and provides a key to the understanding of human nature. (See Reader's Note, page 108). Briefly, some concepts of Romanticism that are reflected in Bryant's poetry are an awareness that the physical world is subject to decline and decay; the belief that while everything changes and dies, God, the Absolute, remains immortal; and the belief that the natural world provides a key to the human world—that humanity is fulfilled through the life cycle of birth, growth, decay, and death. The message in "Thanatopsis," then, is unmistakably Romantic: To those who seek "communion" with her, nature speaks in "a still voice," providing a "healing sympathy."

Bryant's theme of death in "Thanatopsis" is eminently Romantic, since death is the ultimate restriction on the individual. Only when death is seen as one step in the natural process of renewal, can one accept the final fate of mixing forever with the "sluggish clod." Like other Romantics, Bryant emphasized the ancient past as a form of establishing continuity with the present. Thus, in death, the individual joins the "long train/ Of ages," the "innumerable caravan, which moves/ To that mysterious realm."

Stylistically, Bryant also borrowed from the poets of the Romantic Movement. He cast his verse in the dignified unrhymed meter of **blank verse** and used lofty diction and inverted syntax to convey his ideas. Like other Romantic poets, Bryant was fond of using archaic words such as *thou, thy, shalt, couldst,* and *list* (for *listen*) to convey a serious, philosophical tone. Another stylistic technique that appears frequently in his poetry is inversion, or **anastrophe**—the displacement of a word, phrase, or clause from its normal position in a sentence, either for emphasis or poetic effect. Frequently inversion enables a poet to maintain meter and/or rhyme.

Through all these devices, Bryant presents a view of death that is neither morbid nor sentimental. "Thanatopsis," in its structure and philosophy, is perhaps the most characteristic embodiment of the emerging Romantic literature in the National Period.

George Inness, *The Home of the Heron* (1893). The Art Institute of Chicago

BIOGRAPHY

Henry Wadsworth Longfellow
1807–1882

Detail of a portrait of
Longfellow painted by his
son Ernest in 1876.

Henry Wadsworth Longfellow, in his lifetime the best loved of American poets, was born in Portland, Maine. He could trace his ancestry directly to John and Priscilla Alden, who had come over in the *Mayflower* and whom the poet immortalized in the popular narrative, *The Courtship of Miles Standish.* Longfellow, along with his contemporaries James Russell Lowell, Oliver Wendell Holmes, and John Greenleaf Whittier, became known as one of the Fireside Poets—a group of Romantics who entertained the American public with poems about patriotism, nature, and family.

Longfellow was educated at Bowdoin College where, after further study abroad, he taught for six years. He then transferred to Harvard, where he remained for twenty years, combining the teaching of languages with the writing of poems. His first book of poems, *Voices of the Night,* appeared in 1839 and gained a national reputation for him. He finally resigned his professorship in 1855 in order to devote himself exclusively to writing.

Along with Washington Irving, Longfellow provided a young American nation with a body of legend and folklore all its own. Until he immortalized them in verse, the names of Paul Revere, Miles Standish, John and Priscilla Alden, Hiawatha, and Minnehaha were virtually unknown in the United States. In addition, Longfellow introduced foreign poetic forms into America. *Evangeline* (1847), *The Song of Hiawatha* (1855), and *The Courtship of Miles Standish* (1858) were long narrative poems that followed European forms but treated American legends. Occasionally, he looked not only to the quaint and colorful past of his own country, but to the legends of other lands, for poetic inspiration.

No stranger to grief, the poet lost his first wife to illness while he was traveling and studying in Europe. "A voice from my inmost heart at a time when I was rallying from depression" is Longfellow's own description of "A Psalm of Life," written three years afterward. Longfellow reportedly wrote the poem in a single day on the blank margins of a note of invitation he had received.

His second wife burned to death many years later when her dress caught fire. The latter tragedy inspired the moving sonnet "The Cross of Snow," and his most ambitious and significant work, a translation of Dante's *Divine Comedy,* was undertaken as a means of mastering his grief.

Children delighted Longfellow, especially his three daughters. His letters abound with the joyous beauty of the child-world. In "The Children's Hour" his fatherly love expresses itself in one of his best-loved poems.

During a tour of England in his later years, both Oxford and Cambridge universities awarded him honorary degrees, and after his death a bust of him was unveiled in the Poet's Corner of Westminster Abbey. He was the first American poet to attain this honor.

A Psalm of Life

Henry Wadsworth Longfellow

WHAT THE HEART OF THE YOUNG MAN SAID TO THE PSALMIST

Tell me not, in mournful numbers,
    Life is but an empty dream!—
For the soul is dead that slumbers,
    And things are not what they seem.

5 Life is real! Life is earnest!
    And the grave is not its goal;
Dust thou art, to dust returnest,
    Was not spoken of the soul.

Not enjoyment, and not sorrow,
10   Is our destined end or way;
But to act, that each tomorrow
    Find us farther than today.

Art is long, and Time is fleeting,
    And our hearts, though stout and brave,
15 Still, like muffled drums, are beating
    Funeral marches to the grave.

In the world's broad field of battle,
    In the bivouac of Life,

Be not like dumb, driven cattle!
20   Be a hero in the strife!

Trust no Future, howe'er pleasant!
    Let the dead Past bury its dead!
Act—act in the living Present!
    Heart within, and God o'erhead!

25 Lives of great men all remind us
    We can make our lives sublime,
And, departing, leave behind us
    Footprints on the sands of time;

Footprints, that perhaps another,
30   Sailing o'er life's solemn main,
A forlorn and shipwrecked brother,
    Seeing, shall take heart again.

Let us, then, be up and doing,
    With a heart for any fate;
35 Still achieving, still pursuing,
    Learn to labor and to wait.

1838

THINK AND DISCUSS
Understanding
1. What is a *psalm* and how is the word pronounced? (Check the Glossary, if necessary.)
2. How does the speaker feel about the past, present, and future (lines 21–24)?
3. To what process in the life cycle does the phrase "to dust returnest" in stanza 2 refer? Why does this process not apply to the soul?
4. Which meaning of the word *main* is intended in line 30? (Check the Glossary, if necessary.)

Analyzing
5. What sort of person is the speaker of this poem? young or old? optimistic or pessimistic? active or passive?
6. What word would you use to describe the **tone** of the poem? Explain your choice.
7. According to the poem, how should our

lives be led in order to overcome the fact that each day brings us nearer to death?

8. Longfellow refers to life as a *bivouac*. After consulting your Glossary, explain the appropriateness of this **metaphor**.

9. How would you interpret the phrase "Footprints on the sands of time" (line 28)? According to lines 29–32, what purpose can these "footprints" serve?

 See SYNECDOCHE in the Handbook of Literary Terms, page 887.

The Children's Hour

Henry Wadsworth Longfellow

Between the dark and the daylight,
    When the night is beginning to lower,
Comes a pause in the day's occupations,
    That is known as the Children's Hour.

5 I hear in the chamber above me
    The patter of little feet,
The sound of a door that is opened
    And voices soft and sweet.

From my study I see in the lamplight,
10   Descending the broad hall stair,
Grave Alice, and laughing Allegra
    And Edith with golden hair.

A whisper, and then a silence;
    Yet I know by their merry eyes
15 They are plotting and planning together
    To take me by surprise.

A sudden rush from the stairway,
    A sudden raid from the hall!
By three doors left unguarded
20   They enter my castle wall!

They climb up into my turret
    O'er the arms and back of my chair;
If I try to escape, they surround me;
    They seem to be everywhere.

25 They almost devour me with kisses,
    Their arms about me entwine,
Till I think of the Bishop of Bingen[1]
    In his Mouse-Tower on the Rhine!

Do you think, O blue-eyed banditti,
30   Because you have scaled the wall,
Such an old mustache as I am
    Is not a match for you all!

I have you fast in my fortress,
    And will not let you depart,
35 But put you down into the dungeon
    In the round-tower of my heart.

And there will I keep you forever,
    Yes, forever and a day,
Till the walls shall crumble to ruin,
40   And moulder in dust away!

1859

1. *the Bishop of Bingen*. This is a reference to a tenth-century legend about Bishop Hatto who, because he burned poor people so that there would be more food for the rich, was besieged and devoured by an army of mice. Hatto tried to take refuge in what has come to be known as the Mäuseturm or Mouse-Tower, a structure still standing along the Rhine River in Germany.

John Singer Sargent, detail of *The Daughters of Edward D. Boit* (1882). Museum of Fine Arts, Boston

THINK AND DISCUSS
Understanding
1. At what time of the day or night does the children's hour take place? How are these children described in stanza 3?
2. What room is the speaker comparing to a castle? From where have the invading children come?

Analyzing
3. To what does the speaker compare the invading children? What words and phrases sustain this **metaphor** throughout the poem?
4. In what sense are the children captured and imprisoned forever?
5. In what ways is the attack similar to the attack on the Bishop of Bingen? From what source has this **allusion** been drawn?

APPLYING: Synecdoche H汀
See Handbook of Literary Terms, p. 887.

Synecdoche is a figure of speech in which a part is used to suggest the whole ("Give me a hand") or the whole used for the part (calling a policeman "the law"). Synecdoche is generally used to emphasize a particular characteristic. If you refer to someone as "a wagging tongue" or "a sharp tongue," for example, you are highlighting his or her tendency to gossip or criticize.

1. What is the effect of the speaker's describing himself as "an old mustache"?
2. What **tone** do you think he intended?

COMPOSITION

Observing Contemporary Life

Many people have observed that parents, particularly fathers, in modern society do not spend enough quality time with their children. Consequently, family relationships suffer. Write an essay of at least four paragraphs in which you discuss what an average American family would probably be doing during the "children's hour," from 7 to 8 P.M. Then explain whether or not you think this hour is typical of family life in general. Make some concluding observation about contemporary family relationships. Direct your article to a family magazine.

Comparing a Paraphrase with a Poem

Write an essay of at least four paragraphs about "A Psalm of Life." In the first paragraph, paraphrase the ideas expressed in the poem, changing figurative language to literal. In the remaining paragraphs, explain what Longfellow's work has lost in your paraphrase. Note in particular what is lost in the rephrasing of the expression "leave behind us/Footprints on the sands of time." Address your essay to a classmate who had difficulty understanding the poem and did not enjoy reading it. See "Writing About Poetry and Poetic Devices" in the Writer's Handbook.

Comment

Longfellow at Home by Newton Arvin

There were many visitors to Craigie House, Longfellow's home in Cambridge. Although some of the visitors, categorized by the poet as "books, bores, and beggars," made themselves nuisances, they were always received with courtesy. Fortunately Longfellow's humor was usually equal to the occasion, and he could describe some of his guests with characteristic good nature. There was the Englishman who remarked that, in other countries, you know, we go to see ruins and all that—"but you have no ruins in your country, and I thought I would call and see *you*." There was the young Westerner who asked Longfellow how old he was, and when the poet answered "Seventy," rejoined, "I have seen a good many men of your age who looked much younger than you." A German woman, with a strong accent, called to talk with him about "The Building of the Ship," which she was planning to read in public, and which she called "The Lunch of the Sheep." As he was standing at the front door one August morning, a woman in black came up to him and inquired whether this was the house in which Longfellow had been born; when he explained that it was

not, she went on to ask, "Did he die here?"

His correspondence, too, had assumed appalling proportions, and his kindness was too genuine to allow him to turn a deaf ear to any of it. Most of the appeals he received, of course, were requests for his autograph, sometimes for *quantities* of autographs to be sold at benefits and the like; perhaps there were not many appeals, however, though there was one, for "your autograph in your own handwriting." Many of these demands came from people who wished Longfellow to read and criticize their manuscripts, like the man in Maine who had written an epic poem on the Creation, and had "done up" the six days' work "in about six hundred lines." Other appeals were for original poems; a stranger in the West put in an order for two poems "on friendship, or a subject like that, for the album of a young lady who is a very particular friend"; he also directed Longfellow to "send the bill with the articles."

From *Longfellow: His Life and Work* by Newton Arvin. Copyright © 1963 by Newton Arvin. Reprinted by permission of Little, Brown and Company in association with the Atlantic Monthly Press.

BIOGRAPHY

Oliver Wendell Holmes

1809–1894

Oliver Wendell Holmes once wrote: "I like books. I was born and bred among them and have the easy feeling when I get into their presence that a stable boy has among horses." It is not surprising that Holmes would seek to convey that same "easy feeling" in his own writing.

Born in Cambridge, Massachusetts, and educated at Harvard, Holmes received an M.D. from the Harvard School of Medicine in 1836, the same year in which he published *Poems*, his first volume. He did not gain a large practice. His small figure (he was five feet five inches tall) and youthful face inspired little confidence at first. Besides, Holmes jested about his profession, saying that "all small fevers would be gratefully received." But he did win distinction as Professor of Anatomy in Harvard College. This position he held actively for thirty-five years, and by honorary title till his death.

By the mid-1800s Holmes had earned a reputation as a writer of humorous verse. Hardly a celebration was held in the city that was not attended by Holmes, who would write light verse for the occasion. As he explained,

"I'm a florist in verse, and what *would* people say
If I came to a banquet without my bouquet?"

In the year 1857 the *Atlantic Monthly* was started under the editorship of James Russell Lowell, whose work appears in this unit. He had long enjoyed the conversation of Holmes and consented to edit the new periodical only on condition that Holmes contribute. Holmes's essays, published serially, took the form of conversations among people gathered around a boardinghouse table. Collected and titled *The Autocrat of the Breakfast Table*, these sprightly essays contain whims, opinions, and witticisms that cause readers to think about themselves and to observe life more closely.

Although Holmes's occasional poems were light and humorous, his verse could be serious and moralistic. "The Chambered Nautilus," in which he compares the progress of the human soul to a snail-like creature, is an example of such verse. The very name *nautilus*, from the Greek *naus* meaning "ship," suggests a sort of journey. Holmes described the shell as a "series of enlarging compartments successively dwelt in by the animal that inhabits the shell, which is built in a widening spiral." From this "widening spiral" Holmes draws his lesson.

The Chambered Nautilus

Oliver Wendell Holmes

This is the ship of pearl, which, poets feign,
  Sails the unshadowed main—
  The venturous bark that flings
On the sweet summer wind its purpled wings
5 In gulfs enchanted, where the Siren sings,[1]
  And coral reefs lie bare,
Where the cold sea-maids[2] rise to sun their streaming hair.

Its webs of living gauze[3] no more unfurl;
  Wrecked is the ship of pearl!
10 And every chambered cell,
Where its dim dreaming life was wont to dwell,
As the frail tenant shaped his growing shell,
  Before thee lies revealed—
Its irised[4] ceiling rent, its sunless crypt unsealed!

15 Year after year beheld the silent toil
  That spread his lustrous coil;
  Still, as the spiral grew,
He left the past year's dwelling for the new,
Stole with soft step its shining archway through,
20 Built up its idle door,
Stretched in his last-found home, and knew the old no more.

Thanks for the heavenly message brought by thee,
  Child of the wandering sea,
  Cast from her lap, forlorn!
25 From thy dead lips a clearer note is born

Robert Amft, detail of a photograph of a chambered nautilus

---

1. *the Siren sings.* In Greek mythology, the sirens were nymphs who by their sweet singing lured sailors to destruction.
2. *sea-maids,* mermaids.
3. *webs of living gauze,* tentacles.
4. *irised,* containing the colors of the rainbow.

Than ever Triton[5] blew from wreathèd horn!
    While on mine ear it rings,
Through the deep caves of thought I hear a voice that sings:

Build thee more stately mansions, O my soul,
30   As the swift seasons roll!
    Leave thy low-vaulted past!
Let each new temple, nobler than the last,
Shut thee from heaven with a dome more vast,
    Till thou at length art free,
35 Leaving thine outgrown shell by life's unresting sea!

                                        1858

---

5. *Triton*, in Greek mythology, the son of Poseidon, god of the sea. His
conch shell horn makes the roaring of the ocean.

THINK AND DISCUSS
Understanding
1. What is a *nautilus*? (Check the Glossary, if necessary.) What has caused it to be "wrecked" (line 9)?
2. Two words appear in lines 1–3 that are synonyms for *boat*. What are they?
3. What is the "frail tenant" mentioned in stanza 2? By what means does it shape its growing shell?

Analyzing
4. Why is the comparison between the nautilus and the soul appropriate? (In answering, keep in mind the fact that the nautilus yearly grows a new chamber of shell to fit its expanding body.)
5. What is the lesson learned from the nautilus that is expressed in the final stanza? At what point does the human body leave its "outgrown shell" (line 35)?

Extending
6. What lesson might a writer with a less optimistic outlook have derived from viewing the broken shell?

APPLYING: Theme H▨
See Handbook of Literary Terms, p. 914.
    Theme is the underlying meaning in a literary work. A theme may be directly stated, but more often it is implied.

1. Which of the following lines comes closest to expressing the theme of "The Chambered Nautilus"?
   • "Wrecked is the ship of pearl."
   • "Build thee more stately mansions, O my soul."
   • "He left the past year's dwelling for the new."
2. What statement is the speaker of the poem making about human life?

The Ballad of the Oysterman

Oliver Wendell Holmes

It was a tall young oysterman lived by the riverside,
His shop was just upon the bank, his boat was on the tide;
The daughter of a fisherman, that was so straight and slim,
Lived over on the other bank, right opposite to him.

5 It was the pensive oysterman that saw a lovely maid,
Upon a moonlight evening, a-sitting in the shade;
He saw her wave her handkerchief, as much as if to say,
"I'm wide awake, young oysterman, and all the folks away."

Then up arose the oysterman, and to himself said he,
10 "I guess I'll leave the skiff at home, for fear that folks should see;
I read it in the storybook, that, for to kiss his dear,
Leander swam the Hellespont[1]—and I will swim this here."

And he has leaped into the waves, and crossed the shining stream,
And he has clambered up the bank, all in the moonlight gleam;
15 Oh there were kisses sweet as dew, and words as soft as rain—
But they have heard her father's step, and in he leaps again!

Out spoke the ancient fisherman—"Oh, what was that, my daughter?"
" 'T was nothing but a pebble, sir, I threw into the water."
"And what is that, pray tell me, love, that paddles off so fast?"
20 "It's nothing but a porpoise, sir, that's been a-swimming past."

Out spoke the ancient fisherman—"Now bring me my harpoon!
I'll get into my fishing boat, and fix the fellow soon."
Down fell that pretty innocent, as falls a snow-white lamb,
Her hair drooped round her pallid cheeks, like seaweed on a clam.

John Singer Sargent, detail of
Breton Girl with a Basket (1877).
Terra Museum of American Art,
Chicago

---

1. *Leander swam the Hellespont.* Leander, a young man in ancient Greek legend,
nightly swam the Hellespont to be with his beloved Hero. When Leander drowned,
Hero leaped in the Hellespont and also died.

25 Alas for those two loving ones! she waked not from her swound,
And he was taken with the cramp, and in the waves was drowned;
But Fate has metamorphosed them, in pity of their woe,
And now they keep an oyster shop for mermaids down below.

1830

THINK AND DISCUSS
Understanding
1. Why does the oysterman decide to swim rather than take the skiff to cross the stream?
2. How does the daughter of the fisherman try to deceive her father?
3. What happens to the oysterman at the end of the poem? to the maid?

Analyzing
4. What word would you use to describe the **tone** of the poem? Explain your choice.
5. What things are compared in the **simile** in line 24? Think of similes that could describe the hair and pale cheeks of a young girl in a poem that has a serious tone.
6. Is the end of the poem comic or tragic? Explain.
7. A *literary ballad* is a poetic narrative of known authorship with the following characteristics: love or courage as themes, little characterization, action developed largely through dialogue, 4-line stanzas, a final summary stanza. Explain how each of these characteristics is seen in Holmes's ballad.

APPLYING: Rhythm H⫶
See Handbook of Literary Terms, p. 903.

Rhythm is the arrangement of stressed and unstressed syllables in speech or writing. Poets use rhythm for various purposes—to heighten effect, to stress ideas, and to convey a mood. "The Ballad of the Oysterman" has a regular, almost sing-song, rhythm that creates a light-hearted mood. *Scansion* is the process of determining the *meter*, or rhythm, in a poem. This poem consists of seven *feet*, or patterns of rhythm, each one with an unstressed syllable followed by a stressed one. This rhythmic pattern, called *iambic heptameter*, can be indicated thus:

It was/ a tall/ young oy/sterman/ lived by/ the riv/erside.

1. Write line 2 of this poem, indicating the iambic pattern with accents and slashes, as was done for line 1 above.
2. If line 9 were arranged in a normal sentence pattern, it would read this way: "Then the oysterman arose up, and he said to himself." Explain what the use of anastrophe adds.

COMPOSITION
Writing a Comparison
Write a three-paragraph comparison between an object of nature—an insect, plant, animal—and some aspect of human nature. You might, for example, relate a spider spinning its web to the performance of a difficult human task, or compare a plant that opens to sunlight or closes at night to a similar human response.

ENRICHMENT
Oral Reading
Using your school or public library, find a literary ballad that you think the class might enjoy. Practice reading it aloud so that you can present it smoothly to the class. Longfellow's collection *Ballads and Other Poems* contains favorites such as "The Wreck of the Hesperus" and "The Skeleton in Armor." Whittier's *Home Ballads, Poems and Lyrics* contains, among other poems, "Skipper Ireson's Ride."

John Greenleaf Whittier
1807–1892

Unlike the New England writers who were his contemporaries, John Greenleaf Whittier had little formal education. As a country boy, the son of a Quaker farmer near Haverhill, Massachusetts, he could go only now and then for a few weeks to a village school. Equally restricted was his reading, which consisted largely of books by pious Quakers. During his whole life he never got farther away from home than the nation's capital. However, at an early age he did encounter the works of the Scottish rural poet, Robert Burns (1759–1796), which exerted a great influence over him.

When he was nineteen, one of Whittier's poems was published by the abolitionist William Lloyd Garrison in a paper that he edited. This was the beginning of a lifelong association between the two men and marked the start of Whittier's career both as a writer and as a reformer. Under Garrison's influence, Whittier returned to school, spending two terms at the Haverhill Academy. In the years to follow, he was a shoemaker, a teacher, and an editor of journals in Hartford and Boston.

The political excitement of the times roused his ambition. He branded President Jackson as "the blood-thirsty old man at the head of our government," and planned to run for Congress to oppose his policies. But these political aspirations gave way in 1833, when Whittier's love of freedom led him to join the abolitionists, who were regarded at the time as dangerous fanatics. In their cause he remained active, sometimes at the peril of his life, until the amendment abolishing slavery was adopted in 1865. To further the antislavery crusade he wrote verse full of fire and reforming zeal. His ballad, "The Kansas Emigrants," is a rallying cry for the New England abolitionists who traveled cross-country to settle in the Territory of Kansas.

But the masterpiece for which Whittier is renowned is *Snowbound,* a long poem that provides an unrivaled description of a New England household shut in for a week by a snowstorm. In this poem, he draws on childhood memories, recording with vivid images the speech, thoughts, and lives of the people who lived during his time. From the eight hundred lines of *Snowbound* rises also the character of New England's homespun poet, with his sympathy for humble people everywhere.

from Snowbound

John Greenleaf Whittier

The sun that brief December day
Rose cheerless over hills of gray,
And, darkly circled, gave at noon
A sadder light than waning moon.
5 Slow tracing down the thickening sky
Its mute and ominous prophecy,
A portent seeming less than threat,
It sank from sight before it set.
A chill no coat, however stout,
10 Of homespun stuff could quite shut out,
A hard, dull bitterness of cold,
That checked, mid-vein, the circling race
Of lifeblood in the sharpened face,
The coming of the snowstorm told.
15 The wind blew east; we heard the roar
Of Ocean on his wintry shore,
And felt the strong pulse throbbing there
Beat with low rhythm our inland air.

Meanwhile we did our nightly chores—
20 Brought in the wood from out of doors,
Littered the stalls, and from the mows
Raked down the herd's grass for the cows;
Heard the horse whinnying for his corn;
And, sharply clashing horn on horn,
25 Impatient down the stanchion[1] rows
The cattle shake their walnut bows;
While, peering from his early perch
Upon the scaffold's pole of birch
The cock his crested helmet bent
30 And down his querulous challenge sent.

Unwarmed by any sunset light
The gray day darkened into night,

A night made hoary with the swarm
And whirl-dance of the blinding storm,
35 As zigzag, wavering to and fro
Crossed and recrossed the wingèd snow;
And ere the early bedtime came
The white drift piled the window frame,
And through the glass the clothesline posts
40 Looked in like tall and sheeted ghosts.

So all night long the storm roared on:
The morning broke without a sun;
In tiny spherule[2] traced with lines
Of nature's geometric signs,
45 In starry flake, and pellicle,[3]
All day the hoary meteor fell;
And, when the second morning shone,
We looked upon a world unknown,
On nothing we could call our own.
50 Around the glistening wonder bent
The blue walls of the firmament,
No cloud above, no earth below—
A universe of sky and snow!
The old familiar sights of ours
55 Took marvelous shapes; strange domes and towers
Rose up where sty or corncrib stood,
Or garden wall, or belt of wood;
A smooth white mound the brush pile showed,
A fenceless drift that once was road;
60 The bridle post an old man sat
With loose-flung coat and high cocked hat;

---

1. *stanchion,* a device that fits loosely around a cow's neck, allowing only movement sideways.
2. *spherule,* a little sphere.
3. *pellicle,* a thin skin or membrane.

The well-curb had a Chinese roof,[4]
And even the long sweep,[5] high aloof,
In its slant splendor, seemed to tell
65 Of Pisa's leaning miracle,[6] . . .

Shut in from all the world without,
We sat the clean-winged hearth[7] about,
Content to let the north wind roar
In baffled rage at pane and door,
70 While the red logs before us beat
The frost line back with tropic heat;
And ever, when a louder blast
Shook beam and rafter as it passed,
The merrier up its roaring draught
75 The great throat of the chimney laughed;
The house dog on his paws outspread
Laid to the fire his drowsy head,
The cat's dark silhouette on the wall
A couchant[8] tiger's seemed to fall;

80 And, for the winter fireside meet,
Between the andirons' straddling feet,
The mug of cider simmered slow,
The apples sputtered in a row,
And, close at hand, the basket stood
85 With nuts from brown October's wood. . . .

1866

4. *well-curb . . . roof.* The well-curb, or framing around the mouth of the well, was probably "roofed" with snow that curved upwards on the sides in drifts, resembling a pagoda roof.
5. *sweep,* a long pole connected to a bucket used for obtaining water in a well.
6. *Pisa's leaning miracle,* a noted leaning tower in Pisa, Italy.
7. *clean-winged hearth.* Hearths were commonly swept with the wing of a turkey.
8. *couchant* (kou'chənt), lying down, but with head raised. (This term is often used to refer to an animal on a coat of arms.)

Grandma Moses, *Snowed In* (1957). Copyright © 1973
Grandma Moses Properties Company, New York

THINK AND DISCUSS
Understanding

1. How much time elapses in the course of this excerpt? (You may need to reread lines 1–3 and 41–49.)
2. What are the "nightly chores" that the family members perform?
3. How have the "old familiar sights" been transformed (lines 54–65)?

Analyzing

4. Describe the **tone** of the first three stanzas (lines 1–40). List words and phrases that establish this tone.
5. At what point in stanza 4 (lines 41–65) does the tone shift? What words signal this new tone?
6. Name two **images** that describe the "marvelous shapes" of the snow in lines 37–40 and 54–65. To what different senses do these images appeal?
7. What is the **rhythm** pattern of this excerpt? Find a line that does not strictly adhere to this pattern.

APPLYING: Personification H𝕋
See Handbook of Literary Terms, p. 887.

   Personification is a figure of speech in which life or human characteristics are attributed to an animal, object, or concept. When poets speak of the wind singing or a brook babbling they are using personification. Whittier helps us see the wind in a new light by portraying its "strong pulse throbbing."

1. Find in the last stanza (lines 66–85) examples of personification that describe the raging storm.
2. Find in the final stanza examples of personification that portray indoor comfort.

COMPOSITION ✒
Evoking a Mood in Prose

   Imagine yourself and your family and pets snowbound at a luxurious, modern-day lodge or ski resort complete with stereo, microwave oven, television, and other modern conveniences. Reread lines 66–85 of *Snowbound*. Then write a prose paragraph that evokes a similar mood of comfort and contentment.

Recasting a Prose Paragraph into a Poem

   Try recasting the paragraph you have written above into poetry. You may want to use the iambic tetrameter rhythm that Whittier used in *Snowbound*. Include at least one example of personification in your poem, which should be at least 12 lines long.

The Story of American English

In *The American Democrat* (1838), James Fenimore Cooper wrote: "The common faults of American language are an ambition of effect, a want of simplicity, and a turgid abuse of terms." As editor of the New York *Evening Post*, William Cullen Bryant drew up a list of terms that his staff was not to use. This list included Americanisms denounced by the British: *reliable, balance, bogus, lengthy, to jeopardize,* and *to donate.*

But in spite of literature's reluctance to reflect the living language, the vocabulary of spoken American English grew rapidly. The War of 1812 gave us *Uncle Sam* and *The Star-Spangled Banner,* as well as the battle cry, "Don't give up the ship."

The Erie Canal, stretching the 360 miles from the Hudson River to Lake Erie (Albany to Buffalo), was finished in 1825 and christened the *Big Ditch.* It was to make New York City the pre-eminent American port on the Atlantic. And it brought into the language *boat mules* (those pulling the boats), *canalers* (workers on the boats), and *deck passengers* (travelers carried along with the cargo).

As Americans moved across the continent, they came upon the vast stretches of flat, generally treeless land for which they borrowed a name from the French—*prairie.* They combined this word with other words to describe the new environment: *prairie chicken, prairie dog, prairie grass, prairie law, prairie schooner.* Life on the *frontier* gave rise to the terms *rambunctious, hornswoggle,* and *ripsnorter.*

Politics in the fledgling nation became the source of a rich and vivid vocabulary, especially with the presidency of the plain-spoken Democrat, Andrew Jackson (1829–1937), known as *Old Hickory.* The term *logrolling* (mutual aid or conniving among politicians to promote legislation) came from the collaboration of pioneers in disposing of logs that obstructed construction or development.

Much *bunk* (or *bunkum*) was spoken on the floor of Congress (beginning with the rambling speeches of a congressman from Buncombe County, North Carolina). *Political machine, platform, lobbyist,* and *to stump* all originated in this early period.

An important influence on the development of the American language came from the black population. At the beginning of the seventeenth century, slave ships crossed the Atlantic to the ports of Britain's Southern American colonies, Georgia and South Carolina. Because there often existed no common language on these slave ships, pidgin English evolved—a form of English with simplified grammatical structure and a mixed vocabulary.

By the eighteenth century, black pidgin English was well established on the Southern plantations. And it is here that musical traditions, including the spirituals, originated. The slaves were free to hold religious gatherings—one of their few freedoms. These began as acts of religious devotion, but sometimes served as a way to pass along coded messages. *Steal away to Jesus* meant notice of a meeting; *Judgment Day* was the day the slaves were to unite and rebel; and *home* or *heaven* referred to Africa. In addition, words survived from the original African languages. Words such as the following have an African heritage: *voodoo, tote, banjo, banana, goober, gumbo,* and *yam.*

In *Democracy in America* (1835), the French historian Alexis de Tocqueville devoted an entire chapter to "How American Democracy Has Modified the English Language." He wrote: "The continual restlessness of a democracy leads to endless change of language as of all else." As in so much of his commentary on other aspects of American life, Tocqueville was to prove prophetic in his comments on the American language; change would not diminish but quicken.

Born into a London theatrical family, Fanny Kemble began her acting career as Juliet in a family production of *Romeo and Juliet*. At seventeen, she joined her father, who managed the Covent Garden Theatre, and her aunt, Sarah Kemble Siddons, a noted actress, on an American tour. Acclaimed in New York, Boston, and Philadelphia, she remained in the East to marry. Soon she gave up acting to pursue a literary career, writing poems, plays, and journals. After a visit to her husband's plantation in Georgia, Kemble began to protest the injustices of slavery, publishing her *Journal of a Residence on a Georgia Plantation*. Although much of her work was directed toward social reform, "A Wish" dwells on the Romantic themes of death and immortality.

A Wish

Fanny Kemble

Let me not die for ever, when I'm gone
  To the cold earth! but let my memory
Live like the gorgeous western light that shone
  Over the clouds where sank day's majesty.
5 Let me not be forgotten; though the grave
  Has clasped its hideous arms around my brow.
Let me not be forgotten! though the wave
  Of time's dark current rolls above me now.
Yet not in tears remembered be my name;
10   Weep over those ye loved; for me, for me,
Give me the wreath of glory, and let fame
  Over my tomb spread immortality!

THINK AND DISCUSS
Understanding
1. The speaker requests that three things will not happen in lines 1, 5, and 9. What are these things?
2. What does the speaker request in lines 11 and 12?

Analyzing
3. Given the two professions mentioned in her biography, how might Kemble herself have achieved "the wreath of glory"?

Extending
4. Do you think that fame is an effective way to overcome death? Can you think of other ways to gain a kind of immortality? Explain.

BIOGRAPHY

Edgar Allan Poe
1809–1849

Self-portrait by Poe

Orphaned before he was three, Poe was taken into the home of John Allan, a wealthy Richmond, Virginia, merchant. When Poe declined an offer to become a merchant and spoke of a literary career, Mr. Allan disowned him. There were several abortive attempts at reconciliation, but this rejection left permanent scars on the young man. In 1830, after serving two years in the army, Poe received an appointment to West Point but was dismissed within the year for "gross neglect of duty."

Meeting only limited success with his stories and poetry, Poe took on the editorship of a series of magazines. A brilliant and diligent editor, he vastly increased circulation of several leading publications of the time but seldom was adequately paid for his efforts. His fiery temper and emotional outbreaks kept him poor and on the move from one magazine to another.

In 1835 Poe married his fragile, thirteen-year-old cousin, Virginia Clemm. Moving to Philadelphia, he began to enjoy prominence with his poems, stories, and criticisms. But eventually he again suffered personal despair, job upheaval, and poverty. Publication of "The Raven" brought fame but little money. Poe probably received five or ten dollars for the poem. Before the death of his wife Virginia in 1847 from tuberculosis, Poe was plagued by her illness, his emotional troubles, and poverty. With her death, the instability that haunted him intensified. Though his last years were not without periods of achievement ("Annabel Lee," a tribute to his wife, was written during the last months of his life), his sense of persecution increased.

He disappeared one day on a business trip to Philadelphia and was found later on the streets of Baltimore, battered and drunk. After four days of delirium, he died, on October 7, 1849.

American literature found its first real critic in Poe. He led the way in making the magazine a suitable vehicle for criticism, earning a reputation as a critic long before he was recognized as poet and short-story writer.

Poe constructed his poems and tales to create a single effect upon a reader's mind and feelings. Every event, every word, and every detail built toward that effect, whether it be one of horror, madness, irony, or revenge. With this effect in mind, Poe devised and ordered incidents so that they mounted to a frightening climax, drawing the reader in to share the horror experienced by the characters.

As a poet, Poe believed with other Romantic poets that beauty was "the essence of the poem." Along with this beauty, his poems are characterized by a haunting musical quality and a melancholy tone.

Poe's contemporaries differed widely in their appraisals. Alfred, Lord Tennyson, the foremost English poet of the time, saw Poe as "the most American genius," while Ralph Waldo Emerson thought Poe a mere "jingle man." Although Poe's personal reputation remains somewhat controversial, his contributions to literature are universally acknowledged.

See IRONY in the Handbook of Literary Terms, page 893.

The Cask of Amontillado

Edgar Allan Poe

he thousand injuries of Fortunato I had borne as I best could; but when he ventured upon insult, I vowed revenge. You, who so well know the nature of my soul, will not suppose, however, that I gave utterance to a threat. *At length* I would be avenged; this was a point definitively settled—but the very definitiveness with which it was resolved, precluded the idea of risk. I must not only punish, but punish with impunity. A wrong is unredressed when retribution overtakes its redresser. It is equally unredressed when the avenger fails to make himself felt as such to him who has done the wrong.

It must be understood, that neither by word nor deed had I given Fortunato cause to doubt my goodwill. I continued, as was my wont, to smile in his face, and he did not perceive that my smile *now* was at the thought of his immolation.

He had a weak point—this Fortunato—although in other regards he was a man to be respected and even feared. He prided himself on his connoisseurship in wine. Few Italians have the true virtuoso spirit. For the most part their enthusiasm is adopted to suit the time and opportunity—to practice imposture upon the British and Austrian millionaires. In painting and gemmary Fortunato, like his countrymen, was a quack—but in the matter of old wines he was sincere. In this respect I did not differ from him materially: I was skillful in the Italian vintages myself, and bought largely whenever I could.

It was about dusk, one evening during the supreme madness of the carnival season, that I encountered my friend. He accosted me with excessive warmth, for he had been drinking much. The man wore motley.[1] He had on a tight-fitting parti-striped dress, and his head was surmounted by the conical cap and bells. I was so pleased to see him, that I thought I should never have done wringing his hand.

I said to him: "My dear Fortunato, you are luckily met. How remarkably well you are looking today! But I have received a pipe of what passes for Amontillado, and I have my doubts."

"How?" said he. "Amontillado? A pipe? Impossible! and in the middle of the carnival!"

"I have my doubts," I replied; "and I was silly enough to pay the full Amontillado price without consulting you in the matter. You were not to be found, and I was fearful of losing a bargain."

"Amontillado!"

"I have my doubts."

"Amontillado!"

"And I must satisfy them."

"Amontillado!"

"As you are engaged, I am on my way to Luchesi. If anyone has a critical turn, it is he. He will tell me——"

"Luchesi cannot tell Amontillado from sherry."

"And yet some fools will have it that his taste is a match for your own."

"Come, let us go."

Amontillado (ə mon′tə yä′dō), a dry, pale sherry wine.
1. *motley* (mot′lē), the multi-colored costume characteristic of the professional jester.

"Whither?"

"To your vaults."

"My friend, no; I will not impose upon your good nature. I perceive you have an engagement. Luchesi——"

"I have no engagement—come."

"My friend, no. It is not the engagement, but the severe cold with which I perceive you are afflicted. The vaults are insufferably damp. They are encrusted with nitre."[2]

"Let us go, nevertheless. The cold is merely nothing. Amontillado! You have been imposed upon. And as for Luchesi, he cannot distinguish sherry from Amontillado."

Thus speaking, Fortunato possessed himself of my arm. Putting on a mask of black silk, and drawing a *roquelaure*[3] closely about my person, I suffered him to hurry me to my palazzo.

There were no attendants at home; they had absconded to make merry in honor of the time. I had told them that I should not return until the morning, and had given them explicit orders not to stir from the house. These orders were sufficient, I well knew, to insure their immediate disappearance, one and all, as soon as my back was turned.

I took from their sconces two flambeaux,[4] and giving one to Fortunato, bowed him through several suites of rooms to the archway that led into the vaults. I passed down a long and winding staircase, requesting him to be cautious as he followed. We came at length to the foot of the descent, and stood together on the damp ground of the catacombs of the Montresors.

The gait of my friend was unsteady, and the bells upon his cap jingled as he strode.

"The pipe?" said he.

"It is farther on," said I; "but observe the white web-work which gleams from these cavern walls."

He turned toward me, and looked into my eyes with two filmy orbs that distilled the rheum of intoxication.

"Nitre?" he asked, at length.

"Nitre," I replied. "How long have you had that cough?"

"Ugh! ugh! ugh!—ugh! ugh! ugh!—ugh! ugh! ugh!—ugh! ugh! ugh!—ugh! ugh! ugh!"

My poor friend found it impossible to reply for many minutes.

"It is nothing," he said, at last.

"Come," I said, with decision, "we will go back; your health is precious. You are rich, respected, admired, beloved; you are happy, as once I was. You are a man to be missed. For me it is no matter. We will go back; you will be ill, and I cannot be responsible. Besides, there is Luchesi——"

"Enough," he said; "the cough is a mere nothing; it will not kill me. I shall not die of a cough."

"True—true," I replied; "and, indeed, I had no intention of alarming you unnecessarily; but you should use all proper caution. A draught of this Medoc will defend us from the damps."

Here I knocked off the neck of a bottle which I drew from a long row of its fellows that lay upon the mould.

"Drink," I said, presenting him the wine.

He raised it to his lips with a leer. He paused and nodded to me familiarly, while his bells jingled.

"I drink," he said, "to the buried that repose around us."

"And I to your long life."

He again took my arm, and we proceeded.

"These vaults," he said, "are extensive."

"The Montresors," I replied, "were a great and numerous family."

"I forget your arms."

"A huge human foot d'or, in a field azure; the foot crushes a serpent rampant[5] whose fangs are imbedded in the heel."

"And the motto?"

---

2. *nitre* (nī′tər), potassium nitrate. Also spelled *niter*.
3. *roquelaure* (rŏk lôr′), a knee-length cloak buttoned in front.
4. *sconces two flambeaux.* A sconce (skons) is a candlestick projecting from a wall bracket. Flambeaux (flam bōz′) are flaming torches.
5. *arms . . . rampant.* The Montresor coat-of-arms (a shield) shows, on a blue (azure) background, a golden foot crushing a snake reared up to strike.

"Nemo me impune lacessit." [6]

"Good!" he said.

The wine sparkled in his eyes and the bells jingled. My own fancy grew warm with the Medoc. We had passed through walls of piled bones, with casks and puncheons intermingling, into the inmost recesses of the catacombs. I paused again, and this time I made bold to seize Fortunato by an arm above the elbow.

"The nitre!" I said; "see, it increases. It hangs like moss upon the vaults. We are below the river's bed. The drops of moisture trickle among the bones. Come, we will go back ere it is too late. Your cough——"

"It is nothing," he said; "let us go on. But first, another draught of the Medoc."

I broke and reached him a flagon of De Grâve. He emptied it at a breath. His eyes flashed with a fierce light. He laughed and threw the bottle upward with a gesticulation I did not understand.

I looked at him in surprise. He repeated the movement—a grotesque one.

"You do not comprehend?" he said.

"Not I," I replied.

"Then you are not of the brotherhood."

"How?"

"You are not of the masons."[7]

"Yes, yes," I said; "yes, yes."

"You? Impossible! A mason?"

"A mason," I replied.

"A sign," he said.

"It is this," I answered, producing a trowel from beneath the folds of my *roquelaure.*

"You jest," he exclaimed, recoiling a few paces. "But let us proceed to the Amontillado."

"Be it so," I said, replacing the tool beneath the cloak, and again offering him my arm. He leaned upon it heavily. We continued our route in search of the Amontillado. We passed through a range of low arches, descended, passed on, and descending again, arrived at a deep crypt, in which the foulness of the air caused our flambeaux rather to glow than flame.

At the most remote end of the crypt there appeared another less spacious. Its walls had been lined with human remains, piled to the vault overhead, in the fashion of the great catacombs of Paris. Three sides of this interior crypt were still ornamented in this manner. From the fourth the bones had been thrown down, and lay promiscuously upon the earth, forming at one point a mound of some size. Within the wall thus exposed by the displacing of the bones, we perceived a still interior recess, in depth about four feet, in width three, in height six or seven. It seemed to have been constructed for no especial use within itself, but formed merely the interval between two of the colossal supports of the roof of the catacombs, and was backed by one of their circumscribing walls of solid granite.

It was in vain that Fortunato, uplifting his dull torch, endeavored to pry into the depth of the recess. Its termination the feeble light did not enable us to see.

"Proceed," I said; "herein is the Amontillado. As for Luchesi——"

"He is an ignoramus," interrupted my friend, as he stepped unsteadily forward, while I followed immediately at his heels. In an instant he had reached the extremity of the niche, and finding his progress arrested by the rock, stood stupidly bewildered. A moment more and I had fettered him to the granite. In its surface were two iron staples, distant from each other about two feet, horizontally. From one of these depended a short chain, from the other a padlock. Throwing the links about his waist, it was but the work of a few seconds to secure it. He was too much astounded to resist. Withdrawing the key I stepped back from the recess.

"Pass your hand," I said, "over the wall; you cannot help feeling the nitre. Indeed it is *very* damp. Once more let me *implore* you to return. No? Then I must positively leave you. But I must first render you all the little attentions in my power."

---

6. *Nemo me impune lacessit* (nā′mō mā im pü′nā la kes′ sit). "No one can harm me unpunished." [*Latin*]

7. *masons,* a play on words. Fortunato refers to a member of a fraternal society. Montresor implies one who builds with stone or brick.

"The Amontillado!" ejaculated my friend, not yet recovered from his astonishment.

"True," I replied; "the Amontillado."

As I said these words I busied myself among the pile of bones of which I have before spoken. Throwing them aside, I soon uncovered a quantity of building stone and mortar. With these materials and with the aid of my trowel, I began vigorously to wall up the entrance of the niche.

I had scarcely laid the first tier of the masonry when I discovered that the intoxication of Fortunato had in a great measure worn off. The earliest indication I had of this was a low moaning cry from the depth of the recess. It was *not* the cry of a drunken man. There was then a long and obstinate silence. I laid the second tier, and the third, and the fourth; and then I heard the furious vibrations of the chain. The noise lasted for several minutes, during which, that I might hearken to it with the more satisfaction, I ceased my labors and sat down upon the bones. When at last the clanking subsided, I resumed the trowel, and finished without interruption the fifth, the sixth, and the seventh tier. The wall was now nearly upon a level with my breast. I again paused, and holding the flambeaux over the mason-work, threw a few feeble rays upon the figure within.

A succession of loud and shrill screams, bursting suddenly from the throat of the chained form, seemed to thrust me violently back. For a brief moment I hesitated—I trembled. Unsheathing my rapier, I began to grope with it about the recess; but the thought of an instant reassured me. I placed my hand upon the solid fabric of the catacombs, and felt satisfied. I reapproached the wall. I replied to the yells of him who clamored. I reechoed—I aided—I surpassed them in volume and in strength. I did this, and the clamorer grew still.

It was now midnight, and my task was drawing to a close. I had completed the eighth, the ninth, and the tenth tier. I had finished a portion of the last and the eleventh; there remained but a single stone to be fitted and plastered in. I struggled with its weight; I placed it partially in its destined position. But now there came from out the niche a low laugh that erected the hairs upon my head. It was succeeded by a sad voice, which I had difficulty in recognizing as that of the noble Fortunato. The voice said——

"Ha! ha! ha!—he! he!—a very good joke indeed—an excellent jest. We will have many a rich laugh about it at the palazzo—he! he! he!—over our wine—he! he! he!"

"The Amontillado!" I said.

"He! he! he!—he! he! he!—yes, the Amontillado. But is it not getting late? Will not they be awaiting us at the palazzo, the Lady Fortunato and the rest? Let us be gone."

"Yes," I said, "let us be gone."

"For the love of God, Montresor!"

"Yes," I said, "for the love of God!"

But to these words I hearkened in vain for a reply. I grew impatient. I called aloud:

"Fortunato!"

No answer. I called again:

"Fortunato!"

No answer still. I thrust a torch through the remaining aperture and let it fall within. There came forth in return only a jingling of the bells. My heart grew sick—on account of the dampness of the catacombs. I hastened to make an end of my labor. I forced the last stone into its position; I plastered it up. Against the new masonry I reerected the old rampart of bones. For the half of a century no mortal has disturbed them. *In pace requiescat.*[8]

1846

---

8. *In pace requiescat* (in pä'ke re'kwi äs'kät). May he rest in peace. [*Latin*]

![black and white striped bar decoration]

THINK AND DISCUSS
Understanding
1. What is Montresor's goal, as stated at the beginning of the story?
2. Of what nationality is Fortunato? In what area does Montresor consider Fortunato an expert? In what other areas does he say Fortunato is a quack?
3. How does Montresor lure Fortunato to the vault?

Analyzing
4. Why is "the supreme madness of the carnival season" an appropriate setting for this story?
5. When translated from the French, Montresor's name means "my treasure." How does this, along with his coat of arms and its motto, strengthen his motivation?
6. There are several reasons why Fortunato does not suspect Montresor's act of revenge. Discuss two of them.
7. Why do you think that the evils we are

told were committed by Fortunato are never explained?

8. Who is more a victim, Fortunato or Montresor?

Extending

9. What aspects of Romanticism (see Reader's Note, page 108) appear in this story?

APPLYING: Irony HⱫ
See Handbook of Literary Terms, p. 893.

Irony is a contrast between what appears to be and what really is. With *verbal irony* there is a contrast between what is said and what is actually meant. (One might say of a dull movie, "How exciting!") *Irony of situation* occurs when things turn out contrary to what is expected or intended. (A shy, quiet teenager turns out to be a famous comedian.) *Dramatic irony* occurs when a reader or viewer knows more about a situation than the characters do. (A burglar who has not seen the "Beware of Dog" sign is about to climb over a fence.) Everything in "The Cask of Amontillado" contributes to the effect of irony.

1. What is ironic about Fortunato's name? his costume?
2. Explain how each of the following is ironic.
   • Fortunato says of his cough, "It will not kill me."
   • Montresor drinks to Fortunato's long life.
   • Both men are "masons."
3. Poe chooses a carnival setting for his story. Is this an example of verbal irony or of irony of situation?

VOCABULARY
Etymology

An *etymology* is the derivation of a word, an account of the word's origin and history. In the Glossary of this book, the etymologies of some words are given in brackets at the ends of entries. The symbol < means "derived from." Use your Glossary to determine the etymologies of the following words from "A Cask of Amontillado." On a sheet of paper, write a brief explanation of each etymology.

connoisseur	flagon
redress	ejaculate
rheum	gesticulation

COMPOSITION ⬤━
Analyzing a Character

Some critics interpret the line "My heart grew sick" in the final paragraph to mean that Montresor is experiencing remorse for the murder he had committed. Others say he is feeling not remorse, but nausea from the fetid air in the catacombs. Write four paragraphs for your classmates arguing in favor of one of these interpretations. In the first paragraph, explain your reading of these lines, giving some general ideas on what has caused you to form this opinion. In the middle paragraphs, give reasons for your opinion based on the content of the story and on your interpretation of Montresor's character. In the final paragraph, explain whether or not you think that the final sentence, translated as, "May he rest in peace," can be applied to Montresor himself. See "Writing About Characters" in the Writer's Handbook.

Writing About Irony

Write a composition of five paragraphs entitled "Irony in 'The Cask of Amontillado.' " In the first paragraph, discuss irony in general, defining the three kinds of irony. In the second, third, and fourth paragraphs, respectively, point out examples of each kind of irony. (Your answers to the Applying questions should be helpful.) In the final paragraph, discuss how the various uses of irony contribute to the total effect of the story. Assume that your paper will be submitted to a student expository writing contest. See "Writing About Irony" in the Writer's Handbook.

Comment

The Facts Behind "The Cask of Amontillado"
by Edward Rowe Snow

Edgar Allan Poe became a private in the army in 1827, and was sent out to Fort Independence on Castle Island in Boston Harbor. Actually, were it not for Poe's serving at Castle Island, "The Cask of Amontillado" would never have been written.

While at Fort Independence Poe became fascinated with the inscriptions on a gravestone on a small monument outside the walls of the fort. . . .

One Sunday morning he arose early and . . . copied with great care the entire wording on the marble monument. The following inscription was recorded from the western side of the monument:

The officers of the U.S. Regiment of Lt. Art'y erected this monument as a testimony of their respect & friendship for an amiable man & gallant officer.

Then he moved to the eastern panel, where he inscribed in his notebook the famous lines from Collins's ode:[1]

"Here honour comes, a Pilgrim gray, To deck the turf, that wraps his clay."

After resting briefly, he attacked the northern side of the edifice, and then copied the fourth panel facing South Boston:

Beneath this stone are deposited the remains of Lieut. ROBERT F. MASSIE, of the U.S. Regt. of Light Artillery.
Near this spot on the 25th, Decr. 1817, fell Lieut. Robert F. Massie, Aged 21 years.

Extremely interested in the wording of the fourth panel, which said, "Near this spot fell" Lieutenant Massie, he decided to find out all he could about the duel. Interviewing every officer at the fort, he soon learned the unusual tale of the two officers and their fatal combat.

During the summer of 1817, Poe learned, twenty-year-old Lieutenant Robert F. Massie of Virginia had arrived at Fort Independence as a newly appointed officer. Most of the men at the post came to enjoy Massie's friendship, but one officer, Captain Green, took a violent dislike to him. Green was known at the fort as a bully and a dangerous swordsman.

When Christmas vacations were allotted, few of the officers were allowed to leave the fort, and Christmas Eve found them up in the old barracks hall, playing cards. Just before midnight, at the height of the card game, Captain Green sprang to his feet, reached across the table and slapped Lieutenant Massie squarely in the face. "You're a cheat," he roared, "and I demand immediate satisfaction!"

Massie quietly accepted the bully's challenge, naming swords as the weapons for the contest. Seconds[2] arranged for the duel to take place the next morning at dawn.

Christmas morning was clear but bitter. The two contestants and their seconds left the inner walls of the fort at daybreak for Dearborn Bastion. Here the seconds made a vain attempt at reconciliation. The duel began. Captain Green, an expert swordsman, soon had Massie at a disadvantage and ran him through. Fatally wounded, the young Virginian was carried back to the fort, where he died that afternoon. His many friends mourned the passing of a gallant officer.

A few weeks later a fine marble monument was erected to Massie's memory. Placed over his grave at the scene of the encounter, the monument reminded all who saw it that an overbearing bully had killed the young Virginian.

Feeling against Captain Green ran high for many weeks, and then suddenly he completely vanished. Years went by without a sign of him, and Green was written off the army records as a deserter.

According to the story which Poe finally

---

1. *Collins's ode,* "Ode Written in the Year 1746" by William Collins (1721–1759), a British poet.
2. *Seconds,* supporters who arranged combats for duelists, saw to the observance of fair play, and secured the help of a doctor on the scene.

From *Mysterious New England,* Copyright © 1974. *Yankee, Inc.* Reprinted by permission.

gathered together, Captain Green had been so detested by his fellow officers at the fort that they decided to take a terrible revenge on him for Massie's death. . . .

Visiting Captain Green one moonless night, they pretended to be friendly and plied him with wine until he was helplessly intoxicated. Then, carrying the captain down to one of the ancient dungeons, the officers forced his body through a tiny opening which led into the subterranean casemate.[3] . . .

By this time Green had awakened from his drunken stupor and demanded to know what was taking place. Without answering, his captors began to shackle him to the floor, using the heavy iron handcuffs and footcuffs fastened into the stone. Then they all left the dungeon and proceeded to seal the captain up alive inside the windowless casemate, using bricks and mortar which they had hidden close at hand.

Captain Green shrieked in terror and begged for mercy, but his cries fell on deaf ears. The last brick was finally inserted, mortar applied and the room sealed up, the officers believed, forever. Captain Green undoubtedly died a horrible death within a few days. . . .

As Edgar Allan Poe heard this story, he took many notes. . . . Poe was soon asked to report to the post commander, and the following conversation is said to have taken place:

"I understand," began the officer, "that you've been asking questions about Massie's monument and the duel which he fought?"

"I have, sir," replied Poe meekly.

"And I understand that you've learned all about the subsequent events connected with the duel?"

"I have, sir."

"Well, you are never to tell that story outside the walls of this fort."

Poe agreed that he would never *tell* the story, but years afterwards he did *write* the tale based on this incident, transferring the scene across the ocean to Europe and changing both the characters and the story itself. He named the tale "The Cask of Amontillado."

In 1905, eighty-eight years after the duel, when the workmen were repairing a part of the old fort, they came across a section of the

ancient cellar marked on the plans as a small dungeon. They were surprised to find only a blank wall where the dungeon was supposed to be. . . . Several lanterns were brought down and a workman was set to chipping out the old mortar. . . . Eventually it was possible for the smallest man in the group to squeeze through the aperture.

"It's a skeleton!" they heard him cry a moment later, and he rushed for the opening, leaving the lantern behind him.

Several of the others then pulled down the entire brick barrier and went into the dungeon where they saw a skeleton shackled to the floor with a few fragments of an 1812 army uniform clinging to the bones.

The remains could not be identified but they were given a military funeral and placed in the Castle Island cemetery in a grave marked UNKNOWN.

---

3. *casemate,* a vault with openings for the firing of cannon.

Hop-Frog

Edgar Allan Poe

never knew any one so keenly alive to a joke as the king was. He seemed to live only for joking. To tell a good story of the joke kind, and to tell it well, was the surest road to his favor. Thus it happened that his seven ministers were all noted for their accomplishments as jokers. They all took after the king, too, in being large, corpulent, oily men, as well as inimitable jokers. Whether people grow fat by joking, or whether there is something in fat itself which predisposes to a joke, I have never been quite able to determine; but certain it is that a lean joker is a *rara avis in terris*.[1]

About the refinements, or, as he called them, the "ghosts" of wit, the king troubled himself very little. He had an especial admiration for *breadth* in a jest, and would often put up with *length*, for the sake of it. Overniceties wearied him. He would have preferred Rabelais' *Gargantua* to the *Zadig* of Voltaire:[2] and, upon the whole, practical jokes suited his taste far better than verbal ones.

At the date of my narrative, professing jesters had not altogether gone out of fashion at court. Several of the great continental "powers" still retained their "fools," who wore motley, with caps and bells, and who were expected to be always ready with sharp witticisms, at a moment's notice, in consideration of the crumbs that fell from the royal table.

Our king, as a matter of course, retained his "fool." The fact is, he *required* something in the way of folly—if only to counterbalance the heavy wisdom of the seven wise men who were his ministers—not to mention himself.

His fool, or professional jester, was not *only* a fool, however. His value was trebled in the eyes of the king, by the fact of his being also a dwarf and a cripple. Dwarfs were as common at court, in those days, as fools; and many monarchs would have found it difficult to get through their days (days are rather longer at court than elsewhere) without both a jester to laugh *with*, and a dwarf to laugh *at*. But, as I have already observed, your jesters, in ninety-nine cases out of a hundred, are fat, round, and unwieldy—so that it was no small source of self-gratulation with our king that, in Hop-Frog (this was the fool's name), he possessed a triplicate treasure in one person.

I believe the name "Hop-Frog" was *not* that given to the dwarf by his sponsors at baptism, but it was conferred upon him, by general consent of the seven ministers, on account of his inability to walk as other men do. In fact, Hop-Frog could only get along by a sort of interjectional gait—something between a leap and a wriggle,—a movement that afforded illimitable amusement, and of course consolation, to the

---

1. *rara avis in terris* (rä'rä ä'vēs in ter'rēs), "a rare bird on earth." [*Latin*]
2. *Rabelais' Gargantua . . . Zadig of Voltaire* (räb'ə lā'; gär gan'chü ə; zä dēg'; võl ter'). Gargantua, a creation of the French author Rabelais (?1494–1553), had an enormous appetite for eating and drinking and a love of practical jokes. In contrast, Zadig, title character in a novel by the French satirist Voltaire (1694–1778), was a "sensible young man," extremely prudent and virtuous.

king, for (notwithstanding the protuberance of his stomach and a constitutional swelling of the head) the king, by his whole court, was accounted a capital figure.

But although Hop-Frog, through the distortion of his legs, could move only with great pain and difficulty along a road or floor, the prodigious muscular power which nature seemed to have bestowed upon his arms, by way of compensation for deficiency in the lower limbs, enabled him to perform many feats of wonderful dexterity, where trees or ropes were in question, or anything else to climb. At such exercises he certainly much more resembled a squirrel, or a small monkey, than a frog.

I am not able to say, with precision, from what country Hop-Frog originally came. It was from some barbarous region, however, that no person ever heard of—a vast distance from the court of our king. Hop-Frog, and a young girl very little less dwarfish than himself (although of exquisite proportions, and a marvelous dancer), had been forcibly carried off from their respective homes in adjoining provinces, and sent as presents to the king, by one of his ever-victorious generals.

Under these circumstances, it is not to be wondered at that a close intimacy arose between the two little captives. Indeed, they soon became sworn friends. Hop-Frog, who, although he made a great deal of sport, was by no means popular, had it not in his power to render Trippetta many services; but *she*, on account of her grace and exquisite beauty (although a dwarf), was universally admired and petted; so she possessed much influence; and never failed to use it, whenever she could, for the benefit of Hop-Frog.

On some grand state occasion—I forget what—the king determined to have a masquerade; and whenever a masquerade, or any thing of that kind, occurred at our court, then the talents both of Hop-Frog and Trippetta were sure to be called into play. Hop-Frog, in especial, was so inventive in the way of getting up pageants, suggesting novel characters, and arranging costume, for masked balls, that nothing could be done, it seems, without his assistance.

The night appointed for the *fête* had arrived. A gorgeous hall had been fitted up, under Trippetta's eye, with every kind of device which could feasibly give *éclat*[3] to a masquerade. The whole court was in a fever of expectation. As for costumes and characters, it might well be supposed that everybody had come to a decision on such points. Many had made up their minds (as to what *rôles* they should assume) a week, or even a month, in advance; and, in fact, there was not a particle of indecision anywhere—except in the case of the king and his seven ministers. Why they hesitated I never could tell, unless they did it by way of a joke. More probably, they found it difficult, on account of being so fat, to make up their minds. At all events, time flew; and, as a last resort, they sent for Trippetta and Hop-Frog.

When the two little friends obeyed the summons of the king, they found him sitting at his wine with the seven members of his cabinet council; but the monarch appeared to be in a very ill humor. He knew that Hop-Frog was not fond of wine; for it excited the poor cripple almost to madness; and madness is no comfortable feeling. But the king loved his practical jokes, and took pleasure in forcing Hop-Frog to drink and (as the king called it) "to be merry."

"Come here, Hop-Frog," said he, as the jester and his friend entered the room; "swallow this bumper to the health of your absent friends (here Hop-Frog sighed) and then let us have the benefit of your invention. We want characters—*characters*, man,—something novel —out of the way. We are wearied with this everlasting sameness. Come, drink! the wine will brighten your wits."

Hop-Frog endeavored, as usual, to get up a jest in reply to these advances from the king; but the effort was too much. It happened to be the poor dwarf's birthday, and the command to drink to his "absent friends" forced the tears to his eyes. Many large, bitter drops fell into the goblet as he took it, humbly, from the hand of the tyrant.

---

3. *éclat* (ā klä′), brilliant spirit.

"Ah! ha! ha! ha!" roared the latter, as the dwarf reluctantly drained the beaker. "See what a glass of good wine can do! Why, your eyes are shining already!"

Poor fellow! his large eyes *gleamed*, rather than shone; for the effect of wine on his excitable brain was not more powerful than instantaneous. He placed the goblet nervously on the table, and looked round upon the company with a half-insane stare. They all seemed highly amused at the success of the king's "*joke.*"

"And now to business," said the prime minister, a *very* fat man.

"Yes," said the king. "Come, Hop-Frog, lend us your assistance. Characters my fine fellow; we stand in need of characters[4]—all of us—ha! ha! ha!" and as this was seriously meant for a joke, his laugh was chorused by the seven.

Hop-Frog also laughed, although feebly and somewhat vacantly.

"Come, come," said the king, impatiently, "have you nothing to suggest?"

"I am endeavoring to think of something *novel*," replied the dwarf, abstractedly, for he was quite bewildered by the wine.

"Endeavoring!" cried the tyrant, fiercely; "what do you mean by *that?* Ah, I perceive. You are sulky, and want more wine. Here, drink this!" and he poured out another goblet full and offered it to the cripple, who merely gazed at it, gasping for breath.

"Drink, I say!" shouted the monster, "or by the fiends——"

The dwarf hesitated. The king grew purple with rage. The courtiers smirked. Trippetta, pale as a corpse, advanced to the monarch's seat, and, falling on her knees before him, implored him to spare her friend.

The tyrant regarded her, for some moments, in evident wonder at her audacity. He seemed quite at a loss what to do or say—how most becomingly to express his indignation. At last, without uttering a syllable, he pushed her violently from him, and threw the contents of the brimming goblet in her face.

The poor girl got up as best she could, and,
not daring even to sigh, resumed her position at the foot of the table.

There was a dead silence for about half a minute, during which the falling of a leaf, or of a feather, might have been heard. It was interrupted by a low, but harsh and protracted *grating* sound which seemed to come at once from every corner of the room.

"What—what—*what* are you making that noise for?" demanded the king, turning furiously to the dwarf.

The latter seemed to have recovered, in great measure, from his intoxication, and looking fixedly but quietly into the tyrant's face, merely ejaculated:

"I—I? How could it have been me?"

"The sound appeared to come from without," observed one of the courtiers. "I fancy it was the parrot at the window, whetting his bill upon his cage-wires."

"True," replied the monarch, as if much relieved by the suggestion; "but, on the honor of a knight, I could have sworn that it was the gritting of this vagabond's teeth."

Hereupon the dwarf laughed (the king was too confirmed a joker to object to any one's laughing), and displayed a set of large, powerful, and very repulsive teeth. Moreover, he avowed his perfect willingness to swallow as much wine as desired. The monarch was pacified; and having drained another bumper with no very perceptible ill effect, Hop-Frog entered at once, and with spirit, into the plans for the masquerade.

"I cannot tell what was the association of idea," observed he, very tranquilly, and as if he had never tasted wine in his life, "but *just after* your majesty had struck the girl and thrown the wine in her face—*just after* your majesty had done this, and while the parrot was making that odd noise outside the window, there came into my mind a capital diversion—one of my own country frolics —often enacted among us, at our masquerades: but here it will be new altogether. Unfortunately,

---

4. *characters,* a pun, meaning both imaginary roles and good character references.

however, it requires a company of eight persons, and——"

"Here we *are!*" cried the king, laughing at his acute discovery of the coincidence; "eight to a fraction—I and my seven ministers. Come! what is the diversion?"

"We call it," replied the cripple, "the Eight Chained Orang-Outangs, and it really is excellent sport if well enacted."

"*We* will enact it," remarked the king, drawing himself up, and lowering his eyelids.

"The beauty of the game," continued Hop-Frog, "lies in the fright it occasions among the women."

"Capital!" roared in chorus the monarch and his ministry.

"I will equip you as orang-outangs," proceeded the dwarf; "leave all that to me. The resemblance shall be so striking, that the company of masqueraders will take you for real beasts —and of course, they will be as much terrified as astonished."

"Oh, this is exquisite!" exclaimed the king. "Hop-Frog! I will make a man of you."

"The chains are for the purpose of increasing the confusion by their jangling. You are supposed to have escaped, *en masse*, from your keepers. Your majesty cannot conceive the *effect* produced, at a masquerade, by eight chained orang-outangs, imagined to be real ones by most of the company; and rushing in with savage cries, among the crowd of delicately and gorgeously habited men and women. The *contrast* is inimitable."

"It *must* be," said the king: and the council arose hurriedly (as it was growing late), to put in execution the scheme of Hop-Frog.

His mode of equipping the party as orang-outangs was very simple, but effective enough for his purposes. The animals in question had, at the epoch of my story, very rarely been seen in any part of the civilized world; and as the imitations made by the dwarf were sufficiently beastlike and more than sufficiently hideous, their truthfulness to nature was thus thought to be secured.

The king and his ministers were first encased in tight-fitting stockinet shirts and drawers. They were then saturated with tar. At this stage of the process, some one of the party suggested feathers; but the suggestion was at once overruled by the dwarf, who soon convinced the eight, by ocular demonstration, that the hair of such a brute as the orang-outang was much more efficiently represented by *flax*. A thick coating of the latter was accordingly plastered upon the coating of tar. A long chain was now procured. First, it was passed about the waist of the king, *and tied;* then about another of the party, and also tied; then about all successively, in the same manner. When this chaining arrangement was complete, and the party stood as far apart from each other as possible, they formed a circle; and to make all things appear natural, Hop-Frog passed the residue of the chain, in two diameters, at right angles, across the circle, after the fashion adopted, at the present day, by those who capture chimpanzees, or other large apes, in Borneo.

The grand saloon in which the masquerade was to take place, was a circular room, very lofty, and receiving the light of the sun only through a single window at top. At night (the season for which the apartment was especially designed) it was illuminated principally by a large chandelier, depending by a chain from the centre of the skylight, and lowered, or elevated, by means of a counterbalance as usual; but (in order not to look unsightly) this latter passed outside the cupola and over the roof.

The arrangements of the room had been left to Trippetta's superintendence; but, in some particulars, it seems, she had been guided by the calmer judgment of her friend the dwarf. At his suggestion it was that, on this occasion, the chandelier was removed. Its waxen drippings (which, in weather so warm, it was quite impossible to prevent) would have been seriously detrimental to the rich dresses of the guests, who, on account of the crowded state of the saloon, could not *all* be expected to keep from out its centre—that is to say, from under the chandelier. Additional sconces were set in various parts of the hall, out of the way; and a flambeau, emitting sweet

Karl Zerbe, detail of *Harlequin* (1943). Whitney Museum of American Art

While the tumult was at its height, and each masquerader attentive only to his own safety (for, in fact, there was much *real* danger from the pressure of the excited crowd), the chain by which the chandelier ordinarily hung, and which had been drawn up on its removal, might have been seen very gradually to descend, until its hooked extremity came within three feet of the floor.

Soon after this, the king and his seven friends having reeled about the hall in all directions, found themselves, at length, in its centre, and of course, in immediate contact with the chain. While they were thus situated, the dwarf, who had followed noiselessly at their heels, inciting them to keep up the commotion, took hold of their own chain at the intersection of the two portions which crossed the circle diametrically and at right angles. Here, with the rapidity of thought, he inserted the hook from which the chandelier had been wont to depend; and, in an instant, by some unseen agency, the chandelier-chain was drawn so far upward as to take the hook out of reach, and, as an inevitable consequence, to drag the orang-outangs together in close connection, and face to face.

The masqueraders, by this time, had recovered, in some measure, from their alarm; and, beginning to regard the whole matter as a well-contrived pleasantry, set up a loud shout of laughter at the predicament of the apes.

"Leave them to *me!*" now screamed Hop-Frog, his shrill voice making itself easily heard through all the din. "Leave them to *me.* I fancy I know them. If I can only get a good look at them, *I* can soon tell who they are."

Here, scrambling over the heads of the crowd, he managed to get to the wall; when, seizing a flambeau from one of the Caryatides, he returned, as he went, to the centre of the room —leaped, with the agility of a monkey, upon the king's head—and thence clambered a few feet up the chain—holding down the torch to examine

odor, was placed in the right hand of each of the Caryatides[5] that stood against the wall—some fifty or sixty all together.

The eight orang-outangs, taking Hop-Frog's advice, waited patiently until midnight (when the room was thoroughly filled with masqueraders) before making their appearance. No sooner had the clock ceased striking, however, than they rushed, or rather rolled in, all together—for the impediments of their chains caused most of the party to fall, and all to stumble as they entered.

The excitement among the masqueraders was prodigious, and filled the heart of the king with glee. As had been anticipated, there were not a few of the guests who supposed the ferocious-looking creatures to be beasts of *some* kind in reality, if not precisely orang-outangs. Many of the women swooned with affright; and had not the king taken the precaution to exclude all weapons from the saloon, his party might soon have expiated their frolic in their blood. As it was, a general rush was made for the doors; but the king had ordered them to be locked immediately upon his entrance; and, at the dwarf's suggestion, the keys had been deposited with *him.*

---

5. *Caryatides* (kar'ē at'id ēz), statues of women used as columns.

the group of orang-outangs, and still screaming: "*I* shall soon find out who they are!"

And now, while the whole assembly (the apes included) were convulsed with laughter, the jester suddenly uttered a shrill whistle; when the chain flew violently up for about thirty feet—dragging with it the dismayed and struggling orang-outangs, and leaving them suspended in mid-air between the sky-light and the floor. Hop-Frog, clinging to the chain as it rose, still maintained his relative position in respect to the eight maskers, and still (as if nothing were the matter) continued to thrust his torch down toward them, as though endeavoring to discover who they were.

So thoroughly astonished was the whole company at this ascent, that a dead silence, of about a minute's duration, ensued. It was broken by just such a low, harsh, *grating* sound, as had before attracted the attention of the king and his councillors when the former threw the wine in the face of Trippetta. But, on the present occasion, there could be no question as to *whence* the sound issued. It came from the fanglike teeth of the dwarf, who ground them and gnashed them as he foamed at the mouth, and glared, with an expression of maniacal rage, into the upturned countenances of the king and his seven companions.

"Ah, ha!" said at length the infuriated jester. "Ah, ha! I begin to see who these people *are*, now!" Here, pretending to scrutinize the king more closely, he held the flambeau to the flaxen coat which enveloped him, and which instantly burst into a sheet of vivid flame. In less than half a minute the whole eight orang-outangs were blazing fiercely, amid the shrieks of the multitude who gazed at them from below, horror-stricken, and without the power to render them the slightest assistance.

At length the flames, suddenly increasing in virulence, forced the jester to climb higher up the chain, to be out of their reach; and, as he made this movement, the crowd again sank, for a brief instant, into silence. The dwarf seized his opportunity, and once more spoke:

"I now see *distinctly*," he said, "what manner of people these maskers are. They are a great king and his seven privy-councillors,—a king who does not scruple to strike a defenceless girl, and his seven councillors who abet him in the outrage. As for myself, I am simply Hop-Frog, the jester—and *this is my last jest.*"

Owing to the high combustibility of both the flax and the tar to which it adhered, the dwarf had scarcely made an end of his brief speech before the work of vengeance was complete. The eight corpses swung in their chains, a fetid, blackened, hideous, and indistinguishable mass. The cripple hurled his torch at them, clambered leisurely to the ceiling, and disappeared through the skylight.

It is supposed that Trippetta, stationed on the roof of the saloon, had been the accomplice of her friend in his fiery revenge, and that, together, they effected their escape to their own country; for neither was seen again.

1849

THINK AND DISCUSS
Understanding
1. What connection does the narrator make between people's ability to enjoy a joke and their fatness?
2. What was the job of a jester, or fool?
3. Why was Hop-Frog a "triplicate treasure" to the king? How did the jester get his name?

Analyzing
4. What can we infer about the king from the information that "Overniceties wearied him," and "practical jokes suited his taste far better than verbal ones"?
5. Hop-Frog bears many of the king's taunts without apparant malice. What one act of the king's causes Hop-Frog's act of revenge?

6. In what ways is Hop-Frog crippled in spirit? In what respect are the king and his seven ministers more crippled than Hop-Frog?

Extending

7. If **irony** is the "single effect" created in "The Cask of Amontillado," what is the single effect created in "Hop-Frog"? Explain your answer.

APPLYING: Characterization H𝑇
See Handbook of Literary Terms, p. 882.

   Characterization is the means an author uses to develop the personality of a character in a literary work. In order to be believable, fictional characters must have reasons, or motives, for what they do. Motivated action follows from the personality of a character and from the external events surrounding that character.

1. Does Hop-Frog's act of revenge seem consistent with his personality? Why or why not?

2. Is Hop-Frog motivated to seek revenge because of love or of hate? Explain.

3. What do you think motivates Trippetta to be Hop-Frog's accomplice?

VOCABULARY
Context

   Use context clues to determine the meaning of each italicized word below. Then write the letter of the correct definition on your paper.

1. Large, *corpulent* men make better jokers than wiry, slim ones. (**a**) good-looking; (**b**) heavy; (**c**) light; (**d**) depressed.

2. "Trippetta, pale as a corpse, advanced to the monarch's seat, and, falling on her knees before him, *implored* him to spare her friend." (**a**) ignored; (**b**) laughed; (**c**) ordered; (**d**) begged.

3. "He seemed quite at a loss what to do or say . . . to express his *indignation*. At last, without uttering a syllable, he pushed her violently from him, and threw the contents of the brimming goblet in her face." (**a**) anger; (**b**) happiness; (**c**) boredom; (**d**) love.

4. Hop-Frog possessed a "*prodigious* muscular power" that "enabled him to perform many feats of wonderful dexterity." (**a**) great; (**b**) tiny; (**c**) organized; (**d**) boring.

5. The chandelier's waxen drippings "would have been seriously *detrimental* to the rich dresses of the guests." (**a**) harmful; (**b**) helpful; (**c**) unrelated; (**d**) immature.

COMPOSITION ◄━●
Writing About Revenge

   In a four-paragraph essay, explain why you think the theme of revenge is so popular in books, TV shows, and films. In your essay, cite plots that are based on revenge. Assume your writing will be published in a magazine such as *Psychology Today*.

Writing About Author's Technique

   Poe carefully constructs his story so that suspense builds as the plot develops. Write an essay of at least four paragraphs for a literary magazine in which you describe the various details Poe uses to create suspense in "Hop-Frog." Note also how dramatic irony contributes to the building of suspense. See "Writing to Analyze Author's Style" in the Writer's Handbook.

ENRICHMENT
Research

   Many stories and biographies deal with people who have had to contend with unusual physical characteristics. Using the library, rented videotapes, or other resources, prepare a report of at least four paragraphs for your classmates about a real or a fictional character who was physically set apart from the majority of people. Focus on that character's differences from the norm and the way he or she adjusted to those differences. Possible sources might include Swift's *Gulliver's Travels*, Kafka's *The Metamorphosis*, Rostand's *Cyrano de Bergerac*, or the films *Mask* or *The Elephant Man*.

Reading A POEM

Poems are words compressed and arranged into lines having **rhythm,** and often, **rhyme.** Poetry uses musical language to express emotion and ideas that go beyond the literal meanings of words. Because poetry is condensed and non-literal, some people are intimidated by it. Yet reading and understanding a poem need not be difficult if you follow some simple guidelines.

Determine the poet's purpose. Poe's purpose was to produce a single effect in "The Raven"—to portray a mind filled with "fantastic terrors." He chose a subject and devices to reinforce this effect, using details (a bleak December setting, a midnight visitor) and **images** (the gloating lamplight, the oppressive perfumed air) to establish this effect. **Figurative language** suggests the terror brought on by the darkness ("Night's Plutonian shore") and highlights the eerie humanlike qualities of the *lonely, stately, beguiling* raven.

Examine the structure of the poem. Note the relationship of the structure to the content, as well as the stanza divisions and the punctuation within stanzas. Many of the 6-line stanzas in "The Raven" consist of a single sentence that builds in intensity. Read these poetic sentences as you would prose ones, looking for the subject and verb, and determining what each word contributes to the meaning.

Note the poet's word choice. Poe chose certain words to convey an impression, whether it be a sensuous, melancholy effect ("silken, sad, uncertain rustling of each purple curtain") or a suggestion of darkness and evil ("black plume," "ominous bird," "fiend"). Numerous words with *-ing* endings and the repeated final rhyme in each stanza produce a hypnotic effect.

Listen to the rhythm of the poem. The meter, or pattern of stressed and unstressed syllables, is *trochaic* (trō kā′ik)—an accented syllable followed by an unaccented one. There are eight trochaic *feet,* or syllable patterns, in all but

the final line of each stanza. These lines should be read with a break in the middle. Often these internal pauses, or *caesuras* (si zhür′əz), are marked by a comma or other punctuation, but as you settle into Poe's meter, you will automatically read the break even when there is no punctuation. Occasionally, you will have to compress a word to maintain the meter. For example, in line 2 *curious* must be read as two syllables.

Note the sound devices. The following sound devices create a mood of mystery and melancholy.

1. *Rhyme.* Along with *end rhyme,* or rhyme at the end of lines, Poe uses *internal rhyme,* or rhyme within lines. Notice, for example, that *dreary* within line 1 rhymes with *weary* at its end, and that *napping* within line 3 rhymes with *tapping* at the end of this line and with *rapping* within line 4.
2. *Alliteration,* the repetition of the initial sound, usually consonant, of two or more closely related words or accented syllables, enriches the poem ("*w*eak and *w*eary" in line 1; "*n*odded, *n*early, *n*apping" in line 3).
3. *Assonance,* the repetition of similar vowel sounds followed by different consonant sounds in stressed syllables or words, adds to the musical effect of the poem. For example, the long *a* sound is repeated in the words *stately, Raven, saintly,* and *days* in line 38.
4. *Repetition,* the repeating of a word or phrase, is striking in lines 16 and 17 and in the concluding word of each stanza, which is *more* or a variation of it.
5. *Onomatopoeia,* the use of words whose sounds suggest the natural sounds of an object or activity, is apparent in words such as *rapping, tapping,* and *beating.* In addition, these words suggest the pronounced heartbeat of the agitated speaker.

The Raven

Edgar Allan Poe

Once upon a midnight dreary, while I pondered, weak and weary,
Over many a quaint and curious volume of forgotten lore—
While I nodded, nearly napping, suddenly there came a tapping,
As of someone gently rapping, rapping at my chamber door.
5 " 'Tis some visitor," I muttered, "tapping at my chamber door—
Only this and nothing more."

Ah, distinctly I remember it was in the bleak December,
And each separate dying ember wrought its ghost upon the floor.
Eagerly I wished the morrow; vainly I had sought to borrow
10 From my books surcease of sorrow—sorrow for the lost Lenore—
For the rare and radiant maiden whom the angels name Lenore—
Nameless here forevermore.

And the silken, sad, uncertain rustling of each purple curtain
Thrilled me—filled me with fantastic terrors never felt before;
15 So that now, to still the beating of my heart, I stood repeating,
" 'Tis some visitor entreating entrance at my chamber door—
Some late visitor entreating entrance at my chamber door—
That it is and nothing more."

Presently my soul grew stronger; hesitating then no longer,
20 "Sir," said I, "or Madam, truly your forgiveness I implore;
But the fact is I was napping, and so gently you came rapping,
And so faintly you came tapping, tapping at my chamber door,
That I scarce was sure I heard you"—here I opened wide the door—
Darkness there and nothing more.

25 Deep into that darkness peering, long I stood there wondering, fearing,
Doubting, dreaming dreams no mortal ever dared to dream before;
But the silence was unbroken, and the stillness gave no token,
And the only word there spoken was the whispered word, "Lenore?"
This I whispered, and an echo murmured back the word "Lenore!"
30 Merely this and nothing more.

(continued)

Back into the chamber turning, all my soul within me burning,
Soon again I heard a tapping somewhat louder than before.
"Surely," said I, "surely that is something at my window lattice;
Let me see, then, what thereat is, and this mystery explore—
35 Let my heart be still a moment and this mystery explore;
                              'Tis the wind and nothing more!"

Open here I flung the shutter, when, with many a flirt and flutter,
In there stepped a stately Raven of the saintly days of yore;
Not the least obeisance made he; not a minute stopped or stayed he;
40 But, with mien of lord or lady, perched above my chamber door—
Perched upon a bust of Pallas[1] just above my chamber door—
                              Perched, and sat, and nothing more.

Then this ebony bird beguiling my sad fancy into smiling,
By the grave and stern decorum of the countenance it wore,
45 "Though thy crest be shorn and shaven, thou," I said, "art sure no craven,
Ghastly grim and ancient Raven wandering from the Nightly shore—
Tell me what thy lordly name is on the Night's Plutonian[2] shore!"
                              Quoth the Raven, "Nevermore."

Much I marveled this ungainly fowl to hear discourse so plainly,
50 Though its answer little meaning—little relevancy bore;
For we cannot help agreeing that no living human being
Ever yet was blessed with seeing bird above his chamber door—
Bird or beast upon the sculptured bust above his chamber door,
                              With such name as "Nevermore."

55 But the Raven, sitting lonely on the placid bust, spoke only
That one word, as if his soul in that one word he did outpour.
Nothing further then he uttered, not a feather then he fluttered—
Till I scarcely more than muttered, "Other friends have flown before;
On the morrow *he* will leave me, as my hopes have flown before."
60   Then the bird said, "Nevermore."

Startled at the stillness broken by reply so aptly spoken,
"Doubtless," said I, "what it utters is its only stock and store,
Caught from some unhappy master whom unmerciful disaster
Followed fast and followed faster till his songs one burden bore—
65 Till the dirges of his hope that melancholy burden bore
                              Of 'Never—nevermore.' "

---

1. *Pallas* (pal′əs), one of the names of Athena, who, in Greek mythology, was the goddess
of wisdom.
2. *Plutonian* (plü tō′nē ən), of the spirit world ruled over by Pluto, Greek and Roman god
of the lower world.

Glen Loates, *Raven, 1967.*
Private collection

But the Raven still beguiling all my fancy into smiling,
Straight I wheeled a cushioned seat in front of bird and bust and door;
Then, upon the velvet sinking, I betook myself to linking
70 Fancy unto fancy, thinking what this ominous bird of yore—
What this grim, ungainly, ghastly, gaunt, and ominous bird of yore
                         Meant in croaking "Nevermore."

This I sat engaged in guessing, but no syllable expressing
To the fowl, whose fiery eyes now burned into my bosom's core;
75 This and more I sat divining, with my head at ease reclining
On the cushion's velvet lining that the lamplight gloated o'er,[3]
But whose velvet violet lining with the lamplight gloating o'er,
                       She shall press, ah, nevermore!

(continued)

---

3. *the lamplight gloated o'er.* The rays of the light were refracted or turned aside by the velvet material with which the seat was covered.

Then, methought, the air grew denser, perfumed from an unseen censer
80 Swung by seraphim[4] whose footfalls tinkled on the tufted floor.
"Wretch,"[5] I cried, "thy God hath lent thee—by these angels he hath sent thee
Respite—respite and nepenthe—[6] from thy memories of Lenore!
Quaff, oh quaff this kind nepenthe and forget this lost Lenore!"
                                        Quoth the Raven, "Nevermore."

85 "Prophet!" said I, "thing of evil! prophet still, if bird or devil!
Whether Tempter sent, or whether tempest tossed thee here ashore,
Desolate yet all undaunted, on this desert land enchanted—
On this home by Horror haunted—tell me truly, I implore;
Is there—*is* there balm in Gilead?[7]—tell me—tell me, I implore!"
90   Quoth the Raven, "Nevermore."

"Prophet!" said I, "thing of evil! prophet still, if bird or devil!
By that Heaven that bends above us, by that God we both adore,
Tell this soul with sorrow laden if, within the distant Aidenn,[8]
It shall clasp a sainted maiden whom the angels name Lenore—
95 Clasp a rare and radiant maiden whom the angels name Lenore."
                                        Quoth the Raven, "Nevermore."

"Be that word our sign of parting, bird or fiend!" I shrieked, upstarting.
"Get thee back into the tempest and the Night's Plutonian shore!
Leave no black plume as a token of that lie thy soul hath spoken!
100 Leave my loneliness unbroken! quit the bust above my door!
Take thy beak from out my heart, and take thy form from off my door!"
                                        Quoth the Raven, "Nevermore."

And the Raven, never flitting, still is sitting, *still* is sitting
On the pallid bust of Pallas just above my chamber door;
105 And his eyes have all the seeming of a demon's that is dreaming,
And the lamplight o'er him streaming throws his shadow on the floor;
And my soul from out that shadow that lies floating on the floor
                                        Shall be lifted—nevermore!
                                                                    1845

---

4. *seraphim* (ser′ə fim), angels of one of the highest orders.
5. *Wretch.* The narrator is here addressing himself.
6. *nepenthe,* in mythology, a potion believed to relieve sorrow.
7. *is there balm in Gilead* (gil′ē əd)? Is there no comfort for my sorrow? In Jeremiah 8:22
the prophet asks whether no healing ointment (balm) can be found in Gilead, a region in
ancient Palestine east of the Jordan River. Gradually the words came to have the figurative
meaning which Poe uses.
8. *Aidenn* (ā′den), the Moslem paradise.

THINK AND DISCUSS

Understanding

1. In what activity is the speaker involved at the beginning of the poem? At what time of the year and day do the initial events occur?
2. What noise interrupts the speaker? How does he account for this noise?
3. How does the raven finally enter the chamber? Where does he perch?
4. What is the only word the raven speaks? What explanation does the speaker give (lines 62–66) for how the raven learned this word?
5. Rephrase in your own words the question that the speaker asks in line 89, noting footnote 7.
6. What information does the speaker demand of the bird in lines 93–95? How does the speaker react to its answer (line 97)?

Analyzing

7. From the evidence provided in the poem, what can you infer about the speaker's relationship to Lenore?
8. At what point in the poem does the speaker's **tone** shift from melancholy to anger? How does the raven react to the speaker's angry words?
9. Cite words and phrases from the poem that indicate the speaker thinks the raven is sent from hell. What **allusion** reinforces this impression?
10. Explain the meaning of the phrase, "Take thy beak from out my heart" (line 101).
11. Reread the final stanza. Why is it significant that the speaker, not the raven, uses the word *nevermore?* How would you describe the speaker's state of mind at this point?

Extending

12. Why do you think Poe might have chosen a raven rather than another bird (canary, parrot) or animal (dog, mouse) for his poem? In answering, consider the appearance of the raven, as well as the associations it suggests.

COMPOSITION

Imitating a Poetic Style

Poe's distinctive poetic style invites imitation, perhaps even a *parody*, or humorous imitation. Try writing your own poem of at least two stanzas, using Poe's rhyme scheme, rhythm, and meter. You might, for instance, begin with a line such as, "Once upon a noonday fateful, I was caught at something hateful."

Interpreting a Poem

"The Raven" can be interpreted as any of the following: a poem about sadness and loss, a poem about madness, a poem in which music (sound) is more important than meaning. Using one of these topics, write an essay of at least four paragraphs about this poem. In your first paragraph, explain how the interpretation you have chosen creates the single effect of the poem. In the middle paragraphs, reinforce your interpretation with examples from the poem. Although the final paragraph should follow from the preceding ones, try to arrive at some new insight about the poem.

ENRICHMENT

Memorizing Poetry

This poem should be heard to be appreciated. Memorize several stanzas or the entire poem and recite it before the class, adjusting your voice to the various moods of the speaker. You may wish to have a second student recite the final line of each stanza for dramatic effect.

Annabel Lee

Edgar Allan Poe

It was many and many a year ago,
   In a kingdom by the sea,
That a maiden there lived whom you may
   know
By the name of Annabel Lee;—
5 And this maiden she lived with no other
   thought
   Than to love and be loved by me.

She was a child and *I* was a child,
   In this kingdom by the sea,
But we loved with a love that was more than
   love—
10   I and my Annabel Lee—
With a love that the wingèd seraphs of Heaven
   Coveted her and me.

And this was the reason that, long ago,
   In this kingdom by the sea,
15 A wind blew out of a cloud by night
   Chilling my Annabel Lee;
So that her highborn kinsmen came
   And bore her away from me,
To shut her up in a sepulcher
20   In this kingdom by the sea.

The angels, not half so happy in Heaven,
   Went envying her and me:—
Yes! that was the reason (as all men know,
   In this kingdom by the sea)
25 That the wind came out of the cloud, chilling
   And killing my Annabel Lee.

But our love it was stronger by far than the
   love
   Of those who were older than we—
   Of many far wiser than we—
30 And neither the angels in Heaven above
   Nor the demons down under the sea,
Can ever dissever my soul from the soul
   Of the beautiful Annabel Lee:—

For the moon never beams without bringing me
   dreams
35   Of the beautiful Annabel Lee;
And the stars never rise but I see the bright eyes
   Of the beautiful Annabel Lee;
And so, all the night-tide; I lie down by the side
Of my darling, my darling, my life and my
   bride,
40   In her sepulcher there by the sea—
   In her tomb by the side of the sea.

1849

THINK AND DISCUSS
Understanding
1. What was the physical cause of the young bride's death? What spiritual forces caused her death?
2. How does the loss of his bride affect the speaker?
3. What happened to the body of Annabel Lee?

Analyzing

4. Point out words and phrases that give the poem its unreal quality.
5. Cite lines in the poem that indicate the poet has idealized the power of love.
6. What in the poem illustrates the poet's belief in the timelessness of love?

Extending

7. Why do you think Poe titled this poem "Annabel Lee" instead of "Virginia Clemm"?

APPLYING: Sound Devices H
See Handbook of Literary Terms, p. 909.

"Annabel Lee" relies heavily on **sound devices** for its effect. These devices are dis-cussed in the article titled "Reading a Poem" on page 166. Review the article, if necessary, to answer the following questions.

1. Find examples of internal **rhyme** in lines 32 and 34. Examine the end rhyme and chart the rhyme scheme of the first three stanzas of the poem. (See the Handbook of Literary Terms, page 902, if you need help.)
2. What sound is **alliterated** in line 21?
3. Cite examples of **assonance** in lines 36 and 38.
4. What words and phrases are repeated in the final stanza (lines 34–41)? What is the effect of this repetition?
5. What mood is created by the sound devices in this poem?

Reader's Note

"To Helen"

"To Helen" was inspired by the beautiful young mother of one of Poe's boyhood friends —"the first purely ideal love of my soul"—according to the poet. The woman of the title is modeled after Helen of Troy, celebrated both in literature and mythology as the image of ideal beauty. The Greek poet Homer recounts the bloody battles of the Trojan War, which was fought to recover Helen, who had been kidnapped by Paris. No one is sure why Poe chose to compare Helen's beauty to *Nicean* [nī sē′ən: referring to Nicea, an ancient city in Asia Minor] barks, but perhaps the word serves solely for its musical qualities or for its suggestions of remoteness. "The weary, wayworn wanderer" refers to Odysseus, or Ulysses, who was delayed for ten years in returning from the Trojan War. Like the ship, or bark, that carried Ulysses home, Helen's beauty has transported the poet on his early voyages on the sea of life.

Throughout the poem, Poe continues to use classical **images** and **allusions,** in keeping with the Romantic notion that pure beauty can best be captured by references to past "glory" and "grandeur." Helen's features constitute a "classic face," while her hair, like that described in Homeric poems, is "hyacinth," or golden and wavy. "Naiad [nā′ad] airs" refers to the graceful behavior of a mythological nymph who inhabited and sustained lakes, rivers, and fountains. Lines 9 and 10 evoke the greatness of past civilizations, suggesting to the reader images of the serene beauty of classical art and literature.

In the final stanza Helen appears as a statue. Influenced by the preceding classical allusions, the reader recalls the calm facial expression and flowing garments of the Greek and Roman statuary. The "agate lamp" in her hand is connected with the subsequent reference to Psyche [sī′kē], the **personification** of the soul in Greek mythology. Although forbidden to look at her lover Cupid, one night while he was asleep Psyche viewed his face by lamplight, thereby earning his prolonged anger. The Holy Land of the final line is the land of antiquity and for Poe the realm of ideal beauty that is separate from the hardships and ugliness of the workaday world.

To Helen

Edgar Allan Poe

Helen, thy beauty is to me
  Like those Nicean barks of yore,
That gently, o'er a perfumed sea,
  The weary, wayworn wanderer bore
5 To his own native shore.

On desperate seas long wont to roam,
  Thy hyacinth hair, thy classic face,
Thy Naiad airs, have brought me home
To the glory that was Greece
10 And the grandeur that was Rome.

Lo! in yon brilliant window niche
  How statuelike I see thee stand!
The agate lamp within thy hand,
  Ah, Psyche, from the regions which
15 Are Holy Land!

1823   1831

THINK AND DISCUSS
Understanding
1. What is a bark? (Consult your Glossary, if necessary.) What quality do Helen and the Nicean barks have in common?
2. To what does the speaker compare himself in stanzas 1 and 2?
3. In what form does Helen appear in the final stanza? Why do you think she carries a lamp?

Analyzing
4. The woman in the poem is spoken of as a ship and a statue, but never as a flesh-and-blood person. Why?
5. What qualities of Romanticism (see Reader's Note, page 108) does this poem display?

Extending
6. In what sense could an ideal supply people with a guiding force?

COMPOSITION
Writing a Poem to Achieve an Effect
Poe built his poems to express a particular effect or mood for the reader. Think of a mood —surprise, anger, awe, horror, happiness, sadness—you would like to express in a poem. Choose a topic to express this effect —for example, a vast, starry sky to express awe. List words to describe your topic that employ sound devices (*vast, vanquish, victorious*). Think of words or phrases that could be repeated throughout the poem (*scattering starlight*). Decide whether or not rhyme would enhance the effect of your poem. Now put these elements together in a poem of at least 10 lines, to present to a relative on a special occasion. You may wish to give your poem a title that suggests the mood or effect it is designed to achieve. See "Developing Your Style" in the Writer's Handbook.

James Russell Lowell
1819–1891

Born in Cambridge, Massachusetts, James Russell Lowell learned to speak Latin almost as fluently as English before entering Harvard at fifteen. In college he spent more time reading in the library as whim dictated than he did studying prescribed subjects at home. He was elected class poet, but because of his neglect of college regulations the authorities would not permit him to read his poem at commencement. In his senior year, he met Emerson, who impressed him with his so-called "radical" doctrines, and began a lifelong involvement in democratic causes. (Lowell's dedication to social reform and abolition are reflected in "Stanzas on Freedom.") After leaving Harvard, he contributed a number of articles to newspapers and magazines, published two volumes of poetry, and wrote a volume of criticism.

Besides contributing forty articles to Boston periodicals in the single year 1848, this versatile writer published four books: *Poems, Second Series; The Biglow Papers* (First Series); *A Fable for Critics;* and *The Vision of Sir Launfal.* The supposed author of *The Biglow Papers* was a Yankee farmer's son, who used his native dialect, common sense, and shrewd humor to attack in stinging verse the government's policy in the Mexican War. The characters—the rustic youth, his proud father, the pedantic village parson—all remained so true to themselves at every appearance that many readers thought the poems actually were sent in by a country youth. For humor, satire, deep conviction, and genuine power of expression these dialect poems remain Lowell's best.

In 1855, when Longfellow retired from his professorship at Harvard, Lowell succeeded him, teaching there until 1872. In 1857 Lowell helped found the *Atlantic Monthly,* functioning as editor until 1861. Lowell was appointed to diplomatic posts, serving as ambassador to Spain and later to England. Queen Victoria said of him, "During my reign no ambassador or minister has created so much interest or won so much regard."

Lowell's verse, like that of most poets in this unit, was notable for the old Puritan strain of moral earnestness. Concerning his own efforts Lowell declared, "I shall never be a poet till I get out of the pulpit." Although there is much of the pulpit in Lowell's works, there is also the humor and homespun charm that characterize later American literature.

Stanzas on Freedom

James Russell Lowell

Men! whose boast it is that ye
Come of fathers brave and free,
If there breathe on earth a slave,
Are ye truly free and brave?
5 If ye do not feel the chain,
When it works a brother's pain,
Are ye not base slaves indeed,
Slaves unworthy to be freed?

Women! who shall one day bear
10 Sons to breathe New England air,
If ye hear, without a blush,
Deeds to make the roused blood rush
Like red lava through your veins,
For your sisters now in chains—
15 Answer! are ye fit to be
Mothers of the brave and free?

Is true Freedom but to break
Fetters for our own dear sake,
And, with leathern hearts, forget
20 That we owe mankind a debt?
No! true freedom is to share
All the chains our brothers wear,
And, with heart and hand, to be
Earnest to make others free!

25 They are slaves who fear to speak
For the fallen and the weak;
They are slaves who will not choose
Hatred, scoffing, and abuse,
Rather than in silence shrink
30 From the truth they needs must think;
They are slaves who dare not be
In the right with two or three.   1843

THINK AND DISCUSS
Understanding
1. What do the men mentioned in the first stanza boast of? Why might such men not be truly free (lines 3–4)?
2. What should cause the women to blush (lines 11–14)?
3. What kind of people is the speaker calling slaves in the final stanza?

Analyzing
4. What, according to stanza 3, is true freedom?
5. Summarize how the speaker differentiates between slaves and free people in this poem.
6. Locate and discuss the appropriateness of the **simile** in lines 12–13 and the **metaphor** in line 19.

Extending
7. What applications does this poem have in modern life? Explain.

READING LITERATURE SKILLFULLY
Author's Purpose
Every author has a reason or reasons for writing, usually to persuade, to inform, or to entertain. Once an author settles on a purpose, he or she chooses a form, a style, and language that best serves this purpose. As you read, decide what you think the author has set out to accomplish. When you finish reading, determine whether or not you think the author has successfully achieved this purpose.

1. What do you think Lowell's purpose was for writing "Stanzas on Freedom"?
2. How does his use of **figurative language** in lines 12–13 and 19 reinforce this purpose?
3. How does the **rhythm** in this poem serve to convey Lowell's forceful ideas?
4. What word would you use to describe Lowell's **tone**? How do words such as *base* and *unworthy* (lines 7 and 9) and *Hatred, scoffing,* and *abuse* (line 28) contribute to this tone?

BIOGRAPHY

James W. C. Pennington
1809–1870

James Pennington was born a slave in Maryland. Trained as a blacksmith, he continued in that trade until, at twenty-one, he escaped from his master and fled to Pennsylvania where he was taken in by a Quaker family. He spent six months there, receiving his first education. He then moved to Long Island, found work, and continued his education, attending school at night. Finally he became a teacher and a minister and was active in the antislavery movement, attending meetings and writing in support of abolition. After the passage of the Fugitive Slave Law in 1850, fearing recapture, he went abroad until friends had successfully negotiated with his former master to secure his freedom. The account of his early life, *The Fugitive Blacksmith*, was published in 1850. The following excerpt appears in complete form in *Great Slave Narratives*, edited by Arna Bontemps.

Escape: A Slave Narrative

James W. C. Pennington

It was in the month of November, somewhat past the middle of the month. It was a bright day, and all was quiet. Most of the slaves were resting about their quarters; others had leave to visit their friends on other plantations, and were absent. The evening previous I had arranged my little bundle of clothing, and had secreted it at some distance from the house.

It is impossible for me now to recollect all the perplexing thoughts that passed through my mind during that forenoon; it was a day of heart-aching to me. But I distinctly remember the two great difficulties that stood in the way of my flight: I had a father and mother whom I dearly loved—I had also six sisters and four brothers on the plantation. The question was, shall I hide my purpose from them? Moreover, how will my flight affect them when I am gone? Will they not be suspected? Will not the whole family be sold off as a disaffected family, as is generally the case when one of its members flies? But a still more trying question was, how can I expect to succeed, I have no knowledge of distance or direction—I know that Pennsylvania is a free state, but I know not where its soil begins, or where that of Maryland ends? . . .

One of my perplexing questions I had settled—I had resolved to let no one into my secret; but the other difficulty was now to be met. Within my recollection no one had attempted to escape from my master; but I had many cases in my mind's eye, of slaves of other planters who had failed, and who had been made examples of the most cruel treatment, by flogging and selling to the far South, where they were never to see their friends more. I was not without serious apprehension that such would be my fate. The bare possibility was impressively solemn; but the hour was now come, and the man must act and be free, or remain a slave forever. How the impression came to be upon my mind I cannot tell; but there was a strange and horrifying belief, that if I did not meet the crisis that day, I should be self-doomed. Hope, fear, dread, terror, love, sorrow, and deep melancholy were mingled in my mind together; my mental state was one of most painful distraction. When I looked at my numerous family—a beloved father and mother, eleven brothers and sisters, etc.; but when I looked at slavery as such; when I looked at it in its mildest form, with all its annoyances; and above all, when I remembered that one of the chief annoyances of slavery, in the most mild form, is the liability of being at any moment sold into the worst form, it seemed that no consideration, not even that of life itself, could tempt me to give up the thought of flight. . . .

It was now two o'clock. . . . I sallied forth thoughtfully and melancholy, and after crossing the barnyard, a few moments' walk brought me to a small cave, near the mouth of which lay a pile of stones, and into which I had deposited my clothes. From this, my course lay through thick and heavy woods and back lands to—— town, where my brother lived. . . .

I entered the town about dark, resolved, all things in view, *not* to shew myself to my brother. Having passed through the town without being recognized, I now found myself under cover of night, a solitary wanderer from home and friends; my only guide was the *north star*; by this I knew my general course northward, but at what point I should strike Pennsylvania, or when and where I should find a friend I knew not. . . . Only now and then I was cheered by the *wild* hope, that I should somewhere and at some time be free. . . .

The day dawned upon me, in the midst of an open extent of country, where the only shelter I could find, without risking my travel by daylight, was a corn shock, but a few hundred yards from the road, and here I must pass my first day out. The day was an unhappy one; my hiding place was extremely precarious. I had to sit in a squatting position the whole day, without the least chance to rest. Night came again to my relief, and I sallied forth to pursue my journey.

As I traveled I felt my strength failing and my spirits wavered; my mind was in a deep and melancholy dream. It was cloudy; I could not see my star, and had serious misgivings about my course.

In this way the night passed away, and just at the dawn of day I found a few sour apples, and took my shelter under the arch of a small bridge that crossed the road. Here I passed the second day in ambush.

The day passed away again without any further incident, and as I set out at nightfall I felt quite satisfied that I could not pass another twenty-four hours without nourishment. I made but little progress during the night, and often sat down, and slept frequently fifteen or twenty minutes. At the dawn of the third day I continued my travel. As I had found my way to a public turnpike road during the night, I came very early in the morning to a tollgate, where the only person I saw, was a lad about twelve years of age. I inquired of him where the road led to. He informed me it led to Baltimore. I asked him the distance, he said it was eighteen miles.

This intelligence was perfectly astounding to me. My master lived eighty miles from Baltimore. I was now sixty-two miles from home. That distance in the right direction, would have placed me several miles across Mason and Dixon's line,[1] but I was evidently yet in the state of Maryland.

I ventured to ask the lad at the gate another question—Which is the best way to Philadelphia?

_____

1. **Mason and Dixon's line,** the southern border of Pennsylvania, surveyed by Charles Mason and Jeremiah Dixon, British astronomers. The line became part of the boundary between the free and slave states.

Eastman Johnson, detail of *My Old Kentucky Home: Life in the South* (1859).
New York Historical Society

Said he, you can take a road which turns off about half-a-mile below this, and goes to Getsburgh, or you can go on to Baltimore and take the packet.[2] . . .

When I had walked a mile on this road, and when it had now gotten to be about nine o'clock, I met a young man with a load of hay. He drew up his horses, and addressed me in a very kind tone.

"Are you traveling any distance, my friend?"

"I am on my way to Philadelphia."

"Are you free?"

"Yes, sir."

"I suppose, then, you are provided with free papers?"

"No, sir. I have no papers."

"Well, my friend, you should not travel on this road: you will be taken up before you have gone three miles."

He then very kindly gave me advice where to turn off the road at a certain point, and how to find my way to a certain house, where I would meet with an old gentleman who would further advise me whether I had better remain till night, or go on.

I left this interesting young man; and such was my surprise and chagrin at the thought of having so widely missed my way, and my alarm at being in such a dangerous position, that in ten minutes I had so far forgotten his directions as to deem it unwise to attempt to follow them, lest I should miss my way, and get into evil hands. . . .

I went about a mile, making in all two miles from the spot where I met my young friend, and about five miles from the tollgate to which I have referred, and I found myself at the twenty-four miles' stone from Baltimore. It was now about ten o'clock in the forenoon; my strength was greatly exhausted by reason of the want of suitable food. Under ordinary circumstances as a traveler, I should have been glad to see the "Tavern," which was near the mile stone; but as the case stood with me, I deemed it a dangerous place to pass, much less to stop at. I was therefore passing it as quietly and as rapidly as possible, when from the lot just opposite the house, or

signpost, I heard a coarse stern voice cry, "Halloo!"

I turned my face to the left, the direction from which the voice came, and observed that it proceeded from a man who was digging potatoes. I answered him politely; when the following occurred:

"Who do *you* belong to?"

"I am free, sir."

"Have you got papers?"

"No, sir."

"Well, you must stop here."

"My business is onward, sir, and I do not wish to stop."

"I will see then if you don't stop, you black rascal."

He was now in the middle of the road, making after me in a brisk walk.

I saw that a crisis was at hand; I had no weapons of any kind, not even a pocketknife; but I asked myself, shall I surrender without a struggle. The instinctive answer was, No. What will you do? continue to walk; if he runs after you, run; get him as far from the house as you can, then turn suddenly and smite him on the knee with a stone; that will render him, at least, unable to pursue you.

He began to breathe short. He was evidently vexed because I did not halt, and I felt more and more provoked at the idea of being thus pursued by a man to whom I had not done the least injury. At this moment he yelled out "Jake Shouster!" and at the next moment the door of a small house standing to the left was opened, and out jumped a shoemaker girded up in his leather apron, with his knife in hand. He sprang forward and seized me by the collar, while the other seized my arms behind.

Standing in the door of the shoemaker's shop, was a third man; and in the potato lot I had passed, was still a fourth man. Thus surrounded by superior physical force, the fortune of the day it seemed to me was gone.

---

2. **Getsburgh . . . packet.** Gettysburg (Getsburgh) is in southern Pennsylvania. A packet is a scheduled passenger ship.

A few moments after I was taken into the bar-room, the news having gone as by electricity, the house and yard were crowded with gossipers. But among the whole, there stood one whose name I have never known. Said he, "That fellow is a runaway I know; put him in jail a few days, and you will soon hear where he came from." And then fixing a fiendlike gaze upon me, he continued, "If I lived on this road, *you* fellows would not find such clear running as you do, I'd trap more of you."

But now comes the pinch of the case, the case of conscience to me even at this moment. Emboldened by the cruel speech just recited, my captors enclosed me, and said, "Come now, this matter may easily be settled without you going to jail; who do you belong to, and where did you come from?"

I knew according to the law of slavery, who I belonged to and where I came from, and I must now do one of three things—I must refuse to speak at all, or I must communicate the fact, or I must tell an untruth. The first point decided was, the facts in this case are my private property. These men have no more right to them than a highway robber has to my purse. . . .

I resolved, therefore, to insist that I was free. This not being satisfactory without other evidence, they tied my hands and set out, and went to a magistrate who lived about half a mile distant. It so happened, that when we arrived at his house he was not at home. But I soon learned by their conversation, that there was still another magistrate in the neighborhood, and that they would go to him. In about twenty minutes, and after climbing fences and jumping ditches, we, captors and captive, stood before his door, but it was after the same manner as before—he was not at home. By this time the day had worn away to one or two o'clock, and my captors evidently began to feel somewhat impatient of the loss of time. We were about a mile and a quarter from the tavern. As we set out on our return, they began to parley. Finding it was difficult for me to get over fences with my hands tied, they untied me. . . .

We got to the tavern at three o'clock. Here they again cooled down, and made an appeal to me to make a disclosure. I said to them, "If you will not put me in jail, I will now tell you where I am from." They promised. "Well," said I, "a few weeks ago, I was sold from the eastern shore to a slave trader, who had a large gang, and set out for Georgia, but when he got to a town in Virginia, he was taken sick, and died with the smallpox. Several of his gang also died with it, so that the people in the town became alarmed, and did not wish the gang to remain among them. No one claimed us, or wished to have anything to do with us; I left the rest, and thought I would go somewhere and get work."

When I said this, it was evidently believed by those who were present, and notwithstanding the unkind feeling that had existed, there was a murmur of approbation. At the same time I perceived that a panic began to seize some, at the idea that I was one of a smallpox gang. Several who had clustered near me, moved off to a respectful distance. . . .

I was now left alone with the man who first called to me in the morning. In a sober manner, he made this proposal to me: "John, I have a brother living in Risterstown, four miles off, who keeps a tavern; I think you had better go and live with him, till we see what will turn up. He wants an ostler."[3] I at once assented to this. "Well," said he, "take something to eat, and I will go with you." . . .

I sat down to eat; it was Wednesday, four o'clock, and this was the first regular meal I had since Sunday morning. This over, we set out, and to my surprise, he proposed to walk. We had gone about a mile and a half, and we were approaching a wood through which the road passed with a bend. I fixed upon that as the spot where I would either free myself from this man, or die in his arms. I had resolved upon a plan of operation—it was this: to stop short, face about, and commence action; and neither ask or give quarters, until I was free or dead!

---

3. *ostler*, someone who takes care of horses.

We had got within six rods of the spot, when a gentleman turned the corner, meeting us on horseback. He came up, and entered into conversation with my captor. After a few moments, this gentleman addressed himself to me and I then learned that he was one of the magistrates on whom we had called in the morning. . . . I repeated carefully all I had said; at the close, he said, "Well, you had better stay among us a few months, until we see what is to be done with you." It was then agreed that we should go back to the tavern, and there settle upon some further plan. He seemed quite satisfied of the correctness of my statement, and made the following proposition: that I should go and live with him for a short time, stating that he had a few acres of corn and potatoes to get in, and that he would give me twenty-five cents per day. I most cheerfully assented to this proposal. It was also agreed that I should remain at the tavern with my captor that night, and that he would accompany me in the morning. . . .

My captor had left his hired man most of the day to dig potatoes alone; but the wagon being now loaded, it being time to convey the potatoes into the barn, and the horses being all ready for that purpose, he was obliged to go into the potato field and give assistance. . . . This left no one in the house, but a boy, about nine years of age.

The potato lot was across the public road, directly in front of the house; at the back of the house, and about three hundred yards distant, there was a thick wood. The circumstances of the case would not allow me to think for one moment of remaining there for the night—the time had come for another effort—but there were two serious difficulties. One was, that I must either deceive or dispatch this boy who is watching me with intense vigilance. I am glad to say, that the latter did not for a moment seriously enter my mind. To deceive him effectually, I left my coat and went to the back door, from which my course would be direct to the wood. When I got to the door, I found that the barn, to which the wagon must soon come, lay just to the right, and overlooking the path I must take

to the wood. But on looking through the gate, I saw that my captor, being with the team, would see me if I attempted to start before he moved from the position he then occupied. To add to my difficulty the horses had balked; while waiting for the decisive moment, the boy came to the door and asked me why I did not come in. I told him I felt unwell, and wished him to be so kind as to hand me a glass of water; he came with the water and I quickly used it up by gargling my throat and by drinking a part. I asked him to serve me by giving me another glass: he gave me a look of close scrutiny, but went in for the water. I heard him fill the glass, and start to return with it; when the hind end of the wagon cleared the corner of the house. As I passed out the gate, I cast a last glance over my right shoulder, and saw the boy just perch his head above the garden picket to look after me. I felt some assurance that although the boy might give the alarm, my captor could not leave the team until it was in the barn. I heard the horses' feet on the barn floor, just as I leaped the fence, and darted into the wood. . . .

The reader may well imagine how the events of the past day affected my mind. You have seen what was done to me; you have heard what was said to me—you have also seen what I have done, and heard what I have said. If you ask me whether I had expected before I left home, to gain my liberty by shedding men's blood, or breaking their limbs? I answer, No! and as evidence of this, I had provided no weapon whatever; not so much as a penknife—it never once entered my mind. I cannot say that I expected to have the ill fortune of meeting with any human being who would attempt to impede my flight.

If you ask me if I expected when I left home to gain my liberty by fabrications and untruths? I answer, No! my parents, slaves as they were, had always taught me, when they could, that "truth may be blamed but cannot be ashamed"; so far as their example was concerned, I had no habits of untruth. I was arrested, and the demand made upon me, "Who do you belong to?" Knowing the fatal use these men would make of *my* truth, I at once concluded that they had no more right to it than a highwayman has to a traveler's purse. . . .

Whatever my readers may think, therefore, of the history of events of the day, do not admire in it the fabrications; but *see* in it the impediments that often fall into the pathway of the flying bond-man. *See* how when he would do good, evil is thrust upon him. . . .

I penetrated through the wood, thick and thin, and more or less wet, to the distance I should think of three miles. By this time my clothes were all thoroughly soaked through, and I felt once more a gloom and wretchedness; the recollection of which makes me shudder at this distant day. . . .

I was now out of the hands of those who had so cruelly teased me during the day; but a number of fearful thoughts rushed into my mind to alarm me. It was dark and cloudy, so that I could not see the *north star*. How shall I regain the road? How shall I know when I am on the right road again?

At a venture I struck an angle northward in search of the road. After several hours of zigzag and laborious travel, dragging through briars, thorns, and running vines, I emerged from the wood and found myself wading marshy ground and over ditches.

I can form no correct idea of the distance I traveled, but I came to a road, I should think about three o'clock in the morning. It so happened that I came out near where there was a fork in the road of three prongs.

Now arose a serious query—Which is the right prong for me? After a few moments parley with myself, I took the central prong of the road and pushed on with all my speed. . . .

The day dawned upon me when I was near a small house and barn, situated close to the roadside. The barn was too near the road, and too small to afford secure shelter for the day; but as I cast my eye around by the dim light, I could see no wood, and no larger barn. It seemed to be an open country to a wide extent. I therefore took to the mow[4] of the little barn at a great risk, as the events of the day will shew. Besides

inflicting upon my own excited imagination the belief that I made noise enough to be heard by the inmates of the house who were likely to be rising at the time, I had the misfortune to attract the notice of a little house dog. This little creature commenced a fierce barking. I had at once great fears that the mischievous little thing would betray me. It now being entirely daylight, it was too late to retreat from this shelter, even if I could have found another.

It was Thursday morning. It was not until about an hour after the sun rose that I heard any outdoor movements about the house. As soon as I heard those movements, I was satisfied there was but one man about the house, and that he was preparing to go some distance to work for the day. This was fortunate for me; the busy movements about the yard, and especially the active preparations in the house for breakfast, silenced my unwelcome little annoyer until after the man had gone, when he commenced afresh, and continued with occasional intermissions through the day. . . .

In this way I passed the day till about the middle of the afternoon, when there seemed to be an unusual stir about the public road, which passed close by the barn. Men seemed to be passing in parties on horseback, and talking anxiously. From a word which I now and then overheard, I had not a shadow of doubt that they were in search of me. . . . I listened and trembled.

Just before the setting of the sun, the laboring man of the house returned, and commenced his evening duties about the house and barn; chopping wood, getting up his cow, feeding his pigs, etc., attended by the little brute, who continued barking at short intervals. He came several times into the barn below. While matters were passing thus, I heard the approach of horses again, and as they came up nearer, I was led to believe that all I had heard pass were returning in one party. They passed the barn and halted at the house, when I recognized the voice of my old captor; addressing the laborer. . . .

---

4. *mow*, a loft for storing hay.

To my great relief, however, the party rode off, and the laborer after finishing his work went into the house. Hope seemed now to dawn for me once more. About eight o'clock I ventured to descend from the mow of the barn into the road. The little dog the while began a furious fit of barking, so much so, that I was sure that with what his master had learned about me, he could not fail to believe I was about his premises. I quickly crossed the road, and got into an open field opposite. After stepping lightly about two hundred yards, I halted, and on listening, I heard the door open. Feeling about on the ground, I picked up two stones, and one in each hand I made off as fast as I could, but I heard nothing more that indicated pursuit, and after going some distance I discharged my encumbrance. . . .

All I could do was to keep my legs in motion, and this I continued to do with the utmost difficulty. The latter part of the night I suffered extremely from cold. There came a heavy frost; I expected at every moment to fall on the road and perish. I came to a cornfield covered with heavy shocks of Indian corn that had been cut; I went into this and got an ear, and then crept into one of the shocks; ate as much of it as I could, and I sunk to sleep.

When I awoke, the sun was shining around; I started with alarm, but it was too late to think of seeking any other shelter. After recovering a little from my fright, I commenced again eating my whole corn. Grain by grain I worked away at it; when my jaws grew tired, as they often did, I would rest, and then begin afresh. Thus, although I began an early breakfast, I was nearly the whole of the forenoon before I had done. . . .

Friday night came without any other incident worth naming. As I sallied out, I felt evident benefit from the ear of corn I had nibbled away. Thus encouraged, I set out with better speed than I had made since Sunday and Monday night. I had a presentiment, too, that I must be near free soil. I had not yet the least idea where I should find a home or a friend, still my spirits were so highly elated, that I took the whole of the road to myself; I ran, hopped, skipped, jumped, clapped my hands, and talked to myself. But to the old slaveholder I had left, I said, "Ah! ah! old fellow, I told you I'd fix you." . . .

Saturday morning dawned upon me; and although my strength seemed yet considerably fresh, I began to feel a hunger somewhat more destructive and pinching, if possible, than I had before. I resolved, at all risk, to continue my travel by daylight, and to ask information of the first person I met. . . .

I continued my flight on the public road; and a little after the sun rose, I came in sight of a tollgate again. . . . I found it attended by an elderly woman, whom I afterwards learned was a widow, and an excellent Christian woman. I asked her if I was in Pennsylvania. On being informed that I was, I asked her if she knew where I could get employ? She said she did not; but advised me to go to W. W., a Quaker, who lived about three miles from her, whom I would find to take an interest in me.

In about half an hour I stood trembling at the door of W. W. After knocking, the door opened upon a comfortably spread table; the sight of which seemed once to increase my hunger sevenfold. Not daring to enter, I said I had been sent to him in search of employ. "Well," said he, "Come in and take thy breakfast, and get warm, and we will talk about it; thee must be cold without any coat." . . .

From that day to this, whenever I discover the least disposition in my heart to disregard the wretched condition of any poor or distressed persons with whom I meet, I call to mind these words—"*Come in and take thy breakfast, and get warm.*" . . .

1850

THINK AND DISCUSS

Understanding

1. What two difficulties mentioned in the second paragraph stand in the way of Pennington's escape?
2. What probable penalty does he face if he is caught in his escape attempt?
3. Describe the emotions Pennington feels right before his escape. What thoughts about slavery make him leave despite his feelings?
4. What is Pennington's destination?
5. Name three obstacles Pennington encounters in his escape.
6. Describe Pennington's escape from his captor on the journey.

Analyzing

7. On what occasions is Pennington forced to lie in order to maintain his freedom or his life? How does he justify these deceptions?
8. How does each of the following assist Pennington: the north star, Indian corn, a Quaker?
9. What is the **tone** of this selection? Support your answer with examples from the narrative.

Extending

10. In the strict legal sense, Pennington is a fugitive and a lawbreaker. If such a person had come to you for refuge, what would you have done?

COMPOSITION

Writing a Dialogue

Construct a dialogue of at least one page that could have taken place at the breakfast table between Pennington and the Quaker W. W. on the morning that they meet. Try to be true to the characters. Pennington would presumably be weary, nervous, and uneasy in the home of a white man. W. W., who would speak with the Quaker pronouns *thee*, *thou*, *thy*, and *thine*, would be gracious and comforting. In addition, he might quiz Pennington on his skills for possible employment, on the state of his health, or on details about his journey to freedom. Be sure to punctuate the dialogue correctly.

Describing a Character

Using information from the selection, write a four-paragraph description of Pennington's character and personality. Imagine that the description is to be read at a memorial service honoring the 180th anniversary of his birth. Assess his sense of integrity, morality, and honor, along with his intelligence and bravery, citing specific evidence to support your observations. End with a comment on slavery, as it affected Pennington's life.

The five songs that follow include three spirituals, a humorous ballad, and a rallying cry against slavery.

Spirituals can be grouped into plantation songs, songs about events, work songs, and sorrow songs. The work songs helped ease labor by their steady rhythms and by the communal feeling evoked by group chanting. The sorrow songs clearly reveal the longing to escape bondage, a strong religious faith, a passionate hope for a better life, and unyielding defiance of slavery. Many spirituals of all types were used by slaves to send secret messages safely from plantation to plantation. Some critics have speculated that modern black poets owe much to the skill with which the apparently simple language of spirituals conveys complex, multiple meanings. "Follow the Drinking Gourd" is one "coded" spiritual, indicating a northward route to freedom. Passed from generation to generation, the spirituals existed long before they were published in the twentieth century.

With the California gold rush, a new and uniquely American folk character emerged—the lonesome prospector who dreamed of the big strike but knew that failure was more likely. The fatalistic attitudes of these prospectors, hardened by disappointment, are humorously reflected in ballads such as "Clementine."

Whittier wrote "The Kansas Emigrants" as a rallying song for the thousands of New England abolitionists who flocked to the Kansas territory in the mid-1850s to establish that area as a free state.

Deep River

Deep river, my home is over Jordan.
Deep river, Lord, I want to cross over into Campground.
Oh, chillun, oh, don't you want to go
To that gospel feast, that promised land,
5 That land where all is peace?
Walk into heaven and take my seat
And cast my crown at Jesus' feet. Lord,
Deep river, my home is over Jordan.
Deep river, Lord, I want to cross over into Campground.

Swing Low, Sweet Chariot

Swing low, sweet chariot,
Comin' for to carry me home.

I looked over Jordan and what did I see,
Comin' for to carry me home?
A band of angels comin' aftah me,
Comin' for to carry me home.

5 If you git there before I do,
Comin' for to carry me home,
Tell all my frien's I'm a-comin', too,
Comin' for to carry me home.

The brightes' day that ever I saw,
10 Comin' for to carry me home,
When Jesus washed my sins away,
Comin' for to carry me home.

I'm sometimes up an' sometimes down,
Comin' for to carry me home,
15 But still my soul feel heavenly-boun',
Comin' for to carry me home.

John Antrobus, *A Plantation Burial* (c. 1860).
The Historic New Orleans Collection

Follow the Drinking Gourd

When the sun comes back and the first quail calls,
   Follow the drinking gourd,
For the old man is a-waiting for to carry you to freedom
   If you follow the drinking gourd.

5 Follow the drinking gourd,
   Follow the drinking gourd,
For the old man is a-waiting for to carry you to freedom
   If you follow the drinking gourd.

The riverbank will make a very good road,
10   The dead trees show you the way,
Left foot, peg foot traveling on
   Follow the drinking gourd.

The river ends between two hills
   Follow the drinking gourd.
15 There's another river on the other side,
   Follow the drinking gourd.

Where the little river meets the great big river,
   Follow the drinking gourd.
The old man is a-waiting for to carry you to freedom,
20   If you follow the drinking gourd.

"Follow the Drinking Gourd" by B. A. Botkin. Copyright 1949 by B. A. Botkin. Copyright © renewed 1977 by Gertrude Botkin. Reprinted by permission of Curtis Brown Ltd.

Comment

Of the Sorrow Songs by W. E. B. Du Bois

Little of beauty has America given the world save the rude grandeur God himself stamped on her bosom; the human spirit in this new world has expressed itself in vigor and ingenuity rather than in beauty. And so by fateful chance the Negro folk song—the rhythmic cry of the slave —stands today not simply as the sole American music, but as the most beautiful expression of human experience born this side the seas. It has been neglected, it has been, and is, half despised, and above all it has been persistently mistaken and misunderstood; but notwithstanding, it still remains as the singular spiritual heritage of the nation and the greatest gift of the Negro people. . . .

Through all the sorrow of the Sorrow Songs there breathes a hope—a faith in the ultimate justice of things. The minor cadences of despair change often to triumph and calm confidence. Sometimes it is faith in life, sometimes a faith in death, sometimes assurance of boundless justice in some fair world beyond.

Du Bois (dū bois'). Du Bois's biography and writing appear in Unit 4.

The Kansas Emigrants

John Greenleaf Whittier

We cross the prairie as of old
　The Pilgrims crossed the sea,
To make the West, as they the East,
　The homestead of the free.

5　We go to rear a wall of men
　　On Freedom's southern line,
And plant beside the cotton tree
　The rugged Northern pine!

We're flowing from our native hills
10　As our free rivers flow:
The blessing of our Motherland
　Is on us as we go.

We go to plant her common schools
　On distant prairie swells,
15　And give the Sabbaths of the wild
　The music of her bells.

Upbearing, like the Ark of Old,
　The Bible in our van,
We go to test the truth of God
20　Against the fraud of man.

No pause, nor rest, save where the streams
　That feed the Kansas run,
Save where our Pilgrim gonfalon[1]
　Shall flout the setting sun!

25　We'll tread the prairie as of old
　Our fathers sailed the sea,
And make the West, as they the East,
　The homestead of the free!

1854

---

1. *gonfalon* (gon'fə lən), a flag or banner.

Harvey Dunn (1884–1952), *Something for Supper*. South Dakota Art Museum

Thomas Eakins, *Home Ranch* (1892). Philadelphia Museum of Art

Clementine

In a cavern in a canyon, excavating for a mine,
Dwelt a miner, forty-niner, and his daughter, Clementine.

    Oh, my darling, oh, my darling, oh, my darling Clementine,
    You are lost and gone forever, dreadful sorry, Clementine.

5 Light she was and like a fairy, and her shoes were number nine,
Herring boxes without topses, sandals were for Clementine.

Drove her ducklings to the water, every morning just at nine,
Hit her foot against a splinter, fell into the foaming brine.

Ruby lips above the water, blowing bubbles soft and fine,
10 Alas, for me! I was no swimmer, so I lost my Clementine.

In a churchyard, near the canyon, where the myrtle doth entwine,
There grow roses and other posies fertilized by Clementine.

Then the miner, forty-niner, soon began to droop and pine,
Thought he ought to join his daughter, now he's with his Clementine.

15 In my dreams she still doth haunt me, robed in garments soaked in brine,
Though in life I used to kiss her, now she's dead, I draw the line.

                         1849

THINK AND DISCUSS

Understanding
1. To whom does Whittier compare the Kansas emigrants in lines 1–4? What similar purpose did each group of pioneers share?
2. What two trees, representing North and South, are mentioned in lines 7 and 8?

Analyzing
3. Which lines suggest that the abolitionists also had religious and educational goals?
4. Describe the **tone** of this poem. How does the **rhythm** reinforce this tone?

Extending
5. Compare the purpose of Whittier's poem with that of one of the spirituals.

COMPOSITION
Writing a Song

Create your own song, modeling it on one of the spirituals, "Clementine," or Whittier's poem. Decide what purpose the song should accomplish: Is it to be a working song, one that describes a current event, or one that expresses a feeling? Once you have decided on a subject, purpose, and tone, structure your work according to the rhythm of the literary song that best conveys your ideas. For example, the rhythm of "Deep River" suits a pensive tone, while that of "The Kansas Emigrants" suggests a vigorous rallying cry.

THINKING CRITICALLY
ABOUT LITERATURE

UNIT 2   LITERARY NATIONALISM

■ CONCEPT REVIEW

The following excerpt contains many of the important ideas and literary
terms of the period you have just studied. The notes and questions are
designed to help you think critically about your reading. Page numbers
in the notes refer to an application. A more extensive discussion of these
terms is in the Handbook of Literary Terms.

Bryant was only twenty-one when he wrote this lyric about the flight
of a lonely bird. As he meditates on the forces that guide the migrating
bird, he reaches a conclusion about his own life. On a separate piece of
paper, write your answers to the questions following the poem.

To a Waterfowl

William Cullen Bryant

Whither, midst falling dew,
While glow the heavens with the last steps of day,
Far, through their rosy depths, dost thou pursue
     Thy solitary way?

5   Vainly the fowler's eye
Might mark thy distant flight to do thee wrong,
As, darkly seen against the crimson sky,
     Thy figure floats along.

Seek'st thou the plashy brink
10 Of weedy lake, or marge of river wide,
Or where the rocking billows rise and sink
     On the chafed ocean side?

There is a Power whose care
Teaches thy way along that pathless coast—
15 The desert and illimitable air—
     Lone wandering, but not lost.

■ **Whither:** where.

■ **dost:** does.

■ **Synecdoche** (page
137): The "fowler's eye"
represents the hunter who
might "mark" or view the
bird as a moving target.

■ **Lofty diction:** Notice
the types of words used
in this poem: *thou, shalt,
seek'st,* and *thy.*

■ **Teaches:** guides.

■ The Romantic poets
believed that the world of

192 *Literary Nationalism*

John James Audubon (1785–1851),
Great Blue Heron. Newberry Library

All day thy wings have fanned,
At that far height, the cold, thin atmosphere,
Yet stoop not, weary, to the welcome land,
20   Though the dark night is near.

And soon that toil shall end;
Soon shalt thou find a summer home, and rest,
And scream among thy fellows; reeds shall bend,
    Soon, o'er thy sheltered nest.

25   Thou'rt gone, the abyss of heaven
Hath swallowed up thy form; yet, on my heart
Deeply has sunk the lesson thou has given,
    And shall not soon depart.

He who, from zone to zone,
30 Guides through the boundless sky thy certain flight,
In the long way that I must tread alone,
    Will lead my steps aright.

        1818

nature provided a key to the human world. Both worlds are directed by a Divine plan.

■ Notice how the **tone** has changed from the preceding stanza.

■ **Anastrophe** (page 132): This poetic technique is often used by the poets of this period for emphasis or poetic effect. Notice it in lines 2, 3, 9, 22, and 27.

■ Note the **theme** (page 141) of the poem in this last stanza.

THINK AND DISCUSS
Understanding
1. What words and phrases indicate the time of day the action of the poem takes place?
2. To whom are the questions in stanzas 1 and 3 addressed?

Analyzing
3. To whom does the "fowler's eye" in line 5 refer? What harm might the fowler do?
4. Who is the Power mentioned in line 13? How does this Power influence the bird?
5. What feeling do the adjectives in stanzas 4 and 5 (with the exception of *welcome*) convey? What contrasting feeling do the words *summer*, *sheltered*, and *nest* provide in stanza 6?
6. What does stanza 6 describe?

Extending
7. What aspects of Romanticism are reflected in this poem? Refer to the Reader's Note on page 108 if you need help.

REVIEWING LITERARY TERMS
Synecdoche
1. In the poem, why is the fowler's *eye* a better representation of the hunter than the fowler's *arm?*

Anastrophe
2. Select one of the inverted lines in the poem. Explain what effect anastrophe has in this line.

Theme
3. Explain in your own words the theme of the poem.

Alliteration
4. What initial sound is frequently repeated in stanza 6 (lines 21–24)? What effect is achieved by this alliteration?

Rhyme
5. Chart the rhyme scheme for this poem. What type of rhyme does Bryant use?

Rhythm
The rhythm of line 17 can be indicated thus:

Ăll dáy/ thў wíngs/ hăve fánned,

6. Write the remaining three lines of this stanza, indicating its rhythm.

■ CONTENT REVIEW
Classifying
1. Tom Walker, Deerslayer, Montresor, and Hop-Frog are memorable literary characters. Write the name of each character at the top of a separate list. Below the names, write at least three characteristics that you recall about them that make them unique.
2. Some distinctly American themes explored by the authors of this period are the following: *The Frontiersman, Heroism, Nature,* and *Freedom.* List these heads on a sheet of paper. Beneath the appropriate heads, list titles from this unit.

Generalizing
3. Recall three works from this unit that contain irony, and explain how they are ironic.
4. Choose three of the following authors that you consider Romantic, judging from their works in the unit. Discuss the Romantic elements in their works, citing specific examples: Irving, Lowell, Longfellow, Bryant, and Poe. (Refer to the Reader's Note on Romanticism, page 108, if necessary.)
5. An author may write specifically to entertain, to instruct, to provide an explanation, or to create a special effect for a reader. Choose two selections from this unit that are written for two different purposes. Then describe the author's purpose in each selection.

Synthesizing
6. Imagine that Tom Walker, Deerslayer, and Montresor awoke after a prolonged sleep to find themselves in America during the last decade of the twentieth century. What kind of job would each seek? In what part of the country would each live? What type of hous-

ing would each choose? List one organization that each might join. Base your speculations on details and clues provided in the stories in this unit.

7. Imagine that Poe had chosen a waterfowl rather than a raven and that Bryant had chosen a raven rather than a waterfowl as title figures for their respective poems. How would the substitutions have affected their poems? Why are their original choices more appropriate?

Evaluating

8. "In many ways the spirituals best achieved the distinctive literary qualities so eagerly sought by American authors. They have strong emotional appeal, contain excellent imagery, and express the kind of idealism that characterizes America." Discuss the validity of the previous statement, citing examples from spirituals that appear in this unit.

9. Choose one work of art in this unit that you think captures the Romantic spirit. Explain what qualities (use of color and light, for example) make this work Romantic.

■ COMPOSITION REVIEW

Choose one of the following topics for writing.

Writing a Newspaper Article

Imagine that you are an American newspaper writer of the early nineteenth century, writing an article for the *London Times*. Your purpose is to inform the British that America is moving toward a national literature that is increasingly independent from Europe in both its subject matter and its style. To prepare for writing the article, jot down examples from several selections in the unit in which the characters, settings, and situations seem uniquely American. Use a lead sentence that will entice readers and make sure the facts you cite strengthen your position.

Describing Heroism

The tradition of the American hero has its roots in the period of Literary Nationalism. In an essay of at least four paragraphs, sketch out some ideas about heroism, based on questions such as the following: Is heroism a matter of thought, of action, or of both? Do heroes plan out their actions or act spontaneously? Are they realistic or superhuman? Has the concept of heroism changed in the past 150 years? Direct your essay to someone you know who is not American born.

Examining Humor

A love of humor is another aspect of the American character that is revealed in some selections in this unit. Write a three-paragraph essay for a literary magazine that examines humor, as used by Irving, Holmes, and Longfellow. In your prewriting notes, you may want to list answers to the following questions. Is the humor satiric in nature, pointing out human foibles and frailties in the hope of making a better world? Does the humor take the form of gentle self-mockery, making the author seem less pompous and more down-to-earth or human? Does exaggeration contribute to the humorous effect?

Comparing/Contrasting Ideas on Nature

Choose two or three poems from this unit and compare and contrast the uses of nature in them. Write a four-paragraph essay for a nature magazine that sketches out answers to questions such as the following. What qualities are associated with nature? What natural images dominate? What thoughts and lessons are being expressed through these images?

Writing About Revenge

Imagine you are writing a biography on Poe and want to devote a section of four or five paragraphs to his use of the theme of revenge. Using "The Cask of Amontillado" and "Hop-Frog" to illustrate, explain how the main characters are motivated by revenge. Conclude by explaining to the reader the picture of humanity that Poe was trying to create in both stories.

AMERICAN CLASSIC 1840–1870

1840	1845	1850	1855

HISTORY AND THE ARTS

• California Gold Rush

• Compromise of 1850

• Era of "Manifest Destiny" begins

• Planet Neptune sighted (Germany)

• Brook Farm commune

• Howe invents sewing machine

Perry opens trade with Japan •

• Potato famine begins (Ireland)   Morse patents telegraph •

• Treaty of Guadalupe Hidalgo ends Mexican War

• First women's rights convention

PRESIDENTS' ADMINISTRATIONS

• 1849–1850 Zachary Taylor

• 1853–1857 Franklin Pierce

• 1841 William Henry Harrison

• 1841–1845 John Tyler   • 1845–1849 James K. Polk

• 1850–1853 Millard Fillmore

LITERATURE

• Melville: *Moby Dick*

• Transcendental Movement begins

Stowe: *Uncle Tom's Cabin* •

• Emerson: *Essays*

• Douglass: *Narrative of the Life of an American Slave*

Thoreau: *Walden* •

• Hawthorne: *The Scarlet Letter*

• *The North Star* founded by Douglass

Whitman: *Leaves of Grass* •

• Fuller: *Woman in the Nineteenth Century*

• Thoreau: *Civil Disobedience*

Nathaniel Currier, lithograph of California gold hunter (c. 1845)

Louis Schultze, *Dred Scott*

Locomotive weathervane (c. 1860)

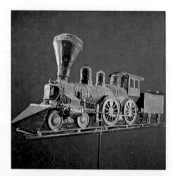

1860	1865	1870

• John Brown's raid on Harper's Ferry

• Dred Scott decision   Transcontinental railroad completed •

• Civil War begins   • First transatlantic cable laid

Homestead Act provides free land •   U.S. steel production mushrooms •

Wars against Plains tribes begin •   • Emancipation Proclamation

Reconstruction Era begins •   U.S. population 38,818,449 •

• Lincoln-Douglas debates   National women's suffrage convention •

• Slavery abolished

• 1857–1861 James Buchanan   • 1865–1869 Andrew Johnson

• 1861–1865 Abraham Lincoln

1869–1877 Ulysses S. Grant •

• *The Atlantic Monthly* founded   • Lincoln: Gettysburg Address

• Alcott: *Little Women*

Civil War drum

Mathew Brady (1823?–1896), photograph of General Grant

Decorative valentine trimmed with ribbon and lace (c. 1860)

PREVIEW

UNIT 3   AMERICAN CLASSIC   1840–1870

Authors

Ralph Waldo Emerson
Henry David Thoreau
Chief Seattle
Harriet Hanson Robinson
Nathaniel Hawthorne
Herman Melville

Louisa May Alcott
Harriet Beecher Stowe
Frederick Douglass
Sojourner Truth
Abraham Lincoln
Robert E. Lee

Sidney Lanier
Josh Billings
Davy Crockett
Mike Fink
Elizabeth Cady Stanton

Features
Reader's Note: Transcendentalism
Reading Essays and Speeches
Comment: What's Become of Walden?
Reader's Note: Ambiguity in "Young
    Goodman Brown"
The Story of American English
Themes in American Literature:
    Moral Struggle
Comment: Women Novelists of the
    Nineteenth Century
Comment: American Humor

Application of Literary Terms
consonance   foreshadowing
epigram   point of view
figurative language

Review of Literary Terms
personification   tone
characterization   sound devices

Reading Literature Skillfully
main idea

Vocabulary Skills
dictionary
affixes
roots

Thinking Skills
classifying
generalizing
synthesizing
evaluating

Composition Assignments Include
Writing About an Author's Philosophy
Writing a Fable
Personifying an Abstract Concept
Analyzing a Poem
Imitating a Writer's Style
Writing Epigrams
Writing About Foreshadowing
Writing an Objective Account
Describing a Change of Character
Using Sound Devices
Writing a Tall Tale

Enrichment
Research
Debate
Making a Poster
Oral Report
Multi-Media Presentation

Thinking Critically About Literature
Concept Review
Content Review
Composition Review

BACKGROUND

AMERICAN CLASSIC 1840–1870

American literature began to flourish as never before during the years 1840 to 1870. For the first time, a genuinely distinctive form of national expression began to emerge with the appearance of a new generation of writers. Earlier, authors like Irving, Cooper, and Bryant had proved that United States artists could create works worthy of respect. But their writing often reflected strong European influences. Ralph Waldo Emerson wrote in 1837: "We have listened too long to the courtly muses of Europe. We will walk on our own feet; we will work with our own hands; and we will speak our own minds."

Emerson's call for independence was prophetic. A few years after he spoke, some of the greatest classics of American literature began to appear. Indeed, so many of them crowded into the 1850s that the period has been variously called America's Golden Day, the Flowering of New England, and the American Renaissance. Whatever the title of the period, it clearly was the era of the American Classic.

During a brief five-year period, 1850–1855, many of the most enduring of American books appeared—1850: Emerson's *Representative Men*, Hawthorne's *The Scarlet Letter;* 1851: Melville's *Moby Dick*, Hawthorne's *The House of the Seven Gables;* 1852: Stowe's *Uncle Tom's Cabin*, Hawthorne's *The Blithedale Romance*, Melville's *Pierre;* 1854: Thoreau's *Walden;* 1855: Whitman's *Leaves of Grass*.

UNITARIANISM AND TRANSCENDENTALISM

In order to understand and appreciate the literature of this period, one must first examine the climate that produced the dominant philosophy of the time, Transcendentalism. Since America's earliest years, there flourished a native relish for intellectual combat. Out of political criticism came reforms that led to self-government. Religious debates had been carried on from the moment of the first settlement in the 1600s down into the nineteenth century.

What began as argument over minor points of Puritan dogma had become by the eighteenth century (sometimes called the Age of Enlightenment) an outright challenge to the dominance of Puritanism. The Quakers, unlike the Puritans, held that individuals did not need a minister to mediate between themselves and God but could know the Deity directly through an Inner Light. The Deists affirmed that Nature, not the Bible, was the principal Revelation of God.

These and other beliefs lay behind the gradual displacement of Puritanism by Unitarianism. Unitarianism derived its name from its rejection of a belief in the Trinity in favor of a belief in a Unitary God; and it rejected the Calvinistic notions of Original Sin and Determinism in favor of beliefs in the basic goodness and innate free will of the individual.

By the time that Emerson went to Harvard Divinity School, it was Unitarian, and the Boston church in which he became a minister was Unitarian. But even Unitarianism was too restrictive for Emerson, and he resigned his ministry in 1832 because he could not in good conscience administer the Christian sacrament of the Lord's Supper. Carrying with him many of the Unitarian beliefs, Emerson began his search for a philosophy in which he could place his faith. Transcendentalism was partly a borrowing and partly his own invention.

Transcendentalism is, as the name implies,

William James Stillman (1828–1901), detail of *Philosophers' Camp in the Adirondacks*. Concord Free Public Library

a belief that the *transcendent* (or spiritual) reality, rather than the material world, is the ultimate reality. This transcendental reality can be known not by the rational faculty or logic, but only by intuition or mystical insight. But all people are open to this higher knowledge, and thus Transcendentalism is a philosophy of individualism and self-reliance, traits that had always been treasured in the American frontier society.

Thoreau, Emerson's friend (and his one-time live-in handyman), expressed his independence characteristically: "I would rather sit on a pumpkin and have it all to myself, than be crowded on a velvet cushion." No writer of the American Classic period escaped the influence of Transcendentalism. Even those who attacked transcendental thought, like Hawthorne and Melville, were affected by it.

REFORM

Widespread feelings of self-sufficiency and trust in the judgment of others led to the establishment of Utopian communities that experimented with new ideas in cooperative living. The most famous was Brook Farm, established in 1841 by some members of the Transcendental Club. Brook Farm attracted many of the leading writers of the day, including Nathaniel Hawthorne and Margaret Fuller. All members of the community shared in the work on the farm, drew similar pay, and participated in the cultural and intellectual life.

Hawthorne was quickly disillusioned with

Brook Farm, left after a few months, and later wrote *The Blithedale Romance* based on his experience: "No sagacious man will long retain his sagacity," he observed, "if he live exclusively among reformers and progressive people, without periodically returning into the settled system of things."

Other issues were debated during this period. There were women like Elizabeth Cady Stanton who spoke up courageously in what has been identified as the first women's rights convention, held in Seneca Falls, New York, in 1848. And there were Indians like Chief Seattle, who spoke out forthrightly to a government that often seemed indifferent to rights of Native Americans. But there is no doubt that the issue that aroused the fiercest emotions was the issue of slavery in the "land of the free."

Throughout the first half of the nineteenth century, tension on the issue grew as the abolitionists of the North confronted the slaveholders of the South. The Mexican War of 1846–1848, though brought about by a number of causes, was viewed by abolitionists as an attempt by slavery advocates to extend slave-holding territory. And the war's treaty ceded two-fifths of Mexico, including California, to the United States. One of the most unpopular wars in American history, the Mexican War inspired indignation and resistance, especially among abolitionists.

Congressional acts frequently inflamed the controversy over slavery and often inspired outright defiance. The Fugitive Slave Law of 1850 compelled the return of runaway slaves to their owners. Many Northerners, including Emerson and Thoreau, swore that they would not uphold this law. Indeed, abolitionists and others in the North participated in setting up stations along an "underground railroad" to assist the slaves to escape to the North and up into Canada. The escape of slaves to Canada provided the climax for Harriet Beecher Stowe's *Uncle Tom's Cabin*, the novel that Abraham Lincoln once credited with bringing on the Civil War.

This long and bitter war involved sides that appeared unevenly matched. The North had more than twice the population of the South

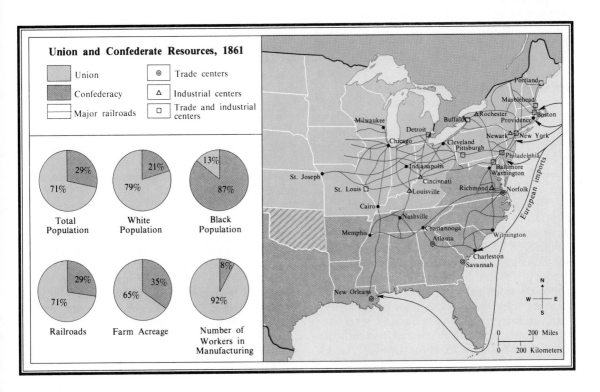

Union and Confederate Resources, 1861

and, consequently, more men to serve in its armies. In addition, the North had a strong industrial system that could support both the military and the civilian population. With few industrial and trade centers, the South was forced to buy most of its war materials from Europe. Although the South did have some strategic and military advantages, it was ultimately ravaged by a war that was the most costly—both in human and material losses—in American history.

In the Revolutionary War the nation was born, and in the Civil War the country survived its severest test and came of age. The events of the period and their dates have been lifted from history and mythologized: in 1861, the Southern states seceded and the firing on Fort Sumter began the conflict; in 1863 the Emancipation Proclamation freed the slaves; and also in 1863, the Union Army won the crucial battle at Gettysburg and Lincoln delivered his Gettysburg Address; in 1864, General Sherman made his march to the sea; Lee surrendered to Grant at Appomattox on April 9, 1865; and on April 14, Abraham Lincoln was assassinated. The Civil War has proved an almost inexhaustible subject for the American imagination; it has been sung in poetry, memorialized in fiction, and endlessly reenacted on stage, screen, and television.

TWO GREAT LITERARY PAIRS

The selections on the following pages offer a rich sampling of the American Classic writers. Thoreau was only twenty-four years old when Emerson, fourteen years his senior, invited him to join the Emerson household, earning his board and room by doing odd jobs. Thoreau read deeply in Emerson's works, and it was Emerson's ideas in large part that inspired Thoreau to retreat to Walden Pond for his experiment in simple living.

Although Emerson has justly been called the fountainhead of American literature, and although Thoreau looked up to Emerson, Thoreau's work enjoys a wider reading public today. Emerson's essays, though studded with brilliant, memorable sentences, tend on the whole to be elusively abstract and difficult to follow. Thoreau's style, on the other hand,

is concrete even as it conveys complex ideas: "I long ago lost a hound, a bay horse, and a turtledove, and am still on their trail." Readers must decide for themselves what, if anything, these items symbolize, but there is no problem conjuring a vivid image from the sentence.

In their essays included here, Emerson and Thoreau exhibit many of the ideas of the Transcendentalists, as well as the fierce independence and individualism that characterized the time. The excerpts from Emerson's "Self-Reliance" represent the kind of theory that inspired Thoreau to concrete action. The excerpts from *Walden* and *Civil Disobedience* may be seen as an account of Thoreau's acting out of Emerson's theory. But the works of Emerson and Thoreau included here serve to illustrate how closely related ideas may be clothed in radically different styles, and how the styles can make a major difference in the impact on the reader.

As with Emerson and Thoreau, the names of Hawthorne and Melville are linked in literary history, with Hawthorne advising and supporting the younger writer. Melville was thirty-one, Hawthorne, forty-six when, in 1850, Melville discovered that he and Hawthorne lived in neighboring towns in the Berkshire Hills of Massachusetts. A friendship quickly developed, and they exchanged ideas and books.

In 1851 Melville dedicated his masterpiece, *Moby Dick*, to Hawthorne. Though the novel was little noted at the time, it has gained in the twentieth century a worldwide reputation that overshadows Hawthorne's masterpiece, *The Scarlet Letter* (1850). As in the case of Thoreau and Emerson, the disciple unwittingly excelled the master.

Hawthorne and Melville are represented here by stories that show the Puritan strain in the American imagination had not entirely faded from the scene. Though neither author could be justly labeled Puritan, they both embody in their fiction a dark view of human nature and fate. This view is obscurely symbolized by the dark forest in "Young Goodman Brown" and embedded in the fate of the title character whose "dying hour was gloom." Melville's concern is with evil that takes the form of social injustice and human squalor in "What Redburn Saw in Launcelott's-Hey."

OTHER AMERICAN CLASSIC WRITERS

Other selections in this unit convey a sense of the times or capture the flavor of American life during the midnineteenth century. Lincoln's Gettysburg Address and Lee's "Letter to His Son" offer a glimpse into the deep passion evoked by the tragedy of the Civil War. Alcott reveals in her diary the demands placed upon a dedicated army nurse during this war.

The other women presented in this unit reveal strong commitments to social causes—Robinson in her picture of women factory workers in Lowell, Massachusetts, Stowe in her indictment of slavery in *Uncle Tom's Cabin*, and Sojourner Truth in her outspoken words on black womanhood.

Two speeches round out the section: Frederick Douglass presents an eloquent case for independence (and the vote) for black people, and Chief Seattle speaks forcefully and poetically for his tribe. Like the other writers represented in this unit, these men demonstrate that independence, individualism, and self-reliance were ideals deeply embedded in the American consciousness.

Sidney Lanier's "Song of the Chattahooche," with its romantic tone and conventional verse form, is a representative lyric of the period (though it was written in 1877). In the next period, Walt Whitman's and Emily Dickinson's radical innovations in poetry would make Lanier seem conservative. But however tradiional Lanier may appear, he is skilled in the writing of verse that is characterized by grace and harmony.

The unit ends with three selections conveying humor that is distinctly American. Davy Crockett's tall tale and Mike Fink's brag depict the extravagant American superhero, while Josh Billings focuses on the lessons his countrymen can learn from an ant. Although these humorists display a lighter side of the American character than other writers depict in this unit, their works portray the qualities of self-reliance and individuality that characterize the spirit of this period.

THINKING ABOUT GRAPHIC AIDS
Using the Time Line

As you study the time line on pages 196 and 197, be prepared to make some generalizations about social, industrial, and literary trends. For example, judging from the conventions held in 1848 and 1869, you can generalize that women's rights were an important social issue of this period. Make some generalizations in order to answer the following questions.

1. Between 1840 and 1870, the telegraph was patented, the first transatlantic cable was laid, and the transcontinental railroad was completed. What effects might you conclude these landmarks would have on the country?
2. How do you think the mushrooming of steel production and the invention of the sewing machine would affect U.S. industry?
3. In what way might the Gold Rush and the Homestead Act influence U.S. expansion?

Using the Map

Use the map on page 201, which shows the Union and the Confederate resources, to answer the following questions.

1. List four advantages that the Union had over the Confederacy.
2. Where is the South's only industrial center?
3. Given the South's limited industrial resources, where would it get its war materials?

BIOGRAPHY

Ralph Waldo Emerson
1803–1882

John Greenleaf Whittier once said of Ralph Waldo Emerson that he was "the one American who is sure of being remembered in a thousand years." Emerson advocated self-reliance, self-trust, and individualism, qualities that formed the basis of a philosophy called Transcendentalism. Dominating an era of American cultural development with his leadership of the New England Transcendental Movement, he revolutionized American literary thought.

Emerson was born in Boston in 1803. His father, descended from six generations of clergymen, was the minister at the First Church of Boston. While Emerson was young, his father died and left his family destitute. In spite of his poverty, Emerson attended the Latin School and entered Harvard College in 1817. During his years there, he began writing bits of personal philosophy in notebooks that he later called *Journals*. Feeling friendless, alone, and without confidence in himself, he wrote these ironic words in 1820: "I find myself often idle, vagrant, stupid. . . . I am indolent and shall be insignificant."

After finishing Harvard, he taught for three years and entered Harvard Divinity School in 1825, but poor health and family difficulties forced him to leave the seminary. In 1829 he became associate pastor at the Unitarian Second Church in Boston (formerly Cotton Mather's church) and married Ellen Tucker. In 1832 he resigned his church position because he believed "the profession was antiquated" and he could no longer perform some of its rituals. It was about this time that Emerson's wife and two of his brothers died. Distressed by these personal tragedies, he decided to go to Europe. While he was abroad, he discovered German Transcendentalism, which he brought back to this country and made distinctively American by combining his ideas of self-reliance and free-thinking with Romantic Idealism. (See Reader's Note: Transcendentalism on page 207.) Emerson's optimistic philosophy, which stressed human goodness and intuition, was considered illogical by some and incomplete by others because it failed to account for the existence of evil in the world.

In 1835 he remarried and moved to his grandfather's home, Old Manse, in Concord, Massachusetts, where he read, wrote, prepared lectures, and influenced others in Transcendentalism. Followers such as Henry Thoreau and Bronson Alcott took up social causes, including the abolition of slavery and reforms in education, labor, suffrage, and women's rights. These followers encouraged communal living experiments (such as Brook Farm) and espoused free expression in a magazine called *The Dial*. Although Emerson supported these endeavors intellectually, he did not actively participate in most of them.

Emerson's optimistic philosophy, found in all of his writings, from the simple poem "Fable" to such essays as "Self-Reliance" and "The Over-Soul," might be summed up in one of his own epigrams: "Trust thyself; every heart vibrates to that iron string."

Maxims of Emerson

Ralph Waldo Emerson

Speak your latent conviction, and it shall be the universal sense.

Society everywhere is in conspiracy against the manhood of every one of its members.

Nothing is at last sacred but the integrity of your own mind.

My life is for itself and not for a spectacle.

A foolish consistency is the hobgoblin of little minds,
Adored by little statesmen and philosophers and divines.

An institution is the lengthened shadow of one man.

Life only avails, not the having lived.

Insist on yourself; never imitate.

The civilized man has built a coach, but has lost the use of his feet.

1841

Fable

Ralph Waldo Emerson

The mountain and the squirrel
Had a quarrel,
And the former called the latter "Little Prig";
Bun replied,
5 "You are doubtless very big;
But all sorts of things and weather
Must be taken in together,
To make up a year
And a sphere.
10 And I think it no disgrace
To occupy my place.
If I'm not so large as you,
You are not so small as I,
And not half so spry.
15 I'll not deny you make
A very pretty squirrel track;
Talents differ; all is well and wisely put;
If I cannot carry forests on my back,
Neither can you crack a nut."

1845

THINK AND DISCUSS

Understanding

1. What does Emerson mean in the first maxim by "latent conviction"? (Consult the Glossary, if necessary.)
2. Rephrase the second maxim in your own words.
3. Which maxim could be paraphrased thus: "Technology has caused people to lose their individual abilities"?

Analyzing

4. How do the third and eighth maxims relate to one another in meaning?
5. Why does Emerson choose the **image** of a "lengthened shadow of one man" to describe an institution? (Keep in mind that a shadow is merely a reflection of a real person.)
6. Emerson uses **figurative language** in the last maxim. What do the "coach" and the "feet" represent?

Extending

7. Do you think that these maxims are more, or less, relevant today than they were a century and a half ago? Explain.
8. Restate the meaning of Emerson's poem "Fable" in the form of a maxim.

THINKING SKILLS

Classifying

The maxims of Emerson that you have read are based on his ideas of the individual versus society. You can arrive at a better understanding of his ideas by classifying, or categorizing, the words he uses to describe each group.

1. Under the heads *Individual* and *Society*, list at least eight words and phrases from the maxims.
2. Add an appropriate word or phrase of your own under each category.

COMPOSITION

Writing Maxims

Write at least six maxims that express your own philosophy about life. Use figurative language in at least one maxim.

Writing About an Author's Philosophy

Write an essay of at least three paragraphs analyzing Emerson's philosophy as stated in his maxims. In the first paragraph, describe the qualities that Emerson admires in an individual. In the middle paragraph(s), explain how this kind of person might function in modern society. In the final paragraph, comment on whether or not you think this kind of person would encounter obstacles in contemporary life.

ENRICHMENT

Research

Short statements expressing a moral or a truth about life appear in works ranging from the Bible and Shakespeare to magazine interviews and newspaper articles. Collect a list of such statements that appeal to you and present them in a report to your class.

Debate

With a classmate, prepare a debate about the pros and cons of pursuing Emerson's philosophy in everyday life. One side should defend the rights of the individual, the other side, the rights of institutions and society in general. You might organize your debate by defending or refuting the following maxim: "Society everywhere is in conspiracy against the manhood of every one of its members."

Transcendentalism

Transcendentalism, a philosophy popular in New England during the 1830s, was an offshoot of the Romantic Movement that preceded it (see Reader's Note on Romanticism, pages 108 and 133). Both philosophies upheld the goodness of humanity, the glories of nature, and the importance of free individual expression. In addition, Transcendentalism maintained that an awareness of reality, or a sense of truth, is reached through intuition rather than through reasoning or logic. Consequently, individuals should act according to their innermost personal beliefs, or spiritual conviction, rather than follow the dictates of society. Closely related to this idea is that of the integrity of the individual, the belief that each person is inherently good, capable of making rational decisions, and worthy of the respect of every other human being. These ideas found a sympathetic response among a people who had long cherished the democratic and individualistic principles of the early settlers, statesmen, and citizens.

Inevitably, these ideas were to clash with the doctrines of organized religion. An earlier group of New England intellectuals broke away from Puritanism and founded the Unitarian Church during the late eighteenth century. Their split with the established church was largely due to the intellectual and commercial trends of the age. In a day when commerce and science had become predominant, when material comfort and social mobility were becoming increasingly accessible to more and more people, the old religion—Puritanism—lost its hold. By the 1830s the Unitarians, yesterday's rebels, had become Boston's establishment, dominating the city's intellectual centers, both the church and Harvard University. But Boston's economic, social, political, and cultural elite found themselves—by the early 1830s—embroiled in yet another intellectual insurrection, though this time it was they who were under attack.

Transcendentalists like Emerson did not limit their attacks solely to questions of theology. To them, sterility in religion had its analogues in both public and private life. They believed that Rationalism, the philosophy from which modern science had sprung, denied the profound sense of mystery that these thinkers found in both nature and humanity. They felt that current thought had reduced God to a watchmaker who once having built and wound up the universe now sat back and detachedly observed it. The individual in this scheme was likewise reduced, as Thoreau said, "to a cog" or wheel in this cosmic machine. Social conformity, materialism, and what they believed to be a lack of moral commitment angered these young men and women. In addition to their writings, their beliefs found expression in various movements: feminism, abolitionism, utopianism, communalism, and even the beginnings of labor unionism.

In opposition to the rationalistic tendencies of the age, Transcendentalism incorporated elements from many philosophies and religions. But Transcendentalism is closest in spirit to the philosophy of Idealism, which held that material objects do not have a real existence of their own. Rather, these objects are diffused parts or aspects of God, the Over-Soul. As the ultimate spiritual force, the Over-Soul encompasses all existence and reconciles all the opposing forces in the world. Material objects therefore mirror or reflect an ideal world. Thus, by contemplating objects in nature, the individual can transcend this world and discover union with God and the Ideal. The key innate quality used by the individual to achieve this state of union is intuition, granted every soul at birth.

from Self-Reliance

Ralph Waldo Emerson

A Nonconformist

Whoso would be a man, must be a nonconformist. He who would gather immortal palms must not be hindered by the name of goodness, but must explore if it be goodness. Nothing is at last sacred but the integrity of your own mind. Absolve you to yourself, and you shall have the suffrage of the world. I remember an answer which when quite young I was prompted to make to a valued adviser who was wont to importune me with the dear old doctrines of the church. On my saying, "What have I to do with the sacredness of traditions, if I live wholly from within?" my friend suggested—"But these impulses may be from below, not from above." I replied, "They do not seem to me to be such; but if I am the Devil's child, I will live then from the Devil." No law can be sacred to me but that of my nature. Good and bad are but names very readily transferable to that or this; the only right is what is after my constitution; the only wrong what is against it. A man is to carry himself in the presence of all opposition as if every thing were titular and ephemeral but he. I am ashamed to think how easily we capitulate to badges and names, to large societies and dead institutions. Every decent and well-spoken individual affects and sways me more than is right. I ought to go upright and vital, and speak the rude truth in all ways. If malice and vanity wear the coat of philanthropy, shall that pass? If an angry bigot assumes this bountiful cause of Abolition, and comes to me with his last news from Barbados,[1] why should I not say to him, "Go love thy infant; love thy wood chopper; be good-natured and modest; have that grace; and never varnish your hard, uncharitable ambition with this incredible tenderness for black folk a thousand miles off. Thy love afar is spite at home." Rough and graceless would be such greeting, but truth is handsomer than the affectation of love. Your goodness must have some edge to it—else it is none. The doctrine of hatred must be preached, as the counteraction of the doctrine of love, when that pules and whines. I shun father and mother and wife and brother when my genius calls me. I would write on the lintels of the doorpost, *Whim*. I hope it is somewhat better than whim at last, but we cannot spend the day in explanation. Expect me not to show cause why I seek or why I exclude company. Then again, do not tell me, as a good man did today, of my obligation to put all poor men in good situations. Are they *my* poor? I tell thee, thou foolish philanthropist, that I grudge the dollar, the dime, the cent I give to such men as do not belong to me and to whom I do not belong. There is a class of persons to whom by all spiritual affinity I am bought and sold; for them I will go to prison if need be; but your miscellaneous popular charities; the education at college of fools; the building of meetinghouses to the vain end to which many now stand; alms to sots, and the thousandfold Relief Societies—though I confess with shame I sometimes succumb and give the dollar, it is a wicked dollar, which by and by I shall have the manhood to withhold.

Traveling

It is for want of self-culture that the superstition of Traveling, whose idols are Italy, England,

---

1. ***Barbados.*** Slaves had arrived in America from Barbados in the West Indies where they had been brought from Africa. The British abolished slavery in the West Indies in 1833.

Egypt, retains its fascination for all educated Americans. They who made England, Italy, or Greece venerable in the imagination, did so by sticking fast where they were, like an axis of the earth. In manly hours we feel that duty is our place. The soul is no traveler; the wise man stays at home, and when his necessities, his duties, on any occasion call him from his house, or into foreign lands, he is at home still and shall make men sensible by the expression of his countenance that he goes, the missionary of wisdom and virtue, and visits cities and men like a sovereign and not like an interloper or a valet.

I have no churlish objection to the circumnavigation of the globe for the purposes of art, of study, and benevolence, so that the man is first domesticated, or does not go abroad with the hope of finding somewhat greater than he knows. He who travels to be amused, or to get somewhat which he does not carry, travels away from himself, and grows old even in youth among old things. In Thebes, in Palmyra,[2] his will and mind have become old and dilapidated as they. He carries ruins to ruins.

Traveling is a fool's paradise. Our first journeys discover to us the indifference of places. At home I dream that at Naples, at Rome, I can be intoxicated with beauty and lose my sadness. I pack my trunk, embrace my friends, embark on the sea and at last wake up in Naples, and there beside me is the stern fact, the sad self, unrelenting, identical, that I fled from. I seek the Vatican and the palaces. I affect to be intoxicated with sights and suggestions, but I am not intoxicated. My giant goes with me wherever I go.

Reliance on Property

And so the reliance on Property, including the reliance on governments which protect it, is the want of self-reliance. Men have looked away from themselves and at things so long that they have come to esteem the religious, learned, and civil institutions as guards of property, and they deprecate assaults on these, because they feel them to be assaults on property. They measure their esteem of each other by what each has, and not

Maxfield Parrish, *The Tourist* (1909). Private collection

by what each is. But a cultivated man becomes ashamed of his property, out of new respect for his nature. Especially he hates what he has if he see that it is accidental—came to him by inheritance, or gift, or crime; then he feels that it is not having; it does not belong to him, has no root in him and merely lies there because no revolution or no robber takes it away. But that which a man is, does always by necessity acquire; and what the man acquires, is living property, which does not wait the beck of rulers, or mobs, or revolutions, or fire, or storm, or bankruptcies, but perpetually renews itself wherever the man breathes. "Thy lot or portion of life," said the Caliph Ali,[3] "is seeking after thee; therefore be at rest from seeking after it." Our dependence on

---

2. *Thebes . . . Palmyra,* ancient cities. Thebes was the capital of ancient Egypt. Palmyra, in Syria, was known as the city of Tadmor in the Bible and was said to have been founded by Solomon.
3. *Caliph Ali,* the fourth successor of Mohammed as civil and spiritual leader of the Moslems. A collection of his sayings had been translated into English in 1832.

these foreign goods leads us to our slavish respect for numbers. The political parties meet in numerous conventions; the greater the concourse and with each new uproar of announcement, The delegation from Essex! The Democrats from New Hampshire! The Whigs of Maine! The young patriot feels himself stronger than before by a new thousand of eyes and arms. In like manner the reformers summon convention and vote and resolve in multitude. Not so, O friends! Will the God deign to enter and inhabit you, but by a method precisely the reverse. It is only as a man puts off all foreign support and stands alone that I see him to be strong and to prevail. He is weaker by every recruit to his banner. Is not a man better than a town? Ask nothing of men, and, in the endless mutation, thou only firm column must presently appear the upholder of all that surrounds thee. He who knows that power is inborn, that he is weak because he has looked for good out of him and elsewhere, and, so perceiving, throws himself unhesitatingly on his thought, instantly rights himself, stands in the erect position, commands his limbs, works miracles; just as a man who stands on his feet is stronger than a man who stands on his head.

1841

THINK AND DISCUSS
Understanding
1. What, according to the third sentence in "A Nonconformist," is the only sacred thing?
2. What advice does Emerson give to the angry bigot?
3. Against what institutions does Emerson rebel, according to the last sentence of "A Nonconformist"?
4. Why do educated Americans travel, according to the first sentence of "Traveling"?
5. What does Emerson consider valid reasons for traveling?
6. In "Reliance on Property," how should men, as represented by "the cultivated man," regard property? How are political parties and reformers inferior to the individual?

Analyzing
7. Emerson uses a form of **synecdoche** in referring to the tendency to "capitulate to badges and names." What do the badges represent? What point does he make about human behavior?
8. At the end of "Traveling," Emerson states that "My giant goes with me wherever I go." What or who is this "giant," and why is it ever present?

VOCABULARY
Affixes
Verbs that end in -ate can often be changed into nouns by dropping e and adding the suffix -ion, which means "in the state, act, or condition of." For example, dilapidation means "in the state of falling apart."

Change each of the following words into a noun by adding the suffix -ion: circumnavigate, delegate, deprecate, mutate, capitulate, domesticate.

Consulting your Glossary if necessary, use either the noun or verb form of each of these six words in a sentence that shows you understand the meaning of that word.

ENRICHMENT
Research
Emerson wrote extensively and effectively throughout his long life. Consult a volume of his collected works and examine one work in depth, such as "Nature." Prepare an oral report to deliver to the class.

from The American Scholar

Ralph Waldo Emerson

Man Thinking

t is one of those fables which out of an unknown antiquity convey an unlooked-for wisdom, that the gods, in the beginning, divided Man into men, that he might be more helpful to himself; just as the hand was divided into fingers, the better to answer its end.

The old fable covers a doctrine ever new and sublime; that there is One Man—present to all particular men only partially, or through one faculty; and that you must take the whole society to find the whole man. Man is not a farmer, or a professor, or an engineer, but he is all. Man is priest, and scholar, and statesman, and producer, and soldier. In the *divided* or social state these functions are parceled out to individuals, each of whom aims to do his stint of the joint work, whilst each other performs his. The fable implies that the individual, to possess himself, must sometimes return from his own labor to embrace all the other laborers. But, unfortunately, this original unit, this fountain of power, has been so distributed to multitudes, has been so minutely subdivided and peddled out, that it is spilled into drops, and cannot be gathered. The state of society is one in which the members have suffered amputation from the trunk, and strut about so many walking monsters—a good finger, a neck, a stomach, an elbow, but never a man.

Man is thus metamorphosed into a thing, into many things. The planter, who is Man sent out into the field to gather food, is seldom cheered by any idea of the true dignity of his ministry. He sees his bushel and his cart, and nothing beyond, and sinks into the farmer, instead of Man on the farm. The tradesman scarcely ever gives an ideal worth to his work, but is ridden by the routine of his craft, and the soul is subject to dollars. The priest becomes a form; the attorney a statute book; the mechanic a machine; the sailor a rope of the ship.

In this distribution of functions the scholar is the delegated intellect. In the right state he is *Man Thinking*. In the degenerate state, when the victim of society, he tends to become a mere thinker, or still worse, the parrot of other men's thinking.

In this view of him, as Man Thinking, the theory of his office is contained. Him Nature solicits with all her placid, all her monitory pictures; him the past instructs; him the future invites. Is not indeed every man a student, and do not all things exist for the student's behoof? And, finally, is not the true scholar the only true master?

1837

THINK AND DISCUSS
Understanding
1. What fable does Emerson mention in the first paragraph?
2. According to the third paragraph, the planter fails to look beyond "his bushel and his cart" in order to recognize "the true dignity" of his work. What other workmen does he mention in this paragraph who focus on the objects rather than on the dignity of their work?
3. What are the roles of the scholar in the "right state" and in the "degenerate state," according to paragraph four?

Analyzing

4. Emerson uses a **metaphor** in paragraph two when he says, "The state of society is one in which the members have suffered amputation from the trunk, and strut about so many walking monsters—a good finger, a neck, a stomach, an elbow, but never a man." Find another sentence in this paragraph that states this idea literally.
5. What is the difference between "a mere thinker" and "Man Thinking"?
6. Judging from this speech, delivered to Harvard students in 1837, how does Emerson characterize the American scholar?

Extending

7. Do you think Emerson's speech would be relevant for a college graduating class of today? Why or why not?

COMPOSITION

Writing a Fable

Write a fable to illustrate a situation in which society is in conflict with the individual. Use animals to present a moral such as the following: "An individual's solution to a problem is better than one that society presents." Use one of the following situations or think of your own for the basis of your fable: gathering food, preventing war, eliminating poverty.

Writing a Commencement Address

Imagine that you have been asked to write a commencement address for the graduating seniors of your school. In four or more paragraphs, outline several points that you consider valuable in dealing with the world at large. Assume a tone of authority as you present your advice.

According to Hindu belief, Brahma is the supreme soul of the universe—a force in whom all opposites are united and all contradictions are reconciled. Brahma resembles Emerson's Over-Soul and is the perfect vehicle by which this author can express his transcendental thoughts. In both "Brahma" and "Days" Emerson speaks of superhuman forces that resolve the mysteries of life, which are beyond human understanding.

Brahma

Ralph Waldo Emerson

If the red slayer think he slays,
  Or if the slain think he is slain,
They know not well the subtle ways
  I keep, and pass, and turn again.

5 Far or forgot to me is near;
  Shadow and sunlight are the same;
The vanished gods to me appear;
  And one to me are shame and fame.

They reckon ill who leave me out;
10   When me they fly, I am the wings;
I am the doubter and the doubt,
  And I the hymn the Brahmin[1] sings.

The strong gods pine for my abode,
  And pine in vain the sacred Seven,[2]
15 But thou, meek lover of the good!
  Find me, and turn thy back on heaven.

1857

---

1. *Brahmin,* a member of the highest, priestly caste in the Hindu religion.
2. *sacred Seven,* the seven most revered saints in the Brahmin's religion.

THINK AND DISCUSS

Understanding
1. How does the speaker identify himself in the third stanza?
2. Who "pine in vain" for Brahma, according to lines 13 and 14? Who will find Brahma, according to lines 15 and 16?

Analyzing
3. What **image** is evoked in the term "red slayer"? Why is red an appropriate color?
4. Name several of the **paradoxes** mentioned in the poem.

5. Why, from the perspective of the speaker, are these paradoxes reconciled?
6. In what sense might death, mentioned in the first stanza, be only an illusion for Brahma?

Extending
7. Read again the Reader's Note on Transcendentalism, especially the last paragraph dealing with the Over-Soul (207b, 2). What similarities do you see between the Over-Soul and Brahma?

 Review PERSONIFICATION in the Handbook of Literary Terms, page 887.

Days

Ralph Waldo Emerson

Daughters of Time, the hypocritic Days,
Muffled and dumb like barefoot dervishes,
And marching single in an endless file,
Bring diadems and fagots in their hands.
5 To each they offer gifts after his will,
Bread, kingdoms, stars, and sky
      that holds them all.
I, in my pleached garden, watched the pomp,
Forgot my morning wishes, hastily
Took a few herbs and apples, and the Day
10 Turned and departed silent. I, too late,
Under her solemn fillet saw the scorn.

               1857

Worthington Whittredge, detail of *Apples* (1867).
Museum of Fine Arts, Boston

THINK AND DISCUSS

Understanding

1. What adjectives are used to describe Days in lines 1 and 2?
2. What gifts do Days offer?
3. What gifts does the speaker offer?
4. What word in the last line expresses the Days' feelings toward the speaker?

Analyzing

5. The conflict in this poem is between Days, which promise infinite gifts, and humanity, hindered by mortality and unable to partake of each day in its fullest sense. In what way are Days, which march in an "endless file," hypocritic, or deceptive?
6. Look up the words *diadem* and *fagot* in your Glossary. If fagots represent the humble and practical aspects of life, what might diadems represent?
7. What progression is there in the list of other gifts that Days offer in line 6? Where in the list of gifts would "a few herbs and apples" fall?
8. What might the speaker's "morning wishes" have been?

Extending

9. Mention one idea expressed in either "Days" or "Brahma" that has presented you with a unique view of the passage of time or the nature of good and evil.

REVIEWING: Personification H2T

See Handbook of Literary Terms, p. 887.

Personification is the presentation of abstractions, ideas, animals, or inanimate objects as human beings by endowing them with human qualities.

1. Days are described as *muffled, dumb,* and *silent.* What qualities of time passing do these words suggest?
2. Why is the picture of Days "Marching single in an endless file" more effective than "marching ten abreast"?

COMPOSITION

Personifying an Abstract Concept

In both "Days" and "Brahma" Emerson expresses an abstract concept through the use of personification. Think of another abstract concept—the arrival or departure of love or the feeling of victory or defeat, for example. Personify this concept for your classmates in a poem or a prose description of several paragraphs, using vivid images and details to make this concept come alive. Try to appeal to at least two different senses in your description.

Analyzing a Poem

Write an essay of at least four paragraphs in which you comment on the meaning of "Days." Use the first sentence of item 5 under Analyzing as your thesis statement, or construct one of your own. Devote each of your middle paragraphs to a different aspect of the poem. Use any of your answers to the Think and Discuss questions to strengthen your essay. In the final paragraph, arrive at some general conclusion about Emerson's concept of time or about the devices he uses to convey his ideas. See "Writing About Poetry and Poetic Devices" in the Writer's Handbook.

The Snowstorm

Ralph Waldo Emerson

Announced by all the trumpets of the sky,
Arrives the snow, and, driving o'er the fields,
Seems nowhere to alight: the whited air
Hides hills and woods, the river, and the heaven,
5   And veils the farmhouse at the garden's end.
The sled and traveler stopped, the courier's feet
Delayed, all friends shut out, the housemates sit
Around the radiant fireplace, enclosed
In a tumultuous privacy of storm.

10   Come see the north wind's masonry.
Out of an unseen quarry evermore
Furnished with tile, the fierce artificer
Curves his white bastions with projected roof
Round every windward stake, or tree, or door.
15   Speeding, the myriad-handed, his wild work
So fanciful, so savage, nought cares he
For number or proportion. Mockingly,
On coop or kennel he hangs Parian[1] wreaths;
A swanlike form invests the hidden thorn;
20   Fills up the farmer's lane from wall to wall,
Maugre the farmer's sighs; and at the gate
A tapering turret overtops the work.
And when his hours are numbered, and the world
Is all his own, retiring, as he were not,
25   Leaves, when the sun appears, astonished Art
To mimic in slow structures, stone by stone,
Built in an age, the mad wind's night work,
The frolic architecture of the snow.

1841

---

1. *Parian* (per'ē ən), of Paros, a Greek island noted for its beautiful white marble.

THINK AND DISCUSS
Understanding
1. What are some of the effects of the snowstorm mentioned in lines 1–9?
2. Is this a city scene or a rural one? How do you know?
3. To what kind of craftsman is the snowstorm compared in lines 10–28?

Analyzing
4. How is the snowstorm **personified** in lines 10–15?
5. What words and **images** reflect the winter artist's unrestrained creativity?
6. What is the difference between this "frolic architecture" and the human art (see lines 26–27) that it mimics?
7. What process in nature is described in lines 23–28?

APPLYING: Consonance
See Handbook of Literary Terms, p. 909.

Consonance is the repetition of consonant sounds that are preceded by different vowel sounds. These different vowels distinguish consonance (fed/fad) from rhyme (fed/bed). Like alliteration, consonance repeats consonant sounds to create an effect or to unify ideas.

1. What words in line 7 provide a pattern of consonance with the word *feet* in line 6?
2. What word, occurring twice in line 26, fits the consonance pattern of the words *when* and *sun* in line 25?

BIOGRAPHY

Henry David Thoreau
1817–1862

Thoreau thought of himself as "a mystic, a Transcendentalist, and a natural philosopher," but he was much more. He acted out the dictates of his conscience with a determination that was unsettling to those who lived more cautious lives. While Emerson and other Transcendentalists discussed the abolition of slavery, Thoreau helped runaway slaves escape to Canada. When it was not popular to do so, he spoke in defense of the abolitionist John Brown. To register his disapproval of slavery and the Mexican War, he refused to pay his poll tax and went to jail. It is said that while Emerson visited Thoreau on his day in jail, he asked, "Henry, why are you here?" Thoreau answered, "Waldo, why are you not here?" From this civil protest came the essay *Civil Disobedience*, still popular today as a manifesto of the individual's right to protest immoral acts of government.

Henry David Thoreau was born in Concord, Massachusetts, in 1817. Although he graduated near the top of his Harvard class in 1837, for most of his life he supported himself by manual labor. Thoreau, who had been at Harvard when Emerson, fourteen years his senior, had given "The American Scholar" address, is said to have once walked eighteen miles from Concord to Boston and back to hear Emerson speak. Thoreau became a follower of Emerson's and at one point lived with his family as a tutor and handyman.

In 1839, on a vacation from teaching, he and his brother John went on a thirteen-day journey down the Concord River and up the Merrimack River. He later wrote about this experience in his first book, *A Week on the Concord and Merrimack Rivers*. The book, however, was not well received by the public, and seven hundred out of one thousand copies were sent back to him unsold. He referred to them in this manner: "I have now a library of nearly nine hundred volumes, over seven hundred of which I wrote myself."

His experiment in living at Walden Pond began in 1845. He explained his action with these words, "I went to the woods because I wished to live deliberately, to front only the essential facts of life, and see if I could not learn what it had to teach, and not when I came to die discover that I had not lived." At Walden he stripped his life to its essentials, noting every aspect of nature around him and putting transcendental ideas to the test. He stayed there for twenty-six months and lived in a cabin he built, ate the vegetables he grew, and gathered the material for *Walden*, a book that would immortalize him, even though in 1854 only two thousand copies were sold.

Thoreau died from tuberculosis at the age of forty-four. A few hours before his death an aunt asked if he had "made his peace with God." Thoreau replied, "I have never quarreled with Him."

Reading ESSAYS AND SPEECHES

An *essay* is a brief work of nonfiction prose that expresses an opinion on a topic. The form is associated with the French philosopher, Montaigne (mon tān'), who called his brief prose pieces *essais* or "attempts." Essays may be classified as formal or informal. The *formal essay*, with its serious tone and persuasive intent, is marked by a dignified style and tight construction. The *informal essay*, which is more intent on entertaining than persuading, has a personal tone, and relies on a looser structure that allows a writer to occasionally digress. Sometimes anecdotal and humorous, this type of essay today takes the form of newspaper and magazine articles.

Earlier American writers such as Franklin, Paine, and Jefferson had recognized the flexibility and range of this genre. Writers of the American Classic period used the essay to probe human behavior and to search for new patterns to live by. Many of the speeches included in this unit can be considered essays that were delivered orally. Use the following guidelines to gain the full benefit from the essays and speeches you are about to read.

Find the main idea. Once you find the main idea, you can direct your reading and determine the relative importance of each sentence. Examine the title or skim the first and last paragraphs, looking for words and ideas that are emphasized or repeated. Often, the main idea is directly expressed, as it is in Thoreau's one-word directive in *Walden*—"Simplify!" At other times, you will have to infer the main idea by synthesizing several sentences into your own words. For example, a reader has to sift through the excerpt from *Civil Disobedience* to find its main idea, which might be summarized thus: "The State must derive its authority from the individual and be molded by the dictates of the people." Once you have found the main idea, note sentences and details that support it.

Note the author's tone. This tone may range from congenial to formal and highly serious. There may be flashes of humor in an essay such as *Walden* or a speech such as Stanton's, but these flashes should be recognized as only a means to highlight a dominant tone that is serious. Note how a writer or a speaker can switch tones for effect, as Sojourner Truth does when she shifts from the homespun, maternal voice of "old Sojourner" to the final admonition, "And now they is asking to do it, the men better let them."

Determine the author's purpose. Although most of these authors are proposing social action, they make their appeal in different ways. Accordingly, each author has chosen a pattern of organization, literary devices, and a style that best states the case. Truth's impromptu speech has an entirely different flavor from Thoreau's works. Relying more on emotional than intellectual appeal, Truth's style is direct, colloquial, and full of phrases such as "out of kilter" and "in a fix." Thoreau, on the other hand, makes his appeal to the intellect in urging reform. His reliance on climactic sentence structure, epigrammatic wit, and allusion makes his work difficult to read. Billings satirizes human follies but without any great seriousness or intent to reform. Once you determine the author's purpose and realize what demands will be made on you as reader, you can adjust your reading rate accordingly.

Establish the audience. Stanton, speaking to what we gather was a supportive audience acquainted with the issues she raises, uses anecdote and figurative language to make her case for women's rights. Lincoln, on the other hand, addresses the patriots at Gettysburg with a tightly constructed argument in language that is formal and almost exclusively literal. Chief Seattle attempts to explain his people and values to a governor who represents an alien culture. Although his tone is generally conciliatory, he cautions that "the dead are not powerless."

from Walden

Henry David Thoreau

Why I Went to the Woods

 went to the woods because I wished to live deliberately, to front only the essential facts of life, and see if I could not learn what it had to teach, and not, when I came to die, discover that I had not lived. I did not wish to live what was not life, living is so dear; nor did I wish to practice resignation, unless it was quite necessary. I wanted to live deep and suck out all the marrow of life, to live so sturdily and Spartanlike as to put to rout all that was not life, to cut a broad swath and shave close, to drive life into a corner, and reduce it to its lowest terms, and, if it proved to be mean, why then to get the whole and genuine meanness of it, and publish its meanness to the world; or if it were sublime, to know it by experience, and be able to give a true account of it in my next excursion.[1] For most men, it appears to me, are in a strange uncertainty about it, whether it is of the devil or of God, and have *somewhat hastily* concluded that it is the chief end of man here to "glorify God and enjoy Him forever."[2]

Still we live meanly, like ants, though the fable tells us that we were long ago changed into men;[3] like pygmies we fight with cranes;[4] it is error upon error, and clout upon clout, and our best virtue has for its occasion a superfluous and evitable wretchedness. Our life is frittered away by detail. An honest man has hardly need to count more than his ten fingers or in extreme cases he may add his ten toes, and lump the rest. Simplicity, simplicity, simplicity! I say, let your affairs be as two or three, and not a hundred or a thousand; instead of a million count half a dozen, and keep your accounts on your thumbnail. In the midst of this chopping sea of civilized life, such are the clouds and storms and quicksands and thousand-and-one items to be allowed for, that a man has to live, if he would not founder and go to the bottom and not make his port at all, by dead reckoning,[5] and he must be a great calculator indeed who succeeds. Simplify, simplify. Instead of three meals a day, if it be necessary eat but one; instead of a hundred dishes, five; and reduce other things in proportion. Our life is like a German Confederacy, made up of petty states,[6] with its boundary forever fluctuating, so that even a German cannot tell you how it is bounded at any moment. The nation itself, with all its so-called internal

---

1. *my next excursion,* my next or future life.
2. *"glorify God and enjoy Him forever,"* the answer in the Westminster Catechism of the Presbyterian Church to the question "What is the chief end of man?"
3. *ants . . . men.* According to Greek legend, the Myrmidons, the followers of Achilles, were ants changed into men.
4. *like pygmies we fight with cranes.* Homer and other ancient writers believed that the pygmies, dwarf inhabitants of Africa, carried on warfare with the cranes.
5. *dead reckoning,* calculation of a ship's position by using a compass and studying the record of the voyage, and without using observations of the sun and stars.
6. *a German Confederacy, made up of petty states.* At the time Thoreau wrote *Walden,* Germany as a nation did not exist. Before 1815, the several hundred German states were each ruled by a prince or duke. After the Congress of Vienna (1814–1815) reduced the German states to thirty-eight, a loose German Confederation was formed.

improvements, which, by the way, are all external and superficial, is just such an unwieldy and overgrown establishment, cluttered with furniture and tripped up by its own traps, ruined by luxury and heedless expense, by want of calculation and a worthy aim, as the million households in the land; and the only cure for it as for them is in a rigid economy, a stern and more than Spartan simplicity of life and elevation of purpose. It lives too fast. Men think that it is essential that the *Nation* have commerce, and export ice, and talk through a telegraph, and ride thirty miles an hour, without a doubt, whether *they* do or not; but whether we should live like baboons or like men is a little uncertain. If we do not get out sleepers, and forge rails, and devote days and nights to the work, but go to tinkering upon our *lives* to improve them, who will build railroads? And if railroads are not built, how shall we get to heaven in season? But if we stay at home and mind our business, who will want railroads? We do not ride on the railroad; it rides upon us. . . .

Why I Left the Woods

I left the woods for as good a reason as I went there. Perhaps it seemed to me that I had several more lives to live, and could not spare any more time for that one. It is remarkable how easily and insensibly we fall into a particular route, and make a beaten track for ourselves. I had not lived there a week before my feet wore a path from my door to the pondside; and though it is five or six years since I trod it, it is still quite distinct. It is true, I fear, that others may have fallen into it, and so helped to keep it open. The surface of the earth is soft and impressible by the feet of men; and so with the paths which the mind travels. How worn and dusty, then, must be the highways of the world, how deep the ruts of tradition and conformity! I did not wish to take a cabin passage, but rather to go before the mast and on the deck of the world, for there I could best see the moonlight amid the mountains. I do not wish to go below now.

I learned this, at least, by my experiment: that if one advances confidently in the direction of his dreams, and endeavors to live the life which he has imagined, he will meet with a success unexpected in common hours. He will put some things behind, will pass an invisible boundary; new, universal, and more liberal laws will begin to establish themselves around and within him; or the old laws be expanded, and interpreted in his favor in a more liberal sense, and he will live with the license of a higher order of beings. In proportion as he simplifies his life, the laws of the universe will appear less complex, and solitude will not be solitude, nor poverty poverty, nor weakness weakness. If you have built castles in the air, your work need not be lost; that is where they should be. Now put the foundations under them. . . .

Why should we be in such desperate haste to succeed and in such desperate enterprises? If a man does not keep pace with his companions, perhaps it is because he hears a different drummer. Let him step to the music which he hears, however measured or far away. It is not important that he should mature as soon as an apple tree or an oak. Shall he turn his spring into summer? If the condition of things which we were made for is not yet, what were any reality which we can substitute? We will not be shipwrecked on a vain reality. Shall we with pains erect a heaven of blue glass over ourselves, though when it is done we shall be sure to gaze still at the true ethereal heaven far above, as if the former were not?

There was an artist in the city of Kouroo who was disposed to strive after perfection. One day it came into his mind to make a staff. Having considered that in an imperfect work time is an ingredient, but into a perfect work time does not enter, he said to himself, It shall be perfect in all respects, though I should do nothing else in my life. He proceeded instantly to the forest for wood, being resolved that it should not be made of unsuitable material; and as he searched for and rejected stick after stick, his friends gradually deserted him, for they grew old in their works and died, but he grew not older by a moment.

His singleness of purpose and resolution, and his elevated piety, endowed him, without his knowledge, with perennial youth. As he made no compromise with Time, Time kept out of his way, and only sighed at a distance because he could not overcome him. Before he had found a stick in all respects suitable the city of Kouroo was a hoary ruin, and he sat on one of its mounds to peel the stick. Before he had given it the proper shape the dynasty of the Candahars[7] was at an end, and with the point of the stick he wrote the name of the last of that race in the sand, and then he resumed his work. By the time he had smoothed and polished the staff Kalpa was no longer the polestar; and ere he had put on the ferule and the head adorned with precious stones, Brahma had awoke and slumbered many times.[8] But why do I stay to mention these things? When the finishing stroke was put to his work, it suddenly expanded before the eyes of the astonished artist into the fairest of all the creations of Brahma. He had made a new system in making a staff, a world with full and fair proportions; in which, though the old cities and dynasties had passed away, fairer and more glorious ones had taken their places. And now he saw by the heap of shavings still fresh at his feet, that, for him and his work, the former lapse of time had been an illusion, and that no more time had elapsed than is required for a single scintillation from the brain of Brahma to fall on and inflame the tinder of a mortal brain. The material was pure, and his art was pure; how could the result be other than wonderful?

No face which we can give to a matter will stead us so well at last as the truth. This alone wears well. For the most part, we are not where we are, but in a false position. Through an infirmity of our natures, we suppose a case, and put ourselves into it, and hence are in two cases at the same time, and it is doubly difficult to get out. In sane moments we regard only the facts, the case that is. Say what you have to say, not what you ought. Any truth is better than make-believe. Tom Hyde, the tinker, standing on the gallows, was asked if he had anything to say. "Tell the tailors," said he, "to remember to make a knot in their thread before they take the first stitch." His companion's prayer is forgotten.

However mean your life is, meet it and live it; do not shun it and call it hard names. It is not so bad as you are. It looks poorest when you are richest. The faultfinder will find faults even in paradise. Love your life, poor as it is. You may perhaps have some pleasant, thrilling, glorious hours, even in a poorhouse. The setting sun is reflected from the windows of the almshouse as brightly as from the rich man's abode; the snow melts before its door as early in the spring. I do not see but a quiet mind may live as contentedly there, and have as cheering thoughts, as in a palace. The town's poor seem to me often to live the most independent lives of any. Maybe they are simply great enough to receive without misgiving. Most think that they are above being supported by the town; but it oftener happens that they are not above supporting themselves by dishonest means, which should be more disreputable. Cultivate poverty like a garden herb, like sage. Do not trouble yourself much to get new things, whether clothes or friends. Turn the old; return to them. Things do not change; we change. Sell your clothes and keep your thoughts. God will see that you do not want society. If I were confined to a corner of a garret all my days, like a spider, the world would be just as large to me while I had my thoughts about me. The philosopher said: "From an army of three divisions one can take away its general, and put it in disorder; from the man the most abject and vulgar one cannot take away his thought." Do not seek so anxiously to be developed, to subject yourself to many influences to be played on; it is all dissipation. Humility like darkness reveals the heavenly lights. The shadows of poverty and meanness gather around us, "and lo! creation

<hr />

7. **Candahars**, Kandahar, an Afghanistan city long ruled by Darius I, king of the Achaemenid dynasty of Persia, and taken by Alexander in 329 B.C.
8. **Kalpa . . . many times.** According to Hindu belief, Brahma is the creator of the world which endures for 2,160,000,000 years and then is destroyed, only to be recreated by him after a like duration. Each 4,320,000,000-year period of this sort constitutes a day and a night of Brahma, or a Kalpa.

widens to our view."[9] We are often reminded that if there were bestowed on us the wealth of Croesus,[10] our aims must still be the same, and our means essentially the same. Moreover, if you are restricted in your range by poverty, if you cannot buy books and newspapers, for instance, you are but confined to the most significant and vital experiences; you are compelled to deal with the material which yields the most sugar and the most starch. It is life near the bone where it is sweetest. You are defended from being a trifler. No man loses ever on a lower level by magnanimity on a higher. Superfluous waste can buy superfluities only. Money is not required to buy one necessary of the soul. . . .

Rather than love, than money, than fame, give me truth: I sat at a table where were rich food and wine in abundance, an obsequious attendance, but sincerity and truth were not; and I went away hungry from the inhospitable board. The hospitality was as cold as the ices. I thought that there was no need of ice to freeze them. They talked to me of the age of the wine and the fame of the vintage; but I thought of an older, a newer, and purer wine, of a more glorious vintage, which they had not got, and could not buy. The style, the house and grounds and "entertainment" pass for nothing with me. I called on the king, but he made me wait in his hall, and conducted like a man incapacitated for hospitality. There was a man in my neighborhood who lived in a hollow tree. His manners were truly regal. I should have done better had I called on him. . . .

There is an incessant influx of novelty into the world, and yet we tolerate incredible dullness. I need only suggest what kind of sermons are still listened to in the most enlightened countries. There are such words as joy and sorrow, but they are only the burden of a psalm, sung with a nasal twang, while we believe in the ordinary and mean. We think that we can change our clothes only. It is said that the British Empire is very large and respectable, and that the United States are a first-rate power. We do not believe that a tide rises and falls behind every man which can float the British Empire like a chip, if he should ever harbor it in his mind. Who knows what sort of seventeen-year locust will next come out of the ground? The government of the world I live in was not framed, like that of Britain, in after-dinner conversations over the wine.

The life in us is like the water in the river. It may rise this year higher than man has ever known it, and flood the parched uplands; even this may be the eventful year, which will drown out all our muskrats. It was not always dry land where we dwell. I see far inland the banks which the stream anciently washed, before science began to record its freshets. Everyone has heard the story which has gone the rounds of New England, of a strong and beautiful bug which came out of the dry leaf of an old table of apple-tree wood, which had stood in a farmer's kitchen for sixty years, first in Connecticut, and afterward in Massachusetts—from an egg deposited in the living tree many years earlier still, as appeared by counting the annual layers beyond it; which was heard gnawing out for several weeks, hatched perchance by the heat of an urn. Who does not feel his faith in a resurrection and immortality strengthened by hearing of this? Who knows what beautiful and winged life, whose egg has been buried for ages under many concentric layers of woodenness in the dead dry life of society, deposited at first in the alburnum of the green and living tree, which has been gradually converted into the semblance of its well-seasoned tomb—heard perchance gnawing out now for years by the astonished family of man, as they sat round the festive board—may unexpectedly come forth from amidst society's most trivial and handselled furniture, to enjoy its perfect summer life at last!

I do not say that John or Jonathan will realize all this; but such is the character of that morrow which mere lapse of time can never make to dawn. The light which puts out our eyes is darkness to us. Only that day dawns to which we are awake. There is more day to dawn. The sun is but a morning star.　　**1854**

---

9. *"and lo . . . view,"* a slight misquotation from "Night," a sonnet by Joseph Blanco White (1775-1841).
10. *Croesus* (krē'səs), a king of Lydia in the 6th century B.C. renowned for his vast wealth.

THINK AND DISCUSS
Understanding
1. Why did Thoreau go to the woods?
2. What are some ways to simplify life, according to the third paragraph, which begins, "Simplicity, simplicity, simplicity"?
3. How does Thoreau regard railroads, according to paragraph three?
4. Why does Thoreau leave the woods? What has he learned from this experiment?

Analyzing
5. In the first paragraph, Thoreau uses the following figurative expressions to illustrate what he hopes to accomplish in his Walden retreat. Explain in your own words what he means in each case.
   - "to live deep and suck out all the marrow of life"
   - "to cut a broad swath and shave close"
   - "to drive life into a corner"
6. What does Thoreau mean in paragraph three when he cautions people to "keep your accounts on your thumbnail"?
7. Thoreau makes many **allusions** in these excerpts from *Walden*. Referring to the footnotes, name an allusion that is drawn from each of the following areas: religion, myth or legend, history.
8. What point about art and time is Thoreau making in the anecdote about the artist from Kouroo?

Extending
9. What are two Transcendental ideas expressed in these excerpts? (Refer to the first paragraph of the Reader's Note on Transcendentalism, page 207.)

APPLYING: Epigram H𝒵
See Handbook of Literary Terms, p. 885.

Epigrams are short, witty sayings (or verses), often ending with a wry twist. One of Thoreau's best-known epigrams is, "If a man does not keep pace with his companions, perhaps it is because he hears a different drummer." Explain what Thoreau means in the following epigrams.

1. "We do not ride on the railroad; it rides upon us."
2. "So is all change for the better, like birth and death, which convulse the body."

READING LITERATURE SKILLFULLY
Main Idea
The *main idea* is the most important point that the author is making in a work. If the main idea in a work is implied rather than directly stated, it is up to the reader to infer it.

1. Find a sentence in each paragraph of "Why I Went to the Woods" that expresses the main idea of that paragraph.
2. List four details in the third paragraph that Thoreau offers as ways to simplify life.
3. State the main idea in paragraph three of "Why I Left the Woods" in a sentence of your own.

COMPOSITION ✐
Imitating a Writer's Style
Thoreau's style is distinctive for, among other things, his construction of sentences that build to a climax. Examine the first paragraph of the excerpt that begins, "I went to the woods because. . . ." Then write your own paragraph, structuring your sentences on Thoreau's model. Choose a topic that lends itself to Thoreau's structure. The following is a model for the first sentence: I bought a new bike because I wished to travel conveniently, to avoid traffic jams, to see if I could not escape exhaust fumes, and not, when I was on my way, discover that I had run out of gas. See "Developing Your Style" in the Writer's Handbook.

ENRICHMENT
Research

Consult a travel book or a reference work on American literary history that has information on Walden Pond near Concord, Massachusetts. Locate maps, illustrations, or photographs of the pond and of such nearby sites as the home of Emerson or Hawthorne. Using this information, make a poster with an outline of the Walden Pond area and fill in as many informative points of the 1840–1860 era as you can. Indicate distances and directions to places like Brook Farm.

Comment

What's Become of Walden?

As we approach the end of the twentieth century, a three-way war is being waged between young people, literary historians, and elderly members of a mobile home park called Walden Breezes. This war is over Walden Pond, located in Concord, Massachusetts, eighteen miles west of Boston. Each faction in the struggle over Thoreau's famous refuge sees the site of his experiment in living as an answer to its particular needs.

To local teenagers, Walden Pond, the only freshwater pond in the area that is open to the public, is a source for recreation. The literary historians, many of them members of the Thoreau Society that runs a bookstore, relic display, and reference library on the site, want to restrict the area to sightseers and to those who revere Thoreau's legend. The elderly residents of Walden Breezes, some of whom have been there for decades, want to protect their living quarters.

It appears that the historical preservationists are winning the battle. Environmentalists, who have fought legal battles to preserve the area, have, with the aid of the state, restocked ponds, banned motorcycles and rubber boats, cleared away debris, and limited beach access. The Concord town dump near Walden Breezes is scheduled to be restored to a green hill. Since the state took over Walden Breezes in 1974, no new mobile home permits have been issued and

Fred MacNeill, *Walden*.
Private collection

the number of homes has dwindled to fewer than two dozen.

Thoreau might applaud the efforts of preservationists and the state government to return his refuge to the kind of simplicity he urges in *Walden*, despite his belief that "That government is best which governs not at all."

from Civil Disobedience

Henry David Thoreau

I heartily accept the motto—"That government is best which governs least"; and I should like to see it acted up to more rapidly and systematically. Carried out, it finally amounts to this, which also I believe—"That government is best which governs not at all" and when men are prepared for it, that will be the kind of government which they will have. Government is at best but an expedient; but most governments are usually, and all governments are sometimes, inexpedient. The objections which have been brought against a standing army, and they are many and weighty, and deserve to prevail, may also at last be brought against a standing government. The standing army is only an arm of the standing government. The government itself, which is only the mode which the people have chosen to execute their will, is equally liable to be abused and perverted before the people can act through it. Witness the present Mexican war, the work of comparatively a few individuals using the standing government as their tool;[1] for, in the outset, the people would not have consented to this measure.

This American government—what is it but a tradition, though a recent one, endeavoring to transmit itself unimpaired to posterity, but each instant losing some of its integrity? It has not the vitality and force of a single living man; for a single man can bend it to his will. It is a sort of wooden gun to the people themselves. But it is not the less necessary for this; for the people must have some complicated machinery or other, and hear its din, to satisfy that idea of government which they have. Governments show thus how successfully men can be imposed on, even impose on themselves, for their own advantage. It is excellent, we must all allow.

Yet this government never of itself furthered any enterprise, but by the alacrity with which it got out of its way. *It* does not keep the country free. *It* does not settle the West. *It* does not educate. The character inherent in the American people has done all that has been accomplished; and it would have done somewhat more, if the government had not sometimes got in its way. For government is an expedient by which men would fain succeed in letting one another alone; and, as has been said, when it is most expedient, the governed are most let alone by it. Trade and commerce, if they were not made of India rubber, would never manage to bounce over the obstacles which legislators are continually putting in their way; and, if one were to judge these men wholly by the effects of their actions and not partly by their intentions, they would deserve to be classed and punished with those mischievous persons who put obstructions on the railroads.

But, to speak practically and as a citizen, unlike those who call themselves no-government men, I ask for, not at once no government, but *at once* a better government. Let every man make known what kind of government would command his respect, and that will be one step toward obtaining it.

After all, the practical reason why, when the power is once in the hands of the people, a majority are permitted, and for a long period continue, to rule is not because they are most likely to be in the right, nor because this seems fairest to the minority, but because they are physically the

---

1. *Mexican war . . . tool.* The Mexican War (1846-1848) ended with the United States taking half of Mexico, which became the Southwestern states. Northern Abolitionists blamed the war on the desire of the Southern planters and Northern merchants to enlarge slave territory.

strongest. But a government in which the majority rule in all cases cannot be based on justice, even as far as men understand it. Can there not be a government in which majorities do not virtually decide right and wrong, but conscience?—in which majorities decide only those questions to which the rule of expediency is applicable? Must the citizen ever for a moment, or in the least decree, resign his conscience to the legislator? Why has every man a conscience, then? I think that we should be men first, and subjects afterward. It is not desirable to cultivate a respect for the law, so much as for the right. The only obligation which I have a right to assume is to do at any time what I think right. . . .

It is not a man's duty, as a matter of course, to devote himself to the eradication of any, even the most enormous wrong; he may still properly have other concerns to engage him; but it is his duty, at least, to wash his hands of it, and, if he gives it no thought longer, not to give it practically his support. If I devote myself to other pursuits and contemplations, I must first see, at least, that I do not pursue them sitting upon another man's shoulders. I must get off him first, that he may pursue his contemplations too. See what gross inconsistency is tolerated. I have heard some of my townsmen say, "I should like to have them order me out to help put down an insurrection of the slaves, or to march to Mexico—see if I would go"; and yet these very men have each, directly by their allegiance, and so indirectly, at least, by their money, furnished a substitute. The soldier is applauded who refuses to serve in an unjust war by those who do not refuse to sustain the unjust government which makes the war; is applauded by those whose own act and authority he disregards and sets at naught; as if the state were penitent to that degree that it hired one to scourge it while it sinned, but not to that degree that it left off sinning for a moment. Thus, under the name of Order and Civil Government, we are all made at last to pay homage to and support our own meanness. After the first blush of sin comes its indifference; and from immoral it becomes, as it were, *un*moral, and not quite unnecessary to that life which we have made. . . .

If the injustice is part of the necessary friction of the machine of government, let it go, let it go: perchance it will wear smooth—certainly the machine will wear out. If the injustice has a spring, or a pulley, or a rope, or a crank, exclusively for itself, then perhaps you may consider whether the remedy will not be worse than the evil; but if it is of such a nature that it requires you to be the agent of injustice to another, then, I say, break the law. Let your life be a counter friction to stop the machine. What I have to do is to see, at any rate, that I do not lend myself to the wrong which I condemn.

As for adopting the ways which the state has provided for remedying the evil, I know not of such ways. They take too much time, and a man's life will be gone. I have other affairs to attend to. I came into this world, not chiefly to make this a good place to live in, but to live in it, be it good or bad. A man has not everything to do, but something; and because he cannot do *everything,* it is not necessary that he should do *something* wrong. It is not my business to be petitioning the Governor or the Legislature any more than it is theirs to petition me; and if they should not hear my petition, what should I do then? But in this case the state has provided no way: its very Constitution is the evil. This may seem to be harsh and stubborn and unconciliatory; but it is to treat with the utmost kindness and consideration the only spirit that can appreciate or deserves it. So is all change for the better, like birth and death, which convulse the body.

I do not hesitate to say, that those who call themselves Abolitionists should at once effectually withdraw their support, both in person and property, from the government of Massachusetts, and not wait till they constitute a majority of one, before they suffer the right to prevail through them. I think that it is enough if they have God on their side, without waiting for that other one. Moreover, any man more right than his neighbors constitutes a majority of one already.

I meet this American government, or its representative, the state government, directly, and face to face, once a year—no more—in the person of its tax-gatherer; this is the only mode in which a man situated as I am necessarily meets it; and it then says distinctly, Recognize me; and the simplest, the most effectual, and, in the present posture of affairs, the indispensablest mode of treating with it on this head, of expressing your little satisfaction with and love for it is to deny it then. My civil neighbor, the tax-gatherer, is the very man I have to deal with—for it is, after all, with men and not with parchment that I quarrel—and he has voluntarily chosen to be an agent of the government. How shall he ever know well what he is and does as an officer of the government, or as a man, until he is obliged to consider whether he shall treat me, his neighbor, for whom he has respect, as a neighbor and well-disposed man, or as a maniac and disturber of the peace, and see if he can get over this obstruction to his neighborliness without a ruder and more impetuous thought or speech corresponding with his action. I know this well, that if one thousand, if one hundred, if ten men whom I could name,—if ten *honest* men only—ay, if *one* HONEST man, in this State of Massachusetts, *ceasing to hold slaves*, were actually to withdraw from this co-partnership, and be locked up in the county jail therefore, it would be the abolition of slavery in America. For it matters not how small the beginning may seem to be: what is once well done is done forever. . . .

I have paid no poll tax for six years. I was put into a jail once on this account, for one night; and, as I stood considering the walls of solid stone, two or three feet thick, the door of wood and iron, a foot thick, and the iron grating which strained the light, I could not help being struck with the foolishness of that institution which treated me as if I were mere flesh and blood and bones, to be locked up. I wondered that it should have concluded at length that this was the best use it could put me to, and had never thought to avail itself of my services in some way. I saw that, if there was a wall of stone between me and my townsmen, there was a still more difficult one to climb or break through before they could get to be as free as I was. I did not for a moment feel confined, and the walls seemed a great waste of stone and mortar. I felt as if I alone of all my townsmen had paid my tax. They plainly did not know how to treat me, but behaved like persons who are underbred. In every threat and in every compliment there was a blunder; for they thought that my chief desire was to stand the other side of that stone wall, I could not but smile to see how industriously they locked the door on my meditations, which followed them out again without let or hindrance, and *they* were really all that was dangerous. As they could not reach me, they had resolved to punish my body; just as boys, if they cannot come at some person against whom they have a spite, will abuse his dog. I saw that the State was half-witted, that it was timid as a lone woman with her silver spoons, and that it did not know its friends from its foes, and I lost all my remaining respect for it, and pitied it. . . .

When I came out of prison—for someone interfered, and paid that tax[2]—I did not perceive that great changes had taken place on the common, such as he observed who went in a youth and emerged a tottering and gray-headed man; and yet a change had to my eyes come over the scene—the town, and State, and country—greater than any that mere time could effect. I saw yet more distinctly the State in which I lived. I saw to what extent the people among whom I lived could be trusted as good neighbors and friends; that their friendship was for summer weather only; that they did not greatly propose to do right; that they were a distinct race from me by their prejudices and superstitions, as the Chinamen and Malays are; that in their sacrifices to humanity they ran no risks, not even to their property; that after all they were not so noble but they treated the thief as he had treated them, and hoped, by a certain outward observance and a few prayers, and by walking in a particular straight though useless path from time to time, to save their souls. This may be to judge my neighbors

---

2. *someone . . . tax.* According to legend, Ralph Waldo Emerson paid the tax, but according to Thoreau family reminiscence, it was paid by Thoreau's Aunt Maria.

harshly; for I believe that many of them are not aware that they have such an institution as the jail in their village. . . .

If others pay the tax which is demanded of me, from a sympathy with the State, they do but what they have already done in their own case, or rather they abet injustice to a greater extent than the State requires. If they pay the tax from a mistaken interest in the individual taxed, to save his property, or prevent his going to jail, it is because they have not considered wisely how far they let their private feelings interfere with the public good. . . .

The authority of government, even such as I am willing to submit to—for I will cheerfully obey those who know and can do better than I, and in many things even those who neither know nor can do so well—is still an impure one: to be strictly just, it must have the sanction and consent of the governed. It can have no pure right over my person and property but what I conceded to it. The progress from an absolute to a limited monarchy, from a limited monarchy to a democracy, is a progress toward a true respect for the individual. Even the Chinese philosopher[3] was wise enough to regard the individual as the basis of the empire. Is a democracy, such as we know it, the last improvement possible in government? Is it not possible to take a step further towards recognizing and organizing the rights of man? There will never be a really free and enlightened State until the State comes to recognize the individual as a higher and independent power, from which all its own power and authority are derived, and treats him accordingly. I please myself with imagining a State at last which can afford to be just to all men, and to treat the individual with respect as a neighbor; which even would not think it inconsistent with its own repose if a few were to live aloof from it, not meddling with it, nor embraced by it, who fulfilled all the duties of neighbors and fellowmen. A State which bore this kind of fruit, and suffered it to drop off as fast as it ripened, would prepare the way for a still more perfect and glorious State, which also I have imagined, but not yet anywhere seen.

1849

---

3. *Chinese philosopher*, Confucius (?551-478 B.C.), whose ethical teachings emphasize dutiful obedience by individuals to their parents, elders, and the state.

THINK AND DISCUSS
Understanding
1. What kind of government is best, according to the first paragraph?
2. What is the only way that government has "furthered any enterprise," according to paragraph two?
3. What, instead of the majority, should decide right and wrong, according to paragraph four?
4. Why was Thoreau put into jail for one night? Why did he consider his jailers foolish?

5. Under what conditions will there be "a really free and enlightened State," according to the final paragraph?

Analyzing
6. Thoreau presents his readers with two major justifications for civil disobedience. Using references to his essay, explain what these justifications are.
7. Thoreau says, "I think we should be men first and subjects afterward." Explain this statement in the light of his essay.
8. Write a sentence in your own words that states the main idea of Thoreau's essay.

Find six sentences from Thoreau's essay that support this idea.

9. Thoreau's essay is a combination of abstract argument and personal anecdote. Which of the two do you think is more effective in illustrating his main idea?

Extending

10. Compose an **epigram** that embodies one of the ideas Thoreau expresses in his essay on civil disobedience.
11. What similarities exist between Thoreau's attitude toward government and Emerson's philosophy in "A Nonconformist"? Support your answer with lines from both essays.

VOCABULARY
Dictionary

Thoreau presents a tightly constructed argument in his essay on civil disobedience. To follow the argument closely, the reader must know the vocabulary Thoreau is using. Check the Glossary for the definitions of the italicized words in the following sentences. Then, using your own words entirely, write a paraphrase of each passage. Be sure you can spell all the italicized words.

1. "Government is at best but an *expedient;* but most governments are usually, and all governments are sometimes, *inexpedient.*"
2. "Yet this government never of itself furthered any enterprise, but by the *alacrity* with which it got out of its way. . . . The character *inherent* in the American people has done all that has been accomplished; and it would have done somewhat more, if the government had not sometimes got in its way."
3. "It is not a man's duty, as a matter of course, to devote himself to the *eradication* of any, even the most enormous wrong. . . . "
4. "The soldier is applauded who refuses to serve in an unjust war by those who do not refuse to sustain the unjust government which makes the war . . . as if the state were *penitent* to that degree that it hired one to *scourge* it while it sinned, but not to that degree that it left off sinning for a moment."

COMPOSITION
Writing Epigrams

Compose a list of topics about which you feel strongly. You might want to consider topics such as fads, clothes, education, leisure, or jobs. Write two or three epigrams based on your chosen topic(s) that could serve as captions accompanying your picture in the school yearbook.

Writing About an Author's Philosophy

Choose one of the following quotations by Thoreau as the topic of a personal essay of at least four paragraphs written for your classmates. Write a thesis statement that expresses your opinion about the quotation. Include vivid images and details from your experience that reinforce your opinion. Decide what tone—humorous, angry, light, serious—will best convey your ideas.

• "Rather than love, than money, than fame, give me truth."
• "That government is best which governs least."
• "If a man does not keep pace with his companions, perhaps it is because he hears a different drummer."
• "There is an incessant influx of novelty into the world, and yet we tolerate incredible dullness."

ENRICHMENT
Making a Poster

Many of Thoreau's statements, as well as those of Emerson, can easily be incorporated into the modern medium of poster art. Choose a statement by one of these authors and design and produce an illustrated poster that dramatically portrays a related idea. Feel free to either draw or paint the graphics, or, if you prefer, to create a collage of illustrations cut out from magazines or newpapers. Ask your teacher to display your work in the classroom.

Seattle was the chief of the Duwamish and Suquamish, who were fishing tribes of the Northwest. The suffix -*amish* in many of the names of tribes indicates that each was located near a river.

The city of Seattle is named after the Chief. Legend has it that he did not want the city to bear his name because he thought that every time his name was spoken after his death, his spirit would be troubled.

Before signing a treaty yielding his tribe's lands near Puget Sound to white settlers, Chief Seattle made the following speech to Isaac Stevens, Governor of Washington Territory, in 1854.

 See **FIGURATIVE LANGUAGE** in the Handbook of Literary Terms, page 886.

This Sacred Soil

Chief Seattle

onder sky that has wept tears of compassion upon my people for centuries untold and which to us appears changeless and eternal, may change. Today is fair. Tomorrow it may be overcast with clouds. My words are like the stars that never change. Whatever Seattle says the great chief at Washington can rely upon with as much certainty as he can upon the return of the sun or the seasons. The White Chief says that Big Chief at Washington sends us greetings of friendship and goodwill. That is kind of him for we know he has little need of our friendship in return. His people are many. They are like the grass that covers vast prairies. My people are few. They resemble the scattering trees of a storm-swept plain. . . . I will not dwell on, nor mourn over, our untimely decay, nor reproach our paleface brothers with hastening it, as we too may have been somewhat to blame. . . .

Your God is not our God. Your God loves your people and hates mine. He folds his strong and protecting arms lovingly about the paleface and leads him by the hand as a father leads his infant son—but He has forsaken His red children—if they really are his. Our God, the Great Spirit, seems also to have forsaken us. Your God makes your people strong every day. Soon they will fill the land. Our people are ebbing away like a

From *Northwest Gateway: The Story of the Port of Seattle* by Archie Binns. Copyright 1941, pp. 100–104. Reprinted by permission of Ellen F. Binns.

rapidly receding tide that will never return. The white man's God cannot love our people or He would protect them. They seem to be orphans who can look nowhere for help. How then can we be brothers? . . . We are two distinct races with separate origins and separate destinies. There is little in common between us.

To us the ashes of our ancestors are sacred and their resting place is hallowed ground. You wander far from the graves of your ancestors and seemingly without regret. Your religion was written upon tables of stone by the iron finger of your God so that you could not forget. The Red Man could never comprehend nor remember it. Our religion is the traditions of our ancestors—the dreams of our old men, given them in solemn hours of night by the Great Spirit; and the visions of our sachems; and it is written in the hearts of our people.

Your dead cease to love you and the land of their nativity as soon as they pass the portals of the tomb and wander way beyond the stars. They are soon forgotten and never return. Our dead never forget the beautiful world that gave them being.

Day and night cannot dwell together. The Red Man has ever fled the approach of the White Man, as the morning mist flees before the morning sun. However, your proposition seems fair and I think that my people will accept it and will retire to the reservation you offer them. Then we will dwell apart in peace. . . . It matters little where we pass the remnant of our days. They will not be many. A few more moons; a few more winters—and not one of the descendants of the mighty hosts that once moved over this broad land or lived in happy homes, protected by the Great Spirit, will remain to mourn over the graves of a people once more powerful and hopeful than yours. But why should I mourn at the untimely fate of my people? Tribe follows tribe, and nation follows nation, like the waves of the sea. It is the order of nature, and regret is useless. Your time of decay may be distant, but it will surely come, for even the White Man whose God walked and talked with him as friend with friend, cannot be exempt from the common destiny. We may be brothers after all. We will see. . . .

Every part of this soil is sacred in the estimation of my people. Every hillside, every valley, every plain and grove, has been hallowed by some sad or happy event in days long vanished. The very dust upon which you now stand responds more lovingly to their footsteps than to yours, because it is rich with the blood of our ancestors and our bare feet are conscious of the sympathetic touch. Even the little children who lived here and rejoiced here for a brief season will love these somber solitudes and at eventide they greet shadowy returning spirits. And when the last Red Man shall have perished, and the memory of my tribe shall have become a myth among the White Men, these shores will swarm with the invisible dead of my tribe, and when your children's children think themselves alone in the field, the store, the shop, upon the highway, or in the silence of the pathless woods, they will not be alone. At night when the streets of your cities and villages are silent and you think them deserted, they will throng with the returning hosts that once filled and still love this beautiful land. The White Man will never be alone.

Let him be just and deal kindly with my people, for the dead are not powerless. Dead, did I say? There is no death, only a change of worlds.

1854

THINK AND DISCUSS

Understanding

1. Who is the Big Chief at Washington? What has he sent Seattle and his people?
2. To what does Seattle agree in the treaty he signs (230a, 3)?

Analyzing

3. How does Seattle's religion differ from that of the "White Man," as described in paragraph three?
4. What has led to the "untimely decay" of Seattle's people?
5. How do Seattle's people view the dead? In what way does this view contribute to his concept of the sacredness of the soil?
6. Seattle's **style** is marked by parallelism: "Tribe follows tribe, and nation follows nation." Find two other examples of parallelism.

Extending

7. In the last line, Seattle says, "There is no death, only a change of worlds." Compare this line with lines 22–29 of "Thanatopsis" (page 129). Explain whether the philosophies are the same or different.
8. The Chief says: ". . . when the last Red Man shall have perished, and the memory of my tribe shall have become a myth among the White Men, these shores will swarm with the invisible dead of my tribe . . . they will throng with the returning hosts that once filled and still love this beautiful land." In what ways has Seattle's prophecy come true in contemporary attitudes toward Native American cultures—past and present?

APPLYING: Figurative Language H*

See Handbook of Literary Terms, p. 886.

Figurative language goes beyond the usual, or literal, meaning of words to express relationships between things that are basically dissimilar. Some of the more frequently used figures of speech are **simile, metaphor, personification,** and **synecdoche.** In his speech, Chief Seattle draws upon nature to create memorable and moving figurative language.

1. In his opening sentence, Seattle observes "Yonder sky that has wept tears of compassion. . . ." What type of figurative language is he using?
2. What items are being compared in the following statement: "My words are like the stars that never change"? What assurance is Seattle making in this simile?
3. How would you rewrite the following lines as a simile—"My people are few. They resemble the scattering trees of a storm-swept plain . . ."?

ENRICHMENT

Oral Report

Just as the Northwest regions of the country were settled by the Duwamish and Suquamish fishing tribes, specific areas all across the rest of the United States were once inhabited by tribes who developed their own distinctive ways of life. Investigate the indigenous people associated with an area near you. Compose a profile of the main points you learn about their history and culture. Prepare an oral report for your classmates supplemented by maps, drawings, graphs, or any other form of illustration that you can create or reproduce.

BIOGRAPHY

Harriet Hanson Robinson
1825–1911

A leader of the women's movement of the nineteenth century, Harriet Robinson worked in the Lowell cotton mills of Massachusetts after finishing school. She contributed to *The Lowell Offering*, a periodical by and for women working in the mills. She and her husband, a journalist, campaigned against slavery and for women's rights and reform of factory working conditions. Her writing in support of these causes was influential and included the plays *Captain Mary Miller* (1887) and *The New Pandora* (1889). *Loom and Spindle, or Life Among the Early Mill Girls* (1898), from which the following excerpt is taken, is her most notable work.

from Loom and Spindle

Harriet Hanson Robinson

t the time the Lowell cotton mills were started, the factory girl was the lowest among women. In England, and in France particularly, great injustice had been done to her real character; she was represented as subjected to influences that could not fail to destroy her purity and self-respect. In the eyes of her overseer she was but a brute, a slave, to be beaten, pinched, and pushed about. It was to overcome this prejudice that such high wages had been offered to women that they might be induced to become mill girls, in spite of the opprobrium that still clung to this "degrading occupation." At first only a few came; for, though tempted by the high wages to be regularly paid in "cash," there were many who still preferred to go on working at some more *genteel* employment at seventy-five cents a week and their board.

But in a short time the prejudice against factory labor wore away, and the Lowell mills became filled with blooming and energetic New England women.

One of the first strikes of cotton-factory operatives that ever took place in this country was that in Lowell, in October, 1836. When it was announced that the wages were to be cut down, great indignation was felt, and it was decided to strike, *en masse*.[1] This was done. The mills

---

1. *en masse* (en mas'), all together. [*French*]

Portions of *Loom and Spindle*, Revised Edition, Copyright © 1976 by Press Pacifica, are reprinted by permission of Press Pacifica, Kailua, Hawaii.

were shut down, and the girls went in procession from their several corporations to the "grove" on Chapel Hill, and listened to "incendiary" speeches from early labor reformers.

One of the girls stood on a pump, and gave vent to the feelings of her companions in a neat speech, declaring that it was their duty to resist all attempts at cutting down the wages. This was the first time a woman had spoken in public in Lowell, and the event caused surprise and consternation among her audience.

Cutting down the wages was not their only grievance, nor the only cause of the strike. Hitherto the corporations had paid twenty-five cents a week towards the board of each operative, and now it was their purpose to have the girls pay the sum; and this, in addition to the cut in wages, would make a difference of at least one dollar a week. It was estimated that as many as twelve or fifteen hundred girls turned out, and walked in procession through the streets. They had neither flags nor music, but sang songs, a favorite (but rather inappropriate) one being a parody on "I Won't Be a Nun."

"Oh! isn't it a pity, such a pretty girl as I—
Should be sent to the factory to pine away
    and die?
Oh! I cannot be a slave,
I will not be a slave,
For I'm so fond of liberty
That I cannot be a slave."

My own recollection of this first strike (or "turn out" as it was called) is very vivid. I worked in a lower room, where I had heard the proposed strike fully, if not vehemently, discussed; I had been an ardent listener to what was said against this attempt at "oppression" on the part of the corporation, and naturally I took sides with the strikers. When the day came on which the girls were to turn out, those in the upper rooms started first, and so many of them left that our mill was at once shut down. Then, when the girls in my room stood irresolute, uncertain what to do, asking each other, "Would you?" or "Shall we turn

out?" and not one of them having the courage to lead off, I, who began to think they would not go out, after all their talk, became impatient, and started on ahead, saying, with childish bravado, "I don't care what you do, *I* am going to turn out, whether anyone else does or not"; and I marched out, and was followed by the others.

As I looked back at the long line that followed me, I was more proud than I have ever been since at any success I may have achieved, and more proud than I shall ever be again until my own beloved State gives to its women citizens the right of suffrage.

The agent of the corporation where I then worked took some small revenges on the supposed ringleaders; on the principle of sending the weaker to the wall, my mother was turned away from her boardinghouse, that functionary saying, "Mrs. Hanson, you could not prevent the older girls from turning out, but your daughter is a child, and *her* you could control."

It is hardly necessary to say that so far as results were concerned this strike did no good. The dissatisfaction of the operatives subsided, or burned itself out, and though the authorities did not accede to their demands, the majority returned to their work, and the corporation went on cutting down the wages.

One of the most curious phases in the life of New England, and one that must always puzzle the historian of its literature, is its sudden intellectual blossoming half a century ago.

Emerson says, "The children of New England between 1820 and 1840 were born with knives in their brains"; and this would seem to be true, since during or very near that time, were born the majority of those writers and thinkers whose lives have been so recently and so nobly rounded out —Emerson, Bryant, Longfellow, Lowell, Whittier, John Pierpont—they whose influence cannot be overestimated in bringing an ideal element into our hitherto prosaic New England life.

And the "literary" girls among us would often be seen writing on scraps of paper which we hid "between whiles" in the waste boxes upon which we sat while waiting for the looms or frames to

Winslow Homer (1836–1910), *Mill Girls Winding Bobbins.*
Merrimack Valley Textile Museum

In January, 1845, the magazine had on its outside cover a vignette, a young girl simply dressed, with feet visible and sleeves rolled up. She had a book in one hand, and her shawl and bonnet were thrown over her arm. She was represented as standing in a very sentimental attitude, contemplating a beehive at her right hand. This vignette was adopted, as the editor said, "To represent the New England schoolgirl, of which our factories are made up, standing near a beehive, emblem of industry and intelligence, and in the background the Yankee schoolhouse, church, and factory." The motto was:

"The worm on the earth
May look up to the star."

This rather abject sentiment was not suited to the independent spirit of most of the contributors, who did not feel a bit like worms; and in the February number it was changed to one from Bunyan.[4]

"And do you think the words of your book are certainly true?"
"Yea, verily."

The magazine finally died, however, under its favorite motto:

"Is Saul also among the prophets?"

The contributions to *The Offering* were on a great variety of subjects. There were allegories, poems, conversations on physiology, astronomy, and other scientific subjects, dissertations on poetry, and on the beauties of nature, didactic pieces on highly moral and religious subjects, translations from French and Latin, stories of factory and other life, sketches of local New Eng-

need attention. Some of these studious ones kept notebooks, with abstracts of their reading and studies, or jotted down what they were pleased to call their "thoughts." It was natural that such a thoughtful life should bear fruit, and this leads me to speak of *The Lowell Offering*, a publication which was the natural outgrowth of the mental habit of the early mill girls, for many of the pieces that were printed there were thought out amid the hum of the wheels, while the skillful fingers and well-trained eyes of the writers tended the loom or the frame.

The Lowell Offering was a small, thin magazine of about thirty pages, with one column to the page. The price of the first number was six and a quarter cents. Its title page was plain, with a motto from Gray;[2] the verse beginning:

"Full many a gem of purest ray serene."

This motto was used for two years, when another was adopted:

"Is Saul also among the prophets?"[3]

2. Gray, Thomas Gray (1716–1771), an English poet best known for his odes and elegies.
3. "Is Saul also among the prophets?" a biblical allusion to the first king of Israel, who was called to leadership by the prophet Samuel. (I Samuel 10:11)
4. Bunyan, John Bunyan (1628–1688), an English writer whose most famous work, *The Pilgrim's Progress*, is an allegorical account of the attainment of heaven.

land history, and sometimes the chapters of a novel. Miss Curtis, in 1840, wrote an article on "Women's Rights," in which were so many familiar arguments in favor of the equality of the sexes, that it might have been the production of the pen of almost any modern advocate of woman's rights; but there was this difference, that the writer, though she felt sure of her ground, was too timid to maintain it against the world, and towards the end throws out the query, "whether public life is, after all, woman's most appropriate and congenial sphere?"

These authors represent what may be called the poetic element of factory life. They were the ideal mill girls, full of hopes, desires, aspirations; poets of the loom, spinners of verse, artists of factory life.

The Lowell Offering did a good work, not only among the operatives themselves, but among the rural population from which they had been drawn. It was almost the only magazine that reached their secluded homes, where it was lent from house to house, read and reread, and thus set the women to thinking, and added its little leaven of progressive thought to the times in which it lived.

1898

THINK AND DISCUSS
Understanding
1. Why was factory work at first considered a "degrading occupation" for a female?
2. What eventually caused the Lowell mills to be "filled with blooming and energetic New England women"?
3. What were the two causes of the Lowell cotton factory strike?
4. What was the author's role in the strike? What "small revenge" was taken on her mother?
5. Which writers and thinkers does the author mention "whose influence cannot be overestimated"?
6. What was *The Lowell Offering?*

Analyzing
7. What is Robinson's attitude toward management and the owners of the mill?
8. What personal qualities does the author demonstrate in her actions during the strike?
9. What do you think Emerson meant when he referred to the children of New England as being "born with knives in their brains"?

Extending
10. Do you think Emerson and Thoreau would have supported Robinson's actions during the factory walkout? Give reasons for your opinion.

COMPOSITION
Writing a Narrative
Write a narrative of several paragraphs about a time when you had to take the initiative while those around you hesitated. First, describe the situation and the choices facing you and your companions. Next, explain their behavior and probable reasons for hesitating, along with your own motivation. Conclude by describing your feelings about the incident.

Planning a Magazine
In the second half of this selection, Robinson describes the authors, design, titles, motto, table of contents, audience, and even the effect of *The Lowell Offering.* Assume that a grant is available for a publication of your own creation and design. Describe in two paragraphs the "magazine of your dreams," indicating the audience to whom it will be directed. Then design a cover and write a table of contents for the first issue.

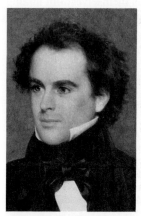

Detail of portrait by
Charles Osgood (1809–1890).
Essex Institute, Salem,
Massachusetts

One of Hawthorne's ancestors was involved in prosecuting the "witches" in Salem, Massachusetts, in the 1690s, and Hawthorne, born in Salem, was haunted by this ancestral guilt. In the introductory essay to his most widely acclaimed work, *The Scarlet Letter*, Hawthorne proclaimed that he took the shame upon himself, and hoped thereby to dispel the family curse.

Hawthorne was the son of a shipmaster who died when the boy was four. Brought up in a disciplined household where his mother took many meals in her room, he acquired what he called the "cursed habits" of solitude. After attending Bowdoin College in Maine, he returned home and devoted himself to writing (and destroying) stories, learning his craft while living in isolation. Although he did make occasional forays into the New England countryside and villages, where he gathered material for his later stories, he romanticized this period as the "twelve dark years." Gradually, Hawthorne's tales began to appear in magazines, and in 1837 he gathered a number of these published pieces into a volume titled *Twice-Told Tales*.

In 1842 when Hawthorne moved to the house in Concord, Massachusetts, known as the "Old Manse," he wrote in the very room where Emerson had written his essay on nature six years earlier. "Young Goodman Brown" is among the stories published in 1846 in the collection called *Mosses from an Old Manse*. Along with Poe, Hawthorne became a leader in the development of the short story.

Hawthorne was acquainted with the leading Transcendentalists of his time, often meeting with Emerson and his group to discuss the philosophy. He spent several months at Brook Farm, the experiment in communal living founded by a number of these Transcendentalists. Hawthorne married Sophia Peabody, an ardent advocate of Transcendentalism, yet he himself never fully adopted the philosophy. His strong sense of the active presence of evil in the world was more compatible with America's Puritan tradition.

In addition to his novel, *The Scarlet Letter* (1850), written a year before Melville's *Moby Dick*, Hawthorne wrote three other notable works: *The House of the Seven Gables*, an account of an ancestral curse; *The Blithedale Romance*, based on Hawthorne's experiences in the ill-fated experiment in communal living at Brook Farm in the early 1840s; and *The Marble Faun*, a tale of "innocent" Americans in "decadent and treacherous" Italy.

However much Hawthorne criticized his Puritan heritage in his work, he never fully emerged from its shadow. Herman Melville, a close friend and kindred spirit, wrote of him: " . . . in spite of all the Indian-summer sunlight on the hither side of Hawthorne's soul, the other side—like the dark half of the physical sphere—is shrouded in a blackness, ten times black."

See FORESHADOWING in the Handbook of Literary Terms, page 889.

Young Goodman Brown

Nathaniel Hawthorne

oung Goodman Brown came forth at sunset into the street at Salem village; but put his head back, after crossing the threshold, to exchange a parting kiss with his young wife. And Faith, as the wife was aptly named, thrust her own pretty head into the street, letting the wind play with the pink ribbons of her cap while she called to Goodman Brown.

"Dearest heart," whispered she, softly and rather sadly, when her lips were close to his ear, "prithee put off your journey until sunrise and sleep in your own bed tonight. A lone woman is troubled with such dreams and such thoughts that she's afeard of herself sometimes. Pray tarry with me this night, dear husband, of all nights in the year."

"My love and my Faith," replied young Goodman Brown, "of all nights in the year, this one night must I tarry away from thee. My journey, as thou callest it, forth and back again, must needs be done 'twixt now and sunrise. What, my sweet, pretty wife, dost thou doubt me already, and we but three months married?"

"Then God bless you!" said Faith, with the pink ribbons; "and may you find all well when you come back."

"Amen!" cried Goodman Brown. "Say thy prayers, dear Faith, and go to bed at dusk, and no harm will come to thee."

So they parted; and the young man pursued his way until, being about to turn the corner by the meetinghouse, he looked back and saw the head of Faith still peeping after him with a melancholy air, in spite of her pink ribbons.

"Poor little Faith!" thought he, for his heart smote him. "What a wretch am I to leave her on such an errand! She talks of dreams, too. Me thought as she spoke there was trouble in her face, as if a dream had warned her what work is to be done tonight. But no, no; 'twould kill her to think it. Well, she's a blessed angel on earth; and after this one night I'll cling to her skirts and follow her to heaven."

With this excellent resolve for the future, Goodman Brown felt himself justified in making more haste on his present evil purpose. He had taken a dreary road, darkened by all the gloomiest trees of the forest, which barely stood aside to let the narrow path creep through, and closed immediately behind. It was all as lonely as could be; and there is this peculiarity in such a solitude, that the traveler knows not who may be concealed by the innumerable trunks and the thick boughs overhead; so that with lonely footsteps he may yet be passing through an unseen multitude.

"There may be a devilish Indian behind every tree," said Goodman Brown to himself; and he glanced fearfully behind him as he added, "What if the devil himself should be at my very elbow!"

His head being turned back, he passed a crook of the road, and, looking forward again, beheld the figure of a man, in grave and decent attire, seated at the foot of an old tree. He arose at Goodman Brown's approach and walked onward side by side with him.

"You are late, Goodman Brown," said he. "The clock of the Old South was striking as I came through Boston, and that is full fifteen minutes agone."

"Faith kept me back a while," replied the young man, with a tremor in his voice, caused by the sudden appearance of his companion, though not wholly unexpected.

It was now deep dusk in the forest, and deepest in that part of it where these two were journeying. As nearly as could be discerned, the second traveler was about fifty years old, apparently in the same rank of life as Goodman Brown, and bearing a considerable resemblance to him, though perhaps more in expression than features. Still they might have been taken for father and son. And yet, though the elder person was as simply clad as the younger, and as simple in manner too, he had an indescribable air of one who knew the world, and who would not have felt abashed at the governor's dinner table or in King William's court,[1] were it possible that his affairs should call him thither. But the only thing about him that could be fixed upon as remarkable was his staff, which bore the likeness of a great black snake, so curiously wrought that it might almost be seen to twist and wriggle itself like a living serpent. This, of course, must have been an ocular deception, assisted by the uncertain light.

"Come, Goodman Brown," cried his fellow traveler, "this is a dull pace for the beginning of a journey. Take my staff, if you are so soon weary."

"Friend," said the other, exchanging his slow pace for a full stop, "having kept covenant by meeting thee here, it is my purpose now to return whence I came. I have scruples touching the matter thou wot'st of."

"Sayest thou so?" replied he of the serpent, smiling apart. "Let us walk on, nevertheless, reasoning as we go; and if I convince thee not thou shalt turn back. We are but a little way in the forest yet."

"Too far! too far!" exclaimed the good man, unconsciously resuming his walk. "My father never went into the woods on such an errand, nor his father before him. We have been a race of honest men and good Christians since the days of the martyrs; and shall I be the first of the name of Brown that ever took this path and kept——"

"Such company, thou wouldst say," observed the elder person, interpreting his pause. "Well said, Goodman Brown! I have been as well acquainted with your family as with ever a one among the Puritans; and that's no trifle to say. I helped your grandfather, the constable, when he lashed the Quaker woman so smartly through the streets of Salem; and it was I that brought your father a pitchpine knot, kindled at my own hearth, to set fire to an Indian village, in King Philip's war.[2] They were my good friends, both; and many a pleasant walk have we had along this path, and returned merrily after midnight. I would fain be friends with you for their sake."

"If it be as thou sayest," replied Goodman Brown, "I marvel they never spoke of these matters; or, verily, I marvel not, seeing that the least rumor of the sort would have driven them from New England. We are a people of prayer, and good works to boot, and abide no such wickedness."

"Wickedness or not," said the traveler with the twisted staff, "I have a very general acquaintance here in New England. The deacons of many a church have drunk the communion wine with me; the selectmen of divers towns make me their chairman; and a majority of the Great and General Court are firm supporters of my interest. The governor and I, too—But these are state secrets."

"Can this be so?" cried Goodman Brown, with a stare of amazement at his undisturbed companion. "Howbeit, I have nothing to do with the governor and council; they have their own ways, and are no rule for a simple husbandman like me. But, were I to go on with thee, how should I

---

1. *King William's court.* William of Orange (1650–1702), was declared William III of England when James II abdicated in 1689. King William ruled as joint sovereign with his wife Mary for the first five years of his reign, which lasted until 1702.

2. *King Philip's war.* King Philip was an Indian chief of New England who led a war against the colonists from 1675 to 1676.

meet the eye of that good old man, our minister, at Salem village? Oh, his voice would make me tremble both Sabbath day and lecture day."

Thus far the elder traveler had listened with due gravity; but now burst into a fit of irrepressible mirth, shaking himself so violently that his snakelike staff actually seemed to wriggle in sympathy.

"Ha! ha! ha!" shouted he again and again; then composing himself, "Well, go on, Goodman Brown, go on; but, prithee, don't kill me with laughing."

"Well, then, to end the matter at once," said Goodman Brown, considerably nettled, "there is my wife, Faith. It would break her dear little heart; and I'd rather break my own."

"Nay, if that be the case," answered the other, "e'en go thy ways, Goodman Brown. I would not for twenty old women like the one hobbling before us that Faith should come to any harm."

As he spoke he pointed his staff at a female figure on the path, in whom Goodman Brown recognized a very pious and exemplary dame, who had taught him his catechism in youth, and was still his moral and spiritual adviser, jointly with the minister and Deacon Gookin.

"A marvel, truly, that Goody[3] Cloyse should be so far in the wilderness at nightfall," said he. "But with your leave, friend, I shall take a cut through the woods until we have left this Christian woman behind. Being a stranger to you, she might ask whom I was consorting with and whither I was going."

"Be it so," said his fellow traveler. "Betake you to the woods, and let me keep the path."

Accordingly the young man turned aside, but took care to watch his companion, who advanced softly along the road until he had come within a staff's length of the old dame. She, meanwhile, was making the best of her way, with singular speed for so aged a woman, and mumbling some indistinct words—a prayer, doubtless—as she went. The traveler put forth his staff and touched her withered neck with what seemed the serpent's tail.

"The devil!" screamed the pious old lady.

"Then Goody Cloyse knows her old friend?" observed the traveler, confronting her and leaning on his writhing stick.

"Ah, forsooth, and is it your worship indeed?" cried the good dame. "Yea, truly is it, and in the very image of my old gossip, Goodman Brown, the grandfather of the silly fellow that now is. But—would your worship believe it?—my broomstick hath strangely disappeared, stolen, as I suspect, by that unhanged witch, Goody Cory, and that, too, when I was all anointed with the juice of smallage, and cinquefoil, and wolf's bane——"

"Mingled with fine wheat and the fat of a newborn babe," said the shape of old Goodman Brown.

"Ah, your worship knows the recipe," cried the old lady, cackling aloud. "So, as I was saying, being all ready for the meeting, and no horse to ride on, I made up my mind to foot it; for they tell me there is a nice young man to be taken into communion tonight. But now your good worship will lend me your arm, and we shall be there in a twinkling."

"That can hardly be," answered her friend. "I may not spare you my arm, Goody Cloyse; but here is my staff, if you will."

So saying, he threw it down at her feet, where, perhaps, it assumed life, being one of the rods which its owner had formerly lent to the Egyptian magi.[4] Of this fact, however, Goodman Brown could not take cognizance. He had cast up his eyes in astonishment, and, looking down again, beheld neither Goody Cloyse nor the serpentine staff, but his fellow traveler alone, who waited for him as calmly as if nothing had happened.

"That old woman taught me my catechism," said the young man; and there was a world of meaning in this simple comment.

They continued to walk onward, while the elder traveler exhorted his companion to make

---

3. **Goody,** Mrs., housewife; feminine equivalent to Goodman.
4. **Egyptian magi.** The Egyptian Pharaoh's magicians cast down rods which changed into snakes. (Exodus 7:11)

good speed and persevere in the path, discoursing so aptly that his arguments seemed rather to spring up in the bosom of his auditor than to be suggested by himself. As they went, he plucked a branch of maple to serve for a walking stick, and began to strip it of the twigs and little boughs, which were wet with evening dew. The moment his fingers touched them they became strangely withered and dried up as with a week's sunshine. Thus the pair proceeded, at a good free pace, until suddenly, in a gloomy hollow of the road, Goodman Brown sat himself down on the stump of a tree and refused to go any farther.

"Friend," said he, stubbornly, "my mind is made up. Not another step will I budge on this errand. What if a wretched old woman do choose to go to the devil when I thought she was going to heaven: is that any reason why I should quit my dear Faith and go after her?"

"You will think better of this by and by," said his acquaintance, composedly. "Sit here and rest yourself a while; and when you feel like moving again, there is my staff to help you along."

Without more words, he threw his companion the maple stick, and was as speedily out of sight as if he had vanished into the deepening gloom. The young man sat a few moments by the roadside, applauding himself greatly, and thinking with how clear a conscience he should meet the minister in his morning walk, nor shrink from the eye of good old Deacon Gookin. And what calm sleep would be his that very night, which was to have been spent so wickedly, but so purely and sweetly now, in the arms of Faith! Amidst these pleasant and praiseworthy meditations, Goodman Brown heard the tramp of horses along the road, and deemed it advisable to conceal himself within the verge of the forest, conscious of the guilty purpose that had brought him thither, though now so happily turned from it.

On came the hoof tramps and the voices of the riders, two grave old voices, conversing soberly as they drew near. These mingled sounds appeared to pass along the road, within a few yards of the young man's hiding place; but, owing doubtless to the depth of the gloom at that particular spot,

neither the travelers nor their steeds were visible. Though their figures brushed the small boughs by the wayside, it could not be seen that they intercepted, even for a moment, the faint gleam from the strip of bright sky athwart which they must have passed. Goodman Brown alternately crouched and stood on tiptoe, pulling aside the branches and thrusting forth his head as far as he durst without discerning so much as a shadow. It vexed him the more, because he could have sworn, were such a thing possible, that he recognized the voices of the minister and Deacon Gookin, jogging along quietly, as they were wont to do, when bound to some ordination or ecclesiastical council. While yet within hearing, one of the riders stopped to pluck a switch.

"Of the two, reverend sir," said the voice like the deacon's, "I had rather miss an ordination dinner than tonight's meeting. They tell me that some of our community are to be here from Falmouth and beyond, and others from Connecticut and Rhode Island, besides several of the Indian powwows, who, after their fashion, know almost as much deviltry as the best of us. Moreover, there is a goodly young woman to be taken into communion."

"Mighty well, Deacon Gookin!" replied the solemn old tones of the minister. "Spur up, or we shall be late. Nothing can be done, you know, until I get on the ground."

The hoofs clattered again; and the voices, talking so strangely in the empty air, passed on through the forest, where no church had ever been gathered or solitary Christian prayed. Whither, then, could these holy men be journeying so deep into the heathen wilderness? Young Goodman Brown caught hold of a tree for support, being ready to sink down on the ground, faint and overburdened with the heavy sickness of his heart. He looked up to the sky, doubting whether there really was a heaven above him. Yet there was the blue arch, and the stars brightening in it.

"With heaven above and Faith below, I will yet stand firm against the devil!" cried Goodman Brown.

While he still gazed upward into the deep arch of the firmament and had lifted his hands to pray, a cloud, though no wind was stirring, hurried across the zenith and hid the brightening stars. The blue sky was still visible, except directly overhead, where this black mass of cloud was sweeping swiftly northward. Aloft in the air, as if from the depths of the cloud, came a confused and doubtful sound of voices. Once the listener fancied that he could distinguish the accents of townspeople of his own, men and women, both pious and ungodly, many of whom he had met at the communion table, and had seen others rioting at the tavern. The next moment, so indistinct were the sounds, he doubted whether he had heard aught but the murmur of the old forest, whispering without a wind. Then came a stronger swell of those familiar tones, heard daily in the sunshine at Salem village, but never until now from a cloud of night. There was one voice of a young woman, uttering lamentations, yet with an uncertain sorrow, and entreating for some favor, which, perhaps, it would grieve her to obtain; and all the unseen multitude, both saints and sinners, seemed to encourage her onward.

"Faith!" shouted Goodman Brown, in a voice of agony and desperation; and the echoes of the forest mocked him, crying, "Faith! Faith!" as if bewildered wretches were seeking her all through the wilderness.

The cry of grief, rage, and terror was yet piercing the night, when the unhappy husband held his breath for a response. There was a scream, drowned immediately in a louder murmur of voices, fading into far-off laughter, as the dark cloud swept away, leaving the clear and silent sky above Goodman Brown. But something fluttered lightly down through the air and caught on the branch of a tree. The young man seized it, and beheld a pink ribbon.

"My Faith is gone!" cried he, after one stupefied moment. "There is no good on earth; and sin is but a name. Come, devil; for to thee is this world given."

And, maddened with despair, so that he laughed loud and long, did Goodman Brown grasp his staff and set forth again, at such a rate that he seemed to fly along the forest path rather than to walk or run. The road grew wilder and drearier and more faintly traced, and vanished at length, leaving him in the heart of the dark wilderness, still rushing onward with the instinct that guides mortal man to evil. The whole forest was peopled with frightful sounds—the creaking of the trees, the howling of wild beasts, and the yell of Indians; while sometimes the wind tolled like a distant church bell, and sometimes gave a broad roar around the traveler, as if all Nature were laughing him to scorn. But he was himself the chief horror of the scene, and shrank not from its other horrors.

"Ha! ha! ha!" roared Goodman Brown when the wind laughed at him. "Let us hear which will laugh loudest. Think not to frighten me with your deviltry. Come witch, come wizard, come Indian powwow, come devil himself, and here comes Goodman Brown. You may as well fear him as he fear you."

In truth, all through the haunted forest there could be nothing more frightful than the figure of Goodman Brown. On he flew among the black pines, brandishing his staff with frenzied gestures, now giving vent to an inspiration of horrid blasphemy, and now shouting forth such laughter as set all the echoes of the forest laughing like demons around him. The fiend in his own shape is less hideous than when he rages in the breast of man. Thus sped the demoniac on his course, until, quivering among the trees, he saw a red light before him, as when the felled trunks and branches of a clearing have been set on fire, and throw up their lurid blaze against the sky, at the hour of midnight. He paused, in a lull of the tempest that had driven him onward, and heard the swell of what seemed a hymn, rolling solemnly from a distance with the weight of many voices. He knew the tune; it was a familiar one in the choir of the village meeting house. The verse died heavily away, and was lengthened by a chorus, not of human voices, but of all the sounds of the benighted wilderness pealing in awful harmony together. Goodman Brown cried out, and

Dan Morrill, photograph
of a forest fire

his cry was lost to his own ear by its unison with the cry of the desert.

In the interval of silence he stole forward until the light glared full upon his eyes. At one extremity of an open space, hemmed in by the dark wall of the forest, arose a rock, bearing some rude, natural resemblance either to an altar or a pulpit, and surrounded by four blazing pines, their tops aflame, their stems untouched, like candles at an evening meeting. The mass of foliage that had overgrown the summit of the rock was all on fire, blazing high into the night and fitfully illuminating the whole field. Each pendent twig and leafy festoon was in a blaze. As the red light arose and fell, a numerous congregation alternately shone forth, then disappeared in shadow, and again grew, as it were, out of the darkness, peopling the heart of the solitary woods at once.

"A grave and dark-clad company," quoth Goodman Brown.

In truth they were such. Among them, quivering to and fro between gloom and splendor, appeared faces that would be seen next day at the council board of the province, and others which, Sabbath after Sabbath, looked devoutly heavenward, and benignantly over the crowded pews, from the holiest pulpits in the land. Some affirm that the lady of the governor was there. At least there were high dames well-known to her, and wives of honored husbands, and widows, a great multitude, and ancient maidens, all of excellent repute, and fair young girls, who trembled lest their mothers should espy them. Either the sudden gleams of light flashing over the obscure field bedazzled Goodman Brown, or he recognized a score of the church members of Salem village famous for their especial sanctity. Good old Deacon Gookin had arrived, and waited at the skirts of that venerable saint, his revered pastor. But, irreverently consorting with these grave, reputable, and pious people, these elders of the church, these chaste dames and dewy virgins, there were men of dissolute lives and women of spotted fame, wretches given over to all mean and filthy vice, and suspected even of horrid crimes. It was strange to see that the good shrank not from the wicked, nor were the sinners abashed by the saints. Scattered also among their palefaced enemies were the Indian priests, or powwows, who had often scared their native forest with more hideous incantations than any known to English witchcraft.

"But where is Faith?" thought Goodman Brown; and, as hope came into his heart, he trembled.

Another verse of the hymn arose, a slow and mournful strain, such as the pious love, but joined to words which expressed all that our nature can conceive of sin, and darkly hinted at far more. Unfathomable to mere mortals is the lore of fiends. Verse after verse was sung; and still the chorus of the desert swelled between like the deepest tone of a mighty organ; and with the final peal of that dreadful anthem there came a sound, as if the roaring wind, the rushing streams, the howling beasts, and every other voice of the unconcerted wilderness were mingling and according with the voice of guilty man in homage to the prince of all. The four blazing pines threw up a loftier flame, and obscurely discovered shapes and visages of horror on the smoke wreaths above the impious assembly. At the same moment the fire on the rock shot redly forth and formed a glowing arch above its base, where now appeared a figure. With reverence be it spoken, the figure bore no slight similitude, both in garb and manner, to some grave divine of the New England churches.

"Bring forth the converts!" cried a voice that echoed through the field and rolled into the forest.

At the word, Goodman Brown stepped forth from the shadow of the trees and approached the congregation, with whom he felt a loathful brotherhood by the sympathy of all that was wicked in his heart. He could have well-nigh sworn that the shape of his own dead father beckoned him to advance, looking downward from a smoke wreath, while a woman, with dim features of despair, threw out her hand to warn him back. Was it his mother? But he had no power to retreat one step, nor to resist, even in thought, when the minister and good old Deacon Gookin seized his arms and led him to the blazing rock. Thither came also the slender form of a veiled female, led between Goody Cloyse, that pious teacher of the catechism, and Martha Carrier, who had received the devil's promise to be queen of hell. A rampant hag was she. And there stood the proselytes beneath the canopy of fire.

"Welcome, my children," said the dark figure, "to the communion of your race. Ye have found thus young your nature and your destiny. My children, look behind you!"

They turned; and flashing forth, as it were, in a sheet of flame, the fiend worshippers were seen; the smile of welcome gleamed darkly on every visage.

"There," resumed the sable form, "are all whom ye have reverenced from youth. Ye deemed them holier than yourselves, and shrank from your own sin, contrasting it with their lives of righteousness and prayerful aspirations heavenward. Yet here are they all in my worshipping assembly. This night it shall be granted you to know their secret deeds: how hoary-bearded elders of the church have whispered wanton words to the young maids of their households; how many a woman, eager for widows' weeds, has given her husband a drink at bedtime and let him sleep his last sleep in her bosom; how beardless youths have made haste to inherit their fathers' wealth; and how fair damsels—blush not, sweet ones—have dug little graves in the garden, and bidden me, the sole guest, to an infant's funeral. By the sympathy of your human hearts for sin ye shall scent out all the places—whether in church, bedchamber, street, field, or forest—where crime has been committed, and shall exult to behold the whole earth one stain of guilt, one mighty blood spot. Far more than this. It shall be yours to penetrate, in every bosom, the deep mystery of sin, the fountain of all wicked arts, and which inexhaustibly supplies more evil impulses than human power—than my power at its utmost—can make manifest in deeds. And now, my children, look upon each other."

They did so; and, by the blaze of the hell-kindled torches, the wretched man beheld his Faith, and the wife her husband, trembling before that unhallowed altar.

"Lo, there ye stand, my children," said the figure, in a deep and solemn tone, almost sad with its despairing awfulness, as if his once angelic nature could yet mourn for our miserable race. "Depending upon one another's hearts, ye had still hoped that virtue were not all a dream. Now are ye undeceived. Evil is the nature of mankind. Evil must be your only happiness. Welcome again, my children, to the communion of your race."

"Welcome," repeated the fiend worshippers, in one cry of despair and triumph.

And there they stood, the only pair, as it

seemed, who were yet hesitating on the verge of wickedness in this dark world. A basin was hollowed, naturally, in the rock. Did it contain water, reddened by the lurid light? Or was it blood? or, perchance, a liquid flame? Herein did the shape of evil dip his hand and prepare to lay the mark of baptism upon their foreheads, that they might be partakers of the mystery of sin, more conscious of the secret guilt of others, both in deed and thought, than they could now be of their own. The husband cast one look at his pale wife, and Faith at him. What polluted wretches would the next glance show them to each other, shuddering alike at what they disclosed and what they saw!

"Faith! Faith!" cried the husband, "look up to heaven, and resist the wicked one."

Whether Faith obeyed he knew not. Hardly had he spoken when he found himself amid calm night and solitude, listening to a roar of the wind which died heavily away through the forest. He staggered against the rock, and felt it chill and damp; while a hanging twig, that had been all on fire, besprinkled his cheek with the coldest dew.

The next morning young Goodman Brown came slowly into the street of Salem village, staring around him like a bewildered man. The good old minister was taking a walk along the graveyard to get an appetite for breakfast and meditate his sermon, and bestowed a blessing, as he passed, on Goodman Brown. He shrank from the venerable saint as if to avoid an anathema. Old Deacon Gookin was at domestic worship, and the holy words of his prayer were heard through the open window. "What God doth the wizard pray to?" quoth Goodman Brown. Goody Cloyse, that excellent old Christian, stood in the early sunshine at her own lattice, catechizing a little girl who had brought her a pint of morning's milk. Goodman Brown snatched away the child as from the grasp of the fiend himself. Turning the corner by the meetinghouse, he spied the head of Faith, with the pink ribbons, gazing anxiously forth, and bursting into such joy at sight of him that she skipped along the street and almost kissed her husband before the whole village. But Goodman Brown looked sternly and sadly into her face, and passed on without a greeting.

Had Goodman Brown fallen asleep in the forest and only dreamed a wild dream of a witch meeting?

Be it so if you will; but alas! it was a dream of evil omen for young Goodman Brown. A stern, a sad, a darkly meditative, a distrustful, if not a desperate man did he become from the night of that fearful dream. On the Sabbath day, when the congregation were singing a holy psalm, he could not listen because an anthem of sin rushed loudly upon his ear and drowned all the blessed strain. When the minister spoke from the pulpit with power and fervid eloquence, and, with his hand on the open Bible, of the sacred truths of our religion, and of saintlike lives and triumphant deaths, and of future bliss or misery unutterable, then did Goodman Brown turn pale, dreading lest the roof should thunder down upon the gray blasphemer and his hearers. Often, waking suddenly at midnight, he shrank from the bosom of Faith; and at morning or eventide, when the family knelt down at prayer, he scowled and muttered to himself, and gazed sternly at his wife, and turned away. And when he had lived long, and was borne to his grave a hoary corpse, followed by Faith, an aged woman, and children and grandchildren, a goodly procession, besides neighbors not a few, they carved no hopeful verse upon his tombstone, for his dying hour was gloom.

1835

THINK AND DISCUSS
Understanding
1. What are the two main settings in the story? At what time of day do the initial events occur?
2. What do the first seven paragraphs reveal about the characters of Goodman Brown and Faith?

3. How do you know that Brown's meeting with the unnamed man was actually prearranged? What are this man's previous associations with the Brown family?
4. Briefly describe the episode in the woods with Goody Cloyse and note Brown's response.
5. What causes Brown to exclaim "My Faith is gone!" (241a, 4)?
6. At the altar scene, which community members does Brown recognize and what are they said to share?
7. At what crucial point does the forest scene end, and under what circumstances does Brown suddenly find himself?

Analyzing
8. Citing specific details from the text, explain whether you think Goodman Brown saw or dreamed the incidents in the forest.
9. Would you consider Goodman Brown's change more plausible if he actually had seen the events in the forest or if he had only imagined or dreamed them? Explain.
10. How has Brown's character changed in the final paragraph of the story?

Extending
11. "Young Goodman Brown" can be considered an **allegory**—that is, a story in which characters, action, and setting represent abstract concepts apart from the literal meaning of the action. Choose from the following interpretations the one you think is most convincing and defend your choice.
   • Hawthorne is revealing the hypocrisy of Puritanism by highlighting the fact that even those who appear to be pious and noble are actually sinners.
   • The story represents one man's disillusionment and loss of faith. Unable to accept either the evils or joys of life, Goodman Brown lives and dies in despair.
   • This is a reenactment of the story of Eden—an allegory of humanity's first fall from innocence and the resulting guilt.

APPLYING: Foreshadowing   H/
See Handbook of Literary Terms, p. 889.
   Foreshadowing is a hint given to the reader of what is to come. Such indications of future events may be direct and obvious, as in "Young Goodman Brown," or quite subtle.

1. Why does Faith first ask Brown to postpone his departure?
2. What two conversations overheard by Brown in the forest hint that both he and Faith will be taken into communion later at the forest ceremony?
3. In the forest, Brown observes something that "fluttered lightly down through the air and caught on the branch of a tree." What is this object and what does it foreshadow?

VOCABULARY
Affixes and Roots
   A word such as *unaccountable* is composed of a prefix meaning "not," a suffix meaning "that can be," and a root. The word *unaccountable* means "that cannot be accounted for or explained." The following words, from "Young Goodman Brown," contain prefixes meaning "not" and suffixes meaning "that can be." See if you can figure out their meanings from their roots. Write each word along with its definition. Use your Glossary if necessary. The words are *indescribable, irrepressible, inexhaustible.*

THINKING SKILLS
Evaluating
   Various readers may view Brown's character in different lights, depending on how they interpret his words and actions. Evaluate the following statement in order to answer the questions.

   Brown is viewed by some as a sympathetic character—an innocent young man whose life is blighted by an encounter with evil. Others consider Brown an unsympathetic character, righteous, unfeeling, and unwilling to accept flawed humanity.

1. Which opinion is closer to your own?
2. Do you think Brown's abrupt change in character is believable? Why or why not?

## Writing About Foreshadowing

In three or four paragraphs, analyze how the use of foreshadowing contributes to the meaning and effect of "Young Goodman Brown." Assume that your work might be published in a student literary magazine. First, discuss how the initial remarks of both main characters cre-ate certain expectations in the reader. Next, discuss how other elements of foreshadowing make Brown's actions seem almost inevitable. Use your answers to the three items under *Applying* to help you write. In a final paragraph, comment on the total effect achieved by foreshadowing.

Reader's Note

Ambiguity in "Young Goodman Brown"

The action of "Young Goodman Brown" appears to come full circle. At sunset Goodman Brown leaves his wife and the Salem town, spends a haunting night in the forest, and returns home at dawn a changed man. This plot, knit tightly by devices such as **foreshadowing,** reappearing characters, and recurring **symbols** (like Faith's pink ribbons), involves dramatic contrasts—day and night, town and forest, calm and chaos, and, most significantly, appearance and reality. The **images,** particularly those in the altar-rock scene of the forest, are vividly drawn, with the predominant colors red (fire, blood) and black (night, evil).

A reader's interpretation of "Young Goodman Brown" hinges on the answers to several crucial questions: Has Goodman Brown rejected his former faith or has he only begun to doubt it? Has his young wife Faith actually participated in the evil ceremony in the forest? Are Brown's suspicions about the townspeople concretely verified, or are they products of his imagination? Is this an allegory designed to show the pitfalls of a shallow and unquestioning faith, or is it a portrayal of a naive man's inability to confront universal evil? The basic question, of course, contains the central ambiguity of the story: Have the strange events in the forest actually occurred, or are they merely a dream?

The story relies on what one critic has called "multiple choice devices," which admit of a double meaning at every turn. Note a passage such as the following:

> "Had Goodman Brown fallen asleep in the forest and only dreamed a wild dream of a witch meeting?
>
> "Be it so if you will; but alas! it was a dream of evil omen for young Goodman Brown."

Hawthorne is equally ambiguous when he observes that the staff of the man in the forest "might almost be seen to twist and wriggle itself like a living serpent," adding, "This, of course, must have been an ocular deception, assisted by the uncertain light." Throughout the story are words and phrases such as *perhaps, seemed, appeared, some affirmed,* and *he could have sworn.* And always the forest scenes are dim, the sounds distant and indistinct, and the figures shadowy. Hawthorne maintains a **tone** that is detached and **ironic,** as if to say, "Reader, interpret for yourself these events."

A reader can assume that Hawthorne has intended his story to be ambiguous in order to produce an atmosphere of doubt and uncertainty, suggesting that there is no simple or clear-cut line between good and evil. Thus, the decisions of Goodman Brown and the outcome of the story are rich in suggestion, open to a variety of interpretations. The story has been variously viewed as an indictment of Puritan hypocrisy, a pre-Freudian study of sexual awareness and guilt, and a reenactment of Adam and Eve's temptation by a fiend of "once angelic nature." A careful reader will, no doubt, find a basis for a wealth of other interpretations.

The Story of American English

Noah Webster once said that the progress of the American language "is like the course of the Mississippi; the motion of which, at times, is scarcely perceptible, yet even then it possesses a momentum quite irresistible. Words and expressions will be forced into use."

To discover some of the forces behind the progress of the American language, consult the time line on pages 196-197. The period from 1840 to 1870 was characterized by new inventions, great expansion, and increased communication. Among the hundreds of new inventions that transformed American production was the use of *interchangeable parts*, pioneered by Eli Whitney, which laid the basis for *mass production* and the modern *assembly line*. Elias Howe's invention of the sewing machine in 1846 created the *ready-to-wear* garment industry. Charles Goodyear's invention of *vulcanized rubber* revolutionized the shoe industry. The completion of the first telegraph lines in 1844 introduced the terms *telegram* and *cablegram*.

Many pioneers followed the admonition, "Go West, young man" and sought their fortunes during the California Gold Rush. In 1849 alone, tens of thousands of *prospectors*, or *forty-niners*, headed for California. These adventurers included poets, bankers, farmers, and clergymen. Their experiences, recorded through letters and newspaper articles, helped move western words east.

Bonanza ("fair weather" in Spanish) became any rich source of profit. *To pan out*, from *panning gold* (washing it in a pan to separate it from dirt and other minerals), came to mean "to be productive" or "to work." *Grubstake* referred to the food, equipment, and money supplied to a prospector on condition of sharing whatever was found. A *strike* was a discovery of gold. The lucky prospector rushed to *stake a claim*, establishing exclusive rights to mining lands.

Cattlemen also provided a rich source for enhancing American English. Herding cattle was a common sight in Texas in 1820, but the word *cowboy* didn't enter into common usage until 1867. During that year over 5,000 cowboys were hired to bring longhorns from Texas up the Chisholm Trail to the railhead in Abilene, Kansas. The word *cow* spawned compounds, including *cowhand*, *cowpoke*, and *cowpuncher*. Cowboys who got *hot under the collar* usually *bit the dust* sooner or later. The first *chuck wagon* was made from a surplus Civil War army wagon in 1867. Cattle were brought home in a *roundup*, unless they were stolen by *rustlers*.

The generating of language, however, was not confined to the West. From New York's financial district—*Wall Street*, or *the Street*—came terms such as *market, common* and *preferred stock, board* (a group of brokers or the stock exchange), and *blue chips* (high quality stock, named from the blue chips in poker). In 1873, America suffered its first major *crash*, but soon recovered during a *boom*, or period of prosperity.

From factories such as the Lowell textile mill that Harriet Hanson Robinson describes in this unit, came words such as *striker, trade union, unionist*, and *lockout* (closing factories during contract negotiations). Workers feared being *fired* or *getting the sack*.

The increasingly popular game of baseball, originally called the *Massachusetts game*, was referred to by 1856 as *the national game*. By midcentury, terms such as *strike, fast ball, hardball, shortstop, balk*, and *bag* had entered the vocabulary. Later in the century, terms such as *pitcher's box, infield, base line, high fly, stolen base*, and *ballpark* were in common usage.

In his 1855 Preface to *Leaves of Grass*, Walt Whitman praised English as a language that "befriends the grand American expression" . . . "brawny enough and limber and full" in portraying the American experience.

Detail of portrait by Francis Day (1863–?). Library of Congress

Herman Melville was born into a middle-class but financially precarious New York family; in his early years he was raised in a genteel environment. But when his father died in 1832, Melville (age 13) left school to take on a series of jobs, finally shipping as cabin boy to Liverpool. This voyage, to be described in *Redburn* (1849), was the beginning of many remarkable experiences that would become the foundation for his novels. He next sailed for the South Seas on a whaling ship, the voyage that would later provide the background for *Moby Dick* (1851). He jumped ship at the Marquesas Islands and, as related in *Typee* (1846), took refuge among the cannibalistic Typees. He lived with them a short while and then left on a passing Australian whaler that dropped him off in Tahiti. His stay in Tahiti resulted in *Omoo* (1847). He then enlisted as an ordinary seaman on the frigate *United States* until the ship's eventual return to Boston. His account of the Navy's cruelty and tyranny in *White Jacket* (1850) added fuel to a movement that would shortly result in the abolition of flogging on U.S. Navy ships.

The colorful descriptions of Melville's experiences in *Typee* and *Omoo* won the interest of a curious and fascinated public. He was widely read and became known as the man who had lived among cannibals. But with succeeding works Melville's fiction became deeper and made more demands on the reader. A public that preferred simple adventure stories had little use for Melville's ambiguities and allegories. As the profundity of his writing increased, his popularity diminished. His criticism of missionaries in *Omoo* had further set segments of the public against him. Thus when his masterpiece *Moby Dick* was published just five years after his initial success, it was generally ignored, and remained largely unread for over seventy years.

The exhausting effort of writing *Moby Dick* and the disappointment of its reception embittered Melville. He wrote other tales but never regained the public's interest. Soon he turned to writing poetry, privately published. In his later years, he supported himself as a customs inspector and died forgotten at the age of seventy-two. Barrett Wendell's *Literary History of America*, published in 1900, reads, "Herman Melville . . . began a career of literary promise, which never came to fruition." Melville was finally rediscovered in the 1920s, and today *Moby Dick* is considered by many to be the greatest American novel ever written.

The following account is from Melville's novel *Redburn*. With the "scent and savor of poverty" upon him, young Wellingborough Redburn sailed as a "ship's boy" on a merchant vessel bound for Liverpool, England. On the voyage over from New York, he learned much from his fellow seamen about hoisting sails and surviving in a wicked world. He learned even more about humanity during his weeks in Liverpool as he roamed the port city's swarming, dirty streets.

See POINT OF VIEW in the Handbook of Literary Terms, page 900.

What Redburn Saw in Launcelott's-Hey

Herman Melville

n going to our boardinghouse, the sign of the Baltimore Clipper, I generally passed through a narrow street called "Launce-lott's-Hey," lined with dingy, prisonlike cotton warehouses. In this street, or rather alley, you seldom see any one but a truck man, or some solitary old warehouse keeper, haunting his smoky den like a ghost.

Once, passing through this place, I heard a feeble wail, which seemed to come out of the earth. It was but a strip of crooked sidewalk where I stood; the dingy wall was on every side, converting the midday into twilight; and not a soul was in sight. I started, and could almost have run, when I heard that dismal sound. It seemed the low, hopeless, endless wail of some one forever lost. At last I advanced to an opening which communicated downward with deep tiers of cellars beneath a crumbling old warehouse; and there, some fifteen feet below the walk, crouching in nameless squalor, with her head bowed over, was the figure of what had been a woman. Her blue arms folded to her livid bosom two shrunken things like children, that leaned toward her, one on each side. At first, I knew not whether they were alive or dead. They made no sign; they did not move or stir; but from the vault came that soul-sickening wail.

I made a noise with my foot, which, in the silence, echoed far and near; but there was no response. Louder still; when one of the children lifted its head, and cast upward a faint glance; then closed its eyes, and lay motionless. The woman also, now gazed up, and perceived me; but let fall her eye again. They were dumb and next to dead with want. How they had crawled into that den, I could not tell; but there they had crawled to die. At that moment I never thought of relieving them; for death was so stamped in their glazed and unimploring eyes, that I almost regarded them as already no more. I stood looking down on them, while my whole soul swelled within me; and I asked myself, What right had anybody in the wide world to smile and be glad, when sights like this were to be seen? It was enough to turn the heart to gall; and make a man hater of a Howard. For who were these ghosts that I saw? Were they not human beings? a woman and two girls? with eyes, and lips, and ears like any queen? with hearts which, though they did not bound with blood, yet beat with a dull, dead ache that was their life.

At last, I walked on toward an open lot in the alley hoping to meet there some ragged old women, whom I had daily noticed groping amid foul rubbish for little particles of dirty cotton, which they washed out and sold for a trifle.

I found them; and accosting one, I asked if she knew of the persons I had just left. She replied, that she did not; nor did she want to. I then asked another, a miserable, toothless old woman, with a tattered strip of coarse baling stuff round her body. Looking at me for an instant, she resumed her raking in the rubbish, and said that she knew who it was that I spoke of; but that she had no time to attend to beggars and their brats. Accosting still another, who seemed to know my errand, I asked if there was no place to which the woman could be taken. "Yes," she replied, "to the churchyard." I said she was alive, and not dead.

"Then she'll never die," was the rejoinder. "She's been down there these three days, with nothing to eat—that I know myself."

"She desarves it," said an old hag, who was just placing on her crooked shoulders her bag of pickings, and who was turning to totter off, "that Betsey Jennings desarves it—was she ever married? Tell me that."

Leaving Launcelott's-Hey, I turned into a more frequented street; and soon meeting a policeman, told him of the condition of the woman and the girls.

"It's none of my business, Jack," said he. "I don't belong to that street."

"Who does then?"

"I don't know. But what business is it of yours? Are you not a Yankee?"

"Yes," said I, "but come, I will help you remove that woman, if you say so."

"There, now, Jack, go on board your ship, and stick to it; and leave these matters to the town."

I accosted two more policemen, but with no better success; they would not even go with me to the place. The truth was, it was out of the way, in a silent, secluded spot; and the misery of the three outcasts, hiding away in the ground, did not obtrude upon any one.

Returning to them, I again stamped to attract their attention; but this time, none of the three looked up, or even stirred. While I yet stood irresolute, a voice called to me from a high, iron-shuttered window in a loft over the way; and asked what I was about. I beckoned to the man, a sort of porter, to come down, which he did; when I pointed down into the vault.

"Well," said he, "what of it?"

"Can't we get them out?" said I, "haven't you some place in your warehouse where you can put them? Have you nothing for them to eat?"

"You're crazy, boy," said he; "do you suppose, that Parkins and Wood want their warehouse turned into a hospital?"

I then went to my boardinghouse, and told Handsome Mary of what I had seen; asking her if she could not do something to get the woman and girls removed; or if she could not do that, let me have some food for them. But though a kind person in the main, Mary replied that she gave away enough to beggars in her own street (which was true enough) without looking after the whole neighborhood.

Going into the kitchen, I accosted the cook, a little shriveled-up old Welshwoman, with a saucy tongue, whom the sailors called *Brandy-Nan;* and begged her to give me some cold victuals, if she had nothing better, to take to the vault. But she broke out in a storm of swearing at the miserable occupants of the vault, and refused. I then stepped into the room where our dinner was being spread; and waiting till the girl had gone out, I snatched some bread and cheese from a stand, and thrusting it into the bosom of my frock, left the house. Hurrying to the lane, I dropped the food down into the vault. One of the girls caught at it convulsively; but fell back, apparently fainting; the sister pushed the other's arm aside, and took the bread in her hand; but with a weak uncertain grasp like an infant's. She placed it to her mouth; but letting it fall again, murmured faintly something like "water." The woman did not stir; her head was bowed over, just as I had first seen her.

Seeing how it was, I ran down toward the docks to a mean little sailor tavern, and begged for a pitcher; but the cross old man who kept it refused, unless I would pay for it. But I had no money. So as my boardinghouse was some way off, and it would be lost time to run to the ship for my big iron pot; under the impulse of the moment, I hurried to one of the Boodle

Hydrants, which I remembered having seen running near the scene of a still smoldering fire in an old rag house; and taking off a new tarpaulin hat, which had been loaned me that day, filled it with water.

With this, I returned to Launcelott's-Hey; and with considerable difficulty, like getting down into a well, I contrived to descend with it into the vault; where there was hardly space enough left to let me stand. The two girls drank out of the hat together; looking up at me with an unalterable, idiotic expression, that almost made me faint. The woman spoke not a word, and did not stir. While the girls were breaking and eating the bread, I tried to lift the woman's head; but feeble as she was, she seemed bent upon holding it down. Observing her arms still clasped upon her bosom, and that something seemed hidden under the rags there, a thought crossed my mind, which impelled me forcibly to withdraw her hands for a moment; when I caught a glimpse of a meager little babe, the lower part of its body thrust into an old bonnet. Its face was dazzlingly white, even in its squalor; but the closed eyes looked like balls of indigo. It must have been dead some hours.

The woman refusing to speak, eat, or drink, I asked one of the girls who they were, and where they lived; but she only stared vacantly, muttering something that could not be understood.

The air of the place was now getting too much for me; but I stood deliberating a moment, whether it was possible for me to drag them out of the vault. But if I did, what then? They would only perish in the street, and here they were at least protected from the rain; and more than that, might die in seclusion.

I crawled up into the street, and looking down upon them again, almost repented that I had brought them any food; for it would only tend to prolong their misery, without hope of any permanent relief; for die they must very soon; they were too far gone for any medicine to help them. I hardly know whether I ought to confess another thing that occurred to me as I stood there; but it was this—I felt an almost irresistible impulse to do them the last mercy, of in some way putting an end to their horrible lives; and I should almost have done so, I think, had I not been deterred by thoughts of the law. For I well knew that the law, which would let them perish of themselves without giving them one cup of water, would spend a thousand pounds if necessary, in convicting him who should so much as offer to relieve them from their miserable existence.

The next day, and the next, I passed the vault three times, and still met the same sight. The girls leaning up against the woman on each side, and the woman with her arms still folding the babe, and her head bowed. The first evening I did not see the bread that I had dropped down in the morning; but the second evening, the bread I had dropped that morning remained untouched. On the third morning the smell that came from the vault was such, that I accosted the same policeman I had accosted before, who was patrolling the same street, and told him that the persons I had spoken to him about were dead, and he had better have them removed. He looked as if he did not believe me, and added, that it was not his street.

When I arrived at the docks on my way to the ship, I entered the guardhouse within the walls, and asked for one of the captains, to whom I told the story; but, from what he said, was led to infer that the Dock Police was distinct from that of the town, and this was not the right place to lodge my information.

I could do no more that morning, being obliged to repair to the ship; but at twelve o'clock, when I went to dinner, I hurried into Launcelott's-Hey, when I found that the vault was empty. In place of the woman and children, a heap of quicklime was glistening.

I could not learn who had taken them away, or whither they had gone; but my prayer was answered—they were dead, departed, and at peace.

But again I looked down into the vault, and in fancy beheld the pale, shrunken forms still crouching there. Ah! What are our creeds, and how do we hope to be saved? Tell me, oh Bible, that story of Lazarus[1] again, that I may find comfort in my heart for the poor and forlorn. Surrounded as we are by the wants and woes of our fellow men, and yet given to follow our own pleasures, regardless of their pains, are we not like people sitting up with a corpse, and making merry in the house of the dead?

1849

---

1. *Lazarus* (laz′ə res), an allusion to Jesus' parable of the beggar Lazarus and the rich man who did not help him. Lazarus is comforted in Heaven (Luke 16:19-31).

THINK AND DISCUSS
Understanding
1. What sound drew Redburn's attention to the opening in the street?
2. Describe Redburn's reaction to what he saw.
3. What is the reaction of the other characters—"the ragged old woman," the policeman, "the sort of porter," Handsome Mary, Brandy-Nan, and the owner of the "mean little sailor tavern"?
4. What thought does Redburn hesitantly confess after he has brought water and food to the dying woman and children? Why does he fail to act on this thought?

Analyzing
5. What new insights has Redburn gained from this experience?
6. In what way does the **allusion** to Lazarus offer a parallel to Redburn's situation?
7. Do you think Redburn has become a better man or a less noble one as a result of his experience? Explain.

APPLYING: Point of View H𝕋
See Handbook of Literary Terms, p. 900.

Point of view is the relationship assumed between the teller of the story and the characters in it. The teller, or *narrator*, is a character in this selection, so the story is told from the *first-person* point of view. Unlike the voice of the "I" we hear in nonfiction, such as in the writings of Emerson or Thoreau, we cannot equate the personality we "hear" in fiction with that of the author. In this piece by Melville, the voice is that of a created, fictional character—young Wellingborough Redburn—who tells us his tale of dismay and revelation in his own words.

1. What remarks in the first three paragraphs express Redburn's feelings for the unfortunate family?
2. Why do you think that Melville chose to tell this story from Redburn's point of view rather than from that of the policeman?
3. How does Melville's choice of narrator affect the **tone** of this story?

COMPOSITION ✎
Writing an Objective Account
Imagine that you are the first policeman whom Redburn meets in Launcelott's-Hey. From the officer's point of view, write a two-paragraph report to the head of your department about the condition and eventual plight of the poor family. Make sure that the report is purely factual and maintain an objective tone.

Describing a Change of Character
The Redburn we meet at the beginning of this narrative is different from the Redburn described at the end. Write a three-paragraph essay describing this change of character for your classmates. In the first paragraph, describe the qualities, actions, and attitudes that the young sailor initially displays. In the second paragraph, describe the same characteristics, as displayed at the end of the narrative. Finally, write a paragraph in which you make a generalization about the influence that his encounter with evil has had on Redburn.

Themes IN AMERICAN LITERATURE

Moral Struggle

Moral struggle—the drama of good versus evil—has been a prominent theme in American literature from its earliest works, in which Satan appears as a flesh-and-blood presence who plots human downfall, to modern works, in which evil is presented as a formidable inner force. According to the Puritan Jonathan Edwards, human beings, innately depraved and prone to sin, were held by God "over the pit of hell much as one holds a spider. . . ." Generations later, Nathaniel Hawthorne examined his Puritan past, probing the psychology of sin. Descended from a judge who officiated at the Salem witch trials, Hawthorne was haunted by the blood of martyred witches whom he felt "had left a stain upon him." Thus the theme of sin and its ensuing guilt became the obsessive center of his fiction. Just as Hawthorne examined the effects of adultery, deception, and betrayal in *The Scarlet Letter*, he focused on the results of the sins of distrust and alienation in "Young Goodman Brown." Goodman Brown, who sees the whole earth as "one stain of guilt," accepts the Puritan view of human depravity: "Evil is the nature of mankind."

Melville's view of life's tragic dimensions was similar to Hawthorne's. As Hawthorne was obsessed with guilt resulting from evil, Melville was concerned with the origin and nature of evil in itself. His novel *Moby Dick* involves a universe where good and evil are inextricably linked. In his attempt to seek revenge on the whale, who has maimed him and become for him the embodiment of evil, Captain Ahab destroyed his ship, his crew, and himself.

This concern about evil accounts for the zeal of many American writers in attacking social injustice—slavery, female subjugation, and other inequalities. Moral struggle, for reformers such as Elizabeth Cady Stanton and Sojourner Truth, took the form of social activism, as they fought for civil liberties and equality. Even Melville, who in *Moby Dick* portrayed good and evil in richly symbolic terms, presented a literal picture of evil in the squalor of nineteenth-century Liverpool in "What Redburn Saw in Launcelott's-Hey." Harriet Beecher Stowe and Frederick Douglass attacked the conscience of a nation that permitted slavery, while Chief Seattle protested the government's confiscation of his land.

It may seem surprising that evil was such an obsessive concern and reform so zealously pursued in an era dominated by the optimistic philosophy of Transcendentalism, which maintained that human nature was essentially good and that evil was merely a part of a divine or cosmic plan beyond human understanding. Yet even Thoreau, who tested the ideas of Transcendentalism while espousing them, sought governmental reforms. Writers like Melville and Hawthorne satirized Transcendentalism and throughout their work devoted themselves to dramatizing the "power of blackness."

Even before Hawthorne and Melville, Edgar Allan Poe created a world controlled by mysterious and sinister forces that seemed beyond rational control and that often led to disaster and death. And later American writers found evil lurking in chance events that determine human fate in a seemingly indifferent universe—as in Stephen Crane's novel *The Red Badge of Courage*.

Modern American writers, following the lead of Mark Twain's *Huckleberry Finn*, have found their way to this theme through a kind of dark comedy, sometimes labeled black humor. Flannery O'Connor has made her fictional trademark the symbolic presence of the devil in an absurd (and violent) world in such stories as "The Life You Save May Be Your Own." (See Unit 7.)

Given America's strong Puritan heritage, with its enduring image of life as a continual struggle with Satan, it is likely that the drama of good versus evil will continue to be central to American literature.

Louisa May Alcott once wrote that life had always puzzled her and that she hoped for greater understanding of it. Her attitude is not surprising since her entire life was spent struggling to become a writer and trying to help her family achieve financial security. Her father, Bronson Alcott, an experimenter in education, was never able to provide satisfactorily for his large family, and his daughter assumed his responsibilities.

As the daughter of a prominent Transcendentalist, she grew up surrounded by some of the time's greatest thinkers—Ralph Waldo Emerson, Henry David Thoreau, Margaret Fuller, and others. Their influence on her thinking can be seen in her choice of a literary occupation and in the social and moral causes that she later espoused—the abolition of slavery and women's suffrage.

In her diary, which she started while her family resided at Fruitlands, her father's experiment in communal farm living, she commented on the farm's general lack of success and the lack of practicality in undertaking this idealistic experiment. She was pleased when her family left the farm three years later and settled in Concord by themselves.

In 1848 her family moved to Boston, where her mother became a social worker. Over the years, Louisa May Alcott tried sewing and teaching as occupations, but gave them up in hopes of becoming a writer. In 1854 she published her first book, which was about fairies and fables and for which she received thirty-two dollars.

With the advent of the Civil War, she went to Union Hospital in Washington, D.C., to nurse wounded soldiers. While she was there, she worked tirelessly, kept a journal, and left only after she became seriously ill with pneumonia.

Her most famous work, *Little Women,* appeared in 1868; it is the story of a family of girls that was based on her personal experiences. Ironically, years before, she had written in her diary, "I am old for my age and don't care much for girl's things." *Little Women* brought her not only personal success, but financial security for her family as well. Other books followed such an *An Old Fashioned Girl* in 1870, and *Little Men* in 1871.

The following excerpt, taken from *Hospital Sketches,* reveals Alcott's compassion for others and her insight into human life. Letters to her family, which corresponded to these journal entries, were published in the *Commonwealth* newspaper, attracting a good deal of attention. Although the six-week stay at the army hospital in Georgetown left Alcott with permanently shattered nerves and a weakened constitution, the experience gave to her writings a sharper understanding of human nature and a greater sense of reality.

from Hospital Sketches

Louisa May Alcott

ovember, 1862—Thirty years old. Decided to go to Washington as nurse if I could find a place. Help needed, and I love nursing, and *must* let out my pent-up energy in some new way. Winter is always a hard and dull time, and if I am away there is one less to feed and warm and worry over.

I want new experiences, and am sure to get 'em if I go. So I've sent in my name, and bide my time writing tales, to leave all snug behind me, and mending up my old clothes—for nurses don't need nice things, thank Heaven!

December—On the 11th I received a note from Miss H. M. Stevenson telling me to start for Georgetown next day to fill a place in the Union Hotel Hospital. Mrs. Ropes of Boston was matron, and Miss Kendall of Plymouth was a nurse there, and though a hard place, help was needed. I was ready, and when my commander said "March!" I marched. Packed my trunk, and reported in B. that same evening.

We had all been full of courage till the last moment came; then we all broke down. I realized that I had taken my life in my hand, and might never see them all again. I said, "Shall I stay, Mother?" as I hugged her close. "No, go! and the Lord be with you!" answered the Spartan woman; and till I turned the corner she bravely smiled and waved her wet handkerchief on the doorstep. Shall I ever see that dear old face again?

So I set forth in the December twilight, with May and Julian Hawthorne[1] as escort, feeling as if I was the son of the house going to war.

Friday, the 12th, was a very memorable day, spent in running all over Boston to get my pass, etc., calling for parcels, getting a tooth filled, and buying a veil—my only purchase. A. C. gave me some old clothes; the dear Sewalls money for myself and boys, lots of love and help; and at 5:00 P.M., saying "good-by" to a group of tearful faces at the station, I started on my long journey, full of hope and sorrow, courage and plans.

A most interesting journey into a new world full of stirring sights and sounds, new adventures, and an evergrowing sense of the great task I had undertaken.

I said my prayers as I went rushing through the country white with tents, all alive with patriotism, and already red with blood.

A solemn time, but I'm glad to live in it; and am sure it will do me good whether I come out alive or dead.

All went well, and I got to Georgetown one evening very tired. Was kindly welcomed, slept in my narrow bed with two other roommates, and on the morrow began my new life by seeing a poor man die at dawn, and sitting all day between a boy with pneumonia and a man shot through the lungs. A strange day, but I did my best; and when I put mother's little black shawl round the boy while he sat up panting for breath, he smiled and said, "You are real motherly, ma'am." I felt as if I was getting on. The man only lay and stared with his big black eyes, and made me very nervous. But all were well-behaved; and I sat looking at the twenty strong faces as they looked back at me—the only new thing they had to amuse them—hoping that I looked "motherly" to them; for my thirty years made me feel old, and the suffering round me made me long to comfort every one.

January, 1863 *Union Hotel Hospital, Georgetown, D.C.*—I never began the year in a stranger place than this: five hundred miles from home,

---

1. *May and Julian Hawthorne.* Nathaniel Hawthorne and his family lived next door to the Alcotts for a time.

alone, among strangers, doing painful duties all day long, and leading a life of constant excitement in this great house, surrounded by three or four hundred men in all stages of suffering, disease, and death. Though often homesick, heartsick, and worn-out, I like it, find real pleasure in comforting, tending, and cheering these poor souls who seem to love me, to feel my sympathy though unspoken, and acknowledge my hearty goodwill, in spite of the ignorance, awkwardness, and bashfulness which I cannot help showing in so new and trying a situation. The men are docile, respectful, and affectionate, with but few exceptions; truly lovable and manly many of them. John Sulie, a Virginia blacksmith, is the prince of patients; and though what we call a common man in education and condition, to me is all I could expect or ask from the first gentleman in the land. Under his plain speech and unpolished manner I seem to see a noble character, a heart as warm and tender as a woman's, a nature fresh and frank as any child's. He is about thirty, I think, tall and handsome, mortally wounded, and dying royally without reproach, repining, or remorse. Mrs. Ropes and myself love him, and feel indignant that such a man should be so early lost; for though he might never distinguish himself before the world, his influence and example cannot be without effect, for real goodness is never wasted.

Monday, 4th—I shall record the events of a day as a sample of the days I spend—

Up at six, dress by gaslight, run through my ward and throw up the windows, though the men grumble and shiver; but the air is bad enough to breed a pestilence; and as no notice is taken of our frequent appeals for better ventilation, I must do what I can. Poke up the fire, add blankets, joke, coax, and command; but continue to open doors and windows as if life depended upon it. Mine does, and doubtless many another, for a more perfect pestilence box than this house I never saw—cold, damp, dirty, full of vile odors from wounds, kitchens, washrooms, and stables. No competent head, male or female, to right matters, and a jumble of good, bad, and indifferent nurses, surgeons, and attendants, to complicate the chaos still more.

After this unwelcome progress through my stifling ward, I go to breakfast with what appetite I may; find the uninvitable fried beef, salt butter, husky bread, and washy coffee; listen to the clack of eight women and a dozen men—the first silly, stupid, or possessed of one idea; the last absorbed with their breakfast and themselves to a degree that is both ludicrous and provoking, for all the dishes are ordered down the table *full* and returned *empty;* the conversation is entirely among themselves, and each announces his opinion with an air of importance that frequently causes me to choke in my cup, or bolt my meals with undignified speed lest a laugh betray to these famous beings that a "chiel's amang them takin' notes."

Till noon I trot, trot, giving out rations, cutting up food for helpless "boys," washing faces, teaching my attendants how beds are made or floors are swept, dressing wounds, taking Dr. F. P.'s orders (privately wishing all the time that he would be more gentle with my big babies), dusting tables, sewing bandages, keeping my tray tidy, rushing up and down after pillows, bed linen, sponges, books, and directions, till it seems as if I would joyfully pay down all I possess for fifteen minutes' rest. At twelve the big bell rings, and up comes dinner for the boys, who are always ready for it and never entirely satisfied. Soup, meat, potatoes, and bread is the bill of fare. Charles Thayer, the attendant, travels up and down the room serving out the rations, saving little for himself, yet always thoughtful of his mates, and patient as a woman with their helplessness. When dinner is over, some sleep, many read, and others want letters written. This I like to do, for they put in such odd things, and express their ideas so comically, I have great fun interiorally, while as grave as possible exteriorally. A few of the men word their paragraphs well and make excellent letters. John's was the best of all I wrote. The answering of letters from friends after someone had died is the saddest and hardest duty a nurse has to do.

Eastman Johnson, *The Letter Home* (1867).
Museum of Fine Arts, Boston

Supper at five sets everyone to running that can run; and when that flurry is over, all settle down for the evening amusements, which consist of newspapers, gossip, and doctor's last round, and, for such as need them, the final doses for the night. At nine the bell rings, gas is turned down, and day nurses go to bed. Night nurses go on duty, and sleep and death have the house to themselves.

My work is changed to night watching, or half night and half day—from twelve to twelve. I like it, as it leaves me time for a morning run, which is what I need to keep well; for bad air, food, and water, work and watching, are getting to be too much for me. I trot up and down the streets in all directions, sometimes to the Heights, then halfway to Washington, again to the hill, over which the long trains of army wagons are constantly vanishing and ambulances appearing. That way the fighting lies, and I long to follow.

Ordered to keep my room, being threatened with pneumonia. Sharp pain in the side, cough, fever, and dizziness. A pleasant prospect for a lonely soul five hundred miles from home! Sit and sew on the boys' clothes, write letters, sleep, and read; try to talk and keep merry, but fail decidedly, as day after day goes, and I feel no better. Dream awfully, and wake unrefreshed, think of home, and wonder if I am to die here, as Mrs. R., the matron, is likely to do. Feel too miserable to care much what becomes of me. Dr. S. creaks up twice a day to feel my pulse, give me doses, and ask if I am at all consumptive, or some other cheering question. Dr. O. examines my lungs and looks sober. Dr. J. haunts the room, coming by day and night with wood, cologne, books, and messes, like a motherly little man as he is. Nurses fussy and anxious, matron dying, and everything very gloomy. They want me to go home, but I *won't* yet.

January 16th—Was amazed to see Father enter the room that morning, having been telegraphed to by order of Mrs. R. without asking leave. I was very angry at first, though glad to see him, because I knew I should have to go. Mrs. D. and Miss Dix came, and pretty Miss W., to take me to Willard's to be cared for by them. I wouldn't go, preferring to keep still, being pretty ill by that time.

On the 21st I suddenly decided to go home, feeling very strangely, and dreading to be worse. Mrs. R. died, and that frightened the doctors about me; for my trouble was the same—typhoid pneumonia. Father, Miss K., and Lizzie T. went with me. Miss Dix brought a basket full of bottles of wine, tea, medicine, and cologne, besides a little blanket and pillow, a fan, and a testament. She is a kind old soul, but very queer and arbitrary.

Was very sorry to go, and "my boys" seemed sorry to have me. Quite a flock came to see me off; but I was too sick to have but a dim idea of what was going on.　　　　　　　　**1863**

THINK AND DISCUSS
Understanding
1. What are Louisa May Alcott's motives for volunteering to be a nurse in a Union hospital?
2. What duties does Alcott describe as part of a typical daily schedule?
3. How much time does she actually spend at the Georgetown hospital?
4. What conditions at the hospital affect her health and why does she finally leave?

Analyzing
5. Judging from this journal account, how would you describe Alcott's character?
6. Which qualities make her a good nurse?

Extending
7. How do you think Alcott would respond to Emerson's comment: "There is an incessant influx of novelty into the world; and yet we tolerate incredible dullness"?

COMPOSITION
Writing a Journal Entry
Assume you are one of the less seriously injured soldiers in Alcott's ward who has witnessed some of the incidents she describes. Write a journal entry describing a hospital scene that you find memorable. Use dialogue and images to make the scene vivid.

Writing a Character Sketch
Write a three-paragraph character sketch that could serve as part of Alcott's biography. In the first paragraph, describe her character. In the second paragraph, focus on characteristics that make her a good nurse. In the final paragraph, speculate on how the insights gained from her nursing may have made her a better writer of fiction. In revising your work, use the checklists included in "The Writing Process" in the Writer's Handbook.

When Harriet Beecher Stowe visited President Lincoln in the White House during the Civil War, it is said that he remarked to her, "So you're the little woman who wrote the book that made this great war!" Her novel, *Uncle Tom's Cabin*, was the most widely sold volume of the nineteenth century; and while it did not start the war, it focused national attention on the immorality and cruelty of slavery.

Harriet Beecher's childhood in Connecticut was intensely religious. For a time she attended the Hartford Female Seminary, a progressive institution established by her sister Catherine. In 1832, her father, a minister of great renown, became the president of Lane Theological Seminary in Cincinnati, Ohio, and the family moved there.

In 1836, she married Calvin Stowe, a professor at Lane. For the next eighteen years, while raising a large family and publishing magazine articles, she watched the dramatic escape attempts of runaway slaves who crossed the nearby Ohio River. She later drew upon her observations in *Uncle Tom's Cabin*.

The first serial installment of *Uncle Tom's Cabin* appeared in the *National Era*, an antislavery newspaper, on June 5, 1851, and the last on April 1, 1852. When the novel was published in book form in 1852, it was an instant triumph. The narration of the cruelties of slavery as seen through the eyes of Uncle Tom and Eliza sold 350,000 copies during the first year and has since been translated into forty languages with a world-wide readership of many millions. Although *Uncle Tom's Cabin* has never been considered a literary masterpiece, it is one of the most influential books of social criticism ever written. When asked to defend her fiction-alized account, Stowe called her book "a very inadequate representation of slavery," which is "too dreadful for the purposes of art."

The following excerpts are taken from the early chapters of *Uncle Tom's Cabin*. In an attempt to save his debt-ridden Kentucky plantation, Mr. Shelby agrees to sell two of his slaves, old Uncle Tom and a child named Harry, to a slave trader named Haley. Eliza, Harry's mother, overhears the plan and decides to flee with her child to Canada and safety.

from Uncle Tom's Cabin

Harriet Beecher Stowe

here was one listener to this conversation whom Mr. and Mrs. Shelby little suspected. Communicating with their apartment was a large closet, opening by a door into the outer passage. When Mrs. Shelby had dismissed Eliza for the night, her feverish and excited mind had suggested the idea of this closet; and she had hidden herself there, and with her ear pressed close against the crack of the door, had lost not a word of the conversation. When the voices died into silence, she rose and crept stealthily away. Pale, shivering, with rigid features and compressed lips, she looked an entirely altered being from the soft and timid creature she had been hitherto. She moved cautiously along the entry, paused one moment at her mistress's door and raised her hands in mute appeal to heaven, and then turned and glided into her own room. It was a quiet, neat apartment, on the same floor with her mistress's. There was the pleasant sunny window where she had often sat singing at her sewing; there was a little case of books, and various little fancy articles ranged by them, the gifts on Christmas holidays; there was her simple wardrobe in the closet and in the drawers; here was, in short, her home, and, on the whole, a happy one it had been to her. But there, on the bed, lay her slumbering boy, his long curls falling negligently around his unconscious face, his rosy mouth half open, his little fat hands thrown out over the bedclothes, and a smile spread like a sunbeam over his whole face.

"Poor boy! Poor fellow!" said Eliza; "they have sold you, but your mother will save you yet!"

No tear dropped over that pillow. In such straits as these the heart has no tears to give; it drops only blood, bleeding itself away in silence. She took a piece of paper and a pencil, and wrote hastily:

"Oh, missis! Dear missis! Don't think me ungrateful—don't think hard of me, anyway. I heard all you and master said tonight. I am going to try and save my boy—you will not blame me! God bless and reward you for all your kindness!"

Hastily folding and directing this, she went to a drawer and made up a little package of clothing for her boy, which she tied with a handkerchief firmly round her waist; and so fond is a mother's remembrance that even in the terrors of that hour she did not forget to put in the little package one or two of his favorite toys, reserving a gaily painted parrot to amuse him when she should be called on to awaken him. It was some trouble to arouse the little sleeper; but after some effort he sat up, and was playing with his bird while his mother was putting on her bonnet and shawl.

"Where are you going, Mother?" said he, as she drew near the bed with his little coat and cap.

His mother drew near, and looked so earnestly into his eyes that he at once divined that something unusual was the matter.

"Hush, Harry," she said; "mustn't speak loud, or they will hear us. A wicked man was coming

For background information on this novel, see the final paragraph of Stowe's biography, page 259.

to take little Harry away from his mother, and carry him 'way off in the dark; but Mother won't let him—she's going to put on her little boy's cap and coat and run off with him, so the ugly man can't catch him."

Saying these words, she had tied and buttoned on the child's simple outfit, and, taking him in her arms, she whispered to him to be very still; and, opening a door in her room which led into the outer verandah, she glided noiselessly out. . . . A few minutes brought them to the window of Uncle Tom's cottage, and Eliza, stopping, tapped lightly on the windowpane.

The prayer meeting at Uncle Tom's had, in the order of hymn singing, been protracted to a very late hour; and, as Uncle Tom had indulged himself in a few lengthy solos afterwards, the consequence was that, although it was between twelve and one o'clock, he and his worthy helpmeet were not yet asleep.

"Good Lord! What's that?" said Aunt Chloe, starting up, and hastily drawing the curtain. "My sakes alive, if it an't Lizzy! Get on your clothes, old man, quick!" . . .

And, suiting the action to the word, the door flew open, and the light of the tallow candle, which Tom had hastily lighted, fell on the haggard face and dark wild eyes of the fugitive.

"Lord bless you! I am skeered to look at ye, Lizzy! Are ye tuck sick, or what's come over ye?"

"I'm running away, Uncle Tom and Aunt Chloe—carrying off my child. Master sold him!"

"Sold him?" echoed both, lifting up their hands in dismay.

"Yes, sold!" said Eliza, firmly; "I crept into the closet by mistress's door tonight, and I heard master tell missis that he had sold my Harry and you, Uncle Tom, both to a trader, and that he was going off this morning on his horse, and that the man was to take possession today."

Tom had stood during this speech with his hands raised and his eyes dilated, like a man in a dream. Slowly and gradually, as its meaning came over him, he collapsed, rather than seated himself, on his old chair, and sunk his head down upon his knees.

"The good Lord have pity on us!" said Aunt Chloe. "Oh, it don't seem as if it was true! What has he done that mas'r should sell *him?*"

"He hasn't done anything—it isn't for that. Master don't want to sell, and missis—she's always good. I heard her plead and beg for us; but he told her 'twas no use—that he was in this man's debt, and that this man had got the power over him—and that if he didn't pay him off clear, it would end in his having to sell the place and all the people, and move off. Yes, I heard him say there was no choice between selling these two and selling all, the man was driving them so hard. Master said he was sorry; but oh!—missis! you ought to have heard her talk! If she an't a Christian and an angel, there never was one. I'm a wicked girl to leave her so; but then I can't help it. She said herself one soul was worth more than the world; and this boy has a soul, and if I let him be carried off who knows what'll become of it? It must be right; but, if it an't right, the Lord forgive me, for I can't help doing it!"

"Well, old man!" said Aunt Chloe. "Why don't you go too? Will you wait to be toted down river, where they kill you with hard work and starving? I'd a heap rather die than go there, any day! There's time for ye; be off with Lizzy—you've got a pass to come and go any time. Come, bustle up, and I'll get your things."

Tom slowly raised his head, and looked sorrowfully but quietly around, and said——

"No, no; I an't going. Let Eliza go—it's her right. I wouldn't be the one to say no. 'Tan't in *natur* for her to stay; but you heard what she said! If I must be sold, or all the people on the place, and everything go to rack, why, let me be sold. I s'pose I can b'ar it as well as any on 'em" he added, while something like a sob and a sigh shook his broad rough chest convulsively. "Mas'r always found me on the spot—he always will. I never have broke trust, nor used my pass noways contrary to my word, and I never will. It's better for me alone to go than to break up the place and sell all. . . . "

"And now," said Eliza, as she stood in the door, "I saw my husband only this afternoon, and I knew little then what was to come. They have pushed him to the very last standing-place, and he told me today that he was going to run away. Do try, if you can, to get word to him. Tell him how I went, and why I went; and tell him I'm going to try and find Canada. You must give my love to him, and tell him, if I never see him again"—she turned away, and stood with her back to them for a moment, and then added, in a husky voice, "tell him to be as good as he can, and try and meet me in the kingdom of heaven. . . . "

A few last words and tears, a few simple adieus and blessings, and, clasping her wondering and affrighted child in her arms, she glided noiselessly away. . . .

It is impossible to conceive of a human creature more wholly desolate and forlorn than Eliza when she turned her footsteps from Uncle Tom's cabin. . . .

The boundaries of the farm, the grove, the wood lot, passed by her dizzily as she walked on; and still she went, leaving one familiar object after another, slackening not, pausing not, till reddening daylight found her many a long mile from all traces of any familiar objects upon the open highway.

She had often been with her mistress to visit some connections in the little village of T——, not far from the Ohio River, and knew the road well. To go thither, to escape across the Ohio River, were the first hurried outlines of her plan of escape; beyond that, she could only hope in God.

When horses and vehicles began to move along the highway, with that alert perception peculiar to a state of excitement, and which seems to be a sort of inspiration, she became aware that her headlong pace and distracted air might bring on her remark and suspicion. She therefore put the boy on the ground, and, adjusting her dress and bonnet, she walked on at as rapid a pace as she thought consistent with the preservation of appearances. . . .

She was many miles past any neighborhood where she was personally known. If she should chance to meet any who knew her, she reflected that the well-known kindness of the family would be of itself a blind to suspicion, as making it an unlikely supposition that she could be a fugitive. As she was also so white as not to be known as of colored lineage without a critical survey, and her child was white also, it was much easier for her to pass on unsuspected.

On this presumption she stopped at noon at a neat farmhouse, to rest herself, and buy some dinner for her child and self; for, as the danger decreased with the distance, the supernatural tension of the nervous system lessened, and she found herself both weary and hungry.

The good woman, kindly and gossiping, seemed rather pleased than otherwise with having someone come in to talk with; and accepted, without examination, Eliza's statement that she "was going on a little piece, to spend a week with her friends"—all of which she hoped in her heart might prove strictly true.

An hour before sunset she entered the village of T——, by the Ohio River, weary and footsore, but still strong in heart. Her first glance was at the river, which lay, like Jordan, between her and the Canaan[1] of liberty on the other side.

It was now early spring, and the river was swollen and turbulent; great cakes of floating ice were swinging heavily to and fro in the turbid waters. Owing to the peculiar form of the shore on the Kentucky side, the land bending far out into the water, the ice had been lodged and detained in great quantities, and the narrow channel which swept round the bend was full of ice, piled one cake over another, thus forming a temporary barrier to the descending ice, which lodged, and formed a great undulating raft, filling up the whole river, and extending almost to the Kentucky shore.

Eliza stood for a moment, contemplating this unfavorable aspect of things, which she saw at once must prevent the usual ferryboat from run-

---

1. *Canaan* (kā′nən). In the Bible, Canaan was the land God promised to Abraham and his descendants. In general, Canaan represents any desirable place.

Robert Scott Duncanson, detail of *Uncle Tom and Little Eva* (1857).
The Detroit Institute of Arts

ning, and then turned into a small public house on the bank, to make a few inquiries.

The hostess, who was busy in various fizzing and stewing operations over the fire, preparatory to the evening meal, stopped, with a fork in her hand, as Eliza's sweet and plaintive voice arrested her.

"What is it?" she said.

"Isn't there a ferry or boat that takes people over to B——y, now?" she said.

"No, indeed!" said the woman; "the boats has stopped running."

Eliza's look of dismay and disappointment struck the woman, and she said, inquiringly——

"Maybe you're wanting to get over?—anybody sick? Ye seem mighty anxious."

"I've got a child that's very dangerous," said Eliza. "I never heard of it till last night, and I've walked quite a piece today, in hopes to get to the ferry."

"Well, now, that's onlucky," said the woman, whose motherly sympathies were much aroused; "I'm re'lly concerned for ye. Solomon!" she called, from the window, towards a small back building. A man in leather apron and very dirty hands appeared at the door.

"I say, Sol," said the woman, "is that ar man going to tote them bar'ls over tonight?"

"He said he should try, if 'twas any way prudent," said the man.

"There's a man a piece down here that's going over with some truck this evening, if he durs' to; he'll be in here to supper tonight, so you'd better sit down and wait. That's a sweet little fellow," added the woman, offering him a cake.

But the child, wholly exhausted, cried with weariness.

"Poor fellow! He isn't used to walking, and I've hurried him on so," said Eliza.

"Well, take him into this room," said the woman, opening into a small bedroom, where stood a comfortable bed. Eliza laid the weary boy upon it, and held his hand in hers till he was fast asleep. For her there was no rest. As a fire in her bones, the thought of the pursuer urged her on; and she gazed with longing eyes on the sullen, surging waters that lay between her and liberty.

1852

THINK AND DISCUSS
Understanding
1. How does Eliza hear of Shelby's plan to sell her son and Uncle Tom? What does she then decide to do?
2. What does Uncle Tom decide to do, on hearing the plan?
3. What is Eliza's proposed destination?
4. Why is Eliza unlikely to attract suspicion on her flight?
5. What obstacles prevent her from crossing the Ohio River?

Analyzing
6. In what way are Eliza's loyalties divided?
7. What is the prevailing atmosphere at the end of this excerpt?
8. Sentimental literature is writing that overemphasizes emotion. In what way, given the language and situation in this excerpt, could Stowe's writing be considered sentimental?

Extending
9. Eliza, Redburn, and Goodman Brown all undergo a moral struggle. Which one of these characters seems best able to cope with the evils encountered?

REVIEWING: Characterization HꞭ
See Handbook of Literary Terms, p. 882.

Characterization is the method an author uses to acquaint a reader with his or her characters. We learn about Eliza's character, for example, by reading descriptions of her appearance, personality, behavior, thoughts, and feelings and by examining her speech. Although memorable, Eliza's character appears at times *flat*—that is, one-dimensional in her range of emotions and lacking in complexity. A *round* character, on the other hand, acts according to complex and realistic patterns of emotion, motivation, and change.

1. Examine the conversation among Eliza, Aunt Chloe, and Uncle Tom when Eliza first arrives at their cabin. Do you feel their dialogue is realistic? Explain.
2. Are the feelings they express convincing? Why or why not?
3. Would you classify each of these three characters as *flat* or *round*?

COMPOSITION ◆■
Writing a News Story
Assume you are a reporter for the local newspaper in the region of Mr. Shelby's Kentucky plantation. Compose a news story recounting the events described in this selection. Include an arresting headline for your story and maintain an objective tone.

Writing About Characters
Reread the first five paragraphs of Stowe's narrative with an eye toward details that make Eliza appear as a flat character. Then write a five-paragraph essay on how the description of her character, her own speech, the letter she writes, and the overall sentimental tone contribute to her flat characterization. In the last paragraph, suggest some specific changes that would have made her a more rounded character. See "Writing About Characters" in the Writer's Handbook.

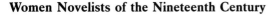

Comment

Women Novelists of the Nineteenth Century

Few modern readers would recognize the names Susanna Rowson, Susan Warner, E. D. E. N. Southworth, Lydia Sigourney, Grace Greenwood, Fanny Forester, or Fanny Fern. Yet these women, contemporaries of Hawthorne, Melville, and Emerson, were among the most popular writers of their day. In fact, most best sellers of the nineteenth century were written by women, although these works survive today mainly in library archives and old book stores.

Ironically, writers such as Herman Melville and Henry David Thoreau, considered literary giants by modern readers, were often neglected by readers of their own times. Published in 1851, Melville's *Moby Dick* was virtually unread for over seventy years. Thoreau's first book, written in 1849, sold only 219 copies in three years, while in that same year readers bought 70,000 copies of *Fern Leaves from Fanny's Portfolio*. In that same year the publishing house of G. P. Putnam paid Hawthorne royalties of $144.01, while paying Susan Warner $4,500 for six months' sales of her novel, *The Wide, Wide World*. Hawthorne, whose works were generally too gloomy and psychological for popular taste, raged about the "mob of scribbling women" who were taking the literate public by storm.

With few exceptions, the most popular fiction of the day took the form of domestic novels with complicated plots comparable to those of modern soap operas. But the virtues extolled were typically those of the nineteenth century —piety, self-sacrifice, sobriety, and domesticity—and the tone was moralistic and sentimental. In these works by and about women, the main characters usually suffered seduction, abandonment, and ultimately death in childbirth. Although this common pattern of events can hardly be considered uplifting, it appealed to a new generation of literate women. The first best-selling American novel, *Charlotte Temple*

by Susanna Rowson (1791), reigned supreme until midcentury, despite challenges from the likes of James Fenimore Cooper and Washington Irving. When Warner's *The Wide, Wide World* appeared in 1849, it was read by most literate women in America, remaining a best seller until *Uncle Tom's Cabin* appeared in 1852.

The causes of this explosion in reading lay beyond the books themselves. The dream of free education was beginning to be realized, and increasing numbers of people were learning to read. Advances in printing made books easier to produce. The oil lamp was replacing the candle, adding hours to the reading day. The increasing number of literate women, whose household duties were somewhat lightened by kitchen stoves and sewing machines, enjoyed more leisure time. And these newly liberated readers chose to read about other women, although their fictional counterparts were largely meek, submissive, and exploited. One notable exception was Capitola, the hero of E. D. E. N. Southworth's *The Hidden Hand*, who was "full of fun, frolic, spirit, and courage." A forerunner of strong women in contemporary fiction, Capitola was so beloved in her time that stores produced Capitola hats and suits, and hotels, towns, and even boats bore her name.

But not all of the women novelists of this period have been forgotten. Harriet Beecher Stowe, whose work had historical impact when it first appeared, continued to command the respect of succeeding generations of readers. Although her perennial best seller, *Uncle Tom's Cabin*, shares the sentimental tone of other novels of the day, it centers on slavery, a subject other "women's novels" avoided. Its themes of freedom, courage, and human dignity and depravity transcend topical subjects. Clearly, a writer having such a profound effect on history must be elevated above Hawthorne's ranks of "scribbling women."

"Right is of no Sex—Truth is of no Color—God is the Father of us all, and we are all Brethren." With these words on the masthead, Frederick Douglass in 1847 established the *North Star,* an antislavery weekly newspaper. Born into slavery, Douglass went on to become a nationally recognized reformer, passionately speaking for black emancipation and economic opportunity.

Douglass's childhood was spent as a slave in the shipyards of Baltimore, Maryland. In 1838 he escaped, married and settled in New Bedford, Massachusetts, with his wife, who was free.

After reading William Lloyd Garrison's newspaper, *The Liberator,* Douglass became active in the antislavery movement. He published his autobiography, *Narrative of the Life of Frederick Douglass,* in 1845 in the hope that his experiences might convince others of the evils of slavery. Popularizing the cause of antislavery, he traveled in England and Ireland.

When the Civil War began, he organized black soldiers for the Union army. After the war was over, he continued to work for black suffrage and civil rights. Later he was appointed Ambassador to Haiti.

So powerful was Douglass's impact on his contemporaries that when he died in 1895, Elizabeth Cady Stanton wrote, "Frederick Douglass is not dead! His grand character will long be an object lesson in our national history, his lofty sentiments of liberty, justice, and equality, echoed on every platform over our broad land, must influence and inspire many coming generations."

An eloquent and persuasive orator, Douglass argued for black suffrage in "What the Black Man Wants." This speech, excerpted here, was delivered at the annual meeting of the Massachusetts Anti-Slavery Society in Boston, 1865.

from What the Black Man Wants

Frederick Douglass

. . . I have had but one idea for the last three years to present to the American people, and the phraseology in which I clothe it is the old Abolition phraseology. I am for the "immediate, unconditional, and universal" enfranchisement of the black man, in every state in the Union. Without this, his liberty is a mockery; without this, you might as well almost retain the old name of slavery for his condition; for, in fact, if he is not the slave of the individual master, he is the slave of society, and holds his liberty as a privilege, not as a right. He is at the mercy of the mob, and has no means of protecting himself.

It may be objected, however, that this pressing of the Negro's right to suffrage is premature. Let us have slavery abolished, it may be said, let us have labor organized, and then, in the natural course of events, the right of suffrage will be extended to the Negro. I do not agree with this. The constitution of the human mind is such, that if it once disregards the conviction forced upon it by a revelation of truth, it requires the exercise of a higher power to produce the same conviction afterward. The American people are now in tears. The Shenandoah has run blood,[1] the best blood of the North. All around Richmond, the blood of New England and of the North has been shed, of your sons, your brothers, and your fathers. We all feel, in the existence of this rebellion, that judgments terrible, widespread, far-reaching, overwhelming, are abroad in the land; and we feel, in view of these judgments, just now, a disposition to learn righteousness. This is the hour. Our streets are in mourning, tears are falling at every fireside, and under the chastisement of this rebellion we have almost come up to the point of conceding this great, this all-important right of suffrage. I fear that if we fail to do it now, if Abolitionists fail to press it now, we may not see, for centuries to come, the same disposition that exists at this moment. Hence, I say, now is the time to press this right.

It may be asked, "Why do you want it? Some men have got along very well without it. Women have not this right." Shall we justify one wrong by another? That is a sufficient answer. Shall we at this moment justify the deprivation of the Negro of the right to vote, because some one else is deprived of that privilege? I hold that women, as well as men, have the right to vote, and my heart and my voice go with the movement to extend suffrage to woman; but that question rests upon another basis than that on which our right rests. We may be asked, I say, why we want it. I will tell you why we want it. We want it because it is our right, first of all. No class of men can, without insulting their own nature, be content with any deprivations of their rights. We want it, again, as a means for educating our race. Men are so constituted that they derive their conviction of their own possibilities largely from the estimate formed of them by others. If nothing is expected of a people, that people will find it difficult to contradict that expectation. By depriving us of suffrage, you affirm our incapacity to form an intelligent judgment respecting public men and public measures; you declare before the world that we are unfit to exercise the elective franchise, and by this means lead us to undervalue ourselves, to put a low estimate upon ourselves, and to feel that we have no possibilities like other men. Again, I want the elective franchise, for one, as a colored man, because ours is a peculiar government, based upon a peculiar idea, and that idea is universal suffrage. If I were in a monarchical government, or an autocratic or aristocratic government, where the few bore rule and the many were subject, there would be no special stigma resting upon me, because I did not exercise the elective franchise. It would do me no great violence. Mingling with the mass, I should partake of the strength of the mass, and I should have the same incentives to endeavor with the mass of my fellow men; it would be no particular burden, no particular deprivation; but here, where universal suffrage is the rule, where that is the fundamental idea of the government, to rule us out is to make us an exception, to brand us with the stigma of inferiority, and to invite to our heads the missiles of those about us; therefore, I want the franchise for the black man. . . .

I ask my friends who are apologizing for not insisting upon this right, where can the black man look in this country for the assertion of this right, if he may not look to the Massachusetts Anti-Slavery Society? Where under the whole heavens can he look for sympathy in asserting this right, if he may not look to this platform? Have

---

1. **Shenandoah . . . blood.** The valley of the Shenandoah River in Virginia was the scene of some of the bloodiest campaigns in the Civil War.

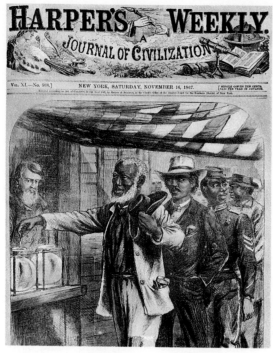

HARPER'S WEEKLY.
A
JOURNAL OF CIVILIZATION.

Vol. XI.—No. 568.]   NEW YORK, SATURDAY, NOVEMBER 16, 1867.   [SINGLE COPIES TEN CENTS. $4.00 PER YEAR IN ADVANCE.

Black voters at the polls in 1867, when the South was occupied by Federal troops.

you lifted us up to a certain height to see that we are men, and then are any disposed to leave us there, without seeing that we are put in possession of all our rights? We look naturally to this platform for the assertion of all our rights, and for this one especially. I understand the antislavery societies of this country to be based on two principles—first the freedom of the blacks of this country; and, second, the elevation of them. Let me not be misunderstood here. I am not asking for sympathy at the hands of Abolitionists, sympathy at the hands of any. I think the American people are disposed often to be generous rather than just. I look over this country at the present time, and I see educational societies, sanitary commissions, freedmen's associations and the like—all very good: but in regard to the colored people there is always more than is benevolent, I perceive, than just, manifested towards us. What I ask for the Negro is not benevolence, not pity, not sympathy, but simple justice. The American

people have always been anxious to know what they shall do with us. . . .

Everybody has asked the question, and they learned to ask it early of the Abolitionists, "What shall we do with the Negro?" I have had but one answer from the beginning. Do nothing with us! Your doing with us has already played the mischief with us. Do nothing with us! If the apples will not remain on the tree of their own strength, if they are worm-eaten at the core, if they are early ripe and disposed to fall, let them fall! I am not for tying or fastening them on the tree in any way, except by nature's plan, and if they will not stay there, let them fall. And if the Negro can not stand on his own legs, let him fall also. All I ask is, give him a chance to stand on his own legs! Let him alone! If you see him on his way to school, let him alone—don't disturb him. If you see him going to the dinner table at a hotel, let him go! If you see him going to the ballot box, let him alone—don't disturb him! If you see him going into a workshop, just let him alone—your interference is doing him a positive injury. . . . Let him fall if he can not stand alone! If the Negro can not live by the line of eternal justice, . . . the fault will not be yours; it will be his who made the Negro, and established that line for his government. Let him live or die by that. If you will only untie his hands, and give him a chance, I think he will live. . . .   1865

THINK AND DISCUSS
Understanding
1. What is the meaning of *suffrage* and *enfranchisement?* (Consult your Glossary, if necessary.)
2. What is the rebellion mentioned in the second paragraph that has caused the American people to suffer?
3. What reasons does Douglass give in paragraph three (267a, 2) for wanting suffrage?

4. What things do blacks *not* want, according to the last sentence in paragraph four? What is it that they *do* want?

Analyzing

5. How does Douglass respond to the assertion that women do not have the right to vote?
6. This speech was delivered in 1865. Given the date, why is Douglass afraid that society will not sustain its zeal in working for black suffrage? Support your answer with passages from the text.
7. Identify three examples of **figurative language** in this speech.
8. One rhetorical technique often used to convince an audience is that of anticipating and stating the arguments that one's opponent is likely to give, and answering these arguments even before the opponent has had a chance to voice them. Douglass makes use of this technique at least three times in his address. What are these arguments and how does Douglass refute them?

COMPOSITION
Writing a Persuasive Letter

Douglass's tactic of anticipating and addressing an opponent's argument requires skill and forethought. Compose a five-paragraph letter to your school newspaper in which you use this tactic in arguing for or against a current issue. In the introductory paragraph, state the issue, along with your feelings about it. In the middle paragraphs, develop three points of your argument. In the final paragraph, summarize your arguments and recommend a plan of action.

BIOGRAPHY

Sojourner Truth
1795–1883

Born a slave in New York, Sojourner Truth was freed at the age of thirty-one under the New York State Emancipation Act. She was deeply religious and had mystical experiences. After one such experience, she recognized a calling to follow a more active path of preaching and enlightening people. At the age of forty-six, she dropped her slave name Isabella and adopted the name Sojourner (one who is a temporary resident; a visitor) Truth. She stopped working as a domestic, and for the next thirty years traveled throughout the country, speaking in support of abolitionist and feminist causes.

Although illiterate, she was a powerful speaker, at times rising from her seat in the audience to counter remarks and arguments with which she disagreed. Gradually she became a known and respected leader in social movements of the time. When, in 1861, she met President Lincoln, she encouraged him to support the enlistment of free blacks to fight in defense of the Union. After the Civil War, she continued her speaking career until she retired in Battle Creek, Michigan, at the age of eighty-six.

The following is an extemporaneous speech at the women's rights convention in Akron, Ohio, in 1851, in response to male speakers who opposed women's rights.

Ain't I a Woman?

Sojourner Truth

Well, children, where there is so much racket there must be something out of kilter. I think that 'twixt the Negroes of the South and the women at the North, all talking about rights, the white men will be in a fix pretty soon. But what's all this here talking about?

That man over there says that women need to be helped into carriages, and lifted over ditches, and to have the best place everywhere. Nobody ever helps me into carriages, or over mud-puddles, or gives me any best place! And ain't I a woman? Look at me! Look at my arm! I have ploughed and planted, and gathered into barns, and no man could head me! And ain't I a woman? I could work as much and eat as much as a man—when I could get it—and bear the lash as well! And ain't I a woman? I have borne thirteen children, and seen them most all sold off to slavery, and when I cried out with my mother's grief, none but Jesus heard me! And ain't I a woman?

Then they talk about this thing in the head; what's this they call it? [Intellect, someone whispers.] That's it, honey. What's that got to do with women's rights or Negro's rights? If my cup won't hold but a pint, and yours holds a quart, wouldn't you be mean not to let me have my little half-measure full?

Then that little man in black there, he says women can't have as much rights as men, 'cause Christ wasn't a woman! Where did your Christ come from? Where did your Christ come from? From God and a woman! Man had nothing to do with Him.

If the first woman God ever made was strong enough to turn the world upside down all alone, these women together ought to be able to turn it back, and get it right side up again! And now they is asking to do it, the men better let them.

Obliged to you for hearing me, and now old Sojourner ain't got nothing more to say.

1851

THINK AND DISCUSS
Understanding
1. According to the first paragraph, what two groups will make part of the audience uncomfortable?
2. What aspects of her difficult life does Truth mention in the second paragraph?
3. How does she counter the point presented that Christ was not a woman?

Analyzing
4. How would you describe the **tone** of Truth's speech?

5. What **allusion** does Truth make in the fifth paragraph?

THINKING SKILLS
Generalizing
You can make several generalizations about Sojourner Truth, based on her biography and her speech.

1. What kind of life has she led?
2. What does her change of name indicate about her?

BIOGRAPHY

Abraham Lincoln
1809–1865

James Russell Lowell once described Abraham Lincoln as "the first American." Well over a hundred years later he remains the foremost figure in our national mythology. Lincoln faced the greatest crisis—the secession of the Southern states from the Union and the resulting Civil War—that this country has ever faced. Hated as well as loved for his war policies, he seemed to grow in stature as national problems mounted—no small accomplishment for a small-town lawyer turned statesman turned military strategist. He suffered patiently through setback after setback before the Union he loved was finally saved. Then, while attending the theater after learning of Lee's surrender, he was assassinated.

One of the bloodiest and most decisive battles of the Civil War was fought near Gettysburg, Pennsylvania, in July, 1863. In November of that year, people gathered for the dedication of a cemetery where thousands of men had died. Unlike the orator who had preceded him and who had spoken for almost two hours, Lincoln spoke for slightly more than two minutes. In his remarks, now known as the Gettysburg Address—once described by Edgar Lee Masters as a prose poem—President Lincoln emerges as a national leader deeply grieved by the tragic conflict between North and South and firmly resolved in his commitment to a better future.

 Review TONE in the Handbook of Literary Terms, page 915.

Gettysburg Address

Abraham Lincoln

our score and seven years ago our fathers brought forth on this continent a new nation, conceived in liberty and dedicated to the proposition that all men are created equal.

Now we are engaged in a great civil war, testing whether that nation or any nation so conceived and so dedicated can long endure. We are met on a great battlefield of that war. We have come to dedicate a portion of that field as a final resting place for those who here gave their lives that that nation might live. It is altogether fitting and proper that we should do this.

But, in a larger sense, we cannot dedicate—

we cannot consecrate—we cannot hallow—this ground. The brave men, living and dead, who struggled here have consecrated it far above our poor power to add or detract. The world will little note nor long remember what we say here, but it can never forget what they did here. It is for us, the living, rather to be dedicated here to the unfinished work which they who fought here have thus far so nobly advanced.

It is rather for us to be here dedicated to the great task remaining before us—that from these honored dead we take increased devotion to that cause for which they gave the last full measure of devotion; that we here highly resolve that these dead shall not have died in vain; that this nation, under God, shall have a new birth of freedom; and that government of the people, by the people, for the people shall not perish from the earth.

1863

THINK AND DISCUSS
Understanding
1. On what occasion does Lincoln deliver his address?
2. Who are the people who have really consecrated the cemetery?
3. What is the "unfinished work" to be done?

Analyzing
4. What emotional effect on the audience is Lincoln trying to create and with what means does he achieve this effect?
5. What is the climactic point of the speech? Explain.
6. Compare the **tone** of Lincoln's speech with that of Douglass and Truth. Explain how the circumstances and audience of each speech influenced each speaker's tone and purpose.

REVIEWING: Tone H⫶
See Handbook of Literary Terms, p. 915.
Tone is the author's attitude toward his or her subject matter and audience. It is often revealed by the choice and arrangement of words and by the use of detail.

1. How would you describe the tone of this speech?
2. Why might Lincoln have chosen to say "Four score and seven" rather than "eighty-seven"? "fitting and proper" rather than "just fine"?

COMPOSITION ✦
Imitating a Writer's Style
Try writing your own address, based on the structure and style of the Gettysburg Address. You may want to adopt a tone that differs from Lincoln's somber one. Your topic, like Lincoln's, must allow for conflict or debate. You may, for example, begin: "_____ years ago our city brought forth a new school (my parents brought forth a new daughter/son; my teacher brought forth a new assignment; our coach brought forth a new rule; Congress brought forth a new law, etc.)." The final sentence, which will probably be the most difficult to construct, should sum things up the way Lincoln's does. See "Developing Your Style" in the Writer's Handbook.

ENRICHMENT
Planning a Multi-Media Presentation
Assume that a grant has been announced providing funds for the production by high-school students of a multi-media presentation of the Gettysburg Address. Prepare a proposal describing what you would envision as a powerful and moving presentation of this historical and literary episode. Suggest a title, graphics, music, and supplementary script.

BIOGRAPHY

Robert E. Lee
1807–1870

Detail of photograph by Mathew Brady (c. 1823–1896). National Archives

Already a distinguished military leader when the Civil War broke out in 1861, Robert E. Lee was originally offered command of the Union's armed forces. Lee rejected the offer although he supported neither slavery (he no longer held any slaves of his own) nor secession from the Union ("secession is nothing but revolution"). Since Lee was a descendant of a noteworthy Virginia family and felt intensely loyal to his home state, he resigned from the Union army, vowing to defend Virginia from attack if necessary, despite his own convictions.

When his native state seceded, he was forced to come to its defense. Eventually his personal qualities and tactical skills as a military strategist (he had graduated second in his class at West Point) made him an inspiring and powerful leader of the confederate forces. Ironically, Lee, one of the most professional and exemplary of all the military commanders in the Confederacy, would ultimately be defeated by President Lincoln, military strategist for the Northern army during much of the Civil War, whom Civil War historian Bruce Catton identified as "a man who never wore a uniform or fought a battle."

Robert E. Lee wrote the letter that follows to his son just four months before the outbreak of the Civil War and his subsequent resignation from what became the Northern army.

Letter to His Son

Robert E. Lee

Fort Mason, Texas
January 23, 1861

 received Everett's *Life of Washington* which you sent me, and enjoyed its perusal. How his spirit would be grieved could he see the wreck of his mighty labors! I will not, however, permit myself to believe, until all ground of hope is gone, that the fruit of his noble deeds will be destroyed, and that his precious advice and virtuous example will so soon be forgotten by his countrymen. As far as I can judge by the papers, we are between a state of anarchy and civil war. May God avert both of these evils from us! I fear that mankind will not for years be sufficiently Christianized to bear the absence of restraint and force. I see that four states[1] have

---

1. *four states*, South Carolina, Mississippi, Florida, and Alabama.

declared themselves out of the Union; four more will apparently follow their example. Then, if the border states are brought into the gulf of revolution, one-half of the country will be arrayed against the other. I must try and be patient and await the end, for I can do nothing to hasten or retard it.

The South, in my opinion, has been aggrieved by the acts of the North, as you say. I feel the aggression and am willing to take every proper step for redress. It is the principle I contend for, not individual or private benefit. As an American citizen, I take great pride in my country, her prosperity and institutions, and would defend any state if her rights were invaded. But I can anticipate no greater calamity for the country than a dissolution of the Union. It would be an accumulation of all the evils we complain of, and I am willing to sacrifice everything but honor for its preservation. I hope, therefore, that all constitutional means will be exhausted before there is a resort to force. Secession is nothing but revolution. The framers of our Constitution never exhausted so much labor, wisdom, and forbearance in its formation, and surrounded it with so many guards and securities, if it was intended to be broken by every member of the confederacy at will. It was intended for "perpetual union," so expressed in the preamble, and for the establishment of a government, not a compact, which can only be dissolved by revolution or the consent of all the people in convention assembled. It is idle to talk of secession. Anarchy would have been established, and not a government, by Washington, Hamilton, Jefferson, Madison, and the other patriots of the Revolution. . . . Still, a Union that can only be maintained by swords and bayonets, and in which strife and civil war are to take the place of brotherly love and kindness, has no charm for me. I shall mourn for my country and for the welfare and progress of mankind. If the Union is dissolved, and the government disrupted, I shall return to my native state and share the miseries of my people; and save in defense will draw my sword on none.

1863

THINK AND DISCUSS
Understanding
1. Which states have already left the Union at the time Lee wrote this letter? What does Lee say to indicate that he thinks more states will leave?
2. What one thing does Lee refuse to sacrifice in preserving the Union?
3. What are the only conditions under which the government can be dissolved, according to Lee?
4. What does Lee promise to do if the Union is dissolved?

Analyzing
5. Give examples from the letter that show Lee's loyalty to both his country and to the South.

6. How would you describe the **tone** of Lee's letter? What reasons would explain its rather unusual quality for a letter from a father to his son?
7. State the main idea of Lee's letter in a sentence of your own.

Extending
8. Both Lee and Lincoln respected the sanctity of the Union, yet their attitudes differed in some respects. How would you explain their differences?

Lanier was born in Macon, Georgia, and educated at Oglethorpe University. After graduation he enlisted in the Confederate army and served for the duration of the war. The last five months of the war he was imprisoned in a Federal camp where, as a result of exposure, his health was impaired for the rest of his life.

After the war, while teaching school and working as a hotel clerk, Lanier found time to revive his earlier interest in writing. He published a novel titled *Tiger-Lilies* in 1867. But he decided he had a greater enthusiasm for poetry than for fiction, and he worked hard to perfect his skill. Lanier was a musician as well as a poet. A flutist of great ability, he was a member of the Peabody Symphony Orchestra in Baltimore in the 1870s. During these same years he was a lecturer in literature at Johns Hopkins University.

Lanier rebelled against what he called the "prim smugness and clean-shaven propriety" of conventional verse. In *The Science of English Verse* (1880), he declared that the principles of music and poetry are the same. His emphasis on sound over meaning resembles the ideas of Poe. He used musical notations to analyze verse rhythms and wrote his most characteristic poems as if he were composing music. Although shocked by the radical departures in the poetry of Whitman and Dickinson, Lanier himself made certain technical innovations.

Lanier finally gained recognition when several of his poems were published in a periodical in 1875. However, *Poems,* a volume that was published in 1877, was not well received, and his hope that his work at Johns Hopkins would result in a professorship was unrealized. The last few years of his life were spent in preparing his lectures and in writing some of his finest poetry.

Try reading the following poem aloud to hear its musical effects. The Chattahoochee (chat′ə hü′chē) River, which originates in the Blue Ridge Mountains of northeastern Georgia, forms the borders between Georgia and Alabama, and Georgia and Florida. This river flows between Habersham and Hall, which are counties in northeast Georgia.

Song of the Chattahoochee

Sidney Lanier

Out of the hills of Habersham,
  Down the valleys of Hall,
I hurry amain to reach the plain,
Run the rapid and leap the fall,
5 Split at the rock and together again,
Accept my bed, or narrow or wide,
And flee from folly on every side
With a lover's pain to attain the plain
    Far from the hills of Habersham,
10   Far from the valleys of Hall.

All down the hills of Habersham,
  All through the valleys of Hall,
The rushes cried *Abide, abide,*
The willful waterweeds held me thrall,
15 The laving laurel turned my tide,
The ferns and the fondling grass said *Stay,*
The dewberry dipped for to work delay,
And the little reeds sighed *Abide, abide,*
    Here in the hills of Habersham,
20   *Here in the valleys of Hall.*

High o'er the hills of Habersham,
  Veiling the valleys of Hall,
The hickory told me manifold
Fair tales of shade, the poplar tall
25 Wrought me her shadowy self to hold,
The chestnut, the oak, the walnut, the pine,
Overleaning, with flickering meaning and sign,
Said, *Pass not, so cold, these manifold*
    Deep shades of the hills of Habersham,
30   *These glades in the valleys of Hall.*

And oft in the hills of Habersham,
  And oft in the valleys of Hall,
The white quartz shone, and the smooth
    brook stone
Did bar me of passage with friendly brawl,
35 And many a luminous jewel lone
—Crystals clear or a-cloud with mist,
Ruby, garnet and amethyst——
Made lures with the lights of streaming stone
    In the clefts of the hills of Habersham,
40   In the beds of the valleys of Hall.

But oh, not the hills of Habersham,
  And oh, not the valleys of Hall
Avail: I am fain for to water the plain.
Downward the voices of Duty call——
45 Downward, to toil and be mixed with the main,[1]
The dry fields burn, and the mills are to turn,
And a myriad flowers mortally yearn,
And the lordly main from beyond the plain
    Calls o'er the hills of Habersham,
50   Calls through the valleys of Hall.
1877   1884

---

1. *the main,* the sea.

From Vol. I of *Centennial Edition of the Works of Sidney Lanier,*
edited by Charles R. Anderson. Copyright 1945, The Johns Hopkins
University Press. Reprinted by permission.

Joseph Rusling Meeker, *The Acadians in the Achafalaya,*
"Evangeline" (1871). The Brooklyn Museum

THINK AND DISCUSS
Understanding
1. Who is the speaker, the "I" in line 3?
2. In the second stanza, what is the speaker urged to do?
3. What voices call the river in line 44? What work awaits the river (line 46)?

Analyzing
4. Chart the **rhyme scheme** of the first stanza.
5. What stanza introduces a turning point in the speaker's thoughts?

Extending
6. The poem can be read as an expression of conflicting desires of the human spirit. What are these desires? Which desire usually wins?

REVIEWING: Sound Devices HⓏ
See Handbook of Literary Terms, p. 909.

Lanier's poem relies heavily on the **sound devices** of **alliteration** and **internal rhyme** to achieve its musical effect.

1. Which words in the first stanza are examples of internal rhyme?
2. Cite examples of alliteration in the second stanza. Note that alliteration makes it necessary to read this stanza slowly. How does this technique reinforce the meaning?

COMPOSITION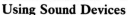
Using Sound Devices
Write a two-paragraph statement or two stanzas of poetry for a student literary magazine about a place that has special meaning or emotional significance for you. First, make a list of words and phrases containing sound devices that reflect your feelings or ideas. Then, using words from your list, compose stanzas or paragraphs reflecting your views about this place. Read your composition aloud to assure that these techniques are creating the sound effects you desire.

Writing About a Poem
Lanier uses sound devices similar to those that Edgar Allan Poe uses in his poems (Unit 2). Write a four-paragraph essay for a classmate comparing the use of sound devices in "The Song of the Chattahoochee" with those in "The Raven." In paragraphs one to three, respectively, describe both poets' use of alliteration, rhyme, and repetition. In the final paragraph, evaluate the effectiveness of these devices in each poem. See "Writing About Poetry and Poetic Devices" in the Writer's Handbook.

Josh Billings   1818–1885

Josh Billings was a personality created by Henry Wheeler Shaw, who was born in Massachusetts but eventually settled in New York. Shaw engaged in various occupations, including farming, selling real estate, and commanding a riverboat, until he began to write relatively late in life. He quickly became a successful author and lecturer, enjoying national popularity after 1867, when he joined the *New York Weekly* as a contributor. Under the pseudonym of Josh Billings, he gained fame with sketches, letters, and an annual *Allminax* of "affurisms" that was issued from 1869 to 1880.

As a popular cracker-barrel philosopher, he employed an earthy, homespun, vernacular English associated with many of the literary comedians of the time. In his various publications, he appears as "Uncle Josh," a humorist and philosopher, defending common sense, fair play, and traditional values.

Davy Crockett   1776–1836

Born in Tennessee, Davy Crockett began his political career as a justice of the peace. After serving in the state legislature, he ran successfully for Congress. There he became a noted figure, combining grass-roots and backwoods democracy with frontier heroism. His picturesque eccentricities, rough-hewn humor, shrewdness, and hearty pioneer spirit helped to mold his colorful national image. Crockett's wilderness exploits were publicized in a biography and in an autobiography titled *A Narrative of the Life of Davy Crockett of the State of Tennessee* (1834).

After his political career in Tennessee, Crockett traveled to Texas where he joined the war for state independence and died a few months later in the Battle of the Alamo.

Mike Fink   c. 1770

The date and place of Mike Fink's birth, along with his ancestry, are uncertain. It is believed that he was born around Fort Pitt, in about 1770, of Scotch-Irish (or perhaps German) parents. Most of what we know today of Fink is culled from stories passed orally for generations along the Western rivers. Fink's legendary strength and boldness form the basis of his brags. In his own words, he was "King of the Rivers," and "a ring-tailed screamer from the old Mississippi."

Fink was one of the last of the Mississippi boatmen, who were replaced when steamships took over the rivers. During his final years, he was a trapper and a mountain man in the Rockies.

from Uncle Josh's Zoo

Josh Billings

The Ant

The ant has no holidays, no eight-hour system, nor never strikes for higher wages. They are cheerful little toilers and have no malice nor back door to their hearts. There is no sedentary loafers among them and you never see one out of a job. They get up early, go to bed late, work all the time, and eat on the run.

You never see two ants arguing some foolish question that neither of them don't understand; they don't care whether the moon is inhabited or not; nor whether a fish weighing two pounds put into a pail of water already full will make the pail slop over or weigh more. They ain't hunting after the philosopher's stone or getting crazy over the cause of the sudden earthquake. They don't care whether Jupiter is thirty or thirty-one millions of miles up in the air nor whether the earth bobs around on its axis or not, so long as it don't bob over their corncrib and spill their barley.

They are simple, little, busy ants, full of faith, working hard, living prudently, committing no sin, praising God by minding their own business, and dying when their time comes, to make room for the next crop of ants.

They are a reproach to the lazy, an encouragement to the industrious, a rebuke to the vicious, and a study to the Christian.

Ants have bylaws and a constitution and they mean something. Their laws ain't like our laws, made with a hole in them so that a man can steal a horse and ride through them on a walk. They don't have any legislators that you can buy, nor any judges, lying around on the half-shell, ready to be swallowed.

I rather like the ants and think now I shall sell out my money and real estate and join them.

THINK AND DISCUSS
Understanding
1. In the first paragraph, Billings describes specific activities the ant does *not* do. What are these activities?
2. What is the ant's only concern, according to paragraph two?
3. How are the ant's laws and legislatures different from ours, according to paragraph five?

Analyzing
4. What qualities of the ants, mentioned in paragraph three, does Billings imply would also characterize good human beings?
5. Billings says that ants have no "back door to their hearts." What does he mean by this **figurative language?**

Extending
6. Most people interpret Billings's remarks as a critique of human—not ant—behavior. What points do you think he is making about people? Do you agree with him?

Tall Tale

Davy Crockett

lmost every boddy that knows the forrest, understands parfectly well that Davy Crockett never loses powder and ball, havin' ben brort up to blieve it a sin to throw away amminition, and that is the benefit of a vartuous eddikation. I war out in the forrest won arternoon, and had jist got to a plaice called the grate gap, when I seed a rakkoon setting all alone upon a tree. I klapped the breech of Brown Betty to my sholder, and war jist a going to put a piece of led between his sholders, when he lifted one paw, and sez he, "Is your name Crockett?"

Sez I, "You are rite for wonst, my name is Davy Crockett."

"Then," sez he, "you needn't take no further trubble, for I may as well cum down without another word"; and the cretur wauked rite down from the tree, for he considered himself shot.

c. 1830

Richard Curtis, *The Genial Idiots: The American Saga as Seen by Our Humorists*. New York: Macmillan Publishing Company, 1968.

John James Audubon (1785–1851), *Raccoon*. Newberry Library

Brag

Mike Fink

The following brag is Fink's challenge to another boatman for a fight. His "WHOOP" echoes the sound of a boat horn.

'm a regular screamer from the Ohio, the Mississippi, and all the streams that run into them! I can strike a blow like a falling tree, and every lick I make in the woods lets in an acre of sunshine! WHOOP! I can out-run, out-shoot, out-brag, and out-fight—rough-and-tumble or fair play, any man on the rivers from Pittsburgh to New Orleans and back again. WHOOP! Come on and see how tough I am! Haven't had a tussle for two whole live-long days, and my muscles are as rusty as an old hinge! Cock-a-doodle-do!"

Walter Blair, *Tall Tale America: A Legendary History Of Our Humorous Heroes.* New York: Coward, McCann & Geoghegan, Inc., 1944.

THINK AND DISCUSS
Understanding
1. What personal ability is Crockett illustrating with the tall tale?
2. What personal qualities are highlighted in Fink's brag?

Analyzing
3. Which piece—Crockett's or Fink's—do you think shows more imagination?
4. Which of the two works displays more humor? Explain.

Extending
5. Every country has its narratives of exaggerated feats by superheroes. What qualities distinguish the American superhero in these two selections?

THINKING SKILLS
Synthesizing
The humor of Mike Fink and Davy Crockett is broad and exaggerated, like that of a cartoon. A cartoon or picture that dramatically exaggerates an outstanding or peculiar feature is called a *caricature.* For example, a greedy person could be portrayed with a huge, grasping fist.

1. What quality of appearance or character seems most prominent about Davy Crockett? Mike Fink?
2. Describe or draw a caricature of each of these characters, based on the tall tale and the brag.

COMPOSITION
Writing a Tall Tale
Using Crockett's work as a model, write a three-paragraph tall tale about a superhero. Try to achieve a humorous effect through stylized vernacular, exaggeration, concrete detail, and dialogue. Assume your tall tale will be published in a student literary magazine.

American Humor

Humor as a pure species of American culture evolved gradually. Although the rigors of early colonial life seldom allowed for humorous writings, the spirit of play awakened with the publishing of Benjamin Franklin's *Poor Richard's Almanack* in 1732. Although Franklin's humor was too closely patterned on British models to be considered thoroughbred American, it included such gems as, "Love your neighbor, but don't pull down your hedges" and "God heals, and the doctor takes the fees." Franklin's creation, Mistress Silence Dogood, began a tradition of literary alter ego identities—Washington Irving's Diedrich Knickerbocker, C. F. Browne's Artemus Ward, and H. W. Shaw's Josh Billings—to name a few. Such stage personalities allowed American humorists the relative freedom and distance to indulge their imaginative fancies.

The election of Andrew Jackson in 1828 marked the triumph of the American common man and signaled the development of a new type of distinctly American humor. Dominant characters emerged—the Western frontiersman, the Down East peddler, the Mississippi boatman, the Yankee cracker-barrel philosopher—figures who mimicked the qualities of natives of various sections of the country.

Tall tales about David Crockett were typical of the picture that the humorous yarn spinners drew of a frontiersman—a man characterized by exuberance, rough activity, and courage to surmount any hardship. The Mississippi boatman, Mike Fink, bragged about similar survival skills of the superhero, which, at times, included violence. Seba Smith, a Down East humorist, created the character of Jack Downing, a quiet, shrewd observer of the public scene. Less exuberant and expansive than that of the Southwest frontier, Down East humor espoused rural values and common sense through characters that were more realistic and practical than their Western counterparts.

In addition to the regional characters, there were other humorous characters whose home, speech, and ways of thinking and acting belonged to no particular section. These well-intentioned blunderers, called "genial idiots" by Mark Twain, spoke in colloquial "misexpressions," once termed "cacophonics" or "deformed writing." Josh Billings used the bizarre spellings, illogical associations, ungrammatical constructions, and outlandish puns popular among literary comedians of the time.

By the second half of the nineteenth century, American humor, although varied, had achieved some standard, recognizable features: a boisterous irreverence for the conventional; an emphasis on incongruity and extravagant exaggeration, a good-natured but often dark view of humanity; a partiality to plain folk at the expense of their superiors; and a disregard for standard English.

These characteristics are typified in the works of America's preeminent literary jester, Mark Twain (Unit 4). Unlike the earlier humorists, Twain often created memorable local-color settings, as well as characters who were three-dimensional rather than stereotypical. With Twain, American humor came of age and merged with literature. His character Huck Finn is a national—even global—expression of definitive American humor and of the American character itself.

It has been observed that American humor parallels the country's exuberant way of life. Although contemporary life, and consequently its humor, has become more sophisticated and urbane than its rollicking, lusty predecessors, the underlying spirit remains unchanged. It is still bold, frank, and irreverent, and provides an antidote to the nation's ills.

THINKING CRITICALLY
ABOUT LITERATURE

UNIT 3   AMERICAN CLASSIC   1840–1870

■ CONCEPT REVIEW

The following speech excerpt contains many of the important ideas and literary terms of the period you have just studied. The notes and questions are designed to help you think critically about your reading. Page numbers in the notes refer to an application. A more extensive discussion of these terms is in the Handbook of Literary Terms.

On July 19, 1848, Elizabeth Cady Stanton was the principal speaker at the first convention of the women's rights movement, held in Seneca Falls, New York. Stanton first became aware that women were denied political and economic rights when she heard the stories of women who came to her father, an attorney, for legal aid. As she grew older, she became increasingly convinced of the need for women to organize to attain those rights. Stanton's keynote address, excerpted here, got the meeting off to a rousing start.

Speech to the First Women's Rights Convention

Elizabeth Cady Stanton

We have met here today to discuss our rights and wrongs, civil and political, and not, as some have supposed, to go into the detail of social life alone. We do not propose to petition the legislature to make our husbands just, generous, and courteous, to seat every man at the head of a cradle, and to clothe every woman in male attire. None of these points, however important they may be considered by leading men, will be touched in this convention. As to their costume, the gentlemen need feel no fear of our imitating that, for we think it in violation of every principle of taste, beauty, and dignity; notwithstanding all the contempt cast upon our loose, flowing

■ Note how Stanton achieves a humorous effect by anticipating and answering arguments.

garments, we still admire the graceful folds, and consider our costume far more artistic than theirs. Many of the nobler sex seem to agree with us in this opinion, for the bishops, priests, judges, barristers, and lord mayors of the first nation on the globe, and the pope of Rome, with his cardinals, too, all wear the loose flowing robes, thus tacitly acknowledging that the male attire is neither dignified nor imposing. No, we shall not molest you in your philosophical experiments with stocks, pants, high-heeled boots, and Russian belts. . . .

But we are assembled to protest against a form of government existing without the consent of the governed—to declare our right to be free as man is free, to be represented in the government which we are taxed to support, to have [abolished] such disgraceful laws as give man the power to chastise and imprison his wife, to take the wages which she earns, the property which she inherits, and, in case of separation, the children of her love; laws which make her the mere dependent on his bounty. It is a protest against such unjust laws as these that we are assembled today, and to have them, if possible, forever erased from our statute books, deeming them a shame and a disgrace to a Christian republic in the nineteenth century. We have met

■ **Tone** (page 272): Stanton becomes serious as she states the purpose for this meeting.

■ Stanton notes the effects of unjust laws.

> To uplift woman's fallen divinity
> Upon an even pedestal with man's.

And, strange as it may seem to many, we now demand our right to vote according to the declaration of the government under which we live. This right no one pretends to deny. We need not prove ourselves equal to Daniel Webster to enjoy this privilege, for the ignorant Irishman in the ditch has all the civil rights he has. We need not prove our muscular power equal to this same Irishman to enjoy this privilege, for the most tiny, weak, ill-shaped stripling of twenty-one has all the civil rights of the Irishman. We have no objection to discuss the question of equality, for we feel that the weight of argument lies wholly with us, but we wish the question of equality kept distinct from the question of rights, for the proof of the one does not determine the truth of the other. All white men in this country have the same rights, however they may differ in mind, body, or estate.

■ **Daniel Webster** (1782–1852): American statesman and orator

The right is ours. The question now is: how shall we get possession of what rightfully belongs to us? We should not feel so sorely grieved if no man who had not attained the full stature of a Webster, Clay, Van Buren, or Gerrit Smith could claim the right of the elective franchise. But to have drunkards, idiots, horse-racing, rum-selling rowdies, ignorant foreigners, and silly boys fully recognized, while we ourselves are thrust out from all the rights that belong to citizens, it is too grossly insulting to the dignity of woman to be longer quietly submitted to. The right is ours. Have it, we must. Use it, we will. The pens, the tongues, the fortunes, the indomitable wills of many women are already pledged to secure this right. The great truth that no just government can be formed without the consent of the

■ **Webster . . . Smith:** Stanton contrasts these noble American statesmen with base men who nonetheless share the right to vote.

■ **Have it . . . we will:** Note Stanton's style, which uses parallelism and balance for dramatic effect.

governed we shall echo and reecho in the ears of the unjust judge, until by continual coming we shall weary him. . . .

There seems now to be a kind of moral stagnation in our midst. Philanthropists have done their utmost to rouse the nation to a sense of its sins. War, slavery, drunkenness, licentiousness, gluttony, have been dragged naked before the people, and all their abominations and deformities fully brought to light, yet with idiotic laugh we hug those monsters to our breasts and rush on to destruction. Our churches are multiplying on all sides, our missionary societies, Sunday schools, and prayer meetings and innumerable charitable and reform organizations are all in operation, but still the tide of vice is swelling, and threatens the destruction of everything, and the battlements of righteousness are weak against the raging elements of sin and death. Verily, the world waits the coming of some new element, some purifying power, some spirit of mercy and love. The voice of woman has been silenced in the state, the church, and the home, but man cannot fulfill his destiny alone, he cannot redeem his race unaided. There are deep and tender chords of sympathy and love in the hearts of the downfallen and oppressed that woman can touch more skillfully than man.

The world has never yet seen a truly great and virtuous nation, because in the degradation of woman the very fountains of life are poisoned at their source. It is vain to look for silver and gold from mines of copper and lead. It is the wise mother that has the wise son. So long as your women are slaves you may throw your colleges and churches to the winds. You can't have scholars and saints so long as your mothers are ground to powder between the upper and nether millstone of tyranny and lust. How seldom, now, is a father's pride gratified, his fond hopes realized, in the budding genius of his son! The wife is degraded, made the mere creature of caprice, and the foolish son is heaviness to his heart. Truly are the sins of the fathers visited upon the children to the third and fourth generation. God, in His wisdom, has so linked the whole human family together that any violence done at one end of the chain is felt throughout its length, and here, too, is the law of restoration, as in woman all have fallen, so in her elevation shall the race be recreated. . . .

We do not expect our path will be strewn with the flowers of popular applause, but over the thorns of bigotry and prejudice will be our way, and on our banners will beat the dark storm clouds of opposition from those who have entrenched themselves behind the stormy bulwarks of custom and authority, and who have fortified their position by every means, holy and unholy. But we will steadfastly abide the result. Unmoved we will bear it aloft. Undauntedly we will unfurl it to the gale, for we know that the storm cannot rend from it a shred, that the electric flash will but more clearly show to us the glorious words inscribed upon it "Equality of Rights." . . .

1848

■ **Personification** (page 214): Note how these abstract ideas come alive as "monsters."

■ Irony: Stanton observes that in the midst of reforms, vice is swelling.

■ **It is vain . . . wise son.** Stanton uses two **epigrams** (page 222) to argue for the elevation of women.

■ Main idea: Note how details in this paragraph serve to develop the main idea stated in the first sentence.

■ **We do not . . . unholy.** Note the use (and perhaps, overuse) of **figurative language** (page 231).

THINK AND DISCUSS
Understanding
1. What do the assembled women want to discuss, according to paragraph one?
2. What do they wish to avoid discussing?
3. To what does *it* refer in the final two sentences?

Analyzing
4. Cite examples of humor in Stanton's speech. Why do you think she included humor in a speech that is essentially serious?
5. What point is Stanton making in paragraph five with her references to fountains and a chain?
6. Restate the first sentence of the last paragraph in a purely literal way.
7. Stanton says, "The *pens*, the *tongues* . . . of the women are already pledged. . . ." What type of figurative language is she using?
8. Write six sentences that state the main idea of each paragraph in this speech.
9. State the main idea of the entire essay in a sentence.

Extending
10. In the first sentence of paragraph two, Stanton mentions laws of her time that were unjust to women. Do such laws exist today? Explain.

REVIEWING LITERARY TERMS
Epigram
1. Explain the following epigram in the light of paragraph five: "It is vain to look for silver and gold from mines of copper and lead."

Figurative Language
2. Stanton uses **synecdoche** in paragraph three when she pledges the *pens* and *tongues* of women to secure their rights. What do these italicized words represent?
3. Which object is *not* used in a metaphor in the fifth paragraph: a mine, a chain, a mill, a ladder?
4. What abstractions are **personified** in the fourth paragraph? Do you consider these personifications appropriate? Why or why not?
5. What are four figurative comparisons that Stanton makes in the first sentence of the final paragraph? Do you think that this sentence would have been more effective or less so with fewer figurative comparisons?

Tone
6. What word would you use to describe Stanton's prevailing tone? Do you feel that the humor she introduces at the beginning of her speech detracts from this tone? Why or why not?

■ CONTENT REVIEW

THINKING SKILLS
Classifying
1. List under the headings *Optimists* and *Pessimists* the names of the authors represented in this unit. Base your classifications on details in the selections. If necessary, create a third heading to indicate authors who seem to fit in neither category.

Generalizing
2. Frederick Douglass and Chief Seattle protest the way blacks and Native Americans are treated. What do you suppose Thoreau might have advised them to do? In what way are these protests relevant today?
3. Lanier, Melville, and Thoreau all convey a keen sense of place in their respective works included in the unit. How do the feelings conveyed about place differ in these works? Which author, for example, emphasizes the mystery of his surroundings? the romance? the horror or evil?
4. Both Lincoln and Lee are noble figures who felt deeply the pain, destruction, and loss of life caused by the Civil War. Examine Lincoln's speech and Lee's letter and describe briefly the positive qualities you feel each contributes to the American heritage.
5. In Alcott's journal and Stanton's speech do you detect any of the traits that Emerson and Thoreau called for in "Self-Reliance" or *Walden?* Explain.

6. Although most works in this unit express concern about social problems, Billings, Crockett, and Fink display a lighter side of the American character. Explain how these humorists display the self-reliance and individuality espoused by writers such as Emerson and Thoreau.

Synthesizing

7. Thoreau said, "We do not ride on the railroad; it rides upon us." Think of a modern invention or trend that, like the railroad in Thoreau's time, controls or obsesses Americans. Then write an epigram about its effect.
8. Imagine that the authors appearing in this unit attended your high school. Decide who you think would be voted "most likely to succeed" after graduation. Then write a caption to appear beneath this author's picture in the yearbook, using either the author's own words or a description of your own.

Evaluating

9. Do you feel that the social concerns expressed by the authors in this unit are still issues at the end of the twentieth century? In answering, focus on three issues mentioned in the works in this unit.
10. Both Redburn and Goodman Brown have undergone a moral struggle. Do you think these characters have become bitter, or are they simply more realistic as a result of their experiences? Explain.

■ COMPOSITION REVIEW

Choose one of the following topics for writing.

Writing About Characters

Some critics have observed that Goodman Brown and Eliza from *Uncle Tom's Cabin* are merely frames on which to hang a writer's ideas, rather than fully drawn, realistic characters. Write a four-paragraph essay for your classmates in which you agree or disagree with this observation. If you feel that these are real flesh-and-blood characters, tell what makes them realistic. If you think they serve only to illustrate an author's ideas, explain what they represent.

Writing to an Author

Write two letters to Thoreau, one complimenting him on the actions he takes and the ideas he expresses in *Civil Disobedience*, the other trying to convince him that he was wrong. Before you write, make an outline of his major ideas and actions. Next to each, write reasons why he might be commended, as well as reasons why he might be criticized. Try to be as objective as possible in thinking of reasons for each view.

Writing About a Social Concern

Many of the social ills mentioned in this unit are still concerns over a hundred years later. Write a three-paragraph essay about one such ill. In the first paragraph, describe the ill as viewed by a nineteenth-century author. In the second paragraph, explain whether you think these evils still exist today. Finally, explain whether a remedy proposed by the author or one that you have thought of yourself would be an effective solution.

Describing an Individualist

Write a three-paragraph character sketch of someone you consider an individualist. Be prepared to give this work to the person you describe. Describe the qualities this person possesses that set him or her apart from the crowd. In the final paragraph describe what you think Thoreau would have thought of this person.

VARIATIONS AND DEPARTURES 1870–1915

1870	1875	1880	1885	1890

HISTORY AND THE ARTS

• Edison invents phonograph   789,000 U.S. immigrants annually •

• Franco-Prussian War begins   • Tolstoy completes *Anna Karenina* (Russia) • Statue of Liberty dedicated

• Black suffrage   • Sioux defeat   • Clara Barton founds American Red Cross
                           Custer's 7th Cavalry   • American Federation of
     Bell patents telephone •   Labor founded

                                   7th Cavalry massacres Sioux at Wounded Knee •

PRESIDENTS' ADMINISTRATIONS   • 1881–1885   1889–1893 •
   1877–1881 Rutherford B. Hayes •   Chester A. Arthur   Benjamin Harrison
              James A. Garfield 1881 •   • 1885–1889 Grover Cleveland

LITERATURE

                                            Freeman: *A New England Nun* •
   • Twain: *Roughing It* • Twain: *The Adventures*   • Twain: *The Adventures of*
                              of Tom Sawyer   *Huckleberry Finn*
               • James: *The American*   • Twain: *Life on the Mississippi*
                        Whitman: *Complete Poems and Prose* •
                                        Dickinson: *Poems* •

Lamp by Louis Comfort Tiffany
(1848–1933)

Wooden woolwinder

Mechanical bank (1885)

1895	1900	1905	1910	1915

- X rays discovered
- First modern Olympic games (Greece)
- Marie Curie discovers radium (France)
- U.S. Steel becomes first billion-dollar corporation
- Ford designs Model T
- Peary at North Pole

Spanish-American War • Wright brothers' flight •   Population 91,972,266 •   World War I •

Gold discovered in Alaska •   • Queen Victoria   The Republic of China established •
                              dies (England)
Marconi sends first transatlantic •   *Titanic* sinks on its maiden voyage •
wireless message (Italy)

Panama Canal opened •

- 1893–1897 Grover Cleveland
- 1901–1909 Theodore Roosevelt
- 1909–1913 William Howard Taft
- 1897–1901 William McKinley
  1913–1921 Woodrow Wilson •

- Crane: *The Red Badge of Courage*
- Dunbar: *Lyrics of Lowly Life*   *The Crisis* founded by Du Bois •
- Robinson: *Children of the Night*   Wharton: *Ethan Frome* •
- James: *The Ambassadors*
- Du Bois: *The Souls of Black Folk*
  Poetry magazine founded by Harriet Monroe •
          Masters: *Spoon River Anthology* •

Early typewriter (1892)

Will Bradley, cover for *The Chap Book* (1894)

Poster for the 1896 Olympic Games

PREVIEW

UNIT 4   VARIATIONS AND DEPARTURES   1870–1915

Authors

Walt Whitman
Emily Dickinson
Mark Twain
Satanta
Chief Joseph

Bret Harte
Ambrose Bierce
Mary E. Wilkins Freeman
Kate Chopin
Paul Laurence Dunbar

W. E. B. Du Bois
Stephen Crane
Edwin Arlington Robinson
Edgar Lee Masters

Features
Reading the Poetry of Whitman and Dickinson
Comment: Walt Whitman and
  Abraham Lincoln
Reader's Note: "I Heard a Fly Buzz
  When I Died"
Comment: Dialect
Themes in American Literature: Individualism
Comment: The Story Behind "El Corrido
  de Gregorio Cortez"
The Story of American English
Reader's Note: Crane's Fictional Techniques

Application of Literary Terms
free verse
symbol
onomatopoeia
slant rhyme
mood
local color
flashback
plot
dramatic monologue

Review of Literary Terms
imagery
figurative language
characterization

Reading Literature Skillfully
summarizing

Vocabulary Skills
dictionary
etymology
context
pronunciation
synonyms

Thinking Skills
classifying
generalizing
synthesizing

Composition Assignments Include
Analyzing a Symbol
Writing a Description
Writing a Biographical Sketch
Writing About Imagery
Writing About a Career Choice
Analyzing Humor
Writing About a Ballad
Defending Your Position
Analyzing a Character
Writing About Style
Responding to a Theme in Poetry

Enrichment
Choric Interpretation
Readers Theater

Thinking Critically About Literature
Concept Review
Content Review
Composition Review

VARIATIONS AND DEPARTURES 1870–1915

The North's victory in the Civil War preserved the Union, freed the slaves, and left the South in anguish and poverty, which would take a century to overcome. But, in the searing experience of war, the nation had gained a lasting, though disillusioned, maturity.

Lincoln had indicated that he would be conciliatory to the defeated South. His assassination therefore heightened tension and strengthened those factions on both sides who wanted revenge rather than reconciliation. The resulting exploitation of the South during the Reconstruction Era did not end until 1877, when federal troops were withdrawn and the area reverted to local rule.

Mark Twain observed in *The Gilded Age:* "The eight years in America from 1860 to 1868 uprooted institutions that were centuries old, changed the politics of a people, transformed the social life of half the country, and wrought so profoundly upon the entire national character that the influence cannot be measured." By this time the nation's energies were focused on the explosive growth of business and industry. Symbolic of this growth was the development of the railroads during this period. The thirty-five thousand miles of track in 1865 had increased to about two hundred thousand miles by the end of the century. In 1869 the Union Pacific Railroad which, in effect, linked America from the Atlantic to the Pacific oceans, was completed.

In "Passage to India," Whitman called for a spiritual achievement to parallel the amazing engineering achievements of the age, and he had good reason. Spiritual reform was urgently needed, for the period was a time of plunder and exploitation, of greedy materialism and political corruption, of financial piracy and labor strife. Great fortunes were accumulated while some people went hungry in the swelling cities. Immigrants from Europe poured into the United States in search of fortune, but most found themselves laboring on railroads or in sweatshop factories for low wages.

The Civil War, the industrial boom that it helped set off, and the flood of immigrants lured by this prosperity—these factors laid the foundations of modern American society and literature. During the war, people from various regions of the country mingled more freely than ever before, and so came to know each other's folk ballads and tall tales. The nation's traditional fascination with the frontier was further enhanced. And the problems of materialism and poverty aroused many writers to social satire and protest.

This period also saw the final stage of the centuries-long displacement of Native Americans, as the army pushed the hunters of the Plains onto reservations to make way for railroads and land-hungry settlers. The buffalo herds, on which the diet and even the culture of the Plains tribes largely depended, were slaughtered to feed railroad workers. Most white Americans at the time saw only one-sided reports denouncing the "savage Indians," or admired romanticized paintings of the "Vanishing Indian" by such artists as Frederic Remington. The contrasting Native American view of these bitter wars is represented in this unit by the speeches of Satanta, the Kiowa "Orator of the Plains," and of Chief Joseph, the great Nez Percé leader, respected even by his enemies.

Magazine and book publishing flourished with the growth of a properous, literate middle class, who thirsted for practical information and for fiction representing "real life." Such writers as Walt Whitman, Mark Twain, Emily Dickinson, Stephen Crane, and W. E. B. Du Bois were largely concerned with finding new points of departure in theme, in content, in form, and in the use of language. The major literary innovations were *free verse*, *Realism* (including *local color*), and *Naturalism*.

THREE LITERARY GIANTS

Walt Whitman, Mark Twain, and Emily Dickinson found the subjects and materials for their works in their own experience and in their own locales. Walt Whitman, the self-proclaimed "poet of America," used bold images and symbols drawn from workaday life to capture a truth greater than the individual—the truth of the American experience. Mark Twain set his greatest works, *The Adventures of Tom Sawyer* and *The Adventures of Huckleberry Finn*, in middle America where he grew up—Hannibal, Missouri, and along the Mississippi River. Emily Dickinson discovered the substance for her poems in the garden next to her house in Amherst, Massachusetts; in the small events of household life; and in the depths of her inquisitive mind.

The variations and departures of Twain, Whitman, and Dickinson are to be found not only in their substance but also in their literary forms and in their astonishing use of language. Twain brought a dimension and humor to the novel that it had not embraced before. Whitman developed and extended the possibilities of free verse. Emily Dickinson adopted slant rhymes and bizarre syntactic patterns that were new to poetry. Each in his or her own way brought the American language—the language of the farms and streets, the language of steamboatmen and Westerners, the language of the New England household—into novels, poems, and essays that Americans would read. The language was simple and direct, sometimes slangy, generally native, different in ways both conspicuous and subtle from the "literary" and British language that previous American writers had used.

These tendencies toward greater naturalness of style in prose and poetry ran parallel to the increased recognition of American folk traditions. Frontier humor, popular even before the Civil War, was shaped into literature, while the wartime ballads aroused interest in the folk songs of all regions. Tales and ballads of the West, such as "Shenandoah" and the legend of Gregorio Cortez, became especially popular. Eastern publishers began to produce a spate of cowboy song books and of tawdry dime novels romanticizing outlaws like Jesse James and the Sundance Kid.

REALISM

Beginning with Twain's writing in the 1860s, Realism dominated most American fiction written up through the 1930s. During the Civil War, readers hungered for detailed accounts of the cataclysm. Accuracy of detail had always been characteristic of most American writing, but Civil War journalism greatly reinforced public taste for truthful representation of daily life.

Realism was partly a reaction against Romanticism, for the proponents of Realism felt that Romantic fiction was too idealized, too neatly patterned, too grandly tragic and heroic to reflect real life. Realists were concerned with the immediate ethical consequences of everyday actions. To help readers "experience" real life, they attempted to re-create everyday reality, for they believed the truth of experience was to be found in events described accurately and objectively, undistorted by the writer's imagination.

One of the currents of realism was local color or regionalism, set in a specific area of the country—New England, the South, the Frontier West. Local-color writers embraced folk speech, local customs and settings, and regional character, temperament, and dress. Bret Harte is considered the first local colorist, and his "Outcasts of Poker Flat" is an affecting representation of life in the California mining camps. Mary E. Wilkins Freeman, in stories like "A New England Nun," concentrated on faithfully representing New England ways of life and talk. Kate Chopin portrayed, particularly in her early stories, the exotic ways of Creole life in Louisiana. But both Freeman and Chopin created characters, notably women, realistically motivated and compellingly believable. Chopin's novel *The Awakening*, long neglected because of adverse criticism received when it first appeared in 1899, has been reinstated in recent times as a classic of American Realism.

W. E. B. Du Bois adapted the techniques of Realism to his materials, exploring the identity and situation of black Americans barely a generation away from slavery. In essays, sociological studies, and fiction, he dealt with the realities of segregation: opportunities lost and talents destroyed.

NATURALISM

Growing concern with social injustice and the gradual acceptance of realistic subject matter and techniques opened the way for naturalistic fiction. The new theories of Darwin, Freud, and Marx were suggesting that biology, psychology, and economics determine each individual's destiny. Naturalistic novelists applied these theories to their presentation and interpretation of human experience. Writers like Stephen Crane and Ambrose Bierce tended to depict life as grim, the universe as cold and spiritless, and the individual as a hapless victim of heredity, society, and natural forces. Naturalism was therefore in direct opposition to Romanticism and Transcendentalism, which envisioned a holy and mystical presence in nature. Crane, along with the novelists Frank Norris and Theodore Dreiser, exposed poverty, cruelty, corruption, and the futility of war.

In method, Naturalism closely resembled Realism. But where the realists often assumed a moral universe in their fiction, and even portrayed the comic side of life, the naturalists selected details to provide a scientifically precise, usually grim, view of the human condition. Humanity—to the naturalistic writer—was at the mercy of an indifferent universe.

POETRY IN TRANSITION

The poetry of Paul Laurence Dunbar, Stephen Crane, Edwin Arlington Robinson, and Edgar Lee Masters, while not so innovative as the poetry of Whitman and Dickinson, revealed both realistic and naturalistic tendencies. These poets all used commonplace images and everyday language to convey their view of the darker side of existence. They depicted human weaknesses, foibles, and vanities. But they also shared a deep sympathy for the plight of ordinary people in the real world. However, instead of denouncing injustice, Dunbar symbolized its effects by accurately detailing the behavior of a caged bird. The selection and arrangement of material in "Miniver Cheevy" readily conveyed—without comment from Robinson—the reality of the embittered dreamer. *Spoon River Anthology* by Masters was realistic both in subject and in technique. The subjects were small-town Midwesterners who, speaking from the grave, recalled their lives with quiet contentment or angry disappointment. The realistic technique Masters employed was to reveal the attitudes and circumstances of his characters directly, through their own language.

The writers of this period captured the new America, which was emerging in its headlong pursuit of world power and of the "American Dream." The spiritual values and social manners of a stable, rural society were being challenged by a nation rushing into an urban, industrial future. New values, new attitudes, new goals were sought to match the new spirit of America; and the writers tested both the old and the new.

THINKING ABOUT GRAPHIC AIDS
Using the Time Line

Use the time line on pages 288–289 to answer these questions.

1. Which Presidents served for the longest terms? Who served for the shortest term?
2. What items on the time line served to expand channels of communication?
3. Which time-line item signifies the expansion of industry?
4. Which time-line item indicates that workers had become united?
5. The U.S. population tripled from 1860 to 1910. What do you think accounts for this tremendous expansion?

Walt Whitman
1819–1892

Walt Whitman by Thomas Eakins. The Pennsylvania Academy of the Fine Arts

Although Whitman was a contemporary of Bryant, Poe, Emerson, Thoreau, Whittier, Lowell, and Longfellow, there is sufficient reason for considering him America's first modern poet. He embraced the ideal of working-class democracy more fully than any of these writers, and his experiments with free-verse rhythms and realistic imagery inspired many twentieth-century poets.

Whitman's family was poor, and his education ceased early in his teens. When Whitman was four, his family moved to the growing village of Brooklyn. Whitman, much later in life, once remarked that his early friendships with the merchants, sailors, farmers, and fishermen of Brooklyn were ". . . my best experiences and deepest lessons in human nature."

Between 1839 and 1848 he worked on Manhattan and Brooklyn newspapers as an editor-reporter. Unconsciously, he was developing much of the material and the crisp, objective reporter's style that would later appear in his poetry.

Whitman's journey to New Orleans in 1848 fired his imagination by showing him the diversity of the young nation. Sometime during 1854 Whitman underwent a great internal turmoil, perhaps brought on by his father's paralysis and subsequent death. By early July of 1855, he published a thin volume of twelve long, untitled poems. This was the first of many editions of *Leaves of Grass*.

Many who read his poetry rejected it as crude or gross. Whittier reportedly threw his copy into a fire. Bryant broke off his friendship with the younger poet. Though the book was a financial failure, some influential readers admired Whitman's revolutionary verse, among them Emerson, Thoreau, and Lincoln. However, Whitman returned to newspaper work to support himself, while writing his greatest poetry in his spare hours.

Whitman was too old to enlist when the Civil War broke out, but he went to care for his brother George, who had been wounded at Fredericksburg. Poems based on his observations of war appeared in later editions of *Leaves of Grass*. After the war, he worked in veterans' hospitals and minor government jobs until 1873, when he suffered a paralytic stroke.

He continued to revise and expand his masterwork, and approved the last edition from his deathbed. Although his later poems decreased in vigor and force, *Leaves of Grass* firmly established him as one of the greatest and most influential American poets—that "inescapable figure," as one critic put it, "in every American poet's heritage."

Reading A POEM

In the poems of Walt Whitman and Emily Dickinson, America finally achieved its own poetic voice—a voice with a distinctly American accent. Whitman's publication of the first edition of *Leaves of Grass* in 1855 constituted a Declaration of Poetic Independence. But Whitman was not widely read during his lifetime, and Emily Dickinson was virtually unknown, having published only some ten poems during her life! Today, however, these two are recognized by many as our greatest poets. As you read their works, keep in mind the following suggestions.

Read their poetry aloud. Read with dramatic emphasis, reflecting the joyful or somber moods of the poems. The rhythm and sounds of the words will help convey the intended feeling—exuberance, calm, or terror. Let lines such as those that catalog nature and people in "There Was a Child Went Forth" build toward a climax. Read the self-contained stanzas of Dickinson with a keen sense of the importance of each word and an awareness of her subtle shifts in thought.

Observe the poetic form. Whitman's free verse sweeps across the page in long lines that defy traditional rhythmic restraints to assert the themes of democracy and individuality. The rhythm of his breath-length phrases is always natural, yet never predictable. Although Whitman avoids regular rhyme, his poetry sings in subtle ways—by chiming repetitions or recurring consonants and -*ing* endings. Dickinson's hymnlike stanzaic patterns suggest terse riddles about life. Her favorite punctuation, the dash (often used at the end of a poem), serves variously to suspend sense or to impel it forward. Her frequent use of capitalization flags important words. And although Dickinson always uses a regular stanzaic rhyme scheme, she strains against it with unusual slant rhymes at surprising turns.

Note the ingenious use of language. Whitman makes it a matter of principle to bring the language of the streets into his poems. "I sound my barbaric yawp over the roofs of the world," he proclaims, as he sprinkles American slang throughout his work. Dickinson's poems are cryptic, leaving out more than they include, using a single image to suggest a world of meaning. She can feel "Zero at the Bone," lean "upon the Awe," and linger "with Before." When the heavens become a bell, she can sense her entire being becoming "but an Ear."

Summarize the poem. One way to make sure you understand a poem is to briefly summarize it. The longer poems of Whitman are generally easier to summarize than Dickinson's brief ones, which rely on paradox, wit, and juxtaposition of the simple with the profound. Consider her poems a kind of written shorthand that you, as reader, must decipher. Observe the words she capitalizes and the details she emphasizes. Be aware of the connotations, or associations, of words such as *zero, door, scar, chair, home,* and *glass.* Once you have put together the pieces of her puzzle-poems, try to state her ideas in your own words.

Contrast the works of these poets with those of earlier poets. Whitman's and Dickinson's poems have been called the beginning of twentieth-century poetry. Both differ radically from predecessors such as Longfellow, Lowell, and Whittier, whose often moralistic poetry is generally easy to understand. Dickinson admonishes, "Tell all the truth but tell it slant." "The greatest poet does not moralize . . . he knows the soul," proclaimed Whitman. Both believed that poetry must be suggestive, requiring mental effort rather than human reform. "The process of reading," Whitman wrote, "is not a half-sleep but, in the highest sense, an exercise, a gymnast's struggle."

Walt Whitman

 See FREE VERSE in the Handbook of Literary Terms, page 890.

I Hear America Singing

I hear America singing, the varied carols I hear,
Those of mechanics, each one singing his as it should be blithe and strong,
The carpenter singing his as he measures his plank or beam,
The mason singing his as he makes ready for work, or leaves off work,
5   The boatman singing what belongs to him in his boat, the deckhand singing on the steamboat deck,
The shoemaker singing as he sits on his bench, the hatter singing as he stands,
The woodcutter's song, the ploughboy's on his way in the morning, or at noon intermission or at sundown,
The delicious singing of the mother, or of the young wife at work, or of the girl sewing or washing,
Each singing what belongs to him or her and to none else,
10 The day what belongs to the day—at night the party of young fellows, robust, friendly,
Singing with open mouths their strong melodious songs.

1860

Winslow Homer (1836–1910), *The Lookout—"All's Well."* Museum of Fine Arts, Boston

THINK AND DISCUSS
Understanding
1. What does the speaker hear?
2. Name seven people that the speaker hears.

Analyzing
3. How do those people introduced in the last two lines differ from those listed before?
4. In general, most poetry written prior to Whitman's day dealt with idealized characters or extraordinary heroes. What kinds of people did Whitman choose to portray?
5. Why is each person "singing what belongs to him or her and to none else" (line 9)?
6. Do you think that the word *singing* is used in a literal or a figurative sense? Explain.

APPLYING: Free Verse
See Handbook of Literary Terms, p. 890.

Free verse differs from conventional verse forms in being "free" from a fixed pattern of rhyme, rhythm, and line length. Free verse achieves its music with poetic devices introduced naturally. Some of these devices are repetition, assonance, alliteration, a speech rhythm of balanced phrases, and a visual rhythm in the ebb and flow of lines.

1. What words are repeated throughout this poem?

2. What sound is alliterated at the beginning of three words in line 5? line 11?

3. Imagine that Whitman had chosen to use a consistent line length, regular rhythm, and end rhyme in a poem that began thus:

> I hear the songs of Americans ring.
> The voice of mechanics and carpenters
>   sing.

What do you think would have been gained or lost with this change?

H🦅   Review IMAGERY in the Handbook of Literary Terms, page 891.

There Was a Child Went Forth

There was a child went forth every day,
And the first object he look'd upon, that object he became,
And that object became part of him for the day or a certain part of the day,
Or for many years or stretching cycles of years.

5 The early lilacs became part of this child,
And grass and white and red morning-glories, and white and red clover, and
    the song of the phoebe-bird,
And the Third-month[1] lambs and the sow's pink-faint litter, and the mare's foal
    and the cow's calf,
And the noisy brood of the barnyard or by the mire of the pond-side,
And the fish suspending themselves so curiously below there, and the beautiful
    curious liquid,
10 And the water-plants with their graceful flat heads, all became part of him.

The field-sprouts of Fourth-month and Fifth-month became part of him,

---

1. *Third-month,* March. Whitman used the Quaker method of referring to months.

Dennis Pearson, *Windpoint Lighthouse*.

Winter-grain sprouts and those of the light-yellow corn, and the esculent roots
    of the garden,
And the apple-trees cover'd with blossoms and the fruit afterward, and
    woodberries, and the commonest weeds by the road,
And the old drunkard staggering home from the outhouse of the tavern whence
    he had lately risen,
15 And the schoolmistress that pass'd on her way to the school,
And the friendly boys that pass'd, and the quarrelsome boys,
And the tidy and fresh-cheek'd girls, and the barefoot Negro boy and girl,
And all the changes of city and country wherever he went.

His own parents, he that had father'd him and she that had conceiv'd him in
    her womb and birth'd him
20 They gave this child more of themselves than that,
They gave him afterward every day, they became part of him.

The mother at home quietly placing the dishes on the supper-table,
The mother with mild words, clean her cap and gown, a wholesome odor
    falling off her person and clothes as she walks by,
The father, strong, self-sufficient, manly, mean, anger'd, unjust,
25 The blow, the quick loud word, the tight bargain, the crafty lure,
The family usages, the language, the company, the furniture, the yearning and
    swelling heart,
Affection that will not be gainsay'd, the sense of what is real, the thought if
    after all it should prove unreal,
The doubts of day-time and the doubts of night-time, the curious whether and how,
Whether that which appears so is so, or is it all flashes and specks?
30 Men and women crowding fast in the streets, if they are not flashes and specks
    what are they?
The streets themselves and the facades of houses, and goods in the windows,
Vehicles, teams, the heavy-plank'd wharves, the huge crossing at the ferries,
The village on the highland seen from afar at sunset, the river between,
Shadows, aureola and mist, the light falling on roofs and gables of white or
    brown two miles off,
35 The schooner near by sleepily dropping down the tide, the little boat
    slack-tow'd astern,
The hurrying tumbling waves, quick-broken crests, slapping,
The strata of color'd clouds, the long bar of maroon-tint away solitary by itself,
    the spread of purity it lies motionless in,
The horizon's edge, the flying sea-crow, the fragrance of salt marsh and shore mud,
These became part of that child who went forth every day, and who now goes,
    and will always go forth every day.

1855

Walt Whitman

THINK AND DISCUSS

Understanding

1. In lines 1–13, Whitman describes objects and animals in nature. What does he describe in lines 19–26? lines 31–35?
2. What is the mother doing in line 22? What words are used to describe the father in line 24?
3. Cite three lines that indicate that the village described is near water.

Analyzing

4. What natural phenomenon is the poet describing in line 37?
5. How long a period of time does the poem encompass literally? metaphorically?
6. How did the child's parents become "part of him" (lines 19–21)?
7. The last line states that the child "will always go forth every day." In what sense can this be true? In answering, consider whether the poem refers to only one child or has universal applications.

Extending

8. Whitman was the great poet of selfhood and individuality. What, according to "There Was a Child Went Forth," is the source of a person's identity and individuality? What, if any, other factors help shape an individual?

REVIEWING: Imagery

See Handbook of Literary Terms, p. 891.

The term **imagery** refers to word pictures that appeal to one or more of the senses involved in seeing, hearing, smelling, tasting, touching, and feeling internally. Whether literal or figurative, an image provides vividness and immediacy in a way that abstract language does not.

1. Find four images in the poem that appeal to four different senses.
2. Cite three images that rely on color.
3. Examine the picture that accompanies this poem. Explain whether or not you think its images and use of color suit the images in this poem.

COMPOSITION

Writing About Contemporary America

Since Whitman wrote "I Hear America Singing," the nature of work in America has changed. The invention of the production line, for example, has changed the relationship of the worker to his or her work. Write a four-paragraph letter addressed to Walt Whitman (but perhaps intended for the local newspaper), in which you begin something like this: "Dear Walt, I have just read how you heard the workers of America singing. In the last 150 years, America has changed. I want to let you know what I hear now." You might include some lines from the song you sang on the last part-time or summer job you had. See "Writing About a Period or Trend" in the Writer's Handbook.

Explaining a Poem

Your friend, who is very literal and practical minded in reading poetry, has written you a note after reading "There Was a Child Went Forth." He says he finds it ridiculous that people could believe that the objects they look upon could become part of them. As he points out to you, "That's physically impossible." In a five-paragraph reply, explain to him that he is taking the statements in the poem too literally. Tell him that he should recognize the psychological, emotional, and spiritual implications of the poem. See "Writing to Persuade an Audience" in the Writer's Handbook.

See SYMBOL in the Handbook of Literary Terms, page 912.

When Lilacs Last in the Dooryard Bloom'd

1

When lilacs last in the dooryard bloom'd,
And the great star early droop'd in the western sky in the night,
I mourn'd, and yet shall mourn with ever-returning spring.

Ever-returning spring, trinity sure to me you bring,
5 Lilac blooming perennial and drooping star in the west,
And thought of him I love.

2

O powerful western fallen star!
O shades of night—O moody, tearful night!
O great star disappear'd—O the black murk that hides the star!
10 O cruel hands that hold me powerless—O helpless soul of me!
O harsh surrounding cloud that will not free my soul.

3

In the dooryard fronting an old farm-house near the white-wash'd palings,
Stands the lilac-bush tall-growing with heart-shaped leaves of rich green,
With many a pointed blossom rising delicate, with the perfume strong I love,
15 With every leaf a miracle—and from this bush in the dooryard,
With delicate-color'd blossoms and heart-shaped leaves of rich green,
A sprig with its flower I break.

4

In the swamp in secluded recesses,
A shy and hidden bird is warbling a song.

20 Solitary the thrush,
The hermit withdrawn to himself, avoiding the settlements,
Sings by himself a song.

Song of the bleeding throat,
Death's outlet song of life, (for well dear brother I know,
25 If thou wast not granted to sing thou would'st surely die).

Currier & Ives lithograph, *The Funeral of President Lincoln,
New York, April 25th, 1865.* Museum of the City of New York

5

Over the breast of the spring, the land, amid cities,
Amid lanes and through old woods, where lately the violets peep'd from the ground, spotting the
    gray debris,
Amid the grass in the fields each side of the lanes, passing the endless grass,
Passing the yellow-spear'd wheat, every grain from its shroud in the dark-brown fields uprisen,
30 Passing the apple-tree blows of white and pink in the orchards,
Carrying a corpse to where it shall rest in the grave,
Night and day journeys a coffin.[1]

---

1. . . . ***journeys a coffin.*** The funeral train bearing Lincoln's body traveled first east to New York and then west to Illinois
for burial—a journey lasting several days and covering over 1,500 miles.

6

Coffin that passes through lanes and streets,
Through day and night with the great cloud darkening the land,
35 With the pomp of the inloop'd flags with the cities draped in black,
With the show of the States themselves as of crape-veil'd women standing,
With processions long and winding and the flambeaus of the night,
With the countless torches lit, with the silent sea of faces and the unbared heads,
With the waiting depot, the arriving coffin, and the somber faces,
40 With dirges through the night, with the thousand voices rising strong and solemn,
With all the mournful voices of the dirges pour'd around the coffin,
The dim-lit churches and the shuddering organs—where amid these you journey,
With the tolling tolling bells' perpetual clang,
Here, coffin that slowly passes,
45 I give you my sprig of lilac.

7

(Nor for you, for one alone,
Blossoms and branches green to coffins all I bring,
For fresh as the morning, thus would I chant a song for you O sane and sacred death.

All over bouquets of roses,
50 O death, I cover you over with roses and early lilies,
But mostly and now the lilac that blooms the first,
Copious I break, I break the sprigs from the bushes,
With loaded arms I come, pouring for you,
For you and the coffins all of you O death.)

8

55 O western orb sailing the heaven,
Now I know what you must have meant as a month since I walk'd,
As I walk'd in silence the transparent shadowy night,
As I saw you had something to tell as you bent to me night after night,
As you droop'd from the sky low down as if to my side, (while the other stars all look'd on),
60 As we wander'd together the solemn night, (for something I know not what kept me from sleep),
As the night advanced, and I saw on the rim of the west how full you were of woe,
As I stood on the rising ground in the breeze in the cool transparent night,
As I watch'd where you pass'd and was lost in the netherward black of the night,
As my soul in its trouble dissatisfied sank, as where you sad orb,
65 Concluded, dropt in the night, and was gone.

9

Sing on there in the swamp,
O singer bashful and tender, I hear your notes, I hear your call,
I hear, I come presently, I understand you,
But a moment I linger, for the lustrous star has detain'd me,
70 The star my departing comrade holds and detains me.

10

O how shall I warble myself for the dead one there I loved?
And how shall I deck my song for the large sweet soul that has gone?
And what shall my perfume be for the grave of him I love?

Sea-winds blown from east and west,
75 Blown from the Eastern sea and blown from the Western sea, till there on the prairies meeting,
These and with these and the breath of my chant,
I'll perfume the grave of him I love.

11

O what shall I hang on the chamber walls?
And what shall the pictures be that I hang on the walls,
80 To adorn the burial-house of him I love?

Pictures of growing spring and farms and homes,
With the Fourth-month[2] eve at sundown, and the gray smoke lucid and bright,
With floods of the yellow gold of the gorgeous, indolent, sinking sun, burning, expanding the air,
With the fresh sweet herbage under foot, and the pale green leaves of the trees prolific,
85 In the distance the flowing glaze, the breast of the river, with a wind-dapple here and there,
With ranging hills on the banks, with many a line against the sky, and shadows,
And the city at hand with dwellings so dense, and stacks of chimneys,
And all the scenes of life and the workshops, and the workmen homeward returning.

12

Lo, body and soul—this land,
90 My own Manhattan with spires, and the sparkling and hurrying tides, and the ships,
The varied and ample land, the South and the North in the light, Ohio's shores and flashing Missouri,
And ever the far-spreading prairies cover'd with grass and corn.

Lo, the most excellent sun so calm and haughty,
The violet and purple morn with just-felt breezes,
95 The gentle soft-born measureless light,
The miracle spreading bathing all, the fulfill'd noon,
The coming eve delicious, the welcome night and the stars,
Over my cities shining all, enveloping man and land.

13

Sing on, sing on you gray-brown bird,
100 Sing from the swamps, the recesses, pour your chant from the bushes,
Limitless out of the dusk, out of the cedars and pines.

---

2. *Fourth-month,* April.

Sing on dearest brother, warble your reedy song,
Loud human song, with voice of uttermost woe.

O liquid and free and tender!
05 O wild and loose to my soul—O wondrous singer!
You only I hear—yet the star holds me, (but will soon depart),
Yet the lilac with mastering odor holds me.

14

Now while I sat in the day and look'd forth,
In the close of the day with its light and the fields of spring, and the farmers preparing their crops,
10 In the large unconscious scenery of my land with its lakes and forests,
In the heavenly aerial beauty, (after the perturb'd winds and the storms),
Under the arching heavens of the afternoon swift passing, and the voices of children and women,
The many-moving sea-tides, and I saw the ships how they sail'd,
And the summer approaching with richness, and the fields all busy with labor,
15 And the infinite separate houses, how they all went on, each with its meals and minutia of daily
    usages,
And the streets how their throbbings throbb'd, and the cities pent—lo, then and there,
Falling upon them all and among them all, enveloping me with the rest,
Appear'd the cloud, appear'd the long black trail,
And I knew death, its thought, and the sacred knowledge of death.

20 Then with the knowledge of death as walking one side of me,
And the thought of death close-walking the other side of me,
And I in the middle as with companions, and as holding the hands of companions,
I fled forth to the hiding receiving night that talks not,
Down to the shores of the water, the path by the swamp in the dimness,
25 To the solemn shadowy cedars and ghostly pines so still.

And the singer so shy to the rest receiv'd me,
The gray-brown bird I know receiv'd us comrades three,
And he sang the carol of death, and a verse for him I love.

From deep secluded recesses,
30 From the fragrant cedars and the ghostly pines so still,
Came the carol of the bird.

And the charm of the carol rapt me,
As I held as if by their hands my comrades in the night,
And the voice of my spirit tallied the song of the bird.

35 *Come lovely and soothing death,*
Undulate round the world, serenely arriving, arriving,
In the day, in the night, to all, to each,
Sooner or later delicate death.

Prais'd be the fathomless universe,
140 *For life and joy, and for objects and knowledge curious,*
And for love, sweet love—but praise! praise! praise!
For the sure-enwinding arms of cool-enfolding death.

Dark mother always gliding near with soft feet,
Have none chanted for thee a chant of fullest welcome?
145 *Then I chant it for thee, I glorify thee above all,*
I bring thee a song that when thou must indeed come, come unfalteringly.

Approach strong deliveress,
When it is so, when thou hast taken them I joyously sing the dead,
Lost in the loving floating ocean of thee,
150 *Laved in the flood of thy bliss O death.*

From me to thee glad serenades,
Dances for thee I propose saluting thee, adornments and feastings for thee,
And the sights of the open landscape and the high-spread sky are fitting,
And life and the fields, and the huge and thoughtful night.

155 *The night in silence under many a star,*
The ocean shore and the husky whispering wave whose voice I know,
And the soul turning to thee O vast and well-veil'd death,
And the body gratefully nestling close to thee.

Over the tree-tops I float thee a song,
160 *Over the rising and sinking waves, over the myriad fields and the prairies wide,*
Over the dense-pack'd cities all and the teeming wharves and ways,
I float this carol with joy, with joy to thee O death.

15
To the tally of my soul,
Loud and strong kept up the gray-brown bird,
165 With pure deliberate notes spreading filling the night.
Loud in the pines and cedars dim,
Clear in the freshness moist and the swamp-perfume,
And I with my comrades there in the night.

While my sight that was bound in my eyes unclosed,
170 As to long panoramas of visions.

And I saw askant the armies,
I saw as in noiseless dreams hundreds of battle-flags,
Borne through the smoke of the battles and pierc'd with missiles I saw them,
And carried hither and yon through the smoke, and torn and bloody,

175 And at last but a few shreds left on the staffs, (and all in silence),
And the staffs all splinter'd and broken.

I saw battle-corpses, myriads of them,
And the white skeletons of young men, I saw them,
I saw the debris and debris of all the slain soldiers of the war,
180 But I saw they were not as was thought,
They themselves were fully at rest, they suffer'd not,
The living remain'd and suffer'd, the mother suffer'd,
And the wife and the child and the musing comrade suffer'd,
And the armies that remain'd suffer'd.

16
185 Passing the visions, passing the night,
Passing, unloosing the hold of my comrades' hands,
Passing the song of the hermit bird and the tallying song of my soul,
Victorious song, death's outlet song, yet varying ever-altering song,
As low and wailing, yet clear the notes, rising and falling, flooding the night,
190 Sadly sinking and fainting, as warning and warning, and yet again bursting with joy,
Covering the earth and filling the spread of the heaven,
As that powerful psalm in the night I heard from recesses,
Passing, I leave thee lilac with heart-shaped leaves,
I leave thee there in the dooryard, blooming, returning with spring.

195 I cease from my song for thee,
From my gaze on thee in the west, fronting the west, communing with thee,
O comrade lustrous with silver face in the night.

Yet each to keep and all, retrievements out of the night,
The song, the wondrous chant of the gray-brown bird,
200 And the tallying chant, the echo arous'd in my soul,
With the lustrous and drooping star with the countenance full of woe,
With the holders holding my hand nearing the call of the bird,
Comrades mine and I in the midst, and their memory ever to keep, for the dead I loved so well,
For the sweetest, wisest soul of all my days and lands—and this for his dear sake,
205 Lilac and star and bird twined with the chant of my soul,
There in the fragrant pines and the cedars dusk and dim.   **1865**

Walt Whitman

THINK AND DISCUSS
Understanding
1. What is the speaker doing in Section 1?
2. How is the lilac bush described in Section 3?
3. What aspects of the city does the speaker mention in lines 87 and 88?
4. Who suffer as a result of death, according to lines 177–184?
5. What words and thoughts are repeated in the first stanza of Section 16?

Analyzing
6. How do the **images** in lines 26–30 contrast with those in lines 33–44?
7. Why do you think Section 7 appears in parentheses?
8. How is the western star **personified** in Section 8?
9. Are the first three lines of Section 11 to be understood literally or **figuratively**? Explain them.
10. To what main sense do the images that appear in Sections 11 and 12 appeal? Why would the things represented in these images be an appropriate homage to Lincoln?
11. Why is Section 13 a transitional section?
12. What is the attitude toward death in the thrush's song that begins, *"Come lovely and soothing death"* (line 135)? From this point on, how does the **tone** differ from that in earlier portions of the poem?
13. Although **free verse** does not rely on consistent line length or rhyme, it uses other devices to emphasize ideas and to unify thought. Examine the shape of the first stanza in Section 16. How does the fact that it builds up in the middle, then subsides, suit the ideas expressed?

Extending
14. When President John Kennedy was assassinated in 1963, "When Lilacs Last in the Dooryard Bloom'd" was read a number of times on radio and television in the period of national mourning. What, in your opinion, made the poem seem suitable as an expression of national feeling on that occasion?

APPLYING: Symbol HⱫ
See Handbook of Literary Terms, p. 912.
A **symbol** is an object or event that represents something beyond itself. Most symbols are concrete images used to designate abstract qualitites. For example, a skull might symbolize death, or a dove, peace.

1. What clues do you find in Section 2 of "Lilacs" that the star symbolizes Lincoln; in Section 3 that the lilacs symbolize the poet's love and memory of Lincoln; in Section 4 that the thrush's song symbolizes immortality?
2. To which sense or senses does each of these three symbols appeal?
3. List one quality each symbol possesses that makes it an appropriate sign of the thing it represents.

COMPOSITION ◀━━▶
Choosing a Symbol
Whitman portrays the assassinated Lincoln, a midwesterner who has achieved a kind of immortality through fame and death, to the western star, a fixed heavenly body temporarily obscured by a cloud. Think of an object in nature that could be used to symbolize someone—either living or dead—whom you regard highly. Write a two-paragraph description of this symbol and the person it represents for your school literary magazine.

Analyzing a Symbol
In an essay of five paragraphs, discuss the symbolism of the lilacs, the thrush's song, or the western star. To prepare for writing, reread the explanation of symbolism under Applying and review your answers to the questions. Note as many qualities as you can that make this an appropriate symbol. Consider why other

items—a tulip, a coyote's cry, or a full moon, for example—would have been less effective as symbols. Devise a thesis statement that expresses your ideas on this symbol as it functions in the poem. Direct your essay to your school literary magazine. See "Writing About Symbolism" in the Writer's Handbook.

ENRICHMENT
Choric Interpretation

Find a copy of Whitman's other poem written on the death of Lincoln, "O Captain! My Captain," composed not in free verse but in traditional meters, rhyme, and stanzaic structure. Practice with your friends reading it and parts of "When Lilacs Last in the Dooryard Bloom'd" aloud. Several voices alternating might be used in reading. When you are ready, volunteer to read both poems before the class. Then lead a discussion of the differences in form of the two poems and the relation of form to the effect of each poem. Discuss which poem has greater impact and why.

Comment

Walt Whitman and Abraham Lincoln

Walt Whitman's deep feelings for Abraham Lincoln, expressed in his elegy "When Lilacs Last in the Dooryard Bloom'd," were not based on personal friendship. But Whitman lived in Washington, D.C., during the Civil War and recorded in his journal his account of seeing the President pass in the streets. August 12, 1863: "I see the President almost every day, as I happen to live where he passes to or from his lodgings out of town. . . . I see very plainly Abraham Lincoln's dark brown face, with the deep-cut lines, the eyes, always to me with a deep latent sadness in the expression. We have got so that we exchange bows, and very cordial ones." The two men never officially met.

In another passage introducing the war years, Whitman wrote: "Of all the days of the war, there are two especially I can never forget. Those were the day[s] of that first Bull Run defeat, and the day of Abraham Lincoln's death. I was home in Brooklyn on both occasions. The day of the murder we heard the news very early in the morning. Mother prepared breakfast—and other meals afterward—as usual; but not a mouthful was eaten all day by either of us. We each drank half a cup of coffee; that was all. Little was said. We got every newspaper morning and evening, and the frequent extras of that period, and pass'd them silently to each other."

"There were many lilacs in full bloom," said Whitman later. "I find myself always reminded of the great tragedy of that day by the sight and odor of these blossoms. It never fails."

This haunting image of the lilacs became the sustaining symbol for "When Lilacs Last in the Dooryard Bloom'd." Like other solemn, reflective poems, or *elegies*, "Lilacs" follows a movement from intense or bitter grief, through some kind of spiritual understanding of death in general, to an ultimate acceptance of the particular death of the person elegized.

The poet's grief for Lincoln's death is expressed in Sections 1–13 (most bitterly in Section 2); the spiritual understanding comes as the poet (holding the hands of his two companions—the "thought of death" and the "sacred knowledge of death") listens to the hermit thrush's carol in Section 14; the comprehension of death in general comes in Section 15 and reconciliation to Lincoln's death is expressed in Section 16. Note that in line 197 the "black murk" of line 9 no longer obscures the star: "O comrade lustrous with silver face in the night."

What Is the Grass?

from **Song of Myself**

A child said *What is the grass?* fetching it to me with full hands,
How could I answer the child? I do not know what it is any more than he.

I guess it must be the flag of my disposition, out of hopeful green stuff woven.

Or I guess it is the handkerchief of the Lord,
5 A scented gift and remembrancer designedly dropped,
Bearing the owner's name someway in the corners, that we may see and remark, and say *Whose?*

Or I guess the grass is itself a child, the produced babe of the vegetation.

Or I guess it is a uniform hieroglyphic,
And it means, Sprouting alike in broad zones and narrow zones,
10 Growing among black folks as among white,
Canuck, Tuckahoe, Congressman, Cuff,[1] I give them the same, I receive them the same.

And now it seems to me the beautiful uncut hair of graves.

Tenderly will I use you curling grass,
It may be you transpire from the breasts of young men,
15 It may be if I had known them I would have loved them,
It may be you are from old people, or from offspring taken soon out of their mothers' laps,
And here you are the mothers' laps.

This grass is very dark to be from the white heads of old mothers,
Darker than the colorless beards of old men,
20 Dark to come from under the faint red roof of mouths.

O I perceive after all so many uttering tongues,
And I perceive they do not come from the roofs of mouths for nothing.

I wish I could translate the hints about the dead young men and women,
And the hints about old men and mothers, and the offspring taken soon out of their laps.

---

1. *Canuck . . . Cuff.* Canuck (kə nuk′) is slang for a Canadian. Tuckahoe (tuk′ə hō) is a nickname for an inhabitant of eastern Virginia. Cuff, from the African word *cuffee* meaning "a black person," is slang for a black American.

25 What do you think has become of the young and old men?
And what do you think has become of the women and children?

They are alive and well somewhere,
The smallest sprout shows there is really no death,
And if ever there was it led forward life, and does not wait at the end to arrest it,
30 And ceased the moment life appeared.

All goes onward and outward, nothing collapses,
And to die is different from what anyone supposed, and luckier.

1855

THINK AND DISCUSS
Understanding
1. To what is the grass compared in line 3? line 4? line 7? line 12?
2. Where and for whom does the grass appear, according to lines 8–11?
3. What questions does the poet address to the grass in lines 25 and 26? What is the answer to these questions, according to lines 27–30?

Analyzing
4. The grass **symbolizes** several things in this poem. What qualities are suggested in the comparison of the grass to a flag "out of hopeful green stuff woven"?
5. What quality of the grass is suggested by calling it "the handkerchief of the Lord"? "a child"?
6. Collectively considered, do these symbols suggest positive or negative associations with the grass? Explain.
7. In lines 8–11, the grass is called a "uniform hieroglyphic" (suggesting it is a kind of secret but universal language). Given this comparison, what does the grass seem to symbolize?

8. The last group of 21 lines is devoted to the **theme** of death. As an extension of people (the "uncut hair of graves"), who, despite death, are "alive and well somewhere," what does the grass appear to symbolize?
9. Explain the last line—"to die is different from what anyone supposed, and luckier."

Extending
10. Why do you imagine Whitman began this passage with a child asking him a question, "What is the grass?"

Cavalry Crossing a Ford

A line in long array where they wind betwixt green islands,
They take a serpentine course, their arms flash in the sun—hark to the musical clank,
Behold the silvery river, in it the splashing horses loitering stop to drink,
Behold the brown-faced men, each group, each person a picture, the negligent
    rest on the saddles,
5 Some emerge on the opposite bank, others are just entering the ford—while,
Scarlet and blue and snowy white,
The guidon flags flutter gaily in the wind.

1865

Bivouac on a Mountain Side

I see before me now a traveling army halting,
Below a fertile valley spread, with barns and the orchards of summer,
Behind, the terraced sides of a mountain, abrupt, in places rising high,
Broken, with rocks, with clinging cedars, with tall shapes dingily seen,
5 The numerous camp-fires scatter'd near and far, some away up on the mountain,
The shadowy forms of men and horses, looming, large-sized, flickering,
And over all the sky—the sky! far, far out of reach, studded, breaking out, the
    eternal stars.

1865

THINK AND DISCUSS
CAVALRY CROSSING A FORD
BIVOUAC ON A MOUNTAINSIDE
Understanding
1. What colors does the poet use to describe the scene in "Cavalry Crossing a Ford"?
2. What words in this poem suggest motion?
3. In "Bivouac on a Mountain Side," where is the speaker in relation to the scene he views?
4. To what are the bivouac campfires compared in the final lines of the second poem?

Analyzing
5. The first poem uses **images** that portray continuous movement in a daylight scene. The second poem uses images that portray a generally static nighttime scene. Point out three images in each poem that convey these impressions.
6. Would you describe the general atmosphere in both poems as restful, tense, menacing, or as something else? Explain.

When I Heard the Learn'd Astronomer

When I heard the learn'd astronomer,
When the proofs, the figures, were ranged in columns before me,
When I was shown the charts and diagrams, to add, divide, and measure them,
When I sitting heard the astronomer where he lectured with much applause in the lecture-room,
5 How soon unaccountable I became tired and sick,
Till rising and gliding out I wander'd off by myself,
In the mystical moist night-air, and from time to time,
Look'd up in perfect silence at the stars.

1865

 See ONOMATOPOEIA in the Handbook of Literary Terms, page 910.

Sparkles from the Wheel

Where the city's ceaseless crowd moves on the livelong day,
Withdrawn I join a group of children watching, I pause aside with them.

By the curb toward the edge of the flagging,
A knife-grinder works at his wheel sharpening a great knife,
5 Bending over he carefully holds it to the stone, by foot and knee,
With measur'd tread he turns rapidly, as he presses with light but firm hand,
Forth issue then in copious golden jets,
Sparkles from the wheel.

The scene and all its belongings, how they seize and affect me,
10 The sad sharp-chinn'd old man with worn clothes and broad shoulder-band of leather,
Myself effusing and fluid, a phantom curiously floating, now here absorb'd and arrested,
The group, (an unminded point set in a vast surrounding),
The attentive, quiet children, the loud, proud, restive base of the streets,
The low hoarse purr of the whirling stone, the light-press'd blade,
15 Diffusing, dropping, sideways-darting, in tiny showers of gold,
Sparkles from the wheel.

1871

THINK AND DISCUSS
WHEN I HEARD THE LEARN'D ASTRONOMER
Understanding
1. According to line 2, what does the astronomer provide to support his lecture?
2. How does the speaker respond to the astronomer's words in line 5?
3. Where does the speaker go to be by himself?

Analyzing
4. What feelings does the speaker get from looking at the stars? Point out words that reflect these feelings.
5. What attitudes does this poem express toward science and toward nature?

SPARKLES FROM THE WHEEL
Understanding
1. How does the speaker describe the knife grinder in line 10?
2. What act does he perform to produce "sparkles"?
3. Who is watching him work?

Analyzing
4. With whom does the speaker identify in line 2? What does this identification suggest about the speaker?
5. This poem is a detailed "snapshot" of a street scene. Explain in your own words the **image** that catches the speaker's attention.

Extending
6. One Whitman critic has asked of this poem: "Does the poet see in the grinder an image of himself as artist—his poetry sending off sparks to illuminate the world to give glimpses into the universe?" What suggestive words and images in lines 9–16 might support a *yes* answer?

APPLYING: Onomatopoeia H𝕋
See Handbook of Literary Terms, p. 910.
   Onomatopoeia is the use of words whose sounds suggest the natural sounds of the object or activity described. Descriptions of water *gurgling* or mud *oozing* are onomatopoetic.

1. Find examples of onomatopoeia in line 14 of "Sparkles from the Wheel."
2. What onomatopoetic words can you find in "Cavalry Crossing a Ford"?
3. In Section 4 of "When Lilacs Last in the Dooryard Bloom'd," Whitman describes the thrush thus: "A shy and hidden bird is warbling a song." Speculate on why Whitman chose *warbling* rather than *whistling, tweeting,* or *chirping.*

VOCABULARY
Dictionary and Etymology
   Use your Glossary to answer the questions about each numbered word from Whitman's poems. Write the answers on your paper, and be sure you can spell and pronounce each word.

1. strata
   What is the singular form of this word?
   What is the meaning of the Latin root *sternere?*
2. copious
   From what Latin root does this word come? What is the meaning of the root?
3. diffuse, effuse
   What is the common Latin root of these two words? Explain the difference in meaning between *diffuse* and *effuse.*
4. restive
   From what language does this word come? What is its definition?

COMPOSITION ◆━━◆
Writing a Description
   "Cavalry Crossing a Ford" and "Bivouac on a Mountain Side" have been called vignettes, or verbal pictures sketched by the poet. Write a free-verse poem of seven lines, or a paragraph in prose, that captures and conveys a scene. Choose a perspective from which you view this scene, describing it with vivid images and colors. Consider one of the following scenes, or choose one of your own: "Looking Down Main Street at Sunrise (or Sunset)," "Seeing the City from the Top of the Tallest Building," "A Farm Scene Viewed from a Country Road."

Dickinson once described her concept of poetry: "If I read a book and it makes my body so cold no fire can ever warm me, I know that is poetry. If I feel physically as if the top of my head were taken off, I know *that* is poetry." During her life, she published only a handful of the 1,775 poems that she wrote, and her complete poetic works were not published until 1955. She and her poetry never fully belonged to their own time.

Dickinson lived all her life in Amherst, Massachusetts. In her youth she was vivacious and fun-loving. But the society in which she grew up was strict, with precise specifications as to the proper manners and beliefs for young women. It was a world where fun itself was officially frowned upon, where intellectual curiosity and agility were deemed most "unladylike." Though religious, Dickinson did not accept the Calvinist views of the New England church; and her attendance at Mount Holyoke Female Seminary, which she had excitedly anticipated, was marred by daily sessions with the school's headmistress who worked tirelessly for her conversion. But while apparently shy, Dickinson had an unrelenting firmness, and never converted. She did not return to Mount Holyoke after her first year.

In her midtwenties Dickinson gradually withdrew from public life and lived thereafter in almost total seclusion from all but the immediate members of her family. Her poetry writing began in earnest in the late fall of 1861. The most direct influence on her style seems to have come from some of Emerson's poetry. Dickinson also took to heart Emerson's admonition for self-reliance, a prerequisite to her unconventional life and poetry. Nevertheless, she at times wished for critical appraisal. Reading an article of advice to beginning writers by Thomas Wentworth Higginson, Dickinson mailed four of her poems to this abolitionist editor and asked, "Are you too deeply occupied to say if my verse is alive?" He found himself puzzled by her quaint diction and punctuation, but intrigued by her genius. Although he regularized her meter and rhyme when he edited her poems after her death, he must be credited with helping to save her poems for posterity.

There are indications that Dickinson realized the quality and possible importance of her work. Yet she had no wish for recognition in her own time and despite the urgings of friends declined to publish, saying her "barefoot rank" was better. She lived out her life in the family home, dressed always in white, and had little interchange with the outside world. But hers was a rich life of the spirit, as her poetry attests. Many critics consider it the beginning of modern, or twentieth-century, poetry.

Emily Dickinson

This Is My Letter to the World

This is my letter to the World
That never wrote to Me—
The simple News that Nature told—
With tender Majesty

5 Her Message is committed
To Hands I cannot see—
For love of Her—Sweet—countrymen—
Judge tenderly—of Me

c. 1862   1890

To Make a Prairie It Takes a Clover

To make a prairie it takes a clover and one bee,
One clover, and a bee,
And revery.
The revery alone will do,
5 If bees are few.

1896

Winslow Homer (1836–
1910), *The Four-Leaf
Clover*. Detroit Institute of
Arts

I Taste a Liquor Never Brewed

I taste a liquor never brewed—
From Tankards scooped in Pearl—
Not all the Vats upon the Rhine
Yield such an Alcohol!

5 Inebriate of Air—am I—
And Debauchee of Dew—
Reeling—thro endless summer days—
From inns of Molten Blue—

When "Landlords" turn the drunken Bee
10 Out of the Foxglove's door—
When Butterflies—renounce their "drams"—
I shall but drink the more!

Till Seraphs swing their snowy Hats—
And Saints—to windows run—
15 To see the little Tippler
Leaning against the—Sun—

c. 1860   1861

A Narrow Fellow in the Grass

A narrow Fellow in the Grass
Occasionally rides—
You may have met Him—did you not
His notice sudden is—

5 The Grass divides as with a Comb—
A spotted shaft is seen—
And then it closes at your feet
And opens further on—

He likes a Boggy Acre
10 A Floor too cool for Corn—
Yet when a Boy, and Barefoot—
I more than once at Noon

Have passed, I thought, a Whip lash
Unbraiding in the Sun
15 When stooping to secure it
It wrinkled, and was gone—

Several of Nature's People
I know, and they know me—
I feel for them a transport
20 Of cordiality—

But never met this Fellow
Attended, or alone
Without a tighter breathing
And Zero at the Bone—

c. 1865   1866

All Dickinson poems are reprinted by permission of the publishers and the Trustees of Amherst College from *The Poems of Emily Dickinson*, edited by Thomas H. Johnson, Cambridge, Mass.: The Belknap Press of Harvard University Press, Copyright 1951, © 1955, 1979, 1983 by the President and Fellows of Harvard College.

I Like to See It Lap the Miles

I like to see it lap the Miles—
And lick the Valleys up—
And stop to feed itself at Tanks—
And then—prodigious step

5 Around a Pile of Mountains—
And supercilious peer
In Shanties—by the sides of Roads—
And then a Quarry pare

To fit its Ribs
10 And crawl between

Complaining all the while
In horrid—hooting stanza—
Then chase itself down Hill—

And neigh like Boanerges[1]—
15 Then—punctual as a Star
Stop—docile and omnipotent
At its own stable door—

c. 1862   1891

1. *Boanerges* (bō′ə nėr′jēz), a loud preacher or orator.
[*Greek*]

THINK AND DISCUSS
THIS IS MY LETTER TO THE WORLD
Understanding
1. Whom is the speaker addressing in this letter?
2. From where does the speaker obtain the News?

Analyzing

This poem has been interpreted to mean that although Dickinson was reluctant to publish her poems during her lifetime, she looked forward to their publication after her death. In the light of this interpretation, answer the following questions.

3. What might the "letter" of line 1 refer to?
4. In what sense did the world never write to the speaker?
5. To what might the "Hands I cannot see" refer?

TO MAKE A PRAIRIE
Understanding
1. What things are needed to "make" a prairie?

2. What is the meaning of *revery*? (Consult your Glossary, if necessary.)

Analyzing
3. In what sense can one "make" a prairie?
4. How can "revery alone" create a prairie?

I TASTE A LIQUOR NEVER BREWED
Understanding
1. According to lines 5 and 6, what is the "liquor never brewed"?
2. What effects does the speaker feel from this "liquor"?

Analyzing
3. What might the "inns of Molten Blue" in line 8 refer to?
4. Explain the **extended metaphor** in this poem.
5. One **stereotyped** portrayal depicts the drunkard leaning against ("holding up") a lamppost. How is this **image** suggested in the last stanza?

A NARROW FELLOW IN THE GRASS

Understanding

1. What is the "narrow Fellow in the Grass"?
2. Where would this creature be likely to appear, according to line 9?

Analyzing

3. Identify some **images** from this poem drawn from everyday experience.
4. Contrast the speaker's responses to the "narrow Fellow" and to others "of Nature's People."
5. How does the **tone** change at the end?
6. What kind of feeling does "Zero at the Bone" describe?

Extending

7. Explore the different attitudes toward nature expressed in this poem and in "I Taste a Liquor Never Brewed."

I LIKE TO SEE IT LAP THE MILES

Understanding

1. This poem is like a riddle: the subject is never named. What is the "it" mentioned in line 1 and throughout the poem? List all the verbs that tell what "it" is doing.
2. Name items in the landscape that "it" passes through.

Analyzing

3. To what is "it" being compared in this **extended metaphor?** To which of these compared things do the verbs in the poem seem better suited? Explain.
4. What is probably happening when "it" is said to "feed itself at Tanks" (line 3)?
5. How can "it" "peer/ In Shanties" (lines 6–7)?
6. About what does "it" complain in lines 8–12? What is the "hooting stanza"?

COMPOSITION ◄━━

Writing About Nature

Write a three-paragraph letter to a friend describing an encounter with nature. Recollect an episode in which you felt joyous, sad, surprised, or depressed. Maybe you saw a squirrel eating an acorn, a worm crawling along a railing, a butterfly hovering over a flower, two dogs fighting, or a cat stalking a bird. Reconstruct the incident, using vivid images and strong verbs to describe your feelings. See "Developing Your Style" in the Writer's Handbook.

The Soul Selects Her Own Society

The Soul selects her own Society—
Then—shuts the Door—
To her divine Majority—
Present no more—

5 Unmoved—she notes the Chariots—pausing—
At her low Gate—
Unmoved—an Emperor be kneeling
Upon her Mat—

I've known her—from an ample nation—
10 Choose One—
Then—close the Valves of her attention—
Like Stone—

c. 1862   1890

Emily Dickinson

 Review FIGURATIVE LANGUAGE in the Handbook of Literary Terms, page 886.

If You Were Coming in the Fall

If you were coming in the Fall,
I'd brush the Summer by
With half a smile, and half a spurn,
As Housewives do, a Fly.

5 If I could see you in a year,
I'd wind the months in balls—
And put them each in separate Drawers,
For fear the numbers fuse—

If only Centuries, delayed,
10 I'd count them on my Hand,
Subtracting, till my fingers dropped
Into Van Diemen's Land.[1]

If certain, when this life was out—
That yours and mine, should be
15 I'd toss it yonder, like a Rind,
And take Eternity—

But, now, uncertain of the length
Of this, that is between,
It goads me, like the Goblin Bee—
20 That will not state—its sting.

c. 1862   1890

---

1. *Van Diemen's* (dē´mənz) *Land,* Tasmania, a large island south of Australia. It was discovered in 1642 by the Dutch explorer Tasman, who originally named it for Antony van Diemen, a Dutch colonial governor.

My Life Closed Twice Before Its Close

My life closed twice before its close—
It yet remains to see
If Immortality unveil
A third event to me

5 So huge, so hopeless to conceive
As these that twice befell.
Parting is all we know of heaven,
And all we need of hell.

1896

Much Madness Is Divinest Sense

Much Madness is divinest Sense—
To a discerning Eye—
Much Sense—the starkest Madness—
'Tis the Majority
5 In this, as All, prevail—
Assent—and you are sane—
Demur—you're straightway dangerous—
And handled with a Chain—

c. 1862   1890

See SLANT RHYME in the Handbook of Literary Terms, page 902.

I Years Had Been from Home

I Years had been from Home
And now before the Door
I dared not enter, lest a Face
I never saw before

5 Stare stolid into mine
And ask my Business there—
"My Business but a Life I left
Was such remaining there?"

I leaned upon the Awe—
10 I lingered with Before—
The Second like an Ocean rolled
And broke against my ear—

I laughed a crumbling Laugh
That I could fear a Door
15 Who Consternation compassed
And never winced before.

I fitted to the Latch
My Hand, with trembling care
Lest back the awful Door should spring
20 And leave me in the Floor—

Then moved my Fingers off
As cautiously as Glass
And held my ears, and like a Thief
Fled gasping from the House—

c. 1872   1891

I Felt a Funeral in My Brain

I felt a Funeral, in my Brain,
And Mourners to and fro
Kept treading—treading—till it seemed
That Sense was breaking through—

5 And when they all were seated,
A Service, like a Drum—
Kept beating—beating—till I thought
My Mind was going numb—

And then I heard them lift a Box
10 And creak across my Soul
With those same Boots of Lead, again,
Then Space—began to toll,

As all the Heavens were a Bell,
And Being, but an Ear,
15 And I, and Silence, some strange Race
Wrecked, solitary, here—

And then a Plank in Reason, broke,
And I dropped down, and down—
And hit a World, at every plunge,
20 And Finished knowing—then—

c. 1861   1896

Emily Dickinson

THINK AND DISCUSS

THE SOUL SELECTS HER OWN SOCIETY
Understanding
1. According to the first two lines, what two things does the soul do?
2. What word, repeated in lines 5 and 7, indicates the soul's reaction to the chariots and the emperor?
3. According to stanza 3, what does the soul choose? What happens then?

Analyzing
4. Find the key verbs in the poem that describe the soul's activity. What do they suggest about the soul?
5. Young people are considered minors until they reach their *majority*, or age of responsibility. Using this context, explain "divine Majority" (line 3).
6. Instead of opening the poem, "I select my own society," the speaker begins "The Soul selects her own Society." What is suggested by this emphasis on the soul as doing the selecting?

IF YOU WERE COMING IN THE FALL
Understanding
1. What would allow the speaker to "brush the Summer by," according to stanza 1?
2. What time span is mentioned in line 2? line 5? line 9? line 16?
3. To what does the speaker compare the uncertainty of the length of time separating her from her beloved (line 19)?

Analyzing
4. What kind of relationship exists between the speaker and the *you* addressed in the poem?
5. What word would you use to describe the **tone** of this poem?
6. Summarize the poem in your own words.

REVIEWING: Figurative Language H7
See Handbook of Literary Terms, p. 886.

Figurative language is the use of words outside their literal, or usual, meanings. Figurative language adds beauty, increases vitality and impact, suggests comparisons, and develops conciseness. "If You Were Coming in the Fall" achieves much of its effect from its use of two figures of speech—**simile** and **hyperbole**.

1. *Similes* are comparisons, usually made with the words *like* or *as*. Identify the similes in stanzas 1, 4, and 5.
2. What is the *it* in line 15 that the speaker will toss like a rind? Why is a rind particularly appropriate in this simile?
3. *Hyperbole* is a figure of speech in which exaggeration is used to heighten effect. The speaker is willing to count the centuries until her fingers drop. What qualities of the speaker does this hyperbole suggest?

MY LIFE CLOSED TWICE BEFORE ITS CLOSE
Understanding
1. The speaker considers two events in her life as a kind of "closing." What word in line 7 provides a clue as to what these events involved?
2. How many more such events does the speaker anticipate?

Analyzing
3. In what respect might separations, losses, or partings be considered forerunners of death?
4. In what sense is parting "all we know of heaven"? How might it be "all we need of hell"?

MUCH MADNESS IS DIVINEST SENSE
Understanding
1. Who determines what is sense and what is madness, according to line 4?
2. What action mentioned in line 6 makes one appear sane?
3. What action mentioned in line 7 makes one appear dangerous? How are dangerous people treated?

Analyzing
4. How might a "discerning Eye" regard madness as divinest sense?

5. What view of society does this poem imply?

Extending

6. Can you think of examples of so-called madness being sense, or so-called sense being madness? Explain.

I YEARS HAD BEEN FROM HOME
Understanding

1. What does the speaker fear, according to lines 3–6, as she stands before the door of her old home?
2. How has she previously reacted in confronting Consternation (paralyzing horror), according to line 16?
3. What does the speaker do in line 13? lines 17–18? line 24?

Analyzing

4. There are a total of three **similes** in the third and the final stanzas. What are they and to what different senses do these similes appeal?
5. Why do you think lines 7–8 are in quotation marks?
6. What word would you use to describe the **tone** of this poem? What details help establish this tone?

APPLYING: Slant Rhyme H𝓏
See Handbook of Literary Terms, p. 902.

   Slant rhyme, sometimes called *off rhyme* or *near rhyme,* is rhyme in which the vowel sounds are similar but not identical (in/stone, telling/calling, eye/me). Since slant rhyme usually occurs in a poem in which a rhyme pattern has been established, its appearance disappoints readers' expectations, jarring them to attention.

1. Identify the slant rhymes in "I Years Had Been from Home."
2. How does slant rhyme in these stanzas mirror the emotional state of the speaker?
3. Imagine that a less accomplished poet had written the final line thus: "Fled gasping through the Grass." What effect does the change in punctuation and wording have on the line and on the poem in general?

I FELT A FUNERAL IN MY BRAIN
Understanding

1. At the "Funeral" in the speaker's brain, what are the mourners doing in stanza 1?
2. According to stanza 2, what is the funeral service like?
3. What does the speaker's "Being" become (line 14) when "all the Heavens were a Bell"?
4. When the "Plank in Reason" breaks and the speaker drops, what does she hit?

Analyzing

5. What **slant rhymes** appear in the poem?
6. To which one of the five senses does the main **imagery** of this poem appeal?
7. This poem uses an **extended metaphor** to describe a state of emotional trauma or mental breakdown. What words and phrases suggest an emotional collapse?

COMPOSITION ◄━●
Describing a Psychological State

   Write a three-paragraph description for a personal circle of friends of an incident in which you felt extreme elation or depression, numbing fear, or some other overwhelming emotion. Sketch out the situation or events that triggered this psychological state, using images that will re-create the scene for your readers. Then describe that state with as vivid a vocabulary and figurative language as you can summon. See "Developing Your Style" in the Writer's Handbook.

Writing a Biographical Sketch

   Judging from the poems by Dickinson that you have just read, speculate on the kind of person she appears to have been. In a five-paragraph sketch that might appear in a biography, discuss how you think she would have felt about topics such as the following: individualism, privacy, friendship, nature, imagination. Use some quotations from her poems to document your work.

Emily Dickinson

Some Keep the Sabbath Going to Church

Some keep the Sabbath going to Church—
I keep it, staying at Home—
With a Bobolink for a Chorister—
And an Orchard, for a Dome—

5 Some keep the Sabbath in Surplice[1]—
I just wear my Wings—
And instead of tolling the Bell, for Church,
Our little Sexton[2]—sings.

God preaches, a noted Clergyman—
10 And the sermon is never long,
So instead of getting to Heaven, at last—
I'm going, all along.

c. 1860   **1864**

---

1. *Surplice* (sèr′plis), a loose, white gown worn by members of the clergy.
2. *Sexton*, church caretaker and bell ringer.

Winslow Homer (1836–1910), *Fresh Air.*
The Brooklyn Museum

"Faith" Is a Fine Invention

"Faith" is a fine invention
When Gentlemen can *see*—
But *Microscopes* are prudent
In an Emergency.
c. 1860   1891

There's a Certain Slant of Light

There's a certain Slant of light,
Winter Afternoons—
That oppresses, like the Heft
Of Cathedral Tunes—

5 Heavenly Hurt, it gives us—
We can find no scar,
But internal difference,
Where the Meanings, are—

None may teach it—Any—
10 'Tis the Seal Despair—
An imperial affliction
Sent us of the Air—

When it comes, the Landscape listens—
Shadows—hold their breath—
15 When it goes, 'tis like the Distance
On the look of Death—
c. 1861   1890

I Heard a Fly Buzz When I Died

I heard a Fly buzz—when I died—
The Stillness in the Room
Was like the Stillness in the Air—
Between the Heaves of Storm—

5 The Eyes around—had wrung them dry—
And Breaths were gathering firm
For that last Onset—when the King
Be witnessed—in the Room—

I willed my Keepsakes—Signed away
10 What portion of me be
Assignable—and then it was
There interposed a Fly—

With Blue—uncertain stumbling Buzz—
Between the light—and me—
15 And then the Windows failed—and then
I could not see to see—
c. 1862   1896

Emily Dickinson

"I Heard a Fly Buzz When I Died"

The extraordinary thing about this poem is that the speaker is remembering the circumstances of her death—and is therefore speaking from beyond the grave. She is remembering that particular moment in the midst of her dying when an ominous "stillness" settled around her—the moment just after the explosive grief of those witnesses gathered around, and just before the agonized and final onset of death. Clearly the assembled friends and relatives are awaiting—and hope to share in—the moment when the dying person will glimpse into the beyond to see a manifestation of God or Christ "in his power." In Emily Dickinson's day, it was common to believe in such visions at death.

But contrary to these high expectations, after the speaker has made her final arrangements for death (willed her "Keepsakes"), there "interposed a Fly." In other words, the speaker sees not the awaited divine vision, but a common household pest often associated with dead creatures, a fly. This fly, with small bulk, interposes itself between the speaker and the light, and with its "Blue—uncertain stumbling Buzz" must also interpose itself between the speaker and the voices of those assembled at the bedside. Immediately, then, the "Windows failed" (all light blotted out), and the speaker "could not see to see." The poem ends, affirming a double failure of vision: the speaker at death has been cut off from vision both in this world and the next.

Because I Could Not Stop for Death

Because I could not stop for Death—
He kindly stopped for me—
The Carriage held but just Ourselves—
And Immortality.

5 We slowly drove—He knew no haste
And I had put away
My labor and my leisure too,
For His Civility—

We passed the School, where Children strove
10 At Recess—in the Ring—
We passed the Fields of Gazing Grain—
We passed the Setting Sun—

Or rather—He passed Us—
The Dews drew quivering and chill—

15 For only Gossamer, my Gown—
My Tippet—only Tulle[1]—

We paused before a House that seemed
A Swelling of the Ground—
The Roof was scarcely visible—
20 The Cornice—in the Ground—

Since then—'tis Centuries—and yet
Feels shorter than the Day
I first surmised the Horses' Heads
Were toward Eternity—

c. 1863   1890

---

1. *Tippet—only Tulle.* The speaker's shawl, or tippet, was made of tulle (túl), a fine net cloth.

THINK AND DISCUSS

SOME KEEP THE SABBATH GOING TO CHURCH

Understanding

1. How do some people keep the Sabbath, according to line 1? Where does the speaker stay on this day?
2. Who is the Chorister, or choir member?
3. Who preaches at this service? What kind of sermon is delivered?

Analyzing

4. What is the source of music at the speaker's service?
5. In what sense could an orchard resemble a church dome?
6. In what sense is the speaker "going" to heaven "all along"?

"FAITH" IS A FINE INVENTION

Understanding

1. When is "Faith" a fine invention?
2. Under what circumstances are microscopes prudent?

Analyzing

3. Why is "Faith" fine "When Gentlemen can see"?
4. In what kind of emergency might a microscope be "prudent"?

THERE'S A CERTAIN SLANT OF LIGHT

Understanding

1. At what time of day and during what season does the slant of light appear? What is its effect, according to lines 3 and 5?
2. What two things is the slant of light called in the third stanza?

Analyzing

3. The slant of light is described in stanza 1 as oppressive, "like the Heft/ Of Cathedral Tunes." Why might such tunes be considered heavy and oppressive?
4. What feelings does the **image** of a slant of

light arouse in the speaker? What words and phrases convey these feelings?
5. What are examples of **personification** in the last stanza?
6. The poem ends with the word *Death*, followed by a dash. What impression do you think this ending was intended to convey?

Extending

7. What do you think would have been gained, or lost, if the poem had been titled "There's a Certain Pool (Stream, Circle) of Light"?

I HEARD A FLY BUZZ WHEN I DIED

Understanding

1. To what is the stillness in the room compared in stanza 1?
2. What preparations for death has the speaker made, according to stanza 3?
3. What interrupts the still scene? What happens after this interruption?

Analyzing

4. The dying speaker sees the mourners around her in stanza 2, not as people but as "Eyes" and "Breaths." What does this use of **synecdoche** indicate about their behavior?
5. Consider both the meanings and the sounds in the phrase "uncertain stumbling Buzz." Then explain whether or not you consider this phrase effective.
6. Why is the fly's appearance **ironic**?
7. What do you think happens when the "Windows failed"?
8. Does the word *see*, repeated in the last line, refer to a physical or a spiritual vision, or to both? Explain.

BECAUSE I COULD NOT STOP FOR DEATH

Understanding

1. Whose carriage stops for the speaker?
2. According to the second stanza, what two things does she give up for Death's "Civility"?
3. Toward what are the horses directed, according to the last line?

Analyzing

4. What role does death, as **personified** in stanza 1, play in calling on the speaker?

5. In stanza 3, the carriage passes a schoolyard, a field of grain, and a setting sun. What stages in life might each of these scenes **symbolize**?

6. What is the "House" in line 17?

7. How is the speaker's vantage point in the last stanza different from that of the first five stanzas?

8. By what means does this poem make death—both the experience and the character "Death"—seem pleasant rather than terrifying?

Extending

9. Compare the attitudes toward death in "Because I Could Not Stop for Death" and "I Heard a Fly Buzz When I Died."

THINKING SKILLS
Classifying

You can classify Dickinson's images and words by categorizing them into similar groups. One system of classification is to group images according to the senses to which they appeal. Another method of classification is to group words according to the associations, or connotations—positive or negative—that they appear to have in the context of the poem.

1. List two images appearing in the poems that you have read by Dickinson under each of the following heads: *Taste, Smell, Sight,* and *Sound.*

2. Under the heads *Positive* and *Negative,* list six nouns that appear in Dickinson's poems. Be prepared to explain your choices.

COMPOSITION
Writing a Poem

Dickinson uses words that have many connotations, or associated meanings, for different readers—*home, chain, glass, door,* and *star,* to name a few. Choose one of these words or a word of your own that has special associations for you. List these associations. Then try to express them with vivid images or through figurative language. Now put your ideas together in a poem of ten lines or so to appear in your journal. See "Developing Your Style" in the Writer's Handbook.

Writing About Imagery

Dickinson uses stunning imagery to express abstractions and feelings—a crumbling laugh, a slant of light, a tossed rind, closed valves, a goblin bee. In an essay of at least five paragraphs directed to a friend, select several images that appeal to various senses from the poems that appear in this unit. Then comment on how these images contribute to their respective poems and on their effect on you as a reader. Begin your essay with a thesis statement about Dickinson's images and end your writing with an observation about their cumulative effect.

Comparing Two Poems

Write an essay of five or more paragraphs for your school literary magazine that compares and contrasts Dickinson's and Whitman's treatment of death in their respective poems, "Because I Could Not Stop for Death" and "When Lilacs Last in the Dooryard Bloom'd." Concentrate on each poet's style, imagery, and use of poetic devices such as figurative language and symbolism. Conclude your essay by commenting on which poet you think treats the theme of death more effectively. See "Writing About Poetry and Poetic Devices" in the Writer's Handbook.

ENRICHMENT
Readers Theater

Emily Dickinson's poems come alive when read aloud. Assemble a group of students and select four or five of her poems to read aloud to each other. In your selection of the poems, emphasize the range of her subjects and themes. With some of her poems, you might have someone pantomime the action (center) while the poem is being read aloud (at the side). Poems that might lend themselves to this team performance are "I Years Had Been from Home" and "I Felt a Funeral in my Brain." Offer your production to the class.

BIOGRAPHY

Mark Twain (Samuel Langhorne Clemens) 1835–1910

Samuel Langhorne Clemens was reared in the Mississippi River town of Hannibal, Missouri. Many of the adventures of Tom Sawyer can be traced back to Clemens's own childhood. His father died when he was twelve, forcing him to leave school to help support the family. He became a printer's devil (apprentice) and for a number of years worked on his brother's paper. In his early twenties Clemens was able to apprentice himself to a steamboat pilot on the Mississippi. After a year and a half he graduated to licensed pilot, and the next few years were perhaps the happiest of his life. They ended when the Civil War put a stop to traffic on the Mississippi.

Torn between regional loyalties and his opposition to slavery, Clemens eventually left with his brother for Nevada. After unsuccessfully trying his hand at prospecting, Clemens became a journalist under the pseudonym of Mark Twain, a name he took from a depth measurement in river navigation. He was a reporter and correspondent in Virginia City and then in California, where in 1865 he wrote "The Celebrated Jumping Frog of Calaveras County." It appeared in a New York magazine and was quickly picked up and reprinted by newspapers across the nation.

Capitalizing on the success of the story, Twain sailed to New York, and in 1867 a collection of sketches headed by the "Jumping Frog" story was published. That same year he joined a group of tourists sailing for the Mediterranean and the Holy Land. His humorous accounts of the Americans taking in the wonders of the Old World were collected and released as *The Innocents Abroad*. It sold prodigiously and made Twain both renowned and rich.

At thirty-five Twain married Olivia Langdon, with whom he settled in Hartford, Connecticut. In the following seventeen years he produced his finest writing: *The Adventures of Tom Sawyer* (1876), *A Tramp Abroad* (1880), *The Prince and the Pauper* (1882), *Life on the Mississippi* (1883), *The Adventures of Huckleberry Finn* (1884), and *A Connecticut Yankee at King Arthur's Court* (1889). He spent his royalty money carelessly, living sumptuously and investing in schemes that all failed. Twain invested in his own publishing firm, which eventually collapsed. He faced bankruptcy, but instead of filing such papers, he insisted he would pay all his creditors in full and set off on an around-the-world lecture tour to raise the money.

Life was especially hard on him in the final years; his wife and two of his three daughters died. Twain seems to have experienced a combination of despair, pity, and resignation. He once said, "Everything human is pathetic. The secret source of humor itself is not joy but sorrow. There is no humor in heaven."

The Celebrated Jumping Frog of Calaveras County

Mark Twain

In compliance with the request of a friend of mine, who wrote me from the East, I called on good-natured, garrulous old Simon Wheeler, and inquired after my friend's friend, Leonidas W. Smiley, as requested to do, and I hereunto append the result. I have a lurking suspicion that *Leonidas W.* Smiley is a myth; that my friend never knew such a personage; and that he only conjectured that if I asked old Wheeler about him, it would remind him of his infamous *Jim* Smiley, and he would go to work and bore me to death with some exasperating reminiscence of him as long and as tedious as it should be useless to me. If that was the design, it succeeded.

I found Simon Wheeler dozing comfortably by the barroom stove of the dilapidated tavern in the decayed mining camp of Angel's, and I noticed that he was fat and baldheaded, and had an expression of winning gentleness and simplicity upon his tranquil countenance. He roused up, and gave me good day. I told him a friend of mine had commissioned me to make some inquiries about a cherished companion of his boyhood named *Leonidas W.* Smiley—*Rev. Leonidas W.* Smiley, a young minister of the Gospel, who he had heard was at one time a resident of Angel's Camp. I added that if Mr. Wheeler could tell me anything about this Rev. Leonidas W. Smiley, I would feel under many obligations to him.

Simon Wheeler backed me into a corner and blockaded me there with his chair, and then sat down and reeled off the monotonous narrative which follows this paragraph. He never smiled, he never frowned, he never changed his voice from the gentle-flowing key to which he tuned his initial sentence, he never betrayed the slightest suspicion of enthusiasm; but all through the interminable narrative there ran a vein of impressive earnestness and sincerity which showed me plainly that, so far from his imagining that there was anything ridiculous or funny about his story, he regarded it as a really important matter, and admired its two heroes as men of transcendent genius in finesse. I let him go on in his own way, and never interrupted him once.

"Rev. Leonidas W. H'm, Reverend Le—well, there was a feller here once by the name of *Jim* Smiley, in the winter of '49—or maybe it was the spring of '50—I don't recollect exactly, somehow, though what makes me think it was one or the other is because I remember the big flume wasn't finished when he first came to the camp. But anyway, he was the curiousest man about always betting on anything that turned up you ever see, if he could get anybody to bet on the other side; and if he couldn't, he'd change sides. Any way that suited the other man would suit *him*—any way just so's he got a bet, *he* was satisfied. But still he was lucky, uncommon lucky; he most always come out winner. He was always ready and laying for a chance; there couldn't be no

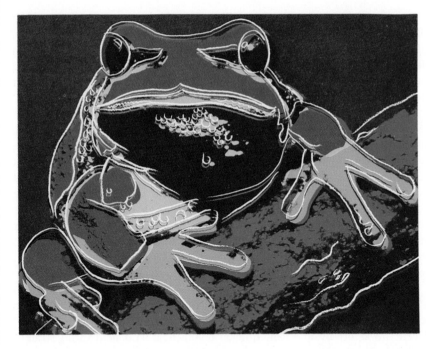

Andy Warhol (1928?–1987),
Pine Barrens Tree Frog

solit'ry thing mentioned but that feller'd offer to bet on it, and take any side you please, as I was just telling you. If there was a horse race, you'd find him flush or you'd find him busted at the end of it; if there was a dogfight, he'd bet on it; if there was a cat fight, he'd bet on it; if there was a chicken fight, he'd bet on it. Why, if there was two birds setting on a fence, he would bet you which one would fly first; or if there was a camp meeting, he would be there reg'lar to bet on Parson Walker, which he judged to be the best exhorter about there, and so he was too, and a good man. If he even see a straddlebug start to go anywheres, he would bet you how long it would take him to get wherever he was going to, and if you took him up, he would foller that straddlebug to Mexico but what he would find out where he was bound for and how long he was on the road.

"Lots of the boys here has seen Smiley, and can tell you about him. Why, it never made no difference to *him*—he'd bet on *any*thing—the dangdest feller. Parson Walker's wife laid very sick once, for a good while, and it seemed as if they warn't going to save her; but one morning he come in, and Smiley asked how she was, and he said she was considerable better—thank the Lord for His inf'nite mercy—and coming on so smart that with the blessing of Prov'dence she'd get well yet; and Smiley, before he thought, says, 'Well, I'll resk two-and-a-half that she don't anyway.'

"This-hyer Smiley had a mare—the boys called her the fifteen-minute nag, but that was only in fun, you know, because of course she was faster than that—and he used to win money on that horse, for all she was so slow and always had the asthma, or the distemper, or the consumption, or something of that kind. They used to give her two or three hundred yards' start, and then pass her underway; but always at the fag end of the race she'd get excited and desperatelike, and come cavorting and straddling up, and scattering her legs around limber, sometimes in the air, and sometimes out to one side among the fences, and kicking up m-o-r-e dust and raising m-o-r-e racket with her coughing and sneezing and blowing her nose—and *always* fetch up at the stand just about a neck ahead, as near as you could cipher it down.

"And he had a little small bull pup, that to look at him you'd think he wan't worth a cent but to set around and look ornery and lay for a chance to steal something. But as soon as money was up on him, he was a different dog; his under jaw'd begin to stick out like the fo'castle of a steamboat, and his teeth would uncover and shine like the furnaces. And a dog might tackle him and bullyrag him, and bite him, and throw him over his shoulder two or three times, and Andrew Jackson—which was the name of the pup—Andrew Jackson would never let on but what *he* was satisfied, and hadn't expected nothing else—and the bets being doubled and doubled on the other side all the time, till the money was all up; and then all of a sudden he would grab that other dog jest by the j'int of his hind leg and freeze to it—not chaw, you understand, but only just grip and hang on till they throwed up the sponge, if it was a year.

"Smiley always come out winner on that pup, till he harnessed a dog once that didn't have no hind legs, because they'd been sawed off by a circular saw, and when the thing had gone along far enough, and the money was all up, and he come to make a snatch for his pet holt, he saw in a minute how he'd been imposed on, and how the other dog had him in the door,[1] so to speak, and he 'peared surprised, and then he looked sorter discouraged like, and didn't try no more to win the fight, and so he got shucked out[2] bad. He give Smiley a look, as much as to say his heart was broke, and it was *his* fault, for putting up a dog that hadn't no hind legs for him to take holt of, which was his main dependence in a fight, and then he limped off a piece and laid down and died. It was a good pup, was that Andrew Jackson, and would have made a name for hisself if he'd lived, for the stuff was in him and he had genius—I know it, because he hadn't had no opportunities to speak of, and it don't stand to reason that a dog could make such a fight as he could under them circumstances if he hadn't no talent. It always makes me feel sorry when I think of that last fight of his'n, and the way it turned out.

"Well, thish-yer Smiley had rat terriers, and chicken cocks, and tomcats and all them kind of things, till you couldn't rest, and you couldn't fetch nothing for him to bet on but he'd match you. He ketched a frog one day, and took him home, and said he calk'lated to edercate him; and so he never done nothing for three months but set in his backyard and learn that frog to jump. And you bet he *did* learn him, too. He'd give him a little punch behind, and the next minute you'd see that frog whirling in the air like a doughnut—see him turn one summer-set, or maybe a couple, if he got a good start, and come down flat-footed and all right, like a cat. He got him up so in the matter of catching flies, and kep' him in practice so constant, that he'd nail a fly every time as far as he could see him.

"Smiley said all a frog wanted was education, and he could do 'most anything—and I believe him. Why, I've seen him set Dan'l Webster down here on this floor—Dan'l Webster was the name of the frog—and sing out, 'Flies, Dan'l, flies!' and quicker'n you could wink he'd spring straight up and snake a fly off'n the counter there, and flop down on the floor ag'in as solid as a gob of mud, and fall to scratching the side of his head with his hind foot as indifferent as if he hadn't no idea he'd been doin' any more'n any frog might do. You never see a frog so modest and straight-for'ard as he was, for all he was so gifted. And when it come to fair and square jumping on a dead level, he could get over more ground at one straddle than any animal of his breed you ever see. Jumping on a dead level was his strong suit, you understand; and when it come to that, Smiley would ante up money on him as long as he had a red.[3] Smiley was monstrous proud of his frog, and well he might be, for fellers that had traveled and been everywheres all said he laid over any frog that ever *they* see.

"Well, Smiley kept the beast in a little lattice box, and he used to fetch him downtown sometimes and lay for a bet. One day a feller—a

---

1. *had him in the door,* had him at a disadvantage.
2. *shucked out,* beaten.
3. *a red,* a red cent, or any money at all.

stranger in the camp, he was—come across him with his box, and says:

" 'What might it be that you've got in the box?'

"And Smiley says, sorter indifferentlike, 'It might be a parrot, or it might be a canary, maybe, but it ain't—it's only just a frog.'

"And the feller took it, and looked at it careful, and turned it around this way and that, and says, 'H'm—so 'tis. Well, what's *he* good for?'

" 'Well,' Smiley says, easy and careless, 'he's good enough for *one* thing, I should judge—he can out-jump ary frog in Calaveras County.'

"The feller took the box again, and took another long, particular look, and give it back to Smiley, and says, very deliberate, 'Well, I don't see no p'ints about that frog that's any better'n any other frog.'

" 'Maybe you don't,' Smiley says. 'Maybe you understand frogs and maybe you don't understand 'em; maybe you've had experience, and maybe you ain't only a amature, as it were. Anyways, I've got *my* opinion, and I'll resk forty dollars that he can outjump any frog in Calaveras County.'

"And the feller studied a minute, and then says, kinder sadlike, 'Well, I'm only a stranger here, and I ain't got no frog; but if I had a frog, I'd bet you.'

"And then Smiley says, 'That's all right—that's all right—if you'll hold my box a minute, I'll go and get you a frog.' And so the feller took the box, and put up his forty dollars along with Smiley's, and set down to wait.

"So he set there a good while thinking and thinking to himself, and then he got the frog out and prized his mouth open and took a teaspoon and filled him full of quail shot—filled him pretty near up to his chin—and set him on the floor.

"Smiley he went to the swamp and slopped around in the mud for a long time, and finally he ketched a frog, and fetched him in, and give him to this feller, and says:

" 'Now, if you're ready, set him alongside of Dan'l, with his forepaws just even with Dan'l's, and I'll give the word.' Then he says, 'One—two—three—jump!' and him and the feller touched up the frogs from behind, and the new frog hopped off, but Dan'l give a heave and hysted up his shoulders—so—like a Frenchman, but it wan't no use—he couldn't budge; he was planted as solid as an anvil, and he couldn't no more stir than if he was anchored out. Smiley was a good deal surprised, and he was disgusted too, but he didn't have no idea what the matter was, of course.

"The feller took the money and started away; and when he was going out at the door, he sorter jerked his thumb over his shoulder—this way—at Dan'l, and says again, very deliberate, 'Well, *I* don't see no p'ints about that frog that's any better'n any other frog.'

"Smiley he stood scratching his head and looking down at Dan'l a long time, and at last he says, 'I do wonder what in the nation that frog throw'd off for—I wonder if there ain't something the matter with him—he 'pears to look mighty baggy somehow.' And he ketched Dan'l by the nap of the neck, and lifted him up, and says, 'Why blame my cats if he don't weight five pound!' and turned him upside down, and he belched out a double handful of shot. And then Smiley see how it was, and he was the maddest man—he set the frog down and took out after that feller, but he never ketched him. And——"

[Here Simon Wheeler heard his name called from the front yard, and got up to see what was wanted.] And turning to me as he moved away, he said: "Just set where you are, stranger, and rest easy—I ain't going to be gone a second."

But, by your leave, I did not think that a continuation of the history of the enterprising vagabond *Jim* Smiley would be likely to afford me much information concerning the Rev. *Leonidas W.* Smiley, and so I started away.

At the door I met the sociable Wheeler returning, and he buttonholed me and recommenced:

"Well, this-hyer Smiley had a yaller one-eyed cow that didn't have no tail, only just a short stump like a bannanner, and——"

However, lacking both time and inclination, I did not wait to hear about the afflicted cow, but took my leave.   1865

THINK AND DISCUSS

Understanding

1. For what reason has the narrator called upon Simon Wheeler?
2. Where does the narrator find Wheeler? How is Wheeler described in paragraphs two and three?
3. Name five things that Smiley bet on, according to paragraph four.
4. How did the pup Andrew Jackson win bets for Smiley?
5. How is Smiley's frog eventually defeated?

Analyzing

6. Twain captures the flavor of the oral yarn by creating a humorous narrator who slowly spins out his tale. What is humorous about Wheeler's character? Cite several examples of his getting sidetracked in his narration.
7. Twain chooses a narrator who tells this story in frontier *dialect*, using peculiar sentence patterns, mispronunciations (represented by misspellings), and grammatical deviations. What **tone** is conveyed by this use of dialect?

8. In his narrative, Wheeler describes the frog as "whirling in the air like a doughnut" and flopping down on the floor as "solid as a gob of mud." How are these **similes** appropriate to the yarn-spinner?
9. An old tradition of literature involves the classic situation of "the trickster tricked." Relate Smiley to this tradition.

APPLYING: Mood H⫶

See Handbook of Literary Terms, p. 897.

Mood is the atmosphere a writer creates through choices of setting, images, figures of speech, and other devices. Mood, which can reinforce a work's meaning and effect, may range from the *nightmarish* to the *awesome*, from the *somber* to the *lighthearted*.

1. Which of the italicized words above best describes the mood of "The Celebrated Jumping Frog"? Explain your choice.
2. Find two similes in paragraph seven used to describe the small bull pup. Explain how these similes contribute to the mood.

Comment

Dialect

In "The Celebrated Jumping Frog," Simon Wheeler tells the story of the frog in his own language: "Well, thish-yer Smiley had rat terriers, and chicken cocks, and tomcats and all them kind of things. . . . He ketched a frog one day, and took him home, and said he calk'lated to edercate him. . . ." Wheeler speaks in a dialect, the language of the American frontier in the far West.

Other dialects were and are spoken in various areas of the country, including the South and New England. Dialects deviate from the norms of standard language in vocabulary, pro-

nunciation, and usage. In Twain's story, for example, the opening and closing paragraphs (the "frame" of the story) are written in standard English, sometimes with a literary flourish. Twain wanted a strong contrast between the "frame" of the story and the colloquial dialect of Simon Wheeler. In the latter part of the nineteenth century, as stories were set in various regions of the U.S., they incorporated various dialects. See, for example, Bret Harte's "The Outcasts of Poker Flat" and Mary E. Wilkins Freeman's "A New England Nun," which both appear in this unit.

To Be a Steamboatman

from **Life on the Mississippi**

Mark Twain

hen I was a boy, there was but one permanent ambition among my comrades in our village on the west bank of the Mississippi River. That was, to be a steamboatman. We had transient ambitions of other sorts, but they were only transient. When a circus came and went, it left us all burning to become clowns; the first Negro minstrel show that ever came to our section left us all suffering to try that kind of life; now and then we had a hope that if we lived and were good, God would permit us to be pirates. These ambitions faded out, each in its turn; but the ambition to be a steamboatman always remained.

Once a day a cheap, gaudy packet arrived upward from St. Louis, and another downward from Keokuk.[1] Before these events, the day was glorious with expectancy; after them, the day was a dead and empty thing. Not only the boys, but the whole village, felt this. After all these years I can picture that old time to myself now, just as it was then: the white town drowsing in the sunshine of a summer's morning; the streets empty, or pretty nearly so; one or two clerks sitting in front of the Water Street stores, with their splint-bottomed chairs[2] tilted back against the walls, chins on breasts, hats slouched over their faces, asleep—with shingle-shavings enough around to show what broke them down; a sow, and a litter of pigs loafing along the sidewalk, doing a good business in watermelon rinds and seeds; two or three lonely little freight piles scattered about the levee; a pile of skids on the slope of the stone-paved wharf, and the fragrant town drunkard asleep in the shadow of them; two or three wood flats[3] at the head of the wharf, but nobody to listen to the peaceful lapping of the wavelets against them; the great Mississippi, the majestic, the magnificent Mississippi, rolling its mile-wide tide along, shining in the sun; the dense forest away on the other side; the point above the town, and the point below, bounding the river glimpse and turning it into a sort of sea, and withal a very still and brilliant and lonely one. Presently a film of dark smoke appears above one of those remote points: instantly a Negro drayman, famous for his quick eye and prodigious voice, lifts up the cry, "S-t-e-a-m-boat a-comin'!" and the scene changes! The town drunkard stirs, the clerks wake up, a furious clatter of drays follows, every house and store pours out a human contribution, and all in a twinkling the dead town is alive and moving. Drays, carts, men, boys, all go hurrying from many quarters to a common center, the wharf. Assembled there, the people fasten their eyes upon the coming boat as upon a wonder they are seeing for the first time. And the boat *is* rather a handsome sight, too. She is long and sharp and trim and pretty; she has two tall, fancy-topped chimneys, with a gilded device of some kind swung between them; a fanciful pilot

---

1. **Keokuk** (kē′ə kuk), a Mississippi River town in the southeastern corner of Iowa, about fifty miles above Hannibal.
2. *splint-bottomed chairs*, chairs with seats woven of thin strips (splints) of wood.
3. *wood flats*, small flat-bottomed boats.

house, all glass and gingerbread, perched on top of the texas deck[4] behind them; the paddle boxes[5] are gorgeous with a picture or with gilded rays above the boat's name; the boiler deck, the hurricane deck,[6] and the texas deck are fenced and ornamented with clean white railings; there is a flag gallantly flying from the jack staff,[7] the furnace doors are open and the fires glaring bravely; the upper decks are black with passengers; the captain stands by the big bell, calm, imposing, the envy of all; great volumes of the blackest smoke are rolling and tumbling out of the chimneys—a husbanded grandeur created with a bit of pitch pine just before arriving at a town; the crew are grouped on the forecastle; the broad stage[8] is run far-out over the port bow; and a deck hand stands picturesquely on the end of it with a coil of rope in his hand; the pent steam is screaming through the gauge cocks; the captain lifts his hand, a bell rings, the wheels stop; then they turn back, churning the water to foam, and the steamer is at rest. Then such a scramble as there is to get aboard, and to get ashore, and to take in freight and to discharge freight, all at one and the same time; and such a yelling and cursing as the mates facilitate it all with! Ten minutes later the steamer is under way again, with no flag on the jack staff and no black smoke issuing from the chimneys. After ten more minutes the town is dead again, and the town drunkard asleep by the skids once more.

My father was a justice of the peace, and I supposed he possessed the power of life and death over all men, and could hang anybody that offended him. This was distinction enough for me as a general thing; but the desire to be a steamboatman kept intruding, nevertheless. I first wanted to be a cabin boy, so that I could come out with a white apron on and shake a tablecloth over the side, where all my old comrades could see me; later I thought I would rather be the deckhand who stood on the end of the stage-plank with the coil of rope in his hand, because he was particularly conspicuous. But these were only daydreams—they were too heavenly to be contemplated as real possibilities.

By and by one of our boys went away. He was not heard of for a long time. At last he turned up as apprentice engineer or "striker" on a steamboat. This thing shook the bottom out of all my Sunday-school teachings. That boy had been notoriously worldly, and I just the reverse; yet he was exalted to this eminence, and I left in obscurity and misery. There was nothing generous about this fellow in his greatness. He would always manage to have a rusty bolt to scrub while his boat tarried at our town, and he would sit on the inside guard[9] and scrub it, where we all could see him and envy him and loathe him. And whenever his boat was laid up he would come home and swell around the town in his blackest and greasiest clothes, so that nobody could help remembering that he was a steamboatman; and he used all sorts of steamboat technicalities in his talk, as if he were so used to them that he forgot common people could not understand them. He would speak of the "lab-board"[10] side of a horse in an easy, natural way that would make one wish he was dead. And he was always talking about "St. Looy" like an old citizen; he would refer casually to occasions when he was "coming down Fourth Street," or when he was "Passing by the Planter's House," or when there was a fire and he took a turn on the brakes of "the old Big Missouri"; and then he would go on and lie about how many towns the size of ours were burned down there that day. Two or three of the boys had long been persons of consideration among us

---

4. *texas deck*. The texas is a range of staterooms adjacent to the pilot house reserved for officers. The texas deck adjoins these living quarters.
5. *paddle boxes*, the wooden coverings built over the upper part of the paddle wheels that propelled the steamer.
6. *the boiler deck, the hurricane deck*. The boiler deck is that part of the upper deck immediately over the boilers; the hurricane deck is the topmost deck.
7. *jack staff*, a short pole erected at the front of the vessel.
8. *forecastle . . . stage*. The forecastle is an upper deck at the forward part of the ship; the stage is a stage-plank or gangplank.
9. *inside guard*, part of the steamboat's deck that curves out over the paddle wheel.
10. *"lab-board,"* larboard, the left or port side of a ship.

Currier & Ives lithograph, *Low Water in the Mississippi* (1868).
Museum of the City of New York

because they had been to St. Louis once and had a vague general knowledge of its wonders, but the day of their glory was over now. They lapsed into a humble silence, and learned to disappear when the ruthless cub engineer approached. This fellow had money, too, and hair oil. Also an ignorant silver watch and a showy brass watch chain. He wore a leather belt and used no suspenders. If ever a youth was cordially admired and hated by his comrades, this one was. No girl could withstand his charms. He "cut out" every boy in the village. When his boat blew up at last, it diffused a tranquil contentment among us such as we had not known for months. But when he came home the next week, alive, renowned, and appeared in church all battered up and bandaged, a shining hero, stared at and wondered over by everybody, it seemed to us that the partiality of Providence for an undeserving reptile had reached a point where it was open to criticism.

This creature's career could produce but one result, and it speedily followed. Boy after boy managed to get on the river. The minister's son became an engineer. The doctor's and the postmaster's sons became mud clerks;[11] the wholesale liquor dealer's son became a barkeeper on a boat; four sons of the chief merchant, and two sons of the county judge, became pilots. Pilot was the grandest position of all. The pilot, even in those days of trivial wages, had a princely salary—from a hundred and fifty to two hundred and fifty dollars a month, and no board to pay. Two months of his wages would pay a preacher's salary for a year. Now some of us were left disconsolate. We could not get on the river—at least our parents would not let us.

---

11. **mud clerks,** second clerks, so called because it was their duty to go ashore at unimportant stops, often mere mudbanks, to receive or check off freight.

So, by and by, I ran away. I said I would never come home again till I was a pilot and could come in glory. But somehow I could not manage it. I went meekly aboard a few of the boats that lay packed together like sardines at the long St. Louis wharf, and humbly inquired for the pilots, but got only a cold shoulder and short words from mates and clerks. I had to make the best of this sort of treatment for the time being, but I had comforting daydreams of a future when I should be a great and honored pilot, with plenty of money, and could kill some of these mates and clerks and pay for them.

1875

THINK AND DISCUSS
Understanding
1. What are three "transient ambitions" of the boys in the village? What is their "permanent ambition"?
2. According to the beginning of the second paragraph, what is the atmosphere in the village just before the "gaudy packet" arrives? How does this atmosphere change, once the packet departs?
3. How do the boys regard the apprentice engineer who returns to the village, according to paragraph four, which begins, "By and by, one of our boys . . .?
4. Paragraph five begins, "This creature's career could produce but one result. . . ." What is that result?

Analyzing
5. How does the appearance of the apprentice engineer shake "the bottom out of all my [the narrator's] Sunday-school teachings"?
6. The boys both admire and despise the visiting apprentice engineer. What causes these conflicting feelings?
7. What examples of humor can you find in this account?
8. The contrasting **moods** of "To Be a Steamboatman" are those of peacefulness and great excitement. Cite three **images** that convey each of these moods in the second paragraph.
9. Twain's **tone** is at times humorous and ironic as he paints a picture of the village. Cite two examples from this narrative that portray the conflicting feelings that the apprentice engineer evokes in the village boys.

Extending
10. Do you think Twain's description of the process of choosing a career is accurate? Explain.

COMPOSITION
Writing About a Career Choice
Write a three- or four-paragraph letter to your parents telling them how you have come to a decision on a career. First you might want to review all the decisions you have made in the past. If you are like most people, you have already selected and discarded several choices. Then explain what has led to your current decision. Conclude by hinting that you might—just might—again change your mind.

Analyzing Humor
Twain's humor is based in part on his use of irony, exaggeration, juxtaposition of the ordinary with the bizarre, unusual images (the "fragrant" town drunkard), and depictions of quirks in human nature. Write a four-paragraph essay for your school newspaper that discusses the humor of "The Celebrated Jumping Frog of Calaveras County" or "To Be a Steamboatman." If you choose to write about the first story, you may wish to discuss the use of dialect and the narrator's "frame" that begins and ends the story.

Individualism

The theme of individualism received its strongest and most vivid expression in the American literature of the nineteenth century. The theme runs throughout Ralph Waldo Emerson's work and inspired such essays as "Self-Reliance"—a call for readers to discover and rely on their selfhood. He exclaimed, "Nothing is at last sacred but the integrity of your own mind."

Emerson's friend and disciple, Henry David Thoreau, took Emerson's theory and put it into practice by going to live alone at a pond near Concord, and out of the experience writing his masterpiece of individualism, *Walden*. He expressed a typical sentiment when he wrote: "I would rather sit on a pumpkin and have it all to myself, than be crowded on a velvet cushion."

Walt Whitman made the theme of individualism so much his own that he is known as its most eloquent poet. His masterpiece, *Leaves of Grass*, opens with the lines: "One's-self I sing, a simple separate person, /Yet utter the word Democratic, the word En-Masse." Whitman was aware that an individualism grown too strong could deteriorate into anarchy, and he therefore always connected it with democracy (the French word *en-masse* evoking the people, the mass). Thus Whitman defined the American ideal as an individualism balanced with equality.

Whitman's greatest poem, and also his most powerful treatment of the theme of individualism, is *Song of Myself*, which opens: "I celebrate myself, and sing myself, /And what I assume you shall assume, /For every atom belonging to me as good belongs to you." The poet no sooner begins celebration of himself than he turns to his readers and proclaims that they are equal to him.

In "What Is the Grass?" (Section 6 of *Song of Myself*) Whitman presents his fullest treatment of the central symbol introduced in the title of his book, *Leaves of Grass*. Obviously the grass is a complex symbol for Whitman, but among its many meanings are those associated directly with individualism and equality.

Mark Twain found the theme of individualism among the frontier motifs that characterized all of his books. An early work, *Roughing It*, suggests by its very title the self-reliance that all settlers needed in order to survive in a land with a minimum of social structures and comforts. His characters (like Huck Finn and Tom Sawyer) always fall back on their own resources, plain common sense or native shrewdness, to endure.

Emily Dickinson sounded the theme of individualism in a number of poems, including "I Taste a Liquor Never Brewed," which is a kind of celebration of self intoxicated in communion with nature. She begins another of her poems thus: "On a Columnar Self—/How ample to rely." And she opens another poem: "You cannot take itself/ From any Human soul."

By no means confined to nineteenth-century literature, individualism is a motif that is found in many of the selections that appear throughout *The United States in Literature*. William Faulkner's "The Bear" celebrates a boy who confronts a mythic animal all by himself. In John Steinbeck's "The Leader of the People," one individual finds his whole life shaped by an instance in which his self-sufficiency enabled him to take his people across the continent. Individualism runs throughout W. E. B. Du Bois's "Of the Meaning of Progress"; it lies at the heart of Teresa Paloma Acosta's poem, "My Mother Pieced Quilts"; and it is the cornerstone of Kurt Vonnegut, Jr.'s story, "Harrison Bergeron."

The theme of individualism is likely to endure in American literature as modern writers celebrate those individuals who resist and struggle to retain their identities and ideals in a mass society. Such writers focus on personal affirmation and individual worth, very much in the tradition of Emerson and Whitman.

In the later nineteenth century, folk songs began to be hailed by many as truly American poetry of the sort Whitman was proclaiming. Two major folk traditions are represented here. "Shenandoah," a chantey or work song sung to the rhythms of a sailor's tasks, originated on American ships and spread to the rivers west of the Mississippi. U.S. cavalrymen in the West sang a similar version titled "The Wild Missourye." In this ballad, *Shenandoah* is the name of an Indian chieftain whose daughter is stolen from him.

"El Corrido de Gregorio Cortez," from the Rio Grande frontier, belongs to a time-honored, worldwide tradition of border ballads from the border of Scotland and England where, as along the Rio Grande long ago, officials of both countries were considered annoying "outsiders." Borderers settled their own feuds according to a strict code of honor, and the hero was the lone underdog "defending his right" against all odds.

Shenandoah

Oh, Missouri, she's a mighty river,
    Away you rolling river.
The Red-skins' camp lies on its borders,
    Ah-ha, I'm bound away 'cross the wide Missouri.

5 The white man loved the Indian maiden,
    Away you rolling river.
With notions sweet his canoe was laden,
    Ah-ha, I'm bound away 'cross the wide Missouri.

"O Shenandoah, I love your daughter,
10   Away you rolling river.
I'll take her 'cross yon rolling water."
    Ah-ha, I'm bound away 'cross the wide Missouri.

The chief disdained the trader's dollars:
    Away you rolling river.
15 "My daughter never you shall follow."
    Ah-ha, I'm bound away 'cross the wide Missouri.

Harry C. Edwards, *Handsome Morning—A Dakota* (1921). The Brooklyn Museum

"Shenandoah" from *Sea Songs and Shanties* by W. B. Whall. Reprinted by permission of Brown, Son & Ferguson, Ltd.

At last there came a Yankee skipper,
   Away you rolling river.
He winked his eye, and he tipped his flipper.
20   Ah-ha, I'm bound away 'cross the wide Missouri.

He sold the chief that firewater,
   Away you rolling river.
And 'cross the river he stole his daughter,
   Ah-ha, I'm bound away 'cross the wide Missouri.

25 "O Shenandoah, I long to hear you,
   Away you rolling river.
Across that wide and rolling river."
   Ah-ha, I'm bound away 'cross the wide Missouri.

El Corrido de Gregorio Cortez

In the county of El Carmen
A great misfortune befell;
The Major Sheriff is dead;
Who killed him no one can tell.

5 At two in the afternoon,
In half an hour or less,
They knew that the man who killed him
Had been Gregorio Cortez.

They let loose the bloodhound dogs;
10 They followed him from afar.
But trying to catch Cortez
Was like following a star.

All the rangers of the county
Were flying, they rode so hard;
15 What they wanted was to get
The thousand-dollar reward.

And in the county of Kiansis
They cornered him after all;
Though they were more than three hundred
20 He leaped out of their corral.

Then the Major Sheriff[1] said,
As if he was going to cry,
"Cortez, hand over your weapons;
We want to take you alive."

25 Then said Gregorio Cortez,
And his voice was like a bell,
"You will never get my weapons
Till you put me in a cell."

Then said Gregorio Cortez,
30 With his pistol in his hand,
"Ah, so many mounted Rangers
Just to take one Mexican!"

El Corrido de Gregorio Cortez (el kôr rē′dô de gre gô′ryô kôr tes′). A *corrido* is a form
of heroic ballad popular in Mexico and along the Rio Grande border.
1. *Major Sheriff.* This refers to the second county sheriff to pursue Cortez, not to the
sheriff he shot.

Reprinted from *With His Pistol in His Hand* by Américo Paredes. Copyright © 1958, renewed in 1986.
By permission of the University of Texas Press.

THINK AND DISCUSS

SHENANDOAH

Understanding

1. What does the white man tell the chief in lines 9–11? How does the chief respond?

2. What does the Yankee skipper do in lines 21–23?

Analyzing

3. Although the narrator is the dominant voice in "Shenandoah," there are several other voices indicated by the quotation marks. Name these other singers and identify their lines.

4. What meaning does *bound* have in lines sung by the narrator? What new meaning is suggested by the word *bound* in the final refrain if the singer is the Indian maid?

5. This poem is a *folk ballad*—a story by an anonymous author arranged in four-line stanzas, which relies on dialogue and contains little characterization. The **theme** of this poem is common to many ballads. What is it?

EL CORRIDO DE GREGORIO CORTEZ

Understanding

1. For what crime is Cortez wanted? Why do the rangers want to catch him, according to stanza 4?

2. Where do they finally corner him?

3. Under what circumstances will Cortez give up his weapons?

Analyzing

4. What do the final stanza and **simile** in line 12 reveal about Cortez?

5. What qualities of a folk ballad does this poem display?

Comment

The Story Behind "El Corrido de Gregorio Cortez"

Cortez was born on June 22, 1875, in Mexico and emigrated in 1887 to Texas, where he joined a brother who had been living there for some time. On June 13, 1901, Sheriff W. T. "Brock" Morris came to their house while looking for a Mexican who had stolen a horse. He asked Cortez and his brother several questions, but one of the sheriff's deputies interpreted Cortez's answers wrongly, and Morris mistakenly concluded that Cortez was defying his authority as a sheriff.

He gave orders for his men to arrest both Cortez and his brother. In the ensuing fight, Morris shot and killed Cortez's brother, and in retaliation Gregorio shot the sheriff and killed him.

Cortez fled, and a posse led by Sheriff Robert M. Glover set out after him. They caught up with Cortez on June 16, 1901, and Cortez killed Glover in the gun battle that followed. In spite of the overwhelming odds against Cortez, he managed to get away again and started out toward Mexico.

But as he approached the border, he stopped in a small town to rest and was betrayed to the Texas Rangers by "El Teco," whose actual name was Jesús González. Cortez was taken back to Corpus Christi, where a jury determined that he had killed Sheriff Morris in self-defense. However, when tried for killing Sheriff Glover, Cortez was found guilty and given a life sentence in prison. He spent the next sixteen years in various jails until Governor Oscar B. Colquitt finally pardoned him.

After the Civil War, a new surge of homesteaders and repeated violations of U.S. government treaties infuriated the Plains tribes. As second chief of the Kiowas, Satanta led attacks on settlers. Chiefs of some nations, including Satanta, the "Orator of the Plains," agreed to the Medicine Lodge treaty. The treaty, signed in 1867, limited where the Plains tribes could live and hunt. Satanta's reluctance to accept the terms of the treaty is evident in the following speech, which he delivered to the United States commissioners at Medicine Lodge Creek, Kansas.

Hostilities soon resumed and Satanta was imprisoned. He killed himself in the Texas state prison, perhaps attempting by his death to inspire the Kiowas to resist total subjugation.

My Heart Feels Like Bursting

Satanta

 love the land and the buffalo and will not part with it. I want you to understand well what I say. Write it on paper. . . . I hear a great deal of good talk from the gentlemen whom the Great Father[1] sends us, but they never do what they say. I don't want any of the medicine lodges[2] within the country. I want the children raised as I was. . . .

I have heard that you intend to settle us on a reservation near the mountains. I don't want to settle. I love to roam over the prairies. There I feel free and happy, but when we settle down, we grow pale and die. I have laid aside my lance, bow, and shield, and yet I feel safe in your presence. I have told you the truth. I have no little lies hid about me, but I don't know how it is with the commissioners. Are they as clear as I am? A long time ago this land belonged to our fathers; but when I go up to the river, I see camps of soldiers on its banks. These soldiers cut down my timber; they kill my buffalo; and when I see that, my heart feels like bursting; I feel sorry. I have spoken.

1867

---

1. *Great Father*, President Andrew Johnson.
2. *medicine lodges*, schools and churches like those of the whites.

THINK AND DISCUSS

Understanding

1. What does Satanta want, according to the end of paragraph one? What does he not want?

2. What does Satanta say will happen to his people if they are forced to settle on a reservation?

3. What have the camps of soldiers destroyed?

Analyzing

4. What are Satanta's ideals of good conduct?

5. Choose a word to describe Satanta's **tone** in this speech and explain your choice.

6. What emotional responses is his speech designed to evoke from the government commissioners?

Extending

7. What would be your response to Satanta's claim, "A long time ago this land belonged to our fathers"?

BIOGRAPHY

Chief Joseph
1832?–1904

At the age of only thirty, Chief Joseph became council leader of the Nez Percé [nez′pėrs′], a tribe of the Pacific Northwest. In 1876, the government ordered the tribe to yield its already restricted lands. Chief Joseph's legal arguments failed, and he left for Canada with 750 followers, few of them warriors. For two months and over 1,600 miles of mountains, his war chiefs brilliantly outfought veteran troops, but the exhausted survivors were trapped barely thirty miles from Canada. The speech that follows was made when Chief Joseph surrendered with his people to General Nelson Miles in 1877.

Exiled first to Oklahoma, then to a reservation in Washington, Chief Joseph visited Washington, D.C., and the East in 1903.

I Will Fight No More Forever

Chief Joseph

Tell General Howard I know his heart. What he told me before, I have in my heart. I am tired of fighting. Our chiefs are killed. Looking Glass is dead. Toohoolhoolzote[1] is dead. The old men are all dead. It is the young men who say yes and no. He who led on the young men is dead. It is cold and we have no blankets. The little children are freezing to death. Many people, some of them, have run away to the hills and have no blankets, no food; no one knows where they are—perhaps freezing to death. I want to have time to look for my children and see how many I can find. Maybe I shall find them among the dead. Hear me, my chiefs. I am tired; my heart is sick and sad. From where the sun now stands I will fight no more forever.

1877

---

1. *Toohoolhoolzote* (tü hül'hül'zōt), a prophet who once served as Chief Joseph's spokesman.

From *Indian Oratory: Famous Speeches by Noted Indian Chieftains*, compiled by W. C. Vanderwerth. Copyright 1971 by the University of Oklahoma Press. Reprinted by permission.

THINK AND DISCUSS

Understanding

1. Which two men does Chief Joseph say are now dead?
2. What ill effects are those people suffering who have run away to the hills?

Analyzing

3. What characteristics of a great leader are revealed in this speech?
4. What phrases suggest that Chief Joseph experienced opposition from his own people?

Extending

5. Imagine that these two speeches had been titled "I Am Sad" and "No More Fighting," respectively. Why are the original titles more effective?

COMPOSITION

Writing About a Ballad

Find a book, a record, or a tape of American ballads and choose one to read, sing, or play for the class. Write a two- or three-paragraph introduction, based on research, explaining the origins of the ballad, the area of the country in which it was popular, and the variations that developed as it was passed on. Then present your introduction and the ballad to your class.

Defending Your Position

Write a four-paragraph letter to the local newspaper pointing out why you believe the U.S. should or should not make restitution to Native Americans for land lost during America's settlement. You might use remarks from the speeches of Chief Joseph or Satanta as a point of departure. In addition, consider what responsibility modern Americans bear for what their ancestors did. See "Writing to Persuade an Audience" in the Writer's Handbook.

BIOGRAPHY

Bret Harte
1836–1902

Bret Harte became in the 1860s the most famous western writer in American literature. His local-color stories portraying the small mining towns of California during the period of the Gold Rush were well known throughout America and even in England. He created stock characters —gamblers, drifters, prospectors, hardened women, and naive youths —who fascinated a large public and took on a mythic life of their own.

The irony in this achievement is that Harte was not originally a westerner, but New York born. His father died in 1845, leaving a wife with four children. Harte went to work at thirteen and was soon supporting himself. Though he left school, he read avidly in his father's large library, where he fell in love with the works of the British novelist, Charles Dickens.

It was not until he was eighteen years old, in 1853, that Harte went to California, then still in the throes of the mad rush to extract fortunes from the mountains and streams. He worked at several jobs, including that of rider for the Wells Fargo Express, and became an editor of the *Overland Monthly* in 1868. It was in this magazine that he began to publish his own fiction: "The Luck of Roaring Camp" in 1868, and "The Outcasts of Poker Flat" in 1869. Suddenly Harte found himself a literary celebrity.

In 1871, Harte pulled up stakes in California and headed back East, where his fame brought a contract from the *Atlantic Monthly* for $10,000 a year (then a princely sum) for regular contributions. But Harte had left behind in the West the materials that had ignited his imagination. Never again would he find such a literary gold mine. His later work turned out to be diluted versions of early successes. Harte went abroad, spending his last years in England, where he continued to write and was much admired by British readers as an American western "original."

Harte's early works, especially stories like "The Outcasts of Poker Flat," have continued to appeal to successive generations. Perhaps the secret of that appeal lies in Harte's ability to capture primal elements of American character and America's mythic past in his frontier tales of the West.

The Outcasts of Poker Flat

Bret Harte

s Mr. John Oakhurst, gambler, stepped into the main street of Poker Flat on the morning of the 23d of November, 1850, he was conscious of a change in its moral atmosphere since the preceding night. Two or three men, conversing earnestly together, ceased as he approached, and exchanged significant glances. There was a Sabbath lull in the air, which, in a settlement unused to Sabbath influences, looked ominous.

Mr. Oakhurst's calm, handsome face betrayed small concern in these indications. Whether he was conscious of any predisposing cause was another question. "I reckon they're after somebody," he reflected; "likely it's me." He returned to his pocket the handkerchief with which he had been whipping away the red dust of Poker Flat from his neat boots, and quietly discharged his mind of any further conjecture.

In point of fact, Poker Flat was "after somebody." It had lately suffered the loss of several thousand dollars, two valuable horses, and a prominent citizen. It was experiencing a spasm of virtuous reaction, quite as lawless and ungovernable as any of the acts that had provoked it. A secret committee[1] had determined to rid the town of all improper persons. This was done permanently in regard of two men who were then hanging from the boughs of a sycamore in the gulch, and temporarily in the banishment of certain other objectionable characters. I regret to say that some of these were ladies. It is but due to the sex, however, to state that their impropriety was professional, and it was only in such easily established standards of evil that Poker Flat ventured to sit in judgment.

Mr. Oakhurst was right in supposing that he was included in this category. A few of the committee had urged hanging him as a possible example and a sure method of reimbursing themselves from his pockets of the sums he had won from them. "It's agin justice," said Jim Wheeler, "to let this yer young man from Roaring Camp—an entire stranger—carry away our money." But a crude sentiment of equity residing in the breasts of those who had been fortunate enough to win from Mr. Oakhurst overruled this narrower local prejudice.

Mr. Oakhurst received his sentence with philosophic calmness, none the less coolly that he was aware of the hesitation of his judges. He was too much of a gambler not to accept fate. With him life was at best an uncertain game, and he recognized the usual percentage in favor of the dealer.

A body of armed men accompanied the deported wickedness of Poker Flat to the outskirts of the settlement. Besides Mr. Oakhurst, who was known to be a coolly desperate man, and for whose intimidation the armed escort was intended, the expatriated party consisted of a young woman familiarly known as "The Duchess;" another who had won the title of

---

1. *secret committee,* a vigilance committee exercising temporarily the authority of law.

"Mother Shipton;"[2] and "Uncle Billy," a suspected sluice-robber[3] and confirmed drunkard. The cavalcade provoked no comments from the spectators, nor was any word uttered by the escort. Only when the gulch which marked the uttermost limit of Poker Flat was reached, the leader spoke briefly and to the point. The exiles were forbidden to return at the peril of their lives.

As the escort disappeared, their pent-up feelings found vent in a few hysterical tears from the Duchess, some bad language from Mother Shipton, and a Parthian[4] volley of expletives from Uncle Billy. The philosophic Oakhurst alone remained silent. He listened calmly to Mother Shipton's desire to cut somebody's heart out, to the repeated statements of the Duchess that she would die in the road, and to the alarming oaths that seemed to be bumped out of Uncle Billy as he rode forward. With the easy good humor characteristic of his class, he insisted upon exchanging his own riding-horse, "Five-Spot," for the sorry mule which the Duchess rode. But even this act did not draw the party into any closer sympathy. The young woman readjusted her somewhat draggled plumes with a feeble, faded coquetry; Mother Shipton eyed the possessor of "Five-Spot" with malevolence, and Uncle Billy included the whole party in one sweeping anathema.

The road to Sandy Bar—a camp that, not having as yet experienced the regenerating influences of Poker Flat, consequently seemed to offer some invitation to the emigrants—lay over a steep mountain range. It was distant a day's severe travel. In that advanced season the party soon passed out of the moist, temperate regions of the foothills into the dry, cold, bracing air of the Sierras. The trail was narrow and difficult. At noon the Duchess, rolling out of her saddle upon the ground, declared her intention of going no farther, and the party halted.

The spot was singularly wild and impressive. A wooded amphitheatre, surrounded on three sides by precipitous cliffs of naked granite, sloped gently toward the crest of another precipice that overlooked the valley. It was, undoubtedly, the most suitable spot for a camp, had camping been advisable. But Mr. Oakhurst knew that scarcely half the journey to Sandy Bar was accomplished, and the party were not equipped or provisioned for delay. This fact he pointed out to his companions curtly, with a philosophic commentary on the folly of "throwing up their hand before the game was played out." But they were furnished with liquor, which in this emergency stood them in place of food, fuel, rest, and prescience. In spite of his remonstrances, it was not long before they were more or less under its influence. Uncle Billy passed rapidly from a bellicose state into one of stupor, the Duchess became maudlin, and Mother Shipton snored. Mr. Oakhurst alone remained erect, leaning against a rock, calmly surveying them.

Mr. Oakhurst did not drink. It interfered with a profession which required coolness, impassiveness, and presence of mind, and, in his own language, he "couldn't afford it." As he gazed at his recumbent fellow exiles, the loneliness begotten of his pariah trade, his habits of life, his very vices, for the first time seriously oppressed him. He bestirred himself in dusting his black clothes, washing his hands and face, and other acts characteristic of his studiously neat habits, and for a moment forgot his annoyance. The thought of deserting his weaker and more pitiable companions never perhaps occurred to him. Yet he could not help feeling the want of that excitement which, singularly enough, was most conducive to that calm equanimity for which he was notorious. He looked at the gloomy walls that rose a thousand feet sheer above the circling pines around him, at the sky ominously clouded, at the valley below, already deepening into shadow; and, doing so, suddenly he heard his own name called.

---

2. **Mother Shipton,** name given to a reputed witch, Ursula Southill (born c. 1488), famous for her extraordinary prophecies.
3. **sluice-robber,** one who steals gold from the trough in which it is sifted from the sand.
4. **Parthian.** The Parthians were an ancient Asian people known for their strategy of pretending flight and then suddenly attacking.

A horseman slowly ascended the trail. In the fresh, open face of the newcomer Mr. Oakhurst recognized Tom Simson, otherwise known as "The Innocent," of Sandy Bar. He had met him some months before over a "little game," and had, with perfect equanimity, won the entire fortune—amounting to some forty dollars—of that guileless youth. After the game was finished, Mr. Oakhurst drew the youthful speculator behind the door and thus addressed him: "Tommy, you're a good little man, but you can't gamble worth a cent. Don't try it over again." He then handed him his money back, pushed him gently from the room, and so made a devoted slave of Tom Simson.

There was a remembrance of this in his boyish and enthusiastic greeting of Mr. Oakhurst. He had started, he said, to go to Poker Flat to seek his fortune. "Alone?" No, not exactly alone; in fact (a giggle), he had run away with Piney Woods. Didn't Mr. Oakhurst remember Piney? She that used to wait on the table at the Temperance House? They had been engaged a long time, but old Jake Woods had objected, and so they had run away, and were going to Poker Flat to be married, and here they were. And they were tired out, and how lucky it was they had found a place to camp, and company. All this the Innocent delivered rapidly, while Piney, a stout, comely damsel of fifteen, emerged from behind the pine-tree, where she had been blushing unseen, and rode to the side of her lover.

Mr. Oakhurst seldom troubled himself with sentiment, still less with propriety; but he had

Winslow Homer (1836–1910), *The Bridle Path* (1868). Sterling and Francine Clark Art Institute, Williamstown, Massachusetts

a vague idea that the situation was not fortunate. He retained, however, his presence of mind sufficiently to kick Uncle Billy, who was about to say something, and Uncle Billy was sober enough to recognize in Mr. Oakhurst's kick a superior power that would not bear trifling. He then endeavored to dissuade Tom Simson from delaying further, but in vain. He even pointed out the fact that there was no provision, nor means of making a camp. But, unluckily, the Innocent met this objection by assuring the party that he was provided with an extra mule loaded with provisions, and by the discovery of a rude attempt at a log house near the trail. "Piney can stay with Mrs. Oakhurst," said the Innocent, pointing to the Duchess, "and I can shift for myself."

Nothing but Mr. Oakhurst's admonishing foot saved Uncle Billy from bursting into a roar of laughter. As it was, he felt compelled to retire up the cañon until he could recover his gravity. There he confided the joke to the tall pine trees, with many slaps of his leg, contortions of his face, and the usual profanity. But when he returned to the party, he found them seated by a fire—for the air had grown strangely chill and the sky overcast—in apparently amicable conversation. Piney was actually talking in an impulsive girlish fashion to the Duchess, who was listening with an interest and animation she had not shown for many days. The Innocent was holding forth, apparently with equal effect, to Mr. Oakhurst and Mother Shipton, who was actually relaxing into amiability. "Is this yer a d——d picnic?" said Uncle Billy, with inward scorn, as he surveyed the sylvan group, the glancing firelight, and the tethered animals in the foreground. Suddenly an idea mingled with the alcoholic fumes that disturbed his brain. It was apparently of a jocular nature, for he felt impelled to slap his leg again and cram his fist into his mouth.

As the shadows crept slowly up the mountain, a slight breeze rocked the tops of the pine-trees and moaned through their long and gloomy aisles. The ruined cabin, patched and covered with pine boughs, was set apart for the ladies. As the lovers parted, they unaffectedly exchanged a kiss, so

honest and sincere that it might have been heard above the swaying pines. The frail Duchess and the malevolent Mother Shipton were probably too stunned to remark upon this last evidence of simplicity, and so turned without a word to the hut. The fire was replenished, the men lay down before the door, and in a few minutes were asleep.

Mr. Oakhurst was a light sleeper. Toward morning he awoke benumbed and cold. As he stirred the dying fire, the wind, which was now blowing strongly, brought to his cheek that which caused the blood to leave it,—snow!

He started to his feet with the intention of awakening the sleepers, for there was no time to lose. But turning to where Uncle Billy had been lying, he found him gone. A suspicion leaped to his brain, and a curse to his lips. He ran to the spot where the mules had been tethered—they were no longer there. The tracks were already rapidly disappearing in the snow.

The momentary excitement brought Mr. Oakhurst back to the fire with his usual calm. He did not waken the sleepers. The Innocent slumbered peacefully, with a smile on his good-humored, freckled face; the virgin Piney slept beside her frailer sisters as sweetly as though attended by celestial guardians; and Mr. Oakhurst, drawing his blanket over his shoulders, stroked his mustaches and waited for the dawn. It came slowly in a whirling mist of snowflakes that dazzled and confused the eye. What could be seen of the landscape appeared magically changed. He looked over the valley, and summed up the present and future in two words, "Snowed in!"

A careful inventory of the provisions, which, fortunately for the party, had been stored within the hut, and so escaped the felonious fingers of Uncle Billy, disclosed the fact that with care and prudence they might last ten days longer. "That is," said Mr. Oakhurst *sotto voce*[5] to the Innocent, "if you're willing to board us. If you

---

5. **sotto voce** (sot'ō vō'chē), in a low voice. [*Italian*]

ain't—and perhaps you'd better not—you can wait till Uncle Billy gets back with provisions." For some occult reason, Mr. Oakhurst could not bring himself to disclose Uncle Billy's rascality, and so offered the hypothesis that he had wandered from the camp and had accidentally stampeded the animals. He dropped a warning to the Duchess and Mother Shipton, who of course knew the facts of their associate's defection. "They'll find out the truth about us *all* when they find out anything," he added significantly, "and there's no good frightening them now."

Tom Simson not only put all his worldly store at the disposal of Mr. Oakhurst, but seemed to enjoy the prospect of their enforced seclusion. "We'll have a good camp for a week, and then the snow'll melt, and we'll all go back together." The cheerful gayety of the young man and Mr. Oakhurst's calm infected the others. The Innocent, with the aid of pine boughs, extemporized a thatch for the roofless cabin, and the Duchess directed Piney in the rearrangement of the interior with a taste and tact that opened the blue eyes of that provincial maiden to their fullest extent. "I reckon now you're used to fine things at Poker Flat," said Piney. The Duchess turned away sharply to conceal something that reddened her cheeks through their professional tint, and Mother Shipton requested Piney not to "chatter." But when Mr. Oakhurst returned from a weary search for the trail, he heard the sound of happy laughter echoed from the rocks. He stopped in some alarm, and his thoughts first naturally reverted to the whiskey, which he had prudently cachéd. "And yet it don't somehow sound like whiskey," said the gambler. It was not until he caught sight of the blazing fire through the still blinding storm, and the group around it, that he settled to the conviction that it was "square fun."

Whether Mr. Oakhurst had cachéd his cards with the whiskey as something debarred the free access of the community, I cannot say. It was certain that, in Mother Shipton's words, he "didn't say 'cards' once" during that evening. Haply the time was beguiled by an accordion, produced somewhat ostentatiously by Tom Simson from his pack. Notwithstanding some difficulties attending the manipulation of this instrument, Piney Woods managed to pluck several reluctant melodies from its keys, to an accompaniment by the Innocent on a pair of bone castanets. But the crowning festivity of the evening was reached in a rude camp-meeting hymn, which the lovers, joining hands, sang with great earnestness and vociferation. I fear that a certain defiant tone and Covenanter's swing[6] to its chorus, rather than any devotional quality, caused it speedily to infect the others, who at last joined in the refrain:—

"I'm proud to live in the service of the Lord,
And I'm bound to die in His army."[7]

The pines rocked, the storm eddied and whirled above the miserable group, and the flames of their altar leaped heavenward, as if in token of the vow.

At midnight the storm abated, the rolling clouds parted, and the stars glittered keenly above the sleeping camp. Mr. Oakhurst, whose professional habits had enabled him to live on the smallest possible amount of sleep, in dividing the watch with Tom Simson somehow managed to take upon himself the greater part of that duty. He excused himself to the Innocent by saying that he had "often been a week without sleep." "Doing what?" asked Tom. "Poker!" replied Oakhurst sententiously. "When a man gets a streak of luck, he don't get tired. The luck gives in first. Luck," continued the gambler reflectively, "is a mighty queer thing. All you know about it for certain is that it's bound to change. And it's finding out when it's going to change that makes you. We've had a streak of bad luck since we left Poker Flat,—you come along, and slap you get into it, too. If you can

---

6. *Covenanter's swing*, the compelling rhythms of songs sung by Scottish Presbyterians, bound by covenants or statements that resisted the rule of the Church of England.
7. *"I'm proud . . . army,"* refrain from the early American spiritual, "Service of the Lord."

hold your cards right along you're all right. For," added the gambler, with cheerful irrelevance—

" 'I'm proud to live in the service of the Lord,
And I'm bound to die in His army.' "

The third day came, and the sun, looking through the white-curtained valley, saw the outcasts divide their slowly decreasing store of provisions for the morning meal. It was one of the peculiarities of that mountain climate that its rays diffused a kindly warmth over the wintry landscape, as if in regretful commiseration of the past. But it revealed drift on drift of snow piled high around the hut,—a hopeless, uncharted, trackless sea of white lying below the rocky shores to which the castaways still clung. Through the marvelously clear air the smoke of the pastoral village of Poker Flat rose miles away. Mother Shipton saw it, and from a remote pinnacle of her rocky fastness hurled in that direction a final malediction. It was her last vituperative attempt, and perhaps for that reason was invested with a certain degree of sublimity. It did her good, she privately informed the Duchess. "Just you go out there and cuss, and see." She then set herself to the task of amusing "the child," as she and the Duchess were pleased to call Piney. Piney was no chicken, but it was a soothing and original theory of the pair thus to account for the fact that she didn't swear and wasn't improper.

When night crept up again through the gorges, the reedy notes of the accordion rose and fell in fitful spasms and long-drawn gasps by the flickering campfire. But music failed to fill entirely the aching void left by insufficient food, and a new diversion was proposed by Piney,—story-telling. Neither Mr. Oakhurst nor his female companions caring to relate their personal experiences, this plan would have failed too, but for the Innocent. Some months before he had chanced upon a stray copy of Mr. Pope's[8] ingenious translation of the *Iliad*.[9] He now proposed to narrate the principal incidents of that poem—having thoroughly mastered the argument and fairly forgotten the words—in the current vernacular of Sandy Bar.

And so for the rest of that night the Homeric demigods again walked the earth. Trojan bully and wily Greek wrestled in the winds, and the great pines in the cañon seemed to bow to the wrath of the son of Peleus.[10] Mr. Oakhurst listened with quiet satisfaction. Most especially was he interested in the fate of "Ash-heels,"[11] as the Innocent persisted in denominating the "swift-footed Achilles."

So, with small food and much of Homer and the accordion, a week passed over the heads of the outcasts. The sun again forsook them, and again from leaden skies the snowflakes were sifted over the land. Day by day closer around them drew the snowy circle, until at last they looked from their prison over drifted walls of dazzling white, that towered twenty feet above their heads. It became more and more difficult to replenish their fires, even from the fallen trees beside them, now half hidden in the drifts. And yet no one complained. The lovers turned from the dreary prospect and looked into each other's eyes, and were happy. Mr. Oakhurst settled himself coolly to the losing game before him. The Duchess, more cheerful than she had been, assumed the care of Piney. Only Mother Shipton—once the strongest of the party—seemed to sicken and fade. At midnight on the tenth day she called Oakhurst to her side. "I'm going," she said, in a voice of querulous weakness, "but don't say anything about it. Don't waken the kids. Take the bundle from under my head, and open it." Mr. Oakhurst did so. It contained Mother Shipton's rations for the last week, untouched. "Give 'em to the child," she said, pointing to the sleeping Piney. "You've starved yourself," said the gambler. "That's what they call it," said the

---

8. *Mr. Pope,* Alexander Pope (1688–1744), an English poet.
9. **Iliad**, a Greek epic poem, attributed to Homer, about the siege of Troy.
10. *son of Peleus.* Achilles (ə kil′ēz), a character in the *Iliad*, was the son of Peleus (pel′yüs).
11. *"Ash-heels,"* a mispronunciation of *Achilles*, who could be wounded only in his heel; thus the mispronunciation is an inadvertent pun.

woman querulously, as she lay down again, and, turning her face to the wall, passed quietly away.

The accordion and the bones were put aside that day, and Homer was forgotten. When the body of Mother Shipton had been committed to the snow, Mr. Oakhurst took the Innocent aside, and showed him a pair of snowshoes, which he had fashioned from the old pack-saddle. "There's one chance in a hundred to save her yet," he said, pointing to Piney; "but it's there," he added, pointing toward Poker Flat. "If you can reach there in two days she's safe." "And you?" asked Tom Simson. "I'll stay here," was the curt reply.

The lovers parted with a long embrace. "You are not going, too?" said the Duchess, as she saw Mr. Oakhurst apparently waiting to accompany him. "As far as the cañon," he replied. He turned suddenly and kissed the Duchess, leaving her pallid face aflame, and her trembling limbs rigid with amazement.

Night came, but not Mr. Oakhurst. It brought the storm again and the whirling snow. Then the Duchess, feeding the fire, found that someone had quietly piled beside the hut enough fuel to last a few days longer. The tears rose to her eyes, but she hid them from Piney.

The women slept but little. In the morning, looking into each other's faces, they read their fate. Neither spoke, but Piney, accepting the position of the stronger, drew near and placed her arm around the Duchess's waist. They kept this attitude for the rest of the day. That night the storm reached its greatest fury, and, rending asunder the protecting vines, invaded the very hut.

Toward morning they found themselves unable to feed the fire, which gradually died away. As the embers slowly blackened, the Duchess crept closer to Piney, and broke the silence of many hours: "Piney, can you pray?" "No, dear," said Piney simply. The Duchess, without knowing exactly why, felt relieved, and, putting her head upon Piney's shoulder, spoke no more. And so reclining, the younger and purer pillowing the head of her soiled sister upon her virgin breast, they fell asleep.

The wind lulled as if it feared to waken them. Feathery drifts of snow, shaken from the long pine boughs, flew like white winged birds, and settled about them as they slept. The moon through the rifted clouds looked down upon what had been the camp. But all human stain, all trace of earthly travail, was hidden beneath the spotless mantle mercifully flung from above.

They slept all that day and the next, nor did they waken when voices and footsteps broke the silence of the camp. And when pitying fingers brushed the snow from their wan faces, you could scarcely have told from the equal peace that dwelt upon them which was she that had sinned. Even the law of Poker Flat recognized this, and turned away, leaving them still locked in each other's arms.

But at the head of the gulch, on one of the largest pine trees, they found the deuce of clubs[12] pinned to the bark with a bowie knife. It bore the following, written in pencil in a firm hand:—

†

BENEATH THIS TREE
LIES THE BODY

of

JOHN OAKHURST,

WHO STRUCK A STREAK OF BAD LUCK
ON THE 23D OF NOVEMBER, 1850,

AND

HANDED IN HIS CHECKS
ON THE 7TH DECEMBER, 1850.

†

And pulseless and cold, with a Derringer[13] by his side and a bullet in his heart, though still calm as in life, beneath the snow lay he who was at once the strongest and yet the weakest of the outcasts of Poker Flat.

1869, 1870

---

12. *deuce of clubs,* the lowest card in the deck, and thus a loser's card.
13. *Derringer,* a small, short-barreled pistol of large caliber invented by the American gunsmith, Henry Derringer (1786–1868).

THINK AND DISCUSS

Understanding

1. At the beginning of the story, when John Oakhurst walks out on the main street in Poker Flat, what change does he notice?
2. What losses had Poker Flat recently suffered?
3. Who are the people banished from Poker Flat? Who later joins the party? Where are the newcomers headed and why?
4. What happens to each of the women in the party? Which of the men may have been survivors?

Analyzing

5. How had Oakhurst been involved with Tom Simson before, and what does the incident reveal about their **characters?**
6. Oakhurst awakens at dawn after the first night camping to make two discoveries. What are they and how do they affect the group's plans?
7. With what diversions does the group amuse itself? In what sense does the group appear to have become a family?
8. On the tenth day, what happens to Mother Shipton? What has she done and what does her action reveal about her character?
9. On the same day, after the burial of Mother Shipton, Oakhurst proposes a plan to Tom Simson, which the youth agrees to. What does the scene reveal about each of their characters?
10. How would you characterize Oakhurst? In what sense is he "the strongest and yet the weakest of the outcasts of Poker Flat"?

Extending

11. Which of the characters and situations in the story are recognizable **stereotypes** that appear in modern fiction, movies, or TV shows about the West?

APPLYING: Local Color H/L
See Handbook of Literary Terms, p. 895.

Local-color writing, a type of regionalism, focuses on a particular locale or area of the country and the peculiarities of speech, dress, custom, and landscape that make it distinctive. Local-color works are often marked by sentimentalism, eccentric characters, and touches of humor. New England, the South, and the West are areas of the U.S. that produced considerable bodies of this type of writing.

1. Cite some examples of western speech that establish this as a local-color story.
2. What do you learn about the moral code, customs, and location of Poker Flat?
3. Do you think the story is marked by sentimentalism? Explain.

COMPOSITION

Describing an Ambiguous Person

Write a four-paragraph essay for your journal describing a friend, relative, or acquaintance who has surprised you with some apparent contradiction of opinion, outlook, act, or behavior pattern. Write a general sketch but come to focus on the contradiction. Then give your view as to what lies beneath the contradiction.

Analyzing a Character

Write a five-paragraph essay for the school literary journal analyzing John Oakhurst's character. Consider the following acts: trading horses with the Duchess, returning money to Tom Simson, giving the Duchess a parting kiss. Consider also Oakhurst's final act, along with the narrator's comment that he was "the strongest and yet the weakest of the outcasts." You may wish to base your thesis statement on this comment by the narrator. See "Writing About Characters" in the Writer's Handbook.

BIOGRAPHY

Ambrose Bierce
1842–1914?

Raised on an Ohio farm, Bierce was the youngest of a large, poor, pious family. He was later reluctant to talk about his beginnings and is said to have despised his relatives. At fifteen he left home and spent two years as a printer's apprentice. There followed a year at the Kentucky Military Institute, the only schooling he would receive, and then the Civil War broke out. He enlisted as a drummer boy, fought bravely in some of the most difficult fighting of the war, and by war's end had earned the honorary rank of major.

Living in San Francisco afterwards, Bierce began writing short satiric pieces for a news weekly, was given his own column, and soon was made editor of the paper. It was a period of fiery personal journalism for which Bierce's biting wit was ideally suited. Bierce was married in 1871, and a few months later he and his wife sailed for England. He stayed there four years, working on the staff of *Fun* magazine. But his wife grew tired of England and returned to California. From there she announced the impending arrival of their third child, and Bierce was soon sailing for San Francisco. For the next ten years, he wrote his famous "Prattler" column for the *Argonaut*. The column was bought in 1887 by William Randolph Hearst and placed on the editorial page of the Sunday *Examiner*.

By this time Bierce's merciless wit had made him the dictator of literary tastes for the West Coast. He was capable of championing the mediocre and attacking the genuine for personal reasons. Though his journalism showed remarkable talent, most critics think he lacked the underlying compassion necessary to make satire more than momentary entertainment.

His fiction, however, won for itself a small but lasting place. He wrote haunting stories, often with strange psychological twists, a few of which have emerged as classics.

Bierce spent a number of his later years in Washington, D.C., exposing for the Hearst newspapers corrupt deals between politicians and industrialists. In 1913, at the age of seventy-one, he seemed weary of it all. He left for Mexico to cover the revolution there and disappeared. Upon leaving, he wrote a friend, "Goodbye, if you hear of my being stood up against a Mexican stone wall and shot to rags, please know that I think it a pretty good way to depart this life. It beats old age, disease, or falling down the cellar stairs."

See FLASHBACK in the Handbook of Literary Terms, page 888.

An Occurrence at Owl Creek Bridge

Ambrose Bierce

man stood upon a railroad bridge in northern Alabama, looking down into the swift water twenty feet below. The man's hands were behind his back, the wrists bound with a cord. A rope closely encircled his neck. It was attached to a stout cross-timber above his head and the slack fell to the level of his knees. Some loose boards laid upon the sleepers supporting the metals of the railway supplied a footing for him and his executioners—two private soldiers of the Federal army, directed by a sergeant who in civil life may have been a deputy sheriff. At a short remove upon the same temporary platform was an officer in the uniform of his rank, armed. He was a captain. A sentinel at each end of the bridge stood with his rifle in the position known as "support," that is to say, vertical in front of the left shoulder, the hammer resting on the forearm thrown straight across the chest—a formal and unnatural position, enforcing an erect carriage of the body. It did not appear to be the duty of these two men to know what was occurring at the center of the bridge; they merely blockaded the two ends of the foot planking that traversed it.

Beyond one of the sentinels nobody was in sight; the railroad ran straight away into a forest for a hundred yards, then, curving, was lost to view. Doubtless there was an outpost farther along. The other bank of the stream was open ground—a gentle acclivity topped with a stockade of vertical tree trunks, loopholed for rifles, with a single embrasure through which protruded the muzzle of a brass cannon commanding the bridge. Midway of the slope between bridge and fort were the spectators—a single company of infantry in line, at "parade rest," the butts of the rifles on the ground, the barrels inclining slightly backward against the right shoulder, the hands crossed upon the stock. A lieutenant stood at the right of the line, the point of his sword upon the ground, his left hand resting upon his right. Excepting the group of four at the center of the bridge, not a man moved. The company faced the bridge, staring stonily, motionless. The sentinels, facing the banks of the stream, might have been statues to adorn the bridge. The captain stood with folded arms, silent, observing the work of his subordinates, but making no sign. Death is a dignitary who when he comes announced is to be received with formal manifestations of respect, even by those most familiar with him. In the code of military etiquette silence and fixity are forms of deference.

The man who was engaged in being hanged was apparently about thirty-five years of age. He was a civilian, if one might judge from his habit, which was that of a planter. His features were good—a straight nose, firm mouth, broad forehead, from which his long, dark hair was combed straight back, falling behind his ears to the collar of his well-fitting frock coat. He wore a mustache and pointed beard, but no whiskers; his eyes were large and dark gray, and had a kindly expression which one would hardly have expected in one whose neck was in the hemp. Evidently this was no vulgar assassin. The liberal military code makes provision for hanging many kinds of persons, and gentlemen are not excluded.

The preparations being complete, the two private soldiers stepped aside and each drew away the plank upon which he had been standing. The sergeant turned to the captain, saluted and placed himself immediately behind that officer, who in turn moved apart one pace. These movements left the condemned man and the sergeant standing on the two ends of the same plank, which spanned three of the crossties of the bridge. The end upon which the civilian stood almost, but not quite, reached a fourth. This plank had been held in place by the weight of the captain; it was now held by that of the sergeant. At a signal from the former the latter would step aside, the plank would tilt and the condemned man go down between two ties. The arrangement commended itself to his judgment as simple and effective. His face had not been covered nor his eyes bandaged. He looked a moment at his "unsteadfast footing," then let his gaze wander to the swirling water of the stream racing madly beneath his feet. A piece of dancing driftwood caught his attention and his eyes followed it down the current. How slowly it appeared to move! What a sluggish stream!

He closed his eyes in order to fix his last thoughts upon his wife and children. The water, touched to gold by the early sun, the brooding mists under the banks at some distance down the stream, the fort, the soldiers, the piece of drift—all had distracted him. And now he became conscious of a new disturbance. Striking through the thought of his dear ones was a sound which he could neither ignore nor understand, a sharp, distinct, metallic percussion like the stroke of a blacksmith's hammer upon the anvil; it had the same ringing quality. He wondered what it was, and whether immeasurably distant or nearby—it seemed both. Its recur-

rence was regular, but as slow as the tolling of a death knell. He awaited each stroke with impatience and—he knew not why—apprehension. The intervals of silence grew progressively longer; the delays became maddening. With their greater infrequency the sounds increased in strength and sharpness. They hurt his ear like the thrust of a knife; he feared he would shriek. What he heard was the ticking of his watch.

He unclosed his eyes and saw again the water below him. "If I could free my hands," he thought, "I might throw off the noose and spring into the stream. By diving I could evade the bullets and swimming vigorously, reach the bank, take to the woods, and get away home. My home, thank God, is as yet outside their lines; my wife and little ones are still beyond the invader's farthest advance."

As these thoughts, which have here to be set down in words, were flashed into the doomed man's brain rather than evolved from it the captain nodded to the sergeant. The sergeant stepped aside.

II

Peyton Farquhar was a well-to-do planter, of an old and highly respected Alabama family. Being a slave owner and like other slave owners a politician, he was naturally an original secessionist and ardently devoted to the Southern cause. Circumstances of an imperious nature, which it is unnecessary to relate here, had prevented him from taking service with the gallant army that had fought the disastrous campaigns ending with the fall of Corinth, and he chafed under the inglorious restraint, longing for the release of his energies, the larger life of the soldier, the opportunity for distinction. That opportunity, he felt, would come, as it comes to all in wartime. Meanwhile he did what he could. No service was too humble for him to perform in aid of the South, no adventure too perilous for him to undertake if consistent with the character of a civilian who was at heart a soldier, and who in good faith and without too much qualification assented to at least

Tom Heflin, detail of *Try to Remember*. Private collection

a part of the frankly villainous dictum that all is fair in love and war.

One evening while Farquhar and his wife were sitting on a rustic bench near the entrance to his grounds, a gray-clad soldier[1] rode up to the gate and asked for a drink of water. Mrs. Farquhar was only too happy to serve him with her own white hands. While she was fetching the water, her husband approached the dusty horseman and inquired eagerly for news from the front.

"The Yanks are repairing the railroads," said the man, "and are getting ready for another advance. They have reached the Owl Creek bridge, put it in order, and built a stockade on the north bank. The commandant has issued an order, which is posted everywhere, declaring that any civilian caught interfering with the railroad, its bridges, tunnels or trains will be summarily hanged. I saw the order."

"How far is it to the Owl Creek bridge?" Farquhar asked.

"About thirty miles."

"Is there no force on this side of the creek?"

"Only a picket post half a mile out, on the railroad, and a single sentinel at this end of the bridge."

"Suppose a man—a civilian and student of

---

1. *a gray-clad soldier.* Confederate soldiers wore gray uniforms.

hanging—should elude the picket post and perhaps get the better of the sentinel," said Farquhar, smiling, "what could he accomplish?"

The soldier reflected. "I was there a month ago," he replied. "I observed that the flood of last winter had lodged a great quantity of driftwood against the wooden pier at this end of the bridge. It is now dry and would burn like tow."

The lady had now brought the water, which the soldier drank. He thanked her ceremoniously, bowed to her husband and rode away. An hour later, after nightfall, he repassed the plantation, going northward in the direction from which he had come. He was a Federal scout.

III

As Peyton Farquhar fell straight downward through the bridge he lost consciousness and was as one already dead. From this state he was awakened—ages later, it seemed to him—by the pain of a sharp pressure upon his throat, followed by a sense of suffocation. Keen, poignant agonies seemed to shoot from his neck downward through every fiber of his body and limbs. These pains appeared to flash along well-defined lines of ramification and to beat with an inconceivably rapid periodicity. They seemed like streams of pulsating fire heating him to an intolerable temperature. As to his head, he was conscious of nothing but a feeling of fullness—of congestion. These sensations were unaccompanied by thought. The intellectual part of his nature was already effaced; he had power only to feel, and feeling was torment. He was conscious of motion. Encompassed in a luminous cloud, of which he was now merely the fiery heart, without material substance, he swung through unthinkable arcs of oscillation, like a vast pendulum. Then all at once, with terrible suddenness, the light about him shot upward with the noise of a loud plash; a frightful roaring was in his ears, and all was cold and dark. The power of thought was restored; he knew that the rope had broken and he had fallen into the stream. There was no additional strangulation; the noose about his neck was already suffocating him and kept the water from his lungs.

To die of hanging at the bottom of a river!—the idea seemed to him ludicrous. He opened his eyes in the darkness and saw above him a gleam of light, but how distant, how inaccessible! He was still sinking for the light became fainter and fainter until it was a mere glimmer. Then it began to grow and brighten, and he knew that he was rising toward the surface—knew it with reluctance, for he was now very comfortable. "To be hanged and drowned," he thought, "that is not so bad; but I do not wish to be shot. No; I will not be shot; that is not fair."

He was not conscious of an effort, but a sharp pain in his wrist apprised him that he was trying to free his hands. He gave the struggle his attention, as an idler might observe the feat of a juggler, without interest in the outcome. What splendid effort!—what magnificent, what superhuman strength! Ah, that was a fine endeavor! Bravo! The cord fell away; his arms parted and floated upward, the hands dimly seen on each side in the growing light. He watched them with a new interest as first one and then the other pounced upon the noose at his neck. They tore it away and thrust it fiercely aside, its undulations resembling those of a water snake. "Put it back, put it back!" He thought he shouted these words to his hands, for the undoing of the noose had been succeeded by the direst pang that he had yet experienced. His neck ached horribly; his brain was on fire; his heart, which had been fluttering faintly, gave a great leap, trying to force itself out at his mouth. His whole body was racked and wrenched with an insupportable anguish! But his disobedient hands gave no heed to the command. They beat the water vigorously with quick, downward strokes, forcing him to the surface. He felt his head emerge; his eyes were blinded by the sunlight; his chest expanded convulsively, and with a supreme and crowning agony his lungs engulfed a great draught of air, which instantly he expelled in a shriek!

He was now in full possession of his physical senses. They were, indeed, preternaturally keen and alert. Something in the awful disturbance of his organic system had so exalted and refined them that they made record of things never before perceived. He felt the ripples upon his face and heard their separate sounds as they struck. He looked at the forest on the bank of the stream, saw the individual trees, the leaves and the veining of each leaf—saw the very insects upon them: the locusts, the brilliant-bodied flies, the gray spiders stretching their webs from twig to twig. He noted the prismatic colors in all the dewdrops upon a million blades of grass. The humming of the gnats that danced above the eddies of the stream, the beating of the dragon-flies' wings, the strokes of the water-spiders' legs, like oars which had lifted their boat—all these made audible music. A fish slid along beneath his eyes and he heard the rush of its body parting the water.

He had come to the surface facing down the stream; in a moment the visible world seemed to wheel slowly round, himself the pivotal point, and he saw the bridge, the fort, the soldiers upon the bridge, the captain, the sergeant, the two privates, his executioners. They were in silhouette against the blue sky. They shouted and gesticulated, pointing at him. The captain had drawn his pistol, but did not fire; the others were unarmed. Their movements were grotesque and horrible, their forms gigantic.

Suddenly he heard a sharp report and something struck the water smartly within a few inches of his head, spattering his face with spray. He heard a second report, and saw one of the sentinels with his rifle at his shoulder, a light cloud of blue smoke rising from the muzzle. The man in the water saw the eye of the man on the bridge gazing into his own through the sights of the rifle. He observed that it was a gray eye and remembered having read that gray eyes were keenest, and that all famous marksmen had them. Nevertheless, this one had missed.

A counter-swirl had caught Farquhar and turned him half round; he was again looking into the forest on the bank opposite the fort. The sound of a clear, high voice in a monotonous singsong now rang out behind him and came across the water with a distinctness that pierced and subdued all other sounds, even the beating of the ripples in his ears. Although no soldier, he had frequented camps enough to know the dread significance of that deliberate, drawling, aspirated chant; the lieutenant on shore was taking a part in the morning's work. How coldly and pitilessly—with what an even, calm intonation, presaging, and enforcing tranquility in the men—with what accurately measured intervals fell those cruel words:

"Attention, company! . . . Shoulder arms! . . . Ready! . . . Aim! . . . Fire!"

Farquhar dived—dived as deeply as he could. The water roared in his ears like the voice of Niagara, yet he heard the dulled thunder of the volley and, rising again toward the surface, met shining bits of metal, singularly flattened, oscillating slowly downward. Some of them touched him on the face and hands, then fell away, continuing their descent. One lodged between his collar and neck; it was uncomfortably warm and he snatched it out.

As he rose to the surface, gasping for breath, he saw that he had been a long time underwater; he was perceptibly farther down stream—nearer to safety. The soldiers had almost finished reloading; the metal ramrods flashed all at once in the sunshine as they were drawn from the barrels, turned in the air, and thrust into their sockets. The two sentinels fired again, independently and ineffectually.

The hunted man saw all this over his shoulder; he was now swimming vigorously with the current. His brain was as energetic as his arms and legs; he thought with the rapidity of lightning.

"The officer," he reasoned, "will not make that martinet's error a second time. It is as easy to dodge a volley as a single shot. He has probably already given the command to fire at will. God help me, I cannot dodge them all!"

An appalling plash within two yards of him was followed by a loud, rushing sound, *diminuendo*,[2] which seemed to travel back through the air to

2. *diminuendo*, with gradually diminishing volume, a term used in music.

the fort and died in an explosion which stirred the very river to its deeps! A rising sheet of water curved over him, fell down upon him, blinded him, strangled him! The cannon had taken a hand in the game. As he shook his head free from the commotion of the smitten water, he heard the deflected shot humming through the air ahead, and in an instant it was cracking and smashing the branches in the forest beyond.

"They will not do that again," he thought; "the next time they will use a charge of grape. I must keep my eye upon the gun; the smoke will apprise me—the report arrives too late; it lags behind the missile. That is a good gun."

Suddenly he felt himself whirled round and round—spinning like a top. The water, the banks, the forests, the now distant bridge, fort and men—all were commingled and blurred. Objects were represented by their colors only; circular horizontal streaks of color—that was all he saw. He had been caught in a vortex and was being whirled on with a velocity of advance and gyration that made him giddy and sick. In a few moments he was flung upon the gravel at the foot of the left bank of the stream—the southern bank—and behind a projecting point which concealed him from his enemies. The sudden arrest of his motion, the abrasion of one of his hands on the gravel, restored him, and he wept with delight. He dug his fingers into the sand, threw it over himself in handfuls and audibly blessed it. It looked like diamonds, rubies, emeralds; he could think of nothing beautiful which it did not resemble. The trees upon the bank were giant garden plants; he noted a definite order in their arrangement, inhaled the fragrance of their blooms. A strange, roseate light shone through the spaces among their trunks and the wind made in their branches the music of aeolian harps.[3] He had no wish to perfect his escape—was content to remain in that enchanting spot until retaken.

A whiz and rattle of grapeshot among the branches high above his head roused him from his dream. The baffled cannoneer had fired him a random farewell. He sprang to his feet, rushed up the sloping bank, and plunged into the forest.

All that day he traveled, laying his course by the rounding sun. The forest seemed interminable; nowhere did he discover a break in it, not even a woodman's road. He had not known that he lived in so wild a region. There was something uncanny in the revelation.

By nightfall he was fatigued, footsore, famishing. The thought of his wife and children urged him on. At last he found a road which led him in what he knew to be the right direction. It was as wide and straight as a city street, yet it seemed untraveled. No fields bordered it, no dwelling anywhere. Not so much as the barking of a dog suggested human habitation. The black bodies of the trees formed a straight wall on both sides, terminating on the horizon in a point, like a diagram in a lesson in perspective. Overhead, as he looked up through this rift in the wood, shone great golden stars looking unfamiliar and grouped in strange constellations. He was sure they were arranged in some order which had a secret and malign significance. The wood on either side was full of singular noises, among which—once, twice, and again—he distinctly heard whispers in an unknown tongue.

His neck was in pain and lifting his hand to it he found it horribly swollen. He knew that it had a circle of black where the rope had bruised it. His eyes felt congested; he could no longer close them. His tongue was swollen with thirst; he relieved its fever by thrusting it forward from between his teeth into the cold air. How softly the turf had carpeted the untraveled avenue—he could no longer feel the roadway beneath his feet!

Doubtless, despite his suffering, he had fallen asleep while walking, for now he sees another scene—perhaps he has merely recovered from a delirium. He stands at the gate of his own home. All is as he left it, and all bright and beautiful in the morning sunshine. He must have traveled the entire night. As he pushes open the gate and

---

3. aeolian harps, musical instruments consisting of a box across which strings are stretched. They are placed at open windows where the wind can produce harmonic, sweet tones.

passes up the wide white walk, he sees a flutter of female garments; his wife, looking fresh and cool and sweet, steps down from the veranda to meet him. At the bottom of the steps she stands waiting, with a smile of ineffable joy, an attitude of matchless grace and dignity. Ah, how beautiful she is! He springs forward with extended arms. As he is about to clasp her, he feels a stunning blow upon the back of the neck; a blinding white light blazes all about him with a sound like the shock of a cannon—then all is darkness and silence!

Peyton Farquhar was dead; his body, with a broken neck, swung gently from side to side beneath the timbers of the Owl Creek bridge.

1890

THINK AND DISCUSS
Understanding
1. What scene is described in the first paragraph? How many people are at this scene?
2. According to the second paragraph, what group is assembled on one bank of the stream? What "forms of deference" are they exhibiting, according to the final sentence in this paragraph?
3. What information, provided in paragraph three, indicates that the man being hanged was "no vulgar assassin"?
4. As Farquhar prepares to die, he becomes conscious of a "sharp, distinct, metallic percussion like the stroke of a blacksmith's hammer upon the anvil." What is really causing this sound?
5. What news does the gray-clad soldier deliver to Farquhar at the beginning of Part II? Who is this soldier later revealed to be?

Analyzing
6. How was Farquhar the victim of a trap?
7. Decide what actually occurred. Did Farquhar escape or did he only imagine it? Explain.
8. How does the title contribute to the ambiguity of the tale?
9. Assuming that Farquhar is hanged at the end of the tale, what hints does the author give the reader that the escape is only a desperate dream?

APPLYING: Flashback   H7
See Handbook of Literary Terms, p. 888.
A **flashback** is an interruption in the action of a story to portray incidents that occurred at an earlier time. The opening scene of "An Occurrence at Owl Creek Bridge," which depicts a hanging, is interrupted with a flashback that provides information essential to the plot.

1. List the events of the story in straightforward chronological sequence. What effects are created by Bierce's rearrangement of time?
2. What does the flashback reveal about Farquhar's motivation? Do you feel the flashback makes him appear more sympathetic or less so? Explain.
3. Why do you suppose Bierce didn't portray Farquhar's attempt to destroy the bridge and his capture by the Union soldiers?

COMPOSITION
Writing a Missing Episode
Write a three-paragraph addition to Part II of "An Occurrence at Owl Creek Bridge" for your classmates, describing Farquhar's actions in trying to destroy the railroad bridge and his capture. Attempt to make your style match Bierce's. Discuss with your classmates whether they think your addition has improved the story or interfered with it.

American English was infused with a special vigor and energy during the period from 1870 to 1915. This was a time of rapid technological progress, tremendous population expansion, and an explosive push westward. Leading writers of the period were using new rhythms, forms, and vocabulary to portray the changing American experience. New words entered the vocabulary; and existing words—those of the farms, the streets, the steamboats, the railways, and especially the West—began to appear in literature.

Mark Twain adopted the vigor and energy of frontier talk with its dialect and slang to enliven his stories. One of his characters is described thus: "He ketched a frog, and . . . calk'lated to edercate him." Slang phrases that came into general usage through Twain's use of them include *dead broke*, *take it easy*, *to get even*, and *a close call*.

More than any other influence, the expanding frontier helped shape the language, as western pioneers coined words to describe their experiences. From cowboys came *stampede*, *ranch*, *maverick*, and *hot under the collar*. Gambling terminology lent colorful phrases such as *put up or shut up*, *hit the jackpot*, *pass the buck*, and *play both ends against the middle*. The transcontinental railroad borrowed the popularized nautical jargon—*berth*, *purser*, *fare*, *freight*, and *cabin*—and introduced many terms of its own. The verb *to railroad*, which meant in 1877 "to convict someone falsely," has come to mean "to coerce." *To be in the clear*, *to make the grade*, *to backtrack*, *to have the right of way*, and *to reach the end of the line* are all phrases with a railroad past.

Between 1865 and 1920, the steamship brought cheap travel to more Europeans, initiating a great wave of immigrants to America. With the influx of Germans, American English acquired words such as *delicatessen*, *ecology*, *hoodlum*, *spiel*, and *kindergarten*. From the Italians, came food words—*pizza*, *broccoli*, *parmesan*, *pasta*, and *spaghetti*. A third group of Europeans who influenced the language were the three million East and Central European Jews who landed between 1880 and 1910. Yiddish produced words such as *kosher* (all right, fine, legitimate); *nebbish* (a timid, inept and colorless person); *schlemiel* (a clumsy person); *schlock* (worthless junk or trash); and *schlep* (to move awkwardly and slowly).

George Caleb Bingham, *Raftsmen Playing Cards* (1847–50). City Museum of St. Louis

Mary E. Wilkins Freeman
1852–1930

Mary E. Wilkins Freeman is remembered primarily as a writer of short stories that chronicle the decline of New England. She wrote her best-known works in the late nineteenth century, when New England, as an aftermath of the Civil War, was becoming economically and industrially stagnant, losing population and business to more dynamic parts of the country, particularly the West. It was a world populated by spinsters whose strong, independent characters were to be drawn by women writers who pioneered in the creation of local-color Realism.

Mary Wilkins was born in Massachusetts, but moved to Brattleboro, Vermont, with her family at the age of fifteen. She attended Mount Holyoke Seminary, withdrawing at the end of a year because of frail health. She continued her education by reading virtually everything that came within her reach and by studying closely New England history, character, and dialect.

By the time she was thirty-one, she found herself without family and with the need to earn a living. She returned to Massachusetts and settled into a literary career. Publication of her work in *Harper's Magazine* in 1884 brought public recognition, and she soon began to publish volumes of her short stories, including *A New England Nun*, in 1891.

She was already established as a successful self-supporting writer when, at the age of forty-nine, she married Dr. Charles Freeman in 1902. The marriage failed, because of his confinement in 1920 for alcoholism, but Freeman went on to receive the Howells Medal for Fiction in 1926. In that same year, she and Edith Wharton became the first women to be elected to membership in the National Institute of Arts and Letters.

Though she published thirty-nine volumes of stories and novels, and one play, she is best known for her local-color stories, characterized by a poignancy verging on the tragic and by a redeeming humor. Her most memorable stories portray the shrewdness and determination of the Yankee character and provide glimpses of life as lived in the New England village. Freeman's people are often those whose lives are limited by circumstance or by chains of their own creation. However, moral correctness gives dignity to their painful adherence to the "right."

A New England Nun

Mary E. Wilkins Freeman

t was late in the afternoon, and the light was waning. There was a difference in the look of the tree shadows out in the yard. Somewhere in the distance, cows were lowing and a little bell was tinkling; now and then a farm wagon tilted by, and the dust flew; some blue-shirted laborers with shovels over their shoulders plodded past; little swarms of flies were dancing up and down before the people's faces in the soft air. There seemed to be a gentle stir arising over everything for the mere sake of subsidence—a very premonition of rest and hush and night.

This soft diurnal commotion was over Louisa Ellis also. She had been peacefully sewing at her sitting-room window all the afternoon. Now she quilted her needle carefully into her work, which she folded precisely, and laid in a basket with her thimble and thread and scissors. Louisa Ellis could not remember that ever in her life she had mislaid one of these little feminine appurtenances, which had become, from long use and constant association, a very part of her personality.

Louisa tied a green apron round her waist, and got out a flat straw hat with a green ribbon. Then she went into the garden with a little blue crockery bowl, to pick some currants for her tea. After the currants were picked she sat on the back doorstep and stemmed them, collecting the stems carefully in her apron and afterward throwing them into the hencoop. She looked sharply at the grass beside the step to see if any had fallen there.

Louisa was slow and still in her movements; it took her a long time to prepare her tea; but when ready it was set forth with as much grace as if she had been a veritable guest to her own self. The little square table stood exactly in the center of the kitchen, and was covered with a starched linen cloth whose border pattern of flowers glistened. Louisa had a damask napkin on her tea tray, where were arranged a cut-glass tumbler full of teaspoons, a silver cream pitcher, a china sugar bowl, and one pink china cup and saucer. Louisa used china every day—something which none of her neighbors did. They whispered about it among themselves. Their daily tables were laid with common crockery, their sets of best china stayed in the parlor closet, and Louisa Ellis was no richer nor better bred than they. Still she would use the china. She had for her supper a glass dish full of sugared currants, a plate of little cakes, and one of light white biscuits. Also a leaf or two of lettuce, which she cut up daintily. Louisa was very fond of lettuce, which she raised to perfection in her little garden. She ate quite heartily, though in a delicate, pecking way; it seemed almost surprising that any considerable bulk of the food should vanish.

After tea she filled a plate with nicely baked thin corn cakes, and carried them out into the backyard.

"Caesar!" she called. "Caesar! Caesar!"

There was a little rush, and the clank of a

From *A New England Nun and Other Stories* by Mary E. Wilkins, published by Harper and Brothers, 1891.

chain, and a large yellow-and-white dog appeared at the door of his tiny hut, which was half hidden among the tall grasses and flowers. Louisa patted him and gave him the corn cakes. Then she returned to the house and washed the tea things, polishing the china carefully. The twilight had deepened; the chorus of the frogs floated in at the open window wonderfully loud and shrill, and once in a while a long sharp drone from a tree toad pierced it. Louisa took off her green gingham apron, disclosing a shorter one of pink-and-white print. She lighted her lamp, and sat down again with her sewing.

In about half an hour Joe Dagget came. She heard his heavy step on the walk, and rose and took off her pink-and-white apron. Under that was still another—white linen with a little cambric edging on the bottom; that was Louisa's company apron. She never wore it without her calico sewing apron over it unless she had a guest. She had barely folded the pink-and-white one with methodical haste and laid it in a table drawer when the door opened and Joe Dagget entered.

He seemed to fill up the whole room. A little yellow canary that had been asleep in his green cage at the south window woke up and fluttered wildly, beating his yellow wings against the wires. He always did so when Joe Dagget came into the room.

"Good evening," said Louisa. She extended her hand with a kind of solemn cordiality.

"Good evening, Louisa," returned the man, in a loud voice.

She placed a chair for him, and they sat facing each other, with the table between them. He sat bolt upright, toeing out his heavy feet squarely, glancing with a good-humored uneasiness around the room. She sat gently erect, folding her slender hands in her white-linen lap.

"Been a pleasant day," remarked Dagget.

"Real pleasant," Louisa assented, softly. "Have you been haying?" she asked, after a little while.

"Yes, I've been haying all day, down in the ten-acre lot. Pretty hot work."

"It must be."

"Yes, it's pretty hot work in the sun."

"Is your mother well today?"

"Yes, Mother's pretty well."

"I suppose Lily Dyer's with her now?"

Dagget colored. "Yes, she's with her," he answered, slowly.

He was not very young, but there was a boyish look about his large face. Louisa was not quite so old as he, her face was fairer and smoother, but she gave people the impression of being older.

"I suppose she's a good deal of help to your mother," she said, further.

"I guess she is; I don't know how Mother'd get along without her," said Dagget, with a sort of embarrassed warmth.

"She looks like a real capable girl. She's pretty-looking too," remarked Louisa.

"Yes, she is pretty fair-looking."

Presently Dagget began fingering the books on the table. There was a square red autograph album, and a Young Lady's Gift Book which had belonged to Louisa's mother. He took them up one after the other and opened them; then laid them down again, the album on the Gift Book.

Louisa kept eyeing them with mild uneasiness. Finally she rose and changed the position of the books, putting the album underneath. That was the way they had been arranged in the first place.

Dagget gave an awkward little laugh. "Now what difference did it make which book was on top?" said he.

Louisa looked at him with a deprecating smile. "I always keep them that way," murmured she.

"You do beat everything," said Dagget, trying to laugh again. His large face was flushed.

He remained about an hour longer, then rose to take leave. Going out, he stumbled over a rug, and trying to recover himself, hit Louisa's workbasket on the table, and knocked it on the floor.

He looked at Louisa, then at the rolling spools; he ducked himself awkwardly toward them, but she stopped him. "Never mind," she said; "I'll pick them up after you're gone."

She spoke with a mild stiffness. Either she was a little disturbed, or his nervousness affected her and made her seem constrained in her effort to reassure him.

When Joe Dagget was outside, he drew in the sweet evening air with a sigh, and felt much as an innocent and perfectly well-intentioned bear might after his exit from a china shop.

Louisa, on her part, felt much as the kind-hearted, long-suffering owner of the china shop might have done after the exit of the bear.

She tied on the pink, then the green apron, picked up all the scattered treasures and replaced them in her workbasket, and straightened the rug. Then she set the lamp on the floor and began sharply examining the carpet. She even rubbed her fingers over it, and looked at them.

"He's tracked in a good deal of dust," she murmured. "I thought he must have."

Louisa got a dustpan and brush, and swept Joe Dagget's track carefully.

If he could have known it, it would have increased his perplexity and uneasiness, although it would not have disturbed his loyalty in the least. He came twice a week to see Louisa Ellis, and every time, sitting there in her delicately sweet room, he felt as if surrounded by a hedge of lace. He was afraid to stir lest he should put a clumsy foot or hand through the fairy web, and he had always the consciousness that Louisa was watching fearfully lest he should.

Still the lace and Louisa commanded perforce his perfect respect and patience and loyalty. They were to be married in a month, after a singular courtship which had lasted for a matter of fifteen years. For fourteen out of the fifteen years the two had not once seen each other, and they had seldom exchanged letters. Joe had been all those years in Australia, where he had gone to make his fortune, and where he had stayed until he made it. He would have stayed fifty years if it had taken so long, and come home feeble and tottering, or never come home at all, to marry Louisa.

But the fortune had been made in the fourteen years, and he had come home now to marry the woman who had been patiently and unquestioningly waiting for him all that time.

Shortly after they were engaged he had announced to Louisa his determination to strike out into new fields and secure a competency[1] before they should be married. She had listened and assented with the sweet serenity which never failed her, not even when her lover set forth on that long and uncertain journey. Joe, buoyed up as he was by his steady determination, broke down a little at the last, but Louisa kissed him with a mild blush, and said good-by.

"It won't be for long," poor Joe had said, huskily; but it was for fourteen years.

In that length of time much had happened. Louisa's mother and brother had died, and she was all alone in the world. But greatest happening of all—a subtle happening which both were too simple to understand—Louisa's feet had turned into a path, smooth maybe under a calm, serene sky, but so straight and unswerving that it could only meet a check at her grave, and so narrow that there was no room for anyone at her side.

Louisa's first emotion when Joe Dagget came home (he had not apprised her of his coming) was consternation, although she would not admit it to herself, and he never dreamed of it. Fifteen years ago she had been in love with him—at least she considered herself to be. Just at that time, gently acquiescing with and falling into the natural drift of girlhood, she had seen marriage ahead as a reasonable feature and a probable desirability of life. She had listened with calm docility to her mother's views upon the subject. Her mother was remarkable for her cool sense and sweet, even temperament. She talked wisely to her daughter when Joe Dagget presented himself, and Louisa accepted him with no hesitation. He was the first lover she had ever had.

She had been faithful to him all these years. She had never dreamed of the possibility of marrying anyone else. Her life, especially for the last

---

1. *a competency* (kom'pə tən sē), a sufficient income on which to live.

seven years, had been full of a pleasant peace; she had never felt discontented nor impatient over her lover's absence; still, she had always looked forward to his return and their marriage as the inevitable conclusion of things. However, she had fallen into a way of placing it so far in the future that it was almost equal to placing it over the boundaries of another life.

When Joe came she had been expecting him, and expecting to be married for fourteen years, but she was as much surprised and taken aback as if she had never thought of it.

Joe's consternation came later. He eyed Louisa with an instant confirmation of his old admiration. She had changed but little. She still kept her pretty manner and soft grace, and was, he considered, every whit as attractive as ever. As for himself, his stent was done; he had turned his face away from fortune seeking, and the old winds of romance whistled as loud and sweet as ever through his ears. All the song which he had been wont to hear in them was Louisa; he had for a long time a loyal belief that he heard it still, but finally it seemed to him that although the winds sang always that one song, it had another name. But for Louisa the wind had never more than murmured; now it had gone down, and everything was still. She listened for a little while with half-wistful attention; then she turned quietly away and went to work on her wedding clothes.

Joe had made some extensive and quite magnificent alterations in his house. It was the old homestead; the newly married couple would live there, for Joe could not desert his mother, who refused to leave her old home. So Louisa must leave hers. Every morning, rising and going about among her neat maidenly possessions, she felt as one looking her last upon the faces of dear friends. It was true that in a measure she could take them with her, but, robbed of their old environments, they would appear in such new guises that they would almost cease to be themselves.

Then there were some peculiar features of her happy solitary life which she would probably be obliged to relinquish altogether. Sterner tasks than these graceful but half-needless ones would probably devolve upon her. There would be a large house to care for; there would be company to entertain; there would be Joe's rigorous and feeble old mother to wait upon; and it would be contrary to all thrifty village traditions for her to keep more than one servant.

Louisa had a little still, and she used to occupy herself pleasantly in summer weather with distilling the sweet and aromatic essences from roses and peppermint and spearmint. By-and-by her still must be laid away. Her store of essences was already considerable, and there would be no time for her to distill for the mere pleasure of it. Then Joe's mother would think it foolishness; she had already hinted her opinion in the matter.

Louisa dearly loved to sew a linen seam, not always for use, but for the simple, mild pleasure which she took in it. She would have been loath to confess how more than once she had ripped a seam for the mere delight of sewing it together again. Sitting at her window during long sweet afternoons, drawing her needle gently through the dainty fabric, she was peace itself. But there was small chance of such foolish comfort in the future. Joe's mother, domineering, shrewd old matron that she was even in her old age, and very likely even Joe himself, with his honest masculine rudeness, would laugh and frown down all these pretty but senseless old maiden ways.

Louisa had almost the enthusiasm of an artist over the mere order and cleanliness of her solitary home. She had throbs of genuine triumph at the sight of the windowpanes which she had polished until they shone like jewels. She gloated gently over her orderly bureau drawers, with their exquisitely folded contents redolent with lavender and sweet clover and very purity. Could she be sure of the endurance of even this? She had visions, so startling that she half repudiated them as indelicate, of coarse masculine belongings strewn about in endless litter; of dust and disorder arising necessarily from a coarse masculine presence in the midst of all this delicate harmony.

Among her forebodings of disturbance, not the least was with regard to Caesar. Caesar was a

George Newell Bowers, *Meditation* (1889).
Museum of Fine Arts, Springfield, Massachusetts

veritable hermit of a dog. For the greater part of his life he had dwelt in his secluded hut, shut out from the society of his kind and all innocent canine joys. Never had Caesar since his early youth watched at a woodchuck's hole; never had he known the delights of a stray bone at a neighbor's kitchen door. And it was all on account of a sin committed when hardly out of his puppyhood. No one knew the possible depth of remorse of which this mild-visaged, although innocent-looking old dog might be capable; but whether or not he had encountered remorse, he had encountered a full measure of righteous retribution. Old Caesar seldom lifted up his voice in a growl or a bark; he was fat and sleepy; there were yellow rings which looked like spectacles around his dim old eyes; but there was a neighbor who bore on his hand the imprint of several of Caesar's sharp white youthful teeth, and for that he had lived at the end of a chain, all alone in a little hut, for fourteen years. The neighbor, who was choleric and smarting with the pain of his wound, had demanded either Caesar's death or complete ostracism. So Louisa's brother, to whom the dog had belonged, had built him his little kennel and tied him up. It was now fourteen years since, in a flood of youthful spirits, he had inflicted that memorable bite, and with the exception of short excursions, always at the end of the chain, under the strict guardianship of his master or Louisa, the old dog had remained a close prisoner. It is doubtful if, with his limited ambition, he took much pride in the fact, but it is certain that he was possessed of considerable cheap fame. He was regarded by all the children in the village and by many adults as a very monster of ferocity. St. George's dragon[2] could hardly have surpassed in evil repute Louisa Ellis's old yellow dog. Mothers charged their children with solemn emphasis not to go too near to him, and the children listened and believed greedily, with a fascinated appetite for terror, and ran by Louisa's house stealthily, with many sidelong and backward glances at the terrible dog. If perchance he sounded a hoarse bark, there was a panic. Wayfarers chancing into Louisa's yard eyed him

with respect, and inquired if the chain were stout. Caesar at large might have seemed a very ordinary dog and excited no comment whatever; chained, his reputation overshadowed him, so that he lost his own proper outlines and looked darkly vague and enormous. Joe Dagget, however, with his good-humored sense and shrewdness, saw him as he was. He strode valiantly up to him and patted him on the head, in spite of Louisa's soft clamor of warning, and even attempted to set him loose. Louisa grew so alarmed that he desisted, but kept announcing his opinion in the matter quite forcibly at intervals. "There ain't a better-natured dog in town," he would say, "and it's downright cruel to keep him tied up there. Some day I'm going to take him out."

Louisa had very little hope that he would not, one of these days, when their interests and possessions should be more completely fused in one. She pictured to herself Caesar on the rampage through the quiet and unguarded village. She saw innocent children bleeding in his path. She was herself very fond of the old dog, because he had belonged to her dead brother, and he was always very gentle with her; still she had great faith in his ferocity. She always warned people not to go too near him. She fed him on ascetic fare of corn mush and cakes, and never fired his dangerous temper with heating and sanguinary diet of flesh and bones. Louisa looked at the old dog munching his simple fare, and thought of her approaching marriage and trembled. Still no anticipation of disorder and confusion in lieu of sweet peace and harmony, no forebodings of Caesar on the rampage, no wild fluttering of her little yellow canary, were sufficient to turn her a hair's-breadth. Joe Dagget had been fond of her and working for her all these years. It was not for her, whatever came to pass, to prove untrue and break his heart. She put the exquisite little stitches into her wedding garments, and the time went on until it was only a week before her

2. *St. George's dragon.* In legend, St. George, patron saint of England, killed a dragon.

wedding day. It was a Tuesday evening, and the wedding was to be a week from Wednesday.

There was a full moon that night. About nine o'clock Louisa strolled down the road a little way. There were harvest fields on either hand, bordered by low stone walls. Luxuriant clumps of bushes grew beside the wall, and trees—wild cherry and old apple trees—at intervals. Presently Louisa sat down on the wall and looked about her with mildly sorrowful reflectiveness. Tall shrubs of blueberry and meadowsweet, all woven together and tangled with blackberry vines and horsebriers, shut her in on either side. She had a little clear space between them. Opposite her, on the other side of the road, was a spreading tree; the moon shone between its boughs, and the leaves twinkled like silver. The road was bespread with a beautiful shifting dapple of silver and shadow; the air was full of a mysterious sweetness. "I wonder if it's wild grapes?" murmured Louisa. She sat there some time. She was just thinking of rising, when she heard footsteps and low voices, and remained quiet. It was a lonely place, and she felt a little timid. She thought she would keep still in the shadow and let the persons, whoever they might be, pass her.

But just before they reached her the voices ceased, and the footsteps. She understood that their owners had also found seats upon the stone wall. She was wondering if she could not steal away unobserved, when the voice broke the stillness. It was Joe Dagget's. She sat still and listened.

The voice was announced by a loud sigh, which was as familiar as itself. "Well," said Dagget, "you've made up your mind, then, I suppose?"

"Yes," returned another voice. "I'm going day after tomorrow."

"That's Lily Dyer," thought Louisa to herself. The voice embodied itself in her mind. She saw a girl tall and full-figured, with a firm, fair face, looking fairer and firmer in the moonlight, her strong yellow hair braided in a close knot. A girl full of a calm rustic strength and bloom, with a masterful way which might have beseemed a princess. Lily Dyer was a favorite with the village folk; she had just the qualities to arouse the admiration. She was good and handsome and smart. Louisa had often heard her praises sounded.

"Well," said Joe Dagget. "I ain't got a word to say."

"I don't know what you could say," returned Lily Dyer.

"Not a word to say," repeated Joe, drawing out the words heavily. Then there was a silence. "I ain't sorry," he began at last, "that that happened yesterday—that we kind of let on how we felt to each other. I guess it's just as well we knew. Of course I can't do anything any different. I'm going right on an' get married next week. I ain't going back on a woman that's waited for me fourteen years, an' break her heart."

"If you should jilt her tomorrow, I wouldn't have you," spoke up the girl, with sudden vehemence.

"Well, I ain't going to give you the chance," said he; "but I don't believe you would, either."

"You'd see I wouldn't. Honor's honor, an' right's right. An' I'd never think anything of any man that went against 'em for me or any other girl; you'd find that out, Joe Dagget."

"Well, you'll find out fast enough that I ain't going against 'em for you or any other girl," returned he. Their voices sounded almost as if they were angry with each other. Louisa was listening eagerly.

"I'm sorry you feel as if you must go away," said Joe, "but I don't know but it's best."

"Of course it's best. I hope you and I have got common sense."

"Well, I suppose you're right." Suddenly Joe's voice got an undertone of tenderness. "Say, Lily," said he, "I'll get along well enough myself, but I can't bear to think—you don't suppose you're going to fret much over it?"

"I guess you'll find out I shan't fret much over a married man."

"Well, I hope you won't—I hope you won't, Lily. God knows I do. And—I hope—one of these days—you'll—come across somebody else——"

"I don't see any reason why I shouldn't." Suddenly her tone changed. She spoke in a sweet, clear voice, so loud that she could have been heard across the street. "No, Joe Dagget," said she, "I'll never marry any other man as long as I live. I've got good sense, an' I ain't going to break my heart nor make a fool of myself; but I'm never going to be married, you can be sure of that. I ain't that sort of a girl to feel this way twice."

Louisa heard an exclamation and a soft commotion behind the bushes; then Lily spoke again—the voice sounded as if she had risen. "This must be put a stop to," said she. "We've stayed here long enough. I'm going home."

Louisa sat there in a daze, listening to their retreating steps. After a while she got up and slunk softly home herself. The next day she did her housework methodically; that was as much a matter of course as breathing; but she did not sew on her wedding clothes. She sat at her window and meditated. In the evening Joe came. Louisa Ellis had never known that she had any diplomacy in her, but when she came to look for it that night she found it, although meek of its kind, among her little feminine weapons. Even now she could hardly believe that she had heard right, and that she would not do Joe a terrible injury should she break her troth plight. She wanted to sound him out without betraying too soon her own inclinations in the matter. She did it successfully, and they finally came to an understanding; but it was a difficult thing, for he was as afraid of betraying himself as she.

She never mentioned Lily Dyer. She simply said that while she had no cause of complaint against him, she had lived so long in one way that she shrank from making a change.

"Well, I never shrank, Louisa," said Dagget. "I'm going to be honest enough to say that I think maybe it's better this way; but if you'd wanted to keep on, I'd have stuck to you till my dying day. I hope you know that."

"Yes, I do," said she.

That night she and Joe parted more tenderly than they had done for a long time. Standing in the door, holding each other's hands, a last great wave of regretful memory swept over them.

"Well, this ain't the way we've thought it was all going to end, is it, Louisa?" said Joe.

She shook her head. There was a little quiver on her placid face.

"You let me know if there's ever anything I can do for you," said he. "I ain't ever going to forget you, Louisa." Then he kissed her, and went down the path.

Louisa, all alone by herself that night, wept a little, she hardly knew why; but the next morning, on waking, she felt like a queen who, after fearing lest her domain be wrested away from her, sees it firmly insured in her possession.

Now the tall weeds and grasses might cluster around Caesar's little hermit hut, the snow might fall on its roof year in and year out, but he never would go on a rampage through the unguarded village. Now the little canary might turn itself into a peaceful yellow ball night after night, and have no need to wake and flutter with wild terror against its bars. Louisa could sew linen seams, and distill roses, and dust and polish and fold away in lavender, as long as she listed. That afternoon she sat with her needlework at the window, and felt fairly steeped in peace. Lily Dyer, tall and erect and blooming, went past; but she felt no qualm. If Louisa Ellis had sold her birthright, she did not know it; the taste of her pottage[3] was so delicious, and had been her sole satisfaction for so long. Serenity and placid narrowness had become to her as the birthright itself. She gazed ahead through a long reach of future days strung together like pearls in a rosary, every one like the others, and all smooth and flawless and innocent, and her heart went up in thankfulness. Outside was the fervid summer afternoon; the air was filled with the sounds of the busy harvest of men and birds and bees; there were halloos, metallic clatterings, sweet calls, and long hummings. Louisa sat, prayerfully numbering her days, like an uncloistered nun.

1891

---

3. *pottage* (pot'ij), a thick soup. This is a reference to the biblical story of Esau, who sold his birthright to his twin brother Jacob for a bowl of pottage (Genesis 25:29–34).

THINK AND DISCUSS
Understanding
1. Who is Caesar and why is he considered dangerous?
2. For how long was Joe Dagget in Australia? Why had he gone there?
3. What two things does Dagget do that appear to disrupt Louisa's orderly house?
4. Who is Lily Dyer? Why does she decide to leave her job?

Analyzing
5. What clues early in the story indicate that both Louisa Ellis and Joe Dagget are uncomfortable in their relationship with each other?
6. What aspects of Louisa's life and personality are **symbolized** by her canary and by Caesar?
7. How does Louisa's reaction to Joe's departure fourteen years earlier **foreshadow** the end of the story?
8. Explain how the ending of the story depends both on chance and on the characters of Louisa, Joe, and Lily.
9. Is Louisa's final decision a noble one? Why or why not? Would you call the ending "happy" or "unhappy"? Explain.

Extending
10. Point out and explain examples of Realism in situations and **characterization** in this story. (See the discussion of Realism in the Unit Background.)

APPLYING: Plot H𝑇
See Handbook of Literary Terms, p. 899.

A **plot** is a sequence of related incidents presenting and resolving a *conflict* that may be internal or external. As the plot unfolds, the conflict builds to an emotional or dramatic peak—the *climax*, which is followed by a *resolution* or denouement. Events occurring before the climax are called the *rising action;* those that follow the climax are called the *falling action.*

1. What is the conflict in the plot of "A New England Nun"?
2. What is the climax of the story? the resolution?
3. Explain how each of the following helps develop the conflict in the story: the description of Louisa's meal, Joe's visit, information about Caesar.

READING LITERATURE SKILLFULLY
Summarizing
Often you can aid your understanding of a work of literature by summarizing the plot. Such a summary should include only main actions or events.

1. In three or four sentences, summarize the plot of "A New England Nun."
2. Do you think that a mention of Louisa's pets, Caesar and the canary, belong in such a summary? Why or why not?

VOCABULARY
Context and Dictionary
In your Glossary look up the definition of each of the following words from "A New England Nun." On your paper write the word next to the number of the sentence that it correctly completes. Be sure you can spell and pronounce all the words.

redolence   docile
methodical   ostracize
premonition   consternation

1. From the moment Carrie got up that morning, she had a feeling that something was going to go wrong, and the _____ grew as she drove to work.
2. The class is so _____ and obedient that the teacher never has to quiet them down.
3. As Carmen walked into the florist's, a sweet _____ drifted into her nostrils. Never before had she experienced a fragrance this pleasant.

4. Raymond was warned that if he kept being a bully, the rest of the class would _____ him for the year.

5. The oxen pulled the plow with the _____ motion of a machine that does its task a thousand times a day.

COMPOSITION

Assessing a Life Lived Alone

Write four paragraphs for your journal on the advantages and disadvantages of living alone. You might consider the lives of people you know, or those of literary characters such as Louisa Ellis. Examine, for example, the benefits of wholehearted devotion to a career, a hobby, or the pursuit of a dream. Then weigh these advantages against those of having continual companionship, a family, or other aspects of close human bonding. Finally, take a position on which kind of life might be best for you.

Describing What Might Have Happened

In a five-paragraph essay written for readers of "A New England Nun," assume that Louisa Ellis has not overheard Joe Dagget talking with Lily and goes ahead with her marriage. What do you imagine happens to her canary and her dog? What conflict develops with Dagget's mother? Does Louisa continue to engage in the activities she has grown to love? Give your imagination free rein and write another ending for this story.

BIOGRAPHY

Kate Chopin
1851–1904

Kate Chopin's literary career is fascinating because it was in eclipse for so long. Her novel, *The Awakening*, published in 1899, outraged readers by its frank treatment of the psychological awakening of the young heroine. Condemned by critics as sordid and "unhealthily introspective," the book sank into oblivion and had to await its time. That time came, and the novel is now recognized as a masterpiece of psychological Realism. Kate Chopin has come into her own as an important American writer.

She was born Katherine O'Flaherty in St. Louis in 1851. When she was twenty years old she married Oscar Chopin and spent the next ten years of her life in New Orleans. After business failure, the family moved to rural Louisiana to take over management of a cotton plantation. When her husband died of swamp fever, Chopin returned to St. Louis in 1884, faced with the problem of taking care of her six children.

She began to write local-color stories based on her Louisiana experiences. In order to look after her children as she wrote, she set to work among them, using a lapboard. She published *Bayou Folk* in 1894, followed by *A Night in Acadie* in 1897. By the time she came to write *The Awakening*, she had come under the influence of Walt Whitman's sensuous lyricism, and it runs throughout the novel. After the attack on *The Awakening*, she wrote little. She died of a brain hemorrhage in 1904.

A Pair of Silk Stockings

Kate Chopin

ittle Mrs. Sommers one day found herself the unexpected possessor of fifteen dollars. It seemed to her a very large amount of money, and the way in which it stuffed and bulged her worn old *porte-monnaie*[1] gave her a feeling of importance such as she had not enjoyed for years.

The question of investment was one that occupied her greatly. For a day or two she walked about apparently in a dreamy state, but really absorbed in speculation and calculation. She did not wish to act hastily, to do anything she might afterwards regret. But it was during the still hours of the night when she lay awake revolving plans in her mind that she seemed to see her way clearly toward a proper and judicious use of the money.

A dollar or two should be added to the price usually paid for Janie's shoes, which would insure their lasting an appreciable time longer than they usually did. She would buy so and so many yards of percale for new shirtwaists for the boys and Janie and Mag. She had intended to make the old ones do by skillful patching. Mag should have another gown. She had seen some beautiful patterns, veritable bargains in the shop windows. And still there would be left enough for new stockings—two pairs apiece—and what darning that would save for a while! She would get caps for the boys and sailor hats for the girls. The vision of her little brood looking fresh and dainty and new for once in their lives excited her and made her restless and wakeful with anticipation.

The neighbors sometimes talked of certain "better days" that little Mrs. Sommers had known before she had ever thought of being Mrs. Sommers. She herself indulged in no such morbid retrospection. She had no time—no second of time to devote to the past. The needs of the present absorbed her every faculty. A vision of the future like some dim, gaunt monster sometimes appalled her, but luckily tomorrow never comes.

Mrs. Sommers was one who knew the value of bargains; who could stand for hours making her way inch by inch toward the desired object that was selling below cost. She could elbow her way if need be; she had learned to clutch a piece of goods and hold it and stick to it with persistence and determination till her turn came to be served, no matter when it came.

But that day she was a little faint and tired. She had swallowed a light luncheon—no! when she came to think of it, between getting the children fed and the place righted, and preparing herself for the shopping bout, she had actually forgotten to eat any luncheon at all!

She sat herself upon a revolving stool before a counter that was comparatively deserted, trying to gather strength and courage to charge through an eager multitude that was besieging breastworks of shirting and figured lawn. An all-gone limp feeling had come over her, and she rested her hand aimlessly upon the counter. She wore no gloves. By degrees she grew aware that her

---

1. **porte-monnaie** (pôrt mô ne′), a small purse. [*French*]

a tiara of diamonds with the ultimate view of purchasing it. But she went on feeling the soft, sheeny luxurious things—with both hands now, holding them up to see them glisten, and to feel them glide serpentlike through her fingers.

Two hectic blotches came suddenly into her pale cheeks. She looked up at the girl.

"Do you think there are any eights-and-a-half among these?"

There were any number of eights-and-a-half. In fact, there were more of that size than any other. Here was a light blue pair; there were some lavender, some all black and various shades of tan and gray. Mrs. Sommers selected a black pair and looked at them very long and closely. She pretended to be examining their texture, which the clerk assured her was excellent.

"A dollar and ninety-eight cents," she mused aloud. "Well, I'll take this pair." She handed the girl a five dollar bill and waited for her change and for her parcel. What a very small parcel it was! It seemed lost in the depths of her shabby old shopping bag.

Mrs. Sommers after that did not move in the direction of the bargain counter. She took the elevator, which carried her to an upper floor into the region of the ladies' waiting rooms. Here, in a retired corner, she exchanged her cotton stockings for the new silk ones which she had just bought. She was not going through any acute mental process or reasoning with herself, nor was she striving to explain to her satisfaction the motive of her action. She was not thinking at all. She seemed for the time to be taking a rest from that laborious and fatiguing function and to have abandoned herself to some mechanical impulse that directed her actions and freed her of responsibility.

How good was the touch of the raw silk to her flesh! She felt like lying back in the cushioned chair and reveling for a while in the luxury of it. She did for a little while. Then she replaced her shoes, rolled the cotton stockings together and thrust them into her bag. After doing this she crossed straight over to the shoe department and took her seat to be fitted.

Maurice Brazil Prendergast, *Lady on the Boulevard*. Terra Museum of American Art, Chicago

hand had encountered something very soothing, very pleasant to touch. She looked down to see that her hand lay upon a pile of silk stockings. A placard nearby announced that they had been reduced in price from two dollars and fifty cents to one dollar and ninety-eight cents; and a young girl who stood behind the counter asked her if she wished to examine their line of silk hosiery. She smiled just as if she had been asked to inspect

She was fastidious. The clerk could not make her out; he could not reconcile her shoes with her stockings, and she was not too easily pleased. She held back her skirts and turned her feet one way and her head another way as she glanced down at the polished, pointed-tipped boots. Her foot and ankle looked very pretty. She could not realize that they belonged to her and were a part of herself. She wanted an excellent and stylish fit, she told the young fellow who served her, and she did not mind the difference of a dollar or two more in the price so long as she got what she desired.

It was a long time since Mrs. Sommers had been fitted with gloves. On rare occasions when she had bought a pair they were always "bargains," so cheap that it would have been preposterous and unreasonable to have expected them to be fitted to the hand.

Now she rested her elbow on the cushion of the glove counter, and a pretty, pleasant young creature, delicate and deft of touch, drew a long-wristed "kid" over Mrs. Sommer's hand. She smoothed it down over the wrist and buttoned it neatly, and both lost themselves for a second or two in admiring contemplation of the little symmetrical gloved hand. But there were other places where money might be spent.

There were books and magazines piled up in the window of a stall a few paces down the street. Mrs. Sommers bought two high-priced magazines such as she had been accustomed to read in the days when she had been accustomed to other pleasant things. She carried them without wrappings. As well as she could she lifted her skirts at the crossings. Her stockings and boots and well-fitted gloves had worked marvels in her bearing—had given her a feeling of assurance, a sense of belonging to the well-dressed multitude.

She was very hungry. Another time she would have stilled the cravings for food until reaching her own home, where she would have brewed herself a cup of tea and taken a snack of anything that was available. But the impulse that was guiding her would not suffer her to entertain any such thought.

There was a restaurant at the corner. She had never entered its doors; from the outside she had sometimes caught glimpses of spotless damask and shining crystal, and soft-stepping waiters serving people of fashion.

When she entered her appearance created no surprise, no consternation, as she had half feared it might. She seated herself at a small table alone, and an attentive waiter at once approached to take her order. She did not want a profusion; she craved a nice and tasty bite—a half dozen bluepoints,[2] a plump chop with cress, a something sweet, a crème-frappée,[3] for instance; a glass of Rhine wine, and after all a small cup of black coffee.

While waiting to be served, she removed her gloves very leisurely and laid them beside her. Then she picked up a magazine and glanced through it, cutting the pages with a blunt edge of her knife.[4] It was all very agreeable. The damask was even more spotless than it had seemed through the window, and the crystal more sparkling. There were quiet ladies and gentlemen, who did not notice her, lunching at the small tables like her own. A soft, pleasing strain of music could be heard, and a gentle breeze was blowing through the window. She tasted a bite, and she read a word or two, and she sipped the amber wine and wiggled her toes in the silk stockings. The price of it made no difference. She counted the money out to the waiter and left an extra coin on his tray, whereupon he bowed before her as if before a princess of royal blood.

There was still money in her purse, and her next temptation presented itself in the shape of a matinée poster.

It was a little later when she entered the theater, the play had begun and the house seemed to her to be packed. But there were vacant seats here and there, and into one of them she was ushered, between brilliantly dressed women who

---

2. **bluepoints,** oysters from Long Island, New York.
3. **crème-frappée,** (krem fra pä´), ice cream. [French]
4. **cutting the pages . . . knife.** Books and magazines used to be printed with their pages unseparated. The pages were cut apart as they were read.

had gone there to kill time and eat candy and display their gaudy attire. There were many others who were there solely for the play and acting. It is safe to say there was no one present who bore quite the attitude which Mrs. Sommers did to her surroundings. She gathered in the whole stage and players and people in one wide impression, and absorbed it and enjoyed it. She laughed at the comedy and wept—she and the gaudy woman next to her wept over the tragedy. And they talked a little together over it. And the gaudy woman wiped her eyes and sniffled on a tiny square of filmy, perfumed lace and passed little Mrs. Sommers her box of candy.

The play was over, the music ceased, the crowd filed out. It was like a dream ended. People scattered in all directions. Mrs. Sommers went to the corner and waited for the cable car.

A man with keen eyes, who sat opposite to her, seemed to like the study of her small, pale face. It puzzled him to decipher what he saw there. In truth, he saw nothing—unless he were wizard enough to detect a poignant wish, a powerful longing that the cable car would never stop anywhere, but go on and on with her forever.

1897

THINK AND DISCUSS
Understanding
1. When Mrs. Sommers finds herself the possessor of fifteen dollars, what plans does she make for spending the money?
2. Why does Mrs. Sommers suddenly feel "a little faint and tired" (paragraph 6)?
3. As she rests her hand upon a counter, Mrs. Sommers becomes aware of "something very soothing" (paragraph 7). What is it? How does this incident trigger a change of plans?
4. How does Mrs. Sommers spend the fifteen dollars?

Analyzing
5. Summarize the story in three or four sentences.
6. Is the conflict in this story internal or external? Explain.
7. When Mrs. Sommers gets on the cable car to go home, the **point of view** shifts to that of a man sitting opposite her. What does he see? What escapes his "keen eyes"?

Extending
8. How would you explain the significance of this story to a classmate who considered it as simply an account of a poor woman's shopping spree?

REVIEWING: Characterization HT
See Handbook of Literary Terms, p. 882.

You have learned that **characterization** is the means an author uses to make a character comprehensible and realistic for a reader. The author may describe a character's physical or personality traits, actions, thoughts, feelings, or the reaction of others to that character. Often characterization is based on all these methods.

1. What do we learn about Mrs. Sommers's previous life before marriage in contrast with her present life? How does this information help explain her behavior?
2. What is Mrs. Sommers's "poignant wish," as she returns home on the cable car? How does this reveal her character?

COMPOSITION
Describing a Self-indulgent Afternoon
Write a description of at least three paragraphs for your journal, describing what you would do were you to find yourself with a hundred dollars from an unexpected source. Would you spend the money on books, clothes, food, cassettes, entertainment, or on something else? Or would you put the money in a savings account for college?

BIOGRAPHY

W. E. B. Du Bois
1868–1963

Born in Massachusetts, William Edward Burghardt Du Bois [dü bois′] graduated from Fisk University in 1888 and in 1895 became the first black student to receive a Ph.D. degree from Harvard University. He then taught history and economics at Atlanta University. In 1909, he helped found the National Association for the Advancement of Colored People and edited its magazine, *The Crisis*, for twenty years before returning to Atlanta University.

Du Bois was regarded by many as one of the most incisive intellectuals in the United States. At the time of his death, he lived in Ghana and was working as editor-in-chief of the *Encyclopedia Africana*.

The Souls of Black Folk (1903), from which the following essay is taken, was a landmark in American literature. In that book, Du Bois treated sociological questions of black identity and pride with a vividness and lyrical style that have made his recollections memorable.

Of the Meaning of Progress

W. E. B. Du Bois

nce upon a time I taught school in the hills of Tennessee, where the broad dark vale of the Mississippi begins to roll and crumple to greet the Alleghenies. I was a Fisk student then, and all Fisk men thought that Tennessee—beyond the Veil[1]—was theirs alone, and in vacation time they sallied forth in lusty bands to meet the county school-commissioners. Young and happy, I too went, and I shall not soon forget that summer, seventeen years ago.

First, there was a Teachers' Institute at the county seat; and there distinguished guests of the superintendent taught the teachers fractions and spelling and other mysteries—white teachers in the morning, Negroes at night. A picnic now and then, and a supper, and the rough world

was softened by laughter and song. I remember how—but I wander.

There came a day when all the teachers left the Institute and began the hunt for schools. I learn from hearsay (for my mother was mortally afraid of firearms) that the hunting of ducks and bears and men is wonderfully interesting, but I am sure that the man who has never hunted a country school has something to learn of the pleasures of the chase. I see now the white, hot roads lazily rise and fall and wind before me under the burning July sun; I feel the deep weariness of heart and limb as ten, eight, six miles stretch relentlessly ahead; I feel my heart sink

---

1. *the Veil*, the barrier of racial segregation.

heavily as I hear again and again, "Got a teacher? Yes." So I walked on and on—horses were too expensive—until I had wandered beyond railways, beyond stage lines, to a land of "varmints" and rattlesnakes, where the coming of a stranger was an event, and men lived and died in the shadow of one blue hill.

Sprinkled over hill and dale lay cabins and farmhouses, shut out from the world by the forests and the rolling hills toward the east. There I found at last a little school. Josie told me of it; she was a thin, homely girl of twenty, with a dark brown face and thick, hard hair. I had crossed the stream at Watertown, and rested under the great willows; then I had gone to the little cabin in the lot where Josie was resting on her way to town. The gaunt farmer made me welcome, and Josie, hearing my errand, told me anxiously that they wanted a school over the hill; that but once since the war[2] had a teacher been there; that she herself longed to learn—and thus she ran on, talking fast and loud, with much earnestness and energy.

Next morning I crossed the tall round hill, lingered to look at the blue and yellow mountains stretching toward the Carolinas, then plunged into the wood, and came out at Josie's home. It was a dull frame cottage with four rooms, perched just below the brow of the hill, amid peach trees. The father was a quiet, simple soul, calmly ignorant, with no touch of vulgarity. The mother was different—strong, bustling, and energetic, with a quick, restless tongue, and an ambition to live "like folks." There was a crowd of children. Two boys had gone away. There remained two growing girls; a shy midget of eight; John, tall, awkward, and eighteen; Jim, younger, quicker, and better looking; and two babies of indefinite age. Then there was Josie herself. She seemed to be the center of the family; always busy at service, or at home, or berry picking; a little nervous and inclined to scold, like her mother, yet faithful, too, like her father. She had about her a certain fineness, the shadow of an unconscious moral heroism that would willingly give all of life to make life broader, deeper, and

fuller for her and hers. I saw much of this family afterwards, and grew to love them for their honest efforts to be decent and comfortable, and for their knowledge of their own ignorance. There was with them no affectation. The mother would scold the father for being so "easy"; Josie would roundly berate the boys for carelessness; and all knew that it was a hard thing to dig a living out of a rocky side hill.

I secured the school. I remember the day I rode horseback out to the commissioner's house with a pleasant young white fellow who wanted the white school. The road ran down the bed of a stream; the sun laughed and the water jingled, and we rode on. "Come in," said the commissioner—"come in. Have a seat. Yes, that certificate will do. Stay to dinner. What do you want a month?" "Oh," thought I, "this is lucky"; but even then fell the awful shadow of the Veil, for they ate first, then I—alone.

The schoolhouse was a log hut, where Colonel Wheeler used to shelter his corn. It sat in a lot behind a rail fence and thorn bushes, near the sweetest of springs. There was an entrance where a door once was, and within, a massive rickety fireplace; great chinks between the logs served as windows. Furniture was scarce. A pale blackboard crouched in the corner. My desk was made of three boards, reinforced at critical points, and my chair, borrowed from the landlady, had to be returned every night. Seats for the children—these puzzled me much. I was haunted by a New England vision of neat little desks and chairs, but, alas! the reality was rough plank benches without backs, and at times without legs. They had the one virtue of making naps dangerous—possibly fatal, for the floor was not to be trusted.

It was a hot morning late in July when the school opened. I trembled when I heard the patter of little feet down the dusty road, and saw the growing row of dark solemn faces and bright eager eyes facing me. First came Josie and her

---

2. *the war,* the Civil War.

brothers and sisters. The longing to know, to be a student in the great school at Nashville, hovered like a star above this child-woman amid her work and worry, and she studied doggedly. There were the Dowells from their farm over toward Alexandria—Fanny, with her smooth black face and wondering eyes; Martha, brown and dull; the pretty girl-wife of a brother, and the younger brood.

There were the Burkes—two brown and yellow lads, and a tiny haughty-eyed girl. Fat Reuben's little chubby girl came, with golden face and old-gold hair, faithful and solemn. 'Thenie was on hand early—a jolly, ugly, good-hearted girl, who slyly dipped snuff and looked after her little bow-legged brother. When her mother could spare her, 'Tildy came—a midnight beauty, with starry eyes and tapering limbs; and her brother, correspondingly homely. And then the big boys—the hulking Lawrences; the lazy Neills, unfathered sons of mother and daughter; Hickman, with a stoop in his shoulders, and the rest.

There they sat, nearly thirty of them, on the rough benches, their faces shading from a pale cream to a deep brown, the little feet bare and swinging, the eyes full of expectation, with here and there a twinkle of mischief, and the hands grasping Webster's blue-black spelling book. I loved my school, and the fine faith the children had in the wisdom of their teacher was truly marvelous. We read and spelled together, wrote a little, picked flowers, sang, and listened to stories of the world beyond the hill. At times the school would dwindle away, and I would start out. I would visit Mun Eddings, who lived in two very dirty rooms, and ask why little Lugene, whose flaming face seemed ever ablaze with the dark red hair uncombed, was absent all last week, or why I missed so often the inimitable rags of Mack and Ed. Then the father, who worked Colonel Wheeler's farm on shares,[3] would tell me how the crops needed the boys; and the thin, slovenly mother, whose face was pretty when washed, assured me that Lugene must mind the baby. "But we'll start them again next week." When the Lawrences stopped, I knew that the doubts of the old folks

about book-learning had conquered again, and so, toiling up the hill, and getting as far into the cabin as possible, I put Cicero's "Pro Archia Poeta"[4] into the simplest English with local applications, and usually convinced them—for a week or so.

On Friday nights I often went home with some of the children—sometimes to Doc Burke's farm. He was a great, loud, thin black, ever working, and trying to buy the seventy-five acres of hill and dale where he lived; but people said that he would surely fail, and the "white folks would get it all." His wife was a magnificent Amazon, with saffron face and shining hair, uncorseted and barefooted, and the children were strong and beautiful. They lived in a one-and-a-half-room cabin in the hollow of the farm, near the spring. The front room was full of great fat white beds, scrupulously neat; and there were bad chromos[5] on the walls, and a tired center-table. In the tiny back kitchen I was often invited to "take out and help" myself to fried chicken and wheat biscuit, "meat" and corn pone, stringbeans and berries. At first I used to be a little alarmed at the approach of bedtime in the one lone bedroom, but embarrassment was very deftly avoided. First, all the children nodded and slept, and were stowed away in one great pile of goose feathers; next, the mother and the father discreetly slipped away to the kitchen while I went to bed; then, blowing out the dim light, they retired in the dark. In the morning all were up and away before I thought of awaking. Across the road, where fat Reuben lived, they all went outdoors while the teacher retired, because they did not boast the luxury of a kitchen.

I liked to stay with the Dowells, for they had four rooms and plenty of good country fare. Uncle Bird had a small, rough farm, all woods and hills, miles from the big road; but he was

---

3. **on shares,** dividing the crop with the landlord, instead of paying rent.
4. **"Pro Archia Poeta"** (prō är′kē ä pō ā′tä), a Latin phrase meaning "on behalf of great poets." This speech by the Roman orator Cicero (sis′e rō; 106–43 B.C.) supported the value of literature.
5. **chromos,** pictures printed in colors.

Edward Lamson Henry, *Kept In* (1888).
New York State Historical Association, Cooperstown

full of tales—he preached now and then—and
with his children, berries, horses, and wheat he
was happy and prosperous. Often, to keep the
peace, I must go where life was less lovely; for
instance, 'Tildy's mother was incorrigibly dirty,
Reuben's larder was limited seriously, and herds
of untamed insects wandered over the Eddingses'
beds. Best of all I loved to go to Josie's, and sit on
the porch, eating peaches, while the mother bustled and talked: how Josie had bought the sewing
machine; how Josie worked at service in winter,
but that four dollars a month was "mighty little"
wages; how Josie longed to go away to school,
but that it "looked like" they never could get far
enough ahead to let her; how the crops failed

and the well was yet unfinished; and, finally, how
"mean" some of the white folks were.

For two summers I lived in this little world;
it was dull and humdrum. The girls looked
at the hill in wistful longing, and the boys
fretted and haunted Alexandria. Alexandria was
"town"—a straggling, lazy village of houses,
churches, and shops, and an aristocracy of Toms,
Dicks, and Captains. Cuddled on the hill to the
north was the village of the colored folks, who
lived in three- or four-room unpainted cottages,
some neat and homelike, and some dirty. The
dwellings were scattered rather aimlessly, but
they centered about the twin temples of the hamlet, the Methodist, and the hard-shell Baptist

churches. These, in turn, leaned gingerly on a sad-colored schoolhouse. Hither my little world wended its crooked way on Sunday to meet other worlds, and gossip, and wonder, and make the weekly sacrifice with frenzied priest at the altar of the "old-time religion." Then the soft melody and mighty cadences of Negro song fluttered and thundered.

I have called my tiny community a world, and so its isolation made it; and yet there was among us but a half-awakened common consciousness, sprung from common joy and grief, at burial, birth, or wedding; from a common hardship in poverty, poor land, and low wages; and, above all, from the sight of the Veil that hung between us and Opportunity. All this caused us to think some thoughts together; but these, when ripe for speech, were spoken in various languages. Those whose eyes twenty-five and more years before had seen "the glory of the coming of the Lord,"[6] saw in every present hindrance or help a dark fatalism bound to bring all things right in His own good time. The mass of those to whom slavery was a dim recollection of childhood found the world a puzzling thing: it asked little of them, and they answered with little, and yet it ridiculed their offering. Such a paradox they could not understand, and therefore sank into listless indifference, or shiftlessness, or reckless bravado. There were, however, some—such as Josie, Jim, and Ben—to whom War, Hell, and Slavery were but childhood tales, whose young appetites had been whetted to an edge by school and story and half-awakened thought. Ill could they be content, born without and beyond the World. And their weak wings beat against their barriers—barriers of caste, of youth, of life; at last, in dangerous moments, against everything that opposed even a whim.

The ten years that follow youth, the years when first the realization comes that life is leading somewhere—these were the years that passed after I left my little school. When they were past, I came by chance once more to the walls of Fisk University, to the halls of the chapel of melody. As I lingered there in the joy and pain of meeting old school friends, there swept over me a sudden longing to pass again beyond the blue hill, and to see the homes and the school of other days, and to learn how life had gone with my schoolchildren; and I went.

Josie was dead, and the gray-haired mother said simply, "We've had a heap of trouble since you've been away." I had feared for Jim. With a cultured parentage and a social caste to uphold him, he might have made a venturesome merchant or a West Point cadet. But here he was, angry with life and reckless; and when Farmer Durham charged him with stealing wheat, the old man had to ride fast to escape the stones which the furious fool hurled after him. They told Jim to run away; but he would not run, and the constable came that afternoon. It grieved Josie, and great awkward John walked nine miles every day to see his little brother through the bars of Lebanon jail. At last the two came back together in the dark night. The mother cooked supper, and Josie emptied her purse, and the boys stole away. Josie grew thin and silent, yet worked the more. The hill became steep for the quiet old father, and with the boys away there was little to do in the valley. Josie helped them to sell the old farm, and they moved nearer town. Brother Dennis, the carpenter, built a new house with six rooms; Josie toiled a year in Nashville, and brought back ninety dollars to furnish the house and change it to a home.

When the spring came, and the birds twittered, and the stream ran proud and full, little sister Lizzie, bold and thoughtless, flushed with the passion of youth, bestowed herself on the tempter, and brought home a nameless child. Josie shivered and worked on, with the vision of school days all fled, with a face wan and tired—worked until, on a summer's day, some one married another; then Josie crept to her mother like a hurt child, and slept—and sleeps.

I paused to scent the breeze as I entered the valley. The Lawrences have gone—father and

---

6. *"the glory . . . Lord,"* from the first line of the "Battle Hymn of the Republic."

son forever—and the other son lazily digs in the earth to live. A new young widow rents out their cabin to fat Reuben. Reuben is a Baptist preacher now, but I fear as lazy as ever, though his cabin has three rooms; and little Ella has grown into a bouncing woman, and is ploughing corn on the hot hillside. There are babies aplenty, and one half-witted girl. Across the valley is a house I did not know before, and there I found, rocking one baby and expecting another, one of my schoolgirls, a daughter of Uncle Bird Dowell. She looked somewhat worried with her new duties, but soon bristled into pride over her neat cabin and the tale of her thrifty husband, and the horse and cow, and the farm they were planning to buy.

My log schoolhouse was gone. In its place stood Progress; and Progress, I understand, is necessarily ugly. The crazy foundation stones still marked the former site of my poor little cabin, and not far away, on six weary boulders, perched a jaunty board house, perhaps twenty by thirty feet, with three windows and a door that locked. Some of the window glass was broken, and part of an old iron stove lay mournfully under the house. I peeped through the window half reverently, and found things that were more familiar. The blackboard had grown by about two feet, and the seats were still without backs. The county owns the lot now, I hear, and every year there is a session of school. As I sat by the spring and looked on the Old and the New, I felt glad, very glad, and yet——

After two long drinks I started on. There was the great double log house on the corner. I remembered the broken, blighted family that used to live there. The strong, hard face of the mother, with its wilderness of hair, rose before me. She had driven her husband away, and while I taught school a strange man lived there, big and jovial, and people talked. I felt sure that Ben and 'Tildy would come to naught from such a home. But this is an odd world; for Ben is a busy farmer in Smith County, "doing well, too," they say, and he had cared for little 'Tildy until last spring, when a lover married her. A hard life the lad had led, toiling for meat, and laughed at

because he was homely and crooked. There was Sam Carlon, an impudent old skinflint, who had definite notions about "niggers," and hired Ben a summer and would not pay him. Then the hungry boy gathered his sacks together, and in broad daylight went into Carlon's corn; and when the hard-fisted farmer set upon him, the angry boy flew at him like a beast. Doc Burke saved a murder and a lynching that day.

The story reminded me again of the Burkes, and an impatience seized me to know who won in the battle, Doc or the seventy-five acres. For it is a hard thing to make a farm out of nothing, even in fifteen years. So I hurried on, thinking of the Burkes. They used to have a certain magnificent barbarism about them that I liked. They were never vulgar, never immoral, but rather rough and primitive, with an unconventionality that spent itself in loud guffaws, slaps on the back, and naps in the corner. I hurried by the cottage of the misborn Neill boys. It was empty, and they were grown into fat, lazy farmhands. I saw the home of the Hickmans, but Albert, with his stooping shoulders, had passed from the world. Then I came to the Burkes' gate and peered through; the inclosure looked rough and untrimmed, and yet there were the same fences around the old farm save to the left, where lay twenty-five other acres. And lo! the cabin in the hollow had climbed the hill and swollen to a half-finished six-room cottage.

The Burkes held a hundred acres, but they were still in debt. Indeed, the gaunt father who toiled night and day would scarcely be happy out of debt, being so used to it. Some day he must stop, for his massive frame is showing decline. The mother wore shoes, but the lionlike physique of other days was broken. The children had grown up. Rob, the image of his father, was loud and rough with laughter. Birdie, my school baby of six, had grown to a picture of maiden beauty, tall and tawny. "Edgar is gone," said the mother, with head half-bowed—"gone to work in Nashville; he and his father couldn't agree."

Little Doc, the boy born since the time of my school, took me horseback down the creek next morning toward Farmer Dowell's. The road and the stream were battling for mastery, and the stream had the better of it. We splashed and waded, and the merry boy, perched behind me, chattered and laughed. He showed me where Simon Thompson had bought a bit of ground and a home; but his daughter Lana, a plump, brown, slow girl, was not there. She had married a man and a farm twenty miles away. We wound on down the stream till we came to a gate that I did not recognize, but the boy insisted that it was "Uncle Bird's." The farm was fat with the growing crop. In that little valley was a strange stillness as I rode up; for death and marriage had stolen youth and left age and childhood there. We sat and talked that night after the chores were done. Uncle Bird was grayer, and his eyes did not see so well, but he was still jovial. We talked of the acres bought—one hundred and twenty-five—of the new guest-chamber added, of Martha's marrying. Then we talked of death: Fanny and Fred were gone; a shadow hung over the other daughter, and when it lifted she was to go to Nashville to school. At last we spoke of the neighbors, and as night fell, Uncle Bird told me how, on a night like that, 'Thenie came wandering back to her home over yonder, to escape the blows of her husband. And next morning she died in the home that her little bow-legged brother, working and saving, had bought for their widowed mother.

My journey was done, and behind me lay hill and dale, and Life and Death. How shall man measure Progress there where the dark-faced Josie lies? How many heartfuls of sorrow shall balance a bushel of wheat? How hard a thing is life to the lowly, and yet how human and real! And all this life and love and strife and failure—is it the twilight of nightfall or the flush of some faint-dawning day?

Thus sadly musing, I rode to Nashville in the Jim Crow car.[7]

1903

---

7. *Jim Crow car,* a segregated car for blacks only. Segregation laws were called Jim Crow laws.

THINK AND DISCUSS
Understanding
1. In the first paragraph, Du Bois reflects on his early teaching experiences. Where and when did the scene he recalls occur?
2. To what does he compare the "hunt for schools" in paragraph three?
3. Reread the paragraph that begins, "There they sat. . . ." (381a, 2) What activities does Du Bois use to teach his class? For what reasons does the class size "dwindle away"?

Analyzing
4. Du Bois says that "all Fisk men thought that Tennessee—beyond the Veil—was theirs alone." What does this reveal about the attitudes of the young men? At what point does Du Bois personally encounter "the Veil"?
5. What pleasures and hardships does Du Bois find in living and teaching?
6. Describe Josie's character and ambitions. What factors destroy her dreams?
7. What does "progress" mean to Du Bois?
8. From the examples Du Bois gives, does he seem optimistic or pessimistic about the possibilities of progress for rural blacks in the late nineteenth century?

Extending
9. Is Du Bois's philosophy mainly naturalistic or realistic? Explain. (Refer to the explanations of these terms in the Unit Background.)

COMPOSITION
Defending Your Position
Write an essay of at least four paragraphs for readers of the Du Bois essay, taking as your starting point one of the following generalizations (or one of your own) for consideration. 1. Du Bois is an incurable Romantic with too rosy a view of human nature. 2. Du Bois is too pessimistic about the ability of people to escape poverty through hard work. 3. Du Bois is a realistic and compassionate observer of the harsh realities of human existence and prejudice.

BIOGRAPHY

Stephen Crane
1871–1900

Crane was born into a family with printer's ink in their veins. Both his parents were writers and two of his brothers were reporters. He attended college for two semesters, spending more time on newspaper reporting and playing baseball than on his studies. The next five years he spent in New York. What little money he had came from occasional free-lance reporting for the *Tribune* and the *Herald*. His beat was the Bowery saloons and the slums around him.

He brought these grim experiences to life in his first book, *Maggie: A Girl of the Streets* (1893), the first American naturalistic novel. Because the story was considered sordid, Crane was unable to find a publisher. Finally, he borrowed $700 and printed it himself but was able to sell only a few copies.

Two years later Crane, who had no war experience, published *The Red Badge of Courage*, a remarkably real war story that many consider the greatest American war novel ever written. As a result of the success of this novel (it made him famous but paid only $100), Crane was hired to cover the Cuban revolt against Spanish colonial rule. However, his ship sank off the coast of Florida. His ordeal in reaching shore in the ship's dinghy is the basis for his most famous short story, "The Open Boat."

Crane later covered the Greco-Turkish War and the Spanish-American War in Cuba. He died at twenty-eight, never having fully recovered from his ordeal when shipwrecked, which aggravated his tuberculosis.

In his brief life, Stephen Crane left a lasting imprint with both his fiction and his poetry. His short, sharply etched poems are often characterized by their sardonic views and ironic twists. The body of his poetry is small, consisting of two small volumes, *The Black Riders and Other Lines* (1895), and *War Is Kind and Other Lines* (1899). His poetic techniques were innovative, utilizing simple forms that were conversational in tone and proselike in sentence structure. In his use of sharp, vivid images he appears to be a link between Emily Dickinson and the later Imagists such as Ezra Pound and William Carlos Williams.

An Episode of War

Stephen Crane

he lieutenant's rubber blanket lay on the ground, and upon it he had poured the company's supply of coffee. Corporals and other representatives of the grimy and hot-throated men who lined the breastwork had come for each squad's portion.

The lieutenant was frowning and serious at this task of division. His lips pursed as he drew with his sword various crevices in the heap, until brown squares of coffee, astoundingly equal in size, appeared on the blanket. He was on the verge of a great triumph in mathematics, and the corporals were thronging forward, each to reap a little square, when suddenly the lieutenant cried out and looked quickly at a man near him as if he suspected it was a case of personal assault. The others cried out also when they saw blood upon the lieutenant's sleeve.

He had winced like a man stung, swayed dangerously, and then straightened. The sound of his hoarse breathing was plainly audible. He looked sadly, mystically, over the breastwork at the green face of a wood, where now were many little puffs of white smoke. During this moment the men about him gazed statuelike and silent, astonished and awed by this catastrophe which happened when catastrophes were not expected—when they had leisure to observe it.

As the lieutenant stared at the wood, they too swung their heads, so that for another instant all hands, still silent, contemplated the distant forest as if their minds were fixed upon the mystery of a bullet's journey.

The officer had, of course, been compelled to take his sword into his left hand. He did not hold it by the hilt. He gripped it at the middle of the blade, awkwardly. Turning his eyes from the hostile wood, he looked at the sword as he held it there, and seemed puzzled as to what to do with it, where to put it. In short, this weapon had of a sudden become a strange thing to him. He looked at it in a kind of stupefaction, as if he had been endowed with a trident, a scepter, or a spade.

Finally he tried to sheathe it. To sheathe a sword held by the left hand, at the middle of the blade, in a scabbard hung at the left hip, is a feat worthy of a sawdust ring.[1] This wounded officer engaged in a desperate struggle with the sword and the wobbling scabbard, and during the time of it he breathed like a wrestler.

But at this instant the men, the spectators, awoke from their stonelike poses and crowded forward sympathetically. The orderly-sergeant took the sword and tenderly placed it in the scabbard. At the time, he leaned nervously backward, and did not allow even his finger to brush the body of the lieutenant. A wound gives strange dignity to him who bears it. Well men shy from this new and terrible majesty. It is as if the wounded man's hand is upon the curtain which hangs before the revelations of all existence—the meaning of ants, potentates, wars, cities, sunshine, snow, a feather dropped from a bird's wing; and the power of it sheds radiance upon a bloody form, and makes the other men understand sometimes that they are little. His comrades look at him with large eyes thoughtfully. Moreover, they fear vaguely that the weight of a finger upon him might send him headlong, precipitate the tragedy, hurl him at once into the dim, gray unknown. And so the orderly-sergeant, while sheathing the sword, leaned nervously backward.

---

1. *sawdust ring*, circus ring.

There were others who proffered assistance. One timidly presented his shoulder and asked the lieutenant if he cared to lean upon it, but the latter waved him away mournfully. He wore the look of one who knows he is the victim of a terrible disease and understands his helplessness. He again stared over the breastwork at the forest, and then, turning, went slowly rearward. He held his right wrist tenderly in his left hand as if the wounded arm was made of very brittle glass.

And the men in silence stared at the wood, then at the departing lieutenant; then at the wood, then at the lieutenant.

As the wounded officer passed from the line of battle, he was enabled to see many things which as a participant in the fight were unknown to him. He saw a general on a black horse gazing over the lines of blue infantry at the green woods which veiled his problems. An aide galloped furiously, dragged his horse suddenly to a halt, saluted, and presented a paper. It was, for a wonder, precisely like a historical painting.

To the rear of the general and his staff a group, composed of a bugler, two or three orderlies, and the bearer of the corps standard, all upon maniacal horses, were working like slaves to hold their ground, preserve their respectful interval, while the shells boomed in the air about them, and caused their chargers to make furious quivering leaps.

A battery, a tumultuous and shining mass, was swirling toward the right. The wild thud of hoofs, the cries of the riders shouting blame and praise, menace and encouragement, and, last, the roar of the wheels, the slant of the glistening guns, brought the lieutenant to an intent pause. The battery swept in curves that stirred the heart; it made halts as dramatic as the crash of a wave on the rocks, and when it fled onward this aggregation of wheels, levers, motors had a beautiful unity, as if it were a missile. The sound of it was a war chorus that reached into the depths of man's emotion.

The lieutenant, still holding his arm as if it were of glass, stood watching this battery until all detail of it was lost, save the figures of the riders, which rose and fell and waved lashes over the black mass.

Later, he turned his eyes toward the battle, where the shooting sometimes crackled like bush fires, sometimes sputtered with exasperating irregularity, and sometimes reverberated like the thunder. He saw the smoke rolling upward and saw crowds of men who ran and cheered, or stood and blazed away at the inscrutable distance.

He came upon some stragglers, and they told him how to find the field hospital. They described its exact location. In fact, these men, no longer having part in the battle, knew more of it than others. They told the performance of every corps, every division, the opinion of every general. The lieutenant, carrying his wounded arm rearward, looked upon them with wonder.

At the roadside a brigade was making coffee and buzzing with talk like a girls' boarding school. Several officers came to him and inquired concerning things of which he knew nothing. One, seeing his arm, began to scold. "Why, man, that's no way to do. You want to fix that thing." He appropriated the lieutenant and the lieutenant's wound. He cut the sleeve and laid bare the arm, every nerve of which softly fluttered under his touch. He bound his handkerchief over the wound, scolding away in the meantime. His tone allowed one to think that he was in the habit of being wounded every day. The lieutenant hung his head, feeling, in this presence, that he did not know how to be correctly wounded.

The low white tents of the hospital were grouped around an old schoolhouse. There was here a singular commotion. In the foreground two ambulances interlocked wheels in the deep mud. The drivers were tossing the blame of it back and forth, gesticulating and berating, while from the ambulances, both crammed with wounded, there came an occasional groan. An interminable crowd of bandaged men were coming and going. Great numbers sat under the trees nursing heads or arms or legs. There was a dispute of some kind raging on the steps of the schoolhouse. Sitting with his back against a tree a man with a face as gray as a new army blanket was serenely smoking a corncob pipe. The lieutenant wished to rush forward and inform him that he was dying.

A busy surgeon was passing near the lieutenant. "Good morning," he said, with a friendly smile. Then he caught sight of the lieutenant's arm, and his face at once changed. "Well, let's have a look at it." He seemed possessed suddenly of a great contempt for the lieutenant. This wound evidently placed the latter on a very low social plane. The doctor cried out impatiently: "What mutton-head had tied it up that way anyhow?" The lieutenant answered, "Oh, a man."

When the wound was disclosed the doctor fingered it disdainfully. "Humph," he said. "You come along with me and I'll 'tend to you." His voice contained the same scorn as if he were saying: "You will have to go to jail."

The lieutenant had been very meek, but now his face flushed, and he looked into the doctor's eyes. "I guess I won't have it amputated," he said.

"Nonsense, man! Nonsense! Nonsense!" cried the doctor. "Come along, now. I won't amputate it. Come along. Don't be a baby."

"Let go of me," said the lieutenant, holding back wrathfully, his glance fixed upon the door of the old schoolhouse, as sinister to him as the portals of death.

And this is the story of how the lieutenant lost his arm. When he reached home, his sisters, his mother, his wife, sobbed for a long time at the sight of the flat sleeve. "Oh, well," he said, standing shamefaced amid these tears, "I don't suppose it matters so much as all that."

1899

THINK AND DISCUSS
Understanding
1. What is the lieutenant doing as the story opens?
2. What happens to the lieutenant before the task is finished?
3. What is the surgeon's reaction to the lieutenant's bandage? What does he ultimately do to the lieutenant?

Analyzing
4. What device does Crane use to bring his scenes to life? Cite **images** from the first three paragraphs.
5. Explain the **irony of situation** suggested by the opening vignette and by the lieutenant's initial response to his wound.
6. How does the lieutenant's being wounded change his men's attitude toward him? Explain their reaction.
7. After the lieutenant is wounded, do the battle and its participants seem less or more vivid to him? less or more "real" to him?

8. What **paradox** is there in the great knowledge of the battle displayed by the wounded soldiers? How does this paradox make sense?
9. What incidents indicate that the lieutenant is a powerless spectator of his own life, both before and after being wounded?

Extending
10. Why is Crane's title more appropriate to the story's presentation than a title like "The Bloody Wound" or "A Victim of Battle"?

VOCABULARY
Pronunciation and Synonyms
Use your Glossary to find the primary accented syllable in each of the following italicized words from "An Episode of War." Then, from the choices that follow each italicized word, select the word that rhymes with that accented syllable and write it on your paper. Be sure you know the definitions of the italicized words.

1. *potentate:* (**a**) dough; (**b**) date; (**c**) den; (**d**) lot.
2. *maniacal:* (**a**) cane; (**b**) ban; (**c**) by; (**d**) bull.
3. *tumultuous:* (**a**) doom; (**b**) dew; (**c**) salt; (**d**) dull.
4. *reverberate:* (**a**) key; (**b**) fir; (**c**) date; (**d**) hat.
5. *disdainful:* (**a**) bliss; (**b**) main; (**c**) bull; (**d**) fine.

On a sheet of paper write each of the preceding words from the story next to its synonym. The synonyms are *scornful, ruler, disorderly, insane, echo.*

THINKING SKILLS
Generalizing

To generalize is to arrive at a conclusion from particular data. Make some broad observations, using Crane's story and the information below.

Amputation was a common form of treatment for soldiers injured in the Civil War. For example, one-fifth of Mississippi's state revenue for 1866 was spent on artificial limbs for Confederate veterans.

1. What can you generalize about medical facilities during the Civil War?
2. Do you consider the lieutenant's reaction to losing his arm, "I don't suppose it matters so much as all that," a typical reaction?

COMPOSITION
Describing a Picture

Crane uses images and details, much as a painter does, to make scenes appear vivid. Choose a scene from "An Episode of War"—perhaps the initial one, or the one described in the paragraph beginning "A battery, a tumultuous and shining mass . . ." (388a, 5) that could be depicted in a painting. In three or four paragraphs, explain what colors, style (abstract, impressionistic, realistic) and medium (watercolor, oil) you would use to portray this scene. Decide whether you would present this scene from a distance or whether you would focus closely on a few details. In the final paragraph, explain the mood you would wish to convey in this picture.

Writing About Style

Write an essay of at least four paragraphs for the school literary journal analyzing Crane's use of imagery, metaphors, and similes in this story. Speculate on how this story would change if it were presented without impressionistic details and figurative language. See "Writing to Analyze Author's Style" in the Writer's Handbook.

Reader's Note

Crane's Fictional Techniques

Impressionism and symbolism are literary techniques often used by Crane in his fiction. In "An Episode of War" the wound suffered by the lieutenant is a symbol of his new vision or understanding of reality. The wound removes him from the struggle so that he can "see many things which as a participant in the fight were unknown to him."

Impressionism is a highly personal and subjective mode of writing, in that the author selects and organizes details strictly according to one character's point of view. "An Episode

of War" is impressionistic because its events are conveyed to the reader through the eyes of the lieutenant who experiences various aspects of war as fixed and static vignettes. Reality seen subjectively seems unreal, something like "a historical painting," and the various participants seem "statuelike and silent."

Crane's use of Impressionism and symbolism to express his grim naturalistic philosophy was a dramatic innovation that later influenced such noted novelists as Steinbeck and Hemingway (see Unit 5).

I Met a Seer

I met a seer.
He held in his hands
The book of wisdom.
"Sir," I addressed him,
5 "Let me read."
"Child——" he began.
"Sir," I said,
"Think not that I am a child,
For already I know much
10 Of that which you hold.
Aye, much."

He smiled.
Then he opened the book
And held it before me.——
15 Strange that I should have grown
    so suddenly blind.

1895

A Man Said
to the Universe

A man said to the universe:
"Sir, I exist!"
"However," replied the universe,
"The fact has not created in me
5 A sense of obligation."

1899

The Wayfarer

The wayfarer
Perceiving the pathway to truth
Was struck with astonishment.
It was thickly grown with weeds.
5 "Ha," he said,
"I see that none has passed here
In a long time."
Later he saw that each weed
Was a singular knife.
10 "Well," he mumbled at last,
"Doubtless there are other roads."

1899

George Segal, *Aerial View* (1970).
Sara Hildén Art Museum, Tampere

THINK AND DISCUSS

I MET A SEER

Understanding
1. What does the seer hold in his hands?
2. What does the speaker request of the seer?
3. When the seer begins to protest, what does the speaker say?

Analyzing
4. In the last lines of "I Met a Seer," the relationship between the seer and the speaker changes. Why does the seer smile?
5. Why does the speaker grow suddenly blind?

THE WAYFARER

Understanding
1. What does the wayfarer perceive? With what feeling is he struck?
2. What is each weed on the pathway?

Analyzing
3. Why does the wayfarer's attitude change?

Extending
4. Is the wayfarer a specific individual, or are we all in some sense wayfarers?

A MAN SAID TO THE UNIVERSE

Understanding
1. What does the man say to the universe?

Analyzing
2. Is the attitude of the man who speaks humble or defiant? Explain.
3. Does the universe's reply express concern or indifference? Explain.

Extending
4. In the brief exchange of "A Man Said to the Universe," what do you imagine the man's reaction was to the universe's reply to him?

BIOGRAPHY

Paul Laurence Dunbar
1872–1906

Dunbar was the son of former slaves who had escaped by way of the Underground Railroad. After graduating from high school in Dayton, Ohio, Dunbar, who could not afford to go to college, went to work as an elevator operator. He was holding this job when his first book of poetry, *Oak and Ivy*, was published in 1893. The book made little impression, but his second collection, *Majors and Minors* (1895), came to the attention of the noted novelist and editor, William Dean Howells. He persuaded Dunbar to combine the best poetry from both books into one volume. The result was *Lyrics of Lowly Life* (1896), which made Dunbar a national literary figure. Although his life was short, Dunbar published six collections of poetry, four collections of short stories, and four novels. His *Complete Poems* was published in 1913 and heralded a new era of black writing in American literature.

Sympathy

Paul Laurence Dunbar

I know what the caged bird feels, alas!
When the sun is bright on the upland slopes;
When the wind stirs soft through the
    springing grass,
And the river flows like a stream of glass;
5 When the first bird sings and the first bud opes,
And the faint perfume from its chalice steals——
I know what the caged bird feels!

I know why the caged bird beats his wing
Till its blood is red on the cruel bars;
10 For he must fly back to his perch and cling
When he fain would be on the bough a-swing;
And a pain still throbs in the old, old scars
And they pulse again with a keener sting——
I know why he beats his wing!

15 I know why the caged bird sings, ah me,
When his wing is bruised and his bosom sore——
When he beats his bars and he would be free;
It is not a carol of joy or glee,
But a prayer that he sends from his heart's
    deep core,
20 But a plea, that upward to Heaven he flings——
I know why the caged bird sings!

                        1893

"Sympathy" by Paul Laurence Dunbar. Reprinted by permission of Dodd, Mead & Company, Inc. from *The Complete Poems of Paul Laurence Dunbar*.

THINK AND DISCUSS

Understanding

1. Why does the bird beat its wings, according to lines 10 and 11?
2. What two things, mentioned in lines 19 and 20, are expressed in the bird's song?

Analyzing

3. Discuss the possible metaphorical meanings of the cage, the bird, and the outdoor scene.
4. What contrast is drawn between the song as it appears in stanza 1 and the song described in stanza 3?
5. Why is the poem entitled "Sympathy"?
6. What is the effect of the repetition of "I know" at the beginning of six lines of the poem?

COMPOSITION

Responding to a Theme in Poetry

Write two or three paragraphs for your journal in which you describe your personal reactions to the theme of one of the poems you have read by Crane or Dunbar. You might begin, "Yes, we are all wayfarers on a quest for truth. . . ." Or you might say, "Indeed, we all occupy cages of some sort." Make your response as personal and as imaginative as you like. See "Writing About Theme" in the Writer's Handbook.

Comparing Protesting Poets

Write a four- or five-paragraph essay for the readers of the poetry of Crane and Dunbar comparing the subjects and effects of their protests. Crane appears to be protesting the human plight in an indifferent universe, while Dunbar is protesting the plight of blacks in a racist society. In comparing and contrasting their poetry, give your views as to the impact of their poems.

BIOGRAPHY

Edwin Arlington Robinson

1869–1935

During the 1920s Edwin Arlington Robinson was generally regarded as America's greatest living poet. Three times during that decade he was awarded the Pulitzer Prize.

Raised in Gardiner, Maine, Robinson attended Harvard for two years and finally settled in New York. There he led a hermitlike, impoverished life, working at odd jobs and writing poetry until in 1916 *The Man Against the Sky* brought him fame. The poems that follow are part of the "Tilbury" portraits that grew out of his New England experiences. This Tilbury Town gallery is composed largely of "cheated dreamers" and "bewildered mediocrities" who withdraw from hard reality. But Robinson's pessimism is always tempered by wit, imagination, and wry humor.

Miniver Cheevy

Miniver Cheevy, child of scorn,
   Grew lean while he assailed the seasons;
He wept that he was ever born,
   And he had reasons.

5 Miniver loved the days of old
   When swords were bright and steeds
    were prancing;
The vision of a warrior bold
   Would set him dancing.

Miniver sighed for what was not,
10   And dreamed, and rested from his labors;
He dreamed of Thebes and Camelot,
   And Priam's neighbors.[1]

Miniver mourned the ripe renown
   That made so many a name so fragrant;
15 He mourned Romance, now on the town,[2]
   And Art, a vagrant.

Miniver loved the Medici,[3]
   Albeit he had never seen one;
He would have sinned incessantly
20   Could he have been one.

Miniver cursed the commonplace
   And eyed a khaki suit with loathing;
He missed the medieval grace
   Of iron clothing.

1. **Thebes . . . neighbors.** Thebes was the capital of ancient Egypt during its period of greatness. Camelot was the legendary site of King Arthur's palace. Priam was the last king of Troy; his neighbors were the Greeks, who conquered Troy in the Trojan War.
2. **on the town,** living on charity, a pauper.
3. **the Medici** (med'ə chē), the ruling family of Florence, Italy, during the fifteenth and sixteenth centuries, who were notable both for their generous patronage of art and for their lavish living and wicked lives.

"Miniver Cheevy" from *The Town Down the River* by Edwin Arlington Robinson. Copyright 1910 Charles Scribner's Sons. Copyright renewed 1938 Ruth Nivision. Reprinted with the permission of Charles Scribner's Sons.

25 Miniver scorned the gold he sought,
    But sore annoyed was he without it;
Miniver thought, and thought, and thought,
    And thought about it.

Miniver Cheevy, born too late,
30   Scratched his head and kept on thinking;
Miniver coughed, and called it fate,
    And kept on drinking.

                  1907

Richard Cory

Whenever Richard Cory went downtown,
    We people on the pavement looked at him:
He was a gentleman from sole to crown,
    Clean-favored, and imperially slim.

5 And he was always quietly arrayed,
    And he was always human when he talked;
But still he fluttered pulses when he said,
    "Good morning," and he glittered when
        he walked.

And he was rich—yes, richer than a king——
10   And admirably schooled in every grace:
In fine, we thought that he was everything
    To make us wish that we were in his place.

So on we worked, and waited for the light,
    And went without the meat, and cursed
        the bread;
15 And Richard Cory, one calm summer night,
    Went home and put a bullet through his head.

                  1897

"Richard Cory" from *The Children of the Night* by Edwin Arlington Robinson. Copyright under the Berne Convention. Reprinted with the permission of Charles Scribner's Sons.

Tinsmith, attributed to J. Krans (c. 1895).
Private collection

THINK AND DISCUSS

MINIVER CHEEVY

Understanding
1. What does Miniver Cheevy love, according to lines 5–8?
2. What does Cheevy do about his dilemma, according to lines 27–28 and 30–32?

Analyzing
3. What complaints does Cheevy make about his own time?
4. What is **ironic** about Cheevy's actions as described in the last two lines?

Extending
5. Would Cheevy have been happy in the other times of which he dreams? Why or why not?

RICHARD CORY

Understanding
1. What do you learn about Richard Cory's physical appearance? his manners? his economic condition?
2. What effect does his greeting have on people?
3. What finally happens to Cory?

Analyzing
4. What feelings do the people have toward Cory? Do they understand him? Explain.
5. Where does **irony** occur in the poem? Do you think the final twist of events makes this a better poem than it would have been otherwise? Why or why not?
6. What possible motive might Cory have had for killing himself?

BIOGRAPHY

Edgar Lee Masters
1868–1950

As a young boy, Masters began writing poems and stories, and continued to do so during his brief sojourn at Knox College in Illinois and his work in his father's law office. In 1891 he was admitted to the bar and became a highly respected lawyer. *Spoon River Anthology*, which first appeared as a series of poems in a St. Louis newspaper in 1914, became so popular that book publication followed the next year, and brought Masters fame. A few years later he abandoned law to devote all his time to writing and in 1924 published *The New Spoon River*.

Since publication, the *Spoon River* epitaphs have maintained their great popularity. Masters continued to write poetry and biographies until his death. Although his later works were interesting and readable, he never again achieved the brilliance of the *Spoon River* poems.

The following poems are set in the graveyard of Spoon River, an imaginary composite of several small towns in central Illinois. The speaker of each poem is a former resident of Spoon River, delivering from the grave an epitaph that gives a verdict on life, shaped by the speaker's feeling of tranquillity or of bitterness.

See DRAMATIC MONOLOGUE in the Handbook of Literary Terms, page 885.

Lucinda Matlock

I went to dances at Chandlerville,
And played snap-out at Winchester.
One time we changed partners,
Driving home in the moonlight of middle June,
5 And then I found Davis.
We were married and lived together for seventy years,
Enjoying, working, raising the twelve children,
Eight of whom we lost
Ere I had reached the age of sixty.
10 I spun, I wove, I kept the house, I nursed the sick,
I made the garden, and for holiday

Rambled over the fields where sang the larks,
And by Spoon River gathering many a shell,
And many a flower and medicinal weed——
15 Shouting to the wooded hills, singing to the green valleys.
At ninety-six I had lived enough, that is all,
And passed to a sweet repose.
What is this I hear of sorrow and weariness,
Anger, discontent, and drooping hopes?
20 Degenerate sons and daughters,
Life is too strong for you——
It takes life to love Life.

1915

"Lucinda Matlock," "Richard Bone," and "Mrs. Charles Bliss" from *Spoon River Anthology* by Edgar
Lee Masters. Copyright 1915, 1916, 1942, 1949 by Edgar Lee Masters. Reprinted by permission of
Ellen C. Masters.

Tom Heflin, *Memories.*
Private collection

Richard Bone

When I first came to Spoon River
I did not know whether what they told me
Was true or false.
They would bring me the epitaph
5 And stand around the shop while I worked
And say "He was so kind," "He was wonderful,"
"She was the sweetest woman," "He was a consistent Christian."
And I chiseled for them whatever they wished,
All in ignorance of its truth.
10 But later, as I lived among the people here,
I knew how near to the life
Were the epitaphs that were ordered for them as they died.
But still I chiseled whatever they paid me to chisel
And made myself party to the false chronicles
15 Of the stones,
Even as the historian does who writes
Without knowing the truth,
Or because he is influenced to hide it.

1915

Mrs. Charles Bliss

Reverend Wiley advised me not to divorce him
For the sake of the children,
And Judge Somers advised him the same.
So we stuck to the end of the path.
5 But two of the children thought he was right,
And two of the children thought I was right.
And the two who sided with him blamed me,
And the two who sided with me blamed him,
And they grieved for the one they sided with.
10 And all were torn with the guilt of judging,
And tortured in soul because they could not admire
Equally him and me.
Now every gardener knows that plants grown in cellars
Or under stones are twisted and yellow and weak.
15 And no mother would let her baby suck
Diseased milk from her breast.
Yet preachers and judges advise the raising of souls
Where there is no sunlight, but only twilight,
No warmth, but only dampness and cold——
20 Preachers and judges!

1915

Rudolph Ohrning, *Old House*. Private collection

THINK AND DISCUSS
LUCINDA MATLOCK
Understanding
1. Under what circumstances does Lucinda Matlock meet her husband?
2. For how long does the couple live together? How many children do they have?
3. What activities does the speaker describe in lines 10–11?
4. How old is Lucinda Matlock when she dies?

Analyzing
5. What kind of life has Lucinda Matlock lived as she describes it in the first 17 lines of the poem? Has it been easy or hard? Explain.
6. How do the last five lines in particular **characterize** Lucinda Matlock?
7. Who are the degenerate children? Paraphrase Lucinda Matlock's message to them in the final line.

RICHARD BONE
Understanding
1. What kind of work does Richard Bone do?

Analyzing

2. What does Bone mean in lines 10–12?
3. According to Bone, how does he resemble a historian? Explain.

MRS. CHARLES BLISS
Understanding

1. What advice have the preacher and the judge given to the Blisses?
2. Who sides with each parent? What are the effects of these loyalties, as expressed in lines 10–12?

Analyzing

3. What **metaphor** most powerfully describes the children's condition? What does it imply about their future?
4. Explain the **irony** in the speaker's married name.
5. How would you describe the **tone** of the poem?
6. How would you read the last line aloud to emphasize Mrs. Bliss's attitude toward preachers and judges?

Extending

7. Each speaker in these Spoon River poems delivers a verdict on life. Which one do you consider most realistic?

APPLYING: Dramatic Monologue HT
See Handbook of Literary Terms, p. 885.

A **dramatic monologue** is a poem in which a character, during a critical moment, reveals his or her personality to a silent audience whose replies are not recorded. The speakers in these three poems by Masters deliver from the grave a commentary on life, presumably to those who read their epitaphs.

1. What advice does Lucinda Matlock offer at the end of her dramatic monologue?
2. What irony does Richard Bone observe about the tombstone inscriptions he carves?
3. Which of the three speakers do you feel expresses the most pessimistic view of life?

THINKING SKILLS
Synthesizing

To synthesize is to organize elements into a new structure. Imagine that Richard Bone were writing an epitaph to appear on the tombstone of Mrs. Charles Bliss's grave.

1. Write an epitaph that represents a "false chronicle" of her life as it might have appeared to those who knew her only superficially. Then write another epitaph that reflects her life as portrayed in the poem.
2. Write an epitaph that reflects on one of the other characters portrayed in another poem by Masters or by Robinson in this unit.

COMPOSITION ◄━━
Thinking About Happiness

Write several paragraphs to a close friend in which you present your views of happiness. You may want to comment on the epigram expressed in "Lucinda Matlock": "It takes life to love Life." Consider these questions: What do you mean by *happiness?* Whom do you know that fits your definition of a truly happy person? What things or qualities could guarantee you a happy life?

Comparing Two Characters

Write a four- or five-paragraph essay for the class comparing and contrasting Miniver Cheevy (or Richard Cory) and Lucinda Matlock—what they did with their lives, how they lived their lives, what they seemed to think about life. You might by your tone imply what you think is the best way to live a fulfilled life. See "Writing About Characters" in the Writer's Handbook.

ENRICHMENT
Readers Theater

Find a copy of Edgar Lee Masters's *Spoon River Anthology.* Assemble a group of fellow students and jointly make a selection of poems to read aloud. Each of the poems represents one of the dead in the Spoon River cemetery telling the story of his or her life. Some of the poems are interrelated—husband and wife, a family group, two friends, two enemies. In a production that you could present to the class, arrange all the characters on "stage" sitting on boxes or stools. One individual can play several characters. If someone in the class plays a guitar, he or she might accompany selections with appropriate folk ballads.

UNIT 4   VARIATIONS AND DEPARTURES   1870–1915

■ CONCEPT REVIEW

The following poems illustrate many of the important ideas and literary terms found in the period you have just studied. The notes and questions are designed to help you think critically about your reading. Page numbers in the notes refer to an application. A more extensive discussion of these terms is in the Handbook of Literary Terms.

She Rose to His Requirement

Emily Dickinson

She rose to His Requirement—dropt
The Playthings of Her Life
To take the honorable Work
Of Woman, and of Wife—

5 If ought She missed in Her new Day,
Of Amplitude, or Awe—
Or first Prospective—Or the Gold
In using, wear away,

It lay unmentioned—as the Sea
10 Develops Pearl, and Weed,
But only to Himself—be known
The Fathoms they abide—

c. 1863   1890

■ Her serious interests are considered "Playthings" by her husband.

■ **Amplitude:** fullness, abundance.

■ Note the simile. Her feelings of loss were hidden (unmentioned), like the oyster's pearl and the weed in the ocean.

■ *Himself* refers to the Sea, which is personified.

■ **Slant rhyme** (page 323): *Weed/abide*. Note also *Awe/away* in lines 6 and 8.

Reprinted by permission of the publishers and the Trustees of Amherst College from *The Poems of Emily Dickinson*, edited by Thomas H. Johnson, Cambridge, Mass.: The Belknap Press of Harvard University Press, Copyright 1951, © 1955, 1979, 1983 by the President and Fellows of Harvard College.

A Noiseless Patient Spider

Walt Whitman

A noiseless patient spider,
I mark'd where on a little promontory it stood isolated,
Mark'd how to explore the vacant vast surrounding,
It launch'd forth filament, filament, filament, out of itself,
5 Ever unreeling them, ever tirelessly speeding them.

And you O my soul where you stand,
Surrounded, detached, in measureless oceans of space,
Ceaselessly musing, venturing, throwing, seeking the spheres to connect
   them,
Till the bridge you will need be form'd, till the ductile anchor hold,
10 Till the gossamer thread you fling catch somewhere,
    O my soul.

1871

■ **Mood** (page 334): Adjectives in lines 1 and 3 establish the atmosphere.

■ **mark'd:** noticed.

■ **Free verse** (page 297): Note repetition and parallelism in lines 4 and 5.

■ In line 6, the speaker addresses the soul in an apostrophe.

■ **Imagery** (page 300): The soul is portrayed as a planet in space.

■ **Symbol** (page 308): A thread catching symbolizes a close human relationship.

THINK AND DISCUSS

SHE ROSE TO HIS REQUIREMENT
Understanding
1. What "honorable Work" does the woman take, according to the first stanza?
2. What must she drop, or give up (line 2)?

Analyzing
3. What do the words *rose* and *Requirement* in line 1 imply about the nature of the relationship in marriage?
4. Why do you think that the woman's interests and activities are referred to as "Playthings"?
5. What is missing in marriage, as suggested by *Amplitude* and *Awe*?

A NOISELESS PATIENT SPIDER
Understanding
1. What words describe the spider in lines 1–2?
2. What is the spider doing in lines 4–5?

Analyzing
3. What two things form the central comparison in this poem?
4. What is the effect of the repetition of *filament* in line 4?

5. What is the **theme** of this poem?

REVIEWING LITERARY TERMS
Mood
1. What mood does Whitman create in "A Noiseless Patient Spider"? What words and images help convey this mood?

Free Verse
2. Free verse depends on subtle patterns of rhythm and sound for its effects. Explain how the sounds of words in lines 4 and 5 of Whitman's poem suggest the process that they are describing.

Figurative Language
3. What human yearning does the isolated spider ceaselessly spinning its web symbolize? What makes this symbol appropriate?

Slant Rhyme
4. In the first stanza of "She Rose to His Requirement," the perfect sound match of *Life/Wife* suggests the harmony of an ideal marriage. Describe how slant rhyme relates to the meaning of stanzas 2 and 3.

■ CONTENT REVIEW

THINKING SKILLS

Classifying

1. Head two lists with the labels *Free Verse* and *Regular Rhymed Verse*. Under the appropriate head, list the names of poets appearing in this unit whose works fit these labels.
2. Two dominant themes of this period are democracy and rugged individualism. Choose three works from this unit that develop each theme and discuss how the themes are reflected in the works.

Generalizing

3. What elements in Bret Harte's "The Outcasts of Poker Flat" and Mary Wilkins Freeman's "A New England Nun" identify them as local-color fiction?
4. Compare the different ways in which the stories by Bierce, Chopin, and Crane explore a "crucial moment" in each protagonist's life.
5. Reread the discussion of Realism and Naturalism in the Unit Backround. Then give examples of these philosophies that are illustrated in the stories by Freeman, Crane, Chopin, and Bierce.
6. Compare the portrayals of and attitudes expressed toward small-town rural life in the selections by Twain, Freeman, Masters, and Du Bois.

Synthesizing

7. Write three one-sentence epitaphs that might appear on the gravestones of three authors represented in this unit. Base your epitaphs on the selections by these authors or on the information presented in the biographies.
8. Choose three works from this unit that illustrate in some respect "variations and departures" from the literature that appears in the first three units. You might consider selections that are expressed in new forms, characters that are more complex or psychologically oriented than their literary predecessors, or topics that did not appear in earlier literature. Explain your choices.

Evaluating

9. Pick two works in this unit that express an optimistic philosophy of life. Then choose two works that offer a view of life that you consider pessimistic. Explain your choices. Finally select the one work of these four that expresses a view of life closest to your own and tell how it fits with your philosophy.

■ COMPOSITION REVIEW

Choose one of the following topics for writing.

Writing a Preface

Suppose that you are putting together a collection of poems by Walt Whitman and Emily Dickinson. Write a preface of at least three paragraphs for the collection that will prepare the reader for the differences in subject matter, theme, style, and tone between the poems of these writers. Refer to specific poems and lines to support your ideas.

Writing About Mood

Mary E. Wilkins Freeman, Ambrose Bierce, and Stephen Crane are all skillful at creating mood. Write an essay of four paragraphs for your classmates that contrasts the dominant moods in two of the following. Refer to those words, images, and actions that create mood.

"A New England Nun" (365a, 1–2)

"An Occurrence at Owl Creek Bridge" (361a, 2)

"An Episode of War" (387a, 1–5)

Comparing Views of Nature

Compare the views of nature held by Whitman, Satanta, and Dickinson. Which authors' views reflect Transcendentalist beliefs? How? Whose attitude resembles modern environmentalist thinking? Your essay should be at least four paragraphs long and directed to a friend who is fond of the outdoors.

Writing About Irony

Write an essay of three or four paragraphs for the school literary journal analyzing the irony in three of the poems from this unit. Decide what type of irony occurs (verbal, dramatic, or situational), as well as the effect this use of irony has on you the reader. In closing, you might speculate on how these poems would be changed if the authors had omitted all ironic touches.

HE MODERN TEMPER

1920	1925	1930

HISTORY AND THE ARTS

- U.S. enters World War I
- Tomb of Tutankhamun discovered (Egypt)
- Treaty of Versailles signed (France)
- First commercial radio broadcast
- Women's suffrage
- Scopes trial
- A. A. Milne: *Winnie the Pooh* (England)
- Transatlantic wireless telephone
- Lindbergh's transatlantic flight
- Stock market crash
- Sinclair Lewis receives Nobel Prize
- Nazi party wins national election (Germany)
- Empire State Building completed

PRESIDENTS' ADMINISTRATIONS

- 1913–1921 Woodrow Wilson
- 1921–1923 Warren G. Harding
- 1923–1929 Calvin Coolidge
- 1929–1933 Herbert Hoover

LITERATURE

- Lowell: *Men, Women, and Ghosts*
- Sandburg: *Chicago Poems*
- Eliot: *Prufrock and Other Observations*
- Cather: *My Ántonia*
- Anderson: *Winesburg, Ohio*
- Toomer: *Cane*
- Fitzgerald: *The Great Gatsby*
- *The New Yorker* founded
- Hughes: *The Weary Blues*
- Johnson: *God's Trombones*
- Faulkner: *The Sound and the Fury*

James M. Flagg (1877–1960), World War I recruiting poster

First *New Yorker* cover (1925)

Cartoon of "flapper" (1928) by John Held, Jr.

1915–1945

UNIT

- World War II begins
- First commercial television
- Frances Perkins, first woman cabinet member
- Pearl Harbor attack: U.S. enters war
- New Deal Era begins
- First American jet plane tested
- Eugene O'Neill receives Nobel Prize
- Nationwide rationing of essential goods
- Atom bomb dropped

- 1933–1945 Franklin D. Roosevelt
- 1945–1953 Harry S. Truman

- Moore: *Selected Poems*
- Wright: *Native Son*
- Sandburg: *The People, Yes*
- Welty: *A Curtain of Green*
- Wilder: *Our Town*
- Walker: *For My People*
- Steinbeck: *The Grapes of Wrath*
- Hemingway: *For Whom the Bell Tolls*

Emblem of the National Recovery Administraton

Depression-era glass of the "Mt. Vernon" pattern

Roosevelt asking Congress to declare war on Japan in 1941

PREVIEW

UNIT 5 THE MODERN TEMPER 1915–1945

Authors in This Unit Include

Willa Cather
Sherwood Anderson
Katherine Anne Porter
F. Scott Fitzgerald
Ernest Hemingway
William Faulkner
John Steinbeck
Richard Wright
Eudora Welty

Amy Lowell
Carl Sandburg
Marianne Moore
Robert Frost
Langston Hughes
Countee Cullen
Jean Toomer
James Weldon Johnson
T. S. Eliot

Vachel Lindsay
Edna St. Vincent Millay
Elinor Wylie
Wallace Stevens
E. E. Cummings
Margaret Walker
James Thurber
Council of American Indians
Dorothy Parker

Features
Reading a Modern Short Story
Themes in American Literature:
    The Frontier
Comment: The Real Hard Terror of Writing
Comment: Reading Modern Poetry
The Story of American English
Reader's Notes: "Patterns"
    "The Love Song of J. Alfred Prufrock"
    "anyone lived in a pretty how town"
    "l(a"

Application of Literary Terms
stream of consciousness
setting
inference
apostrophe
blank verse
connotation/denotation
sonnet

Review of Literary Terms
theme
mood
symbol

Reading Literature Skillfully
cause/effect

Vocabulary Skills
combined skills
context
dictionary

Thinking Skills
evaluating
classifying

Composition Assignments Include
Being a Story Character
Analyzing Imagery
Writing About Theme
Imitating a Writer's Style
Explaining a Symbol
Writing to Persuade
Writing About Poetry
Writing a Prose Poem
Writing a Summary

Enrichment
Research
Oral Reading
Participating in Discussions

Thinking Critically About Literature
Concept Review
Content Review
Composition Review

THE MODERN TEMPER   1915–1945

The period from 1915 to 1945 encompassed two of the most eventful and memorable decades in American history—the Jazz Age of the 1920s and the Great Depression of the 1930s. Separating these decades was the stock market crash of 1929, which drastically changed American life. Quick fortunes, high living, and extravagant dreams gave way to unemployment, poverty, and soup lines; optimism was replaced with despair, and complacency yielded to threats of political and social upheaval. The two World Wars that bracketed this era uprooted people and radically changed their lives, bringing social and political shifts and turns that were often exhilarating, sometimes bewildering, and frequently frightening.

The events of this period were so dramatic, the changes so drastic and disorienting, that they might have overwhelmed sensitive creative talent. But instead the times seemed to inspire literary imaginations and to challenge American writers to ever greater creative achievement. The era has emerged as one of the richest periods in American literary history.

World War I exploded the propriety and stability so cherished by Victorian society. Novelists, poets, and dramatists turned for inspiration to such earlier literary rebels as Herman Melville, Walt Whitman, and Emily Dickinson. Free verse and other innovative poetic forms, though still unacceptable to most readers, became the rallying cry of young poets as diverse as Ezra Pound, Amy Lowell, and Carl Sandburg. At the same time, Sherwood Anderson, Ernest Hemingway, and William Faulkner deliberately disrupted the chronological time sequences found in traditional works and focused on seemingly uneventful but emotionally crucial moments. Hemingway's distinctive prose style stripped descriptions and narrative accounts to the barest—but highly suggestive—minimum.

Writers were influenced by new psychological theories such as those of the Austrian Sigmund Freud (1856–1939) and the American William James (1842–1910). James coined the term *stream of consciousness*, a technique that dramatized the random flow of thoughts running through the minds of characters during particular moments of their lives. This technique, used in embryonic form by Ambrose Bierce (Unit 4), was refined and perfected in the novels of James Joyce, Virginia Woolf, and William Faulkner. The technique is shown at its best in Katherine Anne Porter's "The Jilting of Granny Weatherall," which appears in this unit.

During this period, popular poets like Carl Sandburg, Vachel Lindsay, and Robert Frost gave public readings to large and enthusiastic crowds, thereby expanding the audience for poetry. Prosperous magazines such as *The Saturday Evening Post* paid premium fees for short stories and serialized novels and made household names out of many writers, including F. Scott Fitzgerald. At the same time, a rebellion against "big" publishing (and literary banality) gave birth to dozens of "little magazines" like *Poetry* (1912), *Blast* (1914), *The Fugitive* (1922), and *Opportunity* (1923). The many new outlets for unconventional talents and innovative literary techniques encouraged experimentation and inspired still greater creative activity.

THE NEW FICTION

As in the past during times of crisis, some

inspired American writers turned to humor, offering ironic laughter as a possible though inadequate response to the war, devastation, poverty, and pain of the era. Among the humorists of this period (and a worthy successor to Mark Twain), James Thurber was one of the most ingenious in combining psychological insight and piercing wit. His character Walter Mitty has become the archetype of the henpecked husband who cuts a heroic figure in the world of his daydreams. A character similarly out of step with the world's expectations appears in "University Days" in this unit.

A number of novelists of the period witnessed firsthand the movement from the farm to the city, the "revolt from the village," which characterized this era. Willa Cather memorialized her native Red Cloud, Nebraska, in such novels as *My Ántonia* (1918), and Sherwood Anderson imaginatively transfigured his hometown of Clyde, Ohio, into *Winesburg, Ohio* (1919). Near the end of both works, the "heroes" set off for the big city. Like their longer works, Cather's "A Wagner Matinée" and Anderson's "Sophistication" portray with psychological insight the deprivations and aspirations of small-town people. Both of these short stories appear in this unit. A work often compared with *Winesburg, Ohio*, Jean Toomer's *Cane* (1923), explored the hardships and joys of the Southern black rural experience by weaving together stories, poems, and dramatic sketches in an evocative style; this experience was then contrasted with the more sophisticated black urban experience in the North.

F. Scott Fitzgerald chose a different focus in his works. The protagonist of his first novel, *This Side of Paradise* (1920), lamented that he had "grown up to find all gods dead, all wars fought, all faiths in man shaken." The titles of Fitzgerald's collections of short stories—*Flappers and Philosophers* (1920) and *Tales of the Jazz Age* (1922)—suggest why he was regarded as spokesman for the reckless youth of the '20s. In fact, his masterpiece, *The Great Gatsby* (1925), about the wealthy, who in their carelessness leave destruction and death in their wake, provides one of the best descriptions of this era in American literature. "Winter Dreams" in this unit is typical of his works in portraying the pursuit of the elusive fantasy of idealized love.

Like many other American writers of the '20s, Fitzgerald lived in Paris. There he met Ernest Hemingway, read in manuscript Hemingway's *The Sun Also Rises*, and recommended it to his editor at Scribner's, Maxwell Perkins. Its publication in 1926 created a sensation. It portrayed a "lost generation" of Americans, wounded spiritually and physically by the war, wandering aimlessly around Europe seeking both the pleasures of the moment and meaning for their lives. The style—simple, direct, terse—seemed exactly right for a war-weary, cynical generation. This style is evident in Hemingway's story "In Another Country," which begins "In the fall the war was always there." Hemingway's later works, such as *A Farewell to Arms* (1929), made him an admired and imitated novelist around the world.

With an elaborate, intricate style in direct contrast with Hemingway's spare prose, William Faulkner probed the effects of modern experience and change on Southern traditions and identity. To explore this theme in depth, he chronicled the lives and times of his privately created mythical county of Yoknapatawpha, Mississippi, in many novels, the best-known being *The Sound and the Fury* (1929). His short story "The Bear," which appears in this unit, typifies his attempts to incorporate folk tales and humor, myth and legends into his fiction.

Other Southern writers who became prominent in the 1930s were Katherine Anne Porter, Eudora Welty, and Richard Wright. Porter's reputation rests mainly on her short stories which, like "The Jilting of Granny Weatherall," are noted for emotional subtlety, psychological depth, and technical complexity. Welty, who began publishing late in this period, set her work in her Mississippi birthplace. But she transcended the geographical limits of local-color fiction by portraying the inner solitude of all individuals and the power of love to unite them in human community. "A Worn Path" is typical of her works affirming human dignity and endurance.

Richard Wright's "The Man Who Saw the Flood," rooted in the Southern black experience, provides a first-rate example of the social protest fiction of the 1930s. In *Native Son*, a novel based partly on a 1938 murder case, Wright analyzed the dehumanizing forces of urban slums. His autobiography, *Black Boy* (1945), generally considered to be his masterwork, portrayed his own highly perilous but ultimately successful struggle to escape dehumanization.

Perhaps the foremost protest novel of the Great Depression was John Steinbeck's *The Grapes of Wrath* (1939). It traced in accurate, moving detail the desperate exodus of an Oklahoma family from their ancestral farm, destroyed by dust storms, to the migrant-worker camps of California, where they struggled to hold on to their family ties and self-

Carroll Dickerson's band plays for a jazz floor show in Chicago. (1924)

respect. Steinbeck's short story "The Leader of the People" is likewise based on the motif of the epic journey, but the journey here is a part of the "westering" movement of the frontier period —preserved only in an old man's faltering memory and embattled spirit.

THE NEW POETRY

In vigor and variety, the poetry of 1915–1945 was equal to the fiction, and reflected a number of the same tensions, themes, and feelings. Many of the innovations in poetic style and technique had been foreshadowed by the poetry of Walt Whitman, Emily Dickinson, and (to some extent) Stephen Crane.

The poetic renaissance of this era might be said to have begun in London, before World War I, under the guidance of Ezra Pound, the brilliant and erratic American poet. He encouraged poets to break with the past in order to achieve greater freedom of expression. Pound's theories led to the concept of Imagism, which owed something to French symbolism as well as to ancient Chinese, Japanese, and Greek poetry.

The Imagists, joined enthusiastically by Amy Lowell, had some influence on most modern poets, including Carl Sandburg, T. S. Eliot, Marianne Moore, and Wallace Stevens. Pound defined the principles of Imagism as precision of diction and image, freedom in the choice of subjects, and a controlled freedom of rhythm based on musical cadence and not on traditional meters (free verse, in other words).

The revolt against poetic conventions had started early in the twentieth century. Robert Frost had already produced fresh and original work by the end of the first decade. Ignored at first, he later emerged as a luminary of the poetry revival.

In 1912, Harriet Monroe published the first issue of *Poetry: A Magazine of Verse* in Chicago. This magazine was of strategic importance, providing a medium for the work of poets here and abroad, disseminating the new poetic theories, and bringing them to the attention of the public.

The poetic renaissance, slowed during World War I, gained momentum in the 1920s, a period of drastic social change. Freudian psychology, enlarged economic opportunities and political rights for women, the development of science and technology—all suggested new possibilities for poetry. Religious skepticism, growing since the last century, and the moral disillusionment caused by the war were recurrent themes in the new poetry. The spiritual emptiness of an industrialized civilization and the sense of alienation and futility experienced by many were the themes of T. S. Eliot's "The Love Song of J. Alfred Prufrock" and *The Waste Land*.

But if poets were critics of twentieth-century life, they were also explorers engaged in exciting voyages of personal discovery. Some looked for a genuine "American rhythm," seeking it in jazz and spirituals, and in the poetry and song of the American Indian. Folk heroes and legendary figures were celebrated in ballads and other forms of narrative poetry. DuBose Heyward, a novelist, poet, and dramatist from South Carolina, was one of the first white writers to focus on the experience of black Americans. His novel *Porgy* was a great success in 1925. Working with his playwright wife, he adapted it for the stage as a four-act drama and later collaborated with George Gershwin on the libretto of the memorable folk opera, *Porgy and Bess* (1935), much later made into a movie classic.

By the 1930s the ideals of the new poetry had been accepted and no longer seemed radical or even controversial. Free verse was the preferred technique of many poets, and although Imagism as a distinct movement no longer existed, it was still a minor influence. Significant work in traditional forms continued, of course. Robert Frost pursued what he called his "lover's quarrel with the world" in verse forms (often in blank verse) that were conventional though the poet's vision and tone were highly individual. Edna St. Vincent Millay cast many of her striking love poems in sonnet form. Personal and metaphysical poetry employing conventional meter and rhyme often achieved notable distinction through the artistry of such poets as Countee Cullen and Elinor Wylie.

During the Depression '30s, social consciousness and political awareness gave special impetus to American poetry. Much of the poetry of Carl Sandburg and Archibald MacLeish was written out of a deep concern over injustice and human exploitation. Langston Hughes and Margaret Walker wrote perceptively about the condition of black Americans. Some critics objected to the poet in the role of propagandist, who championed the oppressed victims of an unjust social order. The question of whether a valid distinction between art and propaganda could really be made was hotly debated in these years. Notwithstanding his poems of protest, MacLeish could advocate, in "Ars Poetica," the concept of the "pure poem," detached from social purpose. This debate continued vigorously as the worldwide Depression and the menace of Fascism dragged the world once more toward global war.

T. S. Eliot, looking back in 1953, remarked: "In the nineteenth century, Poe and Whitman stand out as solitary international figures; in the last forty years, for the first time, there has been assembled a *body* of American poetry which has made its total impression in England and Europe." The same could be said of American fiction in these decades, during which the world recognized that American literature had blossomed into full maturity.

THE HARLEM RENAISSANCE

The Harlem Renaissance, known also as the New Negro Movement, was an important cultural manifestation of the midtwenties. With Harlem as its center, the Renaissance was an upsurge of new racial attitudes and ideals and an artistic and political awakening on the part of black Americans. Harlem writers and artists were, like their white counterparts, in quest of new images, forms, and techniques. They too were skeptical and disillusioned. What chiefly differentiated them, however, was their view of artistic endeavor as an extension of the struggle against oppression.

Little magazines like *The Crisis* and *Opportunity* published the Harlem writers, including Langston Hughes, Claude McKay, Countee Cullen, Jean Toomer, Arna Bontemps, and James Weldon Johnson. Writing in both free and conventional verse, the Harlem poets expressed racial pride more boldly than their predecessors, affirming their African heritage.

Jazz rhythms, images from big-city life (Harlem's in particular), and themes from history and folklore were found in the works of the Harlem poets, several of whom, like Jean Toomer, were also novelists. Blues and jazz suggested motifs and verse patterns for Langston Hughes's first book, *The Weary Blues* (1926). In such novels as *Jonah's Gourd Vine* (1934), the anthropologist-novelist Zora Neale Hurston used the folkways of blacks in rural Florida to challenge the extreme materialism of the modern temper.

FACTUAL PROSE

The factual prose that rounds out this unit covers a range of topics. Eudora Welty reveals how her mother and father shaped her art in a selection from *One Writer's Beginnings*. James Thurber reflects on his college experiences with his characteristic ability to focus on humorous misfits. A speech delivered by the Grand Council Fire of American Indians makes a plea for fair representation of Native Americans in the teaching of American History. Aptly concluding an era that witnessed the advent of the Atomic Age is William Faulkner's Nobel Prize speech. To those who ask, "When will I be blown up?" Faulkner provides assurance . . . "Man will not merely endure; he will prevail."

THINKING ABOUT GRAPHIC AIDS
Using the Time Line

Use the time line on pages 404–405 to answer the following items.

1. Which time-line items indicate improved methods of communication and transportation?
2. How many years elapsed between the time of the first commercial radio broadcast and the first commercial television?
3. Which two time-line items represent advancements for women?
4. Which President was in office during the U.S. involvement in World War I?
5. Name two time-line items that directly resulted from U.S. involvement in World War II.

Willa Cather once wrote that for her the world broke in two in 1922. Although she never explained fully what she meant, she may have been referring to the fact that the old world she cherished—the world of the frontier struggle for survival on the Great Plains with all the old-fashioned values the struggle inspired—had given way to a new era dominated by World War I and the Jazz Age.

Born into a genteel, middle-class family in Virginia, Cather moved at age nine with her family to the awesome, empty prairies of frontier Nebraska. There she witnessed firsthand the brutalizing effects of pioneer life on civilized immigrants, forced literally to dig their sod houses out of the land itself and to coax a living out of a hostile—though hauntingly beautiful—environment.

The sensitive, impressionable Willa Cather observed and remembered the little town of Red Cloud, Nebraska, later memorializing it under a variety of names in a series of novels.

While studying at the University of Nebraska, Cather edited a literary magazine and wrote acidic play reviews for the Lincoln *State Journal.* In 1896, she moved to Pittsburgh. There, though busy as a journalist, Cather found time for her main interest, the writing of poems and stories. Her journalistic success and creative writing caught the attention of S. S. McClure, who hired her to come to New York to edit *McClure's,* a successful magazine of the day, famed for its exposés of American institutions.

As editor of *McClure's,* Cather had reached the peak of her profession with a notable career in journalism. But she directed her creative energies more and more into the writing of novels, beginning with *Alexander's Bridge* (1912). In *O Pioneers!* (1913) she fictionalized her Nebraska experiences and memories. With *My Ántonia* (1918) she achieved her first popular success in a novel now widely recognized as her masterpiece. Its nostalgic remembrance of the early Nebraska pioneer days has haunted readers ever since its appearance.

After *My Ántonia,* Cather devoted her career totally to literature, writing an impressive series of novels, including the Pulitzer prizewinning novel, *One of Ours,* (1922), *A Lost Lady* (1923), *The Professor's House* (1925), and *Death Comes for the Archbishop* (1927). In later years her writing lost some of its passionate intensity but none of its lyric simplicity. When she died in 1947, she was recognized as a major figure in modern American literature.

A Wagner Matinée

Willa Cather

received one morning a letter, written in pale ink on glassy, blue-lined notepaper, and bearing the postmark of a little Nebraska village. This communication, worn and rubbed, looking as if it had been carried for some days in a coat pocket that was none too clean, was from my uncle Howard, and informed me that his wife had been left a small legacy by a bachelor relative, and that it would be necessary for her to go to Boston to attend to the settling of the estate. He requested me to meet her at the station and render her whatever services might be necessary. On examining the date indicated as that of her arrival, I found it to be no later than tomorrow. He had characteristically delayed writing until, had I been away from home for a day, I must have missed my aunt altogether.

The name of my Aunt Georgiana opened before me a gulf of recollection so wide and deep that, as the letter dropped from my hand, I felt suddenly a stranger to all the present conditions of my existence, wholly ill at ease and out of place amid the familiar surroundings of my study. I became, in short, the gangling farmer boy my aunt had known, scourged with chilblains and bashfulness, my hands cracked and sore from the cornhusking. I sat again before her parlor organ, fumbling the scales with my stiff, red fingers, while she, beside me, made canvas mittens for the huskers.

The next morning, after preparing my landlady for a visitor, I set out for the station. When the train arrived, I had some difficulty in finding my aunt. She was the last of the passengers to alight, and it was not until I got her into the carriage that she seemed really to recognize me. She had come all the way in a day coach; her linen duster had become black with soot and her black bonnet gray with dust during the journey. When we arrived at my boardinghouse, the landlady put her to bed at once and I did not see her again until the next morning.

Whatever shock Mrs. Springer experienced at my aunt's appearance, she considerately concealed. As for myself, I saw my aunt's battered figure with that feeling of awe and respect with which we behold explorers who have left their ears and fingers north of Franz Josef Land,[1] or their health somewhere along the Upper Congo. My Aunt Georgiana had been a music teacher at the Boston Conservatory, somewhere back in the latter sixties. One summer, while visiting in the little village among the Green Mountains where her ancestors had dwelt for generations, she had kindled the callow fancy of my uncle, Howard Carpenter, then an idle, shiftless boy of twenty-one. When she returned to her duties in Boston, Howard followed her, and the upshot of this infatuation was that she eloped with him, eluding the reproaches of her family and the criticism of her friends by going with him to the Nebraska frontier. Carpenter, who, of course, had no money, took up a homestead in Red Willow County, fifty miles from the railroad. There they had measured off their land themselves, driving across the prairie in a wagon, to the wheel of which they had tied a red cotton handkerchief, and counting its revolutions. They built a dugout in the red hillside, one of those cave dwellings whose inmates so often reverted to primitive conditions. Their water they got from the lagoons where the buffalo drank, and their slender stock of provisions was always at the mercy of bands of roving Indians. For thirty years my aunt had not

---

Wagner (väg′nər), 1813–1883, German composer.

1. *Franz Josef Land,* Arctic archipelago of about eighty islands, uninhabited and mostly ice-covered.

been farther than fifty miles from the homestead.

I owed to this woman most of the good that ever came my way in my boyhood, and had a reverential affection for her. During the years when I was riding herd for my uncle, my aunt, after cooking the three meals—the first of which was ready at six o'clock in the morning—and putting the six children to bed, would often stand until midnight at her ironing board, with me at the kitchen table beside her, hearing me recite Latin declensions and conjugations, gently shaking me when my drowsy head sank down over a page of irregular verbs. It was to her, at her ironing or mending, that I read my first Shakespeare, and her old textbook on mythology was the first that ever came into my empty hands. She taught me my scales and exercises on the little parlor organ which her husband had bought her after fifteen years during which she had not so much as seen a musical instrument. She would sit beside me by the hour, darning and counting, while I struggled with the "Joyous Farmer." She seldom talked to me about music, and I understood why. Once when I had been doggedly beating out some easy passages from an old score of *Euryanthe*[2] I had found among her music books, she came up to me and, putting her hands over my eyes, gently drew my head back upon her shoulder, saying tremulously, "Don't love it so well, Clark, or it may be taken from you."

When my aunt appeared on the morning after her arrival in Boston, she was still in a semisomnambulant state. She seemed not to realize that she was in the city where she had spent her youth, the place longed for hungrily half a lifetime. She had been so wretchedly trainsick throughout the journey that she had no recollection of anything but her discomfort and, to all intents and purposes, there were but a few hours of nightmare between the farm in Red Willow County and my study on Newbury Street. I had planned a little pleasure for her that afternoon, to repay her for some of the glorious moments she had given me when we used to milk together in the straw-thatched cowshed and she, because I was more than usually tired, or because her husband had

spoken sharply to me, would tell me of the splendid performance of the *Huguenots*[3] she had seen in Paris, in her youth.

At two o'clock the Symphony Orchestra was to give a Wagner program, and I intended to take my aunt; though as I conversed with her, I grew doubtful about her enjoyment of it. I suggested our visiting the Conservatory and the Common before lunch, but she seemed altogether too timid to wish to venture out. She questioned me absently about various changes in the city, but she was chiefly concerned that she had forgotten to leave instructions about feeding half-skimmed milk to a certain weakling calf, "old Maggie's calf, you know, Clark," she explained, evidently having forgotten how long I had been away. She was further troubled because she had neglected to tell her daughter about the freshly-opened kit of mackerel in the cellar, which would spoil if it were not used directly.

I asked her whether she had ever heard any of the Wagnerian operas, and found that she had not, though she was perfectly familiar with their respective situations, and had once possessed the piano score of the *The Flying Dutchman*.[4] I began to think it would be best to get her back to Red Willow County without waking her, and regretted having suggested the concert.

From the time we entered the concert hall, however, she was a trifle less passive and inert, and for the first time seemed to perceive her surroundings. I had felt some trepidation lest she might become aware of her queer, country clothes, or might experience some painful embarrassment at stepping suddenly into the world to which she had been dead for a quarter of a century. But, again, I found how superficially I had judged her. She sat looking about her with eyes as impersonal, almost as stony, as those with which the granite Rameses in a museum watches the froth and fret that ebbs and flows

---

2. *Euryanthe* (oi′rē än′tə).
3. *Huguenots* (hyü′gə nots).
4. *The Flying Dutchman,* an early opera by Wagner.

John Singer Sargent, *Rehearsal of the Pasdeloup Orchestra at the Cirque d'Hiver* (1876).
Museum of Fine Arts, Boston

about his pedestal. I have seen this same aloofness in old miners who drift into the Brown Hotel at Denver, their pockets full of bullion, their linen soiled, their haggard faces unshaven; standing in the thronged corridors as solitary as though they were still in a frozen camp on the Yukon.

The matinée audience was made up chiefly of women. One lost the contour of faces and figures, indeed any effect of line whatever, and there was only the color of bodices past counting, the shimmer of fabrics soft and firm, silky and sheer; red, mauve, pink, blue, lilac, purple, écru, rose, yellow, cream, and white, all the colors that an impressionist finds in a sunlit landscape, with here and there the dead shadow of a frock coat. My Aunt Georgiana regarded them as though they had been so many daubs of tube paint on a palette.

When the musicians came out and took their places, she gave a little stir of anticipation, and looked with quickening interest down over the rail at that invariable grouping, perhaps the first wholly familiar thing that had greeted her eye since she had left old Maggie and her weakling calf. I could feel how all those details sank into her soul, for I had not forgotten how they had sunk into mine when I came fresh from ploughing forever and forever between green aisles of corn, where, as in a treadmill, one might walk from daybreak to dusk without perceiving a shadow of change. The clean profiles of the musicians, the gloss of their linen, the dull black of their coats, the beloved shapes of the instruments, the patches of yellow light on the smooth, varnished bellies of the 'cellos and the bass viols in the rear, the restless, wind-tossed forest of fiddle necks and bows—I recalled how, in the first orchestra I ever heard, those long bow strokes seemed to draw the heart out of me, as a conjurer's stick reels out yards of paper ribbon from a hat.

The first number was the *Tannhäuser*[5] overture. When the horns drew out the first strain of the Pilgrim's chorus, Aunt Georgiana clutched my coat sleeve. Then it was I first realized that

for her this broke a silence of thirty years. With the battle between the two motives, with the frenzy of the Venusberg theme and its ripping of strings, there came to me an overwhelming sense of the waste and wear we are so powerless to combat; and I saw again the tall, naked house on the prairie, black and grim as a wooden fortress; the black pond where I had learned to swim, its margin pitted with sun-dried cattle tracks; the rain gullied clay banks about the naked house; the four dwarf ash seedlings where the dishcloths were always hung to dry before the kitchen door. The world there was the flat world of the ancients; to the east, a cornfield that stretched to daybreak; to the west, a corral that reached to sunset; between, the conquests of peace, dearer bought than those of war.

The overture closed, my aunt released my coat sleeve, but she said nothing. She sat staring dully at the orchestra. What, I wondered, did she get from it? She had been a good pianist in her day, I knew, and her musical education had been broader than that of most music teachers of a quarter of a century ago. She had often told me of Mozart's operas and Meyerbeer's, and I could remember hearing her sing, years ago, certain melodies of Verdi.[6] When I had fallen ill with a fever in her house, she used to sit by my cot in the evening—when the cool, night wind blew in through the faded mosquito netting tacked over the window and I lay watching a certain bright star that burned red above the cornfield—and sing "Home to our mountains, O, let us return!" in a way fit to break the heart of a Vermont boy near dead of homesickness already.

I watched her closely through the prelude to *Tristan and Isolde*,[7] trying vainly to conjecture what that seething turmoil of strings and winds might mean to her, but she sat mutely staring at

5. *Tannhäuser* (tän'hoi zər).
6. *Mozart . . . Meyerbeer . . . Verdi,* Mozart (mōt'särt), 1756–1791, Austrian composer; Meyerbeer (mī'ər bir), 1791–1864, German composer of opera; Verdi (ver'dē), 1813–1901, Italian composer of opera.
7. *Tristan and Isolde* (tris'tən, i sōl'də), an opera by Wagner in which the title characters are lovers.

the violin bows that drove obliquely downward, like the pelting streaks of rain in a summer shower. Had this music any message for her? Had she enough left to at all comprehend this power which had kindled the world since she had left it? I was in a fever of curiosity, but Aunt Georgiana sat silent upon her peak in Darien.[8] She preserved this utter immobility throughout the number from *The Flying Dutchman*, though her fingers worked mechanically upon her black dress, as if, of themselves, they were recalling the piano score they had once played. Poor hands! They had been stretched and twisted into mere tentacles to hold and lift and knead with—on one of them a thin, worn band that had once been a wedding ring. As I pressed and gently quieted one of those groping hands, I remembered with quivering eyelids their services for me in other days.

Soon after the tenor began the "Prize Song," I heard a quick drawn breath and turned to my aunt. Her eyes were closed, but the tears were glistening on her cheeks, and I think, in a moment more, they were in my eyes as well. It never really died, then—the soul which can suffer so excruciatingly and so interminably; it withers to the outward eye only; like that strange moss which can lie on a dusty shelf half a century and yet, if placed in water, grows green again. She wept so throughout the development and elaboration of the melody.

During the intermission before the second half, I questioned my aunt and found that the "Prize Song" was not new to her. Some years before there had drifted to the farm in Red Willow County a young German, a tramp cowpuncher, who had sung in the chorus at Bayreuth[9] when he was a boy, along with the other peasant boys and girls. Of a Sunday morning he used to sit on his gingham-sheeted bed in the hands' bedroom which opened off the kitchen, cleaning the leather of his boots and saddle, singing the "Prize Song" while my aunt went about her work in the kitchen. She had hovered over him until she had prevailed upon him to join the country church, though his sole fitness for this step, in so far as I

could gather, lay in his boyish face and his possession of this divine melody. Shortly afterward, he had gone to town on the Fourth of July, been drunk for several days, lost his money at a faro table, ridden a saddled Texas steer on a bet, and disappeared with a fractured collarbone. All this my aunt told me huskily, wanderingly, as though she were talking in the weak lapses of illness.

"Well, we have come to better things than the old *Trovatore*[10] at any rate, Aunt Georgie?" I queried, with a well-meant effort at jocularity.

Her lips quivered and she hastily put her handkerchief up to her mouth. From behind it she murmured, "And you have been hearing this ever since you left me, Clark?" Her question was the gentlest and saddest of reproaches.

The second half of the program consisted of four numbers from the *Ring*, and closed with Siegfried's funeral march. My aunt wept quietly, but almost continuously, as a shallow vessel overflows in a rainstorm. From time to time her dim eyes looked up at the lights, burning softly under their dull glass globes.

The deluge of sound poured on and on; I never knew what she found in the shining current of it; I never knew how far it bore her, or past what happy islands. From the trembling of her face I could well believe that before the last number she had been carried out where the myriad graves are, into the gray, nameless burying grounds of the sea; or into some world of death vaster yet, where, from the beginning of the world, hope has lain down with hope and dream with dream and, renouncing, slept.

The concert was over; the people filed out of the hall chattering and laughing, glad to relax and find the living level again, but my kinswoman made no effort to rise. The harpist slipped the green felt cover over his instrument; the flute

---

8. *peak in Darien.* This phrase from the last line of John Keats's sonnet, "On First Looking into Chapman's Homer," refers to a mountain in Panama from which the Pacific was contemplated in silence and awe.

9. *Bayreuth* (bī′roit), town in Bavaria, Germany, which has been the home of the annual Richard Wagner Festival since 1876.

10. *Trovatore* (trō′və tôr′e).

Mary Cassatt (1845–1926), *Portrait of Miss Harriet Buchanan Dressed for the Matinée.*
Collection of Mr. and Mrs. R. Philip Hanes, Jr.

players shook the water from their mouthpieces; the men of the orchestra went out one by one, leaving the stage to the chairs and music stands, empty as a winter cornfield.

I spoke to my aunt. She burst into tears and sobbed pleadingly. "I don't want to go, Clark, I don't want to go!"

I understood. For her, just outside the concert hall, lay the black pond with the cattle-tracked bluffs; the tall, unpainted house, with weather-curled boards, naked as a tower; the crook-backed ash seedlings where the dishcloths hung to dry; the gaunt, molting turkeys picking up refuse about the kitchen door.   1904

THINK AND DISCUSS
Understanding
1. For what reason does the narrator's aunt leave her "little Nebraska village" to travel to Boston? What is the narrator requested to do in the letter he receives?
2. Why did the narrator's aunt originally move from Boston to Nebraska?
3. What was the aunt's occupation before she moved to Nebraska? How did she occupy herself after the move?

Analyzing
4. The boy's aunt has said of his music, "Don't love it so well, Clark, or it may be taken from you." Why is this statement significant in this story?
5. At the Wagner matinée, the narrator finally realizes that the music is affecting his aunt deeply. How does he know? What is his reaction?
6. How would you **characterize** the aunt? What details serve to reveal her character?

Extending
7. Imagine that you had to move from your hometown and live for an extended period of time in a foreign country. What would you miss most?

COMPOSITION
Being a Story Character
Assume that you are Aunt Georgiana. Write a letter of three or four paragraphs to your husband explaining what has happened to you and why you have decided to stay an extra week in Boston. At the end of the letter, remind your husband to take care of those things that worried you on arrival. Be sure to observe proper letter form and punctuation in writing your friendly letter.

Analyzing Imagery
Central to this story is the contrast between the Nebraska homestead and life in Boston. Write a composition of at least three paragraphs for your classmates in which you analyze Cather's use of imagery to describe setting in this story. Note particularly the final paragraph of the story and the paragraph describing the narrator and his aunt listening to the overture. These and other passages evoke Georgiana's life in Nebraska. Images that relate to Boston appear in descriptions of the matinée audience and the musicians and their instruments.

For some readers, a story like Sherwood Anderson's "Sophistication" can be baffling and unsatisfying. Traditional stories, such as those by James Fenimore Cooper or Washington Irving, present clear conflicts that are resolved in narratives organized with clear beginnings, middles, and ends. Many modern short stories, however, do not conform to this pattern. Instead, they focus on the psychological development of characters within a more loosely constructed plot structure. By following a few simple guidelines, a reader can more easily understand and appreciate a modern short story.

Determine the plot. The **plot** is the pattern that depicts the events of the story. As you look for the plot, determine the main conflict and find the resolution, if any. In "Sophistication," the plot is not presented in step-by-step chronological order. A **flashback** reviews an early walk that George and Helen had taken in the summer; and much of the "action" is actually the characters' inner feelings and thoughts.

Examine the characterizations in the story. Look at how the characters are revealed. In modern short stories, **characterization** is often presented through a character's feelings or thoughts. In "Sophistication," George is characterized as isolated within the crowd. Helen's inner thoughts reveal her struggles against her mother's expectations, and her growing sense of independence.

Analyze the theme of the story, and its relation to the title. In "Sophistication," George becomes aware of the limitations of life and at the same time crosses the line into adulthood. In this sense, he becomes "sophisticated," or more worldly.

Recognize from what point of view the story is told. Note who the narrator is and the vantage point that the story is being told from. "Sophistication" is told from a third-person omniscient **point of view**. Through the information presented by the omniscient narrator, the reader has the opportunity to empathize with a boy and girl poised on the brink of adulthood.

Be on the alert for details, images, and symbols that reinforce the meaning. Sometimes, these details are integral parts of the story's **setting.** An important piece of information is conveyed in the first sentence of "Sophistication." The season is late fall. Not only is it near the conclusion of a calendar year, but it is symbolically the conclusion of childhood in the lives of George and Helen. Linked to the change of seasons is the harvest motif. George sees himself as "merely a leaf blown by the wind . . . a thing destined like corn to wilt in the sun." Like the corn, George and Helen are about to go out into the world, separated from the families that have nurtured them. The small-town, rural setting of "Sophistication" serves to reinforce the story's theme.

Determine any cause-effect relationships that exist in the story. In any pattern of action, just as events are related to one another in time and place, they are also related in terms of *cause and effect.* In tightly woven stories, most events can be traced to other events that have caused them. For example, George's increasing maturity in "Sophistication" is to some extent due to the death of his mother.

As you read, look for effects that result from important acts or events. Do not be concerned if clue words such as *because, if, then, since, therefore,* and *consequently* do not appear in a story to spell out certain cause-and-effect relationships. You can still understand causes by asking yourself why some event happened, and effects by considering what is likely to occur as a result of the event at hand.

Some of the stories in this unit illustrate characteristics of the modern short story; others are more traditional. As you read, look for elements of plot and character that reflect one or the other of these traditions.

Sherwood Anderson was one of a large number of writers in revolt against both the subject matter and form of older stories. Many such writers reflected in their portrayal of characters the descriptions and theories of the new psychology, which was causing people to view human motivation and behavior in a new light. Anderson and his contemporaries exhibited in their styles the plainness, simplicity, and directness characteristic of the earlier experiments in prose by Gertrude Stein, an American expatriot living in Paris.

Anderson's volume of interrelated short stories, *Winesburg, Ohio* (1919), marked a radical change in the American short story in content and style. The work, which opens with "The Book of the Grotesque," portrays ordinary people psychologically warped by their desperately lonely lives in small-town America. Omitting the structure of a traditional plot, which included a climax, Anderson's stories appear rather formless, concentrating on little moments that bring life into sharp focus for the characters. Such moments, seen in "Sophistication," are rendered in a spare style that works a magic in evoking sympathy in a reader.

Anderson knew small-town America well. He grew up in Clyde, Ohio, working at odd jobs ranging from errand boy to stable groom. His father, a wandering house painter and harness maker, never made much money but was an entertaining storyteller and amateur actor. From him, and from a literary idol, Mark Twain, young Anderson learned to use the rhythms of the oral story, an ability that later enabled him to achieve in his writings a deceptively unstudied air of reminiscence.

At the age of fourteen, Anderson quit school. For over twenty years he worked at various jobs both in Clyde and in Chicago, served in the Spanish-American War, returned to school, became a writer of advertising copy, and finally established a manufacturing company specializing in roof paint.

He was thirty-six years old when, married and the father of three children, he suddenly left his factory and departed for Chicago, determined to devote his life to writing. Chicago, at that time, was the scene of a new ferment in the arts—the "Chicago Renaissance," led by Carl Sandburg, Edgar Lee Masters, Vachel Lindsay, and others. Although he was forced to write advertising copy for a living, Anderson joined this circle of writers and honed his craft. Despite his many books, Anderson's most enduring work is *Winesburg, Ohio*. Its frustrated small-town people still speak to later generations confronting the loneliness of urban crowds. With the book's appearance in 1919, the American short story was suddenly opened to new possibilities in subject and form.

Sophistication

Sherwood Anderson

 t was early evening of a day in the late fall and the Winesburg County Fair had brought crowds of country people into town. The day had been clear and the night came on warm and pleasant. On the Trunion Pike, where the road after it left town stretched away between berry fields now covered with dry brown leaves, the dust from passing wagons arose in clouds. Children, curled into little balls, slept on the straw scattered on wagon beds. Their hair was full of dust and their fingers black and sticky. The dust rolled away over the fields and the departing sun set it ablaze with colors.

In the main street of Winesburg, crowds filled the stores and the sidewalks. Night came on, horses whinnied, the clerks in the stores ran madly about, children became lost and cried lustily, an American town worked terribly at the task of amusing itself.

Pushing his way through the crowds in Main Street, young George Willard concealed himself in the stairway leading to Doctor Reefy's office and looked at the people. With feverish eyes he watched the faces drifting past under the store lights. Thoughts kept coming into his head, and he did not want to think. He stamped impatiently on the wooden steps and looked sharply about. "Well, is she going to stay with him all day? Have I done all this waiting for nothing?" he muttered.

George Willard, the Ohio village boy, was fast growing into manhood, and new thoughts had been coming into his mind. All that day, amid the jam of people at the Fair, he had gone about feeling lonely. He was about to leave Winesburg to go away to some city where he hoped to get work on a city newspaper and he felt grown-up. The mood that had taken possession of him was a thing known to men and unknown to boys. He felt old and a little tired. Memories awoke in him. To his mind his new sense of maturity set him apart, made of him a half-tragic figure. He wanted someone to understand the feeling that had taken possession of him after his mother's death.

There is a time in the life of every boy when he for the first time takes the backward view of life. Perhaps that is the moment when he crosses the line into manhood. The boy is walking through the street of his town. He is thinking of the future and of the figure he will cut in the world. Ambitions and regrets awake within him. Suddenly something happens; he stops under a tree and waits as for a voice calling his name. Ghosts of old things creep into his consciousness; the voices outside of himself whisper a message concerning the limitations of life. From being quite sure of himself and his future he becomes not at all sure. If he be an imaginative boy a door is torn open and for the first time he looks out upon the world, seeing, as though they marched in procession before him, the countless figures of men who before his time have come out of nothingness into the world, lived their lives and

"Sophistication," *Winesburg, Ohio* by Sherwood Anderson. Copyright 1919 by B. W. Huebsch, Inc. Copyright renewed 1947 by Eleanor Oppenhaver Anderson. All rights reserved. Reprinted by permission of Viking Penguin Inc. Slightly abridged.

again disappeared into nothingness. The sadness of sophistication has come to the boy. With a little gasp he sees himself as merely a leaf blown by the wind through the streets of his village. He knows that in spite of all the stout talk of his fellows he must live and die in uncertainty, a thing blown by the winds, a thing destined like corn to wilt in the sun. He shivers and looks eagerly about. The eighteen years he has lived seem but a moment, a breathing space in the long march of humanity. Already he hears death calling. With all his heart he wants to come close to some other human, touch someone with his hands, be touched by the hand of another. If he prefers that the other be a woman, that is because he believes that a woman will be gentle, that she will understand. He wants, most of all, understanding.

When the moment of sophistication came to George Willard, his mind turned to Helen White, the Winesburg banker's daughter. Always he had been conscious of the girl growing into womanhood as he grew into manhood. Once on a summer night when he was eighteen, he had walked with her on a country road and in her presence had given way to an impulse to boast, to make himself appear big and significant in her eyes. Now he wanted to see her for another purpose. He wanted to tell her of the new impulses that had come to him. He had tried to make her think of him as a man when he knew nothing of manhood, and now he wanted to be with her and to try to make her feel the change he believed had taken place in his nature.

As for Helen White, she also had come to a period of change. What George felt, she in her young woman's way felt also. She was no longer a girl and hungered to reach into the grace and beauty of womanhood. She had come home from Cleveland, where she was attending college, to spend a day at the Fair. She also had begun to have memories. During the day she sat in the grandstand with a young man, one of the instructors from the college, who was a guest of her mother's. The young man was of a pedantic turn of mind, and she felt at once he would not do

for her purpose. At the Fair she was glad to be seen in his company as he was well dressed and a stranger. She knew that the fact of his presence would create an impression. During the day she was happy, but when night came on she began to grow restless. She wanted to drive the instructor away, to get out of his presence. While they sat together in the grandstand and while the eyes of former schoolmates were upon them, she paid so much attention to her escort that he grew interested. "A scholar needs money. I should marry a woman with money," he mused.

Helen White was thinking of George Willard even as he wandered gloomily through the crowds thinking of her. She remembered the summer evening when they had walked together and wanted to walk with him again. She thought that the months she had spent in the city, the going to theaters and the seeing of great crowds wandering in lighted thoroughfares, had changed her profoundly. She wanted him to feel and be conscious of the change in her nature.

The summer evening together that had left its mark on the memory of both the young man and woman had, when looked at quite sensibly, been rather stupidly spent. They had walked out of town along a country road. Then they had stopped by a fence near a field of young corn, and George had taken off his coat and let it hang on his arm. "Well, I've stayed here in Winesburg—yes—I've not yet gone away but I'm growing up," he had said. "I've been reading books and I've been thinking. I'm going to try to amount to something in life."

"Well," he explained, "that isn't the point. Perhaps I'd better quit talking."

The confused boy put his hand on the girl's arm. His voice trembled. The two started to walk back along the road toward town. In his desperation George boasted, "I'm going to be a big man, the biggest that ever lived here in Winesburg," he declared. "I want you to do something, I don't know what. Perhaps it is none of my business. I want you to try to be different from other women. You see the point. It's none of my business, I tell you. I want you to be a beautiful woman.

Tom Heflin, *The Meeting Place* (1976).
Private collection

You see what I want."

The boy's voice failed and in silence the two came back into town and went along the street to Helen White's house. At the gate he tried to say something impressive. Speeches he had thought out came into his head, but they seemed utterly pointless. "I thought—I used to think—I had it in my mind you would marry Seth Richmond. Now I know you won't," was all he could find to say as she went through the gate and toward the door of her house.

On the warm fall evening as he stood in the stairway and looked at the crowd drifting through Main Street, George thought of the talk beside the field of young corn and was ashamed of the figure he had made of himself. In the street the people surged up and down like cattle confined in a pen. Buggies and wagons almost filled the narrow thoroughfare. A band played and small boys raced along the sidewalk, diving between the legs of men. Young men with shining red faces walked awkwardly about with girls on their arms. In a room above one of the stores, where a dance was to be held, the fiddlers tuned their instruments. The broken sounds floated down through an open window and out across the murmur of voices and the loud blare of the horns of the band. The medley of sounds got on young Willard's nerves. Everywhere, on all sides, the sense of crowding, moving life closed in about him. He wanted to run away by himself and think. "If she wants to stay with that fellow she may. Why should I care? What difference does it make to me?" he growled and went along Main Street and through Hern's grocery into a side street.

George felt so utterly lonely and dejected that he wanted to weep, but pride made him walk rapidly along, swinging his arms. He came to Westley Moyer's livery barn and stopped in the shadows to listen to a group of men who talked of a race Westley's stallion, Tony Tip, had won at the Fair during the afternoon. A crowd had gathered in front of the barn, and before the crowd walked Westley, prancing up and down and boasting. He held a whip in his hand and kept tapping the ground. Little puffs of dust arose in the lamplight. "Quit your talking," Westley exclaimed. "I wasn't afraid, I knew I had 'em beat all the time. I wasn't afraid."

Ordinarily George Willard would have been intensely interested in the boasting of Moyer, the horseman. Now it made him angry. He turned and hurried away along the street. "Old windbag," he sputtered. "Why does he want to be bragging? Why don't he shut up?"

George went into a vacant lot and as he hurried along, fell over a pile of rubbish. A nail protruding from an empty barrel tore his trousers. He sat down on the ground and swore. With a pin he mended the torn place and then arose and went on. "I'll go to Helen White's house, that's what I'll do. I'll walk right in. I'll say that I want to see her. I'll walk right in and sit down, that's what I'll do," he declared, climbing over a fence and beginning to run.

On the veranda of Banker White's house Helen was restless and distraught. The instructor sat between the mother and daughter. His talk wearied the girl. Although he had also been raised in an Ohio town, the instructor began to put on the airs of the city. He wanted to appear cosmopolitan. "I like the chance you have given me to study the background out of which most of our girls come," he declared. "It was good of you, Mrs. White, to have me down for the day." He turned to Helen and laughed. "Your life is still bound up with the life of this town?" he asked. "There are people here in whom you are interested?" To the girl his voice sounded pompous and heavy.

Helen arose and went into the house. At the door leading to a garden at the back she stopped and stood listening. Her mother began to talk. "There is no one here fit to associate with a girl of Helen's breeding," she said.

Helen ran down a flight of stairs at the back of the house and into the garden. In the darkness she stopped and stood trembling. It seemed to her that the world was full of meaningless people saying words. Afire with eagerness she ran through a garden gate and turning a corner by the banker's barn, went into a little side street. "George! Where are you, George?" she cried, filled with nervous excitement. She stopped running, and leaned against a tree to laugh hysterically. Along the dark little street came George Willard, still saying words. "I'm going to walk right into her house. I'll go right in and sit down," he declared as he came up to her. He stopped and stared stupidly. "Come on," he said and took hold of her hand. With hanging heads they walked along the street under the trees. Dry leaves rustled under foot. Now that he had found her George wondered what he had better do and say.

At the upper end of the fairground, in Winesburg, there is a half-decayed old grandstand. It has never been painted and the boards are all warped out of shape. The fairground stands on top of a low hill rising out of the valley of Wine Creek, and from the grandstand one can see at night, over a cornfield, the lights of the town reflected against the sky.

George and Helen climbed the hill to the fairground, coming by the path past Waterworks Pond. The feeling of loneliness and isolation that had come to the young man in the crowded streets of his town was both broken and intensified by the presence of Helen. What he felt was reflected in her.

In youth there are always two forces fighting in people. The warm unthinking little animal struggles against the thing that reflects and remembers, and the older, the more sophisticated thing had possession of George Willard. Sensing his mood, Helen walked beside him filled with respect. When they got to the grandstand they climbed up under the roof and sat down on one of the long bench-like seats.

There is something memorable in the experience to be had by going into a fairground that stands at the edge of a Middle Western town on a night after the annual fair has been held. The sensation is one never to be forgotten. On all sides are ghosts, not of the dead, but of living people. Here, during the day just passed, have come the people pouring in from the town and the country around. Farmers with their wives and children and all the people from the hundreds of little frame houses have gathered within these board walls. Young girls have laughed and men with beards have talked of the affairs of their lives. The place has been filled to overflowing with life. It has itched and squirmed with life and now it is night and the life has all gone away. The silence is almost terrifying. One conceals oneself standing silently beside the trunk of a tree and what there is of a reflective tendency in his nature is intensified. One shudders at the thought of the meaninglessness of life while at the same instant, and if the people of the town are his people, one loves life so intensely that tears come into the eyes.

In the darkness under the roof of the grandstand, George Willard sat beside Helen White and felt very keenly his own insignificance in the scheme of existence. Now that he had come out of town where the presence of the people stirring about, busy with a multitude of affairs, had been so irritating the irritation was all gone. The presence of Helen renewed and refreshed him. It was as though her woman's hand was assisting him to make some minute readjustment of the machinery of his life. He began to think of the people in the town where he had always lived with something like reverence. He had reverence for Helen. He wanted to love and to be loved by her, but he did not want at the moment to be confused by her womanhood. In the darkness he took hold of her hand and when she crept close put a hand on her shoulder. A wind began to blow and he shivered. With all his strength he tried to hold and to understand the mood that had come upon him. In that high place in the darkness the two oddly sensitive human atoms held each other tightly and waited. In the mind of each was the same thought. "I have come to this lonely place and here is this other," was the substance of the thing felt.

In Winesburg the crowded day had run itself out into the long night of the late fall. Farm horses jogged away along lonely country roads pulling their portion of weary people. Clerks began to bring samples of goods in off the sidewalks and lock the doors of stores. In the Opera House a crowd had gathered to see a show, and further down Main Street the fiddlers, their instruments tuned, sweated and worked to keep the feet of youth flying over a dance floor.

In the darkness in the grandstand Helen White and George Willard remained silent. Now and then the spell that held them was broken and they turned and tried in the dim light to see into each other's eyes. They kissed but that impulse did not last. At the upper end of the fairground a half dozen men worked over horses that had raced during the afternoon. The men had built a fire and were heating kettles of water. Only their legs could be seen as they passed back and forth in the light. When the wind blew, the little flames of the fire danced crazily about.

George and Helen arose and walked away into the darkness. They went along a path past a field of corn that had not yet been cut. The wind whispered among the dry corn blades. For a moment during the walk back into town the spell that held them was broken. When they had come to the crest of Waterworks Hill they stopped by a tree and George again put his hands on the girl's shoulders. She embraced him eagerly and then again they drew quickly back from that impulse. They stopped kissing and stood a little apart. Mutual respect grew big in them. They were both embarrassed and to relieve their embarrassment dropped into the animalism of youth. They laughed and began to pull and haul at each other. In some way chastened and purified by the mood they had been in they became, not man and woman, not boy and girl, but excited little animals.

It was so they went down the hill. In the darkness they played like two splendid young things in a young world. Once, running swiftly forward, Helen tripped George and he fell. He squirmed and shouted. Shaking with laughter, he rolled down the hill. Helen ran after him. For just a moment she stopped in the darkness. There is no way of knowing what woman's thoughts went through her mind but, when the bottom of the hill was reached and she came up to the boy, she took his arm and walked beside him in dignified silence. For some reason they could not have explained they had both got from their silent evening together the thing needed. Man or boy, woman or girl, they had for a moment taken hold of the thing that makes the mature life of men and women in the modern world possible.

1919

THINK AND DISCUSS
Understanding
1. What annual event has just been held in the town where the story is set?
2. Why is George Willard planning to leave Winesburg?
3. How old is George? What personal tragedy has he recently experienced?
4. Where has Helen White spent the last few months?

Analyzing
5. Why does the boasting of Westley Moyers make George angry? What similar situation is Helen enduring at about the same time?
6. Before George and Helen encounter one another in the story, there is a **flashback** to an evening they had spent together during the summer a few months earlier. Contrast that experience with the walk that the two take on the evening of the conclusion of the

county fair. Why is George ashamed when he thinks back on that summer evening with Helen?

7. What is the **symbolic** significance of the season? How do the **images** of corn reinforce this symbolism?

8. Check the various definitions of *sophistication* in an unabridged dictionary and select one appropriate to this story. Explain the reasons for your choice.

Extending

9. The instructor asks Helen, "Your life is still bound up with the life of this town?" How has your home town—whether large or small, city, suburb, or rural area—affected you?

REVIEWING: Theme HT
See Handbook of Literary Terms, p. 914.

Although the theme, or underlying meaning of a work, can be directly stated, it is more often implied.

1. Reread the fifth paragraph of "Sophistication," which begins, "There is a time in the life of every boy. . . ." Paraphrase the paragraph in a single sentence of your own that states the theme of "Sophistication."

2. What images in this paragraph convey the sense of uncertainty and helplessness that accompany sophistication?

3. Think back over the stories and poems you have read in this book. Choose one and state its theme in a single sentence.

READING LITERATURE SKILLFULLY
Cause/Effect

A primary focus of Sherwood Anderson's "Sophistication" is George's behavior and the reasons for that behavior. Determining what event causes what behavior can help you understand both George and Helen. To identify cause and effect, first pinpoint the effect. Then look for the cause (or causes) of that effect. Keep in mind that just as an effect can have more than one cause, so an event can result in more than one effect.

1. What event has caused George to face the concept of death and his own mortality?

2. What does he realize about his likely effect on the world? What do these thoughts lead him to want from another human?

3. These realizations and desires culminate in action. What is George driven to do?

COMPOSITION
Writing About Theme

One of the most common themes in literature concerns a person's passage from innocence to experience, from childhood to maturity. Write an essay of at least three paragraphs about a story or book you have read or a movie you have seen that describes a person's entrance into adulthood. Your audience will be your classmates. In your essay, describe the character in his or her state of innocence, discuss the event or ordeal that marks the character's initiation into adulthood, and conclude with a description of the new wisdom or maturity that the character has gained. See "Writing About Theme" in the Writer's Handbook.

Comparing Two Stories

Anderson's stories marked a radical change from the more traditional works of writers like Edgar Allan Poe. In an essay of four or five paragraphs, compare and contrast the structure of "Sophistication" and "The Cask of Amontillado," page 151. Devise a thesis statement that focuses on the structural and thematic differences between the modern and the traditional short story in America. You might wish to review the article titled Reading a Modern Short Story, page 420. See "Writing About Plot and Plot Devices" in the Writer's Handbook.

BIOGRAPHY

Katherine Anne Porter
1890–1980

Although the body of her fiction is small, Katherine Anne Porter made a major contribution to the American short story. She once wrote that the "exercise of memory [is] the chief occupation of my mind. . . . Now and again thousands of memories converge, harmonize, arrange themselves around a central idea in a coherent form, and I write a story."

In 1941, while living in Baton Rouge, Porter was asked for an autobiographical sketch and responded in part as follows: "I was born at Indian Creek, Texas, brought up in Texas and Louisiana, and educated in small Southern convent schools. I was precocious, nervous, rebellious, unteachable, and made life very uncomfortable for myself and, I suppose, for those around me. As soon as I learned to form letters on paper, at about three years, I began to write stories, and this has been the basic and absorbing occupation, the intact line of my life which directs my actions, determines my point of view, and profoundly affects my character and personality, my social beliefs and economic status, and the kind of friendships I form. I did not choose this vocation, and if I had any say in the matter, I would not have chosen it. I made no attempt to publish anything until I was thirty, but I have written and destroyed manuscripts quite literally by the trunkful. I spent fifteen years wandering about, weighted horribly with masses of paper and little else. Yet for this vocation I was and am willing to live and die, and I consider very few other things of the slightest importance. . . ."

There are aspects of her life she does not touch upon. At the age of twenty-one she was working for a newspaper in Chicago; she later played bit parts in motion pictures, and still later went to Mexico to study Aztec and Mayan art, where she became involved in a revolution.

Porter's first published volume was *Flowering Judas and Other Stories*, which appeared in 1930. The stories, "The Jilting of Granny Weatherall" among them, were delicate and precise, sensitive and subtle. The years of preparation had paid off in a technical mastery of the art of impeccable writing. The important place Porter has won for herself among contemporary American writers is based on a comparatively small total output. A slow writer, she produced only a few books in the more than forty years after *Flowering Judas* was first published. Furthermore, some of her works experienced substantial delays in publication because of the exacting care that went into her writing. Her first and only novel, *Ship of Fools*, was begun in 1940 and did not reach completion until 1962. She called it the "hardest thing I ever did in my life."

In 1966 Porter won both the National Book Award and the Pulitzer Prize for *The Collected Short Stories of Katherine Anne Porter*.

HT See STREAM OF CONSCIOUSNESS in the
Handbook of Literary Terms, page 911.

The Jilting of Granny Weatherall

Katherine Anne Porter

She flicked her wrist neatly out of Doctor Harry's pudgy careful fingers and pulled the sheet up to her chin. The brat ought to be in knee breeches. Doctoring around the country with spectacles on his nose! "Get along now, take your schoolbooks and go. There's nothing wrong with me."

Doctor Harry spread a warm paw like a cushion on her forehead where the forked green vein danced and made her eyelids twitch. "Now, now, be a good girl, and we'll have you up in no time."

"That's no way to speak to a woman nearly eighty years old just because she's down. I'd have you respect your elders, young man."

"Well, Missy, excuse me." Doctor Harry patted her cheek. "But I've got to warn you, haven't I? You're a marvel, but you must be careful or you're going to be good and sorry."

"Don't tell me what I'm going to be. I'm on my feet now, morally speaking. It's Cornelia. I had to go to bed to get rid of her."

Her bones felt loose, and floated around in her skin, and Doctor Harry floated like a balloon around the foot of the bed. He floated and pulled down his waistcoat and swung his glasses on a cord. "Well, stay where you are, it certainly can't hurt you."

"Get along and doctor your sick," said Granny Weatherall. "Leave a well woman alone. I'll call for you when I want you. . . . Where were you forty years ago when I pulled through milkleg and double pneumonia? You weren't even born. Don't let Cornelia lead you on," she shouted,

because Doctor Harry appeared to float up to the ceiling and out. "I pay my own bills, and I don't throw my money away on nonsense!"

She meant to wave good-by, but it was too much trouble. Her eyes closed of themselves, it was like a dark curtain drawn around the bed. The pillow rose and floated under her, pleasant as a hammock in a light wind. She listened to the leaves rustling outside the window. No, somebody was swishing newspapers; no, Cornelia and Doctor Harry were whispering together. She leaped broad awake, thinking they whispered in her ear.

"She was never like this, *never* like this!" "Well, what can we expect?" "Yes, eighty years old. . . ."

Well, and what if she was? She still had ears. It was like Cornelia to whisper around doors. She always kept things secret in such a public way. She was always being tactful and kind. Cornelia was dutiful; that was the trouble with her. Dutiful and good: "So good and dutiful," said Granny, "that I'd like to spank her." She saw herself spanking Cornelia and making a fine job of it.

"What'd you say, Mother?" Granny felt her face tying up in hard knots. "Can't a body think, I'd like to know?"

"The Jilting of Granny Weatherall." Copyright 1930, 1958 by Katherine Anne Porter. Reprinted from her volume *Flowering Judas and Other Stories* (British title, *The Collected Stories of Katherine Anne Porter*) by permission of Harcourt Brace Jovanovich, Inc. and Jonathan Cape Ltd.

"I thought you might want something."

"I do. I want a lot of things. First off, go away and don't whisper."

She lay and drowsed, hoping in her sleep that the children would keep out and let her rest a minute. It had been a long day. Not that she was tired. It was always pleasant to snatch a minute now and then. There was always so much to be done, let me see: tomorrow.

Tomorrow was far away and there was nothing to trouble about. Things were finished somehow when the time came; thank God there was always a little margin over for peace: then a person could spread out the plan of life and tuck in the edges orderly. It was good to have everything clean and folded away, with the hair brushes and tonic bottles sitting straight on the white embroidered linen: the day started without fuss and the pantry shelves laid out with rows of jelly glasses and brown jugs and white stone-china jars with blue whirligigs and words painted on them: coffee, tea, sugar, ginger, cinnamon, allspice: and the bronze clock with the lion on top nicely dusted off. The dust that lion could collect in twenty-four hours! The box in the attic with all those letters tied up, well, she'd have to go through that tomorrow. All those letters—George's letters and John's letters and her letters to them both —lying around for the children to find afterward made her uneasy. Yes, that would be tomorrow's business. No use to let them know how silly she had been once.

While she was rummaging around, she found death in her mind and it felt clammy and unfamiliar. She had spent so much time preparing for death there was no need for bringing it up again. Let it take care of itself now. When she was sixty, she had felt very old, finished, and went around making farewell trips to see her children and grandchildren, with a secret in her mind: This is the very last of your mother, children! Then she made her will and came down with a long fever. That was all just a notion like a lot of other things, but it was lucky too, for she had once and for all got over the idea of dying for a long time. Now she couldn't be worried. She hoped she had better sense now. Her father had lived to be one hundred and two years old and had drunk a noggin of strong hot toddy on his last birthday. He told the reporters it was his daily habit, and he owed his long life to that. He had made quite a scandal and was very pleased about it. She believed she'd just plague Cornelia a little.

"Cornelia! Cornelia!" No footsteps, but a sudden hand on her cheek. "Bless you, where have you been?"

"Here, Mother."

"Well, Cornelia, I want a noggin of hot toddy."

"Are you cold, darling?"

"I'm chilly, Cornelia. Lying in bed stops the circulation. I must have told you that a thousand times."

Well, she could just hear Cornelia telling her husband that Mother was getting a little childish and they'd have to humor her. The thing that most annoyed her was that Cornelia thought she was deaf, dumb, and blind. Little hasty glances and tiny gestures tossed around her and over her head saying, "Don't cross her, let her have her way, she's eighty years old," and she sitting there as if she lived in a thin glass cage. Sometimes Granny almost made up her mind to pack up and move back to her own house where nobody could remind her every minute that she was old. Wait, wait, Cornelia, till your own children whisper behind your back!

In her day she had kept a better house and had got more work done. She wasn't too old yet for Lydia to be driving eighty miles for advice when one of the children jumped the track, and Jimmy still dropped in and talked things over: "Now, Mammy, you've a good business head, I want to know what you think of this? . . ." Old. Cornelia couldn't change the furniture around without asking. Little things, little things! They had been so sweet when they were little. Granny wished the old days were back again with the children young and everything to be done over. It had been a hard pull, but not too much for her. When she thought of all the food she had cooked, and all the clothes she had cut and sewed, and all the gardens she had made—well, the children showed it. There they were, made out of her, and they couldn't get away from that. Sometimes she wanted to see John again and point to them and say, Well, I didn't do so badly, did I? But that would have to wait. That was for tomorrow. She used to think of him as a man, but now all the children were older than their father, and he would be a child beside her if she saw him now. It seemed strange and there was something wrong in the idea. Why, he couldn't possibly recognize her. She had fenced in a hundred acres once, digging the postholes herself and clamping the wires with just a Negro boy to help. That changed a woman. John would be looking for a young woman with the peaked Spanish comb in her hair and the painted fan. Digging postholes changed a woman. Riding country roads in the winter when women had their babies was another thing: sitting up nights with sick horses and sick Negroes and sick children and hardly ever losing one. John, I hardly ever lost one of them! John would see that in a minute, that would be something he could understand, she wouldn't have to explain anything!

It made her feel like rolling up her sleeves and putting the whole place to rights again. No matter if Cornelia was determined to be everywhere at once, there were a great many things left undone on this place. She would start tomorrow and do them. It was good to be strong enough for everything, even if all you made melted and changed and slipped under your hands, so that by the time you finished you almost forgot what you were working for. What was it I set out to do? she asked herself intently, but she could not remember. A fog rose over the valley, she saw it marching across the creek swallowing the trees and moving up the hill like an army of ghosts. Soon it would be at the near edge of the orchard, and then it was time to go in and light the lamps. Come in, children, don't stay out in the night air.

Lighting the lamps had been beautiful. The children huddled up to her and breathed like little calves waiting at the bars in the twilight. Their eyes followed the match and watched the flame rise and settle in a blue curve, then they moved away from her. The lamp was lit, they didn't have to be scared and hang on to Mother anymore. Never, never, nevermore. God, for all my life I thank Thee. Without Thee, my God, I could never have done it. Hail, Mary, full of grace.[1]

I want you to pick all the fruit this year and see that nothing is wasted. There's always someone who can use it. Don't let good things rot for want of using. You waste life when you waste good food. Don't let things get lost. It's bitter to lose things. Now, don't let me get to thinking, not when I am tired and taking a little nap before supper. . . .

The pillow rose about her shoulders and pressed against her heart and the memory was being squeezed out of it: oh, push down the pillow, somebody: it would smother her if she tried to hold it. Such a fresh breeze blowing and such a green day with no threats in it. But he had not come, just the same. What does a woman do when she has put on the white veil and set out the white cake for a man and he doesn't come? She tried to remember. No, I swear he never harmed me but in that. He never harmed me but in that . . . and what if he did? There was the day, the day, but a whirl of dark smoke rose and covered it, crept up and over into the bright field where everything was planted so carefully in orderly rows. That was hell, she knew hell when she saw it. For sixty years she had prayed against remembering him and against losing her soul in the deep pit of hell, and now the two things were mingled in one and the thought of him was a smoky cloud from hell that moved and crept in her head when she had just got rid of Doctor Harry and was trying to rest a minute. Wounded vanity, Ellen, said a sharp voice in the top of her mind. Don't let your wounded vanity get the upper hand of you. Plenty of girls get jilted. You were jilted, weren't you? Then stand

---

1. *Hail, Mary, full of grace,* the opening line of a Catholic prayer.

Andrew Wyeth, *Beckie King* (1946). Dallas Museum of Fine Arts

up to it. Her eyelids wavered and let in streamers of blue-gray light like tissue paper over her eyes. She must get up and pull the shades down or she'd never sleep. She was in bed again and the shades were not down. How could that happen? Better turn over, hide from the light, sleeping in the light gave you nightmares. "Mother, how do you feel now?" and a stinging wetness on her forehead. But I don't like having my face washed in cold water!

Hapsy? George? Lydia? Jimmy? No, Cornelia, and her features were swollen and full of little puddles. "They're coming, darling, they'll all be here soon." Go wash your face, child, you look funny.

Instead of obeying, Cornelia knelt down and put her head on the pillow. She seemed to be talking but there was no sound. "Well, are you tongue-tied? Whose birthday is it? Are you going to give a party?"

Cornelia's mouth moved urgently in strange shapes. "Don't do that, you bother me, daughter."

"Oh, no, Mother. Oh, no. . . ."

Nonsense. It was strange about children. They disputed your every word. "No what, Cornelia?"

"Here's Doctor Harry."

"I won't see that boy again. He just left five minutes ago."

"That was this morning, Mother. It's night now. Here's the nurse."

"This is Doctor Harry, Mrs. Weatherall. I never saw you look so young and happy!"

"Ah, I'll never be young again—but I'd be happy if they'd let me lie in peace and get rested."

She thought she spoke up loudly, but no one answered. A warm weight on her forehead, a warm bracelet on her wrist, and a breeze went on whispering, trying to tell her something. A shuffle of leaves in the everlasting hand of God. He blew on them and they danced and rattled. "Mother, don't mind, we're going to give you a little hypodermic." "Look here, daughter, how do ants get in this bed? I saw sugar ants yesterday." Did you send for Hapsy too?

It was Hapsy she really wanted. She had to go a long way back through a great many rooms to find Hapsy standing with a baby on her arm. She seemed to herself to be Hapsy also, and the baby on Hapsy's arm was Hapsy and himself and herself, all at once, and there was no surprise in the meeting. Then Hapsy melted from within and turned flimsy as gray gauze and the baby was a gauzy shadow, and Hapsy came up close and said, "I thought you'd never come," and looked at her very searchingly and said, "You haven't changed a bit!" They leaned forward to kiss, when Cornelia began whispering from a long way off, "Oh, is there anything you want to tell me? Is there anything I can do for you?"

Yes, she had changed her mind after sixty years and she would like to see George. I want you to find George. Find him and be sure to tell him I forgot him. I want him to know I had my husband just the same and my children and my house like any other woman. A good house too and a good husband that I loved and fine children out of him. Better than I hoped for even. Tell him I was given back everything he took away and more. Oh, no, oh, God, no, there was

something else besides the house and the man and the children. Oh, surely they were not all? What was it? Something not given back. . . . Her breath crowded down under her ribs and grew into a monstrous frightening shape with cutting edges; it bored up into her head, and the agony was unbelievable: Yes, John, get the doctor now, no more talk, my time has come.

When this one was born, it should be the last. The last. It should have been born first, for it was the one she had truly wanted. Everything came in good time. Nothing left out, left over. She was strong, in three days she would be as well as ever. Better. A woman needed milk in her to have her full health.

"Mother, do you hear me?"

"I've been telling you——"

"Mother, Father Connolly's here."

"I went to Holy Communion only last week. Tell him I'm not so sinful as all that."

"Father just wants to speak to you."

He could speak as much as he pleased. It was like him to drop in and inquire about her soul as if it were a teething baby, and then stay on for a cup of tea and a round of cards and gossip. He always had a funny story of some sort, usually about an Irishman who made his little mistakes and confessed them, and the point lay in some absurd thing he would blurt out in the confessional showing his struggles between native piety and original sin. Granny felt easy about her soul. Cornelia, where are your manners? Give Father Connolly a chair. She had her secret comfortable understanding with a few favorite saints who cleared a straight road to God for her. All as surely signed and sealed as the papers for the new Forty Acres. Forever . . . heirs and assigns forever. Since the day the wedding cake was not cut, but thrown out and wasted. The whole bottom dropped out of the world, and there she was blind and sweating with nothing under her feet and the walls falling away. His hand had caught her under the breast, she had not fallen, there was the freshly polished floor with the green rug on it, just as before. He had cursed like a sailor's parrot and said, "I'll kill him for you." Don't lay a hand on him, for my sake leave something to God. "Now, Ellen, you must believe what I tell you. . . ."

So there was nothing, nothing to worry about any more, except sometimes in the night one of the children screamed in a nightmare, and they both hustled out shaking and hunting for the matches and calling, "There, wait a minute, here we are!" John, get the doctor now, Hapsy's time has come. But there was Hapsy standing by the bed in a white cap. "Cornelia, tell Hapsy to take off her cap. I can't see her plain."

Her eyes opened very wide and the room stood out like a picture she had seen somewhere. Dark colors with the shadows rising toward the ceiling in long angles. The tall black dresser gleamed with nothing on it but John's picture, enlarged from a little one, with John's eyes very black when they should have been blue. You never saw him, so how do you know how he looked? But the man insisted the copy was perfect, it was very rich and handsome. For a picture, yes, but it's not my husband. The table by the bed had a linen cover and a candle and a crucifix. The light was blue from Cornelia's silk lampshades. No sort of light at all, just frippery. You had to live forty years with kerosene lamps to appreciate honest electricity. She felt very strong and she saw Doctor Harry with a rosy nimbus around him.

"You look like a saint, Doctor Harry, and I vow that's as near as you'll ever come to it."

"She's saying something."

"I heard you, Cornelia. What's all this carrying on?"

"Father Connolly's saying——"

Cornelia's voice staggered and bumped like a cart in a bad road. It rounded corners and turned back again and arrived nowhere. Granny stepped up in the cart very lightly and reached for the reins, but a man sat beside her and she knew him by his hands, driving the cart. She did not look in his face, for she knew without seeing, but looked instead down the road where the trees leaned over and bowed to each other and a thousand birds

were singing a Mass. She felt like singing too, but she put her hand in the bosom of her dress and pulled out a rosary, and Father Connolly murmured Latin in a very solemn voice and tickled her feet.[2] My God, will you stop that nonsense? I'm a married woman. What if he did run away and leave me to face the priest by myself? I found another a whole world better. I wouldn't have exchanged my husband for anybody except St. Michael himself, and you may tell him that for me with a thank you in the bargain.

Light flashed on her closed eyelids, and a deep roaring shook her. Cornelia, is that lightning? I hear thunder. There's going to be a storm. Close all the windows. Call the children in. . . . "Mother, here we are, all of us." "Is that you, Hapsy?" "Oh, no, I'm Lydia. We drove as fast as we could." Their faces drifted above her, drifted away. The rosary fell out of her hands and Lydia put it back. Jimmy tried to help, their hands fumbled together, and Granny closed two fingers around Jimmy's thumb. Beads wouldn't do, it must be something alive. She was so amazed her thoughts ran round and round. So, my dear Lord, this is my death and I wasn't even thinking about it. My children have come to see me die. But I can't, it's not time. Oh, I always hated surprises. I wanted to give Cornelia the amethyst set—Cornelia, you're to have the amethyst set, but Hapsy's to wear it when she wants, and, Doctor Harry, do shut up. Nobody sent for you. Oh, my dear Lord, do wait a minute. I meant to do something about the Forty Acres, Jimmy doesn't need it and Lydia will later on, with that worthless husband of hers. I meant to finish the altar cloth and send six bottles of wine to Sister Borgia for her dyspepsia. I want to send six bottles of wine to Sister Borgia, Father Connolly, now don't let me forget.

Cornelia's voice made short turns and tilted over and crashed. "Oh, Mother, oh, Mother, oh, Mother. . . ."

2. **Father Connolly . . . feet.** The priest is administering the sacrament for the dying, which includes anointing the hands and feet.

"I'm not going, Cornelia. I'm taken by surprise. I can't go."

You'll see Hapsy again. What about her? "I thought you'd never come." Granny made a long journey outward, looking for Hapsy. What if I don't find her? What then? Her heart sank down and down, there was no bottom to death, she couldn't come to the end of it. The blue light from Cornelia's lampshade drew into a tiny point in the center of her brain, it flickered and winked like an eye, quietly it fluttered and dwindled. Granny lay curled down within herself, amazed and watchful, staring at the point of light that was herself; her body was now only a deeper mass of shadow in an endless darkness and this darkness would curl around the light and swallow it up. God, give a sign!

For the second time there was no sign. Again no bridegroom and the priest in the house. She could not remember any other sorrow because this grief wiped them all away. Oh, no, there's nothing more cruel than this—I'll never forgive it. She stretched herself with a deep breath and blew out the light.   **1930**

THINK AND DISCUSS
Understanding
1. How old is Granny and what is her situation at the beginning of the story?
2. Which of Granny's children is at her bedside at the beginning? With whom does Granny now live?
3. What event does Granny recall with anger?

Analyzing
4. How is the seemingly random order in which past events come into Granny's mind related to happenings in the sickroom?
5. To what situations in the past do Granny's thoughts keep returning and why? How do these situations reflect the appropriateness of her last name?
6. Tell in detail the story of the jilting mentioned in the title. How long ago did it occur?
7. Why does the author reveal the facts about the jilting in a **flashback** instead of giving the information straightforwardly and then ending her story?

Extending
8. Granny Weatherall reacted to being jilted by pushing the memory deep into her subconscious and working hard. How else might she have reacted? Could she have avoided carrying her emotional sorrow to her deathbed? How?

APPLYING: Stream of Consciousness H7
See Handbook of Literary Terms, p. 911.
Granny Weatherall's freely flowing thoughts and memories are presented through a technique called **stream of consciousness.** This random flow of mental associations without any attempt at explanation suggests both the vagueness and confusion and also the moments of clarity that characterize Granny.

1. Cite passages that reflect Granny's state of mind.
2. Do most of the clearly visualized scenes relate to the present or the past? Explain why this is so.
3. Find transitions between Granny's shifts in thoughts. Are these transitions logical? Explain.

After Fitzgerald's fame as a novelist had faded, he wrote a long account (*The Crack-Up*, 1936) baring the wretched state of his soul, comparing himself to a cracked plate. He observed, "One should . . . be able to see that things are hopeless and yet be determined to make them otherwise." Many of his fictional characters struggle with these incompatible viewpoints, some of them breaking down under the pressure.

Fitzgerald was born into a middle-class family from St. Paul, Minnesota. After a few years in the schools of St. Paul, he was sent to a private school in New Jersey and from there to four years at Princeton University. Shortly after America's entrance into World War I, he left college without completing his degree and joined the army, serving as an aide-de-camp until demobilized in 1919. Living in New York City after the war, Fitzgerald tried to become a newspaper reporter but instead ended up writing streetcar slogans for an advertising agency. He left the position three months later, encouraged by the sale of a short story, and returned to St. Paul to begin work on a novel, *This Side of Paradise*. Finished in 1920 (the same year he married Zelda Sayre, also a writer), the novel made him a celebrity.

The rest of his life was marked by a struggle between the temptation of a glamorous life, wealth, and fame and a desire to perfect his craft. Fitzgerald and Zelda spent much time with just the sort of people he criticized in his writings. The couple's exploits in New York, their unorthodox life in France, their personal problems—which somehow always became public—were eagerly followed by a sensation-hungry world press. Much of his writing, produced for the popular magazines, consists of little more than shallow ideas dressed in glittering phrases. But when Fitzgerald was at his best, he was exceedingly good. *The Great Gatsby*, which appeared in 1925, is not only a brilliant comment on the twenties but also an ironic treatment of the American success myth.

When the 1930s ushered in the Depression, the American attitude became more serious-minded; but Fitzgerald continued to write in the vein that had brought him fame. In 1934 he published *Tender Is the Night*, a moving novel about Americans in Europe living on the edge of emotional and psychological breakdown.

No longer the idol of the American reading public, beset by personal and financial worries, Fitzgerald accepted work as a Hollywood screen writer. The commercial demands of the film colony only compounded his problems, and his years in Hollywood were tormented ones. Alcohol increasingly became his means of escape from a world he no longer understood. During his last years he tried to write, but the work he produced lacked the magic of his earlier fiction. At the end, he seemed to have found his stride again in an unfinished novel, *The Last Tycoon*. He died of a heart attack in 1940, feeling that he, like many of the "sad young men" he had created, was a failure.

Winter Dreams

F. Scott Fitzgerald

I

Some of the caddies were poor as sin and lived in one-room houses with a neurasthenic cow in the front yard, but Dexter Green's father owned the second best grocery store in Black Bear—the best one was "The Hub," patronized by the wealthy people from Sherry Island—and Dexter caddied only for pocket money.

In the fall when the days became crisp and gray, and the long Minnesota winter shut down like the white lid of a box, Dexter's skis moved over the snow that hid the fairways of the golf course. At these times the country gave him a feeling of profound melancholy—it offended him that the links should lie in enforced fallowness, haunted by ragged sparrows for the long season. It was dreary, too, that on the tees where the gay colors fluttered in summer there were now only the desolate sandboxes, knee-deep in crusted ice. When he crossed the hills the wind blew cold as misery, and if the sun was out he tramped with his eyes squinted up against the hard dimensionless glare.

In April the winter ceased abruptly. The snow ran down into Black Bear Lake scarcely tarrying for the early golfers to brave the season with red and black balls. Without elation, without an interval of moist glory, the cold was gone.

Dexter knew that there was something dismal about this Northern spring, just as he knew there was something gorgeous about the fall. Fall made him clinch his hands and tremble and repeat idiotic sentences to himself, and make brisk abrupt gestures of command to imaginary audiences and armies. October filled him with hope which November raised to a sort of ecstatic triumph, and in this mood the fleeting brilliant impressions of the summer at Sherry Island were ready grist to his mill. He became a golf champion and defeated Mr. T. A. Hedrick in a marvelous match played a hundred times over the fairways of his imagination, a match each detail of which he changed about untiringly—sometimes he won with almost laughable ease, sometimes he came up magnificently from behind. Again, stepping from a Pierce-Arrow automobile, like Mr. Mortimer Jones, he strolled frigidly into the lounge of the Sherry Island Golf Club—or perhaps, surrounded by an admiring crowd, he gave an exhibition of fancy diving from the springboard of the club raft. . . . Among those who watched him in open-mouthed wonder was Mr. Mortimer Jones.

And one day it came to pass that Mr. Jones—himself and not his ghost—came up to Dexter with tears in his eyes and said that Dexter was the —— —— best caddy in the club, and wouldn't he decide not to quit if Mr. Jones made it worth his while, because every other —— —— caddy in the club lost one ball a hole for him—regularly—

"No sir," said Dexter decisively, "I don't want to caddy anymore." Then, after a pause: "I'm too old."

"You're not more than fourteen. Why the devil did you decide just this morning that you wanted to quit? You promised that next week you'd go over to the state tournament with me."

"I decided I was too old."

Dexter handed in his "A Class" badge, collected what money was due him from the caddy master, and walked home to Black Bear Village.

F. Scott Fitzgerald, "Winter Dreams." Copyright 1922 Charles Scribner's Sons; copyright renewed 1950. Reprinted with the permission of Charles Scribner's Sons from *All the Sad Young Men* (British title: *The Bodley Head Scott Fitzgerald*, Vol. V) and The Bodley Head. Slightly abridged.

J. C. Leyendecker, detail of illustration (1910)

"The best —— —— caddy I ever saw," shouted Mr. Mortimer Jones over a drink that afternoon. "Never lost a ball! Willing! Intelligent! Quiet! Honest! Grateful!"

The little girl who had done this was eleven—beautifully ugly as little girls are apt to be who are destined after a few years to be inexpressibly lovely and bring no end of misery to a great number of men. The spark, however, was perceptible. There was a general ungodliness in the way her lips twisted down at the corners when she smiled, and in the—Heaven help us!—in the almost passionate quality of her eyes. Vitality is born early in such women. It was utterly in evidence now, shining through her thin frame in a sort of glow.

She had come eagerly out on to the course at nine o'clock with a white linen nurse and five small new golf clubs in a white canvas bag which the nurse was carrying. When Dexter first saw her, she was standing by the caddy house, rather ill at ease and trying to conceal the fact by engaging her nurse in an obviously unnatural conversation graced by startling and irrelevant grimaces from herself.

"Well, it's certainly a nice day, Hilda," Dexter heard her say. She drew down the corners of her mouth, smiled, and glanced furtively around, her eyes in transit falling for an instant on Dexter.

Then to the nurse:

"Well, I guess there aren't very many people out here this morning, are there?"

The smile again—radiant, blatantly artificial—convincing.

"I don't know what we're supposed to do now," said the nurse looking nowhere in particular.

"Oh, that's all right. I'll fix it up."

Dexter stood perfectly still, his mouth slightly ajar. He knew that if he moved forward a step, his stare would be in her line of vision—if he moved backward, he would lose his full view of her face. For a moment he had not realized how young she was. Now he remembered having seen her several times the year before—in bloomers.

Suddenly, involuntarily, he laughed, a short abrupt laugh—then, startled by himself, he turned and began to walk quickly away.

"Boy!"

Dexter stopped.

"Boy——"

Beyond question he was addressed. Not only that, but he was treated to that absurd smile, that preposterous smile—the memory of which at least a dozen men were to carry into middle age.

"Boy, do you know where the golf teacher is?"

"He's giving a lesson."

"Well, do you know where the caddy master is?"

"He isn't here yet this morning."

"Oh." For a moment this baffled her. She stood alternately on her right and left foot.

"We'd like to get a caddy," said the nurse. "Mrs. Mortimer Jones sent us out to play golf, and we don't know how without we get a caddy."

Here she was stopped by an ominous glance from Miss Jones, followed immediately by the smile.

"There aren't any caddies here except me," said Dexter to the nurse, "and I got to stay here in charge until the caddy master gets here."

"Oh."

Miss Jones and her retinue now withdrew, and at a proper distance from Dexter became involved in a heated conversation, which was concluded by Miss Jones taking one of the clubs and hitting it on the ground with violence. For further emphasis she raised it again and was about to bring it down smartly upon the nurse's bosom, when the nurse seized the club and twisted it from her hands.

"You little mean old *thing!*" cried Miss Jones wildly.

Another argument ensued. Realizing that the elements of the comedy were implied in the scene, Dexter several times began to laugh, but each time restrained the laugh before it reached audibility. He could not resist the monstrous conviction that the little girl was justified in beating the nurse.

The situation was resolved by the fortuitous appearance of the caddy master, who was appealed to immediately by the nurse.

"Miss Jones is to have a little caddy, and this one says he can't go."

"Mr. McKenna said I was to wait here till you came," said Dexter quickly.

"Well, he's here now." Miss Jones smiled cheerfully at the caddy master. Then she dropped her bag and set off at a haughty mince toward the first tee.

"Well?" The caddy master turned to Dexter. "What you standing there like a dummy for? Go pick up the young lady's clubs."

"I don't think I'll go out today," said Dexter.

"You don't——"

"I think I'll quit."

The enormity of his decision frightened him. He was a favorite caddy, and the thirty dollars a month he earned through the summer were not to be made elsewhere around the lake. But he had received a strong emotional shock, and his perturbation required a violent and immediate outlet.

It is not so simple as that, either. As so frequently would be the case in the future, Dexter was unconsciously dictated to by his winter dreams.

II

Now, of course, the quality and the seasonability of these winter dreams varied, but the stuff of them remained. They persuaded Dexter several years later to pass up a business course at the State university—his father, prospering now, would have paid his way—for the precarious advantage of attending an older and more famous university in the East, where he was bothered by his scanty funds. But do not get the impression, because his winter dreams happened to be concerned at first with musings on the rich, that there was anything merely snobbish in the boy. He wanted not association with glittering things and glittering people—he wanted the glittering things themselves. Often he reached out for the best without knowing why he wanted it—and sometimes he ran up against the mysterious denials and prohibitions in which life indulges. It is with one of those denials and not with his career as a whole that this story deals.

He made money. It was rather amazing. After college he went to the city from which Black Bear Lake draws its wealthy patrons. When he was only twenty-three and had been there not quite two years, there were already people who liked to say: "Now *there's* a boy——" All about him rich men's sons were peddling bonds precariously, or investing patrimonies precariously, or plodding through the two dozen volumes of the "George Washington Commercial Course," but Dexter borrowed a thousand dollars on his college degree and his confident mouth, and bought a partnership in a laundry.

It was a small laundry when he went into it, but Dexter made a specialty of learning how the English washed fine woolen golf stockings without shrinking them, and within a year he was catering to the trade that wore knickerbockers.[1] Men were insisting that their Shetland[2] hose and sweaters go to his laundry, just as they had insisted on a caddy who could find golf balls. A little later he was doing their wives' lingerie as well—and running five branches in different parts of the city. Before he was twenty-seven he owned the largest string of laundries in his section of the country. It was then that he sold out and went to New York. But the part of his story that concerns us goes back to the days when he was making his first big success.

When he was twenty-three, Mr. Hart—one of the gray-haired men who like to say "Now there's a boy"—gave him a guest card to the Sherry Island Golf Club for a weekend. So he signed his name one day on the register, and that afternoon played golf in a foursome with Mr. Hart and Mr. Sandwood and Mr. T. A. Hedrick. He did not consider it necessary to remark that he had once carried Mr. Hart's bag over this same links, and

that he knew every trap and gully with his eyes shut—but he found himself glancing at the four caddies who trailed them, trying to catch a gleam or gesture that would remind him of himself, that would lessen the gap which lay between his present and his past.

It was a curious day, slashed abruptly with fleeting, familiar impressions. One minute he had the sense of being a trespasser—in the next he was impressed by the tremendous superiority he felt toward Mr. T. A. Hedrick, who was a bore and not even a good golfer anymore.

Then, because of a ball Mr. Hart lost near the fifteenth green, an enormous thing happened. While they were searching the stiff grasses of the rough, there was a clear call of "Fore!" from behind a hill in their rear. And as they all turned abruptly from their search a bright new ball sliced abruptly over the hill and caught Mr. T. A. Hedrick in the abdomen.

"By Gad!" cried Mr. T. A. Hedrick, "they ought to put some of these crazy women off the course. It's getting to be outrageous."

A head and a voice came up together over the hill:

"Do you mind if we go through?"

"You hit me in the stomach!" declared Mr. Hedrick wildly.

"Did I?" The girl approached the group of men. "I'm sorry. I yelled 'Fore!'"

Her glance fell casually on each of the men—then scanned the fairway for her ball.

"Did I bounce into the rough?"

It was impossible to determine whether this question was ingenuous or malicious. In a moment, however, she left no doubt, for as her partner came up over the hill she called cheerfully:

"Here I am! I'd have gone on the green except that I hit something."

As she took her stance for a short mashie shot, Dexter looked at her closely. She wore a blue gingham dress, rimmed at throat and shoulders

---

1. *knickerbockers*, full breeches gathered and banded just below the knee.
2. *Shetland*, a fine, loosely twisted yarn made from the wool of Shetland sheep.

with a white edging that accentuated her tan. The quality of exaggeration, of thinness, which had made her passionate eyes and down-turning mouth absurd at eleven, was gone now. She was arrestingly beautiful. The color in her cheeks was centered like the color in a picture—it was not a "high" color, but a sort of fluctuating and feverish warmth, so shaded that it seemed at any moment it would recede and disappear. This color and the mobility of her mouth gave a continual impression of flux, of intense life, of passionate vitality—balanced only partially by the sad luxury of her eyes.

She swung her mashie impatiently and without interest, pitching the ball into a sand pit on the other side of the green. With a quick, insincere smile and a careless "Thank you!" she went on after it.

"That Judy Jones!" remarked Mr. Hedrick on the next tee, as they waited—some moments—for her to play on ahead. "All she needs is to be turned up and spanked for six months and then to be married off to an old-fashioned cavalry captain."

"My, she's good-looking!" said Mr. Sandwood, who was just over thirty.

"Good-looking!" cried Mr. Hedrick contemptuously, "she always looks as if she wanted to be kissed! Turning those big cow eyes on every calf in town!"

It was doubtful if Mr. Hedrick intended a reference to the maternal instinct.

"She'd play pretty good golf if she'd try," said Mr. Sandwood.

"She has no form," said Mr. Hedrick solemnly.

"She has a nice figure," said Mr. Sandwood.

"Better thank the Lord she doesn't drive a swifter ball," said Mr. Hart, winking at Dexter.

Later in the afternoon the sun went down with a riotous swirl of gold and varying blues and scarlets, and left the dry, rustling night of western summer. Dexter watched from the veranda of the Golf Club, watched the even overlap of the waters in the little wind, silver molasses under the harvest moon. Then the moon held a finger to her lips and the lake became a clear pool, pale and quiet. Dexter put on his bathing suit and swam out to the farthest raft, where he stretched dripping on the wet canvas of the springboard.

There was a fish jumping and a star shining and the lights around the lake were gleaming. Over on a dark peninsula a piano was playing the songs of last summer and of summers before that— songs from *Chin-Chin* and *The Count of Luxemburg* and *The Chocolate Soldier*[3]—and because the sound of a piano over a stretch of water had always seemed beautiful to Dexter, he lay perfectly quiet and listened.

The tune the piano was playing at that moment had been gay and new five years before when Dexter was a sophomore at college. They had played it at a prom once when he could not afford the luxury of proms, and he had stood outside the gymnasium and listened. The sound of the tune precipitated in him a sort of ecstasy, and it was with that ecstasy he viewed what happened to him now. It was a mood of intense appreciation, a sense that, for once, he was magnificently attuned to life and that everything about him was radiating a brightness and a glamor he might never know again.

A low, pale oblong detached itself suddenly from the darkness of the Island, spitting forth the reverberate sound of a racing motorboat. Two white streamers of cleft water rolled themselves out behind it and almost immediately the boat was beside him, drowning out the hot tinkle of the piano in the drone of its spray. Dexter raising himself on his arms was aware of a figure standing at the wheel, of two dark eyes regarding him over the lengthening space of water—then the boat had gone by and was sweeping in an immense and purposeless circle of spray round and round in the middle of the lake. With equal eccentricity one of the circles flattened out and headed back toward the raft.

"Who's that?" she called, shutting off her motor. She was so near now that Dexter could

---

3. *Chin-Chin and The Count of Luxemburg and The Chocolate Soldier*, popular musicals and light operas of the day.

see her bathing suit, which consisted apparently of pink rompers.

The nose of the boat bumped the raft, and as the latter tilted rakishly, he was precipitated toward her. With different degrees of interest they recognized each other.

"Aren't you one of those men we played through this afternoon?" she demanded.

He was.

"Well, do you know how to drive a motorboat? Because if you do, I wish you'd drive this one so I can ride on the surfboard behind. My name is Judy Jones"—she favored him with an absurd smirk—rather, what tried to be a smirk, for, twist her mouth as she might, it was not grotesque, it was merely beautiful—"and I live in a house over there on the Island, and in that house there is a man waiting for me. When he drove up at the door, I drove out of the dock because he says I'm his ideal."

There was a fish jumping and a star shining and the lights around the lake were gleaming. Dexter sat beside Judy Jones and she explained how her boat was driven. Then she was in the water, swimming to the floating surfboard with a sinuous crawl. Watching her was without effort to the eye, watching a branch waving or a sea gull flying. Her arms, burned to butternut, moved sinuously among the dull platinum ripples, elbow appearing first, casting the forearm back with a cadence of falling water, then reaching out and down, stabbing a path ahead.

They moved out into the lake; turning, Dexter saw that she was kneeling on the low rear of the now uptilted surfboard.

"Go faster," she called, "fast as it'll go."

Obediently he jammed the lever forward and the white spray mounted at the bow. When he looked around again, the girl was standing up on the rushing board, her arms spread wide, her eyes lifted toward the moon.

"It's awful cold," she shouted. "What's your name?"

He told her.

"Well, why don't you come to dinner tomorrow night?"

His heart turned over like the flywheel of the boat, and, for the second time, her casual whim gave a new direction to his life.

III

Next evening while he waited for her to come downstairs, Dexter peopled the soft deep summer room and the sun porch that opened from it with the men who had already loved Judy Jones. He knew the sort of men they were—the men who when he first went to college had entered from the great prep schools with graceful clothes and the deep tan of healthy summers. He had seen that, in one sense, he was better than these men. He was newer and stronger. Yet in acknowledging to himself that he wished his children to be like them, he was admitting that he was but the rough, strong stuff from which they eternally sprang.

When the time had come for him to wear good clothes, he had known who were the best tailors in America, and the best tailors in America had made him the suit he wore this evening. He had acquired that particular reserve peculiar to his university, that set it off from other universities. He recognized the value to him of such a mannerism and he had adopted it; he knew that to be careless in dress and manner required more confidence than to be careful. But carelessness was for his children. His mother's name had been Krimslich. She was a Bohemian of the peasant class and she had talked broken English to the end of her days. Her son must keep to the set patterns.

At a little after seven Judy Jones came downstairs. She wore a blue silk afternoon dress, and he was disappointed at first that she had not put on something more elaborate. This feeling was accentuated when, after a brief greeting, she went to the door of a butler's pantry and pushing it open called: "You can serve dinner, Martha." He had rather expected that a butler would announce dinner, that there would be a cocktail. Then he put these thoughts behind him as they sat down side by side on a lounge and looked at each other.

"Father and Mother won't be here," she said thoughtfully.

He remembered the last time he had seen her father, and he was glad the parents were not to be here tonight—they might wonder who he was. He had been born in Keeble, a Minnesota village fifty miles farther north, and he always gave Keeble as his home instead of Black Bear Village. Country towns were well enough to come from if they weren't inconveniently in sight and used as footstools by fashionable lakes.

They talked of his university, which she had visited frequently during the past two years, and of the nearby city which supplied Sherry Island with its patrons, and whither Dexter would return next day to his prospering laundries.

During dinner she slipped into a moody depression which gave Dexter a feeling of uneasiness. Whatever petulance she uttered in her throaty voice worried him. Whatever she smiled at—at him, at a chicken liver, at nothing—it disturbed him that her smile could have no root in mirth, or even in amusement. When the scarlet corners of her lips curved down, it was less a smile than an invitation to a kiss.

Then, after dinner, she led him out on the dark sun porch and deliberately changed the atmosphere.

"Do you mind if I weep a little?" she said.

"I'm afraid I'm boring you," he responded quickly.

"You're not. I like you. But I've just had a terrible afternoon. There was a man I cared about, and this afternoon he told me out of a clear sky that he was poor as a church mouse. He'd never even hinted it before. Does this sound horribly mundane?"

"Perhaps he was afraid to tell you."

"Suppose he was," she answered. "He didn't start right. You see, if I'd thought of him as poor—well, I've been mad about loads of poor men, and fully intended to marry them all. But in this case, I hadn't thought of him that way, and my interest in him wasn't strong enough to survive the shock. As if a girl calmly informed her fiancé that she was a widow. He might not

object to widows, but——

"Let's start right," she interrupted herself suddenly. "Who are you, anyhow?"

For a moment Dexter hesitated. Then:

"I'm nobody," he announced. "My career is largely a matter of futures."

"Are you poor?"

"No," he said frankly, "I'm probably making more money than any man my age in the Northwest. I know that's an obnoxious remark, but you advised me to start right."

There was a pause. Then she smiled and the corners of her mouth drooped and an almost imperceptible sway brought her closer to him, looking up into his eyes. A lump rose in Dexter's throat, and he waited breathless for the experiment, facing the unpredictable compound that would form mysteriously from the elements of their lips. Then he saw—she communicated her excitement to him, lavishly, deeply, with kisses that were not a promise but a fulfillment. They aroused in him not hunger demanding renewal but surfeit that would demand more surfeit . . . kisses that were like charity, creating want by holding back nothing at all.

It did not take him many hours to decide that he had wanted Judy Jones ever since he was a proud, desirous little boy.

IV

It began like that—and continued, with varying shades of intensity, on such a note right up to the denouement. Dexter surrendered a part of himself to the most direct and unprincipled personality with which he had ever come in contact. Whatever Judy wanted, she went after with the full pressure of her charm. There was no divergence of method, no jockeying for position or premeditation of effects—there was a very little mental side to any of her affairs. She simply made men conscious to the highest degree of her physical loveliness. Dexter had no desire to change her. Her deficiencies were knit up with a passionate energy that transcended and justified them.

When, as Judy's head lay against his shoulder that first night, she whispered, "I don't know what's the matter with me. Last night I thought I was in love with a man and tonight I think I'm in love with you——"—it seemed to him a beautiful and romantic thing to say. It was the exquisite excitability that for the moment he controlled and owned. But a week later he was compelled to view this same quality in a different light. She took him in her roadster to a picnic supper, and after supper she disappeared, likewise in her roadster, with another man. Dexter became enormously upset and was scarcely able to be decently civil to the other people present. When she assured him that she had not kissed the other man, he knew she was lying—yet he was glad that she had taken the trouble to lie to him.

He was, as he found before the summer ended, one of a varying dozen who circulated about her. Each of them had at one time been favored above all others—about half of them still basked in the solace of occasional sentimental revivals. Whenever one showed signs of dropping out through long neglect, she granted him a brief honeyed hour, which encouraged him to tag along for a year or so longer. Judy made these forays upon the helpless and defeated without malice, indeed half unconscious that there was anything mischievous in what she did.

When a new man came to town, everyone dropped out—dates were automatically cancelled.

The helpless part of trying to do anything about it was that she did it all herself. She was

Mort Kunstler, *Silver Ghost, Autumn Leaves* (1976).
Private collection

not a girl who could be "won" in the kinetic sense—she was proof against cleverness, she was proof against charm; if any of these assailed her too strongly, she would immediately resolve the affair to a physical basis, and under the magic of her physical splendor the strong as well as the brilliant played her game and not their own. She was entertained only by the gratification of her desires and by the direct exercise of her own charm. Perhaps from so much youthful love, so many youthful lovers, she had come, in self-defense, to nourish herself wholly from within.

Succeeding Dexter's first exhilaration came restlessness and dissatisfaction. The helpless ecstasy of losing himself in her was opiate rather than tonic. It was fortunate for his work during the winter that those moments of ecstasy came infrequently. Early in their acquaintance it had seemed for a while that there was a deep and spontaneous mutual attraction—that first August, for example—three days of long evenings on her dusky veranda, of strange wan kisses through the late afternoon, in shadowy alcoves or behind the protecting trellises of the garden arbors, of mornings when she was fresh as a dream and almost shy at meeting him in the clarity of the rising day. There was all the ecstasy of an engagement about it, sharpened by his realization that there was no engagement. It was during those three days that, for the first time, he had asked her to marry him. She said "maybe some day," she said "kiss me," she said "I'd like to marry you," she said "I love you"—she said—nothing.

The three days were interrupted by the arrival of a New York man who visited at her house for half September. To Dexter's agony, rumor engaged them. The man was the son of the president of a great trust company. But at the end of a month it was reported that Judy was yawning. At a dance one night she sat all evening in a motorboat with a local beau, while the New Yorker searched the club for her frantically. She told the local beau that she was bored with her visitor, and two days later he left. She was seen with him at the station, and it was reported that he looked very mournful indeed.

On this note the summer ended. Dexter was twenty-four, and he found himself increasingly in a position to do as he wished. He joined two clubs in the city and lived at one of them. Though he was by no means an integral part of the stag lines at these clubs, he managed to be on hand at dances where Judy Jones was likely to appear. He could have gone out socially as much as he liked—he was an eligible young man, now, and popular with downtown fathers. His confessed devotion to Judy Jones had rather solidified his position. But he had no social aspirations and rather despised the dancing men who were always on tap for the Thursday or Saturday parties and who filled in at dinners with the younger married set. Already he was playing with the idea of going East to New York. He wanted to take Judy Jones with him. No disillusion as to the world in which she had grown up could cure his illusion as to her desirability.

Remember that—for only in the light of it can what he did for her be understood.

Eighteen months after he first met Judy Jones, he became engaged to another girl. Her name was Irene Scheerer, and her father was one of the men who had always believed in Dexter. Irene was light-haired and sweet and honorable, and a little stout, and she had two suitors whom she pleasantly relinquished when Dexter formally asked her to marry him.

Summer, fall, winter, spring, another summer, another fall—so much he had given of his active life to the incorrigible lips of Judy Jones. She had treated him with interest, with encouragement, with malice, with indifference, with contempt. She had inflicted on him the innumerable little slights and indignities possible in such a case—as if in revenge for having ever cared for him at all. She had beckoned him and yawned at him and beckoned him again and he had responded often with bitterness and narrowed eyes. She had brought him ecstatic happiness and intolerable agony of spirit. She had caused him untold inconvenience and not a little trouble. She had insulted him, and she had ridden over him, and she had played his interest in her against his interest in his work—for fun. She had done everything to him except to criticize him—this she had not done—it seemed to him only because it might have sullied the utter indifference she manifested and sincerely felt toward him.

When autumn had come and gone again, it occurred to him that he could not have Judy Jones. He had to beat this into his mind but he convinced himself at last. He lay awake at night for a while and argued it over. He told himself the trouble and pain she had caused him, he enumerated her glaring deficiencies as a wife. Then he said to himself that he loved her, and after a while he fell asleep. For a week, lest he imagine her husky voice over the telephone or her eyes opposite him at lunch, he worked hard and late, and at night he went to his office and plotted out his years.

At the end of a week he went to a dance and cut in on her once. For almost the first time since they had met he did not ask her to sit out with him or tell her that she was lovely. It hurt him that she did not miss these things—that was all. He was not jealous when he saw that there was a new man tonight. He had been hardened against jealousy long before.

He stayed late at the dance. He sat for an hour with Irene Scheerer and talked about books and about music. He knew very little about either. But he was beginning to be master of his own time now, and he had a rather priggish notion that he—the young and already fabulously successful Dexter Green—should know more about such things.

That was in October, when he was twenty-five. In January, Dexter and Irene became engaged. It was to be announced in June, and they were to be married three months later.

The Minnesota winter prolonged itself interminably, and it was almost May when the winds came soft and the snow ran down into Black Bear Lake at last. For the first time in over a year Dexter was enjoying a certain tranquility of spirit. Judy Jones had been in Florida, and afterward in Hot Springs, and somewhere she had been engaged, and somewhere she had broken it off. At first, when Dexter had definitely given her up, it had made him sad that people still linked them together and asked for news of her, but when he began to be placed at dinner next to Irene Scheerer, people didn't ask him about her anymore—they told him about her. He ceased to be an authority on her.

May at last. Dexter walked the streets at night when the darkness was damp as rain, wondering that so soon, with so little done, so much of ecstasy had gone from him. May one year back had been marked by Judy's poignant, unforgivable yet forgiven turbulence—it had been one of those rare times when he fancied she had grown to care for him. That old penny's worth of happiness he had spent for this bushel of content. He knew that Irene would be no more than a curtain spread behind him, a hand moving among gleaming teacups, a voice calling to children . . . fire and loveliness were gone, the magic of nights and the wonder of the varying hours and seasons . . . slender lips, down-turning, dropping to his lips and bearing him up into a heaven of eyes. . . . The thing was deep in him. He was too strong and alive for it to die lightly.

In the middle of May when the weather balanced for a few days on the thin bridge that led to deep summer, he turned in one night at Irene's house. Their engagement was to be announced in a week now—no one would be surprised at it. And tonight they would sit together on the lounge at the University Club and look on for an hour at the dancers. It gave him a sense of solidity to go with her—she was so sturdily popular, so intensely "great."

He mounted the steps of the brownstone house and stepped inside.

"Irene," he called.

Mrs. Scheerer came out of the living room to meet him.

"Dexter," she said. "Irene's gone upstairs with a splitting headache. She wanted to go with you but I made her go to bed."

"Nothing serious, I——"

"Oh, no. She's going to play golf with you in the morning. You can spare her for just one night, can't you, Dexter?"

Her smile was kind. She and Dexter liked each other. In the living room he talked for a moment before he said good night.

Returning to the University Club, where he had rooms, he stood in the doorway for a moment and watched the dancers. He leaned against the doorpost, nodded at a man or two—yawned.

"Hello, darling."

The familiar voice at his elbow startled him. Judy Jones had left a man and crossed the room to him—Judy Jones, a slender enameled doll in cloth of gold: gold in a band at her head, gold in two slipper points at her dress's hem. The fragile glow of her face seemed to blossom as she smiled at him. A breeze of warmth and light blew through the room. His hands in the pockets of his dinner jacket tightened spasmodically. He was filled with a sudden excitement.

"When did you get back?" he asked casually.

"Come here and I'll tell you about it."

She turned and he followed her. She had been away—he could have wept at the wonder of her return. She had passed through enchanted streets, doing things that were like provocative music. All mysterious happenings, all fresh and quickening hopes, had gone away with her, come back with her now.

She turned in the doorway.

"Have you a car here? If you haven't, I have."

"I have a coupé."

In then, with a rustle of golden cloth. He slammed the door. Into so many cars she had stepped—like this—like that—her back against the leather, so—her elbow resting on the door—waiting. She would have been soiled long since had there been anything to soil her—except herself—but this was her own self outpouring.

With an effort he forced himself to start the car and back into the street. This was nothing, he must remember. She had done this before, and he had put her behind him, as he would have crossed a bad account from his books.

He drove slowly downtown, and, affecting abstraction, traversed the deserted streets of the business section, peopled here and there where a movie was giving out its crowd or where consumptive or pugilistic youth lounged in front of pool halls. The clink of glasses and the slap of hands on the bars issued from saloons, cloisters of glazed glass and dirty yellow light.

She was watching him closely and the silence was embarrassing, yet in this crisis he could find no casual word with which to profane the hour. At a convenient turning he began to zigzag back toward the University Club.

"Have you missed me?" she asked suddenly.

"Everybody missed you."

He wondered if she knew of Irene Scheerer. She had been back only a day—her absence had been almost contemporaneous with his engagement.

"What a remark!" Judy laughed sadly—without sadness. She looked at him searchingly. He became absorbed in the dashboard.

"You're handsomer than you used to be," she said thoughtfully. "Dexter, you have the most rememberable eyes."

He could have laughed at this, but he did not laugh. It was the sort of thing that was said to sophomores. Yet it stabbed at him.

"I'm awfully tired of everything, darling." She called everyone darling, endowing the endearment with careless, individual camaraderie. "I wish you'd marry me."

The directness of this confused him. He should have told her now that he was going to marry another girl, but he could not tell her. He could as easily have sworn that he had never loved her.

"I think we'd get along," she continued, on the same note, "unless probably you've forgotten me and fallen in love with another girl."

Her confidence was obviously enormous. She had said, in effect, that she found such a thing impossible to believe, that if it were true he had merely committed a childish indiscretion—and probably to show off. She would forgive him, because it was not a matter of any moment but rather something to be brushed aside lightly.

"Of course, you could never love anybody but me," she continued, "I like the way you love me. Oh, Dexter, have you forgotten last year?"

"No, I haven't forgotten."

"Neither have I!"

Was she sincerely moved—or was she carried along by the wave of her own acting?

"I wish we could be like that again," she said, and he forced himself to answer:

"I don't think we can."

"I suppose not. . . . I hear you're giving Irene Scheerer a violent rush."

There was not the faintest emphasis on the name, yet Dexter was suddenly ashamed.

"Oh, take me home," cried Judy suddenly; "I don't want to go back to that idiotic dance—with those children."

Then, as he turned up the street that led to the residence district, Judy began to cry quietly to herself. He had never seen her cry before.

The dark street lightened, the dwellings of the rich loomed up around them, he stopped his coupé in front of the great white bulk of the Mortimer Joneses' house, somnolent, gorgeous, drenched with the splendor of the damp moonlight. Its solidity startled him. The strong walls, the steel of the girders, the breadth and beam and pomp of it were there only to bring out the contrast with the young beauty beside him. It was sturdy to accentuate her slightness—as if to show what a breeze could be generated by a butterfly's wing.

He sat perfectly quiet, his nerves in wild clamor, afraid that if he moved, he would find her irresistibly in his arms. Two tears had rolled down her wet face and trembled on her upper lip.

"I'm more beautiful than anybody else," she said brokenly, "why can't I be happy?" Her moist eyes tore at his stability—her mouth turned slowly downward with an exquisite sadness: "I'd like to marry you if you'll have me, Dexter. I suppose you think I'm not worth having, but I'll be so beautiful for you, Dexter."

A million phrases of anger, pride, passion, hatred, tenderness fought on his lips. Then a perfect wave of emotion washed over him, carrying off with it a sediment of wisdom, of convention, of doubt, of honor. This was his girl who was speaking, his own, his beautiful, his pride.

"Won't you come in?" He heard her draw in her breath sharply.

Waiting.

"All right," his voice was trembling, "I'll come in."

V

It was strange that neither when it was over nor a long time afterward did he regret that night. Looking at it from the perspective of ten years, the fact that Judy's flare for him endured just one month seemed of little importance. Nor did it matter that by his yielding he subjected himself to a deeper agony in the end and gave serious hurt to Irene Scheerer and to Irene's parents, who had befriended him. There was nothing sufficiently pictorial about Irene's grief to stamp itself on his mind.

Dexter was at bottom hard minded. The attitude of the city on his action was of no importance to him, not because he was going to leave the city, but because any outside attitude on the situation seemed superficial. He was completely indifferent to popular opinion. Nor, when he had seen that it was no use, that he did not possess in himself the power to move fundamentally or to hold Judy Jones, did he bear any malice toward her. He loved her, and he would love her until the day he was too old for loving—but he could not have her. So he tasted the deep pain that is reserved only for the strong, just as he had tasted for a little while the deep happiness.

Even the ultimate falsity of the grounds upon which Judy terminated the engagement that she did not want to "take him away" from Irene—Judy who had wanted nothing else—did not revolt him. He was beyond any revulsion or any amusement.

He went East in February with the intention of selling out his laundries and settling in New York—but the war came to America in March and changed his plans. He returned to the West, handed over the management of the business to his partner, and went into the first officers' training camp in late April. He was one of those young thousands who greeted the war with a certain amount of relief, welcoming the liberation from webs of tangled emotion.

VI

This story is not his biography, remember, although things creep into it which have nothing to do with those dreams he had when he was young. We are almost done with them and with him now. There is only one more incident to be related here, and it happens seven years farther on.

It took place in New York, where he had done well—so well that there were no barriers too high for him. He was thirty-two years old, and, except for one flying trip immediately after the war, he had not been West in seven years. A man named Devlin from Detroit came into his office to see him in a business way, and then and there this incident occurred, and closed out, so to speak, this particular side of his life.

"So you're from the Middle West," said the man Devlin with careless curiosity. "That's funny—I thought men like you were probably born and raised on Wall Street. You know—wife of one of my best friends in Detroit came from your city. I was an usher at the wedding."

Dexter waited with no apprehension of what was coming.

"Judy Simms," said Devlin with no particular interest; "Judy Jones she was once."

"Yes, I knew her." A dull impatience spread over him. He had heard, of course, that she was married—perhaps deliberately he had heard no more.

"Awfully nice girl," brooded Devlin meaninglessly, "I'm sort of sorry for her."

"Why?" Something in Dexter was alert, receptive, at once.

"Oh, Lud Simms has gone to pieces in a way. I don't mean he ill-uses her, but he drinks and runs around——"

"Doesn't she run around?"

"No. Stays at home with her kids."

"Oh."

"She's a little too old for him," said Devlin.

"Too old!" cried Dexter. "Why, man, she's only twenty-seven."

He was possessed with a wild notion of rushing out into the streets and taking a train to Detroit. He rose to his feet spasmodically.

"I guess you're busy," Devlin apologized quickly. "I didn't realize——"

"No, I'm not busy," said Dexter, steadying his voice. "I'm not busy at all. Not busy at all. Did you say she was—twenty-seven? No, I said she was twenty-seven."

"Yes, you did," agreed Devlin dryly.

"Go on, then. Go on."

"What do you mean?"

"About Judy Jones."

Devlin looked at him helplessly.

"Well, that's—I told you all there is to it. He treats her like the devil. Oh, they're not going to get divorced or anything. When he's particularly outrageous she forgives him. In fact, I'm inclined to think she loves him. She was a pretty girl when she first came to Detroit."

A pretty girl! The phrase struck Dexter as ludicrous.

"Isn't she—a pretty girl anymore?"

"Oh, she's all right."

"Look here," said Dexter, sitting down suddenly. "I don't understand. You say she was a 'pretty girl' and now you say she's 'all right.' I don't understand what you mean—Judy Jones wasn't a pretty girl, at all. She was a great beauty. Why, I knew her, I knew her. She was——"

Devlin laughed pleasantly.

"I'm not trying to start a row," he said. "I think Judy's a nice girl and I like her. I can't understand how a man like Lud Simms could fall madly in love with her, but he did." Then he added: "Most of the women like her."

Dexter looked closely at Devlin, thinking wildly that there must be a reason for this, some insensitivity in the man or some private malice.

"Lots of women fade just like *that*," Devlin snapped his fingers. "You must have seen it happen. Perhaps I've forgotten how pretty she was at her wedding. I've seen her so much since then, you see. She has nice eyes."

Norman Rockwell (1894–1978), detail of *Guests Arriving at Party*.
The Norman Rockwell Museum at Stockbridge

A sort of dullness settled down upon Dexter. For the first time in his life he felt like getting very drunk. He knew that he was laughing loudly at something Devlin had said, but he did not know what it was or why it was funny. When, in a few minutes, Devlin went he lay down on his lounge and looked out the window at the New York skyline into which the sun was sinking in dull lovely shades of pink and gold.

He had thought that having nothing else to lose he was invulnerable at last—but he knew that he had just lost something more, as surely as if he had married Judy Jones and seen her fade away before his eyes.

The dream was gone. Something had been taken from him. In a sort of panic he pushed the palms of his hands into his eyes and tried to bring up a picture of the waters lapping on Sherry Island and the moonlit veranda, and gingham on the golf links and the dry sun and the gold color of her neck's soft down. And her mouth damp to his kisses and her eyes plaintive with melan-

choly and her freshness like new fine linen in the morning. Why, these things were no longer in the world! They had existed and they existed no longer.

For the first time in years the tears were streaming down his face. But they were for himself now. He did not care about mouth and eyes and moving hands. He wanted to care, and he could not care. For he had gone away and he could never go back anymore. The gates were closed, the sun was gone down, and there was no beauty but the gray beauty of steel that withstands all time. Even the grief he could have borne was left behind in the country of illusion, of youth, of the richness of life, where his winter dreams had flourished.

"Long ago," he said, "long ago, there was something in me, but now that thing is gone. Now that thing is gone, that thing is gone. I cannot cry. I cannot care. That thing will come back no more."

1922

THINK AND DISCUSS

Understanding

1. What are some of the fantasies about summer that Dexter indulges in at the Sherry Island Golf Club?
2. When Dexter sees the young Judy Jones on the golf course, how does she act? What is Dexter's reaction to her behavior?
3. What does the adult Dexter do for a living? How successful is he? How do you know?

Analyzing

4. In giving up caddying, Dexter was "unconsciously dictated to by his winter dreams." Give other examples of decisions made under the influence of those dreams.
5. As Part II ends, the author tells us that for a second time Judy Jones's "casual whim gave a new direction to" Dexter's life. Explain.
6. When Dexter goes to have dinner with Judy Jones, he tells her at one point: "I'm probably making more money than any man my age in the Northwest." Why does he make this statement? What is Judy's reaction?
7. In Part IV, Dexter becomes engaged to Irene Scheerer. Why do you think he does this? How does Judy intervene?
8. In Part V, Dexter is described as being "hard minded." How does this description help explain his reaction both to Irene's grief and to Judy's rejection.
9. Part VI takes place seven years later in New York. What does Dexter learn about Judy and how does he react to this information? What has Dexter lost?

Extending

10. Should Dexter have married Irene? Would he have been happier? Explain your answer.

VOCABULARY

Combined Skills

The italicized words below appear in "Winter Dreams." On a sheet of paper answer the following questions, consulting your Glossary whenever necessary.

1. The French source from which the word *denouement* comes means "to untie." How do you relate the original meaning to its present definition?
2. The first syllable of *poignant* rhymes with (**a**) log; (**b**) boy; (**c**) cow; (**d**) slow.
3. The g in *pugilistic* is the same as the initial sound in (**a**) girl; (**b**) jam.
4. The word most nearly the opposite of *blatant* is (**a**) *incorrigible;* (**b**) *consumptive;* (**c**) *imperceptible;* (**d**) *precarious.*
5. Give a brief example of an event that could be considered *fortuitous.*

ENRICHMENT

Research

1. Most experts feel that the short novel *The Great Gatsby* is Fitzgerald's finest work. Fitzgerald once spoke of "Winter Dreams" as "a sort of first draft of the Gatsby idea." Read the novel and report to the class on similarities in characters, theme, and plot.
2. Much of Fitzgerald's work is autobiographical. Read critical or biographical studies of Fitzgerald and look for similarities between Dexter Green and the author or between Judy Jones and one of Fitzgerald's early loves, Ginevra King. (An excellent sourcebook is *The Far Side of Paradise* by Arthur Mizener.) Share your findings with the class in an oral report.

Ernest Hemingway's deceptively simple, intensely compressed literary style has influenced countless writers around the world. He once explained the style to an interviewer: "I always try to write on the principle of the iceberg. There is seven-eighths of it underwater for every part that shows. Anything you know, you can eliminate and it only strengthens your iceberg. It is the part that doesn't show. If a writer omits something because he does not know it, then there is a hole in the story."

Hemingway grew up in Oak Park, Illinois. During vacations, he hunted with his father, a physician, in northern Michigan. After graduation from high school, he worked as a newspaper reporter in Kansas City, where his interest in boxing acquainted him with prizefighters and gunmen. Before the United States entered World War I, he served in a French ambulance unit and was seriously wounded. After the war, Hemingway went to Paris where he worked as correspondent for American newspapers and became acquainted with other American expatriates, including F. Scott Fitzgerald, who helped him get his works published. Hemingway brought out a book of short stories, *In Our Time*, in 1924, and his first novel, *The Sun Also Rises*, in 1926. This novel described Americans living abroad after the devastation of World War I, searching for the meaning of life. For an epigraph to his novel, Hemingway quoted something that the writer Gertrude Stein once said to him: "You are all a lost generation." The name came to characterize the self-exiled artists and writers who were his contemporaries.

As Hemingway's artistic reputation grew, his activities and interests —fishing, boxing, hunting in Africa, and passion for bullfights—made him familiar to millions who had never read his books. He solidified his reputation as a writer with *A Farewell to Arms* (1929), a love story set in World War I.

He also became a renowned war correspondent. *For Whom the Bell Tolls* (1940), considered by some to be his finest novel, grew out of his experiences in the Spanish Civil War.

When America entered World War II, Hemingway spent two years on a privately organized antisubmarine patrol in the Caribbean and then joined the American forces in Europe as a reporter. In 1952, he published *The Old Man and the Sea*, which was awarded the Pulitzer Prize. The following year he received the Nobel Prize for literature. He died from a gunshot wound. It is generally believed that he committed suicide, as his father had before him.

Works published after his death include his reminiscence of life in Paris during the 1920s, *A Moveable Feast* (1964); a novel titled *Islands in the Stream* (1970); and a heavily edited novel titled *The Garden of Eden* (1986).

In Another Country

Ernest Hemingway

n the fall the war[1] was always there, but we did not go to it any more. It was cold in the fall in Milan and the dark came very early. Then the electric lights came on, and it was pleasant along the streets looking in the windows. There was much game hanging outside the shops, and the snow powdered in the fur of the foxes and the wind blew their tails. The deer hung stiff and heavy and empty, and small birds blew in the wind and the wind turned their feathers. It was a cold fall and the wind came down from the mountains.

We were all at the hospital every afternoon, and there were different ways of walking across the town through the dusk to the hospital. Two of the ways were alongside canals, but they were long. Always, though, you crossed a bridge across a canal to enter the hospital. There was a choice of three bridges. On one of them a woman sold roasted chestnuts. It was warm, standing in front of her charcoal fire, and the chestnuts were warm afterward in your pocket. The hospital was very old and very beautiful, and you entered through a gate and walked across a courtyard and out a gate on the other side. There were usually funerals starting from the courtyard. Beyond the old hospital were the new brick pavilions, and there we met every afternoon and were all very polite and interested in what was the matter, and sat in the machines that were to make so much difference.

The doctor came up to the machine where I was sitting and said: "What did you like best to do before the war? Did you practice a sport?"

I said: "Yes, football."

"Good," he said. "You will be able to play football again better than ever."

My knee did not bend and the leg dropped straight from the knee to the ankle without a calf, and the machine was to bend the knee and make it move as in riding a tricycle. But it did not bend yet, and instead the machine lurched when it came to the bending part. The doctor said: "That will all pass. You are a fortunate young man. You will play football again like a champion."

In the next machine was a major who had a little hand like a baby's. He winked at me when the doctor examined his hand, which was between two leather straps that bounced up and down and flapped the stiff fingers, and said: "And will I too play football, captain-doctor?" He had been a very great fencer, and before the war the greatest fencer in Italy.

The doctor went to his office in the back room and brought a photograph which showed a hand that had been withered almost as small as the major's, before it had taken a machine course, and after was a little larger. The major held the photograph with his good hand and looked at it very carefully. "A wound?" he asked.

"An industrial accident," the doctor said.

"Very interesting, very interesting," the major

---

1. *the war,* World War I (1914–1918).

Ernest Hemingway, "In Another Country" from *Men Without Women.* Copyright 1927 Charles Scribner's Sons; copyright renewed 1955 Ernest Hemingway. Reprinted with the permission of Charles Scribner's Sons and Jonathan Cape Ltd.

said, and handed it back to the doctor.

"You have confidence?"

"No," said the major.

There were three boys who came each day who were about the same age I was. They were all three from Milan, and one of them was to be a lawyer, and one was to be a painter, and one had intended to be a soldier, and after we were finished with the machines, sometimes we walked back together to the Café Cova, which was next door to the Scala.[2] We walked the short way through the communist quarter because we were four together. The people hated us because we were officers, and from a wineshop someone called out, *"A basso gli ufficiali!"*[3] as we passed. Another boy who walked with us sometimes and made us five wore a black silk handkerchief across his face because he had no nose then and his face was to be rebuilt. He had gone out to the front from the military academy and been wounded within an hour after he had gone into the front line for the first time. They rebuilt his face, but he came from a very old family and they could never get the nose exactly right. He went to South America and worked in a bank. But this was a long time ago, and then we did not any of us know how it was going to be afterward. We only knew then that there was always the war, but that we were not going to it anymore.

We all had the same medals, except the boy with the black silk bandage across his face, and he had not been at the front long enough to get any medals. The tall boy with a very pale face who was to be a lawyer had been a lieutenant of Arditi[4] and had three medals of the sort we each had only one of. He had lived a very long time with death and was a little detached. We were all a little detached, and there was nothing that held us together except that we met every afternoon at the hospital. Although, as we walked to the Cova through the tough part of town, walking in the dark, with light and singing coming out of the wineshops, and sometimes having to walk into the street when the men and women would crowd together on the sidewalk so that we would have had to jostle them to get by, we felt held together by there being something that had happened that they, the people who disliked us, did not understand.

We ourselves all understood the Cova, where it was rich and warm and not too brightly lighted, and noisy and smoky at certain hours, and there were always girls at the tables and the illustrated papers on a rack on the wall. The girls at the Cova were very patriotic, and I found that the most patriotic people in Italy were café girls—and I believe they are still patriotic.

The boys at first were very polite about my medals and asked me what I had done to get them. I showed them the papers, which were written in very beautiful language and full of *fratellanza* and *abnegazione*,[5] but which really said, with the adjective removed, that I had been given the medals because I was an American. After that their manner changed a little toward me, although I was their friend against outsiders. I was a friend, but I was never really one of them after they had read the citations, because it had been different with them and they had done very different things to get their medals. I had been wounded, it was true; but we all knew that being wounded, after all, was really an accident. I was never ashamed of the ribbons, though, and sometimes after cocktail hour, I would imagine myself having done all the things they had done to get their medals; but walking home at night through the empty streets with the cold wind and all the shops closed, trying to keep near the street lights, I knew that I would never have done such things, and I was very much afraid to die, and often lay in bed at night by myself, afraid to die and wondering how I would be when I went back to the front again.

The three with the medals were like hunting

---

2. *the Scala,* La Scala, Milan's world-famous opera house.

3. *"a basso gli ufficiali!"* Down with the officers! [*Italian*]

4. *Arditi,* a picked group of volunteers which served as storm troops of the Italian infantry.

5. *fratellanza* (frä tel län′zä) *and abnegazione* (äb′nä-gä tzyō′ne), brotherhood and self-denial. [*Italian*]

hawks; and I was not a hawk, although I might seem a hawk to those who had never hunted; they, the three, knew better and so we drifted apart. But I stayed good friends with the boy who had been wounded his first day at the front, because he would never know now how he would have turned out; so he could never be accepted either, and I liked him because I thought perhaps he would not have turned out to be a hawk either.

The major, who had been the great fencer, did not believe in bravery, and spent much time while we sat in the machines correcting my grammar. He had complimented me on how I spoke Italian, and we talked together very easily. One day I had said that Italian seemed such an easy language to me that I could not take a great interest in it; everything was so easy to say. "Ah, yes," the major said. "Why, then, do you not take up the use of grammar?" So we took up the use of grammar, and soon Italian was such a difficult language that I was afraid to talk to him until I had the grammar straight in my mind.

The major came very regularly to the hospital. I do not think he ever missed a day, although I am sure he did not believe in the machines. There was a time when none of us believed in the machines, and one day the major said it was all nonsense. The machines were new then and it was we who were to prove them. It was an idiotic idea, he said, "a theory, like another." I had not learned my grammar, and he said I was a stupid impossible disgrace, and he was a fool to have bothered with me. He was a small man and he sat straight up in his chair with his right hand thrust into the machine and looked straight ahead at the wall while the straps thumped up and down with his fingers in them.

"What will you do when the war is over if it is over?" he asked me. "Speak grammatically!"

"I will go to the States."

"Are you married?"

"No, but I hope to be."

"The more of a fool you are," he said. He seemed very angry. "A man must not marry."

John Singer Sargent, *A Street in Arras* (1918).
Imperial War Museum, London

"Why, Signor Maggiore?"[6]

"Don't call me 'Signor Maggiore.' "

"Why must not a man marry?"

"He cannot marry. He cannot marry," he said angrily. "If he is to lose everything, he should not place himself in a position to lose that. He should not place himself in a position to lose. He should find things he cannot lose."

He spoke very angrily and bitterly, and looked straight ahead while he talked.

"But why should he necessarily lose it?"

"He'll lose it," the major said. He was looking at the wall. Then he looked down at the machine and jerked his little hand out from between the straps and slapped it hard against his thigh. "He'll lose it." he almost shouted. "Don't argue with me!" Then he called to the attendant who ran the machines. "Come and turn this damned thing off."

He went back into the other room for the light treatment and massage. Then I heard him ask the doctor if he might use his telephone and he shut the door. When he came back into the room, I was sitting in another machine. He was wearing his cape and had his cap on, and he came directly toward my machine and put his arm on my shoulder.

"I am so sorry," he said, and patted me on the shoulder with his good hand. "I would not be rude. My wife has just died. You must forgive me."

"Oh——" I said, feeling sick for him. "I am *so* sorry."

He stood there biting his lower lip. "It is very difficult," he said. "I cannot resign myself."

He looked straight past me and out through the window. Then he began to cry. "I am utterly unable to resign myself," he said, and choked. And then crying, his head up looking at nothing, carrying himself straight and soldierly, with tears on both his cheeks and biting his lips, he walked past the machines and out the door.

The doctor told me that the major's wife, who was very young and whom he had not married until he was definitely invalided out of the war, had died of pneumonia. She had been sick only a few days. No one expected her to die. The major did not come to the hospital for three days. Then he came at the usual hour, wearing a black band on the sleeve of his uniform. When he came back, there were large framed photographs around the wall, of all sorts of wounds before and after they had been cured by the machines. In front of the machine the major used were three photographs of hands like his that were completely restored. I do not know where the doctor got them. I always understood we were the first to use the machines. The photographs did not make much difference to the major because he only looked out of the window.

1927

---

6. *Signor Maggiore* (sē'nyôr mäj jô're), Mr. Major. In Italy it is a sign of respect to prefix an officer's rank with *Signor*.

THINK AND DISCUSS
Understanding
1. What is the nationality of the narrator? In what country does the action take place?
2. What is the purpose of the machines in the hospital?
3. Why does the major warn the narrator to avoid marriage?

Analyzing
4. Not only are the soldiers, as a group, shut off from other groups; as individuals, they are separated from one another. How is the isolation of each man shown?
5. Have their war experiences had anything to do with the loneliness of these men? Explain.

6. How does the major differ from the other invalids?
7. Describe the **tone** of the major's comments about the machines and compare it with his tone in telling of his wife's death. Which hurts him more—her death, or the crippling of his hand?
8. What is the **theme** of the story? Relate the final situation of the major to the theme.
9. Cite examples from this story of Hemingway's terse, understated **style**. Explain how this style is suited to Hemingway's theme.

Extending
10. Reread the article titled "Reading a Modern Short Story," page 420. In what ways is this a modern, rather than a traditional, short story?

REVIEWING: Mood H̶T̶
See Handbook of Literary Terms, p. 897.
   Remember that **mood** is the overall atmosphere in a work of literature. This atmosphere is conveyed through an author's choice of **setting, imagery,** and details.

1. What is the mood created in the first paragraph?
2. What details and images serve to establish this mood?
3. How does this mood reinforce the theme of the story?

THINKING SKILLS
Evaluating
   Critics can differ widely in their interpretations of a work of literature. Taking their cues from the opening paragraph of the story, various critics have offered the following explanations for the word *country* mentioned in the title:

• The country of battle from which the wounded soldiers are exluded.
• The country of peace, glimpsed through lighted windows from dark streets.
• The country of death, suggested by the words *cold, dark,* and *empty,* and reinforced by the stiff, lifeless bodies of game that hang outside the shops.
• Italy, a country that emphasizes the alienation of the American narrator.

   Evaluate these interpretations by measuring them against your own ideas. Then choose the one you consider most plausible, or offer one of your own.

COMPOSITION
Imitating a Writer's Style
   Hemingway's famous prose style is often parodied, or imitated. Think of a simple situation involving a setting and a time of year. Describe it for a Hemingway imitation contest in a paragraph modeled on the opening paragraph of "In Another Country." Note that Hemingway uses many compound sentences joined by *and* and repeats key words like *fall*. Vocabulary is simple, and there is a heavy reliance on the past-tense linking verb *was*.

Writing About Characters
   The major in "In Another Country" and the lieutenant in Stephen Crane's "An Episode of War" (Unit 4) are both seriously wounded in war. Write an essay of three paragraphs or more comparing and contrasting these two characters, directed to someone who is considering a military career. Your essay should explain how you think their army experiences and wounds will affect them for the rest of their lives.

William Faulkner is one of the most original of American writers—in technique, in style, and in subject matter. As a setting for his greatest work, he created Yoknapatawpha County, Mississippi, and peopled it with unforgettable characters of the old and new South. As he suggested in his Nobel Prize acceptance speech, which appears at the end of this unit, his stories dealt with "the problems of the human heart in conflict with itself."

Faulkner was born near Oxford, Mississippi. The family soon moved to Oxford, and Faulkner spent most of his life there. During World War I, he enlisted in the Canadian Air Force; however the war ended before he saw any action. Returning to Mississippi, he enrolled at the state university but left before graduating.

By this time, he had become interested in poetry and spent a good deal of time both reading and writing. In 1924 his first book of poetry, *The Marble Faun*, was published. In the same year, Faulkner went to New Orleans where he met Sherwood Anderson, who encouraged him to write fiction. With Anderson's help, Faulkner's first novel, *Soldier's Pay*, was published in 1926. This novel, dealing with World War I, was followed by *Mosquitoes* in 1927, which portrayed the dissolute life during the Jazz Age of a group of New Orleans intellectuals and their wealthy friends. It was not until the writing of *Sartoris* (1929) that Faulkner discovered his true material—in his own background in rural Mississippi.

The Sound and the Fury (1929) was next in a long succession of distinguished works chronicling the lives of a number of old Southern families, usually in decline. In *As I Lay Dying* (1932), Faulkner demonstrated that he could give an authentic fictional portrayal of life on the lower social levels of his Mississippi locale.

For many years Faulkner's work won little recognition. One exception, *Sanctuary* (1931), created something of a sensation because of its lurid violence. But after World War II Faulkner began to attract both critical and popular acclaim. His reputation abroad grew rapidly, too, especially in France, and in 1950 he was awarded the Nobel Prize for literature.

Faulkner was preoccupied with form and experimented with different means of capturing reality. Most of his novels combine a stream-of-consciousness technique with a scrambling of chronology—resulting in stories difficult to read but rewarding in their profundity. Above all, Faulkner dealt with "the old verities and truths of the heart, the old universal truths" that must be, he said, the subject and goal of every serious writer. Echoing the sentiments expressed in his Nobel speech, his characters embody the qualities of compassion and endurance.

The Bear

William Faulkner

e was ten. But it had already begun, long before that day when at last he wrote his age in two figures and he saw for the first time the camp where his father and Major de Spain and old General Compson and the others spent two weeks each November and two weeks again each June. He had already inherited then, without ever having seen it, the tremendous bear with one trap-ruined foot which, in an area almost a hundred miles deep, had earned for itself a name, a definite designation like a living man.

He had listened to it for years: the long legend of corncribs rifled, of shoats and grown pigs and even calves carried bodily into the woods and devoured, of traps and deadfalls overthrown and dogs mangled and slain, and shotgun and even rifle charges delivered at point-blank range and with no more effect than so many peas blown through a tube by a boy—a corridor of wreckage and destruction beginning back before he was born, through which sped, not fast but rather with the ruthless and irresistible deliberation of a locomotive, the shaggy tremendous shape.

It ran in his knowledge before ever he saw it. It looked and towered in his dreams before he even saw the unaxed woods where it left its crooked print, shaggy, huge, red-eyed, not malevolent but just big—too big for the dogs which tried to bay it, for the horses which tried to ride it down, for the men and the bullets they fired into it, too big for the very country which was its constricting scope. He seemed to see it entire with a child's complete divination before he ever laid eyes on either—the doomed wilderness whose edges were being constantly and punily gnawed at by men with axes and plows who feared it because it was wilderness, men myriad and nameless even to one another in the land where the old bear had earned a name, through which ran not even a mortal animal but an anachronism, indomitable and invincible, out of an old dead time, a phantom, epitome and apotheosis of the old wild life at which the puny humans swarmed and hacked in a fury of abhorrence and fear, like pygmies about the ankles of a drowsing elephant: the old bear solitary, indomitable and alone, widowered, childless, and absolved of mortality—old Priam[1] reft of his old wife and having outlived all his sons.

Until he was ten, each November he would watch the wagon containing the dogs and the bedding and food and guns and his father and Tennie's Jim, the Negro, and Sam Fathers, the Indian, son of a slave woman and a Chickasaw chief, depart on the road to town, to Jefferson where Major de Spain and the others would join them. To the boy, at seven, eight, and nine, they were not going into the Big Bottom to hunt bear and deer, but to keep yearly rendezvous with the bear which they did not even intend to kill. Two

---

1. **Priam** (prī′əm), the last king of Troy. His wife and sons were killed by the Greeks during the Trojan War.

Copyright 1942 and renewed 1970 by Estelle Faulkner and Jill Faulkner Summers. Reprinted from *Go Down, Moses*, by William Faulkner, by permission of Random House, Inc., the Author's Literary Estate and Chatto & Windus Ltd.

weeks later they would return, with no trophy, no head and skin. He had not expected it. He had not even been afraid it would be in the wagon. He believed that even after he was ten and his father would let him go too, for those two weeks in November, he would merely make another one, along with his father and Major de Spain and General Compson and the others, the dogs which feared to bay at it and the rifles and shotguns which failed even to bleed it, in the yearly pageant of the old bear's furious immortality.

Then he heard the dogs. It was in the second week of his first time in the camp. He stood with Sam Fathers against a big oak beside the faint crossing where they had stood each dawn for nine days now, hearing the dogs. He had heard them once before, one morning last week—a murmur, sourceless, echoing through the wet woods, swelling presently into separate voices which he could recognize and call by name. He had raised and cocked the gun as Sam told him and stood motionless again while the uproar, the invisible course, swept up and past and faded; it seemed to him that he could actually see the deer, the buck, blond, smoke-colored, elongated with speed, fleeing, vanishing, the woods, the gray solitude, still ringing even when the cries of the dogs had died away.

"Now let the hammers down," Sam said.

"You knew they were not coming here too," he said.

"Yes," Sam said. "I want you to learn how to do when you didn't shoot. It's after the chance for the bear or the deer has done already come and gone that men and dogs get killed."

"Anyway," he said, "it was just a deer."

Then on the tenth morning he heard the dogs again. And he readied the too-long, too-heavy gun as Sam had taught him, before Sam even spoke. But this time it was no deer, no ringing chorus of dogs running strong on a free scent, but a moiling yapping an octave too high, with something more than indecision and even abjectness in it, not even moving very fast, taking a long time to pass completely out of hearing, leaving them somewhere in the air that echo, thin, slightly hysterical, abject, almost grieving, with no sense of a fleeing, unseen, smoke-colored, grass-eating shape ahead of it, and Sam, who had taught him first of all to cock the gun and take position where he could see everywhere and then never move again, had himself moved up beside him; he could hear Sam breathing at his shoulder and he could see the arched curve of the old man's inhaling nostrils.

"Hah," Sam said. "Not even running. Walking."

"Old Ben!" the boy said. "But up here!" he cried. "Way up here!"

"He do it every year," Sam said. "Once. Maybe to see who in camp this time, if he can shoot or not. Whether we got the dog yet that can bay and hold him. He'll take them to the river, then he'll send them back home. We may as well go back, too; see how they look when they come back to camp."

When they reached the camp the hounds were already there, ten of them crouching back under the kitchen, the boy and Sam squatting to peer back into the obscurity where they huddled, quiet, the eyes luminous, glowing at them and vanishing, and no sound, only that effluvium of something more than dog, stronger than dog and not just animal, just beast, because still there had been nothing in front of that abject and almost painful yapping save the solitude, the wilderness, so that when the eleventh hound came in at noon and with all others watching—even old Uncle Ash, who called himself first a cook—Sam daubed the tattered ear and the raked shoulder with turpentine and axle grease, to the boy it was still no living creature, but the wilderness which, leaning for the moment down, had patted lightly once the hound's temerity.

"Just like a man," Sam said. "Just like folks. Put off as long as she could having to be brave, knowing all the time that sooner or later she would have to be brave to keep on living with herself, and knowing all the time beforehand what was going to happen to her when she done it."

That afternoon, himself on the one-eyed wagon mule which did not mind the smell of blood nor, as they told him, of bear, and with Sam on the other one, they rode for more than three hours through the rapid, shortening winter day. They followed no path, no trail even that he could see; almost at once they were in a country which he had never seen before. Then he knew why Sam had made him ride the mule which would not spook. The sound one stopped short and tried to whirl and bolt even as Sam got down, blowing its breath, jerking and wrenching at the rein, while Sam held it, coaxing it forward with his voice, since he could not risk tying it, drawing it forward while the boy got down from the marred one.

Then, standing beside Sam in the gloom of the dying afternoon, he looked down at the rotted overturned log, gutted and scored with claw marks, and in the wet earth beside it, the print of the enormous warped two-toed foot. He knew now what he had smelled when he peered under the kitchen where the dogs huddled. He realized for the first time that the bear which had run in his listening and loomed in his dreams since before he could remember to the contrary, and which, therefore, must have existed in the listening and dreams of his father and Major de Spain and even old General Compson, too, before they began to remember in their turn, was a mortal animal, and that if they had departed for the camp each November without any actual hope of bringing its trophy back, it was not because it could not be slain, but because so far they had had no actual hope to.

"Tomorrow," he said.

"We'll try tomorrow," Sam said. "We ain't got the dog yet."

"We've got eleven. They ran him this morning."

"It won't need but one," Sam said. "He ain't here. Maybe he ain't nowhere. The only other way will be for him to run by accident over somebody that has a gun."

"That wouldn't be me," the boy said. "It will be Walter or Major or——"

"It might," Sam said. "You watch close in the morning. Because he's smart. That's how come he has lived this long. If he gets hemmed up and has to pick out somebody to run over, he will pick out you."

"How?" the boy said. "How will he know ——" He ceased. "You mean he already knows me, that I ain't never been here before, ain't had time to find out yet whether I——" He ceased again, looking at Sam, the old man whose face revealed nothing until it smiled. He said humbly, not even amazed, "It was me he was watching. I don't reckon he did need to come but once."

The next morning they left the camp three hours before daylight. They rode this time because it was too far to walk, even the dogs in the wagon; again the first gray light found him in a place which he had never seen before, where Sam had placed him and told him to stay and then departed. With the gun which was too big for him, which did not even belong to him, but to Major de Spain, and which he had fired only once—at a stump on the first day, to learn the recoil and how to reload it—he stood against a gum tree beside a little bayou whose black still water crept without movement out of a canebrake and crossed a small clearing and into cane again, where, invisible, a bird—the big woodpecker called Lord-to-God by Negroes—clattered at a dead limb.

It was a stand like any other, dissimilar only in incidentals to the one where he had stood each morning for ten days; a territory new to him, yet no less familiar than that other which, after almost two weeks, he had come to believe he knew a little—the same solitude, the same loneliness through which human beings had merely passed without altering it, leaving no mark, no scar, which looked exactly as it must have looked when the first ancestor of Sam Fathers' Chickasaw predecessors crept into it and looked about, club or stone ax or bone arrow drawn and poised; different only because, squatting at the edge of the kitchen, he smelled the hounds huddled and cringing beneath it and saw the raked ear and shoulder of the one who, Sam said, had had to be brave once in order to live with herself, and saw yesterday in the earth beside the gutted log the print of the living foot.

He heard no dogs at all. He never did hear them. He only heard the drumming of the woodpecker stop short off and knew that the bear was looking at him. He never saw it. He did not know whether it was in front of him or behind him. He did not move, holding the useless gun, which he had not even had warning to cock and which even now he did not cock, tasting in his saliva that taint as of brass which he knew now because he had smelled it when he peered under the kitchen at the huddled dogs.

Then it was gone. As abruptly as it had ceased, the woodpecker's dry, monotonous clatter set up again, and after a while he even believed he could hear the dogs—a murmur, scarce a sound even, which he had probably been hearing for some time before he even remarked it, drifting into hearing and then out again, dying away. They came nowhere near him. If it was a bear they ran, it was another bear. It was Sam himself who came out of the cane and crossed the bayou, followed by the injured bitch of yesterday. She was almost at heel, like a bird dog, making no sound. She came and crouched against his leg, trembling, staring off into the cane.

"I didn't see him," he said. "I didn't, Sam!"

"I know it," Sam said. "He done the looking. You didn't hear him neither, did you?"

"No," the boy said. "I ——"

"He's smart," Sam said. "Too smart." He looked down at the hound, trembling faintly and steadily against the boy's knee. From the raked shoulder a few drops of fresh blood oozed and clung. "Too big. We ain't got the dog yet. But maybe someday. Maybe not next time. But someday."

So I must see him, he thought. *I must look at him.* Otherwise, it seemed to him that it would go on like this forever, as it had gone on with his father and Major de Spain, who was older than his father, and even with old General Compson, who had been old enough to be a brigade commander in 1865. Otherwise, it would go on so forever, next time and next time, after and after and after. It seemed to him that he could

never see the two of them, himself and the bear, shadowy in the limbo from which time emerged, becoming time; the old bear absolved of mortality and himself partaking, sharing a little of it, enough of it. And he knew now what he had smelled in the huddled dogs and tasted in his saliva. He recognized fear. *So I will have to see him,* he thought, without dread or even hope. *I will have to look at him.*

It was in June of the next year. He was eleven. They were in camp again, celebrating Major de Spain's and General Compson's birthdays. Although the one had been born in September and the other in the depth of winter and in another decade, they had met for two weeks to fish and shoot squirrels and turkey and run coons and wildcats with the dogs at night. That is, he and Boon Hoggenback and the Negroes fished and shot squirrels and ran the coons and cats, because the proved hunters, not only Major de Spain and old General Compson, who spent those two weeks sitting in a rocking chair before a tremendous iron pot of Brunswick stew, stirring and tasting, with old Ash to quarrel with about how he was making it and Tennie's Jim to pour whiskey from the demijohn into the tin dipper from which he drank, but even the boy's father and Walter Ewell, who were still young enough, scorned such, other than shooting the wild gobblers with pistols for wagers on their marksmanship.

Or, that is, his father and the others believed he was hunting squirrels. Until the third day, he thought that Sam Fathers believed that too. Each morning he would leave the camp right after breakfast. He had his own gun now, a Christmas present. He went back to the tree beside the bayou where he had stood that morning. Using the compass which old General Compson had given him, he ranged from that point; he was teaching himself to be a better-than-fair woodsman without knowing he was doing it. On the second day he even found the gutted log where he had first seen the crooked print. It was almost completely crumbled now, healing with unbelievable speed, a passionate and almost visible relin-

Winslow Homer, *Gathering Autumn Leaves* (1873). Cooper-Hewitt Museum of Decorative Arts and Design, Smithsonian Institution

the dappling gloom, so that he would not always see them until they moved, returning later and later, first day, second day, passing in the twilight of the third evening the little log pen enclosing the log stable where Sam was putting up the horses for the night.

"You ain't looked right yet," Sam said.

He stopped. For a moment he didn't answer. Then he said peacefully, in a peaceful rushing burst as when a boy's miniature dam in a little brook gives way. "All right. But how? I went to the bayou. I even found that log again. I ——"

"I reckon that was all right. Likely he's been watching you. You never saw his foot?"

"I," the boy said—"I didn't—I never thought——"

"It's the gun," Sam said. He stood beside the fence, motionless—the old man, the Indian, in the battered faded overalls and the five-cent straw hat which in the Negro's race had been the badge of his enslavement and was now the regalia of his freedom. The camp—the clearing, the house, the barn and its tiny lot with which Major de Spain in his turn had scratched punily and evanescently at the wilderness—faded in the dusk, back into the immemorial darkness of the woods. *The gun,* the boy thought. *The gun.*

"Be scared," Sam said. "You can't help that. But don't be afraid. Ain't nothing in the woods going to hurt you unless you corner it, or it smells that you are afraid. A bear or a deer, too, has got to be scared of a coward the same as a brave man has got to be."

The gun, the boy thought.

"You will have to choose," Sam said.

He left the camp before daylight, long before Uncle Ash would wake in his quilts on the kitchen floor and start the fire for breakfast. He had only the compass and a stick for snakes. He could go almost a mile before he would begin to need the compass. He sat on a log, the invisible compass in his invisible hand, while the secret night sounds, fallen still at his movements, scurried again and then ceased for good, and the owls ceased and gave over to the waking of day birds, and he could see the compass. Then he went fast

quishment, back into the earth from which the tree had grown.

He ranged the summer woods now, green with gloom; if anything, actually dimmer than in November's gray dissolution, where, even at noon, the sun fell only in intermittent dappling upon the earth, which never completely dried out and which crawled with snakes—moccasins and water snakes and rattlers, themselves the color of

yet still quietly; he was becoming better and better as a woodsman, still without having yet realized it.

He jumped a doe and a fawn at sunrise, walked them out of the bed, close enough to see them—the crash of undergrowth, the white scut, the fawn scudding behind her faster than he had believed it could run. He was hunting right, upwind, as Sam had taught him; not that it mattered now. He had left the gun; of his own will and relinquishment he had accepted not a gambit, not a choice, but a condition in which not only the bear's heretofore inviolable anonymity but all the old rules and balances of hunter and hunted had been abrogated. He would not even be afraid, not even in the moment when the fear would take him completely—blood, skin, bowels, bones, memory from the long time before it became his memory—all save that thin, clear, immortal lucidity which alone differed him from this bear and from all the other bear and deer he would ever kill in the humility and pride of his skill and endurance, to which Sam had spoken when he leaned in the twilight on the lot fence yesterday.

By noon he was far beyond the little bayou, farther into the new and alien country than he had ever been. He was traveling now not only by the old, heavy, biscuit-thick silver watch which had belonged to his grandfather. When he stopped at last, it was for the first time since he had risen from the log at dawn when he could see the compass. It was far enough. He had left the camp nine hours ago: nine hours from now, dark would have already been an hour old. But he didn't think that. He thought. *All right. Yes. But what?* and stood for a moment, alien and small in the green and topless solitude, answering his own question before it had formed and ceased. It was the watch, the compass, the stick—the three lifeless mechanicals with which for nine hours he had fended the wilderness off; he hung the watch and compass carefully on a bush and leaned the stick beside them and relinquished completely to it.

He had not been going very fast for the last two or three hours. He went no faster now, since distance would not matter even if he could have gone fast. And he was trying to keep a bearing on the tree where he had left the compass, trying to complete a circle which would bring him back to it or at least intersect itself, since direction would not matter now either. But the tree was not there, and he did as Sam had schooled him—made the next circle in the opposite direction, so that the two patterns would bisect somewhere, but crossing no print of his own feet, finding the tree at last, but in the wrong place—no bush, no compass, no watch—and the tree not even the tree, because there was a down log beside it and he did what Sam Fathers had told him was the next thing and the last.

As he sat down on the log he saw the crooked print—the warped, tremendous, two-toed indentation which, even as he watched it, filled with water. As he looked up, the wilderness coalesced, solidified—the glade, the tree he sought, the bush, the watch and the compass glinting where a ray of sunlight touched them. Then he saw the bear. It did not emerge, appear; it was just there, immobile, solid, fixed in the hot dappling of the green and windless noon, not as big as he had dreamed it, but as big as he had expected it, bigger, dimensionless against the dappled obscurity, looking at him where he sat quietly on the log and looked back at it.

Then it moved. It made no sound. It did not hurry. It crossed the glade, walking for an instant into the full glare of the sun; when it reached the other side it stopped again and looked back at him across one shoulder while his quiet breathing inhaled and exhaled three times.

Then it was gone. It didn't walk into the woods, the undergrowth. It faded, sank back into the wilderness as he had watched a fish, a huge old bass, sink and vanish into the dark depths of its pool without even any movement of its fins.

He thought, *It will be next fall.* But it was not next fall, nor the next nor the next. He was fourteen then. He had killed his buck, and Sam Fathers had marked his face with the hot blood, and in the next year he killed a bear. But even before that accolade he had become as competent in the woods as many grown men with the same experience; by his fourteenth year he was a better woodsman than most grown men with more. There was no territory within thirty miles of the camp that he did not know—bayou, ridge, brake, landmark, tree, and path. He could have led anyone to any point in it without deviation, and brought them out again. He knew the game trails that even Sam Fathers did not know; in his thirteenth year he found a buck's bedding place, and unbeknown to his father he borrowed Walter Ewell's rifle and lay in wait at dawn and killed the buck when it walked back to the bed, as Sam had told him how the old Chickasaw fathers did.

But not the old bear, although by now he knew its footprints better than he did his own, and not only the crooked one. He could see any one of the three sound ones and distinguish it from any other, and not only by its size. There were other bears within these thirty miles which left tracks almost as large, but this was more than that. If Sam Fathers had been his mentor and the backyard rabbits and squirrels at home his kindergarten, then the wilderness the old bear ran was his college, the old male bear itself, so long unwifed and childless as to have become its own ungendered progenitor, was his alma mater. But he never saw it.

He could find the crooked print now almost whenever he liked, fifteen or ten or five miles, or sometimes nearer the camp than that. Twice while on stand during the three years he heard the dogs strike its trail by accident; on the second time they jumped it seemingly, the voices high, abject, almost human in hysteria, as on that first morning two years ago. But not the bear itself. He would remember that noon three years ago, the glade, himself and the bear fixed during that moment in the windless and dappled blaze, and it would seem to him that it had never happened, that he had dreamed that too. But it had happened. They had looked at each other, they had emerged from the wilderness old as earth, synchronized to the instant by something more than the blood that moved the flesh and bones which bore them, and touched, pledged something, affirmed something more lasting than the frail web of bones and flesh which any accident could obliterate.

Then he saw it again. Because of the very fact that he thought of nothing else, he had forgotten to look for it. He was still hunting with Walter Ewell's rifle. He saw it cross the end of a long blowdown, a corridor where a tornado had swept, rushing through rather than over the tangle of trunks and branches as a locomotive would have, faster than he had ever believed it could move, almost as fast as a deer even, because a deer would have spent most of that time in the air, faster than he could bring the rifle sights with it. And now he knew what had been wrong during all the three years. He sat on a log, shaking and trembling as if he had never seen the woods before nor anything that ran them, wondering with incredulous amazement how he could have forgotten the very thing which Sam Fathers had told him and the bear itself had proved the next day and had now returned after three years to reaffirm.

And now he knew what Sam Fathers had meant about the right dog, a dog in which size would mean less than nothing. So when he returned alone in April—school was out then, so that the sons of farmers could help with the land's planting, and at last his father had granted him permission, on his promise to be back in four days—he had the dog. It was his own, a mongrel of the sort called by Negroes a fyce, a ratter, itself not much bigger than a rat and possessing that bravery which had long since stopped being courage and had become foolhardiness.

It did not take four days. Alone again, he found the trail on the first morning. It was not a stalk; it was an ambush. He timed the meeting almost as if it were an appointment with a human being. Himself holding the fyce muffled in a feed sack and Sam Fathers with two of the hounds on a piece of a plowline rope, they lay downwind of the trail at dawn of the second morning. They were so close that the bear turned without even running, as if in surprised amazement at the shrill and frantic uproar of the released fyce, turning at bay against the trunk of a tree, on its hind feet; it seemed to the boy that it would never stop rising, taller and taller, and even the two hounds seemed to take a desperate and despairing courage from the fyce, following it as it went in.

Then he realized that the fyce was actually not going to stop. He flung, threw the gun away, and ran; when he overtook and grasped the frantically pinwheeling little dog, it seemed to him that he was directly under the bear.

He could smell it, strong and hot and rank. Sprawling, he looked up to where it loomed and towered over him like a cloudburst and colored like a thunderclap, quite familiar, peacefully and even lucidly familiar, until he remembered: This was the way he had used to dream about it. Then it was gone. He didn't see it go. He knelt, holding the frantic fyce with both hands, hearing the abashed wailing of the hounds drawing farther and farther away, until Sam came up. He carried the gun. He laid it down quietly beside the boy and stood looking down at him.

"You've done seed him twice now with a gun in your hands," he said. "This time you couldn't have missed him."

The boy rose. He still held the fyce. Even in his arms and clear of the ground, it yapped frantically, straining and surging after the fading uproar of the two hounds like a tangle of wire springs. He was panting a little, but he was neither shaking nor trembling now.

"Neither could you!" he said. "You had the gun! Neither did you!"

"And you didn't shoot," his father said. "How close were you?"

"I don't know, sir," he said. "There was a big wood tick inside his right hind leg. I saw that. But I didn't have the gun then."

"But you didn't shoot when you had the gun," his father said. "Why?"

But he didn't answer, and his father didn't wait for him to, rising and crossing the room, across the pelt of the bear which the boy had killed two years ago and the larger one which his father had killed before he was born, to the bookcase beneath the mounted head of the boy's first buck. It was the room which his father called the office, from which all the plantation business was transacted; in it for the fourteen years of his life he had heard the best of all talking. Major de Spain would be there and sometimes old General Compson, and Walter Ewell and Boon Hoggenback and Sam Fathers and Tennie's Jim, too, were hunters, knew the woods and what ran them.

He would hear it, not talking himself but listening—the wilderness, the big woods, bigger and older than any recorded document of white man fatuous enough to believe he had bought any fragment of it or Indian ruthless enough to pretend that any fragment of it had been his to convey. It was of the men, not white nor black nor red, but men, hunters with the will and hardihood to endure and the humility and skill to survive, and the dogs and the bear and deer juxtaposed and reliefed against it, ordered and compelled by and within the wilderness in the ancient and unremitting contest by the ancient and immitigable rules which voided all regrets and brooked no quarter, the voices quiet and weighty and deliberate for retrospection and recollection and exact remembering, while he squatted in the blazing firelight as Tennie's Jim squatted, who stirred only to put more wood on the fire and to pass the bottle from one glass to another. Because the bottle was always present, so that after a while it seemed to him that those fierce instants of heart and brain and courage and wiliness and speed were concentrated and distilled into that brown liquor which not women, not boys and children, but only hunters drank, drinking not of the blood they had spilled but some condensation of the wild immortal spirit, drinking it moderately, humbly even, not with the pagan's base hope of acquiring the virtues of cunning and strength and speed, but in salute to them.

His father returned with the book and sat down again and opened it. "Listen," he said. He read the five stanzas aloud, his voice quiet and deliberate in the room where there was no fire now because it was already spring. Then he looked up. The boy watched him. "All right," his father said. "Listen." He read again, but only the second stanza this time, to the end of it, the last two lines, and closed the book and put it on the table beside him. "She cannot fade, though thou hast not thy bliss, forever wilt thou love, and she be fair,"[2] he said.

"He's talking about a girl," the boy said.

"He had to talk about something," his father said. Then he said, "He was talking about truth. Truth doesn't change. Truth is one thing. It covers all things which touch the heart—honor and pride and pity and justice and courage and love. Do you see now?"

He didn't know. Somehow it was simpler than that. There was an old bear, fierce and ruthless, not merely just to stay alive, but with the fierce pride of liberty and freedom, proud enough of the liberty and freedom to see it threatened without fear or even alarm; nay, who at times even seemed deliberately to put that freedom and liberty in jeopardy in order to savor them, to remind his old strong bones and flesh to keep supple and quick to defend and preserve them. There was an old man, son of a Negro slave and an Indian king, inheritor on the one side of the long chronicle of a people who had learned humility through suffering, and pride through the endurance which survived the suffering and injustice, and on the other side, the chronicle of a people even longer in the land than the first, yet who no longer existed in the land at all save in the solitary brotherhood of an old Negro's alien blood and the wild and invincible spirit of an old bear. There was a boy who wished to learn humility and pride in order to become skillful and worthy in the woods, who suddenly found himself becoming so skillful so rapidly that he feared he would never become worthy because he had not learned humility and pride, although he had tried to, until one day and as suddenly he discovered that an old man who could not have defined either had led him, as though by the hand, to that point where an old bear and a little mongrel of a dog showed

him that, by possessing one thing other, he would possess them both.

And a little dog, nameless and mongrel and many-fathered, grown, yet weighing less than six pounds, saying as if to itself, "I can't be dangerous, because there's nothing much smaller than I am; I can't be fierce, because they would call it just noise; I can't be humble, because I'm already too close to the ground to genuflect; I can't be proud, because I wouldn't be near enough to it for anyone to know who was casting the shadow, and I don't even know that I'm not going to heaven, because they have already decided that I don't possess an immortal soul. So all I can be is brave. But it's all right. I can be that, even if they still call it just noise."

That was all. It was simple, much simpler than somebody talking in a book about a youth and a girl he would never need to grieve over, because he could never approach any nearer her and would never have to get any farther away. He had heard about a bear, and finally got big enough to trail it, and he trailed it four years and at last met it with a gun in his hands and he didn't shoot. Because a little dog——But he could have shot long before the little dog covered the twenty yards to where the bear waited, and Sam Fathers could have shot at any time during that interminable minute while Old Ben stood on his hind feet over them. He stopped. His father was watching him gravely across the spring-rife twilight of the room; when he spoke, his words were as quiet as the twilight, too, not loud, because they did not need to be because they would last. "Courage, and honor, and pride," his father said, "and pity, and love of justice and of liberty. They all touch the heart, and what the heart holds to becomes truth, as far as we know the truth. Do you see now?"

Sam, and Old Ben, and Nip, he thought. And himself too. He had been all right too. His father had said so. "Yes, sir," he said.   **1942**

---

2. *"She cannot ... be fair,"* the last lines of stanza 2 of "Ode on a Grecian Urn" by John Keats (1795–1821).

THINK AND DISCUSS
Understanding
1. On the boy's first hunt, what lesson does Sam Fathers teach him?
2. When the boy is eleven he visits the swamp again. What choice concerning the gun does Sam put to him? What does he find necessary to do before he faces the bear again?
3. What does the boy throw away at his last encounter with the bear? What opportunity do the boy and Sam both fail to take?
4. In his concluding conversation with his father, how does the boy explain his refusal to shoot the bear?

Analyzing
5. The first four paragraphs form the exposition of this story. What has the boy learned about the bear and the hunters' attitude toward it? Describe the **mood** this exposition sets for the story.
6. On what terms does the boy finally face the bear? How do you know?
7. One of the **themes** of the story is a child's growth to maturity. What lessons does the boy learn from his father? the bear? Sam Fathers?
8. What distinctions does Faulkner seem to draw between cowardice, foolhardiness, and true bravery? How is his concept of bravery related to the theme of maturity?

Extending
9. What does the boy's father tell him about truth? Do you think his definition of truth is accurate? Explain your answer.

REVIEWING: Symbol H𝐓
See Handbook of Literary Terms, p. 913.

A **symbol** is an object or event that represents something beyond itself. In this story, the bear is a major symbol.

1. Why does the boy refuse to shoot the bear?
2. How is this bear different from other bears?

How do the hunters treat it differently?
3. What does the bear represent to Sam? to the boy?

VOCABULARY
Context and Dictionary
Use your Glossary to find the meaning of each word below from "The Bear." On your paper write the proper form of the word that correctly completes each statement.

progenitor	abrogate
coalesce	abject
intermittent	interminable
anachronism	retrospection

1. Greg described the sight of a donkey and cart going down the middle of a modern expressway as an _____.
2. The mood of the girl who had lost her house, her car, and her job was _____.
3. The company has _____ its agreement with one supplier in order to use another.
4. Before Father's illness our family bickered constantly, but since then we have _____ in order to solve our problems.
5. The forecast was for _____ showers, ending sometime Tuesday.
6. Beth has spent nearly ten years studying her family tree in an attempt to track down her earliest _____.
7. The dull film seemed _____, and the audience appeared restless.

COMPOSITION ◂━▱
Explaining a Symbol
Assume that your city is seeking a new symbol, and the city council is holding a contest. To enter this contest, you must compose a two-paragraph explanation of why a particular animal should be the symbol for your city. In your first paragraph, state what the symbol is, and what quality or qualities of your city are represented by that animal. In the second paragraph, explain why your symbol embodies those qualities.

The Frontier

At the end of F. Scott Fitzgerald's *The Great Gatsby*, the narrator meditates on how the first explorers of America, on seeing the "fresh, green breast of the new world," must have held their breath "in the presence of this continent." The Frontier as a theme in American culture was born when those first adventurers set eyes on the New World and were enchanted by a vision of verdant wilderness luring them onward to partake of both freedom and the earth's bounty.

John Smith was later to describe Virginia, which he explored in the early 1600s, in terms of an advertising brochure wooing settlers to the empty lands of the New World. His appeal: "Who can desire more . . . than to tread and plant that ground he hath purchased by the hazard of his life?"

This appeal, irresistible to thousands of settlers, endured beyond the next three centuries. It is an appeal that haunts the American imagination today, after most of that original wilderness has disappeared in endless fields of agribusiness, far stretches of suburbia, and ribbons of concrete crisscrossing the continent.

The Frontier came to symbolize much more than just free and abundant land. The Frontier also would build character, turning boys into frontiersmen and girls into pioneer women. The Frontier would provide a new society with freedom, justice, peace, and harmony. And, above all, the Frontier would enable human nature to change, leaving all defects behind.

Emerson in his essay *Nature* explored on a transcendental plane the spiritual resources attainable in communion with the frontier wilderness. Emerson's disciple Thoreau left the town to live alone by Walden Pond and do what many a frontiersman before him had done—"to front only the essential facts of life." And in "When Lilacs Last in the Dooryard Bloom'd," when Whitman identified Lincoln with the "powerful fallen western star," he was in effect conceiving him as one of America's new men created or fostered by the Frontier.

When Huckleberry Finn, at the end of Mark Twain's novel, says, "I reckon I got to light out for the Territory," he was simply repeating what many Americans had said before as they moved west. But in 1890 the U.S. Census Bureau officially declared that, because of the increase in population density of the Western lands, the Frontier no longer existed—the wilderness had all been tamed. Whether the Frontier had vanished physically or not, it certainly endured in the American spirit and imagination, particularly in those indestructible popular art forms, the Western novel and the Western film. John Kennedy adopted the term *New Frontier* to describe the spirit with which he viewed his presidency.

Many of the stories in this unit relate to the frontier myth. The pioneer woman in "A Wagner Matinée" discovers, when she visits Boston, that her hard life on a farm has imposed terrible deprivations. Faulkner's "The Bear," based on the legend of an enormous, elusive, almost mystical bear, is set in a patch of untouched American wilderness. The boy in the story is at last privileged to see and feel the bear's presence. When at the critical moment he refuses to shoot the bear, he completes his rite of passage. The Frontier has once again shaped a boy into a man. John Steinbeck's "The Leader of the People" is set in California—where the West ends. The story is a kind of elegy for the passing of the Frontier. As the grandfather explains to Jody: "It wasn't Indians that were important, nor adventures, nor even getting out here. . . . It was westering and westering." And it is clear from the boy's response that the frontier myth will live on, deeply embedded as it is in Jody's (and the American) imagination.

John Steinbeck once wrote: "Sometimes I have a vision of human personality as a kind of fetid jungle full of monsters and demons and little lights. It seemed to me a dangerous place to venture, a little like those tunnels at Coney Island where 'things' leap out screaming. I have been accused so often of writing about abnormal people." Some of Steinbeck's critics have observed that he often compared human behavior to animal behavior.

Born in Salinas, California, Steinbeck grew up in a rich but strike-tormented valley where the plight of agricultural and factory workers made a deep impression on him. Between 1919 and 1925, he intermittently attended Stanford University, where he developed a lasting interest in marine biology and contributed to university magazines. After leaving Stanford, he worked for a while as a newspaper reporter in New York City. When his first three books were financial failures, he supported himself by such jobs as hod-carrying, surveying, and fruit picking. He finally achieved literary popularity in 1935 with a book that is said to have been rejected by nine publishers: this was *Tortilla Flat,* a series of stories about Mexican Americans on the Monterey Peninsula. His short novel, *Of Mice and Men,* became a best seller in 1937. Two years later a novel dealing with the plight of uprooted farmers in their trek from the Oklahoma dust bowl to California's fruit farms, *The Grapes of Wrath* (1939), earned the Pulitzer Prize.

In 1962, when he was awarded the Nobel Prize, Steinbeck published *Travels with Charley,* the account of a journey he and his dog, Charley, made through the United States. Steinbeck shows compassion for lonely eccentrics and people who live close to the soil. In one way or another, his works probe and question American values. The poetic quality of his vigorous prose, one of his outstanding features as a stylist, is evident in "The Leader of the People."

The Leader of the People

John Steinbeck

n Saturday afternoon Billy Buck, the ranch hand, raked together the last of the old year's haystack and pitched small forkfuls over the wire fence to a few mildly interested cattle. High in the air small clouds like puffs of cannon smoke were driven eastward by the March wind. The wind could be heard whishing in the brush on the ridge crests, but no breath of it penetrated down into the ranch cup.

The little boy, Jody, emerged from the house eating a thick piece of buttered bread. He saw Billy working on the last of the haystack. Jody tramped down scuffling his shoes in a way he had been told was destructive to good shoe leather. A flock of white pigeons flew out of the black cypress tree as Jody passed, and circled the tree and landed again. A half-grown tortoise-shell cat leaped from the bunkhouse porch, galloped on stiff legs across the road, whirled and galloped back again. Jody picked up a stone to help the game along, but he was too late, for the cat was under the porch before the stone could be discharged. He threw the stone into the cypress tree and started the white pigeons on another whirling flight.

Arriving at the used-up haystack, the boy leaned against the barbed-wire fence. "Will that be all of it, do you think?" he asked.

The middle-aged ranch hand stopped his careful raking and stuck his fork into the ground. He took off his black hat and smoothed down his hair. "Nothing left of it that isn't soggy from ground moisture," he said. He replaced his hat and rubbed his dry leathery hands together.

"Ought to be plenty mice," Jody suggested.

"Lousy with them," said Billy. "Just crawling with mice."

"Well, maybe, when you get all through, I could call the dogs and hunt the mice."

"Sure, I guess you could," said Billy Buck. He lifted a forkful of the damp ground hay and threw it into the air. Instantly three mice leaped out and burrowed frantically under the hay again.

Jody sighed with satisfaction. Those plump, sleek, arrogant mice were doomed. For eight months they had lived and multiplied in the haystack. They had been immune from cats, from traps, from poison, and from Jody. They had grown smug in their security, overbearing and fat. Now the time of disaster had come; they would not survive another day.

Billy looked up at the top of the hills that surrounded the ranch. "Maybe you better ask your father before you do it," he suggested.

"Well, where is he? I'll ask him now."

"He rode up to the ridge ranch after dinner. He'll be back pretty soon."

Jody slumped against the fence post. "I don't think he'd care."

As Billy went back to his work he said ominously, "You'd better ask him anyway. You know how he is."

Jody did know. His father, Carl Tiflin, insisted upon giving permission for anything that was done on the ranch, whether it was important or not. Jody sagged farther against the post until he was sitting on the ground. He looked up at the little puffs of wind-driven cloud. "Is it like to rain, Billy?"

"It might. The wind's good for it, but not strong enough."

"Well, I hope it don't rain until after I kill those damn mice." He looked over his shoulder to see whether Billy had noticed the mature profanity. Billy worked on without comment.

"The Leader of the People" from *The Red Pony* by John Steinbeck. Copyright 1938, © 1966 by John Steinbeck. Reprinted by permission of Viking Penguin Inc., McIntosh and Otis, Inc., and William Heinemann Ltd. Publishers.

Jody turned back and looked at the side-hill where the road from the outside world came down. The hill was washed with lean March sunshine. Silver thistles, blue lupins and a few poppies bloomed among the sagebushes. Halfway up the hill Jody could see Doubletree Mutt, the black dog, digging in a squirrel hole. He paddled for a while and then paused to kick bursts of dirt out between his hind legs, and he dug with an earnestness which belied the knowledge he must have had that no dog had ever caught a squirrel by digging in a hole.

Suddenly, while Jody watched, the black dog stiffened, and backed out of the hole and looked up the hill toward the cleft in the ridge where the road came through. Jody looked up too. For a moment Carl Tiflin on horseback stood out against the pale sky and then he moved down the road toward the house. He carried something white in his hand.

The boy started to his feet. "He's got a letter," Jody cried. He trotted away toward the ranch house, for the letter would probably be read aloud and he wanted to be there. He reached the house before his father did, and ran in. He heard Carl dismount from his creaking saddle and slap the horse on the side to send it to the barn where Billy would unsaddle it and turn it out.

Jody ran into the kitchen. "We got a letter!" he cried.

His mother looked up from a pan of beans. "Who has?"

"Father has. I saw it in his hand."

Carl strode into the kitchen then, and Jody's mother asked, "Who's the letter from, Carl?"

He frowned quickly. "How did you know there was a letter?"

She nodded her head in the boy's direction. "Big-Britches Jody told me."

Jody was embarrassed.

His father looked down at him contemptuously. "He *is* getting to be a Big-Britches," Carl said. "He's minding everybody's business but his own. Got his big nose into everything."

Mrs. Tiflin relented a little. "Well, he hasn't enough to keep him busy. Who's the letter from?"

Carl still frowned on Jody. "I'll keep him busy if he isn't careful." He held out a sealed letter. "I guess it's from your father."

Mrs. Tiflin took a hairpin from her head and slit open the flap. Her lips pursed judiciously. Jody saw her eyes snap back and forth over the lines. "He says," she translated, "he says he's going to drive out Saturday to stay for a little while. Why, this is Saturday. The letter must have been delayed." She looked at the postmark. "This was mailed day before yesterday. It should have been here yesterday." She looked up questioningly at her husband, and then her face darkened angrily. "Now what have you got that look on you for? He doesn't come often."

Carl turned his eyes away from her anger. He could be stern with her most of the time, but when occasionally her temper arose, he could not combat it.

"What's the matter with you?" she demanded again.

In his explanation there was a tone of apology Jody himself might have used. "It's just that he talks," Carl said lamely. "Just talks."

"Well, what of it? You talk yourself."

"Sure I do. But your father only talks about one thing."

"Indians!" Jody broke in excitedly. "Indians and crossing the plains!"

Carl turned fiercely on him. "You get out, Mr. Big-Britches! Go on, now! Get out!"

Jody went miserably out the back door and closed the screen with elaborate quietness. Under the kitchen window his shamed, downcast eyes fell upon a curiously shaped stone, a stone of such fascination that he squatted down and picked it up and turned it over in his hands.

The voices came clearly to him through the open kitchen window. "Jody's damn well right," he heard his father say. "Just Indians and crossing the plains. I've heard that story about how the horses got driven off about a thousand times. He just goes on and on, and he never changes a word in the things he tells."

When Mrs. Tiflin answered, her tone was so changed that Jody, outside the window, looked up from his study of the stone. Her voice had become soft and explanatory. Jody knew how her face would have changed to match the tone. She said quietly, "Look at it this way, Carl. That was the big thing in my father's life. He led a wagon train clear across the plains to the coast, and when it was finished, his life was done. It was a big thing to do, but it didn't last long enough. Look!" she continued, "it's as though he was born to do that, and after he finished it, there wasn't anything more for him to do but think about it and talk about it. If there'd been any farther west to go, he'd have gone. He's told me so himself. But at last there was the ocean. He lives right by the ocean where he had to stop."

She had caught Carl, caught him and entangled him in her soft tone.

"I've seen him," he agreed quietly. "He goes down and stares off west over the ocean." His voice sharpened a little. "And then he goes up to the Horseshoe Club in Pacific Grove, and he tells people how the Indians drove off the horses."

She tried to catch him again. "Well, it's everything to him. You might be patient with him and pretend to listen."

Carl turned impatiently away. "Well, if it gets too bad, I can always go down to the bunkhouse and sit with Billy," he said irritably. He walked through the house and slammed the front door after him.

Jody ran to his chores. He dumped the grain to the chickens without chasing any of them. He gathered the eggs from the nests. He trotted into the house with the wood and interlaced it so carefully in the wood-box that two armloads seemed to fill it to overflowing.

His mother had finished the beans by now. She stirred up the fire and brushed off the stove top with a turkey wing. Jody peered cautiously at her to see whether any rancor toward him remained. "Is he coming today?" Jody asked.

"That's what his letter said."

"Maybe I better walk up the road to meet him."

Mrs. Tiflin clanged the stove lid shut. "That would be nice," she said. "He'd probably like to be met."

"I guess I'll just do it then."

Outside, Jody whistled shrilly to the dogs. "Come on up the hill," he commanded. The two dogs waved their tails and ran ahead. Along the roadside the sage had tender new tips. Jody tore off some pieces and rubbed them on his hands until the air was filled with the sharp wild smell. With a rush the dogs leaped from the road and yapped into the brush after a rabbit. That was the last Jody saw of them, for when they failed to catch the rabbit, they went back home.

Jody plodded on up the hill toward the ridge top. When he reached the little cleft where the road came through, the afternoon wind struck him and blew up his hair and ruffled his shirt. He looked down on the little hills and ridges below and then out at the huge green Salinas Valley.[1] He could see the white town of Salinas far out in the flat and the flash of its windows under the waning sun. Directly below him, in an oak tree, a crow congress had convened. The tree was black with crows all cawing at once. Then Jody's eyes followed the wagon road down from the ridge where he stood, and lost it behind a hill, and picked it up again on the other side. On that distant stretch he saw a cart slowly pulled by a bay horse. It disappeared behind the hill. Jody sat down on the ground and watched the place where the cart would reappear again. The wind sang on the hilltops and the puffball clouds hurried eastward.

Then the cart came into sight and stopped. A man dressed in black dismounted from the seat and walked to the horse's head. Although it was so faraway, Jody knew he had unhooked the checkrein, for the horse's head dropped forward. The horse moved on, and the man walked slowly up the hill beside it. Jody gave a glad cry and ran down the road toward them. The squirrels bumped along off the road, and a roadrunner flirted its tail and raced over the edge of the hill and sailed out like a glider.

---

1. *Salinas* (sə lē′nəs) *Valley,* an agriculturally rich valley of California.

Jody tried to leap into the middle of his shadow at every step. A stone rolled under his foot and he went down. Around a little bend he raced, and there, a short distance ahead, were his grandfather and the cart. The boy dropped from his unseemly running and approached at a dignified walk.

The horse plodded stumble-footedly up the hill and the old man walked beside it. In the lowering sun their giant shadows flickered darkly behind them. The grandfather was dressed in a black broadcloth suit and he wore kid congress gaiters and a black tie on a short, hard collar. He carried his black slouch hat in his hand. His white beard was cropped close and his white eyebrows overhung his eyes like mustaches. The blue eyes were sternly merry. About the whole face and figure there was a granite dignity, so that every motion seemed an impossible thing. Once at rest, it seemed the old man would be stone, would never move again. His steps were slow and certain. Once made, no step could ever be retraced; once headed in a direction, the path would never bend nor the pace increase nor slow.

When Jody appeared around the bend, Grandfather waved his hat slowly in welcome, and he called, "Why, Jody! Come down to meet me, have you?"

Jody sidled near and turned and matched his step to the old man's step and stiffened his body and dragged his heels a little. "Yes, sir," he said. "We got your letter only today."

"Should have been here yesterday," said Grandfather. "It certainly should. How are all the folks?"

"They're fine, sir." He hesitated and then suggested shyly, "Would you like to come on a mouse hunt tomorrow, sir?"

"Mouse hunt, Jody?" Grandfather chuckled. "Have the people of this generation come down to hunting mice? They aren't very strong, the new people, but I hardly thought mice would be game for them."

"No, sir. It's just play. The haystack's gone. I'm going to drive out the mice to the dogs. And you can watch, or even beat the hay a little."

The stern, merry eyes turned down on him. "I see. You don't eat them, then. You haven't come to that yet."

Jody explained, "The dogs eat them, sir. It wouldn't be much like hunting Indians, I guess."

"No, not much—but then later, when the troops were hunting Indians and shooting children and burning teepees, it wasn't much different from your mouse hunt."

They topped the rise and started down into the ranch cup, and they lost the sun from their shoulders. "You've grown," Grandfather said. "Nearly an inch, I should say."

"More," Jody boasted. "Where they mark me on the door, I'm up more than an inch since Thanksgiving even."

Grandfather's rich throaty voice said, "Maybe you're getting too much water and turning to pith and stalk. Wait until you head out, and then we'll see."

Jody looked quickly into the old man's face to see whether his feelings should be hurt, but there was no will to injure, no punishing nor putting-in-your-place light in the keen blue eyes. "We might kill a pig," Jody suggested.

"Oh, no! I couldn't let you do that. You're just humoring me. It isn't the time and you know it."

"You know Riley, the big boar, sir?"

"Yes. I remember Riley well."

"Well, Riley ate a hole into that same haystack, and it fell down on him and smothered him."

"Pigs do that when they can," said Grandfather.

"Riley was a nice pig, for a boar, sir. I rode him sometimes, and he didn't mind."

A door slammed at the house below them, and they saw Jody's mother standing on the porch waving her apron in welcome. And they saw Carl Tiflin walking up from the barn to be at the house for the arrival.

The sun had disappeared from the hills by now. The blue smoke from the house chimney hung in flat layers in the purpling ranch cup. The puffball clouds, dropped by the falling wind, hung listlessly in the sky.

Billy Buck came out of the bunkhouse and

flung a washbasin of soapy water on the ground. He had been shaving in midweek, for Billy held Grandfather in reverence, and Grandfather said that Billy was one of the few men of the new generation who had not gone soft. Although Billy was in middle age, Grandfather considered him a boy. Now Billy was hurrying toward the house too.

When Jody and Grandfather arrived, the three were waiting for them in front of the yard gate.

Carl said, "Hello, sir. We've been looking for you."

Mrs. Tiflin kissed Grandfather on the side of his beard, and stood still while his big hand patted her shoulder. Billy shook hands solemnly, grinning under his straw mustache. "I'll put up your horse," said Billy, and he led the rig away.

Grandfather watched him go, and then, turning back to the group, he said as he had said a hundred times before, "There's a good boy. I knew his father, old Mule-tail Buck. I never knew why they called him Mule-tail except he packed mules."

Mrs. Tiflin turned and led the way into the house. "How long are you going to stay, Father? Your letter didn't say."

"Well, I don't know. I thought I'd stay about two weeks. But I never stay as long as I think I'm going to."

In a short while they were sitting at the white oilcloth table eating their supper. The lamp with the tin reflector hung over the table. Outside the dining-room windows the big moths battered softly against the glass.

Grandfather cut his steak into tiny pieces and chewed slowly. "I'm hungry," he said. "Driving out here got my appetite up. It's like when we were crossing. We all got so hungry every night we could hardly wait to let the meat get done. I could eat about five pounds of buffalo meat every night."

"It's moving around does it," said Billy. "My father was a government packer. I helped him when I was a kid. Just the two of us could about clean up a deer's ham."

"I knew your father, Billy," said Grandfather.

"A fine man he was. They called him Mule-tail Buck. I don't know why, except he packed mules."

"That was it," Billy agreed. "He packed mules."

Grandfather put down his knife and fork and looked around the table. "I remember one time we ran out of meat——" His voice dropped to a curious low singsong, dropped into a tonal groove the story had worn for itself. "There was no buffalo, no antelope, not even rabbits. The hunters couldn't even shoot a coyote. That was the time for the leader to be on the watch. I was the leader, and I kept my eyes open. Know why? Well, just the minute the people began to get hungry they'd start slaughtering the team oxen. Do you believe that? I've heard of parties that just ate up their draft cattle. Started from the middle and worked toward the ends. Finally they'd eat the lead pair, and then the wheelers. The leader of a party had to keep them from doing that."

In some manner a big moth got into the room and circled the hanging kerosene lamp. Billy got up and tried to clap it between his hands. Carl struck with a cupped palm and caught the moth and broke it. He walked to the window and dropped it out.

"As I was saying," Grandfather began again, but Carl interrupted him. "You'd better eat some more meat. All the rest of us are ready for our pudding."

Jody saw a flash of anger in his mother's eyes. Grandfather picked up his knife and fork. "I'm pretty hungry, all right," he said. "I'll tell you about that later."

When supper was over, when the family and Billy Buck sat in front of the fireplace in the other room, Jody anxiously watched Grandfather. He saw the signs he knew. The bearded head leaned forward; the eyes lost their sternness and looked wonderingly into the fire; the big lean fingers laced themselves on the black knees.

"I wonder," he began, "I just wonder whether I ever told you how those thieving Piutes drove off thirty-five of our horses."

Frank McCarthy,
Moving On (1972).
Private collection

"I think you did," Carl interrupted. "Wasn't it just before you went up into the Tahoe country?"

Grandfather turned quickly toward his son-in-law. "That's right. I guess I must have told you that story."

"Lots of times," Carl said cruelly, and he avoided his wife's eyes. But he felt the angry eyes on him, and he said, " 'Course I'd like to hear it again."

Grandfather looked back at the fire. His fingers unlaced and laced again. Jody knew how he felt, how his insides were collapsed and empty. Hadn't Jody been called a Big-Britches that very afternoon? He arose to heroism and opened himself to the term Big-Britches again. "Tell about Indians," he said softly.

Grandfather's eyes grew stern again. "Boys always want to hear about Indians. It was a job for men, but boys want to hear about it. Well, let's see. Did I ever tell you how I wanted each wagon to carry a long iron plate?"

Everyone but Jody remained silent. Jody said, "No. You didn't."

"Well, when the Indians attacked, we always put the wagons in a circle and fought from between the wheels. I thought that if every wagon carried a long plate with rifle holes, the men could stand the plates on the outside of the wheels when the wagons were in the circle and they would be protected. It would save lives and that would make up for the extra weight of the iron. But of course the party wouldn't do it. No party had done it before and they couldn't see why they should go to the expense. They lived to regret it, too."

Jody looked at his mother, and knew from her expression that she was not listening at all. Carl picked at a callus on his thumb and Billy Buck watched a spider crawling up the wall.

Grandfather's tone dropped into its narrative groove again. Jody knew in advance exactly what words would fall. The story droned on, speeded up for the attack, grew sad over the wounds, struck a dirge at the burials on the great plains. Jody sat quietly watching Grandfather. The stern blue eyes were detached. He looked as though he were not very interested in the story himself.

When it was finished, when the pause had been politely respected as the frontier of the story, Billy Buck stood up and stretched and hitched his trousers. "I guess I'll turn in," he said. Then he faced Grandfather. "I've got an old powder horn and a cap and ball pistol down to the bunkhouse. Did I ever show them to you?"

Grandfather nodded slowly. "Yes, I think you did, Billy. Reminds me of a pistol I had when I was leading the people across." Billy stood politely until the little story was done, and then he said, "Good night," and went out of the house.

Carl Tiflin tried to turn the conversation then. "How's the country between here and Monterey? I've heard it's pretty dry."

"It is dry," said Grandfather. "There's not a drop of water in the Laguna Seca. But it's a long pull from '87. The whole country was powder then, and in '61 I believe all the coyotes starved to death. We had fifteen inches of rain this year."

"Yes, but it all came too early. We could do with some now." Carl's eye fell on Jody. "Hadn't you better be getting to bed?"

Jody stood up obediently. "Can I kill the mice in the old haystack, sir?"

"Mice? Oh! Sure, kill them all off. Billy said there isn't any good hay left."

Jody exchanged a secret and satisfying look with Grandfather. "I'll kill every one tomorrow," he promised.

Jody lay in his bed and thought of the impossible world of Indians and buffaloes, a world that had ceased to be forever. He wished he could have been living in the heroic time, but he knew he was not of heroic timber. No one living now, save possibly Billy Buck, was worthy to do the things that had been done. A race of giants had lived then, fearless men, men of a staunchness unknown in this day. Jody thought of the wide plains and of the wagons moving across like centipedes. He thought of Grandfather on a huge white horse, marshaling the people. Across his mind marched the great phantoms, and they marched off the earth and they were gone.

He came back to the ranch for a moment, then. He heard the dull rushing sound that space and silence make. He heard one of the dogs, out in the doghouse, scratching a flea and bumping his elbow against the floor with every stroke. Then the wind arose again and the black cypress groaned and Jody went to sleep.

He was up half an hour before the triangle sounded for breakfast. His mother was rattling the stove to make the flames roar when Jody went through the kitchen. "You're up early," she said. "Where are you going?"

"Out to get a good stick. We're going to kill the mice today."

"Who is 'we'?"

"Why, Grandfather and I."

"So you've got him in it. You always like to have someone in with you in case there's blame to share."

"I'll be right back," said Jody. "I just want to have a good stick ready for after breakfast."

He closed the screen door after him and went out into the cool blue morning. The birds were noisy in the dawn and the ranch cats came down from the hill like blunt snakes. They had been hunting gophers in the dark, and although the four cats were full of gopher meat, they sat in a semicircle at the back door and mewed piteously for milk. Doubletree Mutt and Smasher moved sniffing along the edge of the brush, performing the duty with rigid ceremony, but when Jody whistled, their heads jerked up and their tails waved. They plunged down to him, wriggling their skins and yawning. Jody patted their heads seriously, and moved on to the weathered scrap pile. He selected an old broom handle and a short piece of inch-square scrap wood. From his pocket he took a shoelace and tied the ends of the sticks loosely together to make a flail. He whistled his new weapon through the air and struck the ground experimentally, while the dogs leaped aside and whined with apprehension.

Jody turned and started down past the house toward the old haystack ground to look over the field of slaughter, but Billy Buck, sitting patiently on the back steps, called to him, "You better come back. It's only a couple of minutes till breakfast."

Jody changed his course and moved toward the house. He leaned his flail against the steps. "That's to drive the mice out," he said. "I'll bet they're fat. I'll bet they don't know what's going to happen to them today."

"No, nor you either," Billy remarked philosophically, "nor me, nor anyone."

Jody was staggered by this thought. He knew it was true. His imagination twitched away from the mouse hunt. Then his mother came out on the back porch and struck the triangle, and all thoughts fell in a heap.

Grandfather hadn't appeared at the table when they sat down. Billy nodded at his empty chair. "He's all right? He isn't sick?"

"He takes a long time to dress," said Mrs. Tiflin. "He combs his whiskers and rubs up his shoes and brushes his clothes."

Carl scattered sugar on his mush. "A man that's led a wagon train across the plains has got to be pretty careful how he dresses."

Mrs. Tiflin turned on him. "Don't do that, Carl! Please don't!" There was more of threat than of request in her tone. And the threat irritated Carl.

"Well, how many times do I have to listen to the story of the iron plates, and the thirty-five horses? That time's done. Why can't he forget it, now it's done?" He grew angrier while he talked, and his voice rose. "Why does he have to tell them over and over? He came across the plains. All right! Now it's finished. Nobody wants to hear about it over and over."

The door into the kitchen closed softly. The four at the table sat frozen. Carl laid his mush spoon on the table and touched his chin with his fingers.

Then the kitchen door opened and Grandfather walked in. His mouth smiled tightly and his eyes were squinted. "Good morning," he said, and he sat down and looked at his mush dish.

Carl could not leave it there. "Did—did you hear what I said?"

Grandfather jerked a little nod.

"I don't know what got into me, sir. I didn't mean it. I was just being funny."

Jody glanced in shame at his mother, and he saw that she was looking at Carl, and that she wasn't breathing. It was an awful thing that he was doing. He was tearing himself to pieces to talk like that. It was a terrible thing to him to retract a word, but to retract it in shame was infinitely worse.

Grandfather looked sidewise. "I'm trying to get right side up," he said gently. "I'm not being mad. I don't mind what you said, but it might be true, and I would mind that."

"It isn't true," said Carl. "I'm not feeling well this morning. I'm sorry I said it."

"Don't be sorry, Carl. An old man doesn't see things sometimes. Maybe you're right. The crossing is finished. Maybe it should be forgotten, now it's done."

Carl got up from the table. "I've had enough to eat. I'm going to work. Take your time, Billy!" He walked quickly out of the dining room. Billy gulped the rest of his food and followed soon after. But Jody could not leave his chair.

"Won't you tell any more stories?" Jody asked.

"Why, sure I'll tell them, but only when—I'm sure people want to hear them."

"I like to hear them, sir."

"Oh! Of course you do, but you're a little boy. It was a job for men, but only little boys like to hear about it."

Jody got up from his place. "I'll wait outside for you, sir. I've got a good stick for those mice."

He waited by the gate until the old man came out on the porch. "Let's go down and kill the mice now," Jody called.

"I think I'll just sit in the sun, Jody. You go kill the mice."

"You can use my stick if you like."

"No, I'll just sit here a while."

Jody turned disconsolately away, and walked down toward the old haystack. He tried to whip up his enthusiasm with thoughts of the fat juicy mice. He beat the ground with his flail. The dogs coaxed and whined about him, but he could not go. Back at the house he could see Grandfather sitting on the porch, looking small and thin and black.

Jody gave up and went to sit on the steps at the old man's feet.

"Back already? Did you kill the mice?"

"No, sir. I'll kill them some other day."

The morning flies buzzed close to the ground, and the ants dashed about in front of the steps. The heavy smell of sage slipped down the hill. The porch boards grew warm in the sunshine.

Jody hardly knew when Grandfather started to talk. "I shouldn't stay here, feeling the way I do." He examined his strong old hands. "I feel as though the crossing wasn't worth doing." His eyes moved up the side-hill and stopped on a motionless hawk perched on a dead limb. "I tell those old stories, but they're not what I want to tell. I only know how I want people to feel when I tell them.

"It wasn't Indians that were important, nor adventures, nor even getting out here. It was a whole bunch of people made into one big crawling beast. And I was the head. It was westering and westering. Every man wanted something for himself, but the big beast that was all of them wanted only westering. I was the leader, but if I hadn't been there, someone else would have been the head. The thing had to have a head.

"Under the little bushes the shadows were black at white noonday. When we saw the mountains at last, we cried—all of us. But it wasn't getting here that mattered, it was movement and westering.

"We carried life out here and set it down the way those ants carry eggs. And I was the leader. The westering was as big as God, and the slow steps that made the movement piled up and piled up until the continent was crossed.

"Then we came down to the sea, and it was done." He stopped and wiped his eyes until the rims were red. "That's what I should be telling instead of stories."

When Jody spoke, Grandfather stared and looked down at him. "Maybe I could lead the people some day," Jody said.

The old man smiled. "There's no place to go.

There's the ocean to stop you. There's a line of old men along the shore hating the ocean because it stopped them."

"In boats I might, sir."

"No place to go, Jody. Every place is taken. But that's not the worst—no, not the worst. Westering has died out of the people. Westering isn't a hunger any more. It's all done. Your father is right. It is finished." He laced his fingers on his knee and looked at them.

Jody felt very sad. "If you'd like a glass of lemonade, I could make it for you."

Grandfather was about to refuse, and then he saw Jody's face. "That would be nice," he said. "Yes, it would be nice to drink a lemonade."

Jody ran into the kitchen where his mother was wiping the last of the breakfast dishes. "Can I have a lemon to make a lemonade for Grandfather?"

His mother mimicked—"And another lemon to make a lemonade for you."

"No, ma'am. I don't want one."

"Jody! You're sick!" Then she stopped suddenly. "Take a lemon out of the cooler," she said softly. "Here, I'll reach the squeezer down to you."   1937

THINK AND DISCUSS
Understanding
1. Who are the members of the family that live at the ranch? What is Billy Buck's connection to the family?
2. What exciting project does Jody look forward to? Does he carry through with his plans?
3. What does Grandfather like to tell about? How do the various members of the household react to his stories?

Analyzing
4. Why does Grandfather believe that Jody cannot be a "leader of the people"?
5. Find examples of Jody's sensitivity to the feelings and opinions of the adults around him.
6. How might Jody's life on the ranch make him more mature? less mature?
7. Jody's father becomes impatient with the old man's repetitive storytelling. How do you explain Jody's willingness to listen to the stories? For what reason do Jody's mother and Billy Buck listen to them?
8. Jody is **characterized** as immature at the beginning of the story. How does Jody's attitude toward killing mice change between the beginning and the end of the story? What, in your opinion, has brought about this change?
9. At the beginning of the story Jody sees his grandfather as a "giant shadow." Near the end of the story, Jody sees his grandfather looking "small and thin and black." Explain what has brought about this change in Jody's attitude toward his grandfather. How does this change relate to his change in attitude toward the mice?

Extending
10. Imagine that you have been asked to film the two paragraphs beginning "Jody plodded on" and ending "out like a glider" (474b, 3–4). What details and images would you emphasize? Where would you use close-up shots? wide panoramic shots? Would you use color or black and white? From whose **point of view** would you direct the shots? Would you shift this point of view? If so, where?

Richard Wright was born on a plantation near Natchez, Mississippi. He grew up, by his own description, unruly and unwanted. Wright was five years old when his father deserted the family. Within another five years his mother had succumbed to complete paralysis, and he was passed from relative to relative until at the age of fifteen he struck out on his own. He worked in Memphis at various unskilled jobs and then during the Depression traveled all over the country, ending up in Chicago. There he became active in the labor movement and in 1936 joined the Communist Party.

Wright was working in a Memphis post office when his literary interests were awakened by reading the essays of H. L. Mencken. When he reached Chicago, he was able to join a WPA Writers' Project and by 1938 had published *Uncle Tom's Children*, a collection of four stories, one of which had already won the annual *Story* magazine award.

He followed this with *Native Son* (1940), a best seller about a young black man executed for murder. This novel achieved widespread popularity among both black and white readers, becoming a play as well as a movie. Wright's next important work was the autobiographical *Black Boy* (1945), a work that confirmed his position among America's leading writers. Wright had in the meantime broken with the Communist Party and would in a book-length essay, *The God That Failed* (1950), describe his disenchantment.

After World War II, Wright moved to France, living and writing in Paris, with visits to Africa, until his death at the age of fifty-two. "The Man Who Saw the Flood" is taken from *Eight Men*, published posthumously in 1961.

The Man Who Saw the Flood

Richard Wright

t last the flood waters had receded. A black father, a black mother, and a black child tramped through muddy fields, leading a tired cow by a thin bit of rope. They stopped on a hilltop and shifted the bundles on their shoulders. As far as they could see the ground was covered with flood silt. The little girl lifted a skinny finger and pointed to a mud-caked cabin.

"Look, Pa! Ain tha our home?"

The man, round-shouldered, clad in blue, ragged overalls, looked with bewildered eyes. Without moving a muscle, scarcely moving his lips, he said: "Yeah."

For five minutes they did not speak or move. The flood waters had been more than eight feet high here. Every tree, blade of grass, and stray stick had its flood mark; caky, yellow mud. It clung to the ground, cracking thinly here and there in spider web fashion. Over the stark fields came a gusty spring wind. The sky was high, blue, full of white clouds and sunshine. Over all hung a first-day strangeness.

"The henhouse is gone," sighed the woman.

"N the pigpen," sighed the man.

They spoke without bitterness.

"Ah reckon them chickens is all done drowned."

"Yeah."

"Miz Flora's house is gone, too," said the little girl.

They looked at a clump of trees where their neighbor's house had stood.

"Lawd!"

"Yuh reckon anybody knows where they is?"

"Hard t tell."

The man walked down the slope and stood uncertainly.

"There wuz a road erlong here somewheres," he said.

But there was no road now. Just a wide sweep of yellow, scalloped silt.

"Look, Tom!" called the woman. "Here's a piece of our gate!"

The gatepost was half buried in the ground. A rusty hinge stood stiff, like a lonely finger. Tom pried it loose and caught it firmly in his hand. There was nothing particular he wanted to do with it; he just stood holding it firmly. Finally he dropped it, looked up, and said.

"C mon. Les go down n see whut we kin do."

Because it sat in a slight depression, the ground about the cabin was soft and slimy.

"Gimme tha bag o lime, May," he said.

With his shoes sucking in mud, he went slowly around the cabin, spreading the white lime with thick fingers. When he reached the front again he had a little left; he shook the bag out on the porch. The fine grains of floating lime flickered in the sunlight.

"Tha oughta hep some," he said.

"Now, yuh be careful, Sal!" said May. "Don yuh go n fall down in all this mud, yuh hear?"

"Yessum."

"The Man Who Saw the Flood" from *Eight Men* by Richard Wright. Copyright 1937 by Weekly Masses Co., Inc. Copyright 1940, © 1960 by Richard Wright. Reprinted by permission of Harper & Row, Publishers, Inc. and Paul R. Reynolds, Inc.

The steps were gone. Tom lifted May and Sally to the porch. They stood a moment looking at the half-opened door. He had shut it when he left, but somehow it seemed natural that he should find it open. The planks in the porch floor were swollen and warped. The cabin had two colors; near the bottom it was a solid yellow, at the top it was the familiar gray. It looked weird, as though its ghost were standing beside it.

The cow lowed.

"Tie Pat t the pos on the en of the porch, May."

May tied the rope slowly, listlessly. When they attempted to open the front door, it would not budge. It was not until Tom placed his shoulder against it and gave it a stout shove that it scraped back jerkily. The front room was dark and silent. The damp smell of flood silt came fresh and sharp to their nostrils. Only one-half of the upper window was clear, and through it fell a rectangle of dingy light. The floors swam in ooze. Like a mute warning, a wavering flood mark went high around the walls of the room. A dresser sat cater-cornered, its drawers and sides bulging like a bloated corpse. The bed, with the mattress still on it, was like a giant casket forged of mud. Two smashed chairs lay in a corner, as though huddled together for protection.

"Les see the kitchen," said Tom.

The stovepipe was gone. But the stove stood in the same place.

"The stove's still good. We kin clean it."

"Yeah."

"But where's the table?"

"Lawd knows."

"It must've washed erway wid the rest of the stuff, Ah reckon."

They opened the back door and looked out. They missed the barn, the henhouse, and the pigpen.

"Tom, yuh bettah try tha ol pump n see ef eny watah's there."

The pump was stiff. Tom threw his weight on the handle and carried it up and down. No water came. He pumped on. There was a dry hollow cough. Then yellow water trickled. He caught his breath and kept pumping. The water flowed white.

"Thank Gawd! We's got some watah."

"Yuh bettah boil it fo yuh use it," he said.

"Yeah. Ah know."

"Look, Pa! Here's yo ax," called Sally.

Tom took the ax from her. "Yeah. Ah'll need this."

"N here's somethin else," called Sally, digging spoons out of the mud.

"Waal, Ahma git a bucket n start cleanin," said May. "Ain no use in waitin, cause we's gotta sleep on them floors tonight."

When she was filling the bucket from the pump, Tom called from around the cabin. "May, look! Ah done foun mah plow!" Proudly he dragged the silt-caked plow to the pump. "Ah'll wash it n it'll be awright."

"Ahm hongry," said Sally.

"Now, yuh jus wait! Yuh et this mawnin," said May. She turned to Tom. "Now, whutcha gonna do, Tom?"

He stood looking at the mud-filled fields.

"Yuh goin back t Burgess?"

"Ah reckon Ah have to."

"Whut else kin yuh do?"

"Nothin," he said. "Lawd, but Ah sho hate t start all over wid tha white man. Ah'd leave here ef Ah could. Ah owes im nigh eight hundred dollahs. N we needs a hoss, grub, seed, n a lot mo other things. Ef we keeps on like this tha white man'll own us body n soul."

"But, Tom, there ain nothin else t do," she said.

"Ef we try t run erway they'll put us in jail."

"It coulda been worse," she said.

Sally came running from the kitchen. "Pa!"

"Hunh?"

"There's a shelf in the kitchen the flood didn't git!"

"Where?"

"Right up over the stove."

"But, chile, ain nothin up there," said May.

"But there's somethin on it," said Sally.

"C mon. Les see."

High and dry, untouched by the flood water,

John Steuart Curry, *The Mississippi* (1935).
The Saint Louis Museum

was a box of matches. And beside it a half-full sack of Bull Durham tobacco. He took a match from the box and scratched it on his overalls. It burned to his fingers before he dropped it.

"May!"

"Huh?"

"Look! Here's ma bacco n some matches!"

She stared unbelievingly. "Lawd!" she breathed.

Tom rolled a cigarette clumsily.

May washed the stove, gathered some sticks, and after some difficulty, made a fire. The kitchen stove smoked, and their eyes smarted. May put water on to heat and went into the front room. It was getting dark. From the bundles they took a kerosene lamp and lit it. Outside Pat lowed longingly into the thickening gloom and tinkled her cowbell.

"Tha old cow's hongry," said May.

"Ah reckon Ah'll have t be gittin erlong t Burgess."

They stood on the front porch.

"Yuh bettah git on, Tom, fo it gits too dark."

"Yeah."

The wind had stopped blowing. In the east a cluster of stars hung.

"Yuh goin, Tom?"

"Ah reckon Ah have t."

"Ma, Ah'm hongry," said Sally.

"Wait erwhile, honey. Ma knows yuh's hongry."

Tom threw his cigarette away and sighed.

"Look! Here comes somebody!"

"Thas Mistah Burgess now!"

A mud-caked buggy rolled up. The shaggy horse was splattered all over. Burgess leaned his white face out of the buggy and spat.

"Well, I see you're back."

"Yessuh."

"How things look?"

"They don look so good, Mistah."

"What seems to be the trouble?"

"Waal. Ah ain got no hoss, no grub, nothin. The only thing Ah got is tha ol cow there. . . ."

"You owe eight hundred dollahs down at the store, Tom."

"Yessuh, Ah know. But, Mistah Burgess, can't yuh knock somethin off tha, seein as how Ahm down n out now?"

"You ate that grub, and I got to pay for it, Tom."

"Yessuh, Ah know."

"It's going to be a little tough, Tom. But you got to go through with it. Two of the boys tried to run away this morning and dodge their debts, and I had to have the sheriff pick em up. I wasn't looking for no trouble out of you, Tom. . . . The rest of the families are going back."

Leaning out of the buggy, Burgess waited. In the surrounding stillness the cowbell tinkled again. Tom stood with his back against a post.

"Yuh got t go on, Tom. We ain't got nothin here," said May.

Tom looked at Burgess.

"Mistah Burgess, Ah don wanna make no trouble. But this is jus *too* hard. Ahm worse off now than befo. Ah got to start from scratch."

"Get in the buggy and come with me. I'll stake you with grub. We can talk over how you can pay it back." Tom said nothing. He rested his back against the post and looked at the mud-filled fields.

"Well," asked Burgess. "You coming?" Tom said nothing. He got slowly to the ground and pulled himself into the buggy. May watched them drive off.

"Hurry back, Tom!"

"Awright."

"Ma, tell Pa t bring me some 'lasses," begged Sally.

"Oh, Tom!"

Tom's head came out of the side of the buggy.

"Hunh?"

"Bring some 'lasses!"

"*Hunh?*"

"Bring some 'lasses for Sal!"

"Awright!"

She watched the buggy disappear over the crest of the muddy hill. Then she sighed, caught Sally's hand, and turned back into the cabin.

1937

THINK AND DISCUSS

Understanding

1. What has the family lost in the flood? Which objects survived the flood?
2. What is Tom's relationship to Mr. Burgess?
3. What does Mr. Burgess want Tom to do?

Analyzing

4. Compare the language of the black family with the language of Burgess at the end of the story. How does Wright's use of dialogue bring his characters alive and reveal their social relationships?

5. Explain how Burgess keeps the black family in bondage.
6. By what signs does Tom show he is near rebellion toward the end of the story? Why doesn't he rebel?
7. What does the molasses represent to Sally? to Tom?
8. Discuss the meanings—both literal and **figurative**—of the title.

Extending

9. Do you think Tom made the right decision under the circumstances? Why or why not?

APPLYING: Setting
See Handbook of Literary Terms, p. 906.

Setting is the time and place in which the action of a narrative occurs. Setting may be revealed through dialogue and action, or through description. In this story, the setting is crucial since it determines the plot.

1. In what region of the United States is the story set? How do you know?
2. Cite some examples of setting as revealed through dialogue. What other aspects of setting are supplied through description?
3. Could this story have taken place in an urban setting? Why or why not?

The Real Hard Terror of Writing

In describing the experience he had in writing his autobiographical *Black Boy*, Richard Wright said:

"The real hard terror of writing like this came when I found that writing of one's life was vastly different from speaking of it. I was rendering a close and emotionally connected account of my experience, and the ease I had had in speaking from notes at Fisk [University] would not come again. I found that to tell the truth is the hardest thing on earth, harder than fighting in a war, harder than taking part in a revolution. If you try it, you will find that at times sweat will break upon you. You will find that even if you succeed in discounting the attitudes of others to you and your life, you must wrestle with yourself most of all, fight with yourself; for there will surge up in you a strong desire to alter facts, to dress up your feelings. You'll find that there are many things that you don't want to admit about yourself and others. As your record shapes itself, an awed wonder haunts you. And yet there is no more exciting an adventure than trying to be honest in this way. The clean, strong feeling that sweeps you when you've done it makes you know that."

Asked in 1972 whether she wrote for her friends, Eudora Welty said: "At the time of writing, I don't write for my friends or myself, either; I write for *it*, for the pleasure of *it*. I believe if I stopped to wonder what So-and-so would think, or what I'd feel like if this were read by a stranger, I would be paralyzed."

Welty was born in Jackson, Mississippi, and has spent most of her life in her native state. She attended the University of Wisconsin, then went to New York, where she studied journalism at Columbia University and wrote publicity, society news, and radio scripts. After returning to Mississippi, she settled down to a career of writing, with gardening, painting, and photography as hobbies.

Her first volume of short stories, *A Curtain of Green*, was published in 1941. The title story won the O. Henry Memorial Award for that year. Since then she has published several other volumes of short stories and a number of novels, including *Losing Battles* (1970) and *The Optimist's Daughter* (1972). She received the 1973 Pulitzer Prize for *The Optimist's Daughter*. Although her stories are set in the South, her themes extend beyond geographical boundaries, dealing with the problems of adolescence, loneliness, and the failures of personal communication. Her style is a blend of shrewdness, sensitivity, and robust humor.

Recent awards include the National Medal of Arts (1986) and France's Knight of the Order of Arts and Letters (1987). In accepting the coveted French award, Welty responded, "It's not like anything I could have ever imagined—to be a Knight or a Knightess."

Welty lives quietly and alone in her home of over forty years. She treasures her privacy and once commented, "Writing fiction is an interior affair. Novels and stories always will be put down little by little out of personal feeling and personal beliefs arrived at alone and at firsthand over a period of time as time is needed. To go outside and beat the drum is only to interrupt, interrupt. . . . Fiction has, and must keep, a private address. For life is lived in a private place; where it means anything is inside the mind and heart." In the autobiographical *One Writer's Beginnings* (1983), Welty movingly presents scenes from her childhood that helped shape her fiction.

Welty once revealed that the question she most frequently received from students about her work was "Is Phoenix Jackson's grandson really *dead?*" She explains that "A Worn Path" is told through Phoenix's mind, and "as the author at one with the character as I tell it, I must assume that the boy is alive." She adds, however, that readers may believe otherwise. Whether the child is alive or dead doesn't affect the outcome or the meaning of the story, according to Welty. What *is* important is the fact that *Phoenix* is alive.

See INFERENCE in the Handbook of Literary Terms, page 892.

A Worn Path

Eudora Welty

t was December—a bright frozen day in the early morning. Far out in the country there was an old Negro woman with her head tied in a red rag, coming along a path through the pinewoods. Her name was Phoenix Jackson. She was very old and small and she walked slowly in the dark pine shadows, moving a little from side to side in her steps, with the balanced heaviness and lightness of a pendulum in a grandfather clock. She carried a thin, small cane made from an umbrella, and with this she kept tapping the frozen earth in front of her. This made a grave and persistent noise in the still air, that seemed meditative like the chirping of a solitary little bird.

She wore a dark striped dress reaching down to her shoe tops, and an equally long apron of bleached sugar sacks, with a full pocket: all neat and tidy, but every time she took a step she might have fallen over her shoelaces, which dragged from her unlaced shoes. She looked straight ahead. Her eyes were blue with age. Her skin had a pattern all its own of numberless branching wrinkles and as though a whole little tree stood in the middle of her forehead, but a golden color ran underneath, and the two knobs of her cheeks were illumined by a yellow burning under the dark. Under the red rag her hair came down on her neck in the frailest of ringlets, still black, and with an odor like copper.

Now and then there was a quivering in the thicket. Old Phoenix said, "Out of my way, all you foxes, owls, beetles, jack rabbits, coons and wild animals! . . . Keep out from under these feet, little bobwhites. . . . Keep the big wild hogs out of my path. Don't let none of those come running my direction. I got a long way." Under her small black-freckled hand her cane, limber as a buggy whip, would switch at the bush as if to rouse up any hiding things.

On she went. The woods were deep and still. The sun made the pine needles almost too bright to look at, up where the wind rocked. The cones dropped as light as feathers. Down in the hollow was the mourning dove—it was not too late for him.

The path ran up a hill. "Seem like there is chains about my feet, time I get this far," she said, in the voice of argument old people keep to use with themselves. "Something always take a hold of me on this hill—pleads I should stay."

After she got to the top, she turned and gave a full, severe look behind her where she had come. "Up through pines," she said at length. "Now down through oaks."

Her eyes opened their widest, and she started down gently. But before she got to the bottom of the hill a bush caught her dress.

Her fingers were busy and intent, but her skirts were full and long, so that before she could pull them free in one place they were caught in another. It was not possible to allow the dress to tear. "I in the thorny bush," she said. "Thorns, you

"A Worn Path" from *A Curtain of Green and Other Stories* by Eudora Welty. Copyright 1941, 1969 by Eudora Welty. Reprinted by permission of Harcourt Brace Jovanovich, Inc. and Marion Boyars Publishers Ltd.

doing your appointed work. Never want to let folks pass, no sir. Old eyes thought you was a pretty little *green* bush."

Finally, trembling all over, she stood free, and after a moment dared to stoop for her cane.

"Sun so high!" she cried, leaning back and looking, while the thick tears went over her eyes. "The time getting all gone here."

At the foot of this hill was a place where a log was laid across the creek.

"Now comes the trial," said Pheonix.

Putting her right foot out, she mounted the log and shut her eyes. Lifting her skirt, leveling her cane fiercely before her, like a festival figure in some parade, she began to march across. Then she opened her eyes and she was safe on the other side.

"I wasn't as old as I thought," she said.

But she sat down to rest. She spread her skirts on the bank around her and folded her hands over her knees. Up above her was a tree in a pearly cloud of mistletoe. She did not dare to close her eyes, and when a little boy brought her a plate with a slice of marble cake on it she spoke to him. "That would be acceptable," she said. But when she went to take it there was just her own hand in the air.

So she left that tree, and had to go through a barbed-wire fence. There she had to creep and crawl, spreading her knees and stretching her fingers like a baby trying to climb the steps. But she talked loudly to herself; she could not let her dress be torn now, so late in the day, and she could not pay for having her arm or her leg sawed off if she got caught fast where she was.

At last she was safe through the fence and risen up out in the clearing. Big dead trees, like black men with one arm, were standing in the purple stalks of the withered cotton field. There sat a buzzard.

"Who you watching?"

In the furrow she made her way along.

"Glad this not the season for bulls," she said, looking sideways, "and the good Lord made his snakes to curl up and sleep in the winter. A pleasure I don't see no two-headed snake coming around that tree, where it come once. It took a while to get by him, back in the summer."

She passed through the old cotton and went into a field of dead corn. It whispered and shook and was taller than her head. "Through the maze now," she said, for there was no path.

Then there was something tall, black, and skinny there, moving before her.

At first she took it for a man. It could have been a man dancing in the field. But she stood still and listened, and it did not make a sound. It was as silent as a ghost.

"Ghost," she said sharply, "who be you the ghost of? For I have heard of nary death close by."

But there was no answer—only the ragged dancing in the wind.

She shut her eyes, reached out her hand, and touched a sleeve. She found a coat and inside that an emptiness, cold as ice.

"You scarecrow," she said. Her face lighted. "I ought to be shut up for good," she said with laughter. "My senses is gone. I too old. I the oldest people I ever know. Dance, old scarecrow," she said, "while I dancing with you."

She kicked her foot over the furrow, and with mouth drawn down, shook her head once or twice in a little strutting way. Some husks blew down and whirled in streamers about her skirts.

Then she went on, parting her way from side to side with the cane, through the whispering field. At last she came to the end, to a wagon track where the silver grass blew between the red ruts. The quail were walking around like pullets, seeming all dainty and unseen.

"Walk pretty," she said. "This the easy place. This the easy going."

She followed the track, swaying through the quiet bare fields, through the little strings of trees silver in their dead leaves, past cabins silver from weather, with the doors and windows boarded shut, all like old women under a spell sitting there. "I walking in their sleep," she said, nodding her head vigorously.

In a ravine she went where a spring was silently flowing through a hollow log. Old Phoenix bent and drank. "Sweet gum makes the water sweet," she said, and drank more. "Nobody know who made this well, for it was here when I was born."

The track crossed a swampy part where the moss hung as white as lace from every limb. "Sleep on, alligators, and blow your bubbles." Then the track went into the road.

Deep, deep the road went down between the high green-colored banks. Overhead the live oaks met, and it was as dark as a cave.

A black dog with a lolling tongue came up out of the weeds by the ditch. She was meditating, and not ready, and when he came at her she only hit him a little with her cane. Over she went in the ditch, like a little puff of milkweed.

Down there, her senses drifted away. A dream visited her, and she reached her hand up, but nothing reached down and gave her a pull. So she lay there and presently went to talking. "Old woman," she said to herself, "that black dog came up out of the weeds to stall you off, and now there he sitting on his fine tail, smiling at you."

A white man finally came along and found her—a hunter, a young man, with his dog on a chain.

"Well, Granny!" he laughed. "What are you doing there?"

"Lying on my back like a June bug waiting to be turned over, mister," she said, reaching up her hand.

He lifted her up, gave her a swing in the air, and set her down. "Anything broken, Granny?"

"No sir, them old dead weeds is springy enough," said Phoenix, when she had got her breath. "I thank you for your trouble."

"Where do you live, Granny?" he asked, while the two dogs were growling at each other.

"Away back yonder, sir, behind the ridge. You can't even see it from here."

"On your way home?"

"No sir, I going to town."

"Why, that's too far! That's as far as I walk when I come out myself, and I get something for my trouble." He patted the stuffed bag he carried, and there hung down a little closed claw.

It was one of the bobwhites, with its beak hooked bitterly to show it was dead. "Now you go on home, Granny!"

"I bound to go to town, mister," said Phoenix. "The time come around."

He gave another laugh, filling the whole landscape. "I know you old colored people! Wouldn't miss going to town to see Santa Claus!"

But something held old Phoenix very still. The deep lines in her face went into a fierce and different radiation. Without warning, she had seen with her own eyes a flashing nickel fall out of the man's pocket onto the ground.

"How old are you, Granny?" he was saying.

"There is no telling, mister," she said, "no telling."

Then she gave a little cry and clapped her hands and said, "Git on away from here, dog! Look! Look at that dog!" She laughed as if in admiration. "He ain't scared of nobody. He a big black dog." She whispered, "Sic him!"

"Watch me get rid of that cur," said the man. "Sic him, Pete! Sic him!"

Phoenix heard the dogs fighting, and heard the man running and throwing sticks. She even heard a gunshot. But she was slowly bending forward by that time, further and further forward, the lids stretched down over her eyes, as if she were doing this in her sleep. Her chin was lowered almost to her knees. The yellow palm of her hand came out from the fold of her apron. Her fingers slid down and along the ground under the piece of money with the grace and care they would have in lifting an egg from under a setting hen. Then she slowly straightened up, she stood erect, and the nickel was in her apron pocket. A bird flew by. Her lips moved. "God watching me the whole time. I come to stealing."

The man came back, and his own dog panted about them. "Well, I scared him off that time," he said, and then he laughed and lifted his gun and pointed it at Phoenix.

She stood straight and faced him.

"Doesn't the gun scare you?" he said, still pointing it.

"No, sir, I seen plenty go off closer by, in my

day, and for less than what I done," she said, holding utterly still.

He smiled, and shouldered the gun. "Well, Granny," he said, "you must be a hundred years old, and scared of nothing. I'd give you a dime if I had any money with me. But you take my advice and stay home, and nothing will happen to you."

"I bound to go on my way, mister," said Phoenix. She inclined her head in the red rag. Then they went in different directions, but she could hear the gun shooting again and again over the hill.

She walked on. The shadows hung from the oak trees to the road like curtains. Then she smelled wood-smoke, and smelled the river, and she saw a steeple and the cabins on their steep steps. Dozens of little black children whirled around her. There ahead was Natchez shining. Bells were ringing. She walked on.

In the paved city it was Christmas time. There were red and green electric lights strung and crisscrossed everywhere, and all turned on in the daytime. Old Phoenix would have been lost if she had not distrusted her eyesight and depended on her feet to know where to take her.

She paused quietly on the sidewalk where people were passing by. A lady came along in the crowd, carrying an armful of red-, green-, and silver-wrapped presents; she gave off perfume like the red roses in hot summer, and Phoenix stopped her.

"Please, missy, will you lace up my shoe?" She held up her foot.

"What do you want, Grandma?"

"See my shoe," said Phoenix. "Do all right for out in the country, but wouldn't look right to go in a big building."

"Stand still then, Grandma," said the lady. She put her packages down on the sidewalk beside her and laced and tied both shoes tightly.

"Can't lace 'em with a cane," said Phoenix. "Thank you, missy. I doesn't mind asking a nice lady to tie up my shoe, when I gets out on the street."

Moving slowly and from side to side, she went into the big building, and into a tower of steps, where she walked up and around and around until her feet knew to stop.

She entered a door, and there she saw nailed up on the wall the document that had been stamped with the gold seal and framed in the gold frame, which matched the dream that was hung up in her head.

"Here I be," she said. There was a fixed and ceremonial stiffness over her body.

"A charity case, I suppose," said an attendant who sat at the desk before her.

But Phoenix only looked over her head. There was sweat on her face, the wrinkles in her skin shone like a bright net.

"Speak up, Grandma," the woman said. "What's your name? We must have your history, you know. Have you been here before? What seems to be the trouble with you?"

Old Phoenix only gave a twitch to her face as if a fly were bothering her.

"Are you deaf?" cried the attendant.

But then the nurse came in.

"Oh, that's just old Aunt Phoenix," she said. "She doesn't come for herself—she has a little grandson. She makes these trips just as regular as clockwork. She lives away back off the Old Natchez Trace." She bent down. "Well, Aunt Phoenix, why don't you just take a seat? We won't keep you standing after your long trip." She pointed.

The old woman sat down, bolt upright in the chair.

"Now, how is the boy?" asked the nurse.

Old Phoenix did not speak.

"I said, how is the boy?"

But Phoenix only waited and stared straight ahead, her face very solemn and withdrawn into rigidity.

"Is his throat any better?" asked the nurse. "Aunt Phoenix, don't you hear me? Is your grandson's throat any better since the last time you came for the medicine?"

With her hands on her knees, the old woman waited, silent, erect and motionless, just as if she were in armor.

William Holbrook Beard, *In the Forest* (1856).
The Brooklyn Museum

"You mustn't take up our time this way, Aunt Phoenix," the nurse said. "Tell us quickly about your grandson, and get it over. He isn't dead, is he?"

At last there came a flicker and then a flame of comprehension across her face, and she spoke.

"My grandson. It was my memory had left me. There I sat and forgot why I made my long trip."

"Forgot?" The nurse frowned. "After you came so far?"

Then Phoenix was like an old woman begging a dignified forgiveness for waking up frightened in the night. "I never did go to school, I was too old at the Surrender,"[1] she said in a soft voice. "I'm an old woman without an education. It was my memory fail me. My little grandson, he is just the same, and I forgot it in the coming."

"Throat never heals, does it?" said the nurse, speaking in a loud, sure voice to old Phoenix. By now she had a card with something written on it, a little list. "Yes. Swallowed lye. When was it?—January—two-three years ago——"

Phoenix spoke unasked now. "No, missy, he not dead, he just the same. Every little while his throat begin to close up again, and he not able to swallow. He not get his breath. He not able to help himself. So the time come around, and I go on another trip for the soothing medicine."

"All right. The doctor said as long as you came to get it, you could have it," said the nurse. "But it's an obstinate case."

"My little grandson, he sit up there in the house all wrapped up, waiting by himself," Phoenix went on. "We is the only two left in the world. He suffer and it don't seem to put him back at all. He got a sweet look. He going to last. He wear a little patch quilt and peep out holding his mouth open like a little bird. I remembers so plain now. I not going to forget him again, no, the whole enduring time. I could tell him from all the others in creation."

"All right." The nurse was trying to hush her now. She brought her a bottle of medicine. "Charity," she said, making a check mark in a book.

Old Phoenix held the bottle close to her eyes, and then carefully put it into her pocket.

"I thank you," she said.

"It's Christmas time, Grandma," said the attendant. "Could I give you a few pennies out of my purse?"

"Five pennies is a nickel," said Phoenix stiffly.

"Here's a nickel," said the attendant.

Phoenix rose carefully and held out her hand. She received the nickel and then fished the other nickel out of her pocket and laid it beside the new one. She stared at her palm closely, with her head on one side.

Then she gave a tap with her cane on the floor.

"This is what come to me to do," she said. "I going to the store and buy my child a little windmill they sells, made out of paper. He going to find it hard to believe there such a thing in the world. I'll march myself back where he waiting, holding it straight up in this hand."

She lifted her free hand, gave a little nod, turned around, and walked out of the doctor's office. Then her slow step began on the stairs, going down. **1941**

---

1. *the Surrender*, the surrender of the Confederate Army to the Union Army at Appomattox on April 9, 1865.

THINK AND DISCUSS
Understanding
1. Where is Phoenix going at the beginning of the story? Why?
2. For what purpose does she use her makeshift cane?
3. What obstacles does Phoenix encounter on her way?
4. What does she ask of the hunter? the lady carrying presents? the nurse?

Analyzing
5. As you accompany Phoenix Jackson on her solitary trek across the countryside, what kind of person do you discover her to be? In particular, consider the **character** traits she reveals in her encounter with the young hunter.
6. What "worn paths"—both literal and **metaphorical**—do you find in this story?
7. Find elements of **local color**—speech, dress, mannerisms, and geographical qualities that typify the region.
8. Besides the story's regional flavor, what deeper insights into human nature does it offer? How are the regional details useful in making these insights convincing to the reader?

Extending
9. A phoenix is a mythical bird that dies consumed in flames and then rises again from the ashes, fresh and beautiful, to begin a new life. Do you think that Phoenix is an appropriate name for the main character in this story? Why or why not?

APPLYING: Inference   H⫯
See Handbook of Literary Terms, p. 892.

An **inference** is a reasonable conclusion about a character or event based on the limited information presented by the author. Not until the end of the story do we know why the old woman is attempting this long and difficult journey. Even after the nurse reminds Phoenix of what she has come for, readers still must form their own conclusions about certain key points.

1. How does your opinion of Phoenix change when you learn the reason for her trip?
2. What can you infer about the relationship of Phoenix and her grandson from her plan to buy the paper windmill?
3. When Phoenix enters the medical office, "she saw nailed up on the wall the document that had been stamped with the gold seal and framed in the gold frame, which matched the dream that was hung up in her head." What inferences can you draw about the nature of this document and what it means to Phoenix?

COMPOSITION   ◆━⊙
Being a Story Character
Pretend you are the hunter that meets Phoenix and helps her to her feet. You are back in your home. It is dinner time and you are telling your family about the encounter. In a page or two of narrative, try to capture the relaxed, conversational tone that the man would probably use. Before you begin, reread that section of the story to refresh your memory of just what actions take place and what is said.

Writing to Persuade
Some readers feel that the story would be somehow "better" if Phoenix's grandson were dead. Others are sure that the boy must be alive. Still others feel that whether the boy is alive or dead has little bearing on the story. Write an essay for a literary magazine of at least four paragraphs in which you support one of these positions. Consider Phoenix's motivation for her journey, her devotion and single-mindedness, the outcome of the story, and the irony that the boy's death would provide. See "Writing About Plot and Plot Devices" in the Writer's Handbook.

Comment

Reading Modern Poetry

The section that follows represents such a variety of poets, poems, and poetic styles that many arrangements would be possible. The ordering here is meant to enhance pleasure and sharpen awareness by drawing the reader through the various currents and countercurrents of modern poetry.

First appear poems by Ezra Pound, a proponent of Imagism, a doctrine that stresses the precision and emotional impact of carefully selected images. Amy Lowell's "Patterns," which comes next, is a striking example of Imagism used in a dramatic monologue to *reveal* rather than *describe* feelings, resulting in the poem's controlled understatement of emotion.

"Chicago" by Carl Sandburg invests big-city life with a human vitality. Next come two contrasting conceptions of poetry. "Poetry," by Marianne Moore, supports, to some extent, the direct and personal approach to poetic expression; her emphasis is on the "genuine," the "useful," and the "intelligible"—the "real toads" that populate the "imaginary gardens" of poetry. William Carlos Williams's "Spring and All" presents a rather unconventional approach to the subject of seasonal life. Williams's version of the Imagist doctrine was "no ideas but in things." Archibald MacLeish in "Ars Poetica" summarizes the principles of the Imagists and adopts a rather impersonal tone while relying on precise concrete images for emotional impact.

Both the directness and the imagistic subtlety of modernist poetry are embraced in the poetry of Robert Frost, appearing next. In a career spanning seven decades, Frost gave voice to both the optimism and the pessimism that were mingled in the modern temper.

Grimmer social concerns of the Depression and the plight of black people are voiced in the poems of Langston Hughes, Countee Cullen, Arna Bontemps, and Claude McKay. However,

optimism and religious fervor resonate in the poems of Jean Toomer and James Weldon Johnson. These poets are among the array of talented black writers who gravitated to New York during this period and became members of the Harlem Renaissance.

A colossus among poets of the period was T. S. Eliot, represented in this unit by "The Love Song of J. Alfred Prufrock." Eliot's poetry is obsessively self-conscious, highly allusive, world-weary and sophisticated, complex and ironic.

Six highly gifted lyrical poets of this period follow: Vachel Lindsay, DuBose Heyward, Edna St. Vincent Millay, Elinor Wylie, Robinson Jeffers, and Sara Teasdale. Their works demonstrate the vitality of traditional forms in dealing with modern concepts of human relationships; they deal with the psychology of the inner being as well as with social concerns.

In the final group, John Crowe Ransom's "Janet Waking" portrays a young girl's tragic confrontation with death. Wallace Stevens invests profound significance into a simple jar, manipulating language in ways almost as startling as the machinations of E. E. Cummings, who discards conventional punctuation and syntax and scatters lines in visual patterns to mirror his rhythms and images. Alice Walker reflects on a childhood scene.

By the 1930s, poets were preoccupied with the Depression and the rise of Fascism. Nonetheless, some poets maintained a sense of humor. The light verse of Dorothy Parker, Ogden Nash, and Phyllis McGinley (who is represented in this unit) mocked the fads and foibles of the time.

Although it is often useful to read thematically related poems together, poetry is by its very nature individualistic and each poem unique, offering itself on its individual terms.

BIOGRAPHIES

Ezra Pound   1878–1967

Born in Idaho and reared in Pennsylvania, Ezra Pound became a controversial figure in American letters because of his pro-Fascist broadcasts during World War II and his subsequent internment in a mental hospital. Nonetheless, he was the preeminent shaper of modern poetry and a tireless promoter of other poets, including T. S. Eliot, who referred to his peer as "the better craftsman."

Pound fled what he thought was a stifling, provincial America for Europe in 1908 and became involved in many avant-garde movements, including those that opposed capitalism and supported censorship. As foreign correspondent for Chicago's *Poetry* magazine, he helped revitalize American poetry. His own works include *Personae* (1909), *The Chinese Translations in Cathay* (1915), and *The Cantos*, an epic that he defined as a "poem including history." In spite of his exile and his criticism of America, he remained an American poet to the end.

Amy Lowell   1874–1925

Born into one of the wealthiest and most distinguished families in Massachusetts, Amy Lowell counted among her relatives poet James Russell Lowell (Unit 2). Not until she was twenty-eight did she decide to become a poet, and then she studied for eight years before publishing a line. Soon after the publication of her first volume, *A Dome of Many-Colored Glass* (1912), Lowell joined the Imagists, adopting their use of free verse and sensuous language to create strong and concrete images.

Men, Women, and Ghosts (1916), in which "Patterns" first appeared, showed that, in addition to being technically gifted, Lowell was also a superb storyteller. At first ridiculed, the "new poetry" of the Imagists gradually came to be accepted. A well-known poet at the time of her death, Lowell was posthumously awarded the Pulitzer Prize in 1926.

Carl Sandburg   1878–1967

The genius of Carl Sandburg is apparent in his poetry, his children's stories, and his highly regarded biography of Lincoln. In addition, he was a collector of folklore and did much to popularize folk songs by singing them in public appearances, accompanying himself on the guitar. He was awarded two Pulitzer Prizes.

Sandburg was born in Galesburg, Illinois, of Swedish immigrant parents. It was not until he was thirty-eight years old and had tried his hand at many different occupations that fame came to him with the publication of *Chicago Poems* (1916). Written in a free-verse style reminiscent of Walt Whitman, these poems, like those he wrote later, speak in the bold and often earthy idiom of the people. Sensitive to injustice and hypocrisy, fearful of the effects of industrialization on humanity, Sandburg found hope for the future in the common people.

Marianne Moore 1887–1972

Born just outside of St. Louis, Marianne Moore graduated from Bryn Mawr in 1909. Before turning to a full-time career as a writer, she taught at the U.S. Indian School in Carlisle, Pennsylvania, and then moved to New York where she worked as a private tutor, secretary, and assistant at the New York Public Library.

Moore's poetry is highly colored, symbolic, often ironic. Her subjects, which range from animals (she was a frequent visitor at the Bronx Zoo), to laborers, to the craft of poetry, are as varied as the objects—bats, baseball fans, statisticians, and business documents—that she catalogs in "Poetry," which is included in this unit.

Among the many prizes she has won, her *Collected Poems* (1952) was awarded all three of the major American prizes for poetry: the Pulitzer Prize, the National Book Award, and the Bollingen Prize. Her *Complete Poems* was published in 1967.

William Carlos Williams 1883–1963

Although for many years Dr. William Carlos Williams spent much of his time seeing patients and delivering babies in and around Rutherford, New Jersey, he found time to write more than thirty-seven volumes of prose and poetry. For Williams the everyday event had beauty, interest, and significance. His poetry deals with such common things as spring, plums, a wheelbarrow—things that one might see every day yet never notice. His writing reflects the physician's experience of seeing people under all conditions of life—from their birth to the moment of their death. Such observation gave insight and substance to his poetry and stories. His lyric poems have been published in two volumes: *Collected Later Poems* (1950) and *Collected Earlier Poems* (1951).

Archibald MacLeish 1892–1982

Archibald MacLeish was born in Glencoe, Illinois, and educated at Yale and Harvard. He gave up a prosperous law practice claiming he "never could believe in it." In 1923 he left for Paris to discuss theory with contemporary writers and write his own poetry.

After he returned to the United States, he traveled in Mexico, following the route of Cortez. The result was the narrative poem *Conquistador*, which won the Pulitzer Prize in 1933. During World War II as Director of the U.S. Office of Facts and Figures, he was responsible for wartime propaganda.

In 1953 he was awarded both the National Book Award and a second Pulitzer Prize for his *Collected Poems 1917–1952*. And in 1959 he won a third Pulitzer Prize, this time in drama, for his verse play, *J. B.*

The Garden

Ezra Pound

Like a skein of loose silk blown against a wall
She walks by the railing of a path in Kensington Gardens.[1]
And she is dying piece-meal of a sort of emotional anaemia.

And round about there is a rabble
5 Of the filthy, sturdy, unkillable infants of the very poor.
They shall inherit the earth.

In her is the end of breeding.
Her boredom is exquisite and excessive.
She would like some one to speak to her,
10 And is almost afraid that I will commit that indiscretion.

1912

---

1. *Kensington* (ken′zing tən) *Gardens,* beautiful gardens in a palace near London.

The River-Merchant's Wife: A Letter

Ezra Pound

Based on a poem by Li T'ai Po[1]

While my hair was still cut straight across my forehead
I played about the front gate, pulling flowers.
You came by on bamboo stilts, playing horse,
You walked about my seat, playing with blue plums.
5 And we went on living in the village of Chōkan:
Two small people, without dislike or suspicion.

At fourteen I married My Lord you.
I never laughed, being bashful.
Lowering my head, I looked at the wall.
10 Called to, a thousand times, I never looked back.

---

1. *Li T'ai Po* (lē′tī′bō′; 701–762), one of China's greatest poets. His literary name was Li Po.

"The Garden" and "The River-Merchant's Wife: A Letter" by Ezra Pound, *Personae* (British title, *Collected Shorter Poems*). Copyright 1926 by Ezra Pound. Reprinted by permission of New Directions Publishing Corporation and Faber and Faber Ltd.

At fifteen I stopped scowling,
I desired my dust to be mingled with yours
Forever and forever and forever.
Why should I climb the look out?

15 At sixteen you departed,
You went into far Ku-tō-en, by the river of swirling eddies.
And you have been gone five months.
The monkeys make sorrowful noise overhead.
You dragged your feet when you went out.
20 By the gate now, the moss is grown, the different mosses,
Too deep to clear them away!
The leaves fall early this autumn, in wind.
The paired butterflies are already yellow with August
Over the grass in the West garden;
25 They hurt me. I grow older.
If you are coming down through the narrows of the river Kiang,[2]
Please let me know beforehand,
And I will come out to meet you
               As far as Chō-fū-Sa.

                      1915

---

2. **Kiang** (kyäng). The Yangtze (yang'tsē) Kiang River is China's longest.

Patterns

Amy Lowell

I walk down the garden-paths,
And all the daffodils
Are blowing, and the bright blue squills.
I walk down the patterned garden-paths
5 In my stiff, brocaded gown.
With my powdered hair and jeweled fan.
I too am a rare
Pattern. As I wander down
The garden-paths.
10 My dress is richly figured,
And the train
Makes a pink and silver stain

On the gravel, and the thrift
Of the borders.
15 Just a plate of current fashion,
Tripping by in high-heeled, ribboned shoes.
Not a softness anywhere about me,
Only whalebone and brocade.
And I sink on a seat in the shade
20 Of a lime-tree. For my passion
Wars against the stiff brocade.
The daffodils and squills
Flutter in the breeze
As they please.   *(continued)*

"Patterns" from *The Complete Poetical Works of Amy Lowell.* Copyright © 1955 by Houghton Mifflin Company. Reprinted by permission of Houghton Mifflin Company.

25 And I weep;
For the lime-tree is in blossom
And one small flower had dropped upon my bosom.

And the plashing of waterdrops
In the marble fountain
30 Comes down the garden-paths.
The dripping never stops.
Underneath my stiffened gown
Is the softness of a woman bathing in a marble basin,
A basin in the midst of hedges grown
35 So thick, she cannot see her lover hiding,
But she guesses he is near,
And the sliding of the water
Seems the stroking of a dear
Hand upon her.
40 What is Summer in a fine brocaded gown!
I should like to see it lying in a heap upon the ground.
All the pink and silver crumpled up on the ground.

I would be the pink and silver as I ran along the paths,
And he would stumble after,
45 Bewildered by my laughter.
I should see the sun flashing from his sword hilt and
        the buckles on his shoes.
I would choose
To lead him in a maze along the patterned paths,
A bright and laughing maze for my heavy-booted lover.
50 Till he caught me in the shade,
And the buttons of his waistcoat bruised my body as he clasped me
Aching, melting, unafraid.
With the shadows of the leaves and the sundrops,
And the plopping of the waterdrops,
55 All about us in the open afternoon—
I am very like to swoon
With the weight of this brocade,
For the sun sifts through the shade.
Underneath the fallen blossom
60 In my bosom,
Is a letter I have hid.
It was brought to me this morning by a rider from the Duke.[1]
"Madam, we regret to inform you that Lord Hartwell

---

1. *the Duke*, probably John Churchill, Duke of Marlborough (1650–1722), commander of the
united English and Dutch armies during the War of the Spanish Succession (1701–1714). The
initial campaign was fought in Belgium and adjoining countries.

Died in action Thursday se'nnight."[2]
65 As I read it in the white, morning sunlight,
The letters squirmed like snakes.
"Any answer, Madam," said my footman.
"No," I told him.
"See that the messenger takes some refreshment.
70 No, no answer."
And I walked into the garden,
Up and down the patterned paths,
In my stiff, correct brocade.
The blue and yellow flowers stood up proudly in the sun,
75 Each one.
I stood upright too,
Held rigid to the pattern
By the stiffness of my gown.
Up and down I walked,
80 Up and down.

In a month he would have been my husband.
In a month, here, underneath this lime,
We would have broke the pattern;
He for me, and I for him,
85 He as Colonel, I as Lady,
On this shady seat.
He had a whim
That sunlight carried blessing.
And I answered, "It shall be as you have said."
90 Now he is dead.

In Summer and in Winter I shall walk
Up and down
The patterned garden-paths
In my stiff, brocaded gown.
95 The squills and daffodils
Will give place to pillard roses, and to asters, and to snow.
I shall go
Up and down,
In my gown.
100 Gorgeously arrayed,
Bonded and stayed.
And the softness of my body will be guarded from embrace
By each button, hook, and lace.
For the man who should loose me is dead,
105 Fighting with the Duke in Flanders,
In a pattern called a war.
Christ! What are patterns for?   1916

---

2. *se'nnight*, an archaic word meaning a period of seven days and nights.

"Patterns"

"Patterns" is a narrative poem, the story of love unfulfilled because of death. The action of the narrative is only gradually revealed in the poem. As readers, we witness the woman walking in her formal garden, longing for the presence of her absent lover. Not until near the end of the poem do we realize what has caused the lover's absence—his death in war. We then discover that they were engaged to be married within a month. The interest in the poem is thus sustained not only by the action, but by the order in which details of the action are revealed to the reader.

But even more than the action, the motif of "Patterns" helps organize the poem and sustain interest. A *motif* is a pattern itself—a recurring element in a work of literature that gathers meaning as it appears and reappears. Details of setting are intimately fused with this motif. The poem is set in eighteenth-century England, a time when gardens laid out according to a formal pattern were popular. The war to which the poet ultimately refers is just one more war in a dreadful and recurring pattern of wars.

From its title on, the poem gradually reveals more and more patterns—the borders and paths of the garden, the narrator's prescribed dress with its confining whalebone and stiff brocade, along with her admission that she, too, is a rare pattern. Finally all existence appears to be a pattern, and pattern comes to suggest all the restraints and restrictions that prevent emotional fulfillment. After we finish reading this poem, the visual image that is likely to stay with us is related to this motif—a patterned garden with a patterned lady walking up and down in a meaningless pattern, unable to break out of the prison of her patterns.

Howard Chandler Christy, *Liberty Bells of Lexington, 1775* (1912)

See APOSTROPHE in the Handbook of Literary Terms, page 887.

Chicago

Carl Sandburg

Hog Butcher for the World,
Tool Maker, Stacker of Wheat,
Player with Railroads and the Nation's Freight Handler;
Stormy, husky, brawling,
5   City of the Big Shoulders:

They tell me you are wicked and I believe them, for I have seen your painted women under the gas
    lamps luring the farm boys.
And they tell me you are crooked and I answer: Yes, it is true I have seen the gunman kill and go
    free to kill again.
And they tell me you are brutal and my reply is: On the faces of women and children I have seen
    the marks of wanton hunger.
And having answered so I turn once more to those who sneer at this my city, and I give them back
    the sneer and say to them:
10 Come and show me another city with lifted head singing so proud to be alive and coarse and strong
    and cunning.
Flinging magnetic curses amid the toil of piling job on job, here is a tall bold slugger set vivid
    against the little soft cities;
Fierce as a dog with tongue lapping for action, cunning as a savage pitted against the wilderness,
         Bareheaded,
         Shoveling,
15   Wrecking,
         Planning,
         Building, breaking, rebuilding,
Under the smoke, dust all over his mouth, laughing with white teeth,
Under the terrible burden of destiny laughing as a young man laughs,
20 Laughing even as an ignorant fighter laughs who has never lost a battle,
Bragging and laughing that under his wrist is the pulse, and under his ribs the heart of the people,
         Laughing!
Laughing the stormy, husky, brawling laughter of Youth, half-naked, sweating, proud to be Hog
    Butcher, Tool Maker, Stacker of Wheat, Player with Railroads and Freight Handler to the
    Nation.

1914

"Chicago" from *Chicago Poems*, copyright 1916 by Holt, Rinehart and Winston, Inc.; copyright 1944
by Carl Sandburg. Reprinted by permission of Harcourt Brace Jovanovich, Inc.

Poetry

Marianne Moore

I, too, dislike it: there are things that are important beyond all this fiddle.
   Reading it, however, with a perfect contempt for it, one discovers in
   it after all, a place for the genuine.
      Hands that can grasp, eyes
5   that can dilate, hair that can rise
         if it must, these things are important not because a

high-sounding interpretation can be put upon them but because they are
   useful. When they become so derivative as to become unintelligible,
   the same thing may be said for all of us, that we
10   do not admire what
      we cannot understand: the bat
         holding on upside down or in quest of something to

eat, elephants pushing, a wild horse taking a roll, a tireless wolf under
   a tree, the immovable critic twitching his skin like a horse that feels a flea, the base-
15   ball fan, the statistician—
      nor is it valid
         to discriminate against "business documents and

school-books"; all these phenomena are important. One must make a distinction
   however: when dragged into prominence by half poets, the result is not poetry,
20   nor till the poets among us can be
      "literalists of
      the imagination"—above
         insolence and triviality and can present

for inspection, "imaginary gardens with real toads in them," shall we have
25   it. In the meantime, if you demand on the one hand,
   the raw material of poetry in
      all its rawness and
      that which is on the other hand
         genuine, you are interested in poetry.

1921

Reprinted with permission of Macmillan Publishing Co., Inc. and Faber and Faber Limited from *Collected Poems* (British title: *The Complete Poems of Marianne Moore*). Copyright 1935 by Marianne Moore, renewed 1963 by Marianne Moore and T. S. Eliot.

Spring and All

William Carlos Williams

By the road to the contagious hospital
under the surge of the blue
mottled clouds driven from the
northeast—a cold wind. Beyond, the
5 waste of broad, muddy fields
brown with dried weeds, standing and
      fallen

patches of standing water
the scattering of tall trees

All along the road the reddish
10 purplish, forked, upstanding, twiggy
stuff of bushes and small trees
with dead, brown leaves under them
leafless vines—

Lifeless in appearance, sluggish
15 dazed spring approaches—

They enter the new world naked,
cold, uncertain of all
save that they enter. All about them
the cold, familiar wind—
20 Now the grass, tomorrow
the stiff curl of wild carrot leaf
One by one objects are defined—
It quickens: clarity, outline of leaf

But now the stark dignity of
25 entrance—Still, the profound change
has come upon them: rooted they
grip down and begin to awaken

1923

Ars Poetica

Archibald MacLeish

A poem should be palpable and mute
As a globed fruit

Dumb
As old medallions to the thumb

5 Silent as the sleeve-worn stone
Of casement ledges where the moss has grown—

A poem should be wordless
As the flight of birds

A poem should be motionless in time
10 As the moon climbs

Leaving, as the moon releases
Twig by twig the night-entangled trees,

Leaving, as the moon behind the winter leaves,
Memory by memory the mind—

15 A poem should be motionless in time
As the moon climbs

A poem should be equal to:
Not true

For all the history of grief
20 An empty doorway and a maple leaf

For love
The leaning grasses and two lights above the sea—

A poem should not mean
But be

1926

"Spring and All" by William Carlos Williams, *Collected Earlier Poems.* Copyright 1938 by New Directions Publishing Corporation. Reprinted by permission of New Directions Publishing Corporation.

Ars Poetica (ärz pō e′ti kä), the poetic art. [*Latin*]

"Ars Poetica" from *New and Collected Poems 1917–1976* by Archibald MacLeish. Copyright © 1976 by Archibald MacLeish. Reprinted by permission of Houghton Mifflin Company.

THINK AND DISCUSS

THE GARDEN
Understanding
1. What is the **setting** of this poem?
2. How are the infants described in line 5?
3. What would the woman like (line 9)? Of what is she afraid (line 10)?

Analyzing
4. What impression of the woman's appearance is given by the **image** in the first line?
5. Why are the "infants" more likely to "inherit the earth" than the woman?
6. Explain the woman's reaction to the speaker as revealed in the last stanza.
7. Describe the speaker's attitude toward her.

THE RIVER-MERCHANT'S WIFE: A LETTER
Understanding
1. How does the young bride react to her husband in stanza 2?
2. At the age of fifteen, what does she stop doing and what does she desire?
3. How long has her husband been gone? How did he react to leaving (line 19)?

Analyzing
4. What concrete images in stanza 1 suggest the idea of early childhood?
5. The speaker of the poem never says, "I love you." In what ways is her love for her husband revealed?
6. What signs indicate the husband's love?
7. To what does *they* refer in line 25? How do both sentences in this line emphasize the depth of the speaker's grief?

PATTERNS
Understanding
1. Where does the speaker walk? How is she dressed?
2. What are the contents of the letter she receives? Who is the letter from?
3. What specific pattern does the speaker identify in line 106?

Analyzing
4. In what sense is the woman "a rare Pattern"?
5. In line 83, the speaker says, "We would have broke the pattern." What does she mean?
6. In what sense is war a pattern?
7. How do the irregular **rhyme** and **rhythm** reinforce the meaning of the poem?

CHICAGO
Understanding
1. What industries does the speaker mention in lines 1–5?
2. How does the speaker react to those who sneer at his city (lines 9–10)?

Analyzing
3. How would you describe the **tone** of the poem?
4. When "Chicago" was first published before World War I, it created quite a sensation. What qualities might have made the poem exciting at that time? Are the poem's idea, tone, and statement equally appropriate today? Why or why not?
5. As what type of human being(s) is Chicago **personified**?

APPLYING: Apostrophe H𝟕
See Handbook of Literary Terms, p. 887.

An **apostrophe** is a figure of speech in which an absent person, an abstract concept, or an inanimate object is addressed.

1. To whom or what does the speaker address his remarks in lines 6–9? What is the effect of the repeated phrase, "they tell me"?
2. The speaker shifts his address after line 10 to another audience. Who is this audience?
3. Why is this use of apostrophe more effective than a mere description of the city?

ENRICHMENT
Oral Reading
Sandburg's poems are eminently readable and provide an excellent opportunity to practice oral interpretation. "Chicago," "Four Preludes. . . ," "Jazz Fantasia," and others

can be prepared for presentation before a group, with special emphasis on the creation of proper mood in reading. Choose one such poem and read it to your classmates.

POETRY
Understanding
1. What does the speaker discover about poetry, according to lines 2 and 3?
2. What about poetry does one *not* admire, according to lines 9–11?
3. What makes one interested in poetry, according to the final stanza?

Analyzing
4. In what way do the reactions mentioned in lines 4 and 5 indicate the "genuine" in poetry? How does this genuine poetry differ from that written by "half poets"?
5. "Literalists" (line 21) refers to those who use words according to their exact definitions. Why, according to Moore, must poets be "literalists of the imagination"?
6. Why do you think the items in lines 11–15 are cited as poetic subjects rather than, say, flowers, a moonlit evening, or the emotions of love?
7. Why do you think Moore chose the term "real toads" to refer **figuratively** to the "raw material" of poetry?

SPRING AND ALL
Understanding
1. In the first stanza, what adjectives describe the clouds? the fields?
2. What things are described as *cold, dead,* and *lifeless*?

Analyzing
3. What words in stanza 1 have negative **connotations**?
4. How does the description of spring given in the poem differ from conventional descriptions? What aspects of spring does the poem emphasize?
5. What is the double referent of *They* in line 16? What **metaphor** is developed throughout this stanza?
6. How does the poet suggest that the beginning of life is not an easy process?

ARS POETICA
Understanding
1. What are five adjectives the speaker uses to describe poetry in the first ten lines?
2. What does the speaker believe a poem should do and *not* do, according to lines 23–24?

Analyzing
3. MacLeish explains that poetry achieves its subtle and quiet effect on readers through its use of vivid **images**. Why do you think he based his first **simile** on a "globed fruit" rather than, for example, a banana? Why do "old medallions" seem more appropriate than, for example, paper money in his second simile?
4. What qualities of poetry are suggested by the image of the worn ledge overgrown with moss?

Extending
5. Moore says that one needn't necessarily like poetry to be genuinely affected by it. Do you agree or disagree? Which of the seven poems in this group affected you? In what way?

COMPOSITION
Writing a Poem
   Think of an object or emotion that could serve as a subject for a poem of ten or more lines. Then, without naming this subject, write a poem about it, using apostrophe, personification, or metaphor. Add concrete images that will suggest your subject to a reader. When your poem is finished, read it aloud and see if your classmates can identify the subject you are describing.

Writing About Poetry
   Write an essay of five or six paragraphs in which you evaluate a poem, according to criteria that you set up. Choose one of the poems that appears in this group and direct your essay to a literary magazine. Decide what it is about a poem that you find appealing—memorable imagery, a good story, a pertinent message, vivid use of language, or something else. Once you have set up your standards for a good poem, apply them to the poem, explaining why you liked or disliked the work.

As the United States grew to become a world power after World War I, American English increasingly made its mark on the rest of the world.

The 1920s, characterized by flamboyance and prosperity, was variously labeled *The Jazz Age* and *The Roaring Twenties*. Its *flaming youth*, *flappers* with *bobbed* hair, and *sheiks* or *Joe College* types in *raccoon coats*, drank *bootleg* whiskey in private *speakeasies* during *Prohibition* (1919–1933) and danced the *Charleston*.

Jazz music originated in the black culture of New Orleans, but in the 1920s and 1930s, its syncopated rhythms captivated people in Chicago, Paris, and New York's Harlem, where black artists were flourishing in what would be called the Harlem Renaissance. The jazz style developed into *Swing, Boogie-Woogie,* and *Bebop,* each successive wave carrying with it its own *jive talk* (*cat*: musician; *groovy*: fine; *have a ball*: enjoy yourself; *hip*: wise; *in the groove*: perfect; *jam*: improvised music; *mellow*: all right, fine).

By 1930, the prosperous '20s had given way to the severest economic depression in U.S. history. The *Great Depression* ushered in a period of high unemployment, bankruptcies, and mortgage foreclosures. Dire circumstances shaped a new vocabulary: *food stamps, breadlines, soup kitchens, underprivileged,* and *relief*. The homeless lived in shantytowns called *Hoovervilles* (after the President they considered responsible for their plight).

When Franklin Delano Roosevelt took office in 1933, he outlined economic reforms for a *New Deal* in radio talks that came to be known as *fireside chats*. Details of these reforms were implemented by alphabet agencies that, in turn, created large *bureaucracies,* such as the *FHA* (Federal Housing Administration), the *FDIC* (Federal Deposit Insurance Corporation), and the *WPA* (Work Projects Administration).

The world wars that bracketed the Jazz Age and the Depression had a profound effect on the American language. The first world war, called *the Great War*, was eventually called *World War I* with the advent of *World War II*. The *doughboys* or *Yanks*, American soldiers of the first war, came to know the meaning of words like *barrage, bombproof, camouflage, chow line, civvies, dud* (bomb that fails to explode), *grenade, hitch* (period of enlistment), *parachute, red tape* (used on government documents by the English), *sabotage, shell shock,* and *trench warfare*. Soldiers fighting in the trenches or *foxholes* were accustomed to *digging in* before going *over the top* to charge into *no man's land* (the land between two military lines).

The *GI* of World War II took his name from the initials stamped or stenciled on Government *I*ssue underwear or *Jeeps*. *Swabbies* in the navy passed around *scuttlebutt* (gossip) about new inventions such as *radar* and *sonar*. *Flyboys* signaled a code word, *roger* (message received; later it would mean OK). If hit with *flak* (antiaircraft fire; later any criticism), they could be helped with *penicillin*. Servicemen everywhere taped photos of their favorite *pin-up girl*; one of movie idol Rita Hayworth was put on Fat Boy, the *atomic bomb* dropped on Hiroshima in August, 1945. The bomb brought us *fission, countdown, fireball, mushroom cloud, radioactive,* and *fallout*.

The world had entered the *atomic age*. America's influence and language were pervasive. Alistair Cooke, an Englishman turned American, observed in 1974 that a British TV crew working in America became "concerned about preserving the chastity of their native tongue, but they were blissfully unaware that they had been ravished in their cradles; for more than half the slang and much of the idiom they used was American in origin."

BIOGRAPHY

Robert Frost

1874–1963

A man who lived most of his life with great simplicity in New England where nine generations of his ancestors had lived before him, Robert Frost more than most poets was a nationally known figure. Four times winner of the Pulitzer Prize in Poetry, he did much to win acceptance for modern poetry.

Frost was born in San Francisco; and it was not until his newspaper-editor father died that the ten-year-old boy moved with his Scottish-born mother and his sister to his Grandfather Frost's home in Lawrence, Massachusetts. After graduation as valedictorian from high school there, he briefly attended Dartmouth College, worked as a mill hand, wrote for a weekly paper, and taught school. In 1897, after marrying Elinor White, he entered Harvard University.

After two years Frost left Harvard and moved to a farm near Derry, New Hampshire, which had been given to him by his grandfather. For eleven unprofitable years he farmed, then for four more taught school. During all these years he had been writing poems and sending them to magazines. In 1911 Frost added up his accounts and discovered that in twenty years his verses had earned him about two hundred dollars.

Determined to find out once and for all whether he could make a living from his poetry, he resolved to devote several years to concentrated poetic work. According to reports, the cost of living was less in England. Frost sold his farm and in 1912 moved with his wife and four children to Gloucestershire, England.

Frost's first book, *A Boy's Will*, was published in England in 1913. Soon after the first volume came *North of Boston*. Both were enthusiastically received by the British public and the critics, and were shortly republished in the United States.

When Frost returned to this country in 1915, he found himself famous. Lecture invitations poured in. He was appointed a professor of English at Amherst College and in 1916 elected to membership in the National Institute of Arts and Letters.

Like the New Englanders he describes—and like most modern poets—Frost leaves much unsaid. His apparently simple poems often turn out to be rich in hidden meanings. A fine storyteller, he often gives only the fact of an episode and leaves it to the reader to discover the significance.

Part of Frost's popularity with the general reader has no doubt stemmed from the fact that his poetry looks and sounds "like poetry." Readers respond favorably to the familiar iambic pentameter lines he often uses or to other traditional verse forms and stanza patterns. Only on careful reading is the subtly changed rhythm apparent, or the fact that every word carries a particular weight of meaning. Frost once said that art should "clean" life and "strip it to form." There is nothing superfluous in the poetry of Robert Frost.

Robert Frost

 See BLANK VERSE in the Handbook of Literary Terms, page 881.

Birches

When I see birches bend to left and right
Across the lines of straighter darker trees,
I like to think some boy's been swinging them.
But swinging doesn't bend them down to stay
5 As ice storms do. Often you must have seen them
Loaded with ice a sunny winter morning
After a rain. They click upon themselves
As the breeze rises, and turn many-colored
As the stir cracks and crazes their enamel.
10 Soon the sun's warmth makes them shed crystal shells
Shattering and avalanching on the snow crust—
Such heaps of broken glass to sweep away
You'd think the inner dome of heaven had fallen.
They are dragged to the withered bracken by the load,
15 And they seem not to break; though once they are bowed
So low for long, they never right themselves:
You may see their trunks arching in the woods
Years afterwards, trailing their leaves on the ground
Like girls on hands and knees that throw their hair
20 Before them over their heads to dry in the sun.
But I was going to say when Truth broke in
With all her matter of fact about the ice storm,
I should prefer to have some boy bend them
As he went out and in to fetch the cows—
25 Some boy too far from town to learn baseball,
Whose only play was what he found himself,
Summer or winter, and could play alone.
One by one he subdued his father's trees
By riding them down over and over again
30 Until he took the stiffness out of them,
And not one but hung limp, not one was left
For him to conquer. He learned all there was

"Birches," "Out, Out—," "Stopping by Woods on a Snowy Evening," "Fire and Ice," and "Mending Wall" are reprinted from *The Poetry of Robert Frost* edited by Edward Connery Lathem. Copyright © 1969 by Holt, Rinehart, and Winston, Inc. Copyright © 1962 by Robert Frost. Copyright © 1975 by Lesley Frost Ballantine. Reprinted by permission of Henry Holt and Company, Inc., the Estate of Robert Frost, and Jonathan Cape, Ltd.

To learn about not launching out too soon
And so not carrying the tree away
35 Clear to the ground. He always kept his poise
To the top branches, climbing carefully
With the same pains you use to fill a cup
Up to the brim, and even above the brim.
Then he flung outward, feet first, with a swish,
40 Kicking his way down through the air to the ground.
So was I once myself a swinger of birches.
And so I dream of going back to be.
It's when I'm weary of considerations,
And life is too much like a pathless wood
45 Where your face burns and tickles with the cobwebs
Broken across it, and one eye is weeping
From a twig's having lashed across it open.
I'd like to get away from earth awhile
And then come back to it and begin over.
50 May no fate willfully misunderstand me
And half grant what I wish and snatch me away
Not to return. Earth's the right place for love:
I don't know where it's likely to go better.
I'd like to go by climbing a birch tree,
55 And climb black branches up a snow-white trunk
Toward heaven, till the tree could bear no more,
But dipped its top and set me down again.
That would be good both going and coming back.
One could do worse than be a swinger of birches.

1915

Fire and Ice

Some say the world will end in fire,
Some say in ice.
From what I've tasted of desire
I hold with those who favor fire.
5 But if it had to perish twice,
I think I know enough of hate
To say that for destruction ice
Is also great
And would suffice.

1920

Out, Out—"

The buzz saw snarled and rattled in the yard
And made dust and dropped stove-length
    sticks of wood.
Sweet-scented stuff when the breeze drew
    across it.
And from there those that lifted eyes could
    count
5 Five mountain ranges one behind the other
Under the sunset far into Vermont.
And the saw snarled and rattled, snarled
    and rattled.
As it ran light, or had to bear a load.
And nothing happened: day was all but done.
10 Call it a day, I wish they might have said
To please the boy by giving him the half hour
That a boy counts so much when saved from
    work.
His sister stood beside them in her apron
To tell them "Supper." At the word, the saw,
15 As if to prove saws knew what supper meant,
Leaped out at the boy's hand, or seemed to
    leap—
He must have given the hand. However it was,

Neither refused the meeting. But the hand!
The boy's first outcry was a rueful laugh,
20 As he swung toward them holding up the
    hand,
Half in appeal, but half as if to keep
The life from spilling. Then the boy saw all—
Since he was old enough to know, big boy
Doing man's work, though a child at heart—
25 He saw all spoiled. "Don't let him cut my
    hand off—
The doctor, when he comes. Don't let him,
    sister!"
So. But the hand was gone already.
The doctor put him in the dark of ether.
He lay and puffed his lips out with his breath.
30 And then—the watcher at his pulse took
    fright.
No one believed. They listened at his heart.
Little—less—nothing!—and that ended it.
No more to build on there. And they, since
    they
Were not the one dead, turned to their affairs.

1916

Stopping by Woods on a Snowy Evening

Whose woods these are I think I know.
His house is in the village, though;
He will not see me stopping here
To watch his woods fill up with snow.

5 My little horse must think it queer
To stop without a farmhouse near
Between the woods and frozen lake
The darkest evening of the year.

He gives his harness bells a shake
10 To ask if there is some mistake.
The only other sound's the sweep
Of easy wind and downy flake.

The woods are lovely, dark, and deep,
But I have promises to keep,
15 And miles to go before I sleep,
And miles to go before I sleep.

1923

Rudolph Ohrning, *Woods in Snow*.
Private collection

Robert Frost

Mending Wall

Something there is that doesn't love a wall,
That sends the frozen-ground-swell under it
And spills the upper boulders in the sun,
And makes gaps even two can pass abreast.
5 The work of hunters is another thing:
I have come after them and made repair
Where they have left not one stone on a stone,
But they would have the rabbit out of hiding,
To please the yelping dogs. The gaps I mean,
10 No one has seen them made or heard them made,
But at spring mending-time we find them there.
I let my neighbor know beyond the hill;
And on a day we meet to walk the line
And set the wall between us once again.
15 We keep the wall between us as we go.
To each the boulders that have fallen to each.
And some are loaves and some so nearly balls
We have to use a spell to make them balance:
"Stay where you are until our backs are turned!"
20 We wear our fingers rough with handling them.
Oh, just another kind of outdoor game,
One on a side. It comes to little more:
There where it is we do not need the wall:
He is all pine and I am apple orchard.
25 My apple trees will never get across

And eat the cones under his pines, I tell him.
He only says, "Good fences make good
   neighbors."
Spring is the mischief in me, and I wonder
If I could put a notion in his head:
30 "Why do they make good neighbors? Isn't it
Where there are cows? But here there are no
   cows.
Before I built a wall I'd ask to know
What I was walling in or walling out,
And to whom I was like to give offense.
35 Something there is that doesn't love a wall,
That wants it down." I could say "Elves" to
   him,
But it's not elves exactly, and I'd rather
He said it for himself. I see him there,
Bringing a stone grasped firmly by the top
40 In each hand, like an old-stone savage armed.
He moves in darkness as it seems to me,
Not of woods only and the shade of trees.
He will not go behind his father's saying,
And he likes having thought of it so well
45 He says again, "Good fences make good
   neighbors."

1914

THINK AND DISCUSS
BIRCHES
Understanding
1. What effect do ice storms have on birches, according to lines 1–5?
2. What "breaks in" to interrupt the speaker's description (line 21)?
3. When does the speaker want to climb birches (lines 41–49)?

Analyzing
4. What **images, metaphors,** and **similes** of sight and sound describe the effect of ice storms on birches?
5. According to Frost, swinging on birches is a precise art. Describe it in detail.
6. What metaphor is used in lines 37–38 to describe climbing to the top branches? What does this metaphor imply about the satisfaction to be gained from reaching toward high goals?
7. What is the poet's **mood** in lines 42–47? Because of this mood, what does the poet sometimes feel like doing?

APPLYING: Blank Verse H▓
See Handbook of Literary Terms, p. 881.

A line with five beats that moves along this way—ta DUM ta DUM ta DUM ta DUM ta DUM—is called *iambic pentameter*. Unrhymed iambic pentameter lines are called **blank verse**. Frost alternates iambic pentameter with other rhythms to convey a conversational quality.

1. Notice that the beginning lines of the poem strictly adhere to blank-verse rhythm. In which early line does the rhythm begin to deviate from iambic pentameter?
2. In line 23, the iambic pentameter rhythm resumes. In what sense might a lack of regular rhythm convey the kind of emotion felt "when Truth broke in"?

FIRE AND ICE
Understanding
1. What two possible ends for the world are mentioned in the poem?
2. What is the speaker's first choice (line 4)?

Analyzing
3. What two aspects of human nature are represented by fire and ice?
4. In what way is each of these aspects of human nature destructive when it becomes excessive? Which does Frost see as being more destructive, and why?
5. In a single sentence, state the **theme** of the poem.

"OUT, OUT—"
Understanding
1. At what word does the saw leap?
2. What is the boy's initial reaction to his injury? What request does he make of the doctor?

Analyzing
3. What do lines 10–12 imply about the nature of the boy's life?
4. What details are used to **personify** the saw?
5. Some may say that based on lines 33–34, the others were indifferent to the boy. Others may claim that Frost is telling us life must go on in spite of death. Which interpretation do you favor and why?

STOPPING BY WOODS ON A SNOWY EVENING
Understanding
1. Where has the speaker stopped? Why?
2. What time of year is it? What time of day?

Analyzing
3. What differences in attitude are implied among the speaker, his horse, and the owner of the woods?
4. What examples of **alliteration** and **assonance** do you find in the poem? What is the effect of repetition in the last two lines?
5. Do you think this is a poem about a snowy woods or about something else? Explain.

MENDING WALL
Understanding
1. When does the speaker mend the fence? with whom?
2. Which of the menders believes in the need for a wall? For what reasons?

Analyzing
3. How does the speaker **characterize** his neighbor?
4. What meanings does the word *wall* acquire beyond an actual physical wall? In what sense could you describe the neighbor as being "walled in"?

Extending
5. In his poetry, Frost often presents a conflict between two opposing views of life. Cite poems included in this group that present such conflicts and explain what are the opposing forces.

COMPOSITION ✦
Writing a Blank-Verse Description

Choose an event—perhaps something that occurs during an ordinary school day—and narrate it for your classmates in ten lines of blank verse. Remember that you may alter the iambic pattern from time to time to keep the verse from becoming monotonous. A possible opening line might be: "Today I got to school at eight o'clock."

Langston Hughes   1902–1967

Born in Joplin, Missouri, Langston Hughes began writing poetry as a student at Central High School in Cleveland. After graduating, he worked his way on cargo ships to Africa and Europe.

In 1925 he was working as a busboy at a Washington hotel when he was "discovered" by the poet Vachel Lindsay, who was on one of his reading tours. Hughes subsequently became a leading figure in the Harlem Renaissance and, eventually, one of America's best-known poets. After the publication of his first book, *The Weary Blues* (1926), he began traveling across the country giving public readings of his poetry. But he always returned to New York City, to his home in Harlem, where he helped young writers who sought his advice.

Jean Toomer   1894–1967

Jean Toomer wrote: "Racially, I seem to have (who knows for sure) seven blood mixtures: French, Dutch, Welsh, Negro, German, Jewish, and Indian. . . . I have lived equally amid the two race groups. . . . I have strived for a spiritual fusion analogous to the fact of racial intermingling."

Toomer was born in Washington, D.C., the grandson of a black man who had served during Reconstruction as Acting Governor of Louisiana. After college, he taught for a time in the schools of Sparta, Georgia.

In 1923 he published his one book, *Cane*, a mixture of poetry and poetic prose. The innovative book was appreciated by a select few at the time, then disappeared. It reached a wider audience when it was re-issued in 1967, and has come to be recognized as one of the most radical literary experiments of the time.

Countee Cullen   1903–1946

Countee Cullen once said: "Most things I write I do for the sheer joy of the music in them." In his lyrics, he combines an understanding of the joys and sorrows of his race with a thoughtful probing of the attitudes of people in relation to one another.

An adopted son of a Methodist minister, Cullen grew up in New York City, attended New York University, and received a master's degree in English literature from Harvard University. In addition to writing poetry, he taught French and edited *Opportunity: Journal of Negro Life*.

Cullen collected what he considered to be the best verse written by black poets in an anthology titled *Caroling Dusk*. His ability and careful judgment made the book a notable addition to the few such collections that had preceded his.

James Weldon Johnson 1871–1938

Although he will be longest remembered as a poet and essayist, James Weldon Johnson was successful in many fields. He taught school in his home town, Jacksonville, Florida, was admitted to the Florida bar in 1897, and eventually went to New York where he prospered as a writer of songs and light opera. Later he was equally successful as United States consul in Venezuela and Nicaragua.

Still later, he began to edit books of Negro poetry and spirituals. "The Creation," from his collection *God's Trombones*, is cast in the form of a sermon in verse. The speaker of the poem resembles an old-time black preacher who presents a humanized God, looking over His children and concerned for their well-being.

Arna Bontemps 1902–1973

Born in Alexandria, Louisiana, Arna Bontemps graduated from Pacific Union College in 1923 and soon thereafter became associated with what has become known as the Harlem Renaissance. After winning a number of prizes for his poetry in the 1920s, he turned to prose.

In the 1930s he studied at the University of Chicago and earned a degree in library science. For many years he served as librarian at Fisk University and was for a time a member of the faculty at the University of Illinois, Chicago Circle. He also taught at Yale.

His anthologies of black literature and folklore are numerous and widely popular. He also wrote three novels, including *Black Thunder* (1936).

Claude McKay 1890–1948

Claude McKay published two collections of poems just after he turned twenty. Shortly after their publication, McKay came to the United States from his birthplace, Jamaica, to study agriculture, first at Tuskegee Institute, and then at Kansas State University. He soon discovered that he preferred writing and moved to New York, settled in Harlem, and began publishing his poems in small literary magazines. In 1922 his most important collection of poetry, *Harlem Shadows*, was published. In it, he achieved poignant lyricism as well as effective protest.

Although McKay was primarily a poet, he was also a novelist and short-story writer. His writing is noted for his portrayals of black life, his nostalgia for the tropics of his youth, and his demands for unity among blacks in attacking social injustice.

Theme for English B

Langston Hughes

The instructor said,

> *Go home and write*
> *a page tonight.*
> *And let that page come out of you—*
> 5 *Then, it will be true.*

I wonder if it's that simple?
I am twenty-two, colored, born in
    Winston-Salem.
I went to school there, then Durham, then
    here
to this college on the hill above Harlem.
10 I am the only colored student in my class.
The steps from the hill lead down into
    Harlem,
through a park, then I cross St. Nicholas,
Eighth Avenue, Seventh, and I come to the Y,
the Harlem Branch Y, where I take the
    elevator
15 up to my room, sit down, and write this
    page:

It's not easy to know what is true for you
    or me
at twenty-two, my age. But I guess I'm what
I feel and see and hear, Harlem, I hear you:
hear you, hear me—we two—you, me,
    talk on this page.
20 (I hear New York, too.) Me—who?
Well, I like to eat, sleep, drink, and be in love.

I like to work, read, learn, and understand life.
I like a pipe for a Christmas present,
or records—Bessie, bop, or Bach.[1]
25 I guess being colored doesn't make me *not* like
the same things other folks like who are
    other races.

So will my page be colored that I write?
Being me, it will not be white.
But it will be
30 a part of you, instructor.
You are white—
yet a part of me, as I am a part of you.

That's American.
Sometimes perhaps you don't want to be
    a part of me.
35 Nor do I often want to be a part of you.
But we are, that's true!
As I learn from you,
I guess you learn from me—
although you're older—and white—
40 and somewhat more free.

This is my page for English B.

        1951

---

1. *Bessie, bop, or Bach.* Bessie Smith was one of the greatest blues singers of the early twentieth century. Bop is a form of jazz. Johann Sebastian Bach (1685–1750) is considered one of the most important composers of classical music.

"Theme for English B" from *Montage of a Dream Deferred* by Langston Hughes. Reprinted by permission of Harold Ober Associates Incorporated. Copyright 1951 by Langston Hughes. Copyright renewed 1979 by George Houston Bass.

November Cotton Flower

Jean Toomer

Boll-weevil's coming, and the winter's cold,
Made cotton-stalks look rusty, seasons old,
And cotton, scarce as any southern snow,
Was vanishing; the branch, so pinched and slow,
5 Failed in its function as the autumn rake;
Drouth fighting soil had caused the soil to take
All water from the streams; dead birds were
found
In wells a hundred feet below the ground—
Such was the season when the flower bloomed.
10 Old folks were startled, and it soon assumed
Significance. Superstition saw
Something it had never seen before:
Brown eyes that loved without a trace of fear,
Beauty so sudden for that time of year.
                                              1923

"November Cotton Flower" is reprinted from *Cane* by Jean Toomer,
by permission of Liveright Publishing Corporation. Copyright 1923
by Boni & Liveright. Copyright renewed 1951 by Jean Toomer.

Any Human to Another

Countee Cullen

The ills I sorrow at
Not me alone
Like an arrow,
Pierce to the marrow,
5 Through the fat
And past the bone.

Your grief and mine
Must intertwine
Like sea and river,
10 Be fused and mingle,
        Diverse yet single,
Forever and forever.

Let no man be so proud
And confident,
15 To think he is allowed
A little tent
Pitched in a meadow
Of sun and shadow
All his little own.

20 Joy may be shy, unique,
Friendly to a few,
Sorrow never scorned to speak
To any who
Were false or true.

25 Your every grief
Like a blade
Shining and unsheathed
Must strike me down.
Of bitter aloes wreathed,
30 My sorrow must be laid
On your head like a crown.
                                              1929

"Any Human to Another" from *On These I Stand* by Countee Cullen.
Copyright 1935 by Harper & Row, Publishers, Inc.; renewed 1963
by Ida Cullen. Reprinted by permission of Harper & Row, Publishers, Inc.

The Creation

James Weldon Johnson

And God stepped out of space,
And he looked around and said:
I'm lonely—
I'll make a world.

5 And as far as the eye of God could see
Darkness covered everything,
Blacker than a hundred midnights
Down in a cypress swamp.

Then God smiled,
10 And the light broke,
And the darkness rolled up on one side,
And light stood shining on the other,
And God said: That's good!

Then God reached out and took the light
    in his hands,
15 And God rolled the light around in his
    hands
Until he made the sun;
And he set that sun a-blazing in the heavens.
And the light that was left from
    making the sun
God gathered it up in a shining ball
20 And flung it against the darkness,
Spangling the night with the moon and
    stars.
Then down between
The darkness and the light
He hurled the world;
25 And God said: That's good!

Then God himself stepped down—
And the sun was on his right hand,
And the moon was on his left;
The stars were clustered about his head,
30 And the earth was under his feet.
And God walked, and where he trod
His footsteps hollowed the valleys out
And bulged the mountains up.

Then he stopped and looked and saw
35 That the earth was hot and barren.
So God stepped over to the edge of the world
And he spat out the seven seas—
He batted his eyes, and the lightnings
    flashed—
He clapped his hands, and the thunders
    rolled—
40 And the waters above the earth came down,
The cooling waters came down.

Then the green grass sprouted,
And the little red flowers blossomed,
The pine tree pointed his finger to the sky,
45 And the oak spread out his arms,
The lakes cuddled down in the hollows
    of the ground,
And the rivers ran down to the sea;
And God smiled again,
And the rainbow appeared,
50 And curled itself around his shoulder.
Then God raised his arm and he waved his
    hand
Over the sea and over the land,
And he said: Bring forth! Bring forth!
And quicker than God could drop his hand,
55 Fishes and fowls
And beasts and birds
Swam the rivers and the seas,
Roamed the forests and the woods,
And split the air with their wings.
60 And God said: That's good!

Then God walked around,
And God looked around
On all that he had made.

"The Creation" from *God's Trombones* by James Weldon Johnson. Copyright 1927 by The Viking Press, Inc., © renewed 1955 by Grace Nail Johnson. Reprinted by permission of The Viking Press, Inc.

He looked at his sun,
65 And he looked at his moon,
And he looked at his little stars;
He looked on his world
With all its living things,
And God said: I'm lonely still.

70 Then God sat down—
On the side of a hill where he could think;
By a deep, wide river he sat down;
With his head in his hands,
God thought and thought,
75 Till he thought: I'll make me a man!

Up from the bed of the river
God scooped the clay;
And by the bank of the river

He kneeled him down;
80 And there the great God Almighty
Who lit the sun and fixed it in the sky,
Who flung the stars to the most far corner of
the night,
Who rounded the earth in the middle of his
hand;
This Great God
85 Like a mammy bending over her baby,
Kneeled down in the dust
Toiling over a lump of clay
Till he shaped it in his own image;

Then into it he blew the breath of life,
90 And man became a living soul.
Amen. Amen.

1920

Horace Pippin, *Holy Mountain II* (1944). Private collection

A Black Man Talks of Reaping

Arna Bontemps

I have sown beside all waters in my day.
I planted deep, within my heart the fear
That wind or fowl would take the grain away.
I planted safe against this stark, lean year.

5 I scattered seed enough to plant the land
In rows from Canada to Mexico
But for my reaping only what the hand
Can hold at once is all that I can show.

Yet what I sowed and what the orchard yields
10 My brother's sons are gathering stalk and root,
Small wonder then my children glean in fields
They have not sown, and feed on bitter fruit.

1927

"A Black Man Talks of Reaping" by Arna Bontemps from *Personals*.
Reprinted by permission of Harold Ober Associates Incorporated.
Copyright © 1963 by Arna Bontemps.

Bontemps (bôn täN′).

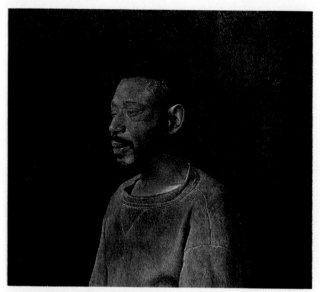

Andrew Wyeth, *Grape Wine* (1976).
The Metropolitan Museum of Art

If We Must Die

Claude McKay

If we must die, let it not be like hogs
Hunted and penned in an inglorious spot,
While round us bark the mad and hungry dogs,
Making their mock at our accursed lot.
5 If we must die, O let us nobly die,
So that our precious blood may not be shed
In vain; then even the monsters we defy
Shall be constrained to honor us though dead!
O kinsmen! we must meet the common foe!
10 Though far outnumbered let us show us brave,
And for their thousand blows deal one deathblow!
What though before us lies the open grave?
Like men we'll face the murderous, cowardly pack,
Pressed to the wall, dying, but fighting back!

1919

"If We Must Die" from *Selected Poems of Claude McKay*, copyright
1953 by Twayne Publishers, Inc. Reprinted with the permission of
Twayne Publishers, A Division of G. K. Hall & Co., Boston.

THINK AND DISCUSS

THEME FOR ENGLISH B

Understanding

1. What is the assignment that the speaker was given by the instructor?
2. What does the speaker wonder?

Analyzing

3. In what sense has the speaker gone beyond or expanded the assignment?
4. How does the speaker feel his world differs from his instructor's? In what way does he feel their worlds are similar?

NOVEMBER COTTON FLOWER

Understanding

1. What threats to the cotton crop are named in lines 1 and 6?
2. What is the season? How do you know?

Analyzing

3. What is the **mood** of the first eight lines? What images contribute to the mood?
4. Why is the event described in the final six lines so startling?
5. What does the event **symbolize** in the lives of the people?

ANY HUMAN TO ANOTHER

Understanding

1. How is joy described in lines 20–21?
2. What "strikes down" the speaker, according to the final stanza?

Analyzing

3. What **images** does the poet use to convey the feelings of grief and pain?
4. What does the "little tent" (line 16) stand for?
5. The ancient Greeks and Romans crowned victors with wreaths of laurel. From early time, grief has been symbolized by aloes, a bitter drug made from the leaves of a plant of the lily family. Using this information, explain what Cullen is saying in the final stanza about the need to share grief.

THE CREATION
Understanding

1. What is God described as doing in this poem?
2. How does God react to His creation at each stage?

Analyzing

3. In the first stanza of this poem, what phrases make God seem extremely human and down-to-earth?
4. According to the poem, how did God bring light out of the darkness that "covered everything"?
5. Describe the **tone** of the poem. What words and descriptions help establish this tone?

A BLACK MAN TALKS OF REAPING
Understanding

1. Why, according to stanza 1, did the speaker plant his seeds deep?
2. What does the speaker have to show for his efforts, according to stanza 2?

Analyzing

3. Who are the "brother's sons" of line 10?
4. What situation is symbolized by the sowing and reaping described in the poem?

IF WE MUST DIE
Understanding

1. To what does the speaker compare his antagonists in line 3?
2. If death is necessary, how should these people die, according to lines 5, 13, and 14?

Analyzing

3. To whom does the speaker address the poem?
4. Why do you think the speaker does not name specifically the dangers that he and his people face?
5. What emotions do you think this poem is intended to arouse? Cite phrases or **figures of speech** that contribute to its emotional effect.

Extending

6. Using the six poems you have just read by writers of the Harlem Renaissance as a basis, make some general observations about the topics and **themes** that these poets chose to develop.

COMPOSITION
Writing a Prose Poem

Suppose you have been given the same instructions for a writing assignment that were given to Langston Hughes when he wrote "Theme for English B." Write a prose poem of a page or so, directed to a creative writing class, that reflects your own experiences. To get started, try to free associate and jot down the images and thoughts that come into your mind. Then revise, giving order and form to your ideas.

Writing a Summary

Assume that you are writing a brief introduction for a collection of poems by the poets of the Harlem Renaissance. Write a four- or five-paragraph essay in which you summarize the topics and techniques that you find in the poems you have just read. Be sure to refer to specific poems in your composition.

ENRICHMENT
Oral Reading

"The Creation" is most effective when read aloud. Your school library may have one or more recordings of *God's Trombones*, of which "The Creation" is a part. Find such a recording and play it for the class, or prepare your own reading, which should reflect the tone and spirit of the poem.

For several decades T. S. Eliot served through his essays and lectures as the main spokesman and theorist of the new poetry of the modern period. From the publication of his first book of poetry in 1917, he dictated the direction and tone for a generation of poets. Indeed, no one has had a greater influence on twentieth-century poetry. His poetry is complex and packed with allusions, based on the idioms and rhythms of natural speech, and full of sense impressions and concrete images. The fact that he both drew from the past and made startling departures from it is seen in one critic's observations that Eliot combined "trivial and tawdry pictures with traditionally poetic subject matter, linking the banalities of conversation to rich rhetoric and interrupting the present with flashbacks of the past."

Eliot was born in St. Louis, Missouri, of New England stock, his grandfather having gone west as a Unitarian minister. From 1906 to 1910 he was an undergraduate at Harvard University, where he published poems in the literary magazine. A formidable scholar, he did graduate work at Harvard, the Sorbonne in France, and Oxford in England.

He was on his way to study in Germany in 1914 when World War I broke out. Instead, he went to England, where he married the daughter of a British artist. He taught, worked as a bank clerk, and eventually became an editor at Faber & Faber. In London, he met Ezra Pound, acting foreign editor for *Poetry* magazine. At Pound's urging, Harriet Monroe, editor of *Poetry* in Chicago, published "The Love Song of J. Alfred Prufrock" in 1915. In 1917 Eliot published a volume of poems titled *Prufrock and Other Observations*. Like most of Eliot's later work, this volume dealt with the frustration and spiritual void of the modern individual.

Acting as Eliot's editor, Pound drastically cut and revised a poem that was published in 1922 as *The Waste Land*, one of the major works of modern literature. This influential and innovative poem immediately became the center of controversy, but gradually won critical acclaim. In vivid images and fragmented sections that mingled many voices, the poem captured the pessimistic mood of the age.

Eliot became a British citizen in 1926 and, shortly after, a convert to the Episcopalian faith. His later works, especially *Four Quartets*, offer strong religious belief as an antidote for the kind of spiritual emptiness described in *The Waste Land*. After publishing *Four Quartets*, Eliot turned to the writing of plays. His poetic dramas such as *The Cocktail Party* created interest as experimental theater. In recognition of his enormous contribution to modern poetry, T. S. Eliot was awarded the Nobel Prize for literature in 1948.

The Love Song of J. Alfred Prufrock

T. S. Eliot

S'io credesse che mia riposta fosse
A persona che mai tornasse al mondo,
Questa fiamma staria senza piu scosse.
Ma perciocche giammai di questo fondo
Non torno vivo alcun, s' i' odo il vero,
Senza tema d' infamia ti rispondo.[1]

Philip Evergood, *Tea for Two* (1927/61). Private collection

Let us go then, you and I,
When the evening is spread out against the sky
Like a patient etherised upon a table;
Let us go, through certain half-deserted streets,
5 The muttering retreats
Of restless nights in one-night cheap hotels
And sawdust restaurants with oyster-shells:
Streets that follow like a tedious argument
Of insidious intent
10 To lead you to an overwhelming question . . .
Oh, do not ask, "What is it?"
Let us go and make our visit.

    In the room the women come and go
Talking of Michelangelo.

15   The yellow fog that rubs its back upon the window-panes,
The yellow smoke that rubs its muzzle on the window-panes
Licked its tongue into the corners of the evening,
Lingered upon the pools that stand in drains,
Let fall upon its back the soot that falls from chimneys,
20 Slipped by the terrace, made a sudden leap,
And seeing that it was a soft October night,
Curled once about the house, and fell asleep.

    And indeed there will be time
For the yellow smoke that slides along the street,

---

1. *S'io credesse . . . ti rispondo.* "If I believed my answer were being made to one who could ever return to the world, this flame would gleam no more; but since, if what I hear is true, never from this abyss [hell] did living man return, I answer thee without fear of infamy." (Dante, *Inferno* XXVII, 61–66)

"The Love Song of J. Alfred Prufrock" from *Collected Poems* 1909–1962 by T. S. Eliot, copyright 1936 by Harcourt Brace Jovanovich, Inc.; copyright © 1963, 1964 by T. S. Eliot. Reprinted by permission of the publishers Harcourt Brace Jovanovich, Inc. and Faber and Faber Publishers.

25 Rubbing its back upon the window-panes;
   There will be time, there will be time
   To prepare a face to meet the faces that you meet;
   There will be time to murder and create,
   And time for all the works and days of hands
30 That lift and drop a question on your plate;
   Time for you and time for me,
   And time yet for a hundred indecisions,
   And for a hundred visions and revisions,
   Before the taking of a toast and tea.

35   In the room the women come and go
   Talking of Michelangelo.

      And indeed there will be time
   To wonder, "Do I dare?" and, "Do I dare?"
   Time to turn back and descend the stair,
40 With a bald spot in the middle of my hair—
   [They will say: "How his hair is growing thin!"]
   My morning coat, my collar mounting firmly to the chin,
   My necktie rich and modest, but asserted by a simple pin—
   [They will say: "But how his arms and legs are thin!"]
45 Do I dare
   Disturb the universe?
   In a minute there is time
   For decisions and revisions which a minute will reverse.

      For I have known them all already, known them all:—
50 Have known the evenings, mornings, afternoons,
   I have measured out my life with coffee spoons;
   I know the voices dying with a dying fall
   Beneath the music from a farther room.
      So how should I presume?

55   And I have known the eyes already, known them all—
   The eyes that fix you in a formulated phrase,
   And when I am formulated, sprawling on a pin,
   When I am pinned and wriggling on the wall,
   Then how should I begin
60 To spit out all the butt-ends of my days and ways?
      And how should I presume?

      And I have known the arms already, known them all—
   Arms that are braceleted and white and bare
   [But in the lamplight, downed with light brown hair!]
65 Is it perfume from a dress

(continued)

That makes me so digress?
Arms that lie along a table, or wrap about a shawl.
    And should I then presume?
    And how should I begin?

                    . . . . .

70 Shall I say, I have gone at dusk through narrow streets
And watched the smoke that rises from the pipes
Of lonely men in shirt-sleeves, leaning out of windows? . . .

    I should have been a pair of ragged claws
Scuttling across the floors of silent seas.

                . . . . .

75 And the afternoon, the evening, sleeps so peacefully!
Smoothed by long fingers,
Asleep . . . tired . . . or it malingers,
Stretched on the floor, here beside you and me.
Should I, after tea and cakes and ices,
80 Have the strength to force the moment to its crisis?
But though I have wept and fasted, wept and prayed,
Though I have seen my head [grown slightly bald] brought in upon a platter,
I am no prophet—and here's no great matter;
I have seen the moment of my greatness flicker,
85 And I have seen the eternal Footman hold my coat, and snicker,
And in short, I was afraid.

    And would it have been worth it, after all,
After the cups, the marmalade, the tea,
Among the porcelain, among some talk of you and me,
90 Would it have been worth while,
To have bitten off the matter with a smile,
To have squeezed the universe into a ball
To roll it toward some overwhelming question,
To say: "I am Lazarus, come from the dead,
95 Come back to tell you all, I shall tell you all"—
If one, settling a pillow by her head,
    Should say: "That is not what I meant at all.
    That is not it, at all."

    And would it have been worth it, after all,
100 Would it have been worth while,
After the sunsets and the dooryards and the sprinkled streets,
After the novels, after the teacups, after the skirts that trail along the floor—
And this, and so much more?—
It is impossible to say just what I mean!
105 But as if a magic lantern threw the nerves in patterns on a screen:

Would it have been worth while
If one, settling a pillow or throwing off a shawl,
And turning toward the window, should say:
    "That is not it at all,
10 That is not what I meant, at all."

                          . . . . .

No! I am not Prince Hamlet,[2] nor was meant to be;
Am an attendant lord, one that will do
To swell a progress, start a scene or two,
Advise the prince; no doubt an easy tool,
15 Deferential, glad to be of use,
Politic, cautious, and meticulous;
Full of high sentence, but a bit obtuse;
At times, indeed, almost ridiculous—
Almost, at times, the Fool.

20   I grow old . . . I grow old . . .
I shall wear the bottoms of my trousers rolled.

    Shall I part my hair behind? Do I dare to eat a peach?
I shall wear white flannel trousers, and walk upon the beach.
I have heard the mermaids singing, each to each.

25   I do not think that they will sing to me.

    I have seen them riding seaward on the waves
Combing the white hair of the waves blown back
When the wind blows the water white and black.

    We have lingered in the chambers of the sea
30 By sea-girls wreathed with seaweed red and brown
Till human voices wake us, and we drown.

                              1915

---

2. *Prince Hamlet*, the hero of William Shakespeare's play *Hamlet*, who set out to prove that his uncle had murdered his father.

THINK AND DISCUSS

Understanding

1. During what time of day does the speaker offer his invitation to go? Where does the speaker want to go?
2. To what is the yellow fog compared in the **metaphor** that begins on line 15?
3. What does Prufrock say he is and is not, in lines 111–119?

Analyzing

4. The words in the epigraph to the poem are spoken by Guido da Montefeltro whom Dante encounters in his imaginary journey through hell. Guido is wrapped in a flame, suffering eternal torment for his sins on earth; he confesses his sins as an evil counselor to Dante on the assumption that Dante, like himself, is a prisoner in hell.

   In what respect is Prufrock's Song likewise the confession of a soul in torment? What kinds of torment might he be suffering?
5. Guido was a worldly man of action. How does Prufrock compare with him in this respect?
6. In what sense could you say that Prufrock, although still alive, is already "dead"?
7. What examples can you find of the **stream-of-consciousness** technique?
8. What kind of "overwhelming question" is Prufrock trying to ask?
9. Why does Prufrock long for the song of the mermaids in the last lines of the poem? What might the mermaids' singing represent? Why does he despair of hearing their song?
10. How would you interpret the **paradoxical** last line of the poem?

Extending

11. In the Bible there are two mentions of men named Lazarus. One is in the gospel of John 11:1–44; the other is in Luke 16:19–31. Look up these references and decide whether one or both apply to the situation of Prufrock.

COMPOSITION

Comparing Yourself to a Character

Find aspects of Prufrock's situation and his feelings that you identify with. In an essay of at least three paragraphs, directed to a relative, explain characteristics of Prufrock that you recognize in yourself. Be sure to refer to specific lines in the poem.

Writing About Allusions

Write an essay of four or five paragraphs in which you discuss the effect that the many allusions have on the meaning of the poem. Consider the epigraph from Dante, the allusions to Michelangelo, Hamlet, John the Baptist, Lazarus, and any others you note. For instance, the reference to Hamlet immediately conjures up the conflicting impulses toward action and hesitation experienced by both Shakespeare's character and Prufrock. Direct your essay to a classmate who had difficulty understanding the allusions in the poem.

"The Love Song of J. Alfred Prufrock"

"The Love Song of J. Alfred Prufrock" is a **dramatic monologue** in which the narrator, Prufrock, is speaking to himself. Thus some parts of the poem are disjointed and fragmentary because we are eavesdropping on Prufrock's random thoughts.

The title is ironic, because Prufrock—isolated, timid, and spiritually numb—is a man unable to love, and the "love song" is sung to nobody. The "you and I" of the first line may be thought of as two parts of Prufrock's personality, one part urging him to go, to participate in experience; the other part holding back, withdrawing, retreating. Thus Prufrock may be seen as a man beset by fears of involvement in life, of relationships with other people. Images of movement and action oppose images of paralysis throughout the poem, reflecting Prufrock's own internal conflict.

The basic story line concerns Prufrock's visit to a woman, his inability to declare his love for her, and his later recollection of this experience. Up to line 61, world-weary Prufrock seems to review his entire life in preparing for the visit. In lines 62–86, he appears to be in the woman's presence (but really wrapped up in his own feelings of timidity and inadequacy). And after line 87 ("And would it have been worth it, after all") the opportunity of the visit seems to have passed, leaving Prufrock to justify the lost opportunity. He rationalizes that the woman would have rejected his proposal by saying: "That is not it at all,/ That is not what I meant, at all."

Prufrock, unlike Hamlet, is unable "to force the moment to its crisis." There is no answer to the questions he poses: "Do I dare?" "And should I then presume?" "How shall I begin?" So he resigns himself to being an "attendant lord," one of life's ineffectual and ridiculous minor characters. The poem abounds with other **allusions:** the biblical Lazarus who was raised from the dead; the prophet John the Baptist whose head was served on a platter to the dancer Salome; a character damned in hell in Dante's *Inferno;* and the eternal Footman, death, ever-present and waiting. All these allusions serve to underscore Prufrock's frustration and sense of futility.

As Prufrock contemplates growing old, with sparse hair and thin limbs, he becomes even more certain that, in his romantic fantasies, the sensual mermaids' song will not be meant for him. Despite attempts to fit in with current fashion, Prufrock remains the outsider. Yet there will always be human intrusions, as suggested in the final line of the poem. The voices, which recall him from his dreams, can have a devastating effect on a man who has so carefully rolled his trousers and metaphorically stayed along the shoreline. The "we" who will "drown" from social contact may be the "you and I" of the poem's opening, the two contradictory parts of Prufrock's inner spirit. At the end Prufrock turns to voices other than his own; we realize that he will never be deeply involved, that he is doomed to live at the edges of life.

BIOGRAPHIES

Vachel Lindsay 1879–1931

Vachel Lindsay was born and died in Springfield, Illinois, home of Abraham Lincoln, whom he celebrates in one of his most famous poems. He began his literary career by reciting and trying to sell his poems on the streets of Springfield. After publishing his first two volumes of poetry in 1913 and 1914, he began touring the country chanting his rhythmic, musical verses to packed audiences in universities, schools, and clubs.

Two of Lindsay's best-known works are "The Congo, A Study of the Negro Race," in which he echoes ragtime rhythms in verse, and "General William Booth Enters into Heaven," written in the rhythmic drumbeats of a marching band. Lindsay's was a new kind of poetry—direct in its approach, democratic in its outlook, and startling in its pulsating, syncopated meters.

DuBose Heyward 1885–1940

DuBose Heyward would have earned fame had he written nothing other than his share of the libretto for *Porgy and Bess*, the famous American opera by George and Ira Gershwin based on Heyward's novel *Porgy* (1925). Collaborating with his wife Dorothy, he also wrote a nonmusical dramatic adaptation of this novel that won for him a Pulitzer Prize in 1927. In addition, he published numerous short stories and poems.

A descendant of a signer of the Declaration of Independence, Heyward spent most of his life in South and North Carolina. He was among the first white writers to concentrate on the lives of blacks in America.

Edna St. Vincent Millay 1892–1950

Born in Maine, Edna St. Vincent Millay began publishing poetry before she entered Vassar College. At nineteen she wrote "Renascence," a long lyric whose quiet beginning builds toward an ecstatic affirmation of life.

Millay moved to Greenwich Village in New York and became the poetic voice of the "flaming youth" of the 1920s. For a few years she abandoned the young and optimistic outlook she had voiced in "Renascence" and began to express the cynicism and disillusionment that followed World War I. In 1923 she was awarded a Pulitzer Prize for *The Harp-Weaver and Other Poems*.

For the last twenty-five years of her life Millay spent most of her time at Steepletop Farm in northern New York. The subdued lyrics and sonnets of this period show genuine poetic power and reveal a striking and intense personality.

Elinor Wylie   1885–1928

One critic has written of Elinor Wylie, "Her images of glass and bronze and gold. . . have the glitter of the world in which she has lived." Wylie herself once announced her aim as a poet was to write "short lines, clean small stanzas, brilliant and compact."

Wylie was born into a wealthy and cultured family and spent much of her childhood in Washington, D.C., where her father served as Assistant Attorney General under Theodore Roosevelt. When she was eighteen, she went to London and Paris for a season of parties and travel.

In the United States she lived in New York City, where she became acquainted with most of the prominent writers of that time. Her poetry, which she constantly revised, was delicate, finely wrought, and painstakingly intelligent.

Robinson Jeffers   1887–1962

Although Robinson Jeffers was born in Pittsburgh and was educated in Europe, most of his life and poetry were shaped by California. His family moved there when he was sixteen, and that is where he went to college, receiving his bachelor's degree at the age of eighteen. He then studied medicine for three years and forestry for one year, but he admitted, "I wasn't deeply interested in anything but poetry." When he married, he and his wife wandered to Carmel, California. There he built a house with his own hands, on the top of a cliff overlooking the Pacific, where they lived out their lives and where he did all his writing.

Jeffers's swelling and ebbing lines resemble Whitman's, but his view of life is dark. Called the most pessimistic of contemporary American poets, he often expresses an aversion for humans and society, and a preference for wild, rugged nature.

Sara Teasdale   1884–1933

After being raised and educated in St. Louis, Sara Teasdale traveled to Europe and the Near East. Upon her return to America, she settled in New York, where she lived in near-seclusion and wrote poetry despite frequent illness. She was truly the independent "solitary" she describes in her poems.

Her first book of poems, *Sonnets to Duse*, appeared in 1907. Other volumes followed, including *Rivers to the Sea* (1915) and *Love Songs* (1917), which went through five editions in one year and won her a special Pulitzer award, the first given to a book of poems in this country. Her poems illustrated her belief that the appeal of poetry should be emotional rather than intellectual so that "the reader will feel and not think while he is reading."

HZ See **CONNOTATION/DENOTATION** in the
Handbook of Literary Terms, page 883.

Abraham Lincoln Walks at Midnight
(In Springfield, Illinois)

Vachel Lindsay

It is portentous,[1] and a thing of state
That here at midnight, in our little town
A mourning figure walks, and will not rest,
Near the old courthouse pacing up and down,

5 Or by his homestead, or in shadowed yards
He lingers where his children used to play,
Or through the market, on the well-worn stones
He stalks until the dawn-stars burn away.

A bronzed, lank man! His suit of ancient black,
10 A famous high top hat and plain worn shawl
Make him the quaint great figure that men love,
The prairie lawyer, master of us all.

He cannot sleep upon his hillside now.
He is among us:—as in times before!
15 And we who toss and lie awake for long
Breathe deep, and start, to see him pass the
      door.

His head is bowed. He thinks on men and kings.
Yea, when the sick world cries, how can he
      sleep?
Too many peasants fight, they know not why,
20 Too many homesteads in black terror weep.

The sins of all the war lords burn his heart.
He sees the dreadnaughts[2] scouring every main.

Photograph of Lincoln by Alexander Gardner (1865). Taken four days before Lincoln died, this is the last known photograph of him.

He carries on his shawl-wrapped shoulders now
The bitterness, the folly and the pain.

25 He cannot rest until a spirit-dawn
Shall come;—the shining hope of Europe free:
The league of sober folk, the Workers' Earth,
Bringing long peace to Cornland, Alp and Sea.

It breaks his heart that kings must murder still,
30 That all his hours of travail[3] here for men
Seem yet in vain. And who will bring white peace
That he may sleep upon his hill again?

1917

1. *portentous,* significant; a sign of something important that is about to happen.
2. *dreadnaughts,* battleships with heavy armor.
3. *travail,* mental suffering and physical labor.

"Abraham Lincoln Walks at Midnight" reprinted with permission of Macmillan Publishing Company from *Collected Poems of Vachel Lindsay* by Vachel Lindsay. Copyright 1914 by Macmillan Publishing Company, renewed 1942 by Elizabeth C. Lindsay.

The Mountain Woman

DuBose Heyward

Among the sullen peaks she stood at bay
And paid life's hard account from her small
    store.
Knowing the code of mountain wives, she bore
The burden of the days without a sigh;
5 And, sharp against the somber winter sky,
I saw her drive her steers afield each day.

Hers was the hand that sunk the furrows deep
Across the rocky, grudging southern slope.
At first youth left her face, and later hope;
10 Yet through each mocking spring and barren
    fall,
She reared her lusty brood, and gave them all
That gladder wives and mothers love to keep.

And when the sheriff shot her eldest son
Beside his still, so well she knew her part,
15 She gave no healing tears to ease her heart;
But took the blow upstanding, with her eyes
As drear and bitter as the winter skies,
Seeing her then, I thought that she had won.

But yesterday her man returned too soon
20 And found her tending, with a reverent touch,
One scarlet bloom; and, having drunk too much,
He snatched its flame and quenched it in the
    dirt.
Then, like a creature with a mortal hurt,
She fell, and wept away the afternoon.

1924

"Mountain Woman" from *Skylines and Horizons* by DuBose Heyward. Copyright 1924 by DuBose Heyward and renewed 1952 by Dorothy Heyward. Reprinted by permission of Henry Holt and Company, Inc.

Harvey Dunn, detail of *The Homesteader's Wife*. South Dakota Memorial Art Center collection, Brookings

Well, I Have Lost You

Edna St. Vincent Millay

Well, I have lost you; and I lost you fairly;
In my own way, and with my full consent.
Say what you will, kings in a tumbrel rarely
Went to their deaths more proud than this one
    went.
5 Some nights of apprehension and hot weeping
I will confess; but that's permitted me;
Day dried my eyes; I was not one for keeping
Rubbed in a cage a wing that would be free.
If I had loved you less or played you slyly
10 I might have held you for a summer more,
But at the cost of words I value highly,
And no such summer as the one before.
Should I outlive this anguish—and men do—
I shall have only good to say of you.

                                      1931

Pretty Words

Elinor Wylie

Poets make pets of pretty, docile words:
I love smooth words, like gold-enamelled fish
Which circle slowly with a silken swish,
And tender ones, like downy-feathered birds:
5 Words shy and dappled, deep-eyed deer in herds,
Come to my hand, and playful if I wish,
Or purring softly at a silver dish,
Blue Persian kittens, fed on cream and curds.

I love bright words, words up and singing early;
10 Words that are luminous in the dark, and sing;
Warm lazy words, white cattle under trees;
I love words opalescent, cool, and pearly,
Like midsummer moths, and honied words like
    bees,
Gilded and sticky, with a little sting.   **1932**

"Well, I Have Lost You . . . ," from *Collected Poems*, Harper &
Row. Copyright 1931, 1958 by Edna St. Vincent Millay and Norma
Millay Ellis.

Copyright 1932 by Alfred A. Knopf, Inc. and renewed 1960 by
Edwina C. Rubenstein. Reprinted from *Collected Poems of Elinor
Wylie*, by permission of Alfred A. Knopf, Inc.

Joseph Stella, *Battle of Lights, Coney Island* (1913). Yale
University Art Gallery, New Haven, Connecticut

Boats in a Fog

Robinson Jeffers

Sports and gallantries, the stage, the arts, the antics of dancers,
The exuberant voices of music,
Have charm for children but lack nobility; it is bitter earnestness
That makes beauty; the mind
5 Knows, grown adult.
                 A sudden fog-drift muffled the ocean,
A throbbing of engines moved in it,
At length, a stone's throw out, between the rocks and the vapor,
One by one moved shadows
10 Out of the mystery, shadows, fishing-boats, trailing each other
Following the cliff for guidance,
Holding a difficult path between the peril of the sea-fog
And the foam on the shore granite.
One by one, trailing their leader, six crept by me,
15 Out of the vapor and into it,
The throb of their engines subdued by the fog, patient and cautious,
Coasting all round the peninsula
Back to the buoys in Monterey harbor. A flight of pelicans
Is nothing lovelier to look at;
20 The flight of the planets is nothing nobler; all the arts lose virtue
Against the essential reality
Of creatures going about their business among the equally
Earnest elements of nature.

1925

"Boats in a Fog" from *The Selected Poetry of Robinson Jeffers* by Robinson Jeffers. Copyright 1925 and renewed 1953 by Robinson Jeffers. Renewed © 1966 by Donnan Jeffers and Garth Jeffers. Reprinted by permission of Random House, Inc.

The Solitary

Sara Teasdale

My heart has grown rich with the passing of
  years,
  I have less need now than when I was young
To share myself with every comer
  Or shape my thoughts into words with my
    tongue.

5 It is one to me that they come or go
  If I have myself and the drive of my will,
And strength to climb on a summer night
  And watch the stars swarm over the hill.

Let them think I love them more than I do,
10   Let them think I care, though I go alone;
If it lifts their pride, what is it to me
  Who am self-complete as a flower or a stone.

1926

"The Solitary." Reprinted with permission of Macmillan Publishing Co., Inc. from *Collected Poems* by Sara Teasdale. Copyright 1926 by Macmillan Publishing Co., Inc., renewed 1954 by Mamie T. Wheless.

THINK AND DISCUSS
ABRAHAM LINCOLN WALKS AT MIDNIGHT
Understanding
1. Why is Lincoln walking? Where does he pace, according to lines 4–7?
2. What breaks his heart, according to the final stanza?
3. How is Lincoln dressed?

Analyzing
4. Bearing in mind the date this poem was published, what historical event do you **infer** might have prompted Lindsay to write this poem?
5. If you did not know the title of this poem, what lines provide clues that the subject is Lincoln?

APPLYING: Connotation/Denotation **H7**
See Handbook of Literary Terms, p. 883.
  Connotations are the emotional associations that surround a word, as opposed to its **denotations,** or dictionary meanings. For example, the term "prairie lawyer" conjures up associations of Lincoln as a common man working for the good of his people.
1. What denotations for the word *travail* make it a more appropriate word than *work* in line 30?
2. Lindsay uses the phrases "*black* terror" (line 20) and "*white* peace" (line 31). What connotations for the words *black* and *white* make them apt descriptions for these abstractions?
3. What connotations for the words *bowed* and *pacing* help characterize Lincoln?

THE MOUNTAIN WOMAN
Understanding
1. What words and phrases in the first two stanzas portray the harsh landscape?
2. What tragedy, mentioned in the third stanza, has the woman survived? What incident causes her to fall and weep?

Analyzing
3. What is the "code of mountain wives" mentioned in line 3?

4. Why do you think the "scarlet bloom" was so important to the woman?

WELL, I HAVE LOST YOU
Understanding
1. To what does the speaker compare the loss of her love in lines 3 and 4?
2. What might the speaker have done to hold her love "for a summer more"?

Analyzing
3. What common human situation does this poem describe? What is the speaker's attitude toward the experience?
4. Explain the **metaphor** in lines 7 and 8. What situation does this metaphor describe?
5. What impression of the speaker's character does this poem create?
6. What are the **connotations** of the words *cage* and *wing*?

PRETTY WORDS
Understanding
1. What do poets do with pretty words, according to line 1?

Analyzing
2. What is the central metaphor developed in this poem?
3. What is different about the last metaphor in the poem—"honied words like bees"?
4. What indication is there in this poem that the poet does indeed love words?

BOATS IN A FOG
Understanding
1. What things do children find charming, according to lines 1–3? What makes beauty, according to lines 3 and 4?
2. What perils do the fishing boats encounter, according to lines 12 and 13?

Analyzing
3. In what ways might the central metaphor of boats in a fog reflect human life?
4. The procession of boats is described as something lovely as the "flight of pelicans" or the "flight of the planets." What quality do all three share? In what significant way is the boats' journey different?

THE SOLITARY
Understanding
1. What does the speaker have less need of as she grows older, according to stanza 1?
2. To what does the speaker compare herself in the last stanza?

Analyzing
3. What word would you use to describe the **tone** of this poem? Explain your choice.
4. How would you characterize the speaker?

Extending
5. The speaker in "The Solitary" claims to be "self-complete as a flower or a stone." Do you think that it is possible for a person to be this independent? Explain. Judging from their poems, do you think that the following would agree or disagree with the philosophy stated in Teasdale's poem: Lindsay, Jeffers, Millay?

THINKING SKILLS
Classifying
Wylie classifies "pretty words" by grouping them according to their sounds and connotations.

1. On a sheet of paper, list these heads: *Smooth, Tender, Shy, Playful, Bright, Lazy, Stinging.* Under these heads, list words and phrases from "Pretty Words" that fit these categories.
2. List at least two words or phrases of your own under each head.

COMPOSITION
Using Connotative Language
Using Wylie's "Pretty Words" as a model, write a poem that begins "I hate hard words. . . ." Find an appropriate simile to conclude the sentence. Use words that have harsh sounds and negative connotations throughout your poem.

BIOGRAPHIES

Wallace Stevens   1879–1955

"Poetry is a search for the inexplicable," wrote Wallace Stevens, and he devoted his entire life to such a search. Born in Reading, Pennsylvania, he spent most of his life as an executive of an insurance company in Hartford, Connecticut. But throughout his career, he wrote poetry. His volumes of poetry were combined in *The Collected Poems of Wallace Stevens*, which received the National Book Award and a Pulitzer Prize in 1955.

Though Stevens's poetry is philosophical, he does not deal with ideas in an abstract manner, but rather represents them with concrete objects, settings, and characters. A recurring subject of his poetry is the role of the imagination in bringing order to a reality that is essentially chaotic. Stevens wrote in his book of essays, *The Necessary Angel* (1951): ". . . the imagination is the power that enables us to perceive the normal in the abnormal, the opposite of chaos in chaos."

John Crowe Ransom   1888–1974

John Crowe Ransom was noted as a poet, literary critic, and teacher. While teaching at Vanderbilt University in Nashville, Tennessee, he and seven other Southern writers formed "The Fugitive Group," which supported the "new poetry" and published poems and critical essays in their periodical, *The Fugitive*. In 1937 Ransom went to Kenyon College, Ohio, where he founded the *Kenyon Review*.

His poems are notable for their gentle irony and lack of sentimentality. The scene is often a domestic one. Unlike some other modern poets such as Cummings, Ransom often worked within regular rhythm patterns, rhyme schemes, and stanza forms. He published several volumes of poetry, including *Chills and Fever* (1924) and *Selected Poems* (1945 and 1963).

E. E. Cummings   1894–1962

E. E. Cummings was brought up according to a rather traditional New England pattern, ending with study at Harvard. During World War I, he served in the ambulance corps in France and was imprisoned by the French as a spy. He later published a book, *The Enormous Room* (1922), describing his experiences and expressing his outrage. After the war, unsettled and disillusioned, he went to Paris. Later he returned to America to live in Greenwich Village, New York, and to write and paint.

Cummings experimented with the ways of representing sounds on paper. He broke compound words into parts and put explanatory words or phrases between the parts. He ran words together to increase the tempo, or separated them, putting one to a line to express slow movement. Through his experiments he created some of the most delightful lyrics in contemporary poetry. Opposite is Cummings's self-portrait (1939).

Phyllis McGinley   1905–1978

A writer of sophisticated light verse, Phyllis McGinley made it her literary business to comment satirically on the modern American scene. In witty poems frequently published in *The New Yorker*, she aimed her pen at the foibles of the upper-middle class—in the suburbs, on the commuter trains, in the offices of business and industry.

She was born in Oregon and educated at the University of Utah and the University of California. She published a large number of volumes, including *A Pocketful of Wry* (1940) and *Husbands Are Difficult* (1941). In 1960 she was awarded the Pulitzer Prize for *Times Three: Selected Verse from Three Decades.*

Margaret Walker   1915–

The daughter of a Methodist minister, Margaret Walker was born and raised in Birmingham, Alabama. She experienced anguish as a black in the South and was confused by the prejudice she found there. When she left Birmingham to attend Northwestern University, she anticipated freer conditions in the North. But she was surprised to find that life was little better for a black in the North than it was in the South. Her poetry is shaped by these experiences.

In 1942 Walker gained prominence when her first book, *For My People*, appeared as a result of her winning the Yale Series of Younger Poets Competition; she was the first black woman poet to win. The poems in this collection are divided into three groups: the public poems in which she speaks directly for the black people; the folk ballads written in the black dialect; and the personal sonnets, one of which appears here.

Anecdote of the Jar

Wallace Stevens

I placed a jar in Tennessee,
And round it was, upon a hill.
It made the slovenly wilderness
Surround that hill.
5 The wilderness rose up to it,
And sprawled around, no longer wild.

The jar was round upon the ground
And tall and of a port in air.
It took dominion everywhere.
10 The jar was gray and bare.
It did not give of bird or bush,
Like nothing else in Tennessee.

1919, 1923

"Anecdote of the Jar" by Wallace Stevens from *Collected Poems of Wallace Stevens*. Copyright 1923 and renewed 1951 by Wallace Stevens. Reprinted by permission of Alfred A. Knopf, Inc. and Faber and Faber Publishers.

Janet Waking

John Crowe Ransom

Beautifully Janet slept
Till it was deeply morning. She woke then
And thought about her dainty-feathered
    hen,
to see how it had kept.

5 One kiss she gave her mother.
Only a small one gave she to her daddy
Who would have kissed each curl of his
    shining baby;
No kiss at all for her brother.

"Old Chucky, old Chucky!" she cried,
10 Running across the world upon the grass
To Chucky's house, and listening. But alas,
Her Chucky had died.

It was a transmogrifying bee
Came droning down on Chucky's old bald
    head
15 And sat and put the poison. It scarcely
    bled,
But how exceedingly

And purply did the knot
Swell with the venom and communicate
Its rigor! Now the poor comb stood up
    straight
20 But Chucky did not.

So there was Janet
Kneeling on the wet grass, crying her
    brown hen
(Translated far beyond the daughters of
    men)
To rise and walk upon it.

25 And weeping fast as she had breath
Janet implored us, "Wake her from her
    sleep!"
And would not be instructed in how deep
Was the forgetful kingdom of death.

1927

Copyright 1927 by Alfred A. Knopf, Inc. and renewed 1955 by
John Crowe Ransom. Reprinted from *Selected Poems*, Third Edition,
Revised and Enlarged, by John Crowe Ransom, by permission of
Alfred A. Knopf, Inc. and Laurence Pollinger Ltd.

anyone lived in a pretty how town

E. E. Cummings

anyone lived in a pretty how town
(with up so floating many bells down)
spring summer autumn winter
he sang his didn't he danced his did.

5 Women and men(both little and small)
cared for anyone not at all
they sowed their isn't they reaped their same
sun moon stars rain

children guessed(but only a few
10 and down they forgot as up they grew
autumn winter spring summer)
that noone loved him more by more

when by now and tree by leaf
she laughed his joy she cried his grief
15 bird by snow and stir by still
anyone's any was all to her

someones married their everyones
laughed their cryings and did their dance
(sleep wake hope and then)they
20 said their nevers they slept their dream

stars rain sun moon
(and only the snow can begin to explain
how children are apt to forget to remember
with up so floating many bells down)

25 one day anyone died i guess
(and noone stooped to kiss his face)
busy folk buried them side by side
little by little and was by was

all by all and deep by deep
30 and more by more they dream their sleep
noone and anyone earth by april
wish by spirit and if by yes.

Women and men(both dong and ding)
summer autumn winter spring
35 reaped their sowing and went their came
sun moon stars rain

1940

"anyone lived in a pretty how town" from *Complete Poems 1913–1962* by E. E. Cummings. Copyright 1940 by E. E. Cummings; renewed 1968 by Marion Morehouse Cummings. Reprinted by permission of Harcourt Brace Jovanovich, Inc. and Grafton Books, London.

Reader's Note

"anyone lived in a pretty how town"

E. E. Cummings nearly always rips language apart and puts it back together again, seemingly in random fashion. But only *seemingly*, because he uses his displaced parts of speech and his disrupted syntax to get more, not less, meaning. This poem can be read as a simple love story between a boy (anyone) and a girl (noone) who lived, loved, married, and died in a small town where other poeple did the same. But the language suggests a general or allegorical meaning: *anyone* might be everyman, his "pretty how town" every place, and such subtly shifting refrains as "sun moon stars rain" might represent all time.

Note how the town (at which we might exclaim "how pretty") is described in the second line: "with up so floating many bells down." The language is very suggestive. Is the town down in a valley, perhaps, with a church whose bells make sounds that float up into the surrounding heights? But note how the line is repeated and its meaning connected with the children's memory in stanza 6. In this stanza the "up so floating" line takes on more the characteristics of mental activity, with experiences standing to the fore and then fading into the past. Note also the suggestiveness of line 4, in which anyone "sang his didn't" and "danced his did." Could this mean, perhaps, that *anyone* sang about the things he did not do, and he danced to the tune of the things he actually did?

"l(a"

Concrete poetry is poetry in which the shape of the poem is related to its subject. In "l(a" the poem is roughly shaped like the first letter of the poem. The key word *loneliness* is broken by a parenthesis. This makes the poem impossible to read aloud. To hear and not see the shape of the poem or the way the words are frag-

mented would be to miss most of the meaning. When reassembled, the words in the parenthesis read "a leaf falls." There is something lonely about the image of a single falling leaf. The odd arrangement of Cummings's letters on the page reinforces this image in subtle ways so that the poem becomes a typographical pun.

Cummings wanted the poem on the page to look like the number one, the loneliest number of all. Note the number of times that the letter "l" (simultaneously the digit one) occurs in the body of the poem. The number is spelled out in the seventh line. The final line "iness" could mean "the state of being first-person singular." The fact that the usually capitalized pronoun is lower case contributes to the sense of insignificance of a lonely person. The narrowness and the spacing of the "stanzas" support the downward movement of the falling leaf until it comes to rest in that climactic and longest line.

Some have seen the parenthesis mark in the first line as a side view of the falling leaf which in line six has turned around in its flight.

Georgia O'Keeffe, *Brown and Tan Leaves* (1928). Private collection

l(a

E. E. Cummings

l(a

le
af
fa

ll

s)
one
l

iness

"l(a" from *Complete Poems 1913–1962* by E. E. Cummings. Copyright © 1958 by E. E. Cummings. Reprinted by permission of Harcourt Brace Jovanovich, Inc. and Grafton Books, London.

Lament of the Normal Child

Phyllis McGinley

The school where I go is a modern school
  With numerous modern graces.
And there they cling to the modern rule
  Of "Cherish the Problem Cases!"
5 From nine to three
I develop Me.
  I dance when I'm feeling dancy,
Or everywhere lay on
With creaking crayon
10 the colors that suit my fancy.
But when the commoner tasks are done,
  Deserted, ignored, I stand.
For the rest have complexes, everyone;
  Or a hyperactive gland.
15 Oh, how can I ever be reconciled
  To my hatefully normal station?
Why couldn't I be a Problem Child
  Endowed with a small fixation?
Why wasn't I trained for a Problem Child
20 With an Interesting Fixation?

I dread the sound of the morning bell.
  The iron has entered my soul.
I'm a square little peg who fits too well
  In a square little normal hole.
25 For seven years
In Mortimer Sears
  Has the Oedipus angle flourished;
And Jessamine Gray,
She cheats at play
30 Because she is undernourished.
The teachers beam on Frederick Knipe
  With scientific gratitude,
For Fred, they claim, is a perfect type
  Of the Antisocial Attitude.
35 And Cuthbert Jones has his temper riled
  In a way professors mention.
But I am a Perfectly Normal Child,
  So I don't get any attention.
I'm nothing at all but a Normal Child,
40 So I don't get the least attention.

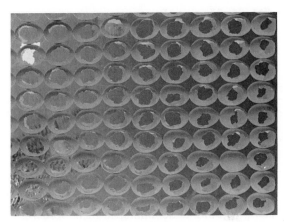

Gene Moore of Tiffany & Company

The others jeer as they pass my way.
  They titter without forbearance.
"He's Perfectly Normal," they shrilly say,
  "With Perfectly Normal parents."
45 I learn to read
With a normal speed.
  I answer when I'm commanded.
Infected antrums
Don't give me tantrums.
50 I don't even write left-handed.
I build with blocks when they give me blocks,
  When it's busy hour, I labor.
And I seldom delight in landing socks
  On the ear of my little neighbor.

55 I sit on the steps alone.
Why couldn't I be a Problem Child
  With a Case to call my own?
Why wasn't I born a Problem Child
  With a Complex of my own?

      1935

"Lament of the Normal Child" from *Times Three* by Phyllis McGinley. Copyright 1935 by Phyllis McGinley. Copyright renewed 1972 by Phyllis McGinley. Reprinted by permission of Viking Penguin Inc. and Martin Secker & Warburg Limited.

Childhood

Margaret Walker

When I was a child I knew red miners
dressed raggedly and wearing carbide lamps.
I saw them come down red hills to their camps
dyed with red dust from old Ishkooda mines.
5 Night after night I met them on the roads,
or on the streets in town I caught their glance;
the swing of dinner buckets in their hands,
and grumbling undermining all their words.

I also lived in low cotton country
10 where moonlight hovered over ripe haystacks,
or stumps of trees, and croppers' rotting shacks
with famine, terror, flood, and plague near by;
where sentiment and hatred still held sway
and only bitter land was washed away.

1942

"Childhood" from *For My People* by Margaret Walker, published by
Yale University Press, 1942. Reprinted by permission of Margaret
Walker Alexander.

THINK AND DISCUSS

ANECDOTE OF THE JAR

Understanding

1. What action does the "I" of the poem perform?
2. What adjectives are used to describe the jar?

Analyzing

3. How is the wilderness of Tennessee characterized? Refer to particular words and phrases.
4. The jar is "round" and "of a port in air," meaning that it has a stately importance. What effect does it have on the surroundings when placed on the ground?
5. Most critics interpret the jar as being a **symbol** of art and the imagination. If so, what does Stevens see as the function of art in relation to reality?

JANET WAKING

Understanding

1. What does Janet think about when she awakens?
2. What happens to Chucky? How?

Analyzing

3. What **mood** is established in the first 10 lines of the poem? What words and **images** help create this mood?
4. How do the speaker and Janet differ in their attitudes toward Chucky's death? Cite words or phrases supporting your opinion.
5. In what sense does the experience awaken Janet from the innocence of childhood? In what lines does it become apparent that she is resisting this process?
6. At first glance, the title seems to refer to Janet as she rises in the morning. In what other sense might Janet be "waking"?

ANYONE LIVED IN A PRETTY HOW TOWN
Understanding
1. What line in stanza 1 suggests the passage of time?
2. What do anyone and noone do in line 14? lines 17–18? lines 25–26?

Analyzing
3. In line 5 what do you think is the difference between "little" and "small"?
4. How are anyone and noone different from other people in the town?
5. In the seventh stanza we learn that "anyone died." Further on we read that "busy folk buried *them*." What can we **infer** has happened to noone?
6. What examples of **paradox** do you find in the poem?

l(a
Understanding
1. Ignoring the title, look at the shape of the poem on the page. What number does it look like?
2. What word is interrupted by the parenthesis? What sentence is in the parentheses?

Analyzing
3. When Cummings wrote this poem, most typewriters did not have a separate key for the numeral *one* but used the lower-case letter *l*. How many times does the word or numeral for *one* appear in the poem? What relationship to loneliness does the number one have?
4. What about a falling leaf makes it a suitable symbol for loneliness?

LAMENT OF THE NORMAL CHILD
Understanding
1. How does the speaker differ from other children, according to stanza 1?
2. What signs of the speaker's normalcy are described in lines 45–54?

Analyzing
3. What elements of meter, **rhyme**, and word choice suggest that this is a humorous poem?
4. What tendency of modern education does the poem **satirize**?

CHILDHOOD
Understanding
1. What kind of workers does the speaker recall from her childhood in stanza 1? stanza 2?
2. What time of day is described in lines 5 and 10?

Analyzing
3. What words with negative **connotations** do you find in the poem?
4. In the last line, the speaker says "only bitter land was washed away." What was *not* washed away?

Extending
5. "Lament of the Normal Child," "Childhood," and "Janet Waking" all deal with some aspect of growing up. What are several scenes or experiences that were significant factors in your childhood?

APPLYING: Sonnet H7
See Handbook of Literary Terms, p. 907.
A **sonnet** is a fourteen-line lyric that expresses an emotion. Most sonnets are written in iambic pentameter and have a fixed rhyme scheme.

1. What emotion is described in "Childhood"?
2. Why is there a break between lines 8 and 9 in the poem?
3. Although Walker's poem lacks a traditional rhyme scheme, some lines do rhyme and other lines end with words that have similar final sounds or vowel sounds. Which lines rhyme and which have near rhymes?

COMPOSITION
Writing a Sonnet
Try your hand at writing a sonnet, using an iambic pentameter rhythm. You may wish to use regular rhyme, a loose pattern of near-rhymes (as Walker does), or no rhyme at all. You may want to write an Italian sonnet form (an eight-line stanza followed by a six-line stanza) or an Elizabethan, or Shakespearean, form (three four-line sections followed by a rhyming couplet). Before you begin writing, review these sonnet forms in the Handbook of Literary Terms. Your teacher may wish to publish a booklet of the class's sonnets.

BIOGRAPHY

James Thurber
1894–1961

The 1930s and '40s had no more popular humorist than James Thurber, whose stories, essays, and cartoons for *The New Yorker* created a style of humor that will probably never be duplicated. He perfected the concept of the neurotic modern man, unable to meet the expectations of family and colleagues. Commenting on the characters he termed "Perfect Neurotics," Thurber said, "They lead an existence of jumpiness and apprehension. In the house of Life they have the feeling that they have never taken off their overcoats."

Born in Columbus, Ohio, Thurber experienced a childhood that had its share of strange incidents, which he later chronicled in *My Life and Hard Times*. After graduating from Ohio State University and working as a journalist, Thurber became a regular contributor to *The New Yorker*, where his stories and cartoons helped establish the style of that magazine. In 1940 he branched out into the theater by collaborating with Elliott Nugent on *The Male Animal*, which was a great success on Broadway.

Thurber was also a talented cartoonist, noted for his whimsical doodles that included drawings of shaggy dogs and portrayals of the battle of the sexes. Because of his failing eyesight, which eventually led to total blindness, Thurber was forced to give up his drawing. Yet he continued to write, dictating his work.

A moody, absent-minded man, Thurber wrote with a casual style that disguised the amount of work that went into all his writing. Indeed, it was not unusual for him to revise a piece ten times. His works were collected and published in a series of books, including *The Seal in the Bedroom and Other Predicaments* (1932), and *My World—and Welcome to It* (1942). *A Thurber Carnival* is the most representative compendium of his work.

University Days

James Thurber

 passed all the other courses that I took at my University, but I could never pass botany. This was because all botany students had to spend several hours a week in a laboratory looking through a microscope at plant cells, and I could never see through a microscope.

I never once saw a cell through a microscope. This used to enrage my instructor. He would

"University Days" from *My Life and Hard Times*, published by Harper & Row, Publishers, Inc. Copyright © 1933, 1961 by James Thurber. (British Title: *Vintage Thurber Volume II.*) Reprinted by permission of Rosemary A. Thurber and Hamish Hamilton Ltd.

wander around the laboratory pleased with the progress all the students were making in drawing the involved and, so I am told, interesting structure of flower cells, until he came to me. I would just be standing there. "I can't see anything," I would say. He would begin patiently enough, explaining how anybody can see through a microscope, but he would always end up in a fury, claiming that I could *too* see through a microscope but just pretended that I couldn't. "It takes away from the beauty of flowers anyway," I used to tell him. "We are not concerned with beauty in this course," he would say. "We are concerned solely with what I may call the *mechanics* of flars." "Well," I'd say, "I can't see anything." "Try it just once again," he'd say, and I would put my eye to the microscope and see nothing at all, except now and again a nebulous milky substance—a phenomenon of maladjustment. You were supposed to see a vivid, restless clockwork of sharply defined plant cells. "I see what looks like a lot of milk," I would tell him. This, he claimed, was the result of my not having adjusted the microscope properly, so he would readjust it for me, or rather, for himself. And I would look again and see milk.

I finally took a deferred pass, as they called it, and waited a year and tried again. (You had to pass one of the biological sciences or you couldn't graduate.) The professor had come back from vacation brown as a berry, bright-eyed, and eager to explain cell-structure again to his classes. "Well," he said to me, cheerily, when we met in the first laboratory hour of the semester, "we're going to see cells this time, aren't we?" "Yes, sir," I said. Students to right of me and to left of me and in front of me were seeing cells; what's more, they were quietly drawing pictures of them in their notebooks. Of course, I didn't see anything.

"We'll try it," the professor said to me, grimly, "with every adjustment of the microscope known to man. As God is my witness, I'll arrange this glass so that you see cells through it or I'll give up teaching. In twenty-two years of botany, I—" He cut off abruptly for he was beginning to quiver all

He Was Beginning to Quiver All Over,
Like Lionel Barrymore

James Thurber, illustration for *My Life and Hard Times* (1933)

over, like Lionel Barrymore,[1] and he genuinely wished to hold onto his temper; his scenes with me had taken a great deal out of him.

So we tried it with every adjustment of the microscope known to man. With only one of them did I see anything but blackness or the familiar lacteal opacity, and that time I saw, to my pleasure and amazement, a variegated constellation of flecks, specks, and dots. These I hastily drew. The instructor, noting my activity, came back from an adjoining desk, a smile on his lips and his eyebrows high in hope. He looked at my cell drawing. "What's that?" he demanded, with a hint of a squeal in his voice. "That's what I saw," I said. "You didn't, you didn't, you *did*n't!" he screamed, losing control of his temper instantly, and he bent over and squinted into the microscope. His head snapped up. "That's your eye!" he shouted. "You've fixed the lens so that it reflects! You've drawn your eye!"

Another course that I didn't like, but somehow managed to pass, was economics. I went to that class straight from the botany class, which didn't help me any in understanding either subject. I used to get them mixed up. But not as mixed up as another student in my economics class who came there direct from a physics laboratory. He was a tackle on the football team, named Bolenciecwcz.[2] At that time Ohio State University had one of the best football teams in the country, and Bolenciecwcz was one of its outstanding stars. In order to be eligible to play it was necessary for him to keep up in his studies, a very difficult matter, for while he was not dumber than an ox he was not any smarter. Most of his professors were lenient and helped him along. None gave him more hints, in answering questions, or asked him simpler ones than the economics professor, a thin, timid man named Bassum. One day when we were on the subject of transportation and distribution, it came Bolenciecwcz's turn to answer a question. "Name one means of transportation," the professor said to him. No light came into the big tackle's eyes. "Just any means of transportation," said the professor. Bolenciecwcz sat staring at him.

"That is," pursued the professor, "any medium, agency, or method of going from one place to another." Bolenciecwcz had the look of a man who is being led into a trap. "You may choose among steam, horse-drawn, or electrically propelled vehicles," said the instructor. "I might suggest the one which we commonly take in making long journeys across land." There was a profound silence in which everybody stirred uneasily, including Bolenciecwcz and Mr. Bassum. Mr. Bassum abruptly broke this silence in an amazing manner. "Choo-choo-choo," he said, in a low voice, and turned instantly scarlet. He glanced appealingly around the room. All of us, of course, shared Mr. Bassum's desire that Bolenciecwcz should stay abreast of the class in economics, for the Illinois game, one of the hardest and most important of the season, was only a week off. "Toot, toot, too-toooooooot!" some student with a deep voice moaned, and we all looked encouragingly at Bolenciecwcz. Somebody else gave a fine imitation of a locomotive letting off steam. Mr. Bassum himself rounded off the little show. "Ding, dong, ding, dong," he said, hopefully. Bolenciecwcz was staring at the floor now, trying to think, his great brow furrowed, his huge hands rubbing together, his face red.

"How did you come to college this year, Mr. Bolenciecwcz?" asked the professor. "*Chuf*fa chuffa, *chuf*fa chuffa."

"M'father sent me," said the football player.

"What on?" asked Bassum.

"I git an 'lowance," said the tackle, in a low, husky voice, obviously embarrassed.

"No, no," said Bassum. "Name a means of transportation. What did you *ride* here on?"

"Train," said Bolenciecwcz.

"Quite right," said the professor. "Now, Mr. Nugent, will you tell us——"

If I went through anguish in botany and economics—for different reasons—gymnasium work was even worse. I don't even like to think about

---

1. *Lionel Barrymore* (1878–1954), a famous actor, one of the celebrated Barrymore family.
2. *Bolenciecwcz* (bō len'sə wits).

Bolenciecwcz Was Trying to Think

James Thurber, illustration for
My Life and Hard Times (1933)

it. They wouldn't let you play games or join in the exercises with your glasses on and I couldn't see with mine off. I bumped into professors, horizontal bars, agricultural students, and swinging iron rings. Not being able to see, I could take it but I couldn't dish it out. Also, in order to pass gymnasium (and you had to pass it to graduate) you had to learn to swim if you didn't know how. I didn't like the swimming pool, I didn't like swimming, and I didn't like the swimming instructor, and after all these years I still don't. I never swam but I passed my gym work anyway, by having another student give my gymnasium number (978) and swim across the pool in my place. He was a quiet, amiable blonde youth, number 473, and he would have seen through a microscope for me if we could have got away with it, but we couldn't get away with it. Another thing I didn't like about gymnasium work was that they made you strip the day you registered. It is impossible for me to be happy when I am stripped and being asked a lot of questions. Still, I did better than a lanky agricultural student who

was cross-examined just before I was. They asked each student what college he was in—that is, whether Arts, Engineering, Commerce, or Agriculture. "What college are you in?" the instructor snapped at the youth in front of me. "Ohio State University," he said promptly.

It wasn't that agricultural student but it was another a whole lot like him who decided to take up journalism, possibly on the ground that when farming went to hell he could fall back on newspaper work. He didn't realize, of course, that that would be very much like falling back full-length on a kit of carpenter's tools. Haskins didn't seem cut out for journalism, being too embarrassed to talk to anybody and unable to use a typewriter, but the editor of the college paper assigned him to the cow barns, the sheep house, the horse pavilion, and the animal husbandry department generally. This was a genuinely big "beat,"[3] for it took up five times as much ground and got ten

3. *"beat,"* the area in which a newspaperman is responsible for reporting all happenings of interest.

times as great a legislative appropriation as the College of Liberal Arts.[4] The agricultural student knew animals, but nevertheless his stories were dull and colorlessly written. He took all afternoon on each of them, on account of having to hunt for each letter on the typewriter. Once in a while he had to ask somebody to help him hunt. "C" and "L," in particular, were hard letters for him to find. His editor finally got pretty much annoyed at the farmer-journalist because his pieces were so uninteresting. "See here, Haskins," he snapped at him one day, "why is it we never have anything hot from you on the horse pavilion? Here we have two hundred head of horses on this campus—more than any other university in the Western Conference[5] except Purdue[6]—and yet you never get any real low down on them. Now shoot over to the horse barns and dig up something lively." Haskins shambled out and came back in about an hour; he said he had something. "Well, start it off snappily," said the editor. "Something people will read." Haskins set to work and in a couple of hours brought a sheet of typewritten paper to the desk; it was a two-hundred word story about some disease that had broken out among the horses. Its opening sentence was simple but arresting. It read: "Who has noticed the sores on the tops of the horses in the animal husbandry building?"

Ohio State was a land grant university[7] and therefore two years of military drill was compulsory. We drilled with old Springfield rifles and studied the tactics of the Civil War even though the World War[8] was going on at the time. At 11 o'clock each morning thousands of freshmen and sophomores used to deploy over the campus, moodily creeping up on the old chemistry building. It was good training for the kind of warfare that was waged at Shiloh[9] but it had no connection with what was going on in Europe. Some people used to think there was German money behind it, but they didn't dare say so or they would have been thrown in jail as German spies. It was a period of muddy thought and marked, I believe, the decline of higher education in the Middle West.

As a soldier I was never any good at all. Most of the cadets were glumly indifferent soldiers, but I was no good at all. Once General Littlefield, who was commandant of the cadet corps, popped up in front of me during regimental drill and snapped, "You are the main trouble with this university!" I think he meant that my type was the main trouble with the university but he may have meant me individually. I was mediocre at drill, certainly—that is, until my senior year. By that time I had drilled longer than anybody else in the Western Conference, having failed at military at the end of each preceding year so that I had to do it all over again. I was the only senior still in uniform. The uniform which, when new, had made me look like an interurban railway conductor, now that it had become faded and too tight made me look like Bert Williams in his bellboy act.[10] This had a definitely bad effect on my morale. Even so, I had become by sheer practise little short of wonderful at squad maneuvers.

One day General Littlefield picked our company out of the whole regiment and tried to get it mixed up by putting it through one movement after another as fast as we could execute them: squads right, squads left, squads on right into line, squads right about, squads left front into line etc. In about three minutes one hundred and nine men were marching in one direction and I was marching away from them at an angle of forty degrees, all alone. "Company, halt!" shouted General Littlefield, "That man is the only man who has it right!" I was made a corporal for my achievement.

---

4. the College of Liberal Arts, the division of the university that included literature, languages, history, philosophy, and other subjects studied for culture rather than for immediate practical use.
5. Western Conference, a group of Midwestern universities organized into a league in athletics.
6. Purdue, a university at Lafayette, Indiana, noted particularly for its schools of agriculture and engineering.
7. a land grant university, a university that received its land as a gift from the government. Such a gift was made to aid public education.
8. the World War, the First World War, 1914–1918.
9. Shiloh (shī′lō), a place in southwestern Tennessee at which one of the important battles of the Civil War was fought in 1862.
10. Bert Williams in his bellboy act. Bert Williams (1876?–1922) was a star of vaudeville and musical comedy.

The next day General Littlefield summoned me to his office. He was swatting flies when I went in. I was silent and he was silent too, for a long time. I don't think he remembered me or why he had sent for me, but he didn't want to admit it. He swatted some more flies, keeping his eyes on them narrowly before he let go with the swatter. "Button up your coat!" he snapped. Looking back on it now I can see that he meant me although he was looking at a fly, but I just stood there. Another fly came to rest on a paper in front of the general and began rubbing its hind legs together. The general lifted the swatter cautiously. I moved restlessly and the fly flew away. "You startled him!" barked General Littlefield, looking at me severely. I said I was sorry. "That won't help the situation!" snapped the General, with cold military logic. I didn't see what I could do except offer to chase some more flies toward his desk, but I didn't say anything. He stared out the window at the faraway figures of co-eds crossing the campus toward the library. Finally, he told me I could go. So I went. He either didn't know which cadet I was or else he forgot what he wanted to see me about. It may have been that he wished to apologize for having called me the main trouble with the university; or maybe he had decided to compliment me on my brilliant drilling of the day before and then at the last minute decided not to. I don't know. I don't think about it much any more.

1933

THINK AND DISCUSS

Understanding

1. Why does Thurber take botany twice? Why does he take military drill?
2. Why does Thurber draw a picture of his eye? How does his professor respond to his drawing?
3. How do the students try to help the athlete in economics class?

Analyzing

4. What other characters are in their own ways as incompetent as the narrator?
5. From what **point of view** is "University Days" told?
6. How is Thurber different from the ideal student?

Extending

7. Thurber has been quoted as saying, "The human species is both horrible and wonderful. I like people and I hate them at the same time." Is this attitude reflected in "University Days"?

COMPOSITION

Determining Tone

Write a five-paragraph essay for your classmates analyzing Thurber's tone in "University Days." Begin by stating your thesis, and then discussing the author's attitude toward any or all of the following: botany, economics, fellow students, military drill, the young Thurber, college in general, journalism. Find evidence, including word choice, hyperbole, imagery, and characterization, to support your points.

ENRICHMENT

Participating in Discussions

Thurber has written many fables that conclude with morals that are witty statements of a theme. Find in your school or public library a copy of Thurber's *Fables for Our Time, Famous Poems Illustrated,* or *Further Fables for Our Time.* Select several to read aloud to the class. Before reading the final sentence of each, allow the class to guess what the moral might be.

Once you have read all the fables, invite the class to discuss the effectiveness of humor as a means to present a moral.

from One Writer's Beginnings

Eudora Welty

hen we set out in our five-passenger Oakland touring car on our summer trip to Ohio and West Virginia to visit the two families, my mother was the navigator. She sat at the alert all the way at Daddy's side as he drove, correlating the AAA Blue Book[1] and the speedometer, often with the baby on her lap. She'd call out, "All right, Daddy: '86-point-2, crossroads. Jog right, past white church. Gravel ends.'—And there's the church!" she'd say, as though we had scored. Our road always became her adversary. "This doesn't surprise me at all," she'd say as Daddy backed up a mile or so into our own dust on a road that had petered out. "I could've told you a road that looked like that had little intention of going anywhere."

"It was the first one we'd seen all day going in the right direction," he'd say. His sense of direction was unassailable, and every mile of our distance was familiar to my father by rail. But the way we set out to go was popularly known as "through the country."

My mother's hat rode in the back with the children, suspended over our heads in a pillowcase. It rose and fell with us when we hit the bumps, thumped our heads and batted our ears in an authoritative manner when sometimes we bounced as high as the ceiling. This was 1917 or 1918; a lady couldn't expect to travel without a hat.

Edward and I rode with our legs straight out in front of us over some suitcases. The rest of the suitcases rode just outside the doors, strapped on the running boards. Cars weren't made with trunks. The tools were kept under the back seat and were heard from in syncopation with the bumps; we'd jump out of the car so Daddy could get them out and jack up the car to patch and vulcanize a tire, or haul out the tow rope or the tire chains. If it rained so hard we couldn't see the road in front of us, we waited it out, snapped in behind the rain curtains and playing "Twenty Questions."

My mother was not naturally observant, but she could scrutinize; when she gave the surroundings her attention, it was to verify something—the truth or a mistake, hers or another's. My father kept his eyes on the road, with glances toward the horizon and overhead. My brother Edward periodically stood up in the back seat with his eyelids fluttering while he played the harmonica, "Old Macdonald Had a Farm" and "Abdul the Bulbul Amir," and the baby slept in Mother's lap and only woke up when we crossed some rattling old bridge. "*There's* a river!" he'd crow to us all. "Why, it certainly *is*," my mother would reassure him, patting him back to sleep. I rode as a hypnotic, with my set gaze on the landscape that vibrated past at twenty-five miles an hour. We were all wrapped by the long ride into some cocoon of our own.

The journey took about a week each way, and each day had my parents both in its grip. Riding behind my father I could see that the road had him by the shoulders, by the hair under his driving cap. It took my mother to make him stop. I inherited his nervous energy in the way I can't stop writing on a story. It makes me understand how Ohio had him around the heart, as West Virginia had my mother. Writers and travelers

See page 488 for Welty's biography.

1. *the AAA Blue Book,* a book of maps and general information about transportation routes in the United States, put out by the American Automobile Association.

Reprinted by permission of the publishers from *One Writer's Beginnings,* by Eudora Welty, Cambridge, Massachusetts: Harvard University Press, Copyright © 1983, 1984 by The President and Fellows of Harvard College.

are mesmerized alike by knowing of their destinations.

And all the time that we think we're getting there so fast, how slowly we do move. In the days of our first car trip, Mother proudly entered in her log, "Mileage today: 161!" with an exclamation mark.

"A Detroit car passed us yesterday." She always kept those logs, with times, miles, routes of the day's progress, and expenses totaled up.

That kind of travel made you conscious of borders; you rode ready for them. Crossing a river, crossing a county line, crossing a state line—especially crossing the line you couldn't see but knew was there, between the South and the North—you could draw a breath and feel the difference.

The Blue Book warned you of the times for the ferries to run; sometimes there were waits of an hour between. With rivers and roads alike winding, you had to cross some rivers three times to be done with them. Lying on the water at the foot of a river bank would be a ferry no bigger than somebody's back porch. When our car had been driven on board—often it was down a roadless bank, through sliding stones and runaway gravel, with Daddy simply aiming at the two-plank gangway—father and older children got out of the car to enjoy the trip. My brother and I got barefooted to stand on wet, sun-warm boards that, weighted with your car, seemed exactly on the level with the water; our feet were the same as in the river. Some of these ferries were operated by a single man pulling hand over hand on a rope bleached and frazzled as if made from cornshucks.

I watched the frayed rope running through his hands. I thought it would break before we could reach the other side.

"No, it's not going to break," said my father. "It's never broken before, has it?" he asked the ferry man.

"No sirree."

"You see? If it never broke before, it's not going to break this time."

His general belief in life's well-being worked either way. If you had a pain, it was "Have you ever had it before? You have? It's not going to kill you, then. If you've had the same thing before, you'll be all right in the morning."

My mother couldn't have more profoundly agreed with that.

"You're such an optimist, dear," she often said with a sigh, as she did now on the ferry.

"You're a good deal of a pessimist, sweetheart."

"I certainly *am*."

And yet I was well aware as I stood between them with the water running over my toes, he the optimist was the one who was prepared for the worst, and she the pessimist was the dare-

Norman Rockwell, detail of *New Car on the Road* (1919)

devil: he the one who on our trip carried chains and a coil of rope and an ax all upstairs to our hotel bedroom every night in case of fire, and she the one—before I was born—when there *was* a fire, had broken loose from all hands and run back—on crutches, too—into the burning house to rescue her set of Dickens[2] which she flung, all twenty-four volumes, from the window before she jumped out after them, all for Daddy to catch.

"I make no secret of my lifelong fear of the water," said my mother, who on ferry boats remained inside the car, clasping the baby to her—my brother Walter, who was destined to prowl the waters of the Pacific Ocean in a minesweeper.[3]

As soon as the sun was beginning to go down, we went more slowly. My father would drive sizing up the towns, inspecting the hotel in each, deciding where we could safely spend the night. Towns little or big had beginnings and ends, they reached to an edge and stopped, where the country began again as though they hadn't happened. They were intact and to themselves. You could see a town lying ahead in its whole, as definitely formed as a plate on a table. And your road entered and ran straight through the heart of it; you could see it all, laid out for your passage through. Towns, like people, had clear identities and your imagination could go out to meet them. You saw houses, yards, fields, and people busy in them, the people that had a life where they were. You could hear their bank clocks striking, you could smell their bakeries. You would know those towns again, recognize the salient detail, seen so close up. Nothing was blurred, and in passing along Main Street, slowed down from twenty-five to twenty miles an hour, you didn't miss anything on either side. Going somewhere "through the country" acquainted you with the whole way there and back.   1983

---

2. *Dickens*, Charles Dickens, English novelist (1812–1870).
3. *destined . . . minesweeper.* During World War II, Walter served on a minesweeper, a naval vessel that cleared underwater explosives.

THINK AND DISCUSS
Understanding
1. Who are the family members on the trip?
2. What is the **setting** (both time and place) of this narrative?
3. With what activities does the family amuse itself on the trip?
4. What quality has the narrator inherited from her father, according to paragraph six?

Analyzing
5. What contrasting attitudes toward life are exhibited by the author's father and mother?
6. What episode reveals the value that the mother places on literature?
7. What is **ironic** about Walter's future occupation?

Extending
8. How is automobile travel different today from what it was at the time the author describes? Do you think that long stretches together in a confined space are good or bad for family relationships? Explain.

COMPOSITION
Writing from a Different Point of View
Imagine that you are Eudora Welty's father. Write a personal essay of three paragraphs or so in which you recall the trip that she describes. Assume that the essay will be read by other members in his family. Try to convey what you think would be his feelings for his wife and children. For instance, do you think he would be entertained or bothered by his young son's harmonica playing?

Writing About a Character
Write a four- or five-paragraph character study of Eudora Welty's mother based on the information contained in the excerpt you have read. Assume that she has asked you for a personal reference for a job as a traveling librarian. Focus on her values, her regard for literature, her relationship with her husband and children, her strengths and weaknesses.

Tell Your Children

The Grand Council Fire of American Indians

You tell all white men "America First." We believe in that. We are the only ones, truly, that are one hundred percent. We therefore ask you while you are teaching school children about America First, teach them truth about the First Americans.

We do not know if school histories are pro-British, but we do know that they are unjust to the life of our people—the American Indian. They call all white victories, battles, and all Indian victories, massacres. The battle with Custer has been taught to school children as a fearful massacre on our part. We ask that this, as well as other incidents, be told fairly. If the Custer battle was a massacre, what was Wounded Knee?[1]

History books teach that Indians were murderers—is it murder to fight in self-defense? Indians killed white men because white men took their lands, ruined their hunting grounds, burned their forests, destroyed their buffalo. White men penned our people on reservations, then took away the reservations. White men who rise to protect their property are called patriots—Indians who do the same are called murderers.

White men call Indians treacherous—but no mention is made of broken treaties on the part of the white man. . . .

White men called Indians thieves—and yet we lived in frail skin lodges and needed no locks or iron bars. White men call Indians savages. What is civilization? Its marks are a noble religion and philosophy, original arts, stirring music, rich story and legend. We had these. . . .

We sang songs that carried in their melodies all the sounds of nature—the running of waters, the sighing of winds, and the calls of the animals. Teach these to your children that they may come to love nature as we love it.

We had our statesmen—and their oratory has never been equalled. Teach the children some of these speeches of our people, remarkable for their brilliant oratory.

We played games—games that brought good health and sound bodies. Why not put these in your schools? We told stories. Why not teach school children more of the wholesome proverbs and legends of our people? Tell them how we loved all that was beautiful. That we killed game only for food, not for fun. Indians think white men who kill for fun are murderers.

Tell your children of the friendly acts of Indians to the white people who first settled here. Tell them of our leaders and heroes and their deeds. . . . Put in your history books the Indian's part in the World War. Tell how the Indian fought for a country of which he was not a citizen, for a flag to which he had no claim, and for a people that have treated him unjustly.

We ask this, Chief,[2] to keep sacred the memory of our people.

1927

---

1. *Custer . . . Wounded Knee.* General George Custer and his forces were killed by the Sioux at the Battle of the Little Big Horn in 1876. At Wounded Knee, South Dakota, in 1890, 200 Sioux were massacred by federal troops.
2. *Chief.* "Big Bill" Thompson (1869–1944), mayor of Chicago, was being addressed.

Reprinted from *I Have Spoken: American History Through the Voices of Indians.* Copyright © 1971 by Virginia Irving Armstrong by permission of Ohio University Press.

THINK AND DISCUSS
Understanding
1. In what ways have school history books misrepresented Native Americans, according to paragraph two?
2. Mention some aspects of Native American culture that should be noted in books, according to the Grand Council's recommendations.

Analyzing
3. Oratory is the art of speaking eloquently or effectively in public. What is your opinion of the eloquence and rhetorical effectiveness of this speech? Explain.

Extending
4. Compare the **tone** of this speech to that of earlier Native American statements in Units 3 and 4.
5. This plea for fair presentation of Native American history was made in 1927. In what ways, if any, has the **stereotype** of Native Americans in history books, fiction, and Western movies changed of late? Give examples.

ENRICHMENT
Research
Using library resources, find information on one of the following topics suggested by "Tell Your Children." Present your findings either in a composition or an oral report:

- Battle of the Little Big Horn
- Battle of Wounded Knee
- Destruction of the buffalo
- Treaties broken by the U.S. government

The following is Faulkner's Nobel Address (1950), a classic of eloquence, which was delivered at a peak of global tension. Faulkner's biography appears on page 459.

Nobel Address

William Faulkner

 feel that this award was not made to me as a man, but to my work—a life's work in the agony and sweat of the human spirit, not for glory and least of all for profit, but to create out of the materials of the human spirit something which did not exist before. So this award is only mine in trust. It will not be difficult to find a dedication for the money part of it commensurate with the purpose and significance of its origin. But I would like to do the same with the acclaim too, by using this moment as a pin-

Nobel Prize Speech from *The Faulkner Reader* by William Faulkner, published by Random House, Inc., 1954.

nacle from which I might be listened to by the young men and women already dedicated to the same anguish and travail, among whom is already that one who will some day stand here where I am standing.

Our tragedy today is a general and universal physical fear so long sustained by now that we can even bear it. There are no longer problems of the spirit. There is only the question: When will I be blown up? Because of this, the young man or woman writing today has forgotten the problems of the human heart in conflict with itself which alone can make good writing because only that is worth writing about, worth the agony and the sweat.

He must learn them again. He must teach himself that the basest of all things is to be afraid; and, teaching himself that, forget it forever, leaving no room in his workshop for anything but the old verities and truths of the heart, the old universal truths lacking which any story is ephemeral and doomed—love and honor and pity and pride and compassion and sacrifice. Until he does so, he labors under a curse. He writes not of love but of lust, of defeats in which nobody loses anything of value, of victories without hope and, worst of all, without pity or compassion. His griefs grieve on no universal bones, leaving no scars. He writes not of the heart but of the glands.

Until he relearns these things, he will write as though he stood among and watched the end of man. I decline to accept the end of man. It is easy enough to say that man is immortal simply because he will endure: that when the last ding-dong of doom has clanged and faded from the last worthless rock hanging tideless in the last red and dying evening, that even then there will still be one more sound: that of his puny inexhaustible voice, still talking. I refuse to accept this. I believe that man will not merely endure: he will prevail. He is immortal, not because he alone among creatures has an inexhaustible voice, but because he has a soul, a spirit capable of compassion and sacrifice and endurance. The poet's, the writer's, duty is to write about these things.

Obverse of the Nobel Medal

It is his privilege to help man endure by lifting his heart, by reminding him of the courage and honor and hope and pride and compassion and pity and sacrifice which have been the glory of his past. The poet's voice need not merely be the record of man, it can be one of the props, the pillars to help him endure and prevail.

1950

THINK AND DISCUSS
Understanding
1. What is our tragedy today, according to paragraph two? What has been forgotten?
2. What major faults does Faulkner criticize in contemporary writers?

Analyzing
3. According to Faulkner, what makes good writing?

Extending
4. Based on what you have read in this unit, do you agree or disagree with Faulkner's criticism of contemporary literature? Explain.

UNIT 5   THE MODERN TEMPER   1915–1945

■ CONCEPT REVIEW

The following narrative illustrates many of the important ideas and literary terms of the period you have just studied. The notes and questions are designed to help you think critically about your reading. Page numbers in the notes refer to an application. A more extensive discussion of these terms is in the Handbook of Literary Terms.

Dorothy Parker visited Spain during the Spanish Civil War. This narrative first appeared in *The New Yorker* in 1938.

Soldiers of the Republic

Dorothy Parker

That Sunday afternoon we sat with the Swedish girl in the big café in Valencia.[1] We had vermouth in thick goblets, each with a cube of honeycombed gray ice in it. The waiter was so proud of that ice he could hardly bear to leave the glasses on the table, and thus part from it forever. He went to his duty—all over the room they were clapping their hands and hissing to draw his attention—but he looked back over his shoulder.

It was dark outside, the quick, new dark that leaps down without dusk on the day; but, because there were no lights in the streets, it seemed as set and as old as midnight. So you wondered that all the babies were still up. There were babies everywhere in the café; babies serious without solemnity and interested in a tolerant way in their surroundings.

At the table next ours, there was a notably small one; maybe six months

■ **Setting** (page 487): This story is set in Spain during the Spanish Civil War (1936–1939).

---

1. *Valencia* (və len′shə). The Loyalist, or Republican, government of Spain moved to this city from Madrid in 1936, during the Spanish Civil War.

"Soldiers of the Republic" from *The Portable Dorothy Parker* (British title: *The Collected Dorothy Parker*). Copyright 1926, 1938 by Dorothy Parker. Copyright renewed 1954, 1966 by Dorothy Parker. Reprinted by permission of Viking Penguin Inc. and Gerald Duckworth & Co. Ltd.

old. Its father, a little man in a big uniform that dragged his shoulders down, held it carefully on his knee. It was doing nothing whatever, yet he and his thin young wife, whose belly was already big again under her sleazy dress, sat watching it in a sort of ecstasy of admiration, while their coffee cooled in front of them. The baby was in Sunday white; its dress was patched so delicately that you would have thought the fabric whole had not the patches varied in their shades of whiteness. In its hair was a bow of new blue ribbon, tied with absolute balance of loops and ends. The ribbon was of no use; there was not enough hair to require restraint. The bow was sheerly an adornment, a calculated bit of dash.

■ This image suggests the large responsibilities of the small soldier.

"Oh, stop that!" I said to myself. "All right, so it's got a piece of blue ribbon on its hair. All right, so its mother went without eating so it could look pretty when its father came home on leave. All right, so it's her business, and none of yours. All right, so what have you got to cry about?"

The big, dim room was crowded and lively. That morning there had been a bombing from the air, the more horrible for broad daylight. But nobody in the café sat tense and strained, nobody desperately forced forgetfulness. They drank coffee or bottled lemonade, in the pleasant, earned ease of Sunday afternoon, chatting of small, gay matters, all talking at once, all hearing and answering.

■ **Mood** (page 458): The festive atmosphere in the café contrasts with the grim backdrop of war.

There were many soldiers in the room, in what appeared to be the uniforms of twenty different armies until you saw that the variety lay in the differing ways the cloth had worn or faded. Only a few of them had been wounded; here and there you saw one stepping gingerly, leaning on a crutch or two canes, but so far on toward recovery that his face had color. There were many men, too, in civilian clothes—some of them soldiers home on leave, some of them governmental workers, some of them anybody's guess. There were plump, comfortable wives, active with paper fans, and old women as quiet as their grandchildren. There were many pretty girls and some beauties, of whom you did not remark, "There's a charming Spanish type," but said, "What a beautiful girl!" The women's clothes were not new, and their material was too humble ever to have warranted skillful cutting.

"It's funny," I said to the Swedish girl, "how when nobody in a place is best-dressed, you don't notice that everybody isn't."

"Please?" the Swedish girl said.

■ **Please?** The Swedish girl has not understood the previous remark.

No one, save an occasional soldier, wore a hat. When we had first come to Valencia, I lived in a state of puzzled pain as to why everybody on the streets laughed at me. It was not because "West End Avenue" was writ across my face as if left there by a customs officer's chalked scrawl. They like Americans in Valencia, where they have seen good ones—the doctors who left their practices and came to help, the calm young nurses, the men of the International Brigade.[2] But when I walked forth, men and women

■ **Connotation** (page 538): Note the associations Valencians have for Americans.

2. *International Brigade,* volunteers from several countries who came to Spain to aid the Loyalist cause during the Spanish Civil War (1936–39).

courteously laid their hands across their splitting faces and little children, too innocent for dissembling, doubled with glee and pointed and cried, "*Ole!*" Then, pretty late, I made my discovery, and left my hat off; and there was laughter no longer. It was not one of those comic hats, either; it was just a hat.

■ **Inference** (page 494): From the information given, readers can infer that hats were rarely worn by civilians and that the narrator's resembles a bullfighter's.

The café filled to overflow, and I left our table to speak to a friend across the room. When I came back to the table, six soldiers were sitting there. They were crowded in, and I scraped past them to my chair. They looked tired and dusty and little, the way that the newly dead look little, and the first things you saw about them were the tendons in their necks. I felt like a prize sow.

■ **prize sow:** Note what this simile reveals about how the narrator views herself.

They were all in conversation with the Swedish girl. She has Spanish, French, German, anything in Scandinavian, Italian, and English. When she has a moment to regret, she sighs that her Dutch is so rusty she can no longer speak it, only read it, and the same is true of her Rumanian.

They had told her, she told us, that they were at the end of forty-eight hours' leave from the trenches, and, for their holiday, they had all pooled their money for cigarettes, and something had gone wrong, and the cigarettes had never come through to them. I had a pack of American cigarettes—in Spain rubies are as nothing to them—and I brought it out, and by nods and smiles and a sort of breaststroke, made it understood that I was offering it to those six men yearning for tobacco. When they saw what I meant, each one of them rose and shook my hand. Darling of me to share my cigarettes with the men on their way back to the trenches. Little Lady Bountiful. The prize sow.

Each one lit his cigarette with a contrivance of yellow rope that stank when afire and was also used, the Swedish girl translated, for igniting grenades. Each one received what he had ordered, a glass of coffee, and each one murmured appreciatively over the tiny cornucopia of coarse sugar that accompanied it. Then they talked.

■ Note the ironic contrasts of the uses for the "yellow rope."

■ Readers can infer that sugar, like ice, is scarce.

They talked through the Swedish girl, but they did to us that thing we all do when we speak our own language to one who has no knowledge of it. They looked us square in the face, and spoke slowly, and pronounced their words with elaborate movements of their lips. Then, as their stories came, they poured them at us so vehemently, so emphatically that they were sure we must understand. They were so convinced we would understand that we were ashamed for not understanding.

But the Swedish girl told us. They were all farmers and farmers' sons, from a district so poor that you try not to remember there is that kind of poverty. Their village was next that one where the old men and the sick men and the women and children had gone, on a holiday, to the bullring; and the planes had come over and dropped bombs on the bullring, and the old men and the sick men and the women and the children were more than two hundred.

They had all, the six of them, been in the war for over a year, and most of the time they had been in the trenches. Four of them were married. One had one child, two had three children, one had five. They had not had word from their families since they had left for the front. There had been no communication; two of them had learned to write from men fighting next them in the trench, but they had not dared to write home. They belonged to a union, and union men, of course, are put to death if taken. The village where their families lived had been captured, and if your wife gets a letter from a union man, who knows but they'll shoot her for the connection?

They told about how they had not heard from their families for more than a year. They did not tell it gallantly or whimsically or stoically. They told it as if—Well, look. You have been in the trenches, fighting, for a year. You have heard nothing of your wife and your children. They do not know if you are dead or alive or blinded. You do not know where they are, or if they are. You must talk to somebody. That is the way they told about it.

One of them, some six months before, had heard of his wife and his three children—they had such beautiful eyes, he said—from a brother-in-law in France. They were all alive then, he was told, and had a bowl of beans a day. But his wife had not complained of the food, he heard. What had troubled her was that she had no thread to mend the children's ragged clothes. So that troubled him, too.

"She has no thread," he kept telling us. "My wife has no thread to mend with. No thread."

■ **Symbol** (page 469): The lack of thread represents all the deprivations suffered by a war-torn country.

We sat there, and listened to what the Swedish girl told us they were saying. Suddenly one of them looked at the clock, and then there was excitement. They jumped up, as a man, and there were calls for the waiter and rapid talk with him, and each of them shook the hand of each of us. We went through more swimming motions to explain to them that they were to take the rest of the cigarettes—fourteen cigarettes for six soldiers to take to war—and then they shook our hands again. Then all of us said "*Salud!*" [3] as many times as could be for six of them and three of us, and then they filed out of the café, the six of them, tired and dusty and little, as men of a mighty horde are little.

■ Note the image of the "little" men who are part of the "mighty horde."

Only the Swedish girl talked, after they had gone. The Swedish girl has been in Spain since the start of the war. She has nursed splintered men, and she has carried stretchers into the trenches and, heavier laden, back to the hospital. She has seen and heard too much to be knocked into silence.

Presently it was time to go, and the Swedish girl raised her hands above her head and clapped them twice together to summon the waiter. He came, but he only shook his head and his hand and moved away.

The soldiers had paid for our drinks.   1938

---

3. **Salud!** (sä lüd'). Good health! [*Spanish*]

THINK AND DISCUSS

Understanding

1. At what time of day does the story take place?
2. What aspect of the baby's outfit particularly impresses the narrator?
3. How are the clothes of the women in the café described?

Analyzing

4. Why is the waiter so proud to have served ice in the drinks?
5. Why are there so many babies in the café?
6. What is the greatest concern or worry of the soldiers?
7. Although the **theme** is never directly stated, a reader can **infer** that the narrator is making a statement about daily life in the midst of war. State this theme in a sentence of your own.

Extending

8. The narrator's **tone** in "Soldiers of the Republic" is involved and emotional. Which passages would have been eliminated in a news story that recounted this episode in a detached, impersonal tone?

REVIEWING LITERARY TERMS

Setting

1. What is it about the setting that makes the narrator feel embarrassed and uncomfortable?

Mood

2. How would you describe the mood or moods conveyed in this narrative?

Inference

3. Explain whether you agree or disagree with the following inference: The narrator feels ill at ease in her surroundings because she is better fed and less affected by war than her companions.
4. What can readers infer about the narrator's feelings and emotions upon learning that the soldiers have paid for the drinks?

Symbol

5. The baby's blue ribbon, acquired through its mother's sacrifice, symbolizes a larger aspect of the war. What is it?

Connotation

6. The word *little*, repeated throughout the story to describe the soldiers, is used at the end to portray the six soldiers: ". . . tired and dusty and little, as men of a mighty horde are little." What connotation do you think the author intended for this word?

■ CONTENT REVIEW

Classifying

1. Write these heads on your paper: *Sonnet, Blank Verse, Stream of Consciousness*. List under the appropriate head the titles of selections from this unit that employ these verse forms or techniques.
2. Much modern poetry reflects the universal fear that Faulkner mentions in his Nobel Address. Consider the following poems and indicate whether you would describe them as expressing optimism, pessimism, or a combination of the two: "The Love Song of J. Alfred Prufrock," "Spring and All," "The Solitary," "Chicago," "Any Human to Another," "November Cotton Flower," and "Boats in a Fog."

Generalizing

3. The Frontier is a motif that runs throughout American literature. (See the article on page 470). Make some broad observations about the American frontier, as reflected in "The Bear," "The Leader of the People," and "A Wagner Matinée."

Synthesizing

4. The selections in this unit are arranged generically—that is, by short stories, poetry, and factual prose or nonfiction. Suppose that you were asked to rearrange this material thematically. Think of several themes such as initiation, freedom, loneliness, nature, or supply themes of your own. Try to list all of the selections under the various themes. Do you think this arrangement is more effective

than a genre grouping, or less so? Explain.

5. Think of stories, novels, poems, plays, television shows, and movies you have seen recently. Which ones could you say focus on the virtues Faulkner espouses—love, honor, pity, pride, compassion, and sacrifice? Which would you say concern themselves not with the heart but with what Faulkner refers to as "the glands"?

Evaluating

6. William Faulkner observes in his Nobel Address that it is "the problems of the human heart in conflict with itself which alone can make good writing." Using this comment for a measuring stick, assess one short story, one poem, and one nonfiction selection that appear in this unit.

■ COMPOSITION REVIEW

Choose one of the following topics for writing.

Writing About Poetic Styles

Some of the poets in this unit rely on the traditional use of rhyme, rhythm, and stanza form and choose topics that are conventionally considered "poetic," such as love, death, and nature. Other poets use more experimental techniques that rely on everyday speech patterns and free verse and choose topics that reflect twentieth-century phenomena. In an essay of several paragraphs directed to a would-be poet, compare and contrast the styles and subjects of a traditional poet and an experimental poet represented in this unit.

Writing About a Period

As a newspaper feature writer, write an article about the attitudes toward love and romance reflected in American literature from 1915 to 1945. Your article, which should be from three to five paragraphs, might focus on works such as the following: "Winter Dreams," "The Love Song of J. Alfred Prufrock," "anyone lived in a pretty how town," "Well, I Have Lost You," and "The Solitary."

Writing About Heroism

In an essay of at least four paragraphs directed to a classmate, compare and contrast a work from Unit 5 that treats some aspect of heroism with a work from a previous unit based on heroism. Before you begin to write, ask yourself questions such as the following: How have the traits considered heroic changed in the past century? Are there still some qualities common to all literary heroes? How has the American concept of heroism changed since the frontier has been settled?

Writing a Personal Reminiscence

In three or four paragraphs, try to capture a memory of someone from your past as Thurber and Welty do in their nonfiction pieces. Through anecdotes, reveal important characteristics of that person. Establish a tone that conveys your feelings toward this person. Put this character in a setting that is appropriate. Remember that the best way to capture a personality is to convey the person's words, quirks, and actions. If you think this person would enjoy your description, share it with him or her.

MODERN DRAMA

1900	1910	1920	1930	1940

- "Little Theater" movement begins
- Film industry moves to Hollywood
- Washington Square Players founded
- Provincetown Players founded
- Theater Guild founded
- Introduction of "talking" movies
- Academy Awards ("Oscars") established
- The Group Theater founded

W.P.A. Federal Theater Project begins •

First feature film entirely in color (*Becky Sharp*) •

Oklahoma! changes nature of American musical plays •

Laurette Taylor as Amanda (1945), Broadway production

Gertrude Lawrence as Amanda (1950), film version

Katherine Hepburn as Amanda (1973), television production

1950	1960	1970	1980	1990

• "Tony" Awards established   Broadway marks 2,000th performance of *Cats* •

• "Golden Age" of live TV drama   • Kennedy Center for the Performing Arts opened in Washington, D.C.

• Arena Stage founded in Washington, D.C.

• Second City improvisational drama group formed in Chicago

• First New York Shakespeare Festival   • *The Fantasticks* enters 23rd year of performance

• First Stratford, Connecticut, Shakespeare Festival

• Lincoln Center for the Performing Arts opened in New York

• The Guthrie Theater Company formed in Minneapolis-St. Paul

• National Endowment for the Arts

• National Black Theater Workshop founded

• American Bicentennial Theater

A Chorus Line breaks long-run record for Broadway show •

Maureen Stapleton as Amanda (1975), Broadway production

Jessica Tandy as Amanda (1983), Broadway production

Joanne Woodward as Amanda (1987), film version

PREVIEW

UNIT 6   MODERN DRAMA

Authors
Tennessee Williams
Lillian Hellman

Features
Reading Modern Drama
Comment: Why It Is Called *The Glass Menagerie* by Tennessee Williams
Reader's Note: Symbolism in *The Glass Menagerie*
Comment: Theater in America Before 1920
The Story of American English
Themes in American Literature:
   The American Dream/ The American Nightmare

Review of Literary Terms
point of view
connotation/denotation

Reading Literature Skillfully
comparison/contrast

Vocabulary Skills
context
pronunciation

Thinking Skills
synthesizing
evaluating

Composition
Writing from a Character's Point of View
Writing a Summary
Writing About Stage Conventions
Writing a Character's Resumé
Writing About a Symbol

Enrichment
Oral Report
Research

Thinking Critically About Literature
Concept Review
Content Review
Composition Review

AMERICAN THEATER IN THE TWENTIETH CENTURY

American drama, as we know it today, was born in a remodeled fish storehouse in Province-town, Massachusetts, in 1916, when a group of Greenwich Village intellectuals staged a few one-act plays, one of which was *Bound East for Cardiff* by Eugene O'Neill. It was the start of the "little theater" movement, which encouraged O'Neill and other dramatists to explore the full possibilities of the modern stage in depicting human experience.

O'Neill's fame soared in the '20s with nearly a score of successful plays that included *The Emperor Jones* (1920), *The Hairy Ape* (1922), *Desire Under the Elms* (1924), and *Strange Interlude* (1928). He was prolific during the decades following, with works (some of them published posthumously) that included *The Iceman Cometh* (1946) and *Long Day's Journey into Night* (1956).

Other American playwrights who helped launch theater in the 1920s were Elmer Rice, whose greatest success was *The Adding Machine* (1923), and Maxwell Anderson, who collaborated with Laurence Stallings in writing the World War I drama *What Price Glory?* (1924).

The growing maturity of American drama is also reflected in the plays of Lillian Hellman, whose work is noted for psychological depth and intensity. *The Little Foxes* (1939) reveals the scheming of a Southern family consumed by its own material and emotional selfishness.

Among the most popular plays written before World War II, two have special significance for high-school audiences. *Our Town* (1938) by Thornton Wilder and *You Can't Take It with You* (1936) by George Kaufman and Moss Hart usually top the list of plays most frequently produced today by students.

Two new forces in American theater emerged after World War II—Arthur Miller and Ten-

nessee Williams. Miller's *The Crucible* (1953) has become an enduring analysis of the demands of conscience. In *Death of a Salesman* (1949), Miller depicts an ordinary man, Willy Loman, who achieves tragic stature in his ruinous pursuit of the American Dream.

In *The Glass Menagerie* (1945), Williams used set and lighting in innovative ways to add poignancy to his account of a family that lives on illusion. Williams's other major plays, *A Streetcar Named Desire* (1947) and *Cat on a Hot Tin Roof* (1955), also deal with emotionally crippled characters who cannot face reality.

With the work of Langston Hughes and other noted playwrights, drama relating to the black experience in America came of age in the 1930s. Since the 1950s, black dramatists such as James Baldwin, Lorraine Hansberry, Imamu Amiri Baraka (LeRoi Jones), and Ed Bullins have developed a vigorously experimental theater. Hansberry's *A Raisin in the Sun* (1959), which transcended racial concerns to address the universal quest for human dignity, became a popular success.

A leader of American experimentation in the theater has been Edward Albee, whose plays often attack the replacement of genuine values with superficial ones in American society. *The Sandbox* (1960), *The American Dream* (1961), and *Who's Afraid of Virginia Woolf?* (1962) all employ grim humor to develop this theme.

Many of the newer dramatic voices got their start in regional theater, which emerged as a strong force during the 1970s and 1980s. Among the recent playwrights who have offered astute, often ironic, commentary on contemporary society are Sam Shepherd, Lanford Wilson, Beth Henley, David Rabe, Ntozake Shange, Arthur Kopit, Marsha Norman, and David Mamet.

Tennessee Williams,
self-portrait (1947)

Thomas Lanier Williams, who listed among his forebears adventurers, an early U.S. senator, and poet Sidney Lanier (Unit 3), grew up in Columbus, Mississippi. He and his older sister Rose were raised in his maternal grandparents' rectory home (his grandfather was an Episcopalian clergyman) in a supportive, bookish atmosphere. When his father, an extroverted traveling shoe salesman, took a desk job in St. Louis, the family was uprooted from its sheltered, genteel existence and transplanted to a cheerless, backstreet apartment. Looking back on the traumatic move (an expulsion from a Southern Eden that became a motif in his plays), Williams observed, "We suddenly discovered that there were two kinds of people, the rich and the poor, and that we belonged more to the latter."

Williams's college education was interrupted during the depression, when he worked for three years in a shoe factory—a job he detested. He resumed his studies and in 1938 received a degree from the University of Iowa. The next few years were lean ones in which he variously wrote, waited on tables, and worked on a pigeon ranch.

The Glass Menagerie opened on Broadway in 1945 and established Williams as a major dramatic talent. The play introduced several motifs that run throughout his works: the vulnerable and anguished woman who lives in a fragile fantasy world; the family hobbled by emotional or physical poverty; the domineering and manipulative parent; and the haunting sense of the old South as a romantic bygone era.

In the next eighteen years, he wrote over a dozen plays, including *A Streetcar Named Desire, Summer and Smoke, The Rose Tattoo, Cat on a Hot Tin Roof,* and *Suddenly Last Summer.* Along with Eugene O'Neill and Arthur Miller, Williams is considered among the greatest of American playwrights. His works have served as vehicles on stage, screen, and TV for Marlon Brando, Elizabeth Taylor, Richard Burton, Katherine Hepburn, Paul Newman, Joanne Woodward, and John Malkovich.

Critic Kenneth Tynan observed of Williams's works, "In his mental battlefield the real is perpetually at war with the ideal; what is public wrestles with what is private; what drags men down fights with what draws them up." Williams's focus on the conflict between good and evil, flesh and spirit, links him to nineteenth-century moral symbolists—Poe, Hawthorne, and Melville. Yet it is not these epic battles but the human beings who fight them that we find memorable in the works of Williams—the outcasts, the odd, the lonely, the vulnerable—who despite their flaws achieve a kind of dignity in their struggle to survive.

Reading MODERN DRAMA

Drama is a general term that includes stage, radio, television, and screen plays—works written to be performed by actors for an audience. Yet great drama offers as many rewards to the reader as to the viewer, and many people will have more opportunity to read plays than to see them as theatrical productions. Use the following guidelines to gain full benefit from reading modern drama.

Note information conveyed in stage directions. Just as stories and novels present information in what is called *exposition* or *description*, plays give information in stage directions. At the beginning of *The Glass Menagerie*, for example, directions establish both setting and mood by describing the grim tenement, flanked by garbage cans, alleys, and fire escapes. These early directions also introduce some of the major props in this play—the daybed, the whatnot that holds the glass objects, and the photograph of the departed father. Note also how stage directions help develop characterization. Not until the end of the play, for example, is Amanda presented with "dignity and tragic beauty."

Stage directions can likewise convey important clues about how you, as reader, should regard a scene. Readers are told early on that this is a memory play and later, that the scene between Jim and Laura, although "apparently unimportant" to him, is to Laura "the climax of her secret life."

Examine the dialogue. Drama relies mainly on *dialogue*, or conversation between characters, to advance the action of the play. Read the lines aloud, trying to "hear" the dialogue as it might be spoken, determining the tone, the pauses, and the words to be emphasized. Note, for example, how Tom as narrator remains more aloof and philosophical than Tom as character, and how Amanda lapses into Southern coquetry in the presence of the gentleman caller.

Recognize comparisons and contrasts among settings, characters, and scenes. Representing the twin worlds of fact and dream, the claustrophobic tenement serves as a foil to both the fragile world of the glass animals and the romantic Deep South of Amanda's past. Any pair of characters offers a contrast—the energetic, domineering Amanda and her dreamy, shy daughter; Tom, the frustrated poet and Jim, the outgoing shipping clerk and aspiring executive. The romantic scene between Laura and Jim pits the introverted hero-worshiper against the extroverted idol. Much of the dramatic effect depends on the general pacing and the shifting emotions of hope and despair in the characters.

Let the conventions enhance your understanding of the play. *Conventions* are mutual agreements about the meaning of gestures, actions, and words. For example, a handshake is a social convention for a sign of greeting. Anyone who reads or sees a play must accept certain dramatic conventions—devices or techniques that substitute for reality. Some conventions are basic, such as the understanding that actors represent characters, stage props are to suggest real settings, and the events on stage are occurring at another time and place. Tom as narrator is an "undisguised convention," who offers crucial information and commentary in his monologues to the audience. The highlighted portrait of the absent father is a convention that reminds us of his "presence" as a fifth character. Gauze curtains, unreal lighting, and haunting music serve to create the mood of a memory play. The convention of the fourth wall gives viewers (and readers) a sense of participation, allowing them to overhear the play as unacknowledged observers. If you accept these conventions, the events happening on stage will be lifelike and authentic, and your reading will be a rewarding experience.

The Glass Menagerie

Tennessee Williams

THE GLASS MENAGERIE was produced by Eddie Dowling and Louis J. Singer at the Playhouse Theatre, New York City, on March 31, 1945, with the following cast:

THE MOTHER	Laurette Taylor
HER SON	Eddie Dowling
HER DAUGHTER	Julie Haydon
THE GENTLEMAN CALLER	Anthony Ross

Pictures accompanying *The Glass Menagerie* in this book are from the 1987 Cineplex Odeon film directed by Paul Newman, starring Joanne Woodward as Amanda, Karen Allen as Laura, John Malkovich as Tom, and James Naughton as the gentleman caller.

SCENE: An alley in St. Louis

PART I: Preparation for a Gentleman Caller
PART II: The Gentleman Calls

TIME: Now and the Past

Ben Rosenthal

THE GLASS MENAGERIE, by Tennessee Williams. Copyright 1945 by Tennessee Williams and Edwina D. Williams and renewed 1973 by Tennessee Williams. Reprinted by permission of Random House, Inc. and International Creative Management.

CAUTION: Professionals and amateurs are hereby warned that *The Glass Menagerie*, being fully protected under the copyright laws of the United States of America, the British Empire, including the Dominion of Canada, and all other countries of the Copyright Union is subject to royalty. All rights, including professional, amateur, motion picture, recitation, lecturing, public reading, radio and television broadcasting, and the rights of translation into foreign languages, are strictly reserved. Particular emphasis is laid on the question of readings, permission for which must be obtained in writing from the author's agent. All inquiries (except for amateur rights) should be addressed to the author's agent, International Creative Management, 40 West 57th St., New York, 10019.

ACT ONE

SCENE 1

The Wingfield apartment is in the rear of the building, one of those vast hivelike conglomerations of cellular living-units that flower as warty growths in overcrowded urban centers of lower middle-class population and are symptomatic of the impulse of this largest and fundamentally enslaved section of American society to avoid fluidity and differentiation and to exist and function as one interfused mass of automatism. The apartment faces an alley and is entered by a fire escape, a structure whose name is a touch of accidental poetic truth, for all of these huge buildings are always burning with the slow and implacable fires of human desperation. The fire escape is included in the set—that is, the landing of it and steps descending from it. (Note that the stage L. *alley may be entirely omitted, since it is never used except for* TOM's *first entrance, which can take place stage* R.) *The scene is memory and is therefore nonrealistic. Memory takes a lot of poetic license. It omits some details, others are exaggerated, according to the emotional value of the articles it touches, for memory is seated predominantly in the heart. The interior is therefore rather dim and poetic.* (MUSIC CUE #1. *As soon as the house lights dim, dance-hall music heard on stage* R. *Old popular music of, say 1915–1920 period. This continues until* TOM *is at fire-escape landing, having lighted cigarette, and begins speaking.*)

AT RISE: *At the rise of the house curtain, the audience is faced with the dark, grim rear wall of the Wingfield tenement. (The stage set proper is screened out by a gauze curtain, which suggests the front part, outside, of the building.) This building, which runs parallel to the footlights, is flanked on both sides by dark, narrow alleys which run into murky canyons of tangled clotheslines, garbage cans and the sinister latticework of neighboring fire escapes. (The alleys are actually in darkness, and the objects just mentioned are not visible.) It is up and down these side alleys that exterior entrances and exits are made, during the play. At the end of* TOM's *opening commentary, the dark tenement wall slowly reveals (by means of a transparency) the interior of the ground-floor Wingfield apartment. (Gauze curtain, which suggests front part of building, rises on the interior set.) Downstage is the living room, which also serves as a sleeping room for* LAURA, *the daybed unfolding to make her bed. Just above this is a small stool or table on which is a telephone. Upstage* C., *and divided by a wide arch or second proscenium with transparent faded portieres (or second curtain, "second curtain" is actually the inner gauze curtain between the living room and the dining room, which is upstage of it), is the dining room. In an old-fashioned whatnot in the living room are seen scores of transparent glass animals. A blown-up photograph of the father hangs on the wall of the living room, facing the audience, to the* L. *of the archway. It is the face of a very handsome young man in a doughboy's First World War cap. He is gallantly smiling, ineluctably smiling, as if to say, "I will be smiling forever." (Note that all that is essential in connection with dance hall is that the window be shown lighting lower part of alley. It is not necessary to show any considerable part of dance hall.) The audience hears and sees the opening scene in the dining room through both the transparent fourth wall (this is the gauze curtain which suggests outside of building) of the building and the transparent gauze portieres of the dining-room arch. It is during this revealing scene that the fourth wall slowly ascends, out of sight. This transparent exterior wall is not brought down again until the very end of the play, during* TOM's *final speech. The narrator is an undisguised convention of the play. He takes whatever license with dramatic convention as is convenient to his purposes.*

TOM *enters, dressed as a merchant sailor, from alley, stage* L. (*i.e., stage* R. *if* L. *alley is omitted), and strolls across the front of the stage to the fire escape. (*TOM *may lean against grillwork of this as he lights cigarette.) There he stops and lights a cigarette. He addresses the audience.*

TOM. I have tricks in my pocket—I have things

up my sleeve—but I am the opposite of the stage magician. He gives you illusion that has the appearance of truth. I give you truth in the pleasant disguise of illusion. I take you back to an alley in St. Louis. The time that quaint period when the huge middle class of America was matriculating from a school for the blind. Their eyes had failed them, or they had failed their eyes, and so they were having their fingers pressed forcibly down on the fiery Braille alphabet of a dissolving economy.—In Spain there was revolution.—Here there was only shouting and confusion and labor disturbances, sometimes violent, in otherwise peaceful cities such as Cleveland—Chicago—Detroit. . . . That is the social background of this play. . . . The play is memory. (MUSIC CUE #2) Being a memory play, it is dimly lighted, it is sentimental, it is not realistic.—In memory everything seems to happen to music.—That explains the fiddle in the wings. I am the narrator of the play, and also a character in it. The other characters in the play are my mother, Amanda, my sister, Laura, and a gentleman caller who appears in the final scenes. He is the most realistic character in the play, being an emissary from a world that we were somehow set apart from.—But having a poet's weakness for symbols, I am using this character as a symbol—as the long-delayed but always expected something that we live for.—There is a fifth character who doesn't appear other than in a photograph hanging on the wall. When you see the picture of this grinning gentleman, please remember this is our father who left us a long time ago. He was a telephone man who fell in love with long distance—so he gave up his job with the telephone company and skipped the light fantastic out of town. . . . The last we heard of him was a picture postcard from the Pacific coast of Mexico, containing a message of two words—"Hello—Good-by!" and no address.

(*Lights up in dining room.* TOM *exits* R. *He goes off downstage, takes off his sailor overcoat and skull-fitting knitted cap and remains offstage by dining-room* R. *door for his entrance cue.* AMANDA's *voice becomes audible through the portieres—i.e., gauze curtains separating dining room and living room.* AMANDA *and* LAURA *are seated at a drop-leaf table.* AMANDA *is sitting in* C. *chair and* LAURA *in* L. *chair. Eating is indicated by gestures without food or utensils.* AMANDA *faces the audience. The interior of the dining room has lit up softly and through the scrim—gauze curtains—we see* AMANDA *and* LAURA *seated at the table in the upstage area.*)

AMANDA. You know, Laura, I had the funniest experience in church last Sunday. The church was crowded except for one pew way down front and in that was just one little woman. I smiled very sweetly at her and said, "Excuse me, would you mind if I shared this pew?" "I certainly would," she said, "this space is rented." Do you know that is the first time that I ever knew that the Lord rented space. (*Dining-room gauze curtains open automatically.*) These Northern Episcopalians! I can understand the Southern Episcopalians, but these Northern ones, no. TOM *enters dining room* R., *slips over to table and sits in chair* R.) Honey, don't push your food with your fingers. If you have to push your food with something, the thing to use is a crust of bread. You must chew your food. Animals have secretions in their stomachs which enable them to digest their food without mastication, but human beings must chew their food before they swallow it down, and chew, chew. Oh, eat leisurely. Eat leisurely. A well-cooked meal has many delicate flavors that have to be held in the mouth for appreciation, not just gulped down. Oh, chew, chew—chew! (*At this point the scrim curtain—if the director decides to use it—the one suggesting exterior wall, rises here and does not come down again until just before the end of the play.*) Don't you want to give your salivary glands a chance to function?

TOM. Mother, I haven't enjoyed one bite of my dinner because of your constant directions on how to eat it. It's you that makes me hurry through my meals with your hawklike atten-

Left to right: Karen Allen, Joanne Woodward, and John Malkovich. All pictures accompanying
The Glass Menagerie in this book are from the movie of the same name. Copyright © 1987 Cineplex Odeon

tion to every bite I take. It's disgusting—all
this discussion of animal's secretion—salivary
glands—mastication! *(Comes down to armchair
in living room* R., *lights cigarette)*

AMANDA. Temperament like a Metropolitan star!
You're not excused from this table.

TOM. I'm getting a cigarette.

AMANDA. You smoke too much.

LAURA *(rising)*. Mother, I'll bring in the coffee.

AMANDA. No, no, no, no. You sit down. I'm
going to be the colored boy today and you're
going to be the lady.

LAURA. I'm already up.

AMANDA. Resume your seat. Resume your seat.
You keep yourself fresh and pretty for the gentlemen callers. *(LAURA sits.)*

LAURA. I'm not expecting any gentlemen callers.

AMANDA *(who has been gathering dishes from table
and loading them on tray)*. Well, the nice thing
about them is they come when they're least
expected. Why, I remember one Sunday afternoon in Blue Mountain when your mother was
a girl . . . *(Goes out for coffee,* U. R.*)*

TOM. I know what's coming now! (LAURA *rises.*)

LAURA. Yes. But let her tell it. *(Crosses to* L. *of
daybed, sits)*

TOM. Again?

LAURA. She loves to tell it.

AMANDA *(entering from* R. *in dining room and
coming down into living room with tray and
coffee)*. I remember one Sunday afternoon in
Blue Mountain when your mother was a girl

she received—seventeen—gentlemen callers! (AMANDA *crosses to* TOM *at armchair* R., *gives him coffee, and crosses* C. LAURA *comes to her, takes cup, resumes her place on* L. *of daybed.* AMANDA *puts tray on small table* R. *of daybed, sits* R. *on daybed. Inner curtain closes, light dims out.*) Why sometimes there weren't chairs enough to accommodate them all and we had to send the colored boy over to the parish house to fetch the folding chairs.

TOM. How did you entertain all those gentlemen callers? (TOM *finally sits in armchair* R.)

AMANDA. I happened to understand the art of conversation!

TOM. I bet you could talk!

AMANDA. Well, I could. All the girls in my day could, I tell you.

TOM. Yes?

AMANDA. They knew how to entertain their gentlemen callers. It wasn't enough for a girl to be possessed of a pretty face and a graceful figure—although I wasn't slighted in either respect. She also needed to have a nimble wit and a tongue to meet all occasions.

TOM. What did you talk about?

AMANDA. Why, we'd talk about things of importance going on in the world! Never anything common or coarse or vulgar. My callers were gentlemen—all! Some of the most prominent men on the Mississippi Delta—planters and sons of planters! There was young Champ Laughlin. (MUSIC CUE #3) He later became Vice-President of the Delta Planter's Bank. And Hadley Stevenson; he was drowned in Moon Lake.—My goodness, he certainly left his widow well provided for—a hundred and fifty thousand dollars in government bonds. And the Cutrere Brothers—Wesley and Bates. Bates was one of my own bright particular beaus! But he got in a quarrel with that wild Wainwright boy and they shot it out on the floor of Moon Lake Casino. Bates was shot through the stomach. He died in the ambulance on his way to Memphis. He certainly left his widow well provided for, too—eight or ten thousand acres, no less. He never loved that woman; she just caught him on the rebound. My picture was found on him the night he died. Oh and that boy, that boy that every girl in the Delta was setting her cap for! That beautiful (*Music fades out.*) brilliant young Fitzhugh boy from Greene County!

TOM. What did he leave his widow?

AMANDA. He never married! What's the matter with you—you talk as though all my old admirers had turned up their toes to the daisies!

TOM. Isn't this the first you've mentioned that still survives?

AMANDA. He made an awful lot of money. He went North to Wall Street and made a fortune. He had the Midas touch—everything that boy touched just turned to gold! (*Gets up*) And I could have been Mrs. J. Duncan Fitzhugh—mind you! (*Crosses* L. C.) But—what did I do?—I just went out of my way and picked your father! (*Looks at picture on* L. *wall. Goes to small table* R. *of daybed for tray*)

LAURA (*rises from daybed*). Mother, let me clear the table.

AMANDA (*crossing* L. *for* LAURA'S *cup, then crossing* R. *for* TOM'S). No, dear, you go in front and study your typewriter chart. Or practice your shorthand a little. Stay fresh and pretty! It's almost time for our gentlemen callers to start arriving. How many do you suppose we're going to entertain this afternoon? (TOM *opens curtains between dining room and living room for her. These close behind her, and she exits into kitchen* R. TOM *stands* U. C. *in living room.*)

LAURA (*to* AMANDA, *offstage*). I don't believe we're going to receive any, Mother.

AMANDA (*offstage*). Not any? Not one? Why, you must be joking! Not one gentleman caller? What's the matter? Has there been a flood or a tornado?

LAURA (*crossing to typing table*). It isn't a flood. It's not a tornado, Mother. I'm just not popular like you were in Blue Mountain. Mother's afraid that I'm going to be an old maid. (MUSIC CUE #4) (*Lights dim out.* TOM *exits* U. C. *in blackout.* LAURA *crosses to menagerie* R.)

SCENE 2

SCENE: *The same. Lights dim up on living room.*
LAURA *discovered by menagerie, polishing glass. Crosses to phonograph, plays record.[1] She times this business so as to put needle on record as* MUSIC CUE #4 *ends. Enter* AMANDA *down alley* R. *Rattles key in lock.* LAURA *crosses guiltily to typewriter and types. (Small typewriter table with typewriter on it is still on stage in living room* L.*)* AMANDA *comes into room* R. *closing door. Crosses to armchair, putting hat, purse and gloves on it. Something has happened to* AMANDA. *It is written in her face: a look that is grim and hopeless and a little absurd. She has on one of those cheap or imitation velvety-looking cloth coats with imitation fur collar. Her hat is five or six years old, one of those dreadful cloche hats that were worn in the late twenties, and she is clasping an enormous black patent-leather pocketbook with nickel clasps and initials. This is her full-dress outfit, the one she usually wears to the* D.A.R.[2] *She purses her lips, opens her eyes very wide, rolls them upward and shakes her head. Seeing her mother's expression,* LAURA *touches her lips with a nervous gesture.*

LAURA. Hello, Mother, I was just . . .

AMANDA. I know. You were just practicing your typing, I suppose. (*Behind chair* R.)

LAURA. Yes.

AMANDA. Deception, deception, deception!

LAURA (*shakily*). How was the D.A.R. meeting, Mother?

AMANDA (*crosses to* LAURA). D.A.R. meeting!

LAURA. Didn't you go to the D.A.R. meeting, Mother?

AMANDA (*faintly, almost inaudibly*). No, I didn't go to any D.A.R. meeting. (*Then more forcibly.*) I didn't have the strength—I didn't have the courage. I just wanted to find a hole in the ground and crawl in it and stay there the rest of my entire life. (*Tears type charts, throws them on floor*)

LAURA (*faintly*). Why did you do that, Mother?

AMANDA (*sits on* R. *end of daybed*). Why? Why? How old are you, Laura?

LAURA. Mother, you know my age.

AMANDA. I was under the impression that you were an adult, but evidently I was very much mistaken. (*She stares at* LAURA.)

LAURA. Please don't stare at me. Mother! (AMANDA *closes her eyes and lowers her head. Pause*)

AMANDA. What are we going to do? What is going to become of us? What is the future? (*Pause*)

LAURA. Has something happened, Mother? Mother, has something happened?

AMANDA. I'll be all right in a minute. I'm just bewildered—by life . . .

LAURA. Mother, I wish that you would tell me what's happened!

AMANDA. I went to the D.A.R. this afternoon, as you know; I was to be inducted as an officer. I stopped off at Rubicam's Business College to tell them about your cold and to ask how you were progressing down there.

LAURA. Oh . . .

AMANDA. Yes, oh—oh—oh. I went straight to your typing instructor and introduced myself as your mother. She didn't even know who you were. Wingfield, she said? We don't have any such scholar enrolled in this school. I assured her she did. I said my daughter Laura's been coming to classes since early January. "Well, I don't know," she said, "unless you mean that terribly shy little girl who dropped out of school after a few days' attendance?" "No," I said, "I don't mean that one. I mean my daughter, Laura, who's been coming here every single day for the past six weeks!" "Excuse me," she said. And she took down the attendance book and there was your name, unmistakable, printed, and all the dates you'd been absent. I still told her she was wrong. I still said, "No, there must have been some mistake! There must have been some mix-up in the records!" "No," she said, "I remember her

---

1. *record.* While "Dardanella" was used in the original production, any other worn and scratchy popular record of the 1920s may be substituted.
2. **D.A.R.**, Daughters of the American Revolution, a society of women who can claim descent from Americans who fought in the Revolutionary War.

perfectly now. She was so shy and her hands trembled so that her fingers couldn't touch the right keys! When we gave a speed-test—she just broke down completely—was sick at the stomach and had to be carried to the washroom! After that she never came back. We telephoned the house every single day and never got any answer." *(Rises from daybed, crosses* R.C.*)* That was while I was working all day long down at that department store, I suppose, demonstrating those——*(With hands indicates brassiere)* Oh! I felt so weak I couldn't stand up! *(Sits in armchair)* I had to sit down while they got me a glass of water! (LAURA *crosses up to phonograph.)* Fifty dollars' tuition. I don't care about the money so much, but all my hopes for any kind of future for you—gone up the spout, just gone up the spout like that. (LAURA *winds phonograph up.)* Oh, don't *do* that, Laura!—Don't play that Victrola!

LAURA. Oh! *(Stops phonograph, crosses to typing table, sits)*

AMANDA. What have you been doing every day when you've gone out of the house pretending that you were going to business college?

LAURA. I've just been going out walking.

AMANDA. That's not true!

LAURA. Yes, it is, Mother, I just went walking.

AMANDA. Walking? Walking? In winter? Deliberately courting pneumonia in that light coat? Where did you walk to, Laura?

LAURA. All sorts of places—mostly in the park.

AMANDA. Even after you'd started catching that cold?

LAURA. It was the lesser of two evils, Mother. I couldn't go back. I threw up on the floor!

AMANDA. From half-past seven till after five every day you mean to tell me you walked around in the park, because you wanted to make me think that you were still going to Rubicam's Business College?

LAURA. Oh, Mother, it wasn't as bad as it sounds. I went inside places to get warmed up.

AMANDA. Inside where?

LAURA. I went in the art museum and the birdhouses at the Zoo. I visited the penguins every day! Sometimes I did without lunch and went to the movies. Lately I've been spending most of my afternoons in the Jewelbox, that big glass house[3] where they raise the tropical flowers.

AMANDA. You did all that to deceive me, just for deception! Why? Why? Why? Why?

LAURA. Mother, when you're disappointed, you get that awful suffering look on your face, like the picture of Jesus' mother in the Museum! *(Rises)*

AMANDA. Hush!

LAURA *(crosses* R. *to menagerie)*. I couldn't face it. I couldn't. (MUSIC CUE #5)

AMANDA *(rising from daybed)*. So what are we going to do now, honey, the rest of our lives? Just sit down in this house and watch the parades go by? Amuse ourselves with the glass menagerie? Eternally play those worn-out records your father left us as a painful reminder of him? *(Slams phonograph lid)* We can't have a business career. *(End* MUSIC CUE #5) No, we can't do that—that just gives us indigestion. *(Around* R. *daybed)* What is there left for us now but dependency all our lives? I tell you, Laura, I know so well what happens to unmarried women who aren't prepared to occupy a position in life. *(Crosses* L., *sits on daybed)* I've seen such pitiful cases in the South—barely tolerated spinsters living on some brother's wife or a sister's husband—tucked away in some mousetrap of a room—encouraged by one in-law to go on and visit the next in-law—little birdlike women—without any nest—eating the crust of humility all their lives! Is that the future that we've mapped out for ourselves? I swear I don't see any other alternative. And I don't think that's a very pleasant alternative. Of course—some girls *do* marry. My goodness, Laura, haven't you ever liked some boy?

LAURA. Yes, Mother, I liked one once.

AMANDA. You did?

LAURA. I came across his picture a while ago.

---

3. *big glass house,* the conservatory at the St. Louis Zoo. Williams emphasizes the identification of Laura with the delicate flowers and the fragile, glass building.

AMANDA. He gave you his picture too? (*Rises from daybed, crosses to chair* R.)

LAURA. No, it's in the yearbook.

AMANDA (*sits in armchair*). Oh—a high-school boy.

LAURA. Yes. His name was Jim. (*Kneeling on floor, gets yearbook from under menagerie*) Here he is in *The Pirates of Penzance*.[4]

AMANDA (*Absently*). The what?

LAURA. The operetta the senior class put on. He had a wonderful voice. We sat across the aisle from each other Mondays, Wednesdays, and Fridays in the auditorium. Here he is with a silver cup for debating! See his grin?

AMANDA. So he had a grin, too! (*Looks at picture of father on wall behind phonograph.[5] Hands yearbook back*)

LAURA. He used to call me—Blue Roses.

AMANDA. Blue Roses? What did he call you a silly name like that for?

LAURA (*still kneeling*). When I had that attack of pleurosis—he asked me what was the matter when I came back. I said pleurosis—he thought that I said "Blue Roses." So that's what he always called me after that. Whenever he saw me, he'd holler, "Hello, Blue Roses!" I didn't care for the girl that he went out with. Emily Meisenbach. Oh, Emily was the best-dressed girl at Soldan. But she never struck me as being sincere . . . I read in a newspaper once that they were engaged. (*Puts yearbook back on a shelf of glass menagerie*) That's a long time ago—they're probably married by now.

AMANDA. That's all right, honey, that's all right. It doesn't matter. Little girls who aren't cut out for business careers sometimes end up married to very nice young men. And I'm just going to see that you do that, too!

LAURA. But, Mother——

AMANDA. What is it now?

LAURA. I'm—crippled!

AMANDA. Don't say that word! (*Rises, crosses to* C. *Turns to* LAURA) How many times have I told you never to say that word! You're not crippled, you've just got a slight defect. (LAURA *rises.*) If you lived in the days when I was a

girl and they had long graceful skirts sweeping the ground, it might have been considered an asset. When you've got a slight disadvantage like that, you've just got to cultivate something else to take its place. You have to cultivate charm—or vivacity—or *charm!* (*Spotlight on photograph. Then dim out*) That's the only thing your father had plenty of—charm! (AMANDA *sits on daybed*. LAURA *crosses to armchair and sits.*) (MUSIC CUE #6) (*Blackout*)

SCENE 3

SCENE: *The same. Lights up again but only on* R. *alley and fire-escape landing, rest of the stage dark.* (*Typewriter table and typewriter have been taken offstage.*) *Enter* TOM, *again wearing merchant sailor overcoat and knitted cap, in alley* R. *As* MUSIC CUE #6 *ends,* TOM *begins to speak.*

TOM (*leans against grill of fire escape, smoking*). After the fiasco at Rubicam's Business College, the idea of getting a gentleman caller for my sister Laura began to play a more and more important part in my mother's calculations. It became an obsession. Like some archetype of the universal unconscious,[6] the image of the gentleman caller haunted our small apartment. An evening at home rarely passed without some allusion to this image, this specter, this hope. . . . And even when he wasn't mentioned, his presence hung in my mother's pre-occupied look and in my sister's frightened, apologetic manner. It hung like a sentence passed upon the Wingfields! But

---

4. *The Pirates of Penzance*, an operetta by William S. Gilbert (1836–1911) and Sir Arthur Sullivan (1842–1900).
5. *picture . . . phonograph.* In the original production this photo was a life-sized head, spotlighted from time to time as indicated. The lighting is optional.
6. *archetype of the universal unconscious*, a key concept of the psychological theory of Carl G. Jung (1875–1961), eminent Swiss psychologist. He believed everyone inherits unconscious memories of experiences that occur in all societies. According to Jung's theory, these "archetypes" give people their idea, for example, of what a parent should be, and they profoundly influence behavior. Tom satirically suggests that the image of a "gentleman caller" became an archetype dominating his mother's thinking.

Comment

Why It Is Called *The Glass Menagerie* by Tennessee Williams

When my family first moved to St. Louis from the South, we were forced to live in a congested apartment neighborhood. It was a shocking change, for my sister and myself were accustomed to spacious yards, porches, and big shade trees. The apartment we lived in was about as cheerful as an Arctic winter. There were outside windows only in the front room and kitchen. The rooms between had windows that opened upon a narrow areaway that was virtually sunless and which we grimly named "Death Valley" for a reason which is amusing only in retrospect.

There were a great many alley cats in the neighborhood which were constantly fighting the dogs. Every now and then some unwary young cat would allow itself to be pursued into this areaway which had only one opening. The end of the cul-de-sac was directly beneath my sister's bedroom window, and it was here that the cats would have to turn around to face their pursuers in mortal combat. My sister would be awakened in the night by the struggle, and in the morning the hideously mangled victim would be lying under her window. Sight of the areaway had become so odious to her, for this reason, that she kept the shade constantly drawn so that the interior of the bedroom had a perpetual twilight atmosphere. Something had to be done to relieve this gloom. So my sister and I painted all her furniture white; she put white curtains at the window and on the shelves around the room she collected a large assortment of little glass articles, of which she was particularly fond. Eventually, the room took on a light and delicate appearance, in spite of the lack of outside illumination, and it became the only room in the house that I found pleasant to enter.

When I left home a number of years later, it was this room that I recalled most vividly and poignantly when looking back to our home life in St. Louis. Particularly the little glass ornaments on the shelves. They were mostly little glass animals. By poetic association they came to represent, in my memory, all the softest emotions that belong to recollection of things past. They stood for all the small and tender things that relieve the austere pattern of life and make it endurable to the sensitive. The areaway where the cats were torn to pieces was one thing—my sister's white curtains and tiny menagerie of glass were another. Somewhere between them was the world that we lived in.

Williams's comment is from the folio accompanying Caedmon's recording of *The Glass Menagerie* as performed by Montgomery Clift, Julie Harris, Jessica Tandy, and David Wayne. Copyright © 1968 Caedmon Records, Inc. Used by permission.

Paul Newman directs John Malkovich, with Joanne Woodward in background in *The Glass Menagerie*, a Cineplex Odeon Films release (1987).

mother was a woman of action as well as words. (MUSIC CUE #7) She began to take logical steps in the planned direction. Late that winter and in the early spring—realizing that extra money would be needed to properly feather the nest and plume the bird—she began a vigorous campaign on the telephone, roping in subscribers to one of those magazines for matrons called *The Homemaker's Companion,* the type of journal that features the serialized sublimations of ladies of letters who think in terms of delicate cuplike breasts, slim, tapering waists, rich creamy thighs, eyes like wood-smoke in autumn, fingers that soothe and caress like soft, soft strains of music. Bodies as powerful as Etruscan sculpture. *(He exits down* R. *into wings. Light in alley* R. *is blacked out, and a head-spot falls on* AMANDA, *at phone in living room.* MUSIC CUE #7 *ends as* TOM *stops speaking.)*

AMANDA. Ida Scott? *(During this speech* TOM *enters dining room* U. R. *unseen by audience, not wearing overcoat or hat. There is an unlighted reading lamp on table. Sits* C. *of dining-room table with writing materials)* This is Amanda Wingfield. We missed you at the D.A.R. last Monday. Oh, first I want to know how's your sinus condition? You're just a Christian martyr. That's what you are. You're just a Christian martyr. Well, I was just going through my little red book, and I saw that your subscription to the *Companion* is about to expire just when that wonderful new serial by Bessie Mae Harper is starting. It's the first thing she's written since "Honeymoon for Three." Now, that was unusual, wasn't it? Why, Ida, this one is even lovelier. It's all about the horsey set on Long Island and a debutante is thrown from her horse while taking him over the jumps at the—regatta. Her spine—her spine is injured. That's what the horse did—he stepped on her. Now, there is only one surgeon in the entire world that can keep her from being completely paralyzed, and that's the man she's engaged to be married to and he's tall and he's blond and he's handsome. That's unusual, too, huh? Oh,

he's not perfect. Of course he has a weakness. He has the most terrible weakness in the entire world. He just drinks too much. What? Oh, no, Honey, don't let them burn. You go take a look in the oven and I'll hold on . . . Why, that woman! Do you know what she did? She hung up on me. *(Dining-room and living-room lights dim in. Reading lamp lights up at same time.)*

LAURA. Oh, Mother, Mother, Tom's trying to write. *(Rises from armchair where she was left at curtain of previous scene, goes to curtain between dining room and living room, which is already open)*

AMANDA. Oh! So he is. So he is. *(Crosses from phone, goes to dining room and up to* TOM*)*

TOM *(at table)*. Now what are you up to?

AMANDA. I'm trying to save your eyesight. *(Business with lamp)* You've got only one pair of eyes and you've got to take care of them. Oh, I know that Milton was blind, but that's not what made him a genius.

TOM. Mother, will you please go away and let me finish my writing?

AMANDA *(squares his shoulders)*. Why can't you sit up straight? So your shoulders don't stick through like sparrows' wings?

TOM. Mother, please go busy yourself with something else. I'm trying to write.

AMANDA *(business with* TOM*)*. Now, I've seen a medical chart, and I know what that position does to your internal organs. You sit up and I'll show you. Your stomach presses against your lungs, and your lungs press against your heart, and that poor little heart gets discouraged because it hasn't got any room left to go on beating for you.

TOM. What in hell! . . . *(Inner curtains between living room and dining room close. Lights dim down in dining room.* LAURA *crosses, stands* C. *of curtains in living room listening to following scene[7] between* TOM *and* AMANDA*.)*

AMANDA. Don't you talk to me like that——

TOM. —am I supposed to do?

---

7. *following scene.* Tom and Amanda remain in the dining room throughout their argument.

AMANDA. What's the matter with you? Have you gone out of your senses?

TOM. Yes, I have. You've driven me out of them.

AMANDA. What is the matter with you lately, you big—big—idiot?

TOM. Look, Mother—I haven't got a thing, not a single thing left in this house that I can call my own.

AMANDA. Lower your voice!

TOM. Yesterday you confiscated my books! You had the nerve to——

AMANDA. I did. I took that horrible novel back to the library—that awful book by that insane Mr. Lawrence.[8] I cannot control the output of a diseased mind or people who cater to them, but I won't allow such filth in my house. No, no, no, no, no!

TOM. House, house! Who pays the rent on the house, who makes a slave of himself to——!

AMANDA. Don't you dare talk to me like that! (LAURA *crosses* D. L. *to back of armchair.*)

TOM. No, *I* mustn't say anything! I've just got to keep quiet and let you do all the talking.

AMANDA. Let me tell you something!

TOM. I don't want to hear any more.

AMANDA. You will hear more——(LAURA *crosses to phonograph.*)

TOM (*crossing through curtains between dining room and living room. Goes upstage of door* R. *where, in a dark spot, there is supposedly a closet*). Well, I'm not going to listen. I'm going out. (*Gets out coat*)

AMANDA (*coming through curtains into living room, stands* C.). You are going to listen to me, Tom Wingfield. I'm tired of your impudence.—And another thing—I'm right at the end of my patience!

TOM (*putting overcoat on back of armchair and crossing back to* AMANDA). What do you think I'm at the end of, Mother? Aren't I supposed to have any patience to reach the end of? I know, I know. It seems unimportant to you, what I'm *doing*—what I'm trying to do—having a difference between them! You don't think that.

AMANDA. I think you're doing things that you're ashamed of, and that's why you act like this. (TOM *crosses to daybed and sits.*) I don't believe that you go every night to the movies. Nobody goes to the movies night after night. Nobody in their right minds goes to the movies as often as you pretend to. People don't go to the movies at nearly midnight and movies don't let out at 2:00 A.M. Come in stumbling, muttering to yourself like a maniac. You get three hours' sleep and then go to work. Oh, I can picture the way you're doing down there. Moping, doping, because you're in no condition.

TOM. That's true—that's very, very true. I'm in no condition!

AMANDA. How dare you jeopardize your job? Jeopardize our security? How do you think we'd manage——? (*Sits armchair* R.)

TOM. Look, Mother, do you think I'm *crazy* about the *warehouse?* You think I'm in love with the Continental Shoemakers? You think I want to spend fifty-five years of my life down there in that—*celotex interior!* with *fluorescent tubes?!* Honest to God, I'd rather somebody picked up a crowbar and battered out my brains—than go back mornings! But I *go!* Sure, every time you come in yelling that bloody *Rise and Shine!* Rise and Shine!! I think how lucky dead people are! But I get up. (*Rises from daybed*) I *go!* For sixty-five dollars a month I give up all that I dream of doing and being *ever!* And you say that is all I think of. Oh, God! Why, Mother, if self is all I ever thought of, Mother, *I'd* be where *he* is—*GONE!* (*Crosses to get overcoat on back of armchair*) As far as the system of transportation reaches! (AMANDA *rises, crosses to him and grabs his arm.*) Please don't grab at me, Mother!

AMANDA (*following him*). I'm not grabbing at you. I want to know where you're going now.

TOM (*taking overcoat and starts crossing to door* R.). I'm going to the movies!

AMANDA (*crosses* C.). I don't believe that lie!

---

8. *Mr. Lawrence*, D. H. Lawrence (1885–1930), English novelist and poet. Some of his works aroused considerable protest on moral grounds. The artistic merit of much of his work, however, is unquestioned.

TOM (*crosses back to* AMANDA). No? Well, you're right. For once in your life you're right. I'm not going to the movies. I'm going to opium dens! Yes, Mother, opium dens, dens of vice and criminals' hangouts, Mother. I've joined the Hogan gang. I'm a hired assassin, I carry a tommy gun in a violin case! I run a string of cathouses in the valley! They call me Killer, Killer Wingfield, I'm really leading a double life. By day I'm a simple, honest warehouse worker, but at night I'm a dynamic czar of the underworld. Why, I go to gambling casinos and spin away a fortune on the roulette table! I wear a patch over one eye and a false mustache, sometimes I wear green whiskers. On those occasions they call me—El Diablo![9] Oh, I could tell you things to make you sleepless! My enemies plan to dynamite this place some night! Some night they're going to blow us all sky-high. And will I be glad! Will I be happy! And so will you be. You'll go up—up—over Blue Mountain on a broomstick! With seventeen gentlemen callers! You ugly babbling old witch! (*He goes through a series of violent, clumsy movements, seizing his overcoat, lunging to* R. *door, pulling it fiercely open. The women watch him, aghast. His arm catches in the sleeve of the coat as he struggles to pull it on. For a moment he is pinioned by the bulky garment. With an outraged groan he tears the coat off again, splitting the shoulder of it, and hurls it across the room. It strikes against the shelf of* LAURA's *glass collection, there is a tinkle of shattering glass.* LAURA *cries out as if wounded.*)

LAURA. My glass!—menagerie . . . (*She covers her face and turns away.* MUSIC CUE #8 *through to end of scene*)

AMANDA (*in an awful voice*). I'll never speak to you again as long as you live unless you apologize to me! (AMANDA *exits through living-room curtains.* TOM *is left with* LAURA. *He stares at her stupidly for a moment. Then he crosses to shelf holding glass menagerie. Drops awkwardly on his knees to collect fallen glass, glancing at* LAURA *as if he would speak, but couldn't. Blackout.* TOM, AMANDA, *and* LAURA *exit in blackout.*)

SCENE 4

SCENE: *The interior is dark: Faint light in alley* R. *A deep-voiced bell in a church is tolling the hour of five as the scene commences.*

TOM *appears at the top of* R. *alley. After each solemn boom of the bell in the tower he shakes a little toy noisemaker or rattle as if to express the tiny spasm of man in contrast to the sustained power and dignity of the Almighty. This and the unsteadiness of his advance make it evident that he has been drinking. As he climbs the few steps to the fire-escape landing, light steals up inside.* LAURA *appears in night-dress, entering living room from* L. *door of dining room, observing* TOM's *empty bed (daybed) in the living room.* TOM *fishes in his pockets for door key, removing a motley assortment of articles in the search, including a perfect shower of movie-ticket stubs and an empty bottle. At last he finds the key, but just as he is about to insert it, it slips from his fingers. He strikes a match and crouches below the door.*

TOM (*bitterly*). One crack—and it falls through! (LAURA *opens door* R.)[10]

LAURA. Tom! Tom, what are you doing?

TOM. Looking for a door key.

LAURA. Where have you been all this time?

TOM. I have been to the movies.

LAURA. All this time at the movies?

TOM. There was a very long program. There was a Garbo picture and a Mickey Mouse and a travelogue and a newsreel and a preview of coming attractions. And there was an organ solo and a collection for the milk fund—simultaneously—which ended up in a terrible fight between a fat lady and an usher!

LAURA (*innocently*). Did you have to stay through everything?

TOM. Of course! And, oh, I forgot! There was a big stage show! The headliner on this stage show was Malvolio the Magician. He performed wonderful tricks, many of them, such as pouring water back and forth between pitch-

9. *El Diablo* (el di äb′lô), the devil. [*Spanish*]
10. *Laura opens door* R. The next few speeches are spoken on fire-escape landing.

John Malkovich and Karen Allen. Copyright © 1987 Cineplex Odeon

ers. First it turned to wine and then it turned to beer and then it turned to whiskey. I know it was whiskey it finally turned into because he needed somebody to come up out of the audience to help him, and I came up—both shows! It was Kentucky Straight Bourbon. A very generous fellow, he gave souvenirs. (*He pulls from his back pocket a shimmering rainbow-colored scarf.*) He gave me this. This is his magic scarf. You can have it, Laura. You wave it over a canary cage and you get a bowl of goldfish. You wave it over the goldfish bowl and they fly away canaries. . . . But the wonderfulest trick of all was the coffin trick. We nailed him into a coffin and he got out of the coffin without removing one nail. (*They enter.*) There is a trick that would come in handy for me—get me out of this two-by-four situation! (*Flops onto daybed and starts removing shoes*)

LAURA. Tom—shhh!

TOM. What're you shushing me for?

LAURA. You'll wake up Mother.

TOM. Goody goody! Pay'er back for all those "Rise an' Shines." (*Lies down groaning*) You know it don't take much intelligence to get yourself into a nailed-up coffin, Laura. But who in hell ever got himself out of one without removing one nail? (*As if in answer, the father's grinning photograph lights up.* LAURA *exits up* L. *Lights fade except for blue glow in dining room. Pause after lights fade, then clock chimes six times. This is followed by the alarm clock. Dim in forestage.*)

SCENE 5

SCENE: *The same. Immediately following. The church bell is heard striking six. At the sixth stroke the alarm clock goes off in* AMANDA's *room off* R. *of dining room and after a few moments we hear her calling, "Rise and shine! Rise and shine!* LAURA, *go tell your brother to rise and shine!"*

TOM (*sitting up slowly in daybed*). I'll rise—but I won't shine. (*The light increases.*)

AMANDA (*offstage*). Laura, tell your brother his coffee is ready. (LAURA, *fully dressed, a cape over her shoulders, slips into living room.* TOM *is still in bed, covered with blanket, having taken off only shoes and coat.*)

LAURA. Tom!—It's nearly seven. Don't make Mother nervous. (*He stares at her stupidly.*) (*Beseechingly*) Tom, speak to Mother this morning. Make up with her, apologize, speak to her!

TOM (*putting on shoes*). She won't to me. It's her that started not speaking.

LAURA. If you just say you're sorry, she'll start speaking.

TOM. Her not speaking—is that such a tragedy?

LAURA. Please—please!

AMANDA (*calling offstage* R. *from kitchen*). Laura, are you going to do what I asked you to do, or do I have to get dressed and go out myself?

LAURA. Going, going—soon as I get on my coat! (*She rises and crosses to door* R.) Butter and what else? (*To* AMANDA)

AMANDA (*offstage*). Just butter. Tell them to charge it.

LAURA. Mother, they make such faces when I do that.

AMANDA (*offstage*). Sticks and stones can break our bones, but the expression on Mr. Garfinkel's face won't harm us! Tell your brother his coffee is getting cold.

LAURA (*at door* R.). Do what I asked you, will you, will you, Tom? (*He looks sullenly away.*)

AMANDA. Laura, go now or just don't go at all!

LAURA (*rushing out* R.). Going—going! (*A second later she cries out. Falls on fire-escape landing.* TOM *springs up and crosses to door* R. AMANDA *rushes anxiously in from dining room, puts dishes on dining-room table.* TOM *opens door* R.)

TOM. Laura?

LAURA. I'm all right, I slipped, but I'm all right. (*Goes up* R. *alley, out of sight*)

AMANDA (*on fire escape*). I tell you if anybody falls down and breaks a leg on those fire-escape steps, the landlord ought to be sued for every cent he——(*Sees* TOM) Who are you? (*Leaves fire-escape landing, crosses to dining room and returns with bowls, coffee cup, cream, etc. Puts them on small table* R. *of daybed, crosses to armchair, sits. Counts 3.* MUSIC CUE #9. *As* TOM *reenters* R., *listlessly for his coffee, she turns her back to him, as she sits in armchair. The light on her face with its aged but childish features is cruelly sharp, satirical as a Daumier print.*[11] TOM *glances sheepishly but sullenly at her averted figure and sits on daybed next to the food. The coffee is scalding hot, he sips it and gasps and spits it back in the cup. At his gasp,* AMANDA *catches her breath and half turns. Then catches herself and turns away.* TOM *blows on his coffee, glancing sidewise at his mother. She clears her throat.* TOM *clears his. He starts to rise. Sinks back down again, scratches his head, clears his throat again.* AMANDA *coughs.* TOM *raises his cup in both hands to blow on it, his eyes staring over the rim of it at his mother for several moments. Then he slowly sets the cup down and awkwardly and hesitantly rises from daybed.*)

TOM (*hoarsely*). I'm sorry, Mother. I'm sorry for all those things I said. I didn't mean it. I apologize.

AMANDA (*sobbingly*). My devotion has made me a witch and so I make myself hateful to my children!

TOM. No, you don't.

AMANDA. I worry so much, I don't sleep, it makes me nervous!

TOM (*gently*). I understand that.

AMANDA. You know I've had to put up a solitary battle all these years. But you're my right hand bower! Now don't fail me. Don't fall down.

TOM (*gently*). I try, Mother.

AMANDA (*with great enthusiasm*). That's all right! You just keep on trying and you're bound to succeed. Why, you're—you're just full of natural endowments! Both my children are —they're very precious children and I've got an awful lot to be thankful for; you just must promise me one thing. (MUSIC CUE #9 *stops.*)

TOM. What is it, Mother?

AMANDA. Promise me you're never going to become a drunkard!

TOM. I promise, Mother. I won't ever become a drunkard!

AMANDA. That's what frightened me so, that you'd be drinking! Eat a bowl of Purina.

TOM. Just coffee, Mother.

AMANDA. Shredded Wheat Biscuit?

TOM. No, no, Mother, just coffee.

AMANDA. You can't put in a day's work on an empty stomach. You've got ten minutes— don't gulp! Drinking too-hot liquids makes cancer of the stomach. . . . Put cream in.

TOM. No, thank you.

AMANDA. To cool it.

TOM. No! No, thank you, I want it black.

AMANDA. I know, but it's not good for you. We have to do all that we can to build ourselves up. In these trying times we live in, all that we have to cling to is—each other . . . That's why it's so important to—Tom, I—I sent out your sister so I could discuss something with you. If you hadn't spoken, I would have spoken to you. (*Sits down*)

TOM (*gently*). What is it, Mother, that you want to discuss?

AMANDA. Laura! (TOM *puts his cup down slowly.* MUSIC CUE #10)

TOM. —Oh.—Laura . . .

AMANDA (*touching his sleeve*). You know how Laura is. So quiet but—still water runs deep! She notices things and I think she—broods about them. (TOM *looks up.*) A few days ago I came in and she was crying.

TOM. What about?

AMANDA. You.

TOM. Me?

AMANDA. She has an idea that you're not happy here. (MUSIC CUE #10 *stops.*)

TOM. What gave her that idea?

AMANDA. What gives her any idea? However, you do act strangely. (TOM *slaps cup down on small table.*) I—I'm not criticizing, understand that! I know your ambitions do not lie in the warehouse, that like everybody in the whole wide world—you've had to—make sacrifices, but—Tom—Tom—life's not easy, it calls for—Spartan endurance! There's so many things in my heart that I cannot describe to

---

11. *Daumier* (dō myā′). Honoré Daumier (1808–1879) was a French caricaturist and painter.

you! I've never told you but I—loved your father . . .

TOM (gently). I know that, Mother.

AMANDA. And you—when I see you taking after his ways! Staying out late—and—well, you had been drinking the night you were in that—terrifying condition! Laura says that you hate the apartment and that you go out nights to get away from it! Is that true, Tom?

TOM. No. You say there's so much in your heart that you can't describe to me. That's true of me, too. There's so much in my heart that I can't describe to you! So let's respect each other's——

AMANDA. But why—why, Tom—are you always so restless? Where do you go to, nights?

TOM. I—go to the movies.

AMANDA. Why do you go to the movies so much, Tom?

TOM. I go to the movies because—I like adventure. Adventure is something I don't have much of at work, so I go to the movies.

AMANDA. But, Tom, you go to the movies entirely too much!

TOM. I like a lot of adventure. (AMANDA *looks baffled, then hurt. As the familiar inquisition resumes, he becomes hard and impatient again.* AMANDA *slips back into her querulous attitude toward him.*)

AMANDA. Most young men find adventure in their careers.

TOM. Then most young men are not employed in a warehouse.

AMANDA. The world is full of young men employed in warehouses and offices and factories.

TOM. Do all of them find adventure in their careers?

AMANDA. They do or they do without it! Not everybody has a craze for adventure.

TOM. Man is by instinct a lover, a hunter, a fighter, and none of those instincts are given much play at the warehouse!

AMANDA. Man is by instinct! Don't quote instinct to me! Instinct is something that people have got away from! It belongs to animals!

Christian adults don't want it!

TOM. What do Christian adults want, then, Mother?

AMANDA. Superior things! Things of the mind and the spirit! Only animals have to satisfy instincts! Surely your aims are somewhat higher than theirs! Than monkeys—pigs——

TOM. I reckon they're not.

AMANDA. You're joking. However, that isn't what I wanted to discuss.

TOM (rising). I haven't much time.

AMANDA (pushing his shoulders). Sit down.

TOM. You want me to punch in red at the warehouse, Mother?

AMANDA. You have five minutes. I want to talk about Laura.

TOM. All right! What about Laura?

AMANDA. We have to be making some plans and provisions for her. She's older than you, two years, and nothing has happened. She just drifts along doing nothing. It frightens me terribly how she just drifts along.

TOM. I guess she's the type that people call home girls.

AMANDA. There's no such type, and if there is, it's a pity! That is unless the home is hers, with a husband!

TOM. What?

AMANDA (crossing D. R. to armchair). Oh, I can see the handwriting on the wall as plain as I see the nose in front of my face! It's terrifying! More and more you remind me of your father! He was out all (Sits in armchair) hours without explanation!—Then left! Good-by! And me with the bag to hold. I saw that letter you got from the Merchant Marine. I know what you're dreaming of. I'm not standing here blindfolded. Very well, then. Then do it! But not till there's somebody to take your place.

TOM. What do you mean?

AMANDA. I mean that as soon as Laura has got somebody to take care of her, married, a home of her own, independent—why, then you'll be free to go wherever you please, (Rises, crosses to TOM) on land, on sea, whichever way the wind blows you! But until that time you've got

Joanne Woodward. Copyright © 1987 Cineplex Odeon

to look out for your sister. (*Crosses* R. *behind armchair*) I don't say me because I'm old and don't matter! I say for your sister because she's young and dependent. I put her in business college—a dismal failure! Frightened her so it made her sick at the stomach! I took her over to the Young People's League at the church. Another fiasco. She spoke to nobody, nobody spoke to her. (*Sits armchair*) Now all she does is fool with those pieces of glass and play those worn-out records. What kind of a life is that for a girl to lead?

TOM. What can I do about it?

AMANDA. Overcome selfishness! Self, self, self is all that you ever think of! (TOM *springs up and crosses* R. *to get his coat and put it on. It is ugly and bulky. He pulls on a cap with earmuffs.*) Where is your muffler? Put your wool muffler on! (*He snatches it angrily from the hook and tosses it around his neck and pulls both ends tight.*) Tom! I haven't said what I had in mind to ask you.

TOM. I'm too late to——

AMANDA (*catching his arm—very importunately. Then shyly*). Down at the warehouse, aren't there some—nice young men?

TOM. No!

AMANDA. There must be—some . . .

TOM. Mother——(*Gesture*)

AMANDA. Find out one that's clean-living—doesn't drink and—ask him out for sister!

TOM. What?

AMANDA. For sister! To meet! Get acquainted!

TOM (*stamping to door* R.). Oh, my go-osh!

AMANDA. Will you? (*He opens door.*) (*Imploringly*) Will you? (*He starts out.*) Will you? Will you, dear? (TOM *exits up alley* R. AMANDA *is on fire-escape landing.*)

TOM (*calling back*). Yes!

AMANDA (*reentering* R. *and crossing to phone.* MUSIC CUE #11.) Ella Cartwright? Ella, this is Amanda Wingfield. First, first, how's that kidney trouble? Oh, it has? It has come back? Well, you're just a Christian martyr, you're just a Christian martyr. I was noticing in my little red book that your subscription to the *Companion* has run out just when that wonderful new serial by Bessie Mae Harper was starting. It's all about the horsey set on Long Island. Oh, you have? You have read it? Well, how do you think it turns out? Oh, no. Bessie Mae Harper never lets you down. Oh, of course, we have to have complications. You have to have complications—oh, you can't have a story without them—but Bessie Mae Harper always leaves you with such an uplift——What's the matter, Ella? You sound so mad. Oh, because it's seven o'clock in the morning. Oh, Ella, I forgot that you never got up until nine. I forgot that anybody in the world was allowed to sleep as late as that. I can't say anymore than I'm sorry, can I? Oh, you will? You're going to take that subscription from me anyhow? Well, bless you, Ella, bless you, bless you, bless you. (MUSIC #11 *fades into* MUSIC CUE #11-A, *dance music, and continues into next scene. Dim out lights.* MUSIC CUE #11-A.)

SCENE 6

SCENE: *The same.—Only* R. *alley lighted, with dim light.*

TOM (*enters* D.R. *and stands as before, leaning against grillwork, with cigarette, wearing merchant sailor coat and cap*). Across the alley was the Paradise Dance Hall. Evenings in spring they'd open all the doors and windows and the music would come outside. Sometimes they'd turn out all the lights except for a large glass sphere that hung from the ceiling. It would turn slowly about and filter the dusk with delicate rainbow colors. Then the orchestra would play a waltz or a tango, something that had a slow and sensuous rhythm. The young couples would come outside, to the relative privacy of the alley. You could see them kissing behind ashpits and telephone poles. This was the compensation for lives that passed like mine, without change or adventure. Changes and adventure, however, were imminent this year. They were waiting around the corner for all these dancing kids. Suspended in the mist over Berchtesgaden, caught in the folds of Chamberlain's umbrella.[12] In Spain there was Guernica![13] Here there was only hot swing music and liquor, dance halls, bars, and movies, and sex that hung in the gloom like a chandelier and flooded the world with brief, deceptive rainbows. . . . While these unsuspecting kids danced to "Dear One, the World Is Waiting for the Sunrise," all the world was really waiting for bombardments. (MUSIC #11-A *stops*. *Dim in dining room: faint glow.* AMANDA *is seen in dining room*.)

AMANDA. Tom, where are you?

TOM (*standing as before*). I came out to smoke. (*Exit* R. *into the wings, where he again changes coats and leaves hat*)

AMANDA (TOM *reenters and stands on fire-escape landing, smoking. He opens door for* AMANDA, *who sits on hassock on landing*.) Oh, you smoke too much. A pack a day at fifteen cents a pack. How much would that be in a month? Thirty times fifteen? It wouldn't be very much. Well, it would be enough to help towards a night-school course in accounting at the Washington U! Wouldn't that be lovely?

TOM. I'd rather smoke.

AMANDA. I know! That's the tragedy of you. This fire-escape landing is a poor excuse for the porch we used to have. What are you looking at?

TOM. The moon.

AMANDA. Is there a moon this evening?

TOM. It's rising over Garfinkel's Delicatessen.

AMANDA. Oh! So it is! Such a little silver slipper of a moon. Have you made a wish on it?

TOM. Um-mm.

AMANDA. What did you wish?

TOM. That's a secret.

AMANDA. All right, I won't tell you what I wished, either. I can keep a secret, too. I can be just as mysterious as you.

TOM. I bet I can guess what you wished.

AMANDA. Why, is my head transparent?

TOM. You're not a sphinx.

AMANDA. No, I don't have secrets. I'll tell you what I wished for on the moon. Success and happiness for my precious children. I wish for that whenever there's a moon, and when there isn't a moon, I wish for it, too.

TOM. I thought perhaps you wished for a gentleman caller.

AMANDA. Why do you say that?

TOM. Don't you remember asking me to fetch one?

AMANDA. I remember suggesting that it would be nice for your sister if you brought home some nice young man from the warehouse. I think that I've made that suggestion more than once.

TOM. Yes, you have made it repeatedly.

AMANDA. Well?

TOM. We are going to have one.

AMANDA. *What?*

TOM. A gentleman caller!

AMANDA. You mean you have asked some nice young man to come over? (*Rising from stool, facing* TOM)

TOM. I've asked him to dinner.

AMANDA. You really did?

TOM. I did.

AMANDA. And did he—accept?

TOM. He did!

AMANDA. He did?

TOM. He did.

AMANDA. Well, isn't that lovely!

TOM. I thought that you would be pleased.

AMANDA. It's definite, then?

TOM. Oh, very definite.

AMANDA. How soon?

TOM. Pretty soon.

AMANDA. How soon?

TOM. Quite soon.

---

12. *Berchtesgaden* (bèrH'təs gä'dən) . . . *Chamberlain's umbrella.* Adolf Hitler, the German Chancellor, was visited at Berchtesgaden, his mountain retreat, by Britain's Prime Minister, Neville Chamberlain, in 1938. Chamberlain agreed to let Hitler annex part of Czechoslovakia in return for a pledge of peace by Hitler. Hitler's breaking of this pledge brought on World War II.
13. *Guernica* (ger në'kä), a town in northern Spain, held by the democratic faction during the Spanish Civil War. It was bombed in 1937 by German airplanes supporting Fascist forces and thus became a symbol of the cruelty of the Fascist overthrow of the Spanish Republic.

AMANDA. How soon?

TOM. Very, very soon.

AMANDA. Every time I want to know anything you start going on like that.

TOM. What do you want to know?

AMANDA. Go ahead and guess. Go ahead and guess.

TOM. All right, I'll guess. You want to know when the gentleman caller's coming—he's coming tomorrow.

AMANDA. Tomorrow? Oh, no, I can't do anything about tomorrow. I can't do anything about tomorrow.

TOM. Why not?

AMANDA. That doesn't give me any time.

TOM. Time for what?

AMANDA. Time for preparations. Oh, you should have phoned me the minute you asked him—the minute he accepted.

TOM. You don't have to make any fuss.

AMANDA. Of course, I have to make a fuss! I can't have a man coming into a place that's all sloppy. It's got to be thrown together properly. I certainly have to do some fast thinking by tomorrow night, too.

TOM. I don't see why you have to think at all.

AMANDA. That's because you just don't know. (Enter living room, crosses to C. Dim in living room) You just don't know, that's all. We can't have a gentleman caller coming into a pigsty! Now, let's see. Oh, I've got those three pieces of wedding silver left. I'll polish that up. I wonder how that old lace tablecloth is holding up all these years? We can't wear anything. We haven't got it. We haven't got anything to wear. We haven't got it. (Goes back to door R.)

TOM. Mother! This boy is no one to make a fuss over.

AMANDA (crossing to C.). I don't know how you can say that when this is the first gentleman caller your little sister's ever had! I think it's pathetic that that little girl has never had a single gentleman caller! Come on inside! Come on inside!

TOM. What for?

AMANDA. I want to ask you a few things.

TOM (from doorway R.). If you're going to make a fuss, I'll call the whole thing off. I'll call the boy up and tell him not to come.

AMANDA. No! You mustn't ever do that. People hate broken engagements. They have no place to go. Come on inside. Come on inside. Will you come inside when I ask you to come inside? Sit down. (TOM comes into living room.)

TOM. Any particular place you want me to sit?

AMANDA. Oh! Sit anywhere. (TOM sits armchair R.). Look! What am I going to do about that? (Looking at daybed) Did you ever see anything look so sad? I know, I'll get a bright piece of cretonne. That won't cost much. And I made payments on a floor lamp. So I'll have that sent out! And I can put a bright cover on the chair. I wish I had time to paper the walls. What's his name?

TOM. His name is O'Connor.

AMANDA. O'Connor—he's Irish and tomorrow's Friday—that means fish. Well, that's all right, I'll make a salmon loaf and some mayonnaise dressing for it. Where did you meet him? (Crosses to daybed and sits)

TOM. At the warehouse, of course. Where else would I meet him?

AMANDA. Well, I don't know. Does he drink?

TOM. What made you ask me that?

AMANDA. Because your father did.

TOM. Now, don't get started on that!

AMANDA. He drinks, then.

TOM. No, not that I know of.

AMANDA. You have to find out. There's nothing I want less for my daughter than a man who drinks.

TOM. Aren't you being a little bit premature? After all, poor Mr. O'Connor hasn't even appeared on the scene yet.

AMANDA. But he will tomorrow. To meet your sister. And what do I know about his character? (Rises and crosses to TOM who is still in armchair, smooths his hair)

TOM (submitting grimly). Now what are you up to?

AMANDA. I always did hate that cowlick. I never could understand why it won't sit down by itself.

Joanne Woodward and John Malkovich. Copyright © 1987 Cineplex Odeon

TOM. Mother, I want to tell you something and I mean it sincerely right straight from my heart. There's a lot of boys who meet girls which they don't marry!

AMANDA. You know you always had me worried because you could never stick to a subject. (*Crosses to daybed*) What I want to know is what's his position at the warehouse?

TOM. He's a shipping clerk.

AMANDA. Oh! Shipping clerk! Well, that's fairly important. That's where you'd be if you had more get-up. How much does he earn? (*Sits on daybed*)

TOM. I have no way of knowing that for sure. I judge his salary to be approximately eighty-five dollars a month.

AMANDA. Eighty-five dollars? Well, that's not princely.

TOM. It's twenty dollars more than I make.

AMANDA. I know that. Oh, how well I know that! How well I know that! Eighty-five dollars a month. No. It can't be done. A family man can never get by on eighty-five dollars a month.

TOM. Mother, Mr. O'Connor is not a family man.

AMANDA. Well, he might be some time in the future, mightn't he?

TOM. Oh, I see. . . . Plans and provisions.

AMANDA. You are the only young man that I know of who ignores the fact that the future becomes the present, the present the past, and the past turns into everlasting regret if you don't plan for it.

TOM. I will think that over and see what I can make of it!

AMANDA. Don't be supercilious with your mother! Tell me some more about this.—What do you call him? Mr. O'Connor, Mr. O'Connor. He must have another name besides Mr. ——?

TOM. His full name is James D. O'Connor. The D. is for Delaney.

AMANDA. Delaney? Irish on both sides and he doesn't drink?

TOM (*rises from armchair*). Shall I call him up and ask him? (*Starts toward phone*)

AMANDA (*crossing to phone*). No!

TOM. I'll call him up and tell him you want to know if he drinks. (*Picks up phone*)

AMANDA (*taking phone away from him*). No, you can't do that. You have to be discreet about that subject. When I was a girl in Blue Mountain, if it was (TOM *sits on* R. *of daybed*.) suspected that a young man was drinking and any girl was receiving his attentions—if any girl *was* receiving his attentions, she'd go to the minister of his church and ask about his character—or her father, if her father was living, then it was his duty to go to the minister of his church and ask about his character, and that's how young girls in Blue Mountain were kept from making tragic mistakes. (*Picture dims in and out.*)[14]

TOM. How come you made such a tragic one?

AMANDA. Oh, I don't know how he did it, but that face fooled everybody. All he had to do was grin and the world was bewitched. (*Behind daybed, crosses to armchair*) I don't know of anything more tragic than a young girl just putting herself at the mercy of a handsome appearance, and I hope Mr. O'Connor is *not* too good-looking.

TOM. As a matter of fact he isn't. His face is covered with freckles and he has a very large nose.

AMANDA. He's not right-down homely?

TOM. No. I wouldn't say right-down—homely —medium homely, I'd say.

AMANDA. Well, if a girl had any sense she'd look for character in a man anyhow.

TOM. That's what I've always said, Mother.

AMANDA. You've always said it—you've always said it! How could you've always said it when you never even thought about it?

TOM. Aw, don't be so suspicious of me.

AMANDA. I am. I'm suspicious of every word that comes out of your mouth, when you talk to me, but I want to know about this young man. Is he up and coming?

TOM. Yes. I really do think he goes in for self-improvement.

AMANDA. What makes you think it?

---

14. *Picture dims in and out.* See note 5, page 579.

TOM. He goes to night school.

AMANDA. Well, what does he do there at night school?

TOM. He's studying radio engineering and public speaking.

AMANDA. Oh! Public speaking! Oh, that shows, that shows that he intends to be an executive some day—and radio engineering. Well, that's coming . . . huh?

TOM. I think it's here.

AMANDA. Well, those are all very illuminating facts. (*Crosses to back of armchair*) Facts that every mother should know about any young man calling on her daughter, seriously or not.

TOM. Just one little warning, Mother. I didn't tell him anything about Laura. I didn't let on we had dark ulterior motives. I just said, "How about coming home to dinner some time?" and he said, "Fine," and that was the whole conversation.

AMANDA. I bet it was, too. I tell you, sometimes you can be as eloquent as an oyster. However, when he sees how pretty and sweet that child is, he's going to be, well, he's going to be very glad he was asked over here to have some dinner. (*Sits in armchair*)

TOM. Mother, just one thing. You won't expect too much of Laura, will you?

AMANDA. I don't know what you mean. (TOM *crosses slowly to* AMANDA. *He stands for a moment, looking at her. Then——*)

TOM. Well, Laura seems all those things to you and me because she's ours and we love her. We don't even notice she's crippled any more.

AMANDA. Don't use that word.

TOM. Mother, you have to face the facts; she is, and that's not all.

AMANDA. What do you mean "that's not all"? (TOM *kneels by her chair.*)

TOM. Mother—you know that Laura is very different from other girls.

AMANDA. Yes, I do know that, and I think that difference is all in her favor, too.

TOM. Not quite all—in the eyes of others—strangers—she's terribly shy. She lives in a world of her own and those things make her seem a little peculiar to people outside the house.

AMANDA. Don't use that word peculiar.

TOM. You have to face the facts.—She is.

AMANDA. I don't know in what way she's peculiar. (MUSIC CUE #12, *till curtain.* TOM *pauses a moment for music, then——*)

TOM. Mother, Laura lives in a world of little glass animals. She plays old phonograph records —and—that's about all——(TOM *rises slowly, goes quietly out the door* R., *leaving it open, and exits slowly up the alley.* AMANDA *rises, goes on to fire-escape landing* R., *looks at moon.*)

AMANDA. Laura! Laura! (LAURA *answers from kitchen* R.)

LAURA. Yes, Mother.

AMANDA. Let those dishes go and come in front! (LAURA *appears with dish towel.*) (*Gaily*) Laura, come here and make a wish on the moon!

LAURA (*entering from kitchen* R. *and comes down to fire-escape landing*). Moon—moon?

AMANDA. A little silver slipper of a moon. Look over your left shoulder, Laura, and make a wish! (LAURA *looks faintly puzzled as if called out of sleep.* AMANDA *seizes her shoulders and turns her at an angle on the fire-escape landing.*) Now! Now, darling, wish!

LAURA. What shall I wish for, Mother?

AMANDA (*her voice trembling and her eyes suddenly filling with tears*). Happiness! And just a little bit of good fortune! (*The stage dims out.*)

Curtain

THINK AND DISCUSS

ACT ONE: SCENES 1 AND 2

Understanding

1. The play begins with a long and detailed set of stage directions. What words and phrases in the first sentence indicate that the Wingfield apartment is not a desirable place to live?
2. What does the apartment face and how is it entered, according to the second sentence?
3. Who is the narrator of the play? In what sense does he serve a double role?
4. Who are the other characters in the play? Which "character" appears only in a photograph?
5. What discovery about Laura angers Amanda at the beginning of scene 2?
6. How does Laura get the nickname "Blue Roses"?

Analyzing

7. What incidents in the first two scenes reveal tension in the family?
8. In what ways does the initial stage setting (music, lighting, scenery) create the **mood** of a memory play?
9. What do you learn about Laura's personality and self image?

Extending

10. In Williams's original script, he explains that there is "much to admire in Amanda, and as much to love and pity as there is to laugh at." Find something about Amanda, as portrayed in the first two scenes, that makes her appear admirable. Find something that makes her appear laughable.

SCENES 3 AND 4

Understanding

1. What job does Amanda perform at home to increase the family income?
2. Where does Tom work? What does he think of his job?
3. At the end of scene 3, Tom hurls his coat. What damage does he do?
4. Where does Tom say he goes each night?

Analyzing

5. How does Tom show his desire for independence in these scenes?
6. According to Williams's notes, the lighting focuses on Laura during the fight between Tom and Amanda in scene 3. Why do you think the playwright wished to highlight Laura?
7. Why is Malvolio the Magician's escape from a nailed coffin a trick that Tom admires?
8. Find three speeches in these scenes that require three different tones of voice. Explain how these tones should differ.

SCENES 5 AND 6

Understanding

1. What does Amanda wish for early in scene 6?
2. What announcement does Tom make in scene 6? How does Amanda react to the news?
3. What does Jim O'Connor look like, according to Tom's description? What is Jim studying?

Analyzing

4. Which of Amanda's **character** traits are revealed in her phone call to Ella Cartwright in scene 5?
5. Point out how Tom teases his mother with his announcement of the impending visit.
6. How does scene 6 serve to advance the action of the **plot?**

Extending

7. A play's humor is much more obvious on stage than in a book. What might actors and actresses do to emphasize humorous moments in scene 6?

REVIEWING: Point of View HLT
See Handbook of Literary Terms, p. 900.

Point of view is the relationship between the narrator of a story and the characters in it. Tom

Wingfield serves both as narrator of *The Glass Menagerie* and as a character within the story. This dual vantage point allows him to be both aloof and involved.

1. What is the difference in time between when Tom narrates the events in the story and their actual occurrence?
2. How would you describe the narrator's tone—*passionate, unconcerned, humorous, distanced,* or something else? Explain.
3. Why do you think that Tom makes a more appropriate choice for narrator-character than Amanda or Laura?

READING LITERATURE SKILLFULLY
Comparison/Contrast

Much of the impact of *The Glass Menagerie* is achieved through Williams's skillful use of contrast. The basic contrast in the play is between the conflicting worlds of reality and illusion. As you read, notice other contrasts— between scenes, between settings, and most of all, between and within characters—that provide dramatic tension.

1. In what ways does Amanda as a youth differ from Laura?
2. What differences do you notice between Tom as narrator and as character?
3. Which habits of Tom and Amanda irritate each other?

VOCABULARY
Context

Try to determine the meaning of each of the italicized words in the sentences below by using the context clues. If there are not enough clues, write *e*. Be sure you can pronounce and spell all the italicized words.

1. "Animals have secretions in their stomachs which enable them to digest their food without *mastication*, but human beings must chew their food before they swallow it down, and chew, chew." (a) gagging; (b) gaining weight; (c) chewing; (d) eating grass; (e) not enough clues.

2. TOM. Yesterday you *confiscated* my books! You had the nerve to _____
   AMANDA. I did. I took that horrible novel back to the library. . . . (a) removed; (b) burned; (c) hid; (d) tore up; (e) not enough clues.
3. "I didn't tell him anything about Laura. I didn't let on we had dark *ulterior* motives." (a) exterior; (b) generous; (c) good; (d) hidden; (e) not enough clues.
4. "Changes and adventure, however, were *imminent* this year. They were waiting around the corner for all these dancing kids." (a) important; (b) about to occur; (c) dangerous; (d) lucky; (e) not enough clues.

COMPOSITION ✑
Writing from a Character's Point of View

Imagine that you are Amanda Wingfield writing a journal entry of several paragraphs that contrasts her fond memories of former days as a Southern belle with her present situation. You might end with some hopeful thoughts on the future that seem in keeping with Amanda's character.

Writing a Summary

Select one scene from *The Glass Menagerie* and summarize it in several paragraphs. Make sure you include the highlights of the scene and omit unimportant details. See "Writing Notes and Summaries" in the Writer's Handbook.

Writing About Stage Directions

Williams uses lighting, curtains, and music to create mood in this play. In three or four paragraphs, explain how these conventions serve to convey atmosphere. Direct your essay to a drama class who is staging this play. See "Writing about Drama" in the Writer's Handbook.

Symbolism in *The Glass Menagerie*

The Glass Menagerie introduces an extensive pattern of symbolism that ranges from the clear-cut to the subtle. Four elements—glass, light, color, and music—are the dominant symbols and motifs, serving to reveal deeper aspects of characters and underlying themes of the play.

The menagerie of glass, Laura's collection of animal figurines, represents the fragile relationships among all the characters. The glass unicorn is most obviously a symbol of Laura—delicate, sadly different, an anomaly in the modern world. But, like Laura and like the shining perfume bottles in the lighted shop windows Tom passes, the unicorn is a beautiful object. When the unicorn is broken by Jim's clumsy but well-meant exuberance, Laura is about to be wounded by news of Jim's engagement. After her brief romantic encounter, Laura gives the unicorn—no longer unique—to Jim and retreats emotionally to her glass case. The glass motif recurs throughout the play in other forms. Laura visits the conservatory at the zoo, a glass house of tropical flowers that are as vulnerable as she is. A glass sphere that hangs from the ceiling of the Paradise Dance Hall reflects rainbow colors and represents the dreams of the dancers. Laura is spoken of as "translucent glass," while the practical and prosaic gentleman caller protests before dancing with Laura, "I'm not made out of glass."

Lighting in the play is significant for several reasons. Dim and poetic, the lighting, along with the gauze curtains, lends an unreal aura to the set, suggesting that this family functions in a world of dreams. Like the tricks Tom professes to have up his sleeve, lighting gives truth "the pleasant disguise of illusion." In another function, lighting serves to punctuate scenes by focusing on absent characters. Several times through lights we are reminded of the "fifth character" in the play, Mr. Wingfield, who appears only through a photograph. When Tom mentions Malvolio the Magician and his trick of escaping from a coffin, Mr. Wingfield's photograph lights up. Tom too will flee, like his father and the magician, beyond the temporary refuge of the fire escape. A more subtle variation of lighting is seen in the lovely, deformed candelabrum (another symbolic representation of Laura), in which Jim's giant shadow is reflected.

There are many references to color in the play, most notably blue, which is associated with Laura, and yellow, commonly linked with Amanda. Jim's nickname for Laura, Blue Roses, suggests a phenomenon that is contrary to nature. There is an opposition between these strange, different flowers ("Blue is—wrong for—roses") and the natural, gay jonquils associated with Amanda. In the original version of the play, Amanda's party dress was described as "a girlish frock of yellow voile" and the light that surrounds her as "lemony." The color comes to suggest Amanda's outgoing and optimistic attitude just as blue connotes the melancholy outlook of Laura.

Music is used throughout *The Glass Menagerie* to evoke mood and haunt memory, reinforcing the symbolism of the play. Williams once described the recurring glass menagerie theme as a tune that is light, delicate, and sad, fragile as spun glass. He added, "It is primarily Laura's music and therefore comes out most clearly when the play focuses upon her and the lovely fragility of glass which is her image."

These elements of glass, light, color, and music are drawn together in the ending scenes of the play. The final appearance of Amanda and Laura is played "as though viewed through soundproof glass." Thus the viewer, like Tom, retreats to another world, leaving the women to their fantasies. But like Tom, who is repeatedly lured back by familiar bits of music, by a piece of transparent glass, or by tiny bottles in delicate colors that suggest "bits of a shattered rainbow," we are drawn back to scenes and characters in the play, settings and people who refuse to be left behind.

Comment

Theater in America Before 1920

American theater began to develop in the middle of the eighteenth century, though most theatrical companies and themes were English imports. Early theaters in America were crude structures—a raised stage, a single curtain suspended from the ceiling, candlelight (which presented a constant fire hazard) and rough benches for the audience. Provident theatergoers brought charcoal foot warmers. In an attempt to gain approval in the eyes of those public officials who considered the theater frivolous, plays were billed as "moral dialogues" and theaters were called "opera houses" or "school houses." Theater was also legitimized by presenting it as an educational vehicle. Thus, some early American theatrical offerings included "lectures" with a single performer dispensing homely wisdom, quoting philosophers, and commenting on current social manners.

By 1800, American theater had gained respectability and a firm foothold along the Atlantic seaboard. Following the westward migration of settlers, a theatrical troupe in 1815 traveled overland from Albany to Pittsburgh and down the Ohio River to Kentucky, establishing a circuit that included Lexington, Louisville, and Frankfort. Other itinerant troupes improvised their repertoire, adopting scripts and sets to suit their numbers and the occasion. One such troupe carried a set of six all-purpose props—a garden, street, wood, palace, parlor, and kitchen—to meet a variety of scenic demands. During the first half of the nineteenth century, most theaters in the West were located on rivers easily reached by boats. (Chicago had no permanent theater until 1847.)

The 1830s introduced the idea of the showboat, or floating theater. Interrupted by the Civil War, showboating, which often staged elaborate musical productions, continued until the 1920s.

By the second half of the nineteenth century, native-born actors and actresses were beginning to enjoy international fame, with some performers developing a distinctively American acting style that was more physical and uninhibited than their English counterparts. Likewise, the subjects exploited by an ever growing number of American playwrights were often distinctly American—Eastern society, the Indian, New England witchcraft, and the outspoken Yankee. Following the leads of popular writers such as Bret Harte and Mark Twain (Unit 4), dramatists were incorporating techniques of Realism and local color into plays that depicted frontier life.

A popular form of play between the Civil War and the early 1900s was *melodrama*—exaggerated, sentimental plays in which the hero eventually triumphed over the villain. In such plays, the audience became active participants, hissing the villain and applauding his overthrow. Also popular were *minstrel shows*, consisting of musical numbers interspersed with witty banter and specialty acts, performed by white actors in blackface.

From the 1880s to the 1920s, *vaudeville* thrived, presenting variety shows that included animal acts, acrobats, singers, dancers, and actors and actresses in short skits. Vaudeville produced some of the greatest American comedians of all time—Ed Wynn, Eddie Cantor, Joe Jackson, and Jimmy Durante, to name a few. By the '20s, however, vaudeville was being supplanted by radio and movies. No longer did existing theatrical forms answer the needs of a country emerging from a world war with a changing outlook and new ideals. After a period of reassessment, new methods, forms, and techniques were introduced to create the modern American theater.

ACT TWO

SCENE 7

SCENE: *The same.*

Inner curtains closed between dining room and living room. Interiors of both rooms are dark as at beginning of play. TOM *has on the same jacket and cap as at first. Same dance-hall music as* CUE #1, *fading as* TOM *begins.*

TOM (*discovered leaning against grill on fire-escape landing, as before, and smoking*). And so the following evening I brought Jim home to dinner. I had known Jim slightly in high school. In high school, Jim was a hero. He had tremendous Irish good nature and vitality with the scrubbed and polished look of white chinaware. He seemed to move in a continual spotlight. He was a star in basketball, captain of the debating club, president of the senior class and the glee club, and he sang the male lead in the annual light opera. He was forever running or bounding, never just walking. He seemed always just at the point of defeating the law of gravity. He was shooting with such velocity through his adolescence that you would just logically expect him to arrive at nothing short of the White House by the time he was thirty. But Jim apparently ran into more interference after his graduation from high school because his speed had definitely slowed. And so, at this particular time in our lives he was holding a job that wasn't much better than mine. He was the only one at the warehouse with whom I was on friendly terms. I was valuable to Jim as someone who could remember his former glory, who had seen him win basketball games and the silver cup in debating. He knew of my secret practice of retiring to a cabinet of the washroom to work on poems whenever business was slack in the warehouse. He called me Shakespeare. And while the other boys in the warehouse regarded me with suspicious hostility, Jim took a humorous attitude toward me. Gradually his attitude began to affect the other boys and their hostility wore off. And so, after a time they began to smile at me too, as people smile at some oddly fashioned dog that trots across their path at some distance. I knew that Jim and Laura had known each other in high school because I had heard my sister Laura speak admiringly of Jim's voice. I didn't know if Jim would remember her or not. Because in high school Laura had been as unobtrusive as Jim had been astonishing. And, if he did remember Laura, it was not as my sister, for when I asked him home to dinner, he smiled and said, "You know, a funny thing, Shakespeare, I never thought of you as having folks!" Well, he was about to discover that I did . . . (MUSIC CUE #13. TOM *exits* R. *Interior living-room lights dim in.* AMANDA *is sitting on small table* R. *of daybed sewing on hem on* LAURA's *dress.* LAURA *stands facing the door* R. AMANDA *has worked like a Turk in preparation for the gentleman caller. The results are astonishing. The new floor lamp with its rose-silk shade is in place,* R. *of living room next to wall, a colored paper lantern conceals the broken light fixture in the ceiling, chintz covers are on chairs and sofa, a pair of new sofa pillows make their initial appearance.* LAURA *stands in the middle of room with lifted arms while* AMANDA *crouches before her, adjusting the hem of the new dress, devout and ritualistic. The dress is colored and designed by memory.*

Karen Allen and Joanne Woodward. Copyright © 1987 Cineplex Odeon

The arrangement of LAURA's *hair is changed; it is softer and more becoming. A fragile, unearthly prettiness has come out in* LAURA; *she is like a piece of translucent glass touched by light, given a momentary radiance, not actual, not lasting.* AMANDA, *still seated, is sewing* LAURA's *dress.* LAURA *is standing* R. *of* AMANDA.)

AMANDA. Why are you trembling so, Laura?

LAURA. Mother, you've made me so nervous!

AMANDA. Why, how have I made you nervous?

LAURA. By all this fuss! You make it seem so important.

AMANDA. I don't understand you at all, honey. Every time I try to do anything for you that's the least bit different you just seem to set yourself against it. Now take a look at yourself. (LAURA *starts for door* R.) No wait! Wait just a minute—I forgot something. (*Picks two powder puffs from daybed*)

LAURA. What is it?

AMANDA. A couple of improvements. (*Business with powder puffs*) When I was a girl we had round little lacy things like that and we called them "Gay Deceivers."

LAURA. I won't wear them!

AMANDA. Of course, you'll wear them.

LAURA. Why should I?

AMANDA. Well, to tell you the truth, honey, you're just a little bit flat-chested.

LAURA. You make it seem like we were setting a trap.

AMANDA. We are. All pretty girls are a trap and

men expect them to be traps. Now look at yourself in that glass. (LAURA *crosses* R. *Looks at mirror, invisible to audience, which is in darkness up* R. *of* R. *door*) See? You look just like an angel on a postcard. Isn't that lovely? Now you just wait. I'm going to dress myself up. You're going to be astonished at your mother's appearance. (*End of* MUSIC CUE. *End of* MUSIC CUE *leads into dance music,*[1] *which then leads in* MUSIC CUE #14, *a few lines below, at stage direction.* AMANDA *exits through curtains upstage off* L. *in dining room.* LAURA *looks in mirror for a moment. Removes "Gay Deceivers," hides them under mattress of daybed. Sits on small table* R. *of daybed for a moment, goes out to fire-escape landing, listens to dance music, until* AMANDA's *entrance.* AMANDA, *off*) I found an old dress in the trunk. But what do you know? I had to do a lot to it but it broke my heart when I had to let it out. Now, Laura, just look at your mother. Oh, no! Laura, come look at me now! (*Enters dining-room* L. *door. Comes down through living-room curtain to living room* C. MUSIC CUE #14)

LAURA (*reenters from fire-escape landing. Sits on* L. *arm of armchair*). Oh, Mother, how lovely! (AMANDA *wears a girlish frock. She carries a bunch of jonquils.*)

AMANDA (*standing* C., *holding flowers*). It used to be. It used to be. It had a lot of flowers on it, but they got awful tired so I had to take them all off. I led the cotillion in this dress years ago. I won the cakewalk twice at Sunset Hill, and I wore it to the Governor's ball in Jackson. You should have seen your mother. You should have seen your mother how she just sashayed around (*Crossing around* L. *of daybed back to* C.) the ballroom, just like that. I had it on the day I met your father. I had malaria fever, too. The change of climate from East Tennessee to the Delta—weakened my resistance. Not enough to be dangerous, just enough to make me restless and giddy. Oh, it was lovely. Invitations poured in from all over. My mother said, "You can't go any place because you have a fever. You have to stay in bed." I said I wouldn't and I took quinine and kept on going and going. Dances every evening and long rides in the country in the afternoon and picnics. That country—that country—so lovely—so lovely in May, all lacy with dogwood and simply flooded with jonquils. My mother said, "You can't bring any more jonquils in this house." I said, "I will," and I kept on bringing them in anyhow. Whenever I saw them, I said, "Wait a minute, I see jonquils," and I'd make my gentlemen callers get out of the carriage and help me gather some. To tell you the truth, Laura, it got to be a kind of a joke. "Look out," they'd say, "here comes that girl and we'll have to spend the afternoon picking jonquils." My mother said, "You can't bring any more jonquils in the house, there aren't any more vases to hold them." "That's quite all right," I said, "I can hold some myself." Malaria fever, your father and jonquils. (AMANDA *puts jonquils in* LAURA's *lap and goes out on to fire-escape landing.* MUSIC CUE #14 *stops. Thunder heard.*) I hope they get here before it starts to rain. I gave your brother a little extra change so he and Mr. O'Connor could take the service car home. (LAURA *puts flowers on armchair* R., *and crosses to door* R.)

LAURA. Mother!

AMANDA. What's the matter now? (*Reentering room*)

LAURA. What did you say his name was?

AMANDA. O'Connor. Why?

LAURA. What is his first name?

AMANDA (*crosses to armchair* R.). I don't remember——Oh, yes, I do too—it was —Jim! (*Picks up flowers*)

LAURA. Oh, Mother, not Jim O'Connor!

AMANDA. Yes, that was it, it was Jim! I've never known a Jim that wasn't nice. (*Crosses* L., *behind daybed, puts flowers in vase*)

LAURA. Are you sure his name was Jim O'Connor?

AMANDA. Why, sure I'm sure. Why?

---

1. *dance music.* Optional. Not on regular record of incidental music to the play.

LAURA. Is he the one that Tom used to know in high school?

AMANDA. He didn't say so. I think he just got to know him—(*Sits on daybed*) at the warehouse.

LAURA. There was a Jim O'Connor we both knew in high school. If that is the one that Tom is bringing home to dinner——Oh, Mother, you'd have to excuse me, I wouldn't come to the table!

AMANDA. What's this now? What sort of silly talk is this?

LAURA. You asked me once if I'd ever liked a boy. Don't you remember I showed you this boy's picture?

AMANDA. You mean the boy in the yearbook?

LAURA. Yes, that boy.

AMANDA. Laura, Laura, were you in love with that boy?

LAURA (*crosses to* R. *of armchair*). I don't know, Mother. All I know is that I couldn't sit at the table if it was him.

AMANDA (*rises, crosses* L. *and walks up* L. *of daybed*). It won't be him! It isn't the least bit likely. But whether it is or not, you will come to the table—you will not be excused.

LAURA. I'll have to be, Mother.

AMANDA (*behind daybed*). I don't intend to humor your silliness, Laura, I've had too much from you and your brother, both. So just sit down and compose yourself till they come. Tom has forgotten his key, so you'll *have* to let them in when they arrive.

LAURA. Oh, Mother—*you* answer the door! (*Sits chair* R.)

AMANDA. How can I when I haven't even finished making the mayonnaise dressing for the salmon?

LAURA. Oh, Mother, please answer the door, don't make me do it! (*Thunder heard offstage*)

AMANDA. Honey, do be reasonable! What's all this fuss about—just one gentleman caller—that's all—just one! (*Exits through living-room curtains.* TOM *and* JIM *enter alley* R., *climb fire-escape steps to landing and wait outside of closed door. Hearing them approach,* LAURA *rises with a panicky gesture. She retreats to living-room curtains. The doorbell rings.* LAURA *catches her breath and touches her throat. More thunder heard offstage*)

AMANDA (*offstage*). Laura, sweetheart, the door!

LAURA. Mother, please, you go to the door! (*Starts for door* R., *then back*)

AMANDA (*offstage, in a fierce whisper*). What is the matter with you, you silly thing? (*Enters through living-room curtains, and stands by daybed*)

LAURA. Please you answer it, please.

AMANDA. Why have you chosen this moment to lose your mind? You go to that door.

LAURA. I can't.

AMANDA. Why can't you?

LAURA. Because I'm sick! (*Crosses to* L. *end of daybed and sits*)

AMANDA. You're sick! Am I sick? You and your brother have me puzzled to death. You can never act like normal children. Will you give me one good reason why you should be afraid to open a door? You go to that door. Laura Wingfield, you march straight to that door!

LAURA (*crosses to door* R.). Yes, Mother.

AMANDA (*stopping* LAURA). I've got to put courage in you, honey, for living. (*Exits through living-room curtains, and exits* R. *into kitchen.* LAURA *opens door.* TOM *and* JIM *enter.* LAURA *remains hidden in hall behind door.*)

TOM. Laura—(LAURA *crosses* C.) this is Jim. Jim, this is my sister Laura.

JIM. I didn't know that Shakespeare had a sister! How are you, Laura?

LAURA (*retreating stiff and trembling. Shakes hands*). How—how do you do?

JIM. Well, I'm okay! Your hand's *cold*, Laura! (TOM *puts hats on phone table.*)

LAURA. Yes, well—I've been playing the Victrola. . . .

JIM. Must have been playing classical music on it. You ought to play a little hot swing music to warm you up. (LAURA *crosses to phonograph.* TOM *crosses up to* LAURA. LAURA *starts phonograph[2]—looks at* JIM. *Exits through living-*

---

2. *LAURA starts phonograph.* A worn record of "Dardanella" or some other popular tune of the 1920s.

room curtains and goes off L.

JIM. What's the matter?

TOM. Oh—Laura? Laura is—is terribly shy. *(Crosses and sits on daybed)*

JIM *(crosses down* C.). Shy, huh? Do you know it's unusual to meet a shy girl nowadays? I don't believe you ever mentioned you had a sister?

TOM. Well, now you know I have one. You want a piece of the paper?

JIM *(crosses to* TOM). Uh-huh.

TOM. Comics?

JIM. Comics? Sports! *(Takes paper. Crosses, sits chair* R.) I see that Dizzy Dean[3] is on his bad behavior.

TOM *(starts to door* R. *Goes out).* Really?

JIM. Yeah. Where are *you* going? *(As* TOM *reaches steps* R. *of fire-escape landing)*

TOM *(calling from fire-escape landing).* Out on the terrace to smoke.

JIM *(rises, leaving newspaper in armchair, goes over to turn off Victrola. Crosses* R. *Exits to fire-escape landing).* You know, Shakespeare—I'm going to sell you a bill of goods!

TOM. What goods?

JIM. A course I'm taking.

TOM. What course?

JIM. A course in public speaking! You know you and me, we're not the warehouse type.

TOM. Thanks—that's good news. What has public speaking got to do with it?

JIM. It fits you for—executive positions!

TOM. Oh.

JIM. I tell you it's done a helluva lot for me.

TOM. In what respect?

JIM. In all respects. Ask yourself: what's the difference between you and me and the guys in the office down front? Brains?—No!—Ability?—No! Then what? Primarily, it amounts to just one single thing——

TOM. What is that one thing?

JIM. Social poise! The ability to square up to somebody and hold your own on any social level!

AMANDA *(offstage).* Tom?

TOM. Yes, Mother?

AMANDA. Is that you and Mr. O'Connor?

TOM. Yes, Mother.

AMANDA. Make yourselves comfortable.

TOM. We will.

AMANDA. Ask Mr. O'Connor if he would like to wash his hands?

JIM. No, thanks, ma'am—I took care of that down at the warehouse. Tom?

TOM. Huh?

JIM. Mr. Mendoza was speaking to me about you.

TOM. Favorably?

JIM. What do you think?

TOM. Well——

JIM. You're going to be out of a job if you don't wake up.

TOM. I'm waking up——

JIM. Yeah, but you show no signs.

TOM. The signs are interior. I'm just about to make a change. I'm right at the point of committing myself to a future that doesn't include the warehouse or Mr. Mendoza, or even a night school course in public speaking.

JIM. Now what are you gassing about?

TOM. I'm tired of the movies.

JIM. The movies!

TOM. Yes, movies! Look at them. *(He waves his hands.)* All of those glamorous people—having adventures—hogging it all, gobbling the whole thing up! You know what happens? People go to the *movies* instead of *moving.* Hollywood characters are supposed to have all the adventures for everybody in America, while everybody in America sits in a dark room and watches them having it! Yes, until there's a war. That's when adventure becomes available to the masses! Everyone's dish, not only Gable's! Then the people in the dark room come out of the dark room to have some adventures themselves—goody—goody! It's our turn now to go to the South Sea Island—to make a safari—to be exotic, far off! . . . But I'm not patient. I don't want to wait till then. I'm tired of the movies and I'm about to move!

JIM *(incredulously).* Move?

---

3. *Dizzy Dean,* a famous baseball pitcher, noted for eccentricity.

TOM. Yes.

JIM. When?

TOM. Soon!

JIM. Where? Where?

TOM. I'm starting to boil inside. I know I seem dreamy, but inside—well, I'm boiling! Whenever I pick up a shoe I shudder a little, thinking how short life is and what I am doing!—Whatever that means, I know it doesn't mean shoes—except as something to wear on a traveler's feet! (*Gets card from inside coat pocket*) Look!

JIM. What?

TOM. I'm a member.

JIM (*reading*). The Union of Merchant Seamen.

TOM. I paid my dues this month, instead of the electric light bill.

JIM. You'll regret it when they turn off the lights.

TOM. I won't be here.

JIM. Yeah, but how about your mother?

TOM. I'm like my father. The bastard son of a bastard. See how he grins? And he's been absent going on sixteen years.

JIM. You're just talking, you drip. How does your mother feel about it?

TOM. Sh! Here comes Mother! Mother's not acquainted with my plans!

AMANDA (*offstage*). Tom!

TOM. Yes, Mother?

AMANDA (*offstage*). Where are you all?

TOM. On the terrace, Mother.

AMANDA (*enters through living-room curtain and stands* C.). Why don't you come in? (*They start inside. She advances to them.* TOM *is distinctly shocked at her appearance. Even* JIM *blinks a little. He is making his first contact with girlish Southern vivacity and in spite of the night-school course in public speaking is somewhat thrown off the beam by the unexpected outlay of social charm. Certain responses are attempted by* JIM *but are swept aside by* AMANDA's *gay laughter and chatter.* TOM *is embarrassed but after the first shock* JIM *reacts very warmly. Grins and chuckles, is altogether won over.* TOM *and* JIM *come in, leaving door open.*)

TOM. Mother, you look so pretty.

AMANDA. You know, that's the first compliment you ever paid me. I wish you'd look pleasant when you're about to say something pleasant, so I could expect it. Mr. O'Connor? (JIM *crosses to* AMANDA.)

JIM. How do you do?

AMANDA. Well, well, well, so this is Mr. O'Connor? Introduction's entirely unnecessary. I've heard so much about you from my boy. I finally said to him, "Tom, good gracious, why don't you bring this paragon to supper finally? I'd like to meet this nice young man at the warehouse! Instead of just hearing you sing his praises so much?" I don't know why my son is so standoffish—that's not Southern behavior. Let's sit down. (TOM *closes door, crosses* U.R., *stands.* JIM *and* AMANDA *sit on daybed,* JIM, R., AMANDA, L.) Let's sit down, and I think we could stand a little more air in here. Tom, leave the door open. I felt a nice fresh breeze a moment ago. Where has it gone to? Mmmm, so warm already! And not quite summer, even. We're going to burn up when summer really gets started. However, we're having—we're having a very light supper. I think light things are better fo' —for this time of year. The same as light clothes are. Light clothes and light food are what warm weather calls fo'. You know our blood gets so thick during th' winter—it takes a while fo' us to adjust ourselves—when the season changes. . . . It's come so quick this year. I wasn't prepared. All of a sudden—Heavens! Already summer!—I ran to the trunk an'—pulled out this light dress—terribly old! Historical almost! But feels so good—so good and cool, why, y' know——

TOM. Mother, how about our supper?

AMANDA (*rises, crosses* R. *to* TOM). Honey, you go ask sister if supper is ready! You know that sister is in full charge of supper. Tell her you hungry boys are waiting for it. (TOM *exits through curtains and off* L. AMANDA *turns to* JIM.) Have you met Laura?

JIM. Well, she came to the door.

AMANDA. She let you in?

JIM. Yes, ma'am.

AMANDA (*crossing to armchair and sitting*). She's very pretty.

JIM. Oh, yes ma'am.

AMANDA. It's rare for a girl as sweet an' pretty as Laura to be domestic! But Laura is, thank heavens, not only pretty but also very domestic. I'm not at all. I never was a bit. I never could make a thing but angel-food cake. Well, in the South we had so many servants. Gone, gone, gone. All vestige of gracious living! Gone completely! I wasn't prepared for what the future brought me. All of my gentlemen callers were sons of planters and so, of course, I assumed that I would be married to one and raise my family on a large piece of land with plenty of servants. But man proposes—and woman accepts the proposal!—To vary that old, old saying a little bit—I married no planter! I married a man who worked for the telephone company!—That gallantly smiling gentleman over there! (*Points to picture*) A telephone man who—fell in love with long-distance!—Now he travels and I don't even know where!—But what am I going on for about my—tribulations? Tell me yours—I hope you don't have any! Tom?

TOM (*reenters through living-room curtains from off* L.). Yes, Mother.

AMANDA. What about that supper?

TOM. Why, supper is on the table. (*Inner curtains between living room and dining room open. Lights dim up in dining room, dim out in living room.*)

AMANDA. Oh, so it is. (*Rises, crosses up to table* C. *in dining room and chair* C.) How lovely. Where is Laura?

TOM (*going to chair* L. *and standing*). Laura is not feeling too well and thinks maybe she'd better not come to the table.

AMANDA. Laura!

LAURA (*offstage. Faintly*). Yes, Mother? (TOM *gestures re:* JIM.)

AMANDA. Mr. O'Connor. (JIM *crosses up* L. *to table and to chair* L. *and stands.*)

JIM. Thank you, ma'am.

AMANDA. Laura, we can't say grace till you come to the table.

LAURA (*enters* U.L., *obviously quite faint, lips trembling, eyes wide and staring. Moves unsteadily toward dining-room table*). Oh, Mother, I'm so sorry. (TOM *catches her as she feels faint. He takes her to daybed in living room.*)

AMANDA (*as* LAURA *lies down*). Why, Laura, you are sick, darling! Laura—rest on the sofa. Well! (*To* JIM) Standing over the hot stove made her ill!—I told her that it was just too warm this evening, but——(*To* TOM) Is Laura all right now?

TOM. She's better, Mother. (*Sits chair* L. *in dining room. Thunder offstage*)

AMANDA (*returning to dining room and sitting at table, as* JIM *does*). My goodness, I suppose we're going to have a little rain! Tom, you say grace.

TOM. What?

AMANDA. What do we generally do before we have something to eat? We say grace, don't we?

TOM. For these and all Thy mercies—God's Holy Name be praised. (*Lights dim out.* MUSIC CUE #15)

SCENE 8

SCENE: *The same. A half-hour later. Dinner is coming to an end in dining room.*

AMANDA, TOM, *and* JIM *sitting at table as at end of last scene. Lights dim up in both rooms, and* MUSIC CUE #15 *ends.*

AMANDA (*laughing, as* JIM *laughs too*). You know, Mr. O'Connor, I haven't had such a pleasant evening in a very long time.

JIM (*rises*). Well, Mrs. Wingfield, let me give you a toast. Here's to the old South.

AMANDA. The old South. (*Blackout in both rooms*)

JIM. Hey, Mr. Light Bulb!

AMANDA. Where was Moses when the lights went out? Do you know the answer to that one, Mr. O'Connor?

JIM. No, ma'am, what's the answer to that one?

AMANDA. Well, I heard one answer, but it wasn't very nice. I thought you might know another one.

JIM. No, ma'am.

AMANDA. It's lucky I put those candles on the table. I just put them on for ornamentation, but it's nice when they prove useful, too.

JIM. Yes, ma'am.

AMANDA. Now, if one of you gentlemen can provide me with a match, we can have some illumination.

JIM (*lighting candles. Dim in glow for candles*). I can, ma'am.

AMANDA. Thank you.

JIM (*crosses back to* R. *of dining-room table*). Not at all, ma'am.

AMANDA. I guess it must be a burnt-out fuse. Mr. O'Connor, do you know anything about a burnt-out fuse?

JIM. I know a little about them, ma'am, but where's the fuse box?

AMANDA. Must you know that, too? Well it's in the kitchen. (JIM *exits* R. *into kitchen.*) Be careful. It's dark. Don't stumble over anything. (*Sound of crash offstage*) Oh, my goodness, wouldn't it be awful if we lost him! Are you all right, Mr. O'Connor?

JIM (*offstage*). Yes, ma'am, I'm all right.

AMANDA. You know, electricity is a very mysterious thing. The whole universe is mysterious to me. Wasn't it Benjamin Franklin who tied a key to a kite? I'd like to have seen that—he might have looked mighty silly. Some people say that science clears up all the mysteries for us. In my opinion they just keep on adding more. Haven't you found it yet?

JIM (*reenters* R.). Yes, ma'am. I found it all right, but them fuses look okay to me. (*Sits as before*)

AMANDA. Tom.

TOM. Yes, Mother?

AMANDA. That light bill I gave you several days ago. The one I got the notice about?

TOM. Oh—yeah. You mean last month's bill?

AMANDA. You didn't neglect it by any chance?

TOM. Well, I——

AMANDA. You did! I might have known it!

JIM. Oh, maybe Shakespeare wrote a poem on that light bill, Mrs. Wingfield?

AMANDA. Maybe he did, too. I might have known better than to trust him with it! There's such a high price for negligence in this world today.

JIM. Maybe the poem will win a ten-dollar prize.

AMANDA. We'll just have to spend the rest of the evening in the nineteenth century, before Mr. Edison found that Mazda lamp!

JIM. Candlelight is my favorite kind of light.

AMANDA. That shows you're romantic! But that's no excuse for Tom. However, I think it was very nice of them to let us finish our dinner before they plunged us into everlasting darkness. Tom, as a penalty for your carelessness you can help me with the dishes.

JIM (*rising.* TOM *rises*). Can I be of some help, ma'am?

AMANDA (*rising*). Oh, no, I couldn't allow that.

JIM. Well, I ought to be good for *something*.

AMANDA. What did I hear?

JIM. I just said, "I ought to be good for something."

AMANDA. That's what I thought you said. Well, Laura's all by her lonesome out front. Maybe you'd like to keep her company. I can give you this lovely old candelabrum for light. (JIM *takes candles*.) It used to be on the altar at the Church of the Heavenly Rest, but it was melted a little out of shape when the church burnt down. The church was struck by lightning one spring, and Gypsy Jones who was holding a revival meeting in the village, said that the church was struck by lightning because the Episcopalians had started to have card parties right in the church.

JIM. Is that so, ma'am?

AMANDA. I never say anything that isn't so.

JIM. I beg your pardon.

AMANDA (*pouring wine into glass—hands it to* JIM). I'd like Laura to have a little dandelion wine. Do you think you can hold them both?

JIM. I can try, ma'am.

AMANDA (*exits* U.R. *into kitchen*). Now, Tom, you get into your apron.

TOM. Yes, Mother. (*Follows* AMANDA. JIM *looks around, puts wineglass down, takes swig from wine decanter, replaces it with thud, takes wine-*

glass—enters living room. Inner curtains close as dining room dims out. LAURA *sits up nervously as* JIM *enters. Her speech at first is low and breathless from the almost intolerable strain of being alone with a stranger. In her speeches in this scene, before* JIM's *warmth overcomes her paralyzing shyness,* LAURA's *voice is thin and breathless as though she has just run up a steep flight of stairs.*)

JIM (*entering holding candelabrum with lighted candles in one hand and glass of wine in other, and stands*). How are you feeling now? Any better? (JIM's *attitude is gently humorous. In playing this scene it should be stressed that while the incident is apparently unimportant, it is to* LAURA *the climax of her secret life.*)

LAURA. Yes, thank you.

JIM (*gives her glass of wine*). Oh, here, this is for you. It's a little dandelion wine.

LAURA. Thank you.

JIM (*crosses* C.). Well, drink it—but don't get drunk. (*He laughs heartily.*) Say, where'll I put the candles?

LAURA. Oh, anywhere . . .

JIM. Oh, how about right here on the floor? You got any objections?

LAURA. No.

JIM. I'll spread a newspaper under it to catch the drippings. (*Gets newspaper from armchair. Puts candelabrum down on floor* C.) I like to sit on the floor. (*Sits on floor*) Mind if I do?

LAURA. Oh, no.

JIM. Would you give me a pillow?

LAURA. What?

JIM. A pillow!

LAURA. Oh . . . (*Puts wineglass on telephone table, hands him pillow, sits* L. *on daybed*)

JIM. How about you? Don't you like to sit on the floor?

LAURA. Oh, yes.

JIM. Well, why don't you?

LAURA. I—will.

JIM. Take a pillow! (*Throws pillow as she sits on floor*) I can't see you sitting way over there. (*Sits on floor again*)

LAURA. I can—see you.

JIM. Yeah, but that's not fair. I'm right here in the limelight. (LAURA *moves a little closer to him.*) Good! Now I can see you! Are you comfortable?

LAURA. Yes. Thank you.

JIM. So am I. I'm comfortable as a cow! Say, would you care for a piece of chewing gum? (*Offers gum*)

LAURA. No, thank you.

JIM. I think that I will indulge. (*Musingly unwraps it and holds it up*) Gee, think of the fortune made by the guy that invented the first piece of chewing gum! It's amazing, huh? Do you know that the Wrigley Building is one of the sights of Chicago?—I saw it summer before last at the Century of Progress.[4] Did you take in the Century of Progress?

LAURA. No, I didn't.

JIM. Well, it was a wonderful exposition, believe me. You know what impressed me most? The Hall of Science. Gives you an idea of what the future will be like in America. Oh, it's more wonderful than the present time is! Say, your brother tells me you're shy. Is that right, Laura?

LAURA. I—don't know.

JIM. I judge you to be an old-fashioned type of girl. Oh, I think that's a wonderful type to be. I hope you don't think I'm being too personal—do you?

LAURA. Mr. O'Connor?

JIM. Huh?

LAURA. I believe I *will* take a piece of gum, if you don't mind. (JIM *peels gum—gets on knees, hands it to* LAURA. *She breaks off a tiny piece.* JIM *looks at what remains, puts it in his mouth, and sits again.*) Mr. O'Connor, have you—kept up with your singing?

JIM. Singing? Me?

LAURA. Yes. I remember what a beautiful voice you had.

JIM. You heard me sing?

---

4. **Century of Progress,** the world's fair held in Chicago in 1933–1934.

LAURA. Oh, yes! Very often. . . . I—don't suppose—you remember me—at all?

JIM (*smiling doubtfully*). You know, as a matter of fact I did have an idea I'd seen you before. Do you know it seemed almost like I was about to remember your name. But the name I was about to remember—wasn't a name! So I stopped myself before I said it.

LAURA. Wasn't it—Blue Roses?

JIM (*grinning*). Blue Roses! Oh, my gosh, yes—Blue Roses! You know, I didn't connect you with high school somehow or other. But that's where it was, it was high school. Gosh, I didn't even know you were Shakespeare's sister! Gee, I'm sorry.

LAURA. I didn't expect you to.—You barely knew me!

JIM. But, we did have a speaking acquaintance.

LAURA. Yes, we—spoke to each other.

JIM. Say, didn't we have a class in something together?

LAURA. Yes, we did.

JIM. What class was that?

LAURA. It was—singing—chorus!

JIM. Aw!

LAURA. I sat across the aisle from you in the auditorium Mondays, Wednesdays, and Fridays.

JIM. Oh, yeah! I remember now—you're the one who always came in late.

LAURA. Yes, it was so hard for me, getting upstairs. I had that brace on my leg then—it clumped so loud!

JIM. I never heard any clumping.

LAURA (*wincing at recollection*). To me it sounded like—thunder!

JIM. I never even noticed.

LAURA. Everybody was seated before I came in. I had to walk in front of all those people. My seat was in the back row. I had to go clumping up the aisle with everyone watching!

JIM. Oh, gee, you shouldn't have been self-conscious.

LAURA. I know, but I was. It was always such a relief when the singing started.

JIM. I remember now. And I used to call you Blue Roses. How did I ever get started calling you a name like that?

LAURA. I was out of school a little while with pleurosis. When I came back, you asked me what was the matter. I said I had pleurosis and you thought I said Blue Roses. So that's what you always called me after that!

JIM. I hope you didn't mind?

LAURA. Oh, no—I liked it. You see, I wasn't acquainted with many—people . . .

JIM. Yeah. I remember you sort of stuck by yourself.

LAURA. I never did have much luck at making friends.

JIM. Well, I don't see why you wouldn't.

LAURA. Well, I started out badly.

JIM. You mean being——?

LAURA. Well, yes, it—sort of—stood between me . . .

JIM. You shouldn't have let it!

LAURA. I know, but it did, and I——

JIM. You mean you were shy with people!

LAURA. I tried not to be but never could——

JIM. Overcome it?

LAURA. No, I—never could!

JIM. Yeah. I guess being shy is something you have to work out of kind of gradually.

LAURA. Yes—I guess it——

JIM. Takes time!

LAURA. Yes . . .

JIM. Say, you know something, Laura? (*Rises to sit on daybed* R.) People are not so dreadful when you know them. That's what you have to remember! And everybody has problems, not just you but practically everybody has problems. You think of yourself as being the only one who is disappointed. But just look around you and what do you see—a lot of people just as disappointed as you are. You take me, for instance. Boy, when I left high school, I thought I'd be a lot further along at this time than I am now. Say, you remember that wonderful write-up I had in *The Torch?*

LAURA. Yes, I do! (*She gets yearbook from under pillow* L. *of daybed.*)

James Naughton and Karen Allen. Copyright © 1987 Cineplex Odeon

JIM. Said I was bound to succeed in anything I went into! Holy Jeez! *The Torch!* (*She opens book, shows it to him, and sits next to him on daybed.*)

LAURA. Here you are in *The Pirates of Penzance!*

JIM. *The Pirates!* "Oh, better far to live and die under the brave black flag I fly!" I sang the lead in that operetta.

LAURA. So beautifully!

JIM. Aw . . .

LAURA. Yes, yes—beautifully—beautifully!

JIM. You heard me then, huh?

LAURA. I heard you all three times!

JIM. No!

LAURA. Yes.

JIM. You mean all three performances?

LAURA. Yes!

JIM. What for?

LAURA. I—wanted to ask you to—autograph my program. (*Takes program from book*)

JIM. Why didn't you ask me?

LAURA. You were always surrounded by your own friends so much that I never had a chance.

JIM. Aw, you should have just come right up and said, "Here is my——"

LAURA. Well, I—thought you might think I was——

JIM. Thought I might think you was—what?

LAURA. Oh——

JIM (*with reflective relish*). Oh! Yeah, I was beleaguered by females in those days.

LAURA. You were terribly popular!

JIM. Yeah . . .

LAURA. You had such a—friendly way——

JIM. Oh, I was spoiled in high school.

LAURA. Everybody liked you!

JIM. Including you?

LAURA. I—why, yes, I—I did, too. . . .

JIM. Give me that program, Laura. (*She does so, and he signs it.*) There you are—better later than never!

LAURA. My—what a—surprise!

JIM. My signature's not worth very much right now. But maybe some day—it will increase in value! You know, being disappointed is one thing and being discouraged is something else. Well, I may be disappointed but I am not discouraged. Say, you finished high school?

LAURA. I made bad grades in my final examinations.

JIM. You mean you dropped out?

LAURA (*rises*). I didn't go back. (*Crosses* R. *to menagerie.* JIM *lights cigarette still sitting on daybed.* LAURA *puts yearbook under menagerie. Rises, picks up unicorn—small glass object—her back to* JIM. *When she touches unicorn,* MUSIC CUE #16-A) How is Emily Meisenbach getting along?

JIM. That kraut-head!

LAURA. Why do you call her that?

JIM. Because that's what she was.

LAURA. You're not still—going with her?

JIM. Oh, I never even see her.

LAURA. It said in the Personal section that you were—engaged!

JIM. Uh-huh. I know, but I wasn't impressed by that—propaganda!

LAURA. It wasn't the truth?

JIM. It was only true in Emily's optimistic opinion!

LAURA. Oh . . . (*Turns* R. *of* JIM. JIM *lights a cigarette and leans indolently back on his elbows, smiling at* LAURA *with a warmth and charm which lights her inwardly with altar candles. She remains by the glass menagerie table and turns in her hands a piece of glass to cover her tumult. Cut* MUSIC CUE #16-A.)

JIM. What have you done since high school?

Huh?

LAURA. What?

JIM. I said what have you done since high school?

LAURA. Nothing much.

JIM. You must have been doing something all this time.

LAURA. Yes.

JIM. Well, then, such as what?

LAURA. I took a business course at business college . . .

JIM. You did? How did that work out?

LAURA (*turns back to* JIM). Well, not very —well. . . . I had to drop out, it gave me—indigestion. . . .

JIM (*laughs gently*). What are you doing now?

LAURA. I don't do anything—much. . . . Oh, please don't think I sit around doing nothing! My glass collection takes a good deal of time. Glass is something you have to take good care of.

JIM. What did you say—about glass?

LAURA (*she clears her throat and turns away again, acutely shy*). Collection, I said—I have one.

JIM (*puts out cigarette. Abruptly*). Say! You know what I judge to be the trouble with you? (*Rises from daybed and crosses* R.) Inferiority complex! You know what that is? That's what they call it when a fellow low-rates himself! Oh, I understand it because I had it, too. Uh-huh! Only my case was not as aggravated as yours seems to be. I had it until I took up public speaking and developed my voice, and learned that I had an aptitude for science. Do you know that until that time I never thought of myself as being outstanding in any way whatsoever!

LAURA. Oh, my!

JIM. Now I've never made a regular study of it—(*Sits armchair* R.) mind you, but I have a friend who says I can analyze people better than doctors that make a profession of it. I don't claim that's necessarily true, but I can sure guess a person's psychology. Excuse me, Laura. (*Takes out gum*) I always take it out when the flavor is gone. I'll just wrap it in a piece of paper. (*Tears a piece of paper off the newspaper under candelabrum, wraps gum in it, crosses to daybed, looks to see if* LAURA *is watching. She isn't. Crosses around daybed)* I know how it is when you get it stuck on a shoe. *(Throws gum under daybed, crosses around L. of daybed. Crosses R. to* LAURA*)* Yep—that's what I judge to be your principal trouble. A lack of confidence in yourself as a person. Now I'm basing that fact on a number of your remarks and on certain observations I've made. For instance, that clumping you thought was so awful in high school. You say that you dreaded to go upstairs? You see what you did? You dropped out of school, you gave up an education all because of a little clump, which as far as I can see is practically nonexistent! Oh, a little physical defect is all you have. It's hardly noticeable even! Magnified a thousand times by your imagination! You know what my strong advice to you is? You've got to think of yourself as *superior* in some way! *(Crosses L. to small table R. of daybed. Sits.* LAURA *sits in armchair.)*

LAURA. In what way would I think?

JIM. Why, man alive, Laura! Look around you a little and what do you see? A world full of common people! All of 'em born and all of 'em going to die! Now, which of them has one-tenth of your strong points! Or mine! Or anybody else's for that matter? You see, everybody excels in some one thing. Well—some in many! You take me, for instance. My interest happens to lie in electrodynamics. I'm taking a course in radio engineering at night school on top of a fairly responsible job at the warehouse. I'm taking that course *and* studying public speaking.

LAURA. Ohhh. My!

JIM. Because I believe in the future of television! I want to be ready to go right up along with it. *(Rises, crosses R.)* I'm planning to get in on the ground floor. Oh, I've already made the right connections. All that remains now is for the industry itself to get under way— full steam! You know, *knowledge*—ZSZZppp! *Money*—Zzzzzzpp! *POWER!* Wham! That's the cycle democracy is built on! *(Pause)* I guess you think I think a lot of myself!

LAURA. No—o-o-o, I don't.

JIM *(kneels at armchair R.).* Well, now how about you? Isn't there some one thing that you take more interest in than anything else?

LAURA. Oh—yes . . .

JIM. Well, then, such as what?

LAURA. Well, I do—as I said—have my—glass collection . . . (MUSIC CUE #16-A)

JIM. Oh, you do. What kind of glass is it?

LAURA *(takes glass ornament off shelf).* Little articles of it, ornaments mostly. Most of them are little animals made out of glass, the tiniest little animals in the world. Mother calls them the glass menagerie! Here's an example of one, if you'd like to see it! This is one of the oldest, it's nearly thirteen. *(Hands it to* JIM*)* Oh, be careful—if you breathe, it breaks! (THE BELL SOLO SHOULD BEGIN HERE. *This is last part of* MUSIC CUE #16-A *and should play to end of record.)*

JIM. I'd better not take it. I'm pretty clumsy with things.

LAURA. Go on, I trust you with him! *(*JIM *takes horse.)* There—you're holding him gently! Hold him over the light, he loves the light! *(*JIM *holds horse up to light.)* See how the light shines through him?

JIM. It sure does shine!

LAURA. I shouldn't be partial, but he is my favorite one.

JIM. Say, what kind of a thing is this one supposed to be?

LAURA. Haven't you noticed the single horn on his forehead?

JIM. Oh, a unicorn, huh?

LAURA. Mmmm-hmmmm!

JIM. Unicorns, aren't they extinct in the modern world?

LAURA. I know!

JIM. Poor little fellow must feel kind of lonesome.

LAURA. Well, if he does, he doesn't complain about it. He stays on a shelf with some horses that don't have horns and they all seem to get along nicely together.

JIM. They do. Say, where will I put him?

LAURA. Put him on the table. *(*JIM *crosses to small*

You needn't be performing in the theater to *steal a scene, prompt someone, appear in the limelight,* or *play to the gallery.* These terms, originating from the theater, serve to describe situations in our everyday life. *Limelight,* for example, once referred to an intense white light produced by lighting the compound lime and used to draw attention to people on stage. Today, anyone in the limelight is the center of attention. During Shakespeare's time and later, inexpensive theater seating could be purchased in the gallery—the very top of the balcony. Thus, those who "played to the gallery" appealed to the low, uncritical tastes of the poor and the rowdy. Today any such base appeal is considered "playing to the gallery."

The word *stage* itself has spawned many compounds: *stage-struck* (very interested in acting), *stage fright* (fear of appearing before an audience), *stage whisper* (a loud whisper), and *upstage* (to draw attention away from someone else), to name a few. Many common slang words are theater bred: the *heavy* (villain in a play), *mug* (to overact), *ham* (bad actor, someone who acts in an exaggerated manner), *scalper* (one who buys and sells theater tickets for profit).

Slapstick originally referred to drama in which characters achieved humorous effects by hitting somebody with two boards or sticks that slapped together loudly. Some silent movies relied on pie-in-the-face slapstick for humor. Today the term refers not only to dramatic comedy but to any horseplay designed to achieve humorous effect.

Broadway, an avenue in the major theater district of New York City, has come to refer to the commercial theater in general. *Off-Broadway* refers to an area outside of the official theater district in which smaller theatrical presentations appear, often in storefronts, basements, or churches. By the same process of metonymy, *the theater,* which once represented a building, now connotes the entire theatrical world. Thus, we speak of famous people in the theater or of recent developments in American theater.

Melodrama, which in the nineteenth century referred to plays in which the characters were stereotypically good or bad, the tone sentimental, and justice eventually triumphant, now refers to any overly emotional writing, speech, or actions. (See picture.)

Many other theatrical expressions have entered our everyday speech, adding color and vividness to our language. The following expressions describe commonplace activities or situations: *standing in the wings, taking a curtain call, missing a cue,* and *bringing down the house.* As the century draws to a close, theater language will continue to move beyond "center stage" to influence American English.

table R. *of daybed, puts unicorn on it.*) They all like a change of scenery once in a while!

JIM (C., *facing upstage, stretching arms*). They do. (MUSIC CUE #16-B: *Dance Music*) Hey! Look how big my shadow is when I stretch.

LAURA (*crossing to* L. *of daybed*). Oh, oh, yes—it stretched across the ceiling!

JIM (*crosses to door* R., *exits, leaving door open, and stands on fire-escape landing. Sings to music. [Popular record of day for dance hall.] When* JIM *opens door, music swells*). It's stopped raining. Where does the music come from?

LAURA. From the Paradise Dance Hall across the alley.

JIM (*reentering room, closing door* R., *crosses to* LAURA). How about cutting the rug a little, Miss Wingfield? Or is your program filled up? Let me take a look at it. (*Crosses back* C. *Music, in dance hall, goes into a waltz. Business here with imaginary dance-program card*) Oh, say! Every dance is taken! I'll just scratch some of them out. Ahhhh, a waltz! (*Crosses to* LAURA)

LAURA. I—can't dance!

JIM. There you go with that inferiority stuff!

LAURA. I've never danced in my life!

JIM. Come on, try!

LAURA. Oh, but I'd step on you!

JIM. Well, I'm not made out of glass.

LAURA. How—how do we start?

JIM. You hold your arms out a little.

LAURA. Like this?

JIM. A little bit higher. (*Takes* LAURA *in arms*) That's right. Now don't tighten up, that's the principal thing about it—just relax.

LAURA. It's hard not to.

JIM. Okay.

LAURA. I'm afraid you can't budge me.

JIM (*dances around* L. *of daybed slowly*). What do you bet I can't?

LAURA. Goodness, yes, you can!

JIM. Let yourself go, now, Laura, just let yourself go.

LAURA. I'm——

JIM. Come on!

LAURA. Trying!

JIM. Not so stiff now—easy does it!

LAURA. I know, but I'm——!

JIM. Come on! Loosen your backbone a little! (*When they get to upstage corner of daybed—so that the audience will not see him lift her—*JIM's *arm tightens around her waist and he swings her around* C. *with her feet off floor about 3 complete turns before they hit the small table* R. *of daybed. Music swells as* JIM *lifts her.*)There we go! (JIM *knocks glass horse off table. Music fades.*)

LAURA. Oh, it doesn't matter——

JIM (*picks horse up*). We knocked the little glass horse over.

LAURA. Yes.

JIM (*hands unicorn to* LAURA). Is he broken?

LAURA. Now he's just like all the other horses.

JIM. You mean he lost his——?

LAURA. He's lost his horn. It doesn't matter. Maybe it's a blessing in disguise.

JIM. Gee, I bet you'll never forgive me. I bet that was your favorite piece of glass.

LAURA. Oh, I don't have favorites—(*Pause*) much. It's no tragedy. Glass breaks so easily. No matter how careful you are. The traffic jars the shelves and things fall off them.

JIM. Still I'm awfully sorry that I was the cause of it.

LAURA. I'll just imagine he had an operation. The horn was removed to make him feel less—freakish! (*Crosses* L., *sits on small table*) Now he will feel more at home with the other horses, the ones who don't have horns. . . .

JIM (*sits on arm of armchair* R., *faces* LAURA). I'm glad to see that you have a sense of humor. You know—you're—different than anybody else I know? (MUSIC CUE #17) Do you mind me telling you that? I mean it. You make me feel sort of—I don't know how to say it! I'm usually pretty good at expressing things, but—this is something I don't know how to say! Did anybody ever tell you that you were pretty? (*Rises, crosses to* LAURA) Well, you are! And in a different way from anyone else. And all the nicer because of the difference. Oh, boy, I wish that you were my sister. I'd teach you to have confidence in yourself. Being different is nothing to be ashamed of. Because other people aren't such wonderful people. They're a hundred times one thousand. You're one times one! They walk all over the earth. You just stay here. They're as common as—weeds, but—you, well you're—*Blue Roses!*

LAURA. But blue is—wrong for—roses . . .

JIM. It's right for you!—You're pretty!

LAURA. In what respect am I pretty?

JIM. In all respects—your eyes—your hair. Your hands are pretty! You think I'm saying this because I'm invited to dinner and have to be nice. Oh, I could do that! I could say lots of things without being sincere. But I'm talking to you sincerely. I happened to notice you had this inferiority complex that keeps you from feeling comfortable with people. Somebody ought to build your confidence up—way up!—and make you proud instead of shy and turning away and—blushing——(JIM *lifts* LAURA *up on small table on "way up."*) Somebody ought to—(*Lifts her down*) somebody ought to kiss you, Laura! (*They kiss.* JIM *releases her and turns slowly away, crossing a little* D. R. *Then, quietly, to himself: As* JIM *turns away, music ends.*) Gee, I shoudn't have done that—that was way off the beam. (*Gives way* D. R. *Turns to* LAURA. LAURA *sits on small table.*) Would you care for a cigarette? You don't smoke, do you? How about a mint? Peppermint—Life-Saver? My pocket's a regular drugstore. . . . Laura, you know, if I had a sister like you, I'd do the same thing as Tom. I'd bring fellows home to meet you. Maybe I shouldn't be saying this. That may not have been the idea in having me over. But what if it was? There's nothing wrong with that.—The only trouble is that in my case—I'm not in a position to——I can't ask for your number and say I'll phone. I can't call up next weekend—ask for a date. I thought I had better explain the situation in case you—misunderstood and I hurt your feelings . . .

LAURA (*faintly*). You—won't—call again?

JIM (*crossing to* R. *of daybed, and sitting*). No, I can't. You see, I've—got strings on me. Lau-ra, I've—been going steady! I go out all the time with a girl named Betty. Oh, she's a nice quiet home girl like you, and Catholic and Irish, and in a great many ways we—get along fine. I met her last summer on a moonlight boat trip up the river to Alton, on the *Majestic.* Well—right away from the start it was—love! Oh, boy, being in love has made a new man of me! The power of love is pretty tremendous! Love is something that—changes the whole world. It happened that Betty's aunt took sick and she got a wire and had to go to Centralia. So naturally when Tom asked me to dinner—naturally I accepted the invitation, not knowing—I mean—not knowing. I wish that you would—say something. (LAURA *gives* JIM *unicorn.*) What are you doing that for? You mean you want me to have him? What for?

LAURA. A—souvenir. (*She crosses* R. *to menagerie,* JIM *rises.*)

AMANDA (*offstage*). I'm coming, children. (*She enters into dining room from kitchen* R.) I thought you'd like some liquid refreshment. (*Puts tray on small table. Lifts a glass*) Mr. O'Connor, have you heard that song about lemonade? It's "Lemonade, lemonade, Made in the shade and stirred with a spade—And then it's good enough for any old maid!"

JIM. No, ma'am, I never heard it.

AMANDA. Why are you so serious, honey? (*To* LAURA)

JIM. Well, we were having a serious conversation.

AMANDA. I don't understand modern young people. When I was a girl, I was gay about everything.

JIM. You haven't changed a bit, Mrs. Wingfield.

AMANDA. I suppose it's the gaiety of the occasion that has rejuvenated me. Well, here's to the gaiety of the occasion! (*Spills lemonade on dress*) Oooo! I baptized myself. (*Puts glass on small table* R. *of daybed*) I found some cherries in the kitchen, and I put one in each glass.

JIM. You shouldn't have gone to all that trouble, ma'am.

AMANDA. It was no trouble at all. Didn't you hear us cutting up in the kitchen? I was so outdone with Tom for not bringing you over sooner, but now you've found your way I want you to come all the time—not just once in a while—but all the time. Oh, I think I'll go back in that kitchen. (*Starts to exit* U.C.)

JIM. Oh, no, ma'am, please don't go, ma'am. As a matter of fact, I've got to be going.

AMANDA. Oh, Mr. O'Connor, it's only the shank of the evening! (JIM *and* AMANDA *stand* U.C.)

JIM. Well, you know how it is.

AMANDA. You mean you're a young working man and have to keep workingmen's hours?

JIM. Yes, ma'am.

AMANDA. Well, we'll let you off early this time, but only on the condition that you stay later next time, much later——What's the best night for you? Saturday?

JIM. Well, as a matter of fact, I have a couple of time clocks to punch, Mrs. Wingfield, one in the morning and another one at night!

AMANDA. Oh, isn't that nice, you're so ambitious! You work at night, too?

JIM. No, ma'am, not work but—Betty!

AMANDA (*crosses* L. *below daybed*). Betty? Who's Betty?

JIM. Oh, just a girl. The girl I go steady with!

AMANDA. You mean it's serious? (*Crosses* D.L.)

JIM. Oh, yes, ma'am. We're going to be married the second Sunday in June.

AMANDA (*sits on daybed*). Tom didn't say anything at all about your going to be married.

JIM. Well, the cat's not out of the bag at the warehouse yet. (*Picks up hat from telephone table*) You know how they are. They call you Romeo and stuff like that.—It's been a wonderful evening. Mrs. Wingfield. I guess this is what they mean by Southern hospitality.

AMANDA. It was nothing. Nothing at all.

JIM. I hope it don't seem like I'm rushing off. But I promised Betty I'd pick her up at the Wabash depot an' by the time I get my jalopy down there her train'll be in. Some women are pretty upset if you keep them waiting.

AMANDA. Yes, I know all about the tyranny of women! Well, good-by, Mr. O'Connor. (AMANDA *puts out hand.* JIM *takes it.*) I wish you happiness—and good fortune. You wish him that, too, don't you, Laura?

LAURA. Yes, I do, Mother.

JIM (*crosses* L. *to* LAURA). Good-by Laura. I'll always treasure that souvenir. And don't you forget the good advice I gave you. So long, Shakespeare! (*Up* C.) Thanks, again, ladies.— Good night! (*He grins and ducks jauntily out* R.)

AMANDA (*faintly*). Well, well, well. Things have a way of turning out so badly——(LAURA *crosses to phonograph, puts on record.*) I don't believe that I would play the Victrola. Well, well—well, our gentleman caller was engaged to be married! Tom!

TOM (*off*). Yes, Mother?

AMANDA. Come out here. I want to tell you something very funny.

TOM (*entering through* R. *kitchen door to dining room and into living room, through curtains,* D.C.). Has the gentleman caller gotten away already?

AMANDA. The gentleman caller made a very early departure. That was a nice joke you played on us, too!

TOM. How do you mean?

AMANDA. You didn't mention that he was engaged to be married.

TOM. Jim? Engaged?

AMANDA. That's what he just informed us.

TOM. I'll be jiggered! I didn't know.

AMANDA. That seems very peculiar.

TOM. What's peculiar about it?

AMANDA. Didn't you tell me he was your best friend down at the warehouse?

TOM. He is, but how did I know?

AMANDA. It seems very peculiar you didn't know your best friend was engaged to be married!

TOM. The warehouse is the place where I work, not where I know things about people!

AMANDA. You don't know things anywhere! You live in a dream; you manufacture illusions! (TOM *starts for* R. *door.*) Where are you going? Where are you going? Where are you going?

TOM. I'm going to the movies.

AMANDA (*rises, crosses up to* TOM). That's right, now that you've had us make such fools of ourselves. The effort, the preparations, all the expense! The new floor lamp, the rug, the clothes for Laura! All for what? To entertain some other girl's fiancé! Go to the movies, go! Don't think about us, a mother deserted, an unmarried sister who's crippled and has no job! Don't let anything interfere with your selfish pleasure! Just go, go, go—to the movies!

TOM. All right, I will, and the more you shout at me about my selfish pleasures, the quicker I'll go, and I won't go to the movies either. (*Gets hat from phone table, slams door* R., *and exits up alley* R.)

AMANDA (*crosses up to fire-escape landing, yelling*). Go, then! Then go to the moon—you selfish dreamer! (MUSIC CUE #18. *Interior light dims out. Reenters living room, slamming* R. *door.* TOM's *closing speech is timed with the interior pantomime. The interior scene is played as though viewed through soundproof glass, behind outer scrim curtain.* AMANDA, *standing, appears to be making a comforting speech to* LAURA *who is huddled on* R. *side of daybed. Now that we cannot hear the mother's speech, her silliness is gone and she has dignity and tragic beauty.* LAURA's *hair hides her face until at the end of the speech she lifts it to smile at her mother.* AMANDA's *gestures are slow and graceful, almost dancelike, as she comforts her daughter.* TOM, *who has meantime put on, as before, the jacket and cap, enters down* R. *from offstage, and again comes to fire-escape landing, stands as he speaks. Meantime lights are upon* AMANDA *and* LAURA, *but are dim.*)

TOM. I didn't go to the moon. I went much farther. For time is the longest distance between two places. . . . I left St. Louis. I descended these steps of this fire escape for the last time and followed, from then on, in my father's footsteps, attempting to find in motion what was lost in space. . . . I traveled around a great deal. The cities swept about me like dead leaves, leaves that were brightly colored but torn away from the branches. I would have stopped, but I was pursued by something. It always came upon me unawares, taking me altogether by surprise. Perhaps it was a familiar bit of music. Perhaps it was only a piece of transparent glass. . . . Perhaps I am walking along a street at night, in some strange city, before I have found companions, and I pass the lighted window of a shop where perfume is sold. The window is filled with pieces of colored glass, tiny transparent bottles in delicate colors, like bits of a shattered rainbow. Then all at once my sister touches my shoulder. I turn around and look into her eyes. . . . Oh, Laura, Laura, I tried to leave you behind me, but I am more faithful than I intended to be! I reach for a cigarette, I cross the street, I run into a movie or a bar. I buy a drink, I speak to the nearest stranger—anything that can blow your candles out!—for nowadays the world is lit by lightning! Blow out your candles, Laura . . . (LAURA *blows out candles still burning in candelabrum and the whole interior is blacked out.*) And so—good-by! (*Exits up alley* R. *Music continues to the end.*)

Curtain 1945

THINK AND DISCUSS
ACT TWO: SCENE 7
Understanding
1. Describe Jim in his high-school days.
2. Why is Tom "valuable" to Jim?
3. What is Jim's nickname for Tom? Why does he give Tom this nickname?
4. What changes has Amanda made in the living room in preparation for the gentleman caller?

5. What union has Tom joined? Where has he gotten the money to pay for his dues?

Analyzing
6. What are Laura's feelings and reactions when her mother tells her to answer the door for Tom and Jim? when she tries to join Jim and the family for dinner?
7. In what ways are both Jim and Tom trying to change the direction of their lives?
8. By what means does Amanda try to charm Jim? Do you think she succeeds? Explain.
9. How does Amanda "promote" Laura to Jim as something different from what she really is?

SCENE 8
Understanding
1. From where has the old candelabrum come? How did it become misshapen?
2. What class did Laura and Jim take together in high school? Why was Laura self-conscious in this class?
3. What two mementos from high school does Laura show Jim? What does he sign and why?
4. Which of Laura's glass figures is her favorite? How does it get broken?
5. Jim explains that he cannot call Laura later for a date. Why is such a call impossible?

Analyzing
6. What is Jim's view of himself and his general outlook on people and life? Do you think his self-confidence is genuine or a pose? Explain.
7. What do you consider the climax of the play? Explain.
8. What do you think the broken unicorn **symbolizes?**
9. All the characters have a private world of illusion to which they retreat. Describe the fantasy world in which each character takes refuge.

Extending
10. In a 1975 production of *The Glass Menagerie*, Williams added the business involving Jim's wrapping of his used chewing gum. Why do you think the playwright added this detail? How does it affect your impression of Jim?

REVIEWING: Connotation/Denotation H⁊
See Handbook of Literary Terms, p. 883.
   Connotation refers to the emotional, imaginative, cultural, or traditional associations surrounding a word, as opposed to its strict, literal dictionary meanings, or **denotation.** For example, *home* has the denotation or dictionary definition of "a dwelling place," although for various people it may have different connotations —a loving family, a bustling kitchen, a noisy, tense mixture of people, or, in the words of poet Robert Frost, "the place where, when you have to go there, /They have to take you in."

1. The Wingfield home is variously called an *apartment* and a *tenement*. What connotations do you associate with each of these words? Which word do you think provides a more accurate description of the Wingfield home?
2. Why does the use of the word *crippled* by both her children to describe Laura displease Amanda? Why is it significant that Amanda herself uses this word to describe Laura in her last speech?
3. What connotations do you associate with the word *glass?* Which of these connotations do you associate with Laura?

VOCABULARY
Pronunciation and Context
   With the help of your Glossary and the pronunciation key in the upper corner of each right-hand Glossary page, answer the following questions, which are based on quotations from the text.
AMANDA. Tom, good gracious, why don't you bring this *paragon* [Jim] to supper. . . ?

1. Does *paragon* rhyme with *marathon* or *telephone?*
2. Does Amanda approve or disapprove of Jim?

AMANDA. Well, in the South we had so many servants. Gone, gone, gone. All *vestige* of gracious living.

3. On which syllable is the accent in *vestige?*
4. Which Glossary definition of *vestige* fits the word in this context?

STAGE DIRECTIONS. JIM lights a cigarette and leans *indolently* back on his elbows, smiling at LAURA with a warmth and charm which lights her inwardly with altar candles.

5. On which syllable does the accent fall in *indolently?*
6. In your own words, describe the manner in which Jim leans back.

AMANDA. You don't know things anywhere! You live in a dream; you manufacture *illusions!*

7. Write a word that rhymes with *illusion.*
8. What is Amanda saying about Tom here?

THINKING SKILLS
Synthesizing

To synthesize is to assemble pieces of information so as to form a new structure. Jim, the gentleman caller, has devised the nicknames "Blue Roses" for Laura and "Shakespeare" for Tom, based on distinguishing features that each character possesses.

1. What nickname would you give to Jim himself?
2. What nickname could you invent for Amanda? for the absent Mr. Wingfield?

Evaluating

To evaluate is to make a judgment based on some kind of standard. For example, in his first speech as narrator, Tom judges Jim to be "the most realistic character in the play."

1. What qualities in Jim's character do you think cause Tom to make this evaluation?
2. What qualities in Jim's character, his self-appraisal, and his outlook on life do you think are unrealistic?
3. Do you think that Jim, in his future life as an adult, can achieve the kind of image he had as a high-school student? Why or why not?

COMPOSITION ◄═══►
Writing a Character's Resumé

Imagine that you are Jim O'Connor writing a resumé in 1945 to a firm that manufactures and sells radios and is expanding into the new industry of television. You might mention the courses you are taking, your belief in the future of television, and the qualities in your personality that would make you a valuable spokesman or salesman for the new TV industry. See "Writing to Persuade an Audience" in the Writer's Handbook.

Writing About a Symbol

Discuss the function of one of the symbols listed below in an essay of several paragraphs directed to your teacher. Emphasize what the symbol reveals about a character or characters, their situation, and the author's attitude toward them. In developing your essay, refer to passages and words in the play. Since several of these symbols are related, you may want to discuss more than one (e.g., the candelabrum and Laura's lameness). See "Writing About Symbolism" in the Writer's Handbook.

- Tom's movie-going
- The glass unicorn
- Jim's giant shadow
- The Paradise Dance Hall
- Laura's lameness
- The candelabrum
- The fire escape

ENRICHMENT
Oral Report

Find a copy of Williams's production notes that accompanied the original script for *The Glass Menagerie.* (You can find these notes in a preface to many texts of the play, including that which appears in *Six Modern American Plays,* published by Random House.) In these notes, Williams elaborates on the musical and lighting effects in the play. In addition, he mentions a screen "on which were projected magic lantern slides bearing images or titles"—a convention that was dropped from the original production. Report on these production notes to the class.

Research

Locate reviews of *The Glass Menagerie* written when the play was first presented in 1945 or reviews of later productions, such as the 1983–1984 revival, starring Jessica Tandy, Amanda Plummer, and John Heard. Or you may want to look at reviews of the 1987 movie version, directed by Paul Newman. In a written report, summarize at least two of these reviews.

Themes IN AMERICAN LITERATURE

The American Dream/The American Nightmare

The American Dream is a combination of the spiritual longing, the material enterprise, and the quest for freedom and equality that led to the founding of this nation. The earliest settlers saw America as an embodiment of their hope, a land of infinite resources and opportunities where they could construct the ideal society and acquire material goods. Although the early colonies fell far short of Utopia, they offered at least the promise of spiritual and material fulfillment. Moreover, Americans such as Benjamin Franklin looked beyond the land to human nature itself as the key to a better world.

With the reformers of the midnineteenth century, the American Dream took a distinctly social direction. The works of Harriet Beecher Stowe and Frederick Douglass address themselves to the question of freedom, while the Gettysburg Address asserts faith in human capabilities.

From the earliest American writings, prosperity has been regarded as God's reward for hard work. The self-improvement maxims in Franklin's *Poor Richard's Almanack* became the guidebook for generations of ambitious Americans. The writer who is most closely associated with the rags-to-riches theme is Horatio Alger (1832–1899), whose books about boys who rose to fame and fortune through hard work, clean living, and bravery have sold some two hundred million copies.

By the turn of the century, the American Dream, as portrayed in literature, had begun to lose its glitter. The fate of Richard Cory (Unit 4) illustrates the discrepancy between appearance and reality discovered by those who pursued the American Dream. W. E. B. DuBois's "Of the Meaning of Progress" (Unit 4) offers little hope for the dreams of rural blacks at the end of the nineteenth century. In Unit 5, F. Scott Fitzgerald deflates the

Winter Dreams of his romantic protagonist, while John Steinbeck's "Leader of the People" delivers a eulogy to those whose dreams died with the end of frontier expansion. J. Alfred Prufrock, who knows the mermaids' song is not for him, is the prototype of the modern fictional antihero, whose dreams have become remote and unattainable.

In *The Glass Menagerie* the American Dream, suggested by gauze curtains and romantic lighting, and its counterpart, the American Nightmare, grounded in the claustrophobic tenement, are pitted as foils. The young narrator's dreams, the mother's attempts to recapture the graceful decorum of the old South, the daughter's fragile fantasies, even the gentleman caller's rosy optimism— like Laura's unicorn—cannot remain intact in this shabby urban setting.

Many writers of modern fiction have produced futuristic works, set in a technological nether world, that explore the American Nightmare. Kurt Vonnegut, Jr.'s "Harrison Bergeron" (Unit 7) portrays a society that forbids variety, talent, beauty, and creative art, a society that enforces mediocrity through a Handicapper General.

World wars, depressions, racial strife, fear of nuclear holocaust, and other events of recent history have caused contemporary writers to reexamine some of the traditional values and dreams that seem overly simple and inadequate as answers to the complexities of modern life. But to those who fear that faith, optimism, and the American Dream have all but disappeared in twentieth-century writing, William Faulkner in his Nobel Prize speech (Unit 5) points toward the aspirations of modern humanity, its compassion, sacrifice, and, above all, its ability to endure and prevail. And he reminds writers of their special duty to lift the heart of humanity by chronicling its nobility and encouraging its dreams.

THINKING CRITICALLY
ABOUT LITERATURE

UNIT 6   MODERN DRAMA

■ CONCEPT REVIEW

The following excerpt from *The Little Foxes* illustrates many of the important ideas and literary terms found in modern drama. The notes and questions are designed to help you think critically about your reading. The page number in the notes refers to a review. A more extensive discussion of these terms is in the Handbook of Literary Terms.

from The Little Foxes, Act I

Lillian Hellman

CHARACTERS

REGINA GIDDENS	A good-looking woman in her forties, she is the sister of Ben and Oscar Hubbard. Her husband is Horace Giddens, a wealthy banker now hospitalized in Baltimore.
ALEXANDRA GIDDENS	She is the seventeen-year-old daughter of the Giddenses.
LEO HUBBARD	He is the twenty-year-old son of Oscar and Birdie.
BEN HUBBARD	Regina's older brother and a partner with Oscar in Hubbard Sons, Merchandise.
ADDIE	She is the black servant in the Giddenses' house.
BIRDIE HUBBARD	She is Oscar's wife and comes from an old Southern aristocratic family.
OSCAR HUBBARD	Regina's other brother, he married Birdie when the Hubbard family took over Birdie's family's cotton estate.

The play is set in the living room of the Giddens house, located in a small town of the deep South. The playwright describes the room as being "good looking, the furniture expensive; but it reflects no particular taste. Everything is of the best and that is all." It is the spring of 1900.

From *The Little Foxes*, by Lillian Hellman. Copyright 1939 and renewed 1967 by Lillian Hellman. Reprinted by permission of Random House, Inc.

CAUTION: Professionals and amateurs are hereby warned that *The Little Foxes*, being fully protected under the copyright laws of the United States of America, the British Empire, including the Dominion of Canada, and all other countries of the Copyright Union, is subject to a royalty. All rights, including professional, amateur, motion picture, recitation, public reading, radio broadcasting and the rights of translation into foreign languages, are strictly reserved. In its present form this play is dedicated to the reading public only. All inquiries regarding this play should be addressed to the author, care of Random House, Inc. 201 East 50th Street, New York City.

In the first part of Act I there is discussion of a business deal that Ben, Oscar, and Regina are anxious to complete. Mr. Marshall, a Northern industrialist, is going to help the Hubbards finance a cotton mill in the South. After celebrating the agreement, he is driven to the train station by Leo and Alexandra.

While they are gone, Oscar and Ben remind Regina that they have raised their shares of $75,000, but the money she has promised from Horace is still not paid. She suggests that Horace is holding out for a greater share of the profits, and she gets Ben and Oscar to agree to give her 40 percent, which will come out of Oscar's share. In exchange Regina agrees to think about having Alexandra marry Leo. Birdie overhears these marriage plans.

REGINA *(calling).* Alexandra? Are you back?

ALEXANDRA. Yes, Mama.

LEO *(comes into the room).* Mr. Marshall got off safe and sound. Weren't those fine clothes he had? You can always spot clothes made in a good place. Looks like maybe they were done in England. Lots of men in the North send all the way to England for their stuff.

BEN *(to LEO).* Were you careful driving the horses?

LEO. Oh, yes, sir. I was. (ALEXANDRA *has come in on* BEN's *question, hears the answer, looks angrily at* LEO.)

ALEXANDRA. It's a lovely night. You should have come, Aunt Birdie.

REGINA. Were you gracious to Mr. Marshall?

ALEXANDRA. I think so, Mama. I like him.

REGINA. Good. And now I have great news for you. You are going to Baltimore in the morning to bring your father home.

ALEXANDRA *(gasps, then delighted).* Me? Papa said I should come? That must mean——(*Turns to* ADDIE) Addie, he must be well. Think of it. He'll be back home again. We'll bring him home.

REGINA. You are going alone, Alexandra.

ADDIE (ALEXANDRA *has turned in surprise*). Going alone? Going by herself? A child that age! Mr. Horace ain't going to like Zan traipsing up there by herself.

REGINA *(sharply).* Go upstairs and lay out Alexandra's things.

ADDIE. He'd expect me to be along——

REGINA. I'll be up in a few minutes to tell you what to pack. (ADDIE *slowly begins to climb the steps. To* ALEXANDRA) I should think you'd like going alone. At your age it certainly would have delighted me. You're a strange girl, Alexandra. Addie has babied you so much.

ALEXANDRA. I only thought it would be more fun if Addie and I went together.

BIRDIE *(timidly).* Maybe I could go with her, Regina, I'd really like to.

REGINA. She is going alone. She is getting old enough to take some responsibilities.

OSCAR. She'd better learn now. She's almost old enough to get married. (*Jovially, to* LEO, *slapping him on shoulder*) Eh, son?

LEO. Huh?

■ Regina is calculating, business-minded, and ruthless.

■ **Connotation/denotation** (page 617): Note the associations various characters have for the word *marriage.*

■ Note what Leo's observation reveals about his values.

■ Alexandra's reaction indicates a genuine fondness for her father.

■ **sharply:** Note how this brief stage direction and those that follow characterize each of the speakers.

OSCAR (*annoyed with* LEO *for not understanding*). Old enough to get married, you're thinking, eh?

LEO. Oh, yes, sir. (*Feebly*) Lots of girls get married at Zan's age. Look at Mary Prester and Johanna and——

REGINA. Well, she's not getting married tomorrow. But she is going to Baltimore tomorrow, so let's talk about that. (*To* ALEXANDRA) You'll be glad to have Papa home again.

ALEXANDRA. I wanted to go before, Mama. You remember that. But you said you couldn't go, and that *I* couldn't go alone.

REGINA. I've changed my mind. (*Too casually*) You're to tell Papa how much you missed him, and that he must come home now—for your sake. Tell him that you need him home.

■ Infer Regina's reasons for wanting Alexandra to make the trip alone.

ALEXANDRA. Need him home? I don't understand.

REGINA. There is nothing for you to understand. You are simply to say what I have told you.

BIRDIE (*rises*). He may be too sick. She couldn't do that——

ALEXANDRA. Yes. He may be too sick to travel. I couldn't make him think he had to come home for me, if he is too sick to——

■ Note the contrast between the motives of Alexandra and Regina.

REGINA (*looks at her, sharply, challengingly*). You *couldn't* do what I tell you to do, Alexandra?

ALEXANDRA (*quietly*). No. I couldn't. If I thought it would hurt him.

REGINA (*after a second's silence, smiles pleasantly*). But you are doing this for Papa's own good. (*Takes* ALEXANDRA's *hand*) You must let me be the judge of his condition. It's the best possible cure for him to come home and be taken care of here. He mustn't stay there any longer and listen to those alarmist doctors. You are doing this entirely for his sake. Tell your papa that I want him to come home, that I miss him very much.

■ Regina uses her husband as a pawn.

ALEXANDRA (*slowly*). Yes, Mama.

REGINA (*to the others. Rises*). I must go and start getting Alexandra ready now. Why don't you all go home?

BEN (*rises*). I'll attend to the railroad ticket. One of the boys will bring it over. Good night, everybody. Have a nice trip, Alexandra. The food on the train is very good. The celery is so crisp. Have a good time and act like a little lady. (*Exits*)

REGINA. Good night, Ben. Good night, Oscar——(*Playfully*) Don't be so glum, Oscar. It makes you look as if you had chronic indigestion.

BIRDIE. Good night, Regina.

REGINA. Good night, Birdie. (*Exits upstairs*)

OSCAR (*starts for hall*). Come along.

LEO (*to* ALEXANDRA). Imagine your not wanting to go! What a little fool you are. Wish it were me. What I could do in a place like Baltimore!

ALEXANDRA (*angrily, looking away from him*). Mind your business. I can guess the kind of things *you* could do.

■ This detail further characterizes Leo and indicates that he would be an unsuitable spouse for Alexandra.

LEO (*laughs*). Oh, no, you couldn't. (*He exits.*)

REGINA (*calling from the top of the stairs*). Come on, Alexandra.

BIRDIE (*quickly, softly*). Zan.

ALEXANDRA. I don't understand about my going, Aunt Birdie. (*Shrugs*) But anyway, Papa will be home again. (*Pats* BIRDIE's *arm*) Don't worry about me. I can take care of myself. Really I can.

BIRDIE (*shakes her head, softly*). That's not what I'm worried about. Zan——

ALEXANDRA (*comes close to her*). What's the matter?

BIRDIE. It's about Leo——

ALEXANDRA (*whispering*). He beat the horses. That's why we were late getting back. We had to wait until they cooled off. He always beats the horses as if——

BIRDIE (*whispering frantically, holding* ALEXANDRA's *hands*). He's my son. My own son. But you are more to me—more to me than my own child. I love you more than anybody else——

ALEXANDRA. Don't worry about the horses. I'm sorry I told you.

BIRDIE (*her voice rising*). *I am not worrying about the horses.* I am worrying about *you.* You are *not* going to marry Leo. I am not going to let them do that to you——

ALEXANDRA. Marry? To Leo? (*Laughs*) I wouldn't marry, Aunt Birdie. I've never even thought about it——

BIRDIE. But they have thought about it. (*Wildly*) Zan, I couldn't stand to think about such a thing. You and——

(OSCAR *has come into the doorway on* ALEXANDRA's *speech. He is standing quietly, listening.*)

ALEXANDRA (*laughs*). But I'm not going to marry. And I'm certainly not going to marry Leo.

BIRDIE. Don't you understand? They'll make you. They'll make you——

ALEXANDRA (*takes* BIRDIE's *hands, quietly, firmly*). That's foolish, Aunt Birdie. I'm grown now. Nobody can make me do anything.

BIRDIE. I just couldn't stand——

OSCAR (*sharply*). Birdie. (BIRDIE *looks up, draws quickly away from* ALEXANDRA. *She stands rigid, frightened. Quietly*) Birdie, get your hat and coat.

ADDIE (*calls from upstairs*). Come on, baby. Your mama's waiting for you, and she ain't nobody to keep waiting.

ALEXANDRA. All right. (*Then softly, embracing* BIRDIE) Good night, Aunt Birdie. (*As she passes* OSCAR) Good night, Uncle Oscar. (BIRDIE *begins to move slowly toward the door as* ALEXANDRA *climbs the stairs.* ALEXANDRA *is almost out of view when* BIRDIE *reaches* OSCAR *in the doorway. As* BIRDIE *quickly attempts to pass him, he slaps her hard, across the face.* BIRDIE *cries out, puts her hand to her face. On the cry,* ALEXANDRA *turns, begins to run down the stairs.*) Aunt Birdie! What happened? What happened? I——

BIRDIE (*softly, without turning*). Nothing, darling. Nothing happened. (*Quickly, as if anxious to keep* ALEXANDRA *from coming close*) Now go to bed. (OSCAR *exits.*) Nothing happened I only—I only twisted my ankle. (*She goes out.* ALEXANDRA *stands on the stairs looking after her as if she were puzzled and frightened.*)

1939

Curtain

■ This explains Alexandra's angry look earlier when Leo assures Ben that he has been careful driving the horses.

■ Alexandra's vow of independence appears ironic in the face of her strong-willed, scheming relatives.

■ Oscar reveals himself to be as ruthless and cruel as his sister Regina. His act of violence offers a parallel to Leo's mistreatment of the horses.

THINK AND DISCUSS
Understanding
1. Where and when does the play take place?
2. Who is Addie?
3. Who is the only family member who shows kindness to Alexandra?
4. What lie does Leo tell Ben?
5. Where does Regina plan to send Alexandra, and for what purpose?

Analyzing
6. What do the following reveal about Regina: her living-room decor, her treatment of Addie, her marriage plans for Alexandra?
7. What words, actions, and stage directions reveal Birdie's concern for Alexandra?
8. During the conversation between Birdie and Alexandra, the audience is aware that Oscar is standing in the doorway, but Birdie is not aware of him. What kind of **irony** does this illustrate?
9. Which word best describes the **mood** of this excerpt—*lighthearted, tense, supernatural,* or *gloomy?* Explain your choice.
10. The central conflict in this play is between which two characters? What about their personalities and situation causes this conflict?

Extending
11. What do you think would happen if a wedding date were set for a marriage between Alexandra and Leo? How would Alexandra react to the news? What chances would there be for a happy union? Explain.

REVIEWING LITERARY TERMS
Connotation/Denotation
1. What is the denotation, or dictionary definition, of *marriage?*
2. What personal connotations do you think Regina Giddens has for this word?
3. The dictionary provides various definitions for the word *aristocratic:* "grand, stylish, snobbish." Which of these definitions applies to Regina Giddens?

■ CONTENT REVIEW
THINKING SKILLS
Classifying
1. There are both schemers and dreamers in *The Glass Menagerie* and the excerpt from *The Little Foxes.* Make two lists, one with the head *Schemers,* the other headed *Dreamers.* Beneath each head, write the names of at least three characters from these two plays who you think fit under these labels. If you consider any characters as fitting both heads, list them twice.

Generalizing
2. Amanda Wingfield and Regina Giddens are both strong-willed mothers who attempt to find husbands for their daughters. Compare and contrast the motives of each woman for finding a suitable match.
3. After Jim's departure at the end of *The Glass Menagerie,* Williams notes in a stage direction that Amanda's "silliness is gone and she has dignity and tragic beauty." How do her final actions reveal this aspect of her character?

Synthesizing
4. Both of these plays present marriages that fall far short of ideal unions. Imagine that Alexandra Giddens from *The Little Foxes* and either Tom Wingfield or Jim O'Connor from *The Glass Menagerie* decide to marry. Judging from what you know of each character, do you think that he or she would be a good marriage partner? Do you see any problems that might arise in this marriage or areas that would require work? Explain.
5. Imagine that you were casting a modern production of *The Glass Menagerie* or *The Little Foxes.* Think of actors and actresses from the theater, movies, or TV that you would consider suitable for the leading roles in the play and briefly explain your choices.

Evaluating

6. To varying degrees, each character in *The Glass Menagerie* cherishes illusions. Describe each character's illusions and determine which character has the best chance of attaining his or her dreams. Then explain what you think the play is implying about illusions, both as aids and as handicaps in coping with life.

7. Amanda Wingfield believes her children will succeed since they are "just full of natural endowments." How are Laura and Tom each affected by their mother's unrealistic expectations of them? Do you find their responses believable? Discuss.

■ COMPOSITION REVIEW

Choose one of the following for a composition.

Writing a Dialogue

Imagine a meeting between Amanda Wingfield and Regina Giddens. Construct a dialogue of a page or so between the two women in which they discuss topics such as the aristocratic South, their daughters, and their husbands. Use stage directions that help reveal the characters of these women. Submit your script to the school literary magazine.

Describing a Character

Think of a character in either play that you find memorable—one that you might recall long after you have read the play. In an essay of several paragraphs to a friend discuss what has impressed you about this character, whether you know someone similar, and whether or not you find this character admirable. See "Writing About Characters" in the Writer's Handbook.

Writing About a Scene

Choose a scene from *The Glass Menagerie* that particularly affected you. What about this scene rang true? Have you ever found yourself in a similar situation? Write about this scene in at least four paragraphs, directed to someone who knows you well.

Elizabeth Taylor as Regina and Ann Talman as Alexandra in the 1981 revival of *The Little Foxes*.

NEW FRONTIERS 1945—

1945	1950	1955	1960	1965

HISTORY AND THE ARTS

- U.N. established
- Orwell: *Nineteen Eighty-Four* (England)
- 12 nations sign NATO pact
- Korean Conflict
- First color television widely available
- Segregation in schools ruled unconstitutional

Martin Luther King, Jr., awarded Nobel Peace Prize •

Indira Gandhi becomes Prime Minister (India) •

- Leonard Bernstein: *West Side Story*
- First copying machine produced by Xerox
- Fidel Castro wins revolution (Cuba)
- Peace Corps started
- Alan Shepard: first American in space
- John F. Kennedy assassinated

PRESIDENTS' ADMINISTRATIONS

1953–1961 Dwight D. Eisenhower •

1961–1963 John F. Kennedy •

• 1963–1969
Lyndon B. Johnson

LITERATURE

- Brooks: *A Street in Bronzeville*
- McCullers: *The Member of the Wedding*
- Miller: *Death of a Salesman*
- Ellison: *Invisible Man*
- Hemingway: *The Old Man and the Sea*
- Salinger: *The Catcher in the Rye*

Baldwin: *Another Country* •

- Hansberry: *A Raisin in the Sun*
- O'Connor: *The Violent Bear It Away*
- Porter: *Ship of Fools*
- Bellow: *Herzog*

Three-dimensional image generated by a PC microcomputer

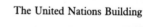

Sandra Day O'Connor, first woman on the Supreme Court

The United Nations Building

1970	1975	1980	1985	1990

- Thurgood Marshall: first black Supreme Court Justice
  - U.S. astronauts walk on moon
    - Solzhenitsyn wins Nobel Prize (Russia)
      - Watergate hearings
      - Vietnam peace treaty signed

- Soviet Union invades Afghanistan; U.S. boycotts Olympics
  - Sandra Day O'Connor: first woman Supreme Court Justice
    - First permanent artificial heart implanted
      - Elie Wiesel granted Nobel Peace Prize

Sally K. Ride: first U.S. woman in space •
Federal deficit reaches 200 billion •
U.S. space shuttle *Challenger* explodes •
End of 20-year rule by Marcos (Philippines) •

- Stock market plunges on Black Monday

- 1969–1974 Richard M. Nixon
  - 1974–1977 Gerald R. Ford
- 1977–1981 Jimmy Carter
  - 1981–1989 Ronald Reagan
- 1989– George Bush

- Momaday: *House Made of Dawn*
  - Vonnegut: *Slaughterhouse-Five*
- Haley: *Roots*
- Plath: *Collected Poems*
  - Rodriguez: *Hunger of Memory*
  - Updike completes *Rabbit* trilogy
- Taylor: *A Summons to Memphis*

Apollo 11 astronaut Edwin Aldrin, Jr., on the moon (1969)

Andy Warhol, detail of *Campbell's Soup Cans*

Avant-garde furniture by Gary Gutterman, New York (1980)

PREVIEW

UNIT 7   NEW FRONTIERS   1945—

Authors in This Unit Include

John Updike
Bernard Malamud
Carson Smith McCullers
Kurt Vonnegut, Jr.
Flannery O'Connor
Robert Hayden
Robert Lowell
May Swenson
Galway Kinnell

Maxine Kumin
Randall Jarrell
Gwendolyn Brooks
Theodore Roethke
James Masao Mitsui
N. Scott Momaday
Leslie Marmon Silko
Simon Ortiz

Linda Pastan
Teresa Paloma Acosta
Garrison Keillor
William Least Heat Moon
Richard Rodriguez
Lorraine Hansberry
Ralph Ellison
Elie Wiesel

Features

Themes in American Literature: The Journey
The Story of American English
Comment: Flannery O'Connor on Her
    Recurring Subject in Fiction
Comment: First Voices
Reader's Note: From the Author:
    "Frederick Douglass"
Reader's Note: "Mr. Edwards and
    the Spider"
Reader's Note: "The Groundhog"
Reader's Note: From the Author:
    "Auto Wreck"
Comment: New Voices
Reading Autobiography and Biography
Comment: Talking with Least Heat Moon
Comment: Sweet Lorraine by James Baldwin

Application of Literary Terms

protagonist
lyric
metonymy

hyperbole
analogy

Review of Literary Terms

point of view
plot
satire
style

setting
rhythm
inference

Reading Literature Skillfully

predicting outcomes

Vocabulary Skills

roots
context
affixes
dictionary

Thinking Skills

evaluating
classifying

Composition Assignments Include

Writing About Male and Female Roles
Analyzing Setting
Analyzing a Story's Ending
Using Imagery in Writing
Writing About a Response to Music
Commenting on Modern Poetry
Explaining the Importance of Words
Describing a Significant Moment
Writing About Tone

Enrichment

Oral Reading
Research

Thinking Critically About Literature

Concept Review
Content Review
Composition Review

NEW FRONTIERS 1945–

World War II, climaxed by the U.S. dropping of the first atomic bombs on Hiroshima and Nagasaki, brought about many social, cultural, and literary changes in America. The war had ended the Great Depression, and the postwar boom gave birth to an affluent society. Millions of Americans found themselves in the middle class, their children taking prosperity for granted.

THE POSTWAR MOOD

Yet through this economic euphoria ran the anxieties created by the Cold War between the United States and the Soviet Union. Intellectuals were preoccupied with the grimness of the recent past, the possibility of nuclear war, and soon with the challenge to intellectual freedom posed by Senator Joseph McCarthy's claims of Communist influence in American government, education, and the arts.

In this social climate, many writers took on a tone of despair and cynicism. But William Faulkner, in his eloquent Nobel Prize Address of 1950, warned against such easy escape from the challenges confronting the human spirit.

In the late 1940s, writers were understandably preoccupied with the war years. There was a succession of war novels, such as Irwin Shaw's *Young Lions*, Norman Mailer's *The Naked and the Dead*, and James Jones's *From Here to Eternity*. Karl Shapiro won the Pulitzer Prize in 1945 for *V-Letter and Other Poems*. Randall Jarrell also won acclaim for poetry focused on the feelings of young soldiers in combat.

At the same time, prewar literary trends resurfaced. Gwendolyn Brooks's poems in *A Street in Bronzeville* (1945) called attention to the joys, sorrows, pride, and vitality of urban black life. In 1952 Ralph Ellison won the National Book Award for *Invisible Man*, a subtle and technically brilliant novel focusing on the problem of identity for American blacks.

William Faulkner, Katherine Anne Porter, Eudora Welty, and a host of talented newcomers reinvigorated the "Southern Renaissance," the creative explosion of Southern writers that had started in the 1920s and 1930s. Among these new authors were Carson McCullers, Flannery O'Connor, Robert Penn Warren, and, later, Truman Capote, William Styron, and Alice Walker. Much of their fiction, like Faulkner's, focused on tightly knit rural communities in the South, although the themes extended beyond geographical boundaries. Later, most of these writers moved on to settings outside the South or to themes reflecting the effect on Southerners, both black and white, of new social patterns and ways of thinking.

Poetry was still dominated by the standards of T. S. Eliot and Ezra Pound: intellectual objectivity, stylistic complexity, and an avoidance of the emotional or the personal. Literature was to be studied without reference to either the life of its authors or the time in which it was created.

Such intellectual detachment matched the mood of the early 1950s, with its avoidance of controversy and its emphasis on materialism and organization. Few writers were willing to commit themselves to any stand. A retreat into obscure, personal symbolism by many poets resulted in a shrinking audience. Novelists such as Capote, Saul Bellow, and John Cheever turned to social satire and comedy, reflecting, analyzing, and ridiculing the "plastic" middle-class culture of status symbols. A typical best-selling novel of the decade was Sloan Wilson's

Man in the Gray Flannel Suit (1955), which depicted the destruction of a marriage by the "status game."

REFORMS AND TRENDS

But a major change was already developing. The civil-rights movement, spurred by the Supreme Court's 1954 decision ordering the end of public-school segregation and by leaders such as Martin Luther King, Jr., gained nationwide attention. Sit-ins, boycotts, and, later, voter registration drives were mounted throughout the South and the North. In *Go Tell It on the Mountain* (1953), James Baldwin chronicled the struggle of rural Southern blacks to adjust their spiritual values to life in the ghetto. Continuing Whitman's tradition of the open road and borrowing from black American culture—especially music, dance, and diction—the Beat Generation became the first large group of middle-class youth eager to "drop out" of the "system." They foreshadowed the hippie counterculture of the 1960s and inspired a new wave in literature. Jack Kerouac's novel *On the Road* (1957), known as the "Beat Bible," was the prototype of many free-flowing narratives that recorded the roaming of young dropouts in search of meaning for their lives beyond what they termed the middle-class "rat race." Although the Beats cultivated "cool"—an attitude of ironic detachment from social conventions and political concerns—their writing was personal, socially committed, and written in the language of the streets. They were joined in scorning poetic artificiality by more established poets such as William Stafford and Denise Levertov. The tuned-in, turned-on verse of Beat poets—Allen Ginsberg, Gregory Corso, and Lawrence Ferlinghetti, to name a few—appealed to the angry young dropouts of the late 1950s. The tone of early Beat poetry is suggested by the title of Ginsberg's best-known poem, "Howl."

Yet, the Beat phenomenon was short-lived. Those Americans in flight from conformity and convention and in search of ideals worthy of commitment found inspiration in a new era promised by the election of President John F. Kennedy and were challenged by his inaugural speech of 1961: "Ask not what your country can do for you; ask what you can do for your country." Young people flocked to register black voters and to join the Peace Corps. Established writers like Gwendolyn Brooks, Robert Lowell, and James Baldwin became prominent champions of various political causes. Younger writers arose to voice the impulse for equality and pride among Hispanics, Native Americans, and other ethnic groups. The women's rights movement began to revive and won literary advocates such as Denise Levertov and Mary McCarthy. The 1960s became a decade of challenge to traditional values and institutions.

Faith in peaceful reform was expressed by the Freedom March of 300,000 civil-rights supporters in Washington, D.C., in 1963. But in the same year, John Kennedy and civil-rights leader Medgar Evers were killed, the first victims of a series of political assassinations. By 1965 hundreds of thousands of American soldiers were pouring into Vietnam. The issues of civil rights and the war were tightly enmeshed. The optimism of the Kennedy years was shattered as clashes between protesters and police mounted into violence on city streets and college campuses.

American literature both affected and was affected by this climate of rage. The tone of much writing became stridently rhetorical. A new type of militant cultural commentary emerged, notably with James Baldwin's *Fire Next Time* (1963).

LITERARY CURRENTS

Truman Capote's *In Cold Blood* (1965), using fictional techniques to analyze a real murder case, gave birth to the "nonfiction novel" and to the "New Journalism." In this type of work, also called "advocacy journalism," writers abandoned the news reporter's traditional objectivity to participate in the events they were observing.

The war novel was revived, notably by Joseph Heller's *Catch-22* (1961) and Kurt Vonnegut, Jr.'s *Slaughterhouse-Five* (1969). The theme of both books is the mindlessness of war. For Heller, the only sane response is madcap, hilarious "insanity." For Vonnegut, the love and compassion of individuals for each other may somehow redeem the world from the madness that views mass bombing as "rational."

In the rich diversity of contemporary fiction, one theme has cropped up regularly. The modern hero often appears as an individual trapped by "the system" or threatened for being an outsider. Some heroes lash out in defiance, maintaining their integrity and asserting their individuality even at the cost of their lives. Such is Randle Patrick McMurphy, the hero of Ken Kesey's *One Flew over the Cuckoo's Nest* (1962). At the other extreme are Bernard Malamud's characters. Frank Alpine of *The Assistant* (1957) and Yakov Bok of *The Fixer* (1966) are silent sufferers. In the middle zone between the rebels and the victims is a group of modern-day Don Quixotes, who joust ridiculously or pathetically with their real and imagined antagonists. In this group are Holden Caulfield of J. D. Salinger's *Catcher in the Rye* (1951), the anonymous hero of Ralph Ellison's *Invisible Man* (1952), Harry Angstrom of John Updike's *Rabbit* trilogy (1960–1982), the title character of John Irving's *World According to Garp* (1978), and Mr. Sammler of Saul Bellow's *Mr. Sammler's Planet* (1969). Close relatives of these characters are the bizarre creations of Carson McCullers and Flannery O'Connor, who, like images in a distorting fun-house mirror, reflect the absurdity of contemporary life.

Science fiction, long associated with the lurid covers of pulp magazines, has risen to literary respectability partly because it appeals to readers faced with the bewildering pace of change. Though long on gimmickry and short on believable characterization, early science fiction dealt with the themes of nuclear power, robots, and space travel long before most people were aware of these possibilities. The proliferation of home computers, the popularity of fantasy games, and the dazzling special effects of science-fiction motion pictures have assured the continuing success of this type of literature. Along with the garish spectacles of intergalactic combat and the fascinating possibilities of extraterrestrial life forms, writers gifted with both literary skills and scientific acumen are offering serious presentations of problems such as pollution, overpopulation, cultural clash, and other facets of the human predicament.

Another aspect of contemporary literature is the reexamination of the American experience. This trend seems to have combined with the ethnic literature that developed so rapidly in the 1960s. But writers such as Lawson Fusao Inada, Gary Soto, Richard Rodriguez, Leslie Silko, and William Least Heat Moon went beyond the political concerns of the 1970s and early 1980s to treat broad universal themes of human striving for identity and desire for connection with one's past.

American literature is vital, always open to experiment in content and form. It is a literature of search—perhaps with more rough edges of style and expression than the literature of older nations. But such is the spirit of quest and experiment, a spirit captured by Thomas Wolfe in his novel *You Can't Go Home Again*: "I believe that we are lost here in America, but I believe we shall be found. . . . I think that the true discovery of America is before us. I think the true fulfillment of our spirit, of our people, of our mighty and immortal land, is yet to come."

Thomas Wolfe. *You Can't Go Home Again.* (New York: Harper & Brothers), 1940.

THINKING ABOUT GRAPHIC AIDS
Using the Time Line

1. Which time-line items are directly related to space exploration?
2. Which items represent breakthroughs for women and minorities?
3. Which item indicates a scientific advancement that can prolong life? Which mentions something found in most American homes? Which mentions something considered a necessity in most large American business offices?
4. Do you feel that the 1954 segregation ruling has had significant impact on your own school today? Why or why not?
5. What time-line event in the 1980s do you consider most important? Explain.

BIOGRAPHY

John Updike

1932–

Born and raised in Shillington, a town in an impoverished area of Pennsylvania, John Updike saw art "as a method of riding a thin pencil line out of Shillington, out of time altogether, into an infinity of unseen and even unborn hearts." His talent for drawing led him upon graduation from Harvard to the Ruskin School of Drawing and Fine Art at Oxford University. But he eventually became a writer, realizing a childhood dream in 1955 when he joined the staff of the *New Yorker*, to which he still contributes poems, stories, and reviews.

Updike has been a highly praised and prolific writer. Among his collections of short stories are *The Same Door* (1959), *Pigeon Feathers* (1962), and *Museums and Women* (1972). His best-known novels include *The Poorhouse Fair* (1959), *Rabbit Run* (1960), and *The Centaur* (1963), for which he received the National Book Award. In 1982 *Rabbit Is Rich*, the third in the "Rabbit" series after *Rabbit Redux* (1971), carried off the triple crown of fiction, winning a Pulitzer Prize, an American Book Award, and a commendation from the National Book Critics Circle. That same year he also published *Bech is Back*, a sequel to *Bech: A Book* (1970). His recent novels are *The Witches of Eastwick* (1984), *Roger's Version* (1986), and *S* (1988). *Assorted Prose* (1965), *Picked-Up Pieces* (1975), and *Hugging the Shore* (1983) contain his numerous essays and criticism.

Updike often writes about ordinary people who struggle vainly to give meaning to their lives but are constantly frustrated by the pettiness and aridity of middle-class existence. His writings powerfully embody the aim of his art: "To transcribe middleness with all its grits, bumps, and anonymities, in all its fullness of satisfaction and mystery."

Review **POINT OF VIEW** in the Handbook of Literary Terms, page 900.

Man and Daughter in the Cold

John Updike

ook at that girl ski!" The exclamation arose at Ethan's side as if, in the disconnecting cold, a rib of his had cried out; but it was his friend, friend and fellow teacher, an inferior teacher but superior skier, Matt Langley, admiring Becky, Ethan's own daughter. It took an effort, in this air like slices of transparent metal interposed everywhere, to make these connections and to relate the young girl, her round face red with windburn as she skimmed down the runout slope, to himself. She was his daughter, age thirteen. Ethan had twin sons, two years younger, and his attention had always been focused on their skiing, on the irksome comedy of their double needs—the four boots to lace, the four mittens to find—and then their cute yet grim competition as now one and now the other gained the edge in the expertise of geländesprungs[1] and slalom[2] form. On their trips north into the mountains, Becky had come along for the ride. "Look how solid she is," Matt went on. "She doesn't cheat on it like your boys—those feet are absolutely together." The girl, grinning as if she could hear herself praised, wiggle-waggled to a flashy stop that sprayed snow over the men's ski tips.

"Where's Mommy?" she asked.

Ethan answered, "She went with the boys into the lodge. They couldn't take it." Their sinewy little male bodies had no insulation; weeping and shivering, they had begged to go in after a single T-bar[3] run.

"What sissies," Becky said.

Matt said, "This wind is wicked. And it's pick-

ing up. You should have been here at nine; Lord, it was lovely. All that fresh powder, and not a stir of wind."

Becky told him, "Dumb Tommy couldn't find his mittens, we spent an *hour* looking, and then Daddy got the Jeep stuck." Ethan, alerted now for signs of the wonderful in his daughter, was struck by the strange fact that she was making conversation. Unafraid, she was talking to Matt without her father's intercession.

"Mr. Langley was saying how nicely you were skiing."

"You're Olympic material, Becky."

The girl perhaps blushed; but her cheeks could get no redder. Her eyes, which, were she a child, she would have instantly averted, remained a second on Matt's face, as if to estimate how much he meant it. "It's easy down here," Becky said. "It's babyish."

Ethan asked, "Do you want to go up to the top?" He was freezing standing still, and the gondola would be sheltered from the wind.

---

1. **geländesprung** (gə len′də sprüng′), jump made by propelling oneself from a crouching position using both poles. [*German*]
2. **slalom** (slä′ləm), a race in which skiers rapidly zigzag downhill.
3. **T-bar**, a ski lift from which metal bars shaped like upside-down letter T's are suspended. The skier holds onto an upright and leans against the crossbar as the lift travels up a slope.

"Man and Daughter in the Cold," Copyright © 1968 by John Updike. Reprinted from *Museums and Women and Other Stories*, by John Updike, by permission of Alfred A. Knopf, Inc. and Andre Deutsch Limited. Originally appeared in *The New Yorker*.

Her eyes shifted to his, with another unconsciously thoughtful hesitation. "Sure. If you want to."

"Come along, Matt?"

"Thanks, no. It's too rough for me; I've had enough runs. This is the trouble with January—once it stops snowing, the wind comes up. I'll keep Elaine company in the lodge." Matt himself had no wife, no children. At thirty-eight, he was as free as his students, as light on his skis and as full of brave know-how. "In case of frostbite," he shouted after them, "rub snow on it."

Becky effortlessly skated ahead to the lift shed. The encumbered motion of walking on skis, not natural to him, made Ethan feel asthmatic: a fish out of water. He touched his parka pocket, to check that the inhalator was there. As a child he had imagined death as something attacking from outside, but now he saw that it was carried within; we nurse it for years, and it grows. The clock on the lodge wall said a quarter to noon. The giant thermometer read two degrees above zero. The racks outside were dense as hedges with idle skis. Crowds, any sensation of crowding or delay, quickened his asthma; as therapy he imagined the emptiness, the blue freedom, at the top of the mountain. The clatter of machinery inside the shed was comforting, and enough teenage boys were boarding gondolas to make the ascent seem normal and safe. Ethan's breathing eased. Becky proficiently handed her poles to the loader points up; her father was always caught by surprise, and often as not fumbled the little maneuver of letting his skis be taken from him. Until, five years ago, he had become an assistant professor at a New Hampshire college an hour to the south, he had never skied; he had lived in those Middle Atlantic cities where snow, its moment of virgin beauty by, is only an encumbering nuisance, a threat of suffocation. Whereas his children had grown up on skis.

Alone with his daughter in the rumbling isolation of the gondola, he wanted to explore her, and found her strange—strange in her uninquisitive child's silence, her accustomed poise in this ascending egg of metal. A dark figure with spreading legs veered out of control beneath them, fell forward, and vanished. Ethan cried out, astonished, scandalized; he imagined the man had buried himself alive. Becky was barely amused, and looked away before the dark spots struggling in the drift were lost from sight. As if she might know, Ethan asked, "Who was that?"

"Some kid." Kids, her tone suggested, were in plentiful supply; one could be spared.

He offered to dramatize the adventure ahead of them: "Do you think we'll freeze at the top?"

"Not exactly."

"What do you think it'll be like?"

"Miserable."

"Why are we doing this, do you think?"

"Because we paid the money for the all-day lift ticket."

"Becky, you think you're pretty smart, don't you?"

"Not really."

The gondola rumbled and lurched into the shed at the top; an attendant opened the door, and there was a howling mixed of wind and of boys whooping to keep warm. He was roughly handed two pairs of skis, and the handler, muffled to the eyes with a scarf, stared as if amazed that Ethan was so old. All the others struggling into skis in the lee of the shed were adolescent boys. Students: after fifteen years of teaching, Ethan tended to flinch from youth—its harsh noises, its cheerful rapacity, its cruel onward flow as one class replaced another, ate a year of his life, and was replaced by another.

Away from the shelter of the shed, the wind was a high monotonous pitch of pain. His cheeks instantly ached, and the hinges linking the elements of his face seemed exposed. His septum tingled like glass—the rim of a glass being rubbed by a moist finger to produce a note. Drifts ribbed the trail, obscuring Becky's ski tracks seconds after she made them, and at each push through the heaped snow his scope of breathing narrowed. By the time he reached the first steep section, the left half of his back hurt as it did only in

Andrew Wyeth (1917–), *From Mt. Kearsarge*. Private collection

the panic of a full asthmatic attack, and his skis, ignored, too heavy to manage, spread and swept him toward a snowbank at the side of the trail. He was bent far forward but kept his balance; the snow kissed his face lightly, instantly, all over; he straightened up, refreshed by the shock, thankful not to have lost a ski. Down the slope Becky had halted and was staring upward at him, worried. A huge blowing feather, a partition of snow, came between them. The cold, unprecedented in his experience, shone through his clothes like furious light, and as he rummaged through his parka for the inhalator he seemed to be searching glass shelves backed by a black wall. He found it, its icy plastic the touch of life, a clumsy key to his insides. Gasping, he exhaled, put it into his mouth, and inhaled; the isoproterenol spray, chilled into drops, opened his lungs enough for him to call on his daughter, "Keep moving! I'll catch up!"

Solid on her skis, she swung down among the moguls and wind-bared ice, and became small, and again waited. The moderate slope seemed a cliff; if he fell and sprained anything, he would freeze. His entire body would become locked tight against air and light and thought. His legs trembled; his breath moved in and out of a narrow slot beneath the pain in his back. The cold and blowing snow all around him constituted an immense crowding, but there was no way out of this white cave but to slide downward toward the dark spot that was his daughter. He had forgotten all his lessons. Leaning backward in an infant's tense snowplow, he floundered through alternating powder and ice.

"You O.K., Daddy?" Her stare was wide, its fright underlined by a pale patch on her cheek.

He used the inhalator again and gave himself breath to tell her, "I'm fine. Let's get down."

In this way, in steps of her leading and waiting, they worked down the mountain, out of the worst wind, into the lower trail that ran between birches and hemlocks. The cold had the quality not of absence but of force: an inverted burning. The last time Becky stopped and waited, the colorless crescent on her scarlet cheek disturbed him, reminded him of some injunction, but he could find in his brain, whittled to a dim determination to persist, only the advice to keep going, toward shelter and warmth. She told him, at a division of trails, "This is the easier way."

"Let's go the quicker way," he said, and in this last descent recovered the rhythm—knees together, shoulders facing the valley, weight forward as if in the moment of release from a diving board—not a resistance but a joyous acceptance of falling. They reached the base lodge, and with unfeeling hands removed their skis. Pushing into the cafeteria, Ethan saw in the momentary mirror of the door window that his face was a specter's; chin, nose, and eyebrows had retained the snow from the near-fall near the top. "Becky, look," he said, turning in the crowded warmth and clatter inside the door. "I'm a monster."

"I know, your face was absolutely white, I didn't know whether to tell you or not. I thought it might scare you."

He touched the pale patch on her cheek. "Feel anything?"

"No."

"Damn. I should have rubbed snow on it."

Matt and Elaine and the twins, flushed and stripped of their parkas, had eaten lunch; shouting and laughing with a strange guilty shrillness, they said that there had been repeated loudspeaker announcements not to go up to the top without face masks, because of frostbite. They had expected Ethan and Becky to come back

down on the gondola, as others had, after tasting the top. "It never occurred to us," Ethan said. He took the blame upon himself by adding, "I wanted to see the girl ski."

Their common adventure, and the guilt of his having given her frostbite, bound Becky and Ethan together in complicity for the rest of the day. They arrived home as sun was leaving even the tips of the hills; Elaine had invited Matt to supper, and while the windows of the house burned golden Ethan shoveled out the Jeep. The house was a typical New Hampshire farmhouse, less than two miles from the college, on the side of a hill, overlooking what had been a pasture, with the usual capacious porch running around three sides, cluttered with cordwood and last summer's lawn furniture. The woodsy sheltered scent of these porches, the sense of rural waste space, never failed to please Ethan, who had been raised in a Newark half-house, then a West Side apartment, and just before college a row house in Baltimore, with his grandparents. The wind had been left behind in the mountains. The air was as still as the stars. Shoveling the light dry snow became a lazy dance. But when he bent suddenly, his knees creaked, and his breathing shortened so that he paused. A sudden rectangle of light was flung from the shadows of the porch. Becky came out into the cold with him. She was carrying a lawn rake.

He asked her. "Should you be out again? How's your frostbite?" Though she was a distance away, there was no need, in the immaculate air, to raise his voice.

"It's O.K. It kind of tingles. And under my chin. Mommy made me put on a scarf."

"What's the lawn rake for?"

"It's a way you can make a path. It really works."

"O.K., you make a path to the garage and after I get my breath I'll see if I can get the Jeep back in."

"Are you having asthma?"

"A little."

"We were reading about it in biology. Dad,

see, it's kind of a tree inside you, and every branch has a little ring of muscle around it, and they tighten." From her gestures in the dark she was demonstrating, with mittens on.

What she described, of course, was classic unalloyed asthma, whereas his was shading into emphysema, which could only worsen. But he liked being lectured to—preferred it, indeed, to lecturing—and as the minutes of companionable silence with his daughter passed he took inward notes on the bright quick impressions flowing over him like a continuous voice. The silent cold. The stars. Orion[4] behind an elm. Minute scintillae in the snow at his feet. His daughter's strange black bulk against the white; the solid grace that had stolen upon her. The conspiracy of love. His father and he shoveling the car free from a sudden unwelcome storm in Newark, instantly gray with soot, the undercurrent of desperation, his father a salesman and must get to Camden. Got to get to Camden, boy, get to Camden or bust. Dead of a heart attack at forty-seven. Ethan tossed a shovelful into the air so the scintillae flashed in the steady golden chord from the house windows. Elaine and Matt sitting flushed at the lodge table, parkas off, in deshabille, as if sitting up in bed. Matt's way of turning a half circle on the top of a mogul, light as a diver. The cancerous unwieldiness of Ethan's own skis. His jealousy of his students, the many-headed immortality of their annual renewal. The flawless tall cruelty of the stars. Orion intertwined with the silhouetted elm. A black tree inside him. His daughter, busily sweeping with the rake, childish yet lithe, so curiously demonstrating this preference for his company. Feminine of her to forgive him her frostbite. Perhaps, flattered on skis,

felt the cold her element. Her womanhood soon enough to be smothered in warmth. A plow a mile away painstakingly scraped. He was missing the point of the lecture. The point was unstated: an absence. He was looking upon his daughter as a woman but without lust. The music around him was being produced, in the zero air, like a finger on crystal, by this hollowness, this generosity of negation. Without lust, without jealousy. Space seemed love, bestowed to be free in, and coldness the price. He felt joined to the great dead whose words it was his duty to teach.

The Jeep came up unprotestingly from the fluffy snow. It looked happy to be penned in the garage with Elaine's station wagon, and the skis, and the oiled chain saw, and the power mower dreamlessly waiting for spring. Ethan was happy, precariously so, so that rather than break he uttered a sound: "Becky?"

"Yeah?"

"You want to know what else Mr. Langley said?"

"What?" They trudged toward the porch, up the path the gentle rake had cleared.

"He said you ski better than the boys."

"I bet," she said, and raced to the porch, and in the precipitate way, evasive and female and pleased, that she flung herself to the top step he glimpsed something generic and joyous, a pageant that would leave him behind.

1968

---

4. *Orion* (ô rī′ən), a constellation, also called the Great Hunter, which appears to have the rough outline of a man wearing a belt and a sword and holding a shield and a club.

THINK AND DISCUSS

Understanding

1. How old is Ethan's daughter? Who are the other members of his family?
2. What is Becky's reaction to Matt Langley's compliment on her skiing?
3. When Ethan and Becky decide to go to the top of the mountain to ski, what does Matt do? What advice does he give?
4. Describe Ethan's home. How does it differ from the places where he was raised?

Analyzing

5. In what ways is Ethan different from his friend Matt Langley?
6. How does the fact that Ethan is a teacher shape his feelings about youth? What does he mean by "the many-headed immorality of their annual renewal"?
7. Review the bits of information given about Ethan's early life. How might Ethan's childhood affect his relationship with his daughter?
8. How and why have Ethan's notions about death changed since he was a child?
9. In a sense, Becky has led her father on a journey (see Themes in American Literature, page 639). How is this literally true? In what respect has she led him to a new awareness?

Extending

10. What is the significance of the title? In your opinion, would "Man and Girl Skiing" be a better title? Why or why not?

REVIEWING: Point of View

See Handbook of Literary Terms, p. 900.

Point of view is the vantage point from which an author presents the actions and characters of a story. The story may be related by a character (first-person point of view) or by a narrator who does not participate in the action (third-person point of view). Further, the third-person narrator may be *omniscient*—able to see into the minds of all characters, or *limited*—confined to a single character's perceptions.

1. From what point of view is the story told?
2. How might the opening paragraph change if the story had been told from Becky's point of view?

COMPOSITION

Changing the Point of View

Rewrite for your journal the opening paragraph of the story from Becky's point of view. Reread the first paragraph and note how the following elements might change from Becky's perspective. Who would the speakers be? How would the dialogue change accordingly? How would Becky describe the sight of the two men? How would she depict her own cold and windburned condition? Would she mention the twins?

Writing About Setting

Write an essay of from three to five paragraphs for a literary magazine analyzing the role setting plays in Updike's story. The setting is hinted at in the "cold" of the title. It is important in relation to Ethan's illness and Becky's developing maturity. Before you write, list details of both time and place that you consider important.

Writing About Point of View

Explain in several paragraphs to a classmate how the story would change if it were told from a third-person limited point of view rather than an omniscient one. In order to gather ideas, you might note answers to the first composition assignment above, titled Changing the Point of View. In addition, think about what information in this story could have been supplied only from an omniscient point of view and what that information adds to the story. See "Writing About Point of View" in the Writer's Handbook.

Themes IN AMERICAN LITERATURE

The Journey

"Drive carefully. The life you save may be your own." This road sign supplies the title of a story by Flannery O'Connor that appears in this unit. The significance of this warning is underscored by an observation of a character in the story: ". . . the spirit, lady, is like a automobile, always on the move, always. . . ." The journey motif in literature has come to represent life itself—the voyage from birth to death or the passage from innocence to maturity and wisdom.

Perhaps one of the most famous journeys in American literature is that of Huckleberry Finn, who grows in wisdom and experience as he travels down the Mississippi and ultimately heads out for the new territory and away from the evil and hypocrisy of civilization. John Steinbeck's *Grapes of Wrath* follows a poor family on its journey from Oklahoma to California, a trip consciously modeled upon the exodus of the Jews from Egypt to the Promised Land.

Many of the selections in *The United States in Literature* deal with voyages and quests, both physical and spiritual. Unit 1 provides the travel narratives of Columbus, De Vaca, and La Salle, as well as Benjamin Franklin's search for moral perfection.

"Follow the Drinking Gourd" in Unit 2 provides a directive to black slaves preparing to escape to freedom. James W. Pennington in *Escape: A Slave Narrative* chronicles his perilous journey to the free state of Pennsylvania. Also included in the unit is "The Kansas Emigrants," in which John Greenleaf Whittier encourages New Englanders to emigrate to Kansas and to keep that territory free from the stain of slavery. The shortest journey in measured distance is that of Oliver Wendell Holmes's chambered nautilus, whose developing shell symbolizes the progress of life toward the ultimate freedom of death.

Several of the stories in Unit 5 are steeped in the frontier myth and, as such, offer memorable illustrations of the journey motif. In John Steinbeck's story "The Leader of the People," Jody's grandfather explains that it wasn't getting *to* the West that mattered to the pioneers, ". . . it was movement and westering." In subsequent literature, the journey increasingly comes to symbolize a quest of the soul. In William Faulkner's story "The Bear," a boy travels through an Edenlike forest in a simultaneous search for a mythic animal and for his own identity. In Eudora Welty's story "A Worn Path," old Phoenix (significantly named) struggles in a kind of endless quest that ultimately signifies human endurance and renewal. The prototype of the modern questing antihero is T. S. Eliot's Prufrock, who wanders "through half-deserted streets" in search of spiritual fulfillment.

Unit 7 includes the modern odyssey of William Least Heat Moon over the "blue highways" of America in search of both himself and the character of the nation. Ralph Ellison and Teresa Paloma Acosta range backward in time to the America of their parents and grandparents. A trip up and down a mountain in Updike's "Man and Daughter in the Cold" represents a stage in the journey from adolescence to adulthood for a girl and a lesson in acceptance of mortality for her father. The journey motif is cleverly inverted in John Morris's poem "Running It Backward," as life reverses itself through a flick of the switch of a movie machine. Tom Shiftlet, in "The Life You Save May Be Your Own," takes a jalopy on a journey in a mad quest for perpetual mobility—a mania that Tom Wingfield describes, in *The Glass Menagerie,* as an attempt "to find in motion what was lost in space."

The theme of the journey has been preeminent in part because the continent is large and much of the population lacks deep roots. There is always space to move on, in hope of renewal.

Bernard Malamud
1914–1986

Bernard Malamud was born to Russian Jewish immigrants who earned a meager living running a grocery store in Brooklyn. The struggles and suffering of the immigrant experience entered the fiction of Malamud, but were transfigured. "I try to see the Jew as universal man," he wrote; "Every man is a Jew though he may not know it." In his "sad and comic tales," the lonely and oppressed often are redeemed through suffering.

Encouraged by parents and teachers, Malamud graduated from the City College of New York in 1936 and began writing, spurred by the rise of fascism, the plight of the Jews in Europe, and the Second World War. From 1940 to 1949 he taught high-school English at night, earning an M.A. at Columbia in 1942. Until his death, he continued to teach, first at Oregon State, then at Bennington College, Vermont.

His first novel, *The Natural* (1952), a comic blend of baseball and myth, was followed by his acknowledged masterpiece, *The Assistant* (1957), a novel about a poor Jewish shopkeeper and his Italian assistant. His collection of short stories, *The Magic Barrel* (1958) won a National Book Award, as did the novel *The Fixer* (1966), also awarded a Pulitzer Prize. In 1983, Malamud was presented with the prestigious Gold Medal for Fiction from the American Academy and Institute of Arts and Letters.

The writer's "most important task," Malamud has said, "is to recapture [man's] image as human being as each of us in his secret heart knows it to be, and as history and literature have from the beginning revealed it. . . . In recreating the humanity of man, in reality his greatness, he will, among other things, hold up the mirror to the mystery of him, in which poetry and possibility live, though he has endlessly betrayed them."

The First Seven Years

Bernard Malamud

eld, the shoemaker, was annoyed that his helper, Sobel, was so insensitive to his reverie that he wouldn't for a minute cease his fanatic pounding at the other bench. He gave him a look, but Sobel's bald head was bent over the last as he worked and he didn't notice. The shoemaker shrugged and continued to peer through the partly frosted window at the near-sighted haze of falling February snow. Neither the shifting white blur outside, nor the sudden deep remembrance of the snowy Polish village where he had wasted his youth could turn his thoughts from Max the college boy, (a constant visitor in the mind since early that morning when Feld saw him trudging through the snowdrifts on his way to school) whom he so much respected because of the sacrifices he had made throughout the years—in winter or direst heat—to further his education. An old wish returned to haunt the shoemaker: that he had had a son instead of a daughter, but this blew away in the snow for Feld, if anything, was a practical man. Yet he could not help but contrast the diligence of the boy, who was a peddler's son, with Miriam's unconcern for an education. True, she was always with a book in her hand, yet when the opportunity arose for a college education, she had said no she would rather find a job. He had begged her to go, pointing out how many fathers could not afford to send their children to college, but she said she wanted to be independent. As for education, what was it, she asked, but books, which Sobel, who diligently read the classics, would as usual advise her on. Her answer greatly grieved her father.

A figure emerged from the snow and the door opened. At the counter the man withdrew from a wet paper bag a pair of battered shoes for repair. Who he was the shoemaker for a moment had no idea, then his heart trembled as he realized, before he had thoroughly discerned the face, that Max himself was standing there, embarrassedly explaining what he wanted done to his old shoes. Though Feld listened eagerly, he couldn't hear a word, for the opportunity that had burst upon him was deafening.

He couldn't exactly recall when the thought had occurred to him, because it was clear he had more than once considered suggesting to the boy that he go out with Miriam. But he had not dared speak, for if Max said no, how would he face him again? Or suppose Miriam, who harped so often on independence, blew up in anger and shouted at him for his meddling? Still, the chance was too good to let by: all it meant was an introduction. They might long ago have become friends had they happened to meet somewhere, therefore was it not his duty—an obligation—to bring them together, nothing more, a harmless connivance to replace an accidental encounter in the subway, let's say, or a mutual friend's introduction in the street? Just let him once see and talk to her and

"The First Seven Years" from *The Magic Barrel* by Bernard Malamud. Copyright 1950, renewed © 1978 by Bernard Malamud. Reprinted by permission of Farrar, Straus and Giroux, Inc. and Chatto & Windus.

he would for sure be interested. As for Miriam, what possible harm for a working girl in an office, who met only loud-mouthed salesmen and illiterate shipping clerks, to make the acquaintance of a fine scholarly boy? Maybe he would awaken in her a desire to go to college; if not—the shoemaker's mind at last came to grips with the truth—let her marry an educated man and live a better life.

When Max finished describing what he wanted done to his shoes, Feld marked them, both with enormous holes in the soles which he pretended not to notice, with large white-chalk x's, and the rubber heels, thinned to the nails, he marked with o's, though it troubled him he might have mixed up the letters. Max inquired the price, and the shoemaker cleared his throat and asked the boy, above Sobel's insistent hammering, would he please step through the side door there into the hall. Though surprised, Max did as the shoemaker requested and Feld went in after him. For a minute they were both silent, because Sobel had stopped banging, and it seemed they understood neither was to say anything until the noise began again. When it did, loudly, the shoemaker quickly told Max why he had asked to talk to him.

"Ever since you went to high school," he said, in the dimly-lit hallway, "I watched you in the morning go to the subway to school, and I said always to myself, this is a fine boy that he wants so much an education."

"Thanks," Max said, nervously alert. He was tall and grotesquely thin, with sharply cut features, particularly a beaklike nose. He was wearing a loose, long slushy overcoat that hung down to his ankles, looking like a rug draped over his bony shoulders, and a soggy, old brown hat, as battered as the shoes he had brought in.

"I am a businessman," the shoemaker abruptly said to conceal his embarrassment, "so I will explain you right away why I talk to you. I have a girl, my daughter Miriam—she is nineteen—a very nice girl and also so pretty that everybody looks on her when she passes by in the street. She is smart, always with a book, and I thought to myself that a boy like you, an educated boy—I

thought maybe you will be interested sometime to meet a girl like this." He laughed a bit when he had finished and was tempted to say more but had the good sense not to.

Max stared down like a hawk. For an uncomfortable second he was silent, then he asked, "Did you say nineteen?"

"Yes."

"Would it be all right to inquire if you have a picture of her?"

"Just a minute." The shoemaker went into the store and hastily returned with a snapshot that Max held up to the light.

"She's all right," he said.

Feld waited.

"And is she sensible—not the flightly kind?"

"She is very sensible."

After another short pause, Max said it was okay with him if he met her.

"Here is my telephone," said the shoemaker, hurriedly handing him a slip of paper. "Call her up. She comes home from work six o'clock."

Max folded the paper and tucked it away into his worn leather wallet.

"About the shoes," he said. "How much did you say they will cost me?"

"Don't worry about the price."

"I just like to have an idea."

"A dollar—dollar fifty. A dollar fifty," the shoemaker said.

At once he felt bad, for he usually charged two twenty-five for this kind of job. Either he should have asked the regular price, or done the work for nothing.

Later, as he entered the store, he was startled by a violent clanging and looked up to see Sobel pounding with all his might upon the naked last. It broke, the iron striking the floor and jumping with a thump against the wall, but before the enraged shoemaker could cry out, the assistant had torn his hat and coat from the hook and rushed out into the snow.

So Feld, who had looked forward to anticipating how it would go with his daughter and Max, instead had a great worry on his mind. Without his temperamental helper he was a lost

Edward Hopper, *Sunday* (1926). The Phillips Collection, Washington, D.C.

man, especially since it was years now that he had carried the store alone. The shoemaker had for an age suffered from a heart condition that threatened collapse if he dared exert himself. Five years ago, after an attack, it had appeared as though he would have either to sacrifice his business upon the auction block and live on a pittance thereafter, or put himself at the mercy of some unscrupulous employee who would in the end probably ruin him. But just at the moment of his darkest despair, this Polish refugee, Sobel, appeared one night from the street and begged for

work. He was a stocky man, poorly dressed, with a bald head that had once been blond, a severely plain face and soft blue eyes prone to tears over the sad books he read, a young man but old—no one would have guessed thirty. Though he confessed he knew nothing of shoemaking, he said he was apt and would work for a very little if Feld taught him the trade. Thinking that with, after all, a landsman,[1] he would have less to fear

1. *landsman*, a fellow countryman.

than from a complete stranger, Feld took him on and within six weeks the refugee rebuilt as good a shoe as he, and not long thereafter expertly ran the business for the thoroughly relieved shoemaker.

Feld could trust him with anything and did, frequently going home after an hour or two at the store, leaving all the money in the till, knowing Sobel would guard every cent of it. The amazing thing was that he demanded so little. His wants were few; in money he wasn't interested—in nothing but books, it seemed—which he one by one lent to Miriam, together with his profuse, queer written comments, manufactured during his lonely rooming house evenings, thick pads of commentary which the shoemaker peered at and twitched his shoulders over as his daughter, from her fourteenth year, read page by sanctified page, as if the word of God were inscribed on them. To protect Sobel, Feld himself had to see that he received more than he asked for. Yet his conscience bothered him for not insisting that the assistant accept a better wage than he was getting, though Feld had honestly told him he could earn a handsome salary if he worked elsewhere, or maybe opened a place of his own. But the assistant answered, somewhat ungraciously, that he was not interested in going elsewhere, and though Feld frequently asked himself what keeps him here? why does he stay? he finally answered it that the man, no doubt because of his terrible experiences as a refugee, was afraid of the world.

After the incident with the broken last, angered by Sobel's behavior, the shoemaker decided to let him stew for a week in the rooming house, although his own strength was taxed dangerously and the business suffered. However, after several sharp nagging warnings from both his wife and daughter, he went finally in search of Sobel, as he had once before, quite recently, when over some fancied slight—Feld had merely asked him not to give Miriam so many books to read because her eyes were strained and red—the assistant had left the place in a huff, an incident which, as usual, came to nothing for he had returned after the shoemaker had talked to him, and taken his seat at the bench. But this time, after Feld had plodded through the snow to Sobel's house—he had thought of sending Miriam but the idea became repugnant to him—the burly landlady at the door informed him in a nasal voice that Sobel was not at home, and though Feld knew this was a nasty lie, for where had the refugee to go? still for some reason he was not completely sure of—it may have been the cold and his fatigue—he decided not to insist on seeing him. Instead he went home and hired a new helper.

Having settled the matter, though not entirely to his satisfaction, for he had much more to do than before, and so, for example, could no longer lie late in bed mornings because he had to get up to open the store for the new assistant, a speechless, dark man with an irritating rasp as he worked, whom he would not trust with the key as he had Sobel. Furthermore, this one, though able to do a fair repair job, knew nothing of grades of leather or prices, so Feld had to make his own purchases; and every night at closing time it was necessary to count the money in the till and lock up. However, he was not dissatisfied, for he lived much in his thoughts of Max and Miriam. The college boy had called her, and they had arranged a meeting for this coming Friday night. The shoemaker would personally have preferred Saturday, which he felt would make it a date of the first magnitude, but he learned Friday was Miriam's choice, so he said nothing. The day of the week did not matter. What mattered was the aftermath. Would they like each other and want to be friends? He sighed at all the time that would have to go by before he knew for sure. Often he was tempted to talk to Miriam about the boy, to ask whether she thought she would like his type —he had told her only that he considered Max a nice boy and had suggested he call her—but the one time he tried she snapped at him—justly—how should she know?

At last Friday came. Feld was not feeling particularly well so he stayed in bed, and Mrs. Feld thought it better to remain in the bedroom with him when Max called. Miriam received the boy, and her parents could hear their voices, his throaty one, as they talked. Just before leaving, Miriam brought Max to the bedroom door and he stood there a minute, a tall, slightly hunched figure wearing a thick, droopy suit, and apparently at ease as he greeted the shoemaker and his wife, which was surely a good sign. And Miriam, although she had worked all day, looked fresh and pretty. She was a large-framed girl with a well-shaped body, and she had a fine open face and soft hair. They made, Feld thought, a first-class couple.

Miriam returned after 11:30. Her mother was already asleep, but the shoemaker got out of bed and after locating his bathrobe went into the kitchen, where Miriam, to his surprise, sat at the table, reading.

"So where did you go?" Feld asked pleasantly.

"For a walk," she said, not looking up.

"I advised him" Feld said, clearing his throat, "he shouldn't spend so much money."

"I didn't care."

The shoemaker boiled up some water for tea and sat down at the table with a cupful and a thick slice of lemon.

"So, how," he sighed after a sip, "did you enjoy?"

"It was all right."

He was silent. She must have sensed his disappointment, for she added, "You can't really tell much the first time."

"You will see him again?"

Turning a page, she said that Max had asked for another date.

"For when?"

"Saturday."

"So what did you say?"

"What did I say?" she asked, delaying for a moment—"I said yes."

Afterwards she inquired about Sobel, and Feld, without exactly knowing why, said the assistant had got another job. Miriam said nothing more and began to read. The shoemaker's conscience did not trouble him; he was satisfied with the Saturday date.

During the week, by placing here and there a deft question, he managed to get from Miriam some information about Max. It surprised him to learn that the boy was not studying to be either a doctor or lawyer but was taking a business course leading to a degree in accountancy. Feld was a little disappointed because he thought of accountants as bookkeepers and would have preferred "a higher profession." However, it was not long before he had investigated the subject and discovered that Certified Public Accountants were highly respected people, so he was thoroughly content as Saturday approached. But because Saturday was a busy day, he was much in the store and therefore did not see Max when he came to call for Miriam. From his wife he learned there had been nothing especially revealing about their meeting. Max had rung the bell and Miriam had got her coat and left with him—nothing more. Feld did not probe, for his wife was not particularly observant. Instead, he waited up for Miriam with a newspaper on his lap, which he scarcely looked at so lost was he in thinking of the future. He awoke to find her in the room with him, tiredly removing her hat. Greeting her, he was suddenly inexplicably afraid to ask anything about the evening. But since she volunteered nothing he was at last forced to inquire how she had enjoyed herself. Miriam began something non-committal but apparently changed her mind, for she said after a minute, "I was bored."

When Feld had sufficiently recovered from his anguished disappointment to ask why, she answered without hesitation, "Because he's nothing more than a materialist."

"What means this word?"

"He has no soul. He's only interested in things."

He considered her statement for a long time but then asked, "Will you see him again?"

"He didn't ask."

"Suppose he will ask you?"

"I won't see him."

He did not argue; however, as the days went by he hoped increasingly she would change her mind. He wished the boy would telephone, because he was sure there was more to him than

Miriam, with her inexperienced eye, could discern. But Max didn't call. As a matter of fact he took a different route to school, no longer passing the shoemaker's store, and Feld was deeply hurt.

Then one afternoon Max came in and asked for his shoes. The shoemaker took them down from the shelf where he had placed them, apart from the other pairs. He had done the work himself and the soles and heels were well built and firm. The shoes had been highly polished and somehow looked better then new. Max's Adam's apple went up once when he saw them, and his eyes had little lights in them.

"How much?" he asked, without directly looking at the shoemaker.

"Like I told you before," Feld answered sadly. "One dollar fifty cents."

Max handed him two crumpled bills and received in return a newly minted silver half dollar.

He left. Miriam had not been mentioned. That night the shoemaker discovered that his new assistant had been all the while stealing from him, and he suffered a heart attack.

Though the attack was very mild, he lay in bed for three weeks. Miriam spoke of going for Sobel, but sick as he was Feld rose in wrath against the idea. Yet in his heart he knew there was no other way, and the first weary day back in the shop thoroughy convinced him, so that night after supper he dragged himself to Sobel's rooming house.

He toiled up the stairs, though he knew it was bad for him, and at the top knocked at the door. Sobel opened it and the shoemaker entered. The room was a small, poor one, with a single window facing the street. It contained a narrow cot, a low table, and several stacks of books piled haphazardly around on the floor along the wall, which made him think how queer Sobel was, to be uneducated and read so much. He had once asked him, Sobel, why you read so much? and the assistant could not answer him. Did you ever study in a college someplace? he had asked, but Sobel shook his head. He read, he said, to know. But to know what, the shoemaker demanded, and to know, why? Sobel never explained, which proved he read much because he was queer.

Feld sat down to recover his breath. The assistant was resting on his bed with his heavy back to the wall. His shirt and trousers were clean, and his stubby fingers, away from the shoemaker's bench, were strangely pallid. His face was thin and pale, as if he had been shut in this room since the day he had bolted from the store.

"So when you will come back to work?" Feld asked him.

To his surprise, Sobel burst out, "Never."

Jumping up, he strode over to the window that looked out upon the miserable street. "Why should I come back?" he cried.

"I will raise your wages."

"Who cares for your wages!"

The shoemaker, knowing he didn't care, was at a loss what else to say.

"What do you want from me, Sobel?"

"Nothing."

"I always treated you like you was my son."

Sobel vehemently denied it. "So why you look for strange boys in the street they should go out with Miriam? Why you don't think of me?"

The shoemaker's hands and feet turned freezing cold. His voice became so hoarse he couldn't speak. At last he cleared his throat and croaked, "So what has my daughter got to do with a shoemaker thirty-five years old who works for me?"

"Why do you think I worked so long for you?" Sobel cried out. "For the stingy wages I sacrificed five years of my life so you could have to eat and drink and where to sleep?"

"Then for what?" shouted the shoemaker.

"For Miriam," he blurted—"for her."

The shoemaker, after a time, managed to say, "I pay wages in cash, Sobel," and lapsed into silence. Though he was seething with excitement, his mind was coldly clear, and he had to admit to himself he had sensed all along that Sobel felt this way. He had never so much as thought it consciously, but he had felt it and was afraid.

"Miriam knows?" he muttered hoarsely.

"She knows."

"You told her?"

"No."

"Then how does she know?"

"How does she know?" Sobel said, "because she knows. She knows who I am and what is in my heart."

Feld had a sudden insight. In some devious way, with his books and commentary, Sobel had given Miriam to understand that he loved her. The shoemaker felt a terrible anger at him for his deceit.

"Sobel, you are crazy," he said bitterly. "She will never marry a man so old and ugly like you."

Sobel turned black with rage. He cursed the shoemaker, but then, though he trembled to hold it in, his eyes filled with tears and he broke into deep sobs. With his back to Feld, he stood at the window, fists clenched, and his shoulders shook with his choked sobbing.

Watching him, the shoemaker's anger diminished. His teeth were on edge with pity for the man, and his eyes grew moist. How strange and sad that a refugee, a grown man, bald and old with his miseries, who had by the skin of his teeth escaped Hitler's incinerators,[2] should fall in love, when he had got to America, with a girl less than half his age. Day after day, for five years he had sat at his bench, cutting and hammering away, waiting for the girl to become a woman, unable to ease his heart with speech, knowing no protest but desperation.

"Ugly I didn't mean," he said half aloud.

Then he realized that what he had called ugly was not Sobel but Miriam's life if she married him. He felt for his daughter a strange and gripping sorrow, as if she were already Sobel's bride, the wife, after all, of a shoemaker, and had in her life no more than her mother had had. And all his dreams for her—why he had slaved and destroyed his heart with anxiety and labor—all these dreams of a better life were dead.

The room was quiet. Sobel was standing by the window reading, and it was curious that when he read he looked young.

"She is only nineteen," Feld said brokenly. "This is too young yet to get married. Don't ask her for two years more, till she is twenty-one, then you can talk to her."

Sobel didn't answer. Feld rose and left. He went slowly down the stairs but once outside, though it was an icy night and the crisp falling snow whitened the street, he walked with a stronger stride.

But the next morning, when the shoemaker arrived, heavy-hearted, to open the store, he saw he needn't have come, for his assistant was already seated at the last, pounding leather for his love.

1950

---

2. *Hitler's incinerators*, the ovens used by the Nazis for the mass disposal of their victims' bodies.

THINK AND DISCUSS
Understanding
1. Where is Max going as he trudges through the snowdrifts past Feld's shop? About what does Feld speak privately to Max?
2. How would you describe Sobel—his background, appearance, and interests? What has he done on two occasions that indicate he is temperamental?
3. What is Miriam's appraisal of Max after their second date?
4. When Feld goes to Sobel's rooming house, what does he offer the assistant to return to his job? What promise finally lures Sobel back?

Analyzing
5. Of Feld, Sobel, Miriam, and Max, who do

you feel is the central character—who most nearly comes to life? Whom can you most easily visualize? Explain.

6. Malamud's characters retain traces of Eastern European culture in some of their mannerisms, speech, and attitudes. Cite examples of their original cultural background.

7. What lesson about life does Feld learn from the events he seeks to control?

8. Malamud's title is an **allusion** to the biblical story of Jacob, who worked two seven-year periods to earn the right to marry Rachel (Genesis 29:13–31). Do you consider this a story about a marriage contract between two men or a love story between a man and a woman? In answering, explain to what degree Miriam has chosen to marry Sobel.

Extending

9. The hope for success in the future that many immigrants to the United States wanted to attain is often called "the American Dream" (see Themes in American Literature, page 619). How does each character seem to interpret this dream?

REVIEWING: Plot HP
See Handbook of Literary Terms, p. 899.

A **plot** is a series of interrelated actions and events in a story. The basis of a plot is a conflict, or struggle—either internal or external—between opposing forces. Every plot builds to an emotional peak, or climax, followed by a resolution or denouement.

1. What is the conflict in "The First Seven Years"?

2. Where does the climax come in the story? What is the resolution?

3. The order of events in a plot is important. Why do you think Sobel does not declare his love for Miriam until the end of the story?

VOCABULARY
Context, Roots, and Affixes

Follow the directions in answering questions about each of the following italicized words. If necessary, use the Glossary.

1. The narrator describes Max as *grotesquely* thin and says that the thought of sending Miriam to Sobel's apartment was *repugnant* to Feld. Though similar in connotation, the words *grotesque* and *repugnant* are not synonyms. Explain the difference in meaning between them.

2. After Feld has had his heart attack, he is afraid he will be at the mercy of some *unscrupulous* employee. What is the root word and its meaning? Using your knowledge of *un-* and *-ous*, what does *unscrupulous* mean?

3. Miriam does not like Max because she thinks he is a *materialist*. What is the root word and its meaning? Using your knowledge of *-ist*, explain what a *materialist* is.

4. Sobel *vehemently* denies that Feld has always treated him as a son. What does *vehement* mean?

5. Sobel's books are piled *haphazardly* around his rooming house. Which of the following words is closest in meaning to *haphazard?* (**a**) insistent; (**b**) inexplicable; (**c**) random; (**d**) devious. Use *haphazard* in a sentence that shows you understand its meaning.

COMPOSITION
Summarizing Plot

Assume that you are a writer for a television guide, and that you are writing a synopsis of a television production of "The First Seven Years." Write a one-paragraph synopsis, including a statement of the conflict, a summary of the complication, and a hint of the climax and resolution. At the same time, don't give the actual plot away.

Analyzing Characterization

Write a three- or four-paragraph analysis of Malamud's characterization of Feld for readers of the story. Examine the techniques Malamud has used and evaluate their success. Note especially how Malamud portrays inner feelings—Feld's dreams, his frustrations, his ambitions for his daughter, his self-deceptions, and his coming to terms with reality. See "Writing About Characters" in the Writer's Handbook.

BIOGRAPHY

Harry Mark Petrakis

1923–

Petrakis was born the son of a Greek Orthodox priest in St. Louis and grew up there and in Chicago's Greek community. He earned his living in a variety of ways—as a steelworker, real-estate salesman, and television scriptwriter.

In his fiction, he has drawn on his boyhood experiences in many different jobs. He has a deep sympathy for ordinary people, often immigrants, struggling for a living; and he is able to paint their portraits vividly because of his keen ear for the inflections of their speech and his sharp eye for the rhythms of their lives.

Petrakis's books include *Lion at My Heart* (1959), *The Odyssey of Kostas Volakis* (1963), and *In the Land of Morning* (1973). His collection of short stories, *Pericles on 31st Street* (1965) was nominated for a National Book Award. *A Petrakis Reader* appeared in 1978, followed in 1983 by the novel *Days of Vengeance* and an autobiography, *Reflections; a Writer's Life, a Writer's Work.*

 See PROTAGONIST/ANTAGONIST in the Handbook of Literary Terms, page 901.

The Wooing of Ariadne

Harry Mark Petrakis

 knew from the beginning she must accept my love—put aside foolish female protestations. It is the distinction of the male to be the aggressor and the cloak of the female to lend grace to the pursuit. Aha! I am wise to these wiles.

I first saw Ariadne at a dance given by the Spartan brotherhood in the Legion Hall on Laramie Street. The usual assemblage of prune-faced and banana-bodied women smelling of virtuous ane-

mia. They were an outrage to a man such as myself.

Then I saw her! A tall stately woman, perhaps in her early thirties. She had firm and slender

---

Ariadne (ar′ē ad′nē).
Petrakis (pe trä′kis).

"The Wooing of Ariadne" from *Pericles on 31st Street* by Harry Mark Petrakis. Copyright © 1965 by Harry Mark Petrakis. Reprinted by permission of Toni Strassman, Author's Representative.

arms bare to the shoulders and a graceful neck. Her hair was black and thick and piled in a great bun at the back of her head. That grand abundance of hair attracted me at once. This modern aberration women have of chopping their hair close to the scalp and leaving it in fantastic disarray I find revolting.

I went at once to my friend Vasili,[1] the baker, and asked him who she was.

"Ariadne Langos," he said. "Her father is Janco Langos, the grocer."

"Is she engaged or married?"

"No," he said slyly. "They say she frightens off the young men. They say she is very spirited."

"Excellent," I said and marveled at my good fortune in finding her unpledged. "Introduce me at once."

"Marko," Vasili said with some apprehension. "Do not commit anything rash."

I pushed the little man forward. "Do not worry, little friend," I said. "I am a man suddenly possessed by a vision. I must meet her at once."

We walked together across the dance floor to where my beloved stood. The closer we came the more impressive was the majestic swell of her breasts and the fine great sweep of her thighs. She towered over the insignificant apple-core women around her. Her eyes, dark and thoughtful, seemed to be restlessly searching the room.

Be patient, my dove! Marko is coming.

"Miss Ariadne," Vasili said. "This is Mr. Marko Palamas.[2] He desires to have the honor of your acquaintance."

She looked at me for a long and piercing moment. I imagined her gauging my mighty strength by the width of my shoulders and the circumference of my arms. I felt the tips of my mustache bristle with pleasure. Finally she nodded with the barest minimum of courtesy. I was not discouraged.

"Miss Ariadne," I said, "may I have the pleasure of this dance?"

She stared at me again with her fiery eyes. I could imagine more timid men shriveling before her fierce gaze. My heart flamed at the passion her rigid exterior concealed.

"I think not," she said.

"Don't you dance?"

Vasili gasped beside me. An old prune-face standing nearby clucked her toothless gums.

"Yes, I dance," Ariadne said coolly. "I do not wish to dance with you."

"Why?" I asked courteously.

"I do not think you heard me," she said. "I do not wish to dance with you."

Oh, the sly and lovely darling. Her subterfuge so apparent. Trying to conceal her pleasure at my interest.

"Why?" I asked again.

"I am not sure," she said. "It could be your appearance, which bears considerable resemblance to a gorilla, or your manner, which would suggest closer alliance to a pig."

"Now that you have met my family," I said engagingly, "let us dance."

"Not now," she said, and her voice rose. "Not this dance or the one after. Not tonight or tomorrow night or next month or next year. Is that clear?"

Sweet, sweet Ariadne. Ancient and eternal game of retreat and pursuit. My pulse beat more quickly.

Vasili pulled at my sleeve. He was my friend, but without the courage of a goat. I shook him off and spoke to Ariadne.

"There is a joy like fire that consumes a man's heart when he first sets eyes on his beloved," I said. "This I felt when I first saw you." My voice trembled under a mighty passion. "I swear before God from this moment that I love you."

She stared shocked out of her deep dark eyes and, beside her, old prune-face staggered as if she had been kicked. Then my beloved did something which proved indisputably that her passion was as intense as mine.

She doubled up her fist and struck me in the eye. A stout blow for a woman that brought a haze to my vision, but I shook my head and moved a step closer.

---

1. *Vasili* (vä sē′lē).
2. *Palamas* (pä lä mäs′).

"I would not care," I said, "if you struck out both my eyes. I would cherish the memory of your beauty forever."

By this time the music had stopped, and the dancers formed a circle of idiot faces about us. I paid them no attention and ignored Vasili, who kept whining and pulling at my sleeve.

"You are crazy!" she said. "You must be mad! Remove yourself from my presence or I will tear out both your eyes and your tongue besides!"

You see! Another woman would have cried, or been frightened into silence. But my Ariadne, worthy and venerable, hurled her spirit into my teeth.

"I would like to call on your father tomorrow," I said. From the assembled dancers who watched there rose a few vagrant whispers and some rude laughter. I stared at them carefully and they hushed at once. My temper and strength of arm were well known.

Ariadne did not speak again, but in a magnificent spirit stamped from the floor. The music began, and men and women began again to dance. I permitted Vasili to pull me to a corner.

"You are insane!" he said. He wrung his withered fingers in anguish. "You assaulted her like a Turk![3] Her relatives will cut out your heart!"

"My intentions were honorable," I said. "I saw her and loved her and told her so." At this point I struck my fist against my chest. Poor Vasili jumped.

"But you do not court a woman that way," he said.

"*You* don't, my anemic friend," I said. "Nor do the rest of these sheep. But I court a woman that way!"

He looked to heaven and helplessly shook his head. I waved good-by and started for my hat and coat.

"Where are you going?" he asked.

"To prepare for tomorrow," I said, "In the morning I will speak to her father."

I left the hall and in the street felt the night wind cold on my flushed cheeks. My blood was inflamed. The memory of her loveliness fed fuel to the fire. For the first time I understood with a terrible clarity the driven heroes of the past performing mighty deeds in love. Paris stealing Helen in passion, and Menelaus pursuing with a great fleet.[4] In that moment if I knew the whole world would be plunged into conflict I would have followed Ariadne to Hades.

I went to my rooms above my tavern. I could not sleep. All night I tossed in restless frenzy. I touched my eye that she had struck with her spirited hand.

Ariadne! Ariadne! my soul cried out.

In the morning I bathed and dressed carefully. I confirmed the address of Langos, the grocer, and started to his store. It was a bright cold November morning, but I walked with spring in my step.

When I opened the door of the Langos grocery, a tiny bell rang shrilly. I stepped into the store piled with fruits and vegetables and smelling of cabbages and greens.

A stooped little old man with white bushy hair and owlish eyes came toward me. He looked as if his veins contained vegetable juice instead of blood, and if he were, in truth, the father of my beloved I marveled at how he could have produced such a paragon of women.

"Are you Mr. Langos?"

"I am," he said and he came closer. "I am."

"I met your daughter last night," I said. "Did she mention I was going to call?"

He shook his head somberly.

"My daughter mentioned you," he said. "In thirty years I have never seen her in such a state of agitation. She was possessed."

"The effect on me was the same," I said. "We met for the first time last night, and I fell passionately in love."

---

3. *like a Turk*, a comparison that reveals the continuous hostility between Greek and Turk during the Ottoman (Turkish) Empire (*c.* 1300–1922).
4. *Paris . . . fleet.* According to Greek legend Paris, the son of Priam, King of Troy, kidnaped Helen, the young wife of Menelaus (men'ə lā'əs), King of Sparta. This incident led to the Trojan War in which Menelaus commanded a fleet that destroyed Troy and rescued Helen.

"Incredible," the old man said.

"You wish to know something about me," I said. "My name is Marko Palamas. I am a Spartan[5] emigrated to this country eleven years ago. I am forty-one years old. I have been a wrestler and a sailor and fought with the resistance movement in Greece in the war. For this service I was decorated by the king. I own a small but profitable tavern on Dart Street. I attend church regularly. I love your daughter."

As I finished he stepped back and bumped a rack of fruit. An orange rolled off to the floor. I bent and retrieved it to hand it to him, and he cringed as if he thought I might bounce it off his old head.

"She is a bad-tempered girl," he said. "Stubborn, impatient, and spoiled. She has been the cause of considerable concern to me. All the eligible young men have been driven away by her temper and disposition."

"Poor girl," I said. "Subjected to the courting of calves and goats."

The old man blinked his owlish eyes. The front door opened and a battleship of a woman sailed in.

"Three pounds of tomatoes, Mr. Langos," she said. "I am in a hurry. Please to give me good ones. Last week two spoiled before I had a chance to put them into Demetri's salad."

"I am very sorry," Mr. Langos said. He turned to me. "Excuse me, Mr. Poulmas."

"Palamas," I said. "Marko Palamas."

He nodded nervously. He went to wait on the battleship, and I spent a moment examining the store. Neat and small. I would not imagine he did more than hold his own. In the rear of the store there were stairs leading to what appeared to be an apartment above. My heart beat faster.

When he had bagged the tomatoes and given change, he returned to me and said, "She is also a terrible cook. She cannot fry an egg without burning it." His voice shook with woe. "She cannot make pilaf or lamb with squash." He paused. "You like pilaf and lamb with squash?"

"Certainly."

"You see?" he said in triumph. "She is useless in the kitchen. She is thirty years old, and I am resigned she will remain an old maid. In a way I am glad because I know she would drive some poor man to drink."

"Do not deride her to discourage me," I said. "You need have no fear that I will mistreat her or cause her unhappiness. When she is married to me she will cease being a problem to you." I paused. "It is true that I am not pretty by the foppish standards that prevail today. But I am a man. I wrestled Zahundos and pinned him two straight falls in Baltimore. A giant of a man. Afterward he conceded he had met his master. This from Zahundos was a mighty compliment."

"I am sure," the old man said without enthusiasm. "I am sure."

He looked toward the front door as if hoping for another customer.

"Is your daughter upstairs?"

He looked startled and tugged at his apron. "Yes," he said. "I don't know. Maybe she has gone out."

"May I speak to her? Would you kindly tell her I wish to speak with her."

"You are making a mistake," the old man said. "A terrible mistake."

"No mistake," I said firmly.

The old man shuffled toward the stairs. He climbed them slowly. At the top he paused and turned the knob of the door. He rattled it again.

"It is locked," he called down. "It has never been locked before. She has locked the door."

"Knock," I said. "Knock to let her know I am here."

"I think she knows," the old man said. "I think she knows."

He knocked gently.

"Knock harder," I suggested. "Perhaps she does not hear."

"I think she hears," the old man said. "I think she hears."

---

5. **Spartan.** Marko Palamas is saying two things: that he comes from an area that was once the ancient city-state of Sparta in southern Greece; and that he adheres to the Spartan credo, famous for its military discipline, physical toughness, and athletic prowess.

William Morris Hunt,
Study of Female Head (1872).
The Brooklyn Museum

"Knock again," I said. "Shall I come up and knock for you?"

"No, no," the old man said quickly. He gave the door a sound kick. Then he groaned as if he might have hurt his foot.

"She does not answer," he said in a quavering voice. "I am very sorry she does not answer."

"The coy darling," I said and laughed. "If that is her game." I started for the front door of the store.

I went out and stood on the sidewalk before the store. Above the grocery were the front windows of their apartment. I cupped my hands about my mouth.

"Ariadne!" I shouted. "Ariadne!"

The old man came out the door running disjointedly. He looked frantically down the street.

"Are you mad?" he asked shrilly. "You will cause a riot. The police will come. You must be mad!"

"Ariadne!" I shouted. "Beloved!"

A window slammed open, and the face of Ariadne appeared above me. Her dark hair tumbled about her ears.

"Go away!" she shrieked. "Will you go away!"

"Ariadne," I said loudly. "I have come as I promised. I have spoken to your father. I wish to call on you."

"Go away!" she shrieked. "Madman! Imbecile! Go away!"

By this time a small group of people had assembled around the store and were watching curiously. The old man stood wringing his hands and uttering what sounded like small groans.

"Ariadne," I said. "I wish to call on you. Stop this nonsense and let me in."

She pushed farther out the window and showed me her teeth.

"Be careful, beloved," I said. "You might fall."

She drew her head in quickly, and I turned then to the assembled crowd.

"A misunderstanding," I said. "Please move on."

Suddenly old Mr. Langos shrieked. A moment later something broke on the sidewalk a foot from where I stood. A vase or a plate. I looked up, and Ariadne was preparing to hurl what appeared to be a water pitcher.

"Ariadne!" I shouted. "Stop that!"

The water pitcher landed closer than the vase, and fragments of glass struck my shoes. The crowd scattered, and the old man raised his hands and wailed to heaven.

Ariadne slammed down the window.

The crowd moved in again a little closer, and somewhere among them I heard laughter. I fixed them with a cold stare and waited for some one of them to say something offensive. I would have tossed him around like sardines, but they slowly dispersed and moved on. In another moment the old man and I were alone.

I followed him into the store. He walked an awkward dance of agitation. He shut the door and peered out through the glass.

"A disgrace," he wailed. "A disgrace. The whole street will know by nightfall. A disgrace."

"A girl of heroic spirit," I said. "Will you speak to her for me? Assure her of the sincerity of my feelings. Tell her I pledge eternal love and devotion."

The old man sat down on an orange crate and weakly made his cross.

"I had hoped to see her myself," I said. "But if you promise to speak to her, I will return this evening."

"That soon?" the old man said.

"If I stayed now," I said, "it would be sooner."

"This evening," the old man said and shook his head in resignation. "This evening."

I went to my tavern for a while and set up the glasses for the evening trade. I made arrangements for Pavlakis to tend bar in my place. Afterward I sat alone in my apartment and read a little of majestic Pindar[6] to ease the agitation of my heart.

Once in the mountains of Greece when I fought with the guerrillas in the last year of the great war, I suffered a wound from which it seemed I would die. For days high fever raged in my body. My friends brought a priest at night secretly from one of the captive villages to read the last rites. I accepted the coming of death and was grateful for many things. For the gentleness and wisdom of my old grandfather, the loyalty of my companions in war, the years I sailed between the wild ports of the seven seas, and the strength that flowed to me from the Spartan earth. For one thing only did I weep when it seemed I would leave life, that I had never set ablaze the world with a burning song of passion for one woman. . . . For that I wept.

In Ariadne I swore before God I had found my woman. I knew by the storm-lashed hurricane that swept within my body. A woman whose

---

6. **Pindar** (522–448? B.C.), a Greek lyrical poet whose poems were mostly written in praise of martial events.

majesty was in harmony with the earth, who would be faithful and beloved to me as Penelope had been to Ulysses.[7]

That evening near seven I returned to the grocery. Deep twilight had fallen across the street, and the lights in the window of the store had been dimmed. The apples and oranges and pears had been covered with brown paper for the night.

I tried the door and found it locked. I knocked on the glass, and a moment later the old man came shuffling out of the shadows and let me in.

"Good evening, Mr. Langos."

He muttered some greeting in answer. "Ariadne is not here," he said. "She is at the church. Father Marlas wishes to speak with you."

"A fine young priest," I said. "Let us go at once."

I waited on the sidewalk while the old man locked the store. We started the short walk to the church.

"A clear and ringing night," I said. "Does it not make you feel the wonder and glory of being alive?"

The old man uttered what sounded like a groan, but a truck passed on the street at that moment and I could not be sure.

At the church we entered by a side door leading to the office of Father Marlas. I knocked on the door, and when he called to us to enter we walked in.

Young Father Marlas was sitting at his desk in his black cassock and with his black goatee trim and imposing beneath his clean-shaven cheeks. Beside the desk, in a dark blue dress sat Ariadne, looking somber and beautiful. A bald-headed, big-nosed old man with flint and fire in his eyes sat in a chair beside her.

"Good evening, Marko." Father Marlas said and smiled.

"Good evening, Father," I said.

"Mr. Langos and his daughter you have met," he said and he cleared his throat. "This is Uncle Paul Langos."

"Good evening, Uncle Paul," I said. He glared at me and did not answer. I smiled warmly at Ariadne in greeting, but she was watching the priest.

"Sit down," Father Marlas said.

I sat down across from Ariadne, and old Mr. Langos took a chair beside Uncle Paul. In this way we were arrayed in battle order as if we were opposing armies.

A long silence prevailed during which Father Marlas cleared his throat several times. I observed Ariadne closely. There were grace and poise even in the way her slim-fingered hands rested in her lap. She was a dark and lovely flower, and my pulse beat more quickly at her nearness.

"Marko," Father Marlas said finally. "Marko, I have known you well for the three years since I assumed duties in this parish. You are most regular in your devotions and very generous at the time of the Christmas and Easter offerings. Therefore, I find it hard to believe this complaint against you."

"My family are not liars!" Uncle Paul said, and he had a voice like hunks of dry hard cheese being grated.

"Of course not," Father Marlas said quickly. He smiled benevolently at Ariadne. "I only mean to say——"

"Tell him to stay away from my niece." Uncle Paul burst out.

"Excuse me, Uncle Paul," I said very politely. "Will you kindly keep out of what is not your business."

Uncle Paul looked shocked. "Not my business?" He looked from Ariadne to Father Marlas and then to his brother. "Not my business?"

"This matter concerns Ariadne and me," I said. "With outside interference it becomes more difficult."

"Not my business" Uncle Paul said. He couldn't seem to get that through his head.

---

7. *Penelope . . . Ulysses.* In Greek mythology, Penelope was the wife of Ulysses, a king of Ithaca, who fought in the Trojan War. During Ulysses's long absence many suitors tried to persuade Penelope to remarry, but she refused and remained faithful to her spouse.

"Marko," Father Marlas said, and his composure was slightly shaken. "The family feels you are forcing your attention upon this girl. They are concerned."

"I understand, Father," I said. "It is natural for them to be concerned. I respect their concern. It is also natural for me to speak of love to a woman I have chosen for my wife."

"Not my business!" Uncle Paul said again, and shook his head violently.

"My daughter does not wish to become your wife," Mr. Langos said in a squeaky voice.

"That is for your daughter to say," I said courteously.

Ariadne made a sound in her throat, and we all looked at her. Her eyes were deep and cold, and she spoke slowly and carefully as if weighing each word on a scale in her father's grocery.

"I would not marry this madman if he were one of the Twelve Apostles,"[8] she said.

"See!" Mr. Langos said in triumph.

"Not my business!" Uncle Paul snarled.

"Marko," Father Marlas said. "Try to understand."

"We will call the police!" Uncle Paul raised his voice. "Put this hoodlum under a bond!"

"Please!" Father Marlas said. "Please!"

"Today he stood on the street outside the store." Mr. Langos said excitedly. "He made me a laughingstock."

"If I were a younger man," Uncle Paul growled, "I would settle this without the police. Zi-ip!" He drew a callused finger violently across his throat.

"Please," Father Marlas said.

"A disgrace!" Mr. Langos said.

"An outrage!" Uncle Paul said.

"He must leave Ariadne alone!" Mr. Langos said.

"We will call the police!" Uncle Paul said.

"Silence!" Father Marlas said loudly.

With everything suddenly quiet he turned to me. His tone softened.

"Marko," he said and he seemed to be pleading a little. "Marko, you must understand."

Suddenly a great bitterness assailed me, and anger at myself, and a terrible sadness that flowed like night through my body because I could not make them understand.

"Father," I said quietly, "I am not a fool. I am Marko Palamas and once I pinned the mighty Zahundos in Baltimore. But this battle, more important to me by far, I have lost. That which has not the grace of God is far better in silence."

I turned to leave and it would have ended there.

"Hoodlum!" Uncle Paul said. "It is time you were silent!"

I swear in that moment if he had been a younger man I would have flung him to the dome of the church. Instead I turned and spoke to them all in fire and fury.

"Listen," I said. "I feel no shame for the violence of my feelings. I am a man bred of the Spartan earth and my emotions are violent. Let those who squeak of life feel shame. Nor do I feel shame because I saw this flower and loved her. Or because I spoke at once of my love."

No one moved or made a sound.

"We live in a dark age," I said. "An age where men say one thing and mean another. A time of dwarfs afraid of life. The days are gone when mighty Pindar sang his radiant blossoms of song. When the noble passions of men set ablaze cities, and the heroic deeds of men rang like thunder to every corner of the earth."

I spoke my final words to Ariadne. "I saw you and loved you," I said gently. "I told you of my love. This is my way—the only way I know. If this way has proved offensive to you I apologize to you alone. But understand clearly that for none of this do I feel shame."

I turned then and started to the door. I felt my heart weeping as if waves were breaking within my body.

"Marko Palamas," Ariadne said. I turned slowly. I looked at her. For the first time the warmth I was sure dwelt in her body radiated within the

---

8. *Twelve Apostles.* Jesus Christ chose twelve disciples to preach the gospel.

circles of her face. For the first time she did not look at me with her eyes like glaciers.

"Marko Palamas," she said and there was a strange moving softness in the way she spoke my name. "You may call on me tomorrow."

Uncle Paul shot out of his chair. "She is mad too!" he shouted. "He has bewitched her!"

"A disgrace!" Mr. Langos said.

"Call the police!" Uncle Paul shouted. "I'll show him if it's my business!"

"My poor daughter!" Mr. Langos wailed.

"Turk!" Uncle Paul shouted. "Robber!"

"Please!" Father Marlas said. "Please!"

I ignored them all. In that winged and zestful moment I had eyes only for my beloved, for Ariadne, blossom of my heart and black-eyed flower of my soul!

1965

THINK AND DISCUSS

Understanding

1. What is the distinction between male and female made by Marko in the first paragraph?
2. How does Ariadne stand out when Marko first sees her at a dance? What especially attracts his attention?
3. What does Marko learn about Ariadne from her father?
4. When Marko muses to himself about having once been close to death, what is it that he at that time regretted never having done?

Analyzing

5. How is Ariadne's father **characterized**? In what respects does he offer a contrast to Ariadne?
6. When Marko finds himself in the presence of the priest, what do each of the opposing characters say to make him feel bitter, sad, angry, and defeated?
7. What statement of Ariadne's indicates a turning point in the **plot**? What causes her to make this statement?

Extending

8. Both "The First Seven Years" and "The Wooing of Ariadne" are love stories. How are the wooers in each case alike? different? Which approach seems more likely to be successful? Why?

APPLYING: Protagonist/Antagonist   H**7**
See Handbook of Literary Terms, p. 901.

A **protagonist** is a leading character in a literary work. An **antagonist** is a character who opposes the leading character, or protagonist.

1. What qualities in Marko's character make him similar to the heroes of his dreams?
2. In his final eloquent speech, Marko says, "We live in a dark age. . . . An age where men say one thing and mean another. A time of dwarfs afraid of life. . . ." Whom or what does he see as his chief opposition?

COMPOSITION

Writing About Male and Female Roles

Write a three- or four-paragraph letter to the editor discussing Marko's comment: "It is the distinction of the male to be the aggressor and the cloak of the female to lend grace to the pursuit." Do you agree or disagree? Is his comment reflected in our society? Should it be? State your position and support it as solidly as possible. See "Writing to Persuade an Audience" in the Writer's Handbook.

Analyzing the Antagonist

Write a three- to five-paragraph essay for class analysis in which you identify the antagonist or antagonists in "The Wooing of Ariadne." In your essay, identify the protagonist, and justify your choice of antagonist with evidence.

The Story of American English

Over one-hundred years ago, a German linguist named Jacob Grimm said of the English language, "In riches, good sense and terse convenience, no other of the living languages may be put beside it." Little did Grimm realize that a century later, English would be a world language, nearly always the second language where it is not the first. And English as a second language tends not to be the British variety, but an American one, with American words and American pronunciation.

No doubt American English has come to be preferred because of the dominant position thrust upon the United States after World War II. The widespread use of American English is illustrated best by *OK*, a small American word that has traveled around the globe and been adopted in many languages as a noun, a verb, an adjective, or simply an exclamation.

World War II spawned a number of words and phrases that became useful in civilian discourse: *booby trap, walkie-talkie, sack time, goof off,* and *snow job,* to name a few. People juggling duties and dodging distractions in modern society might view life as an *obstacle course,* a common component of military training camps.

The *Beat Generation,* or *Beatniks,* of the 1950s gave way to the *hippie* movement of the 1960s, some of them referred to as *flower children.* Power itself became various, as in *flower power, black power,* or *people power,* and *sit-ins* were staged to defend these powers.

Those who didn't elect to drop out in the 1950s or 1960s, may have opted for a *lifestyle* in *suburbia,* buying a *ranch house* with a *rumpus room,* or family room, and a TV that would later be adapted for *videocassettes.*

Many *baby boomers* of the postwar era grew into *preppies*—young people adopting the mannerisms or dress of graduates of preparatory schools. Preppies, in turn, became *yuppies*—young, middle-class professionals, many of them couples referred to as *DINKs* (Double Income, No Kids). Although such labels apply to only a small portion of the American population, they reflect trends and focuses of the 1980s.

Just as *microwave ovens* and *food processors* have become fixtures in many American homes in the '80s, *word processors* and *computers* have become staples in American businesses. Computer terminology such as *hard copy, printout, feedback,* and *input* has pervaded our language, especially in the fields of business and government. Many linguistic purists have waged an unsuccessful battle to ban phrases such as *to impact, to finalize,* and *to channelize.* Nevertheless, there is an increasing trend to change nouns or adjectives into verbs.

H. L. Mencken's *The American Language,* which first appeared in 1919, was revised and reissued by Raven McDavid in 1963. It was the first comprehensive examination of American English as a language different from British English. A still more comprehensive *Dictionary of Americanisms* (some 1946 pages) appeared in 1951, edited by Mitford M. Matthews. These works reassured Americans that their language was really theirs, with its own legitimate pronunciation, vocabulary, and usage patterns.

The modern explosion of new American words to meet the needs of people on the *fast track* make it difficult for dictionaries to keep up. The new *Random House Dictionary of the English Language* published in 1987 added 50,000 new entries and 75,000 definitions to its 1966 edition. New coinages or usages that have found their way into recent dictionaries include the following: *acid fog* (fog laden with sulfuric acid), *green vote* (voters concerned with environmental issues), *headhunter* (personnel agent who searches out gifted executives), *squark* (undetected atomic particle), and *vaporware* (new computer software). More change will come in the next years and decades. Such change is not to be lamented: it is a sign of vitality and life.

BIOGRAPHY

Carson Smith McCullers
1917–1967

From a very early age, Carson McCullers was determined to be famous. Born in Columbus, Georgia, the talented and hard-working Lula Carson Smith at first wanted to be a concert pianist, but at fifteen dedicated herself to writing. At seventeen she set off for New York to attend classes at Columbia University and the Juilliard School of Music. But as the biographical excerpt in this unit relates, a roommate lost her money, forcing Carson to forgo music lessons, work during the day, and go to classes at night. She was fired from her jobs and spent much of her time at the waterfront dreaming of voyages to other lands. But she continued to read voraciously and to write.

At age twenty-three, McCullers was acclaimed for her novel, *The Heart Is a Lonely Hunter* (1940). *Reflections in a Golden Eye* (1941) was less successful, but *The Ballad of the Sad Café* (1943) was included in *Best American Short Stories* and is considered her finest work, along with *The Member of the Wedding* (1946), a novel that later became an award-winning play. Despite strokes—at thirty her left side was paralyzed—and severe illnesses during the rest of her life, McCullers went on to write stories, poems, the play *The Square Root of Wonderful* (1958), and the novel *Clock Without Hands* (1961). For her, writing was a "search for God."

Often placed in the tradition of the Southern gothic because of the grotesque characters in her fiction, McCullers responded, "Nature is not abnormal, only lifelessness is abnormal. . . . I bless the Latin poet Terence who said, 'Nothing human is alien to me.' " Like William Faulkner, McCullers used the grotesque to express universal human problems. The basis of most of her themes, she wrote, is "spiritual isolation." Breaking through that isolation involves the capacity to love or receive love. Thus, communication is paramount, for "communication is the only access to love."

The Haunted Boy

Carson Smith McCullers

Hugh looked for his mother at the corner, but she was not in the yard. Sometimes she would be out fooling with the border of spring flowers—the candytuft, the sweet William, the lobelias (she had taught him the names)—but today the green front lawn with the borders of many-colored flowers was empty under the frail sunshine of the mid-April afternoon. Hugh raced up the sidewalk, and John followed him. They finished the front steps with two bounds, and the door slammed after them.

"Mamma!" Hugh called.

It was then, in the unanswering silence as they stood in the empty, wax-floored hall, that Hugh felt there was something wrong. There was no fire in the grate of the sitting room, and since he was used to the flicker of firelight during the cold months, the room on this first warm day seemed strangely naked and cheerless. Hugh shivered. He was glad John was there. The sun shone on a red piece in the flowered rug. Red-bright, red-dark, red-dead—Hugh sickened with a sudden chill remembrance of "the other time." The red darkened to a dizzy black.

"What's the matter, Brown?" John asked. "You look so white."

Hugh shook himself and put his hand to his forehead. "Nothing. Let's go back to the kitchen."

"I can't stay but just a minute," John said. "I'm obligated to sell those tickets. I have to eat and run."

The kitchen, with the fresh checked towels and clean pans, was now the best room in the house. And on the enameled table there was a lemon pie that she had made. Assured by the everyday kitchen and the pie, Hugh stepped back into the hall and raised his face again to call upstairs.

"Mother! Oh, Mamma!"

Again there was no answer.

"My mother made this pie," he said. Quickly, he found a knife and cut into the pie—to dispel the gathering sense of dread.

"Think you ought to cut it, Brown?"

"Sure thing, Laney."

They called each other by their last names this spring, unless they happened to forget. To Hugh it seemed sporty and grown and somehow grand. Hugh liked John better than any other boy at school. John was two years older than Hugh, and compared to him the other boys seemed like a silly crowd of punks. John was the best student in the sophomore class, brainy but not the least bit a teacher's pet, and he was the best athlete too. Hugh was a freshman and didn't have so many friends that first year of high school—he had somehow cut himself off, because he was so afraid.

"Mamma always has me something nice for after school." Hugh put a big piece of pie on a saucer for John—for Laney.

"This pie is certainly super."

"The crust is made of crunched-up graham crackers instead of regular pie dough," Hugh said, "because pie dough is a lot of trouble. We think this graham-cracker pastry is just as good. Naturally, my mother can make regular pie dough if she wants to."

Hugh could not keep still; he walked up and down the kitchen, eating the pie wedge he carried

---

"The Haunted Boy" from *The Ballad of the Sad Café and Collected Short Stories* by Carson McCullers. Copyright 1936, 1955 by Carson McCullers. Reprinted by permission of Houghton Mifflin Company and The Lantz Office Incorporated.

on the palm of his hand. His brown hair was mussed with nervous rakings, and his gentle gold-brown eyes were haunted with pained perplexity. John, who remained seated at the table, sensed Hugh's uneasiness and wrapped one gangling leg around the other.

"I'm really obligated to sell those Glee Club tickets."

"Don't go. You have the whole afternoon." He was afraid of the empty house. He needed John, he needed someone; most of all he needed to hear his mother's voice and know she was in the house with him. "Maybe Mamma is taking a bath," he said. "I'll holler again."

The answer to his third call too was silence.

"I guess your mother must have gone to the movie or gone shopping or something."

"No," Hugh said. "She would have left a note. She always does when she's gone when I come home from school."

"We haven't looked for a note," John said. "Maybe she left it under the doormat or somewhere in the living room."

Hugh was inconsolable. "No. She would have left it right under this pie. She knows I always run first to the kitchen."

"Maybe she had a phone call or thought of something she suddenly wanted to do."

"She *might* have," he said. "I remember she said to Daddy that one of these days she was going to buy herself some new clothes." This flash of hope did not survive its expression. He pushed his hair back and started from the room. "I guess I'd better go upstairs. I ought to go upstairs while you are here."

He stood with his arm around the newel post; the smell of varnished stairs, the sight of the closed white bathroom door at the top revived again "the other time." He clung to the newel post, and his feet would not move to climb the stairs. The red turned again to whirling, sick dark. Hugh sat down. *Stick your head between your legs,* he ordered, remembering Scout first aid.

"Hugh," John called. "Hugh!"

The dizziness clearing, Hugh accepted a fresh chagrin—Laney was calling him by his ordinary first name; he thought he was a sissy about his mother, unworthy of being called by his last name in the grand, sporty way they used before. The dizziness cleared when he returned to the kitchen.

"Brown," said John, and the chagrin disappeared. "Does this establishment have anything pertaining to a cow? A white, fluid liquid. In French they call it *lait.* Here we call it plain old milk."

The stupidity of shock lightened. "Oh, Laney, I am a dope! Please excuse me. I clean forgot." Hugh fetched the milk from the refrigerator and found two glasses. "I don't think. My mind was on something else."

"I know," John said. After a moment he asked in a calm voice, looking steadily at Hugh's eyes: "Why are you so worried about your mother? Is she sick, Hugh?"

Hugh knew now that the first name was not a slight; it was because John was talking too serious to be sporty. He liked John better than any friend he had ever had. He felt more natural sitting across the kitchen table from John, somehow safer. As he looked into John's gray, peaceful eyes, the balm of affection soothed the dread.

John asked again, still steadily: "Hugh, is your mother sick?"

Hugh could have answered no other boy. He had talked with no one about his mother, except his father, and even those intimacies had been rare, oblique. They could approach the subject only when they were occupied with something else, doing carpentry work or the two times they hunted in the woods together—or when they were cooking supper or washing dishes.

"She's not exactly sick," he said, "but Daddy and I have been worried about her. At least, we used to be worried for a while."

John asked: "Is it a kind of heart trouble?"

Hugh's voice was strained. "Did you hear about that fight I had with that slob Clem Roberts? I scraped his slob face on the gravel walk and nearly killed him sure enough. He's

McCullers 661

still got scars or at least he did have a bandage on for two days. I had to stay in school every afternoon for a week. But I nearly killed him. I would have if Mr. Paxton hadn't come along and dragged me off."

"I heard about it."

"You know why I wanted to kill him?"

For a moment John's eyes flickered away.

Hugh tensed himself; his raw boy hands clutched the table edge; he took a deep, hoarse breath. "That slob was telling everybody that my mother was in Milledgeville. He was spreading it around that my mother was crazy."

"The dirty. . . ."

Hugh said in a clear, defeated voice, "My mother *was* in Milledgeville. But that doesn't mean that she was crazy," he added quickly. "In that big State hospital, there are buildings for people who are crazy, and there are other buildings, for people who are just sick. Mamma was sick for a while. Daddy and me discussed it and decided that the hospital in Milledgeville was the place where there were the best doctors and she would get the best care. But she was the furthest from crazy than anybody in the world. You know Mamma, John." He said again, "I ought to go upstairs."

John said: "I have always thought that your mother is one of the nicest ladies in this town."

"You see, Mamma had a peculiar thing happen, and afterward she was blue."

Confession, the first deep-rooted words, opened the festered secrecy of the boy's heart, and he continued more rapidly, urgent and finding unforeseen relief.

"Last year my mother thought she was going to have a little baby. She talked it over with Daddy and me," he said proudly. "We wanted a girl. I was going to choose the name. We were so tickled. I hunted up all my old toys—my electric train and tracks. . . . I was going to name her Crystal—how does the name strike you for a girl? It reminds me of something bright and dainty."

"Was the little baby born dead?"

Even with John, Hugh's ears turned hot; his cold hands touched them. "No, it was what they call a tumor. That's what happened to my mother. They had to operate at the hospital here." He was embarrassed and his voice was very low. "Then she had something called change of life." The words were terrible to Hugh. "And afterward she was blue. Daddy said it was a shock to her nervous system. It's something that happens to ladies; she was just blue and run-down."

Although there was no red, no red in the kitchen anywhere, Hugh was approaching "the other time."

"One day, she just sort of gave up—one day last fall." Hugh's eyes were wide open and glaring: again he climbed the stairs and opened the bathroom door—he put his hand to his eyes to shut out the memory. "She tried to—hurt herself. I found her when I came in from school."

John reached out and carefully stroked Hugh's sweatered arm.

"Don't worry. A lot of people have to go to hospitals because they are rundown and blue. Could happen to anybody."

"We had to put her in the hospital—the best hospital." The recollection of those long, long months was stained with a dull loneliness, as cruel in its lasting unappeasement as "the other time"—how long had it lasted? In the hospital Mamma could walk around and she always had on shoes.

John said carefully: "This pie is certainly super."

"My mother is a super cook. She cooks things like meat pie and salmon loaf—as well as steaks and hot dogs."

"I hate to eat and run," John said.

Hugh was so frightened of being left alone that he felt the alarm in his own loud heart.

"Don't go," he urged. "Let's talk for a little while."

"Talk about what?"

Hugh could not tell him. Not even John Laney. He could tell no one of the empty house and the horror of the time before. "Do you ever cry?" he asked John. "I don't."

"I do sometimes," John admitted.

"I wish I had known you better when Mother was away. Daddy and me used to go hunting nearly every Saturday. We *lived* on quail and dove. I bet you would have liked that." He added in a lower tone, "On Sunday we went to the hospital."

John said: "It's a kind of a delicate proposition selling those tickets. A lot of people don't enjoy the High School Glee Club operettas. Unless they know someone in it personally, they'd rather stay home with a good TV show. A lot of people buy tickets on the basis of being public-spirited."

"We're going to get a television set real soon."

"I couldn't exist without television," John said.

Hugh's voice was apologetic. "Daddy wants to clean up the hospital bills first because as everybody knows sickness is a very expensive proposition. Then we'll get TV."

John lifted his milk glass. "Skoal," he said. "That's a Swedish word you say before you drink. A good-luck word."

"You know so many foreign words and languages."

"Not so many," John said truthfully. "Just *kaput* and *adios* and *skoal* and stuff we learn in French class. That's not much."

"That's *beaucoup*," said Hugh, and he felt witty and pleased with himself.

Suddenly the stored tension burst into physical activity. Hugh grabbed the basketball out on the porch and rushed into the backyard. He dribbled the ball several times and aimed at the goal his father had put up on his last birthday. When he missed he bounced the ball to John, who had come after him. It was good to be outdoors and the relief of natural play brought Hugh the first line of a poem. "My heart is like a basketball." Usually when a poem came to him he would lie sprawled on the living-room floor, studying to hunt rhymes, his tongue working on the side of his mouth. His mother would call him Shelley-Poe when she stepped over him, and sometimes she would put her foot lightly on his behind. His mother always liked his poems; today the second

line came quickly, like magic. He said it out loud to John: " 'My heart is like a basketball, bouncing with glee down the hall.' How do you like that for the start of a poem?"

"Sounds kind of crazy to me," John said. Then he corrected himself hastily. "I mean it sounds —odd. Odd, I meant."

Hugh realized why John had changed the word, and the elation of play and poems left him instantly. He caught the ball and stood with it cradled in his arms. The afternoon was golden and the wisteria vine on the porch was in full, unshattered bloom. The wisteria was like lavender waterfalls. The fresh breeze smelled of sunwarmed flowers. The sunlit sky was blue and cloudless. It was the first warm day of spring.

"I have to shove off," John said.

"No!" Hugh's voice was desperate. "Don't you want another piece of pie? I never heard of anybody eating just one piece of pie."

He steered John into the house and this time he called only out of habit because he always called on coming in. "Mother!" He was cold after the bright, sunny outdoors. He was cold not only because of the weather but because he was so scared.

"My mother has been home a month and every afternoon she's always here when I come home from school. Always, always."

They stood in the kitchen looking at the lemon pie. And to Hugh the cut pie looked somehow—odd. As they stood motionless in the kitchen the silence was creepy and odd too.

"Doesn't this house seem quiet to you?"

"It's because you don't have television. We put on our TV at seven o'clock and it stays on all day and night until we go to bed. Whether anybody's in the living room or not. There're plays and skits and gags going on continually."

"We have a radio, of course, and a vic."

"But that's not the company of a good TV. You won't know when your mother is in the house or not when you get TV."

Hugh didn't answer. Their footsteps sounded hollow in the hall. He felt sick as he stood on the

John Koch, detail of *Evening* (1957).
Private collection

first step with his arm around the newel post. "If you could just come upstairs for a minute—"

John's voice was suddenly impatient and loud. "How many times have I told you I'm obligated to sell those tickets. You have to be public-spirited about things like Glee Clubs."

"Just for a second—I have something important to show you upstairs."

John did not ask what it was and Hugh sought desperately to name something important enough to get John upstairs. He said finally: "I'm assembling a hi-fi machine. You have to know a lot about electronics—my father is helping me."

But even when he spoke he knew John did not for a second believe the lie. Who would buy a hi-fi when they didn't have television? He hated John, as you hate people you have to need so badly. He had to say something more and he straightened his shoulders.

"I just want you to know how much I value your friendship. During these past months I had somehow cut myself off from people."

"That's O.K., Brown. You oughtn't to be so sensitive because your mother was—where she was."

John had his hand on the door and Hugh was trembling. "I thought if you could come up for just a minute——"

John looked at him with anxious, puzzled eyes. Then he asked slowly: "Is there something you are scared of upstairs?"

Hugh wanted to tell him everything. But he could not tell what his mother had done that September afternoon. It was too terrible and—odd. It was like something a *patient* would do, and not like his mother at all. Although his eyes were wild with terror and his body trembled he said: "I'm not scared."

"Well, so long. I'm sorry I have to go—but to be obligated is to be obligated."

John closed the front door, and he was alone in the empty house. Nothing could save him now. Even if a whole crowd of boys were listening to TV in the living room, laughing at funny gags and jokes, it would still not help him. He had to go upstairs and find her. He sought courage from the last thing John had said, and repeated the words aloud: "To be obligated is to be obligated." But the words did not give him any of John's thoughtlessness and courage; they were creepy and strange in the silence.

He turned slowly to go upstairs. His heart was not like a basketball but like a fast, jazz drum, beating faster and faster as he climbed the stairs. His feet dragged as though he waded through knee-deep water and he held on to the banisters. The house looked odd, crazy. As he looked down at the ground-floor table with the vase of fresh spring flowers that too looked somehow peculiar. There was a mirror on the second floor and his own face startled him, so crazy did it seem to him. The initial of his high-school sweater was backward and wrong in the reflection and his mouth was open like an asylum idiot. He shut his mouth and he looked better. Still the objects he saw—the table downstairs, the sofa upstairs—looked somehow cracked or jarred because of the dread in him, although they were the familiar things of everyday. He fastened his eyes on the closed door at the right of the stairs and the fast, jazz drum beat faster.

He opened the bathroom door and for a moment the dread that had haunted him all that afternoon made him see again the room as he had seen it "the other time." His mother lay on the floor and there was blood everywhere. His mother lay there dead and there was blood every-where, on her slashed wrist, and a pool of blood had trickled to the bathtub and lay dammed there. Hugh touched the doorframe and steadied himself. Then the room settled and he realized that this was not "the other time." The April sun-light brightened the clean white tiles. There was only bathroom brightness and the sunny window. He went to the bedroom and saw the empty bed with the rose-colored spread. The lady things were on the dresser. The room was as it always looked and nothing had happened . . . nothing had happened and he flung himself on the quilted rose bed and cried from relief and a strained, bleak tiredness that had lasted so long. The sobs jerked his whole body and quieted his jazz, fast heart.

Hugh had not cried all those months. He had not cried at "the other time," when he found his mother alone in that empty house with blood everywhere. He had not cried but he made a Scout mistake. He had first lifted his moth-er's heavy, bloody body before he tried to ban-dage her. He had not cried when he called his father. He had not cried those few days when they were deciding what to do. He hadn't even cried when the doctor suggested Milledgeville, or when he and his father took her to the hospi-tal in the car—although his father cried on the way home. He had not cried at the meals they made—steak every night for a whole month so that they felt steak was running out of their eyes, their ears; then they had switched to hot dogs, and ate them until hot dogs ran out of their ears, their eyes. They got in ruts of food and were messy about the kitchen, so that it was never nice except the Saturday the cleaning woman came. He did not cry those lonesome afternoons after he had the fight with Clem Roberts and felt the other boys were thinking queer things of his mother. He stayed at home in the messy kitchen, eat-ing fig newtons or chocolate bars. Or he went to see a neighbor's television—Miss Richards, an old maid who saw old-maid shows. He had not cried when his father drank too much so that it took his appetite and Hugh had to eat alone. He had not even cried on those long, waiting Sundays when they went to Milledgeville and he twice saw a lady on a porch without any shoes on and talking to herself. A lady who was a patient and who struck at him with a horror he could not name. He did not cry when at first his mother would say: *Don't punish me by making me stay here. Let me go home.* He had not cried at the terrible words that haunted him—"change of life"—"crazy"—"Milledgeville"—he could not cry all during those long months strained with dullness and want and dread.

He still sobbed on the rose bedspread which was soft and cool against his wet cheeks. He was sobbing so loud that he did not hear the front door open, did not even hear his mother call or the footsteps on the stairs. He still sobbed when his mother touched him and burrowed his face hard in the spread. He even stiffened his legs and kicked his feet.

"Why, Loveyboy," his mother said, calling him a long-ago child name. "What's happened?"

He sobbed even louder, although his mother tried to turn his face to her. He wanted her to worry. He did not turn around until she had finally left the bed, and then he looked at her. She had on a different dress—blue silk it looked like in the pale spring light.

"Darling, what's happened?"

The terror of the afternoon was over, but he could not tell it to his mother. He could not tell her what he had feared, or explain the horror of things that were never there at all—but had once been there.

"Why did you do it?"

"The first warm day I just suddenly decided to buy myself some new clothes."

But he was not talking about clothes; he was thinking about "the other time" and the grudge that had started when he saw the blood and horror and felt *why did she do this to me*. He thought of the grudge against the mother he loved the most in the world. All those last, sad months the anger had bounced against the love with guilt between.

"I bought two dresses and two petticoats. How do you like them?"

"I hate them!" Hugh said angrily. "Your slip is showing."

She turned around twice and the petticoat showed terribly. "It's supposed to show, goofy. It's the style."

"I still don't like it."

"I ate a sandwich at the tearoom with two cups of cocoa and then went to Mendel's. There were so many pretty things I couldn't seem to get away. I bought these two dresses and look, Hugh! The shoes!"

His mother went to the bed and switched on the light so he could see. The shoes were flat-heeled and *blue*—with diamond sparkles on the toes. He did not know how to criticize. "They look more like evening shoes than things you wear on the street."

"I have never owned any colored shoes before. I couldn't resist them."

His mother sort of danced over toward the window, making the petticoat twirl under the new dress. Hugh had stopped crying now, but he was still angry.

"I don't like it because it makes you look like you're trying to seem young, and I bet you are forty years old."

His mother stopped dancing and stood still at the window. Her face was suddenly quiet and sad. "I'll be forty-three years old in June."

He had hurt her and suddenly the anger vanished and there was only love. "Mamma, I shouldn't have said that."

"I realized when I was shopping that I hadn't been in a store for more than a year. Imagine!"

Hugh could not stand the sad quietness and the mother he loved so much. He could not stand his love or his mother's prettiness. He wiped the tears on the sleeve of his sweater and got up from the bed. "I have never seen you so pretty, or a dress and slip so pretty." He crouched down before his mother and touched the bright shoes. "The shoes are really super."

"I thought the minute I laid eyes on them that you would like them." She pulled Hugh up and kissed him on the cheek. "Now I've got lipstick on you."

Hugh quoted a witty remark he had heard before as he scrubbed off the lipstick. "It only shows I'm popular."

"Hugh, why were you crying when I came in? Did something at school upset you?"

"It was only that when I came in and found you gone and no note or anything—"

"I forgot all about a note."

"And all afternoon I felt—John Laney came in but he had to go sell Glee Club tickets. All afternoon I felt—"

"What? What was the matter?"

But he could not tell the mother he loved about the terror and the cause. He said at last: "All afternoon I felt—odd."

Afterward when his father came home he called Hugh to come out into the backyard with him. His father had a worried look—as though he spied a valuable tool Hugh had left outside. But there was no tool and the basketball was put back in its place on the back porch.

"Son," his father said, "there's something I want to tell you."

"Yes, sir?"

"Your mother said that you had been crying this afternoon." His father did not wait for him to explain. "I just want us to have a close understanding with each other. Is there anything about school—or girls—or something that puzzles you? Why were you crying?"

Hugh looked back at the afternoon and already it was far away, distant as a peculiar view seen at the wrong end of a telescope.

"I don't know," he said. "I guess maybe I was somehow nervous."

His father put his arm around his shoulder. "Nobody can be nervous before they are sixteen years old. You have a long way to go."

"I know."

"I have never seen your mother look so well. She looks so gay and pretty, better than she's looked in years. Don't you realize that?"

"The slip—the petticoat is supposed to show. It's a new style."

"Soon it will be summer," his father said. "And we'll go on picnics—the three of us." The words brought an instant vision of glare on the yellow creek and the summer-leaved, adventurous woods. His father added: "I came out here to tell you something else."

"Yes, sir?"

"I just want you to know that I realize how fine you were all that bad time. How fine, how damn fine."

His father was using a swear word as if he were talking to a grown man. His father was not a person to hand out compliments—always he was strict with report cards and tools left around. His father never praised him or used grown words or anything. Hugh felt his face grow hot and he touched it with his cold hands.

"I just wanted to tell you that, Son." He shook Hugh by the shoulder. "You'll be taller than your old man in a year or so." Quickly his father went into the house, leaving Hugh to the sweet and unaccustomed aftermath of praise.

Hugh stood in the darkening yard after the sunset colors faded in the west and the wisteria was dark purple. The kitchen light was on and he saw his mother fixing dinner. He knew that something was finished; the terror was far from him now, also the anger that had bounced with love, the dread and guilt. Although he felt he would never cry again—or at least not until he was sixteen—in the brightness of his tears glistened the safe, lighted kitchen, now that he was no longer a haunted boy, now that he was glad somehow, and not afraid.

1955

THINK AND DISCUSS
Understanding
1. What grades are Hugh and John in and what is their difference in age? Why does Hugh like John better than he likes the other boys in school?
2. When Hugh calls for his mother and there is no answer, John suggests she may have gone shopping. Why does Hugh assume she has not? Why doesn't Hugh follow John's suggestion to look for a note?

Analyzing
3. Twice before John leaves, Hugh has dizzy spells: first, in the third paragraph, when he sees the sun shining on a spot of red carpet; and again when he is about to go upstairs. What memory causes these spells?

4. What pretext does Hugh use to keep John around? Why doesn't Hugh tell John that he is afraid and that he needs John's help?
5. In what sense is Hugh a "haunted boy"?
6. When Hugh goes upstairs alone, what does he remember and what does he see? Does the experience seem harmful or beneficial? Discuss.
7. What is the effect on Hugh of his mother's arrival and of her conversation about her shopping expedition and purchases?
8. The story concludes with the father having a private talk with Hugh. What is the effect of this talk on Hugh?
9. What techniques does McCullers use to build suspense early in the story? In answering, consider elements such as **mood** and **foreshadowing**.

BIOGRAPHY

Kurt Vonnegut, Jr.
1922–

When asked why he writes, Kurt Vonnegut once quoted the British author George Orwell: "People write the books they can't find on library shelves." Vonnegut didn't always want to write. Born in Indianapolis to an architect father, he was pressed to be a scientist and studied biochemistry at Cornell. "Flunking everything," he was "delighted to join the army and go to war." He then studied anthropology at the University of Chicago, receiving an M.A. twenty years later, not for a thesis, but for his novel *Cat's Cradle* (1963), written long after Vonnegut had turned to full-time writing in the 1950s.

Slaughterhouse-Five (1969), the novel that secured for him a national reputation, depicts the World War II fire-bombing of Dresden, Germany, by Allied bombers—an event unknown at the time to American citizens and ground troops. Vonnegut was there, a prisoner of the Germans. When he emerged from a cellar meat locker after the firestorms, "everything was gone but the cellars where 135,000 Hansels and Gretels had been baked like gingerbread men."

His antiwar stories and novels made a great impact on youthful audiences in the 1960s. Primarily a satirist, mixing "black comedy," science fiction, and a keen sense of the absurd, his works include *Player Piano* (1952), *Breakfast of Champions* (1973), *Jailbird* (1979), *Deadeye Dick* (1982), and *Bluebeard: a Novel* (1987). His nonfiction is collected in *Palm Sunday* (1981).

Disturbed that people "don't think" their own ideas, but accept them from books, Vonnegut thinks "writers are the most important members of society, not just potentially but actually. Good writers must have and stand by their own ideas." As for him, he likes "Utopian talk, speculation about what our planet should be, anger about what our planet is."

Review SATIRE in the Handbook of Literary Terms, page 905.

Harrison Bergeron

Kurt Vonnegut, Jr.

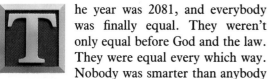

The year was 2081, and everybody was finally equal. They weren't only equal before God and the law. They were equal every which way. Nobody was smarter than anybody else. Nobody was better looking than anybody else. Nobody was stronger or quicker than anybody else. All this equality was due to the 211th, 212th, and 213th Amendments to the Constitution, and to the unceasing vigilance of agents of the United States Handicapper General.

Some things about living still weren't quite right, though. April, for instance still drove people crazy by not being springtime. And it was in that clammy month that the H-G men took George and Hazel Bergeron's fourteen-year-old son, Harrison, away.

It was tragic, all right, but George and Hazel couldn't think about it very hard. Hazel had a perfectly average intelligence, which meant she couldn't think about anything except in short bursts. And George, while his intelligence was way above normal, had a little mental handicap radio in his ear. He was required by law to wear it at all times. It was tuned to a government transmitter. Every twenty seconds or so, the transmitter would send out some sharp noise to keep people like George from taking unfair advantage of their brains.

George and Hazel were watching television. There were tears on Hazel's cheeks, but she'd forgotten for the moment what they were about.

On the television screen were ballerinas.

A buzzer sounded in George's head. His thoughts fled in panic, like bandits from a burglar alarm.

"That was a real pretty dance, that dance they just did," said Hazel.

"Huh?" said George.

"That dance—it was nice," said Hazel.

"Yup," said George. He tried to think a little about the ballerinas. They weren't really very good—no better than anybody else would have been, anyway. They were burdened with sash-weights and bags of birdshot, and their faces were masked, so that no one, seeing a free and graceful gesture or a pretty face, would feel like something the cat drug in. George was toying with the vague notion that maybe dancers shouldn't be handicapped. But he didn't get very far with it before another noise in his ear radio scattered his thoughts.

George winced. So did two out of the eight ballerinas.

Hazel saw him wince. Having no mental handicap herself, she had to ask George what the latest sound had been.

"Sounded like somebody hitting a milk bottle with a ball peen hammer," said George.

Vonnegut (von'ə gət).

"Harrison Bergeron" excerpted from the book *Welcome to the Monkey House* by Kurt Vonnegut, Jr. Copyright © 1961 by Kurt Vonnegut, Jr. Originally published in *Fantasy and Science Fiction*. Reprinted by permission of Delacorte Press/Seymour Lawrence and Jonathan Cape Ltd.

"I'd think it would be real interesting, hearing all the different sounds," said Hazel, a little envious. "All the things they think up."

"Um," said George.

"Only, if I was Handicapper General, you know what I would do?" said Hazel. Hazel, as a matter of fact, bore a strong resemblance to the Handicapper General, a woman named Diana Moon Glampers. "If I was Diana Moon Glampers," said Hazel, "I'd have chimes on Sunday—just chimes. Kind of in honor of religion."

"I could think, if it was just chimes," said George.

"Well—maybe make 'em real loud," said Hazel. "I think I'd make a good Handicapper General."

"Good as anybody else," said George.

"Who knows better'n I do what normal is?" said Hazel.

"Right," said George. He began to think glimmeringly about his abnormal son who was now in jail, about Harrison, but a twenty-one-gun salute in his head stopped that.

"Boy!" said Hazel, "that was a doozy, wasn't it?"

It was such a doozy that George was white and trembling, and tears stood on the rims of his red eyes. Two of the eight ballerinas had collapsed to the studio floor, were holding their temples.

"All of a sudden you look so tired," said Hazel. "Why don't you stretch out on the sofa, so's you can rest your handicap bag on the pillows, honeybunch." She was referring to the forty-seven pounds of birdshot in a canvas bag, which was padlocked around George's neck. "Go on and rest the bag for a little while," she said. "I don't care if you're not equal to me for a while."

George weighed the bag with his hands. "I don't mind it," he said. "I don't notice it anymore. It's just a part of me."

"You been so tired lately—kind of wore out," said Hazel. "If there was just some way we could make a little hole in the bottom of the bag, and just take out a few of them lead balls. Just a few."

"Two years in prison and two thousand dollars fine for every ball I took out," said George. "I don't call that a bargain."

"If you could just take a few out when you came home from work," said Hazel. "I mean—you don't compete with anybody around here. You just set around."

"If I tried to get away with it," said George, "then other people'd get away with it—and pretty soon we'd be right back to the dark ages again, with everybody competing against everybody else. You wouldn't like that, would you?"

"I'd hate it," said Hazel.

"There you are," said George. "The minute people start cheating on laws, what do you think happens to society?"

If Hazel hadn't been able to come up with an answer to this question, George couldn't have supplied one. A siren was going off in his head.

"Reckon it'd fall all apart," said Hazel.

"What would?" said George blankly.

"Society," said Hazel uncertainly. "Wasn't that what you just said?"

"Who knows?" said George.

The television program was suddenly interrupted for a news bulletin. It wasn't clear at first as to what the bulletin was about, since the announcer, like all announcers, had a serious speech impediment. For about half a minute, and in a state of high excitement, the announcer tried to say, "Ladies and gentlemen—"

He finally gave up, handed the bulletin to a ballerina to read.

"That's all right—" Hazel said of the announcer, "he tried. That's the big thing. He tried to do the best he could with what God gave him. He should get a nice raise for trying so hard."

"Ladies and gentlemen—" said the ballerina, reading the bulletin. She must have been extraordinarily beautiful, because the mask she wore was hideous. And it was easy to see that she was the strongest and most graceful of all the dancers, for her handicap bags were as big as those worn by two-hundred-pound men.

And she had to apologize at once for her voice, which was a very unfair voice for a woman to use. Her voice was a warm, luminous, timeless melody. "Excuse me——" she said, and she began again, making her voice absolutely uncompetitive.

"Harrison Bergeron, age fourteen," she said in a grackle squawk, "has just escaped from jail, where he was held on suspicion of plotting to overthrow the government. He is a genius and an athlete, is under-handicapped, and should be regarded as extremely dangerous."

A police photograph of Harrison Bergeron was flashed on the screen, upside down, then sideways, upside down again, then right side up. The picture showed the full length of Harrison against a background calibrated in feet and inches. He was exactly seven feet tall.

The rest of Harrison's appearance was Halloween and hardware. Nobody had ever borne heavier handicaps. He had outgrown hindrances faster than the H-G men could think them up. Instead of a little ear radio for a mental handicap, he wore a tremendous pair of earphones, and spectacles with thick wavy lenses. The spectacles were intended to make him not only half blind, but to give him whanging headaches besides.

Scrap metal was hung all over him. Ordinarily, there was a certain symmetry, a military neatness to the handicaps issued to strong people, but Harrison looked like a walking junkyard. In the race of life, Harrison carried three hundred pounds.

And to offset his good looks, the H-G men required that he wear at all times a red rubber ball for a nose, keep his eyebrows shaved off, and cover his even white teeth with black caps at snaggletooth random.

"If you see this boy," said the ballerina, "do not—I repeat, do not—try to reason with him."

There was the shriek of a door being torn from its hinges.

Screams and barking cries of consternation came from the television set. The photograph of Harrison Bergeron on the screen jumped again and again, as though dancing to the tune of an earthquake.

George Bergeron correctly identified the earthquake, and well he might have—for many was the time his own home had danced to the same crashing tune. "Oh, no——" said George, "that must be Harrison!"

The realization was blasted from his mind instantly by the sound of an automobile collision in his head.

When George could open his eyes again, the photograph of Harrison was gone. A living, breathing Harrison filled the screen.

Clanking, clownish, and huge, Harrison stood in the center of the studio. The knob of the uprooted studio door was still in his hand. Ballerinas, technicians, musicians, and announcers cowered on their knees before him, expecting to die.

"I am the Emperor!" cried Harrison. "Do you hear? I am the Emperor! Everybody must do what I say at once!" He stamped his foot and the studio shook.

"Even as I stand here——" he bellowed, "crippled, hobbled, sickened—I am a greater ruler than any man who ever lived! Now watch me become what I *can* become!"

Harrison tore the straps of his handicap harness like wet tissue paper, tore straps guaranteed to support five thousand pounds.

Harrison's scrap-iron handicaps crashed to the floor.

Harrison thrust his thumbs under the bar of the padlock that secured his head harness. The bar snapped like celery. Harrison smashed his headphones and spectacles against the wall.

He flung away his rubber-ball nose, revealed a man that would have awed Thor, the god of thunder.

"I shall now select my Empress!" he said, looking down on the cowering people. "Let the first woman who dares rise to her feet claim her mate and her throne!"

A moment passed, and then a ballerina arose, swaying like a willow.

Harrison plucked the mental handicap from her ear, snapped off her physical handicaps with marvelous delicacy. Last of all, he removed her mask.

She was blindingly beautiful.

"Now——" said Harrison, taking her hand, "shall we show the people the meaning of the word dance? Music!" he commanded.

The musicians scrambled back into their chairs, and Harrison stripped them of their handicaps, too. "Play your best," he told them, "and I'll make you barons and dukes and earls."

The music began. It was normal at first —cheap, silly, false. But Harrison snatched two musicians from their chairs, waved them like batons as he sang the music as he wanted it played. He slammed them back into their chairs.

The music began again and was much improved.

Harrison and his Empress merely listened to the music for a while—listened gravely, as though synchronizing their heartbeats with it.

They shifted their weights to their toes.

Harrison placed his big hands on the girl's tiny waist, letting her sense the weightlessness that would soon be hers.

And then, in an explosion of joy and grace, into the air they sprang!

Not only were the laws of the land abandoned, but the law of gravity and the laws of motion as well.

They reeled, whirled, swiveled, flounced, capered, gamboled, and spun.

They leaped like deer on the moon.

The studio ceiling was thirty feet high, but each leap brought the dancers nearer to it.

It became their obvious intention to kiss the ceiling.

They kissed it.

And then, neutralizing gravity with love and pure will, they remained suspended in air inches below the ceiling, and they kissed each other for a long, long time.

It was then that Diana Moon Glampers, the Handicapper General, came into the studio with a double-barreled ten-gauge shotgun. She fired twice, and the Emperor and the Empress were dead before they hit the floor.

Diana Moon Glampers loaded the gun again. She aimed it at the musicians and told them they had ten seconds to get their handicaps back on.

It was then that the Bergerons' television tube burned out.

Hazel turned to comment about the blackout to George. But George had gone out into the kitchen for a can of beer.

George came back in with the beer, paused while a handicap signal shook him up. And then he sat down again. "You been crying?" he said to Hazel.

"Yup," she said.

"What about?" he said.

"I forget," she said. "Something real sad on television."

"What was it?" he said.

"It's all kind of mixed up in my mind," said Hazel.

"Forget sad things," said George.

"I always do," said Hazel.

"That's my girl," said George. He winced. There was the sound of a riveting gun in his head.

"Gee—I could tell that one was a doozy," said Hazel.

"You can say that again," said George.

"Gee——" said Hazel, "I could tell that one was a doozy."

1961

THINK AND DISCUSS
Understanding
1. How are all Americans made equal in the year 2081? What handicaps has George been given? Why? Why does Hazel have no handicap?
2. What handicap does the news announcer have? the ballerina who reads the bulletin? Harrison Bergeron?
3. What does Harrison Bergeron do after proclaiming himself emperor? How does he select his empress?
4. What does Diana Moon Glampers do when she finds Harrison and the ballerina dancing?

Analyzing
5. The characters are one-dimensional and the **plot** is deemphasized. Is this deliberate on the part of the author? If so, why?
6. What is Vonnegut **satirizing** in this story?
7. What effect has the system of government of 2081 had on the creative arts? What can you **infer** about its effect on education? on politics?
8. Is the futuristic setting indispensable, or could the story be set equally well in the present or the past? Explain.

Extending
9. Emily Dickinson in "Much Madness Is Divinest Sense" writes:

   Assent—and you are sane—
   Demur—you're straightway dangerous—
   And handled with a Chain—

   How does this quotation apply to the situation of Harrison Bergeron?

REVIEWING: Satire H🖉
See Handbook of Literary Terms, p. 905.
Satire consists of poking fun at, or ridiculing, a human weakness or an injustice or inconsistency in a social, political, or other institution. It might be called criticism with a biting wit. In "Harrison Bergeron," Vonnegut satirizes several modern attitudes.

1. What elements of the comic or ridiculous can you find in the first paragraph of "Harrison Bergeron"?
2. What is the target of the ridicule in this story?

COMPOSITION ✏️
Writing About Equality in Modern America
Write a three- or four-paragraph letter to a citizen of another country in which you explain what equality means in terms of American democracy. Does it mean sameness or conformity? Does it make mediocrity inevitable, or is it compatible with individuality and excellence? Outline your argument before you begin to write.

Analyzing a Story's Ending
Write a three- to five-paragraph analysis for class discussion of the ending of "Harrison Bergeron," considering whether it is consistent with the rest of the story. First, consider an alternate ending—perhaps with Harrison leading a successful rebellion. How would the alternate ending affect the satire of the story? Compare the effect of the present ending with that of your alternate ending. See "Writing About Plot and Plot Devices" in the Writer's Handbook.

Analyzing Irony
Explain to a classmate in at least four paragraphs how the use of irony contributes to the effectiveness of Vonnegut's satire. Consider the use of understatement, exaggeration, verbal irony, and irony of situation (the ballerinas have heavy weight handicaps, announcers have serious speech impediments). Finally, speculate on how the story would change if Vonnegut had adopted a serious tone rather than an ironic one. See "Writing About Irony" in the Writer's Handbook.

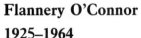

BIOGRAPHY

Flannery O'Connor
1925–1964

Her close friend and literary executor, Robert Fitzgerald, writes of Flannery O'Connor: "She was a girl who started with a gift for cartooning and satire, and found in herself a far greater gift, unique in her time and place, a marvel." The latter gift was storytelling, and mingled with that gift are remnants of her cartooning ability and her satiric bent.

Like so many of the century's influential authors, she was a Southerner. Born in Savannah, Georgia, she was educated in parochial schools and began writing at an early age. Her high-school yearbook lists her chief hobby as "collecting rejection slips." Her fortune changed, however, when her story "The Geranium" appeared in print while she was attending the University of Iowa. Several years after graduation, her first novel and most famous single work, *Wise Blood* (1952), was published. Her second novel was *The Violent Bear It Away* (1960). Her short stories were collected in *A Good Man Is Hard to Find* (1955) and *Everything That Rises Must Converge* (1965). *The Complete Stories* received the National Book Award in 1972.

When O'Connor was only twenty-five, she learned that she had lupus, the same disease that had killed her father. She moved to Milledgeville, Georgia (a town mentioned in Carson McCullers's "The Haunted Boy"), where, despite her suffering, she continued her work. She died at the age of thirty-nine.

O'Connor's characters are usually unsophisticated people whose inability to control their own powerful impulses renders them as bizarre "grotesques." Her stories are often complex in symbolism and psychology, as well as deeply rooted in religion and mythology. With startling intensity, O'Connor's characters emerge from moral polarities. On the one hand, there are the mad prophets, "consumed with an image of Christ"; on the other hand, are con men, concerned only with their own advancement. Often the stories end in death and destruction, yet the horror includes comedy, as well as "the pale light of hope."

O'Connor defended her use of grotesque individuals: "I am interested in making up a good case for distortion, as I am coming to believe it is the only way to make people see."

Review STYLE in the Handbook of Literary Terms, page 912.

The Life You Save May Be Your Own

Flannery O'Connor

he old woman and her daughter were sitting on their porch when Mr. Shiftlet came up their road for the first time. The old woman slid to the edge of her chair and leaned forward, shading her eyes from the piercing sunset with her hand. The daughter could not see far in front of her and continued to play with her fingers. Although the old woman lived in this desolate spot with only her daughter and she had never seen Mr. Shiftlet before, she could tell, even from a distance, that he was a tramp and no one to be afraid of. His left coat sleeve was folded up to show there was only half an arm in it and his gaunt figure listed slightly to the side as if the breeze were pushing him. He had on a black town suit and a brown felt hat that was turned up in the front and down in the back and he carried a tin tool box by a handle. He came on, at an amble, up her road, his face turned toward the sun which appeared to be balancing itself on the peak of a small mountain.

The old woman didn't change her position until he was almost into her yard; then she rose with one hand fisted on her hip. The daughter, a large girl in a short blue organdy dress, saw him all at once and jumped up and began to stamp and point and make excited speechless sounds.

Mr. Shiftlet stopped just inside the yard and set his box on the ground and tipped his hat at her as if she were not in the least afflicted; then he turned toward the old woman and swung the hat all the way off. He had long black slick hair that hung flat from a part in the middle to beyond the tips of his ears on either side. His face descended in forehead for more than half its length and ended suddenly with his features just balanced over a jutting steel-trap jaw. He seemed to be a young man but he had a look of composed dissatisfaction as if he understood life thoroughly.

"Good evening," the old woman said. She was about the size of a cedar fence post and she had a man's gray hat pulled down low over her head.

The tramp stood looking at her and didn't answer. He turned his back and faced the sunset. He swung both his whole and his short arm up slowly so that they indicated an expanse of sky and his figure formed a crooked cross. The old woman watched him with her arms folded across her chest as if she were the owner of the sun, and the daughter watched, her head thrust forward and her fat helpless hands hanging at the wrists. She had long pink-gold hair and eyes as blue as a peacock's neck.

He held the pose for almost fifty seconds and then he picked up his box and came on to the porch and dropped down on the bottom step.

"The Life You Save May Be Your Own." Copyright 1953 by Flannery O'Connor; renewed 1981 by Mrs. Regina O'Connor. Reprinted from *A Good Man is Hard to Find and Other Stories* by Flannery O'Connor by permission of Harcourt Brace Jovanovich, Inc. and Harold Matson Company, Inc.

"Lady," he said in a firm nasal voice, "I'd give a fortune to live where I could see me a sun do that every evening."

"Does it every evening," the old woman said and sat back down. The daughter sat down too and watched him with a cautious sly look as if he were a bird that had come up very close. He leaned to one side, rooting in his pants pocket, and in a second he brought out a package of chewing gum and offered her a piece. She took it and unpeeled it and began to chew without taking her eyes off him. He offered the old woman a piece but she only raised her upper lip to indicate she had no teeth.

Mr. Shiftlet's pale sharp glance had already passed over everything in the yard—the pump near the corner of the house and the big fig tree that three or four chickens were preparing to roost in—and had moved to a shed where he saw the square rusted back of an automobile. "You ladies drive?" he asked.

"That car ain't run in fifteen years," the old woman said. "The day my husband died, it quit running."

"Nothing is like it used to be, lady," he said. "The world is almost rotten."

"That's right," the old woman said. "You from around here?"

"Name Tom T. Shiftlet," he murmured, looking at the tires.

"I'm pleased to meet you," the old woman said. "Name Lucynell Crater and daughter Lucynell Crater. What you doing around here, Mr. Shiftlet?"

He judged the car to be about a 1928 or '29 Ford. "Lady," he said, and turned and gave her his full attention, "lemme tell you something. There's one of these doctors in Atlanta that's taken a knife and cut the human heart—the human heart," he repeated, leaning forward, "out of a man's chest and held it in his hand," and he held his hand out, palm up, as if it were slightly weighted with the human heart, "and studied it like it was a day-old chicken, and, lady," he said, allowing a long significant pause in which his head slid forward and his clay-colored eyes brightened, "he don't know no more about it than you or me."

"That's right," the old woman said.

"Why, if he was to take that knife and cut into every corner of it, he still wouldn't know no more than you or me. What you want to bet?"

"Nothing," the old woman said wisely. "Where you come from, Mr. Shiftlet?"

He didn't answer. He reached into his pocket and brought out a sack of tobacco and a package of cigarette papers and rolled himself a cigarette, expertly with one hand, and attached it in a hanging position to his upper lip. Then he took a box of wooden matches from his pocket and struck one on his shoe. He held the burning match as if he were studying the mystery of flame while it traveled dangerously toward his skin. The daughter began to make loud noises and to point to his hand and shake her finger at him, but when the flame was just before touching him, he leaned down with his hand cupped over it as if he were going to set fire to his nose and lit the cigarette.

He flipped away the dead match and blew a stream of gray into the evening. A sly look came over his face. "Lady," he said, "nowadays, people'll do anything anyways. I can tell you my name is Tom T. Shiftlet and I come from Tarwater, Tennessee, but you never have seen me before: how you know I ain't lying? How you know my name ain't Aaron Sparks, lady, and I come from Singleberry, Georgia, or how you know it's not George Speeds and I come from Lucy, Alabama, or how you know I ain't Thompson Bright from Toolafalls, Mississippi?"

"I don't know nothing about you," the old woman muttered, irked.

"Lady," he said, "people don't care how they lie. Maybe the best I can tell you is, I'm a man; but listen, lady," he said and paused and made his tone more ominous still, "what is a man?"

The old woman began to gum a seed. "What you carry in that tin box, Mr. Shiftlet?" she asked.

"Tools," he said, put back. "I'm a carpenter."

"Well, if you come out here to work, I'll be able to feed you and give you a place to sleep but

I can't pay. I'll tell you that before you begin," she said.

There was no answer at once and no particular expression on his face. He leaned back against the two-by-four that helped support the porch roof. "Lady," he said slowly, "there's some men that some things mean more to them than money." The old woman rocked without comment, and the daughter watched the trigger that moved up and down in his neck. He told the old woman then that all most people were interested in was money, but he asked what a man was made for. He asked her if a man was made for money, or what. He asked her what she thought she was made for but she didn't answer, she only sat rocking and wondered if a one-armed man could put a new roof on her garden house. He asked a lot of questions that she didn't answer. He told her that he was twenty-eight years old and had lived a varied life. He had been a gospel singer, a foreman on the railroad, an assistant in an undertaking parlor, and he had come over the radio for three months with Uncle Roy and his Red Creek Wranglers. He said he had fought and bled in the Arm Service of his country and visited every foreign land and that everywhere he had seen people that didn't care if they did a thing one way or another. He said he hadn't been raised thataway.

A fat yellow moon appeared on the branches of the fig tree as if it were going to roost there with the chickens. He said that a man had to escape to the country to see the world whole and that he wished he lived in a desolate place like this where he could see the sun go down every evening like God made it to do.

"Are you married or are you single?" the old woman asked.

There was a long silence. "Lady," he asked finally, "where would you find you an innocent woman today? I wouldn't have any of this trash I could just pick up."

The daughter was leaning very far down, hanging her head almost between her knees, watching him through a triangular door she had made in her overturned hair; and she suddenly fell in a heap on the floor and began to whimper. Mr. Shiftlet straightened her out and helped her get back in the chair.

"Is she your baby girl?" he asked.

"My only," the old woman said, "and she's the sweetest girl in the world. I wouldn't give her up for nothing on earth. She's smart too. She can sweep the floor, cook, wash, feed the chickens, and hoe. I wouldn't give her up for a casket of jewels."

"No," he said kindly, "don't ever let any man take her away from you."

"Any man come after her," the old woman said, " 'll have to stay around the place."

Mr. Shiftlet's eye in the darkness was focused on a part of the automobile bumper that glittered in the distance. "Lady," he said, jerking his short arm up as if he could point with it to her house and yard and pump, "there ain't a broken thing on this plantation that I couldn't fix for you, one-arm jackleg or not. I'm a man," he said with a sullen dignity, "even if I ain't a whole one. I got," he said, tapping his knuckles on the floor to emphasize the immensity of what he was going to say, "a moral intelligence!" and his face pierced out of the darkness into a shaft of doorlight and he stared at her as if he were astonished himself at this impossible truth.

The old woman was not impressed with the phrase. "I told you you could hang around and work for food," she said, "if you don't mind sleeping in that car yonder."

"Why listen, Lady," he said with a grin of delight, "the monks of old slept in their coffins!"

"They wasn't as advanced as we are," the old woman said.

The next morning he began on the roof of the garden house while Lucynell, the daughter, sat on a rock and watched him work. He had not been around a week before the change he had made in the place was apparent. He had patched the front and back steps, built a new hog pen, restored a fence, and taught Lucynell, who was completely deaf and had never said a word in her life, to say the word *bird*. The big rosy-faced girl followed him everywhere, saying "Burrttddt ddbirrrttdt," and clapping her hands. The old woman watched from a distance, secretly pleased. She was ravenous for a son-in-law.

Mr. Shiftlet slept on the hard narrow back seat of the car with his feet out the side window. He had his razor and a can of water on a crate that served him as a bedside table and he put up a piece of mirror against the back glass and kept his coat neatly on a hanger that he hung over one of the windows.

In the evenings he sat on the steps and talked while the old woman and Lucynell rocked violently in their chairs on either side of him. The old woman's three mountains were black against the dark blue sky and were visited off and on by various planets and by the moon after it had left the chickens. Mr. Shiftlet pointed out that the reason he had improved this plantation was because he had taken a personal interest in it. He said he was even going to make the automobile run.

He had raised the hood and studied the mechanism and he said he could tell that the car had been built in the days when cars were really built. You take now, he said, one man puts in one bolt and another man puts in another bolt and another man puts in another bolt so that it's a man for a bolt. That's why you have to pay so much for a car: you're paying all those men. Now if you didn't have to pay but one man, you could get you a cheaper car and one that had had a personal interest taken in it, and it would be a better car. The old woman agreed with him that this was so.

Mr. Shiftlet said that the trouble with the world was that nobody cared, or stopped and took any trouble. He said he never would have been able to teach Lucynell to say a word if he hadn't cared and stopped long enough.

"Teach her to say something else," the old woman said.

"What you want her to say next?" Mr. Shiftlet asked.

The old woman's smile was broad and toothless and suggestive. "Teach her to say 'sugarpie,' " she said.

Mr. Shiftlet already knew what was on her mind.

The next day he began to tinker with the automobile and that evening he told her that if she would buy a fan belt, he would be able to make the car run.

The old woman said she would give him the money. "You see that girl yonder?" she asked, pointing to Lucynell who was sitting on the floor a foot away, watching him, her eyes blue even in the dark. "If it was ever a man wanted to take her away, I would say, 'No man on earth is going to take that sweet girl of mine away from me!' but if he was to say, 'Lady, I don't want to take her away, I want her right here,' I would say, 'Mister, I don't blame you none. I wouldn't pass up a chance to live in a permanent place and get the sweetest girl in the world myself. You ain't no fool,' I would say."

"How old is she?" Mr. Shiftlet asked casually.

"Fifteen, sixteen," the old woman said. The girl was nearly thirty but because of her innocence it was impossible to guess.

"It would be a good idea to paint it too," Mr. Shiftlet remarked. "You don't want it to rust out."

"We'll see about that later," the old woman said.

The next day he walked into town and returned with the parts he needed and a can of gasoline. Late in the afternoon, terrible noises issued from the shed and the old woman rushed out of the house, thinking Lucynell was somewhere having a fit. Lucynell was sitting on a chicken crate, stamping her feet and screaming, "Burrddttt! bddurrddtttt!" but her fuss was drowned out by the car. With a volley of blasts it emerged from the shed, moving in a fierce and stately way. Mr. Shiftlet was in the driver's seat, sitting very erect. He had an expression of serious modesty on his face as if he had just raised the dead.

That night, rocking on the porch, the old woman began her business at once. "You want you an innocent woman, don't you?" she asked sympathetically. "You don't want none of this trash."

Tom Heflin, *The Old Pump*. Private collection

"No'm, I don't," Mr. Shiftlet said.

"One that can't talk," she continued, "can't sass you back or use foul language. That's the kind for you to have. Right there," and she pointed to Lucynell sitting cross-legged in her chair, holding both feet in her hands.

"That's right," he admitted. "She wouldn't give me any trouble."

"Saturday," the old woman said, "you and her and me can drive into town and get married."

Mr. Shiftlet eased his position on the steps.

"I can't get married right now," he said. "Everything you want to do takes money and I ain't got any."

"What you need with money?" she asked.

"It takes money," he said. "Some people'll do anything anyhow these days, but the way I think, I wouldn't marry no woman that I couldn't take on a trip like she was somebody. I mean take her to a hotel and treat her. I wouldn't marry the Duchesser Windsor,"[1] he said firmly, "unless I could take her to a hotel and give her something good to eat.

"I was raised thataway and there ain't a thing I can do about it. My old mother taught me how to do."

"Lucynell don't even know what a hotel is," the old woman muttered. "Listen here, Mr. Shiftlet," she said, sliding forward in her chair, "you'd be getting a permanent house and a deep well and the most innocent girl in the world. You don't need no money. Lemme tell you something: there ain't any place in the world for a poor disabled friendless drifting man."

The ugly words settled in Mr. Shiftlet's head like a group of buzzards in the top of a tree. He didn't answer at once. He rolled himself a

---

1. ***Duchesser Windsor.*** The Duchess of Windsor, Wallis Warfield Simpson (1896–1986), was the widow of the Duke of Windsor, who was King Edward VIII of England before renouncing the throne to marry Simpson, a divorced American, in 1937.

cigarette and lit it and then he said in an even voice, "Lady, a man is divided into two parts, body and spirit."

The old woman clamped her gums together.

"A body and a spirit," he repeated. "The body, lady, is like a house: it don't go anywhere; but the spirit, lady, is like a automobile: always on the move, always. . . ."

"Listen, Mr. Shiftlet," she said, "my well never goes dry and my house is always warm in the winter and there's no mortgage on a thing about this place. You can go to the courthouse and see for yourself. And yonder under that shed is a fine automobile." She laid the bait carefully. "You can have it painted by Saturday. I'll pay for the paint."

In the darkness, Mr. Shiftlet's smile stretched like a weary snake waking up by a fire. After a second he recalled himself and said, "I'm only saying a man's spirit means more to him than anything else. I would have to take my wife off for the weekend without no regards at all for cost. I got to follow where my spirit says to go."

"I'll give you fifteen dollars for a weekend trip," the old woman said in a crabbed voice. "That's the best I can do."

"That wouldn't hardly pay for more than the gas and the hotel," he said. "It wouldn't feed her."

"Seventeen-fifty," the old woman said. "That's all I got so it isn't any use you trying to milk me. You can take a lunch."

Mr. Shiftlet was deeply hurt by the word *milk*. He didn't doubt that she had more money sewed up in her mattress, but he had already told her he was not interested in her money. "I'll make that do," he said and rose and walked off without treating with her further.

On Saturday the three of them drove into town in the car that the paint had barely dried on and Mr. Shiftlet and Lucynell were married in the Ordinary's office while the old woman witnessed. As they came out of the courthouse, Mr. Shiftlet began twisting his neck in his collar. He looked morose and bitter as if he had been insulted while someone held him. "That didn't satisfy me none," he said. "That was just something a woman in an office did, nothing but paper work and blood tests. What do they know about my blood? If they was to take my heart and cut it out," he said, "they wouldn't know a thing about me. It didn't satisfy me at all."

"It satisfied the law," the old woman said sharply.

"The law," Mr. Shiftlet said and spit. "It's the law that don't satisfy me."

He had painted the car dark green with a yellow band around it just under the windows. The three of them climbed in the front seat and the old woman said, "Don't Lucynell look pretty? Looks like a baby doll." Lucynell was dressed up in a white dress that her mother had uprooted from a trunk and there was a Panama hat on her head with a bunch of red wooden cherries on the brim. Every now and then her placid expression was changed by a sly isolated little thought like a shoot of green in the desert. "You got a prize!" the old woman said.

Mr. Shiftlet didn't even look at her.

They drove back to the house to let the old woman off and pick up the lunch. When they were ready to leave, she stood staring at the window of the car, with her fingers clenched around the glass. Tears began to seep sideways out of her eyes and run along the dirty creases in her face. "I ain't ever been parted with her for two days before," she said.

Mr. Shiftlet started the motor.

"And I wouldn't let no man have her but you because I seen you would do right. Good-by, Sugarbaby," she said, clutching at the sleeve of the white dress. Lucynell looked straight at her and didn't seem to see her there at all. Mr. Shiftlet eased the car forward so that she had to move her hands.

The early afternoon was clear and open and surrounded by pale blue sky. Although the car would go only thirty miles an hour, Mr. Shiftlet imagined a terrific climb and dip and swerve that went entirely to his head so that he forgot his morning bitterness. He had always wanted an automobile but he had never been able to afford one before. He drove very fast because he wanted to make Mobile by nightfall.

Occasionally he stopped his thought long enough to look at Lucynell in the seat beside him. She had eaten the lunch as soon as they were out of the yard and now she was pulling the cherries off the hat one by one and throwing them out the window. He became depressed in spite of the car. He had driven about a hundred miles when he decided that she must be hungry again and at the next small town they came to, he stopped in front of an aluminum-painted eating place called The Hot Spot and took her in and ordered her a plate of ham and grits. The ride had made her sleepy and as soon as she got up on the stool, she rested her head on the counter and shut her eyes. There was no one in The Hot Spot but Mr. Shiftlet and the boy behind the counter, a pale youth with a greasy rag hung over his shoulder. Before he could dish up the food, she was snoring gently.

"Give it to her when she wakes up," Mr. Shiftlet said. "I'll pay for it now."

The boy bent over her and stared at the long pink-gold hair and the half-shut sleeping eyes. Then he looked up and stared at Mr. Shiftlet. "She looks like an angel of Gawd," he murmured.

"Hitchhiker," Mr. Shiftlet explained. "I can't wait. I got to make Tuscaloosa."

The boy bent over again and very carefully touched his finger to a strand of the golden hair and Mr. Shiftlet left.

He was more depressed than ever as he drove on by himself. The late afternoon had grown hot and sultry and the country had flattened out. Deep in the sky a storm was preparing very slowly and without thunder as if it meant to drain every drop of air from the earth before it broke. There were times when Mr. Shiftlet preferred not to be alone. He felt too that a man with a car had a responsibility to others and he kept his eye out for a hitchhiker. Occasionally he saw a sign that warned: "Drive carefully. The life you save may be your own."

The narrow road dropped off on either side into dry fields and here and there a shack or a filling station stood in a clearing. The sun began to set directly in front of the automobile. It was a reddening ball that through his windshield was slightly flat on the bottom and top. He saw a boy in overalls and a gray hat standing on the edge of the road and he slowed the car down and stopped in front of him. The boy didn't have his hand raised to thumb the ride, he was only standing there, but he had a small cardboard suitcase and his hat was set on his head in a way to indicate that he had left somewhere for good. "Son," Mr. Shiftlet said, "I see you want a ride."

The boy didn't say he did or he didn't but he opened the door of the car and got in, and Mr. Shiftlet started driving again. The child held the suitcase on his lap and folded his arms on top of it. He turned his head and looked out the window away from Mr. Shiftlet. Mr. Shiftlet felt oppressed. "Son," he said after a minute, "I got the best old mother in the world so I reckon you only got the second best."

The boy gave him a quick dark glance and then turned his face back to the window.

"It's nothing so sweet," Mr. Shiftlet continued, "as a boy's mother. She taught him his first prayers at her knee, she gave him love when no other would, she told him what was right and what wasn't, and she seen that he done the right thing. Son," he said, "I never rued a day in my life like the one I rued when I left that old mother of mine."

The boy shifted in his seat but he didn't look at Mr. Shiftlet. He unfolded his arms and put one hand on the door handle.

"My mother was a angel of Gawd," Mr. Shiftlet said in a very strained voice. "He took her from heaven and giver to me and I left her." His eyes were instantly clouded over with a mist of tears. The car was barely moving.

The boy turned angrily in the seat. "You go to the devil!" he cried. "My old woman is a flea bag and yours is a stinking polecat!" and with that he flung the door open and jumped out with his suitcase into the ditch.

Mr. Shiftlet was so shocked that for about a hundred feet he drove along slowly with the door still open. A cloud, the exact color of the boy's hat and shaped like a turnip, had descended over the sun, and another, worse looking, crouched behind the car. Mr. Shiftlet felt that the rottenness of the world was about to engulf him. He raised his arm and let it fall again to his breast. "Oh Lord!" he prayed. "Break forth and wash the slime from this earth!"

The turnip continued slowly to descend. After a few minutes there was a guffawing peal of thunder from behind, and fantastic raindrops, like tin-can tops, crashed over the rear of Mr. Shiftlet's car. Very quickly he stepped on the gas and with his stump sticking out the window he raced the galloping shower into Mobile.

1955

THINK AND DISCUSS
Understanding
1. When Mrs. Crater first sees Mr. Shiftlet, where is she and what is her daughter doing?
2. What does Mrs. Crater immediately assume Mr. Shiftlet to be? Does he appear threatening to her?
3. When Mr. Shiftlet walks into the yard, Mrs. Crater greets him. Before saying a word, what does he do?
4. What object most deeply impresses Mr. Shiftlet as he looks around him in the yard? How does he size it up?

Analyzing
5. What is Mrs. Crater's attitude toward her daughter?
6. Mr. Shiftlet's main goal in the story is acquiring the automobile. As he says, "The spirit, lady, is like a automobile: always on the move," and later, "a man's spirit means more to him than anything else." Go back through the story and list concrete details and **figurative language** that reinforce the mechanical nature of Shiftlet.
7. What is Mrs. Crater's main goal? Cite instances in which she goes about achieving that goal.
8. What kind of person has Mr. Shiftlet shown himself to be up to the time of his marriage with Lucynell?
9. Select examples from the story that you

feel are especially effective in contributing to the **mood** of the selection. You may mention **imagery,** details and description, choice of **setting,** and evocative phrases—anything that helps create the atmosphere and feeling.

Extending
10. Flannery O'Conner has written that "Mr. Shiftlet [is] of the Devil. . . . In general the Devil can always be a subject for my kind of comedy one way or another. I suppose this is because he is always accomplishing ends other than his own." What evidence can you find that Shiftlet is "of the Devil"? What evidence can you find that the Devil accomplishes "ends other than his own"?

REVIEWING: Style   H⟨Z⟩
See Handbook of Literary Terms, p. 912.
   Style is the individual shaping of language by a writer to fit a particular purpose or subject. It involves all aspects of language—word choice, figures of speech, sentence length and complexity, rhythms, and harmony of sounds.

1. Cite examples of O'Connor's use of colloquial country speech.
2. O'Connor uses figurative language such as personification, metaphor, and simile in her descriptions. Find two examples of her use of figurative language and discuss their effectiveness.

Flannery O'Connor on Her Recurring Subject in Fiction

To insure our sense of mystery, we need a sense of evil which sees the devil as a real spirit who must be made to name himself, and not simply to name himself as vague evil, but to name himself with his specific personality for every occasion. Literature, like virtue, does not thrive in an atmosphere where the devil is not recognized as existing both in himself and as a dramatic necessity for the writer. . . .

Story-writers are always talking about what makes a story "work." From my own experience in trying to make stories "work," I have discovered that what is needed is an action that is totally unexpected, yet totally believable, and I have found that, for me, this is always an action which indicates that grace has been offered. And frequently it is an action in which the devil has been the unwilling instrument of grace. This is not a piece of knowledge that I consciously put into my stories; it is a discovery that I get out of them.

I have found, in short, from reading my own writing, that my subject in fiction is the action of grace in territory held largely by the devil.

I have also found that what I write is read by an audience which puts little stock either in grace or the devil. You discover your audience at the same time and in the same way that you discover your subject; but it is an added blow.

Excerpt from "On Her Own Work" from *Mystery and Manners* by Flannery O'Connor. Copyright © 1969 by the Estate of Mary Flannery O'Connor. Reprinted by permission of Farrar, Straus and Giroux, Inc.

BIOGRAPHY

Eugenia Collier
1928–

Eugenia Collier has stated that the source of her creativity is her blackness. Nowhere is this more evident than in "Marigolds," which in 1969 won the Gwendolyn Brooks Award for Fiction, presented by *Negro Digest.*

After a traditional education at Howard University, Collier worked as a caseworker for a public welfare department. During this time she came to a new awareness of the importance of her heritage and began to write poems and stories for *Black World, Negro Digest,* and the *New York Times.* In addition, she has contributed to many anthologies portraying life in black America.

Besides her stories, Collier has written several scholarly articles and taught English at the Community College of Baltimore.

Marigolds

Eugenia Collier

hen I think of the home town of my youth, all that I seem to remember is dust—the brown, crumbly dust of late summer—arid, sterile dust that gets into the eyes and makes them water, gets into the throat and between the toes of bare brown feet. I don't know why I should remember only the dust. Surely there must have been lush green lawns and paved streets under leafy shade trees somewhere in town; but memory is an abstract painting—it does not present things as they are, but rather as they *feel*. And so, when I think of that time and that place, I remember only the dry September of the dirt roads and grassless yards of the shanty-town where I lived. And one other thing I remember, another incongruency of memory—a brilliant splash of sunny yellow against the dust—Miss Lottie's marigolds.

Whenever the memory of those marigolds flashes across my mind, a strange nostalgia comes with it and remains long after the picture has faded. I feel again the chaotic emotions of adolescence, illusive as smoke, yet as real as the potted geranium before me now. Joy and rage and wild animal gladness and shame become tangled together in the multi-colored skein of fourteen-going-on-fifteen as I recall that devastating moment when I was suddenly more woman than child, years ago in Miss Lottie's yard. I think of those marigolds at the strangest times; I remember them vividly now as I desperately pass away the time waiting for you, who will not come.

I suppose that futile waiting was the sorrowful background music of our impoverished little community when I was young. The Depression that gripped the nation was no new thing to us, for the black workers of rural Maryland had always been depressed. I don't know what it was that we were waiting for; certainly not for the prosperity that was "just around the corner," for those were white folks' words, which we never believed. Nor did we wait for hard work and thrift to pay off in shining success as the American Dream promised, for we knew better than that, too. Perhaps we waited for a miracle, amorphous in concept but necessary if one were to have the grit to rise before dawn each day and labor in the white man's vineyard until after dark, or to wander about in the September dust offering one's sweat in return for some meager share of bread. But God was chary with miracles in those days, and so we waited—and waited.

We children, of course, were only vaguely aware of the extent of our poverty. Having no radios, few newspapers, and no magazines, we were somewhat unaware of the world outside our community. Nowadays we would be called "culturally deprived" and people would write books and hold conferences about us. In those days everybody we knew was just as hungry and ill-clad as we were. Poverty was the cage in which we all were trapped, and our hatred of it was

Slight abridgment of "Marigolds" by Eugenia Collier. Copyright © November 1969 by *Negro Digest*. Reprinted by permission of Johnson Publishing Company and Eugenia Collier.

still the vague, undirected restlessness of the zoo-bred flamingo who knows that nature created him to fly free.

As I think of those days I feel most poignantly the tag-end of summer, the bright dry times when we began to have a sense of shortening days and the imminence of the cold.

By the time I was fourteen my brother Joey and I were the only children left at our house, the older ones having left home for early marriage or the lure of the city, and the two babies having been sent to relatives who might care for them better than we. Joey was three years younger than I, and a boy, and therefore vastly inferior. Each morning our mother and father trudged wearily down the dirt road and around the bend, she to her domestic job, he to his daily unsuccessful quest for work. After our few chores around the tumble-down shanty, Joey and I were free to run wild in the sun with other children similarly situated.

For the most part, those days are ill-defined in my memory, running together, combining like a fresh water-color painting left out in the rain. I remember squatting in the road drawing a picture in the dust, a picture which Joey gleefully erased with one sweep of his dirty foot. I remember fishing for minnows in a muddy creek and watching sadly as they eluded my cupped hands, while Joey laughed uproariously. And I remember, that year, a strange restlessness of body and of spirit, a feeling that something old and familiar was ending, and something unknown and therefore terrifying was beginning.

One day returns to me with special clarity for some reason, perhaps because it was the beginning of the experience that in some inexplicable way marked the end of innocence. I was loafing under the great oak tree in our yard, deep in some reverie which I have now forgotten except that it involved some secret, secret thoughts of one of the Harris boys across the yard. Joey and a bunch of kids were bored now with the old tire suspended from an oak limb which had kept them entertained for a while.

"Hey, Lizabeth," Joey yelled. He never talked when he could yell. "Hey, Lizabeth, let's us go somewhere."

I came reluctantly from my private world. "Where at, Joey?"

The truth was that we were becoming tired of the formlessness of our summer days. The idleness whose prospect had seemed so beautiful during the busy days of spring now had degenerated to an almost desperate effort to fill up the empty midday hours.

"Let's go see can we find us some locusts on the hill," someone suggested.

Joey was scornful. "Ain't no more locusts there. Y'all got 'em all while they was still green."

The argument that followed was brief and not really worth the effort. Hunting locust trees wasn't fun any more by now.

"Tell you what," said Joey finally, his eyes sparkling. "Let's us go over to Miss Lottie's."

The idea caught on at once, for annoying Miss Lottie was always fun. I was still child enough to scamper along with the group over rickety fences and through bushes that tore our already raggedy clothes, back to where Miss Lottie lived. I think now that we must have made a tragicomic spectacle, five or six kids of different ages, each of us clad in only one garment—the girls in faded dresses that were too long or too short, the boys in patchy pants, their sweaty brown chests gleaming in the hot sun. A little cloud of dust followed our thin legs and bare feet as we tramped over the barren land.

When Miss Lottie's house came into view we stopped, ostensibly to plan our strategy, but actually to reinforce our courage. Miss Lottie's house was the most ramshackle of all our ramshackle homes. The sun and rain had long since faded its rickety frame siding from white to a sullen gray. The boards themselves seemed to remain upright not from being nailed together but rather from leaning together like a house that a child might have constructed from cards. A brisk wind might have blown it down, and the fact that it was still standing implied a kind of enchantment that was stronger than the elements. There it stood, and as far as I know is standing yet—a gray rotting thing with no porch, no shutters, no steps, set on a cramped lot with no grass, not even any weeds —a monument to decay.

In front of the house in a squeaky rocking chair sat Miss Lottie's son, John Burke, completing the impression of decay. John Burke was what was known as "queer-headed." Black and ageless, he sat, rocking day in and day out in a mindless stupor, lulled by the monotonous squeak-squawk of the chair. A battered hat atop his shaggy head shaded him from the sun. Usually John Burke was totally unaware of everything outside his quiet dream world. But if you disturbed him, if you intruded upon his fantasies, he would become enraged, strike out at you, and curse at you in some strange enchanted language which only he could understand. We children made a game of thinking of ways to disturb John Burke and then to elude his violent retribution.

But our real fun and our real fear lay in Miss Lottie herself. Miss Lottie seemed to be at least a hundred years old. Her big frame still held traces of the tall, powerful woman she must have been in youth, although it was now bent and drawn. Her smooth skin was a dark reddish-brown, and her face had Indian-like features and the stern stoicism that one associates with Indian faces. Miss Lottie didn't like intruders either, especially children. She never left her yard, and nobody ever visited her. We never knew how she managed those necessities which depend on human interaction—how she ate, for example, or even whether she ate. When we were tiny children, we thought Miss Lottie was a witch and we made up tales, that we half believed ourselves, about her exploits. We were far too sophisticated now, of course, to believe the witch nonsense. But old fears have a way of clinging like cobwebs, and so when we sighted the tumble-down shack, we had to stop to reinforce our nerves.

"Look, there she is," I whispered, forgetting that Miss Lottie could not possibly have heard me from that distance. "She's fooling with them crazy flowers."

"Yeh, look at 'er."

Miss Lottie's marigolds were perhaps the strangest part of the picture. Certainly they did not fit in with the crumbling decay of the rest of her yard. Beyond the dusty brown yard, in front of the sorry gray house, rose suddenly and shockingly a dazzling strip of bright blossoms, clumped together in enormous mounds, warm and passionate and sun-golden. The old black witch-woman worked on them all summer, every summer, down on her creaky knees, weeding and cultivating and arranging, while the house crumbled and John Burke rocked. For some perverse reason, we children hated those marigolds. They interfered with the perfect ugliness of the place; they were too beautiful; they said too much that we could not understand; they did not make sense. There was something in the vigor with which the old woman destroyed the weeds that intimidated us. It should have been a comical sight—the old woman with the man's hat on her cropped white head, leaning over the bright mounds, her big backside in the air—but it wasn't comical, it was something we could not name. We had to annoy her by whizzing a pebble into her flowers or by yelling a dirty word, then dancing away from her rage, reveling in our youth and mocking her age. Actually, I think it was the flowers we wanted to destroy, but nobody had the nerve to try it, not even Joey, who was usually fool enough to try anything.

"Y'all git some stones," commanded Joey now, and was met with instant giggling obedience as everyone except me began to gather pebbles from the dusty ground. "Come on, Lizabeth."

I just stood there peering through the bushes, torn between wanting to join the fun and feeling that it was all a bit silly.

"You scared, Lizabeth?"

I cursed and spat on the ground—my favorite gesture of phony bravado. "Y'all children get the stones, I'll show you how to use 'em."

I said before that we children were not consciously aware of how thick were the bars of our cage. I wonder now, though, whether we were not more aware of it than I thought. Perhaps we

Hermann Dudley Murphy (b. 1867)
Zinnias and Marigolds.
Museum of Fine Arts, Boston

had some dim notion of what we were, and how little chance we had of being anything else. Otherwise, why would we have been so preoccupied with destruction? Anyway, the pebbles were collected quickly, and everybody looked at me to begin the fun.

"Come on, y'all."

We crept to the edge of the bushes that bordered the narrow road in front of Miss Lottie's place. She was working placidly, kneeling over the flowers, her dark hand plunged into the golden mound. Suddenly *zing*—an expertly aimed stone cut the head off one of the blossoms.

"Who out there?" Miss Lottie's backside came down and her head came up as her sharp eyes searched the bushes.

"You better git!"

We had crouched down out of sight in the bushes, where we stifled the giggles that insisted on coming. Miss Lottie gazed warily across the road for a moment, then cautiously returned to her weeding. *Zing*—Joey sent a pebble into the blooms, and another marigold was beheaded.

Miss Lottie was enraged now. She began struggling to her feet, leaning on a rickety cane and shouting. "Y'all git! Go on home!" Then the rest of the kids let loose with their pebbles, storming the flowers and laughing wildly and senselessly at

Miss Lottie's impotent rage. She shook her stick at us and started shakily toward the road crying, "John Burke! John Burke, come help!"

Then I lost my head entirely, mad with the power of inciting such rage, and ran out of the bushes in the storm of pebbles, straight toward Miss Lottie chanting madly, "Old witch, fell in a ditch, picked up a penny and thought she was rich!" The children screamed with delight, dropped their pebbles and joined the crazy dance, swarming around Miss Lottie like bees and chanting, "Old lady witch!" while she screamed curses at us. The madness lasted only a moment, for John Burke, startled at last, lurched out of his chair, and we dashed for the bushes just as Miss Lottie's cane went whizzing at my head.

I did not join the merriment when the kids gathered again under the oak in our bare yard. Suddenly I was ashamed, and I did not like being ashamed. The child in me sulked and said it was all in fun, but the woman in me flinched at the thought of the malicious attack that I had led. The mood lasted all afternoon. When we ate the beans and rice that was supper that night, I did not notice my father's silence, for he was always silent these days, nor did I notice my mother's absence, for she always worked until well into evening. Joey and I had a particularly bitter argument after supper; his exuberance got on my nerves. Finally I stretched out upon the pallet in the room we shared and fell into a fitful doze.

When I awoke, somewhere in the middle of the night, my mother had returned, and I vaguely listened to the conversation that was audible through the thin walls that separated our rooms. At first I heard no words, only voices. My mother's voice was like a cool, dark room in summer—peaceful, soothing, quiet. I loved to listen to it; it made things seem all right somehow. But my father's voice cut through hers, shattering the peace.

"Twenty-two years, Maybelle, twenty-two years," he was saying, "and I got nothing for you, nothing, nothing."

"It's all right, honey, you'll get something. Everybody out of work now, you know that."

"It ain't right. Ain't no man ought to eat his woman's food year in and year out, and see his children running wild. Ain't nothing right about that."

"Honey, you took good care of us when you had it. Ain't nobody got nothing nowadays."

"I ain't talking about nobody else, I'm talking about *me*. God knows I try." My mother said something I could not hear, and my father cried out louder, "What must a man do, tell me that?"

"Look, we ain't starving. I git paid every week, and Mrs. Ellis is real nice about giving me things. She gonna let me have Mr. Ellis's old coat for you this winter——"

"Damn Mr. Ellis's coat! And damn his money! You think I want white folks' leavings? Damn. Maybelle"—and suddenly he sobbed, loudly and painfully, and cried helplessly and hopelessly in the dark night. I had never heard a man cry before. I did not know men ever cried. I covered my ears with my hands but could not cut off the sound of my father's harsh, painful, despairing sobs. My father was a strong man who could whisk a child upon his shoulders and go singing through the house. My father whittled toys for us and laughed so loud that the great oak seemed to laugh with him, and taught us how to fish and hunt rabbits. How could it be that my father was crying? But the sobs went on, unstifled, finally quieting until I could hear my mother's voice, deep and rich, humming softly as she used to hum to a frightened child.

The world had lost its boundary lines. My mother, who was small and soft, was now the strength of the family; my father, who was the rock on which the family had been built, was sobbing like the tiniest child. Everything was suddenly out of tune, like a broken accordion. Where did I fit into this crazy picture? I do not now remember my thoughts, only a feeling of great bewilderment and fear.

Long after the sobbing and the humming had stopped, I lay on the pallet, still as stone with my hands over my ears, wishing that I too could cry and be comforted. The night was silent now except for the sound of the crickets and of Joey's soft breathing. But the room was too crowded with fear to allow me to sleep, and finally, feeling the terrible aloneness of 4:00 A.M., I decided to awaken Joey.

"Ouch! What's the matter with you? What you want?" he demanded disagreeably when I had pinched and slapped him awake.

"Come on, wake up."

"What for? Go 'way."

I was lost for a reasonable reply. I could not say, "I'm scared and I don't want to be alone," so I merely said, "I'm going out. If you want to come, come on."

The promise of adventure awoke him. "Going out now? Where at, Lizabeth? What you going to do?"

I was pulling my dress over my head. Until now I had not thought of going out. "Just come on," I replied tersely.

I was out the window and halfway down the road before Joey caught up with me.

"Wait, Lizabeth, where you going?"

I was running as if the Furies[1] were after me, as perhaps they were—running silently and furiously until I came to where I had half-known I was headed: to Miss Lottie's yard.

The half-dawn light was more eerie than complete darkness, and in it the old house was like the ruin that my world had become—foul and crumbling, a grotesque caricature. It looked haunted, but I was not afraid because I was haunted too.

"Lizabeth, you lost your mind?" panted Joey.

I had indeed lost my mind, for all the smoldering emotions of that summer swelled in me and burst—the great need for my mother who was never there, the hopelessness of our poverty and degradation, the bewilderment of being neither child nor woman and yet both at once, the fear unleashed by my father's tears. And these feelings combined in one great impulse toward destruction.

"Lizabeth!"

I leaped furiously into the mounds of marigolds and pulled madly, trampling and pulling and destroying the perfect yellow blooms. The fresh smell of early morning and of dew-soaked marigolds spurred me on as I went tearing and mangling and sobbing while Joey tugged my dress or my waist crying, "Lizabeth, stop, please stop!"

And then I was sitting in the ruined little garden among the uprooted and ruined flowers, crying and crying, and it was too late to undo what I had done. Joey was sitting beside me, silent and frightened, not knowing what to say. Then, "Lizabeth, look."

I opened my swollen eyes and saw in front of me a pair of large calloused feet; my gaze lifted to the swollen legs, the age-distorted body clad in a tight cotton night dress, and then the shadowed Indian face surrounded by stubby white hair. And there was no rage in the face now, now that the garden was destroyed and there was nothing any longer to be protected.

"M-miss Lottie!" I scrambled to my feet and just stood there and stared at her, and that was the moment when childhood faded and womanhood began. That violent, crazy act was the last act of childhood. For as I gazed at the immobile face with the sad, weary eyes, I gazed upon a kind of reality which is hidden to childhood. The witch was no longer a witch but only a broken old woman who had dared to create beauty in the midst of ugliness and sterility. She had been born in squalor and lived in it all her life. Now at the end of that life she had nothing except a falling-down hut, a wrecked body, and John Burke, the mindless son of her passion. Whatever verve there was left in her, whatever was of love and beauty and joy that had not been squeezed out by life, had been there in the marigolds she had so tenderly cared for.

Of course I could not express the things that I knew about Miss Lottie as I stood there awkward and ashamed. The years have put words to the things I knew in that moment, and as I look back upon it, I know that the moment marked the end of innocence. Innocence involves an unseeing

---

1. *Furies*, avenging spirits in Greek and Roman myth.

acceptance of things at face value, an ignorance of the area below the surface. In that humiliating moment I looked beyond myself and into the depths of another person. This was the beginning of compassion, and one cannot have both compassion and innocence.

The years have taken me worlds away from that time and that place, from the dust and squalor of our lives and from the bright thing that I destroyed in a blind childish striking out. Miss Lottie died long ago and many years have passed since I last saw her hut, completely barren at last, for despite my wild contrition she never planted marigolds again. Yet, there are times when the image of those passionate yellow mounds returns with a painful poignancy. For one does not have to be ignorant and poor to find that his life is barren as the dusty yards of our town. And I too have planted marigolds.

1969

THINK AND DISCUSS
Understanding
1. According to the first paragraph, what two things does the narrator remember about the home town of her youth?
2. At what stage of life is the narrator when the main events of the story occur?
3. Who is John Burke? How does he react to the children's intrusions?

Analyzing
4. What triggered Lizabeth's second assault on the marigolds?
5. Why was Miss Lottie less enraged by the second attack than she was by the first one?
6. Lizabeth has been initiated—that is, she has gained a new awareness. What has she learned?
7. Why is the incident involving the marigolds so important to the narrator even in her later life?

Extending
8. The narrator concludes that "one cannot have both compassion and innocence." What does this statement mean? In your opinion, is it true? Explain.

REVIEWING: Setting H𝕋
See Handbook of Literary Terms, p. 906.

Setting is the time and place in which the action of a narrative occurs. It may serve only as a backdrop or it may help create mood or atmosphere. In addition, setting, which can be revealed through dialogue and description, sometimes provides clues to events and characters.

1. What is the setting (both time and place) of "Marigolds"?
2. How does the setting help explain the actions of Lizabeth?

COMPOSITION ◄●━
Writing About a Bad Deed
Write several paragraphs in your journal about something you did as a child that you later came to regret. Re-create your feelings at the time and your feelings now as you look back. Include in your discussion the reasons that led you to perform this deed.

Analyzing Setting
Write a four- or five-paragraph essay for a literary magazine analyzing the effect of setting in "Marigolds." What is the time and place of the story? How does the setting contribute to the author's theme? How does the garden of marigolds contrast with the setting as a whole? Answer these and other questions you think of as you take notes before you write.

Comment

First Voices

The first voices heard in American poetry after World War II were from poets steeped in the tenets of the earlier great modernists. Like Eliot, they believed that poetry should be impersonal, showing no trace of the poet's life, and that feelings were to be expressed, not in a subjective way, but through an "objective correlative," some object or image that would evoke the emotion. Like MacLeish in 1929, their "Ars Poetica" was "A poem should not mean/ But be." A poem was conceived as a static "well-wrought urn," to be appreciated as a crafted work of art, not as a meaningful "statement" about the world. Many of the postwar poets and the influential critics of poetry were college professors, immersed in traditional forms and disdainful of the social protest poetry that had emerged in the '30s. But in many of these established poets can be detected the whisper of revolt that would become a "howl" in the late '50s and early '60s.

Preeminent among these academic formalists were Theodore Roethke, Robert Lowell, and Richard Wilbur. Roethke's poetic career, like the motifs in some of his poems, can be seen as a journey. The starting point is a strict formality and technical correctness; the midpoint is rejection of tradition, and the journey's end sees a return to the traditional forms but with adaptations and adjustments. Roethke's most radically inventive poems combine an exploration of his mental and psychological state with echoes and traces of the irony, wit, and gloom of T. S. Eliot, Wallace Stevens, Robinson Jeffers, and other modernists.

Robert Lowell's poem "Mr. Edwards and the Spider" shows the influence of the Puritanism that he both embraced and rejected and the New England traditions of his ancestors, James Russell Lowell and Amy Lowell. Like Roethke, Lowell performed a literary about-face in mid-career, turning from formalism to a poetry that was intensely personal in both form and subject. His finest work is a synthesis of the best facets of the academic and the nonconformist movements.

Lowell characterized the two schools of American poetry as "cooked" and "raw," referring to the division between the traditionalists and the radicals. "Cooked" poetry was exquisite in taste, meticulously measured, and flawless in technique. "Raw" poetry was intense and spontaneous, a vehicle through which poets could bare their souls in emotional outbursts. Richard Wilbur is often spoken of as one of the finest producers of "cooked"—or traditional—poetry.

The clash between convention and revolt is further exemplified in the works of Howard Nemerov and Galway Kinnell, who draw from both factions by blending erudition with passion. The impersonality espoused by Eliot is defied in the "confessional" poetry of Lowell and Roethke, who explored their own mental and psychological states with sometimes painful candor.

Among other poetic currents of the time was the emergence of a large number of accomplished women, often writing from a feminist perspective. Adrienne Rich, Denise Levertov, and Elizabeth Bishop are some of the most notable, each with a large body of distinguished work. Gwendolyn Brooks and Mari Evans are both black women, finding in their heritage rich resources for their probing and sometimes caustic revelations.

But just as we do not recognize a category of "male poets," it is best to drop such categories for female writers. They are in the basic sense *poets*, some female, some black, some both. Their themes and styles are as free-ranging as those of the other poets of the time, and their voices as distinctively individual.

BIOGRAPHIES

Denise Levertov   1923–

Denise Levertov was born in England, where she was educated privately. After serving as a nurse in World War II, she married an American and in 1948 came to this country to live. Her early poems were romantic. But in later years, she moved from purely personal issues to larger political concerns such as opposition to the Vietnam War, women's liberation, and Third World poverty and oppression. Her poems are intensely compact perceptions of people, things, and feelings.

Richard Wilbur   1921–

Richard Wilbur was born in New York City and educated at Amherst College and Harvard. He published his first volume, *The Beautiful Changes*, in 1947. Ten years later, he received both the Pulitzer Prize and the National Book Award. A professor of English at Wesleyan University, he served during 1987–1988 as Poet Laureate Consultant to the Library of Congress. Wilbur's poems are noted for their lyricism, wit, and depth of feeling.

Howard Nemerov   1920–

Howard Nemerov was born and raised in New York City and educated at Harvard. Since 1969 he has been Professor of English at Washington University in St. Louis. For Nemerov, the poet's function is to describe reality precisely and then to "create some kind of comforting order." Many of his poems embody analogies between elements in nature and human characteristics, giving his poetry a philosophical quality. Nemerov won the Pulitzer Prize in 1978 for his *Collected Poems,* and succeeded Richard Wilbur as U.S. Poet Laureate in 1988–1989.

Mona Van Duyn   1921–

Mona Van Duyn grew up in Iowa, where she began writing poems in second grade. After attending Iowa State Teachers College and the State University of Iowa, she taught at the University of Iowa Writers' Workshop, the University of Louisville, and Washington University at St. Louis. In 1947 she and her husband, Jarvis Thurston, co-founded *Perspective, a Quarterly of Literature,* which flourished for twenty years. In 1971, Van Duyn was co-winner of the National Book Award for her volume *To See, To Take.* "The Vision Test" appears in her collection *Letters from a Father and Other Poems* (1982).

The Secret

Denise Levertov

Two girls discover
the secret of life
in a sudden line of
poetry.

5 I who don't know the
secret wrote
the line. They
told me

(through a third person)
10 they had found it
but not what it was,
not even

what line it was. No doubt
by now, more than a week
15 later, they have forgotten
the secret,

the line, the name of
the poem. I love them
for finding what
20 I can't find,

and for loving me
for the line I wrote,
and for forgetting it
so that

25 a thousand times, till death
finds them, they may
discover it again, in other
lines,

in other
30 happenings. And for
wanting to know it,
for

assuming there is
such a secret, yes,
35 for that
most of all.

1964★

Fairfield Porter, *Interior in Sunlight* (1965). Brooklyn Museum

---

Levertov (lev′èr tov).

★This and other dates listed for the poems in Unit 7 correspond to the publication dates that appear in the credits.

Denise Levertov, *Poems 1960–1967*. Copyright © 1964 by Denise Levertov Goodman. Reprinted by permission of New Directions Publishing Corporation.

The Writer

Richard Wilbur

In the room at the prow of the house
Where light breaks, and the windows are tossed with linden,
My daughter is writing a story.

I pause in the stairwell, hearing
5   From her shut door a commotion of typewriter-keys
Like a chain hauled over a gunwale.

Young as she is, the stuff
Of her life is a great cargo, and some of it heavy:
I wish her a lucky passage.

10 But now it is she who pauses,
As if to reject my thought and its easy figure.
A stillness greatens, in which

The whole house seems to be thinking,
And then she is at it again with a bunched clamor
15 Of strokes, and again is silent.

I remember the dazed starling
Which was trapped in that very room, two years ago;
How we stole in, lifted a sash

And retreated, not to affright it;
20 And how for a helpless hour, through the crack of the door,
We watched the sleek, wild, dark

And iridescent creature
Batter against the brilliance, drop like a glove
To the hard floor, or the desk-top,

25 And wait then, humped and bloody,
For the wits to try it again; and how our spirits
Rose when, suddenly sure,

It lifted off from a chair-back,
Beating a smooth course for the right window
30 And clearing the sill of the world.

It is always a matter, my darling,
Of life or death, as I had forgotten. I wish
What I wished you before, but harder.   **1971**

"The Writer." Copyright © 1971 by Richard Wilbur. Reprinted from his volume *The Mind-Reader* by permission of Harcourt Brace Jovanovich, Inc. and Faber and Faber Publishers.

To David, About His Education

Howard Nemerov

The world is full of mostly invisible things,
And there is no way but putting the mind's eye,
Or its nose, in a book, to find them out,
Things like the square root of Everest
5 Or how many times Byron goes into Texas,
Or whether the law of the excluded middle
Applies west of the Rockies. For these
And the like reasons, you have to go to school
And study books and listen to what you are told,
10 And sometimes try to remember. Though I don't know
What you will do with the mean annual rainfall
On Plato's Republic, or the calorie content
Of the Diet of Worms,[1] such things are said to be
Good for you, and you will have to learn them
15 In order to become one of the grown-ups
Who sees invisible things neither steadily nor whole,
But keeps gravely the grand confusion of the world
Under his hat, which is where it belongs,
And teaches small children to do this in their turn.

1962

Photograph by John Hedgecoe

Nemerov (nem′ə rov)

1. *Plato's Republic* . . . *Diet of Worms* (vôrms). *The Republic*
by Plato is a book about just government, based on the teachings
of Socrates; both were philosophers of ancient Greece. In 1521, a
council at the German city of Worms declared Martin Luther, the
Protestant leader, a heretic against Roman Catholicism.

"To David, About His Education" from *The Next Room of the Dream* by
Howard Nemerov. Reprinted by permission of the author.

The Vision Test

Mona Van Duyn

My driver's license is lapsing and so I appear
in a roomful of waiting others and get in line.
I must master a lighted box of far or near,
a highway language of shape, squiggle and sign.
5 As the quarter-hours pass I watch the lady in charge
of the test, and think how patient, how slow, how nice
she is, a kindly priestess indeed, her large,
round face, her vanilla pudding, baked-apple-and-spice
face in continual smiles as she calls each "Dear"
10 and "Honey" and shows first-timers what to see.
She enjoys her job, how pleasant to be in her care
rather than brute little bureaucrat or saleslady.
I imagine her life as a tender placing of hands
on her children's hands as they come to grips with the rocks
15 and scissors of the world. The girl before me stands
in a glow of good feeling. I take my place at the box.
"And how are *you* this lovely morning, Dear?
A few little questions first. Your name?—Your age?—
Your profession?" "Poet." "What?" She didn't hear.
20 "Poet," I say loudly. The blank pink page
of her face is lifted to me. *"What?"* she says.
"POET," I yell, "P-O-E-T."
A moment's silence. *"Poet?"* she asks. "Yes."
Her pencil's still. She turns away from me
25 to the waiting crowd, tips back her head like a hen
drinking clotted milk, and her "Ha ha hee hee hee"
of hysterical laughter rings through the room. Again
"Oh, ha ha ha ha ha hee hee."
People stop chatting. A few titter. It's clear
30 I've told some marvelous joke they didn't quite catch.
She resettles her glasses, pulls herself together,
pats her waves. The others listen and watch.
"And what are we going to call the color of your hair?"
She asks me warily. Perhaps it's turned white
35 on the instant, or green is the color poets declare,
or perhaps I've merely made her distrust her sight.
"Up to now it's always been brown." Her pencil trembles,
then with an almost comically obvious show
of reluctance she lets me look in her box of symbols
40 for normal people who know where they want to go.

1981

"The Vision Test" by Mona Van Duyn
(first published in *The Massachusetts Review*).
Copyright © 1981 by Mona Van Duyn. In
Letters from a Father and Other Poems. Copyright © 1982 by Mona Van Duyn (New York:
Atheneum, 1982). Reprinted with the permission of Atheneum Publishers.

THINK AND DISCUSS

THE SECRET
Understanding
1. What have the two girls discovered in a line of poetry? Who wrote the line?

Analyzing
2. What will the girls forget in a week? Why does the poet love the girls for "assuming there is/ such a secret"?
3. What do you think is the "secret" mentioned in this poem?

THE WRITER
Understanding
1. Who is the speaker observing? What is the writer doing in line 3?

Analyzing
2. What **figure of speech** is introduced in line 1 and extended in lines 6–9? Why is it appropriate?
3. In what way does the incident with the starling offer a parallel to the daughter's attempts at writing?
4. Why does the poet's memory of the starling make him wish even more for his daughter's success?

TO DAVID, ABOUT HIS EDUCATION
Understanding
1. Where must David turn to find out about the "invisible things"?
2. Why is it necessary to learn such things (lines 13–15)?

Analyzing
3. In line 1 the poet speaks of a class of things that share the common characteristic of being "mostly invisible." Judging from the examples of this class of objects given in lines 4–7 and 11–13, what other characteristics do they have in common?
4. Why must "the grand confusion of the world" be kept under the adult's hat? What is the poet's attitude toward this necessity?

THE VISION TEST
Understanding
1. Where is the speaker at the beginning of the poem, and why is she there?
2. What is the speaker's initial evaluation of the lady in charge of the test? What does the speaker imagine the lady's life to be like?

Analyzing
3. Why do you think that the answer "Poet" causes the lady in charge to react the way she does in lines 19–28?
4. In lines 20–21, the speaker says of the lady, "The blank pink page/ of her face is lifted to me." What figure of speech is this and why is it appropriate?
5. Choose one of the following words to describe the **tone** of the woman's question in line 33: *angry, hysterical, cautious, irritated.* Explain your choice.

Extending
6. In the last three lines, the speaker in "The Vision Test" **infers** the lady's attitude toward poets. How does this view compare with the view of Levertov and Wilbur toward writers? Which view is closer to your own? Explain.

COMPOSITION
Describing Your Feelings About Writing
Write a letter of three or four paragraphs to a friend describing your feelings about writing when you are confronted with a blank page. Reread "The Writer" and compare the experience described there with your own experience. Do you ever surprise yourself with what you write?

Comparing Attitudes Toward Poetry
Write an essay of at least three paragraphs comparing and contrasting attitudes toward poetry as expressed in two of the four poems that appear in this group. Identify the attitudes of the speakers and of the characters that they describe. In the last paragraph, explain your own view of poetry and those who write it.

BIOGRAPHIES

Robert Hayden   1913–1980

Robert Hayden was born in Detroit and educated at Wayne State University and the University of Michigan. Before becoming Professor of English at the University of Michigan, he taught for more than twenty years at Fisk University. In 1966 he was awarded the prize for English language poetry at the First World Festival of Negro Arts at Dakar, Senegal. He was elected to the National Academy of American Poets in 1975, and later was twice appointed Poetry Consultant to the Library of Congress.

David Wagoner   1926–

David Wagoner was born in Massillon, Ohio, and attended Penn State University and Indiana University. His poetry, like the titles of his books, evokes images of the outdoors and of self-reliance. His works include *Dry Sun, Dry Wind; A Place to Stand; Staying Alive; Landfall;* and *Through the Forest: New and Selected Poems, 1977–1987.* One fellow poet said that coming to Wagoner's poems after reading the verse of so many modern poets, "One practically has a twinge of Puritan guilt, and feels shamelessly entertained—refreshed instead of exhausted."

William Stafford   1914–

William Stafford was raised in Kansas and educated at the University of Kansas and the University of Iowa. During World War II he was a conscientious objector and is still active in pacifist organizations. He is Professor of Literature Emeritus at Lewis and Clark College in Portland, Oregon. Recent works include *You Must Revise Your Life* (1987) and *An Oregon Message* (1988). Commenting on his work, Stafford said, "My poetry seems to me direct and communicative, with some oddity and variety. It is usually not formal. It is much like talk, with some enhancement. . . . The voice I most consistently hear in my poetry is my mother's voice."

Robert Lowell   1917–1977

A member of the same New England family as James Russell Lowell and Amy Lowell, Robert Lowell was raised in Boston and educated at Harvard and Kenyon College in Ohio. During World War II he was drafted but filed as a conscientious objector and went to prison. His early poetry, difficult and impersonal, is characterized by a concern for corruption in modern society and a search for spiritual values; his later poetry is highly confessional, dealing with personal problems as well as with political issues of the time. He received a Pulitzer Prize in 1947 and a National Book Award in 1960. Lowell once said: ". . . All my poems are written for catharsis; none can cure melancholia or arthritis."

Frederick Douglass

Robert Hayden

When it is finally ours, this freedom, this liberty, this beautiful
and terrible thing, needful to man as air,
usable as earth; when it belongs at last to all,
when it is truly instinct, brain matter, diastole, systole,
5 reflex action; when it is finally won; when it is more
than the gaudy mumbo jumbo of politicians:
this man, this Douglass, this former slave, this Negro
beaten to his knees, exiled, visioning a world
where none is lonely, none hunted, alien,
10 this man, superb in love and logic, this man
shall be remembered. Oh, not with statues' rhetoric,
not with legends and poems and wreaths of bronze alone,
but with the lives grown out of his life, the lives
fleshing his dream of the beautiful, needful thing.

1966

Charles White,
Frederick Douglass (1953).
Private collection

"Frederick Douglass" is reprinted from *Angle of Ascent, New and Selected Poems* by Robert Hayden, by permission of Liveright Publishing Corporation. Copyright © 1975, 1972, 1970, 1966 by Robert Hayden.

Reader's Note

From the Author: "Frederick Douglass"

"Frederick Douglass" was written as part of a sonnet sequence on heroic men and women of the antislavery struggle. . . . I thought of the tribute to Douglass as the climactic poem in the series, but it is now the only one of these sonnets I kept, scrapping the others because I felt they were facile and poorly constructed.

I had intended the sonnets to be one of two sequences in a long poem—an epic of sorts—on slavery and the Civil War, entitled *The Black Spear.* . . . I worked on *The Black Spear* intermittently from about 1941 to 1946, reading biographies, memoirs, histories of slav-ery and the war, poring over Mathew Brady's photographs. . . .

Well, *The Black Spear* did not emerge as the great poem I had struggled to achieve. After tinkering with the manuscript, following its several rejections, I abandoned *The Black Spear,* and it distresses me to realize that I don't know where the manuscript is. However, it is not a complete loss, for certain parts of it have proved viable over the years. And among them "Frederick Douglass" seems to be one of the hardiest survivors. . . .

Since I wished to express my feeling that

the achievements of Douglass were of fundamental value to the entire human race, I tried
to use words and images evoking some sense
of the elemental, the organic, the universal.
Hence, "earth," "air," "diastole," "systole,"
"reflex action," etc. . . .

If I were writing "Douglass" at this stage in
my life, it would be quite different. Or would it?

I would still want to honor Douglass not only as
a hero in the struggle for the freedom of his people but also as a man whose vision of humanity
was all-embracing. This is my vision too. People
of all races and creeds respond warmly to this
poem. I am indeed grateful for that.

*Note: A speech by Frederick Douglass appears
in Unit 3.*

My Father's Garden

David Wagoner

On his way to the open hearth where white-hot steel
Boiled against furnace walls in wait for his lance
To pierce the fire-clay and set loose demons
And dragons in molten tons, blazing
5 Down to the huge satanic cauldrons,
Each day he would pass the scrapyard, his kind of garden.

In rusty rockeries of stoves and brake-drums,
In grottoes of sewing machines and refrigerators,
He would pick flowers for us: small gears and cogwheels
10 With teeth like petals, with holes for anthers,
Long stalks of lead to be poured into toy soldiers,
Ball-bearings as big as grapes to knock them down.

He was called a melter. He tried to keep his brain
From melting in those tyger-mouthed mills
15 Where the same steel reappeared over and over
To be reborn in the fire as something better
Or worse: cannons or cars, needles or girders,
Flagpoles, swords, or ploughshares.

But it melted. His classical learning ran
20 Down and away from him, not burning bright.
His fingers culled a few cold scraps of Latin
And Greek, *Magna sine laude,*[1] for crosswords
And brought home lumps of tin and sewer grills
As if they were his ripe prize vegetables.

1980

---

1. *Magna sine laude* (mag'nə sī'nē
lou'də), without great praise. [*Latin*]

"My Father's Garden" from *Landfall,* by
David Wagoner. Copyright © 1980 by David
Wagoner. First appeared in *Missouri Review.*
By permission of Little, Brown and Company
in association with the Atlantic Monthly Press.

Judgments

William Stafford

I accuse——
    Ellen: you have become forty years old,
    and successful, tall, well-groomed,
    gracious, thoughtful, a secretary.
5   Ellen, I accuse.

George——
    You know how to help others;
    you manage a school. You never
    let fear or pride or faltering plans
10 break your control.
    George, I accuse.

I accuse——
    Tom: you have found a role;
    now you meet all kinds of people
15 and let them find the truth of your
    eminence; you need not push.
    Oh, Tom, I do accuse.

Remember——
    The gawky, hardly to survive students
20 we were: not one of us going to succeed,
    all of us abjectly aware of how cold,
    unmanageable the real world was?
    I remember. And that fear was true.
    And is true.

25 Last I accuse——
    Myself: my terrible poise, knowing
    even this, knowing that then we
    sprawled in the world
    and were ourselves part of it; now
30 we hold it firmly away with gracious
    gestures (like this of mine!) we've
        achieved.

I see it all too well——
    And I am accused, and I accuse.

1964

"Judgments" from *Stories That Could Be True* by William Stafford.
Copyright © 1964 by William Stafford. Reprinted by permission of
Harper & Row, Publishers, Inc.

Mr. Edwards and the Spider

Robert Lowell

I saw the spiders marching through the air,
Swimming from tree to tree that mildewed day
  In latter August when the hay
  Came creaking to the barn. But where
5   The wind is westerly,
Where gnarled November makes the spiders fly
Into the apparitions of the sky,
They purpose nothing but their ease and die
Urgently beating east to sunrise and the sea;

10 What are we in the hands of the great God?
It was in vain you set up thorn and briar
  In battle array against the fire
  And treason crackling in your blood;
    For the wild thorns grow tame
15 And will do nothing to oppose the flame;
Your lacerations tell the losing game
You play against a sickness past your cure.
How will the hands be strong? How will the heart endure?

A very little thing, a little worm,
20 Or hourglass-blazoned spider, it is said,
  Can kill a tiger. Will the dead
  Hold up his mirror and affirm
    To the four winds the smell
And flash of his authority? It's well
25 If God who holds you to the pit of hell,
Much as one holds a spider, will destroy,
Baffle and dissipate your soul. As a small boy

On Windsor Marsh, I saw the spider die
When thrown into the bowels of fierce fire:
30   There's no long struggle, no desire
  To get up on its feet and fly——
    It stretches out its feet
And dies. This is the sinner's last retreat;
Yes, and no strength exerted on the heat
35 Then sinews the abolished will, when sick
And full of burning, it will whistle on a brick.

"Mr. Edwards and the Spider" from *Lord Weary's Castle*, copyright 1946, 1974 by Robert Lowell. Reprinted by permission of Harcourt Brace Jovanovich, Inc. and Faber and Faber Publishers.

But who can plumb the sinking of that soul?
Josiah Hawley,[1] picture yourself cast
    Into a brick-kiln where the blast
40   Fans your quick vitals to a coal——
        If measured by a glass,
How long would it seem burning! Let there pass
A minute, ten, ten trillion; but the blaze
Is infinite, eternal: this is death,
45 To die and know it. This is the Black Widow, death.

                              1944

---

1. *Josiah Hawley,* leader of the faction that got Jonathan Edwards (Unit 1) dismissed from his pastorate in Northampton, Massachusetts.

Reader's Note

"Mr. Edwards and the Spider"

"Mr. Edwards and the Spider" is a **dramatic monologue** in which the austere Calvinist Jonathan Edwards is the speaker. In the poem, Lowell quotes extensively from Edwards's writings and sermons. He thus condemns Edwards and his merciless Calvinism with the preacher's own words and images.

In the first stanza, Lowell draws on Edwards's youthful essay on flying spiders (see page 61), in which he observed how the wind carried the spiders from tree to tree, and eventually to the sea, where they died—although they intended "nothing but their ease" as they flew. Thus the young Edwards drew a Calvinist moral from the spiders' doom, perceiving a stern God carrying the unaware insects to their death. In addition, Edwards's most famous sermon, "Sinners in the Hands of an Angry God" (see page 59), compares sinners to spiders dangling over the flames of Hell's fire, held only by a slender thread and the whim of God.

In lines 13 and 17, "treason crackling in your blood" and a "sickness past your cure" refer to the Calvinist belief that people are inherently sinful; they inherited their sinful character from Adam and Eve, who disobeyed God by eating the forbidden fruit. God has decided people's fate before they are born. Those who are saved, are saved by God's mercy. Those predestined for hell cannot change their fate.

The "hourglass-blazoned spider," line 20, is the poisonous female black widow spider, which has an hourglass-shaped mark on the bottom of its abdomen. Lines 21–24 refer to the custom of holding a mirror in front of a seemingly dead person to see if the person is breathing.

Windsor Marsh mentioned in stanza 4 refers to East Windsor, Connecticut, where Edwards observed the flying spiders. Just as the spider thrown into "fierce fire" realizes that all is lost and goes along with its own death, so too the sinner, regardless of any exertions against the heat of hell, will not be able to give back strength ("sinew") to the "abolished will" but will accept death and succumb to the fire of hell's oven ("whistle on a brick"). Throughout the poem, Lowell uses Edwards's most extreme terms to describe damnation, dwelling on the agonies the sinner will feel without end and in full awareness of what is happening.

THINK AND DISCUSS

FREDERICK DOUGLASS
Understanding
1. For what will Douglass be remembered (lines 13–14)?

Analyzing
2. In lines 1–2, freedom is described as both "beautiful" and a "terrible thing." Explain this **paradox.**
3. What experiences and qualities of Frederick Douglass make him representative of freedom?
4. Describe the **tone** of the poem.

MY FATHER'S GARDEN
Understanding
1. What is the speaker's father called (line 13)? What items does he make to bring home (lines 11–12)?
2. What items are "reborn in the fire" (lines 17–18)?

Analyzing
3. What is the **figure of speech** introduced in lines 2–5? Why is it appropriate?
4. Describe the "garden" of the speaker's father. What sort of "flowers" grow there?
5. What is the father's attitude toward his children? the speaker's attitude toward his father?

JUDGMENTS
Understanding
1. What is the past relationship of the speaker and those he accuses (lines 18–20)?
2. How did they feel about themselves and the world during the time they were together (lines 20–22)?

Analyzing
3. Judging only from the first three stanzas, what is the nature of the accusation the speaker makes against Ellen, George, and Tom?
4. Why does the speaker include himself in his accusation?

5. The speaker observes that "we hold [the world] firmly away with gracious gestures." What does he mean?

MR. EDWARDS AND THE SPIDER
Understanding
1. What is happening to the spiders in stanzas 1 and 4?
2. According to the speaker in the last stanza, what is death?

Analyzing
3. What is meant by the "thorn and briar" of line 11?
4. What religious concepts are expressed by the "fire/ And treason crackling in your blood" and the "sickness past your cure"?
5. If the spiders **symbolize** humanity, what message is the speaker of the poem giving us in these stanzas?

Extending
6. The speakers of these four poems have varying attitudes toward their subjects. Which speakers praise the people whom they describe? Which speakers are critical?

COMPOSITION

Writing a Poem
Write a ten- to twenty-line poem about someone you know. Assume that your poem will be published in a class booklet. If you like, pattern your poem on one of the poems in this cluster. Address this person in your poem, and refer to at least one specific quality of the person or an event in his or her life.

Writing a Character Sketch
Interview someone who has a job to which he or she is particularly well suited or unsuited. Ask questions about the job—its site, the person's view of the work, and details of an ordinary day at work. Then use details from this interview to write a character sketch of this person, as seen through his or her job. Submit this sketch to the person you interviewed to find out if the description is an accurate one.

BIOGRAPHIES

Richard Eberhart   1904–

Richard Eberhart was born in Austin, Minnesota. He studied at Dartmouth and Cambridge, where his poems were first published. From 1933 to 1942 he taught English at two private preparatory schools in Massachusetts. After war service in the U.S. Navy, from which he retired with the rank of commander, he entered a manufacturing business, of which he eventually became vice-president. Meanwhile, his poems appeared in a variety of magazines. In 1952 he returned to academic life. Since 1956 he has been Professor of English at Dartmouth, becoming Professor Emeritus in 1970. Readers can sample a wide variety of Eberhart's poems in his volume, *Collected Poems: 1930–1986*.

May Swenson   1919–

May Swenson was born in Logan, Utah, and went to Utah State University. During most of her professional life she has lived in or near New York City. The hallmark of her poetry is the clarity of her imagery. As she wrote: "The poet works (and plays) with the elements of language, forming and transforming his material to the point where a new perception emerges; something simple or ordinary may be seen as wonderful, something complex or opaque become suddenly clear." Swenson often concerns herself as much with the visual impression of the lines on the page as with the meanings of the words. These shaped poems she calls "iconographs." Swenson's recent collection is titled *In Other Words (1987)*.

Galway Kinnell   1927–

Galway Kinnell was born in Rhode Island and educated at Princeton and the University of Rochester. He has taught in such widely separated places as the University of Chicago, the University of Grenoble in France, and the University of Iran. He is currently director of New York University's creative writing program. In 1983 he won the Pulitzer Prize for his book *Selected Poems* and was also a co-winner of the American Book Award. Believing that a poem does not really enter a person until it has been memorized, Kinnell can recite from memory not only his own works but those of many other poets, old and new.

The Groundhog

Richard Eberhart

In June, amid the golden fields,
I saw a groundhog lying dead.
Dead lay he; my senses shook,
And mind outshot our naked frailty.
5 There lowly in the vigorous summer
His form began its senseless change,
And made my senses waver dim
Seeing nature ferocious in him.
Inspecting close his maggots' might
10 And seething cauldron of his being,
Half with loathing, half with a strange love,
I poked him with an angry stick.
The fever arose, became a flame
And Vigor circumscribed the skies,
15 Immense energy in the sun,
And through my frame a sunless trembling.
My stick had done nor good nor harm.
Then stood I silent in the day
Watching the object, as before;
20 And kept my reverence for knowledge
Trying for control, to be still,
To quell the passion of the blood;
Until I had bent down on my knees
Praying for joy in the sight of decay.
25 And so I left; and I returned
In Autumn strict of eye, to see
The sap gone out of the groundhog,
But the bony sodden hulk remained.
But the year had lost its meaning,

30 And in intellectual chains
I lost both love and loathing,
Mured up in the wall of wisdom.
Another summer took the fields again
Massive and burning, full of life,
35 But when I chanced upon the spot
There was only a little hair left,
And bones bleaching in the sunlight
Beautiful as architecture;
I watched them like a geometer,
40 And cut a walking stick from a birch.
It has been three years, now.
There is no sign of the groundhog.
I stood there in the whirling summer,
My hand capped a withered heart,
45 And thought of China and of Greece,
Of Alexander in his tent;
Of Montaigne in his tower,
Of Saint Theresa[1] in her wild lament

1960

---

1. *Alexander . . . Montaigne . . . Saint Theresa.*
Alexander the Great (356–323 B.C.) conquered the known world of his era. Montaigne (mon tän′), who lived from 1533 to 1592, was a French writer and philosopher. Saint Theresa of Ávila (1515–1582) was a Spanish mystic. These figures represent, respectively, political, intellectual, and spiritual life.

From *Collected Poems 1930–1960* by Richard Eberhart. Copyright © 1960 by Richard Eberhart. Reprinted by permission of Oxford University Press, Inc.

"The Groundhog"

Like many of Eberhart's other works "The Groundhog" deals with the physical cycles of growth and decay and with the universality of death. The first two lines provide a straightforward report that sets the stage. The third line, opening with three stressed words in inverted order, directs the reader's attention to the central fact: "Dead lay he." From then on the poem becomes a meditation on mortality and an analysis of the speaker's reaction to death.

The first encounter with the decaying groundhog, a "seething cauldron," is vividly drawn. Ironically, it is not the sight of death that awes the speaker, but the vigor and energy present at the scene of decay. Reminded of his own mortality, he responds both with loathing and with a strange love (line 11).

In autumn he again visits the groundhog, now a "bony sodden hulk." But he can no longer react emotionally to the scene as he did the previous summer. Thus, "the year had lost its meaning," and autumn becomes a season of the soul.

By the time of the third visit, the speaker has become detached, viewing with the geometrician's eye the bleached bones "beautiful as architecture." Once again he uses a stick, but this time it enables him to walk away rather than to intervene. The speaker's emotions, then, have gradually changed from shock to denial to detachment.

At the final visit the groundhog's body has disappeared, completely entering into the cycle of life. The allusions in lines 45–48 represent people and civilizations that have flourished and then perished. Alexander the Great (356–323 B.C.) conquered the known world. Montaigne (1533–1592) was a French writer and philosopher. Saint Theresa of Ávila (1515–1582) was a Spanish mystic. Respectively, these figures represent the political, intellectual, and spiritual life. Eberhart may be drawing courage from these mighty figures who lived so creatively that they were able to transcend death through their deeds. Similarly, the poet too may transcend death by creating this poem.

Charles Burchfield,
Six O'Clock (1936).
The Syracuse Museum of Fine Arts

Snow by Morning

May Swenson

Some for everyone,
plenty,
and more coming——

fresh, dainty, airily arriving
5 everywhere at once,

transparent at first,
each faint slice——
slow, soundlessly tumbling;

then quickly, thickly, a gracious fleece
10 will spread like youth, like wheat,
over the city.

Each building will be a hill,
all sharps made round——

dark, worn, noisy narrows made still,
15 wide, flat, clean spaces;

streets will be fields,
cars be fumbling sheep;

a deep, bright harvest will be seeded
in a night.

20 By morning we'll be children
feeding on manna,
a new loaf on every doorsill.

1963

"Snow by Morning" by May Swenson, which first appeared in *The New Yorker*, is reprinted with the permission of the author from *To Mix with Time*, copyright © 1963 by May Swenson and Charles Scribner's Sons.

Blackberry Eating

Galway Kinnell

I love to go out in late September
among the fat, overripe, icy, black blackberries
to eat blackberries for breakfast,
the stalks very prickly, a penalty
5 they earn for knowing the black art
of blackberry making; and as I stand among them
lifting the stalks to my mouth, the ripest berries
fall almost unbidden to my tongue,
as words sometimes do, certain peculiar words
10 like *strengths* or *squinched*,
many-lettered, one-syllabled lumps,
which I squeeze, squinch open, and splurge well
in the silent, startled, icy, black language
of blackberry eating in late September.

1980

Photograph by Walter Chandoha

"Blackberry Eating" from *Mortal Acts, Mortal Words* by Galway Kinnell. Copyright © 1980 by Galway Kinnell. Reprinted by permission of Houghton Mifflin Company.

THINK AND DISCUSS

THE GROUNDHOG

Understanding

1. How many encounters does the speaker have with the groundhog's body? How much time elapses between each encounter?
2. How does the animal's body look at each stage?

Analyzing

3. What two meanings might the word *senseless* have in line 6?
4. Why might the sight of such a "seething cauldron" stir "strange love" within the speaker (lines 10–11)?
5. If the stick represents human intervention, what point is being made about people's ability to affect death?
6. With whom does the speaker identify in the final encounter? Why?

SNOW BY MORNING

Understanding

1. What words and phrases describe the snow in lines 4–8?
2. Into what will the snow transform each building? the streets? the cars?

Analyzing

3. How will the snow transform the urban scene into a country scene?

4. Look up *manna* in the Glossary. What does this word suggest about the effects of snow?

BLACKBERRY EATING
Understanding
1. During what season and what time of the day does the speaker like to pick blackberries?
2. What are the four adjectives used to describe the blackberries early in the poem?

Analyzing
3. What is "peculiar" about the words *strengths* and *squinched*?
4. What about the words *squeeze, squinch,* and *splurge* suggests the process of blackberry eating?
5. What adjective is repeated most often in the poem? What do you think is the purpose of this repetition?

Extending
6. These three poems express varying attitudes about things in nature. What are those attitudes? With which do you agree? With which do you disagree? Why?

THINKING SKILLS
Evaluating
To evaluate something is to judge it, based on particular criteria. Poems can be evaluated in several ways. You can evaluate a poem based on qualities such as clarity, emotional appeal, use of poetic language, or originality, to name just a few. A poem that is excellent, as based on one set of criteria, might not rank so highly based on another.

Reread the poems by Eberhart, Swenson, and Kinnell and then answer the following questions.

1. What would be a good set of criteria by which to evaluate these poems?
2. According to these criteria, how would you evaluate each of these poems? Do you consider any of these great poems? Why or why not?

COMPOSITION
Describing a Subject in Nature
Write a three- to five-paragraph description for a nature magazine in which you describe something in nature that you have observed closely—an animal, a snowfall or rainstorm, or a plant. First make a list of appropriate details, including setting, physical description, and images. Then think of a figure of speech that describes your subject. Now organize your notes into a composition. In the final paragraph, express your opinion about the subject you have described. Review your work, correcting mechanical errors and making any necessary revisions to improve your style. See "The Writing Process" in the Writer's Handbook.

Evaluating a Poem
Imagine that you are a textbook editor who, because of lack of space, has to omit one of the poems by Eberhart, Swenson, or Kinnell in the next edition of *The United States in Literature.* Reread each poem, taking notes on the theme, level of difficulty, and degree to which it uses techniques such as sound devices, figurative language, and allusion. In addition, note the appeal, or lack of appeal, each poem has for teenagers. Finally, in a memo of several paragraphs, make a recommendation about which two of the three poems should be retained. See "Writing Notes and Summaries" in the Writer's Handbook.

BIOGRAPHIES

Karl Shapiro 1913–

Karl Shapiro was born in Baltimore and grew up wanting to write poetry. So strong was his interest that he neglected his studies at the University of Virginia to work on his verses. His second volume, *V-Letter and Other Poems,* was awarded the Pulitzer Prize in 1945. The following year he was appointed Poetry Consultant to the Library of Congress. Shapiro has also won fame as critic and editor. From 1950 to 1956 he was editor of *Poetry* magazine, and from 1956 to 1966 he was editor of *The Prairie Schooner.* He has taught at the Chicago Circle Campus of the University of Illinois and at the Davis campus of the University of California. Recent books include *New and Selected Poems* (1987) and the first volume of his *Autobiography* (1988).

Maxine Kumin 1925–

Maxine Kumin was born in Philadelphia and attended Radcliffe. Since 1960 she has published many volumes of poetry, including some for children. Her book *Up Country: Poems of New England* won the Pulitzer Prize in 1973. She became Poetry Consultant to the Library of Congress in 1981. In 1982 she published both a collection of poems, *Our Ground Time Here Will Be Brief,* and a collection of short stories, *Why Can't We Live Together Like Civilized Human Beings?* In 1985, she published another collection of poems titled *The Long Approach.* Kumin sees all her writing as "private experience giving rise to elegy and celebration."

Randall Jarrell 1914–1965

Randall Jarrell was born and raised in Tennessee. After college, he began teaching and writing poetry. In 1942 he entered the Army Air Corps. The poetry he wrote out of his war experience was stark and often violent. In 1946 Jarrell returned to teaching and also became literary editor of *The Nation.* From 1956 to 1958 he served as Poetry Consultant to the Library of Congress. He won the National Book Award in 1961 for *The Woman at the Washington Zoo,* a volume of poetry and translations. Jarrell's uncollected essays and reviews were gathered and published in 1980 under the title *Kipling, Auden & Co.*

Auto Wreck

Karl Shapiro

Its quick soft silver bell beating, beating,
And down the dark one ruby flare
Pulsing out red light like an artery,
The ambulance at top speed floating down
5 Past beacons and illuminated clocks
Wings in a heavy curve, dips down,
And brakes speed, entering the crowd.
The doors leap open, emptying light;
Stretchers are laid out, the mangled lifted
10 And stowed into the little hospital.
Then the bell, breaking the hush, tolls once,
And the ambulance with its terrible cargo
Rocking, slightly rocking, moves away,
As the doors, an afterthought, are closed.

15 We are deranged, walking among the cops
Who sweep glass and are large and composed.
One is still making notes under the light.
One with a bucket douches ponds of blood
Into the street and gutter.
20 One hangs lanterns on the wrecks that cling,
Empty husks of locusts, to iron poles.

Our throats were tight as tourniquets,
Our feet were bound with splints, but now
Like convalescents intimate and gauche,
25 We speak through sickly smiles and warn
With the stubborn saw of common sense,
The grim joke and the banal resolution.
The traffic moves around with care,
But we remain, touching a wound
30 That opens to our richest horror.

Already old, the question Who shall die?
Becomes unspoken Who is innocent?
For death in war is done by hands;
Suicide has cause and stillbirth, logic.
35 But this invites the occult mind,
Cancels our physics with a sneer,
And spatters all we knew of denouement
Across the expedient and wicked stones.

1942

"Auto Wreck," Copyright 1942 and renewed 1970 by Karl Shapiro. Reprinted from *Collected Poems 1940–1978*, by Karl Shapiro, by permission of Random House, Inc.

From the Author: "Auto Wreck"

"Auto Wreck" seems to be my most popular poem. I don't mind really.

Its genesis is partly imaginary, partly composite, partly based on observation, like most poems. Notice that there are no sounds of pain or anguish in the poem. The people are silent, as in a silent film. Even the ambulance bell has a soft almost beautiful music. The accident is at night and the "arterial" light of the ambulance comes and goes through the darkness. And everything is somewhat in slow motion.

The bystander (the Poet) is dissociated from the scene and merely wonders at its meaning and its horror. I watched the police wash the blood down the gutters and sweep away the broken glass, and the rest. I had a particular accident in mind, and the poem was written after witnessing a particularly bad one one midnight in Baltimore, but I drew upon similar scenes such as everyone has experienced from time to time.

The questions asked towards the end of the poem have a certain grisly banality, the very kind of question that loved ones would ask.

Why? Why? For, given another second there would be no accident.

Incidentally, the first line is a deliberate wrenching of an iambic pentameter line, with two reversed feet at the end, "beating, beating." I think the device works well, considering the subject.

I hope these remarks will help.

Eyes

Maxine Kumin

At night Amanda's eyes
are rage red with toy worlds inside.
Head on they rummage the dark
of the paddock like twin cigars
5 but flicker at the edges with
the shyer tongues of the spirit lamp.

There's little enough for her to see:
my white shirt, the sleeves
rolled high, two flaps of stale bread
10 in my fish paws. I can't sleep.
I have come back from
the feed-bag-checkered restaurant
from the pale loose tears of my
    dearest friend
her blue eyes sinking into the highball
    glass
15 her eyeballs clinking on ice
and her mouth drawn down in
    the grand
comedy of anguish.

Today a sparrow has been put
in the hawk's hands and in the net
20 a monarch[1] crazes its wings on gauze.
A doe run down by the dogs
commonly dies of fright before
its jugular opens at the fang hole.
In my friend's eyes the famine victim
25 squats, holding an empty rice bowl.

O Amanda, burn out my dark.
Press the warm suede of your horseflesh
against my cold palm.
Take away all that is human.

1971

Kumin (kü'min).
1. *monarch,* a large orange and black butterfly.

From *House, Bridge, Fountain, Gate* by Maxine Kumin. Copyright © 1971, 1972, 1973, 1974, 1975 by Maxine Kumin. Reprinted by permission of The Viking Press, Inc.

Losses

Randall Jarrell

It was not dying: everybody died.
It was not dying: we had died before
In the routine crashes—and our fields
Called up the papers, wrote home to our folks,
5 And the rates rose, all because of us.
We died on the wrong page of the almanac,
Scattered on mountains fifty miles away;
Diving on haystacks, fighting with a friend,
We blazed up on the lines we never saw.
10 We died like aunts or pets or foreigners.
(When we left high school nothing else had died
For us to figure we had died like.)

In our new planes, with our new crews, we bombed
The ranges by the desert or the shore,
15 Fired at towed targets, waiting for our scores——
And turned into replacements and woke up
One morning, over England, operational.
It wasn't different: but if we died
It was not an accident but a mistake
20 (But an easy one for anyone to make).

We read our mail and counted up our missions——
In bombers named for girls, we burned
The cities we had learned about in school——
Till our lives wore out; our bodies lay among
25 The people we had killed and never seen.
When we lasted long enough they gave us medals;
When we died they said, "Our casualties were low."

They said, "Here are the maps"; we burned the cities.

It was not dying—no, not ever dying;
30 But the night I died I dreamed that I was dead,
And the cities said to me: "Why are you dying?
We are satisfied, if you are; but why did I die?"

1948

"Losses" from *The Complete Poems* by Randall Jarrell. Copyright 1948 by Randall Jarrell. Copyright renewed © 1975 by Mary von Schrader Jarrell. Reprinted by permission of Farrar, Straus & Giroux, Inc. and Faber and Faber Limited.

THINK AND DISCUSS

AUTO WRECK

Understanding

1. What happens after the ambulance arrives in stanza 1?
2. What are the police doing in stanza 2?
3. Stanza 3 describes people reacting. What lines indicate that it is difficult for people to speak or to walk away from the scene?

Analyzing

4. What questions are asked in stanza 4?
5. Find examples of **personification** and **simile** in stanza 1. Explain the **metaphor** presented in lines 29 and 30.
6. Explain the meanings of lines 35–38.

EYES

Understanding

1. What (or who) and where is Amanda?
2. Describe the appearance of Amanda's eyes in the dark (lines 2–6).

Analyzing

3. What is the **mood** of the person described in lines 11–17?
4. How does the list of tragedies in the third stanza fit into the poem?
5. In line 26, the speaker says, "O Amanda, burn out my dark." How does the fire image here relate to that used in describing Amanda's eyes at the opening of the poem?

6. Why does the poem conclude with the speaker's plea to Amanda, "Take away all that is human"?

LOSSES

Understanding

1. Who are the "we" of the poem?
2. What were their specific actions in the war?
3. What did the air fields do when a crew member died (lines 3–4)?

Analyzing

4. What do you think is the attitude of the poet toward war? Which **images** help convey this attitude?

Extending

5. These three poems are about anguish due to accident, depression, and war. Do you consider such subjects appropriate for poetry, or do you consider topics such as nature, love, and beauty more poetic? Explain.

COMPOSITION

Using Imagery in Writing

Shapiro has used images to vividly describe an event that has had a significant impact on his life. Write a description of three or four paragraphs for a classmate of a memorable event in your life. First, list words and images that vividly portray this event. Then, using items from your list, describe your reactions to this event.

Gwendolyn Brooks   1917–

Gwendolyn Brooks was born in Chicago, where she has lived for all but one month of her life. After graduation from Wilson Junior College, she did editorial work on a magazine and held a secretarial job. While working, she took a writing course, submitted a poem to *Poetry* magazine, and had it accepted. Her first volume, *A Street in Bronzeville* (1945), led to an award from the American Academy of Arts and Letters. Her second book of poems, *Annie Allen*, won the Pulitzer Prize in 1950. In 1968 she was named successor to the late Carl Sandburg as Poet Laureate of Illinois and served as Consultant in Poetry at the Library of Congress in 1985–1986. Her recent works include *The Near-Johannesburg Boy* (1986) and *Blacks* (1987).

Elizabeth Bishop   1911–1979

Elizabeth Bishop was born in Worcester, Massachusetts, and educated at Vassar. Her travels took her to Brazil, where she lived for sixteen years. Later, she lived alternately in Brazil and Cambridge, Massachusetts, where she taught part-time at Harvard. Many of her poems were shaped from her experiences in these widely disparate lands. Bishop's poems are distinguished by their precise diction and sharp imagery. Her volume *Poems, North and South* received the Pulitzer Prize in 1956, and she won the National Book Award in 1970. The collection *That Was Then* (1980) was published posthumously.

Theodore Roethke   1908–1963

Theodore Roethke grew up in Saginaw, Michigan, and attended the University of Michigan and Harvard. In his spare time he worked in his father's greenhouse, and his love for plants and flowers appears in his poetry. An extremely skillful technician, Roethke manipulates rhyme and rhythm so subtly that the reader is often engaged by a poem before grasping its meaning. In 1954 Roethke won a Pulitzer Prize for his volume of poems, *The Waking*.

Mari Evans   1923–

Mari Evans was born in Toledo, Ohio, but currently lives in Indianapolis, Indiana. She has taught black literature and been a writer-in-residence at Indiana University, Purdue, and Northwestern. Many of her poems have been choreographed for presentation on TV specials and in off-Broadway productions. Evans also wrote, directed, and produced a TV series titled "The Black Experience" for an Indianapolis station.

To Be in Love

Gwendolyn Brooks

To be in love
Is to touch things with a lighter hand.

In yourself you stretch, you are well.

You look at things
5 Through his eyes.
      A Cardinal is red.
      A sky is blue.
Suddenly you know he knows too.
He is not there but
10 You know you are tasting together
The winter, or light spring weather.

His hand to take your hand is overmuch.
Too much to bear.

You cannot look in his eyes
15 Because your pulse must not say
What must not be said.

When he
Shuts a door——
Is not there——
20 Your arms are water.

And you are free
With a ghastly freedom.

You are the beautiful half
Of a golden hurt.
25 You remember and covet his mouth,
To touch, to whisper on.

Oh when to declare
Is certain Death!

Oh when to apprize
30 Is to mesmerize,

To see fall down, the Column of Gold,
Into the commonest ash.

                    1963

Charles White, *Lovers* (1964). Private collection

"To Be in Love" from *Selected Poems* by Gwendolyn Brooks. Copyright © 1963 by Gwendolyn Brooks
Blakely. Reprinted by permission of Harper & Row, Publishers, Inc.

One Art

Elizabeth Bishop

The art of losing isn't hard to master;
so many things seem filled with the intent
to be lost that their loss is no disaster.

Lose something every day. Accept the
        fluster
5 of lost door keys, the hour badly spent.
The art of losing isn't hard to master.

Then practice losing farther, losing faster;
places, and names, and where it was you
        meant
to travel. None of these will bring disaster.

10 I lost my mother's watch. And look! my
        last, or
next-to-last, of three loved houses went.
The art of losing isn't hard to master.

I lost two cities, lovely ones. And, vaster,
some realms I owned, two rivers, a continent.
15 I miss them, but it wasn't a disaster.

—Even losing you (the joking voice, a
        gesture
I love) I shan't have lied. It's evident
the art of losing's not too hard to master
though it may look like (*Write* it!) like
        disaster.   1955

 Review RHYTHM in the Handbook of Literary Terms, page 903.

Night Journey

Theodore Roethke

Now as the train bears west,
Its rhythm rocks the earth,
And from my Pullman berth
I stare into the night
5 While others take their rest.
Bridges of iron lace,
A suddenness of trees,
A lap of mountain mist
All cross my line of sight,
10 Then a bleak wasted place,
And a lake below my knees.
Full on my neck I feel
The straining at a curve;
My muscles move with steel,

15 I wake in every nerve.
I watch a beacon swing
From dark to blazing bright;
We thunder through ravines
And gullies washed with light.
20 Beyond the mountain pass
Mist deepens on the pane;
We rush into a rain
That rattles double glass.
Wheels shake the roadbed stone,
25 The pistons jerk and shove,
I stay up half the night
To see the land I love.

                    1940

"One Art" reprinted by permission of Farrar, Straus and Giroux, Inc. from *Complete Poems 1927–1979* by Elizabeth Bishop. Copyright © 1955, 1976 by Elizabeth Bishop. Copyright © 1983 by Alice Helen Methfessel.

Roethke (ret′kē).

"Night Journey," copyright © 1940 by Theodore Roethke from the book *The Collected Poems of Theodore Roethke*. Reprinted by permission of Doubleday & Company, Inc. and Faber and Faber Ltd.

. . . and the old women gathered

(The Gospel Singers)

Mari Evans

and the old women gathered
and sang His praises
standing
resolutely together
5 like supply sergeants who
have seen
everything
and are still
Regular Army: It
10 was fierce and
not melodic and
although we ran
the sound of it
stayed in our ears . . .

1970

Prentiss Taylor, *Assembly Church* (1936). National Museum of American Art
(formerly National Collection of Fine Arts), Smithsonian Institution

". . . and the old women gathered" by Mari Evans from *I Am a Black Woman*, published by William
Morrow and Company, 1970, by permission of the author.

THINK AND DISCUSS
TO BE IN LOVE
Understanding
1. According to the first three lines, how does being in love affect the speaker?
2. In what ways does love overwhelm the speaker, according to lines 12–16?

Analyzing
3. What **imagery** does the speaker use to describe the relationship with her loved one?
4. Which lines indicate that the speaker cannot declare her love?

5. What is meant by the gold column becoming ash in the last two lines of the poem?

APPLYING: Lyric H𝄞
See Handbook of Literary Terms, p. 896.
   A poem that expresses some basic emotion or state of mind is a **lyric.** Often short, a lyric may be rhymed or unrhymed. It usually creates a single impression, and is highly personal.

1. What is the state of mind of the speaker in "To Be in Love"?
2. How does the speaker personalize this state of mind?

3. Is this poem rhymed or unrhymed? Explain.

ONE ART
Understanding

1. In lines 4–15, what losses does the speaker mention?

2. What has been lost in the last stanza?

Analyzing

3. How can someone lose a name? a city?

4. In the last stanza, what is the speaker's **tone** and how does it differ from that in the preceding stanzas?

5. What do you think the parenthetical expression in the final line indicates about the speaker's feelings?

NIGHT JOURNEY
Understanding

1. In which direction is the train headed? Where is the speaker of the poem?

2. How do the speaker and the "others" differ in their activities?

Analyzing

3. How does the poet's love of the land become evident in his choice of **imagery**?

4. Why do you think the poet titled his work "Night Journey" rather than "Train Ride"?

REVIEWING: Rhythm HT
See Handbook of Literary Terms, p. 903.

Rhythm is the arrangement of stressed and unstressed syllables in speech and writing. The four most common regular rhythms are iamb (˘ ′), trochee (′ ˘), anapest (˘ ˘ ′), and dactyl (′ ˘ ˘).

1. What is the rhythm used in "Night Journey"?

2. What variation do you find in the rhythm of lines 6, 10, and 11?

3. This poem conveys the impression of a train's movement through sound devices and imagery. Explain how the rhythm, rhyme, line length, and figurative language all combine to convey this impression.

. . . AND THE OLD WOMEN GATHERED
Understanding

1. What are the old women doing?

Analyzing

2. Identify the **simile** in lines 5–9 and discuss its appropriateness.

3. Who do you think the "we" are in line 12? Discuss.

4. The poem, including the title, begins and ends with an ellipsis, a series of marks indicating the omission of one or more words. Why do you suppose the poet did this? What might have gone on before and after?

Extending

5. The poems by Brooks, Bishop, Roethke, and Evans explore different feelings. What has prompted each of these emotions?

COMPOSITION ◄━●
Writing About a Response to Music
In ". . . and the old women gathered," Evans explores the powerful effect of music. Write a three- to five-paragraph essay for your school newspaper describing an experience in which you were deeply moved, excited, or calmed by music. Describe the music, the performers, the setting, the effects on you and others, and your responses.

Writing an Explication
Write several paragraphs explicating "Night Journey" for your classmates. Consider the following questions: What is the significance of the title? How are particular words used to convey the impression of speed and motion? How does the poet use rhythm, rhyme, imagery, and figurative language to enforce ideas? See "Writing About Poetry and Poetic Devices" in the Writer's Handbook.

ENRICHMENT
Oral Reading
Many of the poems you have read in this unit lend themselves well to reading aloud. Choose one of these poems, or find another in this book that you enjoy and feel would be appropriate for reading aloud. Practice reading it so that you adequately convey through tone, pauses, and emphasis, the emotion expressed in the poem. After you practice, present your reading to the class.

Comment

New Voices

In the 1960s and 1970s, the civil rights movement and the "long, dark night of the soul" that was the Vietnam War inspired new voices to employ poetry in a public and political role. Some poets translated their concerns through their ethnic background. Lawson Fusao Inada, Leslie Marmon Silko, and Teresa Paloma Acosta refracted their visions of family relationships through Japanese American, Native American, and Mexican American prisms.

Other poets handled their personal themes in traditional and effective ways. The self-revelations of Sylvia Plath's "Mirror" are concerned with identity and aging. Vern Rutsala's "Words" evokes the contrast between the world of schoolbooks and the world of poverty. Gregory Djanikian reveals how he, as an Egyptian-become-American, solved the perennial problem of the immigrant in "How I Learned English."

The new-found freedom of poetry to say what it wanted or needed to say was accompanied by new freedoms of language and form. The language of poetry became more relaxed, more conversational, more clearly the language of the streets than of the universities. At the same time, poets tended to throw over the old forms and create their own. When Denise Levertov proclaimed that "Form is never more than a revelation of content," she seemed to lay to rest the MacLeish dictum that "A poem must not mean/ But be": content (the meaning) constitutes an important and inseparable aspect of a poem's *being*.

The new freedom breathed new life into poetry. Audiences that had been baffled or bored by poems of the past discovered that poetry could amuse by its wit, dazzle by its revelations, and startle by its cry of pain—in short, perform its old magic still.

BIOGRAPHIES

Jim Wayne Miller   1936–

Jim Wayne Miller possesses the broad range of interests and talents that so often accompany the poetic temperament. Born in rural Leicester, North Carolina, Miller is an expert on the folkways of Appalachia. Additionally, he holds a doctorate from Vanderbilt University and is a professor of German at Western Kentucky University in Bowling Green. Of his poetry, Miller says that he wished to make the verses like the limpid trout streams he knew in North Carolina—crystal clear but deceptively deep. "I want the writing to be so transparent that the reader forgets he is reading and is aware only that he is having an experience. He is suddenly plunged deeper than he expected and comes up shivering."

Vern Rutsala 1934–

Vern Rutsala was born in McCall, Idaho, and educated at Reed College of Oregon and the State University of Iowa. He is currently a professor of English at Lewis and Clark College in Portland, Oregon. Many of his poems recount his anger at the American involvement in Vietnam. Others deal with middle-class society and with the disparity between life's possibilities and the spiritual emptiness of modern existence.

Gregory Djanikian 1949–

Born in Alexandria, Egypt, Gregory Djanikian (jä nē'ke än') came to America and learned English as he describes in his poem. He attended the University of Pennsylvania and Syracuse University. His poems have appeared in *Poetry, The American Scholar,* and many other publications. His first volume of poems, *The Man in the Middle,* was published in 1984. A second collection of verse, titled *Falling Deeply into America,* is scheduled for publication in 1988. Djanikian has taught English at the University of Michigan, Syracuse University, and the University of Pennsylvania.

 See METONYMY in the Handbook of Literary Terms, page 887.

A House of Readers

Jim Wayne Miller

At 9:42 on this May morning
the children's rooms are concentrating too.
Like a tendril growing toward the sun, Ruth
moves her book into a wedge of light
5 that settled on the floor like a butterfly.
She turns a page.
Fred is immersed in magic, cool
as a Black Angus belly-deep in a farm pond.

The only sounds: pages turning softly.
10 This is the quietness
of bottomland where you can hear only the
       young corn
growing, where a little breeze stirs the blades
and then breathes in again.

I mark my place.
15 I listen like a farmer in the rows.

1975

"A House of Readers" by Jim Wayne Miller from *The Mountains Have Come Closer* (Boone, N.C.
Appalachian Consortium Press) 1980. Reprinted by permission of the author.

Words

Vern Rutsala

We had more than
we could use.
They embarrassed us,
our talk fuller than our
5 rooms. They named
nothing we could see——
dining room, study,
mantel piece, lobster
thermidor. They named
10 things you only
saw in movies——
the thin flicker Friday
nights that made us
feel empty in the cold
15 as we walked home
through our only great
abundance, snow.
This is why we said "ain't"
and "he don't."
20 We wanted words to fit
our cold linoleum,
our oil lamps, our
outhouse. We knew
better but it was wrong

25 to use a language
that named ghosts,
nothing you could touch.
We left such words at school
locked in books
30 where they belonged.
It was the vocabulary
of our lives that was
so thin. We knew this
and grew to hate
35 all the words that named
the vacancy of our rooms——
looking here we said
studio couch and saw cot;
looking there we said
40 *venetian blinds* and saw only the yard;
brick meant tarpaper,
fireplace meant wood stove.
And this is why we came to love
the double negative.

1981

"Words" from *Walking Home from the Icehouse* by Vern Rutsala. Copyright © 1981 by Vern Rutsala. Reprinted by permission.

How I Learned English

Gregory Djanikian

It was in an empty lot
Ringed by elms and fir and honeysuckle.
Bill Corson was pitching in his buckskin
    jacket,
Chuck Keller, fat even as a boy, was on
    first,
5 His t-shirt riding up over his gut,
Ron O'Neill, Jim, Dennis, were talking it up
In the field, a blue sky above them
Tipped with cirrus.
                And there I was,
Just off the plane and plopped in the middle
10 Of Williamsport, Pa. and a neighborhood
    game,
Unnatural and without any moves,
My notions of baseball and America
Growing fuzzier each time I whiffed.

So it was not impossible that I,
15 Banished to the outfield and daydreaming
Of water, or a hotel in the mountains,
Would suddenly find myself in the path
Of a ball stung by Joe Barone.
I watched it closing in
20 Clean and untouched, transfixed
By its easy arc before it hit
My forehead with a thud.
                I fell back,
Dazed, clutching my brow,
Groaning, "Oh my shin, oh my shin,"

25 And everybody peeled away from me
And dropped from laughter, and there we
    were,
All of us writhing on the ground for one reason
Or another.
              Someone said "shin" again,
There was a wild stamping of hands on the
    ground,
30 A kicking of feet, and the fit
Of laughter overtook me too,
And that was important, as important
As Joe Barone asking me how I was
Through his tears, picking me up
35 And dusting me off with hands like swatters,
And though my head felt heavy,
I played on till dusk
Missing flies and pop-ups and grounders
And calling out in desperation things like
40 "Yours" and "take it," but doing all right,
Tugging at my cap in just the right way,
Crouching low, my feet set,
"Hum baby" sweetly on my lips.

1987

"How I Learned English" by Gregory Djanikian from *Poetry*, January 1987. Copyright © 1987 by The Modern Poetry Association. Reprinted by permission of the Editor of *Poetry* and the author.

THINK AND DISCUSS

A HOUSE OF READERS

Understanding

1. What time of day and month is it?
2. What are Ruth and Fred doing? What is the speaker doing?

Analyzing

3. What are the three **similes** that describe the narrator and his two children?
4. What is the **metaphor** in stanza 2, describing the children and the activity of reading?

APPLYING: Metonymy H𝒯
See Handbook of Literary Terms, p. 887.

Metonymy is a figure of speech in which one term is substituted for another with which it has some relation, as "crown" for "king." In "John has never read Shakespeare," the name of the author is substituted for his work.

1. What example of metonymy appears in line 7?
2. What related idea does the word *magic* stand for?

WORDS

Understanding

1. Who are the "we" in the first line?
2. What is the only thing the students have in abundance (lines 15–17)?

Analyzing

3. What do the first two lines refer to? more what?
4. Twice the speaker refers to "our rooms" when he seems to be referring to his home. What would be gained or lost in the poem by substituting *home* for rooms?
5. What does the last sentence mean?

REVIEWING: Inference H𝒯
See Handbook of Literary Terms, p. 892.

An **inference** is a reasonable conclusion about the behavior or background of a character or the meaning or implications of an event drawn from the limited information supplied by the author.

1. What inference can you draw about the speaker's life during his school years?
2. What can you infer about the speaker's attitude toward his language lessons, especially vocabulary drills, at school?

HOW I LEARNED ENGLISH

Understanding

1. At the beginning of the poem, what is the speaker doing?
2. In what city and state is the game taking place? Where in the city?

Analyzing

3. What can readers **infer** about the speaker's past from lines 9–14?
4. Why do the other boys laugh at the speaker as he reacts to being hit on the forehead by the ball?
5. The speaker says (lines 30–33) that he is overtaken with laughter too, "And that was important, as important/ As Joe Barone asking me how I was." Why are both reactions important?

Extending

6. The speakers in these poems have differing attitudes about the use and the power of words. With which attitude do you most agree? Why?

COMPOSITION ⚬━

Explaining the Importance of Words

Imagine that a person your age who speaks no English is coming to visit your family for two weeks. Write a composition of several paragraphs explaining the first ten words that you will teach this person. Give reasons why you consider these words important for surviving in today's world. Share your composition with other class members who have made their own lists. After discussing each student's ideas, try to arrive at ten words that the class agrees are most essential.

Lawson Fusao Inada   1938–

Lawson Fusao Inada was one of twenty-one poets, including Gwendolyn Brooks and Robert Penn Warren, asked in 1980 to read poetry at the White House to celebrate A Salute to Poetry and American Poets. He was born in Fresno, California, and studied at Fresno State College, the University of Iowa, and the University of Oregon. Currently, he is a professor of English at Southern Oregon State College. In 1971 he published a book of poems entitled *Before the War* and has received two writing fellowships from the National Endowment for the Arts in 1970 and in 1980. Inada writes that he has been chiefly interested in helping create and uncover Asian-American culture.

James Masao Mitsui   1940–

James Masao Mitsui received his master's degree from the University of Washington and currently teaches high-school English in Renton, Washington. His first volume of poetry, *Journal of the Sun*, received the Pacific Northwest Booksellers' Award for 1974. He was awarded a grant from the National Endowment for the Arts in 1976 and 1977 and published a second volume of poetry, *Crossing the Phantom River*. Another poetry collection, *After the Long Train* (1986), contains family sketches and reflections on Japanese internment during World War II.

N. Scott Momaday   1934–

N. Scott Momaday was born in Lawton, Oklahoma, the son of artists and educators. His father is the distinguished contemporary Kiowa painter and art teacher Alfred Morris Momaday. His mother, Natachee Scott Momaday, is a novelist and writer of juvenile fiction as well as an artist and teacher. Momaday spent his childhood on a number of Indian reservations. He received a Stanford University Creative Writing Fellowship in 1959. In 1969 his novel *House Made of Dawn* won the Pulitzer Prize. Until 1981 Momaday was a professor of English at Stanford. Since then he has served on the faculty of the University of Arizona.

Imamu Amiri Baraka   1934–

Imamu Amiri Baraka grew up in Newark, New Jersey, and graduated from Howard University in Washington, D.C. Early in his career as a playwright, a novelist, and a poet, Baraka—who changed his name from LeRoi Jones in 1964—was often identified as the angry young man of the ghetto. Since then, in addition to his writing, he has led task forces to rebuild the area in Newark, New Jersey, that was ravaged by the ghetto riots of 1967. Baraka founded a black community center, Spirit House, in Newark. His poetry has been variously considered homicidal, caustic and biting, and delicate and gentle.

My Father and Myself Facing the Sun

Lawson Fusao Inada

We are both strong, dark, bright men,
though perhaps you might not notice,
finding two figures flat against the landscape
like the shadowed backs of mountains.

5 Which would not be far from wrong,
for though we both have on western clothes
and he is seated on a yellow spool
of emptied and forgotten telephone cable
and I recline on a green aluminum lounge,

10 we are both facing into the August sun
as august as Hiroshima[1] and the coming
    of autumn.

There are differences, however, if you care
to discover, coming close, respectfully.
You must discover the landscape as you go.

15 Come. It is in the eyes, the face, the way
we would greet you stumbling as you arrive.
He is much the smooth, grass-brown slopes
reaching knee-high around you as you walk;
I am the cracks of cliffs and gulleys,
20 pieces of secret deep in the back of the eye.

But he is still my father, and I his son.

After a while, there is time to go fishing,
both of us squatting on rocks in the dusk,
leaving peaks and treeline responsible for light.
25 There is a lake below, which both of us
acknowledge, by facing, forward, like the sun.

Ripples of fish, moon, luminous insects.
Frogs, owls, crickets at their sound.
Deer, raccoon, badger come down to drink.

30 At the water's edge, the children are fishing,
casting shadows from the enormous shoreline.
Everything functions in the function of summer.

And gradually, and not by chance, the action
stops, the children hush back among rocks
35 and also watch, with nothing to capture but dusk.

There are four of us, together among others.

And I am not at all certain what all this means,
if this mean anything, but feel with all my being
that I must write this down, if I write anything.

40 My father, his son, his grandsons, strong, serene.

Night, night, night, before the following morning.
1976

Fusao Inada (fü sa′ô ē na′da).
1. *Hiroshima* (hir′ō shē′mə), a Japanese city on which
the U.S. dropped an atom bomb in August, 1945, which
killed 92,000 people.

"My Father and Myself Facing the Sun" by Lawson Fusao
Inada from *Bridge, an Asian-American Perspective* (November 1976).
Reprinted by permission of the author.

The Morning My Father Died, April 7, 1963

James Masao Mitsui

Don Nibbelink, Cherry blossoms photographed in
Japan

The youngest son, I left the family inside and stood
alone in the unplanted garden by a cherry tree
we had grown ourselves, next to a trash barrel
smoldering what we couldn't give away or move
5 to Seattle. Looking over the rusty edge I could see
colors of volcano. Feathers of ash floated
up to a sky that was changing. I stared at the sound
of meadowlarks below the water tank
on the pumice-colored hill where the sun would come.
10 I couldn't stop smelling sagebrush, the creosote
bottoms of posts, the dew that was like a thunderstorm
had passed an hour before. Thoughts were trees
under a lake; that moment was sunflower, killdeer
and cheatgrass. Volunteer wheat grew strong
15 on the far side of our place along the old highway.
Undeberg's rooster gave the day its sharper edge,
the top of the sun. Turning to go back inside,
twenty years of Big Bend Country
took off like sparrows from a startled fence.

1974

Masao Mitsui (ma sa′ô mē tsü′ē).

"The Morning My Father Died" from *Journal of the Sun* by James Masao
Mitsui. Copyright © 1974 Copper Canyon Press. Reprinted by permission.

The Stalker

N. Scott Momaday

Sampt'e drew the string back and back until he felt
the bow wobble in his hand, and he let the arrow go.
It shot across the long light of the morning and struck
the black face of a stone in the meadow; it glanced
5 then away towards the west, limping along the air;
and then it settled down in the grass and lay still.
Sampt'e approached; he looked at it with wonder and was
wary; honestly he believed that the arrow might take flight
again; so much of his life did he give into it.

1976

"The Stalker." From *The Gourd Dancer* by N. Scott Momaday. Copyright © 1976 by
N. Scott Momaday. Reprinted by permission of Harper & Row, Publishers, Inc.

Preface to a Twenty Volume Suicide Note

Imamu Amiri Baraka

Lately, I've become accustomed to the way
The ground opens up and envelops me
Each time I go out to walk the dog.
Or the broad edged silly music the wind
5 Makes when I run for a bus——

Things have come to that.

And now, each night I count the stars,
And each night I get the same number.
And when they will not come to be counted
10 I count the holes they leave.

Nobody sings anymore.

And then last night, I tiptoed up
To my daughter's room and heard her
Talking to someone, and when I opened
15 The door, there was no one there . . .
Only she on her knees,
Peeking into her own clasped hands.

1961

Imamu Amiri Baraka (ē mä′mü ä mē′rē bä rä′kä).

"Preface to a Twenty Volume Suicide Note" by LeRoi Jones.
Copyright © 1961 by LeRoi Jones. Reprinted by permission of
Imamu Amiri Baraka.

THINK AND DISCUSS

MY FATHER AND MYSELF FACING THE SUN

Understanding

1. How are the father and son dressed (stanza 2)? Where are they seated? What will they do later (line 22)?
2. How does the speaker feel about the events he has described (line 37)? What does he feel he must do (line 39)?

Analyzing

3. In the first three stanzas, how are the father and the son similar?
4. How does the speaker indicate his ethnic background?
5. In lines 12–20, how do the **images** associated with the father differ from those the speaker associates with himself?

THE MORNING MY FATHER DIED, APRIL 7, 1963

Understanding

1. Where does the speaker stand at the beginning of the poem?
2. Where is the family planning to move?

Analyzing

3. What do you think were the speaker's feelings when his father died? How are these feelings revealed in his description of the sights, smells, and sounds of the unplanted garden?
4. What does the speaker mean in lines 18–19 by the comparison between twenty years and sparrows taking off from a fence?

THE STALKER

Understanding

1. What does the arrow strike? Where does it finally land?

Analyzing

2. What verbs describe the arrow's changing movements?
3. How does Sampt'e feel when he approaches the fallen arrow?

PREFACE TO A TWENTY VOLUME SUICIDE NOTE

Understanding

1. What routine activities does the speaker describe in stanza 1?
2. What does the speaker do each night?

Analyzing

3. The first ten lines of the poem use exaggeration, or **hyperbole**, to make a point about the speaker's condition. What is that condition? What is the speaker's attitude toward his condition?

Extending

4. Each of the poems in this group dramatizes a significant moment in the life of the speaker. Name a moment in your life that was memorable or significant and explain why this point in time held special meaning for you.

COMPOSITION

Describing a Significant Moment

Develop your answer to item number 4 under Extending to write a one-page journal entry about a significant moment in your life. Make the moment vivid by using strong verbs and images to describe your feelings, the setting, or objects associated with your memory.

Commenting on Modern Poetry

Write a letter of at least four paragraphs to someone who has observed that modern poetry is depressing. Using the four poems in this group as a basis, explain whether you agree or disagree with this appraisal. Before writing your letter, review these poems, asking yourself the following questions: Is Baraka's poem really a suicide note? What is the significance of the last lines in this poem? Do the images in Mitsui's poem seem consistent with death? In what ways can people put life into an object, such as Sampt'e does with an arrow in "The Stalker"? What does a poet accomplish by writing about things that he or she doesn't understand?

BIOGRAPHIES

Leslie Marmon Silko   1948–

Leslie Marmon Silko was born in Albuquerque, New Mexico. Her ancestry is a mixture of Laguna Pueblo, Mexican, and white. She claims that all she is as a person and writer results from what she learned on the Laguna Pueblo Indian reservation where she grew up and continues to live. Her earliest memories are of the stories told by her grandmother based on the ancient lore of the Pueblo Indians. Much of this lore appears in Silko's poetry and prose. "I write," she says, "because I love the stories, the feelings, the words." She was awarded the MacArthur Prize Fellowship in 1981.

John N. Morris   1931–

John N. Morris was born in Oxford, England. An American citizen, he graduated from Hamilton College in New York before spending two years in the Marine Corps. He then went on to receive his M.A. and Ph.D. degrees from Columbia. Currently a professor of English at Washington University in St. Louis, he divides his work between writing poetry and short stories and doing scholarly research, especially in eighteenth-century English literature.

Joseph Brodsky   1940–

Winner of the 1987 Nobel Prize for Literature, Joseph Brodsky served time in a Soviet labor camp and later was forced to leave his homeland. Now an American citizen, Brodsky has called his Russian heritage and the freedom he enjoys in the United States "the best possible combination." Writing in both Russian and English, Brodsky has published several volumes of poetry, including *A Part of Speech* (1980), as well as a volume of essays that won the U.S. National Book Critics Award for criticism in 1986.

Sylvia Plath   1932–1963

Sylvia Plath was born in Boston and educated at Smith and Harvard. In 1959, after teaching English at Smith, she moved with her husband, the British poet Ted Hughes, and two children to England. Her volumes of poetry include *The Colossus*, *Ariel*, and *Winter Trees*. Her only novel, *The Bell Jar*, appeared under the pseudonym Victoria Lucas in 1963, the year of her suicide. It was republished in 1966 under her real name and has enjoyed enormous success. Her letters to her mother, written from 1950 to 1963, were published under the title *Letters Home* (1975).

Prayer to the Pacific

Leslie Marmon Silko

Robert Amft, *The Wave*.
Private collection

1
I traveled to the ocean
        distant
                from my southwest land of sandrock
                to the moving blue water
5   Big as the myth of origin.

2
Pale
pale water in the yellow-white light of
                sun floating west
                  to China
10   where ocean herself was born
Clouds that blow across the sand are wet.

3
Squat in the wet sand and speak to Ocean:
        I return to you turquoise the red coral you sent us,
            sister spirit of Earth.
15 Four round stones in my pocket I carry back the ocean
          to suck and to taste.

4
Thirty thousand years ago
           Indians came riding across the ocean
           carried by giant sea turtles.
20 Waves were high that day
        great sea turtles waded slowly out
            from the gray sundown sea.
Grandfather Turtle rolled in the sand four times
        and disappeared
25   swimming into the sun.

5
And so from that time
      immemorial,
          as the old people say,
rainclouds drift from the west
30   gift from the ocean.

6
Green leaves in the wind
Wet earth on my feet
        swallowing raindrops
           clear from China.

1972

"Prayer to the Pacific" by Leslie Silko.
Copyright © 1972 by Leslie Silko.
Reprinted by permission of the author.

Running It Backward

John N. Morris

A simple flick of the switch
And his familiar figure
Steps back out of the doorway,
Out of the fond familiar arms
5 That now drop eagerly to her sides.
Backward he rapidly walks
On the crazy pavement
Into his car whose door
Flies into his hand at a gesture;
10 Expertly staring ahead, he
Reverses quickly out of the picture.

At first it is mildly funny
Watching him perform
With such cheerful address
15 These difficult backward
Easy forward things.
So when the whiskey
Arises into the bottle
And, smiling,
20 He refuses his first job
And returns the diploma
With a firm handshake,
We laugh.
        But suddenly
25 It is turning serious, we see
That he is going
Where we do not wish to follow.
That smile still on his face
But growing doubtful now,
30 He is climbing down
Out of his college,
Through algebra and beginning French
Into a taste for Coca-Cola.

Now quickly he falls
35 Through the grades
Into his shorts
And the birthday parties.
Though a profusion of gifts
Resume their brilliant paper,
40 There, as the breath returns
To him who gave it
And laughter fades
To pure expectancy,
Before the match withdraws
45 That seemed to lean
To seem to put them out,
Out of the dark the candles come
At once alight.

Here with a flick of the switch
50 It is time to be stopping,
For looking ahead
We foresee what is true
But improper to be shown:
How, soon, he is going faster,
55 How he lapses from language
Into helpless tears,
A rage beneath naming
Shaking him as he dwindles;
How, behind his silent scream,
60 He disappears
In a fury of flapping and clicking
Into the dark and shining
Whirring tiny mouth of the machine.

                    1975

John N. Morris, "Running It Backward" (originally in *Hudson Review*) from *The Life Beside This One*. Copyright © 1975 by John N. Morris. Reprinted by permission of Atheneum Publishers.

October Tune

Joseph Brodsky

A stuffed quail
on the mantlepiece minds its tail.
The regular chirr of the old clock's healing,
in the twilight, the rumpled helix.[1]
5   Through the window, birch candles fail.

For the fourth day the sea hits the dike with its hard horizon.
Put aside the book, take your sewing kit;
patch my clothes without turning the light on:
golden hair
10   keeps the corner lit.

1987

"October Tune" by Joseph Brodsky. Copyright © 1987 by Joseph Brodsky. Reprinted by permission of Farrar, Straus and Giroux, Inc. Originally published in *The New Yorker.*

1. **helix,** a three-dimensional spiral in the form of a watchspring or of a cone (or snail).

Mirror

Sylvia Plath

I am silver and exact. I have no preconceptions.
Whatever I see I swallow immediately
Just as it is, unmisted by love or dislike.
I am not cruel, only truthful——
5 The eye of a little god, four-cornered.
Most of the time I meditate on the opposite wall.
It is pink, with speckles. I have looked at it so long
I think it is a part of my heart. But it flickers.
Faces and darkness separate us over and over.

10 Now I am a lake. A woman bends over me,
Searching my reaches for what she really is.
Then she turns to those liars, the candles or the moon.
I see her back, and reflect it faithfully.
She rewards me with tears and an agitation of hands.
15 I am important to her. She comes and goes.
Each morning it is her face that replaces the darkness.
In me she has drowned a young girl, and in me an old woman
Rises toward her day after day, like a terrible fish.

1963

"Mirror" from *Crossing the Water* by Sylvia Plath, published by Faber and Faber Ltd. Copyright © 1971, 1963 by Ted Hughes. Reprinted by permission of Harper & Row, Publishers, Inc. and Olwyn Hughes, Literary Agent.

THINK AND DISCUSS

PRAYER TO THE PACIFIC

Understanding
1. Where is the speaker at the beginning of the poem? From where did the speaker come?
2. According to stanza 4, how long ago did the Indians cross the ocean to America? On what were they transported?

Analyzing
3. What words or phrases show that the speaker regards the ocean as if it were a living being?
4. Describe the relationship between the speaker and the ocean, as well as the speaker's attitude toward it.

RUNNING IT BACKWARD

Understanding
1. What sort of switch is flicked in line 1? Which acts are described in reverse in lines 17–22?
2. What event is described in reverse in lines 37–48?

Analyzing
3. What stages of life are mentioned in the poem?
4. Line 24 signals a shift in **tone**; things turn serious, as the subject goes "Where we do not wish to follow." Why might the "we" who view this scene consider it frightening?
5. What words and **images** convey a backward motion in time?
6. What examples of **onomatopoeia** can you find in the last three lines? What mechanical noise is being approximated in those lines?

OCTOBER TUNE

Understanding
1. What is the time of year and day of this poem?
2. What does the speaker request in lines 7–8?

Analyzing
3. In what way might birch trees resemble candles at twilight?

4. How does the poet use **hyperbole** at the end of the poem?
5. Although the images in this poem appeal primarily to the sense of sight, lines 3 and 6 present auditory images. Explain how these lines appeal to a sense of hearing.
6. How might the visual impression of the poem on the page be related to a helix?

MIRROR

Understanding
1. According to line 2, what does the mirror do with whatever it sees? What is its self-appraisal in line 4?
2. Who looks in the mirror and for what is she searching?

Analyzing
3. In what sense is the mirror "a little god" to the woman? What three stages of life does she imagine seeing in the mirror/lake?
4. In what way are the candles and the moon "liars"?
5. In the final lines, who has drowned? What does the "terrible fish" represent?

Extending
6. Contrast the perspectives on time in "Mirror," "Running It Backward," "October Tune," and "Prayer to the Pacific." In your opinion, which is the most powerful or effective poem? Support your choice.

COMPOSITION

Writing About Tone
What is the attitude of the poet toward the events that take place in "Running It Backward"? Write a three- to four-paragraph essay for class discussion presenting the results of your close reading of the poem, paying special attention to tone. Does the poet's attitude seem to shift at any time in the poem? See "Writing About Mood or Tone" in the Writer's Handbook.

Gary Soto   1952–

Gary Soto was raised in Fresno, California, and educated at the University of California at Irvine. In 1976 his first published collection of poetry, *The Elements of San Joaquin*, was given the U.S. Award of the International Poetry Forum. Since that time, he has written additional collections of poetry, *The Tale of Sunlight* (1978), *Where Sparrows Work Hard* (1981), and *Black Hair* (1984). Soto now teaches Chicano studies at the University of California at Berkeley.

Simon Ortiz   1941–

Simon Ortiz was born in Albuquerque, New Mexico, and has lived all his life in the American Southwest. He has published both poetry and short stories. His first book, *Naked in the Wind*, appeared in 1970. Other books include *Going for the Rain* (1976), *A Poem is a Journey* (1981), and *Fightin': New and Collected Stories* (1983). Among his awards are two fellowships from the National Endowment for the Arts.

Linda Pastan   1932–

Currently living in Maryland, Linda Pastan published her first book, *A Perfect Circle of Sun*, in 1971. Among her other books are *On the Way to the Zoo* (1975), *Waiting for My Life* (1981), *PM/AM: New and Selected Poems* (1982), and *A Fraction of Darkness* (1985).

Teresa Paloma Acosta   1949–

Teresa Paloma Acosta teaches English at St. Edward's University in Austin, Texas, where she is active in student projects that include consulting on a new Chicano play and working with Chicano women's groups. Her first collection of poetry, *A Sheaf of Grain*, is soon to be published. Future projects include working in other literary genres, specifically on short stories. When asked what advice she has for young writers, she said, "Don't be afraid to explore your own experiences and write about them; otherwise a significant part of American literature may be lost forever."

History

Gary Soto

Grandma lit the stove.
Morning sunlight
Lengthened in spears
Across the linoleum floor.
5 Wrapped in a shawl,
Her eyes small
With sleep,
She sliced *papas*,[1]
Pounded chiles
10 With a stone
Brought from Guadalajara.[2]
After Grandpa left for work,
She hosed down
The walk her sons paved
15 And in the shade
Of a chinaberry,
Unearthed her
Secret cigar box
Of bright coins
20 And bills, counted them
In English,
Then in Spanish,
And buried them elsewhere.
Later, back
25 From the market,
Where no one saw her,
She pulled out
Pepper and beet, spines
Of asparagus
30 From her blouse,
Tiny chocolates
From under a paisley bandana,
And smiled.

That was the '50s,
35 And Grandma in her '50s,
A face streaked
From cutting grapes
And boxing plums.

I remember her insides
40 Were washed of tapeworm,
Her arms swelled into knobs

Of small growths——
Her second son
Dropped from a ladder
45 And was dust.
And yet I do not know
The sorrows
That sent her praying
In the dark of a closet,
50 The tear that fell
At night
When she touched
Loose skin
Of belly and breasts.
55 I do not know why
Her face shines
Or what goes beyond this shine,
Only the stories
That pulled her
60 From Taxco to San Joaquin,
Delano to Westside,[3]
The places
In which we all begin.

1977

---

1. *papas* (pä′päs), potatoes. [*Spanish*]
2. *Guadalajara* (gwä′dä lä hä′rä), a city in central Mexico.
3. *Taxco* (tä′skô) *to San Joaquin* (san′ wä kēn′), *Delano to Westside.* Many Chicano families stem from migrants who left Mexican towns like Taxco to work on farms in such areas as the San Joaquin Valley of California. Migrant workers follow the harvest from Delano in the Valley's center to its west side.

"History" from *The Elements of San Joaquin* by Gary Soto, published by the University of Pittsburgh Press, 1977. Reprinted by permission of the author.

My Father's Song

Simon Ortiz

Wanting to say things,
I miss my father tonight.
His voice, the slight catch,
the depth from his thin chest,
5 the tremble of emotion
in something he has just said
to his son, his song:

We planted corn one Spring at Acu—
we planted several times
10 but this one particular time
I remember the soft damp sand
in my hand.

My father had stopped at one point
to show me an overturned furrow;
15 the plowshare had unearthed
the burrow nest of a mouse
in the soft moist sand.

Very gently, he scooped tiny pink animals
into the palm of his hand
20 and told me to touch them.
We took them to the edge
of the field and put them in the shade
of a sand moist clod.

I remember the very softness
25 of cool and warm sand and tiny alive mice
and my father saying things.

1976

"My Father's Song" by Simon J. Ortiz from *Going for the Rain: Poems by Simon J. Ortiz.* Copyright © 1976 by Simon J. Ortiz. Reprinted by permission of the author.

"Grudnow" by Linda Pastan from *Poetry*, October 1986. Copyright © 1986 by the Modern Poetry Association. Reprinted by permission of the Editor of *Poetry* and the author.

Grudnow, also spelled Grodno, had been fought over often by Poland and Russia until it was ceded to Russia after World War II. It is on the Neman River, near the Polish border.

Grudnow

Linda Pastan

When he spoke of where he came from,
my grandfather could have been
clearing his throat
of that name, that town
5 sometimes Poland, sometimes Russia,
the borders pencilled in
with a hand as shaky as his.
He left, I heard him say,
because there was nothing there.

10 I understood what he meant
when I saw the photograph
of his people standing
against a landscape emptied
of crops and trees, scraped raw
15 by winter. Everything
was in sepia, as if the brown earth
had stained the faces,
stained even the air.

I would have died there, I think
20 in childhood maybe
of some fever,
my face pressed for warmth
against a cow with flanks
like those of the great aunts
25 in the picture. Or later
I would have died of history
like the others, who dug

their stubborn heels into that earth,
heels as hard as the heels
30 of the bread my grandfather tore
from the loaf at supper. He always
sipped his tea through a cube of sugar
clenched in his teeth, the way
he sipped his life here, noisily,
35 through all he remembered
that might have been sweet in Grudnow.

1986

My Mother Pieced Quilts

Teresa Paloma Acosta

they were just meant as covers
in winters
as weapons
against pounding january winds

5 but it was just that every morning I awoke
   to these
october ripened canvases
passed my hand across their cloth faces
and began to wonder how you pieced
all these together
10 these strips of gentle communion cotton and
   flannel nightgowns
wedding organdies
dime store velvets
how you shaped patterns square and oblong
   and round
positioned
15 balanced
then cemented them
with your thread
a steel needle
a thimble

20 how the thread darted in and out
galloping along the frayed edges, tucking
   them in
as you did us at night
oh how you stretched and turned and rearranged
your michigan spring[1] faded curtain pieces
25 my father's santa fe work shirt[2]
the summer denims, the tweeds of fall

(continued)

Teresa Paloma Acosta (te re'sä pä lô'mä ä kôs'tä).
1. michigan spring. In spring migrant workers go to
Michigan to pick crops.
2. santa fe work shirt, the work clothes of the Santa Fe
Railroad.

Copyright © 1975 by Teresa Paloma Acosta. From *Festival de Flor
y Canto, an Anthology of Chicano Literature*, published by the University of Southern California Press, 1976. Reprinted by permission
of the author.

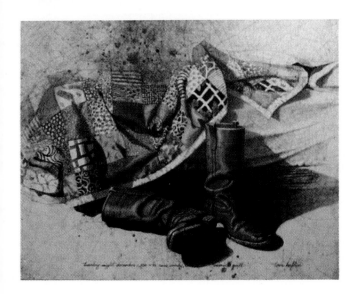

Tom Heflin, *Patchwork* (1981).
Private collection

in the evening you sat at your canvas
—our cracked linoleum floor the drawing
      board
me lounging on your arm
30 and you staking out the plan:
whether to put the lilac purple of easter
      against the red plaid of winter-going-
      into-spring
whether to mix a yellow with blue and white
      and paint the
corpus christi[3] noon when my father held
      your hand
35 whether to shape a five-point star from the
somber black silk you wore to grandmother's
      funeral

you were the river current
carrying the roaring notes
forming them into pictures of a little boy
      reclining
40 a swallow flying
you were the caravan master at the reins
driving your threaded needle artillery across the
      mosaic cloth bridges
delivering yourself in separate testimonies.

oh mother you plunged me sobbing and
      laughing
45 into our past
into the river crossing at five
into the spinach fields
into the plainview[4] cotton rows
into tuberculosis wards
50 into braids and muslin dresses
sewn hard and taut to withstand the thrashings
      of twenty-five years

stretched out they lay
armed/ready/shouting/celebrating

knotted with love
55 the quilts sing on

1976

---

3. *corpus christi* (kôr′pəs kris′tē), a southern Texas
city.
4. *plainview,* a Texas town surrounded by cotton fields.

THINK AND DISCUSS
HISTORY
Understanding
1. What does the speaker's grandmother do
   early in the morning? What other activities
   in her daily routine are described in stanza
   1?
2. What personal tragedies does Grandma suffer, mentioned in lines 39–45?

Analyzing
3. In the second half of the poem, there is
   more emphasis on Grandma's past. How
   does this information help explain the activities described in the first half of the poem?

4. How would you **characterize** Grandma,
   based on details from the poem?

MY FATHER'S SONG
Understanding
1. What is the speaker wanting to do at the
   beginning of the poem? Whom does he miss?

Analyzing
2. Who is speaking in lines 1–7? in lines 8–26?
3. In his "song," the father remembers *his*
   father. What is the incident he remembers?
   What does it reveal of his father's character?
4. How is the title related to the first and last
   lines of the poem?

GRUDNOW

Understanding

1. Why did the speaker's grandfather leave Grudnow?
2. What does the speaker imagine herself dying of in childhood, had she lived there?

Analyzing

3. How did the speaker become convinced that her grandfather was right when he said of Grudnow that there was "nothing there"?
4. The speaker believes if she had survived childhood in Grudnow, she would have died later of history. What do you think she means?

MY MOTHER PIECED QUILTS

Understanding

1. According to the opening lines, what were the quilts meant for?
2. In lines 5–9, what does the speaker do when she wakes up in the morning and what does she begin to wonder?

Analyzing

3. The quilt remembered by the speaker in this poem is a kind of mosaic of the family's history. Look up the word *mosaic* in your Glossary. Then reread lines 5–19 and select words and phrases that are appropriate to the meaning of the word.
4. Of what materials were parts of the quilt composed? What emotional significance did these materials have for the speaker?
5. Throughout this poem, the speaker compares the quilt to a painting. What did her mother use for a drawing board? What were some of the artistic decisions she had to make?

Extending

6. In "History," "My Father's Song," "Grudnow," and "My Mother Pieced Quilts," the speakers present feelings connected with their ancestry and memories. Why do you think the poets felt a need to present these feelings? Do you think these subjects make good poems? Why or why not?

COMPOSITION ◄━━━

Writing About a Family Member

Many of the poems in Unit 7 are recollections of a family member, representing links to the past or clues to the poet's identity. Write a character sketch for members of the next generation, perhaps your future children, describing a relative who has had some impact on you. It may be a relative whom you know only through family stories and photographs. Characterize the relative or ancestor and tell what you might have inherited—spirit, values, physical appearance, skills, talents, and so forth.

Analyzing Modern Poetry

Nearly three dozen poems appear in this unit, all of them written during the past half-century. Using some of these poems as a basis, write at least five paragraphs for a poetry magazine describing some aspects of modern poetry. You might want to concentrate on form and technique (use or nonuse of rhyme and regular rhythm, figurative language, sound devices), subject matter (topics can range from home movies, to an auto wreck, to learning English), and the use of ordinary language once considered "unpoetic." You might want to concentrate on a few poems that "speak" to you in a way that poems written a hundred years ago do not.

Garrison Keillor became famous for a radio show entitled *A Prairie Home Companion* that ran from 1974 to 1987. It was broadcast before a live audience on Saturday nights, presenting country music, gospel singing, yodeling, and even dog acts.

During one regular segment of the show, Keillor delivered a monologue without script, which began, "It has been a quiet week in Lake Wobegon." The monologue usually started with an incident and meandered off on twists and turns—some comic, some sad, all nostalgic—and then surprised listeners by eventually coming back to the beginning incident. The refrain always repeated as the conclusion was: "That's the news from Lake Wobegon, where all the women are strong, the men are good-looking, and all the children are above average."

The monologues appear to be autobiographical reminiscences, based on the small farm town in Minnesota where Keillor grew up. In fact, Lake Wobegon is not on any map, and the Scandinavian Lutherans Keillor describes so well are all invented. But both the town and its people have their imaginative roots in Keillor's past.

Born in Anoka, Minnesota, and educated at the University of Minnesota, Keillor began his radio career in 1963, becoming a producer-announcer on public radio in 1971. Many listeners have been lured away from their TV sets by his variety-show broadcasts. He was awarded the George Foster Peabody Broadcasting Award in 1980, and the Edward R. Murrow Award for Public Broadcasting in 1985. His recent books include *Lake Wobegon Days* (1985) and *Leaving Home: A Collection of Lake Wobegon Stories* (1987).

Keillor maintains that his monologues celebrate "the pleasures of the familiar," adding "one thing I've tried to give myself over to in the course of telling these stories is to stand in praise of common and modest things."

See HYPERBOLE in the Handbook of Literary Terms, page 886.

Easter

Garrison Keillor

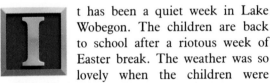

It has been a quiet week in Lake Wobegon. The children are back to school after a riotous week of Easter break. The weather was so lovely when the children were released from confinement, the fresh air went to their heads. Air has a different effect on children: what we merely breathe, children are ignited and launched by. At Our Lady on Sunday morning, Father Emil felt as if he was speaking to a convention of rabbits instead of the usual herd of turtles. Constant movement in the pews. The homily was on new life and it was all around to be seen.

When I was a kid, we sat quietly on Sunday morning sometimes for forty or fifty seconds at a stretch. Fidgety kids were put between two grownups, usually your parents or sometimes a large aunt. Like tying a boat to a dock. Every time you moved they'd grab your shoulder and give you a sharp shake and hiss at you, *Sit*. Death will be like that. I'll be in bed and think, "Well, I think I'll get up and live a little," and death will grab me, shake me, say, "Shhhh. Be quiet. Lie still." I used to think about death on Sunday morning. How hard it would be to lie in your coffin for years with nothing to read, nothing to do, but some grownups I knew probably could manage quite well.

Some former children returned for Easter, bringing their children with them, and some children were shipped earlier to spend the week with grandparents, some of whom are starting to recover to the point where they can sit in a chair and sit back all the way, not lean forward ready to jump when they hear the crash. The grandparents imagined the kiddos leaning against them on the sofa listening to Uncle Wiggily: they forgot how explosive kids can be. Something in the air sets them off. A kid can go all day and hardly eat, then the moon shifts and he's eating like a farmhand. You served baked horse and he eats all of it. Children can lie around for a long time, then a herd of them bursts in the front door and gallops through the kitchen and outside. Children are always on the verge of bursting. They burst six, seven times a day and think nothing of it.

Virginia Ingqvist had two grandkids with her last week. Barbara's two oldest, Doug and Danielle. Hjalmar worked late at the bank. He loves them, but he knows his limit, and it's about thirty minutes. One is four and the other five, an age when you want to find out everything in one day. "Why don't buildings fall?" asked Doug two minutes after he arrived. "Because," Virginia explained, "because they're built to stand." "How?"

Thirty seconds, and already she was into architecture, and knew that biology and astronomy and physics were coming right up. Then theology. "Who's God?" "God is God." "Yeah, but

"Easter" from *Leaving Home* by Garrison Keillor. Copyright © 1987 by Garrison Keillor. Reprinted by permission of Viking Penguin, Inc. and Faber and Faber Limited.

who?" It's never a subject you know something about, such as etiquette.

Barbara came up on Friday with her two-year-old and took all three of them to her friend Ruthie's house to visit. Ruthie has three of her own. Her three and Barbara's three sniffed each other for a moment and then two cats made the mistake of coming around the corner of the house into the backyard. The cats realized it was a mistake and backed away, saying, Uh sorry, didn't know you were here. We'll come back later. But the kids grabbed them, hauled them indoors, got them dressed and into a doll buggy, two little cat children. The cats went limp, waiting for a chance to break out, which they did—two cats in full regalia, one up the tree, one on the garage roof, trying to remove their clothes, five children in pursuit, and the two-year-old investigating the back porch.

Barbara and Ruthie sat in the yard talking about child rearing. Barbara's philosophy is more relaxed than her mother's, less restrictive, a hands-off approach, allowing children freedom to explore and find their own boundaries. As she said this, she watched the little boy climb the porch steps, stand at the top, turn around, and when he took a step forward straight out into space, she leaped up and made a dash for him, too late to catch him, but she almost stepped on his head. When she scooped him up, she came close to spraining his neck. A major cause of injury to children is parents rushing to the scene. The panic reflex. Some children love to scream for the thrill of making immense people move fast. I remember that, on a quiet day, my sister and I in the backyard wondered, "Where's Mom?" Upstairs, we thought. So I screamed, "MOM." She made it down in two seconds. A good pair of wheels for an old lady.

Grandma Tollefson turns off her hearing aid when descendants are around, so a crash is only a whisper to her, boys thundering around upstairs are a distant tapping. One afternoon a sound came out of her house like jets taking off, her grandson practicing his guitar. She was there, knitting, rocking, saying to him, "You know, there was a boy I knew who played the guitar—what was his name? Oh dear. He moved away in 1921, I think. He played his guitar on his porch, and I sat in our porch and listened. I don't think he knew. The screens were so dark, and I could hear him so clear, just like I can hear you. I was in love with him for a whole summer and he didn't know it." Kevin didn't hear a word she said, and she didn't know the music was blowing her hair back.

Selective ignorance, a cornerstone of child rearing. You don't put kids under surveillance: it might frighten you. Parents should sit tall in the saddle and look upon their troops with a noble and benevolent and extremely nearsighted gaze.

The Buehler boy celebrated a birthday last night and ten of his closest friends came over for a party. They danced to alarming music and ate an alarming amount of pizza and told alarming jokes and there were periods of alarming dead silence, which the Buehlers heard from the kitchen, where they remained in quarantine. They whomped up armloads of chow, and passed it to their son, who carried it to his guests. Stayed in the kitchen for five hours, except for one trip to the bathroom, averting their eyes, and the mister snuck up front once to have a look, and when he looked he wished he hadn't. He was dying of curiosity. The party was so quiet and then burst into laughter, and then silence and then whispering and screams of laughter. He tiptoed down the hall and peeked and saw they were huddled over the Buehler's wedding album. Nineteen fifty-nine was a funnier year than he had realized and he was a little hurt. He was quite handsome then in those half-rim glasses, his hair carefully oiled and combed back on the sides, like an ocean wave about to break, and piled high in front. He misses that pompadour. There's not much left where it rose

Winslow Homer, *Snap the Whip* (1872).
Metropolitan Museum of Art

from his head, a little tuft as a souvenir of what a stylish devil he used to be. He was hurt when he heard them laughing about his hair. He thought, "What are these people doing in my house? Why am I feeding them?"

Nothing you do for children is ever wasted. They seem not to notice us, hovering, averting our eyes, and they seldom offer thanks, but what we do for them is never wasted. We know that as we remember some gift given to us long ago. Suddenly it's 1951, I'm nine years old, in the bow of a green wooden rowboat, rocking on Lake Wobegon. It's five o'clock in the morning, dark; I'm shivering; mist comes up off the water, the smell of lake and weeds and Uncle Al's coffee as he puts a worm on my hook and whispers what to do when the big one bites. I lower my worm slowly into the dark water and brace my feet against the bow and wait for the immense fish to strike.

Thousands of gifts, continually returning to us. Uncle Al thought he was taking his nephew fishing, but he made a permanent work of art in my head, a dark morning in the mist, the coffee, the boat rocking, whispering, shivering, waiting for the big one. Still waiting. Still shivering.

1987

THINK AND DISCUSS

Understanding

1. What do the six children do to the two cats? How do the cats react?
2. What happens when Barbara's little boy jumps off the porch?
3. At what do the Buehler boy and his friends laugh? What is his father's reaction?

Analyzing

4. The Easter season is to many people a time of rebirth and new life, the subject of Father Emil's homily. Point out other details in the selection that reinforce this idea.
5. Father Emil feels he is speaking to "a convention of rabbits instead of the usual herd of turtles." On most Sundays what is the atmosphere in his church?
6. Why is having a child sit between two adults in church like "tying a boat to a dock"?
7. Why does Hjalmar Ingqvist work late at the bank during the week of his grandchildren's visit?
8. Why is the anecdote about Grandma Tollefson and her grandson more than just an amusing vignette?
9. What evidence can you find of Keillor's sense of humor?
10. Do you think that Keillor appears to understand the people he portrays? Why or why not?

APPLYING: Hyperbole H/

See Handbook of Literary Terms, p. 886.

Hyperbole is a figure of speech involving great exaggeration. The effect may be satiric, sentimental, or comic.

1. In the third paragraph Keillor speaks about children's appetites. What example of hyperbole do you find in his remarks?
2. When Grandma Tollefson's grandson practices his guitar, a sound "like jets taking off" comes from her house. How is this an example of hyperbole and what is its effect?

COMPOSITION

Writing About a Visit

Write a composition of three or four paragraphs about a visit of some youngsters to your home or a visit you made to your grandparents or other relatives when you were much younger. Use vivid images of sight, sound, smell, and so on, and even hyperbole, to help the reader share the experience.

Writing an Explanation

Keillor says that "selective ignorance" is "a cornerstone of child rearing." In three or four paragraphs explain what he means and what you think might be the advantages and disadvantages resulting from this attitude.

ENRICHMENT

Designing Day-Care Activities

You are going to work part-time in a day-care center that is about to open. The director asks you to suggest games, exercises, and other activities that you might do with the children. After thinking about the children in the selection, what are three suggestions you might make and the benefits to be derived from them?

Reading AUTOBIOGRAPHY AND BIOGRAPHY

Most of us long to know if anybody else has cried, laughed, hoped, and dreamed as we have. Thus the appeal of reading about the lives of others. Autobiographies are written by individuals about themselves; biographies are written by authors about others.

Here are some pointers on what to look for in reading autobiographies and biographies:

Note the organizing principle. Look for the principle guiding the writer in the selection and arrangement of the incidents of the life. In Virginia Spencer Carr's account of the seventeen-year-old Carson McCullers's trip to New York, the episodes are all related to the young Carson's imaginative growth on her way to becoming a writer. Richard Rodriguez constructs his autobiographical excerpt from *Hunger of Memory* with details emphasizing his obsession to become an accomplished reader.

Look ahead to predict outcomes. As the organizing principle becomes clear to you, watch for details from which you can **infer** later actions of the subject of the biography or autobiography. For example, details that appear early in the biographical excerpt about McCullers indicate that she is a survivor who is strongly motivated to become a writer, someone who used her experiences in New York to "transpose reality into fantasy" and "distorted, polished, and embellished" her observations into fiction. When her dreams of success, fan letters, publishing parties, and interviews finally come true, it should be no great surprise.

Examine both the outer and inner events. Keep a sharp eye both on what the subject learns, and what the world learns of the subject. When McCullers is caught reading Proust and fired, the event is a revelation for all the world to see. In contrast, when William Least Heat Moon, in *Blue Highways*, comes upon what he is looking for, it is not a place, but a state of feeling only he can observe. His physical journey is made only for the purpose of his spiritual search.

Watch for telling details that reveal character. They might come in an autobiography in the form of a confession. Ralph Ellison, in "Shadow and Act," reveals much about himself from his discussion of his name. Rodriguez gives a candid appraisal of himself as being "merely bookish" rather than a good reader. Those who read his autobiography must recognize the distinction he makes. Characterizing details might come from a generalization pieced together from scraps of facts, as in the description of the young McCullers's fear and loneliness, her resourcefulness in finding (and changing) jobs, and her keen assessment of her surroundings. Details such as these help round out a memorable character.

Evaluate the openness and reticence of the writer. Be on the lookout for the writer's frankness or evasion. As Lorraine Hansberry says in *To Be Young, Gifted and Black,* those who set out to write their own lives must ask themselves: "How much of the truth to tell?" We might wonder at the tale that could be told by the wife from whom Least Heat Moon has separated, or the pain felt by Richard Rodriguez's inarticulate parents as he enters a world closed to them. A writer's degree of frankness can often reveal his or her attitude toward the subject. Especially in the case of a biography, readers must determine whether the writer's attitude toward his or her subject is favorable or unfavorable. This opinion will affect the tone of the work and influence the choice of details to be included or omitted.

In reading about the lives of others, we learn how we ourselves can live. In understanding another life, we return to our own with deeper insight and a renewed sense of possibility.

from The Lonely Hunter

Virginia Spencer Carr

Virginia Spencer Carr (1929–) began researching the life of Carson McCullers for a Ph.D. dissertation, just prior to McCullers's death in 1967. Carr moved to Columbus, Georgia, where McCullers grew up as Lulu Carson Smith, to research her subject in depth.

Exhibiting an independent spirit, at thirteen McCullers dropped her first name and expressed her determination to become a concert pianist, practicing four or five hours a day. At fifteen, she decided to become a writer and after graduating from high school, she began reading voraciously all the books reputed to be the "greatest literature in the world." Finally she persuaded her mother, Marguerite, that only in New York could she become a writer.

The following excerpts describe the young Carson's apprenticeship in New York and her later triumphant return to that city. McCullers's biography appears on page 659.

ith some five hundred dollars pinned to her underwear, Carson went by train to Savannah, Georgia, 275 miles northeast of Columbus, where she boarded an ocean-going steamer for the three-day voyage to New York. Other than her visit to Cincinnati, Carson had not ventured more than a hundred miles from home. Her trip to Savannah marked the first time she had ever seen the ocean, let alone set sail upon it. A courageous but timorous young woman loped up the gangplank, already a little bit homesick and having no one to wave good-by to. Grasping firmly the two old suitcases, which were her family's legacy, and her friend Helen Jackson's fur coat—for which she had traded a Dresden china dresser set—Carson took heart, for she recalled her mother's parting words at the station in Columbus where her family had seen her off. After a quick hug, Marguerite had pushed her daughter from her and dabbed at a tear. "Lula Carson, don't ever forget who you are. And know that soon you're going to be famous," she had said, beaming.

As the gangling apprentice-author settled uneasily into a deck chair beside dozens of fellow passengers, she wondered how they viewed her—or if they noticed her at all. Would they recognize that it was her first trip to New York, guess that she had never even smelled the ocean before, or seen snow? Surreptitiously she glanced about her, observing and cataloguing every detail offered by her deckmates. Just as she had sat on her front porch throughout childhood and adolescence with book in hand, reading yet not reading, watching her brother and sister at play yet not seeing, dreaming about life, fantasizing situations in which she starred as protagonist and antihero, spinning her thread, weaving, and severing the cord at will, making reality of myth and obliv-

Excerpt from *The Lonely Hunter* by Virginia Spencer Carr, Copyright © 1975 by Virginia Spencer Carr. Reprinted by permission of Doubleday, a division of Bantam, Doubleday, Dell Publishing Group, Inc.

ious of the transubstantiation—so, too, sat Carson aboard her vessel conveying her to the magical land of snow, skyscrapers, and concert halls, of the Metropolitan, Carnegie Hall, Broadway, Fifth Avenue, Washington Square, Tiffany's, and the Brooklyn Bridge. In her mind's eye she worked assiduously, an impressionistic painter whose shapes, textures, colors blurred pointillistically against a canvas of sea and clouds and sky.

Only vaguely did the seventeen-year-old girl know why she was going to New York City. To study at Juilliard,[1] she had told her parents. To take courses at Columbia. And to write. But most of all she wanted to study the city, take its pulse, and, like her idols Walt Whitman and Hart Crane,[2] fuse herself to it.

Steadily Carson's excitement, anticipation, fear, and anxiety mounted, and by the time her steamship entered Manhattan harbor, the lump in her throat had grown to goiterlike dimensions. When her pen pal, Claire Sasser, with whom she was to stay, greeted her at the dock, Carson could only respond inaudibly. Strangers, their single bond was their hometown, for their parents had arranged the meeting. Everyone in Columbus who had heard of "that poor Smith child being sent to New York City, alone and helpless," thought that Marguerite had grievously erred in this last foolish venture. But Carson's mother retorted that her daughter would be secure under the managing eye of a fellow Southerner with whom she had been invited to room until she could settle and decide for herself where she wanted to live.

Claire Sasser, from solid Columbus stock, was several years older than Carson, beautiful and talented. She had been in the city over a year. Miss Sasser wrote to both Marguerite and Carson that she would be delighted to act as mentor to the young novitiate. The relationship, however, proved an unhappy arrangement. Perhaps taking her charge too seriously, Miss Sasser allegedly suggested that Carson had no business carrying all her money about on her person as she tramped around New York, that she should bank it or let a person more experienced with the wiles of the city keep it. Happily Carson combined her money with her roommate's. Almost immediately, however, the purse was lost, either stolen or carelessly left behind on the subway. Now both were penniless.

Feeling responsible for the loss, Claire Sasser phoned her father for money for each of them. Carson had not dared let her father know her predicament. She was sure he would have sent her only a return bus ticket. From her roommate, Carson accepted only enough to survive in the city until she could find work and become self-supporting. If she had had any doubts before about whether to attend Juilliard, Carson's path was at last clear. She would work, take night classes, and write.

But now the cramped bedroom-sitting room that the two girls occupied over a linen store on the Upper West Side seemed even dingier, and Carson's spirits sagged more heavily than the ancient bed they shared. Uneasy, somehow blaming her roommate for her newly fallen state—in spite of the innocence of the incident—Carson decided to strike out on her own. . . .

Fear, loneliness, and a sense of her own anonymity pervaded her consciousness those first few weeks. The cacophony of city noises, the dirt and poverty, the bold stares and curt retorts of waiters, drivers, clerks, and tradesmen, the labyrinth of subways in which she almost daily became lost—juxtaposed with the glitter and elegance of Park Avenue wealth, bediamonded ladies, and gleaming limousines—all fascinated, yet repelled her. Again and again Carson was driven back to the security of her room.

Although the Parnassus Club, a West Side girls' residence that housed many Columbia University students, provided a more stable home for Carson for the next few weeks than the [one] she had left, she still was unhappy; moreover, she was sick much of the time with colds and pleurisy. Still terrified when going out alone, yet feeling desperately the need to be out, to be independent, she discovered safe harbor within the narrow confines of telephone booths. Particularly

---

1. *Juilliard*, School of Music.
2. *Walt Whitman and Hart Crane*, American poets.

in Macy's department store did she revel in the womblike niche in which she could hide away, pull up her knees and hug them to her chest, feel the vibrations of a pounding heart, and then gradually enjoy relaxed breathing. She never left her room without a book; it gave her security. In telephone booths she sat and read, sometimes for hours. At Macy's there were so many booths that she never felt guilty about taking up space or depriving someone of a phone. Here she felt comfortable, the sea of faces not so threatening; the multitudes pressed past, but they were oblivious of her.

"Just call me, Sister, if you need anything. Remember, I'm as close as a telephone," her mother had shouted as Carson's train pulled away from the station. Daily Carson fought off the compulsion to call home—not just home, but her mother—to be caressed by her mother's deep-throated voice, petted by her words, reassured of love, buoyed and strengthened by the old familiar prattle. She wanted to ask what latest prank Brother-Man had been involved in, if Edwin Peacock[3] was still coming regularly to the house evenings, and did Baby Sister miss her? But she would not call—would not dare. Risk being laughed at? Allow the catch in her voice to become a sob? Asked if she were homesick? Tricked into admitting that the city terrified her? Instead, feeling closer to home in a phone booth than anywhere else, Carson sat and read and imagined brave and scintillating conversations over which she had complete control.

Jobs were scarce in New York City in the mid-thirties, especially for unskilled workers and laborers. It was the decade of the Great Depression, and although Carson had seen abject poverty in her mill town, Columbus, Georgia, it had usually been across the tracks or over by the river. . . .

The young Georgia girl, too, was frequently among the unemployed. She got up at dawn, wrote all morning, worked in the afternoon—when she could find a job—and after the first of February, studied and went to school nights and late afternoons. Carson had paid her tuition money to Columbia University the very day before she lost most of her money; thus when the new term began, she was able to take courses in philosophy, psychology, and the art of the short story. . . .

Decrying the fact that she had had no training in anything worthwhile except music, Carson set about to prove how inept she could be on a job. She rarely lasted until the end of a regular pay period. Instead, she took pride in her record of never having resigned from a position; she was always fired. Sometimes she was hired to type, and for a brief period kept the general ledger and answered the phone at a real-estate office. Her employer, Mrs. Louise B. Field—whom Carson described as "a mean old woman"—decided that her company's best interests were not at heart when she discovered Carson devouring *Swann's Way*[4] beneath the giant ledger in which she was supposedly working. "You're fired! You'll never amount to a thing in this world," Mrs. Field reportedly shouted to her errant employee after pounding her head twice with the big book. Carson picked up her thermos and purse and moved sullenly to the door. She had just discovered Marcel Proust and she was not going to be intimidated or allow her enthusiasm to be dampened by what she considered a gross display of vulgarity.

Occasionally Carson worked as a waitress, but she always shunned any opportunity to serve as a short-order cook. She had never cooked at home, she told one prospective employer; furthermore, she did not intend to begin now, and certainly not for someone else. . . .

More palatable to her talents, Carson decided, was an editorial position on a magazine. Such hopes were short lived, however. She found two comic magazines desirous of her services and worked for a short time on each, both of which she soon discovered were rapidly sliding down the fiscal drain into bankruptcy. Just before the creditors closed in on one, *More Fun*, she declined

---

3. *Edwin Peacock,* McCullers's life-long friend.
4. **Swann's Way,** the first book of *Remembrance of Things Past* by French writer Marcel Proust (1871–1922).

the opportunity the owner gave her of buying the magazine for a paltry sum. Whether it was her good sense not to, or the fact that she had no money, Carson was reluctant to speculate on later.

Perhaps Carson succeeded best that first year in New York as a dog walker. She liked dogs, had grown up with a big mongrel she had loved better than did anyone else in the Smith family, and she was always picking up Starke Avenue strays. Frequently she worked at her fiction until midafternoon, left for a class, and then returned home by way of Riverside Drive, where sundry dog lovers hired her to exercise an assortment of boxers, Airedales, chows, and Doberman pinschers. There were always more poodles, Pekingese, dachshunds, and Chihuahuas than she had time for, or wanted, for Carson hated small dogs. They were too poky and inquisitive; rather, she loved a brisk walk with large animals.

Carson's respiratory infections mounted during her first winter in the North. She had little resistance to the cold, although she often was out in it by choice. The piercing wind, sleet, and snow continually assaulted her health, but she was enamored of the snow and spent precious hours walking in it and daydreaming as she watched it settle upon the rooftops, awnings, and sidewalk shrubs.

Gradually she made friends, especially in her musical neighborhood near Juilliard. With music a common denominator, Carson never knew a stranger. Later, she described her aggressiveness in meeting people when music was an entree in her biographical sketch for Whit Burnett, editor of *Story*. She said that she began to hear some wonderful Mozart from a piano near her room and knocked on the door to discover its source. (Carson used the incident fictionally some twenty-five years later in *Clock Without Hands* when Jester Clane, the youthful protagonist, knocked on Sherman Pew's door after he heard his piano playing in the distance.) The musician was a young Jewish boy her age who had recently arrived from Vienna and was on a scholarship in New York City. Carson told Burnett that they immediately became friends. As she explored the city now with a companion, she found that she no longer even thought about telephone booths. Her whole perspective of life in New York City was dramatically altered.

Together they discovered the wharves, their pulse fascinating her, drawing her forward, a sense of urgency almost tangible as she moved among the cargo storage sheds and to the ship's side, activity at fever pitch. Carson watched each sling load of cargo go aboard as though it were the last, the dollies and forklifts in constant motion, carrying pallets from shed to ship, onto the apron, under the crane or boom; the longshoremen constantly chattering when not shouting or whistling signals, the whining of electric motors of the shore cranes barely perceptible over the squealing noises of the ship's winches, the ship impatient to be loaded, to slip her berth and point seaward. The wharf rats—some as large as house cats—startled her, darting from pallet to pallet, pilfering the cargo; and in a moment's lull she could hear the cooing of pigeons fluttering among the shed's rafters, restless until the next longshoremen's break when they could scurry about the floor and feed on grain or flour from a broken sack.

At night Carson frequently returned to the waterfront, watching the light fog drift in, thickening slightly, giving a halo to each light and the water's surface hidden below; listening to the forlorn sounds of fog signals from distant ships, their whistles and bells. At night the longshoremen almost stopped talking, their voices carrying half a ship's length with a whisper, their spirits dampened like the air itself, everyone working more slowly, seemingly lost in his own thoughts. She observed the crew wander back at all hours, looking as though they might collapse into a heap at any moment, smiled at their harsh expletives, listened to their ribald songs and drunken cries, envied their camaraderie, longed to be a part of them. Most of all, she yearned to travel, dreamed of the faraway, the unattainable . . . for now. . . .

No one in Columbus with the possible exception of Edwin Peacock—for they had exchanged letters regularly—knew precisely what had transpired with Carson while she was in New York City alone for the first time. Probably not even Carson herself could ascertain the truth soon after it happened, for she immediately transposed reality into fantasy, distorted, polished, embellished, and presented her wildest imaginings as fact. Once the art had been created, she could not distinguish the tissue between actuality and imagination. She was unconscious, even, of a creative process having gone on, so natural was the flow. . . .

In June, 1935, McCullers returned to Georgia and continued her writing, with intermittent study in New York. In 1937, she married Reeves McCullers and eventually settled in Fayetteville, North Carolina, a town they both found uncongenial. While there, she received word that her novel, *The Heart Is a Lonely Hunter*, would be published in June, 1940, and she was invited to New York to promote the book. Shortly afterwards, accompanied by her husband, the twenty-three-year-old author of a best seller set out once again for New York.

In spite of her eagerness to get away from the South, Carson felt timorous over her impending return North. Self-confidence yielded to doubt as she considered her re-entry into New York City. Today, she would be noticed in a new and exciting way. She had a name and a novel to her credit, yes, but would people like her? Would it be any different from the way it had been in Fayetteville? Regardless of her apparent unconcern over what other people thought, Carson quivered inside and yearned for acceptance. Would they wonder how such a naive young girl could write *The Heart Is a Lonely Hunter*, and would they think any less of the book once they had met its author? En route on the train with Reeves, Carson daydreamed constantly, imagining what life would be like in New York City this time. In most of her dreams she saw a single image: a girl surrounded by admirers, reading fan letters, attending parties hosted by her publisher, granting requests for interviews, receiving the New York literary coterie—whom she saw welcoming her into their sanctum—lunching at the Algonquin[5], being the honored guest at cocktail parties, intimate dinners . . . and the fancies danced on and on. Herself a onesome, not a twosome, she did not see Reeves in the crystal ball.

For once, actuality almost matched Carson's fantasy. She and Reeves arrived in New York City just two weeks after *The Heart Is a Lonely Hunter* burst upon the literary scene amid reviewers' accolades that the book's young author was the most exciting new talent of the decade. Hurriedly settling into their fifth-floor walk-up apartment at 321 West Eleventh Street in Greenwich Village, Carson and Reeves went out to survey their kingdom. Jubilant in her success, they walked arm in arm through midtown Manhattan, pausing at windows of bookshops to thrill at the sight of stacks of her novel and blowups of her picture on prominent display.

She had been photographed at a table as she sat autographing copies of *The Heart Is a Lonely Hunter*, looking like a drowsy-eyed child who had not been long out of bed. Carson did not like the picture, for she thought it made her face appear pouchy—"almost possum-jawed," she called it.

---

5. *Algonquin,* a New York City hotel frequented by writers.

(Later, the British actress Maria Britneva Saint Just referred to Carson as "Choppers.") Her public, however, found Carson freshly appealing and boyish-looking, dressed in Reeves's shirt and a dark man-tailored corduroy jacket. New York's new literary darling had a natural, fresh-scrubbed look. Her straight bangs and long brown hair— tousled and gleamingly clean—well-shaped eyebrows, slightly upturned nose, full lips which parted invitingly into a half smile, all contributed to the wondering look of a sixteen-year-old with captivating charm, a press agent's dream. Both the book and the person took New York by storm.

1975

THINK AND DISCUSS
Understanding

1. According to the second paragraph, what are three things that the young Carson has never done?
2. What has "most of all" motivated her to go to New York City, according to paragraph three?
3. What happened soon after her arrival to the money she brought to New York?

Analyzing

4. What "womblike niche" did McCullers discover where she could feel safe and read? How does this detail help **characterize** her?
5. When McCullers was fired from her job at the real-estate office, her employer exclaimed, "You'll never amount to a thing in this world." Why was she fired and how is her employer's exclamation **ironic**?
6. How did McCullers's musical interests lead to a friendship that dramatically altered her life in New York? How does she use this incident fictionally some twenty-five years later?
7. What insights into McCullers's character are provided by the description of her success as a dog walker and her explorations on the wharves?
8. When McCullers returns to New York, how do her past dreams compare with reality?
9. Why, in the last paragraph, is McCullers described as a "press agent's dream"?

Extending

10. Do you think that writers of fiction generally find their subjects in their everyday lives, in their imaginations, or through their reading? Where do you find your ideas for writing assignments?

READING LITERATURE SKILLFULLY
Predicting Outcomes

As you read about the characters featured in biographies and autobiographies, use clues to make inferences and predictions about what will happen later. Remember that nonfiction selections, like works of fiction, present narratives that progress logically and have a predictable structure.

1. Why does McCullers originally want to live in New York? What is her goal?
2. Judging from the clues to character provided early in this biographical excerpt did you predict her eventual success? Explain.

COMPOSITION
Analyzing Characterization

Select several episodes in this biographical excerpt that reveal important facets of McCullers's character. You might consider her retreat to telephone booths, one of her jobs, or her reaction to the wharves. In an essay of four or five paragraphs for your school literary magazine, explain how these episodes are revealing. See "Writing About Nonfiction" in the Writer's Handbook.

William Least Heat Moon
1940–

William Trogdon of Columbia, Missouri, tells the story behind his pen name in the early pages of *Blue Highways:* "My father calls himself Heat Moon, my elder brother Little Heat Moon. I, coming last, am therefore Least. It has been a long lesson of a name to learn. To the Siouan peoples, the Moon of Heat is the seventh month, a time also known as the Blood Moon because, I think, of its dusky midsummer color." The name William Trogdon is the legacy of a white ancestor who was killed by Tories during the American Revolution for providing food to rebel patriots and thereby "got his name in volume four of *Makers of America.*" As to why he used his tribal name on the book, Least Heat Moon explains that his father always told him to use the name Trogdon when doing Anglo things, such as engaging in business or paying taxes, but to use Heat Moon when he was doing things akin to the spiritual.

In a sense, that is precisely what *Blue Highways* is—the record of a spiritual experience. Least Heat Moon had just been laid off from his job as an English teacher at Stephens College in Missouri. Moreover, his ten-year-old marriage was coming to an end. Filled with a sense of emptiness and a desire for renewal, he decided to embark on a 13,000-mile odyssey. He kept a log of travels which, after three years and eight rewrites, became a best-selling book, full of vivid descriptions and realistic dialogues. But more important, the experience helped Least Heat Moon to overcome his misery, regain a sense of worth, and accept both the Indian and white parts of himself.

William Least Heat Moon decided to follow a circular route in his journey over the back roads of the United States. He travels in a van named Ghost Dancing, a reference to the ceremonies of the 1890s when the Plains Indians danced in the hope of bringing back the buffalo, the grass, and the old way of life that was rapidly dying. The author calls his estranged wife the Cherokee because of her mixed ancestry and labels his marital battles the "Indian wars." Among the town with odd names that he visits are Remote, Oregon; Simplicity, Virginia; New Freedom, Pennsylvania; New Hope, Tennessee; Why, Arizona; Whynot, Mississippi; and Igo, California (just down the road from Ono).

from Blue Highways

William Least Heat Moon

he first highway: Interstate 70 east-bound out of Columbia, Missouri. The road here follows, more or less, the Booneslick Trail, the initial leg of the Oregon Trail; it also parallels both the southern latitude of the last great glacier in central Missouri and the northern boundary of the Osage Nation. The Cherokee and I had skirmished its length in Missouri and Illinois for ten years, and memory made for hard driving that first day of spring. But it was the fastest route east out of the homeland.

Eighty miles on, rain started popping the windshield, and the road became blobby headlights and green interstate signs for this exit, that exit. LAST EXIT TO ELSEWHERE. I crossed the Missouri River not far upstream from where Lewis and Clark on another wet spring afternoon set out for Mr. Jefferson's *terra incognita*.[1] Further to the southeast, under a glowing skullcap of fouled sky, lay St. Louis.

The tumult of St. Louis behind, the Illinois superwide quiet but for the rain, I turned south onto State 4, a shortcut to I-64. After that, the 42,500 miles of straight and wide could lead anywhere; I was going to stay on the 3 million miles of bent and narrow rural American two-lane, the roads that used to be shown in blue on highway maps to distinguish them from the main routes, in red.

The early darkness came on. My headlamps cut only a 40-foot trail through the rain, and the dashboard lights cast a green glow. Sheet lightning behind the horizon of trees made the sky look like a great faded orange cloth being blown about; then darkness soaked up the light, and, for a moment, I was blinder than before.

In the approaching car beams, raindrops spattering the road became little beacons. I bent over the wheel to steer along the divider stripes. A frog, long-leggedy and green, bellyflopped across the road to the side where the puddles would be better. The land, still cold and wintry, was alive with creatures that trusted in the coming of spring.

At Grayville, Illinois, on the Wabash River, I pulled up for the night on North Street and parked in front of the old picture show. The marquee said TRAVELOGUE TODAY, or it would have if both the *o*'s had been there. I should have gone to a café and struck up a conversation, but I stumbled to the bunk in the back of my rig, undressed, zipped into a sleeping bag, and watched things go dark. I fought desolation and wrestled memories of the Indian wars.

First night on the road. I've read that fawns have no scent, so predators cannot track them down. But I heard the past snuffling about somewhere else.

The rain came again in the night and moved on east to leave a morning of cool overcast. Driving through the washed land in my small, self-propelled box—a "wheel estate," a mechanic had called it—I felt clean and almost disentangled. I had what I needed for now, much of it stowed under the wooden bunk:

1 sleeping bag and blanket;

1 Coleman cooler (empty but for a can of chopped liver a friend had given me so there would *always* be something to eat);

1 Rubbermaid basin and a plastic gallon jug (the sink);

---

1. *terra incognita* (ter′ə in kog′nə tə), unknown land. [*Latin*]

From *Blue Highways* by William Least Heat Moon. Copyright © 1982 by William Least Heat Moon. First appeared in *The Atlantic Monthly*. By permission of Little, Brown and Company in association with the Atlantic Monthly Press.

Claes Oldenburg, *Bacon and Eggs* (1961).
Hessisches Landesmuseum, Darmstadt, West Germany

1 Sears Roebuck portable toilet;
1 Optimus 8R white gas cookstove (hardly bigger than a can of beans);
1 knapsack of utensils, a pot, a skillet;
1 U.S. Navy sea bag of clothes;
1 tool kit;
1 satchel full of notebooks, pens, road atlas, and a microcassette recorder;
2 Nikon F2 35mm cameras and five lenses;
2 vade mecums:[2] Whitman's *Leaves of Grass* and Neihardt's *Black Elk Speaks*.

In my billfold were four gasoline credit cards and twenty-six dollars. Hidden under the dash were the remnants of my savings account: $428.

Ghost Dancing, a 1975 half-ton Econoline (the smallest van Ford makes), rode self-contained but not self-containing. So I hoped. It had two worn rear tires and an ominous knocking in the water pump. I had converted the van from a clangy tin box into a six-by-ten place at once a bedroom, kitchen, bathroom, parlor. Everything simple and lightweight: no crushed velvet upholstery, no wine racks, no built-in television. It came equipped with power nothing and drove like what it was—a truck. Your basic plumber's model.

The Wabash divides southern Illinois from Indiana. East of the fluvial flood plain, a sense of the unknown, the addiction of the traveler,

began seeping in. Abruptly, Pokeberry Creek came and went before I could see it. The interstate afforded easy passage over the Hoosierland, so easy it gave no sense of the up and down of the country; worse, it hid away the people. Life doesn't happen along interstates. It's against the law.

At the Huntingburg exit, I turned off and headed for the Ohio River. Indiana 66, a road so crooked it could run for the legislature, took me into the hilly fields of CHEW MAIL POUCH[3] barns, past Christ-of-the-Ohio Catholic Church, through the Swiss town of Tell City, with its statue of William and his crossbow and his nervous son.[4] On past the old stone riverfront houses in Cannelton, on up along the Ohio, the muddy bank sometimes not ten feet from the road. The brown water rolled and roiled. Under wooded bluffs I stopped to stretch among the periwinkles. At the edge of a field, Sulphur Spring bubbled up beneath a cover of dead leaves. Shawnees once believed in the curative power of the water, and settlers even bottled it. I cleared the small spring for a taste. Bad enough to cure something.

I crossed into the Eastern Time Zone and then over the Blue River, which was a brown creek. Blue, Green, Red—yes—but whoever heard of a Brown River? For some reason, the farther west the river and the scarcer the water, the more honest the names become: Stinking Water Branch, Dead Horse Fork, Cutthroat Gulch, Damnation Creek. Perhaps the old trailmen and prospectors figured settlers would be slower to build along a river named Calamity.

I took the nearest Ohio River bridge at Louisville and whipped around the city and went into Pewee Valley and on to La Grange, where seven daily Louisville & Nashville freight trains

<hr>

2. *vade mecum* (vā′dē mē′kəm), useful book. [*Latin*]
3. ***CHEW MAIL POUCH***, an advertisement for chewing tobacco on the side of a barn that is visible from the highway.
4. *with its statue of William . . . nervous son.* After being arrested, William Tell was ordered to shoot an apple from the top of his son's head. He did so successfully and went on to become a legendary hero in the Swiss struggle for independence against Austria.

ran right down Main Street. Then southeast.

Curling, dropping, trying to follow a stream, Kentucky 53 looked as if it needed someone to take the slack out. On that gray afternoon the creek ran full and clear under the rock ledges that dripped out the last meltwater. In spite of snow-packs here and about, a woman bent to the planting of a switch of a tree, one man tilled mulch into his garden, another cleaned a birdhouse.

To walk Main Street in Shelbyville, Kentucky, is to go down three centuries of American architecture: rough-hewn timber, postbellum brick, Victorian fretwork, 1950s plate glass. Founded in 1792, it's an old town for this part of the country.

At the west end of Main, a man stripping siding from a small, two-story house had exposed a log cabin. I stopped to watch him straighten the doorway. To get a better perspective, he came to the sidewalk, eyed the lintel, then looked at me. "It's tilting, isn't it?" he said.

"There's a little list to it, but you could live with that."

"I want it right." He went to the door, set up a jack, measured, and leaned into it. The timbers creaked and squared up. He propped a couple of two-by-fours under the lintel to hold it true and cranked down the jack. "Come in for a look," he said. "After a hundred and fifty years, she's not likely to fall down today."

"That's before people started jacking around with it."

The interior, bare of plaster and lath, leaked a deep smell of old timbers. Bigger than railway ties, the logs lay locked in dovetails, all careful work done only with ax, adz, froe, and wedge. The man, Bob Andriot, asked what I thought.

"It's a beauty. How long have you been at it?"

"Ten days. We want to move in the first of April."

"You're going to live here?"

"My wife and I have a picture-framing and interior-design shop. We're moving it out of our house. We just bought this place."

"Did you know the log cabin was underneath the siding?"

"We thought it possible. Shape of the house and the low windows looked right. We knew some were along Main." He went to the window. "That little house across the street—could be one under the siding. A lot of cabins are still buried under asphalt shingles, and nobody knows it. I've heard Kentucky's got more log houses than any other state."

A squarely solid man stepped through a back window. Andriot said, "Tony here got himself one last year in Spencer County."

"But I knew what I was gettin'," Tony said. "It wasn't sided over. Some fellas clearin' a field were discussin' whether to burn the cabin or push it in the holler. We were lookin' for a house, so we bought it and moved it. Only three inches off square, and I know factually it'd been there since 1807. Good for another couple hundred years now."

"Tony's logs are chestnut and a lot more termite-resistant than these poplar logs here," Andriot said. "Somebody let a gutter leak for a long time on the back corner, and termites came up in the wet wood. Now that end's like a rotted tooth, except we can't pull it. So we'll reinforce."

He took me around to the east wall. "Look at this." He pointed to a worn Roman numeral I cut between adz marks into the bottom log. The eighth tier had a VIII scratched in it. "They're numbered, and we don't know why. I don't think it was ever moved. Maybe precut to a plan."

"A prefab nineteenth-century log house?"

"Don't think this was a house originally. Records show it was a coach stop on the old road to Louisville in 1829, but it's probably older. Main Street's always been the highway."

"What about the gaps between the logs?"

Andriot stuck a crowbar between two timbers and pried out a rock caked with mud as hard as stone. "They chinked with rocks and mud, but we aren't going to be that authentic. We'll leave the rocks but chink with concrete." He locked the crowbar onto a wooden peg, its color much lighter than that of the logs, and pulled it free. "Hand-whittled oak. Sniff it." The peg smelled of freshly cut wood. "You're sniffing a tree from

1776." Andriot touched his nose. "Gives you a real sense of history. Take it with you."

He asked where I was from. Tony listened and asked if I had ever read *Walking Through Missouri on a Mule.*

"Never heard of it, but I like that title."

"It's about an old boy that tramped across the state a hundred years ago. Boy that walked it wrote the book. Now, that's good reading."

A head popped in the window. "Hey, Kirk," Andriot said. "Coke time."

We sat on the plank floor and talked. "You know," Andriot said, "this old place makes a difference here. To us, of course, but to the town, too, before long. I feel it more than I can explain it. I don't know—I guess rescuing this building makes me feel I've done something to last. And people here need to see this old lady. To be reminded."

"Old lady?" Kirk said. "That's not what you were calling her yesterday."

"That was yesterday. She gets better as she gets older."

The men got up to work again, and I shook hands all around.

I drove on east. I thought about how Bob Andriot was rebuilding a past he could see and smell, one he could shape with his hands. He was using it to build something new. I envied him that.

Not out of any plan but just because it lay in front of me, I headed for the bluegrass region. I took an old road, a "pike," the Kentuckians say, since their first highways were toll roads with entrances barred by revolving poles called "turn pikes." I followed the old pike, now Route 421, not out of any plan, either, but because it looked pleasant—a road of white fences around thoroughbred farms.

Along the Leestown Road, near an old white-washed springhouse made useless by a water-district pipeline, I stopped to eat lunch. Downstream from the spring, where butter once got cooled, the clear rill washed around clumps of new watercress under peeling sycamores. I pulled

makings for a sandwich from my haversack: Muenster cheese, a collop of hard salami, sour-dough bread, horseradish. I cut a sprig of watercress, laid it on, and then ate slowly, letting the gurgle in the water and the guttural trilling of red-winged blackbirds do the talking. A noisy, whizzing gnat that couldn't decide whether to eat on my sandwich or my ear joined me.

Had I gone looking for some particular place rather than any place, I would never have found this spring under the sycamores. Since leaving home, I felt for the first time at rest. . . .

There is one almost infallible way to find honest food at just prices in blue-highway America: count the wall calendars in a café.

No calendar: Same as an interstate pit stop.
One calendar: Preprocessed food assembled in New Jersey.
Two calendars: Only if fish trophies are present.
Three calendars: Can't miss on the farmboy breakfasts.
Four calendars: Try the "ho-made" pie, too.
Five calendars: Keep it under your hat, or they'll franchise.

One time I found a six-calendar café in the Ozarks, which served fried chicken, peach pie, and chocolate malts that left me searching for another one ever since. I've never seen a seven-calendar place. But old-time travelers—roadmen in a day when cars had running boards and lunch-room windows said AIR COOLED in blue letters with icicles dripping from the tops—those travelers have told me the golden legends of seven-calendar cafés.

To the rider of back roads, nothing shows the tone, the voice of a small town more quickly than the breakfast grill or the five-thirty tavern. Much of what the people do and believe and share is evident there. The City Café in Gainesboro, Tennessee, had three calendars that I could see from the walk. Inside were no interstate refugees with full bladders and empty tanks, no wild-eyed children just released from the glassy cell of a station wagon back seat, no long-haul truckers talking in CB numbers. There were only townspeople wearing overalls, or catalog-order suits with five-and-dime ties, or uniforms. That is, there were farmers and mill hands, bank clerks, the dry-goods merchant, a policeman, and the chiropractor's receptionist. Because it was Saturday, there were also mothers and children.

I ordered my standard on-the-road breakfast: two eggs up, hashbrowns, tomato juice. The waitress, whose pale, almost translucent skin shifted hue in the gray light like a thin slice of mother-of-pearl, brought the food. Next to the eggs was a biscuit with a little yellow Smiley button stuck in it. She said, "You from the North?"

"I guess I am." A Missourian gets used to southerners thinking him a Yankee, a northerner considering him a cracker, a westerner sneering at his effete easternness, and an easterner taking him for a cowhand.

"So whata you doin' in the mountains?"

"Talking to people. Taking some pictures. Looking, mostly."

"Lookin' for what?"

"A three-calendar café that serves Smiley buttons on the biscuits."

"You needed a smile. Tell me really."

"I don't know. Actually, I'm looking for some jam to put on this biscuit, now you've brought one."

She came back with grape jelly. In a land of quince jelly, apple butter, apricot jam, blueberry preserves, pear conserves, and lemon marmalade, you always get grape jelly.

"Whata you lookin' for?"

Like anyone else, I'm embarrassed to eat in front of a watcher, particularly if I'm getting interviewed. "Why don't you have a cup of coffee?"

"Cain't right now. You gonna tell me?"

"I don't know how to describe it to you. Call it harmony."

She waited for something more. "Is that it?"

Someone called her to the kitchen. I had managed almost to finish by the time she came back. She sat on the edge of the booth. "I started out in life not likin' anything, but then it grew on me.

Maybe that'll happen to you." She watched me spread the jelly. "Saw your van." She watched me eat the biscuit. "You sleep in there?" I told her I did. "I'd love to do that, but I'd be scared spitless."

"I don't mind being scared spitless. Sometimes."

"I'd love to take off cross-country. I like to look at different license plates. But I'd take a dog. You carry a dog?"

"No dogs, no cats, no budgie birds. It's a one-man campaign to show Americans a person can travel alone, without a pet."

"Cain't travel without a dog!"

"I like to do things the hard way."

"Shoot! I'd take me a dog to talk to. And for protection."

"It isn't traveling to cross the country and talk to your pug instead of people along the way. Besides, being alone on the road makes you ready to meet someone when you stop. You get sociable, traveling alone."

She looked out toward the van again. "Time I get the nerve to take a trip, gas'll cost five dollars a gallon."

"Could be. My rig might go the way of the steamboat." I remembered why I'd come to Gainesboro. "You know the way to Nameless?" I had picked Nameless out of my atlas while I sat on my bunk in Livingston, Tennessee, waiting for the rain to stop.

"Nameless? I've heard of Nameless. Better ask the am'lance driver in the corner booth." She pinned the Smiley on my jacket. "Maybe I'll see you on the road somewhere. His name's Bob, by the way."

"The ambulance driver?"

"The Smiley. I always name my Smileys—otherwise they all look alike. I'd talk to him before you go."

"The Smiley?"

"The am'lance driver."

And so I went looking for Nameless, Tennessee, with a Smiley button named Bob.

"I don't know if I got directions for where

you're goin'," the ambulance driver said. "I *think* there's a Nameless down the Shepardsville road."

"When I get to Shepardsville, will I have gone too far?"

"Ain't no Shepardsville."

"How will I know when I'm there?"

"Cain't say for certain."

"What's Nameless look like?"

"Don't recollect."

"Is the road paved?"

"It's possible."

Those were the directions. I was looking for an unnumbered road named after a nonexistent town which would take me to a place called Nameless that nobody was sure existed.

Clumps of wild garlic lined the county highway that I hoped was the Shepardsville road. It scrimmaged with the mountain as it tried to stay on top of the ridges; the hillsides were so steep and thick with oak, I felt as if I were following a trail through the misty treetops. Chickens ran across the road, doing more work with their necks than their legs, and, with a battering of wings, half leaped and half flew into the lower branches of the oaks. A vicious pair of German shepherds raced along trying to eat the tires. After miles, I decided I'd missed the town—assuming there truly *was* a Nameless, Tennessee.

I stopped beside a big man loading tools in a pickup. "I may be lost."

"Where'd you lose the right road?"

"I don't know. Somewhere around 1965."

"Highway 56, you mean?"

"I came down 56. I think I should've turned at the last junction."

"Only thing down that road's stumps and huckleberries, and the berries ain't there in March. Where you tryin' to get to?"

"Nameless. If there is such a place."

"You might not know Thurmond Watts, but he's got him a store down the road. That's Nameless, at his store. Still there, all right, but I might not vouch you that tomorrow."

Nameless, Tennessee, was a town of maybe ninety people if you pushed it, a dozen houses along the road, a couple of barns, same number of churches, a general merchandise store selling Fire Chief gasoline, and a community center with a lighted volleyball court. Behind the center was an open-roofed, rusting metal privy with PAINT ME on the door; in the hollow of a nearby oak lay a full pint of Jack Daniel's. From the houses, the odor of coal smoke.

Next to a red tobacco barn stood the general-merchandise with a poster of Senator Albert Gore, Jr., smiling from the window. I knocked. The door opened a few inches. A tall, thin man said, "Closed up. For good," and started to shut the door.

"Don't want to buy anything. Just a question for Mr. Thurmond Watts."

The man peered through the slight opening. He looked me over. "What question would that be?"

"If this is Nameless, Tennessee, could he tell me how it got that name?"

The man turned back into the store and called out, "Miss Ginny! Somebody here wants to know how Nameless come to be Nameless."

Miss Ginny edged to the door and looked me and my truck over. Clearly, she didn't approve. She said, "You know as well as I do, Thurmond. Don't keep him on the stoop in the damp to tell him." Miss Ginny, I found out, was Mrs. Virginia Watts, Thurmond's wife.

I stepped in and they both began telling the story, adding a detail here, correcting a fact there, both smiling at the foolishness of it all. It seems the hilltop settlement went for years without a name. Then one day the Post Office Department told the people that if they wanted mail up on the mountain, they would have to give the place a name you could properly address a letter to. The community met; there was only a handful, but they commenced debating. Some wanted patriotic names, some names from nature; one man recommended, in all seriousness, his own name. They couldn't agree, and they ran out of names to argue about. Finally, a fellow tired of the talk; he didn't like the mail he received anyway. "Forget the durn post office," he said. "This here's a nameless place if I ever seen one, so leave it be." And that's just what they did.

Watts pointed out the window. "We used to have signs on the road, but the Halloween boys keep tearin' them down."

"You think Nameless is a funny name," Miss Ginny said. "I see it plain in your eyes. Well, you take yourself up north a piece to Difficult or Defeated or Shake Rag. Now them are silly names."

The old store, lighted only by three fifty-watt bulbs, smelled of coal oil and baking bread. In the middle of the rectangular room, where the oak floor sagged a little, stood an iron stove. To the right was a wooden table with an unfinished game of checkers, and a stool made from an apple-tree stump. On shelves around the walls sat earthen jugs with corncob stoppers, a few canned goods, and some of the 2,000 old clocks and clockworks Thurmond Watts owned. Only one was ticking. I asked how long he'd been in the store.

"Thirty-five years, but we closed the first day of the year. We're hopin' to sell it to a churchly couple. Upright people. No athians."[5]

"Did you build this store?"

"I built this one, but it's the third general store on the ground. I fear it'll be the last. I take no pleasure in that. Once you could come in here for a gallon of paint, a pickle, a pair of shoes, and a can of corn."

"Or horehound candy," Miss Ginny said. "Or corsets and salves. We had cough syrups and all that for the body. In season, we'd buy and sell blackberries and walnuts and chestnuts, before the blight got them. And outside, Thurmond milled corn and sharpened plows. Even shoed a horse sometimes."

"We could fix up a horse or a man or a baby," Watts said.

"Thurmond, tell him we had a doctor on the ridge in them days."

"We had a doctor on the ridge in them days. As good as any doctor a-living. He'd cut a crooked toenail or deliver a woman. Dead these last years."

"I got some bad ham meat one day," Miss Ginny said, "and took to vomitin'. All day, all night. Hangin' on the drop edge of yonder. I said to Thurmond, 'Thurmond, unless you want shut of me, call the doctor.'"

"I studied on it," Watts said.

"You never did. You got him right now. He come over and put three drops of iodeen in half a glass of well water. I drank it down and the vomitin' stopped with the last swallow. Would you think iodeen could do that?"

"He put Miss Ginny on one teaspoon of spirits of ammonia in well water for her nerves. Ain't nothin' works better for her to this day."

"Calms me like the hand of the Lord."

Hilda, the Wattses' daughter, came out of the back room. "I remember him," she said. "I was just a baby. Y'all were talkin' to him, and he lifted me up on the counter and gave me a stick of Juicy Fruit and a piece of cheese."

"Knew the old medicines," Watts said. "Only drugstore he needed was a good kitchen cabinet. None of them anteebeeotics that hit you worsen your ailment. Forgotten lore now, the old medicines, because they ain't profit in iodeen."

Miss Ginny started back to the side room where she and her sister Marilyn were taking apart a duck-down mattress to make bolsters. She stopped at the window for another look at Ghost Dancing. "How do you sleep in that thing? Ain't you all cramped and cold?"

"How does the clam sleep in his shell?" Watts said in my defense.

"Thurmond, get the boy a piece of buttermilk pie afore he goes on."

"Hilda, get him some buttermilk pie." He looked at me.

"You like good music?" I said I did. He cranked up an old Edison phonograph, the kind with the big morning-glory blossom for a speaker, and put on a wax cylinder. "This will be "My Mother's Prayer,'" he said.

While I ate buttermilk pie, Watts served as disc jockey of Nameless, Tennessee. "Here's

---

5. *athians,* atheists.

'Mountain Rose.' " It was one of those moments you know at the time will stay with you to the grave—the sweet pie, the gaunt man playing the old music, the coals in the stove glowing orange, the scent of kerosene and hot bread. "Here's 'Evening Rhapsody.' " The music was so heavily romantic we both laughed. I thought: It is for this I have come.

Feathered over and giggling, Miss Ginny stepped from the side room. She knew she was a sight. "Thurmond, give him some lunch. Still looks hungry."

Hilda pulled food off the wood stove in the back room: home-butchered and -canned whole-hog sausage, home-canned June apples, turnip greens, cole slaw, potatoes, stuffing, hot corn-bread. All delicious.

Watts and Hilda sat and talked while I ate.

"Wish you would join me."

"We've ate," Watts said. "Cain't beat a wood stove for flavorful cookin'."

He told me he was raised in a 150-year-old cabin. Still standing in one of the hollows. "How many's left," he said, "that grew up in a log cabin? I ain't the last, surely, but I must be climbin' on the list."

Hilda cleared the table.

"You Watts ladies know how to cook."

"She's in nursin' school at Tennessee Tech. I went over for one of them football games last year there at Coevul." To say "Cookeville," you let the word collapse in upon itself so that it comes out "Coevul."

"Do you like football?" I asked.

"Don't know. I was so high up in that stadium, I never opened my eyes."

Watts went to the back and returned with a fat spiral notebook, which he set on the table. His expression had changed. "Miss Ginny's death-book. She's wrote out twenty years' worth of them. Ever day she listens to the hospital report on the radio and puts the names in. Folks come by to check a date. Or they just turn through the books. Read them like a scrapbook."

Hilda said, "Like Saint Peter at the gates inscribin' the names."

Watts took my arm. "Come along." He led me to the fruit cellar under the store. As we went down, he said, "Always take a newborn baby upstairs afore you take him downstairs, otherwise you'll incline him downwards."

The old cellar was dry and full of cobwebs and jar after jar of home-canned food: sausage, pump-kin, sweet pickles, tomatoes, corn relish, black-berries, peppers, squash, jellies. Watts held a hand out toward the dusty bottles. "Our tomor-rows."

When it was time for me to go, Watts said, "If you find anyone along your way wants a good store, on the road to Cordell Hull Lake, tell them about us."

I said I would. Miss Ginny and Hilda came out to say good-by. It was cold and drizzling again. "Weather to give a man the weary dis-mals," Watts grumbled. "Where you headed from here?"

"I don't know."

"Cain't get lost, then."   1982

THINK AND DISCUSS
Understanding
1. What are blue highways, as described in the third paragraph?
2. What is Ghost Dancing and for what pur-poses does Moon use it on his journey?
3. What is Bob Andriot doing when Moon first encounters him in Shelbyville, Kentucky? What did Andriot discover underneath the siding of the house?
4. What "almost infallible" method does Moon use to find good food at fair prices? What

does a waitress at a restaurant in Gainesboro, Tennessee, give Moon before he leaves?

Analyzing

5. Why do you think Moon chose to travel on blue highways?
6. Not all the things the author takes on his trip are necessary for survival. What do these nonessentials indicate about the purpose(s) of his trip?
7. Cite the passages that show Moon's ability to capture the rhythms and peculiarities of various dialects of American English.
8. After describing his visit with the Watts family in Nameless, Tennessee, the author writes, "It is for this I have come." To what is he referring?

Extending

9. Do you think Moon's description of America and Americans is accurate? Why or why not?

THINKING SKILLS
Classifying

To classify information is to organize it so that it makes sense. When you classify, you sort things into groups according to what they have in common. In "Blue Highways," William Least Heat Moon presents a unique way of classifying restaurants on the road.

1. Explain Moon's way of classifying restaurants.
2. In your experience with restaurants, does Moon's classification system seem plausible?
3. What other ways of classifying restaurants might help a customer find a good meal?

Comment

Talking with Least Heat Moon

In an interview shortly after the publication of *Blue Highways*, Least Heat Moon indicated some of the qualities of the American people that he found over and over again. One was a genuine openness and hospitality. It amazed the author that he was invited into homes so frequently. In the case of the Watts family of Nameless, Tennessee, Least Heat Moon tells how Thurmond Watts even showed the author his fruit cellar. "For him [it] was like showing me his bank account." The only area where this was not true was in the Central Northern states of North Dakota, Minnesota, and Wisconsin. The author attributes this reserve to the Scandinavian background of many of the inhabitants.

Least Heat Moon was also struck by the ease with which people in the South talk. Southerners seem to him to love language for its own sake and to treat it "almost as if it's music." One example of such language was used by a man named Noel Jones in Franklinville, North Carolina. As the author was about to set

off into the woods at dusk, Jones advised him to wait until dawn. "You'll be wiping shadows all the way."

Another aspect that impressed the author was the dignity of the people he met and their attachment to the places where they lived, no matter how small or hot or dusty. Although he found a few lost souls, Least Heat Moon also found many risk takers, still trying to turn their dreams into reality. But then, as he points out, Americans are descendants of risk takers, of people who did not want to stay where they were but preferred to move on in the hope of bettering themselves and their lives.

Perhaps as good a comment as any is his description of the circular route he followed: "There on the map, crudely, was the labyrinth of migration the old Hopis once cut in their desert stone. For me, the migration had been to places and moments of glimpsed clarity. Splendid gifts all."

BIOGRAPHY

Richard Rodriguez
1946–

Richard Rodriguez knew only a few words of English when he entered the first grade in Sacramento, California, at the age of six. His autobiography, *Hunger of Memory: The Education of Richard Rodriguez*, tells the story of how the Roman Catholic nuns taught him English, awakened him to the joys of reading, and set him on a course that would lead him to an undergraduate degree at Stanford University and a graduate degree in English at the University of California at Berkeley.

As both a writer and a teacher, Rodriguez chronicles an intellectual journey that moved him from the comforting intimacy of his family circle to the challenging and sometimes alienating arena of American public life. But Rodriguez says he wishes to be known as a first-rate teacher of English rather than as an American intellectual.

Rodriguez's success as an author and a teacher has been accompanied by a certain amount of pain. As he became more fluent in English, he began to lose his fluency in Spanish and a degree of intimacy with his beloved parents, who have never managed a complete command of English. His autobiography is a modestly stated record of a remarkable personal achievement, glowing with love and gratitude for his elementary school teachers and tinged with regret that his loving and devoted parents may never fully comprehend the book nor the motives that engendered it.

from Hunger of Memory

Richard Rodriguez

rom an early age I knew that my mother and father could read and write both Spanish and English. I had observed my father making his way through what, I now suppose, must have been income tax forms. On other occasions I waited apprehensively while my mother read onion-paper letters air-mailed from Mexico with news of a relative's illness or death. For both my parents, however, reading was something done out of necessity and as quickly as

possible. Never did I see either of them read an entire book. Nor did I see them read for pleasure. Their reading consisted of work manuals, prayer books, newspapers, recipes.

Richard Hoggart[1] imagines how, at home,

---

1. *Richard Hoggart*, British writer Richard Hoggart in *The Uses of Literacy* (1957), Chapter 10.

From *Hunger of Memory* by Richard Rodriguez. Copyright © 1982 by Richard Rodriguez. Reprinted by permission of David R. Godine, Publisher.

". . . [The scholarship boy] sees strewn around, and reads regularly himself, magazines which are never mentioned at school, which seem not to belong to the world to which the school introduces him; at school he hears about and reads books never mentioned at home. When he brings those books into the house, they do not take their place with other books which the family are reading, for often there are none or almost none; his books look, rather, like strange tools."

In our house each school year would begin with my mother's careful instruction: "Don't write in your books so we can sell them at the end of the year." The remark was echoed in public by my teachers, but only in part: "Boys and girls, don't write in your books. You must learn to treat them with great care and respect."

OPEN THE DOORS OF YOUR MIND WITH BOOKS, read the red and white poster over the nun's desk in early September. It soon was apparent to me that reading was the classroom's central activity. Each course had its own book. And the information gathered from a book was unquestioned. READ TO LEARN, the sign on the wall advised in December. I privately wondered: What was the connection between reading and learning? Did one learn something only by reading it? Was an idea only an idea if it could be written down? In June, CONSIDER BOOKS YOUR BEST FRIENDS. Friends? Reading was, at best, only a chore. I needed to look up whole paragraphs of words in a dictionary. Lines of type were dizzying, the eye having to move slowly across the page, then down, and across. . . . The sentences of the first books I read were coolly impersonal. Toned hard. What most bothered me, however, was the isolation reading required. To console myself for the loneliness I'd feel when I read, I tried reading in a very soft voice. Until: "Who is doing all that talking to his neighbor?" Shortly after, remedial reading classes were arranged for me with a very old nun.

At the end of each school day, for nearly six months, I would meet with her in the tiny room that served as the school's library but was actually only a storeroom for used textbooks and a vast collection of *National Geographics*. Everything about our sessions pleased me: the smallness of the room; the noise of the janitor's broom hitting the edge of the long hallway outside the door; the green of the sun, lighting the wall; and the old woman's face blurred white with a beard. Most of the time we took turns. I began with my elementary text. Sentences of astonishing simplicity seemed to me lifeless and drab: "The boys ran from the rain. . . . She wanted to sing. . . . The kite rose in the blue." Then the old nun would read from her favorite books, usually biographies of early American presidents. Playfully she ran through complex sentences, calling the words alive with her voice, making it seem that the author somehow was speaking directly to me. I smiled just to listen to her. I sat there and sensed for the very first time some possibility of fellowship between a reader and a writer, a communication, never *intimate* like that I heard spoken words at home convey, but one nonetheless *personal*.

One day the nun concluded a session by asking me why I was so reluctant to read by myself. I tried to explain; said something about the way written words made me feel all alone—almost, I wanted to add but didn't, as when I spoke to myself in a room just emptied of furniture. She studied my face as I spoke; she seemed to be watching more than listening. In an uneventful voice she replied that I had nothing to fear. Didn't I realize that reading would open up whole new worlds? A book could open doors for me. It could introduce me to people and show me places I never imagined existed. She gestured toward the bookshelves. (African women danced, and the shiny hubcaps of automobiles on the back covers of the *Geographic* gleamed in my mind.) I listened with respect. But her words were not very influential. I was thinking then of another consequence of literacy, one I was too shy to admit but nonetheless trusted. Books were going to make me "educated." *That* confidence enabled me, several months later, to overcome my fear of the silence.

In fourth grade I embarked upon a grandiose reading program. "Give me the names of important books," I would say to startled teachers. They soon found out that I had in mind "adult books." I ignored their suggestion of anything I suspected was written for children. (Not until I was in college, as a result, did I read *Huckleberry Finn* or *Alice's Adventures in Wonderland*.) Instead, I read *The Scarlet Letter* and Franklin's *Autobiography*. And whatever I read I read for extra credit. Each time I finished a book, I reported the achievement to a teacher and basked in the praise my effort earned. Despite my best efforts, however, there seemed to be more and more books I needed to read. At the library I would literally tremble as I came upon whole shelves of books I hadn't read. So I read and I read and I read: *Great Expectations;* all the short stories of Kipling; *The Babe Ruth Story;* the entire first volume of the *Encyclopaedia Britannica* (A-ANSTEY); the *Iliad; Moby Dick; Gone with the Wind; The Good Earth; Ramona; Forever Amber; The Lives of the Saints; Crime and Punishment; The Pearl.* . . . Librarians who initially frowned when I checked out the maximum ten books at a time started saving books they thought I might like. Teachers would say to the rest of the class, "I only wish the rest of you took reading as seriously as Richard obviously does."

But at home I would hear my mother wondering, "What do you see in your books?" (Was reading a hobby like her knitting? Was so much reading even healthy for a boy? Was it the sign of "brains"? Or was it just a convenient excuse for not helping around the house on Saturday mornings?) Always, "What do you see . . . ?"

What *did* I see in my books? I had the idea that they were crucial for my academic success, though I couldn't have said exactly how or why. In the sixth grade I simply concluded that what gave a book its value was some major idea or theme it contained. If that core essence could be mined and memorized, I would become learned like my teachers. I decided to record in a notebook the themes of the books that I read. After reading *Robinson Crusoe*, I wrote that its theme was "the value of learning to live by oneself." When I completed *Wuthering Heights*, I noted the danger of "Letting emotions get out of control." Rereading these brief moralistic appraisals usually left me disheartened. I couldn't believe that they were really the source of reading's value. But for many more years, they constituted the only means I had of describing to myself the educational value of books.

In spite of my earnestness, I found reading a pleasurable activity. I came to enjoy the lonely good company of books. Early on weekday mornings, I'd read in my bed. I'd feel a mysterious comfort then, reading in the dawn quiet—the blue-gray silence interrupted by the occasional churning of the refrigerator motor a few rooms away or the more distant sounds of a city bus beginning its run. On weekends I'd go to the public library to read, surrounded by old men and women. Or, if the weather was fine, I would take my books to the park and read in the shade of a tree. A warm summer evening was my favorite reading time. Neighbors would leave for vacation and I would water their lawns. I would sit through the twilight on the front porches or in backyards, reading to the cool, whirling sounds of the sprinklers.

I also had favorite writers. But often those writers I enjoyed most I was least able to value. When I read William Saroyan's *The Human Comedy*, I was immediately pleased by the narrator's warmth and the charm of his story. But as quickly I became suspicious. A book so enjoyable to read couldn't be very "important." Another summer I determined to read all the novels of Dickens. Reading his fat novels, I loved the feeling I got—after the first hundred pages—of being at home in a fictional world where I knew the names of the characters and cared about what was going to happen to them. And it bothered me that I was forced away at the conclusion, when the fiction closed tight, like a fortuneteller's fist—the futures of all the major characters neatly resolved. I never knew how to take such feelings seriously, however. Nor did I suspect that these experiences could be part of a novel's meaning. Still, there

John Martin, National Book Festival poster (1981)

were pleasures to sustain me after I'd finish my books. Carrying a volume back to the library, I would be pleased by its weight. I'd run my fingers along the edge of the pages and marvel at the breadth of my achievement. Around my room, growing stacks of paperback books reenforced my assurance.

I entered high school having read hundreds of books. My habit of reading made me a confident speaker and writer of English. Reading also enabled me to sense something of the shape, the major concerns, of Western thought. (I was able to say something about Dante and Descartes and Engels and James Baldwin in my high-school term papers.) In these various ways books brought me academic success as I hoped that they would. But I was not a good reader. Merely bookish, I lacked a point of view when I read. Rather, I read in order to acquire a point of view. I vacuumed books for epigrams, scraps of information, ideas, themes—anything to fill the hollow within me and make me feel educated. When one of my teachers suggested to his drowsy tenth-grade English class that a person could not have a "complicated idea" until he had read at least two thousand books, I heard the remark without detecting either its irony or its very complicated truth. I merely determined to compile a list of all the books I had ever read. Harsh with myself, I included only once a title I might have read several times. (How, after all, could one read a book more than once?) And I included only those books over a hundred pages in length. (Could anything shorter be a book?)

There was yet another high-school list I compiled. One day I came across a newspaper article about the retirement of an English professor at a nearby state college. The article was accompanied by a list of the "hundred most important books of Western Civilization." "More than anything else in my life," the professor told the reporter with finality, "these books have made me all that I am." That was the kind of remark I couldn't ignore. I clipped out the list and kept it for the several months it took me to read all of the titles. Most books, of course, I barely understood. While reading Plato's *Republic*, for instance, I needed to keep looking at the book jacket comments to remind myself what the text was about. Nevertheless, with the special patience and superstition of a scholarship boy, I looked at every word of the text. And by the time I reached the last word, relieved, I convinced myself that I had read *The Republic*. In a ceremony of great pride, I solemnly crossed Plato off my list.

1981

THINK AND DISCUSS
Understanding
1. What two languages do the narrator's mother and father read and write? What materials do they read?
2. Why does the narrator's mother tell him not to write in his school books? How does she react when he later "embarked on a grandiose reading program"?
3. What does the narrator do when he comes across a list of the hundred "most important books of Western Civilization"?

Analyzing
4. In what ways do the narrator, as a youngster, and his parents view reading differently?
5. The narrator says, "I was not a good reader, merely bookish." What do you think he means? What in his account seems to indicate that he was reading for the wrong reasons?
6. Reread the final three sentences of this account. What is the narrator's **tone**? How do you know?

BIOGRAPHY

Lorraine Hansberry
1930–1965

Lorraine Hansberry was born in Chicago where she attended public school in a segregated system that opened schools for blacks only for half-day sessions. At the University of Wisconsin, she found her courses dull and irrelevant. But one day she wandered into a rehearsal of Sean O'Casey's *Juno and the Paycock*, an experience that "consumed all my senses." She left college and moved to New York City, where she worked first as a typist and then as a reporter and editor for Paul Robeson's Harlem newspaper, *Freedom*. She married Robert Nemiroff, whom she met at a rally protesting racist practices on the New York University basketball team. The couple was active in the civil rights and peace movements.

When Hansberry was twenty-eight, her first play, *A Raisin in the Sun*, opened on broadway. Two months later she became the youngest American playwright, the fifth woman, and the first black writer to win the New York Drama Critics' Circle Award for the Best Play of the Year. Six years later, at the age of thirty-four, she died of cancer.

The Sign in Sidney Brustein's Window is the only other of her plays performed while she lived. But she left behind three file cabinets of manuscripts of all kinds. Nemiroff and others have been editing the papers, which include the autobiographical pieces that formed the basis for the play and novel *To Be Young, Gifted and Black*.

One of her last notes read: "If anything should happen—before 'tis done—may I trust that all commas and periods will be placed and some-one will complete my thoughts—

"This last should be the least difficult—since there are so many who think as I do——"

from To Be Young, Gifted and Black

Lorraine Hansberry

Chicago: Southside Summers

1

or some time now—I think since I was a child—I have been possessed of the desire to put down the stuff of my life. That is a commonplace impulse, apparently, among persons of massive self-interest; sooner or later we all do it. And, I am quite certain, there is only one internal quarrel: how much of the truth to tell? How much, how much, how much! It *is* brutal, in sober uncompromising moments, to reflect on the comedy of concern we all enact when it comes to our precious images!

Even so, when such vanity as propels the writing of such memoirs is examined, certainly one would wish at least to have some boast of social serviceability on one's side. I shall set down in these pages what shall seem to me to be the truth of my life and essences . . . which are to be found, first of all, on the Southside of Chicago, where I was born. . . .

2

All travelers to my city should ride the elevated trains that race along the back ways of Chicago. The lives you can look into!

I think you could find the tempo of my people on their back porches. The honesty of their living is there in the shabbiness. Scrubbed porches that sag and look their danger. Dirty gray wood steps. And always a line of white and pink clothes scrubbed so well, waving in the dirty wind of the city.

My people are poor. And they are tired. And they are determined to live.

Our Southside is a place apart: each piece of our living is a protest.

3

I was born on May 19, 1930, the last of four children.

Of love and my parents there is little to be written: their relationship to the children was utilitarian. We were fed and housed and dressed and outfitted with more cash than our associates and that was all. We were also vaguely taught certain vague absolutes: that we were better than no one but infinitely superior to everyone; that we were the products of the proudest and most mistreated of the races of man; that there was nothing enormously difficult about life; that one *succeeded* as a matter of course.

Life was not a struggle—it was something that one *did*. One won an argument because, if facts gave out, one invented them—with color! The only sinful people in the world were dull people. And, above all, there were two things which were never to be betrayed: the family and the race. But of love, there was nothing ever said.

If we were sick, we were sternly, impersonally and carefully nursed and doctored back to health. Fevers, toothaches were attended to with urgency and importance; one always felt *important* in my family. Mother came with a tray to your room with the soup and Vick's salve or gave the enemas in a steaming bathroom. But we were not fondled, any of us—head held to breast, fingers about that head—until we were grown, all of us, and my father died.

At his funeral I at last, in my memory, saw my

From the book *To Be Young, Gifted and Black: Lorraine Hansberry in Her Own Words*, adapted by Robert Nemiroff. Copyright © 1969 by Robert Nemiroff and Robert Nemiroff as Executor of the Estate of Lorraine Hansberry. Reprinted by permission of Prentice-Hall, Inc., Englewood Cliffs, New Jersey.

mother hold her sons that way, and for the first time in her life my sister held me in her arms I think. We were not a loving people: we were passionate in our hostilities and affinities, but the caress embarrassed us.

We have changed little. . . .

4

Seven years separated the nearest of my brothers and sisters and myself; I wear, I am sure, the earmarks of that familial station to this day. Little has been written or thought to my knowledge about children who occupy that place: the last born separated by an uncommon length of time from the next youngest. I suspect we are probably a race apart.

The last born is an object toy which comes in years when brothers and sisters who are seven, ten, twelve years older are old enough to appreciate it rather than poke out its eyes. They do not mind diapering you the first two years, but by the time you are five you are a pest that has to be attended to in the washroom, taken to the movies, and "sat with" at night. You are not a person—you are a nuisance who is not particular fun anymore. Consequently, you swiftly learn to play alone. . . .

5

My childhood Southside summers were the ordinary city kind, full of the street games which other rememberers have turned into fine ballets these days, and rhymes that anticipated what some people insist on calling modern poetry:

Oh, Mary Mack, Mack, Mack
With the silver buttons, buttons, buttons
All down her back, back, back.
She asked her mother, mother, mother
For fifteen cents, cents, cents
To see the elephant, elephant, elephant
Jump the fence, fence, fence.
Well, he jumped so high, high, high
'Til he touched the sky, sky, sky
And he didn't come back, back, back
'Til the Fourth of Ju—ly, ly, ly!

I remember skinny little Southside bodies by the fives and tens of us panting the delicious hours away:
"May I?"
And the voice of authority: "Yes, you may—you may take one giant step."

One drew in all one's breath and tightened one's fist and pulled the small body against the heavens, stretching, straining all the muscles in the legs to make—one giant step.

It is a long time. One forgets the reason for the game. (For children's games are always explicit in their reasons for being. To play is to win something. Or not to be "it." Or to be high pointer, or outdoer or, sometimes—just *the winner*. But after a time one forgets.)

Why was it important to take a small step, a teeny step, or the most desired of all—one GIANT step?

A giant step to *where?*

6

Evenings were spent mainly on the back porches where screen doors slammed in the darkness with those really very special summertime sounds. And, sometimes, when Chicago nights got too steamy, the whole family got into the car and went to the park and slept out in the open on blankets. Those were, of course, the best times of all because the grownups were invariably reminded of having been children in the South and told the best stories then. And it was also cool and sweet to be on the grass and there was usually the scent of freshly cut lemons or melons in the air. Daddy would lie on his back, as fathers must, and explain about how men thought the stars above us came to be and how far away they were.

I never did learn to believe that anything could be as far away as *that*. Especially the stars. . . .

7

The man that I remember was an educated soul, though I think now, looking back, that it was as much a matter of the physical bearing of my father as his command of information and

Dong Kingman, *The El and Snow* (1946). Whitney Museum of American Art, New York

of thought that left that impression upon me. I know nothing of the "assurance of kings" and will not use that metaphor on account of it. Suffice it to say that my father's enduring image in my mind is that of a man whom kings might have imitated and properly created their own flattering descriptions of. A man who always seemed to be doing something brilliant and/or unusual to such an extent that to be doing something brilliant and/or unusual was the way I assumed fathers behaved.

He digested the laws of the State of Illinois and put them into little booklets. He invented complicated pumps and railroad devices. He could talk at length on American history and private enterprise (to which he utterly subscribed). And he carried his head in such a way that I was quite certain that there was nothing he was afraid of. Even writing this, how profoundly it shocks my inner sense to realize suddenly that *my father*, like all men, must have known *fear*. . . .

8

April 23, 1964

To the Editor,
The *New York Times:*

With reference to civil disobedience and the Congress of Racial Equality stall-in:
. . . My father was typical of a generation of Negroes who believed that the "American way" could successfully be made to work to democratize the United States. Thus, twenty-five years ago, he spent a small personal fortune, his considerable talents, and many years of his life fighting, in association with NAACP[1] attorneys, Chicago's "restrictive covenants" in one of this nation's ugliest ghettos.

That fight also required that our family occupy

1. **NAACP,** National Association for the Advancement of Colored People.

the disputed property in a hellishly hostile "white neighborhood" in which, literally, howling mobs surrounded our house. One of their missiles almost took the life of the then eight-year-old signer of this letter. My memories of this "correct" way of fighting white supremacy in America include being spat at, cursed, and pummeled in the daily trek to and from school. And I also remember my desperate and courageous mother, patrolling our house all night with a loaded German luger, doggedly guarding her four children, while my father fought the respectable part of the battle in the Washington court.

The fact that my father and the NAACP "won" a Supreme Court decision, in a now famous case which bears his name in the lawbooks, is—ironically—the sort of "progress" our satisfied friends allude to when they presume to deride the more radical means of struggle. The cost, in emotional turmoil, time and money, which led to my father's early death as a permanently embittered exile in a foreign country when he saw that after such sacrificial efforts the Negroes of Chicago were as ghetto-locked as ever, does not seem to figure in their calculations.

That is the reality that I am faced with when I now read that some Negroes my own age and younger say that we must now lie down in the streets, tie up traffic, do whatever we can—take to the hills with guns if necessary—and fight back. Fatuous people remark these days on our "bitterness." Why, of course we are bitter. The entire situation suggests that the nation be reminded of the too little noted final lines of Langston Hughes's mighty poem.[2]

What happens to a dream deferred?
Does it dry up
Like a raisin in the sun?
Or fester like a sore—
And then run?
Does it stink like rotten meat?
Or crust and sugar over—
Like a syrupy sweet?
Maybe it just sags
Like a heavy load.

Or does it explode?

Sincerely,

1969

---

2. *Langston Hughes's mighty poem,* "Harlem," later published under the title "Dream Deferred."

"Dream Deferred" from *The Panther and the Lash* by Langston Hughes. Copyright 1951 by Langston Hughes. Copyright renewed 1979 by George Houston Bass. Reprinted by permission of Alfred A. Knopf, Inc. and Harold Ober Associates Incorporated.

THINK AND DISCUSS

Understanding

1. What, according to Part 1, is the only "internal quarrel" for autobiographers?
2. According to Part 2, what should all visitors to Chicago do? Why?
3. How did the family sometimes spend steamy Chicago nights? Why were these "the best times of all"?

Analyzing

4. Giving examples from the text, describe Hansberry's feelings about growing up in Chicago, her family in general, and her father specifically.
5. What ideals and attitudes did Hansberry's parents instill in their children? In what way does Hansberry relate childhood games to these attitudes?
6. What effect did being by far the youngest child have on Hansberry?
7. What details of the Hansberry family's experiences support the concluding letter of protest in Part 8? In what way do these experiences illustrate the meaning of Langston Hughes's poem?

VOCABULARY
Affixes and Dictionary
A. Hansberry describes her relationship with her parents as *utilitarian*.

1. After reading the definition of *utilitarian* in the Glossary, explain this relationship.

   Utilitarian has been formed by adding to the root word *utility* two suffixes, *-ar* and *-ian*. Answer the following questions about other suffixes that can be added to *utility*.

2. Considering the meaning of *-ize*, what does *utilize* mean?

3. Considering the meaning of *-ism*, what does *utilitarianism* mean?

B. Hansberry says of her father that ". . . he spent a small personal fortune, his considerable talents, and many years of his life fighting . . . Chicago's *'restrictive covenants'* in one of this nation's ugliest ghettos."

Find the Glossary definitions of the two italicized words. Then explain what Hansberry's father was fighting in Chicago.

COMPOSITION
Writing About Progress in Race Relations
Langston Hughes's poem was published in 1951, and Lorraine Hansberry's letter was published in 1964. From your experience or observation, write a three- or four-paragraph essay for your school paper indicating how much has changed since these works were written.

Comparing Childhood Reminiscences
Compare the childhood reminiscences of Hansberry and Rodriguez in their autobiographical excerpts. How would you describe the tone of each work? the incidents these writers recall? their relationship to their parents? their characters? See "Writing About Nonfiction" in the Writer's Handbook.

Comment

Sweet Lorraine by James Baldwin

She was a very young woman, with an overpowering vision, and fame had come to her early—she must certainly have wished, often enough, that fame had seen fit to drag its feet a little. For fame and recognition are not synonyms, especially not here, and her fame was to cause her to be criticized very harshly, very loudly, and very often by both black and white people who were unable to believe, apparently, that a really serious intention could be contained in so glamorous a frame. She took it all with a kind of astringent good humor, refusing, for example, even to consider defending herself when she was being accused of being a "slumlord" because of her family's real-estate holdings in Chicago. I called her during that time, and all she said—with a wry laugh—was, "Jimmy, do you realize you're only the second person who's called me today? And you know how my phone kept ringing *before!*" She was not surprised. She was devoted to the human race, but she was not romantic about it.

When so bright a light goes out so early, when so gifted an artist goes so soon, we are left with a sorrow and wonder which speculation cannot assuage. One is filled for a long time with a sense of injustice as futile as it is powerful. And the vanished person fills the mind, in this or that attitude, doing this or that. Sometimes, very briefly, one hears the exact inflection of the voice, the exact timbre of the laugh—as I have, when watching the dramatic presentation, *To Be Young, Gifted and Black*, and in reading through these pages. But I do not have the heart to presume to assess her work, for all of it, for me, was suffused with the light which was Lorraine.

From "Sweet Lorraine" by James Baldwin. Copyright © 1969 by James Baldwin from *To Be Young, Gifted and Black* published by Prentice-Hall, Inc.

BIOGRAPHY

Ralph Ellison

1914—

In 1953, Ralph Waldo Ellison won the National Book Award for his only published novel, *Invisible Man* (1952), which secured his position as a major modern American writer. His story of a young man's search for identity and humanity in a complex contemporary world was based, in part, on his own experiences. In this work, he went beyond racial commentary on the black experience in America to make a universal statement about all people victimized and denied self-fulfillment.

As a child in Oklahoma City, Ellison studied the trumpet and planned a career in music. Later he attended Tuskegee Institute where he studied symphonic music composition. In his third year he went to New York to study sculpture, and during this time he met Richard Wright and Langston Hughes, who encouraged him to write. In 1937 he wrote a review for *New Challenge*, which was edited by Wright, and began writing literary criticism, essays, and short stories for other periodicals. In 1964 he published a collection of interviews and essays titled *Shadow and Act*, from which the following selection is taken. This selection, first read at the Library of Congress, describes the complex fate of blacks as they continue to define the relationship between an individual and a social identity.

 See ANALOGY in the Handbook of Literary Terms, page 879.

from Shadow and Act

Ralph Ellison

. . . Our names, being the gift of others, must be made our own.

Once while listening to the play of a two-year-old girl who did not know she was under observation, I heard her saying over and over again, at first with questioning and then with sounds of growing satisfaction, "I am Mimi Livisay . . . I am *Mimi* Li-vi-say! I am Mimi. . . ."

And in deed and in fact she was—or became so soon thereafter, by working playfully to establish the unity between herself and her name.

For many of us this is far from easy. We must

From *Shadow and Act* by Ralph Ellison. Copyright © 1964 by Ralph Ellison. Reprinted by permission of Random House, Inc. and William Morris Agency, Inc.

learn to wear our names within all the noise and confusion of the environment in which we find ourselves; make them the center of all of our associations with the world, with man and with nature. We must charge them with all our emotions, our hopes, hates, loves, aspirations. They must become our masks and our shields and the containers of all those values and traditions which we learn and/or imagine as being the meaning of our familial past.

And when we are reminded so constantly that we bear, as Negroes, names originally possessed by those who owned our enslaved grandparents, we are apt, especially if we are potential writers, to be more than ordinarily concerned with the veiled and mysterious events . . . through which our names were handed down unto us. . . .

Perhaps, taken in aggregate, these European names which (sometimes with irony, sometimes with pride, but always with personal investment) represent a certain triumph of the spirit, speaking to us of those who rallied, reassembled and transformed themselves and who under dismembering pressure refused to die. "Brothers and sister," I once heard a Negro preacher exhort, "let us make up our faces before the world, and our names shall sound throughout the land with honor! For we ourselves are our *true* names, not their epithets! So let us, I say, Make Up Our Faces and Our Minds!"

Perhaps my preacher had read T. S. Eliot,[1] although I doubt it. And in actuality, it was unnecessary that he do so, for a concern with names and naming was very much a part of that special area of American culture from which I come, and it is precisely for this reason that this example should come to mind in a discussion of my own experience as a writer.

Undoubtedly, writers begin their *conditioning* as manipulators of words long before they become aware of literature—certain Freudians[2] would say at the breast. Perhaps. But if so, that is far too early to be of use at this moment. Of this, though, I am certain: that despite the misconceptions of those educators who trace the reading difficulties experienced by large numbers of Negro children in Northern schools to their Southern background, these children are, in *their* familiar South, facile manipulators of words. I know, too, that the Negro community is deadly in its ability to create nicknames and to spot all that is ludicrous in an unlikely name or that which is incongruous in conduct. Names are not qualities; nor are words, in this particular sense, actions. To assume that they are could cost one his life many times a day. Language skills depend to a large extent upon a knowledge of the details, the manners, the objects, the folkways, the psychological patterns, of a given environment. Humor and wit depend upon much the same awareness, and so does the suggestive power of names.

"A small brown bowlegged Negro with the name 'Franklin D. Roosevelt Jones' might sound like a clown to someone who looks at him from the outside," said my friend Albert Murray, "but on the other hand he just might turn out to be a fireside operator. He might just lie back in all of that comic juxtaposition of names and manipulate you deaf, dumb and blind—and you not even suspecting it, because you're thrown out of stance by his name! There you are, so dazzled by the FDR image—which you *know* you can't see—and so delighted with your own superior position that you don't realize that it's *Jones* who must be confronted."

Well, as you must suspect, all of this speculation on the matter of names has a purpose, and now, because it is tied up so ironically with my own experience as a writer, I must turn to my own name.

For in the dim beginnings, before I ever thought consciously of writing, there was my own name, and there was, doubtless, a certain magic in it. From the start I was uncomfortable with it, and in my earliest years it caused me much puzzlement. Neither could I understand what a poet was, nor why, exactly, my father had chosen to

---

1. *T. S. Eliot.* See page 525.
2. *Freudians,* people who follow the technique of psychoanalaysis developed by the Austrian physician Sigmund Freud (1856–1939).

name me after one. Perhaps I could have understood it perfectly well had he named me after his own father, but that name had been given to an older brother who died and thus was out of the question. But why hadn't he named me after a hero, such as Jack Johnson,[3] or a soldier like Colonel Charles Young, or a great seaman like Admiral Dewey, or an educator like Booker T. Washington, or a great orator and abolitionist like Frederick Douglass? Or again, why hadn't he named me (as so many Negro parents had done) after President Teddy Roosevelt?

Instead, he named me after someone called Ralph Waldo Emerson,[4] and then, when I was three, he died. It was too early for me to have understood his choice, although I'm sure he must have explained it many times, and it was also too soon for me to have made the connection between my name and my father's love for reading. Much later, after I began to write and work with words, I came to suspect that he was aware of the suggestive powers of names and of the magic involved in naming.

I recall an odd conversation with my mother during my early teens in which she mentioned their interest in, of all things, prenatal culture. But for a long time I actually knew only that my father read a lot, and that he admired this remote Mr. Emerson, who was something called a "poet and philosopher"—so much so that he named his second son after him.

I knew, also, that whatever his motives, the combination of names he'd given me caused me no end of trouble from the moment when I could talk well enough to respond to the ritualized question which grownups put to very young children. Emerson's name was quite familiar to Negroes in Oklahoma during those days when World War I was brewing, and adults, eager to show off their knowledge of literary figures, and obviously amused by the joke implicit in such a small brown nubbin of a boy carrying around such a heavy moniker, would invariably repeat my first two names and then to my great annoyance, they'd add "Emerson."

And I, in my confusion, would reply, "No, no,

I'm not Emerson; he's the little boy who lives next door." Which only made them laugh all the louder. "Oh, no," they'd say, "*you're* Ralph Waldo Emerson," while I had fantasies of blue murder.

For a while the presence next door of my little friend, Emerson, made it unnecessary for me to puzzle too often over this peculiar adult confusion. And since there were other Negro boys named Ralph in the city, I came to suspect that there was something about the combination of names which produced their laughter. Even today I know of only one other Ralph who had as much comedy made out of his name, a campus politician and deep-voiced orator whom I knew at Tuskegee, who was called in friendly ribbing, *Ralph Waldo Emerson Edgar Allan Poe*, spelled Powe. This must have been quite a trial for him, but I had been initiated much earlier.

During my early school years the name continued to puzzle me, for it constantly evoked in the faces of others some secret. It was as though I possessed some treasure or some defect, which was invisible to my own eyes and ears; something which I had but did not *possess*, like a piece of property in South Carolina, which was mine but which I could not have until some future time. I recall finding, about this time, while seeking adventure in back alleys—which possess for boys a superiority over playgrounds like that which kitchen utensils possess over toys designed for infants—a large photographic lens. I remember nothing of its optical qualities, of its speed or color correction, but it gleamed with crystal mystery and it was beautiful.

Mounted handsomely in a tube of shiny brass, it spoke to me of distant worlds of possibility. I played with it, looking through it with squinted eyes, holding it in shafts of sunlight, and tried to use it for a magic lantern. But most of this was as unrewarding as my attempts to make the music

---

3. *Jack Johnson*, American boxing champion from 1908 to 1915.
4. *Ralph Waldo Emerson*. See page 204.

come from a phonograph record by holding the needle in my fingers.

I could burn holes through newspapers with it, or I could pretend that it was a telescope, the barrel of a cannon, or the third eye of a monster—*I* being the monster—but I could do nothing at all about its proper function of making images; nothing to make it yield its secret. But I could not discard it.

Older boys sought to get it away from me by offering knives or tops, agate marbles or whole zoos of grass snakes and horned toads in trade, but I held on to it. No one, not even the white boys I knew, had such a lens, and it was my own good luck to have found it. Thus I would hold on

to it until such time as I could acquire the parts needed to make it function. Finally I put it aside and it remained buried in my box of treasures, dusty and dull, to be lost and forgotten as I grew older and became interested in music.

I had reached by now the grades where it was necessary to learn something about Mr. Emerson and what he had written, such as the "Concord Hymn" and the essay "Self-Reliance," and in following his advice, I reduced the "Waldo" to a simple and, I hoped, mysterious "W," and in my own reading I avoided his works like the plague. I could no more deal with my name—I shall never master it—than I could find a creative use for my lens. . . .

1964

THINK AND DISCUSS
Understanding
1. According to the preacher quoted in paragraph six, what are our *true* names?
2. Who gave the author his name? After whom was he named?

Analyzing
3. In what ways, according to paragraph four, can people establish unity between themselves and their names?
4. Reread the preacher's remarks about names. What does he mean by the following statement? ". . . let us make up our faces before the world, and our names shall sound throughout the land with honor! For we ourselves are our *true* names. . . ."
5. Ellison says he could not deal with or master his name. Why, in the light of his profession, is this statement **ironic**?

Extending
6. Do you believe one's name is as important as Ellison appears to think? Do you know of instances in which a name has made a difference to an individual? Discuss, using specific examples.

APPLYING: Analogy H▨
See Handbook of Literary Terms, p. 879.
An **analogy** is a literal comparison made between two basically different things that share some points in common. Often something simpler or unfamiliar is used to explain something more complex or unfamiliar.

1. Ellison makes an analogy between his name and a lens he finds. What points do these things have in common?
2. Given the fact that a lens is used for making images, why is it an appropriate object to explain the significance of a name?

COMPOSITION
Writing About Your Name
Write a three- to five-paragraph essay for your school literary magazine in response to Ellison's statement, "Our names, being the gift of others, must be made our own." Do you agree or disagree? Describe an experience you have had concerning your own given name or a nickname. Include information about how and why you received your name, your reaction to it, and how others have regarded it. You might speculate on how, given another name, your life might have taken a different direction.

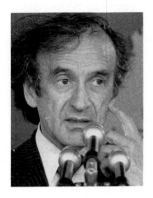

BIOGRAPHY

Elie Wiesel

1928–

In 1944, when Elie Wiesel was fifteen years old, Nazis came to his village in Romania and carried him and his family away to the extermination camp in Auschwitz. He and two older sisters were the only survivors from his family. In war-devastated Europe, Wiesel found a home for a while in France, and began to work with various French and Jewish publications.

He could not at first bring himself to write about the horrors of his experience. But he was finally persuaded to "bear witness" and wrote a semi-autobiographical novel, *Night* (in French, 1956; in English, 1960). It told the story of a boy torn with the guilt of survival of the Holocaust and beset by anguish at the massive destruction of a people.

Wiesel came to the United States in 1956 and was naturalized in 1963. He has been an indefatigable writer ever since, "bearing witness" to the incomprehensible Holocaust. As one critic has written, "he is *the* survivor of the Holocaust. . . . the horror owns him."

Awarded the Nobel Prize in 1986, Weisel gave the eloquent acceptance speech that follows at a ceremony in Oslo, Norway, a pledge not only to the Jewish people but to the oppressed throughout the world. This speech reflects his ongoing fight for the freedom of all people and closes with the assurance that "our survival has meaning for mankind."

Nobel Acceptance Speech

Elie Wiesel

Following is the prepared text of the acceptance speech by Elie Wiesel, the winner of the 1986 Nobel Peace Prize, at a ceremony in Oslo yesterday, as made available by an aide. (*The New York Times*, Dec. 11, 1986)

Reverse of Nobel Medal

It is with a profound sense of humility that I accept the honor you have chosen to bestow upon me. I know: your choice transcends me. This both frightens and pleases me.

It frightens me because I wonder: do I have the right to represent the multitudes who have perished? Do I have the right to accept this great honor on their behalf? I do not. That would be presumptuous. No one may speak for the dead, no one may interpret their mutilated dreams and visions.

It pleases me because I may say that this honor belongs to all the survivors and their children, and through us, to the Jewish people with whose destiny I have always identified.

I remember: it happened yesterday or eternities ago. A young Jewish boy discovered the kingdom of night. I remember his bewilderment, I remember his anguish. It all happened so fast. The ghetto. The deportation. The sealed cattle car. The fiery altar upon which the history of our people and the future of mankind were meant to be sacrificed.

I remember: he asked his father: "Can this be true? This is the twentieth century, not the Middle Ages. Who would allow such crimes to be committed? How could the world remain silent?"

And now the boy is turning to me: "Tell me," he asks. "What have you done with my future? What have you done with your life?"

And I tell him that I have tried. That I have tried to keep memory alive, that I have tried to fight those who would forget. Because if we forget, we are guilty, we are accomplices.

And then I explained to him how naive we were, that the world did know and remain silent. And that is why I swore never to be silent whenever and wherever human beings endure suffering and humiliation. We must always take sides. Neutrality helps the oppressor, never the victim. Silence encourages the tormentor, never the tormented.

Sometimes we must interfere. When human lives are endangered, when human dignity is in jeopardy, national borders and sensitivities become irrelevant. Wherever men or women are persecuted because of their race, religion, or political views, that place must—at that moment —become the center of the universe.

Of course, since I am a Jew profoundly rooted in my people's memory and tradition, my first response is to Jewish fears, Jewish needs, Jewish crises. For I belong to a traumatized generation, one that experienced the abandonment and solitude of our people. It would be unnatural for me not to make Jewish priorities my own: Israel, Soviet Jewry, Jews in Arab lands.

But there are others as important to me. Apartheid[1] is, in my view, as abhorrent as anti-Semitism. To me, Andrei Sakharov's isolation is as much of a disgrace as Iosif Begun's imprisonment. As is the denial of Solidarity and its leader Lech Walesa's right to dissent. And Nelson Mandela's interminable imprisonment.[2]

There is so much injustice and suffering crying out for out attention: victims of hunger, or racism and political persecution, writers and poets, prisoners in so many lands governed by the left and by the right. Human rights are being violated in every continent. More people are oppressed than free.

And then, too, there are the Palestinians[3] to whose plight I am sensitive but whose methods I deplore. Violence and terrorism are not the answer. Something must be done about their suffering, and soon. I trust Israel, for I have faith in the Jewish people. Let Israel be given a chance, let hatred and danger be removed from her horizons, and there will be peace in and around the Holy Land.

Yes, I have faith. Faith in God and even in His creation. Without it no action would be possible. And action is the only remedy to indifference: the most insidious danger of all. Isn't this the meaning of Alfred Nobel's legacy? Wasn't his fear of war a shield against war?

There is much to be done, there is much that can be done. One person—a Raoul Wallenberg,[4]

---

1. *Apartheid* (e pärt'hāt), governmental policy of racial segregation.
2. *Andrei Sakharov. . . imprisonment.* Sakharov, a non-Jewish Russian long forced to live in isolation, was granted freedom in 1987. Begun, a Russian Jew, who suffered long-term imprisonment, also was released in 1987. Walesa was imprisoned for a time by Poland as a Solidarity (Union) leader, and now lives under government imposed restraints. Mandela, a leader of South African blacks, has been imprisoned by South Africa for a long period.
3. *Palestinians,* people who became refugees when Israel was created as a nation in 1948 or in later shifts of Israel's boundaries.
4. *Raoul Wallenberg . . . Albert Schweitzer.* Raoul Wallenberg, a Swedish diplomat who saved many Jews from the holocaust by intervening with the Nazis, died in a Russian prison after World War II. Albert Schweitzer, an Alsatian physicist, philosopher, and missionary, was awarded the Nobel Peace Prize in 1952.

an Albert Schweitzer, one person of integrity, can make a difference, a difference of life and death. As long as one dissident is in prison, our freedom will not be true. As long as one child is hungry, our lives will be filled with anguish and shame.

What all these victims need above all is to know that they are not alone; that we are not forgetting them, that when their voices are stifled we shall lend them ours, that while their freedom depends on ours, the quality of our freedom depends on theirs.

This is what I say to the young Jewish boy wondering what I have done with his years. It is in his name that I speak to you and that I express to you my deepest gratitude. No one is as capable of gratitude as one who has emerged from the kingdom of night.

We know that every moment is a moment of grace, every hour an offering; not to share them would mean to betray them. Our lives no longer belong to us alone; they belong to all those who need us desperately.

Thank you Chairman Aarvik. Thank you, members of the Nobel Committee. Thank you, people of Norway, for declaring on this singular occasion that our survival has meaning for mankind.

1986

THINK AND DISCUSS
Understanding
1. According to the second and third paragraphs, what two conflicting emotions does Wiesel feel on being awarded the Nobel Prize?
2. Who has the right to speak for the dead, according to paragraph two?
3. To whom does the honor bestowed on Wiesel really belong, according to paragraph three?

Analyzing
4. Who might we **infer** is the "young Jewish boy" mentioned in paragraph four? What is the "kingdom of night" he discovers?
5. The boy asks: "What have you done with my future? What have you done with your life?" Judging from the information in this speech, how do you think Wiesel would answer these questions?
6. Wiesel asserts that there is something we must always do and something we must sometimes do. What are these things and why must we do them?
7. On what basis does Wiesel justify making "Jewish priorities" his own? Nevertheless, he asserts that other oppressed people are as important to him as the Jewish people. What are some of the examples he cites?

Extending
8. Near the end of his speech, Wiesel expresses his faith and asserts that "one person of integrity can make a difference." Do you agree? Why or why not?

ENRICHMENT
Research
In his speech, Wiesel asserts that throughout the world, "more people are oppressed than free." To help you better understand the nature and causes of oppression, divide your class into groups by continents. Each student will then choose a country from the designated continent to find examples of oppression, both past and present. Students should present the findings of their research to their group, who will then sift out and organize the major points. Appoint a group representative to present this information to the rest of the class.

BIOGRAPHY

Roger Rosenblatt
1940–

Roger Rosenblatt is a Senior Writer for *Time* and an occasional commentator on the McNeil-Lehrer television news hour on the Public Broadcasting System. Born in New York, he attended Harvard, earning a Ph.D. in 1968 and teaching English there. In addition, he has served as director of education for the National Endowment for the Humanities, literary editor of *The New Republic*, and a columnist for the *Washington Post* (1978–1980). In 1974, his critical work, *Black Fiction*, was published.

The Man in the Water

Roger Rosenblatt

As disasters go, this one was terrible, but not unique, certainly not among the worst on the roster of U.S. air crashes. There was the unusual element of the bridge, of course, and the fact that the plane clipped it at a moment of high traffic, one routine thus intersecting another and disrupting both. Then, too, there was the location of the event. Washington, the city of form and regulations, turned chaotic, deregulated, by a blast of real winter and a single slap of metal on metal. The jets from Washington National Airport that normally swoop around the presidential monuments like famished gulls are, for the moment, emblemized by the one that fell; so there is that detail. And there was the aesthetic clash as well—blue-and-green Air Florida, the name a flying garden, sunk down among gray chunks in a black river. All that was worth noticing, to be sure. Still, there was nothing very special in any of it, except death, which, while always special, does not necessarily bring millions to tears or to attention. Why, then, the shock here?

Perhaps because the nation saw in this disaster something more than a mechanical failure. Perhaps because people saw in it no failure at all, but rather something successful about their makeup. Here, after all, were two forms of nature in collision: the elements and human character. Last Wednesday, the elements, indifferent as ever, brought down Flight 90. And on that same afternoon, human nature—groping and flailing in mysteries of its own—rose to the occasion.

Of the four acknowledged heroes of the event, three are able to account for their behavior. Don-

"The Man in the Water" by Roger Rosenblatt from *Time*, January 25, 1982. Copyright 1982 Time, Inc. All rights reserved. Reprinted by permission of Time, Inc.

ald Usher and Eugene Windsor, a park police helicopter team, risked their lives every time they dipped the skids into the water to pick up survivors. On television, side by side in bright blue jumpsuits, they described their courage as all in the line of duty. Lenny Skutnik, a 28-year-old employee of the Congressional Budget Office, said: "It's something I never thought I would do"—referring to his jumping into the water to drag an injured woman to shore. Skutnik added that "somebody had to go in the water," delivering every hero's line that is no less admirable for its repetitions. In fact, nobody had to go into the water. That somebody actually did so is part of the reason this particular tragedy sticks in the mind.

But the person most responsible for the emotional impact of the disaster is the one known at first simply as "the man in the water. " (Balding, probably in his 50s, an extravagant mustache.) He was seen clinging with five other survivors to the tail section of the airplane. This man was described by Usher and Windsor as appearing alert and in control. Every time they lowered a lifeline and flotation ring to him, he passed it on to another of the passengers. "In a mass casualty, you'll find people like him," said Windsor. "But I've never seen one with that commitment." When the helicopter came back for him, the man had gone under. His selflessness was one reason the story held national attention; his anonymity another. The fact that he went unidentified invested him with a universal character. For a while he was Everyman, and thus proof (as if one needed it) that no man is ordinary.

Still, he could never have imagined such a capacity in himself. Only minutes before his character was tested, he was sitting in the ordinary plane among the ordinary passengers, dutifully listening to the stewardess telling him to fasten his seat belt and saying something about the "no smoking sign." So our man relaxed with the others, some of whom would owe their lives to him. Perhaps he started to read, or to doze, or to regret some harsh remark made in the office that

morning. Then suddenly he knew that the trip would not be ordinary. Like every other person on that flight, he was desperate to live, which makes his final act so stunning.

For at some moment in the water he must have realized that he would not live if he continued to hand over the rope and ring to others. He *had* to know it, no matter how gradual the effect of the cold. In his judgment he had no choice. When the helicopter took off with what was to be the last survivor, he watched everything in the world move away from him, and he deliberately let it happen.

Yet there was something else about the man that kept our thoughts on him, and which keeps our thoughts on him still. He was *there*, in the essential, classic circumstance. Man in nature. The man in the water. For its part, nature cared nothing about the five passengers. Our man, on the other hand, cared totally. So the timeless battle commenced in the Potomac. For as long as that man could last, they went at each other, nature and man; the one making no distinctions of good and evil, acting on no principles, offering no lifelines; the other acting wholly on distinctions, principles and, one supposes, on faith.

Since it was he who lost the fight, we ought to come again to the conclusion that people are powerless in the world. In reality, we believe the reverse, and it takes the act of the man in the water to remind us of our true feelings in this matter. It is not to say that everyone would have acted as he did, or as Usher, Windsor, and Skutnik. Yet whatever moved these men to challenge death on behalf of their fellows is not peculiar to them. Everyone feels the possibility in himself. That is the abiding wonder of the story. That is why we would not let go of it. If the man in the water gave a lifeline to the people gasping for survival, he was likewise giving a lifeline to those who observed him.

The odd thing is that we do not even really believe that the man in the water lost his fight. "Everything in Nature contains all the powers of Nature," said Emerson. Exactly. So the man in the water had his own natural powers. He could not make ice storms, or freeze the water until it froze the blood. But he could hand life over to a stranger, and that is a power of nature too. The man in the water pitted himself against an implacable, impersonal enemy; he fought it with charity; and he held it to a standoff. He was the best we can do.

1982

THINK AND DISCUSS
Understanding
1. Although Rosenblatt begins his essay by observing that the air crash was not unique, he goes on to mention three unusual qualities about it. What was unusual about the bridge that the plane clipped, the location of the crash, and the airplane itself?
2. What, according to the second paragraph, were the "two forms of nature in collision"?
3. Who are the "four acknowledged heroes of the event"? Which one was "most responsible for the emotional impact of the disaster"?

Analyzing
4. How does the heroism of the man in the water differ from that of the other heroes? What in his story caught the attention of the country?
5. Rosenblatt sees this event as part of the "timeless battle" between "nature and man." How does he believe "the elements and human nature" differ?
6. Rosenblatt says that when the man in the water gives the lifeline to others, he was "likewise giving a lifeline to those who observed him." What does he mean?

Extending
7. Do you feel that this essay is more powerful or less so because the hero is unnamed? Explain.

COMPOSITION
Writing About Heroism
Reflect on instances of heroism that impressed you—in the literature you have read, TV or newspaper accounts, or your own life. Then write a journal entry of several paragraphs about this example of heroism. You might want to consider unsung heroes such as the elderly, the disabled, or the disadvantaged who routinely display heroic courage merely to function and to survive. You might even describe those days when the very act of going to school can be a heroic gesture on your part.

Comparing Two Works
Consider how the view of human nature expressed by Rosenblatt or Wiesel differs from that expressed in selections such as "Auto Wreck" (page 712), "The Solitary" (page 538), or "The Love Song of J. Alfred Prufrock" (page 526). In an essay of four paragraphs or more, compare the view of human nature in two contrasting works, supporting your observations with quotations from the works themselves.

Writing About Tone
In three or more paragraphs, describe how the tone of Rosenblatt's essay differs from that of an objective newspaper account. Consider how the writer's attitude toward the man in the water is conveyed—through words, phrases, and images. See "Writing About Mood or Tone" in the Writer's Handbook.

THINKING CRITICALLY ABOUT LITERATURE

UNIT 7   NEW FRONTIERS   1945–

■ CONCEPT REVIEW

The following selections illustrate many of the important ideas and literary terms found in the period you have just studied. The notes and questions are designed to help you think critically about your reading. Page numbers in the notes refer to an application. A more extensive discussion of these terms is in the Handbook of Literary Terms.

Song

Adrienne Rich

You're wondering if I'm lonely:
OK then, yes, I'm lonely
as a plane rides lonely and level
on its radio beam, aiming
5 across the Rockies
for the blue-strung aisle
of an airfield on the ocean

You want to ask, am I lonely?
Well, of course, lonely
10 as a woman driving across country
day after day, leaving behind
mile after mile
little towns she might have stopped
and lived and died in, lonely

■ As you read, note the single emotion expressed in this **lyric** (page 719).

■ Note the similes in lines 3 and 10.

■ **Inference** (page 725): Use clues to infer the speaker's answer to this question.

■ **Rhythm** (page 720): Although irregular, the rhythm has an ebb and flow of its own.

"Song" is reprinted from *The Fact of a Doorframe, Poems Selected and New*, 1950–1984, by permission of W. W. Norton & Company, Inc. Copyright © 1984 by Adrienne Rich. Copyright © 1975, 1978 by W. W. Norton & Company, Inc. Copyright © 1981 by Adrienne Rich.

15 If I'm lonely
it must be the loneliness
of waking first, of breathing
dawn's first cold breath on the city
of being the one awake
20 in a house wrapped in sleep

If I'm lonely
it's with the rowboat ice-fast on the shore
in the last red light of the year
that knows what it is, that knows it's neither
25 ice nor mud nor winter light
but wood, with a gift for burning

1973

■ The "gift for burning" suggests potential for consummation of self in some great endeavor.

from Pilgrim at Tinker Creek

Annie Dillard

Once, when I was ten or eleven years old, my friend Judy brought in a Polyphemus moth[1] cocoon. It was January; there were doily snowflakes taped to the schoolroom panes. The teacher kept the cocoon in her desk all morning and brought it out when we were getting restless before recess. In a book we found what the adult moth would look like; it would be beautiful. With a wingspread of up to six inches, the Polyphemus is one of the few huge American silk moths, much larger than, say, a giant or tiger swallowtail butterfly. The moth's enormous wings are velveted in a rich, warm brown, and edged in bands of blue and pink delicate as a watercolor wash. A startling "eyespot," immense, and deep blue melding to an almost translucent yellow, luxuriates in the center of each hind wing. The effect is one of a masculine splendor foreign to the butterflies, a fragility unfurled to

■ **Setting** (page 690): Note details about time and place that appear here and later in the narrative.

■ **Style** (page 682): The vivid imagery in this description characterizes Dillard's writing.

---

1. *Polyphemus* (pol′ə fē′məs) *moth,* a large moth usually having a buff or pink color.

Abridgment from pages 59–61 from *Pilgrim at Tinker Creek* by Annie Dillard. Copyright © 1974 by Annie Dillard. Reprinted by permission of Harper & Row, Publishers, Inc. and Blanche C. Gregory, Inc.

strength. The Polyphemus moth in the picture looked like a mighty wraith, a beating essence of the hardwood forest, alien-skinned and brown, with spread, blind eyes. This was the giant moth packed in the faded cocoon. We closed the book and turned to the cocoon. It was an oak leaf sewn into a plump oval bundle; Judy had found it loose in a pile of frozen leaves.

■ The moth gets its name from the monstrous one-eyed giant Polyphemus in classic myth, who was blinded by Ulysses.

We passed the cocoon around; it was heavy. As we held it in our hands, the creature within warmed and squirmed. We were delighted, and wrapped it tighter in our fists. The pupa began to jerk violently, in heart-stopping knocks. Who's there? I can still feel those thumps, urgent through a muffling of spun silk and leaf, urgent through the swaddling of many years, against the curve of my palm. We kept passing it around. When it came to me again it was hot as a bun; it jumped half out of my hand. The teacher intervened. She put it, still heaving and banging, in the ubiquitous Mason jar.

■ Imagery and figurative language lend a sense of immediacy.

It was coming. There was no stopping it now, January or not. One end of the cocoon dampened and gradually frayed in a furious battle. The whole cocoon twisted and slapped around in the bottom of the jar. The teacher fades, the classmates fade, I fade: I don't remember anything but that thing's struggle to be a moth or die trying. It emerged at last, a sodden crumple. It was a male; his long antennae were thickly plumed, as wide as his fat abdomen. His body was very thick, over an inch long, and deeply furred. A gray, furlike plush covered his head; a long, tan furlike hair hung from his wide thorax over his brown-furred, segmented abdomen. His multijointed legs, pale and powerful, were shaggy as a bear's. He stood still, but he breathed.

■ This description is at once poetic and scientifically precise.

He couldn't spread his wings. There was no room. The chemical that coated his wings like varnish, stiffening them permanently, dried, and hardened his wings as they were. He was a monster in a Mason jar. Those huge wings stuck on his back in a torture of random pleats and folds, wrinkled as a dirty tissue, rigid as leather. They made a single nightmare clump still wracked with useless, frantic convulsions.

The next thing I remember, it was recess. The school was in Shadyside, a busy residential part of Pittsburgh. Everyone was playing dodgeball in the fenced playground or racing around the concrete schoolyard by the swings. Next to the playground a long delivery drive sloped downhill to the sidewalk and street. Someone—it must have been the teacher—had let the moth out. I was standing in the driveway, alone, stock-still, but shivering. Someone had given the Polyphemus moth his freedom, and he was walking away.

■ alone . . . shivering: Her inner chill is brought on by the event, not the weather.

He heaved himself down the asphalt driveway by infinite degrees, unwavering. His hideous crumpled wings lay glued and rucked on his back, perfectly still now, like a collapsed tent. The bell rang twice; I had to go. The moth was receding down the driveway, dragging on. I went; I ran inside. The Polyphemus moth is still crawling down the driveway, crawling down the driveway hunched, crawling down the driveway on six furred feet, forever.

■ Hyperbole (page 746): The moth "is still crawling," permanently etched in the narrator's memory.

1964

THINK AND DISCUSS
SONG
Understanding
1. How does the plane "ride," according to line 3?
2. What does the "woman driving across country," in the second stanza, leave behind?

Analyzing
3. In each stanza, the speaker uses one central image to describe herself. What are these images?
4. Do you feel that the speaker is really admitting to loneliness in lines 2 and 9? Why or why not?
5. Do you think the following is a good paraphrase for the final stanza? If so, explain why; if not, offer your own paraphrase. "I am aware of my identity and have the potential for self-fulfillment."

Extending
6. How do you think the speaker in this poem would respond to this statement: "*Aloneness* and *loneliness* are synonymous."

PILGRIM AT TINKER CREEK
Understanding
1. Who had found the moth? Where and when?
2. How does the creature in the cocoon react to being passed among the children? How, in turn, do the children react?

Analyzing
3. In the first paragraph, the moth is described as looking like a "mighty wraith." What is this **figure of speech**? Why is the comparison appropriate?
4. The sight of the freed moth leaves the narrator standing "alone, stock-still, but shivering." Why do you think the sight has this effect on her?

REVIEWING LITERARY TERMS
Hyperbole
1. In what sense is the moth crawling down the driveway *forever*?
2. How might the narrator have made this point other than by hyperbole?

Style
3. Find two sentences that characterize Dillard's style and explain why they are representative.

Setting
4. In what sense is the setting of Dillard's narrative appropriate to her theme?

Lyric
5. What is the basic state of mind conveyed by the speaker in "Song"?

Rhythm
6. Although the rhythm in "Song" is irregular, it seems carefully chosen to flow with the speaker's emotions. What is its effect on the reader?

Inference
7. What can you infer about the narrator of "Pilgrim at Tinker Creek" from the description of the crippled moth?

■ CONTENT REVIEW
THINKING SKILLS
Classifying
1. Write the following heads to represent the three genres you have studied in this unit: *Short Story, Poetry, Factual Prose*. List titles from five different works under each of the appropriate heads. Then think of two other ways that you could classify the works in this unit.
2. In this unit, many poems deal with family relationships. What poems can you find that fit this classification? Does bringing the poems together serve to illuminate some aspect of human experience? Explain.

Generalizing
3. Review the poems in the list you made for item 2 under Classifying. Note poems by members of identifiable ethnic groups that capture the routines, values, and customs of a specific group. What generalization might you make about the fact that family relationships seem to be a dominant and recurring theme in modern ethnic poetry?

4. Flannery O'Connor has commented that Mr. Shiftlet in "The Life You Save May Be Your Own" is "of the devil." Compare Mr. Shiftlet to characterizations of the devil that appear in earlier works such as "The Devil and Tom Walker" (Unit 2) and "Young Goodman Brown" (Unit 3). Then make some generalizations about how the theme of evil has changed in American literature during the past hundred years.

5. The characters in several of the works in this unit make a journey of some kind—either a physical one or a figurative one in which the character arrives at a new level of awareness, perhaps by reflecting on the past or the future. Choose three selections from the unit that have a journey motif. Make some generalizations about the effect of the journey on each character. Then arrive at some conclusion as to why the journey motif lends itself so well to modern American literature.

Synthesizing

6. Imagine that one of the authors represented in this unit could visit your class. Which author would you choose and why? What questions would you ask this author? What thoughts of your own would you like to share with this author?

Evaluating

7. What personality types, attitudes, or institutions are satirized in "Harrison Bergeron," "The Vision Test," and "To David, About His Education"? Would you consider each satire harsh or affectionate? Decide which selection you consider most effective in its use of satire and explain your choice.

8. Suppose Karl Shapiro's "Auto Wreck" and Richard Eberhart's "The Groundhog" have been submitted to a poetry contest in which the theme is death. You are a judge. To which poet do you award the prize? Explain.

■ COMPOSITION REVIEW

Choose one of the following topics for a composition.

Writing About a Group's Identity

Imagine that you are the narrator of a TV documentary and must give an introduction that examines what it means to be a member of a particular group in America. Write out your remarks in three paragraphs or more, basing your observations on three of the selections in this unit. Consider these questions: What characteristics distinguish life as presented in each selection? What are the unique problems of these people in America? What are their reassuring sources of pride?

Writing About Contemporary Literature

Choose the selection, either prose or poetry, that seems to you to be the most accurate reflection of the world in which you have grown up. Then choose the selection that gives the least accurate picture. Write an essay of several paragraphs to a classmate explaining your choices. Use quotations from the works to back up your ideas.

Explicating a Poem

An explication titled Reader's Note accompanies some of the more difficult poems in this unit. Write your own explication on one of the following poems for a classmate who has not understood the poem: "October Tune," "My Father's Garden," "To David, About His Education," "Words," "My Mother Pieced Quilts," and "Running It Backward." Before you write, jot down ideas on the following questions: What contribution do figurative language, sound, and rhythm make to the poem? What is the significance of the title? Does the poet use humor, irony, or puns? What is the poet's tone? What images are particularly vivid? Are there any other factors that contribute to the poem's effect? Once you have answered these questions, you should be able to make a generalization about the poem and its meaning.

THE RED BADGE OF COURAGE

Howard Pyle, *The Battle of Nashville*. This battle was fought December 15–16, 1864.

PREVIEW

UNIT 8   THE RED BADGE OF COURAGE

Author
Stephen Crane

Features
Reading a Novel
Comment: The Movie
The Story of American English
Themes in American Literature:
    Initiation

Review of Literary Terms
flashback
irony
characterization

Reading Literature Skillfully
sequence

Vocabulary Skills
pronunciation
context
dictionary

Thinking Skills
classifying
evaluating
synthesizing

Composition
Writing About a Scene of War
Writing a Summary
Writing a Character Sketch
Shifting a Point of View

Enrichment
Research
Oral Report

Thinking Critically About Literature
Concept Review
Content Review
Composition Review

THE RED BADGE OF COURAGE

With no firsthand experience of war, Stephen Crane wrote *The Red Badge of Courage*, acclaimed by many as one of the greatest war novels ever written. Born six years after the end of the Civil War, Crane interviewed war veterans, studied war photographs, and read accounts of the war in order to learn historical details. But aside from its accuracy of detail, this novel could have been about any battle in any war, since the battlefield is merely a backdrop for a psychological study of a soldier's reactions to warfare. At the core of this study is an examination of the ambiguous nature of the motives behind bravery. In Henry's case, bravery is prompted by a mixture of anger, pride, instinct, compulsion, and, ironically, fear.

Other themes such as personal integrity, isolation, failure, fear, guilt, and death are dramatized as the youth attempts to understand and survive internal and external conflicts. Crane's later experiences as newspaper correspondent covering the Greco-Turkish War in 1897 and the Spanish-American War in 1898 confirmed for him that his portrayal of the psychological reactions of a soldier in battle was an accurate one.

Although Crane does not mention actual places or dates, the combat that he describes resembles that which took place in Chancellorsville, Virginia, in the spring of 1863. This battle, between the Union forces led by General Joseph Hooker and the Confederate forces led by Lieutenant-General Thomas J. "Stonewall" Jackson, was distinguished by military mistakes, strategic errors, and general confusion. Henry's

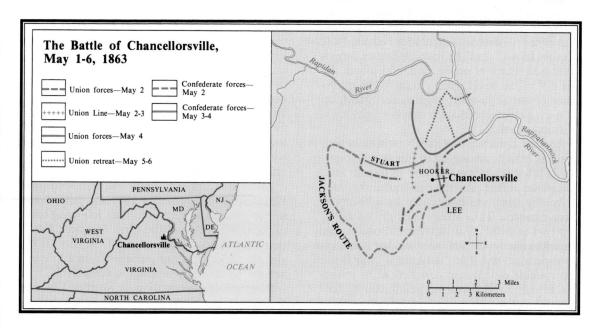

ordeal in *The Red Badge of Courage* coincides with documented statements from actual participants in the battle.

Like their historical counterparts, Henry and the other men are often troubled in the novel by a sense of the confusion of the fighting and a feeling that they are marching back and forth in meaningless patterns. As they watch their fellow soldiers die, they periodically lose faith in the leadership and competence of their officers. At one point, Henry thinks "the generals were stupids." The descriptions in the novel of "an interminable roar," shells with "rows of cruel teeth that grinned at him," and "men screaming like maniacs" reflect accounts of actual Civil War veterans.

IMPRESSIONISM AND NATURALISM

Crane's novel reflects the influence on him of two literary movements of the time—Impressionism and Naturalism. The story is narrated in the third person, but scenes and events are filtered through Henry's impressions. Thus the action is seen not objectively but subjectively, imbued with his feelings and perceptions. Through this technique, called Impressionism, Crane's use of highly selective details conveys a sense of the war in general, much the way a painter's suggestive brushstrokes convey truth through a fleeting impression. In Henry's eyes the entire regiment appears as "grunting bundles of blue," deserting comrades become "a few fleeting forms," and the ensuing battles form a combined image of smoke, fire, and blood. At the end of the novel, Henry regards the experience of war as "a sultry nightmare." Much of Crane's memorable imagery derives from his use of Impressionism.

Another influence on Crane's writing is Naturalism, which, among other things, portrays the indifference of the universe to human fate. Characters, often presented as animallike, are driven by their own instincts or by arbitrary circumstances. Thus Henry is described as "a pestered animal," "a driven beast," one of many "machinelike fools" who are "welded into a common personality." The "red animal" war is itself the epitome of inhuman destruction; its relentless brutality and horror are reinforced by the repetition of words such as *cruel, insolent, futile,*

doomed, and *ludicrous.* Even nature, going "tranquilly on with her golden process in the midst of so much devilment," seems oblivious to the cruelty of war.

Technique in the novel, however, should be studied not in isolation but in relation to its contribution to the narrative's central focus, the complex nature of Henry Fleming. When the novel ends, many questions remain for the reader: Has Henry really grown up under the assault of enemy fire? Has he gained compassion for others? And perhaps most importantly, has Henry gained genuine self-understanding? There is considerable critical debate on the answers to these questions. As you read the novel and work through the editorial material, you will undoubtedly form your own opinions about Henry's character.

ILLUSTRATIONS

The illustrations that accompany the text are rendered as "combat art," complete with notations and water blotches that convey a sense of immediacy and at-the-scene reportage. The artist has re-created visual impressions of combat in much the same way as newspaper artists did during the Civil War. Their sketches, rapidly drawn and immediately dispatched by rider to eastern newspapers and magazines, were engraved and reproduced. Pictures and accompanying newspaper articles by war correspondents were then devoured by a public eager for Civil War news. This kind of on-the-spot sketching is still done today, on battlefields, in courtrooms, in hospitals, anywhere newsworthy events are being reported. Commenting on his artwork, Ted Lewin said, "I tried to see the incidents so vividly described by Crane through the eyes of a combat artist of that time. Drawing with a brush is direct and spontaneous and catches the essence of the action."

The Red Badge of Courage was serialized in a Philadelphia newspaper in 1894 and published in book form the next year. The following text of the novel is that of the First American Edition (New York: Appleton and Company, 1895), slightly abridged. Four passages from a longer version have been reinstated in Chapter 24.

Biographical information on Stephen Crane appears on page 386.

Reading A NOVEL

A novel is an extended piece of narrative prose fiction. As you read a novel, you will recognize many of the elements present in a short story—**plot, characterization, setting,** and **theme.** But because a novel unfolds in a more leisurely manner, the plot is more involved, the characters more fully developed, and the theme more complex, weaving in and out of the narrative.

The following guidelines will help you enjoy and appreciate the *Red Badge of Courage* and other novels that you read.

Identify the theme. Initiation emerges as a dominant theme, as Henry Fleming wages his own private battle on the road to maturity. Often the theme of a novel is implied in its title and reinforced with details appearing throughout. Think of **connotations** for the word *red* (bloody, raw, inflamed) and determine what Henry's badge really represents. Note also details, such as those provided in the **flashbacks,** which highlight the romantic nature of the young initiate.

Note the development and interrelationship of characters. Henry's character is complex; some readers feel he has earned his red badge, while others consider it fraudulent. Henry, like the loud soldier, undergoes a change as the narrative progresses. Characters such as Wilson and Conklin at times operate as foils, thus adding dramatic tension. Other characters, especially the tattered man and the cheerful soldier, serve as gauges against which to measure Henry's own moral behavior.

Determine the function of setting. The battlefield is a fitting backdrop for a story of initiation, reflecting exterior conflict and chaos that underscore Henry's inner turmoil. Crane's vivid **imagery** intensifies the effect of a setting that becomes a vast, smoky, impressionistic clash of noise and color—the "sputter of musketry," "the belchings of yellow smoke," "the battle flags flying like crimson foam." Note that the locale is not outlined in detail but rather functions as a universal arena for conflict.

Pinpoint the major conflict. Determine whether the conflict is external or internal. Although the conflict in *Red Badge* is essentially an internal one, many external conflicts do appear—between characters themselves, and between individuals and the forces of nature and war. To consider this exclusively as a war story would be an inaccurate interpretation; yet the physical battlefield provides large-scale conflict that mirrors Henry's own private war.

Put events in the proper sequence. Note the order of events and the effect one action has on a later one. In a story with frequent flashbacks, recognize what certain details, presented out of chronological order, contribute to the background. Although the story begins after Henry has enlisted, the narrative backtracks to explain what motivated his rash decision.

Appreciate the author's style. Every storyteller puts a personal stamp on a narrative. Crane's style is full of imagery, and he "paints" his scenes in broad, colorful strokes, filtering pictures through Henry's eyes. His choice of a third-person omniscient narrator suits his impressionistic style, lending a sense of on-the-scene immediacy to his story. Thus perceptions are those of a terror-stricken youngster: "The dragons were coming with invincible strides. The army, helpless in the matted thickets and blinded by the overhanging night, was going to be swallowed."

Other techniques that distinguish Crane's style are his frequent use of flashback, his choice of highly connotative words (wound, friend, flag, manhood, blood), and his effective use of dialect. In the opening paragraph of the novel and throughout, Crane uses **sound devices** and **figurative language** to establish a **mood.** All these techniques contribute to Crane's naturalistic portrayal of a universe that is indifferent to human fate. Such a portrayal depicts the soldiers as "Methodical idiots! Machinelike fools" driven by "War, the red animal, the blood-swollen god."

The Red Badge of Courage

Stephen Crane

An Episode of the American Civil War

CHAPTER 1

he cold passed reluctantly from the earth, and the retiring fogs revealed an army stretched out on the hills, resting. As the landscape changed from brown to green, the army awakened, and began to tremble with eagerness at the noise of rumors. It cast its eyes upon the roads, which were growing from long troughs of liquid mud to proper thoroughfares. A river, amber-tinted in the shadow of its banks, purled at the army's feet; and at night, when the stream had become of a sorrowful blackness, one could see across it the red, eyelike gleam of hostile campfires set in the low brows of distant hills.

Once a certain tall soldier developed virtues and went resolutely to wash a shirt. He came flying back from a brook waving his garment bannerlike. He was swelled with a tale he had heard from a reliable friend, who had heard it from a truthful cavalryman, who had heard it from his trustworthy brother, one of the orderlies at division headquarters. He adopted the important air of a herald in red and gold.

"We're goin' t' move t'-morrah—sure," he said pompously to a group in the company street. "We're goin' 'way up the river, cut across, an' come around in behint 'em."

To his attentive audience he drew a loud and elaborate plan of a very brilliant campaign. When he had finished, the blue-clothed men scattered into small arguing groups between the rows of squat brown huts. A negro teamster who had been dancing upon a cracker box with the hilarious encouragement of two score soldiers was deserted. He sat mournfully down. Smoke drifted lazily from a multitude of quaint chimneys.

"It's a lie! That's all it is—a thunderin' lie!" said another private loudly. His smooth face was flushed, and his hands were thrust sulkily into his trousers' pockets. He took the matter as an affront to him. "I don't believe the derned old army's ever going to move. We're set. I've got ready to move eight times in the last two weeks, and we ain't moved yet."

The tall soldier felt called upon to defend the truth of a rumor he himself had introduced. He and the loud one came near to fighting over it.

A corporal began to swear before the assemblage. He had just put a costly board floor in his house, he said. During the early spring he had refrained from adding extensively to the comfort of his environment because he had felt that the army might start on the march at any moment. Of late, however, he had been impressed that they were in a sort of eternal camp.

Many of the men engaged in a spirited debate. One outlined in a peculiarly lucid manner all the plans of the commanding general. He was opposed by men who advocated that there were other plans of campaign. They clamored at each other, numbers making futile bids for the popular attention. Meanwhile, the soldier who had fetched the rumor bustled about with much importance. He was continually assailed by questions.

"What's up, Jim?"

"Th' army's goin' t' move."

"Ah, what yeh talkin' about? How yeh know it is?"

"Well, yeh kin b'lieve me er not, jest as yeh like. I don't care a hang."

There was much food for thought in the manner in which he replied. He came near to convincing

wood
and
mud
chimneys

camp
life

young
Fleming

mobile
command
post

them by disdaining to produce proofs. They grew much excited over it.

There was a youthful private who listened with eager ears to the words of the tall soldier and to the varied comments of his comrades. After receiving a fill of discussions concerning marches and attacks, he went to his hut and crawled through an intricate hole that served it as a door. He wished to be alone with some new thoughts that had lately come to him.

He lay down on a wide bunk that stretched across the end of the room. In the other end, cracker boxes were made to serve as furniture. They were grouped about the fireplace. A picture from an illustrated weekly was upon the log walls, and three rifles were paralleled on pegs. Equipments hung on handy projections, and some tin dishes lay upon a small pile of firewood. A folded tent was serving as a roof. The sunlight, without, beating upon it, made it glow a light yellow shade. A small window shot an oblique square of whiter light upon the cluttered floor. The smoke from the fire at times neglected the clay chimney and wreathed into the room, and this flimsy chimney of clay and sticks made endless threats to set ablaze the whole establishment.

The youth was in a little trance of astonishment. So they were at last going to fight. On the morrow, perhaps, there would be a battle, and he would be in it. For a time he was obliged to labor to make himself believe. He could not accept with assurance an omen that he was about to mingle in one of those great affairs of the earth.

He had, of course, dreamed of battles all his life—of vague and bloody conflicts that had thrilled him with their sweep and fire. In visions he had seen himself in many struggles. He had imagined peoples secure in the shadow of his eagle-eyed prowess. But awake he had regarded battles as crimson blotches on the pages of the past. He had put them as things on the bygone with his thought-images of heavy crowns and high castles. There was a portion of the world's history which he had regarded as the time of wars, but it, he thought, had been long gone over the horizon and had disappeared forever.

From his home his youthful eyes had looked upon the war in his own country with distrust. It must be some sort of a play affair. He had long despaired of witnessing a Greeklike struggle. Such would be no more, he had said. Men were better, or more timid. Secular and religious education had effaced the throat-grappling instinct, or else firm finance held in check the passions.

He had burned several times to enlist. Tales of great movements shook the land. They might not be distinctly Homeric, but there seemed to be much glory in them. He had read of marches, sieges, conflicts, and he had longed to see it all. His busy mind had drawn for him large pictures extravagant in color, lurid with breathless deeds.

But his mother had discouraged him. She had affected to look with some contempt upon the quality of his war ardor and patriotism. She could calmly seat herself and with no apparent difficulty give him many hundreds of reasons why he was of vastly more importance on the farm than on the field of battle. She had had certain ways of expression that told him that her statements on the subject came from a deep conviction. Moreover, on her side, was his belief that her ethical motive in the argument was impregnable.

At last, however, he had made firm rebellion against this yellow light thrown upon the color of his ambitions. The newspapers, the gossip of the village, his own picturings, had aroused him to an uncheckable degree. They were in truth fighting finely down there. Almost every day the newspapers printed accounts of a decisive victory.

One night, as he lay in bed, the winds had carried to him the clangoring of the church bell as some enthusiast jerked the rope frantically to tell the twisted news of a great battle. This voice of the people rejoicing in the night had made him shiver in a prolonged ecstasy of excitement. Later, he had gone down to his mother's room and

A recruiting poster calling for volunteers from New York

had spoken thus: "Ma, I'm going to enlist."

"Henry, don't you be a fool," his mother had replied. She had then covered her face with the quilt. There was an end to the matter for that night.

Nevertheless, the next morning he had gone to a town that was near his mother's farm and had enlisted in a company that was forming there. When he had returned home, his mother was milking the brindle cow. Four others stood waiting. "Ma, I've enlisted," he had said to her diffidently. There was a short silence. "The Lord's will be done, Henry," she had finally replied, and had then continued to milk the brindle cow.

When he had stood in the doorway with his

soldier's clothes on his back, and with the light of excitement and expectancy in his eyes almost defeating the glow of regret for the home bonds, he had seen two tears leaving their trails on his mother's scarred cheeks.

Still, she had disappointed him by saying nothing whatever about returning with his shield or on it. He had privately primed himself for a beautiful scene. He had prepared certain sentences which he thought could be used with touching effect. But her words destroyed his plans. She had doggedly peeled potatoes and addressed him as follows: "You watch out, Henry, an' take good care of yerself in this here fighting business—you watch out, an' take good care of yerself. Don't go a-thinkin' you can lick the hull rebel army at the start, because yeh can't. Yer jest one little feller amongst a hull lot of others, and yeh've got to keep quiet an' do what they tell yeh. I know how you are, Henry.

"I've knet yeh eight pair of socks, Henry, and I've put in all yer best shirts, because I want my boy to be jest as warm and comf'able as anybody in the army. Whenever they get holes in 'em, I want yeh to send 'em rightaway back to me, so's I kin dern 'em.

"An' allus be careful an' choose yer comp'ny. There's lots of bad men in the army, Henry. The army makes 'em wild, and they like nothing better than the job of leading off a young feller like you, as ain't never been away from home much and has allus had a mother, an' a-learning 'em to drink and swear. Keep clear of them folks, Henry. I don't want yeh to ever do anything, Henry, that yeh would be 'shamed to let me know about. Jest think as if I was a'watchin' yeh. If yeh keep that in yer mind allus, I guess yeh'll come out about right.

"Yeh must allus remember yer father, too, child, an' remember he never drunk a drop of licker in his life, and seldom swore a cross oath.

"I don't know what else to tell yeh, Henry, excepting that yeh must never do no shirking, child, on my account. If so be a time comes when yeh have to be kilt or do a mean thing, why, Henry, don't think of anything 'cept what's right, because there's many a woman has to bear up 'ginst sech things these times, and the Lord'll take keer of us all. Don't fergit about the socks and the shirts, child; and I've put a cup of blackberry jam with yer bundle, because I knew yeh like it above

all things. Good-by, Henry. Watch out, and be a good boy."

He had, of course, been impatient under the ordeal of this speech. It had not been quite what he expected, and he had borne it with an air of irritation. He departed feeling vague relief.

Still, when he had looked back from the gate, he had seen his mother kneeling among the potato parings. Her brown face, upraised, was stained with tears, and her spare form was quivering. He bowed his head and went on, feeling suddenly ashamed of his purposes.

From his home he had gone to the seminary to bid adieu to many schoolmates. They had thronged about him with wonder and admiration. He had felt the gulf now between them and had swelled with calm pride. He and some of his fellows who had donned blue were quite overwhelmed with privileges for all of one afternoon, and it had been a very delicious thing. They had strutted.

A certain light-haired girl had made vivacious fun at his martial spirit, but there was another and darker girl whom he had gazed at steadfastly, and he thought she grew demure and sad at sight of his blue and brass. As he had walked down the path between the rows of oaks, he had turned his head and detected her at a window watching his departure. As he perceived her, she had immediately begun to stare up through the high tree branches at the sky. He had seen a good deal of flurry and haste in her movement as she changed her attitude. He often thought of it.

On the way to Washington his spirit had soared. The regiment was fed and caressed at station after station until the youth had believed that he must be a hero. There was a lavish expenditure of bread and cold meats, coffee, and pickles and cheese. As he basked in the smiles of the girls and was patted and complimented by the old men, he had felt growing within him the strength to do mighty deeds of arms.

After complicated journeyings with many pauses, there had come months of monotonous life in a camp. He had had the belief that real war was a series of death struggles with small time in between for sleep and meals; but since his regiment had come to the field, the army had done little but sit still and try to keep warm.

He was brought then gradually back to his

old ideas. Greeklike struggles would be no more. Men were better, or more timid. Secular and religious education had effaced the throat-grappling instinct, or else firm finance held in check the passions.

He had grown to regard himself merely as a part of a vast blue demonstration. His province was to look out, as far as he could, for his personal comfort. For recreation he could twiddle his thumbs and speculate on the thoughts which must agitate the minds of the generals. Also, he was drilled and drilled and reviewed, and drilled and drilled and reviewed.

The only foes he had seen were some pickets along the riverbank. They were a suntanned, philosophical lot, who sometimes shot reflectively at the blue pickets. When reproached for this afterward, they usually expressed sorrow, and swore by their gods that the guns had exploded without their permission. The youth, on guard duty one night, conversed across the stream with one of them. He was a slightly ragged man, who spat skillfully between his shoes and possessed a great fund of bland and infantile assurance. The youth liked him personally.

"Yank," the other had informed him, "yer a right dum good feller." This sentiment, floating to him upon the still air, had made him temporarily regret war.

Various veterans had told him tales. Some talked of gray, bewhiskered hordes who were advancing with relentless curses and chewing tobacco with unspeakable valor; tremendous bodies of fierce soldiery who were sweeping along like the Huns. Others spoke of tattered and eternally hungry men who fired despondent powders. "They'll charge through hell's fire an' brimstone t' git a holt on a haversack, an' sech stomachs ain't a-lastin' long," he was told. From the stories, the youth imagined the red, live bones sticking out through slits in the faded uniforms.

Still, he could not put a whole faith in veterans' tales, for recruits were their prey. They talked much of smoke, fire, and blood, but he could not tell how much might be lies. They persistently yelled, "Fresh fish!" at him, and were in no wise to be trusted.

However, he perceived now that it did not greatly matter what kind of soldiers he was going to fight, so long as they fought, which fact no one disputed. There was a more serious problem. He lay in his bunk pondering upon it. He tried to mathematically prove to himself that he would not run from a battle.

Previously he had never felt obliged to wrestle too seriously with this question. In his life he had taken certain things for granted, never challenging his belief in ultimate success, and bothering little about means and roads. But here he was confronted with a thing of moment. It had suddenly appeared to him that perhaps in a battle he might run. He was forced to admit that as far as war was concerned he knew nothing of himself.

A sufficient time before he would have allowed the problem to kick its heels at the outer portals of his mind, but now he felt compelled to give serious attention to it.

A little panic-fear grew in his mind. As his imagination went forward to a fight, he saw hideous possibilities. He contemplated the lurking menaces of the future, and failed in an effort to see himself standing stoutly in the midst of them. He recalled his visions of broken-bladed glory, but in the shadow of the impending tumult he suspected them to be impossible pictures.

He sprang from the bunk and began to pace nervously to and fro. "Good Lord, what's th' matter with me?" he said aloud.

He felt that in this crisis his laws of life were useless. Whatever he had learned of himself was here of no avail. He was an unknown quantity. He saw that he would again be obliged to experiment as he had in early youth. He must accumulate information of himself, and meanwhile he resolved to remain close upon his guard lest those qualities of which he knew nothing should everlastingly disgrace him. "Good Lord!" he repeated in dismay.

After a time the tall soldier slid dexterously through the hole. The loud private followed. They were wrangling.

"That's all right," said the tall soldier as he entered. He waved his hand expressively. "You can believe me or not, jest as you like. All you got to do is to sit down and wait as quiet as you can. Then pretty soon you'll find out I was right."

His comrade grunted stubbornly. For a moment he seemed to be searching for a formidable reply. Finally he said: "Well, you don't know everything in the world, do you?"

"Didn't say I knew everything in the world,"

retorted the other sharply. He began to stow various articles snugly into his knapsack.

The youth, pausing in his nervous walk, looked down at the busy figure. "Going to be a battle, sure, is there, Jim?" he asked.

"Of course, there is," replied the tall soldier. "Of course, there is. You jest wait 'til tomorrow, and you'll see one of the biggest battles ever was. You jest wait."

"Thunder!" said the youth.

"Oh, you'll see fighting this time, my boy, what'll be regular out-and-out fighting," added the tall soldier, with the air of a man who is about to exhibit a battle for the benefit of his friends.

"Huh!" said the loud one from a corner.

"Well," remarked the youth, "like as not this story'll turn out jest like them others did."

"Not much it won't," replied the tall soldier, exasperated. "Not much it won't. Didn't the cavalry all start this morning?" He glared about him. No one denied his statement. "The cavalry started this morning," he continued. "They say there ain't hardly any cavalry left in camp. They're going to Richmond, or some place, while we fight all the Johnnies. It's some dodge like that. The regiment's got orders, too. A feller what seen 'em go to headquarters told me a little while ago. And they're raising blazes all over camp—anybody can see that."

"Shucks!" said the loud one.

The youth remained silent for a time. At last he spoke to the tall soldier. "Jim!"

"What?"

"How do you think the reg'ment 'll do?"

"Oh, they'll fight all right, I guess, after they once get into it," said the other with cold judgment. He made a fine use of the third person. "There's been heaps of fun poked at 'em because they're new, of course, and all that; but they'll fight all right, I guess."

"Think any of the boys 'll run?" persisted the youth.

"Oh, there may be a few of 'em run, but there's them kind in every regiment, 'specially when they first goes under fire," said the other in a tolerant way. "Of course it might happen that the hull kit-and-boodle might start and run, if some big fighting came first-off, and then again they might stay and fight like fun. But you can't bet on nothing. Of course they ain't never been under fire yet, and

it ain't likely they'll lick the hull rebel army all-to-oncet the first time; but I think they'll fight better than some, if worse than others. That's the way I figger. They call the reg'ment 'Fresh fish' and everything; but the boys come of good stock, and most of 'em 'll fight like sin after they oncet git shootin'." he added, with a mighty emphasis on the last four words.

"Oh, you think you know—" began the loud soldier with scorn.

The other turned savagely upon him. They had a rapid altercation, in which they fastened upon each other various strange epithets.

The youth at last interrupted them. "Did you ever think you might run yourself, Jim?" he asked. On concluding the sentence he laughed as if he had meant to aim a joke. The loud soldier also giggled.

The tall private waved his hand. "Well," said he profoundly, "I've thought it might get too hot for Jim Conklin in some of them scrimmages, and if a whole lot of boys started and run, why, I s'pose I'd start and run. And if I once started to run, I'd run like the devil, and no mistake. But if everybody was a-standing and a-fighting, why, I'd stand and fight. Be jiminey, I would. I'll bet on it."

"Huh!" said the loud one.

The youth of this tale felt gratitude for these words of his comrade. He had feared that all of the untried men possessed a great and correct confidence. He now was in a measure reassured.

CHAPTER 2

The next morning the youth discovered that his tall comrade had been the fast-flying messenger of a mistake. There was much scoffing at the latter by those who had yesterday been firm adherents of his views, and there was even a little sneering by men who had never believed the rumor. The tall one fought with a man from Chatfield Corners[1] and beat him severely.

The youth felt, however, that his problem was

---

1. **Chatfield Corners**, probably a fictional town.

in nowise lifted from him. There was, on the contrary, an irritating prolongation. The tale had created in him a great concern for himself. Now, with the newborn question in his mind, he was compelled to sink back into his old place as part of a blue demonstration.

For days he made ceaseless calculations, but they were all wondrously unsatisfactory. He found that he could establish nothing. He finally concluded that the only way to prove himself was to go into the blaze, and then figuratively to watch his legs to discover their merits and faults. He reluctantly admitted that he could not sit still and with a mental slate and pencil derive an answer. To gain it, he must have blaze, blood, and danger, even as a chemist requires this, that, and the other. So he fretted for an opportunity.

Meanwhile he continually tried to measure himself by his comrades. The tall soldier, for one, gave him some assurance. This man's serene unconcern dealt him a measure of confidence, for he had known him since childhood, and from his intimate knowledge he did not see how he could be capable of anything that was beyond him, the youth. Still, he thought that his comrade might be mistaken about himself. Or, on the other hand, he might be a man heretofore doomed to peace and obscurity, but, in reality, made to shine in war.

The youth would have liked to have discovered another who suspected himself. A sympathetic comparison of mental notes would have been a joy to him.

He occasionally tried to fathom a comrade with seductive sentences. He looked about to find men in the proper mood. All attempts failed to bring forth any statement which looked in any way like a confession to those doubts which he privately acknowledged in himself. He was afraid to make an open declaration of his concern, because he dreaded to place some unscrupulous confidant upon the high plane of the unconfessed from which elevation he could be derided.

In regard to his companions his mind wavered between two opinions, according to his mood. Sometimes he inclined to believing them all heroes. In fact, he usually admitted in secret the superior development of the higher qualities in others. He could conceive of men going very insignificantly about the world bearing a load of courage unseen, and, although he had known many of his comrades through boyhood, he began to fear that his judgment of them had been blind. Then, in other moments, he flouted these theories, and assured himself that his fellows were all privately wondering and quaking.

His emotions made him feel strange in the presence of men who talked excitedly of a prospective battle as of a drama they were about to witness, with nothing but eagerness and curiosity apparent in their faces. It was often that he suspected them to be liars.

He did not pass such thoughts without severe condemnation of himself. He dinned reproaches at times. He was convicted by himself of many shameful crimes against the gods of traditions.

In his great anxiety his heart was continually clamoring at what he considered the intolerable slowness of the generals. They seemed content to perch tranquilly on the riverbank, and leave him bowed down by the weight of a great problem. He wanted it settled forthwith. He could not long bear such a load, he said. Sometimes his anger at the commanders reached an acute stage, and he grumbled about the camp like a veteran.

One morning, however, he found himself in the ranks of his prepared regiment. The men were whispering speculations and recounting the old rumors. In the gloom before the break of the day their uniforms glowed a deep purple hue. From across the river the red eyes were still peering. In the eastern sky there was a yellow patch like a rug laid for the feet of the coming sun; and against it, black and patternlike, loomed the gigantic figure of the colonel on a gigantic horse.

From off in the darkness came the trampling of feet. The youth could occasionally see dark shadows that moved like monsters. The regiment stood at rest for what seemed a long time. The youth grew impatient. It was unendurable the way these affairs were managed. He wondered how long they were to be kept waiting. As he looked all about him and pondered upon the mystic gloom, he began to believe that at any moment the ominous distance might be aflare, and the rolling crashes of an engagement come to his ears. Staring once at the red eyes across the river, he conceived them to be growing larger, as the orbs of a row of dragons advancing. He turned toward the colonel and saw him lift his gigantic arm and calmly stroke his mustache.

At last he heard from along the road at the foot of the hill the clatter of a horse's galloping hoofs. It must be the coming of orders. He bent forward, scarce breathing. The exciting clickety-click, as it grew louder and louder, seemed to be beating upon his soul. Presently a horseman with jangling equipment drew rein before the colonel of the regiment. The two held a short, sharp-worded conversation. The men in the foremost ranks craned their necks.

As the horseman wheeled his animal and galloped away, he turned to shout over his shoulder, "Don't forget that box of cigars!" The colonel mumbled in reply. The youth wondered what a box of cigars had to do with war.

A moment later the regiment went swinging off into the darkness. It was now like one of those moving monsters wending with many feet. The air was heavy, and cold with dew. A mass of wet grass, marched upon, rustled like silk.

There was an occasional flash and glimmer of steel from the backs of all these huge crawling reptiles. From the road came creakings and grumblings as some surly guns were dragged away.

The men stumbled along still muttering speculations. There was a subdued debate. Once a man fell down, and as he reached for his rifle, a comrade, unseeing, trod upon his hand. He of the injured fingers swore bitterly and aloud. A low, tittering laugh went among his fellows.

Presently they passed into a roadway and marched forward with easy strides. A dark regiment moved before them, and from behind also came the tinkle of equipments on the bodies of marching men.

The rushing yellow of the developing day went on behind their backs. When the sun rays at last struck full and mellowingly upon the earth, the youth saw that the landscape was streaked with two long, thin, black columns which disappeared on the brow of a hill in front and rearward vanished in a wood. They were like two serpents crawling from the cavern of the night.

The river was not in view. The tall soldier burst into praises of what he thought to be his powers of perception.

Some of the tall one's companions cried with emphasis that they, too, had evolved the same thing, and they congratulated themselves upon it. But there were others who said that the tall one's plan was not the true one at all. They persisted with other theories. There was a vigorous discussion.

The youth took no part in them. As he walked along in careless line, he was engaged with his own eternal debate. He could not hinder himself from dwelling upon it. He was despondent and sullen, and threw shifting glances about him. He looked ahead, often expecting to hear from the advance the rattle of firing.

But the long serpents crawled slowly from hill to hill without bluster of smoke. A dun-colored cloud of dust floated away to the right. The sky overhead was of a fairy blue.

The youth studied the faces of his companions, ever on the watch to detect kindred emotions. He suffered disappointment. Some ardor of the air which was causing the veteran commands to move with glee—almost with song—had infected the new regiment. The men began to speak of victory as of a thing they knew. Also, the tall soldier received his vindication. They were certainly going to come around in behind the enemy. They expressed commiseration for that part of the army which had been left upon the riverbank, felicitating themselves upon being a part of a blasting host.

The youth, considering himself as separated from the others, was saddened by the blithe and merry speeches that went from rank to rank. The company wags all made their best endeavors. The regiment tramped to the tune of laughter.

The blatant soldier often convulsed whole files by his biting sarcasms aimed at the tall one.

And it was not long before all the men seemed to forget their mission. Whole brigades grinned in unison, and regiments laughed.

A rather fat soldier attempted to pilfer a horse from a dooryard. He planned to load his knapsack upon it. He was escaping with his prize when a young girl rushed from the house and grabbed the animal's mane. There followed a wrangle. The young girl, with pink cheeks and shining eyes, stood like a dauntless statue.

The observant regiment, standing at rest in the roadway, whooped at once, and entered wholesouled upon the side of the maiden. The men became so engrossed in this affair that they entirely ceased to remember their own large war. They jeered the piratical private, and called attention to various defects in his personal appearance; and they were wildly enthusiastic in support of the young girl.

To her, from some distance, came bold advice. "Hit him with a stick."

There were crows and catcalls showered upon him when he retreated without the horse. The regiment rejoiced at his downfall. Loud and vociferous congratulations were showered upon the maiden, who stood panting and regarding the troops with defiance.

At nightfall the column broke into regimental pieces, and the fragments went into the fields to camp. Tents sprang up like strange plants. Campfires, like red, peculiar blossoms, dotted the night.

The youth kept from his companions as much as circumstances would allow him. In the evening he wandered a few paces into the gloom. From this little distance the many fires, with the black forms of men passing to and fro before the crimson rays, made weird and satanic effects.

He lay down in the grass. The blades pressed tenderly against his cheek. The moon had been lighted and was hung in a treetop. The liquid stillness of the night enveloping him made him feel vast pity for himself. There was a caress in the soft winds; and the whole mood of the darkness, he thought, was one of sympathy for himself in his distress.

He wished, without reserve, that he was at home again making the endless rounds from the house to the barn, from the barn to the fields, from the fields to the barn, from the barn to the house. He remembered he had often cursed the brindle cow and her mates, and had sometimes flung milking stools. But, from his present point of view, there was a halo of happiness about each of their heads, and he would have sacrificed all the brass buttons on the continent to have been enabled to return to them. He told himself that he was not formed for a soldier. And he mused seriously upon the radical differences between himself and those men who were dodging implike around the fires.

As he mused thus, he heard the rustle of grass, and, upon turning his head, discovered the loud soldier. He called out, "Oh, Wilson!"

The latter approached and looked down. "Why, hello, Henry; is it you? What you doing here?"

"Oh, thinking," said the youth.

The other sat down and carefully lighted his pipe. "You're getting blue, my boy. You're looking thundering peeked. What the dickens is wrong with you?"

"Oh, nothing," said the youth.

The loud soldier launched then into the subject of the anticipated fight. "Oh, we've got 'em now!" As he spoke, his boyish face was wreathed in a gleeful smile, and his voice had an exultant ring. "We've got 'em now. At last, by the eternal thunders, we'll lick 'em good!"

"If the truth was known," he added, more soberly, "*they've* licked *us* about every clip up to now; but this time—this time—we'll lick 'em good!"

"I thought you was objecting to this march a little while ago," said the youth coldly.

"Oh, it wasn't that," explained the other. "I don't mind marching, if there's going to be fighting at the end of it. What I hate is this getting moved here and moved there; with no good coming of it, as far as I can see, excepting sore feet and short rations."

"Well, Jim Conklin says we'll get a plenty of fighting this time."

"He's right for once, I guess, though I can't see how it come. This time we're in for a big battle, and we've got the best end of it, certain sure. Gee rod! How we will thump 'em!"

He arose and began to pace to and fro excitedly. The thrill of his enthusiasm made him walk with an elastic step. He was sprightly, vigorous, fiery in his belief in success. He looked into the future with clear, proud eye, and he swore with the air of an old soldier.

The youth watched him for a moment in silence. When he finally spoke, his voice was as bitter as dregs. "Oh, you're going to do great things, I s'pose!"

The loud soldier blew a thoughtful cloud of smoke from his pipe. "Oh, I don't know," he remarked with dignity; "I don't know. I s'pose I'll do as well as the rest. I'm going to try like thunder." He evidently complimented himself upon the modesty of this statement.

"How do you know you won't run when the time comes?" asked the youth.

"Run?" said the loud one; "run?—of course not!" He laughed.

"Well," continued the youth, "lots of good-a-'nough men have thought they was going to do great things before the fight, but when the time come they skedaddled."

"Oh, that's all true, I s'pose," replied the other; "but I'm not going to skedaddle. The man that bets on my running will lose his money, that's all." He nodded confidently.

"Oh, shucks!" said the youth. "You ain't the bravest man in the world, are you?"

"No, I ain't," exclaimed the loud soldier indignantly; "and I didn't say I was the bravest man in the world, neither. I said I was going to do my share of fighting—that's what I said. And I am, too. Who are you, anyhow? You talk as if you thought you was Napoleon Bonaparte."[2] He glared at the youth for a moment, and then strode away.

The youth called in a savage voice after his comrade: "Well, you needn't git mad about it!" But the other continued on his way and made no reply.

He felt alone in space when his injured comrade had disappeared. His failure to discover any mite of resemblance in their viewpoints made him more miserable than before. No one seemed to be wrestling with such a terrific personal problem. He was a mental outcast.

He went slowly to his tent and stretched himself on a blanket by the side of the snoring tall soldier. In the darkness he saw visions of a thousand-tongued fear that would babble at his back and cause him to flee, while others were going coolly about their country's business. He admitted that he would not be able to cope with this monster. He felt that every nerve in his body would be an ear to hear the voices, while other men would remain stolid and deaf.

And as he sweated with the pain of these thoughts, he could hear low, serene sentences. "I'll bid five." "Make it six." "Seven." "Seven goes."

He stared at the red, shivering reflection of a fire on the white wall of his tent until, exhausted and ill from the monotony of his suffering, he fell asleep.

CHAPTER 3

When another night came, the columns, changed to purple streaks, filed across two pontoon bridges. A glaring fire wine-tinted the waters of the river. Its rays, shining upon the moving masses of troops, brought forth here and there sudden gleams of silver or gold. Upon the other shore a dark and mysterious range of hills was curved against the sky. The insect voices of the night sang solemnly.

After this crossing the youth assured himself that at any moment they might be suddenly and fearfully assaulted from the caves of the lowering woods. He kept his eyes watchfully upon the darkness.

But his regiment went unmolested to a camping place, and its soldiers slept the brave sleep of wearied men. In the morning they were routed out with early energy, and hustled along a narrow road that led deep into the forest.

It was during this rapid march that the regiment lost many of the marks of a new command.

The men had begun to count the miles upon their fingers, and they grew tired. "Sore feet an' short rations, that's all," said the loud soldier. There was perspiration and grumblings. After a time they began to shed their knapsacks. Some tossed them unconcernedly down; others hid them carefully, asserting their plans to return for them at some convenient time. Men extricated themselves from thick shirts. Presently few carried anything but their necessary clothing, blankets, haversacks, canteens, and arms and ammunition. There was sudden change from the ponderous infantry of theory to the light and speedy infantry of practice. The regiment, relieved of a burden, received a new impetus. But there was much loss of valuable knapsacks, and, on the whole, very good shirts.

But the regiment was not yet veteranlike in appearance. Veteran regiments in the army were

---

2. **Napoleon Bonaparte** (bō′nə pärt), French general and emperor of France from 1804 to 1815.

likely to be very small aggregations of men. Once, when the command had first come to the field, some perambulating veterans, noting the length of their column, had accosted them thus: "Hey, fellers, what brigade is that?" And when the men had replied that they formed a regiment and not a brigade, the older soldiers had laughed.

Also, there was too great a similarity in the hats. The hats of a regiment should properly represent the history of headgear for a period of years. And, moreover, there were no letters of faded gold speaking from the colors. They were new and beautiful, and the color bearer habitually oiled the pole.[1]

Presently the army again sat down to think. The odor of the peaceful pines was in the men's nostrils. The sound of monotonous ax blows rang through the forest, and the insects, nodding upon their perches, crooned like old women. The youth returned to his theory of a blue demonstration.

One gray dawn, however, he was kicked in the leg by the tall soldier, and then, before he was entirely awake, he found himself running down a wood road in the midst of men who were panting from the first effects of speed. His canteen banged rhythmically upon his thigh, and his haversack bobbed softly. His musket bounced a trifle from his shoulder at each stride and made his cap feel uncertain upon his head.

He could hear the men whisper jerky sentences: "Say—what's all this—about?" "What th' thunder—we—skedaddlin' this way fer?" "Billie—keep off m' feet. Yeh run—like a cow." And the loud soldier's shrill voice could be heard: "What th' devil they in sich a hurry for?"

The youth thought the damp fog of early morning moved from the rush of a great body of troops. From the distance came a sudden spatter of firing.

He was bewildered. As he ran with his comrades, he strenuously tried to think, but all he knew was that if he fell down, those coming behind would tread upon him. All his faculties seemed to be needed to guide him over and past obstructions. He felt carried along by a mob.

The sun spread disclosing rays, and, one by one, regiments burst into view like armed men just born of the earth. The youth perceived that the time had come. He was about to be measured. For a moment he felt in the face of his great trial like a babe, and the flesh over his heart seemed very thin.

He seized time to look about him calculatingly.

But he instantly saw that it would be impossible for him to escape from the regiment. It inclosed him. And there were iron laws of tradition and law on four sides. He was in a moving box.

As he perceived this fact, it occurred to him that he had never wished to come to the war. He had not enlisted of his free will. He had been dragged by the merciless government. And now they were taking him out to be slaughtered.

The regiment slid down a bank and wallowed across a little stream. The mournful current moved slowly on, and from the water, shaded black, some white bubble eyes looked at the men.

As they climbed the hill, on the farther side artillery began to boom. Here the youth forgot many things as he felt a sudden impulse of curiosity. He scrambled up the bank with a speed that could not be exceeded by a bloodthirsty man.

He expected a battle scene.

There were some little fields girted and squeezed by a forest. Spread over the grass and in among the tree trunks, he could see knots and waving lines of skirmishers who were running hither and thither and firing at the landscape. A dark battle line lay upon a sunstruck clearing that gleamed orange color. A flag fluttered.

Other regiments floundered up the bank. The brigade was formed in line of battle, and after a pause started slowly through the woods in the rear of the receding skirmishers, who were continually melting into the scene to appear again farther on. They were always busy as bees, deeply absorbed in their little combats.

The youth tried to observe everything. He did not use care to avoid trees and branches, and his forgotten feet were constantly knocking against stones or getting entangled in briers. He was aware that these battalions with their commotions were woven red and startling into the gentle fabric of softened greens and browns. It looked to be a wrong place for a battlefield.

The skirmishers in advance fascinated him. Their shots into thickets and at distant and prominent trees spoke to him of tragedies—hidden, mysterious, solemn.

---

1. *oiled the pole.* The color bearer who carried the flag may have polished the pole to preserve the wood and enhance the general appearance or to prevent splinters.

Once the line encountered the body of a dead soldier. He lay upon his back staring at the sky. He was dressed in an awkward suit of yellowish brown. The youth could see that the soles of his shoes had been worn to the thinness of writing paper, and from a great rent in one the dead foot projected piteously. And it was as if fate had betrayed the soldier. In death it exposed to his enemies that poverty which in life he had perhaps concealed from his friends.

The ranks opened covertly to avoid the corpse. The invulnerable dead man forced a way for himself. The youth looked keenly at the ashen face. The wind raised the tawny beard. It moved as if a hand were stroking it. He vaguely desired to walk around and around the body and stare; the impulse of the living to try to read in dead eyes the answer to the Question.

During the march the ardor which the youth had acquired when out of view of the field rapidly faded to nothing. His curiosity was quite easily satisfied. If an intense scene had caught him with its wild swing as he came to the top of the bank, he might have gone roaring on. This advance upon Nature was too calm. He had opportunity to reflect. He had time in which to wonder about himself and to attempt to probe his sensations.

Absurd ideas took hold upon him. He thought that he did not relish the landscape. It threatened him. A coldness swept over his back, and it is true that his trousers felt to him that they were no fit for his legs at all.

A house standing placidly in distant fields had to him an ominous look. The shadows of the woods were formidable. He was certain that in this vista there lurked fierce-eyed hosts. The swift thought came to him that the generals did not know what they were about. It was all a trap. Suddenly those close forests would bristle with rifle barrels. Ironlike brigades would appear in the rear. They were all going to be sacrificed. The generals were stupids. The enemy would presently swallow the whole command. He glared about him, expecting to see the stealthy approach of his death.

He thought that he must break from the ranks and harangue his comrades. They must not all be killed like pigs; and he was sure it would come to pass unless they were informed of these dangers. The generals were idiots to send them marching into a regular pen. There was but one pair of eyes in the corps. He would step forth and make a speech. Shrill and passionate words came to his lips.

The line, broken into moving fragments by the ground, went calmly on through fields and woods. The youth looked at the men nearest him, and saw, for the most part, expressions of deep interest, as if they were investigating something that had fascinated them. One or two stepped with overvaliant airs as if they were already plunged into war. Others walked as upon thin ice. The greater part of the untested men appeared quiet and absorbed. They were going to look at war, the red animal—war, the blood-swollen god. And they were deeply engrossed in this march.

As he looked, the youth gripped his outcry at his throat. He saw that even if the men were tottering with fear, they would laugh at his warning. They would jeer him, and, if practicable, pelt him with missiles. Admitting that he might be wrong, a frenzied declamation of the kind would turn him into a worm.

He assumed, then, the demeanor of one who knows that he is doomed alone to unwritten responsibilities. He lagged, with tragic glances at the sky.

He was surprised presently by the young lieutenant of his company, who began heartily to beat him with a sword, calling out in a loud and insolent voice: "Come, young man, get up into ranks there. No skulking 'll do here." He mended his pace with suitable haste. And he hated the lieutenant, who had no appreciation of fine minds. He was a mere brute.

After a time the brigade was halted in the cathedral light of a forest. The busy skirmishers were still popping. Through the aisles of the wood could be seen the floating smoke from their rifles. Sometimes it went up in little balls, white and compact.

During this halt many men in the regiment began erecting tiny hills in front of them. They used stones, sticks, earth and anything they thought might turn a bullet. Some built comparatively large ones, while others seemed content with little ones.

This procedure caused a discussion among the men. Some wished to fight like duelists, believing it to be correct to stand erect and be, from their feet to their foreheads, a mark. They said they scorned the devices of the cautious. But the others scoffed in reply, and pointed to the veterans on the flanks who were digging at the ground like terriers. In a short time there was quite a barricade along the regimental fronts. Directly, however, they were ordered to withdraw from that place.

This astounded the youth. He forgot his stewing over the advance movement. "Well, then, what did they march us out here for?" he demanded of the tall soldier. The latter with calm faith began a heavy explanation, although he had been compelled to leave a little protection of stones and dirt to which he had devoted much care and skill.

When the regiment was aligned in another position, each man's regard for his safety caused another line of small intrenchments. They ate their noon meal behind a third one. They were moved from this one also. They were marched from place to place with apparent aimlessness.

The youth had been taught that a man became another thing in a battle. He saw his salvation in such a change. Hence this waiting was an ordeal to him. He was in a fever of impatience. He considered that there was denoted a lack of purpose on the part of the generals. He began to complain to the tall soldier. "I can't stand this much longer," he cried. "I don't see what good it does to make us wear out our legs for nothin'." He wished to return to camp, knowing that this affair was a blue demonstration; or else to go into a battle and discover that he had been a fool in his doubts, and was, in truth, a man of traditional courage. The strain of present circumstances he felt to be intolerable.

The philosophical tall soldier measured a sandwich of cracker and pork and swallowed it in a nonchalant manner. "Oh, I suppose we must go reconnoitering around the country jest to keep 'em from getting too close, or to develop 'em, or something."

"Huh!" said the loud soldier.

"Well," cried the youth, still fidgeting, "I'd rather do anything 'most than go tramping 'round the country all day doing no good to nobody and jest tiring ourselves out."

"So would I," said the loud soldier. "It ain't right. I tell you if anybody with any sense was a-runnin' this army it——"

"Oh, shut up!" roared the tall private. "You little fool. You little cuss. You ain't had that there coat and them pants on for six months, and yet you talk as if——"

"Well, I wanta do some fighting anyway," interrupted the other. "I didn't come here to walk. I could 'ave walked to home—'round and 'round the barn, if I jest wanted to walk."

The tall one, red-faced, swallowed another sandwich as if taking poison in despair.

But gradually, as he chewed, his face became again quiet and contented. He could not rage in fierce argument in the presence of such sandwiches. During his meals he always wore an air of blissful contemplation of the food he had swallowed. His spirit seemed then to be communing with the viands.

He accepted new environment and circumstance with great coolness, eating from his haversack at every opportunity. On the march he went along with the stride of a hunter, objecting to neither gait nor distance. And he had not raised his voice when he had been ordered away from three little protective piles of earth and stone, each of which had been an engineering feat worthy of being made sacred to the name of his grandmother.

In the afternoon the regiment went out over the same ground it had taken in the morning. The landscape then ceased to threaten the youth. He had been close to it and become familiar with it.

When, however, they began to pass into a new region, his fears of stupidity and incompetence reassailed him, but this time he doggedly let them babble. He was occupied with his problem, and in his desperation he concluded that the stupidity did not greatly matter.

Once he thought he had concluded that it would be better to get killed directly and end his troubles. Regarding death thus out of the corner of his eye, he conceived it to be nothing but rest, and he was filled with a momentary astonishment that he should have made an extraordinary commotion over the mere matter of getting killed. He would die; he would go to some place where he would be understood. It was useless to expect appreciation of his profound and fine senses from such men as the lieutenant. He must look to the grave for comprehension.

The skirmish-fire increased to a long clattering sound. With it was mingled faraway cheering. A battery spoke.

Directly the youth would see the skirmishers

running. They were pursued by the sound of musketry fire. After a time the hot, dangerous flashes of the rifles were visible. Smoke clouds went slowly and insolently across the fields like observant phantoms. The din became crescendo, like the roar of an oncoming train.

A brigade ahead of them and on the right went into action with a rending roar. It was as if it had exploded. And thereafter it lay stretched in the distance behind a long gray wall, that one was obliged to look twice at to make sure that it was smoke.

The youth, forgetting his neat plan of getting killed, gazed spellbound. His eyes grew wide and busy with the action of the scene. His mouth was a little ways open.

Of a sudden he felt a heavy and sad hand laid upon his shoulder. Awakening from his trance of observation he turned and beheld the loud soldier.

"It's my first and last battle, old boy," said the latter, with intense gloom. He was quite pale and his girlish lip was trembling.

"Eh?" murmured the youth in great astonishment.

"It's my first and last battle, old boy," continued the loud soldier. "Something tells me——"

"What?"

"I'm a gone coon this first time and—and I w-want you to take these here things—to—my—folks." He ended in a quavering sob of pity for himself. He handed the youth a little packet done up in a yellow envelope.

"Why, what the devil——" began the youth again.

But the other gave him a glance as from the depths of a tomb, and raised his limp hand in a prophetic manner and turned away.

CHAPTER 4

The brigade was halted in the fringe of a grove. The men crouched among the trees and pointed their restless guns out at the fields. They tried to look beyond the smoke.

Out of this haze they could see running men. Some shouted information and gestured as they hurried.

The men of the new regiment watched and listened eagerly, while their tongues ran on in gossip of the battle. They mouthed rumors that had flown like birds out of the unknown.

"They say Perry has been driven in with big loss."

"Yes, Carrott went t' th' hospital. He said he was sick. That smart lieutenant is commanding 'G' Company. Th' boys say they won't be under Carrott no more if they all have t' desert. They allus knew he was a——"

"Hannis's batt'ry is took."

"It ain't either. I saw Hannis's batt'ry off on th' left not more 'n fifteen minutes ago."

"Well——"

"Th' general, he ses he is goin' t' take th' hull cammand of th' 304th when we go inteh action, an' then he ses we'll do sech fightin' as never another one reg'ment done."

"They say we're catchin' it over on th' left. They say th' enemy driv' our line inteh a devil of a swamp an' took Hannis's batt'ry."

"No sech thing. Hannis's batt'ry was 'long here 'bout a minute ago."

"That young Hasbrouck, he makes a good off'cer. He ain't afraid 'a nothin'."

"I met one of th' 148th Maine boys an' he ses his brigade fit th' hull rebel army fer four hours over on th' turnpike road an' killed about five thousand of 'em. He ses one more sech fight as that an' th' war 'll be over."

"Bill wasn't scared either. No, sir! It wasn't that. Bill ain't a-gittin' scared easy. He was jest mad, that's what he was. When that feller trod on his hand, he up an' sed that he was willin' t' give his hand t' his country, but he be dumbed if he was goin' t' have every dumb bushwhacker in th' kentry walkin' 'round on it. So he went t' th' hospital disregardless of th' fight. Three fingers was crunched. Th' dern doctor wanted t' amputate 'm, an' Bill, he raised a row, I hear. He's a funny feller."

The din in front swelled to a tremendous chorus. The youth and his fellows were frozen to silence. They could see a flag that tossed in the smoke angrily. Near it were the blurred and agitated forms of troops. There came a turbulent stream of men across the fields. A battery changing position at a frantic gallop scattered the stragglers right and left.

A shell screaming like a storm banshee went over the huddled heads of the reserves. It landed in the grove, and exploding redly flung the brown earth. There was a little shower of pine needles.

Bullets began to whistle among the branches and nip at the trees. Twigs and leaves came sailing down. It was as if a thousand axes, wee and invisible, were being wielded. Many of the men were constantly dodging and ducking their heads.

The lieutenant of the youth's company was shot in the hand. He began to swear so wondrously that a nervous laugh went along the regimental line. The officer's profanity sounded conventional. It relieved the tightened senses of the new men. It was as if he had hit his fingers with a tack hammer at home.

He held the wounded member carefully away from his side so that the blood would not drip upon his trousers.

The captain of the company, tucking his sword under his arm, produced a handkerchief and began to bind with it the lieutenant's wound. And they disputed as to how the binding should be done.

The battle flag in the distance jerked about madly. It seemed to be struggling to free itself from an agony. The billowing smoke was filled with horizontal flashes.

Men running swiftly emerged from it. They grew in numbers until it was seen that the whole command was fleeing. The flag suddenly sank down as if dying. Its motion as it fell, was a gesture of despair.

Wild yells came from behind the walls of smoke. A sketch in gray and red dissolved into a moblike body of men who galloped like wild horses.

The veteran regiments on the right and left of the 304th immediately began to jeer. With the passionate song of the bullets and the banshee shrieks of shells were mingled loud catcalls and bits of facetious advice concerning places of safety.

But the new regiment was breathless with horror. "Saunders's got crushed!" whispered the man at the youth's elbow. They shrank back and crouched as if compelled to await a flood.

The youth shot a swift glance along the blue ranks of the regiment. The profiles were motionless, carven; and afterward he remembered that the color sergeant was standing with his legs apart, as if he expected to be pushed to the ground.

The following throng went whirling around the flank. Here and there were officers carried along on the stream like exasperated chips. They were striking about them with their swords and with their left fists, punching every head they could reach. They cursed like highwaymen.

A mounted officer displayed the furious anger of a spoiled child. He raged with his head, his arms, and his legs.

Another, the commander of the brigade, was galloping about bawling. His hat was gone and his clothes were awry. He resembled a man who has come from bed to go to a fire. The hoofs of his horse often threatened the heads of the running men, but they scampered with singular fortune. In this rush they were apparently all deaf and blind. They heeded not the largest and longest of the oaths that were thrown at them from all directions.

Frequently over this tumult could be heard the grim jokes of the critical veterans; but the retreating men apparently were not even conscious of the presence of an audience.

The battle reflection that shone for an instant in the faces on the mad current made the youth feel that forceful hands from heaven would not have been able to have held him in place if he could have got intelligent control of his legs.

There was an appalling imprint upon these faces. The struggle in the smoke had pictured an exaggeration of itself on the bleached cheeks and in the eyes wild with one desire.

The sight of this stampede exerted a floodlike force that seemed able to drag sticks and stones and men from the ground. They of the reserves had to hold on. They grew pale and firm, and red and quaking.

The youth achieved one little thought in the midst of this chaos. The composite monster which had caused the other troops to flee had not then appeared. He resolved to get a view of it, and then, he thought he might very likely run better than the best of them.

THINK AND DISCUSS

CHAPTERS 1–4

Understanding

1. With what news does the tall soldier return to camp? How do the other men react to this information?
2. What question does Henry ask Jim Conklin at the end of Chapter 1? What is Jim's response?
3. In Chapter 3, paragraph six, Henry's regiment is described as "not yet veteranlike in appearance." Why?
4. When Henry's regiment encounters a dead soldier (Chapter 3), how do the men react? How is Henry's reaction different?
5. At the end of Chapter 3, what does Wilson give Henry? Why?

Analyzing

6. What **mood** is established in the opening paragraph of the first chapter? What colors and **images** help establish this mood?
7. In what way is Henry an "unknown quantity"? How do Jim Conklin's remarks at the end of the first chapter reassure him?
8. Reread the two paragraphs that describe Henry before battle, beginning "But he instantly . . ." and ending ". . . to be slaughtered" (806b, 1–2). What does the description "He was in a moving box" indicate about Henry's feelings?
9. What words and phrases in the final six paragraphs of Chapter 4 indicate that the retreating men have no control over their flight? What aspects of Naturalism (see Unit Background) are portrayed here?

Extending

10. How do the characters and situations portrayed thus far compare to ideas of war that you have read about or seen on film?

REVIEWING: Flashback H 7

See Handbook of Literary Terms, p. 888.

Flashback is the interruption of the narrative to show an episode that happened earlier. The flashback in Chapter 1 provides important details about Henry.

1. What information does the flashback provide about Henry's background?
2. How does Henry's mother react to his enlistment? How do his former classmates react?
3. What is Henry's conception of war before he enlists? On what has he based his ideas?

VOCABULARY

Pronunciation

Use your Glossary to answer the following questions about the italicized words. Be sure you know the meaning of each italicized word.

1. Which syllable in *vindication* receives the primary accent or stress? (**a**) first; (**b**) second; (**c**) third; (**d**) fourth.
2. Which of the following words rhymes with *trough?* (**a**) cough; (**b**) rough; (**c**) dough; (**d**) bough.
3. How many syllables has *reconnoitering?* (**a**) three; (**b**) four; (**c**) five; (**d**) six.
4. The second vowel sound in *vivacious* is the same as the vowel sound in which word? (**a**) cake; (**b**) man; (**c**) yard; (**d**) learn.
5. Which syllable in *resolutely* receives the secondary accent or stress? (**a**) first; (**b**) second; (**c**) third; (**d**) fourth.

THINKING SKILLS

Classifying

Jim Conklin and Wilson emerge as two very different characters in these early chapters. You can classify, or categorize, these two characters by examining the descriptions of each man.

1. Under the headings *The Tall Soldier* and *The Loud Soldier*, write words and phrases from the first four chapters that serve to characterize these men.
2. Do you think that these two men represent types of soldiers or individuals? Explain.

The Movie

Taken from John Huston's film version of *The Red Badge of Courage* (1951), the scene in the photograph shows raw Union recruits on the march during the Civil War. Newly outfitted for duty, "the youth," played by Audie Murphy, who was the most-decorated United States soldier of World War II, is preoccupied with the thought that he may become a coward on the battlefield. Cartoonist Bill Mauldin, who played "the loud soldier," is seen marching behind Murphy. Like Murphy, Mauldin gained a national reputation in World War II, creating the memorable image of G(overnment) I(ssue) Joe in his sketches. It may seem ironic that Huston cast Murphy and Mauldin, men whose reputations were launched in World War II, to play recruits in the Civil War. Ironic too was Huston's choice to portray Crane's novel, so full of color imagery even in its title, in black and white. Perhaps the director wished to convey the uncompromising starkness of war.

From the motion picture *The Red Badge of Courage*, starring Audie Murphy. Springer/Bettman Film Archive

the general lost his hat

CHAPTER 5

There were moments of waiting. The youth thought of the village street at home before the arrival of the circus parade on a day in the spring. He remembered how he had stood, a small, thrillful boy, prepared to follow the dingy lady upon the white horse, or the band in its faded chariot. He saw the yellow road, the lines of expectant people, and the sober houses. He particularly remembered an old fellow who used to sit upon a cracker box in front of the store and feign to despise such exhibitions. A thousand details of color and form surged in his mind. The old fellow upon the cracker box appeared in middle prominence.

Someone cried, "Here they come!"

There was rustling and muttering among the men. They displayed a feverish desire to have every possible cartridge ready to their hands. The boxes were pulled around into various positions, and adjusted with great care. It was as if seven hundred new bonnets were being tried on.

The tall soldier, having prepared his rifle, produced a red handkerchief of some kind. He was engaged in knitting it about his throat with exquisite attention to its position, when the cry was repeated up and down the line in a muffled roar of sound.

"Here they come! Here they come!" Gunlocks clicked.

Across the smoke-infested fields came a brown swarm of running men who were giving shrill yells. They came on, stooping and swinging their rifles at all angles. A flag, tilted forward, sped near the front.

As he caught sight of them, the youth was momentarily startled by a thought that perhaps his gun was not loaded. He stood trying to rally his faltering intellect so that he might recollect the moment when he had loaded, but he could not.

A hatless general pulled his dripping horse to a stand near the colonel of the 304th. He shook his fist in the other's face. "You've got to hold 'em back!" he shouted, savagely; "you've got to hold 'em back!"

In his agitation the colonel began to stammer. "A-all r-right, General, all right. We-we'll do our—we-we'll d-d-do—do our best, General."

The general made a passionate gesture and galloped away. The colonel, perchance to relieve his feelings, began to scold like a wet parrot. The youth, turning swiftly to make sure that the rear was unmolested, saw the commander regarding his men in a highly resentful manner, as if he regretted above everything his association with them.

The man at the youth's elbow was mumbling, as if to himself: "Oh, we're in for it now! Oh, we're in for it now!"

The captain of the company had been pacing excitedly to and fro in the rear. He coaxed in schoolmistress fashion, as to a congregation of boys with primers. His talk was an endless repetition. "Reserve your fire, boys—don't shoot till I tell you—save your fire—wait till they got close up—don't be fools——"

Perspiration streamed down the youth's face, which was soiled like that of a weeping urchin. He frequently, with a nervous movement, wiped his eyes with his coat sleeve. His mouth was still a little ways open.

He got the one glance at the foe-swarming field in front of him, and instantly ceased to debate the question of his piece being loaded. Before he was ready to begin—before he had announced to himself that he was about to fight—he threw the obedient, well-balanced rifle into position and fired a first wild shot. Directly he was working at his weapon like an automatic affair.

He suddenly lost concern for himself, and forgot to look at a menacing fate. He became not a man but a member. He felt that something of which he was a part—a regiment, an army, a cause, or a country—was in a crisis. He was welded into a common personality which was dominated by a single desire. For some moments he could not flee no more than a little finger can commit a revolution from a hand.

If he had thought the regiment was about to be annihilated perhaps he could have amputated himself from it. But its noise gave him assurance. The regiment was like a firework that, once ignited, proceeds superior to circumstances until its blazing vitality fades. It wheezed and banged with a mighty power. He pictured the ground before it as strewn with the discomfited.

There was a consciousness always of the presence of his comrades about him. He felt the sub-tle battle brotherhood more potent even than the cause for which they were fighting. It was a mysterious fraternity born of the smoke and danger of death.

He was at a task. He was like a carpenter who has made many boxes, making still another box, only there was furious haste in his movements. He, in his thought, was careering off in other places, even as the carpenter who as he works, whistles and thinks of his friend or his enemy, his home or a saloon. And these jolted dreams were never perfect to him afterward, but remained a mass of blurred shapes.

Presently he began to feel the effects of the war atmosphere—a blistering sweat, a sensation that his eyeballs were about to crack like hot stones. A burning roar filled his ears.

Following this came a red rage. He developed the acute exasperation of a pestered animal, a well-meaning cow worried by dogs. He had a mad feeling against his rifle, which could only be used against one life at a time. He wished to rush forward and strangle with his fingers. He craved a power that would enable him to make a world-sweeping gesture and brush all back. His impotency appeared to him, and made his rage into that of a driven beast.

Buried in the smoke of many rifles his anger was directed not so much against men whom he knew were rushing toward him as against the swirling battle phantoms which were choking him, stuffing their smoke robes down his parched throat. He fought frantically for respite for his senses, for air, as a babe being smothered attacks the deadly blankets.

There was a blare of heated rage mingled with a certain expression of intentness on all faces. Many of the men were making low-toned noises with their mouths, and these subdued cheers, snarls, imprecations, prayers, made a wild, barbaric song that went as an undercurrent of sound, strange and chantlike with the resounding chords of the war march. The man at the youth's elbow was babbling. In it there was something soft and tender like the monologue of a babe. The tall soldier was swearing in a loud voice. From his lips came a black procession of curious oaths. Of a sudden another broke out in a querulous way like a man who has mislaid his hat. "Well, why don't they support us? Why don't they send supports? Do they think——"

The youth in his battle sleep heard this as one who dozes hears.

There was a singular absence of heroic poses. The men bending and surging in their haste and rage were in every impossible attitude. The steel ramrods clanked and clanged with incessant din as the men pounded them furiously into the hot rifle barrels. The flaps of the cartridge boxes were all unfastened, and bobbed idiotically with each movement. The rifles, once loaded, were jerked to the shoulder and fired without apparent aim into the smoke or at one of the blurred and shifting forms which upon the field before the regiment had been growing larger and larger like puppets under a magician's hand.

The officers, at their intervals, rearward, neglected to stand in picturesque attitudes. They were bobbing to and fro roaring directions and encouragements. The dimensions of their howls were extraordinary. They expended their lungs with prodigal wills. And often they nearly stood upon their heads in their anxiety to observe the enemy on the other side of the tumbling smoke.

The lieutenant of the youth's company had encountered a soldier who had fled screaming at the first volley of his comrades. Behind the lines these two were acting a little isolated scene. The man was blubbering and staring with sheeplike eyes at the lieutenant, who had seized him by the collar and was pommeling him. He drove him back into the ranks with many blows. The soldier went mechanically, dully, with his animal-like eyes upon the officer. Perhaps there was to him a divinity expressed in the voice of the other—stern, hard, with no reflection of fear in it. He tried to reload his gun, but his shaking hands prevented. The lieutenant was obliged to assist him.

The men dropped here and there like bundles. The captain of the youth's company had been killed in an early part of the action. His body lay stretched out in the position of a tired man resting, but upon his face there was an astonished and sorrowful look, as if he thought some friend had done him an ill turn. The babbling man was grazed by a shot that made the blood stream widely down his face. He clapped both hands to his head. "Oh!" he said, and ran. Another grunted suddenly as if he had been struck by a club in the stomach. He sat down and gazed ruefully. In his eyes there was

mute, indefinite reproach. Farther up the line a man standing behind a tree, had had his knee joint splintered by a ball. Immediately he had dropped his rifle and gripped the tree with both arms. And there he remained, clinging desperately and crying for assistance that he might withdraw his hold upon the tree.

At last an exultant yell went along the quivering line. The firing dwindled from an uproar to a last vindictive popping. As the smoke slowly eddied away, the youth saw that the charge had been repulsed. The enemy were scattered into reluctant groups. He saw a man climb to the top of the fence, straddle the rail, and fire a parting shot. The waves had receded, leaving bits of dark *débris* upon the ground.

Some in the regiment began to whoop frenziedly. Many were silent. Apparently they were trying to contemplate themselves.

After the fever had left his veins, the youth thought that at last he was going to suffocate. He became aware of the foul atmosphere in which he had been struggling. He was grimy and dripping like a laborer in a foundry. He grasped his canteen and took a long swallow of the warmed water.

A sentence with variations went up and down the line. "Well, we've helt 'em back. We've helt 'em back; derned if we haven't." The men said it blissfully, leering at each other with dirty smiles.

The youth turned to look behind him and off to the right and off to the left. He experienced the joy of a man who at last finds leisure in which to look about him.

Underfoot there were a few ghastly forms motionless. They lay twisted in fantastic contortions. Arms were bent and heads were turned in incredible ways. It seemed that the dead men must have fallen from some great height to get into such positions. They looked to be dumped out upon the ground from the sky.

From a position in the rear of the grove a battery was throwing shells over it. The flash of the guns startled the youth at first. He thought they were aimed directly at him. Through the trees he watched the black figures of the gunners as they worked swiftly and intently. Their labor seemed a complicated thing. He wondered how they could remember its formula in the midst of confusion.

The guns squatted in a row like savage chiefs. They argued with abrupt violence. It was a grim powwow. Their busy servants ran hither and thither.

A small procession of wounded men were going drearily toward the rear. It was a flow of blood from the torn body of the brigade.

To the right and to the left were the dark lines of other troops. Far in front he thought he could see lighter masses protruding in points from the forest. They were suggestive of unnumbered thousands.

Once he saw a tiny battery go dashing along the line of the horizon. The tiny riders were beating the tiny horses.

From a sloping hill came the sound of cheerings and clashes. Smoke welled slowly through the leaves.

Batteries were speaking with thunderous oratorical effort. Here and there were flags, the red in the stripes dominating. They splashed bits of warm color upon the dark lines of troops.

The youth felt the old thrill at the sight of the emblem. They were like beautiful birds strangely undaunted in a storm.

As he listened to the din from the hillside, to a deep pulsating thunder that came from afar to the left, and to the lesser clamors which came from many directions, it occurred to him that they were fighting, too, over there, and over there, and over there. Heretofore he had supposed that all the battle was directly under his nose.

As he gazed around him the youth felt a flash of astonishment at the blue, pure sky and the sun-gleamings on the trees and fields. It was surprising that Nature had gone tranquilly on with her golden process in the midst of so much devilment.

CHAPTER 6

The youth awakened slowly. He came gradually back to a position from which he could regard himself. For moments he had been scrutinizing his person in a dazed way as if he had never before seen himself. Then he picked up his cap from the ground. He wriggled in his jacket to make a more comfortable fit, and kneeling relaced his shoe. He thoughtfully mopped his reeking features.

So it was all over at last! The supreme trial had been passed. The red, formidable difficulties of war had been vanquished.

He went into an ecstasy of self-satisfaction. He had the most delightful sensations of his life. Standing as if apart from himself, he viewed that last scene. He perceived that the man who had fought thus was magnificent.

He felt that he was a fine fellow. He saw himself even with those ideals which he had considered as far beyond him. He smiled in deep gratification.

Upon his fellows he beamed tenderness and goodwill. "Gee! ain't it hot, hey?" he said affably to a man who was polishing his streaming face with his coat sleeves.

"You bet!" said the other, grinning sociably. "I never seen sech dumb hotness." He sprawled out luxuriously on the ground. "Gee, yes! An' I hope we don't have no more fightin' till a week from Monday."

There were some handshakings and deep speeches with men whose features were familiar, but with whom the youth now felt the bonds of tied hearts. He helped a cursing comrade to bind up a wound of the shin.

But, of a sudden, cries of amazement broke out along the ranks of the new regiment. "Here they come ag'in! Here they come ag'in!" The man who had sprawled upon the ground started up and said, "Gosh!"

The youth turned quick eyes upon the field. He discerned forms begin to swell in masses out of a distant wood. He again saw the tilted flag speeding forward.

The shells, which had ceased to trouble the regiment for a time, came swirling again, and exploded in the grass or among the leaves of the trees. They looked to be strange war flowers bursting into fierce bloom.

The men groaned. The luster faded from their eyes. Their smudged countenances now expressed a profound dejection. They moved their stiffened bodies slowly, and watched in sullen mood the frantic approach of the enemy. The slaves toiling in the temple of this god began to feel rebellion at his harsh tasks.

They fretted and complained each to each. "Oh, say, this is too much of a good thing!

Why can't somebody send us supports?"

"We ain't never goin' to stand this second banging. I didn't come here to fight the hull rebel army."

There was one who raised a doleful cry. "I wish Bill Smithers had trod on my hand, insteader me treddin' on his'n." The sore joints of the regiment creaked as it painfully floundered into position to repulse.

The youth stared. Surely, he thought, this impossible thing was not about to happen. He waited as if he expected the enemy to suddenly stop, apologize, and retire bowing. It was all a mistake.

But the firing began somewhere on the regimental line and ripped along in both directions. The level sheets of flame developed great clouds of smoke that tumbled and tossed in the mild wind near the ground for a moment, and then rolled through the ranks as through a gate. The clouds were tinged an earthlike yellow in the sunrays and in the shadow were a sorry blue. The flag was sometimes eaten and lost in this mass of vapor, but more often it projected, suntouched, resplendent.

Into the youth's eyes there came a look that one can see in the orbs of a jaded horse. His neck was quivering with nervous weakness and the muscles of his arms felt numb and bloodless. His hands, too, seemed large and awkward as if he was wearing invisible mittens. And there was a great uncertainty about his knee joints.

The words that comrades had uttered previous to the firing began to recur to him. "Oh, say, this is too much of a good thing! What do they take us for—why don't they send supports? I didn't come here to fight the hull rebel army."

He began to exaggerate the endurance, the skill, and the valor of those who were coming. Himself reeling from exhaustion, he was astonished beyond measure at such persistency. They must be machines of steel. It was very gloomy struggling against such affairs, wound up perhaps to fight until sundown.

He slowly lifted his rifle and catching a glimpse of the thick-spread field he blazed at a cantering cluster. He stopped then and began to peer as best he could through the smoke. He caught changing views of the ground covered with men who were all running like pursued imps, and yelling.

To the youth it was an onslaught of redoubtable dragons. He became like the man who lost his legs at the approach of the red and green monster. He waited in a sort of a horrified, listening attitude. He seemed to shut his eyes and wait to be gobbled.

A man near him who up to this time had been working feverishly at his rifle suddenly stopped and ran with howls. A lad whose face had borne an expression of exalted courage, the majesty of he who dares give his life, was, at an instant, smitten abject. He blanched like one who has come to the edge of a cliff at midnight and is suddenly made aware. There was a revelation. He, too, threw down his gun and fled. There was no shame in his face. He ran like a rabbit.

Others began to scamper away through the smoke. The youth turned his head, shaken from his trance by this movement as if the regiment was leaving him behind. He saw the few fleeting forms.

He yelled then with fright and swung about. For a moment, in the great clamor, he was like a proverbial chicken. He lost the direction of safety. Destruction threatened him from all points.

Directly he began to speed toward the rear in great leaps. His rifle and cap were gone. His unbuttoned coat bulged in the wind. The flap of his cartridge box bobbed wildly, and his canteen, by its slender cord, swung out behind. On his face was all the horror of those things which he imagined.

The lieutenant sprang forward bawling. The youth saw his features wrathfully red, and saw him make a dab with his sword. His one thought of the incident was that the lieutenant was a peculiar creature to feel interested in such matters upon this occasion.

He ran like a blind man. Two or three times he fell down. Once he knocked his shoulder so heavily against a tree that he went headlong.

Since he had turned his back upon the fight, his fears had been wondrously magnified. Death about to thrust him between the shoulder blades was far more dreadful than death about to smite him between the eyes. When he thought of it later, he conceived the impression that it is better to view the appalling than to be merely within hearing. The noises of the battle were like stones; he believed himself liable to be crushed.

As he ran on he mingled with others. He dimly saw men on his right and on his left, and he heard footsteps behind him. He thought that all the

Rifle and cap
gone —
absolute panic!

regiment was fleeing, pursued by these ominous crashes.

In his flight the sound of these following footsteps gave him his one meager relief. He felt vaguely that death must make a first choice of the men who were nearest; the initial morsels for the dragons would be then those who were following him. So he displayed the zeal of an insane sprinter in his purpose to keep them in the rear. There was a race.

As he, leading, went across a little field, he found himself in a region of shells. They hurtled over his head with long wild screams. As he listened, he imagined them to have rows of cruel teeth that grinned at him. Once one lit before him and the livid lightning of the explosion effectually barred the way in his chosen direction. He groveled on the ground and then springing up went careering off through some bushes.

He experienced a thrill of amazement when he came within view of a battery in action. The men there seemed to be in conventional moods, altogether unaware of the impending annihilation. The battery was disputing with a distant antagonist and the gunners were wrapped in admiration of their shooting. They were continually bending in coaxing postures over the guns. They seemed to be patting them on the back and encouraging them with words. The guns, stolid and undaunted, spoke with dogged valor.

The precise gunners were coolly enthusiastic. They lifted their eyes every chance to the smoke-wreathed hillock from whence the hostile battery addressed them. The youth pitied them as he ran. Methodical idiots! Machinelike fools! The refined joy of planting shells in the midst of the other battery's formation would appear a little thing when the infantry came swooping out of the woods.

The face of a youthful rider, who was jerking his frantic horse with an abandon of temper he might display in a placid barnyard, was impressed deeply upon his mind. He knew that he looked upon a man who would presently be dead.

Too, he felt a pity for the guns, standing, six good comrades, in a bold row.

He saw a brigade going to the relief of its pestered fellows. He scrambled upon a wee hill and watched it sweeping finely, keeping formation in difficult places. The blue of the line was crusted with steel color, and the brilliant flags projected. Officers were shouting.

This sight also filled him with wonder. The brigade was hurrying briskly to be gulped into the infernal mouths of the war god. What manner of men were they, anyhow? Ah, it was some wondrous breed! Or else they didn't comprehend—the fools.

A furious order caused commotion in the artillery. An officer on a bounding horse made maniacal motions with his arms. The teams went swinging up from the rear, the guns were whirled about, and the battery scampered away. The cannon with their noses poked slantingly at the ground grunted and grumbled like stout men, brave but with objections to hurry.

The youth went on, moderating his pace since he had left the place of noises.

Later he came upon a general of division seated upon a horse that pricked its ears in an interested way at the battle. There was a great gleaming of yellow and patent leather about the saddle and bridle. The quiet man astride looked mouse-colored upon such a splendid charger.

A jingling staff was galloping hither and thither. Sometimes the general was surrounded by horsemen and at other times he was quite alone. He looked to be much harassed. He had the appearance of a business man whose market is swinging up and down.

The youth went slinking around this spot. He went as near as he dared trying to overhear words. Perhaps the general, unable to comprehend chaos, might call upon him for information. And he could tell him. He knew all concerning it. Of a surety the force was in a fix, and any fool could see that if they did not retreat while they had opportunity—why——

He felt that he would like to thrash the general, or at least approach and tell him in plain words exactly what he thought him to be. It was criminal to stay calmly in one spot and make no effort to stay destruction. He loitered in a fever of eagerness for the division commander to apply to him.

As he warily moved about, he heard the general call out irritably: "Tompkins, go over an' see Taylor, an' tell him not t' be in such an all-fired hurry; tell him t' halt his brigade in th' edge of th' woods; tell him t' detach a reg'ment—say I think th' center 'll break if we don't help it out some; tell him t' hurry up."

A slim youth on a fine chestnut horse caught these swift words from the mouth of his superior. He made his horse bound into a gallop almost from a walk in his haste to go upon his mission. There was a cloud of dust.

A moment later the youth saw the general bounce excitedly in his saddle.

"Yes, by heavens, they have!" The officer leaned forward. His face was aflame with excitement. "Yes, by heavens, they've held 'im! They've held 'im!"

He began to blithely roar at his staff: "We'll wallop 'im now. We'll wallop 'im now. We've got 'em sure." He turned suddenly upon an aide: "Here—you—Jones—quick—ride after Tompkins—see Taylor—tell him t' go in—everlastingly—like blazes—anything."

As another officer sped his horse after the first messenger, the general beamed upon the earth like a sun. In his eyes was a desire to chant a paean. He kept repeating, "They've held 'em, by heavens!"

His excitement made his horse plunge, and he merrily kicked and swore at it. He held a little carnival of joy on horseback.

CHAPTER 7

The youth cringed as if discovered in a crime. By heavens, they had won after all! The imbecile line had remained and become victors. He could hear cheering.

He lifted himself upon his toes and looked in the direction of the fight. A yellow fog lay wallowing on the treetops. From beneath it came the clatter of musketry. Hoarse cries told of an advance.

He turned away amazed and angry. He felt that he had been wronged.

He had fled, he told himself, because annihilation approached. He had done a good part in saving himself, who was a little piece of the army. He had considered the time, he said, to be one in which it was the duty of every little piece to rescue itself if possible. Later the officers could fit the little pieces together again, and make a battle-front. If none of the little pieces were wise enough to save themselves from the flurry of death at such a time, why, then, where would be the army? It was all plain that he had proceeded according to very correct and commendable rules. His actions had been sagacious things. They had been full of strategy. They were the work of a master's legs.

Thoughts of his comrades came to him. The brittle blue line had withstood the blows and won. He grew bitter over it. It seemed that the blind ignorance and stupidity of those little pieces had betrayed him. He had been overturned and crushed by their lack of sense in holding the position, when intelligent deliberation would have convinced them that it was impossible. He, the enlightened man who looks afar in the dark, had fled because of his superior perceptions and knowledge. He felt a great anger against his comrades. He knew it could be proved that they had been fools.

He wondered what they would remark when later he appeared in camp. His mind heard howls of derision. Their destiny would not enable them to understand his sharper point of view.

He began to pity himself acutely. He was ill-used. He was trodden beneath the feet of an iron injustice. He had proceeded with wisdom and from the most righteous motives under heaven's blue only to be frustrated by hateful circumstances.

A dull, animal-like rebellion against his fellows, war in the abstract, and fate grew within him. He shambled along with bowed head, his brain in a tumult of agony and despair. When he looked loweringly up, quivering at each sound, his eyes had the expression of those of a criminal who thinks his guilt and his punishment great, and knows that he can find no words.

He went from the fields into a thick woods, as if resolved to bury himself. He wished to get out of hearing of the crackling shots which were to him like voices.

The ground was cluttered with vines and bushes, and the trees grew close and spread out like bouquets. He was obliged to force his way with much noise. The creepers, catching against his legs, cried out harshly as their sprays were torn from the barks of trees. The swishing saplings tried to make known his presence to the world. He could not conciliate the forest. As he made his way, it was always calling out protestations. When he separated embraces of trees and vines, the disturbed foliages waved their arms and turned their face leaves toward him. He dreaded lest these noisy motions and cries should bring men to look at him. So he went far, seeking dark and intricate places.

After a time the sound of musketry grew faint and the cannon boomed in the distance. The sun, suddenly apparent, blazed among the trees. The insects were making rhythmical noises. They seemed to be grinding their teeth in unison. A woodpecker stuck his impudent head around the side of a tree. A bird flew on lighthearted wing.

Off was the rumble of death. It seemed now that Nature had no ears.

This landscape gave him assurance. A fair field holding life. It was the religion of peace. It would die if its timid eyes were compelled to see blood. He conceived Nature to be a woman with a deep aversion to tragedy.

He threw a pine cone at a jovial squirrel, and he ran with chattering fear. High in a treetop he stopped, and, poking his head cautiously from behind a branch, looked down with an air of trepidation.

The youth felt triumphant at this exhibition. There was the law, he said. Nature had given him a sign. The squirrel, immediately upon recognizing danger, had taken to his legs without ado. He did not stand stolidly baring his furry belly to the missile, and die with an upward glance at the sympathetic heavens. On the contrary, he had fled as fast as his legs could carry him; and he was but an ordinary squirrel, too—doubtless no philosopher of his race. The youth wended, feeling that Nature was of his mind. She reenforced his argument with proofs that lived where the sun shone.

Once he found himself almost into a swamp. He was obliged to walk upon bog tufts and watch his feet to keep from the oily mire. Pausing at one time to look about him he saw, out at some black water, a small animal pounce in and emerge directly with a gleaming fish.

The youth went again into the deep thickets. The brushed branches made a noise that drowned the sounds of cannon. He walked on, going from obscurity into promises of a greater obscurity.

At length he reached a place where the high, arching boughs made a chapel. He softly pushed the green doors aside and entered. Pine needles were a gentle brown carpet. There was a religious half light.

Near the threshold he stopped, horror stricken at the sight of a thing.

He was being looked at by a dead man who was seated with his back against a columnlike tree. The corpse was dressed in a uniform that once had been blue, but was now faded to a melancholy shade of green. The eyes, staring at the youth, had changed

half light
chapel like

The American Civil War, called the first modern war, utilized weaponry and technology that revolutionized warfare. Troops, using mass produced weapons such as *machine guns* and *carbines*, were transported by *railroads*. Military innovations included the *telegraph, hand grenades, land mines*, and *trench warfare*. The nearly indestructible armored ships called *ironclads*, along with *submarines*, made wooden ships obsolete, thus drastically changing naval tactics. This was the first major war to be *photographed*, and photographers such as Mathew Brady communicated the grimness and poignancy of the battle to the public. As to be expected, these far-reaching changes had a profound impact on the American language.

Among the many terms popularized by the Civil War were *pup tent, draftee, ensign, rebel, antebellum*, and *muster (out)*. In *The Red Badge of Courage*, a soldier asks "What th' thunder—we—skedaddlin' this way fer?" The term *skedaddle* was commonly used to describe the flight of Confederate troops from the battlefield. The term *A.W.O.L.* (absent without leave) originated during this war, although these letters did not become an acronym pronounced as a single word until World War II. *The Medal of Honor* was established by Congress in 1862 to honor the Union dead. *Dixie*, popularized in a song written in 1859, became a term for the South.

The Confederate Army, variously referred to as *Gray, Graycoats, Butternuts, Rebs*, and *Rebels*, fought the Union Army, called the *Blue, Blue Bellies, Yanks*, and *The Federals*. Banknotes issued by Congress were called *greenbacks*, while Confederate bills were called *bluebacks* or *graybacks*. Northerners who sympathized with the South were known as *Copperheads* after the stealthy, poisonous copperhead snake. The term later came to refer to anyone who sympathized with the enemy during wartime. Interestingly, Union sympathizers in the South were called *Loyalists*, proving that language can carry its own bias.

The names of battlefields—*Bull Run, Shiloh, Chancellorsville, Antietam, Fredricksburg, Gettysburg*—became immortalized, as did the names of famous generals—*Grant, Lee, Beauregard, "Stonewall" Jackson, Meade, Sherman, McClellan*, and *Pickett*. One American general, Ambrose *Burnside*, lent his transposed name to the facial whiskers known as *sideburns*.

New technology and mass production introduced Americans to *canned rations*, the *sewing machine*, and the *mechanical reaper* and *harvester*. Workers left home and farm for factories that provided the troops with food, uniforms, and weapons.

Issues of slavery and human rights, by no means resolved by the Civil War, brought forth their own terminology. Racially integrated troops were referred to as *mixed* army units. The derogatory terms *Simon Legree* and *Uncle Tom* (from the novel *Uncle Tom's Cabin* by Harriet Beecher Stowe, published in 1852) referred, respectively, to sadistic slaveowners or cruel people and subservient slaves. Black people freed by the Emancipation Proclamation and the Civil War were called *freedmen*. People who picked cotton or farmed land for the owner in return for part of the crops were called *sharecroppers*.

The end of the Civil War saw *carpetbaggers* (Northerners who went to the South after the Civil War for political or financial gain) and *scalawags* (white Southerners who cooperated with the Republican Party after the Civil War, usually for personal gain). It also introduced plans for *Reconstruction*, which, in the words of Lincoln, meant a reunion of North and South "with malice toward none; with charity toward all." As the war-torn nation began to heal, people paid tribute to the war dead by placing flowers on their graves. Thus was born the holiday known as *Memorial Day*, which now commemorates the dead from all American wars.

to the dull hue to be seen on the side of a dead fish. The mouth was open. Its red had changed to an appalling yellow. Over the gray skin of the face ran little ants. One was trundling some sort of a bundle along the upper lip.

The youth gave a shriek as he confronted the thing. He was for moments turned to stone before it. He remained staring into the liquid-looking eyes. The dead man and the living man exchanged a long look. Then the youth cautiously put one hand behind him and brought it against a tree. Leaning upon this he retreated, step by step, with his face still toward the thing. He feared that if he turned his back, the body might spring up and stealthily pursue him.

The branches, pushing against him, threatened to throw him over upon it. His unguided feet, too, caught aggravatingly in brambles; and with it all he received a subtle suggestion to touch the corpse. As he thought of his hand upon it, he shuddered profoundly.

At last he burst the bonds which had fastened him to the spot and fled, unheeding the underbrush. He was pursued by a sight of the black ants swarming greedily upon the gray face and venturing horribly near to the eyes.

After a time he paused, and, breathless and panting, listened. He imagined some strange voice would come from the dead throat and squawk after him in horrible menaces.

The trees about the portals of the chapel moved soughingly in a soft wind. A sad silence was upon the little guarding edifice.

CHAPTER 8

The trees began softly to sing a hymn of twilight. The sun sank until slanted bronze rays struck the forest. There was a lull in the noises of insects as if they had bowed their beaks and were making a devotional pause. There was silence save for the chanted chorus of the trees.

Then, upon this stillness, there suddenly broke a tremendous clangor of sounds. A crimson roar came from the distance.

The youth stopped. He was transfixed by this terrific medley of all noises. It was as if worlds were being rended. There was the ripping sound of musketry and the breaking crash of the artillery.

His mind flew in all directions. He conceived the two armies to be at each other panther fashion. He listened for a time. Then he began to run in the direction of the battle. He saw that it was an ironical thing for him to be running thus toward that which he had been at such pains to avoid. But he said, in substance, to himself that if the earth and the moon were about to clash, many persons would doubtless plan to get upon the roofs to witness the collision.

As he ran, he became aware that the forest had stopped its music, as if at last becoming capable of hearing the foreign sounds. The trees hushed and stood motionless. Everything seemed to be listening to the crackle and clatter and ear-shaking thunder. The chorus pealed over the still earth.

It suddenly occurred to the youth that the fight in which he had been was, after all, but perfunctory popping. In the hearing of this present din he was doubtful if he had seen real battle scenes. This uproar explained a celestial battle; it was tumbling hordes a-struggle in the air.

Reflecting, he saw a sort of a humor in the point of view of himself and his fellows during the late encounter. They had taken themselves and the enemy very seriously and had imagined that they were deciding the war. Individuals must have supposed that they were cutting the letters of their names deep into everlasting tablets of brass, or enshrining their reputations forever in the hearts of their countrymen, while, as to fact, the affair would appear in printed reports under a meek and immaterial title. But he saw that it was good, else, he said, in battle everyone would surely run save forlorn hopes and their ilk.

He went rapidly on. He wished to come to the edge of the forest that he might peer out.

As he hastened, there passed through his mind pictures of stupendous conflicts. His accumulated thought upon such subjects was used to form scenes. The noise was as the voice of an eloquent being, describing.

Sometimes the brambles formed chains and tried to hold him back. Trees, confronting him, stretched out their arms and forbade him to pass. After its previous hostility this new resistance of the forest filled him with a fine bitterness. It seemed that Nature could not be quite ready to kill him.

But he obstinately took roundabout ways, and presently he was where he could see long gray walls of vapor where lay battle lines. The voices of cannon shook him. The musketry sounded in long irregular surges that played havoc with his ears. He stood regardant for a moment. His eyes had an awe-struck expression. He gawked in the direction of the fight.

Presently he proceeded again on his forward way. The battle was like the grinding of an immense and terrible machine to him. Its complexities and powers, its grim processes, fascinated him. He must go close and see it produce corpses.

He came to a fence and clambered over it. On the far side, the ground was littered with clothes and guns. A newspaper, folded up, lay in the dirt. A dead soldier was stretched with his face hidden in his arm. Farther off there was a group of four or five corpses keeping mournful company. A hot sun had blazed upon the spot.

In this place the youth felt that he was an invader. This forgotten part of the battleground was owned by the dead men, and he hurried, in the vague apprehension that one of the swollen forms would rise and tell him to be gone.

He came finally to a road from which he could see in the distance dark and agitated bodies of troops, smoke-fringed. In the lane was a blood-stained crowd streaming to the rear. The wounded men were cursing, groaning, and wailing. In the air, always, was a mighty swell of sound that it seemed could sway the earth. With the courageous words of the artillery and the spiteful sentences of the musketry mingled red cheers. And from this region of noises came the steady current of the maimed.

One of the wounded men had a shoeful of blood. He hopped like a schoolboy in a game. He was laughing hysterically.

One was swearing that he had been shot in the arm through the commanding general's misman-agement of the army. One was marching with an air imitative of some sublime drum major. Upon his features was an unholy mixture of merriment and agony. As he marched he sang a bit of doggerel in a high and quavering voice:

"Sing a song 'a vic'try,
  A pocketful 'a bullets,
Five an' twenty dead men
  Baked in a—pie."

Parts of the procession limped and staggered to this tune.

Another had the gray seal of death already upon his face. His lips were curled in hard lines and his teeth were clinched. His hands were bloody from where he had pressed them upon his wound. He seemed to be awaiting the moment when he should pitch headlong. He stalked like the specter of a soldier, his eyes burning with the power of a stare into the unknown.

There were some who proceeded sullenly, full of anger at their wounds, and ready to turn upon anything as an obscure cause.

An officer was carried along by two privates. He was peevish. "Don't joggle so, Johnson, yeh fool," he cried. "Think m' leg is made of iron? If yeh can't carry me decent, put me down an' let someone else do it."

He bellowed at the tottering crowd who blocked the quick march of his bearers. "Say, make way there, can't yeh? Make way, dickens take it all."

They sulkily parted and went to the roadsides. As he was carried past, they made pert remarks to him. When he raged in reply and threatened them, they told him to be gone.

The shoulder of one of the tramping bearers knocked heavily against the spectral soldier who was staring into the unknown.

The youth joined this crowd and marched along with it. The torn bodies expressed the awful machinery in which the men had been entangled.

Orderlies and couriers occasionally broke through the throng in the roadway, scattering wounded men right and left, galloping on, fol-lowed by howls. The melancholy march was con-tinually disturbed by the messengers, and some-times by bustling batteries that came swinging and thumping down upon them, the officers shouting orders to clear the way.

There was a tattered man, fouled with dust, blood and powder stain from hair to shoes, who trudged quietly at the youth's side. He was lis-tening with eagerness and much humility to the lurid descriptions of a bearded sergeant. His lean features wore an expression of awe and admiration. He was like a listener in a country store to wondrous tales told among the sugar barrels. He eyed the storyteller with unspeakable wonder. His mouth was agape in yokel fashion.

The sergeant, taking note of this, gave pause to his elaborate history while he administered a sardonic comment. "Be keerful, honey, you'll be a-ketchin' flies," he said.

The tattered man shrank back abashed.

After a time he began to sidle near to the youth, and in a different way try to make him a friend. His voice was gentle as a girl's voice and his eyes were pleading. The youth saw with surprise that the soldier had two wounds, one in the head, bound with a blood-soaked rag, and the other in the arm, making that member dangle like a broken bough.

After they had walked together for some time, the tattered man mustered sufficient courage to speak. "Was pretty good fight, wa'n't it?" he timidly said. The youth, deep in thought, glanced up at the bloody and grim figure with its lamblike eyes. "What?"

"Was pretty good fight, wa'n't it?"

"Yes," said the youth shortly. He quickened his pace.

But the other hobbled industriously after him. There was an air of apology in his manner, but he evidently thought that he needed only to talk for a time, and the youth would perceive that he was a good fellow.

"Was pretty good fight, wa'n't it?" he began in a small voice, and then he achieved the fortitude to continue. "Dern me if I ever see fellers fight so. Laws, how they did fight! I knowed th' boys 'd like when they onct got square at it. Th' boys ain't had no fair chanct up t' now, but this time they showed what they was. I knowed it'd turn out this way. Yeh can't lick them boys. No, sir! They're fighters, they be."

He breathed a deep breath of humble admiration. He had looked at the youth for encouragement several times. He received none, but gradually he seemed to get absorbed in his subject.

"I was talkin' 'cross pickets with a boy from Georgie, onct, an' that boy, he ses, 'Your fellers 'll all run when they onct hearn a gun,' he ses. 'Mebbe they will,' I ses, 'but I don't b'lieve none of it,' I ses; 'an b' jiminey,' I ses back t' 'um, 'mebbe your fellers 'll all run when they onct hearn a gun,'

I ses. He larfed. Well, they didn't run t'-day, did they, hey? No, sir! They fit, an' fit, an' fit."

His homely face was suffused with a light of love for the army which was to him all things beautiful and powerful.

After a time he turned to the youth, "Where yeh hit, ol' boy?" he asked in a brotherly tone.

The youth felt instant panic at this question, although at first its full import was not borne in upon him.

"What?" he asked.

"Where yeh hit?" repeated the tattered man.

"Why," began the youth, "I—I—that is—why—I——"

He turned away suddenly and slid through the crowd. His brow was heavily flushed, and his fingers were picking nervously at one of his buttons. He bent his head and fastened his eyes studiously upon the button as if it were a little problem.

The tattered man looked after him in astonishment.

CHAPTER 9

The youth fell back in the procession until the tattered soldier was not in sight. Then he started to walk on with the others.

But he was amid wounds. The mob of men was bleeding. Because of the tattered soldier's question he now felt that his shame could be viewed. He was continually casting sidelong glances to see if the men were contemplating the letters of guilt he felt burned into his brow.

At times he regarded the wounded soldiers in an envious way. He conceived persons with torn bodies to be peculiarly happy. He wished that he, too, had a wound, a red badge of courage.

The spectral soldier was at his side like a stalking reproach. The man's eyes were still fixed in a stare into the unknown. His gray, appalling face had attracted attention in the crowd, and men, slowing to his dreary pace, were walking with him. They were discussing his plight, questioning him and giving him advice. In a dogged way he repelled them, signing to them to go on and leave him alone. The shadows of his face were deepening and his tight lips seemed holding in check the moan of great despair. There could be seen a certain stiffness in the movements of his body, as if he were taking infinite care not to arouse the passion of his wounds. As he went on, he seemed always looking for a place, like one who goes to choose a grave.

Something in the gesture of the man as he waved the bloody and pitying soldiers away made the youth start as if bitten. He yelled in horror. Tottering forward he laid a quivering hand upon the man's arm. As the latter slowly turned his waxlike features toward him, the youth screamed:

"Jim Conklin!"

The tall soldier made a little commonplace smile. "Hello, Henry," he said.

The youth swayed on his legs and glared strangely. He stuttered and stammered. "Oh, Jim—oh, Jim—oh, Jim——"

The tall soldier held out his gory hand. There was a curious red and black combination of new blood and old blood upon it. "Where yeh been, Henry?" he asked. He continued in a monotonous voice, "I thought mebbe yeh got keeled over. There's been thunder t' pay t'-day. I was worryin' about it a good deal."

The youth still lamented. "Oh, Jim—oh, Jim—oh, Jim——"

"Yeh know," said the tall soldier, "I was out there." He made a careful gesture. "An', Lord, what a circus! An', b'jiminey, I got shot—I got shot. Yes, b'jiminey, I got shot." He reiterated this fact in a bewildered way, as if he did not know how it came about.

The youth put forth anxious arms to assist him, but the tall soldier went firmly on as if propelled. Since the youth's arrival as a guardian for his friend, the other wounded men had ceased to display much interest. They occupied themselves again in dragging their own tragedies toward the rear.

Suddenly, as the two friends marched on, the tall soldier seemed to be overcome by a terror. His face turned to a semblance of gray paste. He clutched the youth's arm and looked all about him, as if dreading to be overheard. Then he began to speak in a shaking whisper:

"I tell yeh what I'm 'fraid of, Henry—I'll tell yeh what I'm 'fraid of. I'm 'fraid I'll fall down—an' then yeh know—them artillery wagons—they like as not 'll run over me. That's what I'm 'fraid of——"

The youth cried out to him hysterically: "I'll take care of yeh, Jim! I'll take care of yeh! I swear I will!"

"Will yeh, Henry?" the tall soldier beseeched.

"Yes—yes—I tell yeh—I'll take care of yeh, Jim!" protested the youth. He could not speak accurately because of the gulpings in his throat.

But the tall soldier continued to beg in a lowly way. He now hung babelike to the youth's arm. His eyes rolled in the wildness of his terror. "I was allus a good friend t' yeh, wa'n't I, Henry? I've allus been a pretty good feller, ain't I? An' it ain't much t' ask, is it? Jest t' pull me along outer th' road? I'd do it fer you, wouldn't I, Henry?"

He paused in piteous anxiety to await his friend's reply.

The youth had reached an anguish where the sobs scorched him. He strove to express his loyalty, but he could only make fantastic gestures.

However, the tall soldier seemed suddenly to forget all those fears. He became again the grim, stalking specter of a soldier. He went stonily forward. The youth wished his friend to lean upon him, but the other always shook his head and strangely protested. "No—no—no—leave me be—leave me be——"

His look was fixed again upon the unknown. He moved with mysterious purpose, and all of the youth's offers he brushed aside. "No—no—leave me be—leave me be——"

The youth had to follow.

Presently the latter heard a voice talking softly near his shoulders. Turning he saw that it belonged to the tattered soldier. "Ye'd better take 'im outa th' road, pardner. There's a batt'ry comin' helitywhoop down th' road an' he'll git runned over. He's a goner anyhow in about five minutes—yeh kin see that. Ye'd better take 'im outa th' road. Where th' blazes does he git his stren'th from?"

"Lord knows!" cried the youth. He was shaking his hands helplessly.

He ran forward presently and grasped the tall soldier by the arm. "Jim! Jim!" he coaxed, "come with me."

The tall soldier weakly tried to wrench himself

free. "Huh," he said vacantly. He stared at the youth for a moment. At last he spoke as if dimly comprehending. "Oh! Inteh th' fields? Oh!"

He started blindly through the grass.

The youth turned once to look at the lashing riders and jouncing guns of the battery. He was startled from this view by a shrill outcry from the tattered man.

"He's runnin'!"

Turning his head swiftly, the youth saw his friend running in a staggering and stumbling way toward a little clump of bushes. His heart seemed to wrench itself almost free from his body at this sight. He made a noise of pain. He and the tattered man began a pursuit. There was a singular race.

When he overtook the tall soldier, he began to plead with all the words he could find. "Jim—Jim—what are you doing—what makes you do this way—you'll hurt yerself."

The same purpose was in the tall soldier's face. He protested in a dulled way, keeping his eyes fastened on the mystic place of his intentions. "No—no—don't tech me—leave me be—leave me be——"

The youth, aghast and filled with wonder at the tall soldier, began quaveringly to question him. "Where yeh goin', Jim? What you thinking about? Where you going? Tell me, won't you, Jim?"

The tall soldier faced about as upon relentless pursuers. In his eyes there was a great appeal. "Leave me be, can't yeh? Leave me be fer a minnit."

The youth recoiled. "Why, Jim," he said, in a dazed way, "what's the matter with you?"

The tall soldier turned and, lurching dangerously, went on. The youth and the tattered soldier followed, sneaking as if whipped, feeling unable to face the stricken man if he should again confront them. They began to have thoughts of a solemn ceremony. There was something ritelike in these movements of the doomed soldier. And there was a resemblance in him to a devotee of a mad religion, blood-sucking, muscle-wrenching, bone-crushing. They were awed and afraid. They hung back lest he have at command a dreadful weapon.

At last, they saw him stop and stand motionless. Hastening up, they perceived that his face wore an expression telling that he had at last found the place for which he had struggled. His spare figure was erect; his bloody hands were quietly at his side. He was waiting with patience for something that he had come to meet. He was at the rendezvous. They paused and stood, expectant.

There was a silence.

Finally, the chest of the doomed soldier began to heave with a strained motion. It increased in violence until it was as if an animal was within and was kicking and tumbling furiously to be free.

This spectacle of gradual strangulation made the youth writhe, and once as his friend rolled his eyes, he saw something in them that made him sink wailing to the ground. He raised his voice in a last supreme call.

"Jim—Jim—Jim——"

The tall soldier opened his lips and spoke. He made a gesture. "Leave me be—don't tech me—leave me be——"

There was another silence while he waited.

Suddenly, his form stiffened and straightened. Then it was shaken by a prolonged ague. He stared into space. To the two watchers there was a curious and profound dignity in the firm lines of his awful face.

He was invaded by a creeping strangeness that slowly enveloped him. For a moment the tremor of his legs caused him to dance a sort of hideous hornpipe. His arms beat wildly about his head in expression of implike enthusiasm.

His tall figure stretched itself to its full height. There was a slight rending sound. Then it began to swing forward, slow and straight, in the manner of a falling tree. A swift muscular contortion made the left shoulder strike the ground first. The body seemed to bounce a little way from the earth.

The youth had watched, spellbound, this ceremony at the place of meeting. His face had been twisted into an expression of every agony he had imagined for his friend.

He now sprang to his feet and, going closer, gazed upon the pastelike face. The mouth was opened and the teeth showed in a laugh.

As the flap of the blue jacket fell away from the body, he could see that the side looked as if it had been chewed by wolves.

The youth turned, with sudden, livid rage, toward the battlefield. He shook his fist. He seemed about to deliver a philippic.

The red sun was pasted in the sky like a wafer.

THINK AND DISCUSS
CHAPTERS 5–9
Understanding

1. What childhood memory does Henry recall as Chapter 5 opens? What interrupts his reverie?

2. How does Henry feel about himself at the beginning of Chapter 6, after he has fought in battle? What change of events occurs suddenly? How does Henry respond?

3. At the end of Chapter 6, what does Henry learn about the outcome of the battle? Why does he feel wronged (Chapter 7, paragraph three)?

4. In Chapter 7, what lesson does he draw from his encounter with a squirrel? What sight in the thickets horrifies him?

5. Who does Henry meet as he walks along the road? Why do they part company?

6. In Chapter 9, Henry meets the spectral soldier. Who is he? What happens to him?

Analyzing

7. At the end of Chapter 5 we read: "It was surprising that Nature had gone tranquilly on with her golden process in the midst of so much devilment." What influence does nature seem to have in the lives of the men?

8. Both the men and the officers display "a singular absence of heroic poses" and a lack of "picturesque attitudes" (815a, 2–3). How does their behavior in battle fall short of Henry's romantic idea of warfare?

9. Naturalism emphasizes that humans act by instinct, much like animals, or are compulsively driven by circumstances beyond their control. Reread the passage beginning "He suddenly lost . . ." and ending ". . . a driven beast" (814a, 5–814b–3). Then find in this passage three **figurative** comparisons that suggest either the animal nature of Henry or the compulsive nature of his actions. Explain your choices as examples of Naturalism.

Extending

10. After Henry witnesses Jim Conklin's death, he feels a "livid rage, toward the battlefield," and shakes his fist in anger. Do you consider this a realistic response to death? Why or why not?

COMPOSITION ◆━●
Writing About a Scene of War

Imagine that you are a Civil War correspondent describing a scene from Chapters 1–9. Choose a scene such as the encampment, a march, or the soldiers in battle; or select an incident such as the tall soldier's death or Henry's desertion as the subject for a newspaper article of several paragraphs. Decide whether you want to present your article in the form of an editorial, a human-interest feature, or an obituary. Use quoted dialogue and vivid imagery to set the tone and mood of your composition. See "Developing Your Style" in the Writer's Handbook.

Writing a Summary

Write a summary of at least five paragraphs of the plot of Chapters 1–9. Summarize only the highlights of the plot, omitting superfluous details. Direct your summary to a classmate with the intention of encouraging him or her to read the rest of the novel. See "Writing Notes and Summaries" in the Writer's Handbook.

ENRICHMENT
Research

The battle described in *The Red Badge of Courage* is generally acknowledged to be that of Chancellorsville. Do some research on this battle and report your findings to the class. Explain the route of the Union army with the help of the map that appears on page 793.

red sun
duskapproaching

CHAPTER 10

The tattered man stood musing.

"Well, he was reg'lar jim-dandy fer nerve, wa'n't he," said he finally in a little awestruck voice. "A reg'lar jim-dandy." He thoughtfully poked one of the docile hands with his foot. "I wonner where he got 'is stren'th from? I never seen a man do like that before. It was a funny thing. Well, he was a reg'lar jim-dandy."

The youth desired to screech out his grief. He was stabbed, but his tongue lay dead in the tomb of his mouth. He threw himself again upon the ground and began to brood.

The tattered man stood musing.

"Look-a-here, pardner," he said, after a time. He regarded the corpse as he spoke. "He's up an' gone, ain't 'e, an' we might as well begin t' look out fer ol' number one. This here thing is all over. He's up an' gone, ain't 'e? An' he's all right here. Nobody won't bother 'im. An' I might say I ain't enjoying any great health m'self these days."

The youth, awakened by the tattered soldier's tone, looked quickly up. He saw that he was swinging uncertainly on his legs and that his face had turned to a shade of blue.

"Good Lord!" he cried, "you ain't goin' t'—not you, too."

The tattered man waved his hand. "Nary die," he said. "All I want is some pea soup an' a good bed. Some pea soup," he repeated dreamfully.

The youth arose from the ground. "I wonder where he came from. I left him over there." He pointed. "And now I find 'im here. And he was coming from over there, too." He indicated a new direction. They both turned toward the body as if to ask of it a question.

"Well," at length spoke the tattered man, "there ain't no use in our stayin' here an' tryin' t' ask him anything."

The youth nodded an assent wearily. They both turned to gaze for a moment at the corpse.

Chapter 10 **829**

The youth murmured something.

"Well, he was a jim-dandy, wa'n't 'e?" said the tattered man as if in response.

They turned their backs upon it and started away. For a time they stole softly, treading with their toes. It remained laughing there in the grass.

"I'm commencin' t' feel pretty bad," said the tattered man, suddenly breaking one of his little silences. "I'm commencin' t' feel pretty bad."

The youth groaned. "O Lord!" He wondered if he was to be the tortured witness of another grim encounter.

But his companion waved his hand reassuringly. "Oh, I'm not goin' t' die yit! There's too much dependin' on me fer me t' die yit. No sir! Nary die! I *can't!* Ye'd oughta see th' swad a' chil'ren I've got, an' all like that."

The youth glancing at his companion could see by the shadow of a smile that he was making some kind of fun.

As they plodded on, the tattered soldier continued to talk. "Besides, if I died, I wouldn't die th' way that feller did. That was th' funniest thing. I'd jest flop down, I would. I never seen a feller die th' way that feller did.

"Yeh know Tom Jamison, he lives next door t' me up home. He's a nice feller, he is, an' we was allus good friends. Smart, too. Smart as a steel trap. Well, when we was a-fightin' this afternoon, all-of-a-sudden he begin t' rip up an' cuss an' beller at me. 'Yer shot, yeh blamed infernal!'—he swear horrible—he ses t' me. I put up m' hand t' m' head an' when I looked at m' fingers, I seen, sure 'nough, I was shot. I give a holler an' begin t' run, but b'fore I could git away another one hit me in th' arm an' whirl' me clean 'round. I got skeared when they was all a-shoot-in' b'hind me an' I run t' beat all, but I cotch it pretty bad. I've an idee I'd a' been fightin' yit, if t'wasn't fer Tom Jamison."

Then he made a calm announcement: "There's two of 'em—little ones—but they're beginnin' t' have fun with me now. I don't b'lieve I kin walk much furder."

They went slowly on in silence. "Yeh look pretty peeked yerself," said the tattered man at last. "I bet yeh 've got a worser one than yeh think. Ye'd better take keer of yer hurt. It don't do t' let sech things go. It might be inside mostly, an' them plays thunder. Where is it located?" But he continued his harangue without waiting for a reply.

"I see' a feller git hit plum in th' head when my reg'ment was a-standin' at ease onct. An' everybody yelled out to 'im: Hurt, John? Are yeh hurt much? 'No,' ses he. He looked kinder surprised, an' he went on tellin' 'em how he felt. He sed he didn't feel nothin'. But, by dad, th' first thing that feller knowed he was dead. Yes, he was dead—stone dead. So, yeh wanta watch out. Yeh might have some queer kind 'a hurt yerself. Yeh can't never tell. Where is your'n located?"

The youth had been wriggling since the introduction of this topic. He now gave a cry of exasperation and made a furious motion with his hand. "Oh, don't bother me!" he said. He was enraged against the tattered man, and could have strangled him. His companions seemed ever to play intolerable parts. They were ever upraising the ghost of shame on the stick of their curiosity. He turned toward the tattered man as one at bay. "Now, don't bother me," he repeated with desperate menace.

"Well, Lord knows I don't wanta bother anybody," said the other. There was a little accent of despair in his voice as he replied, "Lord knows I've gota 'nough m' own t' tend to."

The youth, who had been holding a bitter debate with himself and casting glances of hatred and contempt at the tattered man, here spoke in a hard voice. "Good-by," he said.

The tattered man looked at him in gaping amazement. "Why—why, pardner, where ye goin'?" he asked unsteadily. The youth looking at him, could see that he, too, like that other one, was beginning to act dumb and animal-like. His thoughts seemed to be floundering about in his head. "Now—now—look—a—here, you Tom Jamison—now—I won't have this—this here won't do. Where—where yeh goin'?"

The youth pointed vaguely. "Over there," he replied.

"Well, now look—a—here—now," said the tattered man, rambling on in idiot fashion. His head was hanging forward and his words were slurred. "This thing won't do, now, Tom Jamison. It won't do. I know yeh, yeh pig-headed devil. Yeh wanta go trompin' off with a bad hurt. It ain't right—now—Tom Jamison—it ain't. Yeh wanta leave me take keer of yeh, Tom Jamison. It ain't—right—it ain't—fer yeh t' go—trompin' off—with a bad hurt—it ain't—ain't—ain't right—it ain't."

In reply the youth climbed a fence and started away. He could hear the tattered man bleating plaintively.

Once he faced about angrily. "What?"

"Look—a—here, now, Tom Jamison—now—it ain't——"

The youth went on. Turning at a distance he saw the tattered man wandering about helplessly in the field.

He now thought that he wished he was dead. He believed that he envied those men whose bodies lay strewn over the grass of the fields and on the fallen leaves of the forest.

The simple questions of the tattered man had been knife thrusts to him. They asserted a society that probes pitilessly at secrets until all is apparent. His late companion's chance persistency made him feel that he could not keep his crime concealed in his bosom. It was sure to be brought plain by one of those arrows which cloud the air and are constantly pricking, discovering, proclaiming those things which are willed to be forever hidden. He admitted that he could not defend himself against this agency. It was not within the power of vigilance.

CHAPTER 11

He became aware that the furnace roar of the battle was growing louder. Great brown clouds had floated to the still heights of air before him. The noise, too, was approaching. The woods filtered men and the fields became dotted.

As he rounded a hillock, he perceived that the roadway was now a crying mass of wagons, teams, and men. From the heaving tangle issued exhortations, commands, imprecations. Fear was sweeping it all along. The cracking whips bit and horses plunged and tugged. The white-topped wagons strained and stumbled in their exertions like fat sheep.

The youth felt comforted in a measure by this sight. They were all retreating. Perhaps, then, he was not so bad after all. He seated himself and watched the terror-stricken wagons. They fled like soft, ungainly animals. All the roarers and lashers served to help him to magnify the dangers and horrors of the engagement that he might try to prove to himself that the thing with which men could charge him was in truth a symmetrical act. There was an amount of pleasure to him in watching the wild march of this vindication.

Presently the calm head of a forward-going column of infantry appeared in the road. It came swiftly on. Avoiding the obstructions gave it the sinuous movement of a serpent. The men at the head butted mules with their musket stocks. They prodded teamsters indifferent to all howls. The men forced their way through parts of the dense mass by strength. The blunt head of the column pushed. The raving teamsters swore many strange oaths.

The commands to make way had the ring of a great importance in them. The men were going forward to the heart of the din. They were to confront the eager rush of the enemy. They felt the pride of their onward movement when the remainder of the army seemed trying to dribble down this road. They tumbled teams about with a fine feeling that it was no matter so long as their column got to the front in time. This importance made their faces grave and stern. And the backs of the officers were very rigid.

As the youth looked at them, the black weight of his woe returned to him. He felt that he was regarding a procession of chosen beings. The separation was as great to him as if they had marched with weapons of flame and banners of sunlight. He could never be like them. He could have wept in his longings.

He searched about in his mind for an adequate malediction for the indefinite cause, the thing upon which men turn the words of final blame. It—whatever it was—was responsible for him, he said. There lay the fault.

The haste of the column to reach the battle seemed to the forlorn young man to be something much finer than stout fighting. Heroes, he thought, could find excuses in that long, seething lane. They could retire with perfect self-respect and make excuses to the stars.

He wondered what those men had eaten that they could be in such haste to force their way to grim chances of death. As he watched, his envy grew until he thought that he wished to change lives with one of them. He would have liked to have used a tremendous force, he said, throwing off himself and become a better. Swift pictures of himself, apart, yet in himself, came to him—a blue desperate figure leading lurid charges with one knee forward and a broken blade high—a blue, determined figure standing before a crimson and steel assault, getting calmly killed on a high place before the eyes of all. He thought of the magnificent pathos of his dead body.

These thoughts uplifted him. He felt the quiver of war desire. In his ears, he heard the ring of victory. He knew the frenzy of a rapid successful charge. The music of the trampling feet, the sharp voices, the clanking arms of the column near him made him soar on the red wings of war. For a few moments he was sublime.

He thought that he was about to start for the front. Indeed, he saw a picture of himself, dust-stained, haggard, panting, flying to the front at the proper moment to seize and throttle the dark, leering witch of calamity.

Then the difficulties of the thing began to drag at him. He hesitated, balancing awkwardly on one foot.

He had no rifle; he could not fight with his hands, said he resentfully to his plan. Well, rifles could be had for the picking. They were extraordinarily profuse.

Also, he continued, it would be a miracle if he found his regiment. Well, he could fight with any regiment.

He started forward slowly. He stepped as if he expected to tread upon some explosive thing. Doubts and he were struggling.

He would truly be a worm if any of his comrades should see him returning thus, the marks of his flight upon him. There was a reply that the intent fighters did not care for what happened rearward saving that no hostile bayonets appeared there. In the battle-blur his face would in a way be hidden, like the face of a cowled man.

But then he said that his tireless fate would bring forth, when the strife lulled for a moment, a man to ask of him an explanation. In imagination he felt the scrutiny of his companions as he painfully labored through some lies.

Eventually, his courage expended itself upon these objections. The debates drained him of his fire.

He was not cast down by this defeat of his plan, for, upon studying the affair carefully, he could not but admit that the objections were very formidable.

Furthermore, various ailments had begun to cry out. In their presence he could not persist in flying high with the wings of war; they rendered it almost impossible for him to see himself in a heroic light. He tumbled headlong.

He discovered that he had a scorching thirst. His face was so dry and grimy that he thought he could feel his skin crackle. Each bone of his body had an ache in it, and seemingly threatened to break with each movement. His feet were like two sores. Also, his body was calling for food. It was more powerful than a direct hunger. There was a dull, weightlike feeling in his stomach, and, when he tried to walk, his head swayed and he tottered. He could not see with distinctness. Small patches of green mist floated before his vision.

While he had been tossed by many emotions, he had not been aware of ailments. Now they beset him and made clamor. As he was at last compelled to pay attention to them, his capacity for self-hate was multiplied. In despair, he declared that he was not like those others. He now conceded it to be impossible that he should ever become a hero. He was a craven loon. Those pictures of glory were piteous things. He groaned from his heart and went staggering off.

A certain mothlike quality within him kept him in the vicinity of the battle. He had a great desire to see, and to get news. He wished to know who was winning.

He told himself that, despite his unprecedented suffering, he had never lost his greed for a victory, yet, he said, in a half-apologetic manner to his conscience, he could not but know that a defeat for the army this time might mean many favorable things for him. The blows of the enemy would splinter regiments into fragments. Thus, many men of courage, he considered, would be obliged to desert the colors and scurry like chickens. He would appear as one of them. They would be sullen brothers in distress, and he could then easily believe he had not run any farther or faster than they. And if he himself could believe in his virtuous perfection, he conceived that there would be small trouble in convincing all others.

He said, as if in excuse for this hope, that previously the army had encountered great defeats and in a few months had shaken off all blood and tradition of them, emerging as bright and valiant as a new one; thrusting out of sight the memory of disaster, and appearing with the valor and confidence of unconquered legions. The shrilling voices of the people at home would pipe dismally for a time, but various generals were usually compelled to listen to these ditties. He of course felt no compunctions for proposing a general as a sacrifice. He could not tell who the chosen for the barbs might be, so he could center no direct sympathy upon him. The people were afar and he did not conceive public opinion to be accurate at long range. It was quite probable they would hit the wrong man who, after he had recovered from his amazement would perhaps spend the rest of his days in writing replies to the songs of his alleged failure. It would be very unfortunate, no doubt, but in this case a general was of no consequence to the youth.

In a defeat there would be a roundabout vindication of himself. He thought it would prove, in a manner, that he had fled early because of his superior powers of perception. A serious prophet upon predicting a flood should be the first man to climb a tree. This would demonstrate that he was indeed a seer.

A moral vindication was regarded by the youth as a very important thing. Without salve, he could not, he thought, wear the sore badge of his dishonor through life. With his heart continually assuring him that he was despicable, he could not exist without making it, through his actions, apparent to all men.

If the army had gone gloriously on, he would be lost. If the din meant that now his army's flags were tilted forward, he was a condemned wretch. He would be compelled to doom himself to isolation. If the men were advancing, their indifferent feet were trampling upon his chances for a successful life.

As these thoughts went rapidly through his mind, he turned upon them and tried to thrust them away. He denounced himself as a villain. He said that he was the most unutterably selfish man in existence. His mind pictured the soldiers who would place their defiant bodies before the spear of the yelling battle fiend, and as he saw their dripping corpses on an imagined field, he said that he was their murderer.

Again he thought that he wished he was dead. He believed that he envied a corpse. Thinking of the slain, he achieved a great contempt for some of them, as if they were guilty for thus becoming lifeless. They might have been killed by lucky chances, he said, before they had had opportunities to flee or before they had been really tested. Yet they would receive laurels from tradition. He cried out bitterly that their crowns were stolen and their robes of glorious memories were shams. However, he still said that it was a great pity he was not as they.

A defeat of the army had suggested itself to him as a means of escape from the consequences of his fall. He considered, now, however, that it was useless to think of such a possibility. His education had been that success for that mighty blue machine was certain; that it would make victories as a contrivance turns out buttons. He presently discarded all his speculations in the other direction. He returned to the creed of soldiers.

When he perceived again that it was not possible for the army to be defeated, he tried to bethink him of a fine tale which he could take back to his regiment, and with it turn the expected shafts of derision.

But, as he mortally feared these shafts, it became impossible for him to invent a tale he felt he could trust. He experimented with many schemes, but threw them aside one by one as flimsy. He was quick to see vulnerable places in them all.

Furthermore, he was much afraid that some arrow of scorn might lay him mentally low before he could raise his protecting tale.

He imagined the whole regiment saying: "Where's Henry Fleming? He run, didn't 'e? Oh, my!" He recalled various persons who would be quite sure to leave him no peace about it. They would doubtless question him with sneers, and laugh at his stammering hesitation. In the next engagement they would try to keep watch of him to discover when he would run.

Wherever he went in camp, he would encounter insolent and lingeringly cruel stares. As he imagined himself passing near a crowd of comrades, he could hear someone say, "There he goes!"

Then, as if the heads were moved by one muscle, all the faces turned toward him with wide, derisive grins. He seemed to hear someone make a humorous remark in a low tone. At it the others all crowded and cackled. He was a slang phrase.

CHAPTER 12

The column that had butted stoutly at the obstacles in the roadway was barely out of the youth's sight before he saw dark waves of men come sweeping out of the woods and down through the fields. He knew at once that the steel fibers had been washed from their hearts. They were bursting from their coats and their equipments as from entanglements. They charged down upon him like terrified buffaloes.

Behind them blue smoke curled and clouded above the treetops, and through the thickets he could sometimes see a distant pink glare. The voices of the cannon were clamoring in interminable chorus.

The youth was horror stricken. He stared in agony and amazement. He forgot that he was engaged in combating the universe. He threw aside his mental pamphlets on the philosophy of the retreated and rules for the guidance of the damned.

The fight was lost. The dragons were coming with invincible strides. The army, helpless in the matted thickets and blinded by the overhanging night, was going to be swallowed. War, the red animal, war, the blood-swollen god, would have bloated fill.

Within him something bade to cry out. He had the impulse to make a rallying speech, to sing a battle hymn, but he could only get his tongue to call into the air: "Why—why—what—what's th' matter?"

Soon he was in the midst of them. They were leaping and scampering all about him. Their blanched faces shone in the dusk. They seemed, for the most part, to be very burly men. The youth turned from one to another of them as they galloped along. His incoherent questions were lost. They were heedless of his appeals. They did not seem to see him.

*artillery flashes
were light*

They sometimes gabbled insanely. One huge man was asking of the sky: "Say, where de plank road? Where de plank road!" It was as if he had lost a child. He wept in his pain and dismay.

Presently, men were running hither and thither in all ways. The artillery booming, forward, rearward, and on the flanks made jumble of ideas of direction. Landmarks had vanished into the gathered gloom. The youth began to imagine that he had got into the center of the tremendous quarrel, and he could perceive no way out of it. From the mouths of the fleeing men came a thousand wild questions, but no one made answers.

The youth, after rushing about and throwing interrogations at the heedless bands of retreating infantry, finally clutched a man by the arm. They swung around face to face.

"Why—why——" stammered the youth struggling with his balking tongue.

The man screamed: "Let go me! Let go me!" His face was livid and his eyes were rolling uncontrolled. He was heaving and panting. He still grasped his rifle, perhaps having forgotten to release his hold upon it. He tugged frantically, and the youth being compelled to lean forward was dragged several paces.

"Let go me! Let go me!"

"Why—why——" stuttered the youth.

"Well, then!" bawled the man in a lurid rage. He adroitly and fiercely swung his rifle. It crushed upon the youth's head. The man ran on.

The youth's fingers had turned to paste upon the other's arm. The energy was smitten from his muscles. He saw the flaming wings of lightning flash before his vision. There was a deafening rumble of thunder within his head.

Suddenly his legs seemed to die. He sank writhing to the ground. He tried to arise. In his efforts against the numbing pain he was like a man wrestling with a creature of the air.

There was a sinister struggle.

Sometimes he would achieve a position half erect, battle with the air for a moment, and then fall again, grabbing at the grass. His face was of a clammy pallor. Deep groans were wrenched from him.

At last, with a twisting movement, he got upon his hands and knees, and from thence, like a babe trying to walk, to his feet. Pressing his hands to his temples he went lurching over the grass.

He fought an intense battle with his body. His dulled senses wished him to swoon and he opposed them stubbornly, his mind portraying unknown dangers and mutilations if he should fall upon the field. He went tall soldier fashion. He imagined secluded spots where he could fall and be unmolested. To search for one he strove against the tide of his pain.

Once he put his hand to the top of his head and timidly touched the wound. The scratching pain of the contact made him draw a long breath through his clinched teeth. His fingers were dabbled with blood. He regarded them with a fixed stare.

Around him he could hear the grumble of jolted cannon as the scurrying horses were lashed toward the front. Once, a young officer on a besplashed charger nearly ran him down. He turned and watched the mass of guns, men, and horses sweeping in a wide curve toward a gap in a fence. The officer was making excited motions with a gauntleted hand. The guns followed the teams with an air of unwillingness, of being dragged by the heels.

Some officers of the scattered infantry were cursing and railing like fishwives. Their scolding voices could be heard above the din. Into the unspeakable jumble in the roadway rode a squadron of cavalry. The faded yellow of their facings shone bravely. There was a mighty altercation.

The artillery were assembling as if for a conference.

The blue haze of evening was upon the field. The lines of forest were long purple shadows. One cloud lay along the western sky partly smothering the red.

As the youth left the scene behind him, he heard the guns suddenly roar out. He imagined them shaking in black rage. They belched and howled like brass devils guarding a gate. The soft air was filled with the tremendous remonstrance. With it came the shattering peal of opposing infantry. Turning to look behind him, he could see sheets of orange light illumine the shadowy distance. There were subtle and sudden lightnings in the far air. At times he thought he could see heaving masses of men.

He hurried on in the dusk. The day had faded until he could barely distinguish a place for his feet. The purple darkness was filled with men who lectured and jabbered. Sometimes he could see them gesticulating against the blue and somber sky. There seemed to be a great ruck of men and munitions spread about in the forest and in the fields.

The little narrow roadway now lay lifeless. There were overturned wagons like sun-dried boulders. The bed of the former torrent was choked with the bodies of horses and splintered parts of war machines.

It had come to pass that his wound pained him but little. He was afraid to move rapidly, however, for a dread of disturbing it. He held his head very still and took many precautions against stumbling. He was filled with anxiety, and his face was pinched and drawn in anticipation of the pain of any sudden mistake of his feet in the gloom.

His thoughts, as he walked, fixed intently upon his hurt. There was a cool, liquid feeling about it and he imagined blood moving slowly down under his hair. His head seemed swollen to a size that made him think his neck to be inadequate.

The new silence of his wound made much worriment. The little blistering voices of pain that had called out from the scalp were, he thought, definite in their expression of danger. By them he believed that he could measure his plight. But when they remained ominously silent, he became frightened and imagined terrible fingers that clutched into his brain.

Amid it he began to reflect upon various incidents and conditions of the past. He bethought him of certain meals his mother had cooked at home, in which those dishes of which he was particularly fond had occupied prominent positions. He saw the spread table. The pine walls of the kitchen were glowing in the warm light from the stove. Too, he remembered how he and his companions used to go from the schoolhouse to the bank of a shaded pool. He saw his clothes in disorderly array upon the grass of the bank. He felt the swash of the fragrant water upon his body. The leaves of the overhanging maple rustled with melody in the wind of youthful summer.

He was overcome presently by a dragging weariness. His head hung forward and his shoulders were stooped as if he were bearing a great bundle. His feet shuffled along the ground.

He held continuous arguments as to whether he should lie down and sleep at some near spot, or force himself on until he reached a certain haven. He often tried to dismiss the question, but his body persisted in rebellion and his senses nagged at him like pampered babies.

At last he heard a cheery voice near his shoulder: "Yeh seem t' be in a pretty bad way, boy?"

The youth did not look up, but he assented with thick tongue. "Uh!"

The owner of the cheery voice took him firmly by the arm. "Well," he said, with a round laugh, "I'm goin' your way. Th' hull gang is goin' your way. An' I guess I kin give yeh a lift." They began to walk like a drunken man and his friend.

As they went along, the man questioned the youth and assisted him with the replies like one manipulating the mind of a child. Sometimes he interjected anecdotes. "What reg'ment do yeh b'long teh? Eh? What's that? Th' 304th N'York? Why, what corps is that in? Oh, it is? Why, I thought they wasn't engaged t'-day—they're 'way over in th' center. Oh, they was, eh? Well, pretty nearly everybody got their share 'a fightin' t'-day. By dad, I give myself up fer dead any number 'a times. There was shootin' here an' shootin' there, an' hollerin' here an' hollerin' there, in th' darkness, until I couldn't tell t' save m' soul which side I was on. Sometimes I thought I was sure 'nough from Ohier, an' other times I could a' swore I was from th' bitter end of Florida. It was th' most mixed up dern thing I ever see. An' these here hull woods is a reg'lar mess. It'll be a miracle if we find our reg'ments t'-night. Pretty soon, though, we'll meet a-plenty of guards an' provost-guards, an' one thing an' another. Ho! There they go with an off'cer, I guess. Look at his hand a-draggin'. He's got all th' war he wants, I bet. He won't be talkin' so big about his reputation an' all when they go t' sawin' off his leg. Poor feller! My brother's got whiskers jest like that. How did yeh git 'way over here, anyhow? Your reg'ment is a long way from here, ain't it? Well, I guess we can find it. Yeh know there was a boy killed in my comp'ny t'-day that I thought th' world an' all of. Jack was a nice feller. By ginger, it hurt like thunder t' see ol' Jack jest git knocked flat. We was a-standin' purty peaceable fer a spell, 'though there was men runnin' ev'ry way all 'round us, an' while we was a-standin' like that, 'long come a big fat feller. He began t' peck at Jack's elbow, an' he ses: 'Say, where's th' road t' th' river?' An' Jack, he never paid no attention, an' th' feller kept on a-peckin' at his elbow an' sayin': 'Say, where's th' road t' th' river?' Jack was a-lookin' ahead all th' time tryin' t' see th' Johnnies comin' through th' woods, an' he never paid no attention t' this big fat feller fer a long time, but at last he turned 'round an' he ses: 'Ah, go an' find th' road t' th' river!' An' jest then a shot slapped him bang on th' side th' head. He was a sergeant, too. Them was his last words. Thunder, I wish we was sure 'a findin' our reg'-ments t'-night. It's goin' t' be long huntin'. But I guess we kin do it."

In the search that followed, the man of the cheery voice seemed to the youth to possess a wand of a magic kind. He threaded the mazes of the tangled forest with a strange fortune. In encounter with guards and patrols he displayed the keenness of a detective and the valor of a gamin. Obstacles fell before him and became of assistance. The youth, with his chin still on his breast, stood wood-enly by while his companion beat ways and means out of sullen things.

The forest seemed a vast hive of men buzzing about in frantic circles, but the cheery man con-ducted the youth without mistakes, until at last he began to chuckle with glee and self-satisfaction. "Ah, there yeh are! See that fire?"

The youth nodded stupidly.

"Well, there's where your reg'ment is. An' now, good-by, ol' boy, good luck t' yeh."

A warm and strong hand clasped the youth's languid fingers for an instant, and then he heard a cheerful and audacious whistling as the man strode away. As he who had so befriended him was thus passing out of his life, it suddenly occurred to the youth that he had not once seen his face.

CHAPTER 13

The youth went slowly toward the fire indicated by his departed friend. As he reeled, he bethought him of the welcome his comrades would give him. He had a conviction that he would soon feel in his sore heart the barbed missiles of ridicule. He had no strength to invent a tale; he would be a soft target.

He made vague plans to go off into the deeper darkness and hide, but they were all destroyed by the voices of exhaustion and pain from his body. His ailments, clamoring, forced him to seek the place of food and rest, at whatever cost.

He swung unsteadily toward the fire. He could see the forms of men throwing black shadows in the red light, and as he went nearer it became known to him in some way that the ground was strewn with sleeping men.

Of a sudden he confronted a black and mon-strous figure. A rifle barrel caught some glint-ing beams. "Halt! halt!" He was dismayed for a moment, but he presently thought that he rec-ognized the nervous voice. As he stood tottering before the rifle barrel, he called out: "Why, hello, Wilson, you—you here?"

The rifle was lowered to a position of caution and the loud soldier came slowly forward. He peered into the youth's face. "That you, Henry?"

"Yes, it's—it's me."

"Well, well, ol' boy," said the other, "by ginger, I'm glad t' see yeh! I give yeh up fer a goner. I thought yeh was dead sure enough." There was husky emotion in his voice.

The youth found that now he could barely stand upon his feet. There was a sudden sinking of his forces. He thought he must hasten to produce his tale to protect him from the missiles already at the lips of his redoubtable comrades. So, stagger-ing before the loud soldier, he began: "Yes, yes, I've—I've had an awful time. I've been all over. Way over on th' right. Ter'ble fightin' over there. I had an awful time. I got separated from th' reg'-ment. Over on th' right, I got shot. In th' head. I never see sech fightin'. Awful time. I don't see how I could a' got separated from th' reg'ment. I got shot, too."

His friend had stepped forward quickly. "What? Got shot? Why didn't yeh say so first? Poor ol' boy, we must—hol' on a minnit; what am I doin'. I'll call Simpson."

Another figure at that moment loomed in the gloom. They could see that it was the corporal. "Who yeh talkin' to, Wilson?" he demanded. His voice was anger-toned. "Who yeh talkin' to? Yeh th' derndest sentinel—why—hello, Henry, you here? Why, I thought you was dead four hours ago! Great Jerusalem, they keep turnin' up every ten minutes or so! We thought we'd lost forty-two men by straight count, but if they keep on a-comin' this way, we'll get th' comp'ny all back by mornin' yit. Where was yeh?"

"Over on th' right. I got separated"—began the youth with considerable glibness.

But his friend had interrupted hastily. "Yes, an' he got shot in th' head an' he's in a fix, an' we must see t' him right away." He rested his rifle in the hollow of his left arm and his right around the youth's shoulder.

"Gee, it must hurt like thunder!" he said.

The youth leaned heavily upon his friend. "Yes, it hurts—hurts a good deal," he replied. There was a faltering in his voice.

"Oh," said the corporal. He linked his arm in the youth's and drew him forward. "Come on, Henry, I'll take keer 'a yeh."

As they went on together the loud private called out after them: "Put 'im t' sleep in my blanket, Simpson. An'—hol' on a minnit—here's my canteen. It's full 'a coffee. Look at his head by th' fire an' see how it looks. Maybe it's a pretty bad un. When I git relieved in a couple 'a minnits, I'll be over an' see t' him."

The youth's senses were so deadened that his friend's voice sounded from afar and he could scarcely feel the pressure of the corporal's arm. He submitted passively to the latter's directing strength. His head was in the old manner hanging forward upon his breast. His knees wobbled.

The corporal led him into the glare of the fire. "Now, Henry," he said, "let's have look at yer ol' head."

The youth sat down obediently and the corporal, laying aside his rifle, began to fumble in the bushy hair of his comrade. He was obliged to turn the other's head so that the full flush of the firelight would beam upon it. He puckered his mouth with a critical air. He drew back his lips and whistled through his teeth when his fingers came in contact with the splashed blood and the rare wound.

"Ah, here we are!" he said. He awkwardly made further investigations. "Jest as I thought," he added, presently. "Yeh've been grazed by a ball. It's raised a queer lump just as if some feller had lammed yeh on th' head with a club. It stopped a-bleedin' long time ago. Th' most about it is that in th' mornin' yeh'll feel that a number ten hat wouldn't fit yeh. An' your head 'll be all het up an' feel as dry as burnt pork. An' yeh may git a lot 'a other sicknesses, too, by mornin'. Yeh can't never tell. Still, I don't much think so. It's jest a good belt on th' head, an' nothin' more. Now, you jest sit here an' don't move, while I go rout out th' relief. Then I'll send Wilson t' take keer 'a yeh."

The corporal went away. The youth remained on the ground like a parcel. He stared with a vacant look into the fire.

After a time he aroused, for some part, and the things about him began to take form. He saw that the ground in the deep shadows was cluttered with men, sprawling in every conceivable posture. Glancing narrowly into the more distant darkness, he caught occasional glimpses of visages that loomed pallid and ghostly, lit with a phosphorescent glow. These faces expressed in their lines the deep stupor of the tired soldiers. They made them appear like men drunk with wine. This bit of forest might have appeared to an ethereal wanderer as a scene of the result of some frightful debauch.

On the other side of the fire the youth observed an officer asleep, seated bolt upright, with his back against a tree. There was something perilous in his position. Badgered by dreams, perhaps, he swayed with little bounces and starts, like an old, toddy-stricken grandfather in a chimney corner. Dust and stains were upon his face. His lower jaw hung down as if lacking strength to assume its normal position. He was the picture of an exhausted soldier after a feast of war.

He had evidently gone to sleep with his sword in his arms. These two had slumbered in an embrace, but the weapon had been allowed in time to fall unheeded to the ground. The brass-mounted hilt lay in contact with some parts of the fire.

Within the gleam of rose and orange light from the burning sticks were other soldiers, snoring and heaving, or lying deathlike in slumber. A few pairs of legs were stuck forth, rigid and straight. The shoes displayed the mud or dust of marches and bits of rounded trousers, protruding from the blankets, showed rents and tears from hurried pitchings through the dense brambles.

The fire crackled musically. From it swelled light smoke. Overhead the foliage moved softly.

The leaves, with their faces turned toward the blaze, were colored shifting hues of silver, often edged with red. Far-off to the right, through a window in the forest, could be seen a handful of stars lying, like glittering pebbles, on the black level of the night.

Occasionally, in this low-arched hall, a soldier would arouse and turn his body to a new position, the experience of his sleep having taught him of uneven and objectionable places upon the ground under him. Or, perhaps, he would lift himself to a sitting posture, blink at the fire for an unintelligent moment, throw a swift glance at his prostrate companion, and then cuddle down again with a grunt of sleepy content.

The youth sat in a forlorn heap until his friend, the loud young soldier, came, swinging two canteens by their light strings. "Well, now, Henry ol' boy," said the latter, "we'll have yeh fixed up in jest about a minnit."

He had the bustling ways of an amateur nurse. He fussed around the fire and stirred the sticks to brilliant exertions. He made his patient drink largely from the canteen that contained the coffee. It was to the youth a delicious draught. He tilted his head afar back and held the canteen long to his lips. The cool mixture went caressingly down his blistered throat. Having finished, he sighed with comfortable delight.

The loud young soldier watched his comrade with an air of satisfaction. He later produced an extensive handkerchief from his pocket. He folded it into a manner of bandage and soused water from the other canteen upon the middle of it. This crude arrangement he bound over the youth's head, tying the ends in a queer knot at the back of the neck.

"There," he said, moving off and surveying his deed, "yeh look like th' devil, but I bet yeh feel better."

The youth contemplated his friend with grateful eyes. Upon his aching and swelling head the cold cloth was like a tender woman's hand.

"Yeh don't holler ner say nothin'," remarked his friend approvingly. "I know I'm a blacksmith at takin' keer 'a sick folks, an' yeh never squeaked. Yer a good un, Henry. Most 'a men would a' been in th' hospital long ago. A shot in th' head ain't foolin' business."

The youth made no reply, but began to fumble with the buttons of his jacket.

"Well, come, now," continued his friend, "come on. I must put yeh t' bed an' see that yeh git a good night's rest."

The other got carefully erect, and the loud young soldier led him among the sleeping forms lying in groups and rows. Presently he stooped and picked up his blankets. He spread the rubber one upon the ground and placed the woolen one about the youth's shoulders.

"There now," he said, "lie down an' git some sleep."

The youth, with his manner of doglike obedience, got carefully down like a crone stooping. He stretched out with a murmur of relief and comfort. The ground felt like the softest couch.

But of a sudden he ejaculated: "Hol' on a minnit! Where you goin' t' sleep?"

His friend waved his hand impatiently. "Right down there by yeh."

"Well, but hol' on a minnit," continued the youth. "What yeh goin' t' sleep in? I've got your—"

The loud young soldier snarled: "Shet up an' go on t' sleep . Don't be makin' a fool 'a yerself," he said severely.

After the reproof the youth said no more. An exquisite drowsiness had spread through him. The warm comfort of the blanket enveloped him and made a gentle languor. His head fell forward on his crooked arm and his weighted lids went slowly down over his eyes. Hearing a splatter of musketry from the distance, he wondered indifferently if those men sometimes slept. He gave a long sigh, snuggled down into his blanket, and in a moment was like his comrades.

THINK AND DISCUSS
CHAPTERS 10–13
Understanding
1. What question does the tattered man ask Henry? Why does this question disturb him?
2. How does Henry receive his wound?
3. What does the cheerful soldier who befriends Henry in Chapter 12 do for him?
4. What familiar figure does Henry encounter when he returns to his regiment? What kind of reception does Henry receive?

Analyzing
5. Describe Henry's thoughts early in Chapter 11 as he watches the troops retreat on the roadway (831a, 2–3). How does he feel about the "forward-going column" that he sees next?
6. In the second half of Chapter 11, Henry argues that a defeat would be "a moral vindication" for him. Explain his reasoning.
7. How does the encampment scene in Chapter 13 differ from the one described at the beginning of the novel? Point out images that contribute to the mood of the latter scene.

Extending
8. Imagine that Henry had received his "red badge" on the battlefield from a gun rather than from the butt of a fleeing soldier's rifle. How would this change affect the plot thus far?

REVIEWING: Irony H⫯
See Handbook of Literary Terms, p. 893.

Irony is a contrast between what appears to be and what actually is. Three kinds of irony are *verbal, dramatic,* and *situational*.

1. Explain the irony of the following words spoken by the tattered man to Henry about his wound: "It don't do t' let sech things go. It might be inside mostly, an' them plays thunder."
2. What is ironic about the manner in which Henry is injured?

3. Which kind of irony is illustrated in each of the preceding examples?

VOCABULARY
Context
Try to determine the meaning of each of the italicized words in the following sentences by using context clues. If there are not enough context clues, write "no clues." Be sure that you can pronounce and spell all the italicized words.

1. "In the battle-blur his face would in a way be hidden, like the face of a *cowled* man." (a) hooded; (b) masked; (c) desperate; (d) cautious.
2. "Wherever he went in camp, he would encounter *insolent* and lingeringly cruel stares." (a) inspiring; (b) insulting; (c) somber; (d) reckless.
3. "Avoiding the obstructions gave it the *sinuous* movement of a serpent." (a) gliding; (b) striking; (c) abrupt; (d) curving.
4. "He now gave a cry of *exasperation* and made a furious motion with his hand." (a) delight; (b) hope; (c) irritation; (d) agreement.
5. "He thought he must hasten to produce his tale to protect him from the missiles already at the lips of his *redoubtable* comrades." (a) vulnerable; (b) cheerful; (c) sullen; (d) formidable.

THINKING SKILLS
Evaluating
The cheerful soldier provides a kind of moral measuring stick for evaluating Henry's own behavior. Although both soldiers have been separated from their regiments and have lost a friend in battle, they respond very differently to their plights.

1. Compare and contrast Henry's treatment of the tattered soldier with the cheerful soldier's treatment of Henry.
2. Why do you think it significant that the cheerful soldier's face is never revealed?

Initiation

Like many young protagonists in American literature, Henry Fleming in *The Red Badge of Courage* has undergone an initiation, moving from innocence to maturity. But the initiation motif takes an ironic twist as Henry becomes a hero through a minor wound administered by a retreating soldier from his own army. Torn between panic and "broken-bladed glory," Henry finally confronts death and gains knowledge far beyond the hollow concepts of bravery he has previously held. Only after he receives his wound does he learn some complex truths—that cowardice and courage are remarkably similar impulses, that he is small but not insignificant, that his sufferings are, in fact, "the bludgeon of correction." In gaining a genuine insight into his personality, he has achieved "a quiet manhood." But he has paid a price for this insight. The image of the tattered soldier dogs him as a constant reminder of his act of human betrayal, tempering his pride with humility.

The title character of Mark Twain's novel *The Adventures of Huckleberry Finn* is another youthful initiate, who wrestles with his conscience as he travels down the Mississippi River with a runaway slave. Ultimately, he decides he cannot betray Jim by turning him in, even though his decision may be considered wrong by society. Through this decision he gains a new sense of identity and awareness but at the cost (he thinks) of his soul.

Ishmael, the narrator of Herman Melville's *Moby Dick*, overcomes his sense of isolation and achieves a "fellow-feeling," a love for humanity. In addition, he emerges from his initiation with an awareness that good and evil are inextricably intertwined. In J. D. Salinger's *Catcher in the Rye*, a modern initiate, Holden Caulfield, gains from his encounters in a senseless, phony world a new-found sympathy for everyone he has known. Ultimately, he relinquishes his self-image as a Catcher in the Rye, realizing that he must plunge into experience and allow others to do so.

Other American classics that focus on initiation include Louisa May Alcott's *Little Women*, Sherwood Anderson's *Winesburg, Ohio*, Richard Wright's *Black Boy*, and John Steinbeck's *Red Pony*.

The initiation motif takes many forms in the works appearing in *The United States in Literature*. Goodman Brown in Nathaniel Hawthorne's "Young Goodman Brown" (Unit 3) witnesses the pervasive presence of evil in the world by attending a midnight witches' meeting; Redburn in Herman Melville's "What Redburn Saw in Launcelott's-Hey" (Unit 3) witnesses the cruelty of humankind as a starving family dies in the midst of a thriving city. Both Goodman Brown and Redburn move toward maturity by perceiving the fundamental and paradoxical relationship of good and evil in human nature.

William Faulkner's story "The Bear" (Unit 5) is an archetypal initiation story that depicts a boy who, in a moment of truth, recognizes the sanctity of a mysterious and mythic bear and the necessity of allowing it to live. In Sherwood Anderson's "Sophistication" (Unit 5), a young man "crosses the line into manhood" and sadly realizes that "he must live and die in uncertainty." A boy who survives a family crisis learns that he has the strength to live without fear in Carson McCullers's "The Haunted Boy" (Unit 7). And Eugenia Collier's "Marigolds" (Unit 7) portrays a young girl who learns compassion through a mindless act of destruction.

Whatever form initiation takes in these stories, it usually results in a move from innocence to maturity, a new sense of identity and purpose, a deeper understanding or awareness, or a new vision. The initiation may be gradual, or it may come in an apocalyptic moment. However it comes, initiation brings to the character a new knowledge about being human that is basic; and it brings to the reader a new awareness of the patterns of human experience that is profound.

gray mist

CHAPTER 14

When the youth awoke, it seemed to him that he had been asleep for a thousand years, and he felt sure that he opened his eyes upon an unexpected world. Gray mists were slowly shifting before the first efforts of the sun rays. An impending splendor could be seen in the eastern sky. An icy dew had chilled his face, and immediately upon arousing he curled farther down into his blankets. He stared for a while at the leaves overhead, moving in a heraldic wind of the day.

The distance was splintering and blaring with the noise of fighting. There was in the sound an expression of a deadly persistency, as if it had not begun and was not to cease.

About him were the rows and groups of men that he had dimly seen the previous night. They were getting a last draught of sleep before the awakening. The gaunt, careworn features and dusty figures were made plain by this quaint light at the dawning, but it dressed the skin of the men in corpselike hues and made the tangled limbs appear pulseless and dead. The youth started up with a little cry when his eyes first swept over this motionless mass of men, thick-spread upon the ground, pallid, and in strange postures. His disordered mind interpreted the hall of the forest as a charnel place. He believed for an instant that he was in the house of the dead, and he did not dare to move lest these corpses start up, squalling and squawking. In a second, however, he achieved his proper mind. He swore a complicated oath at himself. He saw that this somber picture was not a fact of the present, but a mere prophecy.

He heard then the noise of a fire crackling briskly in the cold air, and, turning his head, he saw his friend pottering busily about a small blaze. A few other figures moved in the fog, and he heard the hard cracking of ax blows.

Suddenly there was a hollow rumble of drums. A distant bugle sang faintly. Similar sounds, varying in strength, came from near and far over the forest. The bugles called to each other like brazen gamecocks. The near thunder of the regimental drums rolled.

The body of men in the woods rustled. There was a general uplifting of heads. A murmuring of voices broke upon the air. In it there was much bass of grumbling oaths. Strange gods were addressed in condemnation of the early hours necessary to correct war. An officer's peremptory tenor rang out and quickened the stiffened movement of the men. The tangled limbs unraveled. The corpse-hued faces were hidden behind fists that twisted slowly in the eye sockets.

The youth sat up and gave vent to an enormous yawn. "Thunder!" he remarked petulantly. He rubbed his eyes, and then putting up his hand felt carefully of the bandage over his wound. His friend, perceiving him to be awake, came from the fire. "Well, Henry, ol' man, how do yeh feel this mornin'?" he demanded.

The youth yawned again. Then he puckered his mouth to a little pucker. His head, in truth, felt precisely like a melon, and there was an unpleasant sensation at his stomach.

"Oh, Lord, I feel pretty bad," he said.

"Thunder!" exclaimed the other. "I hoped ye'd feel all right this mornin'. Let's see th' bandage—I guess it's slipped." He began to tinker at the wound in rather a clumsy way until the youth exploded.

"Gosh-dern it!" he said in sharp irritation; "you're the hangdest man I ever saw! You wear muffs on your hands. Why in good thunderation can't you be more easy? I'd rather you'd stand off an' throw guns at it. Now, go slow, an' don't act as if you was nailing down carpet."

He glared with insolent command at his friend, but the latter answered soothingly. "Well, well, come now, an' git some grub," he said. "Then, maybe, yeh'll feel better."

At the fireside the loud young soldier watched over his comrade's wants with tenderness and care. He was very busy marshaling the little black vagabonds of tin cups and pouring into them the streaming, iron colored mixture from a small and sooty tin pail. He had some fresh meat, which he roasted hurriedly upon a stick. He sat down then and contemplated the youth's appetite with glee.

The youth took note of a remarkable change in his comrade since those days of camp life upon the river bank. He seemed no more to be continually regarding the proportions of his personal prowess. He was not furious at small words that pricked his conceits. He was no more a loud young soldier. There was about him now a fine reliance. He showed a quiet belief in his purposes and his abilities. And this inward confidence evidently enabled him to be indifferent to little words of other men aimed at him.

The youth reflected. He had been used to regarding his comrade as a blatant child with an audacity grown from his inexperience, thoughtless, headstrong, jealous, and filled with a tinsel courage. A swaggering babe accustomed to strut in his own dooryard. The youth wondered where had been born these new eyes; when his comrade had made the great discovery that there were many men who would refuse to be subjected by him. Apparently, the other had now climbed a peak of wisdom from which he could perceive himself as a very wee thing. And the youth saw that ever after it would be easier to live in his friend's neighborhood.

His comrade balanced his ebony coffee cup on his knee. "Well, Henry," he said, "what d'yeh think th' chances are? D'yeh think we'll wallop 'em?"

The youth considered for a moment. "Day-b'fore-yestirday," he finally replied, with boldness, "you would 'a' bet you'd lick the hull kit-an'-boodle all by yourself."

His friend looked a trifle amazed. "Would I?" he asked. He pondered. "Well, perhaps I would," he decided at last. He stared humbly at the fire.

The youth was quite disconcerted at this surprising reception of his remarks. "Oh, no, you wouldn't either," he said, hastily trying to retrace.

But the other made a deprecating gesture. "Oh, yeh needn't mind, Henry," he said. "I believe I was a pretty big fool in those days." He spoke as after a lapse of years.

There was a little pause.

"All th' officers say we've got th' rebs in a pretty tight box," said the friend, clearing his throat in a commonplace way. "They all seem t' think we've got 'em just where we want 'em."

"I don't know about that," the youth replied. "What I seen over on th' right makes me think it was th' other way about. From where I was, it looked as if we was gettin' a good poundin' yestirday."

"D'yeh think so?" inquired the friend. "I thought we handled 'em pretty rough yestirday."

"Not a bit!" said the youth. "Why, lord, man, you didn't see nothing of the fight. Why!" Then a sudden thought came to him. "Oh! Jim Conklin's dead."

His friend started. "What? Is he? Jim Conklin?"

The youth spoke slowly. "Yes. He's dead. Shot in th' side."

"Yeh don't say so. Jim Conklin . . . poor cuss!"

All about them were other small fires surrounded by men with their little black utensils. From one of these near came sudden sharp voices in a row. It appeared that two light-footed soldiers had been teasing a huge, bearded man, causing him to spill coffee upon his blue knees. The man had gone into a rage and had sworn comprehensively. Stung by his language, his tormentors had immediately bristled at him with a great show of resenting unjust oaths. Possibly there was going to be a fight.

The friend arose and went over to them, making pacific motions with his arms. "Oh, here, now, boys, what's th' use?" he said. "We'll be at th' rebs in less'n an hour. What's th' good fightin' 'mong ourselves?"

One of the light-footed soldiers turned upon him red-faced and violent. "Yeh needn't come around here with yer preachin'. I s'pose yeh don't approve 'a fightin' since Charley Morgan licked yeh; but I don't see what business this here is 'a yours or anybody else."

"Well, it ain't," said the friend mildly. "Still I hate t' see——"

That was a tangled argument.

"Well, he——," said the two, indicating their opponent with accusative forefingers.

The huge soldier was quite purple with rage. He pointed at the two soldiers with his great hand, extended clawlike. "Well, they——"

But during this argumentative time the desire to deal blows seemed to pass, although they said much to each other. Finally the friend returned to his old seat. In a short while the three antagonists could be seen together in an amiable bunch.

"Jimmie Rogers ses I'll have t' fight him after th' battle t'-day," announced the friend as he again seated himself. "He ses he don't allow no interferin' in his business. I hate t' see th' boys fightin' 'mong themselves."

The youth laughed. "Yer changed a good bit. Yeh ain't at all like yeh was. I remember when you an' that Irish feller——" He stopped and laughed again.

"No, I didn't use t' be that way," said his friend thoughtfully. "That's true 'nough."

"Well, I didn't mean——" began the youth.

The friend made another deprecatory gesture. "Oh, yeh needn't mind, Henry."

There was another little pause.

"Th' reg'ment lost over half th' men yestirday," remarked the friend eventually. "I thought 'a course they was all dead, but, laws, they kep' a-comin' back last night until it seems, after all, we didn't lose but a few. They'd been scattered all over, wanderin' around in th' woods, fightin' with other reg'ments, an' everything. Jest like you done."

"So?" said the youth.

CHAPTER 15

The regiment was standing at order arms at the side of a lane, waiting for the command to march, when suddenly the youth remembered the little packet enwrapped in a faded yellow envelope which the loud young soldier with lugubrious words had entrusted to him. It made him start. He uttered an exclamation and turned toward his comrade.

"Wilson!"

"What?"

His friend, at his side in the ranks, was thoughtfully staring down the road. From some cause his expression was at that moment very meek. The youth, regarding him with sidelong glances, felt impelled to change his purpose. "Oh, nothing," he said.

His friend turned his head in some surprise. "Why, what was yeh goin' t' say?"

"Oh, nothing," repeated the youth.

He resolved not to deal the little blow. It was sufficient that the fact made him glad. It was not necessary to knock his friend on the head with the misguided packet.

He had been possessed of much fear of his friend, for he saw how easily questionings could make holes in his feelings. Lately, he had assured himself that the altered comrade would not tantalize him with a persistent curiosity, but he felt certain that during the first period of leisure his friend would ask him to relate his adventures of the previous day.

He now rejoiced in the possession of a small weapon with which he could prostrate his comrade at the first signs of a cross-examination. He was master. It would now be he who could laugh and shoot the shafts of derision.

The friend had, in a weak hour, spoken with sobs of his own death. He had delivered a melancholy oration previous to his funeral, and had doubtless in the packet of letter, presented various keepsakes to relatives. But he had not died, and thus he had delivered himself into the hands of the youth.

The latter felt immensely superior to his friend, but he inclined to condescension. He adopted toward him an air of patronizing good humor.

His self-pride was now entirely restored. In the shade of its flourishing growth he stood with braced and self-confident legs, and since nothing could now be discovered, he did not shrink from an encounter with the eyes of judges, and allowed no thoughts of his own to keep him from an attitude of manfulness. He had performed his mistakes in the dark, so he was still a man.

Indeed, when he remembered his fortunes of yesterday and looked at them from a distance, he began to see something fine there. He had license to be pompous and veteranlike.

His panting agonies of the past he put out of his sight. In the present, he declared to himself that it was only the doomed and the damned who roared with sincerity at circumstance. Few but they ever did it. A man with a full stomach and the respect of his fellows had no business to scold about anything he might think to be wrong in the ways of the universe, or even with the ways of society. Let the unfortunates rail; the others may play marbles.

He did not give a great deal of thought to these battles that lay directly before him. It was not essential that he should plan his ways in regard to them. He had been taught that many obligations of a life were easily avoided. The lessons of yesterday had been that retribution was a laggard and blind. With these facts before him he did not deem it necessary that he should become feverish over the possibilities of the ensuing twenty-four hours. He could leave much to chance. Besides, a faith in himself had secretly blossomed. There was a little flower of confidence growing within him. He was now a man of experience. He had been out among the dragons, he said, and he assured himself that they were not so hideous as he had imagined them. Also, they were inaccurate; they did not sting with precision. A stout heart often defied, and defying, escaped.

And, furthermore, how could they kill him who was the chosen of the gods and doomed to greatness?

He remembered how some of the men had run from the battle. As he recalled their terror-struck faces, he felt a scorn for them. They had surely been more fleet and more wild than was absolutely necessary. They were weak mortals. As for himself, he had fled with discretion and dignity.

He was aroused from this reverie by his friend, who, having hitched about nervously and blinked at the trees for a time, suddenly coughed in an introductory way, and spoke.

"Fleming!"

"What?"

The friend put his hand up to his mouth and coughed again. He fidgeted in his jacket.

"Well," he gulped, at last, "I guess yeh might as well give me back them letters." Dark, prickling blood had flushed into his cheeks and brow.

"All right, Wilson," said the youth. He loosened two buttons of his coat, thrust in his hand, and brought forth the packet. As he extended it to his friend, the latter's face was turned from him.

He had been slow in the act of producing the packet because during it he had been trying to invent a remarkable comment upon the affair. He could conjure nothing of sufficient point. He was compelled to allow his friend to escape unmolested with his packet. And for this he took unto himself considerable credit. It was a generous thing.

His friend at his side seemed suffering great shame. As he contemplated him, the youth felt his heart grow more strong and stout. He had never been compelled to blush in such manner for his acts; he was an individual of extraordinary virtues.

He reflected, with condescending pity: "Too bad! Too bad! The poor devil, it makes him feel tough!"

After this incident, and as he reviewed the battle pictures he had seen, he felt quite competent to return home and make the hearts of the people glow with stories of war. He could see himself in a room of warm tints telling tales to listeners. He could exhibit laurels. They were insignificant; still, in a district where laurels were infrequent, they might shine.

He saw his gaping audience picturing him as the central figure in blazing scenes. And he imagined the consternation and the ejaculations of his mother and the young lady at the seminary as they drank his recitals. Their vague feminine formula for beloved ones doing brave deeds on the field of battle without risk of life would be destroyed.

CHAPTER 16

A sputtering of musketry was always to be heard. Later, the cannon had entered the dispute. In the fog-filled air their voices made a thudding sound. The reverberations were continued. This part of the world led a strange, battleful existence.

The youth's regiment was marched to relieve a command that had lain long in some damp trenches. The men took positions behind a curving line of rifle pits that had been turned up, like a large furrow, along the line of woods. Before them was a level stretch, peopled with short, deformed stumps. From the woods beyond came the dull popping of the skirmishers and pickets, firing in the fog. From the right came the noise of a terrific fracas.

The men cuddled behind the small embankment and sat in easy attitudes awaiting their turn. Many had their backs to the firing. The youth's friend lay down, buried his face in his arms, and almost instantly, it seemed, he was in a deep sleep.

The youth leaned his breast against the brown dirt and peered over at the woods and up and down the line. Curtains of trees interfered with his ways of vision. He could see the low line of trenches but for a short distance. A few idle flags were perched on the dirt hills. Behind them were rows of dark bodies with a few heads sticking curiously over the top.

Always the noise of skirmishers came from the woods on the front and left, and the din on the right had grown to frightful proportions. The guns were roaring without an instant's pause for breath.

It seemed that the cannon had come from all parts and were engaged in a stupendous wrangle. It became impossible to make a sentence heard.

The youth wished to launch a joke—a quotation from newspapers. He desired to say, "All quiet on the Rappahannock,"[1] but the guns refused to permit even a comment upon their uproar. He never successfully concluded the sentence. But at last the guns stopped, and among the men in the rifle pits rumors again flew, like birds, but they were now for the most part black creatures who flapped their wings drearily near to the ground and refused to rise on any wings of hope. The men's faces grew doleful from the interpreting of omens. Tales of hesitation and uncertainty on the part of those high in place and responsibility came to their ears. Stories of disaster were borne into their minds with many proofs. This din of musketry on the right, growing like a released genie of sound, expressed and emphasized the army's plight.

The men were disheartened and began to mutter. They made gestures expressive of the sentence: "Ah, what more can we do?" And it could always be seen that they were bewildered by the alleged news and could not fully comprehend a defeat.

Before the gray mists had been totally obliterated by the sun-rays, the regiment was marching in a spread column that was retiring carefully through the woods. The disordered, hurrying lines of the enemy could sometimes be seen down through the groves and little fields. They were yelling, shrill and exultant.

At this sight the youth forgot many personal matters and became greatly enraged. He exploded in loud sentences. "B'jiminey, we're generaled by a lot 'a lunkheads."

"More than one feller has said that t'-day," observed a man.

His friend, recently aroused, was still very drowsy. He looked behind him until his mind took in the meaning of the movement. Then he sighed. "Oh, well, I s'pose we got licked," he remarked sadly.

The youth had a thought that it would not be handsome for him to freely condemn other

---

1. *Rappahannock* (rap′ä han′uk), a river located in northeastern Virginia. During the Civil War the Union Army frequently crossed this river on its way south.

men. He made an attempt to restrain himself, but the words upon his tongue were too bitter. He presently began a long and intricate denunciation of the commander of the forces.

"Mebbe, it wa'n't all his fault—not all together. He did th' best he knowed. It's our luck t' git licked often," said his friend in a weary tone. He was trudging along with stooped shoulders and shifting eyes like a man who has been caned and kicked.

"Well, don't we fight like the devil? Don't we do all that men can?" demanded the youth loudly.

He was secretly dumbfounded at this sentiment when it came from his lips. For a moment his face lost its valor and he looked guiltily about him. But no one questioned his right to deal in such words, and presently he recovered his air of courage. He went on to repeat a statement he had heard going from group to group at the camp that morning. "The brigadier said he never saw a new reg'ment fight the way we fought yestirday, didn't he? And we didn't do better than many another reg'ment, did we? Well, then, you can't say it's th' army's fault, can you?"

In his reply, the friend's voice was stern. " 'A course not," he said. "No man dare say we don't fight like th' devil. No man will ever dare say it. Th' boys fight like roosters. But still—still, we don't have no luck."

"Well, then, if we fight like the devil an' don't ever whip, it must be the general's fault," said the youth grandly and decisively. "And I don't see any sense in fighting and fighting and fighting, yet always losing through some derned old lunkhead of a general."

A sarcastic man who was tramping at the youth's side, then spoke lazily. "Mebbe yeh think yeh fit th' hull battle yestirday, Fleming," he remarked.

The speech pierced the youth. Inwardly he was reduced to an abject pulp by these chance words. His legs quaked privately. He cast a frightened glance at the sarcastic man.

"Why, no," he hastened to say in a conciliating voice, "I don't think I fought the whole battle yesterday."

But the other seemed innocent of any deeper meaning. Apparently, he had no information. It was merely his habit. "Oh!" he replied in the same tone of calm derision.

The youth, nevertheless, felt a threat. His mind shrank from going near to the danger, and there-

after he was silent. The significance of the sarcastic man's words took from him all loud moods that would make him appear prominent. He became suddenly a modest person.

There was low-toned talk among the troops. The officers were impatient and snappy, their countenances clouded with the tales of misfortune. The troops, sifting through the forest, were sullen. In the youth's company once a man's laugh rang out. A dozen soldiers turned their faces quickly toward him and frowned with vague displeasure.

The noise of firing dogged their footsteps. Sometimes, it seemed to be driven a little way, but it always returned again with increased insolence. The men muttered and cursed, throwing black looks in its direction.

In a clear space the troops were at last halted. Regiments and brigades, broken and detached through their encounters with thickets, grew together again and lines were faced toward the pursuing bark of the enemy's infantry.

This noise, following like the yellings of eager, metallic hounds, increased to a loud and joyous burst, and then, as the sun went serenely up the sky, throwing illuminating rays into the gloomy thickets, it broke forth into prolonged pealings. The woods began to crackle as if afire.

"Whoop-a-dadee," said a man, "here we are! Everybody fightin'. Blood an' destruction."

"I was willin' t' bet they'd attack as soon as th' sun got fairly up," savagely asserted the lieutenant who commanded the youth's company. He jerked without mercy at his little mustache. He strode to and fro with dark dignity in the rear of his men, who were lying down behind whatever protection they had collected.

A battery had trundled into position in the rear and was thoughtfully shelling the distance. The regiment, unmolested as yet, awaited the moment when the gray shadows of the woods before them should be slashed by the lines of flame. There was much growling and swearing.

The youth grumbled, "We're always being chased around like rats! It makes me sick. Nobody seems to know where we go or why we go. We just get fired around from pillar to post and get licked here and get licked there, and nobody knows what it's done for. It makes a man feel like a kitten in a bag. Now, I'd like to know what the eternal thunders we was marched into these woods for anyhow, unless it was to give the rebs a regular potshot at us. We came in here and got our legs all tangled up in these cussed briers, and then we begin to fight and the rebs had an easy time of it. Don't tell me it's just luck! I know better. It's this derned old——"

The friend seemed jaded, but he interrupted his comrade with a voice of calm confidence. "It'll turn out all right in th' end," he said.

"Oh, the devil it will! You always talk like a dog-hanged parson. Don't tell me! I know——"

At this time there was an interposition by the savage-minded lieutenant, who was obliged to vent some of his inward dissatisfaction upon his men. "You boys shut right up! There no need 'a your wastin' your breath in long-winded arguments about this an' that an' th' other. You've been jawin' like a lot 'a old hens. All you've got t' do is to fight, an' you'll get plenty 'a that t' do in about ten minutes. Less talkin' an' more fightin' is what's best for you boys. I never saw sech gabbling jackasses."

He paused, ready to pounce upon any man who might have the temerity to reply. No words being said, he resumed his dignified pacing.

"There's too much chin music an' too little fightin' in this war, anyhow," he said to them, turning his head for a final remark.

The day had grown more white, until the sun shed his full radiance upon the thronged forest. A sort of a gust of battle came sweeping toward that part of the line where lay the youth's regiment. The front shifted a trifle to meet it squarely. There was a wait. In this part of the field there passed slowly the intense moments that precede the tempest.

A single rifle flashed in a thicket before the regiment. In an instant it was joined by many others. There was a mighty song of clashes and crashes that went sweeping through the woods. The guns in the rear, aroused and enraged by shells that had been thrown burrlike at them, suddenly involved themselves in a hideous altercation with another band of guns. The battle roar settled to a rolling thunder, which was a single, long explosion.

In the regiment there was a peculiar kind of hesitation denoted in the attitudes of the men. They were worn, exhausted, having slept but little and labored much. They rolled their eyes toward the advancing battle as they stood awaiting the shock. Some shrank and flinched. They stood as men tied to stakes.

CHAPTER 17

This advance of the enemy had seemed to the youth like a ruthless hunting. He began to fume with rage and exasperation. He beat his foot upon the ground, and scowled with hate at the swirling smoke that was approaching like a phantom flood. There was a maddening quality in this seeming resolution of the foe to give him no rest, to give him no time to sit down and think. Yesterday he had fought and had fled rapidly. There had been many adventures. For today he felt that he had earned opportunities for contemplative repose. He could have enjoyed portraying to uninitiated listeners various scenes at which he had been a witness or ably discussing the processes of war with other proved men. Too it was important that he should have time for physical recuperation. He was sore and stiff from his experiences. He had received his fill of all exertions, and he wished to rest.

But those other men seemed never to grow weary; they were fighting with their old speed. He had a wild hate for the relentless foe. Yesterday, when he had imagined the universe to be against him, he had hated it, little gods and big gods; today he hated the army of the foe with the same great hatred. He was not going to be badgered of his life, like a kitten chased by boys, he said. It was not well to drive men into final corners; at those moments they could all develop teeth and claws.

He leaned and spoke into his friend's ear. He menaced the woods with a gesture. "If they keep on chasing us, they'd better watch out. Can't stand *too* much."

The friend twisted his head and made a calm reply. "If they keep on a-chasin' us they'll drive us all inteh th' river."

The youth cried out savagely at this statement. He crouched behind a little tree, with his eyes burning hatefully and his teeth set in a curlike snarl. The awkward bandage was still about his head, and upon it, over his wound, there was a spot of dry blood. His hair was wondrously tousled, and some straggling, moving locks hung over the cloth of the bandage down toward his forehead. His jacket and shirt were open at the throat, and exposed his young bronzed neck. There could be seen spasmodic gulpings at his throat.

His fingers twined nervously about his rifle. He wished that it was an engine of annihilating power. He felt that he and his companions were being taunted and derided from sincere convictions that they were poor and puny. His knowledge of his inability to take vengeance for it made his rage into a dark and stormy specter, that possessed him and made him dream of abominable cruelties. The tormentors were flies sucking insolently at his blood, and he thought that he would have given his life for a revenge of seeing their faces in pitiful plights.

The winds of battle had swept all about the regiment, until the one rifle, instantly followed by others, flashed in its front. A moment later the regiment roared forth its sudden and valiant retort. A dense wall of smoke settled slowly down. It was furiously slit and slashed by the knifelike fire from the rifles.

To the youth the fighters resembled animals tossed for a death struggle into a dark pit. There was a sensation that he and his fellows, at bay, were pushing back, always pushing fierce onslaughts of creatures who were slippery. Their beams of crimson seemed to get no purchase upon the bodies of their foes; the latter seemed to evade them with ease, and come through, between, around, and about with unopposed skill.

When, in a dream, it occurred to the youth that his rifle was an impotent stick, he lost sense of everything but his hate, his desire to smash into pulp the glittering smile of victory which he could feel upon the faces of his enemies.

The blue smoke-swallowed line curled and writhed like a snake stepped upon. It swung its ends to and fro in an agony of fear and rage.

The youth was not conscious that he was erect upon his feet. He did not know the direction of the ground. Indeed, once he even lost the habit of balance and fell heavily. He was up again immediately. One thought went through the chaos of his brain at the time. He wondered if he had fallen because he had been shot. But the suspicion flew away at once. He did not think more of it.

He had taken up a first position behind the little tree, with a direct determination to hold it against the world. He had not deemed it possible that his army could that day succeed, and from this he felt the ability to fight harder. But the throng had surged in all ways, until he lost directions and locations, save that he knew where lay the enemy.

The flames bit him, and the hot smoke broiled his skin. His rifle barrel grew so hot that ordinarily he could not have borne it upon his palms; but he kept on stuffing cartridges into it, and pounding them with his clanking, bending ramrod. If he aimed at some changing form through the smoke, he pulled his trigger with a fierce grunt, as if he were dealing a blow of the fist with all his strength.

When the enemy seemed falling back before him and his fellows, he went instantly forward, like a dog who, seeing his foes lagging, turns and insists upon being pursued. And when he was compelled to retire again, he did it slowly, sullenly, taking steps of wrathful despair.

Once he, in his intent hate, was almost alone, and was firing, when all those near him had ceased. He was so engrossed in his occupation that he was not aware of a lull.

He was recalled by a hoarse laugh and a sentence that came to his ears in a voice of contempt and amazement. "Yeh infernal fool, don't yeh know enough t' quit when there ain't anything t' shoot at?"

He turned then and, pausing with his rifle thrown half into position, looked at the blue line of his comrades. During this moment of leisure they seemed all to be engaged in staring with astonishment at him. They had become spectators. Turning to the front again he saw, under the lifted smoke, a deserted ground.

He looked bewildered for a moment. Then there appeared upon the glazed vacancy of his eyes a diamond point of intelligence. "Oh," he said, comprehending.

He returned to his comrades and threw himself upon the ground. He sprawled like a man who had been thrashed. His flesh seemed strangely on fire, and the sounds of the battle continued in his ears. He groped blindly for his canteen.

The lieutenant was crowing. He seemed drunk with fighting. He called out to the youth: "By heavens, if I had ten thousand wildcats like you, I could tear th' stomach outa this war in less'n a week!" He puffed out his chest with large dignity as he said it.

Some of the men muttered and looked at the youth in awestruck ways. It was plain that as he

crouched
behind trees

had gone on loading and firing and cursing without the proper intermission, they had found time to regard him. And they now looked upon him as a war devil.

The friend came staggering to him. There was some fright and dismay in his voice. "Are yeh all right, Fleming? Do yeh feel all right? There ain't nothin' th' matter with yeh, Henry, is there?"

"No," said the youth with difficulty. His throat seemed full of knobs and burrs.

These incidents made the youth ponder. It was revealed to him that he had been a barbarian, a beast. He had fought like a pagan who defends his religion. Regarding it, he saw that it was fine, wild, and, in some ways, easy. He had been a tremendous figure, no doubt. By this struggle he had overcome obstacles which he had admitted to be mountains. They had fallen like paper peaks, and he was now what he called a hero. And he had not been aware of the process. He had slept and, awakening, found himself a knight.

He lay and basked in the occasional stares of his comrades. Their faces were varied in degrees of blackness from the burned powder. Some were utterly smudged. They were reeking with perspiration, and their breaths came hard and wheezing. And from these soiled expanses they peered at him.

"Hot work! Hot work!" cried the lieutenant deliriously. He walked up and down, restless and eager. Sometimes his voice could be heard in a wild, incomprehensible laugh.

When he had a particularly profound thought upon the science of war, he always unconsciously addressed himself to the youth.

There was some grim rejoicing by the men. "By thunder, I bet this army'll never see another new reg'ment like us!"

"You bet!"

"A dog, a woman, an' a walnut tree,
Th' more yeh beat 'em, th' better they be!"

That's like us."

"Lost a piler men, they did. If an' ol' woman swep' up th' woods, she'd git a dustpanful."

"Yes, an' if she'll come around ag'in in 'bout an' hour, she'll git a pile more."

The forest still bore its burden of clamor. From off under the trees came the rolling clatter of the musketry. Each distant thicket seemed a strange porcupine with quills of flame. A cloud of dark smoke, as from smoldering ruins, went up toward the sun now bright and gay in the blue, enameled sky.

CHAPTER 18

The ragged line had respite for some minutes, but during its pause the struggle in the forest became magnified until the trees seemed to quiver from the firing and the ground to shake from the rushing of the men. The voices of the cannon were mingled in a long and interminable row. It seemed difficult to live in such an atmosphere. The chests of the men strained for a bit of freshness, and their throats craved water.

There was one shot through the body, who raised a cry of bitter lamentation when came this lull. Perhaps he had been calling out during the fighting also, but at that time no one had heard him. But now the men turned at the woeful complaints of him upon the ground.

"Who is it? Who is it?"

"It's Jimmie Rogers. Jimmie Rogers."

When their eyes first encountered him, there was a sudden halt, as if they feared to go near. He was thrashing about in the grass, twisting his shuddering body into many strange postures. He was screaming loudly. This instant's hesitation seemed to fill him with a tremendous, fantastic contempt.

The youth's friend had a geographical illusion concerning a stream, and he obtained permission to go for some water. Immediately canteens were showered upon him. "Fill mine, will yeh?" "Bring me some, too." "And me, too." He departed, ladened. The youth went with his friend, feeling a desire to throw his heated body onto the stream and, soaking there, drink quarts.

They made a hurried search for the supposed stream, but did not find it. "No water here," said the youth. They turned without delay and began to retrace their steps.

From their position as they again faced toward the place of the fighting, they could of course comprehend a greater amount of the battle than when their visions had been blurred by the hurling smoke of the line. They could see dark stretches winding along the land, and on one cleared space there was a row of guns making gray clouds, which were filled with large flashes of orange-colored flame. Over some foliage they could see the roof of a house. One window, glowing a deep murder red, shone squarely through the leaves. From the edifice a tall leaning tower of smoke went far into the sky.

Looking over their own troops, they saw mixed masses slowly getting into regular form. The sunlight made twinkling points of the bright steel. To the rear there was a glimpse of a distant roadway as it curved over a slope. It was crowded with retreating infantry. From all the interwoven forest arose the smoke and bluster of the battle. The air was always occupied by a blaring.

Near where they stood shells were flip-flapping and hooting. Occasional bullets buzzed in the air and spanged into tree trunks. Wounded men and other stragglers were slinking through the woods.

Looking down an aisle of the grove, the youth and his companion saw a jangling general and his staff almost ride upon a wounded man, who was crawling on his hands and knees. The general reined strongly at his charger's opened and foamy mouth and guided it with dexterous horsemanship past the man. The latter scrambled in wild and torturing haste. His strength evidently failed him as he reached a place of safety. One of his arms suddenly weakened, and he fell, sliding over upon his back. He lay stretched out, breathing gently.

A moment later the small, creaking cavalacade was directly in front of the two soldiers. Another officer, riding with the skillful abandon of a cowboy, galloped his horse to a position directly before the general. The two unnoticed foot soldiers made a little show of going on, but they lingered near in the desire to overhear the conversation. Perhaps, they thought, some great inner historical things would be said.

The general, whom the boys knew as the commander of their division, looked at the other officer and spoke coolly, as if he were criticizing his clothes. "Th' enemy's formin' over there for another charge," he said. "It'll be directed against Whiterside, an' I fear they'll break through there unless we work like thunder t' stop them."

The other swore at his restive horse, and then cleared his throat. He made a gesture toward his cap. "It'll be hard stoppin' them," he said shortly.

"I presume so," remarked the general. Then he began to talk rapidly and in a lower tone. He frequently illustrated his words with a pointing finger. The two infantrymen could hear nothing until finally he asked: "What troops can you spare?"

The officer who rode like a cowboy reflected for an instant. "Well," he said, "I had to order in th' 12th to help th' 76th, an' I haven't really got any. But there's th' 304th. They fight like a lot 'a mule drivers. I can spare them best of any."

The youth and his friend exchanged glances of astonishment.

The general spoke sharply. "Get 'em ready, then. I'll watch developments from here, an' send you word when t' start them. It'll happen in five minutes."

As the other officer tossed his fingers toward his cap and wheeling his horse, started away, the general called out to him in a sober voice: "I don't believe many of your mule drivers will get back."

The other shouted something in reply. He smiled.

With scared faces, the youth and his companion hurried back to the line.

These happenings had occupied an incredibly short time, yet the youth felt that in them he had been made aged. New eyes were given to him. And the most startling thing was to learn suddenly that he was very insignificant. The officer spoke of the regiment as if he referred to a broom. Some part of the woods needed sweeping, perhaps, and he merely indicated a broom in a tone properly indifferent to its fate. It was war, no doubt, but it appeared strange.

As the two boys approached the line, the lieutenant perceived them and swelled with wrath. "Fleming—Wilson—how long does it take yeh to git water, anyhow—where yeh been to?"

But his oration ceased as he saw their eyes, which were large with great tales. "We're goin' t' charge—we're goin' t' charge!" cried the youth's friend, hastening with his news.

"Charge?" said the lieutenant. "Charge? Now, this is real fightin'." Over his soiled countenance there went a boastful smile.

A little group of soldiers surrounded the two youths. "Are we, sure 'nough? Well, I'll be derned! Charge? What fer? What at? Wilson, you're lyin'."

"I hope to die," said the youth, pitching his tones to the key of angry remonstrance. "Sure as shooting, I tell you."

And his friend spoke in reenforcement. "Not by a blame sight, he ain't lyin'. We heard 'em talkin'."

They caught sight of two mounted figures a short distance from them. One was the colonel of the regiment and the other was the officer who had received orders from the commander of the division. They were gesticulating at each other. The soldier, pointing at them, interpreted the scene.

One man had a final objection: "How could yeh hear 'em talkin'?" But the men, for a large part, nodded, admitting that previously the two friends had spoken truth.

They settled back into reposeful attitudes with airs of having accepted the matter. And they mused upon it, with a hundred varieties of expression. It was an engrossing thing to think about. Many tightened their belts carefully and hitched at their trousers.

A moment later the officers began to bustle among the men, pushing them into a more compact mass and into a better alignment. They chased those that straggled and fumed at a few men who seemed to show by their attitudes that they had decided to remain at that spot. They were like critical shepherds struggling with sheep.

Presently, the regiment seemed to draw itself up and heave a deep breath. None of the men's faces were mirrors of large thoughts. The soldiers were bended and stooped like sprinters before a signal. Many pairs of glinting eyes peered from the grimy faces toward the curtains of the deeper woods. They seemed to be engaged in deep calculations of time and distance.

They were surrounded by the noises of the monstrous altercation between two armies. The world was fully interested in other matters. Apparently, the regiment had its small affair to itself.

The youth, turning, shot a quick, inquiring glance at his friend. The latter returned to him the same manner of look. They were the only ones who possessed an inner knowledge. "Mule drivers— don't believe many will get back." It was an ironical secret. Still, they saw no hesitation in each other's faces, and they nodded a mute and unprotesting assent when a shaggy man near them said in a meek voice: "We'll git swallowed."

CHAPTER 19

The youth stared at the land in front of him. Its foliages now seemed to veil powers and horrors. He was aware of the machinery of orders that started the charge, although from the corners of his eyes he saw an officer, who looked like a boy a-horseback, come galloping, waving his hat. Suddenly he felt a straining and heaving among the men. The line fell slowly forward like a toppling wall, and, with a convulsive gasp that was intended for a cheer, the regiment began its journey. The youth was pushed and jostled for a moment before he understood the movement at all, but directly he lunged ahead and began to run.

He fixed his eye upon a distant and prominent clump of trees where he had concluded the enemy were to be met, and he ran toward it as toward a goal. He had believed throughout that it was a mere question of getting over an unpleasant matter as quickly as possible, and he ran desperately, as if pursued for a murder. His face was drawn hard and tight with the stress of his endeavor. His eyes were fixed in a lurid glare. And with his soiled and disordered dress, his red and inflamed features surmounted by the dingy rag with its spot of blood, his wildly swinging rifle and banging accouterments, he looked to be an insane soldier.

As the regiment swung from its position out into a cleared space, the woods and thickets before it awakened. Yellow flames leaped toward it from many directions. The forest made a tremendous objection.

The line lurched straight for a moment. Then the right wing sprung forward; it in turn was surpassed by the left. Afterward the center careered to the front until the regiment was a wedge-shaped mass, but an instant later the opposition of the bushes, trees, and uneven places on the ground split the command and scattered it into detached clusters.

The youth, light-footed, was unconsciously in advance. His eyes still kept note of the clump of trees. From all places near it the clannish yell of the enemy could be heard. The little flames of rifles leaped from it. The song of the bullets was in the air and shells snarled among the treetops. One tumbled directly into the middle of a hurrying group and exploded in crimson fury. There was an instant's spectacle of a man, almost over it, throwing up his hands to shield his eyes.

Other men, punched by bullets, fell in grotesque agonies. The regiment left a coherent trail of bodies.

They had passed into a clearer atmosphere. There was an effect like a revelation in the new appearance of the landscape. Some men working madly at a battery were plain to them, and the opposing infantry's lines were defined by the gray walls and fringes of smoke.

It seemed to the youth that he saw everything. Each blade of the green grass was bold and clear. He thought that he was aware of every change in the thin, transparent vapor that floated idly in sheets. The brown or gray trunks of the trees showed each roughness of their surfaces. And the men of the regiment, with their starting eyes and sweating faces, running madly, or falling, as if thrown headlong, to queer, heaped-up corpses—all were comprehended. His mind took a mechanical but firm impression, so that afterward everything was pictured and explained to him, save why he himself was there.

But there was a frenzy made from this furious rush. The men, pitching forward insanely, had burst into cheerings, moblike and barbaric, but tuned in strange keys that can arouse the dullard and the stoic. It made a mad enthusiasm that, it seemed, would be incapable of checking itself before granite and brass. There was the delirium that encounters despair and death, and is heedless and blind to the odds. It is a temporary but sublime absence of selfishness. And because it was of this order was the reason, perhaps, why the youth wondered, afterward, what reasons he could have had for being there.

Presently the straining pace ate up the energies of the men. As if by agreement, the leaders began to slacken their speed. The volleys directed against them had had a seeming windlike effect. The regiment snorted and blew. Among some stolid trees it began to falter and hesitate. The men, staring intently, began to wait for some of the distant walls of smoke to move and disclose to them the scene.

Since much of their strength and their breath had vanished, they returned to caution. They were become men again.

The youth had a vague belief that he had run miles, and he thought, in a way, that he was now in some new and unknown land.

The moment the regiment ceased its advance the protesting splutter of musketry became a steadied roar. Long and accurate fringes of smoke spread out. From the top of a small hill came level belchings of yellow flame that caused an inhuman whistling in the air.

The men, halted, had opportunity to see some of their comrades dropping with moans and shrieks. A few lay underfoot, still or wailing. And now for an instant the men stood, their rifles slack in their hands, and watched the regiment dwindle. They appeared dazed and stupid. This spectacle seemed to paralyze them, overcome them with a fatal fascination. They stared woodenly at the sights, and, lowering their eyes, looked from face to face. It was a strange pause, and a strange silence.

Then, above the sounds of the outside commotion, arose the roar of the lieutenant. He strode suddenly forth, his infantile features black with rage.

"Come on, yeh fools!" he bellowed. "Come on! Yeh can't stay here. Yeh must come on." He said more, but much of it could not be understood.

He started rapidly forward, with his head turned toward the men. "Come on," he was shouting. The men stared with blank and yokel-like eyes at him. He was obliged to halt and retrace his steps. He stood then with his back to the enemy and delivered gigantic curses into the faces of the men. His body vibrated from the weight and force of his imprecations. And he could string oaths with the facility of a maiden who strings beads.

The friend of the youth aroused. Lurching suddenly forward and dropping to his knees, he fired an angry shot at the persistent woods. This action awakened the men. They huddled no more like sheep. They seemed suddenly to bethink them of their weapons, and at once commenced firing. Belabored by their officers, they began to move forward. The regiment, involved like a cart involved in mud and muddle, started unevenly with many jolts and jerks. The men stopped now every few paces to fire and load, and in this manner moved slowly on from trees to trees.

The flaming opposition in their front grew with their advance until it seemed that all forward ways were barred by the thin leaping tongues, and off to the right an ominous demonstration could sometimes be dimly discerned. The smoke lately generated was in confusing clouds that made it difficult for the regiment to proceed with intelligence. As he passed through each curling mass, the youth wondered what would confront him on the farther side.

The command went painfully forward until an open space interposed between them and the lurid lines. Here, crouching and cowering behind some trees, the men clung with desperation, as if threatened by a wave. They looked wild-eyed, and as if amazed at this furious disturbance they had stirred. In the storm there was an ironical expression of their importance. The faces of the men, too, showed a lack of a certain feeling of responsibility for being there. It was as if they had been driven. It was the dominant animal failing to remember in the supreme moments the forceful causes of various superficial qualities. The whole affair seemed incomprehensible to many of them.

As they halted thus, the lieutenant again began to bellow profanely. Regardless of the vindictive threats of the bullets, he went about coaxing, berating, and bedamning. His lips, that were habitually in a soft and childlike curve, were now writhed into unholy contortions. He swore by all possible deities.

Once he grabbed the youth by the arm. "Come on, yeh lunkhead!" he roared. "Come on! We'll all git killed if we stay here. We've on'y got t' go across that lot. An' then"—the remainder of his idea disappeared in a blue haze of curses.

The youth stretched forth his arm. "Cross there?" His mouth was puckered in doubt and awe.

"Certainly. Jest 'cross th' lot! We can't stay here," screamed the lieutenant. He poked his face close to the youth and waved his bandaged hand. "Come on!" Presently he grappled with him as if for a wrestling bout. It was as if he planned to drag the youth by the ear on to the assault.

The private felt a sudden unspeakable indignation against his officer. He wrenched fiercely and shook him off.

"Come on yerself, then," he yelled. There was a bitter challenge in his voice.

They galloped together down the regimental front. The friend scrambled after them. In front of the colors the three men began to bawl: "Come on! Come on!" They danced and gyrated like tortured savages.

The flag, obedient to these appeals, bended its glittering form and swept toward them. The men wavered in indecision for a moment, and then with a long, wailful cry the dilapidated regiment surged forward and began its new journey.

Over the field went the scurrying mass. It was a handful of men splattered into the faces of the enemy. Toward it instantly sprang the yellow tongues. A vast quantity of blue smoke hung before them. A mighty banging made ears valueless.

The youth ran like a madman to reach the woods before a bullet could discover him. He ducked his head low, like a football player. In his haste his eyes almost closed, and the scene was a wild blur. Pulsating saliva stood at the corners of his mouth.

Within him, as he hurled himself forward, was born a love, a despairing fondness for this flag which was near him. It was a creation of beauty and invulnerability. It was a goddess, radiant, that bended its form with an imperious gesture to him. It was a woman, red and white, hating and loving, that called him with the voice of his hopes. Because no harm could come to it, he endowed it with power. He kept near, as if it could be a saver of lives, and an imploring cry went from his mind.

In the mad scramble he was aware that the color sergeant flinched suddenly, as if struck by a bludgeon. He faltered, and then became motionless, save for his quivering knees.

He made a spring and a clutch at the pole. At the same instant his friend grabbed it from the other side. They jerked at it, stout and furious, but the color sergeant was dead, and the corpse would not relinquish its trust. For a moment there was a grim encounter. The dead man, swinging with bended back, seemed to be obstinately tugging, in ludicrous and awful ways, for the possession of the flag.

It was past in an instant of time. They wrenched the flag furiously from the dead man, and, as they turned again, the corpse swayed forward with bowed head. One arm swung high, and the curved hand fell with heavy protest on the friend's unheeding shoulder.

THINK AND DISCUSS
CHAPTERS 14–19
Understanding
1. What does Henry return to Wilson in Chapter 15?
2. What unexpected act of Henry's during the battle in Chapter 17 draws praise from the lieutenant? How do Henry's companions react?
3. What information do Henry and Wilson overhear as they go for water? What effect does this information have on Henry?
4. How does Henry gain possession of the flag?

Analyzing
5. What evidence of change does Henry find in Wilson's personality? What indications can you find that Wilson now regards himself differently and relates in a new way to his companions?
6. When Henry contemplates returning Wilson's packet in Chapter 15, he thinks of it as a possible "small weapon." How does he anticipate using this weapon? Why does he deem the actual return of the packet "a generous thing"?
7. Henry slowly begins to develop a different perspective on his own conduct. What kind of rationalization gives him new confidence?

Extending
8. Identify examples of Naturalism in Chapter 19. Consider how Crane depicts the soldiers in battle, the role that fate plays in their lives, and the use of **figurative language**.

THINKING SKILLS
Synthesizing
When you recast one medium, such as a novel, into another form, such as a film, you are synthesizing. Imagine that you were making a contemporary movie of *The Red Badge of Courage.*

1. Who would you choose for the role of Henry? Wilson? Jim Conklin?
2. Choose a scene whose **images** afford rich cinematic possibilities. If you were filming this scene, which details would you focus on? From what vantage point would you film the scene? Would you use slow motion or quick camera shifts? What sound effects would you use?
3. What overall impression or **mood** would you want to convey in this scene?

COMPOSITION
Writing a Character Sketch
Write a character sketch of several paragraphs about one of the following: the tall soldier (Jim Conklin, whom some critics have interpreted as a Christ symbol because of his initials and the way he dies), the loud soldier, the tattered man, the cheery man, or the lieutenant. Include passages from the text about this character's appearance, personality, and any other distinctive features. Don't forget that character clues are often found in a person's speech. See "Writing About Characters" in the Writer's Handbook.

Shifting a Point of View
Choose a scene that is presented from Henry's point of view (for example, the first two paragraphs in Chapters 14, 17, or 19). Rewrite one of these passages from an objective point of view, recording scenes and events like a video camera without interpreting or seeing into his mind. In a final paragraph, explain how this shift in point of view affects the story.

ENRICHMENT
Oral Report
Born six years after the Civil War ended, Stephen Crane gathered the material for this novel by interviewing war veterans, studying war pictures, and reading war accounts. In your local library, try to locate accounts of the Civil War, photographs by Mathew Brady, and paintings by Winslow Homer. Present your findings to the class.

flag—red
and
white.
officers screaming
orders

CHAPTER 20

When the two youths turned with the flag, they saw that much of the regiment had crumbled away, and the dejected remnant was coming back. The men, having hurled themselves in projectile fashion, had presently expended their forces. They slowly retreated, with their faces still toward the spluttering woods, and their hot rifles still replying to the din. Several officers were giving orders, their voices keyed to screams.

"Where yeh goin'?" the lieutenant was asking in a sarcastic howl. And a red-bearded officer, whose voice of triple brass could plainly be heard, was commanding: "Shoot into 'em! Shoot into 'em!" There was a melee of screeches, in which the men were ordered to do conflicting and impossible things.

The youth and his friend had a small scuffle over the flag. "Give it t' me!" "No, let me keep it!" Each felt satisfied with the other's possession of it, but each felt bound to declare, by an offer to carry the emblem, his willingness to further risk himself. The youth roughly pushed his friend away.

The regiment fell back to the stolid trees. There it halted for a moment to blaze at some dark forms that had begun to steal upon its track. Presently it resumed its march again, curving among the tree trunks. By the time the depleted regiment had again reached the first open space, they were receiving a fast and merciless fire. There seemed to be mobs all about them.

The greater part of the men, discouraged, their spirits worn by the turmoil, acted as if stunned. They accepted the pelting of the bullets with bowed and weary heads. It was of no purpose to strive against walls. It was of no use to batter themselves against granite. And from this consciousness that they had attempted to conquer an unconquerable thing, there seemed to arise a feeling that they had betrayed. They glowered with bent brows, but dangerously, upon some of the officers, more particularly upon the red-bearded one with the voice of triple brass.

However, the rear of the regiment was fringed with men, who continued to shoot irritably at the advancing foes. They seemed resolved to make every trouble. The youthful lieutenant was perhaps the last man in the disordered mass. His forgotten back was toward the enemy. He had been shot in the arm. It hung straight and rigid. Occasionally he would cease to remember it, and be about to emphasize an oath with a sweeping gesture. The multiplied pain caused him to swear with incredible power.

The youth went along with slipping, uncertain feet. He kept watchful eyes rearward. A scowl of mortification and rage was upon his face. He had thought of a fine revenge upon the officer who had referred to him and his fellows as mule drivers. But he saw that it could not come to pass. His dreams had collapsed when the mule drivers, dwindling rapidly, had wavered and hesitated on the little clearing, and then had recoiled. And now the retreat of the mule drivers was a march of shame to him.

A dagger-pointed gaze from without his blackened face was held toward the enemy, but his greater hatred was riveted upon the man, who, not knowing him, had called him a mule driver.

When he knew that he and his comrades had failed to do anything in successful ways that might bring the little pangs of a kind of remorse upon the officer, the youth allowed the rage of the baffled to possess him. This cold officer upon a monument, who dropped epithets unconcernedly down, would be finer as a dead man, he thought. So grievous did he think it that he could never possess the secret right to taunt truly in answer.

He had pictured red letters of curious revenge. "We *are* mule drivers, are we?" And now he was compelled to throw them away.

He presently wrapped his heart in the cloak of his pride and kept the flag erect. He harangued his fellows, pushing against their chests with his free hand. To those he knew well he made frantic appeals, beseeching them by name. Between him and the lieutenant, scolding and near losing his

mind with rage, there was felt a subtle fellowship and equality. They supported each other in all manner of hoarse, howling protests.

But the regiment was a machine run down. The two men babbled at a forceless thing. The soldiers who had heart to go slowly were continually shaken in their resolves by a knowledge that comrades were slipping with speed back in the lines. It was difficult to think of reputation when others were thinking of skins. Wounded men were left crying on this black journey.

The smoke fringes and flames blustered always. The youth, peering once through a sudden rift in a cloud, saw a brown mass of troops, interwoven and magnified until they appeared to be thousands. A fierce-hued flag flashed before his vision.

Immediately, as if the uplifting of the smoke had been prearranged, the discovered troops burst into a rasping yell, and a hundred flames jetted toward the retreating band. A rolling gray cloud again interposed as the regiment doggedly replied. The youth had to depend again upon his misused ears, which were trembling and buzzing from the melee of musketry and yells.

The way seemed eternal. In the clouded haze men became panic-stricken with the thought that the regiment had lost its path, and was proceeding in a perilous direction. Once the men who headed the wild procession turned and came pushing back against their comrades, screaming that they were being fired upon from points which they had considered to be toward their own lines. At this cry a hysterical fear and dismay beset the troops. A soldier, who heretofore had been ambitious to make the regiment into a wise little band that would proceed calmly amid the huge-appearing difficulties, suddenly sank down and buried his face in his arms with an air of bowing to a doom. From another a shrill lamentation rang out filled with profane allusions to a general. Men ran hither and thither, seeking with their eyes roads of escape. With serene regularity, as if controlled by a schedule, bullets buffed into men.

The youth walked stolidly into the midst of the mob, and with his flag in his hands took a stand as if he expected an attempt to push him to the ground. He unconsciously assumed the attitude of the color bearer in the fight of the preceding day. He passed over his brow a hand that trembled. His breath did not come freely. He was choking during this small wait for the crisis.

His friend came to him. "Well, Henry, I guess this is good-bye—John."

"Oh, shut up, you fool!" replied the youth, and he would not look at the other.

The officers labored like politicians to beat the mass into a proper circle to face the menaces. The ground was uneven and torn. The men curled into depressions and fitted themselves snugly behind whatever would frustrate a bullet.

The youth noted with vague surprise that the lieutenant was standing mutely with his legs far apart and his sword held in the manner of a cane. The youth wondered what had happened to his vocal organs that he no more cursed.

There was something curious in this little intent pause of the lieutenant. He was like a babe which, having wept its fill, raises its eyes and fixes upon a distant toy. He was engrossed in this contemplation, and the soft under lip quivered from self-whispered words.

Some lazy and ignorant smoke curled slowly. The men, hiding from the bullets, waited anxiously for it to lift and disclose the plight of the regiment.

The silent ranks were suddenly thrilled by the eager voice of the youthful lieutenant bawling out: "Here they come! Right on to us!" His further words were lost in a roar of wicked thunder from the men's rifles.

The youth's eyes had instantly turned in the direction indicated by the awakened and agitated lieutenant, and he had seen the haze of treachery disclosing a body of soldiers of the enemy. They were so near that he could see their features. There was a recognition as he looked at the types of faces. Also he perceived with dim amazement that their uniforms were rather gay in effect, being light gray, accented with a brilliant-hued facing. Too, the clothes seemed new.

These troops had apparently been going forward with caution, their rifles held in readiness, when the youthful lieutenant had discovered them and their movement had been interrupted by the volley from the blue regiment. From the moment's glimpse, it was derived that they had been unaware of the proximity of their dark-suited foes or had mistaken the direction. Almost instantly they were shut utterly from the youth's sight by the smoke from the energetic rifles of his companions. He strained his vision to learn the accomplishment of the volley, but the smoke hung before him.

The two bodies of troops exchanged blows in the manner of a pair of boxers. The fast angry firings went back and forth. The men in blue were intent with the despair of their circumstances and they seized upon the revenge to be had at close range. Their thunder swelled loud and valiant. Their curving front bristled with flashes and the place resounded with the clangor of their ramrods. The youth ducked and dodged for a time and achieved a few unsatisfactory views of the enemy. There appeared to be many of them and they were replying swiftly. They seemed moving toward the blue regiment, step by step. He seated himself gloomily on the ground with his flag between his knees.

As he noted the vicious, wolflike temper of his comrades, he had a sweet thought that if the enemy was about to swallow the regimental broom as a large prisoner, it could at least have the consolation of going down with bristles forward.

But the blows of the antagonist began to grow more weak. Fewer bullets ripped the air, and finally, when the men slackened to learn of the fight, they could see only dark, floating smoke. The regiment lay still and gazed. Presently some chance whim came to the pestering blur, and it began to coil heavily away. The men saw a ground vacant of fighters. It would have been an empty stage if it were not for a few corpses that lay thrown and twisted into fantastic shapes upon the sward.

At sight of this tableau, many of the men in blue sprang from behind their covers and made an ungainly dance of joy. Their eyes burned and a hoarse cheer of elation broke from their dry lips.

It had begun to seem to them that events were trying to prove that they were impotent. These little battles had evidently endeavored to demonstrate that the men could not fight well. When on the verge of submission to these opinions, the small duel had showed them that the proportions were not impossible, and by it they had revenged themselves upon their misgivings and upon the foe.

The impetus of enthusiasm was theirs again. They gazed about them with looks of uplifted pride, feeling new trust in the grim, always confident weapons in their hands. And they were men.

CHAPTER 21

Presently they knew that no fighting threatened them. All ways seemed once more opened to them. The dusty blue lines of their friends were disclosed a short distance away. In the distance there were many colossal noises, but in all this part of the field there was a sudden stillness.

They perceived that they were free. The depleted band drew a long breath of relief and gathered itself into a bunch to complete its trip.

In this last length of journey the men began to show strange emotions. They hurried with nervous fear. Some who had been dark and unfaltering in the grimmest moments now could not conceal an anxiety that made them frantic. It was perhaps that they dreaded to be killed in insignificant ways after the times for proper military deaths had passed. Or, perhaps, they thought it would be too ironical to get killed at the portals of safety. With backward looks of perturbation, they hastened.

As they approached their own lines, there was some sarcasm exhibited on the part of a gaunt and bronzed regiment that lay resting in the shade of trees. Questions were wafted to them.

"Where yeh been?"

"What yeh comin' back fer?"

"Why didn't yeh stay there?"

"Was it warm out there, sonny?"

"Goin' home now, boys?"

One shouted in taunting mimicry: "Oh, mother, come quick an' look at th' sojers!"

There was no reply from the bruised and battered regiment, save that one man made broadcast challenges to fist fights and the red-bearded officer walked rather near and glared in great swashbuckler style at a tall captain in the other regiment. But the lieutenant suppressed the man who wished to fist fight, and the tall captain, flushing at the little fanfare of the redbearded one, was obliged to look intently at some trees.

The youth's tender flesh was deeply stung by these remarks. From under his creased brows he glowered with hate at the mockers. He meditated upon a few revenges. Still, many in the regiment hung their heads in criminal fashion, so that it came to pass that the men trudged with sudden heaviness, as if they bore upon their bended shoulders the coffin of their honor. And the youthful lieutenant, recollecting himself, began to mutter softly in black curses.

They turned, when they arrived at their old position, to regard the ground over which they had charged.

The youth in this contemplation was smitten with a large astonishment. He discovered that the distances, as compared with the brilliant measurings of his mind, were trivial and ridiculous. The stolid trees, where much had taken place, seemed incredibly near. The time, too, now that he reflected, he saw to have been short. He wondered at the number of emotions and events that had been crowded into such little spaces. Elfin thoughts must have exaggerated and enlarged everything, he said.

It seemed, then, that there was bitter justice in the speeches of the gaunt and bronzed veterans. He veiled a glance of disdain at his fellows who strewed the ground, choking with dust, red from perspiration, misty-eyed, disheveled.

They were gulping at their canteens, fierce to wring every mite of water from them, and they polished at their swollen and watery features with coat sleeves and bunches of grass.

However, to the youth there was a considerable joy in musing upon his performances during the charge. He had had very little time previously in which to appreciate himself, so that there was now much satisfaction in quietly thinking of his actions. He recalled bits of color that in the flurry had stamped themselves unawares upon his engaged senses.

As the regiment lay heaving from its hot exertions, the officer who had named them as mule drivers came galloping along the line. He had lost his cap. His tousled hair streamed wildly, and his face was dark with vexation and wrath. His temper was displayed with more clearness by the way in which he managed his horse. He jerked and wrenched savagely at his bridle, stopping the hard-breathing animal with a furious pull near the colonel of the regiment. He immediately exploded in reproaches which came unbidden to the ears of the men. They were suddenly alert, being always curious about black words between officers.

"Oh, thunder, MacChesnay, what an awful bull you made of this thing!" began the officer. He attempted low tones, but his indignation caused certain of the men to learn the sense of his words. "What an awful mess you made! Good Lord, man, you stopped about a hundred feet this side of a very pretty success! If your men had gone a hundred feet farther, you would have made a great charge, but as it is—what a lot of mud diggers you've got anyway!"

The men, listening with bated breath, now turned their curious eyes upon the colonel. They had a ragamuffin interest in this affair.

The colonel was seen to straighten his form and put one hand forth in oratorical fashion. He wore an injured air; it was as if a deacon had been accused of stealing. The men were wiggling in an ecstasy of excitement.

But of a sudden the colonel's manner changed from that of a deacon to that of a Frenchman. He shrugged his shoulders. "Oh, well, general, we went as far as we could," he said calmly.

"As far as you could? Did you?" snorted the other. "Well, that wasn't very far, was it?" he added, with a glance of cold contempt into the other's eyes. "Not very far, I think. You were intended to make a diversion in favor of Whiterside. How well you succeeded your own ears can now tell you." He wheeled his horse and rode stiffly away.

The colonel, bidden to hear the jarring noises of an engagement in the woods to the left, broke out in vague damnations.

The lieutenant, who had listened with an air of impotent rage to the interview, spoke suddenly in firm and undaunted tones. "I don't care what a man is—whether he is a general or what—if he says th' boys didn't put up a good fight out there he's a fool."

"Lieutenant," began the colonel, severely, "this is my own affair, and I'll trouble you—"

The lieutenant made an obedient gesture. "All right, colonel, all right," he said. He sat down with an air of being content with himself.

The news that the regiment had been reproached went along the line. For a time the men were bewildered by it. "Good thunder!" they ejaculated, staring at the vanishing form of the general. They conceived it to be a huge mistake.

Presently, however, they began to believe that in truth their efforts had been called light. The youth could see this conviction weigh upon the entire regiment until the men were like cuffed and cursed animals, but withal rebellious.

The friend, with a grievance in his eye, went to the youth. "I wonder what he does want," he said. "He must think we went out there an' played marbles! I never see sech a man!"

The youth developed a tranquil philosophy for these moments of irritation. "Oh, well," he rejoined, "he probably didn't see nothing of it all and got mad as blazes, and concluded we were a lot of sheep, just because we didn't do what he wanted done. It's a pity old Grandpa Henderson got killed yestirday—he'd have known that we did our best and fought good. It's just our awful luck, that's what."

"I should say so," replied the friend. He seemed to be deeply wounded at an injustice. "I should say we did have awful luck! There's no fun in fightin' fer people when everything yeh do—no matter what—ain't done right. I have a notion t' stay behind next time an' let 'em take their ol' charge an' go t' th' devil with it."

The youth spoke soothingly to his comrade. "Well, we both did good. I'd like to see the fool what'd say we both didn't do as good as we could!"

"Of course we did," declared the friend stoutly. "An' I'd break th' feller's neck if he was as big as a church. But we're all right, anyhow, for I heard one feller say that we two fit th' best in th' reg'ment, an' they had a great argument 'bout it. Another feller, 'a course, he had t' up an' say it was a lie—he seen all what was goin' on an' he never seen us from th' beginnin' t' th' end. An' a lot more struck in an' ses it wasn't a lie—we did fight like thunder, an' they give us quite a send-off. But this is what I can't stand—these everlastin' ol' soldiers, titterin' an' laughin', an' then that general, he's crazy."

The youth exclaimed with sudden exasperation: "He's a lunkhead! He makes me mad. I wish he'd come along next time. We'd show 'im what——"

He ceased because several men had come hurrying up. Their faces expressed a bringing of great news.

"O Flem, yeh jest oughta heard!" cried one, eagerly.

"Heard what?" said the youth.

"Yeh jest oughta heard!" repeated the other, and he arranged himself to tell his tidings. The others made an excited circle. "Well, sir, th' colonel met your lieutenant right by us . . . an' he ses: 'Ahem! ahem!' he ses. 'Mr. Hasbrouck!' he ses, 'by th' way, who was that lad what carried th' flag?' he ses. There, Flemin', what d' yeh think 'a that? 'Who was th' lad what carried th' flag?' he ses, an' th' lieutenant, he speaks up right away: 'That's Flemin', an' he's a jimhickey,' he ses, right away. What? I say he did. 'A jimhickey,' he ses—those 'r his words. He did, too. I say he did. If you kin tell this story better than I kin, go ahead an' tell it. Well, then, keep yer mouth shet. Th' lieutenant, he ses: 'He's a jimhickey,' an' th' colonel, he ses: 'Ahem! Ahem! He is, indeed, a very good man t' have, ahem! He kep' th' flag 'way t' th' front. I saw 'im. He's a good un,' ses th' colonel. 'You bet,' ses th' lieutenant, 'he an' a feller named Wilson was at th' head 'a th' charge, an' howlin' like Indians all th' time,' he ses. 'Head a' th' charge all th' time,' he ses. 'A feller named Wilson,' he ses. There, Wilson, m'boy, put that in a letter an' send it hum t' yer mother, hay? 'A feller named Wilson,' he ses. An' th' colonel, he ses: 'Were they, indeed? Ahem! Ahem! My sakes!' he ses. 'At th' head a' th' reg'ment?' he ses. 'They were,' ses th' lieutenant. 'My sakes!' ses th' colonel. He ses: 'Well, well, well,' he ses, 'those two babies?' 'They were,' ses th' lieutenant. 'Well, well,' ses th' colonel, 'they deserve t' be major generals,' he ses. 'They deserve t' be major generals.' "

Lt. Hasbrouck and the colonel

The youth and his friend had said: "Huh!" "Yer lyin', Thompson." "Oh go t' blazes!" "He never sed it." "Oh, what a lie!" "Huh!" But despite these youthful scoffings and embarrassments, they knew that their faces were deeply flushing from thrills of pleasure. They exchanged a secret glance of joy and congratulation.

They speedily forgot many things. The past held no pictures of error and disappointment. They were very happy, and their hearts swelled with grateful affection for the colonel and the youthful lieutenant.

CHAPTER 22

When the woods again began to pour forth the dark-hued masses of the enemy, the youth felt serene self-confidence. He smiled briefly when he saw men dodge and duck at the long screechings of shells that were thrown in giant handfuls over them. He stood, erect and tranquil, watching the attack begin against a part of the line that made a blue curve along the side of an adjacent hill. His vision being unmolested by smoke from the rifles of his companions, he had opportunities to see parts of the hard fight. It was a relief to perceive at last from whence came some of these noises which had been roared into his ears.

Off a short way he saw two regiments fighting a little separate battle with two other regiments. It was in a cleared space, wearing a set-apart look. They were blazing as if upon a wager, giving and taking tremendous blows. The firings were incredibly fierce and rapid. These intent regiments apparently were oblivious of all larger purposes of war, and were slugging each other as if at a matched game.

In another direction he saw a magnificent brigade going with the evident intention of driving the enemy from a wood. They passed in out of sight and presently there was a most awe-inspiring racket in the wood. The noise was unspeakable. Having stirred this prodigious uproar, and, apparently, finding it too prodigious, the brigade, after a little time, came marching airily out again with its fine formation in nowise disturbed. There were no traces of speed in its movements. The brigade was jaunty and seemed to point a proud thumb at the yelling wood.

On a slope to the left there was a long row of guns, gruff and maddened, denouncing the enemy, who, down through the woods, were forming for another attack in the pitiless monotony of conflicts. The round red discharges for the guns made a crimson flare and a high, thick smoke. Occasional glimpses could be caught of groups of the toiling artillerymen. In the rear of this row of guns stood a house, calm and white, amid bursting shells. A congregation of horses, tied to a long railing, were tugging frenziedly at their bridles. Men were running hither and thither.

The detached battle between the four regiments lasted for some time. There chanced to be no interference, and they settled their dispute by themselves. They struck savagely and powerfully at each other for a period of minutes, and then the lighter-hued regiments faltered and drew back, leaving the dark-blue lines shouting. The youth could see the two flags shaking with laughter amid the smoke remnants.

Presently there was a stillness, pregnant with meaning. The blue lines shifted and changed a trifle and stared expectantly at the silent woods and fields before them. The hush was solemn and churchlike, save for a distant battery that, evidently unable to remain quiet, sent a faint rolling thunder over the ground. It irritated, like the noises of unimpressed boys. The men imagined that it would prevent their perched ears from hearing the first words of the new battle.

Of a sudden the guns on the slope roared out a message of warning. A spluttering sound had begun in the woods. It swelled with amazing speed to a profound clamor that involved the earth in noises. The splitting crashes swept along the lines until an interminable roar was developed. To those in the midst of it it became a din fitted to the universe. It was the whirring and thumping of gigantic machinery, complications among the smaller stars. The youth's ears were filled up. They were incapable of hearing more.

On an incline over which a road wound he saw wild and desperate rushes of men perpetually backward and forward in riotous surges. These parts of the opposing armies were two long waves that pitched upon each other madly at dictated points. To and fro they swelled. Sometimes, one side by its yells and cheers would proclaim decisive blows, but a moment later the other side would be all yells and cheers. Once the youth saw a spray of light forms go in houndlike leaps toward the waving blue lines. There was much howling, and presently it went away with a vast mouthful of prisoners. Again, he saw a blue wave dash with such thunderous force against a gray obstruction that it seemed to clear the earth of it and leave nothing but trampled sod. And always in their swift and deadly rushes to and fro the men screamed and yelled like maniacs.

Particular pieces of fence or secure positions behind collections of trees were wrangled over, as gold thrones or pearl bedsteads. There were desperate lunges at these chosen spots seemingly every instant, and most of them were bandied like light toys between the contending forces. The youth could not tell from the battle flags flying like crimson foam in many directions which color of cloth was winning.

His emaciated regiment bustled forth with undiminished fierceness when its time came. When assaulted again by bullets, the men burst out in a barbaric cry of rage and pain. They bent their heads in aims of intent hatred behind the projected hammers of their guns. Their ramrods clanged loud with fury as their eager arms pounded the cartridges into the rifle barrels. The front of the regiment was a smoke-wall penetrated by the flashing points of yellow and red.

Wallowing in the fight, they were in an astonishingly short time resmudged. They surpassed in stain and dirt all their previous appearances. Moving to and fro with strained exertion, jabbering the while, they were, with their swaying bodies, black faces, and glowing eyes, like strange and ugly fiends jigging heavily in the smoke.

The lieutenant, returning from a tour after a bandage, produced from a hidden receptacle of his mind new and portentous oaths suited to the emergency. Strings of expletives he swung lashlike over the backs of his men, and it was evident that his previous efforts had in nowise impaired his resources.

The youth, still the bearer-of-the-colors, did not feel his idleness. He was deeply absorbed as a spectator. The crash and swing of the great drama made him lean forward, intent-eyed, his face working in small contortions. Sometimes he prattled, words coming unconsciously from him in grotesque exclamations. He did not know that he breathed; that the flag hung silently over him, so absorbed was he.

A formidable line of the enemy came within dangerous range. They could be seen plainly—tall, gaunt men with excited faces running with long strides toward a wandering fence.

At sight of this danger the men suddenly ceased their cursing monotone. There was an instant of strained silence before they threw up their rifles and fired a plumping volley at the foes. There had been no order given; the men, upon recognizing the menace, had immediately let drive their flock of bullets without waiting for word of command.

But the enemy were quick to gain the protection of the wandering line of fence. They slid down behind it with remarkable celerity, and from this position they began briskly to slice up the blue men.

These latter braced their energies for a great struggle. Often, white clinched teeth shone from the dusky faces. Many heads surged to and fro, floating upon a pale sea of smoke. Those behind the fence frequently shouted and yelped in taunts and gibelike cries, but the regiment maintained a stressed silence. Perhaps, at this new assault the men recalled the fact that they had been named mud diggers, and it made their situation thrice bitter. They were breathlessly intent upon keeping the ground and thrusting away the rejoicing body of the enemy. They fought swiftly and with a despairing savageness denoted in their expressions.

The youth had resolved not to budge whatever should happen. Some arrows of scorn that had buried themselves in his heart had generated strange and unspeakable hatred. It was clear to him that his final and absolute revenge was to be achieved by his dead body lying, torn and gluttering, upon the field. This was to be a poignant retaliation upon the officer who had said "mule drivers," and later "mud diggers," for in all the wild graspings of his mind for a unit responsible for his sufferings and commotions he always seized upon the man who had dubbed him wrongly. And it was his idea, vaguely formulated, that his corpse would be for those eyes a great and salt reproach.

The regiment bled extravagantly. Grunting bundles of blue began to drop. The orderly sergeant of the youth's company was shot through the cheeks. Its supports being injured, his jaw hung afar down, disclosing in the wide cavern of his mouth a pulsing mass of blood and teeth. And withal he made attempts to cry out. In his endeavor there was a dreadful earnestness, as if he conceived that one great shriek would make him well.

The youth saw him presently go rearward. His strength seemed in nowise impaired. He ran swiftly, casting wild glances for succor.

Others fell down about the feet of their companions. Some of the wounded crawled out and away, but many lay still, their bodies twisted into impossible shapes.

The youth looked once for his friend. He saw a vehement young man, powder-smeared and frowzled, whom he knew to be him. The lieutenant, also, was unscathed in his position at the rear. He had continued to curse, but it was now with the air of a man who was using his last box of oaths.

For the fire of the regiment had begun to wane and drip. The robust voice, that had come strangely from the thin ranks, was growing rapidly weak.

CHAPTER 23

The colonel came running along back of the line. There were other officers following him. "We must charge'm!" they shouted. "We must charge'm!" they cried with resentful voices, as if anticipating a rebellion against this plan by the men.

The youth, upon hearing the shouts, began to study the distance between him and the enemy. He made vague calculations. He saw that to be firm soldiers they must go forward. It would be death to stay in the present place, and with all the circumstances to go backward would exalt too many others. Their hope was to push the galling foes away from the fence.

Fleming with colors
to the front —
sky — sapphire blue

He expected that his companions, weary and stiffened, would have to be driven to this assault, but as he turned toward them, he perceived with a certain surprise that they were giving quick and unqualified expressions of assent. There was an ominous, clanging overture to the charge when the shafts of the bayonets rattled upon the rifle barrels. At the yelled words of command the soldiers sprang forward in eager leaps. There was new and unexpected force in the movement of the regiment. A knowledge of its faded and jaded condition made the charge appear like a paroxysm, a display of the strength that comes before a final feebleness. The men scampered in insane fever of haste, racing as if to achieve a sudden success before an exhilarating fluid should leave them. It was a blind and despairing rush by the collection of men in dusty and tattered blue, over a green sward and under a sapphire sky, toward a fence, dimly outlined in smoke, from behind which spluttered the fierce rifles of enemies.

The youth kept the bright colors to the front. He was waving his free arm in furious circles, the while shrieking mad calls and appeals, urging on those that did not need to be urged, for it seemed that the mob of blue men hurling themselves on the dangerous group of rifles were again grown suddenly wild with an enthusiasm of unselfishness. From the many firings starting toward them, it looked as if they would merely succeed in making a great sprinkling of corpses on the grass between their former position and the fence. But they were in a state of frenzy, perhaps because of forgotten vanities, and it made an exhibition of sublime recklessness. There was no obvious questioning, nor figurings, nor diagrams. There were, apparently, no considered loopholes. It appeared that the swift wings of their desires would have shattered against the iron gates of the impossible.

He himself felt the daring spirit of a savage religion mad. He was capable of profound sacrifices, a tremendous death. He had no time for dissections, but he knew that he thought of the bullets only as things that could prevent him from reaching the place of his endeavor. There were subtle flashings of joy within him that thus should be his mind.

He strained all his strength. His eyesight was shaken and dazzled by the tension of thought and muscle. He did not see anything excepting the mist of smoke gashed by the little knives of fire, but he knew that in it lay the aged fence of a vanished farmer protecting the snuggled bodies of the gray men.

As he ran, a thought of the shock of contact gleamed in his mind. He expected a great concussion when the two bodies of troops crashed together. This became a part of his wild battle madness. He could feel the onward swing of the regiment about him and he conceived of a thunderous, crushing blow that would prostrate the resistance and spread consternation and amazement for miles. The flying regiment was going to have a catapultian effect. This dream made him run faster among his comrades, who were giving vent to hoarse and frantic cheers.

But presently he could see that many of the men in gray did not intend to abide the blow. The smoke, rolling, disclosed men who ran, their faces still turned. These grew to a crowd, who retired stubbornly. Individuals wheeled frequently to send a bullet at the blue wave.

But at one part of the line there was a grim and obdurate group that made no movement. They were settled firmly down behind posts and rails. A flag, ruffled and fierce, waved over them and their rifles dinned fiercely.

The blue whirl of men got very near, until it seemed that in truth there would be a close and frightful scuffle. There was an expressed disdain in the opposition of the little group, that changed the meaning of the cheers of the men in blue. They became yells of wrath, directed, personal. The cries of the two parties were now in sound an interchange of scathing insults.

They in blue showed their teeth; their eyes shone all white. They launched themselves as at the throats of those who stood resisting. The space between dwindled to an insignificant distance.

The youth had centered the gaze of his soul upon that other flag. Its possession would be high pride. It would express bloody minglings, near blows. He had a gigantic hatred for those who made great difficulties and complications. They caused it to be as a craved treasure of mythology, hung amid tasks and contrivances of danger.

He plunged like a mad horse at it. He was resolved it should not escape if wild blows and darings of blows could seize it. His own emblem, quivering and aflare, was winging toward the other. It seemed there would shortly be an encounter of strange beaks and claws, as of eagles.

The swirling body of blue men came to a sudden halt at close and disastrous range and roared a swift volley. The group in gray was split and broken by this fire, but its riddled body still fought. The men in blue yelled again and rushed in upon it.

The youth, in his leapings, saw, as through a mist, a picture of four or five men stretched upon the ground or writhing upon their knees with bowed heads as if they had been stricken by bolts from the sky. Tottering among them was the rival color bearer, whom the youth saw had been bitten vitally by the bullets of the last formidable volley. He perceived this man fighting a last struggle, the struggle of one whose legs are grasped by demons. It was a ghastly battle. Over his face was the bleach of death, but set upon it was the dark and hard lines of desperate purpose. With this terrible grin of resolution he hugged his precious flag to him and was stumbling and staggering in his design to go the way that led to safety for it.

But his wounds always made it seem that his feet were retarded, held, and he fought a grim fight, as with invisible ghouls fastened greedily upon his limbs. Those in advance of the scampering blue men, howling cheers, leaped at the fence. The despair of the lost was in his eyes as he glanced back at them.

The youth's friend went over the obstruction in a tumbling heap and sprang at the flag as a panther at prey. He pulled at it and, wrenching it free, swung up its red brilliancy with a mad cry of exultation even as the color bearer, gasping, lurched over in final throes and, stiffening convulsively, turned his dead face to the ground. There was much blood upon the grass blades.

At the place of success there began more wild clamorings of cheers. The men gesticulated and bellowed in an ecstasy. When they spoke, it was as if they considered their listener to be a mile away. What hats and caps were left to them they often slung high in the air.

At one part of the line four men had been swooped upon, and they now sat as prisoners. Some blue men were about them in an eager and curious circle. The soldiers had trapped strange birds, and there was an examination. A flurry of fast questions was in the air.

One of the prisoners was nursing a superficial wound in the foot. He cuddled it, baby-wise, but

The youth seized the flag much smoke and yelling

he looked up from it often to curse with an astonishing utter abandon straight at the noses of his captors. He consigned them to red regions; he called upon the pestilential wrath of strange gods. And with it all he was singularly free from recognition of the finer points of the conduct of prisoners of war. It was as if a clumsy clod had trod upon his toe and he conceived it to be his privilege, his duty, to use deep, resentful oaths.

Another, who was a boy in years, took his plight with great calmness and apparent good nature. He conversed with the men in blue, studying their faces with his bright and keen eyes. They spoke of battle and conditions. There was an acute interest in all their faces during this exchange of viewpoints. It seemed a great satisfaction to hear voices from where all had been darkness and speculation.

The third captive sat with a morose countenance. He preserved a stoical and cold attitude. To all advances he made one reply without variation, "Ah, go t' the devil!"

The last of the four was always silent, and, for the most part, kept his face turned in unmolested directions. From the views the youth received he seemed to be in a state of absolute dejection. Shame was upon him, and with it profound regret that he was, perhaps, no more to be counted in the ranks of his fellows. The youth could detect no expression that would allow him to believe that the other was giving a thought to his narrowed future, the pictured dungeons, perhaps, and starvations and brutalities, liable to the imagination. All to be seen was shame for captivity and regret for the right to antagonize.

After the men had celebrated sufficiently, they settled down behind the old rail fence, on the opposite side to the one from which their foes had been driven. A few shot perfunctorily at distant marks.

There was some long grass. The youth nestled in it and rested, making a convenient rail support the flag. His friend, jubilant and glorified, holding his treasure with vanity, came to him there. They sat side by side and congratulated each other.

CHAPTER 24

The roarings that had stretched in a long line of sound across the face of the forest began to grow intermittent and weaker. The stentorian speeches of the artillery continued in some distant encounter, but the crashes of the musketry had almost ceased. The youth and his friend of a sudden looked up, feeling a deadened form of distress at the waning of these noises, which had become a part of life. They could see changes going on among the troops. There were marchings this way and that way. A battery wheeled leisurely. On the crest of a small hill was the thick gleam of many departing muskets.

The youth arose, "Well, what now, I wonder?" he said. By his tone he seemed to be preparing to resent some new monstrosity in the way of dins and smashes. He shaded his eyes with his grimy hand and gazed over the field.

His friend also arose and stared. "I bet we're goin' t' git along out of this an' back over th' river," said he.

"Well, I swan!" said the youth.

They waited, watching. Within a little while the regiment received orders to retrace its way. The men got up grunting from the grass, regretting the soft repose. They jerked their stiffened legs, and stretched their arms over their heads. One man swore as he rubbed his eyes. They all groaned "O Lord!" They had as many objections to this change as they would have had to a proposal for a new battle.

They trampled slowly back over the field across which they had run in a mad scamper. The regiment marched until it had joined its fellows. The reformed brigade, in column, aimed through a wood at the road. Directly they were in a mass of dust-covered troops, and were trudging along in a way parallel to the enemy's lines as these had been defined by the previous turmoil.

They passed within a view of a stolid white house, and saw in front of it groups of their comrades lying in wait behind a neat breastwork. A row of guns were booming at a distant enemy. Shells thrown in reply were raising clouds of dust and splinters. Horsemen dashed along the lines of intrenchments.

At this point of its march the division curved away from the field and went winding off in the direction of the river. When the significance of this movement had impressed itself upon the youth, he turned his head and looked over his shoulder toward the trampled and debris-strewed ground. He breathed a breath of new satisfaction. He finally nudged his friend. "Well, it's all over," he said to him.

His friend gazed backward. "It is," he assented. They mused.

For a time the youth was obliged to reflect in a puzzled and uncertain way. His mind was undergoing a subtle change. It took moments for it to cast off its battleful ways and resume its accustomed course of thought. Gradually his brain emerged from the clogged clouds, and at last was enabled to more closely comprehend himself and circumstance.

He understood then that the existence of shot and countershot was in the past. He had dwelt in a land of strange, squalling upheavals and had come forth. He had been where there was red of blood and black of passion, and he was escaped. His first thoughts were given to rejoicings at this fact.

Later he began to study his deeds, his failures, and his achievements. Thus, fresh from scenes where many of his usual machines of reflection had been idle, from where he had proceeded sheeplike, he struggled to marshal all his acts.

At last they marched before him clearly. From this present viewpoint he was enabled to look at them in spectator fashion and to criticize them with some correctness, for his new condition had already defeated certain sympathies.

But the youth, regarding his procession of memory, felt gleeful and unregretting, for in it his public deeds were paraded in great and shining prominence. Those performances which had been witnessed by his fellows marched now in wide purple and gold, having various deflections. They went gayly with music. It was pleasure to watch these things. He spent delightful minutes viewing the gilded images of memory.

He saw that he was good. He recalled with a thrill of joy the respectful comments of his fellows upon his conduct. Nevertheless, the ghost of his flight from the first engagement appeared to him and danced. There were small shoutings in his brain about these matters. For a moment he blushed, and the light of his soul flickered with shame.

However, he presently procured an explanation and an apology. He said that those tempestuous moments were of the wild mistakes and ravings of a novice who did not comprehend. He had been a mere man railing at a condition, but now he was out of it and could see that it had been very proper and just. It had been necessary for him to swallow swords that he might have a better throat for grapes. Fate had in truth been kind to him; she had stabbed him with benign purpose and diligently cudgeled him for his own sake. In his rebellion, he had been very portentious, no doubt, and sincere, and anxious for humanity, but now that he stood safe, with no lack of blood, it was suddenly clear to him that he had been wrong not to kiss the knife and bow to the cudgel. He had foolishly squirmed.

But the sky would forget. It was true, he admitted, that in the world it was the habit to cry devil at persons who refused to trust what they could not trust, but he thought that perhaps the stars dealt differently. The imperturbable sun shines on insult and worship.

As Fleming was thus fraternizing again with nature, a specter of reproach came to him. There loomed the dogging memory of the tattered soldier—he who, gored by bullets and faint for blood, had fretted concerning an imagined wound in another; he who had loaned his last of strength and intellect for the tall soldier; he who, blind with weariness and pain, had been deserted in the field.

For an instant a wretched chill of sweat was upon him at the thought that he might be detected in the thing. As he stood persistently before his vision, he gave vent to a cry of sharp irritation and agony.

His friend turned. "What's the matter, Henry?" he demanded. The youth's reply was an outburst of crimson oaths.

As he marched along the little branch-hung roadway among his prattling companions, this vision of cruelty brooded over him. It clung near him always and darkened his view of these deeds in purple and gold. Whichever way his thoughts turned they were followed by the somber phantom of the desertion in the fields. He looked stealthily at his companions, feeling sure that they must discern in his face evidences of this pursuit. But they were plodding in ragged array, discussing with quick tongues the accomplishments of the late battle.

"Oh, if a man should come up an' ask me, I'd say we got a dum good lickin'."

"Lickin'—in yer eye! We ain't licked, sonny. We're going down here aways, swing aroun', an' come in behint 'em."

"Oh, hush, with your comin' in behint 'em. I've seen all 'a that I wanta. Don't tell me about comin' in behint——"

"Bill Smithers, he ses he'd rather been in ten hundred battles than been in that hospital. He ses they got shootin' in th' nighttime, an' shells dropped plum among 'em in th' hospital. He ses sech hollerin' he never see."

"Hasbrouck? He's th' best off'cer in this here reg'ment. He's a whale."

"Didn't I tell yeh we'd come aroun' in behint 'em? Didn't I tell yeh so? We——"

"Oh, shet yer mouth!"

For a time this pursuing recollection of the tattered man took all elation from the youth's veins.

He saw his vivid error, and he was afraid that it would stand before him all his life. He took no share in the chatter of his comrades, nor did he look at them or know them, save when he felt sudden suspicion that they were seeing his thoughts and scrutinizing each detail of the scene with the tattered soldier.

Yet gradually he mustered force to pull the sin at a distance. And then he regarded it with what he thought to be great calmness. At last, he concluded that he saw in it quaint uses. He exclaimed that its importance in the aftertime would be great to him if it even succeeded in hindering the workings of his egotism. It would make a sobering balance. It would become a good part of him. He would have upon him often the consciousness of a great mistake. And he would be taught to deal gently and with care. He would be a man.

This plan for the utilization of a sin did not give him complete joy but it was the best sentiment he could formulate under the circumstances, and when it was combined with his success, or public deeds, he knew that he was quite contented. And at last his eyes seemed to open to some new ways. He found that he could look back upon the brass and bombast of his earlier gospels and see them truly. He was gleeful when he discovered that he now despised them.

He was emerged from his struggles, with a large sympathy for the machinery of the universe. With his new eyes, he could see that the secret and open blows which were being dealt about the world with such heavenly lavishness were in truth blessings. It was a deity laying about him with the bludgeon of correction.

His loud mouth against these things had been lost as the storm ceased. He would no more stand upon places high and false, and denounce the distant planets. He beheld that he was tiny but not inconsequent to the sun. In the space-wide whirl of events no grain like him would be lost.

With this conviction came a store of assurance. He felt a quiet manhood, nonassertive but of sturdy and strong blood. He knew that he would no more quail before his guides wherever they should point. He had been to touch the great death, and found that, after all, it was but the great death. He was a man.

So it came to pass that as he trudged from the place of blood and wrath his soul changed. He came from hot plowshares to prospects of clover tranquilly, and it was as if hot plowshares were not. Scars faded as flowers.

It rained. The procession of weary soldiers became a bedraggled train, despondent and muttering, marching with churning effort in a trough of liquid brown mud under a low, wretched sky. Yet the youth smiled, for he saw that the world was a world for him, though many discovered it to be made of oaths and walking sticks. He had rid himself of the red sickness of battle. The sultry nightmare was in the past. He had been an animal blistered and sweating in the heat and pain of war. He turned now with a lover's thirst to images of tranquil skies, fresh meadows, cool brooks—an existence of soft and eternal peace.

Over the river a golden ray of sun came through the hosts of leaden rain clouds.   **1895**

THINK AND DISCUSS
CHAPTERS 20–24
Understanding
1. After the battle in Chapter 21, what do the "gaunt and bronzed" veterans say to Henry's returning regiment? What do the colonel and lieutenant say about Henry and Wilson?
2. In the battle of the rail fence that occurs in Chapter 23, how does Wilson take a Confederate flag?

Analyzing
3. Feelings in Henry's regiment seem to change dramatically in Chapter 20. How do the soldiers feel about themselves at the beginning of the chapter? at the conclusion?
4. Impressionistic writing presents scenes and events from a particular vantage point rather than as they are in actuality. Filtered through Henry's eyes, the enemy viewed through "smoke fringes and flames" is "a brown mass of troops" bearing a "fierce-hued flag." Find three other examples of impressionistic detail in Chapter 20.

5. Henry imagines his comrades as a "regimental broom" which, if swallowed by the enemy, would go down "with bristles forward." Explain the appropriateness of this comparison.
6. Describe the movements of the armies in Chapter 22 as expressed through color **imagery, metaphors,** and **personification.**
7. When Henry reviews his past conduct in the final chapter of the novel, what does he consider his "deeds in purple and gold"? How does he feel about these deeds?
8. How does Henry feel about himself in general at the conclusion of the novel?
9. Why is a war setting appropriate for a story of initiation?

Extending

10. This novel has been variously described as a psychological study of fear, an investigation of maturation (see Themes in American Literature, page 841), an examination of human weakness and heroism, and a commentary on the solitary nature of human existence. Explain which interpretation seems most valid to you.

REVIEWING: Characterization   H𝓩
See Handbook of Literary Terms, p. 882.

Major **characters** in a novel are usually more complex and fully developed than those in shorter works. Most readers will agree that Henry has undergone significant changes during the brief but intense time span covered in the novel.

1. At the end of the novel, what major changes do you see in Henry's character?
2. In what respects have other characters changed their view of him by the end of the novel?
3. Are the changes in Henry believable? Why or why not?

READING LITERATURE SKILLFULLY
Sequence

Although every story has a sequence, or chronological order of events, authors may choose to rearrange the order in which they present these events. A reader must see the relationship between the pattern of events in a narrative and determine why they are presented in a certain order.

1. Why do you think Crane chose to open this novel on the battlefield, rather than with Henry's enlisting, which is presented as a flashback?
2. Why is it important that Henry sees others desert before he does so himself?
3. How is it appropriate that the narrative ends where it does, rather than after Henry returns home?

VOCABULARY
Dictionary

Use your Glossary to find the meaning of each of the following words. On your paper write the word that correctly answers each question. The words are *agitated, harangue, faltering, bandying,* and *emaciated.*

1. Since the prisoner had not eaten for three weeks, his face was drawn and his ribs showed. How would you describe his appearance?
2. The television host was excluded from the conversation between her guests, who continually made brief remarks back and forth to one another. Which word describes the way the guests were talking?
3. If you threw a rock into a still stream, the water would be disturbed. What word would you use to describe the appearance of the water's surface?
4. As the horse approached the final jump, it hesitated, losing its timing. What word describes the horse's hesitation?
5. The speaker in the park was known for his noisy, forceful speeches. What word refers to the way he spoke to his audience?

UNIT 8   THE RED BADGE OF COURAGE

■ CONCEPT REVIEW

The following excerpt contains many of the important ideas and literary terms in the novel you have just studied. The notes and questions are designed to help you think critically about your reading. Page numbers in the notes refer to an application. A more extensive discussion of these terms is in the Handbook of Literary Terms.

"The Bride Comes to Yellow Sky" is the story of an ironic confrontation that takes place in the small Texas town of Yellow Sky during the late 1890s. The confrontation occurs as Jack Potter, the town marshal who is returning from San Antonio where he has gotten married, encounters Scratchy Wilson, an old foe who is on a drunken shooting spree.

from The Bride Comes to Yellow Sky

Stephen Crane

A man in a maroon-colored flannel shirt, which had been purchased for purposes of decoration, and made principally by some Jewish women on the East Side of New York, rounded a corner and walked into the middle of the main street of Yellow Sky. In either hand the man held a long, heavy, blue-black revolver. Often he yelled, and these cries rang through a semblance of a deserted village, shrilly flying over the roofs in a volume that seemed to have no relation to the ordinary vocal strength of a man. It was as if the surrounding stillness formed the arch of a tomb over him. These cries of ferocious challenge rang against walls of silence. And his boots had red tops with gilded imprints, of the kind beloved in winter by little sledding boys on the hillsides of New England.

The man's face flamed in a rage begot of whisky. His eyes, rolling, and yet keen for ambush, hunted the still doorways and windows. He walked with the creeping movement of the midnight cat. As it occurred to him, he

■ **Characterization** (page 871): Note the telling details of dress and behavior that describe Scratchy Wilson.

■ These boots are incongruous with the image of a gun-toting madman.

roared menacing information. The long revolvers in his hands were as easy as straws; they were moved with an electric swiftness. The little fingers of each hand played sometimes in a musician's way. Plain from the low collar of the shirt, the cords of his neck straightened and sank, straightened and sank, as passion moved him. The only sounds were his terrible invitations. The calm adobes preserved their demeanor at the passing of this small thing in the middle of the street.

There was no offer of fight—no offer of fight. The man called to the sky. There were no attractions. He bellowed and fumed and swayed his revolvers here and everywhere.

The dog of the barkeeper of the Weary Gentleman saloon had not appreciated the advance of events. He yet lay dozing in front of his master's door. At sight of the dog, the man paused and raised his revolver humorously. At sight of the man, the dog sprang up and walked diagonally away, with a sullen head, and growling. The man yelled, and the dog broke into a gallop. As it was about to enter an alley, there was a loud noise, a whistling, and something spat the ground directly before it. The dog screamed, and, wheeling in terror, galloped headlong in a new direction. Again there was a noise, a whistling, and sand was kicked viciously before it. Fear-stricken, the dog turned and flurried like an animal in a pen. The man stood laughing, his weapons at his hips.

Ultimately the man was attracted by the closed door of the Weary Gentleman saloon. He went to it and, hammering with a revolver, demanded drink.

The door remaining imperturbable, he picked a bit of paper from the walk, and nailed it to the framework with a knife. He then turned his back contemptuously upon this popular resort and, walking to the opposite side of the street and spinning there on his heel quickly and lithely, fired at the bit of paper. He missed it by a half inch. He swore at himself, and went away. Later he comfortably fusilladed the windows of his most intimate friend. The man was playing with this town; it was a toy for him.

But still there was no offer of fight. The name of Jack Potter, his ancient antagonist, entered his mind, and he concluded that it would be a glad thing if he should go to Potter's house, and by bombardment induce him to come out and fight. He moved in the direction of his desire, chanting Apache scalp-music.

When he arrived at it, Potter's house presented the same still front as had the other adobes. Taking up a strategic position, the man howled a challenge. But this house regarded him as might a great stone god. It gave no sign. After a decent wait, the man howled further challenges, mingling with them wonderful epithets.

Presently there came the spectacle of a man churning himself into deepest rage over the immobility of a house. He fumed at it as the winter wind attacks a prairie cabin in the North. To the distance there should have gone the sound of a tumult like the fighting of two hundred Mexicans. As necessity bade him, he paused for breath or to reload his revolvers.

■ Personification interjects a note of calm indifference amid this menacing scene.

■ The dozing dog, along with the saloon and drunken gunman, are stock features in Westerns.

■ The Western locale, use of dialect, and descriptions of dress and customs all identify this as a local-color story.

■ Wilson is a humorous eccentric—a common type in local-color stories.

Potter and his bride walked sheepishly and with speed. Sometimes they laughed together shame-facedly and low.

"Next corner, dear," he said finally.

They put forth the efforts of a pair walking bowed against a strong wind. Potter was about to raise a finger to point the first appearance of the new home when, as they circled the corner, they came face to face with a man in a maroon-colored shirt, who was feverishly pushing cartridges into a large revolver. Upon the instant the man dropped his revolver to the ground and, like lightning, whipped another from its holster. The second weapon was aimed at the bridegroom's chest.

There was a silence. Potter's mouth seemed to be merely a grave for his tongue. He exhibited an instinct to at once loosen his arm from the woman's grip, and he dropped the bag to the sand. As for the bride, her face had gone as yellow as old cloth. She was a slave to hideous rites, gazing at the apparitional snake.

The two men faced each other at a distance of three paces. He of the revolver smiled with a new and quiet ferocity.

"Tried to sneak up on me," he said. "Tried to sneak up on me!" His eyes grew more baleful. As Potter made a slight movement, the man thrust his revolver venomously forward. "No; don't you do it, Jack Potter. Don't you move a finger toward a gun just yet. Don't you move an eyelash. The time has come for me to settle with you, and I'm goin' to do it my own way, and loaf along with no interferin'. So if you don't want a gun bent on you, just mind what I tell you."

Potter looked at his enemy. "I ain't got a gun on me, Scratchy," he said. "Honest, I ain't." He was stiffening and steadying, but yet somewhere at the back of his mind a vision of the Pullman floated; the sea-green figured velvet, the shining brass, silver, and glass, the wood that gleamed as darkly brilliant as the surface of a pool on oil—all the glory of the marriage, the environment of the new estate. "You know I fight when it comes to fighting, Scratchy Wilson; but I ain't got a gun on me. You'll have to do all the shootin' yourself."

His enemy's face went livid. He stepped forward, and lashed his weapon to and fro before Potter's chest. "Don't you tell me you ain't got no gun on you, you whelp. Don't tell me no lie like that. There ain't a man in Texas ever seen you without no gun. Don't take me for no kid." His eyes blazed with light, and his throat worked like a pump.

"I ain't takin' you for no kid," answered Potter. His heels had not moved an inch backward. "I'm takin' you for a fool. I tell you I ain't got a gun, and I ain't. If you're goin' to shoot me up, you better begin now; you'll never get a chance like this again."

So much enforced reasoning had told on Wilson's rage; he was calmer. "If you ain't got a gun, why ain't you got a gun?" he sneered. "Been to Sunday school?"

"I ain't got a gun because I've just come from San Anton' with my wife. I'm married," said Potter. "And if I'd thought there was going to be any

874 *The Red Badge of Courage*

■ Note the shift in focus and abrupt change in mood.

■ grave . . . tongue. Note the appropriateness of this metaphor, given Wilson's intent to kill.

■ apparitional snake: an allusion to the snake or devil in the biblical Garden of Eden.

■ "Been . . . school?" Wilson's tone changes from rage to sarcasm.

galoots like you prowling around when I brought my wife home, I'd had a gun, and don't you forget it."

"Married!" said Scratchy, not at all comprehending.

"Yes, married. I'm married," said Potter, distinctly.

"Married?" said Scratchy. Seemingly for the first time, he saw the drooping, drowning woman at the other man's side. "No!" he said. He was like a creature allowed a glimpse of another world. He moved a pace backward, and his arm, with the revolver, dropped to his side. "Is this the lady?" he asked.

"Yes; this is the lady," answered Potter.

There was another period of silence.

"Well," said Wilson at last, slowly, "I s'pose it's all off now."

"It's all off if you say so, Scratchy. You know I didn't make the trouble." Potter lifted his valise.

"Well, I 'low it's off, Jack," said Wilson. He was looking at the ground. "Married!" He was not a student of chivalry; it was merely that in the presence of this foreign condition he was a simple child of the earlier plains. He picked up his starboard revolver, and, placing both weapons in their holsters, he went away. His feet made funnel-shaped tracks in the heavy sand.   1898

■ **Irony** (page 840): Note the effect of the word *marriage* on this outlaw.

■ **His feet . . . sand.** This detail reveals that Wilson's spirit is broken.

THINK AND DISCUSS
Understanding
1. How is the character we later learn is Scratchy Wilson dressed, according to the first paragraph? How does he behave?
2. Who is Wilson's "ancient antagonist"?
3. Where has Jack Potter been? Why?

Analyzing
4. What are several ways that Wilson shows his contempt for the town?
5. In what respect would marriage have been a "foreign condition" in this Western **setting**?
6. What is the climax of this story?

Extending
7. Wilson shoots out the windows of "his most intimate friend." Name two other acts of his that suggest the broadly comic antics of a typical antagonist in a TV or movie Western.

REVIEWING LITERARY TERMS
Characterization
1. Potter's wife is characterized mainly through her reactions to Wilson. What can you **infer** about her by her responses?
2. Judging from this excerpt, do you think that Crane was more concerned with developing character or with the plot and setting of this story? Explain.

Irony
3. Wilson appears unafraid of anything until he hears that Potter is married. Why is he disarmed (literally) at the mention of marriage?
4. Put the following explanation of Wilson's ironic reversal into your own words: "He was not a student of chivalry; it was merely that in the presence of this foreign condition he was a simple child of the earlier plains."

■ CONTENT REVIEW

THINKING SKILLS

Classifying

1. Under the headings *Red*, *Badge*, and *Courage*, list words and phrases, both connotative and denotative, that you associate with these words. Circle any of your words or phrases that seem to apply to Crane's novel.

2. Although many of Crane's descriptions depict battlefield frenzy, other descriptions portray a mood of calm. Find three passages from *Red Badge* that portray each of these moods. Then explain how Crane's word choice, use of figurative language, and images help establish these moods.

Generalizing

3. Each of the four minor characters—the tall soldier, the loud soldier, the tattered man, and the cheerful man—makes a contribution to the story. Why are they identified by these labels? What influence does each character have on Henry?

Synthesizing

4. Think of an epithet comparable to that of his companions (the tall soldier, the tattered man) to describe Henry at the beginning of the novel. Do you think this label still describes Henry at the end? If not, think of a new one.

5. Suggest another appropriate title for this novel. Then explain whether or not you consider your title as effective as the original.

Evaluating

6. Does *The Red Badge of Courage* contain enough military action to qualify as a war novel? Why or why not?

7. Some critics feel that *The Red Badge of Courage* is a series of loosely related incidents rather than a traditionally structured novel with a central conflict, a **plot** that has a climax and a resolution, and a main character who develops throughout the course of the narration. Explain whether or not you agree with this critical opinion. In forming your opinion, remember that a novel must have continuity and development.

■ COMPOSITION REVIEW

Choose one of the following topics for a composition.

Examining a Character

In an essay of three or four paragraphs, explain whether or not you think Henry Fleming has really changed during the course of the novel. Consider his self-knowledge, his regard for others, his values, his ability to survive, and whether or not he has earned his red badge. Submit your essay to a literary magazine.

Developing Dialogue

One of the novel's striking effects comes from the dialogue, which is a realistic expression of the characters' regional backgrounds. Compose a narrative of several paragraphs depicting a group such as soldiers, classmates, or teachers through dialogue. Focus on a single incident with a limited number of characters. Before you start to write, assemble a collection of phrases and expressions typical of the informal and everyday language used by this group. If possible, show your narrative to members of the group portrayed and ask if your dialogue is realistic.

Writing from a Character's Point of View

Imagine that you are Henry Fleming and have been keeping a journal since the time the novel begins. Compose several entries that chronicle your feelings and impressions in two or three major scenes of the novel. Try to use color, details, and imagery that will make your impressions vivid for a reader.

Analyzing Style

Write at least four paragraphs that might serve as an introduction to the novel, discussing Crane's style. At the prewriting stage, jot down ideas on questions such as the following: To what degree and how effectively are figurative language and imagery used? Is there a conscious use of devices such as alliteration and rhythm? How effective is the use of flashback? What is the point of view and how does it affect the presentation of material? How does the author create mood? What effect do Naturalism and Impressionism have on the narration?

Francis Luis Mora, *Morning News* (c. 1912). San Diego Museum of Art

HANDBOOK OF LITERARY TERMS

■ ALLUSION

A Different Image

The age
requires this task:
create
a different image;
5 re-animate
the mask.

Shatter the icons of slavery and fear.
Replace the leer
of the minstrel's burnt-cork face
10 with a proud, serene
and classic bronze of Benin.

Dudley Randall

"Trust me—enigmatic is better."

© Punch/Rothco

Do you understand the references in the last stanza of the poem above? The "minstrel's burnt-cork face" refers to the performers in a minstrel show, whites posing in blackface and using burnt cork to achieve a dark complexion. The "bronze of Benin" refers to art work from the ancient culture of Benin in Nigeria, Africa. The images present opposing pictures of black culture. An understanding of these references helps reinforce the meaning of this poem—the necessity of replacing the crude, erroneous stereotype of blacks with an image that is nobler and more realistic.

An **allusion** is a brief reference to a person, event, or place, real or fictitious, or to a work of art. These references, which a reader is expected to know, may be drawn from myth, literature, history, religion, or any aspect of ancient or modern culture. Along with creating mood and adding vividness to a work, allusion may be a means of achieving conciseness, since much can be suggested by a single reference. Sometimes, understanding an allusion is crucial to a reader's understanding of a work. In such cases, it may be necessary to research an allusion.

The following cartoon is humorous only to someone familiar with the famous portrait of the *Mona Lisa*, by Leonardo da Vinci, which is noted for her mystical, puzzling smile.

Recognizing allusions increases a reader's enjoyment and understanding of works by building on their surface meanings. For example, readers can better appreciate the almost superhuman endurance of Phoenix Jackson in "A Worn Path" by Eudora Welty (page 489) by recognizing the phoenix as a mythical bird that lives hundreds of years, is then consumed by fire, and rises magically to begin another long life.

■ ALLUSION

A reference to a person, thing, event, situation, or aspect of culture, real or fictional, past or present. Allusions may be drawn from art, myth, literature, history, religion, or any aspect of culture. An allusion may be incidental or central to the meaning of a literary work.

"A Different Image" from *Cities Burning* by Dudley Randall. Copyright © 1968 by Dudley Randall. Reprinted by permission of Broadside Press.

■ Apply to *The History of Plymouth Plantation*, page 39.

■ ANALOGY

Read the following description of the process of writing:

Writing is, for most, laborious and slow. The mind travels faster than the pen; consequently, writing becomes a question of learning to make occasional wing shots, bringing down the bird of thought as it flashes by. A writer is a gunner, sometimes waiting in his blind for something to come in, sometimes roaming the countryside hoping to scare something up. Like other gunners, he must cultivate patience: he may have to work many covers to bring down one partridge.

William Strunk and *E. B. White*
from *The Elements of Style*

In the passage above, to what is writing compared? What aspects of writing does this comparison highlight?

This particular comparison is an example of **analogy**—a rather detailed comparison made between two basically unlike things that have something in common. Frequently an unfamiliar or complex object or idea is compared to a familiar or simpler one to explain the first. Strunk and White set up their analogy by comparing writers, who seek the right words to express their thoughts, to gunners, who wait "to bring down one partridge." Both efforts require patience and risk frequent missed shots. Analogies are often stated like this: a writer is to a thought as a hunter is to a partridge; or, more briefly, *writer: thought :: hunter: partridge.*

What is compared in the following poem?

Fame Is a Bee

Fame is a bee.
It has a song—
It has a sting—
Ah, too, it has a wing.

Emily Dickinson

■ ANALOGY

A comparison drawn between two basically different things, usually one more simple than the other, in order to explain the more complex or unfamiliar one.

William Strunk, Jr., *The Elements of Style*. New York: Macmillan Publishing Co., Inc., 1972.

Reprinted by permission of the publishers and the Trustees of Amherst College from *The Poems of Emily Dickinson*, edited by Thomas H. Johnson, Cambridge, Mass.: The Belknap Press of Harvard University Press, Copyright 1951, © 1955, 1979, 1983 by The President and Fellows of Harvard College.

■ Apply to "**Shadow and Act**," page 775.

■ ANASTROPHE

See mother earth her offspring's fate bemoan,
And nations gaze at scenes before unknown!

Phillis Wheatley
**from "To His Excellency,
General Washington"**

Restate the lines above in a normal sentence pattern. How has this rearrangement of words affected the lines?

Wheatley has used **anastrophe**—the inversion of the usual word order in a sentence. A writer who says, "Rust and gold were the leaves" is reversing the normal sentence order of subject-verb-complement (The leaves were rust and gold). The word *anastrophe* comes from a Greek word meaning "to turn upside-down." Writers use anastrophe, or inversion, for emphasis or to achieve a certain rhythm or rhyme.

Find examples of anastrophe in the following poem. Rephrase inverted lines and see how the change affects the poem.

In a branch of a willow hid
Sings the evening Caty-did:
From the lofty locust bough
Feeding on a drop of dew,
5 In her suit of green array'd
Hear her singing in the shade
   Caty-did, Caty-did, Caty-did!

While upon a leaf you tread,
Or repose your little head,
10 On your sheet of shadows laid,
All the day you nothing said:
Half the night your cheery tongue
Revell'd out its little song,
   Nothing else but Caty-did.

Philip Freneau
from "To a Caty-Did"

■ ANASTROPHE

The reversal of the conventional order of words in a sentence for emphasis or effect.

■ Apply to **"Thanatopsis,"** page 129.

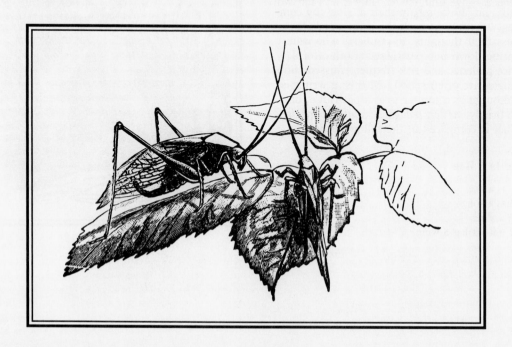

■ BLANK VERSE

Iowa Farmer

I talked to a farmer one day in Iowa.
We looked out far over acres of wheat.
He spoke with pride and yet not boastfully;
he had no need to fumble for his words.
5　He knew his land and there was love for home
within the soft serene eyes of his son.
His ugly house was clean against the storm;
there was no hunger deep within the heart
nor burning riveted within the bone,
10　but here they ate a satisfying bread.
Yet in the Middle West where wheat was
　　plentiful;
where grain grew golden under sunny skies
and cattle fattened through the summer heat
I could remember more familiar sights.

Margaret Walker

Read the poem softly to yourself. What is the predominant rhythm? Are the lines rhymed or unrhymed?

The meter, or rhythm, of this poem is *iambic pentameter*—five units or feet in a line, each with an unaccented syllable followed by an accented one (⌣ ╱). You can sound out the meter of a blank-verse line this way: ta DUM ta DUM ta DUM ta DUM ta DUM. Note, however, that these lines do not rhyme. Unrhymed iambic pentameter lines are called **blank verse**. Blank verse is a form popularized in the sixteenth century by English poets and playwrights who discovered that this cadence reflects the natural, conversational rhythms of the English language.

Read the following poetry excerpts. Which uses blank verse?

The impact of a dollar upon the heart
Smiles warm red light
Sweeping from the hearth rosily upon the
　　white table,
With the hanging cool velvet shadows
Moving softly upon the door.

Stephen Crane
**from "The Impact of a Dollar
upon the Heart"**

Then higher on the glistering sun I gazed
Whose beams was shaded by the leafy tree;
The more I looked the more I grew amazed,
And softly said, "What glory's like to thee?"

Anne Bradstreet
from "Contemplations"

Whose night it was, I had forgot, I fear.
The children marched in dread procession, help!
I saw a gnome, an evil, lurking thing—
Ah yes! It was the eve of Halloween.

S. G. Weinhorn
from "March of the Children"

A line or lines of a blank-verse passage may, at times, depart from a regular iambic pattern. Such shifts in meter enable a poet or playwright to achieve a great variety of dramatic effects. Note how the first two lines of "Iowa Farmer" depart from strict iambic pentameter as they set the stage for the rest of the poem. For additional examples of blank verse, see "Thanatopsis" (page 129) and "The Snowstorm" (page 215).

■ BLANK VERSE

Unrhymed poetry in iambic pentameter—lines of five feet, each foot with an unstressed syllable followed by a stressed one. Blank verse reflects the natural rhythms of the English language.

"Iowa Farmer" from *For My People* by Margaret Walker. Copyright 1942 by Yale University Press. Reprinted by permission of the author.

■ Apply to **"Birches,"** page 510.

■ CHARACTERIZATION

A green hunting cap squeezed the top of the fleshy balloon of a head. The green earflaps, full of large ears and uncut hair and the fine bristles that grew in the ears themselves, stuck out on either side like turn signals indicating two directions at once. Full, pursed lips protruded beneath the bushy black moustache and, at their corners, sank into little folds filled with disapproval and potato chip crumbs. In the shadow under the green visor of the cap Ignatius J. Reilly's supercilious blue and yellow eyes looked down upon the other people waiting under the clock at the D. H. Holmes department store, studying the crowd of people for signs of bad taste in dress. Several of the outfits, Ignatius noticed, were new enough and expensive enough to be properly considered offenses against taste and decency.

John Kennedy Toole
from *A Confederacy of Dunces*

The description of Ignatius J. Reilly presents more than a simple picture of the man. What can you infer about this character's personality from the description? What is ironic about his behavior, as described in the final sentence?

Characterization is the technique writers use to create lifelike characters. Writers may acquaint readers with a character by describing his or her physical appearance, personality, behavior, thoughts, feelings, and speech. In addition, a writer may describe the reactions of some characters to another character.

How does the author develop the character of Ignatius J. Reilly in the following passage?

Shifting from one hip to the other in his lumbering, elephantine fashion, Ignatius sent waves of flesh rippling beneath the tweed and flannel, waves that broke upon buttons and seams. Thus rearranged, he contemplated the long while that he had been waiting for his mother. Principally he considered the discomfort he was beginning to feel. It seemed as if his whole being was ready to burst from his swollen suede desert boots, and, as if to verify this, Ignatius turned his singular eyes toward his feet. The feet did indeed look swollen. He was prepared to offer the sight of those bulging boots to his mother as evidence of her thoughtlessness. Looking up, he saw the sun beginning to descend over the Mississippi at the foot of Canal Street. The Holmes clock said almost five. Already he was polishing a few carefully worded accusations designed to reduce his mother to repentance or, at least, confusion. He often had to keep her in her place.

What additional information is provided about this character's appearance? his personality? his thoughts? How does he appear to regard his mother?

The following passage occurs later in the novel when Ignatius learns from his mother that the family is destitute and that he must find a job. What additional information about this character is provided through his dialogue?

"I hardly thought that we were existing so precariously. However, it is fortunate that you have kept this from me. Had I known how close we were to total penury, my nerves would have given out long ago." Ignatius scratched his paws. "I must admit, though, that the alternative for me is rather grim. I doubt very seriously whether anyone will hire me.". . .

"Employers sense in me a denial of their values." He rolled over onto his back. "They fear me. I suspect that they can see that I am forced to function in a century which I loathe. That was true even when I worked for the New Orleans Public Library."

How does Ignatius's dialogue further characterize him? Note in particular his word choice or *diction*—for example, his reference to a lack of money as "total penury."

Although these passages represent only a small portion of the novel, they should give you a fairly good picture of its main character.

1. What is Ignatius's self-image?
2. What does his observation, "I am forced to live in a century which I loathe," reveal about him?
3. Ignatius says, "I doubt seriously that any-

John Kennedy Toole, *A Confederacy of Dunces.* New York: Grove Press, Inc., 1980.

one will hire me." What makes him a poor prospect for a job?

4. Which characteristics establish Ignatius as a comic figure? Is there anything about him that arouses your pity?

There are two basic types of characters—*flat* and *round*. Flat characters are one-dimensional and lacking in complexity, like cartoon figures. Some flat characters are nonetheless memorable, such as Eliza in *Uncle Tom's Cabin* (page 260).

Round characters are fully developed, realistic characters, who act according to complex and believable patterns of emotion, motivation, and behavior. One critic describes such characters as "capable of surprising a reader in a convincing manner." Although Ignatius Reilly is not the kind of person you would encounter often, he is believable and complex; thus, *round*.

Stereotypes

When flat characters behave in predictable patterns or present a standardized mental picture, they are called **stereotypes**. You have probably come across stereotypes in your reading—the starving poet, the scheming, greedy businessman, the good-humored sidekick. Although amateur writers sometimes unwittingly create stereotypes, skilled writers may purposely use stereotypes to serve as immediately recognizable types or as foils to more fully developed characters.

■ CHARACTERIZATION

The method by which an author describes the personality of a character in a written work. A writer may describe a character's physical appearance, personality, behavior, thoughts, feelings, and speech. *Flat characters*, **which are sometimes** *stereotypes*, **are one-dimensional and lacking in complexity.** *Round characters* **act according to complex and realistic patterns of emotion and behavior.**

■ Apply to "**A Pair of Silk Stockings**," page 375.

■ CONNOTATION/ DENOTATION

What things do you associate with the words *mother* and *home*? How do these associations differ from the dictionary definitions below?

moth er (muᵀH′ər), *n.* **1** a female parent. **2** cause or source of anything. **3** mother superior. **4** person exercising control and responsibility like that of a mother. **5** a familiar name for an old woman. —*v.t.* **1** be mother of; act as mother to: *She mothers her baby sister.* **2** give birth to; bring forth as a mother. —*adj.* **1** of or like a mother; *mother love, the mother church.* **2** native: *one's mother country.*

home (hōm), *n., adj., adv., v.,* **homed, hom ing.** —*n.* **1** place where a person or family lives; one's own house or dwelling place: *a beautiful home.* **2** a family or other group living together: *a happy home.* **3** place where a person was born or brought up; one's own town or country. **4** place where a thing is native or very common; habitat: *Alaska is the home of fur seals.* **5** place where a person can rest and be safe.

Many words have a double significance—dictionary definitions, or **denotations**, and personal or universal associations known as **connotations**. To understand a work of literature, readers must understand not only the denotations of words, but their connotations, which enhance the overall meaning. The following poem contains many words that conjure up personal and universal associations. Look for these words as you read.

Threes

I was a boy when I heard three red words
a thousand Frenchmen died in the streets
for: Liberty, Equality, Fraternity—I asked
why men die for words.

5 I was older; men with mustaches, sideburns,
lilacs, told me the high golden words are:
Mother, Home, and Heaven—other older men with
face decorations said: God, Duty, Immortality
—they sang these threes slow from deep lungs.

(continued)

"Threes" from *Smoke and Steel* by Carl Sandburg. Copyright 1920 by Holt, Rinehart and Winston, Inc.; renewed 1948 by Carl Sandburg. Reprinted by permission of Harcourt Brace Jovanovich, Inc.

10 Years ticked off their say-so on the great clocks
  of doom and damnation, soup and nuts: meteors
    flashed
  their say-so: and out of great Russia came three
  dusky syllables workmen took guns and went out to
    die
  for: Bread, Peace, Land.

15 And I met a marine of the U.S.A., a leatherneck with
  a girl on his knee for a memory in ports circling the
  earth and he said: Tell me how to say three things
  and I always get by—gimme a plate of ham and
    eggs—
  how much?—and, do you love me, kid?

Carl Sandburg

1. What are the "three red words" mentioned in stanza 1? Why are these words called "red"?
2. What connotations for the words *Mother*, *Home*, and *Heaven* make them "high golden words"?
3. What connotations do you have for the word *Bread*? In what sense might this word have more practical associations than *Liberty* or *Heaven*?
4. The first three stanzas mention words with associations that people have died for throughout history. What are the three things that the leatherneck in stanza 4 considers most important?

■ CONNOTATION

The emotional associations surrounding a word, as opposed to its strict, literal dictionary meaning. A connotation may be universal or personal.

■ DENOTATION

The strict dictionary meaning of a word, presented objectively, without emotional associations.

■ Apply to "Abraham Lincoln Walks at Midnight," page 534.

■ COUPLET

Thou blossom bright with autumn dew,
And colored with the heaven's own blue,
That openest when the quiet light
Succeeds the keen and frosty night—

William Cullen Bryant
from "To the Fringed Gentian"

Hail, happy day, when, smiling like the morn,
Fair *Freedom* rose *New-England* to adorn:
The northern clime beneath her genial ray,
Dartmouth, congratulates thy blissful sway:

Phillis Wheatley
from "To the Right Honorable William, Earl of Dartmouth"

Up from the meadows rich with corn,
Clear in the cool September morn,
The clustered spires of Frederick stand
Green-walled by the hills of Maryland.

John Greenleaf Whittier
from "Barbara Frietchie"

What is the rhyme scheme of each of the excerpts above? What is the meter or rhythm?

In poetry, any two consecutive rhymed lines of parallel meter can be considered a **couplet**. One special kind of couplet is the **heroic couplet**: two rhymed iambic pentameter lines, usually containing a complete thought, and hence with the second line end-stopped. The name *heroic* comes from the notion that this meter is appropriate for the serious subjects that characterize epic or "heroic" verse. Which of the preceding examples uses heroic couplets?

■ COUPLET

A pair of rhyming lines with identical meter. A *heroic couplet* is two rhymed iambic pentameter lines that contain a complete thought.

■ Apply to "To S. M., A Young African Painter on Seeing His Works," page 71.

■ DRAMATIC MONOLOGUE

George Gray

I have studied many times
The marble which was chiseled for me—
A boat with a furled sail at rest in a harbor.
In truth it pictures not my destination
5 But my life.
For love was offered me, and I shrank from its
    disillusionment;
Sorrow knocked at my door, but I was afraid;
Ambition called to me, but I dreaded the chances.
Yet all the while I hungered for meaning in my life.
10 And now I know that we must lift the sail
And catch the winds of destiny
Wherever they drive the boat.
To put meaning in one's life may end in madness,
But life without meaning is the torture
15 Of restlessness and vague desire—
It is a boat longing for the sea and yet afraid.

Edgar Lee Masters

    What inferences can you make about the kind
of person the speaker is? How does the image
of the boat with the furled (rolled) sail represent
Gray's life?

    A poem such as "George Gray," in which a
fictional character addresses a silent audience,
is called a **dramatic monologue**. Delivered at
a critical moment, the dramatic monologue
reveals the speaker's personality as well as
the circumstances that led to this discourse.
Although silent, the audience is usually identifiable or even present. George Gray delivers
his epitaph-monologue from the grave, presumably to passers-by who read his tombstone.

■ DRAMATIC MONOLOGUE

**A poem in which the speaker, usually at a crit-
ical moment in life, addresses someone whose
replies are not recorded.**

"George Gray" from *Spoon River Anthology* by Edgar Lee Masters.
Copyright 1915, 1916, 1942, 1949 by Edgar Lee Masters. Reprinted
by permission of Ellen C. Masters.

■ Apply to "**Lucinda Matlock**," page 397.

■ EPIGRAM

He knows the cost of everything, but
    the value of nothing.

Anonymous

Let us all be happy and live within our
    means,
Even if we have to borrow the money to do
    it with.

Artemus Ward

    Restate each saying above in your own words.
In each case, is your restatement as concise and
forceful as the orginal? What turn of thought
occurs at the end of each saying?

    Any saying that states something true, wise,
or witty as briefly and pointedly as possible is
called an **epigram**. Epigrams often end with a
wry or satiric twist. They may either be prose or
poetry, independent statements or units within
larger works. Thoreau's *Walden* is full of epigrams such as the following: "That government
is best which governs not at all."

    Epigrams, whose name orginally referred to
an inscription on a monument, are related to
proverbs and maxims. A *proverb* is a brief, traditional saying that makes an observation about
character or conduct or contains some bit of
popular wisdom: "Red sky at morning, sailors
take warning" or "A watched pot never boils."
A *maxim* is a brief saying embodying a moral or
a piece of advice: "Look before you leap." A
maxim is sometimes called an aphorism.

■ EPIGRAM

A short, witty statement, often in couplet form.

■ Apply to *Walden,* page 218.

HANDBOOK OF LITERARY TERMS

■ FIGURATIVE LANGUAGE

Where Children Live

Homes where children live exude a pleasant
    rumpledness,
like a bed made by a child, or a yard littered with
    balloons.

To be a child again one would need to shed details
till the heart found itself dressed in the coat with a
    hood.
5 Now the heart has taken on gloves and mufflers,
the heart never goes outside to find something to
    "do."
And the house takes on a new face, dignified.
No lost shoes blooming under bushes.
No chipped trucks in the drive.
10 Grown-ups like swings, leafy plants, slow-motion
    back and forth.
While the yard of a child is strewn with the corpses
of bottle-rockets and whistles,
anything whizzing and spectacular, brilliantly short-
    lived.

Trees in children's yards speak in clearer tongues.
15 Ants have more hope. Squirrels dance as well as hide.
The fence has a reason to be there, so children can
    go in and out.
Even when the children are at school, the yards glow
with the leftovers of their affection,
the roots of the tiniest grasses curl toward one another
20 like secret smiles.

Naomi Shihab Nye

1. The speaker says that the adult "heart has taken on gloves and mufflers." What do you think she means?
2. To what are lost shoes compared in line 8?
3. What word in line 11 suggests broken toys and things "outlived"?
4. In what way can the yards inhabited by children be said to flow "with the leftovers of their affection"?

The poem uses imaginative descriptions and comparisons to portray children and their influence. These descriptions are not to be taken literally; that is, a heart doesn't wear clothes, a house has no face, and trees cannot speak. Yet these images function figuratively to convey the magical world of children. Try making the same point that the poet does in purely literal terms. What does Nye's description add to yours?

Nye has used words and phrases to create startling pictures that help readers see things in new ways. Such use of words, called **figurative language**, provides conciseness, vividness, clarity, and impact. Words used apart from their literal meanings are called **figures of speech**. Some common figures of speech are **hyperbole, simile, metaphor, personification, apostrophe, synecdoche,** and **metonymy**.

Hyperbole: exaggeration for effect. The effect may be humorous, satiric, or sentimental. Annie Dillard uses hyperbole for dramatic effect in the excerpt from *Pilgrim at Tinker Creek* (page 785) when she pictures the Polyphemus moth crawling down the driveway "forever." The cartoon below uses hyperbole for humorous effect.

"Popcorn's done, honey."

Drawing by Ziegler; © 1987 *The New Yorker* Magazine, Inc.

Simile: a stated comparison, usually indicated by the words *like, as, appears, than,* or *seems,* between two basically dissimilar things that nonetheless have something in common. A simile at the end of Nye's poem compares the curling roots of grass to "secret smiles."

"Where Children Live" from *Hugging the Jukebox* by Naomi Shihab Nye (The National Poetry Series, 1982). Reprinted by permission of the author.

Metaphor: a comparison between two basically unlike things. There is no connective such as *like* or *as* in a metaphor, which can be direct (Her face was a map) or implied (Worry and suffering were mapped on her face). In line 8, the phrase "shoes blooming" is an implied metaphor that suggests a comparison to flowers.

Extended metaphor: a figurative comparison that is developed throughout an entire work or a great part of it. Two things are compared at some length and in several ways in an extended metaphor, which can appear in prose as well as in poetry.

The silken tent in the following poem is a colorful, stately pavilion used in the Middle Ages for tournaments. It was anchored by a central pole and supporting ropes, whose movements are affected by the wind. In what ways does the silken tent offer parallels to the speaker's beloved in this extended metaphor?

The Silken Tent

She is as in a field a silken tent
At midday when a sunny summer breeze
Has dried the dew and all its ropes relent,
So that in guys[1] it gently sways at ease,
5 And its supporting central cedar pole,
That is its pinnacle to heavenward
And signifies the sureness of the soul,
Seems to owe naught to any single cord,
But strictly held by none, is loosely bound
10 By countless silken ties of love and thought
To everything on earth the compass round,
And only by one's going slightly taut
In the capriciousness of summer air
Is of the slightest bondage made aware.

Robert Frost

Personification: the attributing of human qualities to nonhuman or nonliving things—abstractions, ideas, animals, or objects. Nye's poem relies heavily on personification—the heart clad in gloves and mufflers, the trees speaking in "clearer tongues," the ants with hope. Personification is an especially effective device in this poem because it conveys the power of children to invest nonhuman things with vitality.

Apostrophe: the direct address of a person not living or present, of inanimate objects, or of abstract qualities. Carl Sandburg addresses a city in "Chicago" (page 503); Oliver Wendell Holmes addresses his soul in "The Chambered Nautilus" (page 140). The following poem uses apostrophe for humorous effect.

Beware, O asparagus, you've stalked my last meal.
You look like a snake and slip down like an eel.
I'd prefer drinking a bottle of turpentine,
Rather than eating a tidbit so serpentine.

Wanda Fergus
from "Vegetables I Hate"

Synecdoche: the use of a part to suggest the whole or of the whole to suggest a part. In "the dying year," the whole is used to stand for a part, "autumn." The use of "Wall Street" to refer to the money market or financial affairs of the entire U.S. is an example of the second— using a part to stand for the whole. The word *heart* appears three times in the second stanza of "Where Children Live." Why do you think the poet emphasized this part of adults and children?

Metonymy: the naming of one thing to suggest another associated with it, as when the term "city hall" is used to refer to a mayor, or "the bench" is used to refer to persons who sit as judges.

■ FIGURATIVE LANGUAGE

Words used apart from their ordinary, literal meanings in such a way as to add freshness, conciseness, and vitality to them. The more common figures of speech include hyperbole, simile, metaphor, personification, apostrophe, synecdoche, and metonymy.

---

1. *guys,* poles or ropes used to anchor or steady anything.

From *The Poetry of Robert Frost* edited by Edward Connery Lathem. Copyright © 1969 by Holt, Rinehart and Winston, Inc. Copyright © 1962 by Robert Frost. Copyright © 1975 by Lesley Frost Ballantine. Reprinted by permission of Henry Holt and Company, Inc., the Estate of Robert Frost, and Jonathan Cape Ltd.

■ Apply to **"This Sacred Soil,"** page 229.

■ FLASHBACK

Not all stories are told in strict chronological order. Sometimes, there is an interruption in the progress of a story, a place and time when the author backtracks and relates something that happened before the story began. This technique is called a **flashback**.

A flashback, which can cover years of chronological time, helps the reader better understand characters and events in a story. Flashbacks also help the reader anticipate what will occur when the major action is resumed.

Read the following passage from a novel about a woman who is forced to leave the rural South of her girlhood and migrate to the industrial North. As she whittles on a piece of wood, she recalls former times.

She lifted her glance from a fold of the cloth drawn over the shoulders, and, the knife open in her hand, stared at the window; rain mixed with snow made a moving sheet against it. She watched it, her brows drawn together in puzzlement. Then, the look of wonder deepening, she looked upward, sidewise, an ear turned ceilingward, and listened, frowning, wondering why she could not hear the rain. Then gradually the ceiling drifted into shape, and became the sickly green cardboard, smoke-grimed and darker now at the ending of the winter. The Detroit home shut out the sound of the rain.

Strange, she hadn't noticed the rain on the window until now. Back home she would have known it: a spring rain blown in on a red, windy dawn with thunder growling far across the ridges, the pines crying out the warning, and the sugar tree flowers blowing down the hillside all when the poplar blooms were like yellow lilies unfolding. But better than anything had been the sound of the rain on the roof shingles when the early potatoes and peas and lettuce showed, and the early cabbage was set. Tomorrow she would hunt wild greens; wild sweet potato vine would be high by the creek banks, and she would linger, listening, watching the white water——

A train blew. She shivered, the knife clattered to the floor, but no longer did she go springing toward the window. She only backed away and stood a long moment, her body pressed against the door, her hands pressed hard against her eyes. She was able at last to look again at the window, gray white under the moving sheets of rain. Seemed like the last time she had looked, the window had been a square of quivering red light. It was daylight now—another night was through—and now another day.

Harriette Arnow
from *The Dollmaker*

How does the childhood setting the woman recollects differ from her present surroundings? What insights into the woman's character does this flashback provide?

Flashbacks occur in several of the stories in *The United States in Literature*. In "The Jilting of Granny Weatherall" (page 430), most of the story's narrative is provided through flashback, while in "Sophistication" (page 422) insights into the main characters are provided in several brief flashbacks.

■ FLASHBACK

An interruption of the narrative to show an episode that happened before that particular point in the story. A flashback can shed light on characters and events of the present by providing background information.

Harriette Arnow, *The Dollmaker*. New York: The Macmillan Company, 1954.

■ Apply to **"An Occurrence at Owl Creek Bridge,"** page 356.

■ FORESHADOWING

The companions followed the shady wood road, the cow taking slow steps and the child very fast ones. The cow stopped long at the brook to drink, as if the pasture were not half a swamp, and Sylvia stood still and waited, letting her bare feet cool themselves in the shoal water, while the great twilight moths stuck softly against her. She waded on through the brook as the cow moved away, and listened to the thrushes with a heart that beat fast with pleasure. There was a stirring in the great boughs overhead. They were full of little birds and beasts that seemed to be wide awake, and going about their world, or else saying good night to each other in sleepy twitters. Sylvia herself felt sleepy as she walked along. However, it was not much farther to the house, and the air was soft and sweet. She was not often in the woods so late as this, and it made her feel as if she were a part of the gray shadows and the moving leaves. She was just thinking how long it seemed since she first came to the farm a year ago, and wondering if everything went on in the noisy town just the same as when she was there; the thought of the great red-faced boy who used to chase and frighten her made her hurry along the path to escape from the shadow of the trees.

Sarah Orne Jewett
from "A White Heron"

1. How would you describe the mood of the first half of this passage?
2. How does the mood change in the last two sentences?
3. What words and phrases in these final sentences suggest that something is about to happen to Sylvia?

The technique of giving the reader, listener, or viewer of a story hints of what is to come is called **foreshadowing**. Foreshadowing creates suspense and builds expectations. Readers are eager to see if the inferences they draw are accurate. Foreshadowing also sets the stage for future events. It makes the events to come seem reasonable—even inevitable.

In addition, foreshadowing can reinforce the mood of a literary work. For example, the second paragraph of "An Occurrence at Owl Creek Bridge" (page 356) serves to create an atmosphere, or mood, of foreboding.

■ FORESHADOWING

A hint given to the reader of what is to come. Foreshadowing helps create suspense and convince the reader of the inevitability of the story's outcome.

■ Apply to **"Young Goodman Brown,"** page 237.

■ FREE VERSE

The Rock (Fragment of a Ritual)

unmoved
from time without
end
you rest
5 there in the midst of the paths
in the midst of the winds
you rest
covered with the droppings of birds
grass growing from your feet
10 your head decked with the down of birds
you rest
in the midst of the winds
you wait
Aged one

Omaha

Examine the line length and rhythm of the preceding poem. Is the rhythm regular or irregular? Do the lines rhyme?

The preceding poem is considered **free verse:** poetry that breaks from fixed stanzaic patterns and makes use of unpatterned or irregular rhythms rather than uniform metrical feet. In free verse the unit of rhythmic control is the rise and fall within the entire poem rather than the metric line or stanza. Although free verse has gained great popularity in the past century, it is not a new form.

The term *free verse* explains itself—it is free from the demands of rhyme (although rhyme may occur), free from the necessity of following regular metrical patterns. Walt Whitman was the first recognized American poet to use free verse extensively. Advocates of free verse argue that this form frees the poet from the constraints of rhyme and meter, and so allows scope for greater creativity.

Free verse allows for a variety of rhythmical effects; such free-verse rhythms are less regular than those of conventional verse, and are achieved through a subtle handling of the cadences of words, phrases, and lines. Line length may vary.

Writers of free verse may use imagery, as well as sound devices, to bind lines together and to help create mood. Note the use of repetition (*in the midst*), alliteration (*grass/growing, decked/down, winds/wait*), assonance (*midst/winds, head/decked/rest*), and consonance (*rest/midst*) in "The Rock."

Examine the patterns of rhythm and sound in the following poem.

For You O Democracy

Come, I will make the continent indissoluble,
I will make the most splendid race the sun
   ever shone upon,
I will make divine magnetic lands,
     With the love of comrades,
5   With the life-long love of comrades.

I will plant companionship thick as trees
   along all the rivers of America,
   and along the shores of the great lakes,
   and all over the prairies,
I will make inseparable cities with their
   arms about each other's necks,
     By the love of comrades,
10   By the manly love of comrades.

For you these from me, O Democracy, to
   serve you ma femme!
For you, for you I am trilling these songs.

Walt Whitman

1. What words and phrases are repeated?
2. What examples of alliteration can you find?
3. What sounds provide assonance in line 11?
4. In what way is free verse suited to the poet's expansive, exuberant tone?

■ FREE VERSE

A type of poetry written with rhythm and other poetic devices but without a fixed pattern of meter and rhyme. Free verse depends for its effects on more subtle patterns of rhythm and sound.

Alice C. Fletcher and Francis LaFlesche, "The Omaha Tribe," in *Twenty-seventh Annual BAE Report*, Washington, D.C., 1911.

■ Apply to "**I Hear America Singing,**" page 296.

■ IMAGERY

They were all three silent, reading the typewritten sheets behind the plastic, the combinations of eggs and hashbrowns and toast. The waitress seemed to have forgotten them, however, and they sat, suspended among the other customers, farmers and construction workers already on their coffee breaks. Across the street a new building of tan aluminum was rising. Hammering and the muffled whine of electric saws filled the street. The sun shone on the stacks of candy under the counter, on the coffee urns and the spigots of the milk machine. The waitresses had just come on their shifts. The cook, a large blond woman in an orange bib apron, said things that made the men at the counter laugh into their cups. The radio blared livestock futures and farm reports into the bacon-smelling air. But none of this suggested anything that the three in the booth might say to one another.

Louise Erdrich
from *The Beet Queen*

What sounds, sights, and smells are described in the preceding passage? Is the scene vague or clear?

This passage gains its vividness and immediacy from its **imagery,** word pictures that appeal to any of the senses. The description of sights and smells captures a memorable morning restaurant scene. The insistence of the sounds—hammering, sawing, laughing, talking—serves to underscore the silence of the characters.

An image may appeal to sight, hearing, taste, smell, touch, internal feelings, or the so-called motor sense that has to do with motion or muscle activity. An image may be a simple, literal representation; that is, it may use a word to call up the sight, sound, or feeling it usually evokes. Most of the images in the preceding passage from *Beet Queen* are literal. Images may also be figurative, relying for their effect on unexpected associations or figures of speech.

Read the following poem and note its images, both figurative and literal.

Stray Animals

This is the beauty of being alone
toward the end of summer:
a dozen stray animals asleep on the porch
in the shade of my feet,
5 and the smell of leaves burning
in another neighborhood.
It is late morning,
and my forehead is alive with shadows,
some bats rock back and forth
10 to the rhythm of my humming,
the mimosa flutters with bees.
This is a house of unwritten poems,
this is where I am unborn.

James Tate

What images appeal to the sense of sight? smell? sound? "My forehead is alive with shadows" presents both a literal and a figurative image. In what sense might a poet's head be "alive with shadows"? Speculate on the meaning of the word *unborn* ("looking to the future"? "reunited"? "returning to a former state"?) in the final line.

Effective imagery, whether literal or figurative, seldom appeals to one sense only. When skillfully used, imagery not only presents sensory details but also helps communicate mood, tone, and meaning.

■ IMAGERY

The sensory details in a literary work. Whether literal or figurative, an image provides vividness and immediacy, evoking in the reader a complex of emotional suggestions.

Louise Erdrich, *The Beet Queen*. New York: Henry Holt and Company, Inc., 1986.

"Stray Animals" from *The Oblivion Ha-Ha* by James Tate. Copyright © 1967, 1968, 1969, 1970 by James Tate. Reprinted by permission of the author.

■ Apply to "**A Dancing Song,**" page 16.

Drawing by Vietor; © 1976 *The New Yorker* Magazine, Inc.

■ INFERENCE

Given the "props" of the man in the cartoon—the big cigar and large desk—readers might conclude that he is a successful businessman. What does the artwork in his office suggest about him? By considering the clues in the cartoon and drawing a conclusion from them, you are making an inference. **Inferences** are reasonable conclusions, which may or may not be accurate, based on the evidence provided. In literature, readers draw inferences about the behavior of a character or the meaning of an event from the limited information presented by a writer.

Read the following passage and be prepared to make inferences about the characters based on clues provided by the author.

A newly married pair had boarded this coach at San Antonio. The man's face was reddened from many days in the wind and sun, and a direct result of his new black clothes was that his brick-colored hands were constantly performing in a most conscious fashion. From time to time he looked down respectly at his attire. He sat with a hand on each knee, like a man waiting in a barber's shop. The glances he devoted to other passengers were furtive and shy.

The bride was not pretty, nor was she very young. She wore a dress of blue cashmere, with small reservations of velvet here and there, and with steel buttons abounding. She continually twisted her head to regard her puff sleeves, very stiff, straight, and high. They embarrassed her. It was quite apparent that she had cooked, and that she expected to cook, dutifully. The blushes caused by the careless scrutiny of some passengers as she had entered the car were strange to see upon this plain, underclass countenance, which was drawn in placid, almost emotionless lines.

Stephen Crane
from "The Bride Comes to Yellow Sky"

1. What do the following details reveal about the groom and his life: his new clothes? his reddened face and brick-colored hands? his furtive glances and "constantly performing" hands?
2. What can you infer about the bride from these details: her embarrassment at her puff sleeves? her blushes? the fact that "she had cooked, and that she expected to cook"?

Read the following passage, which appears later in the story.

As a matter of truth, Jack Potter was beginning to find the shadow of a deed weigh upon him like a leaden slab. He, the town marshal of Yellow Sky, a man known, liked, and feared in his corner, a prominent person, had gone to San Antonio to meet a girl he believed he loved, and there, after the usual prayers, had actually induced her to marry him, without consulting Yellow Sky for any part of the transaction. He was now bringing his bride before an innocent and unsuspecting community.

Of course people in Yellow Sky married as it pleased them, in accordance with a general custom; but such was Potter's thought of his duty to his friends, or of their idea of his duty, or of an unspoken form which does not control men in these matters, that he felt he was heinous. He had committed an extraordinary crime. Face to face with this girl in San Antonio, and spurred by his sharp impulse, he had gone headlong over all the social hedges.

1. What was Jack Potter's "extraordinary crime"?
2. What do you infer are the "social hedges" he had "gone headlong over"?

■ INFERENCE

A reasonable conclusion drawn by a reader from clues provided by a writer.

■ Apply to **"A Worn Path,"** page 489.

■ IRONY

Green Memory

A wonderful time—the War:
when money rolled in
and blood rolled out.

But blood
5   was far away
from here—

Money was near.

Langston Hughes

1. Do you think that the speaker really considers this a "wonderful time"? Why or why not?
2. What kind of people might be willing to sacrifice blood for money?

The first line of the poem above is an example of **verbal irony**—saying one thing but meaning the opposite. Often, it is necessary to consider an author's tone to detect verbal irony in which the surface meaning is different from the actual meaning. "The Cask of Amontillado" (page 151) is full of verbal irony, including the pun that Montresor makes on the word *mason*.

Another kind of irony is **irony of situation,** which occurs when events turn out contrary to what is expected or what seems appropriate. This kind of irony is illustrated in "Richard Cory" (page 395) when the title character, who is graceful, rich, and admired by all, commits suicide.

Read the following passage and explain how it illustrates irony of situation.

Seated in a stenographer's chair, tapping away at a typewriter that had served him through four years of college, he wrote a series of guidebooks for people forced to travel on business. Ridiculous,

"Green Memory" by Langston Hughes from *Montage of a Dream Deferred.* Copyright 1951 by Langston Hughes. Copyright renewed 1979 by George Houston Bass. Reprinted by permission of Harold Ober Associates.

when you thought about it: Macon hated travel. He careened through foreign territories on a desperate kind of blitz—squinching his eyes shut and holding his breath and hanging on for dear life, he sometimes imagined—and then settled back home with a sigh of relief to produce his chunky, passport-sized paperbacks. *Accidental Tourist in France. Accidental Tourist in Germany. In Belgium.* No author's name, just a logo: a winged armchair on the cover.

Anne Tyler
from *The Accidental Tourist*

1. Why is Macon's choice of work ironic?
2. What is ironic about the logo of his books, mentioned in the last sentence?

A third type of irony is called **dramatic irony.** This type of irony occurs when the reader or viewer knows more about the actual situation than the speaker or characters do. Often found in drama, this type of irony occurs when important information, hidden from the characters involved, is conveyed in an offhanded remark or an aside. Contemporary readers recognize the dramatic irony of Lincoln's words in the Gettysburg Address, "The world will little note nor long remember what we say here."

The following cartoon relies for its humor on dramatic irony.

"Oh, I'll print it all right, Mr. Paine—but a title like 'Common Sense' isn't going to appeal to very many people."

Explain which type of irony occurs in the following poem.

Back-to-Nature Writer

In books and articles he hymns the pleasures
    Of simple, golden days of long ago.
He quotes at length, and obviously treasures,
    Bucolic thoughts of Wordsworth and Thoreau.
5 He sometimes grieves, he sometimes shouts defiance
    At man too mechanized, enthralled with chrome.
Deploring deeds of industry and science,
    He writes of rustic woodlands as his home.
But do not shed for him a tear of pity
10 Or hasten by his written word to judge him.
He lives where born, amidst a bustling city
    From which a team of horses couldn't budge him.

Richard Armour

■ IRONY

A contrast between what appears to be and what really is. In verbal irony, words imply the opposite of what they literally mean. Irony of situation presents a state of affairs that is the opposite of what is expected. Dramatic irony occurs in fiction or drama when the reader (or viewer) knows more than the characters do.

Anne Tyler, *The Accidental Tourist.* New York: Alfred A. Knopf, Inc., 1985.

"Back-to-Nature Writer" from *Light Armour* by Richard Armour. Copyright 1954 by Richard Armour. Reprinted by permission of the author.

■ Apply to **"The Cask of Amontillado,"** page 151.

Reprinted from *Through History with J. Wesley Smith* by Burr Shafer. Copyright, 1950, by The Vanguard Press, Inc. Copyright, 1953, by Burr Shafer. All rights reserved.

■ LOCAL COLOR

The following excerpt is from "The Luck of Roaring Camp," a story set in a mining camp during the California Gold Rush. The once-hardened miners have become reformed and domesticated by an Indian baby whom they have adopted and call The Luck.

Such was the golden summer of Roaring Camp. They were flush times—and The Luck was with them. The claims had yielded enormously. The camp was jealous of its privileges and looked suspiciously on strangers. No encouragement was given to immigration, and, to make their seclusion more perfect, the land on either side of the mountain wall that surrounded the camp they duly preempted. This, and a reputation of singular proficiency with the revolver, kept the reserve of Roaring Camp inviolate. The expressman—their only connecting link with the surrounding world—sometimes told wonderful stories of the camp. He would say, "They've a street up there in Roaring, that would lay over any street up there in Red Dog. They've got vines and flowers round their houses, and they wash themselves twice a day. But they're mighty rough on strangers, and they worship an Injun baby." . . .

The winter of '51 will long be remembered in the foothills. The snow lay deep on the sierras, and every mountain creek became a river, and every river a lake. Each gorge and gulch was transformed into a tumultuous watercourse that descended the hillsides, tearing down giant trees and scattering its drift and debris along the plain. Red Dog had been twice under water, and Roaring Camp had been forewarned. "Water put the gold into them gulches," said Stumpy; "it's been here once and will be here again!" And that night the North Fork suddenly leaped over its banks, and swept up the triangular valley of Roaring Camp.

Bret Harte
from "The Luck of Roaring Camp"

1. What do you learn about the lives of the miners in this excerpt?
2. What examples of dialect appear?
3. What atmosphere is conveyed by names such as *Stumpy, Roaring Camp, Red Dog,* and *North Fork?*

This passage is an example of **local-color** writing, a form of regionalism that focuses on a particular locale, with its distinctive dress, customs, speech, and landscape. Like other regional works, local-color writing is based on actions, characters, and settings that could not be transplanted to another geographical setting without significant harm to the story. The works of local-color writers such as Bret Harte are often marked by sentimentalism, eccentric characters, and touches of humor.

Writers such as Willa Cather, Kate Chopin, and Mary Wilkins Freeman, whose works are set, respectively, in the West, the South, and New England, explore the effects that setting has on character. Although these writers are often considered local colorists, their characters are apt to be more complex and subtly drawn than the broadly sketched characters created by writers like Bret Harte.

■ LOCAL COLOR

A type of regional writing that focuses on a particular locale and the peculiarities of speech, dress, custom, and landscape that make it distinctive.

■ Apply to **"The Outcasts of Poker Flat,"** page 347.

HANDBOOK OF LITERARY TERMS

■ LYRIC

If You Should Go

Love, leave me like the light,
  The gently passing day;
We would not know, but for the night,
  When it has slipped away.
5 Go quietly; a dream,
  When done, should leave no trace
That it has lived, except a gleam
  Across the dreamer's face.

Countee Cullen

1. Do you think the speaker is primarily concerned with telling a story or expressing an
emotion?
2. Is the speaker's tone personal or impersonal?

"If You Should Go" belongs to a broad classification of poetry called **lyric.** Usually short,
the lyric is a personal reflection by a speaker,
either the poet or some voice adopted by the
poet, that presents a single emotion such as
grief, love, or happiness.

Though the term *lyric* has come a long way
from its original definition—poetry intended to
be sung to the accompaniment of a lyre—it still
retains the characteristic of music in its sounds
and its structural pattern, which may be as formal as a sonnet or as irregular as free verse.
Because of its emotional quality, lyric poetry
relies heavily on sound and mood to reinforce
its ideas.

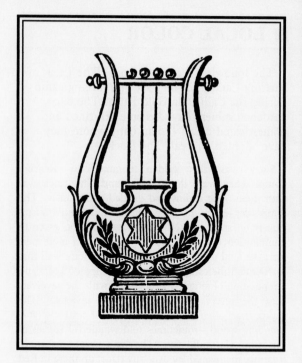

■ LYRIC

**A short poem in which a speaker expresses a
basic personal emotion such as grief, joy, or
love.**

"If You Should Go" from *On These I Stand* by Countee Cullen.
Copyright 1925 by Harper & Row, Publishers, Inc., renewed 1953
by Ida M. Cullen. Reprinted by permission of Harper & Row,
Publishers, Inc.

■ Apply to **"To Be in Love,"** page 717.

■ MOOD

A single hay cart down the dusty road
Creaks slowly, with its driver fast asleep
On the load's top. Against the neighboring hill,
Huddled along the stone wall's shady side,
5 The sheep show white, as if a snowdrift still
Defied the dog-star. Through the open door
A drowsy smell of flowers—gray heliotrope,
And white sweet clover, and shy mignonette—
Comes faintly in, and silent chorus lends
10 To the pervading symphony of peace.

John Greenleaf Whittier
from "Among the Hills"

1. How do these poetic lines make you feel?
2. What words and images in the poem help
   convey this feeling?
3. Think of a word that describes the general
   atmosphere of this work.

Whittier has created a picture that progresses
in slow motion—a hay cart creaking down a
dusty road with its driver asleep. Words such
as *drifting, drowsy,* and *silent* build an atmosphere, or **mood,** of peace. Poets and artists
in general create mood through their choice
of setting, imagery, details, connotations, and
descriptions. Details in "An Occurrence at Owl
Creek Bridge" establish an eerie, unreal mood,
while those in "The Celebrated Jumping Frog
of Calaveras County" convey a lighthearted,
humorous atmosphere.

Mood is not confined to poetry, nor to
the printed word. Examine details that convey
mood in the following passage by Garrison Keillor and in the picture to the right. Then think
of a word to describe the mood in each.

It has been a quiet week in Lake Wobegon. Spring
has come, grass is green, the trees are leafing out,
birds arriving every day by the busload, and now the
Norwegian bachelor farmers are washing their sheets.
In town the windows are open, so, as you pause in
your walk to admire Mrs. Hoglund's rock garden, you
can smell her floor wax and hear the piano lesson she
is giving, the tune that goes "da da Da da Da da da,"
and up by school, smell the macaroni cheese hotdish
for lunch and hear from upstairs the voices of Miss
Melrose's class reciting Chaucer.

Garrison Keillor
from *Leaving Home*

■ MOOD

**The overall climate of a work, as created by
choice of setting, objects, details, images, and
the sounds and connotations of words.**

Garrison Keillor, "Aprille," *Leaving Home.* New York: Viking
Penguin, Inc., 1987.

■ Apply to "**The Celebrated Jumping Frog of Calaveras
County,**" page 330.

Childe Hassam, detail of *Rainy Day, Boston* (1885).
The Toledo Museum of Art

■ PARADOX

Success Is Counted Sweetest

Success is counted sweetest
By those who ne'er succeed.
To comprehend a nectar
Requires sorest need.

5 Not one of all the purple Host
Who took the Flag today
Can tell the definition
So clear of Victory

As he defeated—dying—
10 On whose forbidden ear
The distant strains of triumph
Burst agonized and clear!

Emily Dickinson

The first two lines of this poem make a statement that appears contradictory and, on the surface, impossible. Yet throughout the rest of the poem, Dickinson illustrates that to understand success most profoundly, one must be denied it. A statement that seems self-contradictory yet has valid meaning is called a **paradox.** Paradox can serve to emphasize a point or to create a sense of irony.

Dickinson explores another paradox in "Much Madness Is Divinest Sense" (page 320), which points up the thin line between sanity and insanity. The term *paradox* also applies to people or situations that seem to have contradictory elements, such as a rich, admired individual who is nonetheless miserable (see "Richard Cory," page 395).

The passage that follows examines the paradox of the individual who is lonely in a crowd.

I never found the companion that was so companionable as solitude. We are for the most part more lonely when we go abroad among men that when we stay in our chambers. A man thinking or working is always alone, let him be where he will. Solitude is not measured by the miles of space that intervene between a man and his fellows.

Henry David Thoreau
from *Walden*

How does Thoreau distinguish *lonely* from *alone*? Why might an individual be lonely even when surrounded by people?

■ PARADOX

An apparent contradiction that is nevertheless true. A paradox shocks a reader into paying attention to a truth hidden in a seemingly contradictory statement.

Reprinted by permission of the publishers and the Trustees of Amherst College from *The Poems of Emily Dickinson,* edited by Thomas H. Johnson, Cambridge, Mass.: The Belknap Press of Harvard University Press, Copyright 1951, © 1955, 1979, 1983 by The President and Fellows of Harvard College.

■ Apply to **"To My Dear and Loving Husband,"** page 62.

■ PLOT

Plot refers to a sequence of interrelated actions and events presenting and resolving a conflict. As the plot unfolds, the *conflict* builds to an emotional or dramatic peak—the *climax,* which is followed by a *resolution* or denouement. The first part of a plot is the *exposition.* In the exposition, the author introduces the main character or characters, establishes the setting, and gives whatever background information the reader needs. Sometimes exposition is achieved through *flashbacks,* narratives or scenes out of chronological order, presenting events that happened before the opening of the work. The structure of a plot can be indicated this way:

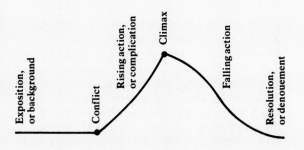

Conflict is the struggle between two opposing forces. The four basic kinds of conflict are the following:

• a person against another person ("The Cask of Amontillado," page 151)
• a person against nature ("The Bear," page 460)
• a person against society ("Harrison Bergeron," page 669)
• two elements within a person that struggle for mastery ("The Haunted Boy," page 660)

The first three kinds of conflict are called *external* conflict; the fourth is called *internal* conflict. More than one kind of conflict is often present in a work. As Robert Penn Warren put it, "No conflict, no story."

The *climax* is the decisive point in a story or play in which the problem must be resolved in one way or another. In "The Bear," the climax occurs when the boy confronts the bear and must decide whether or not to shoot him. In some stories, especially modern ones, the climax may be more subtle and less dramatic—perhaps a moment of insight. Events that precede and build toward the climax are called the *rising action.* Events that follow the climax and serve to resolve the conflict are called the *falling action.*

Denouement, a word derived from a French word that means "the untying," refers to the *resolution* of the plot. The resolution in "The Bear," occurs when the boy refuses to shoot the bear and begins to understand what the animal represents. The climax and the denouement may come very close together, or, in a novel, several chapters may intervene.

■ PLOT

A sequence of interrelated incidents that present and revolve a conflict.

■ Apply to "**A New England Nun,**" page 365.

■ POINT OF VIEW

Every story can be told from more than one perspective. For example, accounts of an automobile accident can vary dramatically, as related by the two parties involved. In literature, a story is told by a narrator from a particular **point of view,** or vantage point. The author's choice of a narrator will affect how the actions and characters are presented. The story may be related by a character in his or her own words *(first-person point of view)* or by a narrator who is not a character and stands anonymously outside the story's action *(third-person point of view)*. The third-person point of view may be either *omniscient* (all-knowing), *limited* (confined to one character), or *objective* (a factual, eyewitness account).

In the *first-person point of view,* the narrator, who is a character within the story, uses pronouns such as *I, we,* and *our.* Examine the following passage:

Call me Ishmael. Some years ago—never mind how long precisely—having little or no money in my purse, and nothing particular to interest me on shore, I thought I would sail about a little and see the watery part of the world. It is a way I have of driving off the spleen, and regulating the circulation. Whenever I find myself growing grim about the mouth; whenever it is a damp, drizzly November in my soul; whenever I find myself involuntarily pausing before coffin warehouses, and bringing up the rear of every funeral I meet; and especially whenever my hypos get such an upper hand of me, that it requires a strong moral principle to prevent me from deliberately stepping into the street, and methodically knocking people's hats off—then, I account it high time to get to sea as soon as I can.

Herman Melville
from *Moby Dick*

1. For what reasons does Ishmael set sail?
2. What else do you learn about this character?

First-person narrators provide a personal account of what happens to them and to others. In such narratives, details are colored by their perspective and restricted to their knowledge. Eugenia Collier uses the first-person point of view in "Marigolds" (page 684).

Now read the following passage.

Her name was really Joy but as soon as she was twenty-one and away from home, she had had it legally changed. Mrs. Hopewell was certain that she had thought and thought until she had hit upon the ugliest name in any language. Then she had gone and had the beautiful name, Joy, changed without telling her mother until after she had done it. Her legal name was Hulga.

When Mrs. Hopewell thought the name, Hulga, she thought of the broad blank hull of a battleship. She would not use it. She continued to call her Joy to which the girl responded but in a purely mechanical way.

Flannery O'Connor
from "Good Country People"

The narrator has insights into the thoughts, actions, and motives of both characters described in this passage. Such an all-knowing narrator tells a story from the *third-person omniscient point of view,* relying on pronouns such as *she, he,* or *they.* This type of narrator, who is not a character in the story, knows everything that occurs to each character in the story, understanding their thoughts, feelings, and motives for acting as they do. In "Sophistication" (page 422), the narrator provides psychological insights into the minds of both of the young protagonists.

Sometimes a third-person narrator knows and relates the thoughts of only one character. Such a narrator presents a *third-person limited point of view.* This point of view, used by Eudora Welty in "A Worn Path" (page 489), is illustrated in the following passage. Note how events are presented from Livvie's perspective.

Flannery O'Connor, "Good Country People," *A Good Man Is Hard to Find and Other Stories.* Orlando, Florida: Harcourt Brace Jovanovich, Inc., 1955.

Livvie knew she made a nice girl to wait on anybody. She fixed things to eat on a tray like a surprise. She could keep from singing when she ironed, and to sit by a bed and fan away the flies, she could be so still she could not hear herself breathe. She could clean up the house and never drop a thing, and wash the dishes without a sound, and she would step outside to churn, for churning sounded too sad to her, like sobbing, and if it made her home-sick and not Solomon, she did not think of that.

But Solomon scarcely opened his eyes to see her, and scarcely tasted his food. He was not sick or paralyzed or in any pain that he mentioned, but he was surely wearing out in the body, and no matter what nice hot thing Livvie would bring him to taste, he would only look at it now, as if he were past seeing how he could add anything more to himself. Before she could beg him, he would go fast asleep.

Eudora Welty
from "Livvie"

Still another kind of third-person narrator may describe only what can be seen, recording events and reactions like a camera. This is called a *third-person objective (or dramatic) point of view,* with the narrator functioning as an eyewitness reporter.

■ POINT OF VIEW

The vantage point from which an author presents the characters and events in a story. This vantage point is established through an author's choice of narrator. The story may be related by a character (*first-person point of view*) or by a narrator who does not participate in the action (*third-person point of view*). Further, the third-person narrator may present a point of view that is *omniscient*—able to see into the minds of all characters, *limited*—confined to a single character's perceptions, or *objective*—describing only what can be seen, like a camera.

■ Apply to **"Man and Daughter in the Cold,"** page 633.

■ PROTAGONIST/ ANTAGONIST

The central character of a story, play, or novel is called a **protagonist**. Always involved in the main action of the plot, the protagonist may or may not be the narrator. Originally, the protagonist (from a Greek word meaning "first actor") was the actor who played the leading part in a Greek drama.

Usually the protagonist is in conflict against an opponent, or **antagonist**. This antagonist may be another character; for example, Diana Moon Glampers, who destroys the title character in "Harrison Bergeron" (page 669) or the Devil, who defeats Tom Walker in "The Devil and Tom Walker" (page 110). On the other hand, the protagonist may be opposed, not by another person, but by external forces ("A Worn Path," page 489) or a thing or animal ("The Bear," page 460).

Occasionally, a character possesses traits that provide a contrast to those of the protagonist. Such a character, called a *foil*, points up the strengths and weaknesses of the protagonist. In *The Glass Menagerie* (page 572), the outgoing, ambitious gentleman caller provides a foil to the introspective, romantic character of Tom Wingfield.

■ PROTAGONIST

The central character in a literary work.

■ ANTAGONIST

The character or force against which the protagonist is in conflict.

Eudora Welty, "Livvie," *The Wide Net and Other Stories.* Orlando, Florida: Harcourt Brace Jovanovich, Inc., 1942.

■ Apply to **"The Wooing of Ariadne,"** page 649.

■ RHYME

Hush little baby don't say a word
Papa's gonna buy you a mocking bird.
If that mocking bird don't sing
Papa's gonna buy you a diamond ring.

Since infancy, most of us have recognized the power of rhyme to soothe and enchant. Lullabies, nursery rhymes, and children's songs are based on **rhyme**—words having the same sound in their stressed syllables *(thought/brought; trying/crying)*. Rhyme can serve to establish a line as a rhythmic unit or to unify an entire stanza or poem.

Like all sound, rhyme should complement and reinforce the sense of what is being said. Like other poetic devices, rhyme contributes toward the total effect communicated in a poem.

There are several types of rhyme. The most common of these are *end rhyme, internal rhyme, slant rhyme,* and *feminine rhyme.* Poets such as Edgar Allan Poe combine several kinds of rhyme for a heightened musical effect.

End rhyme

End rhyme is the rhyming of words at the end of lines of poetry. The *rhyme scheme,* or pattern of rhyme, can be charted. In the poetic excerpt below, the rhyme scheme is indicated by italicized letters on the right. The first rhyme is labeled *a* (and all the words that rhyme with it); the second rhyme, *b*; the third rhyme, *c*; and so on.

My childhood's earliest thoughts are linked with thee;	*a*
The sight of thee calls back the robin's song,	*b*
Who, from the dark old tree	*a*
Beside the door, sang clearly all day long,	*b*
5 And I, secure in childish piety,	*a*
Listened as if I heard an angel sing	*c*
With news from heaven, which he could bring	*c*
Fresh every day to my untainted ears,	*d*
When birds and flowers and I were happy peers.	*d*

James Russell Lowell
from "To the Dandelion"

Internal Rhyme

A poet may rhyme a word within a line with the word that ends it. This kind of rhyme, called *internal rhyme,* can be used to achieve emphasis or variety within a line, as in the following excerpt.

A year has gone, as the tortoise goes,
  Heavy and slow;
And the same rose blows, and the same sun
    glows,
And the same brook sings of a year ago.

John Greenleaf Whittier
from "Telling the Bees"

Slant rhyme

Yet another kind of rhyme, called *slant rhyme,* or half rhyme, occurs when the sounds of words are similar but not identical. Emily Dickinson frequently used this kind of rhyme to jar readers to attention or to create a mood of discord. Note the use of slant rhyme in the following description of the wind by Whittier.

Within our beds awhile we heard
The wind that round the gables roared,
With now and then a ruder shock,
Which made our very bedsteads rock.

John Greenleaf Whittier
from *Snowbound*

Feminine rhyme

A rhyme scheme may involve words of more than one syllable such as *shimmer/dimmer* or *listening/glistening.* This kind of rhyme, in which stressed rhyming syllables are followed by identical unstressed syllables, is called *feminine rhyme.* Following is an example of feminine rhyme.

How they tinkle, tinkle, tinkle,
  In the icy air of night!
While the stars that oversprinkle
All the heavens, seem to twinkle
5   With a crystalline delight;

Edgar Allan Poe
from "The Bells"

Some critics classify any patterns in sound as rhyme. Techniques such as alliteration and assonance might be considered a form of rhyme under this very broad classification.

"What rhymes with *BZLNXXTKBCOƒƒHNPC?*"

© Punch/Rothco

■ RHYME

The repetition of similar or identical sounds. Rhyme serves to unify a poem, and to reinforce its meaning. Common types of rhyme include *end rhyme, internal rhyme, slant rhyme,* and *feminine rhyme.*

■ Apply to "**Upon the Burning of Our House, July 10, 1666,**" page 63.

■ RHYTHM

The rhythm of a poem makes an important contribution to the pleasure with which we read it. We take it for granted that all poems have rhythm, regular or irregular, and that many poems use rhyme. However, some knowledge of the regular rhythms, called *meters,* that are used in all but free verse, will add to our enjoyment of poetry by helping us see precisely how the poet uses them.

The basis of meter is the *foot.* Each foot contains one accented syllable and one or more unaccented syllables. The arrangement of accented and unaccented syllables in a foot gives us four basic meters:

IAMB: This metrical foot, which consists of an unaccented syllable followed by an accented syllable (˘ ′), as in the word *delight,* is the measure most commonly used in verse written in the English language. Notice how the accents fall in the lines from Freneau's poem "The Wild Honeysuckle":

No róv / ing foót / shall crúsh / thee hére, /

No bús / y hánd / pro vóke / a teár. /

TROCHEE: This two-syllabled metrical foot is the opposite of the iamb. Here the accented syllable precedes the unaccented syllable (′ ˘), as in the word *golden.* Longfellow used this meter in *Hiawatha:*

Óut of / child hóod / ín to / mán hood /

Nów had / grówn my / Hí a / wáth a. /

ANAPEST: This three-syllabled measure consists of two short or unaccented syllables followed by one long or accented syllable (˘ ˘ ′), as in the word *introduce.* It is seldom sustained throughout an entire poem, but many poets gain variety and a swift-moving effect by combining anapestic with iambic feet. The following lines from "Sandolphon," by Longfellow, illustrate this meter:

From the spir / its on earth / that a dore /

From the souls / that en treat / and im plore. /

DACTYL: Like the anapest, the dactyl is a three-syllabled foot, but in the dactyl the long or accented syllable precedes the two unaccented syllables (′ ◡ ◡), as in the word *happiness*. Few poems are written entirely in dactylic feet, but Longfellow used this meter frequently in *The Courtship of Miles Standish:*

Noth ing was / heard in the / room but the /

hur ry ing / pen of the / strip ling. /

Few poems are written in metrical feet of a single kind. Poets tend to avoid the monotony of a completely regular beat by using substitute feet. For example, *stripling* is a trochee at the end of a dactylic line by Longfellow quoted above. Poets may also use *spondees*, poetic feet composed of two accented syllables. Most spondees, like the phrase "sweet words" in Wylie's poem "Pretty Words" (page 536), are made up of two monosyllabic words, both of which receive emphasis. Departures from regular rhythm not only prevent monotony; they also may emphasize important words. In addition, variations in meter can signal a shifting mood or introduce a new idea. For example, in lines 8–9 of Emerson's "The Snowstorm" (page 215), a break in meter indicates that the farm family's movement is halted while the storm continues outside.

Poetry varies not only in meter but also in the number of small patterns of accent within lines. Such patterns of accent, called feet, can range from one to eight in a line. The following terms are used to represent the number of feet that occupy a line of poetry.

one foot: *monometer*
two feet: *dimeter*
three feet: *trimeter*
four feet: *tetrameter*
five feet: *pentameter*
six feet: *hexameter*
seven feet: *heptameter*
eight feet: *octameter*

Pentameter, tetrameter, and trimeter are probably the most common line lengths in regular English verse.

Determining the metrical pattern (pattern of accents and number of feet per line) is called *scansion*. Thus, the lines quoted on the previous page from "The Wild Honeysuckle" are called *iambic tetrameter*, while those from "Sandolphon" are called *anapest trimeter*.

The iamb is often used to echo the rhythms of everyday speech in the English language. Thus, it is a popular choice of poets. Iambic pentameter is also used in the dignified unrhymed lines we call blank verse. Bryant's "Thanatopsis" (page 129) and Frost's "Birches" (page 510) are written in this meter.

Examine the meters of some of the poems in this book. You might wish to indicate on the blackboard the scansion of several lines from various poems, noting any substitute feet or spondees. See if you can find examples of poems in which the meter frequently varies and explain why you think the poet changes the metrical pattern.

Read aloud a poem to determine its rhythm, stopping only at the end of a complete thought. Let punctuation guide you. An *end-stopped line* is a line of poetry that contains a complete thought, thus necessitating the use of a strong punctuation mark such as a semicolon or period at the end. Examine these lines from Thoreau's "Though All the Falls."

The ship, becalmed, at length stands still;
The steed must rest beneath the hill;

When the thought continues beyond the end of the poetic line, the result is a *run-on line*. There should be no pause after *might* in the stanza below from Whittier's "Icabod," the unbroken rhythm making a run-on line.

Oh, dumb be passion's stormy rage,
   When he who might
Have lighted up and led his age,
   Falls back in night.

■ RHYTHM

The arrangement of stressed and unstressed syllables in speech or writing. Rhythm, or meter, may be regular, or it may vary within a line or work. The four most common meters are iamb, trochee, anapest, and dactyl.

■ Apply to **"The Ballad of the Oysterman,"** page 142.

■ SATIRE

"I'm not going to be the one to tell 'em it's a ventilator."

Drawing by R. Taylor; © 1947, 1975 *The New Yorker* Magazine, Inc.

1. Do you think the cartoonist is making fun of modern art, of the people who pretend to understand it, or of both?
2. Is the purpose of this cartoon to change people's behavior or merely to entertain them?

This cartoon relies on **satire**—a technique that ridicules some aspect of life or human nature. Although designed to instruct or inform, satire, with its sharp, incisive wit, also serves to entertain. Satire may range in its intensity from a gentle prodding to a savage attack; it may include exaggeration, humor, ridicule, or irony.

Read the following passage in which Mark Twain satirizes James Fenimore Cooper's literary techniques, in *The Leatherstocking Tales*.

Cooper's gift in the way of invention was not a rich endowment; but such as it was he liked to work it, he was pleased with the effects, and indeed he did some quite sweet things with it. In his little box of stage-properties he kept six or eight cunning devices, tricks, artifices for his savages and woodsmen to deceive and circumvent each other with, and he was never so happy as when he was working these innocent things and seeing them go. A favorite one was to make a moccasined person tread in the tracks of the moccasined enemy, and thus hide his own trail. Cooper wore out barrels and barrels of moccasins in working that trick. Another stage-property that he pulled out pretty frequently was his broken twig. He prized his broken twig above all the rest of his effects and worked it the hardest. . . . Every time a Cooper person is in peril, and absolute silence is worth four dollars a minute, he is sure to step on a dry twig. There may be a hundred handier things to step on, but that wouldn't satisfy Cooper. Cooper requires him to turn out and find a dry twig; and if he can't do it, go and borrow one. In fact, the Leatherstocking Series ought to have been called the Broken Twig Series.

Mark Twain
from *Fenimore Cooper's Literary Offenses*

1. What clues do you have that Twain is being satiric?
2. What examples of irony and hyperbole do you find?
3. What might be Twain's goal in presenting this satire?

Burlesque and parody are loosely related to satire. *Parody* is humorous imitation of serious writing. In parody, the writer exaggerates the characteristics of the work being parodied.

■ SATIRE

Criticism of human nature or any aspect of life. Satire uses techniques of exaggeration, ridicule, sarcasm, irony, humor, or absurdity to instruct or inform. Satire can range in degree from a gentle needling to a fierce attack.

■ Apply to **"Traveling in the New Land,"** page 44.

■ SETTING

There was something about the coast town of Dunnet which made it seem more attractive than other maritime villages of eastern Maine. Perhaps it was the simple fact of acquaintance with that neighborhood which made it so attaching, and gave such interest to the rocky shore and dark woods, and the few houses which seemed to be securely wedged and tree-nailed in among the ledges by the Landing. These houses made the most of their seaward view, and there was a gayety and determined floweriness in their bits of garden ground; the small-paned high windows in the peaks of their steep gables were like knowing eyes that watched the harbor and the far sea-line beyond, or looked northward all along the shore and its background of spruces and balsam firs. When one really knows a village like this and its surroundings, it is like becoming acquainted with a single person. The process of falling in love at first sight is as final as it is swift in such a case, but the growth of true friendship may be a lifelong affair.

After a first brief visit made two or three summers before in the course of a yachting cruise, a lover of Dunnet Landing returned to find the unchanged shores of the pointed firs, the same quaintness of the village with its elaborate conventionalities; all that mixture of remoteness, and childish certainty of being the center of civilization of which her affectionate dreams had told. One evening in June, a single passenger landed upon the steamboat wharf. The tide was high, there was a fine crowd of spectators, and the younger portion of the company followed her with subdued excitement up the narrow street of the salt-aired, white-clapboarded little town.

Sarah Orne Jewett
from "The Country of the Pointed Firs"

Sarah Orne Jewett, "The Country of the Pointed Firs," 1896.

1. What is the time and place of the preceding passage?
2. What mood is conveyed in this description?
3. What parts of the passage suggest that the town has cast a spell on "the lover of Dunnet"?

Setting is the time and place in which the action of a narrative occurs. It can be general (somewhere in Italy during World War II) or specific (noon on July 4, 1988, on Maxwell Street in Chicago). In Jewett's description, the setting is Dunnet, Maine, on an evening in June.

Setting may be suggested through dialogue and action, or it may be described by the narrator or one of the characters. Setting contributes to the mood, or atmosphere, and the plausibility of a work and serves to reveal details about character. The detailed, precise description of the eerie swamp in "The Devil and Tom Walker" (page 110), is an appropriate setting for the appearance of the devil. In "Marigolds" (page 684), the shanty-town setting during the Depression is a revealing backdrop for the young narrator who experiences the "chaotic emotions of childhood," providing clues to her behavior and feelings.

■ SETTING

The time and place in which the action of a narrative occurs. Setting helps establish mood and reveal character. It may directly affect the development of the plot and provide important clues about events and motivation.

■ Apply to "**The Man Who Saw the Flood**," page 483.

■ SONNET

A **sonnet** is a lyric poem with a traditional form of fourteen iambic pentameter lines and one of several fixed rhyme schemes.

Nature

As a fond mother, when the day is o'er,
    Leads by the hand her little child to bed,
    Half willing, half reluctant to be led,
    And leave his broken playthings on the floor,
5 Still gazing at them through the open door,
    Nor wholly reassured and comforted
    By promises of others in their stead,
    Which, though more splendid, may not please
       him more;
So Nature deals with us, and takes away
10   Our playthings one by one, and by the hand
Leads us to rest so gently, that we go
Scarce knowing if we wish to go or stay,
    Being too full of sleep to understand
    How far the unknown transcends the what we
      know.

Henry Wadsworth Longfellow

Chart the rhyme scheme of the sonnet above. This sonnet appears to fall into two parts. Judging from the rhyme scheme and punctuation, where do you think this break occurs? What is the difference in emphasis between the first and the second part?

This type of sonnet originated with Italian poets during the thirteenth century. It reached perfection a century later in the work of Petrarch (pē'trärk), and came to be known as the Petrarchan, or Italian, sonnet. The fourteen lines of the Italian sonnet impose a rigid rhyme scheme: the first eight lines, called the *octave*, rhyme *abbaabba* and present the poet's subject; the concluding six lines, or *sestet*, rhyme *cdecde* and indicate the significance of the facts set forth, or resolve the problem posed, in the octave.

Read the following sonnet and decide how it differs from "Nature."

Pity Me Not

Pity me not because the light of day
At close of day no longer walks the sky;
Pity me not for beauties passed away
From field and thicket as the year goes by;
5 Pity me not the waning of the moon,
Nor that the ebbing tide goes out to sea,
Nor that a man's desire is hushed so soon,
And you no longer look with love on me.
This have I known always: Love is no more
10 Than the wide blossom which the wind assails,
Than the great tide that treads the shifting shore,
Strewing fresh wreckage gathered in the gales:
Pity me that the heart is slow to learn
What the swift mind beholds at every turn.

Edna St. Vincent Millay

What is the rhyme scheme of Millay's poem? This poem is an example of the Shakespearean, or English, sonnet, which is composed of three *quatrains* (groups of four lines with a rhyming pattern) and a final rhyming *couplet*. The rhyme scheme can be charted *abab/cdcd/efef/gg*. The concluding couplet usually provides a comment or a mental twist to the preceding train of thought. Note the shift in thought in the last two lines of Millay's sonnet.

The structure and rhyme scheme of both types of sonnets are closely related to the ideas conveyed. Modern sonneteers may use variations on traditional rhyme schemes and metric patterns.

■ SONNET

A lyric poem of fourteen lines, usually iambic pentameter, and having a fixed rhyme scheme. Depending upon the patterns of rhyme and organization of thought, the sonnet may be classified as Shakespearean (English; Elizabethan) or Petrarchan (Italian).

From *Collected Poems* by Edna St. Vincent Millay. Copyright 1923, 1928, 1951, 1955 by Edna St. Vincent Millay and Norma Millay Ellis. Reprinted by permission of the Estate of Edna St. Vincent Millay.

■ Apply to "**Childhood**," page 546.

© Punch/Rothco

"The muse is upon me, Samantha—
I'm loading the sonnet programme."

■ SOUND DEVICES

The purpose of some poems is to create an impression through sound rather than to express a theme or convey deep meaning. Read the following poem.

Counting-Out Rhyme

Silver bark of beech, and sallow
Bark of yellow birch and yellow
   Twig of willow.

Stripe of green in moosewood maple,
5 Color seen in leaf of apple,
   Bark of popple.

Wood of popple pale as moonbeam,
Wood of oak for yoke and barn-beam
   Wood of hornbeam.

10 Silver bark of beech, and hollow
Stem of elder, tall and yellow
   Twig of willow.

Edna St. Vincent Millay

1. What general quality of trees does the poem express?
2. What impression or mood does this poem convey?
3. What words and sounds contribute to this mood?

Millay's poem is an exercise in sound devices, using the musical effects of sounds and words to express the exquisite beauty of trees. Although some poets may not use exact rhymes in their works, all poets rely on one sound device or another to communicate a mood, to unify ideas, and to reinforce meaning. Some of the specific sound devices employed by poets are *alliteration, assonance, consonance, onomatopoeia,* and *repetition.*

Alliteration is the repetition of consonant sounds at the beginnings of words or accented syllables. Alliteration may appear in one line of a poem or it may run through several lines. More than one sound can be alliterated in a given line or lines. What sounds are alliterated in the following lines? How would you describe the effect of these sounds?

Sinuous southward and sinuous northward
   the shimmering band
Of the sand-beach fastens the fringe of
   the marsh to the folds of the land.

Sidney Lanier
from "The Marshes of Glynn"

Assonance
Assonance is the repetition of similar vowel sounds followed by different consonant sounds in stressed syllables or words. *Made* and *played* are examples of rhyme; *made* and *mail,* examples of assonance. In the following line from Poe's "Annabel Lee," the italicized words provide assonance: "And so, all the *night-tide,* I lie down by the *side.* . . . "

Consonance
The repetition of consonant sounds that are preceded by different vowel sounds is called **consonance** (*bear/more, letter/mutter, frail/feel*). Consonance is sometimes synonymous with *slant rhyme,* as in the lines by Dickinson that follow. Note how consonance substitutes for exact rhyme at the end of these lines.

The Wind—tapped like a tired Man
And like a Host—"Come in"
I boldly answered—entered then
My Residence within. . .

Emily Dickinson
from "The Wind Tapped Like a Tired Man"

From *Collected Poems* by Edna St. Vincent Millay. Copyright 1923, 1928, 1951, 1955 by Edna St. Vincent Millay and Norma Millay Ellis. Reprinted by permission of the Estate of Edna St. Vincent Millay.

Reprinted by permission of the publishers and the Trustees of Amherst College from *The Poems of Emily Dickinson,* edited by Thomas H. Johnson, Cambridge, Mass.: The Belknap Press of Harvard University Press, Copyright 1951, © 1955, 1979, 1983 by The President and Fellows of Harvard College.

Onomatopoeia

Onomatopoeia is the use of words whose sounds imitate the natural sounds of an object or activity. Words such as *hiss*, *mumble*, *caw*, and *mew* are onomatopoetic words. In the following example, the author conveys the sound of rustling leaves.

The treetops faintly rustle beneath the
    breeze's flight,
A soft and soothing sound, yet it
    whispers of the night. . . .

William Cullen Bryant
from "Waiting by the Gate"

Repetition

Repetition of a sound, word, or phrase is also a sound device. In a way, rhyme, alliteration, assonance, and consonance are all forms of repetition. Found extensively in free verse, repetition serves to unify a poem and emphasize important ideas. Note the haunting effect of repeated sounds, words, and phrases in the following lines:

Back into the chamber turning, all my soul within me
    burning,
Soon again I heard a tapping somewhat louder than
    before.
"Surely," said I, "surely that is something at my
    window lattice;
Let me see, then, what thereat is, and this mystery
    explore—
5 Let my heart be still a moment and this mystery
    explore—
             'Tis the wind and nothing more!"

Edgar Allan Poe
from "The Raven"

Give examples of three sound devices used by Millay in "Counting-Out Rhyme."

Note how a variety of sound devices combine to create a portrait of an exuberant poet in the following poem. What specific sound devices can you find that convey this picture?

Mediterranean Beach, Day After Storm

How instant joy, how clang
And whang the sun, how
Whoop the sea, and oh
Sun, sing, as whiter than
5 Rage of snow, let sea the spume
Fling.

Let sea the spume, white, fling,
White on blue wild
With wind, let sun
10 Sing, while the world
Scuds, clouds boom and belly,
Creak like sails, whiter than,
Brighter than,
Spume in sun-song, oho!
15 The wind is bright.

Wind the heart winds
In constant coil, turning
In the—forever—light.

Give me your hand.

Robert Penn Warren

■ SOUND DEVICES

The use of words for their auditory effect to convey mood, establish meaning, create music, and unify a work. Some common sound devices other than exact rhyme are alliteration, assonance, consonance, onomatopoeia, and repetition.

"Mediterranean Beach, Day After Storm" from *Selected Poems 1923–1975* by Robert Penn Warren. Copyright © 1966 by Robert Penn Warren. Reprinted by permission of Random House, Inc. and William Morris Agency.

■ Apply to **"Annabel Lee,"** page 172.

STREAM OF CONSCIOUSNESS

Some writers reveal characters by presenting the illogical, random flow of their thoughts. Such a re-creation of the uneven flow of a character's thoughts, memories, sensations, emotions, and mental associations without any attempt on the part of the author to explain them is called **stream of consciousness.** The term itself suggests that the thoughts represented flow like a body of water.

The following description appears in William Faulkner's novel *The Sound and the Fury*. Part of the passage is presented as straightforward narrative, and part is disclosed through the broken thoughts of Benjy Compson, a thirty-three-year-old idiot who is incapable of speech and apprehends things according to his acute senses.

"What are you doing, Jason."

"Nothing." Jason said.

"Suppose you come over here to do it, then." Father said.

Jason came out of the corner.

"What are you chewing." Father said.

"Nothing." Jason said.

"He's chewing paper again." Caddy said.

Jason threw into the fire. It hissed, uncurled, turning black. Then it was gray. Then it was gone. Caddy and Father and Jason were in Mother's chair. Jason's eyes were puffed shut and his mouth moved, like tasting. Caddy's head was on Father's shoulder. Her hair was like fire, and little points of fire were in her eyes, and I went and Father lifted me into the chair too, and Caddy held me. She smelled like trees.

She smelled like trees. In the corner it was dark, but I could see the window. I squatted there, holding the slipper. I couldn't see it, but my hands saw it, and I could hear it getting night, and my hands saw the slipper but I couldn't see myself, but my hands could see the slipper, and I squatted there, hearing it getting dark.

William Faulkner
from *The Sound and the Fury*

Jackson Pollock, *Echo* (Number 25, 1951). Collection, The Museum of Modern Art, New York

1. Where does the passage shift from narrative to Benjy's disjointed thoughts?
2. Which senses does Benjy use to apprehend the objects and people around him?
3. How can Benjy's hands "see the slipper"?

Through the stream-of-consciousness technique, a writer can examine a character's psychology, recording not only what the character thinks but how that character thinks.

STREAM OF CONSCIOUSNESS

A technique of writing that records or re-creates the random, illogical flow of a character's thoughts, sensations, memories, emotions, and mental associations without any attempt at explanation.

Excerpt from *The Sound and the Fury* by William Faulkner. Copyright 1929, renewed 1956, by William Faulkner. Reprinted by permission of Random House, Inc.

■ Apply to "**The Jilting of Granny Weatherall**," page 430.

■ STYLE

The way in which writers use words and sentences to suit their ideas is called *style*. Once authors choose a purpose for writing, they shape words and ideas to serve that purpose. Style involves an author's particular choice and arrangement of words, as well as the tone, mood, imagery, sound effects, and other literary devices in a work.

The first paragraph below is from a psychology textbook; the second, from a novel. As you read these paragraphs, try to determine what makes them different.

First, the mother gratifies the child's instinctual needs, participating in his pleasure. Then the child achieves a sublimated, tender relation to his mother, who enjoys his need to lean on her and his tenderness, and responds to them. In the end, the mother, as a result of educational and emotional influences, becomes a part of his ego ideal and thus is reunited with him.

Helene Deutsch
from *Psychology of Women*

I was the son of a beautiful, word-struck mother and I longed for her touch many years after she felt no obligation to touch me. But I will praise her for the rest of my life for teaching me to seek out the beauty of nature in all its shapes and fabulous designs. It was my mother who taught me to love the lanterns of night fishermen in the starry darkness and the flights of brown pelicans skimming the curling breakers at dawn. It was she who made me take notice of the perfect coinage of sand dollars, the shapes of flounders inlaid in sand like the silhouettes of ladies in cameos, the foundered wreck near the Colleton Bridge that pulsed with the commerce of otters. She saw the world through the dazzling prism of authentic imagination.

Pat Conroy
from *The Prince of Tides*

1. What is the purpose of the first paragraph? the second?
2. Which paragraph uses figurative language and imagery to establish a mood?
3. How would you describe this mood?
4. Which paragraph uses language that is literal and, at times, technical?
5. Choose a word to describe the tone of each paragraph.

The first paragraph describes successive stages in relationships between mother and child. The second paragraph describes how a specific and memorable mother has influenced her son. Why is the style of the first paragraph appropriate for a textbook, while that of the second paragraph is suitable for a novel?

Jonathan Swift defined style as "proper words in proper places." Note how Henry Thoreau chooses and arranges words to achieve their utmost effect in the following: "We do not ride on the railroad; it rides upon us. . . ." Think about why Thoreau's words are more effective than the following restatement: "Modern technology often controls us."

Some writers have a style that is unique and distinguishable from other writers. Such a style might be labeled *poetic, conversational, terse,* or *flamboyant.* A particular writer can likewise display a variety of styles, depending on the purpose of each work.

■ STYLE

The manner in which writers use language to express their ideas. Style involves an author's choice and arrangement of words, as well as the tone, mood, imagery, sound effects, and other literary devices that may or may not appear in a work.

Helene Deutsch, *Psychology of Women.* New York: Grune & Stratton, Inc., 1945.

Pat Conroy, *The Prince of Tides.* Boston: Houghton Mifflin Company, 1986.

■ Apply to **The Declaration of Independence,** page 92.

■ SYMBOL

A **symbol** is an object or event that represents something other than itself, frequently an abstract idea or concept. The use in literature of objects or events to represent something other than themselves is called **symbolism**. In "The Chambered Nautilus" (page 140), the shell symbolizes the body, and the animal in the shell, the soul.

What does the evening star symbolize in the following poem?

The Evening Star

Lo! in the painted oriel of the West,
  Whose panes the sunken sun incarnadines,
  Like a fair lady at her casement, shines
  The evening star, the star of love and
    rest!
5 And then anon she doth herself divest
  Of all her radiant garments, and reclines
  Behind the sombre screen of yonder pines,
  With slumber and soft dreams of love
    oppressed.
O my beloved, my sweet Hesperus!
10 My morning and my evening star of love!
  My best and gentlest lady! even thus,
As that fair planet in the sky above,
  Dost thou retire unto thy rest at night,
  And from thy darkened window fades the
    light.

Henry Wadsworth Longfellow

1. What abstract concept does the evening star represent?
2. What is actually happening in the sky when the star is said to divest "her radiant garments" and sleep?

Originally, the word **symbol** meant a throwing together or fusion. Such a fusion or association occurs in symbolism when one element, usually concrete (a person or object) is used to represent an abstraction.

A symbol may form the framework of an entire poem. Some symbols are based on traditional associations—a dove for peace, for example, or a skull for death or poison. Others are less universal in the associations they evoke.

To determine whether a poem or passage contains symbolic meaning, consider the following:
● Does the author equate something concrete with something abstract?
● Does emphasis upon certain words suggest a symbolic interpretation?
● Does characterization or imagery suggest a symbolic interpretation?
● Is a particular idea or image stressed, perhaps through repetition?

■ SYMBOL

Something used to represent something else. In literature the term *symbol* usually refers to a concrete image used to designate an abstract quality or concept.

■ Apply to "**When Lilacs Last in the Dooryard Bloom'd**," page 301.

■ THEME

A Man Saw a Ball of Gold in the Sky

A man saw a ball of gold in the sky;
He climbed for it,
And eventually he achieved it—
It was clay.
5 Now this is the strange part:
When the man went to the earth
And looked again,
Lo, there was the ball of gold.
Now this is the strange part:
10 It was a ball of gold.
Ay, by the heavens, it was a ball of gold.

Stephen Crane

1. Where does the man actually find the ball of gold?
2. What is significant about the fact that the man had to pursue the ball of gold a second time on Earth?
3. What might the ball of gold represent?

This brief poem is about pursuits and perseverance. One might sum up its meaning thus: People must continue to try after failing and direct their quests closer to home.

The deeper, underlying meaning of a poem is its **theme**. A theme is usually not stated explicitly; instead, it is implied through characterization, action, image, or tone. Theme differs from subject in that the subject is simply the topic or thing described in a work. In "The Wild Honeysuckle" (page 74), for example, the topic or subject is a flower, but the theme is the poet's final recognition of the fleeting nature of human existence.

Not every work has a theme. Works with no theme are most likely to be those written entirely for entertainment. Some mystery novels, for example, have no real themes. Other literary works have more than one theme.

What is the subject of the following poem? What is its theme?

Fossils

The fossils of the warm
bright sunlight of the year
flicker from these dry leaves
falling through the garden air.

5 And we who would find comfort
in shards we might retrieve,
find—whirling at our feet
out of a sky of leaves—

past days are no less past:
10 however near they are,
they touch us with the bright,
cold comfort of the stars.

Alan Shapiro

■ THEME

The main idea or underlying meaning of a literary work. A theme may be directly stated but is more often implied. Theme differs from the subject of a literary work in that it usually makes an observation about the subject. Some literary works have no theme; others have more than one.

"Fossils" from *The Courtesy* by Alan Shapiro. Copyright © 1983 by The University of Chicago. Reprinted by permission.

■ Apply to "**The Chambered Nautilus,**" page 140.

■ TONE

The following passage is from Upton Sinclair's novel, *The Jungle*. Sinclair is describing a meat factory and its workers. As you read, try to determine Sinclair's attitude toward his subject.

The sausage room was an interesting place to visit, for two or three minutes, and provided that you did not look at the people; the machines were perhaps the most wonderful things in the entire plant . . . . There was only a mist of motion, and tangle after tangle of sausages appearing. In the midst of the mist, however, the visitor would suddenly notice the tense set face, with the two wrinkles graven in the forehead, and the ghastly pallor of the cheeks; and then he would suddenly recollect that it was time he was going on. The woman did not go on; she stayed right there—hour after hour, day after day, year after year, twisting sausage links and racing with death. It was piece work, and she was apt to have a family to keep alive; and stern and ruthless economic laws had arranged it that she could only do this by working just as she did, with all her soul upon her work, and with never an instant for a glance at the well-dressed ladies and gentlemen who came to stare at her, as at some wild beast in a menagerie.

Upton Sinclair
from *The Jungle*

1. What does the visitor notice that reminds him "it was time he was going"?
2. What words and phrases suggest the working conditions in this factory?
3. What adjective best describes Sinclair's attitude toward his subject: *disinterested, amused, affectionate, distressed*?

Through his arrangement of details and use of language, Sinclair reveals his concern for the workers and his anger at those who have created what he sees as inhuman working conditions. His attitude is revealed in the tone of his novel.

Tone is an author's relationship to his or her material, to the audience, or to both. By recognizing tone, a reader can determine whether a writer views a subject with sympathy, aloofness, apprehension, ridicule, or admiration. Sometimes a writer's tone will involve a mixture of feelings, or it may change within a given work. Tone conveys the emotional significance of a work and is therefore an essential key to understanding the total meaning.

When we speak, we convey tone through inflection and facial expression. In written language, the author must rely on the use of language to convey the desired impression. Any of the following might provide a clue to the tone of a work: point of view, word choice, style, choice of images, treatment of characters and events—even sound and rhythm. Further, all of the elements of poetry can help convey tone: connotation, imagery, metaphor, irony, understatement, and so on.

Determine the tone of the following poem. What phrases and details help convey this tone?

Upton Sinclair, *The Jungle*, 1905.

After the Dentist

My left upper
lip and half

my nose is gone.
I drink my coffee

5 on the right from
a warped cup

whose left lip dips.
My cigarette's

thick as a finger.
10 Somebody else's.

I put lip-
stick on a cloth-

stuffed doll's
face that's

15 surprised when one
side smiles.

May Swenson

■ TONE

The author's attitude toward his or her subject and audience. Tone, which may be stated directly or implied, conveys the emotional meaning of a work. It may be revealed by the author's word choice, the details included, or the arrangement of ideas and descriptions.

"After the Dentist" from *New & Selected Things Taking Place* by May Swenson. Copyright © 1967 by May Swenson. Reprinted by permission of the author.

■ Apply to "**A Witch Trial at Mount Holly,**" page 84.

Samuel F. B. Morse, *The Muse—Susan Walker Morse* (c. 1835–37). The Metropolitan Museum of Art

WRITER'S HANDBOOK

The Writing Process

Whether you are at home writing a long essay or in class responding to an essay test question, the strategy for writing about literature is the same. It is essential that you read the assignment carefully and do what is asked. Equally important is to find and organize your material, to get it down on paper, and to refine your writing until it expresses exactly what you want to say as clearly as possible. This article will give you specific tips on how to apply three steps of the **writing process**—prewriting, writing, and revising. In the course of your writing, you will find that these steps are recursive and overlapping and that you may shift back and forth from one step to another on the often circuitous way to a finished product.

PREWRITING

Sample Assignment

Below is a sample assignment for writing a literary essay. Following the assignment are some suggestions on how the writing process can be used to write the essay.

"The Love Song of J. Alfred Prufrock" abounds with literary and biblical allusions. In an essay of four or five paragraphs, analyze how the character of Prufrock is developed through the use of allusion.

1. Identify the Task

When you are asked to write about a piece of literature, your first task is to determine exactly what you are required to do. Read the assignment and note key words that will direct you in your writing task.

analyze: examine critically in order to single out the components of a piece of writing.

compare/contrast: point out similarities and differences.

illustrate: make clear by examples, comparisons, quotations, or other textual evidence.

describe: give a picture or account of something.

explain: make clear something not evident or understood.

discuss: consider all sides of a question.

interpret: explain, construe, or understand a selection and support your interpretation with references to the text.

convince: persuade by argument or proof.

imagine: form an image or idea; put yourself or someone else into a hypothetical situation.

defend: write in favor of an opinion.

support: prove ideas, claims, or opinions with evidence or argument.

In addition, look for and underline key words in the assignment and identify the intended audience. Your audience will determine the amount of background you need to supply, and also the sophistication of your style and vocabulary.

2. Form a Thesis Statement

Assignments that ask for a single-paragraph response can be developed around a topic sentence stating the main point of the paragraph. Longer papers, however, are nearly always founded on a thesis statement, generally placed in the opening paragraph, that explains your subject and the aspects of it that you will be covering in the paragraphs that follow. Such a sentence can provide a structure for organizing your ideas.

Often the wording of the assignment will supply much of the wording of your thesis statement. Note how the following thesis statement incorporates words and ideas from the preceding assignment:

The many allusions in this poem serve to characterize Prufrock and to emphasize the frustration, futility, and alienation of his life.

3. Brainstorm

Think about your reading and about the assignment. Class discussion, conversations with friends who have read the poem, and brainstorming with yourself may spark ideas. Charts and cluster diagrams are often helpful in the preliminary phase of getting ideas down on paper.

4. Take Notes

Note the various allusions in the poem and make sure you understand them, using information provided in the footnotes and in the Reader's Note on page 531. If your thesis statement is well worded, it will direct you in finding relevant information for note taking. Your note taking may take any of the following forms.

Use direct quotations. Copy exact words from the selections, in the order in which they appear. The quotation is set off by quotation marks. Ellipses (. . .) are used to show where words have been left out. Quote only words and phrases that will support your thesis. When poetry is quoted, a slash is used to indicate the end of a line. Following is an example of the correct use of ellipses and slash:

> ". . . I am Lazarus, come from the dead,/Come back to tell you all. . . ."

Paraphrase. Extract the sense of a passage and express it in your own words. Usually the source is indicated right with the paraphrase:

> In lines 111–119, Prufrock says that he is not Prince Hamlet but rather an attendant lord—a deferential, cautious advisor who may appear foolish.

Make lists. Jot down images, words and details that you find significant. Your list of allusions and details may look something like this:

> Guido—tormented soul, confesses sins
> Lazarus—raised from the dead (Prufrock is dead too, but not raised.)
> Footman—death, snickers
> Hamlet—unlike Prufrock, who cannot "force the moment to its crisis"
> "I am no prophet"—John the Baptist

Interpret. Note your reactions and generalizations that occur to you, testing them for use later. You can always discard those that you don't need. Be prepared to read between the lines and make inferences based on details provided in the work. Some ideas that occur "off the top of your head" may prove to be important insights:

> Prufrock is an observer rather than a participant in life. It seems appropriate that a character who leads a second-hand, vicarious life is portrayed through allusions to others.

5. Organize Your Notes

Your thesis can help you organize your notes. For this assignment, the obvious divisions are the separate allusions. Because this is to be a four- or five-paragraph essay, you will have an opening and a closing paragraph, and two or three body paragraphs. You may wish to devote an entire paragraph to some of the allusions, and to group others into a single paragraph. Or you could group biblical allusions and literary allusions into two separate paragraphs.

WRITING

6. Write a Rough Draft

Try to write out your first draft quickly so that you can get your main ideas down on paper. Rewriting and polishing can come later. During the first writing, don't bother with misspellings, punctuation, or even a few sentences that seem awkward and unclear. When you've completed your rough draft, you're ready for what many writers consider to be real writing: revising.

REVISING

Bernard Malamud once said of his writing: "I know it's finished when I can no longer stand working on it." His words are testimony to the painstaking process of revision that even the most skilled writer has to experience. Like Malamud, you must recast, reshape, and refine your writing until an inner voice says, "Enough. It's as good as I can make it."

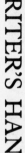

WRITER'S HANDBOOK

Is there a strategy for revision? A checklist that reminds you what to look for when reading over your manuscript can be helpful, especially a series of questions such as the following:

Content, Organization, and Style
- Is the main point of the essay expressed in a strong thesis statement? Will the introduction catch the reader's interest?
- Does the paper have a sense of progression, a steady movement toward the most important ideas, which should always be saved for last?
- Does the paper read well aloud? Where could sentences be combined, *and*'s be eliminated, or similar sentence openings be changed to reduce choppiness and monotony?
- What needs to be cut? (Be ruthless! Don't use five words, such as "due to the fact that," where you could use one—"because." Strike out any sentence that doesn't illuminate your subject, or that repeats what you have just said.)
- Are your paragraphs proportional? Except when used for surprise effect, a paragraph of two sentences next to one of ten or twelve sentences implies a need for more detail or better organization of material.
- Are the opening and closing paragraphs forceful, interesting, and complementary? (Make sure that the last paragraph is not simply a restatement of the first paragraph but a summation and resolution of all that has been discussed.)
- Which sentences, now in passive voice, could be more effectively phrased in active voice? (Not: "Tom Walker's avarice is appealed to and his soul is bought by the devil in exchange for worldly goods" but rather, "The devil appeals to Tom Walker's avarice and buys his soul in exchange for worldly goods.")

Grammar, Mechanics, and Usage
Before typing or writing your paper in its final form, you should edit it carefully to catch errors in grammar, mechanics, or usage.
- Are all the words spelled correctly?
- Is all of the punctuation logical and helpful in making the meaning clear?
- Have you used capitals, italics, numerals, and abbreviations correctly?

- Have you checked pronouns and verbs for common errors, such as faulty agreement, incorrect pronoun form or reference, incorrect form of the verb?
- Can you spot any errors in word choice or usage?

Before handing in your paper, proofread the completed manuscript to catch whatever errors might have slipped in while you were typing or rewriting.

You will find this article helpful in completing most of the composition assignments in this book, including those on pages 17, 258, and 710.

OUTLINE

1. Introduction
   (include thesis statement)
2. Allusions referring to
   death/damnation:
   Guido
   Lazarus
   eternal Footman
3. Hamlet
   Prufrock as foil to Hamlet
   Prufrock—
   "attendant lord," fool
4. John the Baptist
   head on platter
   Prufrock is no prophet
   Prufrock lacks
   nobility and wisdom
5. Allusion—
   appropriate method
   of characterization
   —Prufrock unable
   to express himself

Model

Allusion in "The Love Song of J. Alfred Prufrock"

The many allusions in this poem serve to characterize Prufrock and to emphasize the frustration, futility, and alienation of his life. The poem abounds in biblical and literary allusions that generally refer to characters who are damned, murdered, or cynical in their views of life.

Many of the allusions refer to some aspect of death or damnation. Like Guido, speaker of the epigraph, Prufrock is a tormented soul, condemned to suffer for his transgressions and to confess them. Unlike the biblical Lazarus, Prufrock will not be raised from his state of death. And the eternal Footman—Death—snickers as he makes his inevitable claim on Prufrock.

The indecisive Prufrock serves as a foil to Hamlet, the title character of Shakespeare's play, who avenges his father's death. Unable to "force the moment to its crisis," the indecisive Prufrock will instead be an "attendant Lord"—cautious and deferential, but ultimately ineffectual and "at times, the Fool."

Yet another allusion mentions the prophet John the Baptist whose head was served on a platter to the dancer Salome. Although Prufrock visualizes his own balding head served on a platter, he says, "I am no prophet," thus denying the nobility and wisdom of his biblical counterpart.

Ironically, the character of a man unable to express himself is brilliantly communicated through allusions to other people. Such a method of characterization seems especially appropriate to someone whose life is removed, remote, and vicariously lived.

WRITER'S HANDBOOK

Developing Your Style

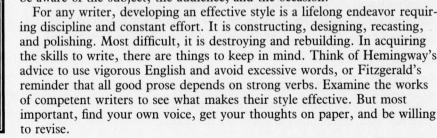

Style, in the words of Jonathan Swift, is putting "proper words in proper places." Every serious writer has a purpose for writing, and to this end arranges words, images, and details. In determining a style, a writer should be aware of the subject, the audience, and the occasion.

For any writer, developing an effective style is a lifelong endeavor requiring discipline and constant effort. It is constructing, designing, recasting, and polishing. Most difficult, it is destroying and rebuilding. In acquiring the skills to write, there are things to keep in mind. Think of Hemingway's advice to use vigorous English and avoid excessive words, or Fitzgerald's reminder that all good prose depends on strong verbs. Examine the works of competent writers to see what makes their style effective. But most important, find your own voice, get your thoughts on paper, and be willing to revise.

1. Find Your Own Voice

Use words and images that are natural and clear to you. Avoid expressions that seem intellectually impressive or sophisticated but do not ring true for you. Simplicity and honesty have always been the hallmark of good style. Know your audience and adjust your tone accordingly. Obviously you will not assume the same tone in an essay on patriotism that you use in a written explanation of team strategy for a classmate.

2. Strive for Flair

In "Of the Meaning of Progress," Du Bois states: "How hard a thing is life to the lowly, and yet how human and real! And all this life and love and strife and failure—is it the twilight of nightfall or the flush of some faint-dawning day?" Note Du Bois's use of the exact word, the right image, and the telling detail. Observe the rhythms of his sentences—one an exclamation, one a question. Writing with a flair, like any skill, is acquired only after painstaking practice.

3. Get Your Reader's Attention

Consider the opening sentence of Kurt Vonnegut, Jr.'s story "Harrison Bergeron": "The year was 2081, and everybody was finally equal." The writer has set the bait; few readers could resist continuing. Don't begin, "My paper will be about. . . ." Rather, launch into your subject in a vivid, inviting way: "Have you ever read

about a literary character who bore an uncanny resemblance to someone in your family?"

4. Use Fresh Images and Figures of Speech

In "An Episode of War," Stephen Crane uses memorable imagery to convey the impression of war: "the wild thud of hoofs," "an interminable crowd of bandaged men," "the roar of the wheels, the slant of the glistening guns." Crane's use of figurative language is likewise fresh and precise: the lieutenant holds his wounded arm "as if it was made of very brittle glass"; "the shooting sometimes crackled like bush fires." Like skilled writers, you should reject the inevitable and easy comparison such as "blue as the sky." Flannery O'Connor describes the eyes of one of her characters as being "blue as a peacock's neck." Eudora Welty describes an old lady's wrinkled face as looking like "a whole little tree stood in the middle of her forehead." Aim for comparisons like these that are unusual, though never contrived.

5. Rely on Strong and Vivid Verbs

F. Scott Fitzgerald once said that "all fine prose is based on verbs carrying the sentence." In "The Celebrated Jumping Frog . . ." Mark Twain writes: "Simon Wheeler *backed* me into a corner and *blockaded* me there with his chair, and then sat down and *reeled off* the monotonous narrative. . . ." Twain's sentence gains much of its impact from the use of strong action verbs. Your writing will likewise be enhanced by vivid verbs—*blockaded* rather than *stopped*, *reeled off* rather than *said*.

6. Vary Sentence Patterns

An accomplished writer is able to construct crisp, compact sentences. Stephen Crane, in "An Episode of War," states: "A wound gives strange dignity to him who bears it."

Crane follows this maxim with a long, flowing sentence that conveys a cumulative sequence of meaningful details: "It is as if the wounded man's hand is upon the curtain which hangs before the revelations of all existence—the meaning of ants, potentates, wars, cities, sunshine, snow, a feather dropped from a bird's wing; and the power of it sheds radiance upon a bloody form, and makes the other men understand sometimes that they are little."

Thus Crane telescopes life and its lesson. Occasionally, Crane inserts an appositive between subject and verb: "A battery, a tumultuous and shining mass, was swirling toward the right."

Skillful writers recognize the need to vary the pace of their sentences. Similarly, you will want to alternate short sentences with more leisurely ones and vary the subject-verb-object format with an occasional appositive, a question, a periodic sentence that saves the subject till last, or an introductory phrase.

7. Strive for Clarity

Being clear is a courtesy to your reader, who usually does not have the patience to dig for your meaning. Do this by constructing sentences for concise, easy reading.

- Avoid circumlocutions.
- Place modifiers within reach of what they modify.
- Keep pronoun references, verb tenses, and sequence clear.
- Use transitions that link precisely but unobtrusively.
- Introduce quotations, paraphrases, and examples clearly.

Finally, remember that even the most famous writers occasionally develop blocks and experience frustration. If you take a step-by-step approach to writing, however, you will find that the result is a well-organized paper that fulfills the assignment.

No matter what the assignment, keep matters of style in mind as you review and evaluate your writing. The following questions may help you.

- Does the opening sentence attract a reader's attention?
- Is your language strong, direct, and concise?
- Have you chosen words, images, and figures of speech that make your style crisp and effective?
- Have you used a variety of sentence patterns?
- Have you expressed your ideas clearly and forcefully?

You will find this article helpful in completing the assignments on pages 174, 222, 272, 319, 323, and 328.

Developing Your Style 923

WRITER'S HANDBOOK

Writing to Persuade an Audience

Good literature presents issues and ideas that are open to various interpretations—all of them defensible. Many writing assignments based on literature offer a statement (a judgment, a position) with which you are invited to agree or disagree and asked to convince others to accept your position. When you write to **persuade** readers, you must follow three steps: carefully consider various interpretations; decide which one makes most sense to you; persuade the audience that your conclusion is a valid one. If the primary purpose for your paper is to persuade an audience, you should find the following tips for developing an argument helpful.

PREWRITING

Sample Assignment

A critic has written that Ernest Hemingway's "In Another Country" is profoundly pessimistic in its portrayal of human experience. Refute or support this interpretation and defend your position.

1. Go to the Source

Don't make any decisions about refuting or supporting the critic's statement until you have carefully reread the story. As you read, look for items that will help you document an interpretation—in this case, words and phrases that convey a tone of optimism or pessimism. Take notes on these items. You might divide your notes, listing details that suggest optimism in one column, and details that convey pessimism in another column.

2. State Your Position

Once you know your material thoroughly, take a stand and make your position clear to your readers. After careful consideration, suppose that you have decided to support the critic's statement. You might state your position in a sentence such as this:

Despite some suggestions of beauty and camaraderie, the tone in Hemingway's "In Another Country" is profoundly pessimistic.

This statement may eventually be refined into a thesis statement. For now, it can direct your search for supporting evidence.

3. Adopt a Tone

After setting forth your position with some precision, you must decide how to go about defending it. Early in the assignment decide what tone to strive for. Do not attempt to use a bludgeon or to attack other positions with sarcasm. Perhaps the tone called for is one of openness and directness, showing respect for other positions but defending your own with convincing evidence.

4. Evaluate Your Evidence

Examine the notes you took when you reread the story. Jot down whatever else you can think of that serves to reinforce your opinion. Now go back and decide which evidence serves you best, eliminating any weak items. Keep in mind the following, as you select your evidence.

Select strong evidence. Remember that the most persuasive evidence will be factual details that unambiguously support your view.

Lonely, alienated, and misunderstood by the townspeople, the soldiers are all either physically or emotionally wounded. No longer participants in the ever-present war, these characters really belong to no country.

Be prepared to make inferences. Make reasonable conclusions based on hints provided. In addition, decide whether the author's tone is serious, playful, or ironic. Note, for example, that although the girls at the Cova are described as "very patriotic," readers might infer that

Hemingway's tone is ironic and that the girls, like the woman selling chestnuts, are interested in making money rather than benefiting their country.

Reject unsupported opinions. Examine the following statement:

There is no hope that the hospital's machines will ever rehabilitate any of the wounded men.

Eliminate such sweeping generalizations and be careful of words like *always, never,* and *no* that lack documentation.

5. Consider Opposing Evidence

Consider the other viewpoint. By becoming aware of why others hold different positions, you are better able to support your own. For instance, at some point in your essay you might admit that there are images of beauty ("The hospital was very old and very beautiful.") and suggestions of pleasant camaraderie among the wounded. However, you might argue, these are overpowered by images of death and isolation. Funerals originate from the beautiful hospital, and the soldiers band together mainly as a defense against alienation and the hostility of the townspeople.

6. Use Evidence Fairly

A careless reading of a text can lead to an improper inference:

The before-and-after pictures of hands like the major's that were completely restored proves that the therapy machines work.

Such a statement overlooks the fact that the soldiers in the story were the first ones to use the machines, thus suggesting the photographs are fraudulent.

WRITING

7. Make Your Main Points

You should have firmly in mind, or on paper, a list of points you want to emphasize in supporting your view. Remember that the places of emphasis are first and last in your composition. If you start off with a solid piece of evidence, keep something equally persuasive in reserve to close with.

8. Finish Strong and Fast

After presenting your main points, conclude with some kind of summary, in fresh language, of your position. Do not repeat or weakly echo the first paragraph. Leave your reader with a sense of closure. Clinch your argument in a final paragraph such as the following one.

Model

Although there are elements of beauty in the setting and attempts at meaningful human relationships, the overpowering message of Hemingway's story is that the human condition is one of loneliness and alienation in a cold and joyless universe. Throughout, Hemingway's stark, terse style strips away all hope and adornment that might make existence bearable. At the story's end, the reader, like the major, stares vacantly out a window into a bleak and hopeless future.

REVISING

Check your preliminary draft, using the checklist on page 920. Also consider the following criteria.
- Read the first sentence of each paragraph. Do these sentences clearly express the points in your argument?
- Do the points seem to flow in a definite direction?
- Is each paragraph adequately developed? Are there unsupported generalizations that need either shoring up or deletion?
- Reread the first and last paragraph. Does the last expand upon the points made in the first?
- Is your tone consistent and convincing?

You will find this article helpful in completing the assignments on pages 36, 300, 345, and 618.

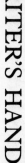

WRITER'S HANDBOOK

Writing Notes and Summaries

Notes and **summaries** are in a sense part of the preparation for writing about literature. They serve as a kind of shorthand for evaluating and selecting materials, for condensing and storing information and ideas. They are ways of learning, for with such writing you attempt to get at the essential, to choose the important and organize it for use later, and to ferret out thoughts and clarify them by putting them into your own words. While summarizing usually serves as a prewriting skill, an assignment such as a book review may request that you briefly summarize a work before you focus on some specific aspect of it.

PREWRITING

Sample Assignments

Summarize the plot of "Harrison Bergeron" in one paragraph.

Summarize William Faulkner's Nobel Address.

1. Think It Through

The following guidelines will help you write your summary.

Be brief. Remember that both note taking and summarizing require you to reduce a narrative or distill ideas down to their bare bones. Imagine that you are writing a telegram and are charged by the word. Decide what information is crucial for your summary and eliminate all superfluous details. If your summary need include only certain aspects of a plot—for example, those that contribute to the irony of the story—hone your material accordingly.

Be complete. Include major events and ideas. Although a summary of "Harrison Bergeron" should not include a detailed description of the handicaps imposed on people, some mention of the handicaps is essential. Likewise, an adequate summary of Faulkner's Nobel Address should note his final optimistic observation that mankind will endure and prevail.

Use the present tense. In summarizing literary works, use the present tense: Harrison *flings* away his heavy handicaps and *dances* with his Empress. Using present tense will help you avoid awkward tense shifts.

2. Take Notes

Note taking is an excellent prewriting tool for even the briefest summary. Before you take notes, have a direction in mind. For a plot summary, list the major events and actions in a narrative. If you are summarizing an entire book, you might write a one-sentence summary as you complete each chapter. Combined with transitional words and phrases, these sentences would form a useful first-draft summary of the whole book. For nonfiction selections such as Faulkner's speech, list major ideas with subordinating ideas underneath them. Keep your notes brief but make them complete enough to be useful. Cite material adequately, so that you do not have to backtrack to fill in information when you begin to write. The following notes can be used to supply information for the two sample assignments.

Harrison Bergeron
Premise of story: 2081—all equal
Main character: Harrison Bergeron
    14-year-old genius
    overhandicapped
    imprisoned and dangerous
Major events:
    Harrison escapes
    declares self Emperor
    rejects handicaps
    takes Empress
    shot dead
    "equality" restored

> *Nobel Address*
> Universal fear: "When will I be blown up?"
> Writers' mission: heart not glands
>   "the problem of the human heart in
>   conflict with itself."
> Faulkner refuses to accept the end of man.
>
> Main idea: Mankind will prevail if inspired
>   by the writer.

WRITING

3. Shape Your Notes into a Summary

Is all the necessary information there? If so, flesh it out into a summary. When you've finished, read it to a classmate who is familiar with the work to see if you have included the high points. You might also read your summary to someone who is not familiar with the work. Then see if that person can reconstruct the plot or restate the main ideas from the information you have supplied.

Note, in addition, that in a work that is satiric or ironic, you should acknowledge the author's purpose or tone since these elements go beyond pure plot summary. Note how the final sentence in the summary of "Harrison Bergeron" below adds information that is essential in understanding the story.

Model: Story Summary

In 2081, everyone is made equal through the use of handicaps that are supervised by agents of the U.S. Handicapper General. Harrison Bergeron, a fourteen-year-old genius who is imprisoned and considered extremely dangerous, has escaped. He appears on television, throws off his heavy handicaps, and declares himself Emperor. As he and his Empress defy gravity in a joyful dance, they are shot dead by the Handicapper General, who quells anarchy and restores society to complete equality. Thus Vonnegut satirizes a society that sacrifices individualism for equality.

Model: Speech Summary

In his Nobel Address (1950), Faulkner identifies a universal physical fear and outlines the mission of the writer in dispelling that fear. With the help of the writer, humanity must overcome its fear of universal destruction and once again confront "the problems of the human heart in conflict with itself." Faulkner insists that writers restore the old universal truths to literature—love, honor, pity, pride, compassion, and sacrifice. Such literature will enable mankind not merely to endure, but to prevail.

REVISING

In addition to reviewing the checklist on page 920, ask yourself these questions:
- Are there any unnecessary words or phrases that can be eliminated?
- In fiction, are the important elements of setting, character identification and character relationships, and plot clear?
- In nonfiction, are the main idea and the author's purpose made clear?
- Are the main points to be covered complete?
- Would the author recognize the plot or ideas?

You will find this article helpful in completing the assignments on pages 596 and 710.

WRITER'S HANDBOOK

Writing About Plot and Plot Devices

The **plot** of a story is usually divided into the following components: *Exposition*—the establishment of the atmosphere, tone, and setting and the supplying of information necessary for the reader to understand the plot. *Sequence of Events*—a set of related happenings. *Conflict*—an interior or exterior struggle involving the main character or characters. *Resolution*—the working out of the conflict. Essay questions dealing with plot may ask you to discuss the plot of a work as a whole or may focus on a single aspect of plot. In any case you will have to understand the whole story or play and its components before responding to the question.

PREWRITING

Sample Assignment

Write a five- or six-paragraph composition about whether or not the role of chance, coincidence, and irony weakens or enhances the plot of "The Cask of Amontillado."

The following tips will help you tackle assignments both on plot and on other aspects of literature.

1. Think It Through

You might find it helpful to refer to Plot in the Handbook of Literary Terms, page 899. Consider the work carefully before committing yourself to a thesis. In this instance, you need to review the events of the story and decide if they are likely or unlikely, natural or contrived.

Here are some obvious points to consider about Poe's story.

- Are the events consistent with the natures of the two characters?
- What examples of chance and coincidence appear?
- Do any of the details of plot seem improbable?
- Does the climax seem natural in view of the types of people involved?
- Is the resolution satisfactory, or do you wish the story had ended differently?
- To what extent is the story suspenseful and by what means is the suspense generated?
- What does irony contribute to the plot?

Make notes on these and other pertinent questions before formulating your opinion.

2. Look for Chains of Cause and Effect

In a well-plotted narrative, even one that relies heavily on coincidence, events do not simply occur; they are *caused*. An action by one character will cause another character to act; that character's action will cause further actions, and so on throughout the entire plot. In skillful hands, such plotting can seem natural and inevitable.

3. Organize Your Material

Here is one way to outline the plot of "The Cask of Amontillado."

Exposition
Montresor's character is established.
Revenge motif is revealed.
Fortunato boasts of wine connoisseurship.
Carnival setting is established.

Sequence of Events
Montresor seeks Fortunato's advice on wines.
The two advance into the catacombs.
Fortunato is fettered and entombed.

Climax
Fortunato realizes he is to die and pleads for mercy.

Resolution
Montresor refuses Fortunato's request.

WRITING

4. Develop Your Thesis Statement

Decide whether or not you think the plot of Poe's story relies too heavily on coincidence and irony or whether these devices serve to enhance the plot. Then formulate your ideas into a thesis statement. If you feel that events in the story are generally believable although a few strain credibility, devise a thesis statement that accommodates your ideas.

Here is an example of the beginning of a paper written to fulfill the assignment on "The Cask of Amontillado."

Model

In "The Cask of Amontillado" the working out of Montresor's murderous revenge is reasonable, given the nature of his character and that of his antagonist, although certain details of plot strain credibility. Once we accept Montresor's self-description in the famous first sentence of the story, we can also accept as plausible the fiendish pleasure he takes in duping and entombing Fortunato. In striving for irony of situation, however, Poe asks us to accept some unlikely plot manipulations.

Montresor explains that his palazzo is empty because he had told his servants that he would be away all night and that they should not stir from the house. This reverse psychology is consonant with other similar examples of situational irony, but one must wonder why he did not simply give the servants the night off and tell them to enjoy the carnival. One might also wonder at Fortunato's gullibility and willingness to be led to his doom, although his drunkenness and pride might account for his eagerness.

Then continue with your analysis, focusing on your specific topic rather than merely presenting a plot summary. For instance, you might explore some of the "unlikely plot manipulations" that "strain credibility," noting items such as the following:

The fact that Montresor's vault does double duty as wine cellar and repository for dead ancestors

The ready availability of building stone and mortar

The handy iron staples complete with chain and padlock

The bodies of Montresor's ancestors being scattered in piles rather than buried

REVISING

When you have completed your first draft, evaluate it by going through the checklist on page 920. Here are some specific points that may be pertinent to consideration of plot.

- Is the connection between story events made clear to the reader?
- Have you correctly identified the climax?
- Do you understand the author's purpose?
- Do you understand how the author achieves that purpose?
- Have you given enough specific examples from the text to support your generalizations?
- Have any unusual aspects of plot structure, such as a frame story or flashbacks, been accounted for?

You will find this article helpful in completing the assignments on pages 428, 494, and 673.

Writing About Characters

Writing about fictional characters involves two rather different processes. You may be asked to describe a character as a human being, covering physical characteristics, personality, actions, motivations, reactions to other characters, and so on. Or, you may be asked to analyze the techniques of characterization a writer uses to create believable characters in a work.

PREWRITING

Sample Assignment

Assignments about characterization may simply ask you to discuss the character traits of a main character or explain how that character changes during the course of a story. Often, you will be asked to compare and contrast one character with another. Still other assignments require you to analyze the author's various methods of characterization.

In a composition of at least five paragraphs directed to a classmate, analyze the character of Carl Tiflin in Steinbeck's story, "The Leader of the People." Note how he is revealed through authorial description, through his own words and actions, and through the observations of others. Finally, explain how this character underscores the personality and maturation of his son, Jody.

1. Think It Through

First review the various techniques of characterization available to writers. As you look back through the story, take notes on the different ways you learn about the characters—descriptions, speeches, actions, and so on. Keep in mind that an author may not use all the methods in one work. As you read, ask yourself the following questions.

What details of physical description are given? Physical appearance may or may not be important to characterization. In Steinbeck's story, Carl Tiflin is first described from Jody's perspective: "For a moment, Carl Tiflin on horseback stood out against the pale sky. . . ." The point of view and imagery are both significant since this description establishes the character as a dominating figure in Jody's life.

What personality traits and feelings are described? Often, an author tells you directly about a character's personality. For example, we are directly told that Carl Tiflin is contemptuous, impatient, and rude. We learn that "it was a terrible thing for him to retract a word" and that in making such a retraction in shame he "was tearing himself to pieces."

What do the character's speech and behavior tell you? These elements are vitally important in understanding characterization. (In a drama, they may be all you have to go on.) Both speech and behavior express the character's thoughts and emotions—unless, of course, the character feels a need to hide his or her real feelings.

Is the character believable? A character may represent an idealized embodiment of humanity, or an Everyman who represents a prototype of mankind, with its flaws and virtues. Is the character stereotypical, like Tom Walker, or a vehicle for expressing an author's ideas, like Goodman Brown? Or is this a three-dimensional, realistic figure, allowed a wide range of human feelings and behavior?

What purpose does the character serve in terms of the work as a whole? Might he or she be a minor character who provides a foil to the main character, highlighting that character's salient qualities by providing similarity or contrast? Might the minor character function as a plot device to provide conflict or to propel events to a climax? Jody's father functions in both of the preceding capacities.

Are the characters' names significant? The name of the title character Granny Weatherall is significant as are those of Mr. Shiftlet and the Craters in "The Life You Save May Be Your Own."

How do the reactions of other characters serve to reveal a character? Mrs. Tiflin's reactions reveal that she is experienced in dealing with her difficult husband. She displays a "flash of anger" and addresses him in a tone "more of threat than of request." She reprimands him for his treatment of Grandfather. "You might be patient with him and pretend to listen." Jody, on the other hand, is embarrassed and made miserable by his father's taunts, responding to his rudeness with "shamed, downcast eyes."

2. Summarize Your Findings

You may by this point have a lot of isolated notes. Take time to organize them carefully—perhaps in a chart like the following one:

Exposition and Description	Character's Speeches
• Carl "insisted on giving permission for anything." • Turns his eyes from his wife's anger; reacts lamely to her reprimands • "It was a terrible thing to him to retract a word."	• Calls Jody "Big-Britches" • "Go on now! Get out!" • Says Jody "got his big nose into everything." • "Your father only talks about one thing." • Speaks irritably
Character's Actions	*Other Characters' Reactions*
• Taunts Jody • Slams door • Turns fiercely • Frowns quickly • "Caught the moth and broke it" • Impatient • Makes sarcastic remarks • Looks at Jody contemptuously	• Mrs. Tiflin asks, "What's the matter with you?" • Flash of anger • Billy tells Jody: "You'd better ask him anyway. You know how he is." • Jody reacts with "shamed, downcast eyes."

3. Analyze the Characterization

Having collected and organized your evidence, you are ready to analyze it. Keep the assignment in mind. Think of how Carl Tiflin affects the theme and plot of this story. For example, how does his cruelty underscore Jody's kindness and growing maturity?

4. Develop Your Thesis Statement

Your thesis statement will help you establish the scope of your paper. In addition, it will help you set up the rest of your essay. Note that the divisions of the chart you made lend themselves to four body paragraphs.

Model

John Steinbeck reveals Carl Tiflin to be a callous, unfeeling person who serves as a foil to his sensitive, maturing son. Tiflin's personality is revealed not only through his own speech and actions, but through authorial description as well as through the reactions of others. Jody, in particular, understands and empathizes with his grandfather's humiliation and tries to smooth over his father's insensitivity with an act of pure generosity and love at the story's conclusion.

Subsequent paragraphs would point to the different methods of characterization employed by the author.

REVISING

Evaluate your first draft, using the checklist on page 920. Also consider these points:
• Does the thesis statement mention the title and author and the points to be considered or the characters to be discussed?
• Are examples from the story included to support the points made?
• Are quotations exact and accurate?

You will find this article helpful in completing the assignments on pages 156, 264, 354, 400, and 648.

WRITER'S HANDBOOK

Writing About Point of View

The author behind every piece of fiction chooses a **point of view,** a perspective from which to tell the story. The author's choice of a narrator determines how the actions and characters are presented. Depending on the point of view, a narrator may be distanced from the events of the plot, or an active participant in the action.

The story may be related by a character in his or her own words (*first-person* point of view) or by a narrator who is not a character and stands anonymously outside the story's action (*third-person* point of view). The third-person point of view may be either *omniscient* (all-knowing), *limited* (confined to one character), or *objective* (a factual, eyewitness account).

PREWRITING
Sample Assignment
Composition assignments about point of view may ask you to show how the author's choice of narrator affects characterization, plot, or theme. Here is one such assignment.

> Write a four-paragraph composition in which you identify the point of view used in "A Worn Path" and explain why it is particularly suitable to the author's purpose.

Here are some points to consider before writing a paper on point of view.

1. Think It Through
In the *first-person* point of view, the narrator, who is a character within the story, uses pronouns such as *I, we,* and *our.* "Marigolds," page 684, is told from the first-person point of view. "A Rescue," page 120, has a *third-person omniscient* narrator who is able to read the minds of all the characters. In "The Jilting of Granny Weatherall," page 430, the narration is limited to the viewpoint of the title character. This is the *third-person limited* point of view. Occasionally, a narrator is like a video camera eye, seeing and hearing everything but making no comment or interpretation. Called the *objective* or *dramatic* point of view, this type of narration appears rather infrequently.

Note any shifts in the point of view. Sometimes the same incident is told from the point of view of more than one character. Be aware of such shifts in narrator and the effect they have on the story.

Decide how point of view affects the following elements.

Theme. How is the theme colored and presented from the vantage point of the narrator? For example, if a story about the Civil War is narrated by a front-line soldier, the theme will probably be different than if it were narrated by a general safely removed from the action. The detached narrator of "An Episode of War," page 387, reinforces the theme that war is impersonal and its destruction is arbitrary.

Characterization. Decide how one character's perceptions filter the information provided about other characters. For example, note how the poetic streak in Dexter of "Winter Dreams," page 438, affects the way other characters are presented.

Plot. Note how the first-person narrator in "The Wooing of Ariadne," page 649, shapes the plot of this story. Note also how involved a reader becomes in the apparently hopeless pursuit of his beloved as a result of hearing Marko tell his own story.

Tone. The objective tone of the narrator in "Harrison Bergeron," page 669, provides a dual atmosphere of humor and irony in a story that could appear tragic from another point of view. Authors choose a narrator who will convey a tone most appropriate to their story.

2. Consider Alternatives
How would the story be changed if a third-person narrator, rather than Marko, had told the story in "The Wooing of Ariadne" or if Harrison

Bergeron were the narrator of *his* story? If you were to write a composition based on the sample assignment in this lesson, you might try to duplicate the thought process that Welty used in choosing the narrator in "A Worn Path." How would the focus have changed with an omniscient narrator? Why would Welty have rejected the possibility of having Phoenix tell her story as a first-person narrator?

WRITING

When writing about point of view, always refer to the *narrator* (or the *speaker*, in poetry) rather than the author. While the author's voice may intrude here and there, readers cannot assume that the narrator's views are the author's.

Here is a composition responding to the sample assignment at the beginning of this lesson.

As Phoenix Sees It

In "A Worn Path," Welty uses the third-person limited point of view to restrict the reader's perceptions to those of the protagonist, Old Phoenix. Through this point of view, the author is best able to achieve her main purpose—the portrayal of an aged, uneducated black woman whose love for her sick grandson enables her to overcome tremendous obstacles during a heroic journey. From the beginning, the reader is absorbed in the old woman's struggle to survive.

The first three paragraphs present a detailed description of Phoenix—her neat-but-humble clothes, her tapping cane, her eyes "blue with age," and her fearless, persistent dialogue with the animals she meets in the thickets. Although at this point readers do not know the purpose of her errand, they are engrossed and sympathetic to the spirited old woman. As the story unfolds, Phoenix's character is further revealed—her determination, her self-mockery, her cunning, and her conscience. Readers see each object portrayed from Phoenix's vantage point, from the flashing nickel dropped by the hunter, to the document nailed on the wall of the clinic—stamped and framed in gold, "which matched the dream that was hung up in her head."

Imagine how Welty came to choose the narrator for this story. Obviously, the inarticulate and sometimes incoherent or speechless Phoenix could not have told her own story as a first-person narrator. An omniscient narrator, on the other hand, would be able to see into the minds of all characters, thus losing the central focus on Phoenix. It required a third-person limited narrator to record her unconscious actions and mutterings, along with all the other details that make her vivid to readers.

When Phoenix finally reaches the clinic in Natchez, we realize that in her mental vagueness she has momentarily forgotten the reason for her journey. In fact, we are not even sure that the grandson is alive. Yet, we delight in her resolve to buy the windmill and wonder, as she slowly descends the stairs, whether this will be her last journey.

REVISING

Evaluate your first draft, using the checklist on page 920. Also consider these questions:
- Have you correctly identified the point of view?
- Do you understand the effect this point of view has on the story?

- Have you referred to the narrator or speaker (not the author)?
- Have you used quotations or specific references to the story to support your statements?

You will find this article helpful in completing the assignments on pages 638 and 816.

WRITER'S HANDBOOK

Writing About Theme

Theme is the underlying meaning in a work of literature. Do not confuse theme, which is often a generalization about life or human nature, with subject or a plot summary. Seldom is a theme stated explicitly; instead it is implied through characterization, setting, symbol, image, and tone. We come to grasp the theme of a work by extracting the central idea of that work. Writing assignments about theme may require you to identify the theme of a literary work, or they may state the theme and ask you to explain how the author has reinforced this theme through particular literary devices.

PREWRITING

Sample Assignment

In Oliver Wendell Holmes's "The Chambered Nautilus," the poet suggests that the soul will outgrow and transcend the mortal body. In a paper of four or five paragraphs, explain to a classmate by what means Holmes establishes and reinforces this theme. Use words and images from the poem to illustrate your observations.

1. Think It Through

Theme differs from subject matter. For example, the subject of Holmes's "The Chambered Nautilus" is a marine creature housed in a spiral shell. The theme, however, is the ability of the soul to outgrow and transcend the mortal body. Likewise, theme is more than a mere plot summary. Welty's "A Worn Path" is about a very old woman who regularly makes a long and difficult journey in order to provide medicine for a child. The theme to be extracted from this story is the power of love to overcome the restraints of old age and physical weakness.

2. Review the Work

Reread the poem and examine it closely. Keep the title in mind, since it is often a clue to theme. Make sure that you understand the words *chambered* and *nautilus*. Refer to a dictionary, your Glossary, or to editorial aids such as the final paragraph on page 139 or the Applying questions on page 141.

Pay particular attention to words and images. Note words and phrases such as *venturous*, *growing*, *shining archway*, and *wings* that suggest an upward movement of the soul toward the spiritual afterlife. In addition, observe images such as "lustrous coil" and "spiral grew" that convey the idea of expansion.

Examine setting, tone, symbolism, and point of view. Elements such as these can be clues to theme. Take note of the interplay of these elements, especially in stories and longer works. Remember that skilled writers adopt a tone and point of view that best conveys a theme. Note, for example, that the humorous tone that Holmes adopts in "The Ballad of the Oysterman" would be inappropriate in this poem about immortality. In discussing theme in "The Chambered Nautilus," one cannot overlook the physical qualities of this sea creature that make it an effective symbol of the human quest for immortality.

3. State the Theme in a Single Declarative Sentence

Do not make it too broad ("People grow spiritually"), too narrow ("Both the body and the nautilus shell become wrecked"), or too unfocused ("Year after year the lustrous coil of the nautilus grows, building 'new temples' and vast new lodgings"). Distill the essence of the theme so that readers can readily identify it. Remember that although the theme is usually implied, it is sometimes stated by the author. "Build thee more stately mansions, O my soul" expresses the essence of Holmes's theme. In cases where the theme is stated in a work, acknowledge such a statement in your essay.

As you analyze the theme of a work, recognize how each element relates to the theme. Look closely at the images created by phrases such as "Wrecked is the ship of pearl" and "sunless crypt" that seem out of keeping with the generally uplifting images in the poem. Determine that such word pictures ultimately connote growth, not destruction. Further, they refer to the outer, temporary housing (body) rather than the immortal "frail tenant" (soul).

Keep in mind that not every work has a theme. Occasionally works are written purely for entertainment. Some mysteries, for example, have no real theme. Other works, such as an informational piece, are to be taken at surface value; that is, they have no underlying meaning. Yet, one of the distinguishing characteristics of good literature is that there is some deeper meaning that can teach us more about life and about ourselves.

4. Organize Your Material

If you use a system of questions to analyze a story, your notes will organize themselves naturally as answers and serve as the basis for the body paragraphs of your paper.

In dealing with longer works such as a novel or play, you will find it helpful to write summaries of each section of the work and establish the thematic contribution of each part. Long works may deal with several themes, which may or may not be connected.

In analyzing the theme of a poem such as "The Chambered Nautilus," you might make a chart to indicate words and phrases that describe both the inhabitant of the nautilus and the soul, and those that describe the shell and the human body.

WRITING

In the sample assignment, the theme has already been identified. The assignment requires an explanation of how this theme is established and reinforced through words and images. Following is an introduction and body paragraph that fulfills the assignment.

Model

Throughout "The Chambered Nautilus," Holmes uses words and images to compare the progress of the human soul to a snail-like creature whose shell expands in a widening spiral. Like the "frail tenant" who inhabits the shell, the soul spirals upward, building "more stately mansions" until, in death, it is finally freed from its body-shell.

Such spiritual expansion is conveyed through words such as *venturous, growing,* and *wings,* and images such as "shining archways," "spiral grew," "lustrous coil," and "dome more vast." Contrasting with images of the soul's growth are those that portray the body's destruction. Verbs such as *wrecked, unsealed,* and *rent* strongly convey the repeated casting off of the body for "each new temple."

REVISING

Use the checklist on page 920 to evaluate your work. In addition, ask yourself the following questions.
• Is the theme stated? If so, have you correctly identified the statement of theme?
• Is the theme implied? If so, have you correctly inferred it?
• Have you supported your thesis statement by referring to literary techniques and devices such as images, symbols, setting, tone, and characterization?
• Have you distinguished theme from mere plot summary or subject?

You will find this article helpful in completing the assignments on pages 72, 393, and 428.

WRITER'S HANDBOOK

Writing to Analyze Author's Style

Style is the distinct way a writer handles language. Occasionally, you will be asked to write about an author's style, or to compare the styles of two authors. Assignments that require you to analyze a writer's style call for more than "I like it" or "It's difficult." In order for you to have some basis for your opinion, you might review Lesson 2, "Developing Your Style." In addition, consider literary devices such as point of view, theme, tone, mood, and symbolism, which are discussed both in the Writer's Handbook and the Handbook of Literary Terms. Most importantly, note the choice of words, the way they are arranged, and the sounds and images they convey.

PREWRITING

Sample Assignment

In a composition of not more than seven paragraphs, show how in "Winter Dreams," the style of the narrator changes from ornately romantic to tersely objective depending on the thing described.

1. Think It Through

Notice how different writers portray the approach of evening.

"The dark came very early." (Hemingway)

". . . While glow the heavens with the last steps of day." (Bryant)

"Later in the afternoon the sun went down with a riotous swirl of gold and varying blues and scarlets, and left the dry, rustling night of western summer." (Fitzgerald)

Which writer relies most heavily on images? Which writer provides a purely literal description? Which writer personifies the departing day? In which description are words inverted from their natural order of subject-verb?

If you are familiar with the works from which these excerpts are taken, you will recognize that Hemingway's spare, unadorned style suits his subject of alienation, while Bryant's lofty formal style portrays God's providence, and Fitzgerald's romantic style aptly conveys his idealistic protagonist's view of the world.

In preparing the assignment on "Winter Dreams," reread the story and make notes. In which descriptions is the narrative voice romantic or poetic? What is the narrator describing when the style loses its embellishments? Your thesis statements will depend on what you decide about the situation in which the different styles appear.

In addition, consider the following elements.

Diction. Note the author's vocabulary. What is the level of the language—plain, difficult, obscure, formal? Does the author use specific, concrete words, or is the language general and abstract? Is language vivid, fresh, or dull, even turgid?

Sentence structure. Are sentences long or short, simple or complex? What can you determine about number, kinds, and placement of modifiers? word order to provide emphasis? use of parallelism to balance thoughts? economy and repetition?

Imagery. Examine words conveying sense impressions—What images dominate? How do these contribute to description, impression, mood? Are some images repeated and to what effect? Is there a pattern of images that can be identified?

Figures of speech. Does the author use simile, metaphor, personification? To what purpose? What makes figures of speech effective or ineffective? Note that the style of many prose writers can be considered poetic. The works of Flannery O'Connor, for example, are characterized by arresting imagery and heavy reliance on figurative language.

Symbols. Do some images or figures take on significance as symbols? If so, are these obvious or subtle? Do they occur singly or repeatedly? To what effect?

Tone. How does tone affect the style? Is the voice serious, satiric, objective, didactic, reportorial, bitter, happy, sad, and so on?

Dialogue. Consider the amount and frequency of dialogue. What makes it natural or artificial? How does it (or does it not) further plot, reflect the characters as individuals, or help distinguish among them?

Sound and rhythm. Read a passage or two aloud. Identify features of sound—alliteration, assonance, onomatopoeia—and words that describe sounds. Determine the pace, the fluency of prose, the rhyme or meter of poetry.

2. Make Some Generalizations

By now you have some labels to identify an author's style. Is it lean or fat? formal or informal? spare or poetic? Is it one that you would like to read more of or imitate? Once you have a feeling for an author's style, you might see if this style is identifiable in another work by him or her.

WRITING

Following are the beginning and ending paragraphs of an essay that responds to the sample assignment.

Model

Narrative Voices in "Winter Dreams"

In "Winter Dreams," Fitzgerald's narrator switches from a richly poetic style to a spare, objective style, depending on the point of view. The first style belongs to Dexter Green. It is used when characters and situations are seen through Dexter's romantic eyes. The second style comes into play when Dexter becomes the subject of discussion rather than the narrator, and when he loses his dreams.

The contrasting styles in the story represent the romanticism of youth and the cynicism of the mature realist. In the end, as Dexter acknowledges the loss of his youthful dreams, there is none of the earlier poetry in his words.

"Long ago," he said, "long ago, there was something in me, but now that thing is gone. Now that this is gone, that thing is gone. I cannot cry. I cannot care. That thing will come back no more."

REVISING

In addition to reviewing the revision checklist on page 920, check your work for the following points:

• Have you avoided mere plot summary?
• Have you adequately illustrated the points in your thesis statement with quotes or specific references to the text?
• Have you pinpointed the major stylistic elements in the story?

You will find this article helpful in completing the assignments on pages 165 and 390.

WRITER'S HANDBOOK

Writing About Poetry and Poetic Devices

Poetry has been called the language of compression. Another definition of poetry is "the best words in the best order." Composition assignments about poetry usually require closer scrutiny of individual words and phrases than do assignments about prose. Assignments on writing about poetry may ask you to analyze an entire poem and explain what makes it work, or they may focus on one or more specific elements of a poem. Sometimes you may be asked to compare how two or more poets use a certain poetic device. Occasionally, you may be asked to write an explication of a poem—that is, a full analysis of all the elements in a poem and how they operate together.

PREWRITING

Sample Assignment

Show how the *connotations* of words chosen by the author of "Richard Cory" support the theme of the poem.

Your task here is twofold. You must provide a precise statement of the theme of the poem. Then you must analyze the connotative force of the language used by Edwin Arlington Robinson and show how individual words and phrases produce specific effects that would be lost or diminished if other choices had been selected. Use the following guidelines to help you complete the sample assignment.

1. Understand the Assignment

In the preceding assignment, you must understand the difference between the denotative meaning and the connotative meaning of words. Both the Handbook of Literary Terms and the Glossary of Literary Terms at the back of this book should help you understand the distinction between these terms. In addition, you must correctly identify the theme: a person's outward show of happiness and success may be an illusion. Broader assignments may ask you to *analyze* or *explicate* the meaning of a poem. In such cases you will have to determine on your own which are the devices to discuss.

2. Read the Poem Closely

A good poem will give more delight in subsequent readings than it does the first time. Images and the full significance of words will become apparent only after close analysis. As you read, ask yourself the following questions.

What is the poem about? Determine the subject and what is being said about the subject.

Who is the speaker? How do I know? The speaker is not the same as the poet. The phrase in line 2, "We people on the pavement," identifies the speaker of "Richard Cory" and establishes a distinction between the regal Cory and the commonfolk who observe him. Sometimes it can be hard to distinguish between persona and poet, for many poems are quite autobiographical, but to be on the safe side use the term *speaker* unless you are discussing the poet's writing techniques. Thus, you might refer to *Robinson's* use of figurative language but *the speaker's* attitude toward Cory.

What is the overall mood, controlling image, or dramatic situation? Robinson's poem is dramatic—the speaker provides a setting and situation, rather like the exposition in a drama. Because this poem is a narrative, it has an outcome. Consider that outcome. In what way is it ironic?

In a lyric poem, you will need to look instead for imagery and the way that one or more images contribute to the mood or to the ideas being expressed.

What can you tell from the diction? Note how phrases such as "clean-favored" and "imperially slim" serve to characterize Richard Cory as an admired person.

3. Examine the Effect of Poetic Devices

The poem is written in four-line iambic pentameter rhymed stanzas that create a sing-song effect. Such meter adds to the ironic effect of the shocking news conveyed at the end of the poem. The images in the poem develop the contrast between the poor townspeople and the elegant title character.

4. Make Notes

For the sample assignment, note words and phrases that contrast the regal Richard Cory with the commonfolk:

Common People	Richard Cory
pavement	gentleman
meat	soul to crown
cursed	clean-favored
bread	imperially slim
	arrayed, glittered
	rich, king, grace

Formulate a thesis statement, based on your lists and other prewriting activities. Then decide how you want to present your ideas.

WRITING

Here are the first two paragraphs of a paper responding to the assignment at the beginning of this article.

Model

"Richard Cory" illustrates the theme that appearances are sometimes deceptive. Thus Cory, well-bred, wealthy, and respected by the "people on the pavement," is in reality a man so miserable that he is driven to suicide. The language chosen to describe Cory reinforces through connotation the sense of his genteel aristocracy, making his final act appear all the more ironic.

Numerous word choices reinforce the elegance and refinement of Cory through connotative suggestion. His first name not only contains the word *rich,* but is also the name of three English kings. The word *gentleman* in line 3 suggests a member of the landed gentry. "*Sole* (echoing *soul*) to crown" is more evocative of grandeur than, for instance, "head to foot." The same can be said for "Clean-favored." Compared to a more commonplace description such as "nice featured," Robinson's choice of words imparts the sense of a character who is not merely handsome but who enjoys special advantages. *Imperially* suggests an emperor and *slim* connotes a positive quality that would not apply to *thin* or *lean.*

REVISING

Evaluate your first draft, using the checklist on page 920. Also consider these questions:

- Have you identified poetic techniques and explained their function?
- Have you avoided unnecessary repetition?
- Have you correctly interpreted the theme of the poem?
- Have you correctly identified the speaker?
- Have you provided reasonable explanations of the poem's meaning and of the connotative force of the words.

You will find this article helpful in completing the assignments on pages 138, 214, 277, and 720.

WRITER'S HANDBOOK

Writing About Drama

Drama shares many characteristics with other genres such as narrative poems, short stories, and novels; each literary form presents characters in a dramatic situation in which events in a plot build toward a climax and are eventually resolved. Yet, because it is meant to be acted, drama differs in some respects from these other literary forms. It relies more heavily on dialogue; it depends upon stage conventions, or devices that represent reality; it focuses on and telescopes a part of action that will "play well" for the audience; it uses stage directions for exposition and description; it derives its effect from shifts in pace and tone from confrontations between characters to engross the audience. Writing assignments may ask you to concentrate on any of these elements.

PREWRITING

Assignments that require you to write about drama may ask you to analyze a particular character or, more likely, to describe the relationships and dynamics among characters. Other assignments may ask you to write about the total effect of the plot or to concentrate on one or more of the elements of plot—exposition, conflict, rising action, climax, falling action, and resolution. Still other assignments may require that you analyze the function of stage conventions such as soliloquies or asides, the use of lighting or curtains, or scenery.

Sample Assignment

Discuss how each character in *The Glass Menagerie* serves as a foil to another character in the play. Then observe how these contrasts supply dramatic tension in the play.

1. Think It Through

Quickly review the play mentally, grouping characters into contrasting pairs according to dominant characteristics. For example, Amanda and Jim, although different, do not function as foils; Amanda and Laura, however, have contrasting personalities that supply dramatic tension in the play. Jim and Tom serve likewise as foils. As you think through other aspects of the play, ask yourself the following questions.

What information is supplied by the stage directions? Remember that stage directions present the exposition in a play. Early in *The Glass Menagerie*, for example, stage directions establish the grim tenement setting, as well as intro- duce props such as the whatnot that holds Laura's glass objects and the photograph of the absent Mr. Wingfield. Stage directions likewise provide clues about how readers should regard a scene. For example, readers are told that the scene between Laura and Jim is "apparently unimportant" to him, although to her it is "the climax of her secret life."

What tone and gestures would characters use in speaking their lines? Because you often will read a play rather than see it acted, you must interpret tone yourself. Appoint yourself director of the play. Taking your cues from the dialogue and stage directions, what tones, gestures, and body language would you instruct your actors to use in the various scenes?

What changes occur in the sets, lighting, or music? These changes may often indicate new emphases, the passage of time, or changes in the characters or situations—information that would be easily related by the narrator in a story but have to be presented dramatically in a play. Note how Tom is clothed when he acts as narrator.

What is the function of dramatic conventions? Anyone who reads a play must accept certain dramatic conventions—the various devices that the audience accepts as reality. The most basic substitutions for reality in a play, of course, are the use of actors to represent real characters and props to suggest actual settings—for example, a black ribbon to represent a road or a suspended gold disk to suggest the sun. Gauze curtains, unreal lighting, and haunting music, along with the highlighted portrait of Mr. Wingfield, all serve as conventions.

What is the theme or overall significance of the play? The dominant theme in *The Glass Menagerie* is illusion versus reality. Once you establish the theme in a play, you can determine how characters, setting, and mood serve to reinforce this theme.

By what means does the playwright heighten dramatic impact? Williams creates tension by highlighting the contrasting personalities of characters. The sample assignment capitalizes on how each character functions as a foil to another character.

2. Organize Your Thoughts

As you answered the preceding questions, you probably noted bits of information. Now it's time to organize your notes in preparation for writing. A chart such as the following might be helpful.

CONTRASTING CHARACTERS	
Amanda domineering, flirtatious practical tough-minded	*Laura* painfully shy impractical fragile

Tom
romantic
introverted
aspires to be a
   poet
pessimistic
	Jim
	realistic
	extroverted
	aspires to be an
	   executive
	optimistic

You might expand on this chart. For example, Jim and Laura provide interesting contrasts, especially in the romantic scene.

3. Develop Your Thesis Statement

Review your notes once again and devise a thesis statement that fulfills the sample assignment.

WRITING

Following is the first paragraph in an essay that responds to the sample assignment.

Model

Characters in *The Glass Menagerie* are pitted against each other as foils in order to heighten dramatic effect and to reveal their distinguishing attributes. Amanda doggedly strives to mold Tom and Laura into the children of her dreams, and they, just as persistently, rebuff her efforts to transform them. Laura—painfully shy, impractical, and fragile—escapes the manipulations of her realistic, tough-minded mother by retreating into her world of fantasy. Tom becomes a merchant sailor in his effort to escape his family, yet he is pulled back to his family by his irrevocable memories.

REVISING

Evaluate your first draft, using the checklist on page 920. Also consider these questions:
- Have you correctly identified the tone of the speakers?
- Have you analyzed the work as a drama, noting areas of tension created by the playwright?
- Have you quoted accurately?

You will find this article helpful in completing the assignments on page 596.

WRITER'S HANDBOOK

Writing About Mood or Tone

Mood is the overall atmosphere of a literary work. It is created by the choice of setting, objects, details, images, and the sounds and connotations of words. Mood, which may be described with words such as *peaceful* or *eerie,* is the effect that a reader carries away from a work. **Tone** is the author's attitude toward his or her subject and audience. The voice of the writer determines tone, which can vary from straightforward to ironic. Although mood and tone are related, they should not be confused. For example, the mood of "The Cask of Amontillado" is one of horror, although the tone is coldly matter-of-fact. Writing assignments may ask you to identify and analyze the mood or the tone of a work and to explain how it contributes to the overall meaning.

PREWRITING

Sample Assignments

In a paragraph directed to someone who has read the poem, identify the mood in Jim Wayne Miller's "A House of Readers," discussing the images and choice of words that contribute to this mood.

Describe in several paragraphs for a classmate the tone of Elizabeth Cady Stanton's "Speech to the First Women's Rights Convention." Note the word choice, the use of imagery and figurative language, and the audience to whom this speech is directed, along with the speaker's purpose. In addition, note any shifts in tone and the effect such shifts are designed to achieve.

1. Think It Through

Mood can be described by any number of terms that run the spectrum from *light* and *playful* to *somber* or *tragic.* Tone can generally be described by those same words, but also by terms like *objective* or *emotional, optimistic* or *pessimistic, formal* or *informal, ironic, satiric, cynical,* or *bitter.* To gain a sense of mood or tone, read the work holistically—to get a feeling for the whole—before attempting any close analysis. Ask yourself the following questions.

Does any of the above descriptive words come to mind as you read? If so, it is a good candidate for the descriptive word you want. Trust your instincts. Just as you can usually tell when someone in conversation is being sarcastic, dryly humorous, and so on, you can often sense the same thing in writing.

Does the work maintain the same mood or tone throughout? If not, try to define the shifting moods or tones. See if you can spot at what points these shifts occur. This will help you figure out the reasons for them.

Does the author use irony, hyperbole, understatement, or satire? The identification of such techniques is essential in determining the tone of a work. Recognizing that a work has satiric or ironic elements may help you understand passages that otherwise seem puzzling or even outrageous. A reader who fails to recognize the irony in "The Cask of Amontillado" when Montresor drinks to Fortunato's health will probably misread the entire work.

What does the tone or mood add to your understanding of the work? Depending upon the type of writing, tone or mood can be either vital to comprehension, or relatively unimportant and practically unnoticeable. If either tone or mood is particularly prominent, consider it important.

2. Gather Your Evidence

While all the elements in a work may help produce a certain effect, pay attention to the author's diction—particularly to the use of connotative language or "loaded" words. Vivid imagery and figurative language contribute significantly to mood, as well.

You might organize information for the assignment on mood into a chart such as the one on the following page. A similar chart, a list, or a cluster could be constructed for the assignment on tone.

IMAGES OF SIGHT
tendril growing toward the sun
wedge of light
butterfly
cool as a Black Angus belly-deep
   in a farm pond
farmer in the rows

IMAGES OF SOUND
pages turning softly
quietness of bottomland
young corn growing
little breeze stirs the blades

FIGURATIVE LANGUAGE
similes (lines 3, 5, 8, 15)
metaphor (lines 11,12)
hyperbole (line 2)
metonymy (line 7)

CONNOTATIVE WORDS
growing
tendril
light
magic
breathes

WRITING

Now put your information together in a paragraph that addresses itself to the assignment. Remember that you are asked both to identify and to illustrate with examples the mood of this poem.

Model

Jim Wayne Miller establishes a mood of peaceful growth in "A House of Readers" by using images from nature, often those from a quiet rural setting. Images of growth abound —the reaching tendril, the thriving bottomland, the growing corn. Significantly, the month is May—the season of new beginnings of life. The children, metaphorically portrayed as "young corn growing," thrive in their intellectual environment, as their father, "like a farmer in the rows," notes their progress. The poem is rich with connotative words such as *growing, tendril, light,* and *breathes* that convey a sense of vitality and enlightenment. In addition, words such as *concentrating, softly,* and *quietness* convey a sense of peace and well-being in this pursuit by "A House of Readers."

If you chose to write about the assignment on tone, you might consider constructing a chart that answers questions such as these: How does Stanton use both anecdote and figurative language to make her case for women's rights? Can we gather that her audience was supportive or antagonistic? What is her tone at the beginning of her speech? during the remainder of her speech? How do you account for this change in tone? What is the speaker's purpose? How does her word choice reflect this purpose?

REVISING

As you evaluate your first draft, consider whether or not you have managed to be specific about a topic that may in itself be vague. Use the checklist on page 920. In addition, ask yourself these questions:

- Are quotations well chosen to demonstrate specific points?
- Are quotations accurate?
- Do any sections tend to ramble or to repeat the same thing in different words?
- Are quotations and other examples explained in terms of significance or application to your thesis?
- Have you accurately distinguished between mood and tone?

You will find this article helpful in completing the assignments on pages 735 and 784.

WRITER'S HANDBOOK

Writing About Irony

Irony is a contrast between what appears to be and what actually is. It is this contrast that gives certain works an added dimension and requires a reader to look beyond surface meanings. Composition assignments dealing with irony may ask you to identify and explain an ironic statement or situation, to analyze an author's use of irony, or to point out how irony contributes to overall meaning. In any event, as you identify and analyze irony, you must correctly interpret the author's tone, especially when the irony is subtle or present in only part of a work.

PREWRITING

Sample Assignment

In five or six paragraphs, discuss verbal, dramatic, and situational irony in "The Cask of Amontillado." Defend the observation that the compounding of ironies is the single effect that Poe was seeking.

1. Think It Through

Determine what type of irony is used in a work. In *verbal irony*, words imply the opposite of what they literally mean. *Irony of situation* presents a state of affairs that is the opposite of what is expected. *Dramatic irony* occurs when the reader or viewer knows more than the characters do. Occasionally a work may contain several different kinds of irony.

Read the work closely. Be aware and wary in your search for irony. As you read, use the following questions to direct you.

What evidence of irony can you find? Look especially for statements that don't seem to say what they really mean or for unexpected twists in the plot. Humorous works often have an ironic tone. In a work such as "Harrison Bergeron," when the overall effect is different from what might be suggested by a plot summary, you can expect the use of irony.

Is the irony subtle or obvious? Readers have been known to miss the use of irony in a work, thereby misunderstanding that work completely. You may not, in fact, be able to pinpoint just where an author is being ironic, or just what devices are being used to achieve irony. Your feeling about the overall effect of a work may be all you have to go on. Occasionally, you will finish reading a story before you know it is iron-ic. In such cases, once you have come to the end, backtrack as you would in a mystery story, looking for clues that suggest irony.

What is the overall tone of an ironic work? Irony may serve to convey the total effect and prevailing tone in a work, such as "The Cask of Amontillado," or it may be just one of several tones. It may be used to supply a surprise or shocking ending, as in the case of "Richard Cory," or provide gentle mockery, as in Twain's description of his youthful companions in *Life on the Mississippi.*

How is irony conveyed? An author may achieve irony through hyperbole, paradox, understatement, or satire. Mention of George Bergeron's ear radio, which emits noises that resemble at times "somebody hitting a milk bottle with a ball peen hammer," as a "little mental handicap" is an example of understatement.

How does irony fulfill the author's purpose? In "Harrison Bergeron," Vonnegut uses irony as a satiric tool. The ironic failure of Hazel and George Bergeron to lament the death of their son Harrison underscores the terrible effects of government-imposed equality. In *The Glass Menagerie,* irony heightens dramatic tension, as when Tom challenges his mother with the words, "I could tell you things to make you sleepless," and continues with a litany of preposterous escapades, including visits to opium dens and the underworld. In this play when the blackout at dinner occurs, we (but not Amanda) know that Tom has used the money for the electric light bill to pay dues to join the Union of Merchant Seamen. Such irony of situation is particularly effective in a play.

2. Organize Your Thoughts

Refer to the original assignment to be sure that you are addressing yourself to it. In the sample assignment for "The Cask of Amontillado," you would reread the directions, noting the points you have been asked to make, especially the words *discuss* and *defend*. Remember that the assignment is twofold: to identify the types of irony in the story and to establish convincingly that irony is the single effect of the story. You might organize your ideas by making a chart to categorize the three kinds of irony in the story.

Here is an abbreviated version of such a chart.

VERBAL IRONY
Montresor's remarks:
"I will not impose upon your good nature."
"Your health is precious."
"Come, we will go back ere it is too late."
"I cannot be responsible."
"In pace requiescat."

Fortunato's remarks:
"I shall not die of a cough."
"A very good joke indeed."

IRONY OF SITUATION
Montresor drinks to Fortunato's long life.
Carnival season setting
Fortunato's name and costume
Montresor's coat of arms

DRAMATIC IRONY
Montresor announces his plans to reader, but Fortunato is unaware of his fate.

---

3. Formulate and Test Your Thesis

Now use your ideas and the chart to devise a thesis statement that addresses the assignment. Ask a peer or classmate who is familiar with the selection if you have missed any important points on your chart or have failed to cover the requirements of the assignment in your thesis statement.

WRITING

Notice how the following opening paragraph addresses itself to the assignment. The body paragraphs would probably focus on and develop the three kinds of irony in the story.

Model

Like Poe's other works, "The Cask of Amontillado" is designed to achieve a single effect: in this case, the accumulation of every kind of irony. All types of irony pervade this work, but the most frequently used are verbal (Montresor constantly inquires after Fortunato's health and well being) and situational (the carnival setting provides a festive backdrop for a story of murder). The ironic premise is, of course, essentially dramatic, since readers learn Montresor's plans immediately, while Fortunato remains unaware of his fate until the very end of the narrative. The prevalence and layers of irony have a cumulative effect of horror since nothing really is what it seems to be.

REVISING

Evaluate your first draft, using the checklist on page 920. Also consider these points:
- Is each example given in its context?
- Is each quotation explained as to meaning and function?
- Have examples been identified as to literary device—hyperbole, paradox, and so on—whenever possible?
- Have you correctly identified the types of irony in the selection?

You will find this article helpful in completing the composition assignments on pages 156 and 673.

WRITER'S HANDBOOK

Writing About Symbolism

Interpreting **symbolism** requires you to look beyond the surface of a work to identify something that represents something else. A symbol is a relatively concrete object, action, character, scene, and so on that takes on another dimension of meaning. This meaning will be generally abstract—a concept or idea that goes beyond the literal statement on the page. In order to arrive at the symbolic meaning in a work, you must be a sensitive reader who is able to follow the writer's intent in using words and images as representational devices.

PREWRITING

Some assignments on writing about symbolism may tell you what symbol to look for and ask you to interpret it. Other assignments may ask you to decide whether an item is symbolic or not. In either case, you will have to document your ideas with evidence.

Sample Assignment

In several paragraphs, explain what is symbolized by the flower in Jean Toomer's poem "November Cotton Flower." In your essay, explain how Toomer's imagery in the octave and the sestet of his sonnet serves to highlight this symbolism.

1. Read the Work Closely

As you read and reread the work, consider whether images or word combinations are stressed or repeated—or perhaps stand out as being unique or unusual. Consider also whether any character in a work (or the speaker in a poem) seems to feel particular significance in an object, action, and so on. If so, the object may or may not carry the same symbolic meaning for the reader. As you read, ask yourself the following questions.

What clues suggest that there is indeed a symbol? Distinguish between images and objects, and items that function as symbols. Remember, first of all, that a symbol must have significance beyond itself. Look for items that are repeated, such as the corn that is mentioned in "Sophistication." Does an item such as the forest in "Young Goodman Brown" receive special emphasis? Sometimes a symbolic item such as the glass menagerie is incorporated into the title

of a work. Sometimes several symbols may be developed in a single work.

What does the symbol represent? Keep in mind that because a symbol can be an object, action, character—or something else—it will always be something relatively concrete. Determine what the symbol represents: an abstraction or a whole complex of associations. In some cases, you may want to offer more than one interpretation of a symbol, showing the relative strengths and weaknesses of each interpretation.

Is this a universal symbol, or one that is particular to the specific work? Some symbols are based on traditional associations—a dove for peace or a skull for death. Others, such as the unicorn in *The Glass Menagerie*, function in the context of a work. Keep in mind that an author may use a traditional symbol, but give it a new twist, one that you should take into account in examining a particular work.

How does the symbolic meaning extend through the rest of the work? The symbol may form the entire framework of a selection, or it may merely highlight some aspect of a subject.

2. Organize Your Thoughts

Any or all of the above questions may apply to the work you are analyzing. The most important thing about symbols is the way in which their meanings add depth and complexity to a work. By this time, you should have established how an item functions as a symbol. Now, organize your supporting evidence into a structure that will form your essay. Given the sample assignment, notes might be organized according to the octave and the sestet of Toomer's poem. Following is a sample list.

WRITER'S HANDBOOK

OCTAVE	SESTET

boll-weevil
winter cold
rusty stalks
seasons old
cotton scarce
branch—pinched,
   slow
drouth
dead birds
	folks startled
	flower "assumed/
	  Significance"
	  new insight: love,
	   no trace of fear
	sudden beauty

Generalization: Images of death and cold in octave give way to images of beauty and love in sestet.

WRITING

Devise a thesis statement that immediately establishes the identity of the symbol you will discuss and tell what it signifies. The rest of your essay will develop the meaning of the symbol, using textual evidence that explains how you arrived at this meaning.

In the example that follows, note how the thesis is stated generally, with subsequent paragraphs devoted to the images portrayed in the octave and the sestet of this sonnet.

Model

The blooming of the November cotton flower in Toomer's poem symbolizes a renewal of faith among the people during a bleak season. The images of death and cold projected in the octave give way to those of beauty and love in the sestet, as the cotton flower is introduced.

Words and images in the octave convey a mood of sterility and despair. Negative connotations resonate in the first eight lines: the boll-weevil, winter cold, rusty stalks, old seasons, scarce cotton, pinched, slow branches, drouth, and dead birds. The season—November—represents the death of the year, a time when there is no growth.

The mood shifts at line nine, which introduces the sestet and the cotton flower. The word *startled* conveys the change in mood. The blooming flower "assumed/ Significance," bringing with it a new insight, something "never seen before." Once again there is love, "without a trace of fear." The beauty of the flower is "sudden" and unexpected. The image of startling life and beauty amid death signals hope. Thus, the cotton flower represents a dual symbol—both within the poem and within the larger context of humanity, serving to inspire hope and the promise of rebirth to a once-despairing people.

REVISING

Symbolic meanings can be complex, but that doesn't mean that your analysis should become so complex that it is difficult for a reader to follow. Have a classmate evaluate your first draft for clarity; then go over it yourself, using the checklist on page 920. Also consider these points:
- Is the straightforward, literal meaning of the symbol presented, as well as the symbolic meaning?
- Is there a demonstration of how the symbolic meaning reflects on the meaning of the work as a whole?

You will find this article helpful in completing the assignments on pages 309 and 618.

WRITER'S HANDBOOK

Writing About a Period or Trend

History, as it is lived, does not divide itself neatly into periods; yet, with the advantage of retrospect, we often can classify people, events, and works of art according to certain shared characteristics. The units in this book represent such classification. Assignments on writing about a literary period may ask you to describe a literary trend (fashion; style; vogue) and choose writings to exemplify it. Or, you may be asked to trace the evolution of a trend, showing what caused it and how it progressed to a final stage or culmination. At other times, you may be given several authors or works and asked to observe a trend—to find and define features common to the works and to give a name to their commonality.

PREWRITING

Sample Assignment

Unit 4 in *The United States in Literature* is titled "Variations and Departures." Choose one author whose works appear in this unit and explain how his or her works constitute a variation and a departure from those works of earlier units. In answering, consider both the form and content of that author's works.

1. Think It Through

Such an assignment requires not only that you are familiar with the selections in Unit 4 but also that you recognize how they differ from works in previous units. The unit time line, Background, authors' biographies, and Reader's Notes and Comments will be invaluable here. As you review these materials, ask yourself the following questions.

What are the most important characteristics of the literary period? List these characteristics as you encounter them. From the Background and authors' biographies you will note that some of these characteristics are a spirit of freedom and expansion; the use of simple, direct language in poetry; the introduction of new verse forms such as free verse; the consideration of new subjects such as working-class America, democracy, individualism, and the Frontier; and so on. Any one, or a combination, of these features might serve as the subject for a composition.

Are causes and effects important? Any information you can glean about what prompted an author to write about a certain subject or why that author wrote in a certain form or style might be useful. You may or may not be able to use the information in your paper, but at the least it will contribute to your own general understanding of the period or trend.

Is biographical information significant? Note, for example, in Whitman's biography that some readers considered his poetry crude or gross. Others, among them Emerson and Thoreau, admired his "revolutionary verse." One can infer that Whitman's innovations in verse form, language, and subject matter, although controversial, were widely recognized and accepted by at least some traditional writers.

What information on the time line can be helpful in supporting your thesis? A quick review of items on the time line reveals that the historical period itself was one of "variations and departures." Note the inventions and discoveries, the improved channels of communication, the "firsts" that make this period unique. Think about how such events and trends might affect the literature of the period. Remember that writers and literary trends do not exist in a vacuum but rather are part of a historical and cultural context. Note also the art that appears beneath the time line. Do the objects and people portrayed provide insights into the period or serve to influence certain literary trends?

Do any selections in a unit seem more in keeping with those of previous periods? Remember that some writers are more experimental than others. A writer such as Edwin Arlington Robinson uses traditional verse forms and rhymes, while Twain harks back to the tall tales used by his literary predecessors. Keep in mind that every literary period encompasses a variety of styles and subjects and that even the most radical writers borrow from earlier literature.

Does the author's tone reflect an attitude about the period? Pay particular note to the author's tone—whether it is satiric, skeptical, optimistic, or supportive of current ideas and trends. For example, Thoreau is extremely critical of government policies in midnineteenth-century America.

2. Gather Your Evidence

The assignment asks you to consider literary works—not the authors' lives or other cultural influences. Turn now to the selections in Unit 4 and review them, looking for the selections that provide the best examples of the characteristics you consider "variations and departures." Try to find at least one example for each characteristic.

3. Organize Your Thoughts

Because you are dealing with a generalization (the period or trend) and with specific examples that support that generalization, it will pay you to plan your paper carefully. Use your first paragraph or your thesis statement to limit the scope of your paper. The assignment itself may suggest an organizational pattern. For example, your first paragraph might give an overall view of one poet's innovations, with subsequent body paragraphs focusing on each of the following areas of change: form, language, and subject matter.

WRITING

Note how the following introductory paragraph establishes the thesis and sets up the rest of the essay.

Model

Walt Whitman, who defied traditional verse forms and turned to new language and subject matter in his poetry, can truly be called the first modern poet. No poet before him had used free verse so effectively to capture the speech rhythms of the American language. Nor had any American poet relied so completely on the simple, direct language of common people, sprinkling verse with idiom and slang. Whitman introduced new subjects into his poems, celebrating democracy, individualism, and working people. His exuberant, breathless lines seem appropriate for conveying the emerging spirit of America.

REVISING

Evaluate your first draft, using the checklist on page 920. Also consider these questions:
- Have you identified major characteristics of the period or trend that you are describing?
- Can certain points be combined?
- Are paragraphs parallel and equal? Do they discuss elements that are of approximately equal weight?
- Are quotation marks used to provide examples of observations?
- Are titles and authors' names spelled correctly? Are titles indicated by underlining (for complete works) or quotation marks (for individual poems and shorter works)?

You will find this article helpful in completing the assignments on pages 11, 42, 56, and 300.

WRITER'S HANDBOOK

Writing About Nonfiction

The **nonfiction** you will read and write about includes essays, historical narratives, biography, autobiography, speeches, and formal published letters. Unlike fiction, in which characters and plot devices are created, nonfiction deals with real characters and events. Often, when you are asked to write about nonfiction, you will be expected to analyze the ideas expressed and to evaluate the truth or validity of a work, determining which parts express the writer's opinions and personal feelings. In such an analysis, you must establish the author's main idea, purpose, tone, and audience, as well as the method of organization and reasons for inclusion (or omission) of particular details.

PREWRITING

Sample Assignment

In an essay of four or five paragraphs, to be read by your teacher, discuss how Roger Rosenblatt's essay, "The Man in the Water," differs from an objective news account. Consider the following elements as you review the selection: the author's inclusion of opinions and personal feelings, the main idea, the selection and presentation of details, the tone, and the author's purpose.

1. Review the Work

Reread the selection, noting details that will fulfill the assignment and help you devise a thesis statement. As you read, ask yourself the following questions.

What is the author's purpose? Much fiction is written primarily to entertain, but nonfiction may have a variety of purposes, including to inform, persuade, or to preserve thoughts and experiences. To identify the author's purpose, it may help to consider the audience the author was writing for.

How is the author's purpose reflected in the structure and development of the work? Purpose can shape both choice of subject and method of organization. Different methods of organization include the following: (1) an illustration or explanation, followed by supporting details or examples; (2) an analysis of causes and effects; (3) an account of events in chronological order; (4) a comparison or contrast.

In "What the Black Man Wants," page 266, Douglass argues for "immediate, unconditional, and universal" enfranchisement of the black man. His case is carefully constructed, as he anticipates and answers his opponents' arguments even before they are voiced.

Determine the author's tone. Be sure you know whether the author is serious or humorous. Note any shifts in tone: an ironic statement in an otherwise humorous piece, a serious note in a comical sketch, or a sustained tone of irony or satire that negates the whole surface meaning of the work.

Which elements of the author's style are most apparent? Generally, nonfiction style will be straightforward, but great differences are still possible. Consider, for example, the differences between Thoreau's style in *Civil Disobedience* and Least Heat Moon's in *Blue Highways*. Here, the styles are influenced by the subjects and the historical periods, as well as by the authors' personalities.

What are the main ideas put forth? An assignment may ask you to analyze ideas and the arguments used to support them or to respond to the ideas with your own ideas. In either case, be sure you can identify the main idea and understand other ideas and details that support it.

2. Assemble Your Information

Make lists, notes, clusters, or diagrams to assemble and organize your information. As you gather information, keep in mind what the assignment asks you to do. In fulfilling the sample assignment, which requires a writer to differentiate between Rosenblatt's essay and a news story, you might compare and contrast in lists like those on the following page.

News Story	Rosenblatt's Essay
objective tone	personal tone
sticks to facts	expresses opinions
straight, chrono-	presents events in
logical narrative	a sequence that
	builds emotion
	and drama
presents a story	conveys a main idea
purpose: to inform	purpose: to instruct
style: direct and	style: literary and
free from figurative	uses images and
language	figurative language
gives names	man is anonymous
dwells on the	dwells on universals
particular	

WRITING

3. Develop a Thesis Statement

The sample assignment should help shape the thesis statement. Make sure the thesis statement encompasses the thrust of your essay. Refer to your notes, lists, or charts as you develop your composition.

The model that follows shows an initial paragraph that responds to the assignment.

Model

In "The Man in the Water," Rosenblatt goes beyond objective news reportage to express not one man's actions, but the courage that represents the best instincts of modern mankind. The fact that the man is anonymous adds to his image as Everyman, who throws a lifeline not only to those he saved but to all who have been inspired by his heroic act. Unlike news reporters who use facts to inform, Rosenblatt offers symbols that serve to teach humanity about its nobler side.

REVISING

Evaluate your first draft, using the checklist on page 920. Then consider these questions:
• Does the thesis statement express the main focus of your essay?
• Have you established the author's purpose?
• Have you identified the main idea of the piece?
• Does the author's tone and organization of material reinforce the main idea?
• Has the author used a writing style that appropriately conveys his or her ideas?
• Have you presented the author's ideas fairly, without taking them out of context?

You will find this article helpful in completing the assignments on pages 753 and 774.

WRITER'S HANDBOOK

GLOSSARY OF LITERARY TERMS

Words within entries in SMALL CAPITAL LETTERS refer to other entries in the Glossary of Literary Terms. Numbers after the titles of examples refer to pages in the text where these selections can be found. Some entries are followed by a cross-reference to the Handbook of Literary Terms, where a more detailed explanation may be found.

allegory (al′ə gôr′ē), a NARRATIVE, either in verse or prose, in which characters, action, and sometimes SETTING represent abstract concepts apart from the literal meaning of a story. The underlying meaning usually has moral, social, religious, or political significance, and the characters are often PERSONIFICATIONS of abstract ideas such as charity, hope, greed, and so on. Though more clearly based in reality than such classic English allegories as John Bunyan's *Pilgrim's Progress*, "Young Goodman Brown," page 237, is sometimes viewed as an allegory (or as having an allegorical level of meaning) as are some other works by Hawthorne.

alliteration (ə lit′ə rā′shən), the repetition of consonant sounds at the beginnings of words or within words, particularly in accented syllables. It can be used to reinforce meaning, unify thought, or create a musical effect. (See also page 909.)

Sinuous southward and sinuous northward
   the shimmering band
Of the sand-beach fastens the fringe of
   the marsh to the folds of the land.
       Lanier, "The Marshes of Glynn"

allusion (ə lü′zhən), a brief reference to a person, event, or place, real or fictitious, or to a work of art. In T. S. Eliot's "The Love Song of J. Alfred Prufrock," page 526, lines 94–95, there is a biblical allusion to Lazarus, the brother of Mary and Martha, whom Jesus raised from the dead. (See also page 878.)

analogy (ə nal′ə jē), a literal comparison made between two items, situations, or ideas that are somewhat alike but unlike in most respects. Frequently an unfamiliar or complex object or idea will be compared to a familiar or simpler one in order to explain the first. Edward Taylor's "Huswifery," page 67, compares cloth making to salvation. (See also page 879.)

anapest (an′ə pest), a three-syllable metrical FOOT consisting of two unaccented syllables followed by an accented syllable, as in the word *buccaneer*. In the following line, the feet are divided by slashes, and since there are four feet, the line can be described as anapestic TETRAMETER.

For the moón / never beáms, / without bring/
ing me dreáms . . .
       Poe, "Annabel Lee," page 172

anastrophe (ə nas′trə fē), inversion of the usual order of the parts of a sentence, primarily for emphasis or to achieve a certain rhythm or rhyme. Oliver Wendell Holmes's line "Wrecked is the ship of pearl," page 140, is a reversal or inversion of the normal order of subject-verb-object (complement), "The ship of pearl is wrecked." (See also page 880.)

antagonist (an tag′ə nist), a character in a story or play who opposes the chief character or PROTAGONIST. In "The Devil and Tom Walker," page 110, the devil is the antagonist. (See also page 901.)

aphorism (af′ə riz′əm) (See MAXIM.)

apostrophe (ə pos′trə fē), a figure of speech in which an absent person, an abstract concept, or an inanimate object is directly addressed. Poe's line "Helen, thy beauty is to me . . ." is an example of the first ("To Helen," page 174); Holmes's line "Build thee more stately mansions, O my soul . . ." is an example of the second ("The Chambered Nautilus," page 140); and "O Shenandoah, I long to hear you" (page 340) an example of the third. (See also page 887.)

assonance (as′n əns), the repetition of similar vowel sounds followed by different consonant sounds in stressed syllables or words. It is used instead of RHYME. *Fade* and *stayed* are examples of rhyme; *fade* and *pale*, examples of assonance. In Poe's "And so, all the night-tide, I lie down by the side . . ." the words *night* and *tide* are assonant. ("Annabel Lee," page 172.) (See also page 909.)

atmosphere, the MOOD of a literary work. An author establishes atmosphere partly through description of SETTING and partly by the objects chosen to be described. For example, in the first three paragraphs of "An Occurrence at Owl Creek Bridge," page 356, Bierce creates an atmosphere of foreboding. (See also page 897.)

autobiography (See BIOGRAPHY.)

ballad, a NARRATIVE of unknown authorship passed on in the oral tradition. It often makes use of repetition and DIALOGUE. "El Corrido de Gregorio Cortez," page 341, and "The Ballad of the Oysterman," page 142, are ballads. A ballad whose author is known is called a literary ballad.

ballad stanza, a STANZA usually consisting of four alternating lines of IAMBIC TETRAMETER and TRIMETER and rhyming the second and fourth lines.

> We cross the prairie as of old
>   The Pilgrims crossed the sea,
> To make the West, as they the East,
>   The homestead of the free.
>   Whittier, "The Kansas Emigrants"

biography, an account of a person's life. (See Carr's *The Lonely Hunter*; page 748.) Autobiography is the story of all or part of a person's life written by the person who lived it. (See Hansberry's "To Be Young, Gifted and Black," page 770.)

blank verse, unrhymed IAMBIC (⌣ ′) PENTAMETER, a line of five feet. (See the first four lines of "Birches," page 510.)

brag, a wildly exaggerated boasting speech, usually associated with frontiersmen like Mike Fink, page 281.

cacophony (kə kof′ə nē), a succession of harsh, discordant sounds in either poetry or prose, used to achieve a specific effect. Note the harsh, somewhat explosive sounds in these lines:

> Too much horrified to speak,
> They can only shriek, shriek,
>   Out of tune,
> In a clamorous appealing to the mercy of the fire,
> In a mad expostulation with the deaf and frantic
>   fire. . . .
>   Poe, "The Bells"

caesura (si zhùr′ə, si zyùr′ə), a pause in a line of verse, usually dictated by the sense of the line and often greater than a normal pause. For purposes of study, the mark indicating a caesura is two short vertical lines (‖). A caesura can be indicated by punctuation, the grammatical construction of a sentence, or the placement of lines on a page. It is used to add variety to regular meter and to add emphasis to certain words.

> And from its station in the hall
> An ancient timepiece says to all,——
>   "Forever— ‖ never!
> Never— ‖ forever!"
>   Longfellow,
>   "The Old Clock on the Stairs"

caricature (kar′ə kə chùr), exaggeration of prominent features of appearance or character. The characters of the miserly Tom Walker and his shrewish wife in Irving's "The Devil and Tom Walker," page 110, are essentially caricatures.

characterization, the method an author uses to acquaint a reader with his or her characters. A character's physical traits and personality may be described, as in the first two paragraphs of "A Worn Path," page 489; a character's speech and behavior may be presented, as in "The Man Who Saw the Flood," page 483; or the thoughts and feelings of a character or the reactions of other characters to an individual may be shown, as in "The Jilting of Granny Weatherall," page 430. Any or all of these methods may be used in the same story or novel. Characters can be described as either round or flat. A round character is fully developed and exhibits a variety of human traits. Caroline Spencer in James's story "Four Meetings," page 796, is a round character. A flat character displays few, if any, distinguishing features. The saintly Uncle Tom in Stowe's *Uncle Tom's Cabin*, page 260, is a flat character. (See also page 882.)

Classicism, a style of literature characterized by attention to form and influenced by the classical writers of Greece and Rome. Classicism flourished in the seventeenth and eighteenth centuries. "To S. M., a Young African Painter on Seeing His Works," page 71, shows the influence of Classicism.

climax, the decisive point in a story or play when the problem must be resolved in one way or another. In "The Bear," page 460, the immediate problem to be resolved is whether or not the boy will shoot the bear. The climax occurs when, given the opportunity, he does not kill the animal. Not every story or play has this kind of dramatic climax. Sometimes a character may simply resolve a problem in his or her mind. At times there is no resolution of the plot; the climax then comes when a character realizes that a resolution is impossible. (See also page 899.)

comedy, a literary work, especially a drama, that has a happy ending and is written primarily to amuse.

comic relief, an amusing episode in a serious or tragic literary work that is introduced to relieve tension.

conceit, an elaborate and surprising *figure of speech* comparing two very dissimilar things. It usually involves intellectual cleverness and ingenuity. In Edward Taylor's "Huswifery," page 67, an intricate comparison is made between cloth making and salvation using a spinning wheel as a central image in his comparison.

concrete poetry, poetry in which the appearance of the verse on the page suggests the subject of the poem. "l(a" on page 544 is a concrete poem that suggests a falling leaf.

conflict, the struggle between two opposing forces. The four basic kinds of conflict are: (**1**) a person against another person ("The Cask of Amontillado," page 151); (**2**) a person against nature ("The Bear," page 460); (**3**) a person against society ("Harrison Bergeron," page 669); and (**4**) two elements within a person struggling for mastery ("The Haunted Boy," page 660). More than one kind of conflict can be and often is present in a work. As Robert Penn Warren put it, "no conflict, no story." (See also page 899.)

connotation, the emotional associations surrounding a word or phrase, as opposed to its literal meaning or DENOTATION. Some connotations are fairly universal, others quite personal. The author of "My Mother Pieced Quilts," page 739, has built her poem around the many personal connotations that *mother* and *quilt* have for her. (See also page 883.)

consonance (kon′sə nəns), the repetition of consonant sounds that are preceded by different vowel sounds.

> The autu*m*n-ti*m*e has co*m*e;
> On woods that drea*m* of bloo*m* . . .
> Whittier, "My Triumph"

Consonance is an effective device for reinforcing MOOD and meaning. In the lines above, the *m* sounds contribute to the drowsy, end-of-summer feeling. (See also page 909.)

couplet, a pair of rhyming lines with identical METER.

> Thou blossom bright with autumn dew,
> And colored with the heaven's own blue,
> That opened when the quiet light
> Succeeds the keen and frosty night——
> Bryant, "To the Fringed Gentian"

The last two lines of "Well, I Have Lost You," page 536, are in couplet form. (See also page 884.)

dactyl (dak′tl), a three-syllable metrical FOOT, consisting of one accented syllable followed by two unaccented syllables, as in the word *merrily*. In the following line, the feet are divided by slashes. The first five feet are dactylic, and the last is spondaic.

> Meánwhile had / spréad in the / víllage
> the / tídings of /íll, and on / áll sídes . . .
> Longfellow, *Evangeline*

denotation, the strict, literal meaning of a word. (See CONNOTATION.)

denouement (dā′nü mäN′), the resolution of the PLOT. In a mystery story, for example, it is the explanation or summation of clues, motives, red herrings, and any loose ends not explained earlier. The CLIMAX and the denouement may come very close together, or, in a novel, several chapters may intervene. (See also page 899.)

dialect, a form of speech characteristic to a particular region or class, differing from the standard language in pronunciation, vocabulary, and grammatical form. Stowe's *Uncle Tom's Cabin*, page 260, contains examples of dialect.

dialogue, the conversation between two or more people in a literary work. Dialogue can serve many purposes, among them: (**1**) CHARACTERIZATION, both of those speaking and of those spoken about, as in "Winter Dreams," page 438; (**2**) the creation of MOOD or ATMOSPHERE, as in "Hop-Frog," page 159; (**3**) the advancement of the PLOT, as in "The Cask of Amontillado," page 151; and (**4**) the development of a THEME, as in "The Leader of the People," page 472.

diction, the author's choice of words or phrases in a literary work. This choice involves both the connotative and denotative meaning of a word as well as levels of usage. In "The Devil and Tom Walker," page 110, Irving refers to Mrs. Tom Walker as "a tall termagant," a choice of words that reveals something about Irving as well as about Walker's wife, whom another writer might have chosen to describe as a common scold.

drama, a literary work in verse or prose, written to be acted, that tells a story through the speech and actions of the characters. A drama may be a TRAGEDY or a COMEDY, or contain elements of both. Williams's *The Glass Menagerie*, page 572, is a drama.

dramatic convention, any of several devices that the audience accepts as a substitution for reality in a dramatic work. For instance, the audience accepts that an interval between acts is a substitute for a passage of time greater than the interval, that a bare stage may be a meadow, that a balcony is attached to a house instead of an invisible scaffold, that an audible dialogue is really supposed to be whispered, or that dawn approaches with a rosy spotlight.

dramatic irony (See IRONY and page 893.)

dramatic monologue (mon′l ôg), a LYRIC poem in which the speaker, usually at a critical moment in life, addresses someone whose replies are not recorded. Sometimes the one addressed seems to be present, sometimes not. See "Well, I Have Lost You," page 536, and "The Love Song of J. Alfred Prufrock," page 526. A dramatic monologue differs from a SOLILOQUY in that a soliloquy usually occurs in a drama and is a speech delivered when a speaker is alone on stage. (See also page 885.)

elegy, a solemn, reflective poem, usually about death, written in a formal style. "When Lilacs Last in the Dooryard Bloom'd," page 301, is Walt Whitman's elegy written on the death of Abraham Lincoln.

end rhyme, the rhyming of words at the ends of lines

of poetry as in "Richard Cory," page 395. (See also INTERNAL RHYME.)

end-stopped line, a line of poetry that contains a complete thought, thus necessitating the use of a semicolon or period at the end.

The ship, becalmed, at length stands still;
The steed must rest beneath the hill;

Thoreau, "Though All the Fates"

(See also RUN-ON LINE.)

epigram, any short, witty verse or saying, often ending with a wry twist.

Let us all be happy and live within our means, even if we have to borrow the money to do it with.

Artemus Ward

(Compare with MAXIM and PROVERB. See also page 885.)

epistle (i pis′əl), in general, any letter; specifically, a long, formal, and instructional composition in prose or verse. Crèvecoeur's "What Is an American?" page 88, is an example of the literary epistle or letter.

epitaph (ep′ə taf), a brief statement commemorating a dead person, often inscribed on a tombstone. Masters's poems in the *Spoon River Anthology*, page 397, are epitaphs about imaginary persons.

epithet (ep′ə thet), a descriptive expression, usually mentioning a quality or attribute of the person or thing being described. "Honest Abe" is an epithet for Lincoln.

essay, a prose composition that presents a personal point of view. An essay may present a viewpoint through formal analysis and argument, as in "Civil Disobedience" by Thoreau, page 224, or it may be informal in style and loosely structured, as in "Easter," page 743.

exposition, the beginning of a work of fiction, particularly a play, in which the author sets the ATMOSPHERE and TONE, explains the SETTING, introduces the characters, and provides the reader with any other information needed in order to understand the PLOT.

extended metaphor, a figure of speech that is used throughout an entire work or a great part of it. It is common in poetry but is often used in prose as well. The spiritual "Swing Low, Sweet Chariot," page 187, contains an extended metaphor, with *home* representing "heaven" throughout and the chariot representing the means by which the believer will be transported to heaven. (See also page 887.)

fable, a brief tale, in which the characters are often animals, told to point out a MORAL truth. (See Emerson's "Fable," page 205.)

falling action, the RESOLUTION of a dramatic PLOT, which takes place after the CLIMAX. (See also page 899.)

fantasy, a work that takes place in an unreal world and that often concerns incredible characters. Science fiction, a kind of fantasy, tends to deal chiefly with events that take place in the future or on other planets and employs physical and scientific principles not yet discovered or proven but distinctly possible. Washington Irving was the first American author to write fantasy, with such stories as "Rip Van Winkle" and "The Legend of Sleepy Hollow," and this tradition continues today in the works of Ray Bradbury, Ursula Le Guin, Isaac Asimov, and others.

fiction, a type of literature drawn from the imagination of the author that tells about imaginary people and happenings. Stowe's NOVEL *Uncle Tom's Cabin*, page 260, and Hawthorne's SHORT STORY "Young Goodman Brown," page 237, are examples of fiction.

figurative language, language used in a nonliteral way to express a suitable relationship between essentially unlike things. When Twain compares the jaw of a bulldog to the "fo'castle of a steamboat" or says that a frog whirled in the air "like a doughnut," he is using a figure of speech or figurative language. Some common figures of speech are APOSTROPHE, SIMILE, METAPHOR, PERSONIFICATION, HYPERBOLE, METONYMY, and SYNECDOCHE. (See also page 886.)

flat character (See CHARACTERIZATION.)

flashback, interruption of the narrative to show an episode that happened before that particular point in the story. In "An Occurrence at Owl Creek Bridge," there is a flashback that begins with section II on page 357. (See also page 888.)

foil, a character whose traits are the opposite of those of another character and who thus points up the strengths or weaknesses of another character. In *The Glass Menagerie*, page 572, the outgoing, ambitious gentleman caller serves as a foil to the romantic, introspective Tom Wingfield.

folk literature, a type of early literature that was passed orally from generation to generation, and written down later. The authorship of folk literature is unknown. Folk literature includes MYTHS, FABLES, fairy tales, BALLADS, and LEGENDS. The border ballad "El Corrido de Gregorio Cortez," page 341, is an example of folk literature.

folklore, the customs, proverbs, legends, superstitions, songs, and tales of a people or nation. Literature often borrows elements from folklore. For instance, the belief that the devil can assume human form and the old legend (common to the folklore of many countries) of someone who strikes a bargain with the devil were incorporated into "The Devil and Tom Walker" by Washington Irving, page 110.

GLOSSARY OF LITERARY TERMS

folk tale (See FOLK LITERATURE and FOLKLORE.)

foot, in verse, a group of syllables usually consisting of one accented syllable and all unaccented syllables associated with it. (A foot may occasionally, for variety, have two accented syllables. See SPONDEE.) In the following lines the feet are divided by slashes:

At mid / night, in / the month / of June.

I stand / beneath / the mys / tic moon.

> Poe, "The Sleeper"

It is probable that this use of the word *foot* refers to the movement of the foot in beating time. The most common line lengths are five feet (PENTAMETER), four feet (TETRAMETER), and three feet (TRIMETER). The quoted lines above are IAMBIC TETRAMETER. (See also RHYTHM.)

foreshadowing, a hint given to the reader of what is to come. In "The First Seven Years," page 641, the reader knows, even if Feld does not, that when Sobel breaks the last and runs out, this foreshadows the revelation of his love for Miriam. (See also page 889.)

free verse, a type of poetry written with RHYTHM and other poetic devices but without a fixed pattern of METER and RHYME. Walt Whitman, page 294, was the first recognized poet to use free verse extensively. (See also page 890.)

genre (zhän′rə), a form or type of literary work. For example, the novel, the short story, and the poem are all genres. The term is a very loose one, however, so that subheadings under these would themselves also be called genres, for instance, the MYTH and the epic.

gothic novel, type of novel that aims at evoking terror through a gloomy SETTING and sensational, sometimes supernatural, action. The English writer Horace Walpole is credited with writing the first gothic novel, *The Castle of Otranto* (1764). The term *Gothic* referred at first to a style of architecture developed in western Europe during the Middle Ages. Since the setting of Walpole's novel is a medieval castle, the term was extended to apply to this type of writing. The term is likewise used to describe a type of present-day novel which, though it may not have a medieval setting, takes place in a terrifying and mysterious place and often involves a love story.

gothic tale (See GOTHIC NOVEL.)

Harlem Renaissance, a cultural movement among black Americans during the 1920s. With the Harlem district of New York City as its center, the Renaissance was an upsurge of new racial, political, and artistic ideals. The Harlem writers included Langston Hughes, Claude McKay, Countee Cullen, Jean Toomer, Arna Bontemps, and James Weldon Johnson, pages 516–517.

hero, the central character in a NOVEL, SHORT STORY, DRAMA, or other work of FICTION. When the central character is a woman, she is usually called a *heroine*. Redburn is the hero of Melville's novel *Redburn*, page 249; Eliza is the heroine of Stowe's novel *Uncle Tom's Cabin*, page 260.

heroic couplet, a pair of rhymed verse lines in IAMBIC PENTAMETER. Wheatley's poem "To S. M., a Young African Painter on Seeing His Works," page 71, is written in heroic couplets.

hexameter (hek sam′ə tər), a verse line of six feet.

Ye who be / lieve in af / fection that / hopes,

and en / dures and is / patient . . .

> Longfellow, *Evangeline*

The first five feet of the line are dactylic; the last foot is spondaic. Hexameter is not very common in American poetry.

historical narrative, a nonfiction prose account of real people, places, and events.

humor, in literature, writing whose purpose is to amuse or evoke laughter. Humorous writing can be sympathetic to human nature or satirical. Some forms of humor are IRONY, SATIRE, PARODY, and CARICATURE.

hyperbole (hī pėr′bə lē), a figure of speech involving great exaggeration. The effect may be satiric, sentimental, or comic. American folklore abounds with hyperbole, such as the story about the man who was so stingy that he stood on one foot at a time to avoid wearing out his shoes. Dickinson's poem "If You Were Coming in the Fall," page 320, makes use of hyperbole. (See also page 886.)

iamb (ī′amb), a two-syllable metrical FOOT consisting of one unaccented syllable followed by one accented syllable, as in the word *decide*.

imagery, the sensory details that provide vividness in a literary work and tend to arouse emotions or feelings in a reader that abstract language does not. The following paragraph illustrates the use of details that appeal to the senses, in this case sight, hearing, and touch:

> When he came to the well, he flung himself face downward and peered into its darkness. There were furtive silver glintings some feet from the surface. He grabbed one of the canteens and, unfastening its cap, swung it down by the cord. The water flowed slowly in with an indolent gurgle.
>
> Stephen Crane, "A Mystery of Heroism"

(See also page 891.)

Imagism (im′ə jiz′əm), a movement in American poetry during the early 1900s, led by Ezra Pound (page 496), Amy Lowell (page 496), and others, which endorsed the use of precise IMAGERY and freedom of subject selection and metrical rhythms.

Impressionism, a manner of writing in which scenes, characters, or moods are presented from a particular vantage point rather than as they actually are. The sights and events in *The Red Badge of Courage*, page 796, are filtered through Henry Fleming's impressions so that, for example, the entire regiment appears as "grunting bundles of blue."

inference, a reasonable conclusion about the behavior of a character or the meaning of an event drawn from the limited information presented by the author. After reading "In Another Country," page 454, one might infer that this is a story, not about war, but about human isolation. Further, one could conclude that the physical wounds of the soldiers symbolize the emotional scars of alienation. (See also page 892.)

interior monologue, a technique used by writers to present the STREAM OF CONSCIOUSNESS of a fictional character, either directly by presenting what is passing through the character's mind or indirectly by the author's selection of and comments upon the character's thoughts.

internal rhyme, rhyming words within lines that also may or may not rhyme at the end: "I spy a fly upon the rye."

inversion (See ANASTROPHE.)

irony, the term used to describe a contrast between what appears to be and what really is. In *verbal irony*, the actual meaning of a statement is different from (often the opposite of) what the statement literally says. *Understatement*, in which a fact is expressed less emphatically than it could be, is a form of verbal irony, usually used for humorous effect. *Irony of situation* refers to an occurrence that is contrary to what is expected or intended, as in "Miniver Cheevy," page 394. *Dramatic irony* refers to a situation in which events or facts not known to a character on stage or in a fictional work are known to another character and the audience or reader. In "The Cask of Amontillado," page 151, Fortunato is unaware of the narrator's plans for him, although the narrator of course knows and the reader suspects. (See also page 893.)

journal, a formal record of a person's daily experiences. It is less intimate or personal than a DIARY and more chronological than an AUTOBIOGRAPHY. The entry from Sarah Kemble Knight's "Traveling in the New Land," page 44, is an example of this type of writing.

legend, a traditional anonymous story, sometimes of a national or folk hero, which has a basis in fact but which also includes imaginative material. There are many legends about Johnny Appleseed, for example, who was a real person named John Chapman, but about whom relatively little is actually known. Places, too, sometimes prompt legends—cliffs from which unhappy lovers are said to have leaped, for instance. (See also MYTH.)

literary ballad (See BALLAD.)

literary letter (See EPISTLE.)

local color (See REGIONALISM.)

lyric, a poem, usually short, that expresses some basic emotion or state of mind. A lyric usually creates a single impression and is highly personal. It may be rhymed or unrhymed. "To Be in Love," page 717, fulfills the qualifications of a lyric. (See also page 896.)

maxim, a brief saying embodying a moral, such as "Diligence is the mother of good luck" [Franklin]. It is sometimes also called an aphorism.

metaphor, a figure of speech involving an implied or stated comparison. In "The Jilting of Granny Weatherall," page 430, Porter makes a comparison between the plan of life and a sheet or comforter: ". . . then a person could spread out the plan of life and tuck in the edges orderly." (See also page 887.)

meter, the pattern of stressed and unstressed syllables in poetry. (See RHYTHM and FOOT.)

metonymy (mə ton′ə mē), a figure of speech in which a term is substituted for another with which it is closely associated, as when the term "city hall" is used to refer to a mayor or "the bench" is used to refer to persons who sit as judges. (See also page 887.)

mock epic, a SATIRE using the form and STYLE of an epic poem to treat a trivial incident. Holmes adopts a mock-epic TONE in "The Ballad of the Oysterman," page 142.

monologue (mon′l ôg), an extended speech given by one speaker. Sometimes a distinction is made between a SOLILOQUY and a monologue, with the term *soliloquy* describing the extended speech of a character on stage who is in effect talking to himself or herself and expressing inner thoughts aloud. These musings are supposed to be known only to the audience and not to other characters. The term *monologue* is usually used to express any rather long speech given by one person—a character in a story or a real person. Amanda's lengthy speech about her social life in her youth, made to Laura as they await the arrival of Tom and Jim for dinner in *The Glass Menagerie*, page 601, is a monologue.

mood, the overall ATMOSPHERE of a work. The mood of "An Occurrence at Owl Creek Bridge," page 356, might be said to be eerie, while the mood of "The Celebrated Jumping Frog of Calaveras County," page 330, is lighthearted. (See also page 897.)

moral, the lesson taught in a work such as a FABLE. A moral, such as "let sleeping dogs lie," directs that the reader should act in a certain way.

motif (mō tēf'), a character, incident, or idea that recurs in various works or in various parts of the same work. In the poem "Patterns," page 499, the motif is patterns—the patterns of a garden, a dress, a fan, paths, and of life itself.

motivation, the portrayal of circumstances and aspects of personality that makes a character's actions and reactions plausible or believable. In "A New England Nun," page 365, Louisa Ellis's decision not to marry Joe seems plausible because of the author's description of events and Louisa's thoughts about her future.

myth, a traditional tale of unknown authorship involving gods and goddesses or other supernatural beings. A myth often attempts to explain aspects of nature such as the seasons or creation.

narrative, a story or account of an event or a series of events. It may be told either in poetry or prose; it may be either fictional or true. Amy Lowell's "Patterns," page 499; Sarah Kemble Knight's account, page 44, and "Winter Dreams," page 438, are all examples of narratives.

narrative poetry, a poem that tells a story or recounts a series of events. "Patterns," page 499, is a narrative. It may be either long or short. Epics and BALLADS are types of narrative poetry.

narrator, the teller of a story. The teller may be a character in the story, as in "The Cask of Amontillado," page 151; the author himself, as in "Escape: A Slave Narrative," page 177; or an anonymous voice outside the story, as in "A Worn Path," page 489. A narrator's attitude toward his or her subject is capable of much variation; it can range from one of apparent indifference to one of extreme conviction and feeling. When a narrator appears to have some bias regarding his or her subject, as in "Soldiers of the Republic," page 560, it becomes especially important to determine whether the narrator and the author are to be regarded as the same person. (See also PERSONA and POINT OF VIEW.)

Naturalism, writing that depicts events as rigidly determined by the forces of heredity and environment. Stephen Crane has been called a naturalist because his writing expounds the philosophy that the world can be understood by examining cause-and-effect relationships and that all events are determined by antecedent causes.

nonfiction, any writing that is not fiction; any type of prose that deals with real people and happenings. BIOGRAPHY and history are types of nonfiction. The excerpt from *The Lonely Hunter*, page 748, Virginia Spencer Carr's biography of Carson McCullers, is nonfiction.

novel, a long work of prose fiction dealing with characters, situations, and SETTINGS that imitate those of real life.

novella, a brief tale, especially the early tales of French and Italian writers, considered to be the form that engendered the later NOVEL. *Novella* is also used as a synonym for novelette, or short novel.

omniscient point of view (See POINT OF VIEW.)

onomatopoeia (on'ə mat'ə pē'ə), use of a word or words whose sounds imitate the sound of the thing spoken about. Words such as *hiss*, *mumble*, *caw*, and *mew* are onomatopoetic words. In the following example, the author has tried to convey the sound of rustling leaves.

> The treetops faintly rustle beneath the
>   breeze's flight,
> A soft and soothing sound, yet it whispers
>   of the night . . .
>
> Bryant, "Waiting by the Gate"

See also page 910.

oral literature, literature passed from one generation to the next by word-of-mouth or by performance. The Native American poems on pages 14, 16, and 17 were sung or chanted long before they were recorded.

parable, a brief fictional work that concretely illustrates an abstract idea or teaches some lesson or truth. It differs from a FABLE in that the characters in it are generally people rather than animals; it differs from an ALLEGORY in that its characters do not necessarily represent abstract qualities.

paradox, a statement, often metaphorical, that seems to be self-contradictory but which has valid meaning. "In death there is life" is a paradox. (See also page 898.)

parallelism, the use of phrases or sentences that are similar in structure. In The Declaration of Independence, page 92, Thomas Jefferson uses parallelism to describe the offenses of King George III: "For imposing taxes . . ., For depriving us . . ., For transporting us. . . ."

parody (See SATIRE.)

pentameter (pen tam'ə tər), a metrical line of five feet. (See also FOOT.)

> O star / of morn / ing and / of lib / erty!
> O bring / er of / the light, / whose splen / dor shines
> Above / the dark / ness of / the Ap / pennines,
> Forerun / ner of / the day / that is / to be!
>
> Longfellow, *Divina Commedia*

persona (pər sō'nə), the mask or voice that a writer assumes in a particular work. *Persona* is derived from a Latin word meaning "mask." Eliot is the author of "The Love Song of J. Alfred Prufrock," page 526, but the persona is Prufrock, through whom Eliot speaks.

In "The Devil and Tom Walker," page 110, Irving has assumed a voice or persona, gently ironic, somewhat indulgent, in telling the story.

personification (pər son′ə fə kā′shən), the representation of abstractions, ideas, animals, or inanimate objects as human beings by endowing them with human qualities. Death is personified in Dickinson's "Because I Could Not Stop for Death," page 326. (See also page 887.)

play (See DRAMA.)

plot, in the simplest sense, a series of happenings in a literary work; but the word is often used to refer to the action as it is organized around a CONFLICT and builds through complication to a CLIMAX followed by a DENOUEMENT or resolution. (See also page 899.)

poetry, a type of literature that creates an emotional response by the imaginative use of words to produce a desired effect through RHYTHM, sound, and meaning. Poetry may be RHYMED or unrhymed. Among the many forms of poetry are the LYRIC, SONNET, BALLAD, ELEGY, BLANK VERSE, and FREE VERSE.

point of view, the author's choice of a narrator; hence, the vantage point from which the actions and characters of a story are presented. The teller, or NARRATOR, may be a character, in which case the story is told from the *first-person* point of view, as in "In Another Country," page 454. A writer who describes, in the third person, both the thoughts and actions of one or all of the characters is said to use the *omniscient* (om nish′ənt) point of view. "The First Seven Years," page 641, is told from the omniscient point of view. Writers who confine themselves, in the third person, to describing thoughts and actions of a single character are sometimes said to use the *third-person limited* point of view. (See "The Jilting of Granny Weatherall," page 430.) An author who describes only what can be seen, like a newspaper reporter, is said to use the *dramatic* point of view. The narrator may then be a minor character in the story who plays the roles of eyewitness and confidant. (See also page 900.)

prose poem, a piece of writing set down as prose but having the rhythms, language, and imaginative quality usually associated with poetry.

protagonist (prō tag′ə nist), the leading character in a literary work. (See also page 901.)

proverb, a brief, traditional saying that makes an observation on character or conduct or contains some bit of popular wisdom such as "Red sky at morning, sailors take warning," or "A watched pot never boils," or "Cold hands, warm heart." (Compare MAXIM and EPIGRAM.)

quatrain (kwot′rān), verse STANZA of four lines. Emerson's poem "Brahma" (page 212) is written in quatrains, as are Robinson's poems "Miniver Cheevy" (page 394) and "Richard Cory" (page 395).

Realism, a way of representing life as it seems to the common reader. The material selected tends to represent, with almost photographic precision and detail, ordinary people in everyday speech, experiences, and settings. Much of the work of Mark Twain and Edith Wharton has realistic aspects, as does the writing of Sherwood Anderson, Eudora Welty, William Dean Howells, Henry James, and Ernest Hemingway.

refrain, the repetition of one or more lines in each STANZA of a poem. "Clementine," page 191, has a refrain.

regionalism, the emphasis in fiction on the dialect, dress, customs, and traditions of a particular region and on the effect that setting has on character development. In "A Wagner Matinée" (page 413), Aunt Georgiana's character is revealed through descriptions of her life on a Nebraska homestead. Local-color writing, as practiced by Bret Harte, Kate Chopin, and Mary Wilkins Freeman during the 1800s, was a less complex form of regional writing which described the West, the South, and New England, respectively. (See also page 895.)

repetition, a poetic device in which a sound, word, or phrase is repeated for STYLE and emphasis, as in Carl Sandburg's poem "Chicago," page 503, with its repeated phrase "they tell me."

resolution (See FALLING ACTION. See also page 899.)

rhyme, exact repetition of sounds in at least the final accented syllable of two or more words. (See also INTERNAL RHYME, END RHYME, SLANT RHYME, FEMININE RHYME, and page 902.)

rhyme scheme, any pattern of end rhyme in a STANZA. For purposes of study, the pattern is labeled as shown below, with the first rhyme labeled *a*, as are all the words rhyming with it; the second rhyme labeled *b*, the third rhyme labeled *c*, and so on.

And what is so rare as a day in June?	*a*
Then, if ever, come perfect days;	*b*
Then Heaven tries earth if it be in tune,	*a*
And over it softly her warm ear lays:	*b*
Whether we look, or whether we listen,	*c*
We hear life murmur, or see it glisten;	*c*

Lowell, *The Vision of Sir Launfal*

rhythm, the arrangement of stressed and unstressed syllables in speech or writing. Rhythm, or METER, may be regular, taDUM, taDUM, taDUM, or it may vary within a line or work. The four most common meters are IAMB or *iambus* (⏑ ′), TROCHEE (′ ⏑), ANAPEST (⏑ ⏑ ′), and DACTYL (′ ⏑ ⏑). (See also page 904.)

rising action, the building of tension between opposing characters or forces toward a CLIMAX. In "An Episode of War," page 387, the climax falls so near the end that nearly the whole story constitutes the rising action.

Romanticism, unlike REALISM, Romanticism tends to portray the uncommon. The material selected tends to deal with extraordinary people in unusual experiences. In Romantic literature there is often a stress on the past (as in the writings of James Fenimore Cooper) and an emphasis on nature (as in the works of William Cullen Bryant).

round character (See CHARACTERIZATION.)

run-on line, a line in which the thought continues beyond the end of the poetic line. There should be no pause after *might* in the stanza below, the unbroken rhythm making a run-on line.

Oh, dumb be passion's stormy rage,
  When he who might
Have lighted up and led his age,
  Falls back in night.

Whittier, "Ichabod"

(See also END-STOPPED LINE.)

sarcasm, the use of language to hurt, wound, or ridicule. It is less subtle in TONE than IRONY.

satire, the TECHNIQUE that employs wit to ridicule a subject, usually some social institution or human foible, with the intention to inspire reform. SARCASM and IRONY are often used in writing satire. *Burlesque* and *parody* are closely related to satire. *Burlesque* is a literary or dramatic composition that treats a serious subject ridiculously or a trivial subject as if it were important. Either way, exaggeration is used. *Parody* is humorous imitation of serious writing. (See also page 905.)

scansion (skan'shən), the marking off of lines of poetry into feet. (See also RHYTHM and FOOT.)

sermon, a written version of a speech on some aspect of religion, morality, conduct, or the like, meant to be delivered in a church. Jonathan Edwards's "Sinners in the Hands of an Angry God," page 59, is a famous sermon from the Colonial period.

setting, the time (both time of day or season and period in history) and place in which the action of a NARRATIVE occurs. The setting may be suggested through DIALOGUE and action, or it may be described by the NARRATOR or one of the characters. Setting contributes strongly to the MOOD or ATMOSPHERE and plausibility of a work. The detailed, precise description of the swamp in "The Devil and Tom Walker," page 110, for example, convinces us that if the devil is ever going to appear in the flesh, he will do so in this fiendish setting. (See also page 906.)

short story, a fairly short prose NARRATIVE that is carefully crafted and usually tightly constructed. The short story form developed in the nineteenth century. This book includes short stories by Poe, Harte, Bierce, Fitzgerald, Hemingway, Faulkner, Steinbeck, Wright, Updike, and others.

simile (sim'ə lē), a figure of speech involving a comparison between two basically unlike things that nonetheless have something in common, using *like* or *as*.

". . . like mourning weeds, dark festoons of sea-grass slimily swept to and fro over the name, with every hearselike roll of the hull."

Melville, Benito Cereno

In the preceding example the similarity between the festoons of sea-grass and mourning clothes (weeds) is based, at least partly, on the dark color of both. The death image is reinforced by the "hearse*like* roll of the hull." (See also page 886.)

slant rhyme, rhyme in which the vowel sounds are not quite identical, as in the first and third lines that follow.

By the rude bridge that arched the flood,
  Their flag to April's breeze unfurled,
Here once the embattled farmers stood
  And fired the shot heard round the world.

Emerson, "Concord Hymn"

soliloquy (sə lil'ə kwē), a DRAMATIC CONVENTION that allows a character to speak his or her thoughts aloud. If someone else is on stage, a soliloquy becomes an *aside*. (Compare with MONOLOGUE.)

sonnet, a LYRIC poem with a traditional form of fourteen IAMBIC PENTAMETER lines and one of several fixed RHYME schemes. (See "Well, I Have Lost You," page 536. See also page 907.)

speaker, the person who is speaking in a poem, as in Amy Lowell's "Patterns," page 499. (See NARRATOR.)

spondee (spon'dē), a metrical FOOT of two accented syllables (′ ′). It serves occasionally as a substitute foot to vary the meter, as in the first foot below.

Tóm, Tóm,/ thĕ pí / pĕr's són . . .

stage directions, directions given by the author of a DRAMA to indicate the action, costumes, SETTING, arrangement of the stage, and so on. Stage directions are usually printed in italics. (See Williams's *The Glass Menagerie*, page 572.)

stanza, a group of lines that are set off and form a division in a poem.

stereotype, a conventional character, plot, or setting, that thus possesses little or no individuality. There are some situations, characters, and settings that are frequently predictable, usually because of the author's treatment. Examples of such stereotypes include "the dead body in the library," "the wandering, lone hero," or "the poet starving in a garret."

stream of consciousness, the recording or re-creation of the uneven and illogical flow of a character's thoughts, sensations, memories, and emotional and mental associations without any attempt at explanation, as in "The Jilting of Granny Weatherall," page 430. (See also page 911.)

style, the distinctive handling of language by an author. Style involves the specific choices made with regard to DICTION, FIGURATIVE LANGUAGE, etc. For a comparison of two very different styles, see "In Another Country" by Ernest Hemingway, page 454, and "The Bear" by William Faulkner, page 460. (See also page 912.)

symbol, an object or event used in a literary work to represent something other than itself, frequently an abstract idea or concept. In "The Chambered Nautilus," page 140, the shell symbolizes the body and the animal in the shell, the soul. (See also page 913.)

synecdoche (si nek'də kē), a type of FIGURATIVE LANGUAGE in which the whole is used for the part or the part used for the whole. In "the dying year," the whole is used to stand for a part, "autumn"; the use of "Wall Street" to refer to the money market or financial affairs of the entire U.S. is an example of the second—using a part to stand for the whole (or the specific to stand for the general). (See also page 887.)

tale, a simple prose or verse NARRATIVE, either true or fictitious. Twain's "The Celebrated Jumping Frog of Calaveras County," page 330, is a tale.

tall tale, a humorous, simple NARRATIVE that recounts extraordinary, impossible happenings. A distinctly American GENRE, it originated on the American frontier when "yarn-spinners" passed on the legendary feats of such folk heroes as Paul Bunyan and Babe the Blue Ox, Mike Fink, and John Henry. The tall tale found its way into the American literary tradition after the Civil War, and its form is preserved in "The Celebrated Jumping Frog of Calaveras County," page 330.

tercet (tėr'sit), a stanza of three rhyming lines.

Maiden! with the meek, brown eyes,
In whose orbs a shadow lies
Like the dusk in evening skies!
    Longfellow, "Maidenhood"

terza rima (ter'tsä rē'mä), a VERSE form with a three-line STANZA, RHYMING *aba, bcb, cdc,* and so on.

tetrameter (te tram'ə tər), a metrical line of four feet.

One au/ tumn night, / in Sud / bury town,
Across / the mead / ows bare / and brown.
    Longfellow, *Tales of a Wayside Inn*

theme, the underlying meaning of a literary work. A theme may be directly stated but more often is implied. In Freneau's "The Wild Honeysuckle," page 74, the topic or subject is a flower, but the theme is the poet's final recognition of the fleeting nature of human existence. (See also page 914.)

tone, the author's attitude toward his or her subject matter or audience. Cabeza de Vaca's tone, page 23, is sometimes matter-of-fact, sometimes wondering. Satanta's tone, page 343, is firm and forthright. (See also page 915.)

tragedy, dramatic or narrative writing in which the main character suffers disaster after a serious and significant struggle but faces his or her downfall in such a way as to attain heroic stature.

Transcendentalism, a mystical philosophy that expresses the belief that within human beings there is an insight or intuition which transcends sensory experience and logic and makes it possible to recognize universal truths. Romantic idealism and self-determination are characteristics of transcendental writing. The works of Emerson and Thoreau are representative of American Transcendentalism.

trimeter (trim'ə tər), metrical line of three feet.

"Oft to / his fro / zen lair
Tracked I / the gris / ly bear . . ."
    Longfellow, "The Skeleton in Armor"

triplet (See TERCET.)

trochee (trō'kē), metrical foot made up of one accented syllable followed by an unaccented syllable, as in the word *pumpkin.* In the following lines the feet are divided by slashes, and since there are four feet, the line can be described as trochaic TETRAMETER.

L'urid / seemed the / sky a / bove him,
L'urid / seemed the / earth be / neath him.
    Longfellow, *The Song of Hiawatha*

verbal irony (See IRONY.)

vignette (vin yet'), a brief NARRATIVE or description written with precision and grace, and intended to give a vivid impression of a personality or scene. Whitman's "Cavalry Crossing a Ford," page 312, is a vignette.

villanelle (vil'ə nel'), a poetic form normally consisting of five three-line STANZAS and a final QUATRAIN, RHYMING *aba aba aba aba aba abaa,* and with lines 1 and 3 repeating alternately as REFRAINS throughout.

voice (See PERSONA.)

Glossary

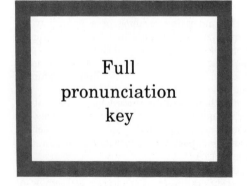

Full pronunciation key

The pronunciation of each word is shown just after the word, in this way: **ab bre vi ate** (ə brē′vē āt). The letters and signs used are pronounced as in the words below. The mark ′ is placed after a syllable with primary or heavy accent, as in the example above. The mark ′ after a syllable shows a secondary or lighter accent, as in **ab bre vi a tion** (ə brē′vē ā′shən).

Some words, taken from foreign languages, are spoken with sounds that do not otherwise occur in English. Symbols for these sounds are given in the key as "foreign sounds."

a	hat, cap	j	jam, enjoy	u	cup, butter	**foreign sounds**
ā	age, face	k	kind, seek	u̇	full, put	
ä	father, far	l	land, coal	ü	rule, move	Y as in French *du.*
		m	me, am			Pronounce (ē) with the lips rounded as for (ü).
b	bad, rob	n	no, in	v	very, save	
ch	child, much	ng	long, bring	w	will, woman	à as in French *ami.*
d	did, red			y	young, yet	Pronounce (ä) with the lips
		o	hot, rock	z	zero, breeze	spread and held tense.
e	let, best	ō	open, go	zh	measure, seizure	
ē	equal, be	ô	order, all			œ as in French *peu.*
ėr	term, learn	oi	oil, voice	ə	represents:	Pronounce (ā) with the lips
		ou	house, out		a in about	rounded as for (ō).
f	fat, if				e in taken	
g	go, bag	p	paper, cup		i in pencil	N as in French *bon.*
h	he, how	r	run, try		o in lemon	The N is not pronounced,
		s	say, yes		u in circus	but shows that the vowel
i	it, pin	sh	she, rush			before it is nasal.
ī	ice, five	t	tell, it			
		th	thin, both			H as in German *ach.*
		ᴛʜ	then, smooth			Pronounce (k) without closing the breath passage.

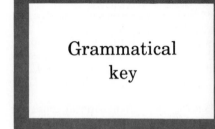

Grammatical key

adj.	adjective	*prep.*	preposition
adv.	adverb	*pron.*	pronoun
conj.	conjunction	*v.*	verb
interj.	interjection	*v.i.*	intransitive verb
n.	noun	*v.t.*	transitive verb
sing.	singular	*pl.*	plural
pt.	past tense	*pp.*	past participle

GLOSSARY

a bash (ə bash′), *v.t.* embarrass and confuse; make uneasy and somewhat ashamed. [< Old French *esbaïss-*, a form of *esbaïr* astonish]

ab di cate (ab′də kāt), *v.t.,* **-cat ed, -cat ing.** give up or relinquish (office, power, or authority) formally; renounce; resign. [< Latin *abdicatum* renounced < *ab-* away + *dicare* proclaim]

a bey ance (ə bā′əns), *n.* temporary inactivity. [< Anglo-French *abeiance* expectation < Old French *abeër* covet]

ab hor (ab hôr′), *v.t.,* **-horred, -hor ring.** regard with horror or disgust; hate completely; detest; loathe. [< Latin *abhorrere* < *ab-* from + *horrere* to shudder, shrink]

ab ject (ab′jekt, ab jekt′), *adj.* **1** so low or degraded as to be hopeless; wretched; miserable: *to live in abject poverty.* **2** deserving contempt; despicable: *the most abject flattery.* **3** slavish: *abject submission.* [< Latin *abjectum* cast down < *ab-* down + *jacere* to throw] **—ab ject′ly,** *adv.* **—ab ject′ness,** *n.*

-able, *suffix forming adjectives from verbs and nouns.* **1** that can be ___ed: *Enjoyable = that can be enjoyed.* **2** giving ___; suitable for ___: *Comfortable = giving comfort.* **3** inclined to ___: *Peaceable = inclined to peace.* **4** deserving to be ___ed: *Lovable = deserving to be loved.* **5** liable to be ___: *Breakable = liable to be broken.*

a bom i na ble (ə bom′ə nə bəl), *adj.* **1** arousing disgust and hatred; detestable; loathsome. **2** very unpleasant; disagreeable.

ab ro gate (ab′rə gāt), *v.t.,* **-gat ed, -gat ing. 1** abolish or annul by an authoritative act; repeal; cancel. **2** do away with. [< Latin *abrogatum* repealed < *ab-* away + *rogare* propose (a law)]

ab scond (ab skond′), *v.i.* go away hurriedly and secretly, especially to avoid punishment; go off and hide. [< Latin *abscondere* < *abs-* away + *condere* store up]

a bys mal (ə biz′məl), *adj.* too deep or great to be measured; bottomless: *abysmal ignorance.*

ac cen tu ate (ak sen′chü āt), *v.t.,* **-at ed, -at ing.** call special attention to; emphasize: *Her white dress accentuated her sunburn.*

ac cli mate (ə klī′mit, ak′lə māt), *v.t., v.i.,* **-mat ed, -mat ing.** accustom or become accustomed to a new climate, surroundings, or conditions.

ac cliv i ty (ə kliv′ə tē), *n., pl.* **-ties.** an upward slope of ground; ascent. [< Latin *acclivitatem* < *acclivis* ascending < *ad-* toward + *clivus* a slope]

ac com plice (ə kom′plis), *n.* person who knowingly aids another in committing a crime or other wrong act. [< earlier *a complice* a confederate < Middle French *complice* < Late Latin *complicem* < Latin *complicare* fold together]

ac cost (ə kôst′, ə kost′), *v.t.* approach and speak to first; address. [< Middle French *accoster* < Latin *ad-* to + *costa* side, rib]

ac cou ter ment (ə kü′tər mənt), *n.* **accouterments,** *pl.* a soldier's equipment with the exception of weapons and clothing.

ac qui esce (ak′wē es′), *v.i.,* **-esced, -esc ing.** give consent by keeping silent or by not making objections; accept (the conclusions or arrangements of others); accede. [< Latin *acquiescere* < *ad-* to + *quies* rest, quiet]

ac qui es cence (ak′wē es′ns), *n.* consent given without making objections; assent.

a cute (ə kyüt′), *adj.* **1** quick in perceiving and responding to impressions; keen. **2** quick in discernment; sharp-witted; clever. [< Latin *acutum* sharpened < *acuere* sharpen]

a dept (*adj.* ə dept′; *n.* ad′ept), *adj.* thoroughly skilled; expert. — *n.* person thoroughly skilled in some art, science, occupation, etc. [< Medieval Latin *adeptum* skilled (in alchemy) < Latin < *ad-* to + *apisci* reach]

a dieu (ə dü′, ə dyü′), *interj., n., pl.* **a dieus** or **a dieux** (ə düz′, ə dyüz′). good-by. [< Middle French < *à Dieu* to God]

ad her ent (ad hir′ənt), *n.* a faithful supporter or follower.

a droit (ə droit′), *adj.* **1** resourceful in reaching one's objective; ingenious; clever. **2** skillful in the use of the hands or body; dexterous. [< French < *à droit* rightly] **—a droit′ly,** *adv.*

ad ver si ty (ad vėr′sə tē), *n., pl.* **-ties.** condition of being in unfavorable circumstances, especially unfavorable financial circumstances; misfortune; distress.

ad vo cate (ad′və kāt), *v.t.,* **-cat ed.** speak or write in favor of; recommend publicly (a measure, policy, etc.); support. [< Latin *advocatum* summoned < *ad-* to + *vocare* to call]

adz or **adze** (adz), *n., pl.* **adz es.** a cutting tool for shaping heavy

agate (def. 1)

a hat	i it	oi oil	ch child	(a in about
ā age	ī ice	ou out	ng long	e in taken
ä far	o hot	u cup	sh she	ə = { i in pencil
e let	ō open	u̇ put	th thin	o in lemon
ē equal	ô order	ü rule	ᴛʜ then	(u in circus
ėr term			zh measure	< = derived from

timbers, similar to an ax but with a blade set across the end of the handle and curving inward. [Old English *adesa*]

aes thet ics (es thet′iks), *n.* study of beauty in art and nature; philosophy of beauty or taste; theory of the fine arts. Also, **esthetics.**

af fin i ty (ə fin′ə tē), *n., pl.* **-ties. 1** a natural attraction to a person or liking for a thing. **2** relation; connection. [< Latin *affinitatem* relation < *affinis* related, bordering on < *ad-* on + *finis* border]

a flare (ə fler′), *adj.* flaring, flaming.

a gape (ə gāp′, ə gap′), *adj.* open-mouthed with wonder or surprise; gaping.

ag ate (ag′it), *n.* **1** a variety of quartz with variously colored stripes, clouded colors, or mosslike formations. **2** a playing marble that looks like this. [< Old French *agathe* < Latin *achates* < Greek *achatēs*]

ag gre gate (ag′rə git, ag′rə gāt), *n.* **1** total amount; sum: *The aggregate of all the gifts was $100.* **2 in the aggregate,** taken together; considered as a whole. **3** mass of separate things joined together; collection. [< Latin *aggregatum* added to < *ad-* to + *grex* flock] **—ag′gre ga′tion,** *n.*

a ghast (ə gast′), *adj.* struck with surprise or horror; filled with shocked amazement. [past participle of obsolete *agast* terrify < Old English *on-* on + *gæstan* frighten. Related to GHOST.]

ag i tate (aj′ə tāt), *v.t.,* **-tat ed, -tat ing. 1** move or shake violently. **2** disturb or upset very much. **3** argue about; discuss vigorously and publicly. [< Latin *agitatum* moved to and fro < *agere* to move]

a gue (ā′gyü), *n.* **1** a malarial fever with chills and sweating that alternate at regular intervals. **2** any fit of shaking or shivering; chill. [< Middle French *ague* < Latin (*febris*) *acuta* severe (fever)]

-al, *suffix forming adjectives from nouns.* of; like; having the nature of: *Ornamental = having the nature of ornament.* Also, **-ial.**

à la chin oise (a la chē nwäz′), FRENCH. in the Chinese manner.

a lac ri ty (ə lak′rə tē), *n.* **1** brisk and eager action; liveliness: *move with alacrity.* **2** cheerful willingness. [< Latin *alacritatem* < *alacer* brisk]

al i bi (al′ə bī), *n.* **1** the plea or fact that a person accused of an offense was somewhere else when the offense was committed. **2** U.S. INFORMAL. an excuse. [< Latin, elsewhere]

al lay (ə lā′), *v.t.,* **-layed, -lay ing.** put at rest; quiet. [Old English *ālecgan* < *ā-* away, off + *lecgan* to lay]

al le vi ate (ə lē′vē āt), *v.t.,* **-at ed, -at ing. 1** make easier to endure (suffering of the body or mind); relieve; mitigate. **2** lessen or lighten; diminish. [< Late Latin *alleviatum* lightened < Latin *ad-* up + *levis* light]

al le vi a tion (ə lē′vē ā′shən), *n.* **1** an alleviating. **2** a being alleviated. **3** thing that alleviates.

al lude (ə lüd′), *v.i.,* **-lud ed, -lud ing.** refer indirectly *(to);* mention slightly in passing. [< Latin *alludere* < *ad-* + *ludere* to play]

al ma ma ter or **Al ma Ma ter** (al′mə mä′tər; äl′mə mä′tər), school, college, or university at which one is or has been a student. [< Latin *alma mater* fostering mother]

am bi ent (am′bē ənt), *adj.* all around; surrounding; encompassing. [< Latin *ambientem* < *ambi-* around + *ire* go]

a men i ty (ə men′ə tē, ə mē′nə tē), *n., pl.* **-ties. 1 amenities,**

GLOSSARY

pl. pleasant ways; polite acts. Saying "Thank you" and holding the door open for a person to pass through are amenities. **2** something which makes life easier and more pleasant; pleasant feature. **3** quality of being pleasant; agreeableness. [< Latin *amoenitatem* < *amoenus* pleasant]

a mor phous (ə môr′fəs), *adj.* **1** having no definite form; shapeless; formless. **2** of no particular type or pattern; not classifiable; anomalous. [< Greek *amorphos* < *a-* without + *morphē* shape]

am pli tude (am′plə tüd, am′plə tyüd), *n.* **1** a being ample in size; largeness. **2** a being ample in amount; abundance: *an amplitude of money.* **3** intellectual scope; breadth of mind.

-an, *suffix forming adjectives and nouns, especially from proper nouns.* **1** of or having to do with ____: *Mohammedan = of or having to do with Mohammed.* **2** of or having to do with ____ or its people: *Asian = of or having to do with Asia or its people.* **3** person who knows much about or is skilled in ____: *Magician = person skilled in magic.* Also, **-ian, -ean.**

a nach ro nism (ə nak′rə niz′əm), *n.* anything out of keeping with a specified time, especially something proper to a former age but not to the present. [< Greek *anachronismos* < *ana-* back + *chronos* time]

a nal o gy (ə nal′ə jē), *n., pl.* **-gies.** **1** a partial or limited similarity or correspondence in some special qualities, circumstances, etc., of two or more things in other respects essentially different. **2** likeness of one thing to another or others; similarity.

a nath e ma (ə nath′ə mə), *n., pl.* **-mas.** **1** a solemn curse by church authorities excommunicating some person from the church. **2** denunciation of some person or thing as evil; curse. **3** person or thing that has been cursed or is utterly detested. [< Latin < Greek]

-ance, *suffix forming nouns chiefly from verbs.* **1** act or fact of ____ ing: *Avoidance = act or fact of avoiding.* **2** quality or state of being ____ed: *Annoyance = quality or state of being annoyed.* **3** thing that ____s: *Conveyance = thing that conveys.* **4** what is ____ed: *Contrivance = what is contrived.* **5** quality or state of being ____ant: *Importance = quality or state of being important.* [< Old French < Latin *-antia, -entia*]

-ancy, *suffix.* variant of **-ance,** as in *ascendancy, buoyancy.*

a ne mi a (ə nē′mē ə), *n.* **1** condition resulting from an insufficiency of hemoglobin or red blood cells or by a loss of blood, characterized by weakness, pallor, palpitation of the heart, and a tendency to fatigue. **2** lack of vigor or strength; weakness. Also, **anaemia.** [< Greek *anaimia* < *an-* not + *haima* blood]

an ni hi la tion (ə nī′ə lā′shən), *n.* complete destruction.

a nom a ly (ə nom′ə lē), *n., pl.* **-lies.** **1** something anomalous. **2** deviation from the rule; irregularity.

an tag o nis tic (an tag′ə nis′tik), *adj.* actively opposed to each other; opposing; hostile.

an ther (an′thər), *n.* the part of the stamen of a flower that bears the pollen. It is usually a double-celled sac situated at the end of the filament. [< Greek *antheros* flowery < *anthos* flower]

an vil (an′vəl), *n.* **1** an iron or steel block on which metals are hammered and shaped. **2** incus. [Old English *anfilt*]

aph o rism (af′ə riz′əm), *n.* a short sentence expressing a general truth or some practical wisdom; maxim. [< Greek *aphorismos* definition < *apo-* off + *horos* boundary]

a poth e o sis (ə poth′ē ō′sis, ə poth′ə sis), *n., pl.* **-ses** (-sēz′). **1** a glorified ideal. **2** the raising of a human being to the rank of a god; deification. [< Greek *apotheōsis* < *apo-* + *theos* god]

ap pa ri tion (ap′ə rish′ən), *n.* **1** a supernatural sight or thing; ghost or phantom. **2** the appearance of something strange, remarkable, or unexpected. [< Late Latin *apparitionem*]

ap pease (ə pēz′), *v.t.,* **-peased, -peas ing.** **1** put an end to by satisfying (an appetite or desire). **2** make calm or quiet; pacify. [< Old French *apaisier* < *a-* to + *pais* peace]

ap pease ment (ə pēz′mənt), *n.* an appeasing or a being appeased; pacification; satisfaction.

a pel la tion (ap′ə lā′shən), *n.* **1** name or title describing or identifying someone. In "John the Baptist," the appellation of *John* is *the Baptist.* **2** act of calling by a name.

ap praise (ə prāz′), *v.t.,* **-praised, -prais ing.** estimate the value of; fix a price for; value. [< Middle French *apriser* < Latin *appretiare* < *ad-* to + *pretium* price]

ap pre ci a ble (ə prē′shē ə bəl, ə prē′shə bəl), *adj.* enough to be felt or estimated; noticeable; perceptible.

ap pre hen sion (ap′ri hen′shən), *n.* **1** expectation of misfortune; dread of impending danger; fear. **2** arrest. **3** understanding.

ap pre hen sive (ap′ri hen′siv), *adj.* afraid that some misfortune is about to occur; anxious about the future; fearful.

ap prize (ə prīz′), *v.t.,* **-prized, -priz ing.** give notice to; let know; inform; notify; advice. [< French *appris,* past participle of *apprendre* learn < Latin *apprehendere*]

ap pro ba tion (ap′rə bā′shən), *n.* **1** favorable opinion; approval. **2** act of formally and authoritatively approving; sanction. [< Latin *approbationem*]

ap pro pri a tion (ə prō′prē ā′shən), *n.* sum of money or other thing set aside for a special purpose.

ap pur te nance (ə pėrt′n əns), *n.* addition to something more important; added thing; accessory. [< Anglo-French *apurtenance.* Related to APPERTAIN.]

ar a besque (ar′ə besk′), *n.* an elaborate and fanciful design of flowers, leaves, geometrical figures, etc. [< French < Italian *arabesco* < *Arabo* Arab]

ar bi trar y (är′bə trer′ē), *adj.* **1** based on one's own wishes, notions, or will; not going by rule or law. **2** using or abusing unlimited power; tyrannical; despotic.

ar che type (är′kə tīp), *n.* an original model or pattern from which copies are made, or out of which later forms develop; prototype. [< Greek *archetypon* < *archein* begin + *typos* type]

ar dent (ärd′nt), *adj.* **1** glowing with passion; passionate; impassioned: *ardent love.* **2** eager; keen. **3** burning; fiery; hot: *an ardent fever.* **4** glowing [< Latin *ardentem* burning]

ar du ous (är′jü əs), *adj.* **1** hard to do; requiring much effort; difficult: *an arduous lesson.* **2** using up much energy; strenuous: *an arduous climb.* [< Latin *arduus* steep]

a ris to crat ic (ə ris′tə krat′ik), *adj.* **1** of or connected with aristocrats: *the aristocratic class.* **2** in keeping with the character of an aristocrat; stylish or grand. **3** snobbish; exclusive. **4** favoring aristocrats or government by aristocrats.

ar o matic (ar′ə mat′ik), *adj.* sweet-smelling; fragrant; spicy.

ar rears (ə rirz′), *n.pl.* **1** money due but not paid; unpaid debts. **2** unfinished work; things not done on time. [< Old French *arere* < Popular Latin *ad retro* to the rear]

ar ro gant (ar′ə gənt), *adj.* excessively proud and contemptuous of others. [< Latin *arrogantem* < *ad-* to + *rogare* ask]

ar tic u late (är tik′yə lit), *adj.* consisting of sections united by joints; jointed. The backbone is an articulate structure.

ar ti fact (är′tə fakt), *n.* anything made by human skill or work, especially a tool or weapon. Also, **artefact.** [< Latin *artem* art + *factum* made]

ar ti fice (är′tə fis), *n.* **1** a clever device or trick. **2** trickery; craft. **3** skill or ingenuity. [< Latin *artificium* < *artem* art + *facere* make]

ar tif i cer (är tif′ə sər), *n.* a skilled workman; craftsman.

ar ti fi cial (är′tə fish′əl), *adj.* **1** produced by human skill or labor; not natural: *artificial light.* **2** made to imitate and compete with or as a substitute for something natural. **3** put on for effect; assumed; affected: *an artificial laugh.* [< Latin *artificialis* < *artificium* artifice] **—ar′ti fi′cial ly,** *adv.*

as cer tain (as′ər tān′), *v.t.* find out for certain by trial and research; make sure of; determine. [< Old French *ascertener* < *a-* to + *certain* certain]

as cet ic (ə set′ik), *n.* **1** person who practices unusual self-denial or self-discipline, especially for religious reasons. Fasting is a common practice of ascetics. **2** person who refrains from pleasures and comforts. —*adj.* refraining from pleasures and comforts; practicing unusual self-denial. [< Greek *askētikos* exercised < *askein* to exercise, discipline]

a skance (ə skans′), *adv.* **1** with suspicion or disapproval: *The students looked askance at the suggestion for having classes on Saturday.* **2** to one side; sideways. [origin uncertain]

as sail (ə sāl′), *v.t.* **1** attack repeatedly with violent blows. **2** attack with hostile words, arguments, or abuse. **3** (of a feeling) come over (a person) strongly; beset; trouble. [< Old French *asalir* < Latin *ad-* at + *salire* to leap] —**as sail′a ble,** *adj.* —**assail′er,** *n.* —**as sail′ment,** *n.*

as sent (ə sent′), *n.* acceptance of a proposal, statement, etc.; agreement. [< Latin *assentire* < *ad-* along with + *sentire* feel, think]

as sid u ous (ə sij′ü əs), *adj.* careful and attentive; diligent. [< Latin *assiduus* < *assidere* sit by] —**as sid′u ous ly,** *adv.* —**as sid′u ous ness,** *n.*

asth matic (az mat′ik), *adj.* **1** of or having to do with asthma, a chronic disease of respiration, characterized by intermittent paroxysms of breathing with a wheezing sound, a sense of constriction in the chest, and coughing. [< Greek]

a sun der (ə sun′dər), *adv.* in pieces; into separate parts: *Lightning split the tree asunder.* —*adj.* apart or separate from each other: *miles asunder.* [Old English *on sundran*]

-ate, *suffix forming adjectives, verbs, and nouns.* **1** of or having to do with ___: *Collegiate = having to do with college.* **2** having or containing ___: *Compassionate = having compassion.* **3** having the form of ___; like ___: *Stellate = having the form of a star.* **4** become ___: *Maturate = become mature.* **5** cause to be ___: *Alienate = cause to be alien.* **6** produce ___: *Ulcerate = produce ulcers.*

at trib ute (ə trib′yüt), *v.,* **-ut ed, -ut ing.** **1** regard as an effect or product of; think of as caused by. **2** think of as belonging to or appropriate to. [< Latin *attributum* assigned < *ad-* to + *tribuere* divide] —**at trib′ut a ble,** *adj.*

au dac i ty (ô das′ə tē), *n.* **1** reckless daring; boldness. **2** rude boldness; impudence; presumption. [< Latin *audacia* < *audax* bold < *audere* to dare]

au di bil i ty (ô′də bil′ə tē), *n.* quality of being audible.

au di ble (ô′də bəl), *adj.* that can be heard; loud enough to be heard. [< Latin *audire* hear]

au re o la (ô rē′ə lə), *n.* aureole

au re ole (ôr′ē ōl), *n.* **1** ring of light surrounding a figure or object, especially in religious paintings. **2** ring of light surrounding the sun. [< Late Latin *aureola* golden < Latin *aurum* gold]

aus tere (ô stir′), *adj.* **1** stern in manner or appearance; harsh. **2** severe in self-discipline; strict in morals. **3** severely simple. [< Greek *austēros* < *auos* dry]

au then tic (ô then′tik), *adj.* **1** worthy of acceptance, trust, or belief. **2** coming from the source stated; not copied; real. [< Greek *authentikos* < *auto-* by oneself + *-hentēs* one who acts]

au to crat (ô′tə krat), *n.* ruler who claims or exerts unrestricted power and uncontrolled authority over his subjects. [< Greek *autokratēs* ruling by oneself < *auto-* + *kratos* strength]

au to crat ic (ô′tə krat′ik), *adj.* of or like an autocrat; absolute in power or authority; despotic; dictatorial.

au tom a tism (ô tom′ə tiz′əm), *n.* action not controlled by the will; involuntary action; automatic action.

av ar ice (av′ər is), *n.* too great a desire for money or property; greed for wealth. [< Old French < Latin *avaritia* < *avarus* greedy]

az ure (azh′ər), *n.* the clear blue color of the unclouded sky; sky blue. —*adj.* sky-blue. [< Old French *l′azur* the azure < Arabic *lāzuward* < Persian *lajward* lapis lazuli]

ba nal (bā′nl, bə nal′, ban′l), *adj.* not new or interesting; commonplace; trite. [< French]

ban dy (ban′dē), *v.t.,* **-died, -dying.** **1** hit or throw back and forth; toss about: *bandy a tennis ball.* **2** give and take; exchange. **3** pass from one to another in a circle or group. [apparently < French *bander*]

bane (bān), *n.* **1** cause of death, ruin, or harm. **2** destruction of any kind; ruin; harm. **3** deadly poison. [Old English *bana* murderer]

ban shee or **ban shie** (ban′shē, ban shē′), *n.* (in Irish and Scottish folklore) a female spirit whose wail means that there will soon be a death in the family. [< Irish *bean sidhe* woman of the fairies]

bar bar ous (bär′bər əs), *adj.* **1** not civilized; savage. **2** savagely cruel; brutal. **3** rough and rude; coarse; unrefined.

bog

a hat	i it	oi oil	ch child		a in about
ā age	ī ice	ou out	ng long		e in taken
ä far	o hot	u cup	sh she	ə =	i in pencil
e let	ō open	u̇ put	th thin		o in lemon
ē equal	ô order	ü rule	ŦH then		u in circus
ėr term			zh measure	<	= derived from

bark (bärk), *n.* **1** a three-masted ship, square-rigged on the first two masts and fore-and-aft-rigged on the other. **2** ARCHAIC. boat; ship. Also, **barque.** [< Middle French *barque* < Italian *barca* < Late Latin]

bas tion (bas′chən, bas′tē ən), *n.* **1** a projecting part of a fortification made so that the defenders can fire at attackers from several angles. **2** any strongly fortified or defended place. [< Middle French < *bastille* fort, building < *bastir* to build]

beck (bek), *n.* motion of the head or hand meant as a call or command. [< *beck,* verb, short for *beckon*]

be get (bi get′), *v.t.,* **be got** or (ARCHAIC) **be gat, be got ten** or **be got, be get ting.** cause to be; produce. [Old English *begitan*]

be guile (bi gīl′), *v.t.,* **-guiled, -guil ing.** **1** trick or mislead (a person); deceive; delude. **2** take away from deceitfully or cunningly. **3** win the attention of; entertain; amuse. **4** while away (time) pleasantly.

be hoof (bi hüf′), *n.* advantage; benefit. [Old English *behōf* need]

bel li cose (bel′ə kōs), *adj.* fond of fighting and quarreling; inclined to war; warlike; pugnacious. [< Latin *bellicosus* < *bellum* war] —**bel′li cose ly,** *adv.*

bel lows (bel′ōz, bel′əs), *n. sing. or pl.* device for producing a strong current of air, used for blowing fires or sounding an organ, accordion, etc.

be think (bi thingk′), *v.,* **-thought, -think ing.** —*v.t.* **bethink oneself of, a** consider; reflect on: *I bethought myself of the need to study.* **b** remember: *You should bethink yourself of your duty to them.* —*v.i.* ARCHAIC. to deliberate; consider.

bit tern (bit′ərn), *n.* any of several small herons found chiefly in marshes, characterized by a peculiar booming cry. [< Old French *butor*]

biv ouac (biv′wak, biv′ü ak), *n., v.,* **-ouacked, -ouack ing.** —*n.* a temporary, outdoor camp of soldiers, mountaineers, hikers, etc., usually without tents or with very small tents. —*v.i.* camp outdoors without tents. [< French]

Black An gus (ang′gəs), any of a breed of small, entirely black, hornless cattle raised for beef and originally bred in Scotland.

blas phe my (blas′fə mē), *n., pl.* **-mies.** abuse or contempt for God or sacred things; profanity.

bla tant (blāt′nt), *adj.* **1** offensively loud or noisy; loudmouthed. **2** showy in dress, manner, etc. **3** obvious; flagrant: *blatant hypocrisy, blatant lies.* [coined by Spenser, apparently < Latin *blatire* babble] —**bla′tant ly,** *adv.*

bla zon (blā′zn), *v.t.* **1** make known; proclaim. **2** decorate; adorn. **3** describe or paint (a coat of arms). **4** display; show. — *n.* **1** coat of arms, or a shield with a coat of arms on it. **2** description or painting of a coat of arms. **3** display; show. [< Old French *blason* shield]

blight (blīt), *n.* **1** disease of plants that causes leaves, stems, fruits, and tissues to wither and die. **2** anything that withers hope or causes destruction or ruin. **3** decay; deterioration.

blithe (blīŦH, blīth), *adj.* **1** happy and cheerful; gay; joyous. **2** heedless. [Old English *blīthe*]

blow (blō), *n.* **1** a state of blossoming; bloom. **2** display of blossoms. —*v.i.* blossom. [Old English *blōwan*]

bludg eon (bluj′ən), *n.* a short club with a heavy end, used as a weapon. —*v.t.* **1** strike with a bludgeon. **2** bully or threaten. [origin unknown]

bod ice (bod′is), *n.* **1** the close-fitting upper part of a dress. **2** a kind of vest worn over a dress or blouse and laced up the front.

bog (bog, bôg), *n., v.,* **bogged, bog ging.** —*n.* piece of wet, spongy ground, consisting chiefly of decayed or decaying moss and

GLOSSARY

965

other vegetable matter, too soft to bear the weight of any heavy body on its surface; marsh; swamp. —*v.t., v.i.* **1** sink or get stuck in a bog. **2 bog down,** sink in or get stuck so that one cannot get out without help.

brack en (brak′ən), *n.* **1** a large, coarse fern common on hillsides, in woods, etc. **2** thicket of these ferns. [Middle English *braken,* apparently < Scandinavian (Swedish) *bräken*]

bran dish (bran′dish), *v.t.* wave or shake threateningly; flourish. —*n.* a threatening shake; flourish. [< Old French *brandiss-,* a form of *brandir* to brand < *brand* sword]

breast work (brest′werk′), *n.* a low, sometimes hastily built wall for defense.

brusque (brusk), *adj.* abrupt in manner or speech; blunt. [< French < Italian *brusco* coarse]

buck a roo (buk′ə rü′, buk′ə rü′), *n., pl.* **-roos.** cowboy. [probably < Gullah *buckra* a white man, of west African origin; ending altered after Spanish *vaquero* vaquero]

bul lion (bul′yən), *n.* gold or silver in the form of ingots or bars. [< Anglo-French < Old French *bouillir* to boil; influenced by Old French *billon* debased metal]

bul wark (bul′wərk), *n.* **1** person, thing, or idea that is a defense or protection. **2** wall of earth or other material for defense against an enemy; rampart. **3** breakwater. **4** Usually, **bulwarks,** *pl.* side of a ship extending like a fence above the deck. —*v.t.* **1** defend; protect. **2** provide with a bulwark or bulwarks. [Middle English *bulwerk*]

bur eau crat (byur′ə krat), *n.* **1** official in a bureaucracy. **2** a government official who insists on rigid routine.

cache (kash), *n.* **1** a hiding place, especially of goods, treasure, food, etc. **2** the store of food or supplies hidden. [< French < *cacher* to hide]

ca coph o ny (kə kof′ə nē), *n., pl.* **-nies.** succession of harsh, clashing sounds; dissonance; discord. [< Greek *kakophōnia* < *kakos* bad + *phōnē* sound]

ca dav er ous (kə dav′ər əs), *adj.* **1** pale and ghastly. **2** thin and worn. **3** of or like a cadaver. —**ca dav′er ous ness,** *n.*

ca dence (kād′ns), *n.* **1** fall of the voice. **2** a rising and falling sound; modulation. [< French < Italian *cadenza* < Latin *cadere* to fall]

ca lam i ty (kə lam′ə tē), *n., pl.* **-ties.** **1** a great misfortune, such as a flood, a fire, the loss of one's sight or hearing. **2** serious trouble; misery. [< Latin *calamitatem*]

cal dron (kôl′drən), *n.* a large kettle or boiler. Also, **cauldron.** [< Old French *caudron* < Late Latin *caldaria* < Latin *calidus* hot]

cal i brate (kal′ə brāt), *v.t.,* **-brat ed, -brat ing.** **1** determine, check or adjust the scale of (a thermometer, gauge, or other measuring instrument). Calibrating is usually done by comparison with a standard instrument. **2** find the caliber of. **3** INFORMAL. measure.

cal lous (kal′əs), *adj.* unfeeling; insensitive. —**cal′lous ness,** *n.*

ca pa cious (kə pā′shəs), *adj.* able to hold much; large and roomy; spacious: *a capacious closet.*

ca pit u late (kə pich′ə lāt), *v.i.,* **-lat ed, -lat ing.** surrender on certain terms or conditions. [< Medieval Latin *capitulatum* arranged under headings or chapters < Latin *capitulum* small head < *caput* head]

ca pit u la tion (kə pich′ə lā′shən), *n.* a surrender on certain terms or conditions.

ca price (kə prēs′), *n.* **1** a sudden change of mind without reason; unreasonable notion or desire; whim. **2** tendency to change suddenly and without reason. **3** capriccio. [< French < Italian *capriccio,* literally, a shiver]

ca pri cious (kə prish′əs, kə prē′shəs), *adj.* likely to change suddenly without reason; changeable; fickle. —**ca pri′cious ly,** *adv.*

car i ca ture (kar′ə kə chur, kar′ə kə chər), *n., v.,* **-tured,**

-turing. **1** picture, cartoon, or description that exaggerates the peculiarities of a person or the defects of a thing. **2** imitation or rendering of something by ridiculous exaggeration of flaws in the original. [< French < Italian *caricatura* < *caricare* exaggerate < Late Latin *carricare* to load < Latin *carrus* wagon]

car niv or ous (kär niv′ər əs), *adj.* **1** of or having to do with an order of mammals that feed chiefly on flesh. **2** using other animals as food; flesh-eating: *the strong carnivorous eagle.* [< Latin *carnivorus* < *carnem* flesh + *vorare* devour]

car ri on (kar′ē ən), *adj.* **1** feeding on dead and decaying flesh. **2** rotten; filthy. [< Old French *caroine* carcass < Popular Latin *caronia* < Latin *carnem* flesh. Doublet of CRONE.]

cas sock (kas′ək), *n.* a long outer garment, usually black, worn by a clergyman. [< French *casaque* < Italian *casacca*]

caste (kast), *n.* **1** an exclusive social group; distinct class. **2** a social system having distinct classes separated by differences of birth, rank, wealth, or position. [< Portuguese *casta* race, class, animal species < Latin *castus* pure, chaste]

cat a comb (kat′ə kōm), *n.* Usually, **catacombs,** *pl.* an underground gallery forming a burial place, especially a network of such galleries with recesses in which to place the dead. [< Late Latin *catacumbae,* plural]

cat a pult (kat′ə pult), *n.* an ancient weapon for shooting stones, arrows, etc. —*v.t.* throw; hurl. —*v.i.* shoot up suddenly; spring. [< Latin *catapulta* < Greek *katapeltēs,* probably < *kata-* down + *pallein* to hurl]

cat e chize (kat′ə kīz), *v.t.,* **-chized, -chiz ing.** question closely. [< Greek *katēchizein.*]

caulk (kôk), *v.t.* fill up (a seam, crack, or joint) so that it will not leak; make watertight. Sailors caulk wooden boats with oakum and tar. Also, **calk.** [< Old French *cauquer* press in, tread < Latin *calcare* < *calcem* heel]

cau ter y (kôt′ə rē), *n., pl.* **-ies.** a heated iron with which dead tissue is burned away.

ca vort (kə vôrt′), *v.* prance about; jump around.

ce les tial (sə les′chəl), *adj.* **1** of the sky; having to do with the heavens. **2** of or belonging to heaven as the place of God and the angels; heavenly; divine. **3** very good or beautiful. [< Latin *caelestis* < *caelum* heaven]

cel i ba cy (sel′ə bə sē), *n.* unmarried state; single life.

cen ser (sen′sər), *n.* container in which incense is burned, especially during religious ceremonies. [ultimately < Latin *incensum* incense]

chafe (chāf), *v.,* **chafed, chaf ing.** wear away by rubbing.

char nel (chär′nl), *adj.* **1** of or used for a charnel. **2** like a charnel; deathlike; ghastly. [< Middle French, ultimately < Latin *carnalem* < CARNAL.]

char y (cher′ē, char′ē), *adj.,* **char i er, char i est.** **1** showing caution; careful; wary. **2** shy. **3** sparing; stingy. [< Old English *cearig* sorrowful < *caru* care]

chas ten (chā′sn), *v.t.* **1** punish to improve; discipline. **2** restrain from excess or crudeness; moderate. **3** make chaste in character or style; purify; refine. —**chas′ten er,** *n.* —**chas′ten ing ly,** *adv.* —**chas′ten ment,** *n.*

chas tise ment (cha stīz′mənt, chas′tiz ment), *n.* punishment.

chère belle (sher bel′), FRENCH. dear beautiful one.

chide (chīd), *v.,* **chid ed, chid, chid ing.** —*v.t.* find fault with; reproach or blame; scold. —*v.i.* find fault; speak in rebuke. [Old English *cīdan*] —**chid′er,** *n.* —**chid′ing ly,** *adv.*

chil blain (chil′blān′), *n.* Usually, **chilblains,** *pl.* an itching sore or redness on the hands or feet caused chiefly by exposure to cold.

chiv al ry (shiv′əl rē), *n.* **1** qualities of an ideal knight in the Middle Ages; bravery, honor, courtesy, protection of the weak, respect for women, generosity, and fairness to enemies. **2** gallant warriors or gentlemen. [< Old French *chevalerie* < *chevalier*]

choc o late (chôk′ə lit, chôk′ə lit; chok′ə lit, chok′ə lit), *n.* **1** substance made by roasting and grinding cacao seeds. It has a strong, rich flavor and much value as food. **2** drink made of chocolate with hot milk or water and sugar. **3** candy made of chocolate. **4** a dark brown. —*adj.* **1** made of or flavored with chocolate. **2** dark-brown. [< Mexican Spanish < Nahuatl *chocolatl*]

chol er ic (kol′ər ik), *adj.* **1** having an irritable disposition; easily made angry. **2** enraged; angry; wrathful.

churl ish (chèr′lish), *adj.* rude or surly; bad-tempered.

cinque foil (singk′foil′), *n.* any of a genus of plants of the rose family, having small, five-petaled yellow, white, or red flowers and leaves divided into five parts. [< Latin *quinquefolium* < *quinque* five + *folium* leaf]

cir cum lo cu tion (sėr′kəm lō kyü′shən), *n.* **1** the use of several or many words instead of one or a few. **2** a roundabout expression.

cir cum nav i gate (sėr′kəm nav′ə gāt), *v.t.*, **-gat ed, -gat ing.** sail around: *Magellan's ship circumnavigated the earth.*

cir cum nav i ga tion (sėr′kəm nav′ə gā′shən), *n.* act of sailing around.

cir cum scribe (sėr′kəm skrīb′, sėr′kəm skrīb′), *v.t.*, **-scribed, -scrib ing.** **1** draw a line around; mark the boundaries of; bound. **2** surround. **3** limit; restrict. [< Latin *circumscribere* < *circum* around + *scribere* write]

cir cum spect (sėr′kəm spekt), *adj.* watchful on all sides; cautious or prudent; careful. [< Latin *circumspectum* < *circum* around + *specere* look]

cir rus (sir′əs), *n., pl.* **cir ri** (sir′ī). **1** cloud formation consisting of thin, detached, featherlike, white clouds of ice crystals occurring at heights of 20,000 feet (7000 meters) and above. **2** (in zoology) a slender process or appendage. **3** (in botany) a tendril. [< Latin, curl]

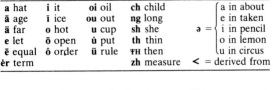

cirrus (def. 1)

ci ta tion (sī tā′shən), *n.* honorable mention for bravery in war.

clem en cy (klem′ən sē), *n., pl.* **-cies.** **1** gentleness in the use of power or authority; mercy or leniency.

clois ter (kloi′stər), *n.* **1** place of religious retirement; convent or monastery. **2** a quiet place shut away from the world. —*v.t.* shut away in a quiet place.

clot (klot), *v.i.*, **clot ted, clot ting.** form into clots; coagulate: *Milk clots when it turns sour.* [< Old English *clott*]

cloy (kloi), *v.t., v.i.* **1** make or become weary by too much, too sweet, or too rich food. **2** make or become weary by too much of anything pleasant.

co a lesce (kō′ə les′), *v.i.*, **-lesced, -lesc ing. 1** grow together. **2** unite into one body, mass, party, etc.; combine. [< Latin *coalescere* < *co-* together + *alescere* grow]

cog ni zance (kog′nə zəns, kon′ə zəns), *n.* **1.** knowledge; perception; awareness. **2 take cognizance of,** take notice of; give attention to: *She took cognizance of her faults.* **3** in law: **a** jurisdiction; responsibility; charge. **4** official notice. **b** right or power to deal with judicially. [< Old French *conoissance* < *conoistre* know < Latin *cognoscere*]

coign (koin), *n.* a projecting corner. [variant of *coin*]

col lat er al (kə lat′ər əl), *adj.* **1** related but less important; secondary; indirect. **2** side by side; parallel. **3** in a parallel line of descent; descended from the same ancestors, but in a different line. Cousins are collateral relatives. [< Medieval Latin *collateralem* < Latin *com-* + *lateralem* lateral]

col lop (kol′əp), *n.* **1** a small portion or slice, especially of meat. **2** a roll of flesh on the body. [Middle English *coloppe, colhoppe*]

col lo quy (kol′ə kwē), *n., pl.* **-quies.** a talking together; conversation; conference. [< Latin *colloquium* < *colloqui* talk together < *com-* with + *loqui* speak]

com bus ti bil i ty (kəm bus′tə bil′ə tē), *n.* flammability.

comme ce la se fait (kôm sə la sə fā′), FRENCH. that's how it's usually done.

com men da tion (kom′ən dā′shən), *n.* **1** praise; approval. **2** recommendation. **3** a handing over to another for safekeeping; entrusting.

com men sur ate (kə men′shər it, kə men′sər it), *adj.* **1** in the

a hat	i it	oi oil	ch child	{ a in about
ā age	ī ice	ou out	ng long	e in taken
ä far	o hot	u cup	sh she	ə = { i in pencil
e let	ō open	u̇ put	th thin	o in lemon
ē equal	ô order	ü rule	ᴛʜ then	u in circus
ėr term			zh measure	< = derived from

proper proportion; proportionate: *The pay should be commensurate with the work.* **2** of the same size or extent; equal. **3** commensurable. [< Late Latin *commensuratum* < Latin *com-* together + *mensura* measure]

com mon (kom′ən), *n.* land owned or used by all the people of a town, village, etc. [< Old French *comun* < Latin *communem* < *com-* together + *munia* duties]

com mune (kə myün′), *v.i.*, **-muned, -mun ing. 1** talk intimately. **2** receive Holy Communion. [< Old French *communer* make common, share < *comun*]

com mun ion (kə myü′nyən), *n.* **1** act of sharing; a having in common. **2** exchange of thoughts and feelings; intimate talk; felllowship. **3** a close spiritual relationship. [< Latin *communionem* < *communis* common]

com pas sion (kəm pash′ən), *n.* feeling for another's sorrow or hardship that leads to help; sympathy; pity. [< Latin *compassionem* < *compati* suffer with < *com-* with + *pati* suffer]

com plai sant (kəm plā′snt, kəm plā′znt), *adj.* **1** obliging; gracious; courteous. **2** compliant. [< French] —**com plai′sant ly,** *adv.*

com pul sion (kəm pul′shən), *n.* **1** a compelling or a being compelled; use of force; force; coercion. **2** impulse that is hard to resist. [< Late Latin *compulsionem* < Latin *compellere*]

com punc tion (kəm pungk′shən), *n.* **1** uneasiness of the mind because of wrongdoing; pricking of conscience; remorse. **2** a slight or passing regret. [< Late Latin *compunctionem* < Latin *compungere* to prick, sting < *com-* + *ungere* to prick]

con ceiv a ble (kən sē′və bəl), *adj.* that can be conceived or thought of; imaginable.

con cen tric (kən sen′trik), *adj.* having the same center.

con cert ed (kən sėr′tid), *adj.* **1** arranged by agreement; planned or made together; combined: *a concerted effort.* **2** (in music) arranged in parts for several voices or instruments.

con duce (kən düs′, kən dyüs′), *v.i.*, **-duced, -duc ing.** be favorable; lead; contribute: *Darkness and quiet conduce to sleep.* [< Latin *conducere.* See CONDUCT.]

con du cive (kən dü′siv, kən dyü′siv), *adj.* favorable; helpful: *Exercise is conducive to health.* —**con du′cive ness,** *n.*

con duct (kən dukt′), *v.t.* **1** direct the course of; manage. **2** guide; lead. [< Latin *conductum* < *conducere* to lead together < *com-* together + *ducere* lead]

con fab u late (kən fab′yə lāt), *v.i.*, **-lat ed, -lat ing.** talk together informally and intimately; chat. [ultimately < Latin *com-* together + *fabulari* talk < *fabula* fable] —**con fab′u la′tion,** *n.*

con fis cate (kon′fə skāt), *v.t.*, **-cat ed, -cat ing. 1** seize for the public treasury. **2** seize by authority; take and keep. [< Latin *confiscatum* laid away in a chest < *com-* + *fiscus* chest, public treasury]

con fla gra tion (kon′flə grā′shən), *n.* a great and destructive fire. [< Latin *conflagrationem* < *conflagrare* burn up < *com-* up + *flagrare* burn]

con glom e ra tion (kən glom′ə rā′shən), *n.* a mixed-up mass of various things or persons; mixture.

con jec ture (kən jek′chər), *n.* **1** formation of an opinion admittedly without sufficient evidence for proof; guessing. **2** a guess. [< Latin *conjectura* < *conjicere* discuss, throw together < *com-* together + *jacere* throw]

con niv ance (kə nī′vəns), *n.* a conniving; pretended ignorance or secret encouragement of wrongdoing.

con nois seur (kon′ə sėr′), *n.* a critical judge of art or of matters of taste; expert. [< Old French < *connoistre* know < Latin *cognoscere*] —**con′nois seur′ship,** *n.*

GLOSSARY

967

con san guin i ty (kon′sang gwin′ə tē), *n.* relationship by descent from the same parent or ancestor; relationship by blood.

con serv a to ry (kən sėr′və tôr′ē, kən sėr′və tōr′ē), school for instruction in music.

con spic u ous (kən spik′yü əs), *adj.* **1** easily seen; clearly visible. **2** worthy of notice; remarkable. [< Latin *conspicuus* visible < *conspicere* look at < *com-* + *specere* look]

con spire (kən spīr′), *v.i.,* **-spired, -spir ing. 1** plan secretly with others to do something unlawful or wrong; plot. **2** act together.

con ster na tion (kon′stər nā′shən), *n.* great dismay; paralyzing terror. [< Latin *consternationem* < *consternare* terrify]

con strain (kən strān′), *v.t.* **1** force; compel. **2** confine; imprison. **3** repress; restrain. [< Old French *constreindre* < Latin *constringere* < *com-* together + *stringere* pull tightly]

con strained (kən strānd′), *adj.* **1** forced. **2** restrained; stiff; unnatural: *a constrained smile.*

con strict (kən strikt′), *v.t.* draw together; contract; compress. [< Latin *constrictum* constricted < *com-* together + *stringere* pull tightly]

con sum mate (kən sum′it), *adj.* in the highest degree; complete; perfect. [< Latin *consummatum* brought to a peak < *com-* + *summa* peak]

con sump tive (kən sump′tiv), *adj.* **1** of, having, or likely to have consumption. **2** tending to consume; destructive; wasteful.

con ta gious (kən tā′jəs), *adj.* **1** spreading by direct or indirect contact; catching: *Scarlet fever is a contagious disease.* **2** causing contagious diseases. **3** used for contagious diseases.

con temn (kən tem′), *v.t.* treat with contempt; scorn. [< Latin *contemnere* < *com-* + *temnere* to scorn]

con tempt (kən tempt′), *n.* **1** the feeling that a person, act, or thing is mean, low, or worthless; scorn; despising; disdain. **2** a being scorned; disgrace. [< Latin *contemptus* < *contemnere*]

con temp tu ous (kən temp′chü əs), *adj.* showing contempt; scornful: *a contemptuous look.*

con tin gen cy (kən tin′jən sē), *n., pl.* **-cies. 1** a happening or event depending on something that is uncertain; possibility. **2** an accidental happening; unexpected event; chance. **3** uncertainty of occurrence; dependence on chance.

con tri tion (kən trish′ən), *n.* **1** sorrow for one's sins or guilt; being contrite; penitence. **2** deep regret.

con triv ance (kən trī′vəns), *n.* **1** thing invented; mechanical device. **2** act or manner of contriving. **3** power or ability of contriving. **4** plan; scheme.

con trive (kən trīv′), *v.t.* **-trived, -triv ing. 1** plan with cleverness or skill; invent; design. **2** plan; scheme; plot: *contrive a robbery.* [< Old French *controver* < Late Latin *contropare* compare]

con ver sa zio ne (kō′ver sä′tsyō′ne), *n.* ITALIAN. social gathering.

con vic tion (kən vik′shən), *n.* **1** act of proving or declaring guilty. **2** condition of being proved or declared guilty. **3** act of convincing (a person). **4** a being convinced. **5** firm belief; certainty.

con vul sive (kən vul′siv), *adj.* **1** violently disturbing. **2** having convulsions. **3** producing convulsions. **—con vul′sive ly,** *adv.*

co pi ous (kō′pē əs), *adj.* **1** more than enough; plentiful; abundant: *a copious harvest.* **2** containing much matter. **3** containing many words. [< Latin *copiosus* < *copia* plenty < *co-* with + *ops* resources]

co que try (kō′kə trē, kō ket′rē), *n., pl.* **-tries. 1** flirting. **2** trifling.

co quette (kō ket′), *n.* woman who tries to attract men; flirt. [< French, feminine of *coquet,* diminutive of *coq* cock]

cor ner stone (kôr′nər stōn′), *n.* **1** stone at the corner of two walls that holds them together. **2** such a stone built into the corner of a building as its formal beginning. The laying of a cornerstone is often accompanied by ceremonies. **3** something of fundamental importance; foundation; basis.

cor nice (kôr′nis), *n.,* **-niced, -nic ing. 1** an ornamental, horizontal molding along the top of a wall, pillar, building, etc. **2** a molding around the walls of a room just below the ceiling or over the top of a window. [< French *corniche* < Italian *cornice*]

cor nu co pi a (kôr′nə kō′pē ə), *n.* **1** a horn-shaped container represented as overflowing with fruits, vegetables, and flowers; horn of plenty. **2** a horn-shaped container or ornament. [< Late Latin, for Latin *cornu copiae* horn of plenty]

cor pu lent (kôr′pyə lənt), *adj.* large or bulky of body; fat. — **cor′pu lent ly,** *adv.*

cor rect (kə rekt′), *adj.* **1** free from mistakes or faults; right: *the correct answer.* **2** agreeing with a recognized standard, especially of good taste; proper: *correct manners.* [< Latin *correctum* made straight < *com-* + *regere* to guide]

cor rup tion (kə rup′shən), *n.* rot; decay.

coun te nance (koun′tə nəns), *n., v.,* **-nanced, -nanc ing. —** *n.* **1** expression of the face. **2** face; features.

cou pé (kü pā′), *n.* a closed, two-door automobile, usually seating two to six people. [< French *coupé,* past participle of *couper* to cut]

cour i er (kėr′ē ər, kùr′ē ər), *n.* **1** messenger sent in haste. **2** a secret agent who transfers information to and from other agents. [< Middle French *courrier* < Italian *corriere* < *correre* to run < Latin *currere*]

cov e nant (kuv′ə nənt), *n.* **1** a solemn agreement between two or more persons or groups to do or not to do a certain thing; compact. **2** a formal agreement that is legal; legal contract. **3** (in the Bible) the solemn promises of God to man; compact between God and man. [< Old French, present participle of *covenir* agree < Latin *convenire*]

cov et (kuv′it), *v.t.* desire eagerly (something that belongs to another).

cowl (koul), *n.* **1** a monk's cloak with a hood. **2** the hood itself. **3** anything shaped like a cowl. —*v.t.* **1** put a monk's cowl on. **2** cover with a cowl or something resembling a cowl. [Old English *cūle, cugele* < Late Latin *cuculla,* variant of Latin *cucullus* hood]

coy o te (kī ō′tē, kī′ōt), *n., pl.* **-tes** or **-te.** a small wolflike mammal of the dog family living on the prairies of western North America; prairie wolf. It is noted for loud howling at night. [< Mexican Spanish < Nahuatl *coyotl*]

cowl (def. 2)

cra ven (krā′vən), *adj.* cowardly. [< Old French *cravente* overcome < Popular Latin *crepantare* < Latin *crepare* crush; burst]

cre o sote (krē′ə sōt), *n.* **1** a poisonous oily liquid with a penetrating odor, obtained by distilling wood tar and used to preserve wood. **2** a similar substance obtained by distilling wood tar and used as an antiseptic. [originally, a meat preservative < German *kreosot* < Greek *kreōs* flesh + *sōzein* to save]

cre scen do (krə shen′dō), *adj., adv., n., pl.* **-dos.** a gradual increase in force or loudness, especially in music. [< Italian, literally, increasing]

cro quet (krō kā′), *n.* an outdoor game played by driving wooden balls through wickets with mallets. [< French, dialectal variant of *crochet*.]

cross bow (krôs′bō′, kros′bō′), *n.* a medieval weapon for shooting arrows, stones, etc., with a bow fixed across a wooden stock, and a groove in the middle to direct the arrows, stones, etc.

cup (kup), *n.* any of various beverages, usually combining wine, fruit, and spices.

cu po la (kyü′pə lə), *n.* **1** a rounded roof; dome. **2** a small dome or tower on a roof. [< Italian < Late Latin *cupula,* diminutive of Latin *cupa* tub]

cur i o (kyùr′ē ō), *n., pl.* **cur i os.** object valued as a curiosity; a strange, rare, or novel object: *oriental curios.* [short for *curiosity*]

dame de comp toir (dam də kômp twär′), FRENCH. woman in charge of running a café.

daunt less (dônt′lis, dänt′lis), *adj.* not to be frightened or discouraged; brave.

de bauch (di bôch′), *n.* period or bout of excessive indulgence in sensual pleasures; excess in eating, drinking, etc. [< French *débaucher* entice from duty]

deb au chee (deb′ô chē′, deb′ô shē′), *n.* person who indulges excessively in sensual pleasures.

de bris or **dé bris** (də brē′, dā′brē′), *n.* the remains of anything broken down or destroyed; ruins; rubbish: *the debris from an explosion.* [< French *débris*]

deb u tante or **dé bu tante** (deb′yə tänt, deb′yə tant, deb′ yə tänt′), *n.* **1** a young woman during her first season in society. **2** woman making a debut. [< French *débutante*]

dec a dence (dek′ə dəns, di kād′ns), *n.* a falling off; growing worse; decline; decay. [< Middle French *décadence* < Medieval Latin *decadentia* < Latin *de-* + *cadere* to fall]

de co rum (di kôr′əm, di kōr′əm), *n.* **1** proper behavior; good taste in conduct, speech, dress, etc. **2** observance or requirement of polite society.

def e ren tial (def′ə ren′shəl), *adj.* showing deference; respectful.

de fin i tive (di fin′ə tiv), *adj.* **1** that decides or settles a question; conclusive; final. **2** authoritative; completely reliable. **3** limiting; defining. —**de fin′i tive ly,** *adv.* **de fin′i tive ness,** *n.*

de i fy (dē′ə fī), *v.t.,* **-fied, -fy ing. 1** make a god of. **2** worship or regard as a god: *deify wealth.* [< Old French *deifier* < Late Latin *deificare* < Latin *deus* god + *facere* make]

de i ty (dē′ə tē), *n., pl.* **-ties. 1** one of the gods worshiped by a people or a tribe; god or goddess. **2** divine nature; being a god. [< Old French *deite* < Late Latin *deitatem* < Latin *deus* god]

del e gate (del′ə gāt, del′ə git), *n.* person given power or authority to act for others; representative to a convention, meeting, etc. [< Latin *delegatum* delegated < *de-* + *legare* send with a commission]

del e ga tion (del′ə gā′shən), *n.* **1** act of delegating. **2** fact of being delegated. **3** group of delegates.

de lin e ate (di lin′ē āt), *v.t.,* **-at ed, -at ing. 1** trace the outline of. **2** draw; sketch. **3** describe in words; portray. [< Latin *delineatum* delineated < *de-* + *linea* line]

de lu sion (di lü′zhən), *n.* **1** a false belief or opinion. **2** a fixed belief maintained in spite of unquestionable evidence to the contrary. People with mental disorders often have delusions. [< Latin *delusionem* < *deludere*]

de mean or (di mē′nər), *n.* way a person looks and acts; behavior; manner.

de mur (di mėr′), *v.,* **-murred, -mur ring.** show disapproval or dislike; take exception; object. [< Old French *demurer* < Latin *demorari* < *de-* + *morari* to delay]

de mure (di myùr′), *adj.,* **-mur er, -mur est.** reserved or composed in demeanor; serious and sober. [< *de-* + Old French *meür* discreet, mature < Latin *maturus*]

de noue ment or **dé noue ment** (dā′nü mäN′, dā nü′mäN), *n.* **1** solution of a plot in a story, play, situation, etc. **2** outcome; end. [< French *dénouement* < *dénouer* untie]

de nun ci a tion (di nun′sē ā′shən), *n.* **1** expression of strong disapproval; public condemnation; denouncing. **2** an informing against; accusation. **3** a formal notice of the intention to end a treaty, etc.

de plete (di plēt′), *v.t.,* **-plet ed, -plet ing.** empty or exhaust by drawing away or using up resources, strength, vitality, etc. [< Latin *depletum* emptied out < *de-* + *-plere* fill]

dep re cate (dep′rə kāt), *v.t.,* **-cat ed, -cat ing. 1** express strong disapproval of. **2** depreciate; belittle. [< Latin *deprecatum* pleaded in excuse, averted by prayer < *de-* + *precari* pray] —**dep′re ca′tion,** *n.*

dep ri va tion (dep′rə vā′shən), *n.* **1** act of depriving. **2** condition of being deprived; loss; privation.

de ride (di rīd′), *v.t.,* **-rid ed, -rid ing.** make fun of; laugh at in scorn. [< Latin *deridere* < *de-* + *ridere* to laugh]

de riv a tive (di riv′ə tiv), *adj.* coming from a source; not origi-nal; derived. —*n.* something derived.

der vish (dėr′vish), member of a Moslem religious order that practices self-denial and devotion. Some dervishes dance and spin about violently. [< Turkish *derviş* < Persian *darvīsh*]

de scry (di skrī′), *v.t.,* **-scried, -scry ing. 1** catch sight of; be able to see; make out. **2** discover by observation; detect. [< Old French *descrier* proclaim < des- dis- + *crier* to cry]

des ha bille (dez′ə bēl′), *n.* See *dishabille.*

des ig na tion (dez′ig nā′shən), *n.* a descriptive title; name: *"Your Honor"* is a designation given to a judge.

des pot ic (des pot′ik), *adj.* of a despot; having unlimited power; tyrannical.

des pot ism (des′pə tiz′əm), *n.* **1** government by a despot. **2** tyranny or oppression.

des ti tu tion (des′tə tü′shən, des′tə tyü′shən), *n.* **1** destitute condition; extreme poverty. **2** a being without; lack.

det ri men tal (det′rə men′tl), *adj.* causing loss or damage; injurious; harmful. —**det′ri men′tal ly,** *adv.*

de vi ous (dē′vē əs), *adj.* **1** out of the direct way; winding; roundabout. **2** straying from the right course; not straightforward. [< Latin *devius* turning aside < *de-* out of + *via* way]

de volve (di volv′), *v.i.,* **-volved, -volv ing.** be handed down to someone else; be transferred. [< Latin *devolvere* < *de-* down + *volvere* to roll]

di a dem (dī′ə dem), *n.* **1** a crown. **2** an ornamental band of cloth formerly worn as a crown. **3** royal power or authority. [< Latin *diadema* < Greek *diadēma* < *diadein* bind across < *dia-* + *dein* bind]

di as to le (dī as′tl ē), *n.* the normal, rhythmical dilation of the heart, especially that of the ventricles. During diastole the chambers of the heart fill up with blood.

di dac tic (dī dak′tik, di dak′tik), *adj.* **1** intended to instruct. **2** inclined to instruct others; teacherlike.

dif fi dent (dif′ə dənt), *adj.* lacking in self-confidence; shy. [< Latin *diffidentem* < *dis-* + *fidere* to trust] —**dif′fi dent ly,** *adv.*

dif fuse (di fyüs′), *adj.* not concentrated together at a single point; spread out: *diffuse light.* [< Latin *diffusum* poured forth < *dis-* + *fundere* to pour]

di lap i da tion (də lap′ə dā′shən), *n.* partial ruin; falling to pieces.

dil a to ry (dil′ə tôr′ē, dil′ə tōr′ē), *adj.* **1** tending to delay; not prompt. **2** causing delay. [< Latin *dilatorius* < *dilatum* brought apart < *dis-* apart + *latum* brought]

di min u tive (də min′yə tiv), *adj.* very small; tiny; minute.

din (din), *n., v.,* **dinned, din ning.** —*n.* a continuing loud, confused noise. —*v.i.* make a din. —*v.t.* **1** strike with a din. **2** say over and over again; repeat in a tiresome way. [Old English *dynn*]

dirge (dėrj), *n.* a funeral song or tune.

dis ar ray (dis′ə rā′), *n.* lack of order; disorder; confusion.

dis con cert (dis′kən sėrt′), *v.t.* **1** disturb the self-possession of; embarrass greatly; confuse. **2** upset or frustrate (plans, etc.).

dis con so late (dis kon′sə lit), *adj.* **1** without hope; forlorn; unhappy. **2** causing discomfort; cheerless. [< Medieval Latin *disconsolatus* < Latin *dis-* + *consolari* to console]

dis cord (dis′kôrd), *n.* disagreement of opinions and aims; dissension. [< Old French < *discorder* disagree < Latin *discordare* < *discordem* discordant < *dis-* apart + *cordem* heart]

dis cord ant (dis kôrd′nt), *adj.* **1** not in agreement; differing. **2** not in harmony. **3** harsh; clashing.

dis creet (dis krēt′), *adj.* very careful and sensible in speech and action; having or showing good judgment; wisely cautious. [< Old

a hat	**i** it	**oi** oil	**ch** child	a in about
ā age	**ī** ice	**ou** out	**ng** long	e in taken
ä far	**o** hot	**u** cup	**sh** she	**ə** = i in pencil
e let	**ō** open	**u̇** put	**th** thin	o in lemon
ē equal	**ô** order	**ü** rule	**ᵺ** then	u in circus
ėr term			**zh** measure	< = derived from

GLOSSARY

French *discret* < Late Latin *discretus* discerning < Latin *discernere* discern]

dis dain (dis dān′), *v.t.* think unworthy of oneself or one's notice; regard or treat with contempt; scorn. —*n.* a disdaining; feeling of scorn. [< Old French *desdeignier* < *des-* dis- + *deignier* deign]

dis dain ful (dis dān′fəl), *adj.* feeling or showing disdain; scornful. —**dis dain′ful ly,** *adv.*

dis ha bille (dis′ə bēl′), *n.* 1 informal; careless dress. 2 condition of being partly undressed: *be caught in a state of dishabille.* Also, **deshabille.** [< French *déshabillé* undressed]

di shev eled or **di shev elled** (də shev′əld), *adj.* not neat; rumpled; mussed; disordered: *disheveled hair.*

dis pas sion ate (dis pash′ə nit), *adj.* free from emotion or prejudice; calm and impartial.

dis po si tion (dis′pə zish′ən), *n.* 1 one's habitual ways of acting toward others or of thinking about things; nature: *a cheerful disposition.* 2 tendency; inclination.

dis qui e tude (dis kwī′ə tüd, dis kwī′ə tyüd), *n.* uneasiness; anxiety.

dis qui si tion (dis′kwə zish′ən), *n.* a long or formal speech or writing about a subject; dissertation. [< Latin *disquisitionem* < *disquirere* inquire < *dis-* + *quaerere* seek]

dis sem ble (di sem′bəl), *v.,* **-bled, -bling.** —*v.t.* 1 hide (one's real feelings, thoughts, plans, etc.); disguise. 2 pretend; feign. —*v.i.* conceal one's opinions, motives, etc.

dis si dent (dis′ə dənt), *adj.* disagreeing in opinion; dissenting —*n.* person who disagrees or dissents. [< Latin *dissidentem* < *dis-* apart + *sedere* sit]

dis si pate (dis′ə pāt), *v.,* **-pat ed, -pat ing.** —*v.t.* 1 spread in different directions; scatter. 2 cause to disappear; dispel. —*v.i.* scatter so as to disappear; disperse. [< Latin *dissipatum* scattered < *dis-* apart + *supare* to throw]

dis so lute (dis′ə lüt), *adj.* living an immoral life; loose in morals; licentious; dissipated. [< Latin *dissolutum* loosened, loose < *dis-* apart + *solvere* to loosen]

dis so lu tion (dis′ə lü′shən), *n.* 1 a breaking up or ending of an association of any kind. 2 the breaking up of an assembly by ending its session. 3 ruin; destruction. 4 death.

di ver gence (də vėr′jəns, dī vėr′jəns), *n.* act or fact of diverging; a deviating or differing: *divergence from the rules, a wide divergence of opinion.*

di vers (dī′vərz), *adj.* more than one; several different; various. [< Old French < Latin *diversum* turned aside, diverted]

div i na tion (div′ə nā′shən), *n.* 1 act of foreseeing the future or discovering what is hidden or obscure by supernatural or magical means. 2 augury; prophecy.

di vulge (də vulj′, dī vulj′), *v.t.,* **-vulged, -vulg ing.** make known or tell openly (something private or secret); reveal. [< Latin *divulgare* make common < *dis-* + *vulgus* common people]

doc ile (dos′əl), *adj.* 1 easily managed or trained; obedient. 2 easily taught; willing to learn. [< Middle French < Latin *docilem* < *docere* teach]

dole ful (dōl′fəl), *adj.* very sad or dreary; mournful; dismal. —**dole′ful ly,** *adv.*

dole some (dōl′səm), *adj.* ARCHAIC. doleful.

do mes ti cate (də mes′tə kāt), *v.t.,* **-cat ed, -cat ing.** 1 change (animals, plants, etc.) from a wild to a tame or cultivated state. 2 make fond of home and family life. 3 cause to be or feel at home; naturalize. —**do mes′ti ca′tion,** *n.*

do min ion (də min′yən), *n.* 1 power or right of governing and controlling; rule; control. 2 territory under the control of one ruler or government.

dough boy (dō′boi′), *n.* U.S. INFORMAL. an infantryman in the United States Army during World War I.

dow a ger (dou′ə jər), *n.* 1 woman who holds some title or property from her dead husband. 2 INFORMAL. a dignified, elderly woman, usually of high social position. [< Old French *douagere* < *douage* dower < *douer* endow < Latin *dotare* < *dotem* dowry]

draft (draft), *n.* 1 a single act of drinking: *I emptied the glass at one draft.* 2 amount taken in a single drink; drink or dose.

draught (draft), *n., v.t., adj.* draft

dray (drā), *n.* a low, strong cart or wagon for carrying heavy loads. —*v.t.* transport or carry on a cart. [Old English *dræge* dragnet < *dragan* to draw]

drone (drōn), *v.i.,* **droned, dron ing.** 1 make a deep, continuous humming sound: *Bees droned among the flowers.* 2 talk in a dull, monotonous voice. [Old English *drān*]

duc tile (duk′təl), *adj.* 1 capable of being hammered out thin or drawn out into a wire. 2 capable of being easily molded or shaped; pliant. 3 easily managed or influenced; docile.

dun (dun), *adj.* dull, grayish-brown. [Old English *dunn*]

dust er (dus′tər), *n.* a long, light garment worn over the clothes to keep dust off them.

dys pep si a (dis pep′sē ə, dis pep′shə), *n.* indigestion. [< Greek < *dys-* bad + *peptein* digest]

eb on y (eb′ə nē), *n., pl.* **-on ies,** *adj.* —*n.* a hard, durable, black wood, used for the black keys of a piano, for the backs and handles of brushes, for ornamental woodwork, etc. —*adj.* like ebony; black; dark. [< Greek *ebenos* ebony < Egyptian *hbnj*]

ec ru or **é cru** (ek′rü, ā′krü), *adj.* pale-brown; light-tan. —*n.* a pale brown; light tan. [< French *écru* raw, unbleached]

ef face (ə fās′), *v.t.,* **-faced, -fac ing.** 1 rub out; blot out; wipe out; obliterate. 2 keep (oneself) from being noticed; make inconspicuous. [< Middle French *effacer* < *es-* away + *face* face]

ef fi ca cy (ef′ə kə sē), *n., pl.* **-cies.** power to produce the effect wanted; effectiveness. [< Latin *efficacia* < *efficere* accomplish < *ex-* + *facere* do, make]

ef flu vi um (i flü′vē əm), *n., pl.* **-vi a** (-vē ə), **-vi ums.** vapor or odor, usually unpleasant. [< Latin, a flowing out]

ef fuse (i fyüz′), *v.t.,* **-fused, -fus ing.** pour out; spill; shed. [< Latin *effusum* poured out < *ex-* out + *fundere* pour]

e gre gious (i grē′jəs), *adj.* 1 remarkably or extraordinarily bad; outrageous; flagrant. 2 remarkable; extraordinary. [< Latin *egregius* < *ex-* out + *gregem* herd, flock]

e jac u late (i jak′yə lāt), *v.t., v.i.,* **-lat ed, -lat ing.** say suddenly and briefly; exclaim. [< Latin *ejaculatum* thrown out < *ex-* out + *jacere* to throw]

e jac u la tion (i jak′yə lā′shən), *n.* something said suddenly and briefly; exclamation.

e la tion (i lā′shən), *n.* high spirits; joy or pride.

el o cu tion (el′ə kyü′shən), *n.* 1 art of speaking or reading clearly and expressively in public, including the use of the voice, gestures, etc. 2 manner of speaking or reading in public; delivery. [< Latin *elocutionem* < *eloqui* speak out]

e lon gate (i lông′gāt, i long′gāt), *v.,* **-gat ed, -gat ing,** *adj.* —*v.t., v.i.* make or become longer; lengthen; extend; stretch. —*adj.* lengthened. [< Latin *elongatum* lengthened < *ex-* out + *longus* long]

e lu ci date (i lü′sə dāt), *v.t.,* **-dat ed, -dat ing.** make clear; explain; clarify. [< Late Latin *elucidatum* made clear < Latin *ex-* out + *lucidus* bright] —**e lu′ci da′tion,** *n.*

e ma ci ate (i mā′shē āt), *v.t.,* **-at ed, -at ing.** make unnaturally thin; cause to lose flesh or waste away; *A long illness had emaciated the patient.* [< Latin *emaciatum* made lean < *ex-* + *macies* leanness]

em bra sure (em brā′zhər), *n.* an opening in a wall for a gun, with sides that spread outward to permit the gun to fire through a greater arc. [< French]

em i nent (em′ə nənt), *adj.* 1 above all or most others; outstanding; distinguished. 2 conspicuous; noteworthy: *The judge was a man of eminent fairness.* 3 high; lofty. [< Latin *eminentem* standing out, prominent < *ex-* out + *minere* jut]

embrasure (def. 1)

em is sar y (em′ə ser′ē), *n., pl.* **-saries.** 1 person sent on a mission or errand. 2 a secret agent; spy. [< Latin *emissarius* < *emittere*]

em phy se ma (em′fə sē′mə), *n.* an abnormal enlargement of the air sacs in the lungs caused by a loss of elasticity in the walls of the air sacs and a resulting inability to expel carbon dioxide. Emphysema makes breathing difficult. [< Greek *emphysēma* swelling]

-ence, *suffix forming nouns chiefly from verbs.* **1** act or fact of ___ing: *Abhorence = act or fact of abhorring.* **2** quality or condition of being ___ent: *Prudence = quality of being prudent.* Also, **-ency.**

en cum ber (en kum′bər), *v.t.* **1** hold back (from running, doing, etc.); hinder; hamper: *Heavy shoes encumber a runner in a race.* **2** burden with weight, difficulties, cares, debt, etc. [< Old French *encombrer* < *en-* in + *combre* barrier]

en cum brance (en kum′brəns), *n.* **1** something useless or in the way; hindrance; burden. **2** claim, mortgage, etc., on property.

en deav or (en dev′ər), *v.i.*, *v.t.* make an effort; try hard; attempt earnestly. —*n.* an earnest attempt; hard try; effort; [< *en-* + Old French *devoir* duty]

en fran chise (en fran′chīz), *v.t.*, **-chised, -chis ing. 1** give the rights of citizenship to, especially the right to vote. **2** set free. —**en fran′chise ment,** *n.*

e nor mi ty (i nôr′mə tē), *n.*, *pl.* **-ties. 1** extreme wickedness; outrageousness. **2** an extremely wicked crime; outrageous offense. **3** INFORMAL. great size, especially of a problem, job, etc.

e nu me rate (i nü′mə rāt′, i nyü′mə rāt′), *v.t.*, **-rat ed, -rat ing. 1** name one by one; list: *He enumerated the capitals of the 50 states.* **2** find out the number of; count. [< Latin *enumeratum* counted < *ex-* out + *numerus* number] —**e nu′me ra′tion,** *n.*

e nun ci ate (i nun′sē āt), *v.*, **-at ed, -at ing.** —*v.i.* speak or pronounce words. —*v.t.* speak or pronounce; articulate. [< Latin *enuntiatum* announced < *ex-* out + *nuntius* messenger]

e phem er al (i fem′ər əl), *adj.* **1** lasting for only a very short time; very short-lived; transitory. **2** lasting for only a day. [< Greek *ephēmeros* < *epi-* upon + *hēmera* day]

ep i thet (ep′ə thet), *n.* **1** a descriptive expression; word or phrase expressing some quality or attribute. In "crafty Ulysses" and "Richard the Lion-Hearted" the epithets are "crafty" and "the Lion-Hearted." **2** an insulting or contemptuous word or phrase used in place of a person's name. [< Greek *epitheton* added < *epi-* upon + *tithenai* to place]

e pit o me (i pit′ə mē), *n.* **1** a condensed account; summary. An epitome contains only the most important points of a literary work, subject, etc. **2** person or thing that is typical or representative of something. [< Greek *epitomē* < *epitemnein* cut short < *epi-* + *temnein* to cut]

ep och (ep′ək, ē′pok), *n.* **1** period of time; era; age. **2** period of time in which striking things happened.

e qua nim i ty (ē′kwə nim′ə tē, ek′wə nim′ə tē), *n.* evenness of mind or temper; calmness; composure. [< Latin *aequanimitatem* < *aequus* even + *animus* mind, temper]

e quiv o cal (i kwiv′ə kəl), *adj.* **1** having two or more meanings; intentionally vague or ambiguous. **2** undecided; uncertain. **3** questionable; suspicious. [< Late Latin *aequivocus* ambiguous < Latin *aequus* equal + *vocare* to call]

e rad i ca tion (i rad′ə kā′shən), *n.* an eradicating; complete destruction.

es cu lent (es′kyə lənt), *adj.* suitable for food; edible. —*n.* anything that is fit for food, especially vegetables. [< Latin *esculentus* < *esca* food]

es pal ier (e spal′yər), *n.* **1** trellis or framework of stakes upon which fruit trees and shrubs are trained to grow. **2** plant or row of plants trained to grow up a wall or an espalier. —*v.t.* train or furnish with an espalier. [< French]

es sence (es′ns), *n.* **1** that which makes a thing what it is; necessary part or parts; important feature or features: *Being thoughtful of others is the essence of politeness.* **2** a concentrated substance that has the characteristic flavor, fragrance, or effect of the plant, fruit, etc.,

espalier (def. 2)

a	hat	i	it	oi	oil	ch child
ā	age	ī	ice	ou	out	ng long
ä	far	o	hot	u	cup	sh she
e	let	ō	open	ů	put	th thin
ē	equal	ô	order	ü	rule	ŦH then
ėr	term					zh measure

ə = { a in about / e in taken / i in pencil / o in lemon / u in circus }

< = derived from

from which it is taken. [< Latin *essentia* < *esse* be]

es teem (e stēm′), *v.t.* **1** have a very favorable opinion of; think highly of. **2** think; consider. —*n.* a very favorable opinion; high regard.

e ther (ē′thər), *n.* a colorless, volatile, flammable, sweet-smelling liquid, produced by the action of sulfuric acid on ethyl alcohol. Because its fumes cause unconsciousness when deeply inhaled, ether is used as an anesthetic. [< Latin *aether* < Greek *aithēr* upper air]

e ther e al (i thir′ē əl), *adj.* **1** light; airy; delicate: *the ethereal beauty of a butterfly.* **2** not of the earth; heavenly.

etherise See *etherize.*

e ther ize (ē′thə rīz′), *v.t.*, **-ized, iz ing. 1** make unconscious with ether fumes. **2** change into ether.

E trus can (i trus′kən), *adj.* of or having to do with Etruria, its people, their language, art, or customs.

et y mol o gy (et′ə mol′ə jē), *n.*, *pl.* **-gies. 1** the derivation of a word. **2** account or explanation of the origin and history of a word. **3** study dealing with linguistic changes, especially with individual word origins. [< Greek *etymologia* < *etymon* the original sense or form of a word (neuter of *etymos* true, real) + *-logos* treating of]

eu lo gy (yü′lə jē), *n.*, *pl.* **-gies. 1** speech or writing in praise of a person or thing, especially a set oration in honor of a deceased person. **2** high praise. [< Greek *eulogia* < *eu-* well + *legein* speak]

e va sive (i vā′siv, i vā′ziv), *adj.* tending or trying to evade.

ev i ta ble (ev′ə tə bəl), *adj.* avoidable.

ex as pe ra tion (eg zas′pə rā′shən), *n.* extreme annoyance; irritation; anger.

ex cru ci at ing (ek skrü′shē ā′ting), *adj.* **1** causing great suffering; very painful; torturing. **2** excessively elaborate; extreme: *excruciating politeness.* —**ex cru′ci at′ing ly,** *adv.*

ex e crate (ek′sə krāt), *v.*, **-crat ed, -crat ing.** —*v.t.* **1** feel intense loathing for; abhor; detest. **2** pronounce a curse upon. —*v.i.* curse. [< Latin *exsecratum* declared accursed < *ex-* out + *sacer* sacred]

ex e cra tion (ek′sə krā′shən), *n.* **1** act of execrating. **2** a curse. **3** person or thing execrated.

ex ec u tor (eg zek′yə tər), *n.* person named in a will to carry out the provisions of the will.

ex em plar y (eg zem′plər ē, eg′zəm pler′ē), *adj.* **1** worth imitating; serving as a model or pattern. **2** serving as a warning to others. **3** serving as an example; typical.

ex hort (eg zôrt′), *v.t.* urge strongly; advise or warn earnestly. [< Latin *exhortari* < *ex-* + *hortari* urge strongly]

ex on e rate (eg zon′ə rāt′), *v.t.*, **-rat ed, -rat ing.** free from blame; prove or declare innocent. [< Latin *exoneratum* freed from burden < *ex-* off + *oneris* burden]

ex pa tri ate (v. eks pā′trē āt; n., *adj.* eks pā′trē it, eks pā′trē āt), *v.*, **-at ed, -at ing,** *n.*, *adj.* —*v.t.* **1** force to leave one's country; banish; exile. **2** withdraw (oneself) from one's country; renounce one's citizenship. —*n.* an expatriated person; exile. —*adj.* expatriated. [ultimately < Latin *ex-* out of + *patria* fatherland] —**ex pa′tri a′tion,** *n.*

ex pe di en cy (ek spē′dē ən sē), *n.*, *pl.* **-cies. 1** a helping to bring about a desired result; desirability or fitness under the circumstances; usefulness. **2** personal advantage; self-interest.

ex pe di ent (ek spē′dē ənt), *adj.* **1** helping to bring about a desired result; desirable or suitable under the circumstances; useful; advantageous. **2** giving or seeking personal advantage; based on self-interest. —*n.* means of bringing about a desired result.

ex pi ate (ek′spē āt), *v.t.*, **-at ed, -at ing.** pay the penalty of; make amends for a wrong, sin, etc.; atone for. [< Latin *expiatum* atoned completely < *ex-* completely + *piare* appease < *pius* devout] —**ex′pi a′tor,** *n.*

ex po si tion (ek′spə zish′ən), *n.* **1** a detailed explanation. **2** speech or writing explaining a process, thing, or idea. **3** part of a work of literature in which the theme is introduced. **4** where something is placed in relation to the sun.

ex qui site (ek′skwi zit, ek skwiz′it), *adj.* **1** very lovely; delicate. **2** sharp; intense. **3** of highest excellence; most admirable. [< Latin *exquisitus* sought out < *ex-* out + *quaerere* seek]

ex tem po rize (ek stem′pə rīz′), *v.i., v.t.,* **-rized, -riz ing. 1** speak, play, sing, or dance, composing as one goes along; improvise. **2** prepare offhand; make for the occasion. —**extem′por i za′tion,** *n.* —**ex tem′po riz′er,** *n.*

ex tra ne ous (ek strā′nē əs), *adj.* **1** from outside; not belonging or proper to a thing; foreign. **2** not essential. [< Latin *extraneus* < *extra* outside]

ex u ber ant (eg zü′bər ənt), *adj.* **1** profuse in growth; luxuriant. **2** abounding in health and spirits; overflowing with good cheer. [< Latin *exuberantem* growing luxuriantly < *ex-* thoroughly + *uber* fertile] —**ex u′ber ance,** *n.*

ex ul tant (eg zul′tənt), *adj.* joyful; jubilant; triumphant.

ex ul ta tion (eg′zul tā′shən), *n.* also **ex ul tance** (eg-zul′təns). great rejoicing; triumph.

fab ri cate (fab′rə kāt), *v.t.,* **-cat ed, -cat ing. 1** make (anything that requires skill); build or manufacture. **2** make by fitting together standardized parts. **3** make up; invent (a story, lie, excuse, etc.).

fab ri ca tion (fab′rə kā′shən), *n.* **1** a fabricating. **2** something fabricated.

fa cade or **fa çade** (fə-säd′), *n.* **1** the front part of a building. **2** any side of a building that faces a street or an open space. [< French *façade,* ultimately < Latin *facies* a form, face]

fac ile (fas′əl), *adj.* moving, acting, working, etc., easily or rapidly: *a facile hand, a facile tongue, a facile pen.* [< French < Latin *facilis* easy < *facere* do]

fac ing (fā′sing), *n.*

facade (def. 1)
of a Romanesque church

fac ings, *pl.* cuffs, collar, and trimmings of a military coat.

fag ot (fag′ət), *n.* **1** bundle of sticks or twigs tied together for fuel. **2** bundle of iron rods or pieces of iron or steel to be welded. —*v.t.* [< Old French]

fal low (fal′ō), *adj.* **1** plowed and left unseeded for a season or more. **2** (of the mind) uncultivated or inactive. —*n.* **1** land plowed and left unseeded for a season or more. **2** the plowing of land without seeding it for a season in order to destroy weeds, improve the soil, etc.; inactive period. [Old English *fealg*] —**fal′low ness,** *n.*

fal ter (fôl′tər), *v.i.* hesitate in action from lack of courage; draw back; waver; *falter before making a difficult decision.*

far o (fer′ō, far′ō), *n,* a gambling game played by betting on the order in which certain cards will appear. [apparently alteration of *Pharaoh*]

fath om (faŦH′əm), *v.* get to the bottom of; understand fully. [Old English *fæthm* width of the outstretched arms]

fat u ous (fach′ü əs), *adj.* stupid but self-satisfied; foolish; silly. [< Latin *fatuus*]

fe lic i tate (fə lis′ə tāt), *v.t.,* **-tat ed, -tat ing.** express good wishes to formally; congratulate.

fer ule (fer′əl, fer′ül), *n.* stick or ruler for punishing children by striking them, especially on the hand. [< Latin *ferula* rod]

fes ter (fes′tər), *v.i.* **1** form pus. **2** cause soreness or pain; rankle. **3** decay; rot. —*v.t.* cause to rankle: *Time festered the insult to his pride.* [< Old French *festre* < Latin *fistula* ulcer]

fet id (fet′id, fē′tid), *adj.* smelling very bad; stinking. [< Latin *foetidus* < *foetere* to stink]

fi as co (fē as′kō), *n., pl.* **-cos** or **-coes.** a complete or ridiculous failure; humiliating breakdown. [< Italian, literally, flask]

fil a ment (fil′ə mənt), *n.* **1** a very fine thread; very slender, threadlike part. **2** the threadlike wire that becomes incandescent by the passage of a current in an electric light bulb. [< Late Latin *filamentum* < Latin *filum* thread]

fil i al (fil′ē əl), *adj.* of a son or daughter; due from a son or daughter toward a mother or father: *filial affection.* [< Late Latin *filialis* < Latin *filius* son and *filia* daughter]

fil let (fil′it; *usually* fi lā′), *n.* **1** slice of fish or meat without bones or fat; filet. **2** a narrow band, ribbon, etc., worn around the head to hold the hair in place or as an ornament. [< Old French *filet,* diminutive of *fil* thread < Latin *filum*]

flag on (flag′ən), *n.* **1** container for liquids, usually having a handle, a spout, and a cover. **2** a large bottle, holding about two quarts (1.9 liters). [< Old French *flacon, flascon* < Late Latin *flasconem.* Related to FLASK.]

flail (flāl), *n.* instrument for threshing grain by hand, consisting of a wooden handle at the end of which a stouter and shorter pole or club is fastened so as to swing freely.

flu vi al (flü′vē əl), *adj.* of, found in, or produced by a river. [< Latin *fluvialis* < *fluvius* river < *fluere* to flow]

fop (fop), *n.* a vain man who is very fond of fine clothes and has affected manners; dandy.

fop per y (fop′ər ē), *n., pl.* **-per ies.** behavior or dress of a fop.

fo ray (fôr′ā, for′ā), *n.* a raid for plunder. —*v.t.* lay waste; plunder; pillage. [< Old French *forrer* to forage]

for bear (fôr ber′, fôr bar′), *v.i.,* **-bore, -borne, -bear ing. 1** hold back; keep from doing, saying, using, etc. **2** be patient; control oneself. [Old English *forberan*]

fore cas tle (fōk′səl, fôr′kas′əl, fōr′kas′əl), *n.* **1** the upper deck in front of the foremast. **2** the sailors' quarters in the forward part of a merchantman.

for mi da ble (fôr′mə də bəl), *adj.* hard to overcome; hard to deal with; to be dreaded. [< Latin *formidabilis* < *formidare* to dread < *formido* terror, dread] —**for′mi da bly,** *adv.*

for mu late (fôr′myə lāt), *v.t.,* **-lat ed, -lat ing. 1** state definitely or systematically. **2** express in a formula; reduce to a formula.

for tu i tous (fôr tü′ə təs, fôr tyü′ə təs), *adj.* **1** happening by chance; accidental. **2** bringing good luck or favorable results; fortunate. [< Latin *fortuitus* < *forte* a chance]

fowl er (fou′lər), *n.* person who hunts, shoots, catches, or traps wild birds.

free boot er (frē′bü′tər), *n.* pirate; buccaneer. [< Dutch *vrijbuiter* < *vrij* free + *buit* booty]

fret work (fret′werk′), *n.* ornamental openwork or carving.

frip per y (frip′ər ē), *n., pl.* **-per ies. 1** cheap, showy clothes; gaudy ornaments. **2** a showing off; foolish display. [< Middle French *friperie,* ultimately < Old French *frepe* rag]

froe (frō), *n.* a cleaving tool having a heavy blade set at right angles to the handle. [origin uncertain]

frol ic some (frol′ik səm), *adj.* full of fun; playful; merry.

fru gal i ty (frü gal′ə tē), *n., pl.* **-ties.** avoidance of waste; thrift.

fur tive (fer′tiv), *adj.* **1** done quickly and with stealth to avoid being noticed; sly: *a furtive glance into the forbidden room.* **2** sly; stealthy: *a furtive manner.* [< Latin *furtivus* < *furtum* theft < *fur* thief] —**fur′tive ly,** *adv.*

fu sil lade (fyü′zə lād′), *n., v.,* **-lad ed, -lad ing.** —*n.* **1** a rapid or continuous discharge of many firearms at the same time. **2** any rapid discharge or burst. —*v.t.* attack or shoot down by a fusillade.

ga loot (gə lüt′), *n.* SLANG. an awkward or foolish person. [origin uncertain]

gam in (gam′ən), *n.* **1** a neglected child left to roam about the streets. **2** a small, lively person. [< French]

gar ru lous (gar′ə les, gar′yə ləs), *adj.* **1** talking too much; talkative. **2** using too many words; wordy. [< Latin *garrulus* < *garrire* to chatter]

gem ma ry (jem′ər ē), *n.* the science of gems. [< Late Latin *gemmarius* < Latin *gemma* jewel; bud]

gen der (jen′dər), *n.* **1** the grouping of nouns into certain classes, such as masculine, feminine, or neuter. **2** sex: *the female gender.* [< Old French *gendre* < Latin *generis* kind, sort, class]

ge ner ic (jə ner′ik), *adj.* **1** characteristic of a genus, kind, or class. **2** having to do with a class of similar things; general.

gen teel (jen tēl′), *adj.* **1** belonging or suited to polite society. **2** polite; well-bred; fashionable; elegant. **3** artificially polite and courteous. [< Middle French *gentil* < Latin *gentilis.* Doublet of GENTILE, GENTLE, JAUNTY.]

ges tic u late (je stik′yə lāt), *v.i.,* **-lat ed, -lat ing.** make or use gestures to show ideas or feelings. [< Latin *gesticulatum* gesticulated, ultimately < *gestus* gesture]

ges tic u la tion (je stik′yə lā′shən), *n.* **1** a making lively or excited gestures. **2** a lively or excited gesture.

gild (gild), *v.t.,* **gild ed** or **gilt, gild ing. 1** cover with a thin layer of gold or similar material; make golden. **2** make (something) look bright and pleasing. [Old English *-gyldan* < *gold* gold]

gin ger ly (jin′jər lē), *adv.* with extreme care or caution.

girt (gėrt), *v.t.* **1** put a belt, girdle, or girth around; gird. **2** fasten with a belt, girdle, or girth. [variant of *girth*]

gnarled (närld), *adj.* containing gnarls; knotted; twisted.

goi ter or **goi tre** (goi′tər). *n.* enlargement of the thyroid gland which is often seen as a large swelling in the front of the neck, usually caused by a diet with too little iodine. [< French *goitre,* ultimately < Latin *guttur* throat]

gon do la (gon′dl ə), *n.* a spherical enclosure suspended from cables by which passengers are transported up and down a mountain. < Italian]

gos sa mer (gos′ə mər), *n.* **1** film or thread of cobweb spun by small spiders, which is seen floating in the air in calm weather. **2** anything very light and thin. —*adj.* like gossamer; very light and thin; filmy. [Middle English *gossomer* goose summer, name for "Indian summer," as the season for goose and cobwebs]

gran di ose (gran′dē ōs), *adj.* **1** grand in an imposing or impressive way; magnificient. **2** grand in a showy or pompous way; not really magnificient, but trying to seem so. [< French < Italian *grandioso* < Latin *grandis* big]

grap ple (grap′əl), *v.t.,* **-pled, -pling.** seize and hold fast; grip or hold firmly. [< Old French *grapil* a hook]

griev ous (grē′vəs), *adj.* **1** hard to bear; causing great pain or suffering; severe. **2** very evil or offensive; outrageous. **3** causing grief.

gro tesque (grō tesk′), *adj.* **1** odd or unnatural in shape, appearance, manner, etc.; fantastic. **2** ridiculous; absurd. [< French < Italian *grottesco,* literally, of caves, cavelike < *grotta*] —**gro tes′que′ly,** *adv.*

grot to (grot′ō), *n., pl.* **-toes** or **-tos. 1** cave or cavern. **2** an artificial cave made for coolness and pleasure. [< Italian *grotto, grotta* < Latin *crypta* < Greek *kryptē* vault. Doublet of CRYPT.]

gui don (gīd′n, gī′don), *n.* **1** a small flag or streamer carried as a guide by soldiers, or used for signaling. **2** flag, steamer, or pennant of a company, regiment, etc. [< Italian *guidone* < *guidare* to direct]

guile less (gīl′lis), *adj.* without guile; honest; frank; straightforward. —**guile′less ly,** *adv.* —**guile′less ness,** *n.*

gy rate (jī′rāt, jī rāt′), *v.i.,* **-rat ed, -rat ing.** move in a circle or spiral; whirl; rotate. [< Latin *gyrus* circle < Greek *gyros*]

gy ra tion (jī rā′shən), *n.* circular or spiral motion; whirling; rotation.

hab i tude (hab′ə tüd, hab′ə tyüd) *n.* **1** characteristic condition of body or mind. **2** habit; custom.

a hat	**i** it	**oi** oil	**ch** child		⎧a in about
ā age	**ī** ice	**ou** out	**ng** long		⎪e in taken
ä far	**o** hot	**u** cup	**sh** she	**ə** = ⎨i in pencil
e let	**ō** open	**ů** put	**th** thin		⎪o in lemon
ē equal	**ô** order	**ü** rule	**ŦH** then		⎩u in circus
ėr term			**zh** measure		**<** = derived from

hal yard (hal′yərd), *n.* rope or tackle used on a ship to raise or lower a sail, yard, flag, etc. [Middle English *hallyer* < *hale;* form influenced by *yard*]

hap haz ard (hap′haz′ərd), *adj.* not planned; random. —**hap′haz′ard ly,** *adv.*

ha rangue (hə rang′), *n., v.,* **-rangued, -rangu ing.** —*n.* **1** a noisy, vehement speech. **2** a long, pompous, formal speech. —*v.t.* address (someone) with a harangue. —*v.i.* deliver a harangue. [< Middle French]

har ass (har′əs, hə ras′), *v.t.* **1** trouble by repeated attacks; harry. **2** distress with annoying labor, care, misfortune, etc.; disturb; worry; torment. [< French *harasser* < Old French *harer* set a dog on < *hare* a shout to excite dogs to attack]

haugh ty (hô′tē), *adj.,* **-ti er, -ti est.** too proud and scornful of others. [Middle English *haute* < Middle French *haut* < Latin *altus* high]

hav er sack (hav′ər sak), *n.* bag used by soldiers and hikers for carrying food, utensils, etc., when on a march or hike. [< French *havresac* < German *Habersack* oat sack]

he lix (hē′liks), *n., pl.* **hel i ces** or **he lix es. 1** anything having a spiral, coiled form such as a screw thread, a watch spring, or a snail shell. **2** a spiral ornament.

hemp (hemp), *n* **1** a tall annual plant of the same family as the mulberry, native to Asia and extensively cultivated elsewhere for its tough fibers, which are made into heavy string, rope, coarse cloth, etc.; cannabis. **2** the tough fibers obtained from the bark of this plant.

hi er o glyph ic (hī′ər ə glif′-ik), *n.* **1** picture, character, or symbol standing for a word, idea, or sound; hieroglyph. The ancient Egyptians used hieroglyphics instead of an alphabet like ours. **2** letter or word that is hard to read. [< Late Latin *hieroglyphicus* < Greek *hieroglyphikos* < *hieros* sacred + *glyphē* a carving]

A KINGLY	𓋴
GIFT OF AN	𓎙
OFFERING TABLE	𓊵
TO	𓊪
RA-HORUS	𓅊
THE GREAT	𓉐
GOD	𓊹
LORD OF	𓎟
HEAVEN	𓇯

hieroglyphic (def. 1)
Egyptian hieroglyphics

hin drance (hin′drəns), *n.* **1** person or thing that hinders. **2** act of hindering.

hoar y (hôr′ē, hōr′ē), *adj.,* **hoar i er, hoar i est. 1** white or gray. **2** white or gray with age. **3** old; ancient.

hob ble (hob′əl), *v.,* **-bled, -bling.** *v.i.* **1** walk awkwardly or lamely; limp. **2** move unsteadily. —*v.t.* **1** cause to walk awkwardly or limp. **2** tie the legs of (a horse, etc.) together in order to prevent free motion. **3** hinder. [Middle English *hobelen*]

hob gob lin (hob′gob′lən), *n.* **1** goblin or elf. **2** bogy.

hom age (hom′ij, om′ij), *n.* **1** dutiful respect; reverence: *Everyone paid homage to the great leader.* **2** (in the Middle Ages) a pledge of loyalty and service by a vassal to a lord.

horn pipe (hôrn′pīp′), *n.* a lively dance done by one person, formerly popular among sailors.

host (hōst), *n.* **1** a large number; multitude: *As it grew dark, a few stars appeared, then a host of them.* **2** army of soldiers. [< Old French < Late Latin *hostis* army < Latin, stranger, enemy]

how be it (hou bē′it), *adv.* ARCHAIC. nevertheless. —*conj.* though.

GLOSSARY

hus band (huz′bənd), *v.t.* **1** manage carefully; be saving of: *husband one's strength.* **2** marry. [Old English *hūsbōnda* < Scandinavian (Old Icelandic) *hūsbōndi* < *hūs* house + *bōndi* freeholder]

hus band ry (huz′bən drē), *n.* **1** farming: *animal husbandry.* **2** careful management of one's affairs or resources; thrift.

-ible *suffix added to verbs to form adjectives.* that can be _____ed: *Reducible = that can be reduced.*

-ic, *suffix added to nouns to form adjectives.* **1** of or having to do with: *Atmospheric = of the atmosphere.* **2** having the nature of: *Heroic = having the nature of a hero.* **3** constituting or being: *Bombastic = constituting bombast.*

i dol a ter (ī dol′ə tər), *n.* **1** person who worships idols. **2** admirer; adorer.

ill-got ten (il′got′n), *adj.* acquired by evil or unfair means; dishonestly obtained.

il lim it a ble (i lim′ə tə bəl), *adj.* without limit; boundless; infinite.

il lu mi nate (i lü′mə nāt), *v.t.,* **-nat ed, -nat ing. 1** make clear; explain. **2** enlighten; inform; instruct.

il lu sion (i lü′zhən), *n.* **1** appearance or feeling that misleads because it is not real; thing that deceives by giving a false idea. **2** a false impression or perception: *an optical illusion.* **3** false notion or belief. [< Latin *illusionem* < *illudere* mock < *in-* at + *ludere* play]

il lu sive (i lü′siv), *adj.* illusory.

il lu sor y (i lü′sər ē), *adj.* due to an illusion; misleading; deceptive.

im mi nent (im′ə nənt), *adj.* likely to happen soon; about to occur. [< Latin *imminentem* overhanging, threatening] **—im′mi nence,** *n.*

im mit i ga ble (i mit′ə gə bəl), *adj.* that cannot be softened or mitigated.

im mo late (im′ə lāt), *v.t.,* **-lat ed, -lat ing. 1** kill as a sacrifice. **2** offer in sacrifice; sacrifice. [< Latin *immolatum* sacrificed, (originally) sprinkled with sacrificial meal < *in-* on + *mola* sacrificial meal] **—im′mo la′tion,** *n.*

im pal pa ble (im pal′pə bəl), *adj.* that cannot be felt by touching; intangible.

im ped i ment (im ped′ə mənt), *n.* **1** hindrance; obstruction. **2** some physical defect, especially a defect in speech.

im pel (im pel′), *v.t.,* **-pelled, -pel ling. 1** drive or force; cause: *The cold impelled her to go indoors.* **2** cause to move; drive forward; push along.

im per cep ti ble (im′pər sep′tə bəl), *adj.* that cannot be perceived or felt; very slight, gradual, subtle, or indistinct.

im per i al (im pir′ē əl), *adj.* **1** of an empire or its ruler: *the imperial palace.* **2** of or having to do with the rule or authority of one country over other countries and colonies. **3** having the rank of an emperor. **4** supreme.

im per i ous (im pir′ē əs), *adj.* **1** haughty or arrogant; domineering; overbearing. **2** not to be avoided; necessary; urgent.

im pla ca ble (im plā′kə bəl, im plak′ə bəl), *adj.* unable to be appeased; refusing to be reconciled; unyielding.

im plore (im plôr′, im plōr′), *v.t.,* **-plored, -plor ing. 1** beg or pray earnestly for. **2** beg (a person) to do something. [< Latin *implorare* < *in-* toward + *plorare* cry] **—im plor′er,** *n.* **—im plor′ing ly,** *adv.*

im por tune (im′pôr tün′, im′pôr tyün′, im pôr′chən), *v.,* **-tuned, -tun ing.** *adj.* —*v.t.* ask urgently or repeatedly; annoy with pressing demands. —*adj.* importunate. [< Latin *importunus* inconvenient]

im pose (im pōz′), *v.t.,* **-posed, -pos ing. 1** force or thrust (oneself or one's company) on another or others; obtrude; presume. **2 impose on** or **impose upon, a** take advantage of; use for selfish purposes. **b** deceive; cheat; trick. [< Middle French *imposer* < *in-* on + *poser* put, place]

im po ten cy (im′pə tən sē), *n.* helplessness.

im po tent (im′pə tənt), *adj.* not having power; helpless.

im prac ti ca ble (im prak′tə kə bəl), *adj.* **1** impossible to put into practice; not practicable. **2** not usable; unfit for use.

im pre ca tion (im′prə kā′shən), *n.* **1** an imprecating; cursing. **2** curse.

im preg na ble (im preg′nə bəl), *adj.* able to resist attack; not yielding to force, persuasion, etc.: *an impregnable fortress.*

im prov i sa tion (im′prov ə zā′shən, im′prə vi zā′shən), *n.* **1** an improvising. **2** something made up on the spur of the moment, without preparation.

im pu dence (im′pyə dəns), *n.* **1** a being impudent; shameless boldness; great rudeness; insolence. **2** impudent conduct or language.

im pu dent (im′pyə dənt), *adj.* shamelessly bold; very rude and insolent. [< Latin *impudentem* < *in-* not + *pudere* be modest]

im pu ni ty (im pyü′nə tē), *n.* freedom from punishment, injury, or other bad consequences: *If laws are not enforced, crimes are committed with impunity.* [< Latin *impunitatem,* ultimately < *in* without + *poena* punishment]

in-[1], *prefix.* not; the opposite of; the absence of: *Inexpensive = not expensive. Inattention = the absence of attention.* Also **i-, il-, im-,** and **ir-.**

in-[2], *prefix.* in; into; on; upon: *Incase = (put) into a case. Intrust = (give) in trust.* Also **il-, im-, ir-.**

in-[3], *prefix.* in; within; into; toward: *Indoors = within doors. Inland = toward land.*

in ac ces si ble (in′ak ses′ə bəl), *adj.* **1** hard to get at; hard to reach or enter. **2** not accessible; that cannot be reached or entered at all.

in al ien a ble (in ā′lyə nə bəl, in ā′lē ə nə bəl), *adj.* that cannot be given or taken away; that cannot be transferred to another: *an inalienable right.* Also, **unalienable.**

in ar tic u late (in′är tik′yə lit), *adj.* **1** not uttered in distinct syllables or words: *an inarticulate mutter.* **2** unable to speak in words; dumb. **—in′ar tic′u late ness,** *n.*

in can ta tion (in′kan tā′shən), *n.* **1** set of words spoken as a magic charm or to cast a magic spell. **2** the use of such words. [< Latin *incantationem* < *incantare* enchant < *in-* against + *cantare* to chant]

in cen di ar y (in sen′dē er′ē), *adj.* deliberately stirring up strife, violence, or rebellion: *incendiary speeches.* [< Latin *incendiarius* causing fire < *incendium* fire < *incendere* to set on fire]

in ces sant (in ses′nt), *adj.* never stopping; continued or repeated without interruption; continual: *the incessant noise from the factory.* [< Late Latin *incessantem* < Latin *in-* not + *cessare* cease]

in com mode (in′kə mōd′), *v.t.,* **-mod ed, -mod ing.** cause trouble, difficulty, etc., to; inconvenience. [< Latin *incommodare* < *incommodus* inconvenient < *in-* not + *commodus* convenient]

in com mod i ty (in′kə mod′ə tē), *n., pl.* **-ties. 1** inconvenience; discomfort. **2** something that is inconvenient.

in con gru ence (in kong′grü əns), *n.* lack of agreement.

in con gru en cy (in′kong grü′ən sē), *n.* lack of agreement; incongruity.

in con gru ous (in kong′grü əs), *adj.* **1** out of keeping; not appropriate; out of place. **2** lacking in agreement or harmony; not consistent.

in cor ri gi ble (in kôr′ə jə bəl, in kor′ə jə bəl), *adj.* **1** too firmly fixed in bad ways, an annoying habit, etc., to be reformed or changed: *an incorrigible liar.* **2** so fixed that it cannot be changed or cured. **—in cor′ri gi bly,** *adv.*

in cred u lous (in krej′ə ləs), *adj.* **1** not ready to believe; doubting; skeptical. **2** showing a lack of belief. **—in cred′u lous ly,** *adv.*

in cur i ous (in kyùr′ē əs), *adj.* lacking curiosity; uninquiring; indifferent.

in de scrib a ble (in′di skrī′bə bəl), *adj.* that cannot be described; beyond description.

in dict (in dīt′), *v.t.* **1** charge with an offense or crime; accuse. **2** (of a grand jury) find enough evidence against (an accused person) to charge formally with a crime. [< Anglo-French *enditer,* in Old French, indite, dicate < Latin *in-* in + *dictare* declare, dictate < *dicere* say, speak]

in dict ment (in dīt′mənt), *n.* **1** a formal written accusation, especially one presented by a grand jury. **2** accusation.

in dig na tion (in′dig nā′shən), *n.* anger at something unworthy, unjust, unfair, or mean; anger mixed with scorn; righteous anger.

in dis cre tion (in′dis kresh′ən), *n.* lack of good judgment; unwiseness; imprudence.

in dis sol u ble (in′di sol′yə bəl), *adj.* that cannot be dissolved, undone, or destroyed; lasting; firm.

in do lent (in′dl ənt), *adj.* disliking work; lazy; idle. **—in′do lent ly,** *adv.*

in dom i ta ble (in dom′ə tə bəl), *adj.* that cannot be conquered; unyielding.

in e bri ate (in ē′brē ət), *n.* one who is drunk.

in ef fec tu al (in′ə fek′chü əl), *adj.* **1** without effect; useless. **2** not able to produce the effect wanted; powerless. **—in′ef fec′-tu al ly,** *adv.*

in ex haust i ble (in′ig zô′stə bəl), *adj.* **1** that cannot be exhausted; very abundant. **2** that cannot be wearied; tireless.

in ex pe di ent (in′ik spē′dē ənt), *adj.* not expedient; not practicable, suitable, or wise.

in ex plic a ble (in′ik splik′ə bəl, in ek′splə kə bəl), *adj.* that cannot be explained, understood, or accounted for; mysterious.

in fir mi ty (in fėr′mə tē), *n., pl.* **-ties.** **1** weakness; feebleness. **2** sickness; illness. **3** weakness, flaw, or defect in a person's character.

in flex i ble (in flek′sə bəl), *adj.* **1** not to be turned from a purpose by persuasion or argument; not yielding; firm; steadfast. **2** that cannot be changed; unalterable. **—in flex′i bly,** *adv.*

in ge nu i ty (in′jə nü′ə tē, in′jə nyü′ə tē), *n., pl.* **-ties.** **1** skill in planning or making something; cleverness. **2** skillfulness of contrivance or design: *the ingenuity of a puzzle.* [< Latin *ingenuitatem* frankness < *ingenuus* ingenuous; influenced by *ingenious*]

in gen u ous (in jen′yü əs), *adj.* **1** free from restraint or reserve; frank and open; sincere. **2** simple and natural; innocent; naïve. [< Latin *ingenuus,* originally, native < *in-* in + *gignere* beget]

in her ent (in hir′ənt, in her′ənt), *adj.* belonging to a person or thing as a permanent and essential quality or attribute; intrinsic: *inherent honesty, the inherent sweetness of sugar.*

in im i ta ble (in im′ə tə bəl), *adj.* impossible to imitate or copy; matchless. **—in im′i ta ble ness,** *n.* **—in im′i ta bly,** *adv.*

in junc tion (in jungk′shən), *n.* **1** a formal order from a court of law ordering a person or group to do, or refrain from doing, something. **2** an authoritative or emphatic order; command: *Injunctions of secrecy did not prevent the news from leaking out.* [< Late Latin *injunctionem* < Latin *injungere* enjoin < *in-* in + *jungere* join]

in noc u ous (i nok′yü əs), *adj.* not hurtful or injurious; harmless.

in nu en do (in′yü en′dō), *n., pl.* **-does.** an indirect hint or reference; insinuation. [< Latin, literally, by nodding to < *innuere* nod to, hint < *in-* + *-nuere* to nod]

in qui si tion (in′kwə zish′ən), *n.* **1** a thorough investigation; searching inquiry. **2** an official investigation; judicial inquiry. [< Latin *inquisitionem* < *inquirere*]

in sen sate (in sen′sāt, in sen′sit), *adj.* **1** without sensation; lifeless; inanimate: *insensate stones.* **2** unfeeling; brutal: *insensate cruelty.* **3** senseless; stupid: *insensate folly.*

in sid i ous (in sid′ē əs), *adj.* **1** seeking to entrap or ensnare; wily or sly; crafty; tricky. **2** working secretly or subtly; developing without attracting attention. [< Latin *insidiosus* < *insidiae* ambush < *insidere* sit in < *in-* in + *sedere* sit]

in sist ent (in sis′tənt), *adj.* **1** insisting. **2** compelling attention or notice; pressing; urgent: *an insistent knocking on the door.*

in so lence (in′sə ləns), *n.* bold rudeness; insulting behavior or speech.

in so lent (in′sə lənt), *adj.* boldly rude; intentionally disregarding the feelings of others; insulting. [< Latin *insolentem* arrogant, contrary to custom < *in-* not + *solere* be accustomed] **—in′so lent ly,** *adv.*

in stan ta ne ous (in′stən tā′nē əs), *adj.* coming or done in an instant; happening or made in an instant: *instantaneous applause.* **—in′stan ta′ne ous ly,** *adv.* **—in′stan ta′ne ous ness,** *n.*

in stinc tive (in stingk′tiv), *adj.* of or having to do with instinct. **—in stinc′tive ly,** *adv.*

in suf fer a ble (in suf′ər ə bəl), *adj.* intolerable; unbearable: *insufferable rudeness.* **—in suf′fer a bly,** *adv.*

a hat	i it	oi oil	ch child	⎧ a in about
ā age	ī ice	ou out	ng long	⎪ e in taken
ä far	o hot	u cup	sh she	ə = ⎨ i in pencil
e let	ō open	ů put	th thin	⎪ o in lemon
ē equal	ô order	ü rule	ᴛ<small>H</small> then	⎩ u in circus
ėr term			zh measure	< = derived from

in sup port a ble (in′sə pôr′tə bəl, in′sə pōr′tə bəl), *adj.* not endurable; unbearable; intolerable.

inter-, *prefix.* **1** one with the other; together: *Intercommunicate = communicate with each other.* **2** between: *Interpose = put between.* **3** between or among a group: *International = between or among nations.*

in ter ces sion (in′tər sesh′ən), *n.* **1** act or fact of interceding. **2** prayer pleading for others. [< Latin *intercessionem* < *intercedere.*]

in ter jec tion al (in′tər jek′shə nəl), *adj.* **1** of an interjection; used as an interjection. **2** containing an interjection.

in ter lop er (in′tər lō′pər), *n.* person who interferes, unasked and unwanted; intruder.

in ter me di ar y (in′tər mē′dē er′ē), *n., pl.* **-ar ies,** *adj.* **—n.** person who acts between others to bring about an agreement; person who acts for another; go-between. **—adj.** acting between others; mediating.

in ter mi na ble (in tėr′mə nə bəl), *adj.* **1** never stopping; unceasing; endless. **2** so long as to seem endless; very long and tiring. **—in ter′mi na bly,** *adv.*

in ter mit tent (in′tər mit′nt), *adj.* stopping for a time and beginning again; pausing at intervals.

in ter pose (in′tər pōz′), *v.,* **-posed, -pos ing.** **—v.t.** **1** put between; insert. **2** put forward; break in with. **—v.i.** **1** come or be between other things. **2** interrupt. **3** interfere in order to help; intervene; interceded. [< Middle French *interposer* < *inter-* between + *poser* to place]

in ter ro gate (in ter′ə gāt), *v.,* **-gat ed, -gat ing. —v.t.** ask questions of; examine or get information from by asking questions; question thoroughly or in a formal manner. **—v.i.** ask a series of questions. [< Latin *interrogatum* interrogated < *inter-* between + *rogare* ask]

in tim i date (in tim′ə dāt), *v.t.,* **-dat ed, -dat ing. 1** make afraid; frighten. **2** influence or force by fear.

in var i a ble (in ver′ē ə bəl, in var′ē ə bəl), *adj.* always the same; unchanging; unchangeable; constant. **—in var′i a bly,** *adv.*

in vi o la ble (in vī′ə lə bəl), *adj.* that must not be violated or injured; sacred.

in vul ner a ble (in vul′nər ə bəl), *adj.* **1** that cannot be wounded or hurt; safe from attack. **2** proof against attack; not easily assailable.

-ion, *suffix forming nouns chiefly from verbs.* **1** act of ____ing: *Attraction = act of attracting.* **2** condition of being ____ed: *Adoption = condition of being adopted.* **3** result of ____ing: *Abbreviation = result of abbreviating.* Also, **-tion, -ation.**

i ras ci ble (i ras′ə bəl), *adj.* **1** easily made angry; with a quick temper; irritable. **2** showing anger. [< Late Latin *irascibilis* < Latin *irasci* grow angry < *ira* anger]

ir i des cent (ir′ə des′nt), *adj.* displaying changing colors; changing color when moved or turned. [< Latin *iris, iridis* rainbow]

irk some (ėrk′səm), *adj.* tiresome; tedious; annoying: *an irksome task.*

i ron i cal (ī ron′ə kəl), *adj.* **1** expressing one thing and meaning the opposite. **2** contrary to what would naturally be expected. **3** using or given to using irony. **—i ron′i cal ly,** *adv.*

ir re deem a ble (ir′i dē′mə bəl), *adj.* **1** that cannot be redeemed or bought back. **2** that cannot be exchanged for coin. **3** impossible to change; beyond remedy; hopeless.

ir re press i ble (ir′i pres′ə bəl), *adj.* that cannot be repressed or restrained; uncontrollable: *irrepressible laughter.*

ir res o lute (i rez′ə lüt), *adj.* not resolute; unable to make up one's mind; not sure of what one wants; hestitating; vacillating.

-ism, *suffix forming nouns from other nouns and from adjectives and verbs.* **1** act or practice of _____ing: *Baptism = act or practice of baptizing.* **2** quality or condition of being a _____: *Heroism = quality of being a hero.* **3** illustration or instance of being _____: *Witticism = instance of being witty.* **4** an unhealthy condition caused by _____: *Alcoholism = an unhealthy condition caused by alcohol.* **5** doctrine, theory, system, or practice of _____: *Darwinism = theory of Charles Darwin.*

i so pro te re nol (ī′sə prō tə rē′nəl), *n.* a crystalline compound that is used in the treatment of asthma.

-ist, *suffix forming nouns chiefly from other nouns.* **1** person who does or makes: *Tourist = a person who tours.* **2** an expert in an art or science: *Botanist = an expert in botany.* **3** person who plays a musical instrument: *Organist = person who plays the organ.* **4** person engaged in or working with: *Journalist = a person engaged in journalism.* **5** person who believes in.

-ity *suffix forming nouns from adjectives.* quality, condition, or fact of being _____: *Sincerity = quality or condition of being sincere.*

-ive, *suffix forming adjectives from nouns.* **1** of or having to do with, as in *interrogative, inductive.* **2** tending to; likely to, as in *active, appreciative.*

-ize, *suffix forming verbs from adjectives and nouns.* **1** make _____; *Legalize = make legal.* **2** become _____: *Crystallize = become crystal.* **3** engage in or use _____: *Criticize = engage in criticism.*

---

jad ed (jā′did), *adj.* **1** worn out; tired; weary. **2** dulled from continual use; surfeited; satiated: *a jaded appetite.*

jo cose (jō kōs′), *adj.* full of jokes; given to joking; jesting; humorous. [< Latin *jocosus* < *jocus* jest]

joc u lar (jok′yə lər), *adj.* speaking or acting in jest; said or done in jest; funny; joking. [< Latin *jocularis* < *joculus,* diminutive of *jocus* jest]

joc u lar i ty (jok′yə lar′ə tē), *n., pl.* **-ties.** **1** jocular quality. **2** jocular talk or behavior. **3** a jocular remark or act.

ju di cious (jü dish′əs), *adj.* having, using, or showing good judgment; wise; sensible. **—ju di′cious ly,** *adv.*

jug u lar (jug′yə lər, jü′gyə lər), *n.* jugular vein. **jugular vein,** one of the two large veins in each side of the neck and head that return blood from the head and neck to the heart.

jux ta pose (juk′stə pōz′), *v.t.,* **-posed, -pos ing.** put close together; place side by side. [< French *juxtaposer* < Latin *juxta* beside + French *power* to place]

jux ta po si tion (juk′stə pə zish′ən), *n.* position close together or side by side.

---

ki net ic (ki net′ik), *adj.* **1** of motion. **2** caused by motion. **3** full of energy; dynamic: *a kinetic movie director.* [< Greek *kinētikos* < *kinein* to move]

knell (nel), *n.* **1** sound of a bell rung slowly after a death or at a funeral. **2** a warning sign of death, failure, etc.: *Their refusal rang the knell of our hopes.* [Old English *cnyllan* to knell]

---

lab y rinth (lab′ə rinth′), *n.* **1** number of connecting passages so arranged that it is hard to find one's way from point to point; maze. **2 Labyrinth** (in Greek legends) the maze built by Daedalus for King Minos of Crete to imprison the Minotaur. **3** any confusing, complicated arrangement.

la belle dé cou verte (lä bel′ dā kü vert′), beautiful discovery; amazing. [French]

lac e rate (*v.* las′ə rāt′; *adj.* las′ər it), *v.,* **-rat ed, -rat ing,** *adj.* **—v.t.** **1** tear roughly; mangle: *The bear's claws lacerated the*

hunter's arm. **2** wound; hurt (the feelings, etc.). **—adj.** deeply or irregularly indented as if torn: *lacerate leaves.* [< Latin *laceratum* torn, mangled]

lac e ra tion (las′ə rā′shən), *n.* **1** a lacerating. **2** a rough tear; mangled place.

lac te al (lak′tē əl), *adj.* **1** of milk; like milk; milky. **2** carrying chyle, a milky liquid formed from digested food. **—n.** any of the tiny lymphatic vessels that carry chyle from the small intestine to the blood.

lan guid (lang′gwid), *adj.* **1** without energy; drooping; weak; weary. **2** without interest or enthusiasm; indifferent; listless. [< Latin *languidus* < *languere* be faint]

las si tude (las′ə tüd, las′ə tyüd), *n.* lack of energy; weariness; languor. [< Latin *lassitudo* < *lassus* tired]

la tent (lāt′nt), *adj.* present but not active; hidden; concealed. [< Latin *latentem* lying hidden] **—la′tent ly,** *adv.*

lathe (lāᴛʜ), *n.* machine for holding pieces of wood, metal, etc., and turning them rapidly against a cutting tool which shapes them. [origin uncertain]

lat tice (lat′is), *n.,* **1** structure of crossed wooden or metal strips with open spaces between them. **2** window, gate, etc., having a lattice.

lau rel (lôr′əl, lor′əl), *n.* **laurels,** *pl.* **1** high honor; fame. **2** victory. [< Old French *lorier, laurier* < *lor* laurel < Latin *laurus*]

lave (lāv), *v.,* **laved, lav ing.** **—v.t.** **1** wash; bathe. **2** wash or flow against: *The stream laves its banks.* **—v.i.** ARCHAIC. bathe. [Old English *lafian* < Latin *lavare*]

lawn (lôn), *n.* kind of thin, sheer linen or cotton cloth. [probably < *Laon,* town in France, an important center of linen manufacture]

li cen tious (lī sen′shəs), *adj.* **1** unrestrained in sexual activities; immoral. **2** disregarding commonly accepted rules or principles; lawless. [< Latin *licentiosus* < *licentia.*] **—li cen′tious ness,** *n.*

lin den (lin′dən), *n.* **1** any of a genus of shade trees with heart-shaped leaves and clusters of small, fragrant, yellowish flowers. **2** the light, white wood of any of these trees.

lin e a ment (lin′ē ə mənt), *n.* part or feature, especially a part or feature of a face with attention to its outline.

lin en (lin′ən), *n.* **1** cloth, thread, or yarn woven from flax. **2** household articles or clothing made of linen or some substitute. **—adj.** made of linen. [Old English *līnen* of flax < *līn* flax]

lin tel (lin′tl), *n.* a horizontal beam or stone over a door, window, etc., to support the structure above it. [< Old French, threshold, ultimately < Latin *limitem* limit]

list (list), ARCHAIC. **—v.t.** be pleasing to; please. **—v.i.** like; wish. [Old English *lystan* < *lust* pleasure]

LINTEL / SILL

lit er al ist (lit′ər ə list), *n.* **1** person who adheres to the exact literal meaning. **2** person who represents or portrays without idealizing.

li ti gious (lə tij′əs), *adj.* **1** having the habit of going to law. **2** that can be disputed in a court of law. **3** of or having to do with litigation. **4** quarrelsome: *litigious neighbors.* **—li ti′gious ness,** *n.*

loam (lōm), *n.* rich, fertile earth in which much humus is mixed with clay and sand.

loath some (lōᴛʜ′səm, lōth′səm), *adj.* making one feel sick; disgusting.

lob ster ther mi dor (thėr′mə dôr′), a dish consisting of cooked lobster meat mixed with a cream sauce and then returned to its shell, sprinkled with cheese, and browned.

lock (lok), *n.* **1** means of fastening doors, boxes, etc., consisting of a bolt and usually needing a key of special shape to open it. **2** an enclosed section of a canal, dock, etc., in which the level of the water can be changed by letting water in or out to raise or lower ships. **3** gunlock. **4** device to keep a wheel from turning.

lu cra tive (lü′krə tiv), *adj.* yielding gain or profit; profitable. [< Latin *lucrativus* < *lucrum* gain]

lu di crous (lü′də krəs), *adj.* causing derisive laughter; amusingly absurd; ridiculous. [< Latin *ludicrus* < *ludus* sport]

lu gu bri ous (lü gyü′brē əs, lü gü′brē əs), *adj.* too sad; overly

GLOSSARY

mournful: *the lugubrious howl of a dog.* [< Latin *lugubris* < *lugere* mourn]

lu mi nous (lü′mə nəs), *adj.* **1** shining by its own light. **2** full of light; shining; bright.

lur id (lùr′id), *adj.* **1** lighted up with a red or fiery glare. **2** glaring in brightness or color: *a lurid red.* **3** shockingly terrible, repulsive, etc.; sensational ; startling. **4** pale and dismal in color; wan and sallow. [< Latin *luridus* pale yellow, ghastly]

a hat	i it	oi oil	ch child	⎧ a in about
ā age	ī ice	ou out	ng long	e in taken
ä far	o hot	u cup	sh she	ə = ⎨ i in pencil
e let	ō open	ù put	th thin	o in lemon
ē equal	ô order	ü rule	ᴛʜ then	⎩ u in circus
ėr term			zh measure	< = derived from

mag na nim i ty (mag′nə nim′ə tē), *n.* magnanimous nature or quality; nobility of soul or mind; generosity.

main (mān), *adj.* **1** most important; chief or principal; largest. **2** exerted to the utmost; full; sheer. —*n.* **1** a large pipe for water, gas, sewage, electricity, etc. **2** the open sea; ocean. **3** (in nautical use) mainmast or mainsail.

maize (māz), *n.* corn; Indian corn. [< Spanish *maíz* < Taino *mahiz*]

mal e dic tion (mal′ə dik′shən), *n.* invocation of evil upon someone; curse. [< Latin *maledictionem* < *maledicere* speak evil < *male* badly + *dicere* speak]

ma lev o lent (mə lev′ə lənt), *adj.* wishing evil to happen to others; showing ill will; spiteful. [< Latin *malevolentem* < *male* badly + *velle* to wish]

ma lin ger (mə ling′gər), *v.i.* pretend to be sick, injured, etc., in order to escape work or duty; shirk. [< French *malingre* sickly]

man gle (mang′gəl), *v.t.,* **-gled, -gling.** cut or tear (the flesh) roughly; lacerate.

ma ni a cal (mə nī′ə kəl), *adj.* violently insane.

man i fold (man′ə fōld), *adj.* of many kinds; many and various: *manifold duties.*

man na (man′ə), *n.* **1** (in the Bible) the food miraculously supplied to the Israelites in the wilderness. **2** food for the soul or mind.

man ner ism (man′ə riz′əm), *n.* **1** too much use of some manner in speaking, writing or behaving; affectation. **2** an odd trick or habit; a peculiar way of acting.

mar a thon (mar′ə thon), *n.* **1** a footrace of 26 miles, 385 yards (42.2 kilometers). **2** any race over a long distance. **3** any activity that calls for endurance.

marge (märj), *n.* ARCHAIC. margin; edge.

mar ti net (märt′n et′), *n.* person who upholds and enforces very strict discipline. [< J. *Martinet,* died 1672, French general and drillmaster]

mast (mast), *n.* acorns, chestnuts, beechnuts, etc., on the ground; fruit of certain forest trees. [Old English *mæst*]

mas ti cate (mas′tə kāt), *v.t.,* *v.i.,* **-cat ed, -cat ing.** grind (food) to a pulp with the teeth; chew. [< Late Latin *masticatum* chewed < Greek *mastichan* gnash the teeth] —**mas′ti ca′tion,** *n.*

ma ter i al ism (mə tir′ē ə liz′əm), *n.* **1** the philosophical theory that all action, thought, and feeling can be explained by the movements and changes of matter. **2** tendency to care too much for the things of this world and to neglect spiritual needs. **3** the ethical doctrine that material self-interest should and does determine conduct.

ma ter i al ist (mə tir′ē ə list), *n.* person who cares too much for the things of this world and neglects spiritual needs. —*adj.* materialistic.

ma ter nal (mə tėr′nl), *adj.* of or like a mother; motherly. [< Middle French *maternel* < Latin *maternus* < *mater* mother]

ma tric u late (mə trik′yə lāt), *v.t.,* *v.i.,* **-lat ed, -lat ing.** enroll, especially in a college or university, as a candidate for a degree.

maud lin (môd′lən), *adj.* **1** sentimental in a weak, silly way: *We saw a maudlin movie about a child's lost dog.* **2** tearfully silly because of drunkenness or excitement. [alteration of Mary *Magdalene,* often painted as weeping]

mau gre (mô′gər), *prep.* ARCHAIC. in spite of. [< Old French]

me dal lion (mə dal′yən), *n.* **1** a large medal. **2** design, ornament, etc., shaped like a medal.

med ley (med′lē), *n., pl.* **-leys,** *adj.* —*n.* **1** mixture of things that ordinarily do not belong together. **2** piece of music made up of parts from other pieces. —*adj.* made up of parts that are not alike; mixed. [< Old French *medlee, meslee* < *mesler* to mix, ultimately < Latin *miscere.* Doublet of MELEE.]

mel an chol y (mel′ən kol′ē), *n.* condition of sadness and low spirits; gloominess; dejection. [< Greek *melancholia* < *melanos* black + *cholē* bile]

meld (meld), *v.t., v.i.* merge; blend. [perhaps blend of *melt* and *weld*]

me lee or **mê lée** (mā′lā, mā lā′), *n.* a confused fight; hand-to-hand fight among a number of fighters. [< French *mêlée* (in Old French *meslee*). Doublet of MEDLEY.]

mel io rate (mē′lyə rāt′, mē′lē ə rāt′), *v.t., v.i.,* **-rat ed, -rat ing.** improve; ameliorate. [< Latin *melior* better] —**mel′io ra′tion,** *n.*

me men to (mə men′tō), *n., pl.* **-tos** or **-toes.** something serving as a reminder of what is past or gone; souvenir.

-ment, *suffix added to verbs to form nouns.* **1** act, process, or fact of ____ing: *Enjoyment* = act of enjoying. **2** condition of being ____ed: *Amazement* = condition of being amazed. **3** product or result of ____ing: *Pavement* = product of paving. **4** means of or instrument for ____ing: *Inducement* = means of inducing.

men tor (men′tər), *n.* a wise and trusted adviser. [< *Mentor,* friend of Ulysses, and adviser of Ulysses' son Telemachus]

mer ce nar y (mėr′sə ner′ē), *n., pl.* **-nar ies.** **1** soldier serving for pay in a foreign army. **2** person who works merely for pay. [< Latin *mercenarius* < *merces* wages < *merx, mercis* wares]

me sa (mā′sə), *n.* a small, isolated, high plateau with a flat top and steep sides, common in dry regions of the western and southwestern United States. [< Spanish < Latin *mensa* table]

mesa

mes mer ize (mez′mə rīz′, mes′mə rīz′), *v.t., v.i.,* **-ized, -iz ing,** hypnotize. [< Franz A. *Mesmer,* 1734-1815, Austrian physician who made hypnotism popular]

met a mor phose (met′ə môr′fōz), *v.,* **-phosed, -phos ing.** change in form, structure, or substance by or as if by witchcraft; transform.

me thod i cal (mə thod′ə kəl), *adj.* **1** done according to a method; systematic; orderly. **2** acting with method or order: *a methodical person.* —**me thod′i cal ly,** *adv.*

me tic u lous (mə tik′yə ləs), *adj.* extremely or excessively careful about small details. [< Latin *meticulosus* fearful, timid < *metus* fear]

mez zo tint (met′sō tint′, mez′ō tint′), *n.* **1** engraving on copper or steel made by polishing and scraping away parts of a roughened surface, so as to produce the effect of light and shade. **2** this method of engraving pictures. [< Italian *mezzotinto* half-tint]

mo gul (mō′gəl), *n.* a small bump or ridge of packed snow on a ski slope. [probably < Scandinavian (Norwegian) *muge* a heap]

moil (moil), *v.i.* work hard; drudge. —*n.* **1** hard work; drudgery. **2** confusion, turmoil, or trouble.

mol ten (mōlt′n), *adj.* **1** made liquid by heat; melted: *molten steel.* **2** made by melting and casting: *a molten image.* —*v.* a pp. of **melt.**

mon i ker (mon′ə kər), *n.* INFORMAL. **1** a person's name or signature. **2** a nickname. [origin unknown]

mon i to ry (mon'ə tôr'ē, mon'ə tōr'ē), *adj.* serving to admonish; warning.

mo rass (mə ras'), *n.* **1** piece of low, soft, wet ground; swamp; marsh. **2** a difficult situation; puzzling mess. [< Dutch *moeras*]

mor bid (môr'bid), *adj.* **1** not wholesome; unhealthy. **2** caused by disease; characteristic of disease; diseased. **3** horrible; gruesome; grisly. [< Latin *morbidus* < *morbus* disease]

mo rose (mə rōs'), *adj.* gloomy; sullen; ill-humored. [< Latin *morosus*, originally, set in one's ways < *morem* custom, habit]

mor ti fi ca tion (môr'tə fə kā'shən), *n.* a feeling of shame; humiliation: *mortification at having spilled food on the table.*

mo sa ic (mō zā'ik), *n.* **1** decoration made of small pieces of stone, glass, wood, etc., of different colors inlaid to form a picture or design. **2** art or process of making such a picture or design. **3** anything like a mosaic. [< Medieval Latin *mosaicus, musaicus* of the Muses, artistic]

mot tle (mot'l), *v.t.,* **-tled, -tling.** mark with spots or streaks of different colors or shades.

mul lion (mul'yən), *n.* a vertical bar between the panes of a window, the panels in the wall of a room, etc. —*v.t.* divide or provide with mullions. [alteration of Middle English *muniall, monial* < Old French *moienel, meienel* < *meien* in the middle < Latin *medianus*]

mum mer y (mum'ər ē), *n., pl.* **-mer ies. 1** performance of mummers. **2** any useless or silly show or ceremony.

mun dane (mun'dān), *adj.* commonplace; ordinary.

mu nif i cent (myü nif'ə sənt), *adj.* extremely generous; bountiful; bounteous.

mu ni tion (myü nish'ən), *n.* Usually, **munitions,** *pl.* material used in war. Munitions are military supplies, such as guns, ammunition, or bombs.

mure (myur'), *v.t.,* **mured, mur ing. 1** shut up within walls; put into prison; confine. **2** build up or entomb in a wall. [< Medieval Latin *immurare* < Latin *murus* wall]

muse (myüz), *v.,* **mused, mus ing.** —*v.i.* **1** be completely absorbed in thought; ponder; meditate. **2** look thoughtfully. —*v.t.* say thoughtfully. [< Old French *muser,* apparently (originally) put one's nose in the air < *muse* muzzle]

Muse (myüz), *n.* **1** (in Greek myths) one of the nine goddesses of the fine arts and sciences. **2** Sometimes, **muse.** spirit that inspires a poet, composer, writer, etc.; source of inspiration.

mu tate (myü'tāt), *v.t., v.i.,* **-tat ed, -tat ing. 1** change. **2** undergo or produce mutation.

mu ta tion (myu tā'shən), *n.* act or process of changing; change; alteration [< Latin *mutationem* < *mutare* to change]

myr i ad (mir'ē əd), *n.* a very great number. —*adj.* countless; innumerable. [< Greek *myriados* ten thousand, countless]

mys tic (mis'tik), *adj.* **1** mystical. **2** having to do with the ancient religious mysteries or other occult rites: *mystic arts.* —*n.* person who believes that union with God or knowledge of truths inaccessible to the ordinary powers of the mind can be attained through faith, spiritual insight, intuition, or exaltation of feeling. [< Latin *mysticus* < Greek *mystikos* < *mystēs* an initiate]

mys ti cal (mis'tə kəl), *adj.* **1** having some secret meaning; beyond human understanding; mysterious. **2** spiritually symbolic.

nau ti lus (nô'tl əs), *n., pl.* **-lus es, -li** (-lī). either of two kinds of cephalopod. The **pearly nautilus** or **chambered nautilus** has a spiral shell divided into many compartments which have a pearly lining. The **paper nautilus** resembles the octopus and has a thin shell. [< Greek *nautilos,* originally, sailor < *naus* ship]

neb u lous (neb'yə ləs), *adj.* **1** hazy; vague; confused. **2** cloudlike.

neg li gence (neg'lə jəns), *n.* **1** lack of proper care or attention; neglect. **2** carelessness; indifference. [< Latin *negligentia* < *negligere* to disregard, neglect < *nec* not + *legere* pick up]

neth er ward (neᴛʜ'ər wərd), *adv.* in a downward direction.

neur as the ni a (nur'əs thē'nē ə, nyur'əs thē'nē ə), *n.* a neu-

rosis with feelings of mental and physical exhaustion, often accompanied by varying aches and pains with no discernible organic cause; nervous breakdown.

neur as then ic (nur'əs then'ik, nyur'əs then'ik), *adj.* of or having to do with neurasthenia. —*n.* person who has neurasthenia.

new el (nü'əl, nyü'əl), *n.* the post at the top or bottom of a stairway that supports the railing.

noc tur nal (nok tér'nl), *adj.* **1** of the night. **2** active in the night. [< Latin *nocturnus* of the night < *noctem* night]

non cha lant (non'shə lənt, non'shə länt'), *adj.* without enthusiasm; coolly unconcerned; indifferent. [< French < *non-* not + *chaloir* care about]

non con form ist (non'kən fôr'mist), *n.* person who refuses to be bound by or accept the established customs or practices of a social group, business, or church.

non de script (non'də skript), *adj.* not easily classified; not of any one particular kind: *She had nondescript eyes, neither brown, blue, nor gray.* —*n.* a nondescript person or thing. [< *non-* + Latin *descriptum* (to be) described]

no vi ti ate or **no vi ci ate** (nō vish'ē it, nō vish'ē āt), *n.* **1** period of trial and preparation in a religious order. **2** novice. **3** house or rooms occupied by religious novices. **4** state or period of being a beginner in anything.

no wise (nō'wīz), *adv.* noway.

nub bin (nub'ən), *n.* a small, not fully developed object or person.

Num bers (num'bərz), *n.* the fourth book of the Old Testament. It tells about the counting of the Israelites after they left Egypt.

o bei sance (ō bā'sns, ō bē'sns), *n.* **1** movement of the body expressing deep respect or reverence; deep bow or curtsy. **2** deference; homage.

o blique (ə blēk'), *adj.* **1** slanting. **2** not straightforward; indirect.

o blit e rate (ə blit'ə rāt'), *v.t.,* **-rat ed, -rat ing. 1** remove all traces of; blot out; efface. **2** blot out so as to leave no distinct traces; make unrecognizable. [< Latin *obliteratum* struck out < *ob literas (scribere)* (draw) through the letters, strike out]

ob se qui ous (əb sē'kwē əs), *adj.* polite or obedient from hope of gain or from fear; servile; fawning. [< Latin *obsequiosus* < *obsequium* dutiful service < *ob-* after + *sequi* follow]

ob tuse (əb tüs', əb tyüs'), *adj.* **1** slow in understanding; stupid. **2** not sensitive; dull. [< Latin *obtusum* blunted < *ob-* against + *tundere* to beat]

oc cult (ə kult', ok'ult), *adj.* **1** beyond the bounds of ordinary knowledge; mysterious. **2** outside the laws of the natural world; magical. **3** not disclosed; secret. [< Latin *occultum* hidden < *ob-* up + *celare* to hide]

oc u lar (ok'yə lər), *adj.* **1** of or having to do with the eye: *an ocular muscle.* **2** like an eye; eyelike. [< Latin *oculus* eye]

om i nous (om'ə nəs), *adj.* unfavorable; threatening: *ominous clouds.* —**om'i nous ly,** *adv.*

om nip o tence (om nip'ə təns), *n.* complete power; unlimited power.

om nip o tent (om nip'ə tənt), *adj.* **1** having all power; almighty. **2** having very great power or influence.

o pac i ty (ō pas'ə tē), *n., pl.* **-ties. 1** a being opaque; being impervious to light; darkness. **2** a being impervious to sound, heat, etc. **3** obscurity of meaning. **4** something opaque. **5** denseness or stupidity. [< Latin *opacitatem* < *opacus* dark]

o pal es cent (ō'pə les'nt), *adj.* having a play of colors like that of an opal. [< *opal* + *-escent*]

o pi ate (ō'pē it, ō'pē āt), *n.* anything that quiets, soothes, etc. —*adj.* bringing sleep or ease.

op pres sion (ə presh'ən), *n.* cruel or unjust treatment; tyranny; persecution; despotism.

op pro bri um (ə prō'brē əm), *n.* disgrace or reproach caused by shameful conduct; infamy; scorn; abuse. [< Latin < *opprobare* to reproach < *ob-* at, against + *probrum* infamy; reproach]

op ti cal (op'tə kəl), *adj.* of the eye or the sense of sight; visual.

GLOSSARY

o rang-ou tang (ô rang′ u̇ tang′), *n.* orangutan.

o rang u tan (ô rang′ u̇-tan′), *n.* a large anthropoid ape of the forests of Borneo and Sumatra, that has very long arms and long, red-dish-brown hair. [< Malay < *orang* man + *utan* of the woods]

orangutan
about 4½ ft. (1.4 m.) tall

orb (ôrb), *n.* **1** anything round like a ball; sphere; globe. **2** sun, moon, planet, or star. **3** the eye-ball or eye. [< Latin *orbis* circle]

or tho dox (ôr′thə doks), *adj.* **1** generally accepted, especially in religion. **2** having generally accepted views or opinions, especially in reli-gion; adhering to established customs and traditions. **3** approved by convention; usual; customary. [< Greek *orthodoxos* < *orthos* correct + *doxa* opinion]

os cil la tion (os′l ā′shən), *n.* **1** fact or process of oscillating. **2** a single swing of a vibrating body.

os ten si ble (o sten′sə bəl), *adj.* according to appearances; de-clared as genuine; apparent; pretended; professed. [< Latin *osten-sum* shown, ultimately < *ob-* toward + *tendere* to stretch] —**os-ten′si bly,** *adv.*

os ten ta tion (os′ten tā′shən), *n.* a showing off; display intended to impress others. [< Latin *ostentationem,* ultimately < *ob-* toward + *tendere* to stretch]

os ten ta tious (os′ten tā′shəs), *adj.* **1** done for display; in-tended to attract notice. **2** showing off; liking to attract notice.

os tra cism (os′trə siz′əm), *n.* **1** banishment from one's native country. **2** a being shut out from society, favor, privileges, or as-sociation with one's fellows.

os tra cize (os′trə sīz), *v.t.,* **-cized, -ciz ing. 1** banish by ostracism. **2** shut out from society, favor, privileges, etc.: *The children ostracized the classmate who had lied.* [< Greek *ostraki-zein* < *ostrakon* tile, potsherd (because originally potsherds were used in balloting)]

-ous, *suffix forming adjectives from nouns.* **1** full of; having much; having: *Joyous = full of joy.* **2** characterized by: *Zealous = char-acterized by zeal.*

pa cif ic (pə sif′ik), *adj.* **1** tending to make peace; making peace; peaceable. **2** loving peace; not warlike. **3** peaceful; calm; quiet.

pad dock (pad′ək), *n.* a small, enclosed field near a stable or house, used for exercising animals or as a pasture.

pa laz zo (pä lät′sō), *n., pl.* **-zi** (-sē). palace, mansion, or large town house in Italy. [< Italian]

pall (pôl), *n.* **1** a heavy, dark cloth, often made of velvet, spread over a coffin, a hearse, or a tomb. **2** a dark, gloomy covering. [Old English *pæll* < Latin *pallium* cloak]

pal let[1] (pal′it), *n.* bed of straw; small or poor bed. [< Old French *paillet* < *paille* straw < Latin *palea*]

pal let[2] (pal′it), *n.* **1** a flat blade used by potters and others for shaping their work. **2** a painter's palette. **3** a low, portable plat-form on which loads are stacked to keep them off the ground in storage and to make the entire stack, including the pallet, easy to pick up. [variant of *palette*]

pal lid (pal′id), *adj.* lacking normal color; wan; pale.

pal pa ble (pal′pə bəl), *adj.* **1** readily seen or heard and recog-nized; obvious. **2** that can be touched or felt; tangible. [< Late Latin *palpabilis* < *palpare* to feel, pat]

pan o ply (pan′ə plē), *n., pl.* **-plies. 1** complete equipment or covering. **2** any splendid array. [< Greek *panoplia* < *pan-* + *hopla* arms]

pan to mime (pan′tə mīm), *n., v.,* **-mimed, -mim ing.** —*n.* **1** a play without words, in which the actors express themselves by gestures. **2** gestures without words; dumb show. —*v.t.* express by gestures. [< Greek *pantomimos* < *pantos* all + *mimos* mimic]

par a gon (par′ə gon), *n.* model of excellence or perfection. [< Middle French, comparison < Italian *paragone* touchstone < Greek *parakonan* to whet < *para-* + *akonē* whetstone]

par ley (pär′lē), *n., pl.* **-leys.** conference or informal talk. —*v.i.* **1** discuss terms, especially with an enemy. **2** ARCHAIC. speak; talk. [< Old French *parlee,* past participle of *parler* speak < Late Latin *parabolare* < *parabola* speech, story. Doublet of PALAVER, PARABLE, PARABOLA, PAROLE.]

par ox ysm (par′ək siz′əm), *n.* **1** a sudden, severe attack of the symptoms of a disease, usually recurring periodically: *a paroxysm of coughing.* **2** a sudden outburst of emotion or activity. [< Greek *paroxysmos* < *para-*[1] + *oxynein* make sharp < *oxys* sharp]

par si mo ni ous (pär′sə mō′nē əs), *adj.* too economical; stingy; miserly.

par si mo ny (pär′sə mō′nē), *n.* extreme economy; stinginess. [< Latin *parsimonia* < *parcere* to spare]

par ti tion (pär tish′ən), *n.* **1** division into parts; apportionment: *the partition of a person's estate after death.* **2** portion; part; section. **3** wall between rooms, etc.

pa thos (pā′thos), *n.* quality in speech, writing, music, events, or a scene that arouses a feeling of pity or sadness; power of evoking tender or melancholy emotion. [< Greek, suffering, feeling < *path-,* stem of *paschein* suffer]

pat ri mo ny (pat′rə mō′nē), *n., pl.* **-nies.** property inherited from one's father or ancestors. [< Latin *patrimonium* < *pater* fa-ther]

peak ed (pē′kid), *adj.* sickly in appearance; wan; thin. [< earlier *peak* look sick; origin uncertain] Also, **peeked.**

pe dan tic (pi dan′tik), *adj.* **1** displaying one's knowledge more than is necessary. **2** tediously learned; scholarly in a dull and nar-row way. —**pe dan′ti cal ly,** *adv.*

pen i tent (pen′ə tənt), *adj.* sorry for sinning or doing wrong; re-penting; repentant. —*n.* **1** person who is sorry for sin or wrongdoing. **2** person who confesses and does penance under the direction of a church. —**pen′i tent ly,** *adv.*

pen ur y (pen′yər ē), *n.* great poverty; extreme want; destitution. [< Latin *penuria* want, need]

per cep ti ble (pər sep′tə bəl), *adj.* that can be perceived: *a per-ceptible improvement.* —**per cep′ti bly,** *adv.*

pe remp tor y (pə remp′tər ē, per′əmp tôr′ē, per′əmp tōr′ē), *adj.* **1** leaving no choice; decisive; final; absolute. **2** allowing no denial or refusal. [< Latin *peremptorius* that puts an end to, ulti-mately < *per-* to the end + *emere* to take]

per fi dy (pèr′fə dē), *n., pl.* **-dies.** a breaking faith; base treach-ery; being false to a trust. [< Latin *perfidia* < *perfidus* faithless < *per-* + *fides* faith]

per me ate (pèr′mē āt), *v.t.,* **-at ed, -at ing. 1** spread through the whole of; pass through; pervade. **2** penetrate through pores or openings; soak through. [< Latin *permeatum* passed through < *per-* through + *meare* to pass] —**per′me a′tion,** *n.*

per tain (pər tān′), *v.i.* **1** belong or be connected as a part, pos-session, etc. **2** have to do with; be related; refer. [< Old French *partenir* < Latin *pertinere* reach through, connect < *per-* through + *tenere* to hold]

per tur ba tion (pèr′tər bā′shən), *n.* **1** a perturbed condition. **2** thing, act, or event that causes disturbance or agitation.

per verse (pər vèrs′), *adj.* **1** contrary and willful; obstinately op-posing what is wanted, reasonable, or required. **2** morally bad; perverted; depraved. [< Latin *perversum* turned away, perverted] —**per verse′ly,** *adv.* —**per verse′ness,** *n.*

pes ti len tial (pes′tl en′shəl), *adj.* **1** like a pestilence; having to do with pestilences. **2** morally harmful; pernicious.

Pronunciation key:

a hat	i it	oi oil	ch child	a in about
ā age	ī ice	ou out	ng long	e in taken
ä far	o hot	u cup	sh she	ə = i in pencil
e let	ō open	u̇ put	th thin	o in lemon
ē equal	ô order	ü rule	ŦH then	u in circus
ėr term			zh measure	< = derived from

petrify

pet ri fy (pet′rə fī), v.t., **-fied, -fy ing. 1** turn into stone; change (organic matter) into a substance like stone. **2** make hard as stone; stiffen; deaden. **3** paralyze with fear, horror, or surprise. [< French *pétrifier* < Latin *petra* stone + *facere* make]

pet u lance (pech′ə ləns), n. a being petulant; peevishness.

phi lan thro py (fə lan′thrə pē), n., pl. **-pies. 1** love of humanity shown by practical kindness and helpfulness. **2** thing that benefits humanity. [< Greek *philanthrōpia* < *philos* loving + *anthrōpos* man]

phi lip pic (fə lip′ik), n. a bitter attack in words.

pi laf or **pi laff** (pi läf′), n. an Oriental dish consisting of rice or cracked wheat boiled often with mutton, fowl, or fish, and flavored with spices, raisins, etc. Also, **pilau, pilaw.** [< Persian *pilāw*]

pil fer (pil′fər), v.i., v.t. steal in small quantities; commit petty theft. [< Old French *pelfrer* rob < *pelfre* booty]

pin ion (pin′yən), n. **1** the last joint of a bird's wing. **2** wing. **3** any one of the stiff flying feathers of the wing; quill. [< Middle French *pignon* < Popular Latin *pinnionem* < Latin *penna* feather and *pinna* wing]

pipe (pīp), n. **1** cask, varying in size, for wine, etc. **2** as much as such a cask holds, now usually reckoned as four barrels or 126 (wine) gallons.

pique (pēk), v.t., **piqued, pi quing.** cause a feeling of anger in; wound the pride of. [< French *piquer* to prick, sting]

pit tance (pit′ns), n. **1** a small allowance of money. **2** a small amount or share. [< Old French *pitance* portion of food allotted to a monk, piety, pity, ultimately < Latin *pietatem* piety]

piv ot al (piv′ə təl), adj. **1** of, having to do with, or serving as a pivot. **2** being that on which something turns, hinges, or depends; very important.

plac id (plas′id), adj. pleasantly calm or peaceful; quiet: *a placid lake.* [< Latin *placidus* < *placere* to please] —**plac′id ly,** adv.

plain tive (plān′tiv), adj. expressive of sorrow; mournful; sad. [< Old French *plaintif* < *plaint* plaint] —**plain′tive ly,** adv.

plait (plāt, plat for 1; plāt, plēt for 2), n., v.t. **1** braid. **2** pleat. [< Old French *pleit,* ultimately < Latin *plicare* to fold]

plash y (plash′ē), adj. abounding with pools or puddles.

pleached (plēcht, plācht), adj. bordered or shaded with interlaced branches or vines: *a pleached walk.*

pleur i sy (plùr′ə sē), n. inflammation of the pleura, often marked by fever, chest pains, and difficulty in breathing.

pleur o sis (plùr ō′sis), n. inflammation of a membrane covering the lungs, often marked by fever, chest pains, and difficulty in breathing.

pli ant (plī′ənt), adj. **1** bending easily; flexible; supple. **2** easily influenced; yielding: *a pliant nature.* **3** changing easily to fit different conditions; adaptable.

poign ant (poi′nyənt), adj. **1** very painful; piercing. **2** stimulating to the mind, feelings, or passions; keen; intense. [< Old French, present participle of *poindre* to prick < Latin *pungere*] —**poign′ant ly,** adv.

poin til list (pwan′tl ist), n. artist who uses pointillism. —adj. of, having to do with, or characteristic of pointillism.

por ti co (pôr′tə kō, pōr′tə kō), n., pl. **-coes** or **-cos.** roof supported by columns, forming a porch or a covered walk. [< Italian < Latin *porticus.* Doublet of PORCH.]

po ten tate (pōt′n tāt), n. **1** person having great power. **2** ruler.

pre am ble (prē′am′bəl), n. **1** a preliminary statement; introduction to a speech or a writing. **2** a preliminary or introductory fact or circumstance, especially one showing what is to follow. [< Medieval Latin *praeambulum* < Late Latin, walking before < Latin *prae-*

portico

pre- + *ambulare* to walk]

pre car i ous (pri ker′ē əs, pri kar′ē əs), adj. **1** not safe or secure; uncertain; dangerous; risky. **2** dependent on chance or circumstance. [< Latin *precarius* obtainable by prayer, uncertain < *precem* prayer] —**pre car′i ous ly,** adv.

pre cip i tate (v. pri sip′ə tāt; adj. pri sip′ə tit), v., **-tat ed, -tat ing.** —v.t. **1** hasten the beginning of; bring about suddenly: *precipitate an argument.* **2** throw headlong; hurl: *precipitate a rock down a cliff.* —adj. **1** very hurried; sudden: *A cool breeze caused a precipitate drop in the temperature.* **2** with great haste and force. [< Latin *praecipitatum* thrown headlong < *praecipitem* headlong.] —**pre cip′i tate ly,** adv.

pre cip i tous (pri sip′ə təs), adj. like a precipice; very steep: *precipitous cliffs.*

pre con cep tion (prē′kən sep′shən), n. idea or opinion formed beforehand.

pre cur sor (pri kėr′sər, prē′kər sər), n. **1** forerunner. **2** predecessor. [< Latin *praecursor* < *praecurrere* run before < *prae-* pre- + *currere* run]

pre dis pose (prē′dis pōz′), v.t., **-posed, -pos ing.** give an inclination or tendency to; make liable or susceptible: *A cold predisposes a person to other diseases.*

pre med i ta tion (prē′med ə tā′shən), n. previous deliberation or planning.

pre mo ni tion (prē′mə nish′ən, prem′ə nish′ən), n. notification or warning of what is to come; forewarning: *a vague premonition of disaster.* [< Latin *praemonitionem* < *praemonere* warn beforehand < *prae-* pre- + *monere* warn]

pre rog a tive (pri rog′ə tiv), n. **1** right or privilege that nobody else has. **2** special superiority of right or privilege, such as may derive from an official position, office, etc. [< Latin *praerogativa* allotted to vote first < *praerogare* ask for a vote first < *prae-* pre- + *rogare* ask]

pre sci ence (prē′shē əns, presh′ē əns; prē′shəns, presh′əns), n. knowledge of things before they exist or happen; foreknowledge; foresight. [< Late Latin *praescientia* < Latin *praescientem* foreknowing < *prae-* pre- + *scire* know]

pre sen ti ment (pri zen′tə mənt), n. a feeling or impression that something, especially something evil, is about to happen; vague sense of approaching misfortune; foreboding.

pre sume (pri züm′), v.i., **-sumed, -sum ing. 1** take an unfair advantage. **2** act with improper boldness; take liberties. [< Latin *praesumere* take for granted < *prae-* pre- + *sumere* take] —**pre sum′er,** n. —**pre sum′ing ly,** adv.

pre sump tu ous (pri zump′chü əs), adj. acting without permission or right; too bold; forward. —**pre sump′tu ous ly,** adv. —**pre sump′tu ous ness,** n.

pre ten sion (pri ten′shən), n. **1** claim. **2** a doing things for show or to make a fine appearance; showy display.

pre ter nat ur al (prē′tər nach′ər əl), adj. **1** out of the ordinary course of nature; abnormal. **2** due to something above or beyond nature; supernatural. [< Latin *praeter* beyond + *natura* nature]

prev a lent (prev′ə lənt), adj. **1** in general use; widespread; common. **2** predominant; victorious.

prig gish (prig′ish), adj. particular about speech and manners to an offensive degree.

pris mat ic (priz mat′ik), adj. **1** of or like a prism. **2** varied in color; brilliant.

pro cure (prə kyùr′), v.t., **-cured, -cur ing. 1** obtain by care or effort; secure. **2** bring about; cause: *procure a person's death.* [< Latin *procurare* manage < *pro-* before + *cura* care]

prod i gal (prod′ə gəl), adj. **1** given to extravagant or reckless spending; wasteful: *America has been progidal of its forests.* **2** abundant; lavish: *Nature's prodigal beauties.* [< Latin *prodigus* wasteful < *prodigere* drive forth, squander < *prod-, pro-* forth + *agere* to drive] —**prod′i gal ly,** adv.

pro di gious (prə dij′əs), adj. **1** very great; huge; vast: *The ocean contains a prodigious amount of water.* **2** wonderful; marvelous. [< Latin *prodigiosus* < *prodigium* prodigy, omen]

pro fane (prə fān′), adj., v., **-faned, -fan ing.** —adj. **1** characterized by contempt or disregard for God or holy things; irreverent: *profane language.* **2** not sacred; worldly: *profane literature.* —v.t. **1** treat (holy things) with contempt or disregard; desecrate. **2** put to wrong or unworthy use. [< Latin *profanus* not sacred <

GLOSSARY

pro- in front (outside) of + *fanum* temple, shrine] —**pro-fane′ly,** *adv.*

prof fer (prof′ər), *v.t.* offer for acceptance; present; tender: *We proffered regrets at having to leave so early.* [< Anglo-French *proffrir* < Old French *pro-* forth + *offrir* to offer]

pro fuse (prə fyüs′), *adj.* very abundant: *profuse thanks.* [< Latin *profusum* poured forth < *pro-* forth < *fundere* pour] —**pro-fuse′ly,** *adv.*

pro fu sion (prə fyü′zhən), *n.* great abundance.

pro gen i tor (prō jen′ə tər), *n.* ancestor in the direct line; forefather.

pro mis cu ous (prə mis′kyü əs), *adj.* 1 mixed and in disorder: *a promiscuous heap of clothing on your closet floor.* 2 making no distinctions; not discriminating. [< Latin *promiscuus* < *pro-* forth + *miscere* to mix] —**pro mis′cu ous ly,** *adv.*

prom on to ry (prom′ən tôr′ē, prom′ən tōr′ē), *n., pl.* -ries. a high point of land extending from the coast into the water. [< Latin *promonturium,* probably < *pro-* forward + *montem* mountain]

pro pi ti ate (prə pish′ē āt), *v.t.,* -at ed, -at ing. prevent or reduce the anger of; win the favor of; appease or conciliate.

pro pi ti a to ry (prə pish′ē ə tôr′ē, prə pish′ē ə tōr′ē), *adj.* intended to propitiate.

prop o si tion (prop′ə zish′ən), *n.* 1 what is offered to be considered; proposal. 2 INFORMAL. a business enterprise; an undertaking: *a paying proposition.*

pros e lyte (pros′ə līt), *n.* person who has been converted from one opinion, religious belief, etc., to another. [< Greek *prosēlytos* having arrived < *pros* toward + *ely-* come]

pros trate (pros′trāt), *v.,* -trat ed, -trat ing, *adj.* —*v.t.* 1 lay down flat; cast down: *The captives prostrated themselves before the conqueror.* 2 make very weak or helpless; exhaust. —*adj.* lying flat with face downward. [< Latin *prostratum* thrown down flat < *pro-* forth + *sternere* spread out]

pro tract (prō trakt′), *v.t.* 1 draw out; lengthen in time; prolong: *protract a visit.* 2 slide out; thrust out; extend. [< Latin *protractum* drawn out < *pro-* forward + *trahere* to draw]

pro tu ber ance (prō tü′bər əns, prō tyü′bər əns), *n.* 1 part that sticks out; bulge; swelling. 2 a protuberant quality or condition.

pro tu ber ant (prō tü′bər ənt, prō tyü′bər ənt), *adj.* bulging out; sticking out; prominent. [< Late Latin *protuberantem* bulging < *pro-* forward + *tuber* lump]

pro ver bi al (prə vėr′bē əl), *adj.* well-known: *the proverbial loyalty of dogs.* —**pro ver′bi al ly,** *adv.*

prov i dence (prov′ə dəns), *n.* 1 God's care and help. 2 **Providence,** God. 3 instance of God's care and help. 4 a being provident; prudence.

prov i dent (prov′ə dənt), *adj.* 1 having or showing foresight; careful in providing for the future; prudent. 2 economical; frugal.

psalm (säm, sälm), *n.* 1 a sacred song or poem. 2 **Psalm,** any of the 150 sacred songs or hymns that together form a book of the Old Testament. —*v.t.* sing or celebrate in psalms.

psalm ist (sä′mist, säl′mist), *n.* 1 author of a psalm or psalms. 2 **the Psalmist,** King David, who according to tradition wrote many of the Psalms.

pu er ile (pyü′ər əl), *adj.* foolish for a grown person to say or do; childish. [< Latin *puerilis* < *puer* boy, child]

pu gi lis tic (pyü′jə lis′tik), *adj.* of or having to do with boxing.

pule (pyül), *v.i.,* **puled, pul ing.** cry in a thin voice, as a sick child does; whimper; whine. [perhaps imitative]

pul let (pùl′it), *n.* a young hen, usually less than a year old. [< Old French *poulet,* diminutive of *poule* hen]

Pull man (pùl′mən), *n.* 1 sleeping car. 2 parlor car. [< George M. *Pullman,* 1831-1897, American inventor who designed railroad cars]

pum mel (pum′əl), *v.t., v.i.,* **-meled, -mel ing** or **-melled, -mel ling.** strike or beat; beat with the fists. Also, **pommel.**

pun cheon (pun′chən), *n.* 1 a large cask for liquor, varying in size from 70 to 120 gallons (265 to 454 liters). 2 amount that it holds, used as a unit of capacity. [< Old French *poinchon, poinçon, ponson*]

pu pa (pyü′pə), *n., pl.* -pae (-pē), -pas. 1 stage between the larva and the adult in the development of many insects. 2 insect in this stage. Most pupae are inactive and some, such as those of many moths, are enclosed in a tough case or cocoon. [< Latin,

girl, doll]

pur chase (pėr′chəs), *n.* a firm hold to help move something or to keep from slipping: *Wind the rope twice around the tree to get a better purchase.* [< Anglo-French *purchacer* pursue < Old French *pur-* forth + *chacier* to chase]

purl (pėrl), *v.i.* flow with rippling motions and a murmuring sound. [perhaps < Scandinavian (Norwegian) *purla* to ripple]

quaff (kwäf, kwaf, kwôf), *v.i., v.t.* drink in large swallows; drink deeply and freely. —*n.* a quaffing. [origin uncertain]

quag mire (kwag′mīr′, kwog′mīr′), *n.* 1 soft, muddy ground; boggy or miry place; quag. 2 a difficult situation.

qua tri eme (kä′trē əm), FRENCH. fourth (floor).

quell (kwel), *v.t.* 1 put down (disorder, rebellion, etc.): *quell a riot.* 2 put an end to; overcome. [Old English *cwellan* to kill]

quelle ex is tence (kel ek zēs täns′), FRENCH. What a life.

quer u lous (kwer′ə ləs, kwer′yə ləs), *adj.* complaining; fretful; peevish. [< Latin *querulus* < *queri* complain]

ra di ant (rā′dē ənt), *adj.* shining; bright; beaming.

rail (rāl), *v.i.* complain bitterly; use violent and reproachful language. [< Middle French *railler* to mock, ridicule, ultimately < Late Latin *ragere* to bray, brawl. Doublet of RALLY.]

ram pant (ram′pənt), *adj.* 1 growing without any check. 2 passing beyond restraint or usual limits. 3 angry; excited; violent.

ram rod (ram′rod′), *n.* 1 rod for ramming down the charge in a gun that is loaded from the muzzle. 2 rod for cleaning the barrel of a gun.

ran cor (rang′kər), *n.* bitter resentment or ill will; extreme hatred or spite. [Late Latin, *rankness* < Latin *rancere* be rank]

ra pac i ty (rə pas′ə tē), *n.* rapacious spirit or practice; greed.

ra pi er (rā′pē ər), *n.* a long and light sword used for thrusting. [< Middle French *rapière*]

ra tion al ize (rash′ə nə līz), *v.t.,* -ized, -iz ing. find (often unconsciously) an explanation or excuse for. —**ra′tion al i za′tion,** *n.*

rav en ous (rav′ə nəs), *adj.* 1 very hungry. 2 greedy.

re-, prefix. 1 again; anew; once more: *Reappear = appear again.* 2 back: *Repay = pay back.* Also, sometimes before vowels, **red-.**

re ac tion ar y (rē ak′shə ner′ē), *adj.* having to do with or favoring a return to a previous, usually more conservative, state of affairs.

re buke (ri byük′), *n.* expression of disapproval; scolding. [< Anglo-French *rebuker* < Old French *rebuchier* < *re-* back + *buchier* to strike]

rec om pense (rek′əm pens), *v.,* -pensed, -pens ing, *n.* —*v.t.* 1 pay (a person); pay back; reward. 2 make a fair return for (an action, anything lost, damage done, or hurt received). —*n.* 1 payment; reward. 2 return; amends. [< Late Latin *recompensare* < Latin *re-* back + *compensare* compensate]

rec on noi ter (rek′ə noi′tər, rē′kə noi′tər), *v.t.* approach and examine or observe in order to learn something; make a first survey of (the enemy, the enemy's strength or position, a region, etc.) in order to gain information for military purposes. —*v.i.* approach a place and make a first survey of it. [< French *reconnoître* < Old

GLOSSARY

French *reconoistre* recognize. Doublet of RECOGNIZE.]

rec tan gle (rek′tang′gəl), *n.* a four-sided plane figure with four right angles. [< Medieval Latin *rectangulus* rectangular, ultimately < Latin *rectus* right + *angulus* angle]

rec ti fy (rek′tə fī), *v.t.,* **-fied, fy ing. 1** make right; put right; adjust; remedy. **2** change into a direct current. [< Late Latin *rectificare* < Latin *rectus* right + *facere* to make]

rec ti tude (rek′tə tüd, rek′tə tyüd), *n.* **1** upright conduct or character; honesty; righteousness. **2** direction in a straight line; straightness. [< Late Latin *rectitudo* < Latin *rectus* straight]

re cum bent (ri kum′bənt), *adj.* lying down; reclining; leaning. [< Latin *recumbentem* < *re-* back + *-cumbere* lie down] **—re cum′bent ly,** *adv.*

red o lence (red′l əns), *n.* redolent condition or quality.

red o lent (red′l ənt), *adj.* **1** having a pleasant smell; fragrant; aromatic. **2** smelling strongly; giving off an odor. [< Latin *redolentem* emitting scent < *re-, red-* back + *olere* to smell]

re doubt a ble (ri dou′tə bəl), *adj.* that should be feared or dreaded; formidable: *a redoubtable warrior.* [< Old French *redoutable* < *redouter* to dread < *re-* again + *douter* to doubt]

re dress (*v.* ri dres′; *n.* rē′dres, ri dres′), *v.t.* set right; repair; remedy. *—n.* a setting right; reparation; relief. [< Middle French *redresser* < *re-* again + *dresser* straighten, arrange] **—re dress′er,** *n.*

re du pli cate (ri dü′plə kāt, ri dyü′plə kāt), *v.t.,* **-cat ed, -cat ing.** double; repeat.

re gat ta (ri gat′ə, ri gät′ə), *n.* a boat race or a series of boat races. [< Italian]

re join der (ri join′dər), *n.* an answer to a reply; response.

re ju ve nate (ri jü′və nāt), *v.t.,* **-nat ed, -nat ing.** make young or vigorous again; give youthful qualities to. [< *re-* + Latin *juvenis* young]

ren dez vous (rän′də vü), *n., pl.* **-vous** (-vüz). an appointment or engagement to meet at a fixed place or time; meeting by agreement. [< Middle French < *rendez-vous* present yourself!]

re pine (ri pīn′), *v.i.,* **-pined, -pin ing.** be discontented; fret; complain. **—re pin′er,** *n.*

re proach (ri prōch′), *n.* blame or censure. *—v.t.* blame or censure: upbraid. [< Middle French *reproche* < *reprocher* < Popular Latin *repropiare* lay at the door of, ultimately < Latin *re-* again + *prope* near]

re prove (ri prüv′), *v.t.,* **-proved, -prov ing.** show disapproval of; find fault with; blame. [< Old French *reprover* < Late Latin *reprobare* < Latin *re-* + *probare* to test]

re pu di ate (ri pyü′dē āt), *v.t.,* **-at ed, -at ing. 1** refuse to accept; reject. **2** refuse to acknowledge or pay. [< Latin *repudiatum* divorced < *repudium* divorce]

re pug nant (ri pug′nənt), *adj.* **1** disagreeable or offensive; distasteful; objectionable. **2** objecting; averse; opposed. [< Latin *repugnantem* resisting, opposing < *re-* back + *pugnare* to fight]

re quite (ri kwīt′), *v.t.,* **-quit ed, -quit ing. 1** pay back; make return for: *requite kindness with love.* **2** reward.

res o lute (rez′ə lüt), *adj.* **1** having a fixed resolve; determined; firm. **2** constant in pursuing a purpose; bold. [< Latin *resolutum* resolved] **—res′o lute′ly,** *adv.*

res pite (res′pit), *n.* time of relief and rest; lull: *a respite from the heat.* [< Old French *respit* < Late Latin *respectus* expectation < Latin, regard. See RESPECT.]

re splend ent (ri splen′dənt), *adj.* very bright; splendid: *the resplendent sun.* [< Latin *resplendentem* < *re-* back + *splendere* to shine]

res tive (res′tiv), *adj.* **1** restless; uneasy. **2** hard to manage. **3** refusing to go ahead; balky. [< Old French *restif* motionless < *rester* remain.]

re stric tive (ri strik′tiv), *adj.* restricting; limiting.

ret i nue (ret′n ü, ret′n yü), *n.* group of attendants or retainers; following: *The queen's retinue accompanied her on the journey.* [< Old French, originally past participle of *retenir* retain]

ret ri bu tion (ret′rə byü′shən), *n.* a deserved punishment; return for wrongdoing. [< Latin *retributionem*, ultimately < *re-* back + *tribuere* assign]

re trieve (ri trēv′), *n.* act of retrieving; recovery. [< Old French *retruev-*, a form of *retrouver* find again < *re-* again + *trouver* to find] **—re trieve′ment,** *n.*

ret ro spect (ret′rə spekt), *n.* **1** survey of past time, events, etc.; thinking about the past. **2 in retrospect,** when looking back. [< Latin *retro-* back + *specere* to look] **—ret′ro spec′tive,** *adj.*

ret ro spec tion (ret′rə spek′shən), *n.* **1** act of looking back on things past. **2** survey of past events or experiences.

re ver be rate (ri vėr′bə rāt′), *v.,* **-rat ed, -rat ing.** *—v.i.* echo back. *—v.t.* reecho (a sound or noise). [< Latin *reverberatum* beaten back < *re-* back + *verber* a blow] **—re ver′be ra′tion,** *n.*

rev er ence (rev′ər əns), *n.* a feeling of deep respect, mixed with wonder, awe, and love; veneration.

rev e ren tial (rev′ə ren′shəl), *adj.* deeply respectful.

rev er ie (rev′ər ē), *n.* **1** dreamy thoughts; dreamy thinking of pleasant things. **2** condition of being lost in dreamy thoughts. Also, **revery.** [< French *rêverie* < *rêver* to dream]

rheum (rüm), *n.* **1** a watery discharge, such as mucus or tears. **2** a cold; catarrh. [< Greek *rheuma* a flowing < *rhein* to flow]

rib ald (rib′əld), *adj.* offensive in speech; coarsely mocking; irreverent; indecent; obscene. [< Old French *ribauld*]

ro de o (rō′dē ō, rō dā′ō), *n., pl.* **-de os. 1** contest or exhibition of skill in roping cattle, riding horses and steers, etc. **2** (in the western United States) the driving together of cattle; roundup. [< Spanish < *rodear* go around, ultimately < Latin *rota* wheel]

ro guish (rō′gish), *adj.* **1** having to do with or like rogues; dishonest; rascally. **2** playfully mischievous.

ro se ate (rō′zē it, rō′zē āt), *adj.* rose-colored; rosy.

ruck[1] (ruk), *n.* crowd; the great mass of common people or things. [< Scandinavian (Norwegian) *ruka*]

ruck[2] (ruk), *v.t.,* **-ed, -ing.** to make a fold in; to crease. [Old Norse *hrukka* wrinkle, crease]

rue (rü), *v.t.,* **rued, ru ing.** be sorry for; regret. [< Old English *hrēowan*]

rue ful (rü′fəl), *adj.* **1** sorrowful; unhappy; mournful: *a rueful expression.* **2** causing sorrow or pity. **—rue′ful ly,** *adv.*

ru mi nate (rü′mə nāt), *v.,* **-nat ed, -na ting.** *—v.i.* **1** chew the cud. **2** think or ponder; meditate; reflect. *—v.t.* **1** chew again (food which has been previously chewed and swallowed). **2** turn over in the mind; meditate on.

Sab bath (sab′əth), *n.* **1** day of the week used for rest and worship. Sunday is the Sabbath for most Christians; Saturday is the Jewish Sabbath. **2 sabbath,** period of rest, quiet, etc. [< Latin *sabbatum* < Greek *sabbaton* < Hebrew *shabbāth* ro rest]

sab bat i cal (sə bat′ə kəl), *n.* sabbatical leave or sabbatical year.

sabbatical leave, leave of absence for a year or half year given to teachers, commonly once in seven years, for rest, study, or travel.

sa chem (sā′chəm), *n.* (among some North American Indians) the chief of a tribe or confederation. [of Algonquian origin]

sa ga cious (sə gā′shəs), *adj.* **1** wise in a keen, practical way; shrewd. **2** intelligent. [< Latin *sagacem*]

sa gac i ty (sə gas′ə tē), *n.* keen, sound judgment; mental acuteness; shrewdness.

salivary gland, any of various glands that empty their secretions into the mouth. The salivary glands of human beings and certain other vertebrates are digestive glands that secrete saliva containing the digestive enzyme ptyalin, salts, mucus, etc.

salle à man ger (sal′ä män zhā′), FRENCH. dining room.

sal ly (sal′ē), *v.,* **-lied, -ly ing,** *n., pl.* **-lies.** *—v.i.* **1** set out briskly or boldly. **2** go on an excursion. *—n.* **1** a going forth; trip; excursion. **2** a sudden start into activity. **3** outburst. **4** a witty remark. [< Old French *saillie* a rushing forth < *saillir* to leap < Latin *salire*]

sanc ti fy (sangk′tə fī), *v.t.,* **-fied, -fy ing. 1** make holy; make legitimate or binding by a religious sanction. **2** set apart as sacred; observe as holy. [< Latin *sanctificare* < *sanctus* holy + *facere* to make]

sanc tu ar y (sangk′chü er′ē), *n., pl.* **-ar ies.** place of refuge.

san gui nar y (sang′gwə ner′ē), *adj.* **1** with much blood or bloodshed; bloody: *a sanguinary battle.* **2** delighting in bloodshed; bloodthirsty. [< Latin *sanguinarius* < *sanguinem* blood]

sar don ic (sär don′ik), *adj.* bitterly sarcastic, scornful, or mocking: *a sardonic outlook.* [< Greek *sardonios,* alteration of *sardanios,* perhaps influenced by *sardonion,* a supposed Sardinian plant that produced hysterical convulsions]

sav in or **sav ine** (sav′ən), *n.* **1** a juniper shrub whose tops yield an oily drug used in medicine. **2** any of various junipers, such as the red cedar. [ultimately < Latin *(herba) Sabina* Sabine (herb)]

sa voir-faire (sav′wär fer′, sav′wär far′), *n.* knowledge of just what to do; tact. [< French, literally, knowing how to do]

scab bard (skab′ərd), *n.* sheath or case for the blade of a sword, dagger, etc. [< Anglo-French *escaubers,* plural; of Germanic origin]

scar i fy (skar′ə fī), *v.t.,* **-fied, -fy ing.** make scratches or cuts in the surface of (the skin, etc.). [< Old French *scarifier* < Late Latin *scarificare* < Greek *skariphasthai* to scratch < *skariphos* stylus]

scep ter (sep′tər), *n.* the rod or staff carried by a ruler as a symbol of royal power or authority. Also, **sceptre.** [< Latin *sceptrum* < Greek *skēptron* staff]

scin til la (sin til′ə), *n.* spark; particle; trace. [< Latin, spark. Doublet of TINSEL.]

scin til la tion (sin′tl ā′shən), *n.* **1** a sparkling; flashing. **2** a spark; flash.

sconce (skons), *n.* bracket projecting from a wall, used to hold a candle or other light. [< Medieval Latin *sconsa* < Latin *abscondere* abscond, hide]

sconce

-scope, *combining form.* instrument for viewing or observing: *Telescope = instrument for viewing distant objects.* [< New Latin *-scopium* < Greek *-skopion* < *skopein* look at]

score (skôr, skōr), *v.,* **scored, scor ing.** cut; scratch; stroke; mark; line: *The carpenter used a nail to score the board.*

scourge (skėrj), *v.t.,* **scourged, scourg ing.** **1** whip; flog; punish severely. **2** trouble very much; afflict; torment. [< Old French *escorge,* ultimately < Latin *ex-* out + *corium* a hide]

scru ple (skrü′pəl), *n.* a feeling of doubt about what one ought to do.

scru ti ny (skrüt′n ē), *n., pl.* **-nies.** close examination; careful inspection. [< Late Latin *scrutinium* < Latin *scrutari* ransack]

scull er (skul′ər), *n.* person who works the oars to propel a boat.

sea son a ble (sē′zn ə bəl), *adj.* **1** suitable to the season. **2** coming at the right or proper time: *The Red Cross brought seasonable aid to the flood victims.* —**sea′son a bil′i ty,** *n.*

se ces sion ist (si sesh′ə nist), *n.* a person who believed that eleven Southern states should formally leave the United States in 1860–1861, an event which resulted in the Civil War.

sec u lar (sek′yə lər), *adj.* not religious or sacred; worldly: *secular music.* [< Latin *saecularis* < *saeculum* age, world]

sedge (sej), *n.* any of a large family of monocotyledonous herbs growing chiefly in wet places, resembling grasses but having solid, three-sided stems and small, inconspicuous flowers usually in spikes or heads.

seer (sir *for 1;* sē′ər *for 2*), *n.* **1** person who foresees or foretells future events; prophet. **2** person who sees.

self-re li ance (self′ri lī′əns), *n.* dependence on one's own acts, abilities, etc.

sem i nar y (sem′ə ner′ē), *n., pl.* **-nar ies.** **1** school or college for training students to be priests, ministers, rabbis, etc. **2** academy or boarding school. [< Latin *seminarium.* Doublet of SEMINAR.]

se nil i ty (sə nil′ə tē), *n.* **1** old age. **2** the mental and physical deterioration often characteristic of old age.

sen su ous (sen′shü əs), *adj.* **1** of or derived from the senses; having an effect on the senses; perceived by the senses. **2** enjoying the pleasures of the senses.

sen tence (sen′təns), *n.* **1** group of words (or sometimes a single word) that is grammatically complete and expresses a statement, request, command, exclamation, etc. **2** a short, wise saying.

a hat	i it	oi oil	ch child		a in about
ā age	ī ice	ou out	ng long		e in taken
ä far	o hot	u cup	sh she	ə = {	i in pencil
e let	ō open	ù put	th thin		o in lemon
ē equal	ô order	ü rule	ŦH then		u in circus
ėr term			zh measure	< = derived from

sen ten tious (sen ten′shəs), *adj.* **1** full of meaning; saying much in few words; pithy. **2** inclined to give advice in a self-righteous way. **3** inclined to make wise sayings; abounding in proverbs.

sen ti men tal (sen′tə men′tl), *adj.* **1** having or showing much tender feeling: *sentimental poetry.* **2** likely to act from feelings rather than from logical thinking.

se pi a (sē′pē ə), *n.* **1** a dark-brown pigment prepared from the inky secretion of cuttlefish. **2** a dark brown. **3** a drawing, photograph, etc., in tones of brown. —*adj.* **1** dark-brown. **2** done in sepia. [< Greek *sēpia* cuttlefish]

sep tum (sep′təm), *n., pl.* **-ta** (-tə). a dividing wall; partition. There is a septum of bone and cartilage between the nostrils. [< Latin *saeptum* a fence < *saepire* hedge in]

sep ul cher (sep′əl kər), *n.* **1** place of burial; tomb; grave Also **sepulchre.**

se pul chral (sə pul′krəl), *adj.* **1** of sepulchers or tombs. **2** of burial. **3** deep and gloomy; dismal; suggesting a tomb. [< Latin *sepulchrum* (< *sepelire* to bury) + English *-al*]

se ques ter (si kwes′tər), *v.t.* remove or withdraw from public use or from public view; seclude: *She sequestered herself while writing her book.* [< Latin *sequestrare* < *sequester* trustee, mediator < *sequi* follow]

ser aph (ser′əf), *n., pl.* **-aphs** or **-a phim.** one of the highest order of angels. [< *seraphim,* plural, < Late Latin < Hebrew *sĕrāphīm*]

se raph ic (sə raf′ik), *adj.* **1** of seraphs. **2** like a seraph; angelic.

se rene (sə rēn′), *adj.* **1** peaceful; calm. **2** not cloudy; clear; bright. —*n.* an expanse of clear sky or calm sea. [< Latin *serenus*]

ser pen tine (sėr′pən tēn′, sėr′pən tīn), *adj.* **1** of or like a serpent. **2** winding; twisting. **3** cunning; sly; treacherous.

ser vile (sėr′vəl), *adj.* like that of slaves; mean; base. [< Latin *servilis* < *servus* slave]

sex ton (sek′stən), *n.* person who takes care of a church building. A sexton's duties sometimes include ringing the church bell, arranging burials, etc.

shal lop (shal′əp), *n.* a small, light, open boat with sail or oars. [< French *chaloupe* < Dutch *sloepe.* Doublet of SLOOP.]

sheathe (shēŦH), *v.t.,* **sheathed, sheath ing.** put (a sword, etc.) into a sheath.

shoal (shōl), *n.* **1** place in a sea, lake, or stream where the water is shallow. **2** sandbank or sandbar that makes the water shallow, especially one which can be seen at low tide.

shroud (shroud), *n.* **1** cloth or garment in which a dead person is wrapped or dressed for burial. **2** something that covers, conceals, or veils. [Old English *scrūd*]

si dle (sī′dl), *v.i.,* **-dled, -dling.** move sideways slowly so as not to attract attention. [< *sideling,* variant of *sidelong*]

sig nale ment (sē nyàl man′), FRENCH. in the form of a detailed description. [variant of *signalment*]

sin ew (sin′yü), *n.* **1** tendon. **2** strength; energy; force. **3** Often, **sinews,** *pl.* means of strength; source of power: *Men and money are the sinews of war.* [Old English *sionu*]

sin gu lar (sing′gyə lər), *adj.* **1** extraordinary; unusual: *a person of singular ability, a story of singular interest.* **2** strange; odd; peculiar. [< Latin *singularis* < *singulus* single]

sin u ous (sin′yü əs), *adj.* **1** having many curves or turns; winding: *the sinuous motion of a snake.* **2** indirect; devious. [< Latin *sinuosus* < *sinus* a curve]

skein (skān), *n.* **1** a small, coiled bundle of yarn or thread. There are 120 yards in a skein of cotton yarn. **2** a confused tangle. [< Old French *escaigne*]

slea zy (slē′zē), *adj.*, **-zi er, -zi est.** flimsy and poor.

sloth (slôth, slōth), *n.* unwillingness to work or exert oneself; laziness; idleness: *His sloth keeps him from engaging in sports.*

slough (slou *for 1 and 3;* slü *for 2*), *n.* **1** a soft, deep, muddy place. **2** a swampy place; marshy inlet; slew; slue. **3** hopeless discouragement; degradation. [Old English *slōh*]

smal lage (smôl′ij), *n.* a variety of wild parsley.

smite (smīt), *v.t.*, **smote, smit ten** or **smit, smit ing.** **1** give a hard blow to (a person, etc.) with the hand, a stick, or the like; strike. **2** to affect sharply with deep feeling. [Old English *smītan*]

smol der (smōl′dər), *v.i.* **1** burn and smoke without flame. **2** exist or continue in a suppressed condition. **3** show suppressed feeling. Also, **smoulder.** [Middle English]

so bri quet (sō′brə kā), *n.* nickname. Also, **soubriquet.** [< French]

sol ace (sol′is), *n.* **1** comfort or relief: *She found solace from her troubles in music.* **2** that which gives comfort or consolation. [< Latin *solacium* < *solari* to console]

so lic i tude (sə lis′ə tüd, sə lis′ə tyüd), *n.* anxious care; anxiety; concern.

som no lent (som′nə lənt), *adj.* **1** sleepy; drowsy. **2** tending to produce sleep. [< Latin *somnolentus* < *somnus* sleep]

sore (sôr, sōr), *adj.*, **sor er, sor est.** **1** causing misery, anger, or offense; vexing: *Their defeat is a sore subject with the team.* **2** severe; distressing.

spang (spang), *v.i.*, **-ed, -ing.** to make a sharp, loud, and often whining sound.

Spar tan (spärt′n), *n.* **1** native or inhabitant of Sparta. The Spartans were noted for simplicity of life, severity, courage, and brevity of speech. **2** person who is like the Spartans.

spe cious (spē′shəs), *adj.* **1** seeming desirable, reasonable, or probable, but not really so: *The teacher saw through that specious excuse.* **2** making a good outward appearance in order to deceive: *a specious friendship.* [< Latin *speciosus* < *species* appearance, sort]

spec ter (spek′tər), *n.* **1** phantom or ghost, especially one of a terrifying nature or appearance. **2** thing causing terror or dread. Also, **spectre.** [< Latin *spectrum* appearance.]

spec tral (spek′trəl), *adj.* **1** of or like a specter; ghostly: *the spectral form of a ship surrounded by fog.* **2** of or produced by a spectrum: *spectral colors.*

spectro-, *combining form.* spectrum; of a spectrum: *Spectrogram = photograph or picture of a spectrum.* [< *spectrum*]

spec u late (spek′yə lāt), *v.i.*, **-lat ed, -lat ing.** **1** think carefully; reflect; meditate; consider.

squal or (skwol′ər), *n.* **1** misery and dirt; filth. **2** quality or condition of being morally squalid. [< Latin]

squeam ish (skwē′mish), *adj.* **1** too proper, modest, etc.; easily shocked; prudish. **2** too particular; too scrupulous. **3** slightly sick at one's stomach; nauseated. [< Anglo-French *escoymous*] — **squeam′ish ness,** *n.*

staunch (stônch, stänch), *adj.* **1** strong or firm: *a staunch defense.* **2** loyal; steadfast: *a staunch supporter of the law.* **3** watertight: *a staunch boat.* [< Middle French *estanche* < *estanchier* to stop, hinder]

sten to ri an (sten tôr′ē ən, sten tōr′ē ən), *adj.* very loud or powerful in sound. <*Stentor,* a Greek herald in the Trojan War, whose voice was extremely loud.

ste ril i ty (stə ril′ə tē), *n.* sterile condition or character; barrenness.

still (stil), *n.* **1** apparatus for distilling liquids, especially alcoholic liquors. **2** distillery. [noun use of *still,* short for *distill*]

sto ic (stō′ik), *n.* person who remains calm and self-controlled, and appears to be indifferent to pleasure and pain.

sto i cal (stō′ə kəl), *adj.* like a stoic; indifferent to pleasure and pain; self-controlled. —**sto′i cal ly,** *adv.*

sto i cism (stō′ə siz′əm), *n.* patient endurance; indifference to pleasure and pain.

stol id (stol′id), *adj.* hard to arouse; not easily excited; showing no emotion; seeming dull; impassive. [< Latin *stolidus*] — **stol′id ly,** *adv.*

stra ta (strā′tə, strat′ə), *n.* a pl. of **stratum.**

stra tum (strā′təm, strat′əm), *n.*, *pl.* **-ta** or **-tums.** layer of material, especially one of several parallel layers placed one upon another. [< Latin, something spread out < *sternere* to spread]

stu por (stü′pər, styü′pər), *n.* **1** a dazed condition; loss or lessening of the power to feel. **2** intellectual or moral numbness. [< Latin < *stupere* be dazed]

sub-, *prefix.* **1** under; below: *Subnormal = below normal.* **2** down; further; again: *Subdivide = divide again.* **3** near; nearly: *Subtropical = nearly tropical.* **4** lower; subordinate: *Subcommittee = a lower or subordinate committee.*

sub due (səb dü′, səb dyü′), *v.t.*, **-dued, -du ing.** **1** overcome by force; conquer: *The Romans subdued all the peoples of the Mediterranean.* **2** keep down; hold back; suppress: *We subdued a desire to laugh.* **3** tone down; soften: *Pulling down the shades subdued the light in the room.*

sub lime (sə blīm′), *adj.* lofty or elevated in thought, feeling, language, etc.; noble; grand; exalted: *sublime devotion.* [< Latin *sublimis,* originally, sloping up (to the lintel). < *sub-* up to + *liminis* threshold]

sub sid ence (səb sīd′ns, sub′sə dəns), *n.* act or process of subsiding; settling down; becoming quiet.

sub sist ence (səb sis′təns), *n.* **1** a keeping alive; living. **2** means of keeping alive; livelihood: *The sea provides a subsistence for fishermen.* **3** existence; continuance.

sub ter fuge (sub′tər fyüj), *n.* trick, excuse, or expedient used to escape something unpleasant. [< Late Latin *subterfugium,* ultimately < Latin *subter-* from under + *fugere* flee]

sub ter ra ne an (sub′tə rā′nē ən), *adj.* underground. [< Latin *subterraneus* < *sub-* under + *terra* earth]

suc cor (suk′ər), *n.* person or thing that helps or assists; help; aid. [< Old French *sucurs,* ultimately < Latin *succurrere* run to help < *sub-* up to + *currere* to run]

suc co tash (suk′ə tash), *n.* kernels of sweet corn and beans, usually lima beans, cooked together. [of Algonquian origin]

suf fer ance (suf′ər əns), *n.* **1** permission or consent given only by a failure to object or prevent. **2** power to bear or endure; patient endurance.

suf frage (suf′rij), *n.* **1** the right to vote; franchise. **2** a vote, usually in support of a proposal, candidate, etc.

suf fuse (sə fyüz′), *v.t.*, **-fused, -fus ing.** overspread (with a liquid, dye, etc.): *eyes suffused with tears.* [< Latin *suffusum* poured under < *sub-* under + *fundere* to pour]

sulk y (sul′kē), *adj.*, **sulk i er, sulk i est,** *n.*, *pl.* **sulk ies.** — *adj.* silent and bad-humored because of resentment; sullen. [origin uncertain] —**sulk′i ly,** *adv.*

sul len (sul′ən), *adj.* **1** silent because of bad humor or anger. **2** gloomy; dismal: *The sullen skies threatened rain.* [Middle English *soleine,* ultimately < Latin *solus* alone]

sul try (sul′trē), *adj.*, **-tri er, -tri est.** **1** hot, close, and moist: *We expect sultry weather during July.* **2** hot or fiery: *sultry glances.* [< obsolete *sulter* (verb) swelter; related to *swelter*]

sump tu ous (sump′chü əs), *adj.* lavish and costly; magnificent; rich: *a sumptuous banquet.* [< Latin *sumptuosus* < *sumptus* expense < *sumere* spend]

sun dry (sun′drē), *adj.* several; various. [Old English *syndrig* separate < *sundor* apart]

su per cil i ous (sü′pər sil′ē əs), *adj.* haughty, proud, and contemptuous; disdainful; showing scorn or indifference because of a feeling of superiority. [< Latin *superciliosus* < *supercilium* eyebrow, pride < *super-* above + *-cilium* < *celare* to cover, conceal]

su per flu ous (sù pèr′flü əs), *adj.* **1** more than is needed. **2** needless; unnecessary: *A raincoat is superfluous on a clear day.* [< Latin *superfluus,* ultimately < *super-* over + *fluere* to flow]

su per nu me rary (sü′pər nü′mə rer′ē, sü′pər nyü′mə rer′ē), *adj.*, *n.*, *pl.* **-rar ies.** —*adj.* more than the usual or necessary number; extra. —*n.* **1** an extra person or thing. **2** person who appears on the stage but usually has no lines to speak. [< Late Latin *supernumerarius* excessive in number < Latin *super numerum* beyond the number]

su per sede (sü′pər sēd′), *v.t.*, **-sed ed, -sed ing.** **1** take the place of; cause to be set aside; displace. **2** succeed and supplant; replace. [< Latin *supersedere* be superior to, refrain from < *super-* above + *sedere* sit]

sup pli cate (sup′lə kāt), *v.*, **-cat ed, -cat ing.** —*v.t.* beg humbly and earnestly. —*v.i.* pray humbly. [< Latin *supplicatum* bent down, suppliant < *sub-* down + *plicare* to bend]

sup po si tion (sup′ə zish′ən), *n.* **1** act of supposing. **2** thing supposed; belief; opinion.

sur cease (sèr′sēs′ sər sēs′), *n.* end; cessation. [< Old French *sursis,* past participle of *surseoir* refrain < Latin *supersedere.* See SUPERSEDE.]

sur feit (sèr′fit), *n.* **1** too much; excess. **2** disgust or nausea caused by too much of anything. —*v.t.* feed or supply to excess. [< Old French *surfait,* originally, overdone < *sur-* over + *faire* to do]

sur ly (sèr′lē), *adj.*, **-li er, -li est.** bad-tempered and unfriendly; rude; gruff. —**sur′li ness,** *n.*

sur mount (sər mount′), *v.t.* **1** rise above. **2** be above or on top of. **3** go up and across. **4** overcome. [< Old French *surmonter* < *sur-* over + *monter* to mount]

sur rep ti tious (sèr′əp tish′əs), *adj.* **1** stealthy; secret: *a surreptitious glance.* **2** secret and unauthorized; clandestine: *surreptitious meetings.* [< Latin *surrepticius* < *surripere* seize secretly < *sub-* under + *rapere* to seize] —**sur′rep ti′tious ly,** *adv.* —**sur′rep ti′tious ness,** *n.*

sus cep ti ble (sə sep′tə bəl), *adj.* **1** easily influenced by feelings or emotions; very sensitive. **2** susceptible of, a capable of receiving, undergoing, or being affected by. **b** sensitive to. **3** susceptible to, easily affected by; liable to; open to. [< Late Latin *susceptibilis,* ultimately < Latin *sub-* up + *capere* to take]

swan (swon), *v.i.*, DIALECT. to swear.

sward (swôrd), *n.* a grassy surface; turf. [Old English *sweard* skin]

syl van (sil′vən), *adj.* of, in, or having woods: *live in a sylvan retreat.* Also, **silvan.** [< Latin *sylvanus, silvanus* < *silva* forest]

sym me try (sim′ə trē), *n.*, *pl.* **-tries.** **1** a regular, balanced arrangement on opposite sides of a line or plane, or around a center or axis. **2** pleasing proportions between the parts of a whole; well-balanced arrangement of parts; harmony. [< Greek *symmetria* < *syn-* together + *metron* measure]

syn chro nize (sing′krə nīz), *v.i.*, **-nized, -niz ing.** **1** occur at the same time; agree in time. **2** move or take place at the same rate and exactly together. [< Greek *synchronizein* < *synchronos* syncronous]

sys to le (sis′tl ē), *n.* the normal rhythmical contraction of the heart, especially that of the ventricles, when blood is pumped from the heart into the arteries. [< Greek *systolē* contraction < *syn-* together + *stellein* to put]

tab leau (tab′lō), *n.*, *pl.* **-leaux** (-lōz), **-leaus.** **1** a striking scene; picture. **2** representation of a picture, statue, scene, etc., by a person or group posing in appropriate costume. [< French, diminutive of *table* table]

te mer i ty (tə mer′ə tē), *n.* reckless boldness; rashness; foolhardiness. [< Latin *temeritatem* < *temere* heedlessly]

tem per a ment (tem′pər ə mənt), *n.* **1** a person's nature or disposition. **2** an easily irritated, sensitive nature. An artist, singer, or actress often has temperament.

tem per a men tal (tem′pər ə men′tl), *adj.* subject to moods and whims; easily irritated. —**tem′per a men′tal ly,** *adv.*

tem per ance (tem′pər əns), *n.* **1** a being moderate in action, speech, habits, etc.; self-control. **2** a being moderate in use of alcoholic drinks.

ten e ment (ten′ə mənt), *n.* **1** tenement house. **2** any house or building to live in; dwelling house. [< Old French, ultimately < Latin *tenere* to hold]

ten ta tive (ten′tə tiv), *adj.* **1** done as a trial or experiment; experimental. **2** hesitating. [< Medieval Latin *tentativus* < Latin *tentare* to try] —**ten′ta tive ly,** *adv.*

ter ma gant (tèr′mə gənt), *n.* a violent, quarreling, scolding woman. —*adj.* violent, quarreling, or scolding. [< *Termagant,* a fictitious Moslem deity in Medieval plays]

---

a hat	i it	oi oil	ch child		a in about
ā age	ī ice	ou out	ng long		e in taken
ä far	o hot	u cup	sh she	ə =	i in pencil
e let	ō open	u̇ put	th thin		o in lemon
ē equal	ô order	ü rule	ŦH then		u in circus
ėr term			zh measure	< = derived from

tes ty (tes′tē), *adj.*, **-ti er, -ti est.** easily irritated; impatient; petulant. [< Anglo-French *testif* headstrong < Old French *teste* head]

tho rax (thôr′aks, thōr′aks), *n.*, *pl.* **tho rax es, tho ra ces** (thôr′ə sēz′, thōr′ə sēz′). **1** part of the body between the neck and the abdomen; chest. **2** the second of the three main divisions of an arthropod's body, between the head and the abdomen. [< Latin < Greek *thōrax*]

tim or ous (tim′ər əs), *adj.* **1** easily frightened; timid. **2** characterized by or indicating fear. [< Latin *timor* fear < *timere* to fear] —**tim′or ous ly,** *adv.* —**tim′or ous ness,** *n.*

tink er (ting′kər), *n.* person who mends pots, pans, etc., usually wandering from place to place. [Middle English *tynekere,* perhaps ultimately < *tin*]

tit ter (tit′ər), *v.i.* laugh in a half-restrained manner, because of nervousness or silliness; giggle. —*n.* a tittering laugh. [imitative]

tit u lar (tich′ə lər, tit′yə lər), *adj.* **1** in title or name only; nominal. **2** having a title. **3** having to do with a title. [< Latin *titulus* title]

trag i com e dy (traj′i kom′ə dē), *n.*, *pl.* **-dies.** incident or situation in which serious and comic elements are blended.

trag i com ic (traj′i kom′ik), *adj.* having both tragic and comic elements.

trans-, *prefix.* **1** across; over; through, as in *transcontinental, transmit.* **2** on the other side of; beyond, as in *transatlantic.* **3** to a different place, condition, etc., as in *transmigration, transform.* [< Latin *trans* across]

trans gres sion (trans gresh′ən, tranz gresh′ən), *n.* breaking a law, command, etc.; sin. [< Latin *transgressum* gone beyond + English *-ion*]

tran sient (tran′shənt), *adj.* **1** passing soon; fleeting; not lasting. **2** passing through and not staying long. —*n.* visitor or boarder who stays for a short time. [< Latin *transientem* going through < *trans-* + *ire* go] —**tran′sient ly,** *adv.*

trans lu cent (tran slü′snt, tranz lü′snt), *adj.* letting light through without being transparent. [< Latin *translucentem* < *trans-* through + *lucere* to shine]

trans mog ri fy (tran smog′rə fī, tranz mog′rə fī), *v.t.*, **-fied, -fying.** change in form or appearance; transform in a surprising or grotesque manner. [< *trans-* + *mogrify* (origin unknown)]

tran sub stan ti a tion (tran′səb stan′shē ā′shən), *n.* **1** a changing of one substance into another; transmutation. **2** in Christian theology: **a** a changing of the substance of the bread and wine of the Eucharist into the substance of the body and blood of Christ, only the appearance of the bread and wine remaining. **b** the doctrine that this change occurs, held by the Roman Catholic and Eastern Churches.

tra vail (trə vāl′, trav′āl), *n.* **1** toil; labor. **2** trouble, hardship, or suffering. **3** severe pain; agony; torture. **4** the labor and pain of childbirth. —*v.i.* **1** toil; labor. **2** suffer the pains of childbirth; be in labor. [< Old French < Late Latin *trepalium* torture device, ultimately < Latin *tri-* three + *palus* stake]

tra verse (trə vėrs′, trav′ərs), *v.t.*, **-versed, -vers ing.** **1** pass across, over, or through: *We traversed the desert.* **2** go to and fro over or along (a place, etc.); cross.

trem u lous (trem′yə ləs), *adj.* **1** trembling; quivering: *a voice tremulous with sobs.* **2** timid; fearful. **3** that wavers; shaky: *tremulous writing.* [< Latin *tremulus* < *tremere* to tremble]

trep i da tion (trep′ə dā′shən), *n.* **1** nervous dread; fear; fright. **2** a trembling. [< Latin *trepidationem* < *trepidare* to tremble < *trepidus* alarmed]

tri dent (trīd′nt), *n.* a three-pronged spear. [< Latin *tridentem* < *tri-* three + *dentem* tooth]

---

troth (trôth, trōth), *n.* ARCHAIC. **1** faithfulness or fidelity; loyalty. **2** promise. **3 plight one's troth,** promise to marry. [Old English *trēowth < trēow* faith]

trough (trôf, trof), *n.* **1** a narrow, open, boxlike container for holding food or water, especially for farm stock or other animals. **2** something shaped like this. **3** a channel for carrying water; gutter. [Old English *trog*]

trun dle (trun′dl), *v.,* **-dled, -dling.** —*v.t.* **1** roll along; push along. **2** cause to rotate; twirl; spin; whirl. —*v.i.* **1** move or be moved by trundling. **2** whirl; revolve. [Old English *trendel* ring, disk]

tum brel (tum′brəl), *n.* **1** any of various two-wheeled carts, especially one used on a farm for hauling and dumping manure. **2** cart that carried prisoners to be executed during the French Revolution. [< Old French *tomberel* cart < *tomber* to fall; of Germanic origin]

tu mult (tü′mult, tyü′mult), *n.* **1** noise or uproar; commotion. **2** a violent disturbance or disorder. **3** a violent disturbance of mind or feeling; confusion or excitement. [< Latin *tumultus*]

tu mul tu ous (tü mul′chü əs, tyü mul′chü əs), *adj.* **1** characterized by tumult; very noisy or disorderly; violent. **2** greatly disturbed. **3** rough; stormy. —**tu mul′tu ous ly,** *adv.*

tur bu lent (tėr′byə lənt), *adj.* **1** causing disorder; disorderly; unruly; violent. **2** stormy. [< Latin *turbulentus < turba* turmoil]

tur ret (tėr′it) *n.* a small tower, often on the corner of a building. [< Old French *touret,* ultimately < Latin *turris* tower]

u biq ui tous (yü bik′wə təs), *adj.* that is everywhere at the same time; present everywhere.

ul te ri or (ul tir′ē ər), *adj.* beyond what is seen or expressed; hidden. [< Latin, comparative of root of *ultra* beyond] —**ul te′ri or ly,** *adv.*

um bra geous (um brā′jəs), *adj.* **1** likely to take offense. **2** shady.

un-[1], *prefix.* not ____; the opposite of ____; *Unequal = not equal; the opposite of equal. Unchanged = not changed.*

un-[2], *prefix.* do the opposite of ____; do what will reverse the act: *Unfasten = do the opposite of fasten.*

un ac count a ble (un′ə koun′tə bəl), *adj.* **1** that cannot be accounted for or explained; inexplicable. **2** not responsible.

un al ien a ble (un ā′lyə nə bəl), *adj.* that cannot be given or taken away. inalienable.

un al ter a ble (un ôl′tər ə bəl), *adj.* not changeable; permanent.

un daunt ed (un dôn′tid, un dän′tid), *adj.* not afraid; not dismayed or discouraged; fearless.

un der ling (un′dər ling), *n.* a person of lower rank or position; inferior.

un du late (un′jə lāt, un′dyə lāt), *v.i.,* **-lat ed, -lat ing. 1** move in waves: *undulating water.* **2** have a wavy form or surface: *undulating hair.* [< Latin *undulatus* wavy < *unda* wave]

un gain ly (un gān′lē), *adj.* not gainly; awkward; clumsy.

un re mit ting (un′ri mit′ing), *adj.* never stopping; not slackening; maintained steadily.

un scru pu lous (un skrü′pyə ləs), *adj.* not careful about right or wrong; without principles or conscience.

un seem ly (un sēm′lē), *adj.* not suitable; improper: *unseemly haste.* —*adv.* improperly; unsuitably.

un wont ed (un wun′tid, un wōn′tid, un wôn′tid), *adj.* **1** not customary; not usual. **2** not accustomed; not used.

u sur er (yü′zhər ər), *n.* person who lends money at an extremely high or unlawful rate of interest.

u sur pa tion (yü′zər pā′shən, yü′sər pā′shən), *n.* a usurping; the seizing and holding of the place or power of another by force or without right: *the usurpation of the throne by a pretender.*

u til i tar i an (yü til′ə ter′ē ən), *adj.* aiming at or designed for usefulness rather than beauty, style, etc.

u til i tar i an ism (yü til′ə ter′ē ə niz′əm), *n.* **1** the doctrine or belief that the greatest good of the greatest number should be the

purpose of human conduct. **2** the doctrine or belief that actions are good if they are useful.

u til i ty (yü til′ə tē), *n., pl.* **-ties. 1** power to satisfy people's needs; usefulness. **2** a useful thing. **3** company that performs a public service; public utility. Railroads, bus lines, and gas and electric companies are utilities. [< Latin *utilitatem < utilis* usable < *uti* to use]

u ti lize (yü′tl īz), *v.t.,* **-lized, -liz ing.** make use of; put to some practical use: *utilize leftovers in cooking.*

vag a bond (vag′ə bond), *n.* **1** an idle wanderer; tramp; vagrant. **2** a disreputable person; rascal. —*adj.* **1** wandering. **2** shiftless; disreputable. **3** moving hither and thither; drifting. [< Old French < Latin *vagabundus < rambling*]

vain glo ry (vān′glôr′ē, vān′glōr′ē), *n.* **1** an extreme pride in oneself; boastful vanity. **2** worthless pomp or show.

va moose (va müs), *v.t., v.i.,* **-moosed, -moos ing.** SLANG. go away quickly. [< Spanish *vamos* let us go]

van quish (vang′kwish, van′kwish), *v.t.* **1** conquer, defeat, or overcome in battle or conflict. **2** overcome or subdue by other than physical means: *vanquish fear.* [< Old French *vainquiss-,* a form of *vainquir* vanquish < Latin *vincere*]

ve he ment (vē′ə mənt), *adj.* **1** having or showing strong feeling; caused by strong feeling; eager; passionate. **2** forceful; violent. [< Latin *vehementem* being carried away < *vehere* carry] —**ve′he ment ly,** *adv.*

ven er y (ven′ər ē), *n.* practice or pursuit of sexual pleasure; gratification of sexual desire. [< Latin *Venus*]

ven om ous (ven′ə məs), *adj.* **1** poisonous. **2** spiteful; malicious.

ves tige (ves′tij), *n.* **1** a slight remnant; trace; mark. **2** (in biology) a part, organ, etc., that is no longer fully developed or useful but performed a definite function in an earlier stage of the existence of the same organism or in lower preceding organisms. [< French < Latin *vestigium* footprint]

vex (veks), *v.t.* **1** anger by trifles; annoy; provoke. **2** worry; trouble; harass. **3** disturb by commotion. [< Latin *vexare*]

vex a tion (vek sā′shən), *n.* **1** a vexing. **2** a being vexed: *His face showed his vexation at the delay.* **3** thing that vexes.

vi and (vī′ənd), *n.* **1** article of food. **2 viands,** *pl.* articles of choice food. [< Old French *viande* < Late Latin *vivenda* things for living < Latin, to be lived < *vivere* to live]

vict ual (vit′l), *n.* **victuals,** *pl.* food or provisions. [< Latin *victualia,* plural of *victualis* of food < *victus* food, sustenance < *vivere* to live]

vig i lance (vij′ə ləns), *n.* **1** watchfulness; alertness; caution. **2** sleeplessness.

vin di ca tion (vin də kā′shən), *n.* a vindicating or a being vindicated; defense; justification.

vin dic tive (vin dik′tiv), *adj.* **1** feeling a strong tendency toward revenge; bearing a grudge. **2** showing a strong tendency toward revenge. [< Latin *vindicta* revenge < *vindex* avenger]

vir tu o so (vėr′chü ō′sō), *n., pl.* **-sos, -si** (sē). —*n.* **1** person skilled in the techniques of an art, especially in playing a musical instrument. **2** person who has a cultivated appreciation of artistic excellence; connoisseur. —*adj.* showing the artistic qualities and skills of a virtuoso. [< Italian, learned, virtuous]

vir u lence (vir′ə ləns, vir′yə ləns), *n.* **1** quality of being very poisonous or harmful; deadliness. **2** intense bitterness or spite; violent hostility.

vis age (viz′ij), *n.* **1** face. **2** appearance or aspect. [< Old French < *vis* face < Latin *visus* sight < *videre* to see]

vi tu pe ra tive (vī tü′pə rā′tiv, vī tyü′pə rā′tiv), *adj.* abusive; reviling. —**vi tu′pe ra′tive ly,** *adv.*

vi va cious (vī vā′shəs, vi vā′shəs), *adj.* lively; sprightly; animated; gay.

vi vac i ty (vī vas′ə tē, vi vas′ə tē), *n., pl.* **-ties.** liveliness; sprightliness; animation; gaiety. [< Latin *vivacitatem < vivacis* lively < *vivere* to live]

vo cif e rate (vō sif′ə rāt′), *v.t., v.i.,* **-rat ed, -rat ing.** cry out loudly or noisily; shout; clamor.

GLOSSARY

vo cif er ous (vō sif′ər əs), *adj.* loud and noisy; shouting; clamoring: *a vociferous person, vociferous cheers.*

voi là (vwá lá′), *interj.* FRENCH. there it is; see there; look; behold.

vol ley (vol′ē), *n., pl.* **-leys.** **1** shower of stones, bullets, arrows, etc. **2** the discharge of a number of guns or other weapons firing missiles at once. [< Middle French *volée* flight < *voler* to fly < Latin *volare*]

vul gar (vul′gər), *adj.* **1** showing a lack of good breeding, manners, taste, etc.; not refined; coarse; low. **2** of the common people. [< Latin *vulgaris* < *vulgus* common people]

vul ner a ble (vul′nər ə bəl), *adj.* **1** that can be wounded or injured; open to attack. **2** sensitive to criticism, temptations, influences, etc. [< Late Latin *vulnerabilis* < Latin *vulnerare* to wound < *vulnus* wound]

wam pum (wom′pəm, wôm′pəm), *n.* **1** beads made from shells, formerly used by North American Indians as money and for ornament. **2** SLANG. money. [of Algonquian origin]

wane (wān), *v.t.,* **waned, wan ing.** **1** lose size; become smaller gradually. **2** decline in power or importance. **3** decline in strength or intensity. **4** draw to a close. [Old English *wanian*]

wan ton (won′tən), *adj.* **1** reckless, heartless, or malicious: *wanton cruelty.* **2** without reason or excuse. [Middle English *wantowen* < Old English *wan-* not, lacking + *togen* brought up]

wax (waks), *v.i.,* **waxed, waxed** or (ARCHAIC) **wax en, wax ing.** **1** grow bigger or greater; increase: *The moon waxes till it becomes full, and then wanes.* **2** become: *The party waxed merry.* [Old English *weaxan*]

wend (wend), *v.,* **wend ed** or **went, wend ing.** —*v.t.* direct (one's way). —*v.i.* go. [Old English *wendan*]

wher ry (hwer′ē), *n., pl.* **-ries.** **1** a light, shallow rowboat for carrying passengers and goods on rivers, used especially in England. **2** any of several types of boats used locally in England, such as a barge, fishing vessel, sailboat, etc. [origin unknown]

wile (wīl), *n., v.,* **wiled, wil ing.** —*n.* **1** a trick to deceive; cunning way: *The serpent by his wiles persuaded Eve to eat the apple.* **2** subtle trickery; slyness; craftiness. —*v.t.* **1** coax; lure; entice. **2 wile away,** while away; pass easily or pleasantly. [Old English *wigle* magic]

wis ter i a (wi stir′ē ə), *n.* any of a genus of climbing shrubs of

a hat	i it	oi oil	ch child		a in about
ā age	ī ice	ou out	ng long		e in taken
ä far	o hot	u cup	sh she	ə =	i in pencil
e let	ō open	ù put	th thin		o in lemon
ē equal	ô order	ü rule	ŦH then		u in circus
ėr term			zh measure	< = derived from

the pea family, with large, drooping clusters of showy purple, blue, or white flowers.

with al (wi ŦHôl′, wi thôl′), *adv.* **1** with it all; as well; besides; also: *I am tired and hungry and hurt withal.* **2** ARCHAIC. **a** in spite of all; nevertheless. **b** therewith. —*prep.* ARCHAIC. with. [Middle English < *with* + *all*]

wit ti cism (wit′ə siz′əm), *n.* a witty remark.

wraith (rāth), *n.* **1** ghost of a person seen before or soon after the person's death. **2** specter; ghost. [origin uncertain]

wran gle (rang′gəl), *v.,* **-gled, -gling.** dispute noisily; quarrel angrily.

wrench (rench), *v.t.* **1** twist or pull violently: *The policeman wrenched the gun out of the man's hand.* **2** injure by twisting. **3** distress or pain greatly. [Old English *wrencan* to twist]

yo kel (yō′kəl), *n.* (often considered offensive) an awkward or unsophisticated person from the country; bumpkin; rustic. [origin uncertain]

yuc ca (yuk′ə), *n.* any of a genus of plants of the same family as the agave, found in dry, warm regions of North and Central America, having stiff, sword-shaped, evergreen leaves at the base.

ze nith (zē′nith), *n.* the point in the heavens directly overhead; point opposite the nadir. [< Old French or Medieval Latin *cenith* < Arabic *samt (ar-rās)* the way (over the head)]

GLOSSARY

INDEX OF AUTHORS AND TITLES

988

INDEX OF FEATURES

INDEX OF READING AND LITERATURE SKILLS

INDEX OF THINKING SKILLS

INDEX OF VOCABULARY EXERCISES

INDEX OF COMPOSITION ASSIGNMENTS

INDEX OF ENRICHMENT ACTIVITIES

INDEX OF GENRES

INDEX OF THEMES

This index is based partly on "Themes in American Literature" articles appearing on pages 76, 127, 253, 339, 470, 619, 639, 843 (in "Three Long Stories" edition), and 841 (in The *Red Badge of Courage* edition). Selections are shown in the order in which they appear in the text. Many selections are shown under more than one theme. A few works are omitted.

*Date of composition. Dates not asterisked are publication dates.

INDEX OF GRAPHIC AIDS

INDEX OF ILLUSTRATIONS AND FINE ART

ILLUSTRATION ACKNOWLEDGMENTS

Illustrations not credited are from Scott, Foresman and Company.

UNIT 1

1—(l to r) Pilgrim Society, Plymouth, MA: Essex Institute, Salem, MA; Courtesy The Colonial Williamsburg Collection; Museum of Fine Arts, Boston, Gift of Joseph W., William B. and Edward H. R. Revere; Independence National Historical Park Collection; 19—Albany Institute of History and Art, Collection of Mr. John B. Knox; 22—Historical Society of Pennsylvania; 23—Collier's, October 14, 1905; 27—Chicago Historical Society code #1883.2; 29—National Gallery of Art, Washington, DC, Paul Mellon Collection, 1965; 32—Reid Lewis; 33—Courtesy The Newberry Library, Chicago; 38—The Bettmann Archive; 50—© Glen Loates; 52—American Antiquarian Society; 60—Ann Parker/Avon Neal; 63—Museum of Fine Arts, Boston, Gift of Samuel Bradstreet; 67—Photo: Courtesy Christie, Manson & Woods, International, Inc.; 70—Library of Congress; 73—Culver Pictures; 74—Reprinted by permission from Addisonia, Vol. II, Plate 370, Copyright 1926, The New York Botanical Garden; 78—Historical Society of Pennsylvania; 87—The Bettmann Archive; 89—The National Gallery, Washington, DC, Index of the Treasury of Design

UNIT 2

102, 103—(l to r) National Gallery of Art, Washington, DC, Index of American Design; Henry Ford Museum; Philadelphia Museum of Art, Photo: Alfred J. Wyatt; Carnegie Library, Pittsburgh; Whitney Museum of American Art; Woolaroc Museum, Bartlesville, Oklahoma; 128—Culver Pictures; 131—Metropolitan Museum of Art, Gift of J. Pierpont Morgan, 1911(11.156); 133—Art Institute of Chicago, Edward B. Butler Collection; 134—Longfellow House Trust; 137—Boston Museum of Fine Arts, Gift of the Daughters of Edward D. Boit in memory of their father, 1919; 139, 144—Culver Pictures; 142—Study for Oyster Gatherers of Cancale, John Singer Sargent, 1877, Daniel J. Terra Collection, Terra Museum of American Art; 149—Pennsylvania Academy of the Fine Arts; 150—Poe, mss. Manuscripts Dept., Lilly Library, Indiana University, Bloomington, IN; 154—British Library 12703 i43; 158—Culver Pictures; 169—© Glen Loates; 175, 177—Culver Pictures; 187—The Historic New Orleans Collection, 533 Royal Street; 190—Philadelphia Museum of Art, Gift of Mrs. Thomas Eakins and Miss Mary Adeline Williams

UNIT 3

196—(l to r) Nathaniel Currier, The Independent Gold Hunter on His Way to California, c. 1845, American Museum in Britain; Louis Schultze, "Dred Scott," Missouri Historical Society, St. Louis; Abby Aldrich Rockefeller Folk Art Collection, Colonial Williamsburg; 197—(l to r) National Gallery of Art, Washington, DC, Index of American Design; Library of Congress; The Mansell Collection; 204—George Eastman House Collection; 213—Museum of Fine Arts, Boston, M. and M. Karolik Collection; 216—Culver Pictures; 229—Suquamish Museum; 236—Essex Institute; 242—© Dan Morrill; 248—Library of Congress; 254—The Newberry Library; 259—George Cush-

ing; 263—The Detroit Institute of Arts, Gift of Mrs. Jefferson Butler and Miss Grace R. Conover; 266—National Portrait Gallery, Smithsonian Institution; 268—Harper's Weekly, November 16, 1867; 269—The Sophia Smith Collection, Women's History Archive, Smith College; 271—Library of Congress; 273—Brady Collection, U.S. Signal Corp. photo in the National Archives No. 111-B-1564; 275—Courtesy MacMillan; 278—The Bettmann Archive; 280—The Newberry Library, Chicago. Gift of Hugh J. Grant, 1974.

UNIT 4

288—(l to r) Metropolitan Museum of Art; Museum of American Folk Art, Gift of Eva and Morris Feld Folk Art Acquisition Fund; Leonard W. Dunham Collection: A.C. Cooper; 289—(l to r) Robin Wyatt: A.C. Cooper; Library of Congress; Historical Pictures Service; 296—Museum of Fine Arts, Boston, William Wilkins Warren Fund; 298—Private Collection; 302—Museum of the City of New York, Harry T. Peters Collection; 315—Trustees of Amherst College; 316—Detroit Institute of Arts. Bequest of Robert H. Tannahill; 329—Charles Noel Flagg, "Mark Twain," Metropolitan Museum of Art, Gift of Miss Ellen Earle Flagg; 331—Courtesy Ronald Feldman Fine Arts, New York; 343—Smithsonian Institution; 344—Philadelphia Museum of Art/Photo: A.J. Wyatt, Staff Photographer; 346—The Bettmann Archive; 358—© Tom Heflin; 363—The St. Louis Art Museum, Ezra H. Linley Fund; 364—The Bettmann Archive; 376—Daniel J. Terra Collection, Terra Museum of American Art, Chicago; 379—UPI/Bettmann Newsphotos; 386—The Newark Public Library; 391—Sara Hildén Art Museum, Tampere, Suomi, Finland. Collection Sara Hildén. 392—The Bettmann Archive; 394—AP/Wide World Photos; 396—Culver Pictures; 398—© Tom Heflin

UNIT 5

404—(l to r) Library of Congress; Copyright © 1925, 1962 The New Yorker Magazine, Inc.; AP/Wide World Photos; 405—(l to r) Culver Pictures; Photo: Curtis & May Studio, Paducah, KY; AP/Wide World Photos; 409—Jazzmen Photo, Ramsey Archives; 412—Willa Cather Pioneer Memorial Collection, Nebraska State Historical Society; 415—Museum of Fine Arts, Boston, Charles Henry Hayden Fund; 421—Historic New Orleans Collection, 533 Royal Street; 424—© Tom Heflin; 429—UPI/Bettmann Newsphotos; 433—Dallas Museum of Art, Gift of Everett L. DeGolyer; 437—Ian Massar/Black Star; 439—Courtesy Cluett, Peabody; 445—Painting by American artist Mort Künstler; photo courtesy Hammer Galleries; 451—Reproduced by permission of the Estate of Norman Rockwell; 453—UPI/Bettmann Newsphotos; 456—Trustees of the Imperial War Museum, London; 459—U.S. Postal Service; 471—Culver Pictures; 482—AP/Wide World Photos; 488—AP/Wide World Photos; 496—(top to btm) New Directions Publishing Corporation, Photo: Boris De Rachewiltz; University of Chicago Library, Department of Special Collections; AP/Wide World Photos; 497—(top to btm) UPI/Bettmann Newsphotos © Rollie McKenna; New York Times Photo; 502—Published by The Bobbs Mer-rill Company; **509**—Frank Donato/Impact Photos, Inc.; **516**—UPI/Bettmann Newsphotos; **517**—(top to btm) Brown Brothers; AP/Wide World Photos; New York Public Library, Schomburg Collection; **521**—Photo courtesy The Philadelphia Museum of Art; **522**—Metropolitan Museum of Art, Gift of Amanda K. Berls, 1967; **525**—Radio Times Hulton Picture Library/Bettmann; **532**—(top to btm) Bettmann Archive; AP/Wide World Photos; Courtesy Vassar College; **533**—(top to btm) Culver Pictures; Lee Blaisdell; UPI/Bettmann Newsphotos; Lincoln National Life Foundation, Fort Wayne; **536**—Yale University Art Gallery, New Haven, CT, Gift of the Société Anonyme; **540**—(top to btm) Culver Pictures; Brown Brothers; Harry Ransom Humanities Research Center, The University of Texas at Austin; **541**—The Bettmann Archive; New York Public Library, Schomburg Collection; **544**—Gerald Peters Gallery; **545**—Gene Moore of Tiffany & Company; **548**—Acme Newspictures; **549, 551**—Copyright © 1933, 1961 by James Thurber, Reprinted by permission of Rosemary A. Thurber and Hamish Hamilton, Ltd.; **555**—Reproduced by permission of the Estate of Norman Rockwell; **559**—Courtesy Nobel Foundation, Stockholm, Sweden

UNIT 6
566—(l to r) The Bettmann Archive; Springer/Bettmann Film Archive; Kobal Collection; **567**—(l to r) Springer/Bettmann Film Archive; Kobal Collection; © 1983 Ken Howard; Kobal Collection; **570**—Harry Ransom Humanities Research Center Art Collection, University of Texas at Austin; **572**—Ben Rosenthal; **575–609**—Museum of Modern Art/Film Stills Archive; **612**—Museum of the City of New York; **625**—Martha Swope

UNIT 7
626—(l to r) Tom Kovacs; Courtesy The White House; Courtesy United Air Lines; **627**—(l to r) NASA; Courtesy the Leo Castelli Gallery, NY; Designer Gary Gutterman; **632**—AP/Wide World Photos; **635**—Courtesy Brandywine River Museum; **640**—Courtesy Farrar, Straus & Giroux, Inc./Janna Malamud; **649**—AP/Wide World Photos; **653**—The Brooklyn Museum, John B. Woodward Memorial Fund; **659**—AP/Wide World Photos; **664**—Photo courtesy Kraushaar Galleries, NY/Photo: © Geoffrey Clements; **668, 674**—AP/Wide World Photos; **679**—© Tom Heflin; **683**—Black America; **687**—Museum of Fine Arts, Boston, Charles Henry Hayden Fund; **692**—(top) © Rollie McKenna, (second from top) © Rollie McKenna, (second from btm) Lloyd Studio, (btm) Washington University, Photo Service/Photo: Herb Weitman; **693**—Brooklyn Museum, Gift of Mr. and Mrs. John Koch; **695**—From *John Hedgecoe's Advanced Photography*, by John Hedgecoe. Copyright © Mitchell Beazley Publishers, 1982; Photographs © John Hedgecoe, 1982. Reprinted by permission of Simon and Schuster; **698**—(second from top) Photo: Copyright © Layle Silbert, (second from btm) AP/Wide World Photos, (btm) UPI/Bettmann Newsphotos; **699**—Photo courtesy Heritage Gallery, L.A.; **705**—(top) Pack Bros., NY, (mdle) © Rollie McKenna, (btm) AP/Wide World Photos; **709**—© Walter Chandoha; **711**—(top to btm) University of Nebraska/Dept. of Public Relations, AP/Wide World Photos, Courtesy

The Dial Press; **716**—(top to btm) Harper & Row, AP/Wide World Photos, Courtesy Doubleday & Company/Photo: Imogen Cunningham, Courtesy William Morrow; **717**—Heritage Gallery, L.A.; **719**—National Museum of American Art (formerly National Collection of Fine Arts) Smithsonian Institution. Gift of Trina A. Reed. Access #1974.44.21; **721**—Courtesy Jim W. Miller; **722**—Joan Rutsala; Gregory Djanikian; **726**—(top) Christopher Briscoe, (second from top) James Mitsui, (second from btm) Courtesy Harper & Row, (btm) UPI/Bettmann Newsphotos; **728**—Don Nibbelink; **731**—(top to btm) 1981 Linda Fry Poverman, Courtesy John Morris, Reuters/Bettmann Newsphotos, Gordon Lameyer; **736**—(top to btm) University of Pittsburgh Press, Marlene Foster-Ortiz; Linda Paston/Photo George Murphy; Teresa P. Acosta/Photo: © 1983 Sharon Steward; **739**—© Tom Heflin; **742**—UPI/Bettmann Newsphotos; **744**—Gift of Christian A. Zabriskie; **754**—Alan Borrud; **764**—David R. Godine Publisher, Inc./Photo: Robert Messick; **769**—AP/Wide World Photos; **775**—Courtesy Random House; **779**—UPI/Bettmann Newsphotos; **779**—Nobel Foundation, Stockholm, Sweden; **782**—Time, Inc.

UNIT 8 (Three Long Stories)
801—Photo Laurie Platt Winfrey, Inc./Carousel; **806**—Cincinnati Art Museum. The J.J. Emery Fund; **813**—Metropolitan Museum of Art, Amelia B. Lazarus Fund, by exchange, 1917; **817**—Beinecke Rare Book & Manuscript Library, Yale University; **823**—© Corcoran Gallery of Art, Museum Purchase, Gallery Fund, 1919; **824**—Metropolitan Museum of Art, New York. Gift of George A. Hearn, 1910; **839**—Private Collection; **852**—© 1986 Jerry Jacka. All rights reserved; **857–870**—© David Muench

UNIT 8 (*The Red Badge of Courage*)
798—New-York Historical Society; **797, 813, 818, 821, 829, 834, 842, 850, 857, 862, 865, 867**—Ted Lewin; **812**—Springer/Bettmann Film Archive

HANDBOOK OF LITERARY TERMS
877—San Diego Museum of Art, Bequest of Mrs. Henry A. Everett; **897**—The Toledo Museum of Art, Gift of Florence Scott Libbey; **911**—Museum of Modern Art, New York. Acquired through the Lillie P. Bliss Bequest and the Mr. and Mrs. David Rockefeller Fund

GLOSSARY
967 (cirrus)—NOAA; **968** (cowl)—Alinari/Art Reference Bureau; **972** (facade)—University Prints, Boston; **977** (mesa)—National Park Service; **979** (orangutan)—Animals, Animals/Miriam Austerman; **980** (portico)—courtesy of Virginia State Travel Service

WRITER'S HANDBOOK
917—Metropolitan Museum of Art, Bequest of Herbert L. Pratt, 1945